THE DEVELOPMENT OF WESTERN MUSIC

A HISTORY

Third Edition

THE DEVELOPMENT OF WESTERN MUSIC

A HISTORY

K MARIE STOLBA

*Professor of Music, Emerita
Indiana University—
Purdue University Fort Wayne*

Boston, Massachusetts   Burr Ridge, Illinois   Dubuque, Iowa
Madison, Wisconsin   New York, New York   San Francisco, California   St. Louis, Missouri

McGraw-Hill

A Division of The **McGraw·Hill** *Companies*

THE DEVELOPMENT OF WESTERN MUSIC

This book is printed on acid-free paper.

8 9 0 VNH/VNH 9 0 9 8 7 6 5 4

ISBN 0–697–29379–3

Publisher: Phil Butcher
Sponsoring Editor: Christopher Freitag
Developmental Editor: JoElaine Retzler
Marketing Manager: Margaret Metz
Project Manager: Marilyn Rothenberger
Production Supervisor: Mary Jess
Designer: Maureen McCutcheon
Photo research coordinator: John Leland
Art Editor: Joyce Watters
Compositor: A-R Editions, Inc.
Typeface: Berkeley
Printer: Von Hoffman Press, Inc.

Library of Congress Catalog Card Number 96–79544

www.mhhe.com

S. D. G.

Table of Contents

Insights

Preface to the Third Edition

Since the time of Pierre Michon, known as Abbé Bourdelot (1610–85), interested persons have gathered information preparatory to writing the history of music "from the earliest times down to the present day." And from 1690, when Wolfgang Printz brought out his *Historische Beschreibung der edelen Sing-und-Klingkunst . . .*, histories of music have been written and published. Historians, musicologists, and even archaeologists continue to delve into the past in a seemingly insatiable quest for knowledge. Their research broadens the spectrum; their finds cast new light on persons, places, and productions. This necessitates repainting the panorama to include new features, alter shadings to conform to facts, and remove details no longer pertinent. The result is a historical picture more meaningful, more enlightening, and, it is hoped, more comprehensible to the observer. This third edition of *The Development of Western Music: A History* incorporates data from recent research in a number of areas and updates the accounts of accomplishments of significant late-twentieth-century composers.

Maps are vital to any historical study, and chronologies and comparative charts that summarize concisely the main developments of an era should be included in both specialized and generalized histories. Such items are features of this music history text.

Music is not a cloistered art. It reflects and is directly affected by contemporary conditions and world affairs. Therefore, a music history must take into account important events in areas other than music. In this book, most of the chapters begin with a general historical overview, and each chapter concludes with a summary of the developments in music discussed therein. Chronologies, in the form of charts, place musical developments in proper perspective with world events and thus help present a true picture of the relationship between music and government, politics,

economics, science, literature, art, and so on. Some color plates correlate artworks with specific compositions and/or historical developments in music; other color plates show significant manuscript folios.

A history text should be interesting to read as well as accurate and informative. As history was being made, the participants were interested in and probably excited about what they were doing; the same kind of interest and enthusiasm should pervade the study of the history they made. Music history is not an account of dead people in a dull past but a recounting of the endeavors and accomplishments of persons going about their daily affairs, coping with the demands of earning a living, composing and performing to meet contemporary needs, whether those needs were their own or those of others. Moreover, music history is not merely a study of the arrangement of symbols on staff paper; it is also a consideration of all that went into making musical compositions that were performed and enjoyed when they were created and that can be re-created for the same kind of enjoyment in modern performances. Biographies provide glimpses of the conditions under which composers worked and the particular circumstances that prompted them to create specific compositions.

This third edition of *The Development of Western Music: A History* traces the development of Western art music from antiquity to the present—from c. 18,000 B.C. into the mid-1990s. Throughout the book, the contributions made by women—as authors, composers, copyists, engravers, performers, and patrons—are duly considered. Music in the Americas is introduced in chapter 16, in connection with seventeenth-century instrumental music, and is a regular part of the discussion thereafter. A chapter is devoted to nationalism in nineteenth-century music; two complete chapters, and almost all of another, concern twentieth-century music. Included is an account of the technological discoveries, inventions, and advances that enabled avant-garde musicians to create the variety of styles that have colored the twentieth century. An abundance of figures and music examples illustrate the text, and "Insights" present interesting and enlightening material closely related to the text.

The historical coverage is full, and headings clearly designate topics under discussion. The Table of Contents constitutes a general outline of the book. Therefore, instructors who wish to omit certain sections (e.g., Scandinavian, Canadian, or Latin American music or that of minor composers) should find it relatively easy to do so.

Analyses of a sufficient number of compositions are included in the text to represent a composer's output and style characteristics and to permit the instructor to select those he or she wishes to emphasize.

Titles of compositions are stated in the original language with English translation in parentheses, except for Cyrillic Slavic and Russian titles, which are given only in English. The date of composition and, where appropriate, the instrumentation of the work are stated when the composition is first mentioned. A few abbreviations are used: LU for *Liber Usualis,* KJV for King James Version of the Bible, and standard abbreviations for voices and instruments. References to *LU* are to the 1959 edition.

Terms, when introduced, are presented in boldface type and then defined. Definitions also appear in the Glossary. A Guide to the Correct Pronunciation of Church Latin is in the Appendix. The Select Bibliography is designed to provide for students' further reading and research on the subject matter presented in the text.

Auxiliary to the history text is *The Development of Western Music: An Anthology,* in two volumes, whose selections are recorded and are obtainable in CD or cassette form. In the text, the letters DWMA followed by a number indicate the presence and location of a composition in the Anthology. Volume 1 of the Anthology contains representative selections of music from ancient times through the Baroque era, and volume 2 contains music from the Classic era through the twentieth century.

Available ancillaries include a set of transparencies, an Instructor's Manual with Test Item File, and a computerized TestPak for use with Macintosh and IBM computers.

Particular thanks are due to Robert Roubos, formerly my department chairman at Indiana University–Purdue University Fort Wayne (IPFW), who urged me to write this text; to the late Ruth Harrod, who constantly encouraged me during the first stages of the writing; and to Karen Speerstra, who was quick to recognize the worth of the project and to further its publication. Thanks are due also to the many students in my music history classes who requested that I put in writing the interesting details that made music history live for them.

It is impossible to name everyone who contributed to this project. From time to time, several of my colleagues have given me the benefit of their specialized knowledge and have loaned me music from their personal libraries. Many librarians assisted in procuring materials for my research. Great demands have been made on the Music Library at Indiana University, Bloomington, and thanks are due especially to R. Michael Fling and David Lasocky, Music Librarians, who have responded promptly to my requests for materials. The InterLibrary Loan/Document Delivery Department at IPFW and the reference librarians at Helmke Library, IPFW, and the Allen County Public Library were helpful, efficient, and generous with their time. I wish to express my gratitude to Kenneth Balthaser, who made available the services of the technicians at the IPFW Learning Resource Center for the preparation of specialized illustrations, particularly cartographer artist Melvin E. Stewart, graphics artist Roberta Sandy Shadle, and photographers James Whitcraft and Elmer Denman.

I wish to express my appreciation to my editors at McGraw-Hill who carefully considered my requests. I appreciate the work of the many reviewers who read these chapters in their various stages, offered valuable suggestions, and occasionally made pertinent comments that sent my thoughts in new directions, sometimes in ways the reviewers probably had not intended.

K Marie Stolba
Fort Wayne, Indiana

Reviewers for Third Edition

James M. Anthony
Towson State University

Sandra Barnes
University of Cincinnati

Daniel Beller-McKenna
University of South Carolina

Linda Cockey
Salisbury State University

Polly Elizabeth Detels
East Texas State University

Peter M. Gano
The Ohio State University

Sharon E. Girard
San Francisco State

Ernest Harriss II
University of Tennessee at Martin

Dane Heuchemer
Kenyon College

Scott Messing
Alma College

Timothy Roden
Ohio Wesleyan University

ABOUT THE AUTHOR

Violinist, composer, musicologist, and educator, K Marie Stolba is Professor of Music, Emerita, at Indiana University—Purdue University Fort Wayne (IPFW) and Visiting Distinguished Lecturer in Music at Colorado Christian University, Lakewood. She received her B.A. from Monmouth College, Monmouth, Illinois; her M.A. from the University of Northern Colorado, Greeley; and her Ph.D. in Musicology from the University of Iowa, Iowa City. In May 1990, Monmouth College conferred on her the degree of Doctor of Humane Letters and in May 1995 inducted her into their Hall of Achievement.

Dr. Stolba has taught a variety of music courses for over 40 years. She is the author of several scholarly articles and monographs, including *A History of the Violin Étude to about 1800.*

THE
DEVELOPMENT
OF WESTERN
MUSIC

A HISTORY

The system of pitch identification used throughout this book:

PRELUDE

$\mathcal{M}$usic has existed from time immemorial. Archaeologists have unearthed traces of music in the most ancient civilizations, ethnomusicologists have found it in even the most primitive tribal cultures, and scientists have claimed it is present in space. Yet no one has been able to establish precisely when, where, why, or how music originated.

In both Oriental and Occidental cultures there are numerous assertions and inferences that music is of divine origin. Plato placed the origin of music in creation, and numerous legends present music as the gift of the gods or the invention of one of them. Some peoples (e.g., the Hebrews and the Hindus) firmly root music's origin in their sacred scriptures. The Hindus believe that Brahma, the creator, placed music in the Vedas, their four sacred writings, to be interpreted and revealed to man by an ascetic brotherhood called Munis. Vedic psalmody, a type of sung recitation, was an essential element in the worship of the Aryans in India approximately 1,500 years before the Christian era. The Hebrews account for the origin of music by tracing in the scrolls of the Torah the genealogy from Cain, son of Adam and Eve, through the

A relief of a musician discovered in Khafajah, Mesopotamia; dated c. 2000 B.C. *(NAD) National Archeological Museum, Athens (Greek TAP Service)*

seventh generation to Jubal, who was "the father of all such as handle the lyre and pipe [flute]" (Gen. 4:17–21). The Hebrew words used for those instruments account for both serene and sensuous music, and the instrument types are comparable with those of the ancient Greeks.

Our noun *music* was originally an adjective derived from *Muse,* a Greek term denoting any one of nine goddesses who collectively presided over song and prompted the memory and each of whom individually governed a particular realm of literature, art, or science. Apollo, guardian of the Muses, was god of "music" (*mousikē,* arts presided over by the Muses). He played the lyre, which Hermes (Mercury) supposedly invented by boring nine holes into each end of a tortoise shell and threading cords through them, one cord representing each Muse. It was natural, then, that the representative instrument of the Greek cult of Apollo was the lyre.

According to Greek mythology, Athena (Minerva), patroness of arts and trades, invented the *aulos,* which she threw to earth when Eros (Cupid) taunted her because she made faces when playing it. This was the instrument associated with the orgiastic cult of Dionysus (Bacchus), god of wine in all its aspects—social, benevolent, and intoxicating.

A more recent theory (**monogenesis**) proposes that in all cultures music originated in a similar manner, that is, from a universal source. The investigations of these theorists are comparable with linguists' search for a universal source of language through a study of features common to all tongues. Certainly, the fact that ethnomusicologists report finding basic similarities in the musical beginnings of various cultures in widely separated parts of the world lends credence to such a theory. There is also the possibility that music originated from the desire of primitive people to communicate, vocally or instrumentally, with their neighbors; that primitive people first sang because they wanted to imitate the sound of a bird or other creature; or that in exultation or sorrow a primitive person produced sounds that relieved emotions and that were pleasurable to repeat.

Each theory concerning the origin of music—whether fact, fiction, or still unproven scientific investigation—has its place in the history of Western music. Mythology, legends, and the musics of ancient cultures have influenced Western art music significantly. Therefore, this historical account of the development of Western music will begin with a consideration of our musical heritage from ancient peoples.

HERITAGE FROM ANTIQUITY

Our heritage of written music from antiquity is meager. Much of this **primary source** material is fragmentary and undecipherable. The few pieces to be located were fairly recent finds and consist mainly of vocal music. Archaeologists continue to find evidence of music in very ancient civilizations—instruments made from mammoth bones c. 18,000 B.C. were discovered in the Ukraine—but they rarely find actual music.

In Paris, Mme Haïk-Vantoura has transcribed the little marks that appear both above and below the words in some scrolls containing the Hebrew Old Testament of the Bible. She believes these marks correspond to melodic formulas or symbols known as *ta'amim* (fig. 1.1). Those Bible verses may be more than 3,000 years old. Probably, Hebrew *ta'amim* symbols served as models for some of the earliest notation of Christian church chants.

MESOPOTAMIAN MUSIC

During the last third of the twentieth century, research by scientists studying ancient Near Eastern civilizations indicates that Mesopotamia, often referred to as "the cradle of Eurasian civilization," may be the cradle of Western music theory. Assyriologists' translations of the cuneiform writing on several of the many clay tablets that archaeologists

FIGURE 1.1 Psalm 137, from Hebrew Scriptures, with **ta'amim** markings. (*Source: Psalm 137, "By the Waters of Babylon," Hebrew Scriptures*)

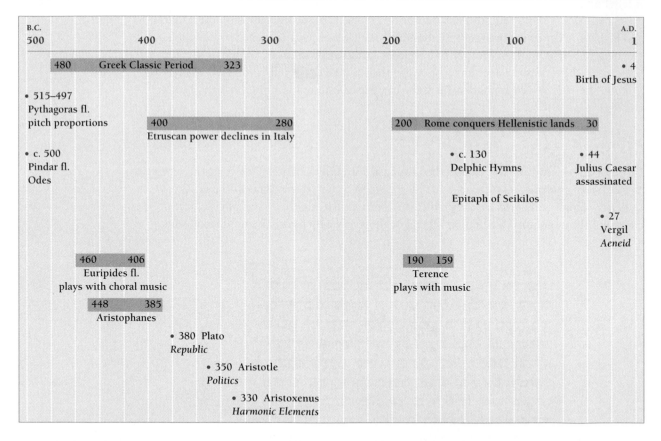

B.C. 2500	2000	1500	1000	B.C 500

Sumerian City-States

• c. 2300 Ebla: singers

• c. 1790–1750 Babylon: Hammurabi
• c. 1760 Code of Laws

• c. 1330 Egypt: Tutankhamen Pharaoh

• c. 1000 Israel: King David *Psalms*

• 753 Rome founded • 660 Byzantium founded

700 510 Etruscan domination of north-central Italy

• c. 1500 India: Vedic psalmody

• c. 1600 Mesopotamia: diatonic scale modes modulation

• c. 1400 Ugarit: Hymn to Nikkal lyre, kithara

• c. 790 Homer *Iliad* • 586 Sakadas programmatic aulos solo at Pythian games

B.C. 500	400	300	200	100	A.D. 1

480 Greek Classic Period 323

• 515–497 Pythagoras fl. pitch proportions

400 Etruscan power declines in Italy 280

• c. 500 Pindar fl. Odes

200 Rome conquers Hellenistic lands 30

• c. 130 Delphic Hymns

Epitaph of Seikilos

• 4 Birth of Jesus

• 44 Julius Caesar assassinated

• 27 Vergil *Aeneid*

460 406 Euripides fl. plays with choral music

448 385 Aristophanes

190 159 Terence plays with music

• 380 Plato *Republic*

• 350 Aristotle *Politics*

• 330 Aristoxenus *Harmonic Elements*

unearthed at the ancient city-states of Assur, Ebla, Nippur, Ugarit, and Ur (fig. 1.2)—tablets dating from the third and second millenia B.C.—have yielded a list of professions that includes instrumentalists and sing-ers, lexical texts containing musicological terms, instructions for tuning a lyra or kithara, a catalog of songs listed according to type and tuning (mode), and lyrics, music, and performance instructions for at least

FIGURE 1.2 The ancient Near East.

Babylonian Music Theory

INSIGHT

Combined research by Assyriologists, philologists, and musicologists indicates that the Babylonian method of determining musical pitches is identical with the Greek method, the discovery of which has been credited (erroneously) to Pythagoras. The Babylonians' basic tuning of the 9-stringed lyra produces a scale pattern that is identical with the Greek Dorian; extension of that tuning on the 15-stringed lyra or kithara produces the same scale as the Greeks' Greater Perfect system (see p. 15). Babylonians used a diatonic heptatonic scale whose first pitch, when its vibrations were doubled, produced the octave. The Babylonians gave the same special significance to the *qablītu,* the middle pitch in their heptatonic scale, that the Greeks gave to the *mese* (p. 16).

The Babylonians used a system of seven scale species that was identical with the Greek system described by Ptolemy. The Babylonians modulated in a manner that produced results identical with those described and illustrated by Ptolemy (p. 16).

32 Hurrian cult hymns, one which has been transcribed (fig. 1.3). This song, our most ancient example of music (DWMA1), is a hymn to Nikkal, wife of the moon god. Cracks in the tablet have obliterated some of the text. The hymn has four stanzas, each with refrain: stanzas 1 and 4 use the same music, and stanzas 2 and 3 are identical musically. The refrains have different texts but use the same music or an abbreviated version of it. The singer is accompanied by lyra; the harmony includes many thirds and sixths, a few fourths, and one fifth.

When combined and tested, data from these tablets revealed startling similarities between Babylonian principles of music theory and those used by the Greeks.

(Insights, "Babylonian Music Theory"; "Greek Music Theory.") Moreover, the Babylonian principles *antedate the Greek ones by more than a millenium.*

The Babylonians seem to have used music exclusively in connection with religious observances and festivals. The names of lyra/kithara strings and musical pitches were related to their cult deities and to the

FIGURE 1.3 Hurrian hymn to Nikkal, in cuneiform notation on a clay tablet from Ugarit; dated c. 1400 B.C. *(National Museum, Damascus, Syria)*

planets in a cosmology that was similar to Greek philosophers' "harmony of the spheres" (p. 13).

It is believed that the Semite, Hittite, and various other tribes who conquered Mesopotamian city-states transmitted the elements of Babylonian music to their civilizations. Eventually, these Babylonian materials were absorbed and adapted by the Greeks.

GREEK MUSIC

Approximately 15 examples of ancient Greek music survive, all from comparatively late periods in Greek history. The most important of these are as follows:

1. Two *Delphic Hymns to Apollo* (c. 130 B.C.). Both hymns are incomplete because the stones on which they are incised have been damaged. The *First Delphic Hymn* is the most extensive example of Greek music we have and is written in the "vocal" notation of that era (fig. 1.4; DWMA2). Probably, this hymn was sung by a priestess at the Delphic oracle. The *Second Delphic Hymn,* ascribed to Limenius of Athens, is in "instrumental" notation. Both notation types use Greek letters as symbols in a kind of tablature.

2. *Epitaph of Seikilos* (second century B.C. or later). This *skolion,* or drinking song, carved into a tombstone, was discovered near Tralles in Asia Minor in 1883. The short song is complete—every syllable of text is set to music, and rhythmic signs are chiseled above pitches (fig. 1.5; DWMA3). The music is in Phrygian mode (see p. 16).

3. *Hymn to the Muse* (actually two poems): *Hymn to the Sun* and *Hymn to Nemesis* (fig. 1.6). The latter two are attributed to Mesomedes of Crete (d. A.D. 138). These hymns were located by Girolamo Mei in a library in Italy. He sent them to Vincenzo Galilei, who published them untranscribed in his *Dialogo della musica antica et della moderna* (Dialogue about ancient and modern music; 1581).

Papyrus fragments in Greek notation, probably from the third century A.D., were located at Oxyrhynchos, Egypt (fig. 1.7). One of these contains the earliest notated example of a Christian hymn. Among other papyrus fragments are some lines from Euripides' tragedy *Orestes* with music from a choral antistrophe (the second of two paired verses) written down sometime

FIGURE 1.4 *First Delphic Hymn,* in ancient Greek notation incised in stone; dated c. 130 B.C. *(National Archaeological Museum, Delphi, Greece)*

FIGURE 1.5 *Epitaph of Seikilos,* in ancient Greek notation incised in tomb stele. *(Copenhagen, Danish National Museum)*

between 250 and 150 B.C.; a portion of a paean to Apollo; some lines, presumably from a tragedy, concerning the suicide of Ajax the elder; and some bits of instrumental music. Also, Friedrich Bellermann included some Greek instrumental music in *Anonymi scriptio de musica* (Anonymous writings about music; 1841).

These items constitute the **primary sources** available for a study of Greek music—items that were all located after c. 1565. Fortunately, our knowledge of Greek music is not limited to these few extant pieces of music, because **secondary sources** are available: surviving artifacts such as vases decorated with paintings of persons holding instruments or performing on them, actual musical instruments, literary writings, and treatises. Scholars have studied these materials and have pieced together a picture of the Greek view of music, its place in society, and a little about

the theoretical processes to which it was subjected. Admittedly, this collage is neither complete nor definitive.

MUSICAL INSTRUMENTS

In ancient Greece, vocal music was preferred and musical virtuosity discouraged. Though instrumental solos were comparatively rare, instrumental music was functional, and several types of instruments were in use.

The main string instruments were the *lyra* (fig. 1.8), used by amateurs, and the *kithara* (fig. 1.9), favored by professionals. Both instrument types had been borrowed from Ur or Sumeria. Basically, the two instruments were of similar construction, each having a resonator from which projected two curved arms connected by a crossbar. A variable number of gut strings (from 3 to 11 on the kithara) were stretched from the resonator across a bridge to the crossbar. The soundbox of the lyra was a tortoise-shell bowl topped with a skin belly; the kithara's resonator was a square, rather flat wooden box. The strings were plucked with either the fingers or a plectrum. In performance, the lyra was held tilted, but the larger and more cumbersome kithara was held more or less upright. The player probably used "gapped" tuning (not strictly pentatonic), which was determined by the

FIGURE 1.7 Location of Oxyrhynchos in the Nile valley.

FIGURE 1.6 *Hymn to Nemesis*, attributed to Mesomedes. *(Source: Vincenzo Galilei, Dialogo della musica antico et della moderna, 1581)*

HERITAGE FROM ANTIQUITY

FIGURE 1.8 Interior of a white kylix: Apollo holding lyra and pouring libations. *(National Archaeological Museum, Delphi, Greece)*

FIGURE 1.9 Greek youth playing kithara and singing. *(Greek Vases, Attic. Early V c. B.C. Attributed to the Berlin painter, said to be from Nola. Metropolitan Museum of Art, New York City, Fletcher Fund, 1956)*

requirements of the music, and made whatever adjustments or adaptations were necessary by stopping the strings.

The most important wind instrument was the *aulos,* a double-reed instrument composed of a pair of even pipes, usually with four finger holes each. The player held one pipe in each hand and inserted the reeds into the mouth through slits in a wide leather band (*phorbeia*) that covered the mouth and was fastened at the back of the head (plate 1). The *phorbeia* provided support for both the pipes and the inflated cheeks of the performer. The aulos player probably controlled pitches in much the same manner as a modern oboist, that is, by the devices of "lipping" and over- or underblowing the pitches.

The *syrinx* was a shepherd's pipe made by fastening together reed pipes of equal length to form a raftlike shape. These reeds were closed at one end and were stopped with wax at graduated intervals so that different pitches could be produced from the individual reeds. From 3 to 13 reeds might be included, though generally 7 were used.

Brass instruments served military purposes but were considered secondary to the aulos. They included the *salpinx,* a straight trumpet, and the *keras,* a curved brass horn. Both had mouthpieces of horn.

Around the third century B.C., the *hydraulos* (*hydōr,* "water"; *aulos,* "pipe") was invented. In this early type of organ, the wind supply was regulated by the weight of the water in a partially filled reservoir.

Percussion instruments included the *tympanon,* a two-headed frame drum; *kymbala,* cymbals approximately 12 inches in diameter played in pairs, especially used in orgiastic rites; and *krotala,* clappers constructed in pairs. The *kroupalon* was a conductor's device that was used percussively to beat time. It consisted of a wooden clapper attached to a sandal that was worn on the player's right foot.

THE GREEK VIEW OF MUSIC

The Greeks regarded music in three ways: (1) as an abstract science, a branch of mathematics whose elements could be computed; (2) as a power, a shaping force that could influence both the individual and the state; and (3) as an art, to be understood, enjoyed, and practiced by the citizens as intelligent amateurs but not as professionals. Music was associated with melody, words, and rhythm, including dancing; instrumental accompaniment to song was by duplicating the melodic line and adding occasional heterophony but without counterpoint to or chordal accompaniment of the melody. This view of music and these features of the music itself seem to have remained constant through the ages. However, musical conditions were not identical in all periods of ancient Greek history.

From the eighth century B.C., poets associated their lines with music, called the sections of their epics "cantos," included in their verses references to music, and presented their poems (wholly or partially) in song. Homer, in the *Iliad,* treated music as an accomplishment of both gods and men; in the *Odyssey,* the power of song was invoked to staunch the bleeding of a wound. Vergil, writing in Latin some centuries later, commenced his *Aeneid* with the words *Arma virumque canō . . .* ("I sing of arms and the man . . ."). There is no reason to doubt that Vergil sang his epic, even though no actual music survives. Music was created anew for each performance, so preservation of notation was unnecessary.

At Pythia (Delphi) in the sixth century B.C., games were designed for competition in music and poetry. At the Pythian Games held in 586 B.C., a person named Sakadas was awarded a prize for playing on the aulos a *nome* (a solo) describing the fight between Apollo and the dragon. Also, the **strophic dithyramb** stems from the sixth century B.C., when it was used by a circular chorus of 50 males to commemorate in song and dance the birth of Dionysus. A strophic dithyramb is a wildly emotional poem constructed in verses, according to a special formal pattern. This poetic form, combined with song and the sounds of the aulos, remained a part of the cult of Dionysus from that time; in combination with choric dance, it gave rise to that drama known as tragedy.

Skolia (sing., *skolion*) were sung by men at drinking parties, each man in turn contributing a line as he quaffed a goblet of wine and then passing the responsibility zigzag (hence the name *skolion,* "zigzag") across the table to a colleague.

In Aeolia, Pindar created odes that were performed with kithara accompaniment. He used the terms *Aeolian* and *Dorian* interchangeably when describing music. By the end of the fifth century B.C., the term *Aeolian* had virtually disappeared from musical use,

and the prevalent types of tunings were Dorian and Phrygian. The Dorian mode, which was diatonic, stable, and classic, was associated with the ode and the kithara (or lyra) and was used to create lyric music for the worship of Apollo. The Phrygian mode, which was described as "chromatic" and considerably less stable, was combined with the somewhat wavering and more pliable tones of the aulos to present, through the dithyramb, the ecstatic music of Dionysian rites.

The Athenians frequented the theater to witness or to participate in performances of tragedy and comedy. These dramas incorporated a citizen chorus that was composed of amateurs whose knowledge of music and choreography was limited to the training they received as part of the three years of such education required by the state. The tones of a single aulos played by a professional supported such a chorus, which performed a melodic line either in unison or in octaves. Euripides, in his later plays, and Aristophanes reduced the size of the chorus and inserted pieces of lyric **monody** (Greek *monōdos,* solo song) to be sung by an actor. From time to time, in composing lyrics for these songs, Euripides and Aristophanes deviated from the classic norm by writing **through-composed** rather than **strophic** monodies. (A through-composed setting has new music for each line of a poem; in a strophic song, all stanzas are sung to the same music.) No music for these survives; doubtless the actor-singer improvised the melodies. That accompanied solo song existed is clear from references to *nomos kitharōdikos,* a solo sung by an actor who accompanied himself on the kithara, and *nomos aulōdikos,* which required two performers: a vocal soloist and his accompanist (an aulos player).

Classic Greek comedy served also as a vehicle for music criticism. Directly and in parody, Aristophanes inserted into some of his plays lines that voiced his displeasure with the music presented by some of his contemporaries. For example, in *Frogs,* he parodied Euripides' manner of repeating syllables of a word, a kind of musical stuttering.

In the fourth century B.C., virtuoso performers rose to prominence but, though admired, were not accorded high social standing. The aristocratic Greeks did not pursue music to the extent that they were considered professionals. Choral singing was still taught to boys, who at that time received only two years of required music education, but adult participation in music declined so much that it became necessary to import professionals to serve in the "citizen" chorus.

PHILOSOPHY AND THE DOCTRINE OF *ETHOS*

Greek philosophers who wrote in the fourth century B.C. said a great deal about music: what it had been, what it was in their time, and what they wished it to be. Plato, in *Laws,* wrote about the changes that had occurred in music: (1) the classic purity of former times had succumbed to popular taste; (2) professional virtuosi who adhered to traditional practices were scorned by the public, who preferred the vulgarity of "modern" music; and (3) musical forms—prayers (*hymnia*), dirges, paeans, dithyrambs, and others—once held inviolate had been carelessly intermingled. For Plato, the "sung poem" was the important part of music, not the strumming of the lyra or kithara that duplicated or varied the melodic line.

In the *Republic,* Plato discoursed on the organization of a utopia in which music would build harmonious personalities and calm human passions and gymnastics would build healthy bodies. Music and gymnastics were divine gifts to mankind that provided the proper degree of tension and relaxation to adjust the soul and the body harmoniously. Music without gymnastics would completely dissolve a man's spirit; gymnastics untempered by contact with the Muse would foster in man a beastly nature—violence and savagery. And what constituted musicianship? According to Plato, the most perfect and most harmonious musician was the man who could best blend gymnastics with music and apply them to the soul, not the person who played the kithara well. In Plato's utopia, music and gymnastics would form an important part of the education of boys—an education carefully regulated by the government.

In *Politics,* Aristotle discussed the studies that should be included in education in the ideal state and justified music as one of these not only because of its value as a leisure pastime but also because it had the power to produce a certain effect on the moral character of the soul. All men should be educated in music, but only the young should take part in it as performers because professional musicians were considered vul-

gar people. Older persons should not make music but merely listen and judge what they heard.

Athenaeus recorded in *Deipnosophists* daily conversations of the Sophists concerning music, mentioning and commenting on treatises written by more ancient Greek authors. *Deipnosophists* is especially valuable because Athenaeus specified those treatises by title and author and quoted from some writings that have not survived. The matter of the mysterious power of music to influence and shape character (*ethos*) entered into the discussions of the Sophists.

The doctrine of **ethos** received considerable attention from the Greek philosophers. For the Greeks, the term *ethos* had a dual meaning: (a) the morals and character of the people (thus it was related to ethics) and (b) the specific character of a musical mode or tuning that affected the morals and character of the people. The morals and character (*ethos*) of the people were important, for the welfare of the state was determined by the ethics of its people. Music, through its influential power, was a shaping force in determining the nature of the moral character of the populace; therefore, music should be included in education and regulated carefully by the state. Music's power to affect persons favorably or adversely was derived from its structure in that music was constructed according to the same mathematical principles by which the universe had been formed. Thus, music stood in direct relationship to the universe as microcosm to macrocosm. The so-called golden equations written down by Plato in *Timaeus* support the philosophy that God created the universe musico-mathematically, using the same proportions that determine the intervals of the musical scale.

Athenaeus wrote that each mode possessed a specific character (*ethos*) or feeling (*pathos*). Any philosopher who devoted any attention to music gave some consideration to the peculiar attributes that each of the different modes possessed and that each mode was capable of instilling into listeners. The various rhythms affected persons in similar ways, and instrumental timbres could depress, stabilize, or excite performers and auditors. For example, it was thought that the Mixolydian mode produced mournful and restrained reactions; the Lydian was considered effeminate; the Dorian was sober yet intense and fostered composure, bravery, and virility; and the Phrygian and the aulos were violently exciting and emotional, especially suited for Bacchic versification, the dithyramb, and choric dance. Aristotle stated that it was not easy to explain precisely what potency music expressed, but it was clear that the various kinds of melodies, rhythms, and tunings affected persons in dramatically different ways. Music was peculiar among the arts in that it alone had the ability to influence character, and exposure to certain modal tunings over long periods of time brought about the characteristics of that mode in the nature of the listener. Because of its stabilizing and virile attributes, Dorian was the preferred tuning and the one thought to produce in citizens the most desirable character. Inasmuch as the factors of music are melody and rhythm, Aristotle wrote, music with a "good" rhythm and a "good" melody was to be preferred. Music could help in defeating an enemy, for by exposing the enemy to music with weakening attributes one could weaken his defenses. (No one mentioned what might happen to the performers.)

MUSIC OF THE SPHERES

The association of music with astronomy and the relationship of certain modes with certain heavenly bodies was a natural outgrowth of the classification of music as one of the mathematical sciences: arithmetic, geometry, astronomy, and music—the four sciences that later became the *quadrivium* of the university curriculum. In the *Republic* and in *Timaeus,* Plato wrote about the "music of the spheres," a phrase and a topic that would be taken up in later centuries by several authors and composers, including Shakespeare and Paul Hindemith (See p. 22). Claudius Ptolemy (second century A.D.), in his *Harmonics,* presented first the theoretical principles of music. He then applied the same ratios and proportions to a consideration of astronomic features of the cosmos and explained the universe as being bound together by mathematico-musical principles.

From the time of Pythagoras of Samos (sixth century B.C.), the Greeks regarded music as a branch of mathematics (Insight, "Greek Music Theory"). Intervals computed mathematically were visibly demonstrated by means of the monochord, a device consisting of a single string stretched, over a movable

FIGURE 1.10 Guido d'Arezzo, *seated at left,* demonstrates use of monochord marked with pitches of the scale from Γ through a (modern G – a′), including both square and round b. Miniature in twelfth-century MS Wn 51, fol. 35v. *(Österreichische Nationalbibliothek, Vienna)*

bridge, across the calibrated upper surface of a long rectangular box (fig. 1.10).

MUSIC IN ANCIENT ROME

Present knowledge of Rome's early music is based entirely on secondary sources; no ancient Roman music has been located. Undoubtedly, some indigenous Roman music was produced, but nothing seems to have survived. What music the Romans played or sang, how they performed it, and what techniques were used in its production are unknown to us, but play and sing they did! Literary accounts describe instruments and performances; cues for music (without music notation) are included in the prefaces of some of Terence's plays; statutes regulated the number and kinds of musicians permitted to perform on certain occasions (e.g., the number of pipers who might be employed to provide music at a funeral); artists depicted in fresco, relief, and mosaic various musical instruments as well as performers playing instruments

(continued on page 17)

Much remains to be learned about Greek music theory. There is still confusion and disagreement concerning what has been uncovered so far, but a core of data is regarded as factual.

RHYTHM

The rhythm of Greek music was that of its poetry. Quantitative rather than qualitative, it is comparable with the long and short patterns known as "iambic," "trochaic," and so on. The matter of stress or accent seems to have been of little importance. For compositions in free verse, such as the skolion of Seikilos, the temporal unit (*chronos*) might be stated above the notation (fig. 1.5). No marking indicated the *chronos protos,* or one beat; a single line ⎯ two beats; ⌐ or ∟ three beats; ⊔ four beats; and ⊔⊔ five beats. A complete or partial *lambda* (λ or \ ) designated a rest.

TETRACHORDS AND SYSTEMS

The extant portions of Aristoxenus's (born c. 360 B.C.) *Harmonics* and *Elements* are the oldest theoretical writings on Greek scales. Aristoxenus systematically presented the theoretical principles of his era, which probably were based, to a considerable extent, on the teaching of his predecessors. To Aristoxenus, the range of sound was a line like a monochord string, containing pitches, and the distance from one pitch to another was an interval. He divided the octave into six equal tones, the tone into two equal semitones, and the semitone into two equal quarter tones. However, in contrast with the Pythagoreans, who calculated and expressed musical intervals as mathematical ratios, Aristoxenus believed that musical intervals should be measured by the trained ear.

The basis of practical Greek music theory was the **tetrachord,** a descending succession of four tones, the highest and lowest of which were a perfect fourth apart. The highest and lowest pitches of this fundamental four-tone unit remained constant, but the location of the two pitches within these limits was variable. The two inner tones might be arranged in any one of three different patterns to form three different *genera,* or types, of tetrachord: diatonic, chromatic, or enharmonic. The diatonic *genus* exhibited the normal (natural) arrangement of the four tones, the first or highest interval containing two semitones (a whole tone), followed by another whole tone and a semitone (ex. 1.1a). This tone-tone-semitone (T T S) pattern corresponded with the first segment of the characteristic octave of the Greater Perfect System (ex. 1.2).

In the chromatic genus, the first interval was expanded to contain three semitones, and the space remaining was divided into two semitones (ex. 1.1b). In the enharmonic genus, the first interval was widened still further to contain four semitones, and the division of the remaining space produced two quarter tones (ex. 1.1c). Possibly, in performance this remaining space was sometimes divided unequally, producing microtones of varying proportions rather than two actual quarter tones. Tones such as b♯ and c′ were not identical in Greek theory. The modern piano produces such tones as identical pitches, but wind and brass players can "lip" the tones to differentiate them, and string players can adjust fingers to achieve this.

Tetrachords were combined to form scale patterns. This joining

might be disjunct, with the lowest note of one tetrachord being placed just above the highest note of the other, or conjunct, with the lowest note of the upper tetrachord being identical with the highest note of the lower tetrachord. Two diatonic tetrachords joined disjunctly formed a diatonic octave, or diatonic scale (ex. 1.2; central octave e′–e).

Two scale systems were formed: the Greater Perfect System and the Lesser Perfect System (ex. 1.2). The Greater consisted of a two-octave scale formed from two pairs of conjunct tetrachords joined disjunctly, with the neighboring tone A, called *Proslambanomenos,* added as the last pitch. At the center of the system was the note a, called *Mese* ("middle"). Each tetrachord in the scale system was named according to its position within the system, and each pitch within each tetrachord bore a double name indicating the tetrachord to which it belonged and its position within that tetrachord. These names did *not* designate actual pitch but were merely terms of reference for locations within the system. The fact that the names were assigned on the basis of the position of the kithara when played (the lowest pitches being at the top of the instrument when held in playing position) explains the peculiarity of the Greek scale patterns seeming to proceed downward from highest pitch to lowest—just the opposite of our modern scales.

Central within the Greater Perfect System was the octave e′–e, called the Dorian octave or mode and frequently referred to by modern theorists as the "characteristic octave." Its central location may explain the preference of Plato, Aristotle, and other

EXAMPLE 1.1 The three Greek tetrachords: (*a*) diatonic, (*b*) chromatic, and (*c*) enharmonic.

EXAMPLE 1.2 The Greater Perfect and the Lesser Perfect Systems.

Greek writers for this particular arrangement of tones.

The Lesser Perfect System was formed from three conjunct tetrachords plus the *Proslambanomenos*. The top tetrachord (*synemmenon*, "hooked") may be represented by the pitches d'–c'–b♭–a.

MODES, OR *TONOI*

No discussion of Greek music theory can be considered complete without some discussion of modes, or *tonoi*. Yet this is the area of least established fact and of the most confusion and disagreement. Several theories have been proposed, two of which are derived from Ptolemy's *Harmon-ics*, which is considered the best scientific treatise on the theory of musical scales that we possess in Greek.

One theory presents a mode as a definite pattern of tones and semitones within the compass of an octave and having a definite tonal center. Each mode was distinctive. Thus, the Dorian scale or mode proceeded from e' down to e, the Phrygian from d' down to d, and so on in scale patterns using no chromatically altered tones (ex. 1.3, col. 3). The Dorian scale presented the sequence of tones (T) and semitones (S): T T S T T T S; the Phrygian presented the succession: T S T T T S T; and other modes had particular suc-

cessions. This theory is based on Ptolemy's description of the scale patterns by functional position within the Greater Perfect System, for example, the Dorian proceeding from *Nete Diezeugmenon* to *Hypate Meson* and the Phrygian from *Paranete Diezeugmenon* to *Lichanos Hypaton*. (Example 1.2 shows the functional names.) It is believed that the Greeks did not confine themselves to the tones in their systems or scales as absolute pitches but that the pitches were relative and could be adjusted to fit the vocal range of the singer. However, the arrangement of tones and semitones within a mode was carefully observed.

A more recent theory, also based on Ptolemy's *Harmonics*, states that (1) only one octave series had practical use, e'–e, the central octave of the Greater Perfect System; (2) this was a characteristic pattern of tones and semitones that was transposed upward and downward along the pitches of the Greater Perfect System; and (3) those tones that overflowed the range of the e'–e octave were transferred from the top to the bottom of the scale (or vice versa) so that they would fit within the central octave. This would create a different arrangement of the tones and semitones within that central octave for each adjusted transposed scale. For example, according to the newer theory, the Phrygian pattern was obtained by first transposing the scale pattern of the central (Dorian) octave to the pitches

$$f\sharp'-e'-d'-c\sharp'-b-a-g-f\sharp$$
$$T\ T\ S\ T\ T\ T\ S$$

and then fitting those pitches within the e'–e octave. This transposition process chromatically altered some

THE SEVEN SPECIES OF *TONOI*
according to Ptolemy's *Harmonics*

EXAMPLE 1.3 Comparison: The two interpretations of the Greeks' use of the seven species of *tonoi*.

pitches within the e′–e octave and changed the tone-semitone pattern to T S T T T S T, or Phrygian:

e′–d′–c#′–b–a–g–f#–e
T S T T T S T

This also happens in modern music theory when the major scale pattern is transposed round the circle of fifths and the pitches are lowered to usable range.

Ptolemy stated that transposition of the Dorian scale (which he called "modulation") was practiced to produce an impression of an altered ethos by shifting the position of the

Mese within the scale. Transposition of the Dorian scale pattern does not change the melodic scale form; it is only when the scale is adjusted to fit within the boundaries of the central octave that the Mese shifts to a high or a low position within the e′–e octave. This, according to Ptolemy, is the primary reason for transposing the scale pattern. One can see in the choice of the Dorian octave as the pattern the importance attached to the ethical character (ethos) of this particular mode. Ptolemy indicated that the term Mese was assigned to the fifth pitch in the octave scale, whatever

that pitch might be. (This differs from the older belief that the pitch a in the middle of the Greater Perfect System was always designated Mese.) When the transposed scale was adjusted to fit within the central octave, the position of the Mese shifted; it would not always *remain* as the fifth pitch. If the Mese were in a low location within the central octave, the ethos of that mode would be considered "low"; if the Mese happened to be in a high position, the ethos would be considered "high."

The first two columns of example 1.3 illustrate the transposition process and the relocation of the pitches within the central octave. Comparison of columns 2 and 3 reveals that the scales produced by the transposition theory exhibit the same tone-semitone patterns set forth in the older theory. Moreover, whether the pitch of the Mese is considered to change (as in the newer interpretation) or whether it remains constant as the pitch a (according to the older theory), its location within the individual scales is identical. The matter of high or low *ethos* is achieved by either interpretation—*the end results do not differ.*

The Greek principle of transposition corresponds with a similar practice in modern music theory: A mode would be comparable to a key, with different modes being created by transposition of the basic octave pattern of tones and semitones (T T S T T T S) to different pitch levels. An even closer similarity is recognizable; that is, the T T S T T T S Dorian (central) octave pattern of the Greeks, if employed to proceed upward in pitch rather than downward as it is be-

lieved they used it, is the same as the pattern of our major scale:

e′ d′ c′ b a g f e
T T S T T T S
Greek Dorian pattern

c′ d′ e′ f′ g′ a′ b′ c″
T T S T T T S
17th–20th c. Major pattern

Was the central octave in practical use in Greek music? Or was it only theoretical? That it had some practical use is evidenced by the *Skolion of Seikilos,* which was written in the Phrygian mode, using the pitches of that modal scale pattern as they appear within the e′–e central octave. The choice of mode and octave is unmistakable: (a) the skolion uses every note of the Phrygian scale within the central octave, and (b) the music does not exceed the limits of the e′–e octave. When one realizes that vocal music was of prime import to the Greeks—that instrumental music was used mainly as accompaniment (i.e., accessory) to the voice or to drama—the matter of vocal range certainly would be of utmost consideration in establishing a practi-

cal system of music. Those melodies and fragments of Greek music that have survived are monophonic and lie within the range of an octave (if modern transcriptions of them are correct). Instrumentalists accompanying singers did not merely duplicate the pitches being sung; rather, it is believed that they improvised heterophonically, that is, ornamenting or varying the melody. Most of the instruments then in use had a compass of about one octave. To some degree instrument tunings were adjustable, and as more strings were added to the kithara, by stopping strings the player could produce all the notes in the Greater Perfect System plus chromatically altered pitches and microtones.

"Modulation" was not done merely to place a melody in a range more in accord with a singer's vocal range. Ptolemy made this clear in *Harmonics.* That kind of adjustment was done automatically: the singer sang where he could and the instrumentalist retuned his instrument to match the singer's range. Remember that for the Greeks all pitch was relative.

(fig. 1.11); and some actual instruments have been found. It seems likely that the musicians either improvised or relied on memory when performing, as none of the artistic depictions or literary accounts indicate the presence of notated music at a performance, nor do any of the writings divulge information concerning the techniques used in playing the instruments.

Rome was a conqueror, and as the Romans subdued nations they borrowed from those cultures items of value, many of which were renamed, adapted, and developed so that they became, in a sense, Roman. Musically, Rome was indebted to the Etruscans, the Greeks, and peoples of Near Eastern lands; borrow-

ings from them are apparent in the instruments the Romans used.

MUSICAL INSTRUMENTS

Though vocal music reigned supreme, a variety of instruments existed in ancient Rome. Aerophones included the animal-horn *bucina* and several instruments made from bronze: the *tuba,* a type of long, straight trumpet (made in sections that fit together) equipped with a conical mouthpiece; the large G-shaped *cornu,* also with a conical mouthpiece; and the J-shaped *lituus* (fig. 1.11). Both the cornu and the lituus were of Etruscan origin.

FIGURE 1.11 A sarcophagus relief from Amiternum, Italy, depicts a Roman funeral procession in the early first century A.D. At the uper right are two cornu players and a lituus player; at the lower right are four tibia players. *(Aquila, Museo Aquilano)*

Graduated lengths of true reeds bound together formed the Pan pipes, or *syrinx*. Double reeds comprised the *tibia* (as the Romans called the Greek aulos) and the Phrygian pipes. The latter consisted of a pair of uneven pipes, the right instrument being straight and the left instrument longer and J-shaped, terminating in an upturned bell made from horn.

Both *hydraulos* and pneumatic organs were used. Harps of various kinds and sizes existed, including the Greek lyra and kithara; soloists preferred the latter. The Roman kithara was much larger than the original Greek kithara.

Numerous percussion instruments were employed, including cymbals, tambourine, drums, and rattles of various kinds. The *scabellum* resembled the Greek kroupalon and served to beat time.

MUSIC IN ROMAN LIFE

Music was a part of everyday life in Rome, where musicians seem to have enjoyed a rather high social status. Trade guilds established during the reign of Numa, second king of Rome, placed pipers first in the hierarchy and tuba and cornu players second. Pipers participated in sacred rites; tuba players supplied ceremonial music for imperial festivities, occasions of honor, and gladiatorial games; and the cornu and tuba had definite military functions. Pipers and trumpeters provided music at funerals. The colloquialism *ad tubicines mittas* (send for the trumpeters) indicated an impending funeral.

The Capitoline Games, founded by Domitian around the end of the first century, provided competitions every fourth year and attracted virtuosi. Rome imported professional artists to concertize; Mesomedes of Crete enjoyed an active career at Hadrian's court. The Romans accorded considerable adulation to virtuosi, who commanded large fees, which even greedy Vespasian paid.

Music in the theater varied from a simple stage play with musical accompaniment, to lengthy dramas with musical interludes between scenes and acts. Pantomimes, extremely popular but of low quality, favored choreography over music.

Musical entertainment was provided at private dinner parties. Sometimes guests at a large dinner party were provided a choice of entertainment: music, choreography, or a reading by an author. Ensemble music, both vocal and instrumental, was frequently enjoyed, especially at homes of the wealthy, and duets between aulos and kithara were not uncommon.

Many of society's elite were musical amateurs, and talented slaves served as both teachers and performers. Lucian reports that many women participated in music, as did several rulers. Nero's musical aspirations were sincere. Contrary to legend, his "fiddle" was probably a kithara, but he received singing and instrumental lessons, practiced diligently, performed (frequently before a captive audience), and participated in contests—always with the fear of infringing on the rules and always with the hope of winning first prize.

Ancient Romans seem to have been interested primarily in secular music, but sacred music was not neglected, as it was an important part of the religious cults. In succeeding centuries, Rome would concentrate on the sacred, particularly the music of the Christian church. With the rise of Christianity and the establishment of the papacy near Rome, it is quite possible that the church's zeal to remove all traces of paganism was a great factor in successfully eradicating all evidence of notated music that was indigenous to Roman culture.

SUMMARY

Archaeologists have unearthed musical instruments dating from c. 18,000 B.C., but very little written music survives from antiquity, and much of that is fragmentary. *Ta'amim* symbols inscribed in scrolls of Hebrew Scripture probably served as notation models for the earliest written chant music of the Christian church. The oldest extant music is a Hurrian cult hymn from c. 1400 B.C. The Babylonians used diatonic modal scales and other theoretical principles of music at least a millennium before the Greeks' use of them is documented, yet it was the Greeks whose views and practices were transmitted to later generations. For centuries—in fact, well into the Baroque era—the theoretical practices and principles and the philosophical views of the Greeks were a benchmark for Western art music.

Approximately 15 pieces of ancient Greek music survive, all located after c. A.D. 1565. Through treatises, musical instruments, and artifacts, the ancient Greeks left a considerable legacy: (1) an acoustical theory established by Pythagoras, stated in mathematical terms and demonstrated audibly and visibly by means of the monochord; (2) the concept of the scale, together with a theory of transposition of a scale pattern; (3) the doctrine of *ethos,* a belief that music is a powerful force capable of affecting character, thought, and conduct; and (4) constructional principles for several types of musical instruments. Certain features and views were transmitted by the ancients that cannot be assigned to any particular ethnic group: (1) the idea of music as monophony, associated with words and rhythm, including dance; (2) a practical view of music in performance as a commodity to be created anew for each use, thus placing value on improvisation; and (3) a philosophy that regarded music as a microcosm closely related to the universe as macrocosm, since music was structured according to the same mathematical principles as the cosmos.

No examples of Roman music have been located. The Romans were conquerors who borrowed from the cultures of the peoples they subdued and then adapted, renamed, and developed those cultural items to the extent that they seemed Roman. Conquered Greeks became slaves who taught their Roman masters the features and philosophical views of Greek music. In antiquity, Romans seem to have been interested mainly in secular music, though music was important in the religious rites of pagan cults. In succeeding centuries, Rome seems to have concentrated on sacred music, particularly the music of the Christian church.

THE EARLY CHRISTIAN ERA

Christianity grew from its humble beginnings largely as a result of the work of Saul of Tarsus, who, converted, renamed and transformed into Paul, preached this faith as a universal brotherhood of mankind without national or racial limitations. Paul maintained contact with small Christian communities and kept them in communication with one another by means of his letters, some of which became the Bible Epistles. Paul personally carried the gospel message to Rome, where he was joined by other evangelists and Peter. Traditionally, the Roman government considered religious beliefs a matter of private concern as long as citizens remained loyal to the state. However, Christians found the expected loyalty to the state incompatible with allegiance to God and refused to burn incense before the imperial image or to serve as soldiers. The classical world had difficulty understanding the Christians' attitude and their regard for God as the supreme authority of heaven and earth.

The degree of oppression Christians suffered varied with the times, but not even the severe persecution that occurred under Diocletian (r. 303–5) could wipe out this faith; rather, oppression unified and strengthened the church. Christianity was practiced in the household of Emperor Constantine I (r. 306–37), who, by the Edict of Milan (313), provided religious toleration throughout his empire and recognized the church as an institution with the right to own property. However, that edict established the political ruler as head of the church. Theodosius I (r. 379–95), by the Edict of Thessalonica (380), established Christianity as the state religion to be practiced by all Roman citizens except Jews. Thereafter, all Roman emperors were Christians.

After Theodosius's death, the Roman empire split apart. In the face of Visigoth invasions, the Western emperor, Honorius I (r. 395–422), who was little more than a puppet ruler, fled north to Ravenna for refuge; in 410 the Visigoths sacked Rome and moved westward through Gaul to settle in Spain. The Romans were increasingly confronted with the necessity of defending their lands and repelling barbarian invaders. For a time, mercenaries were procured to augment Roman military forces, but often these hired soldiers turned situations to their own advantage, making Romans the losers. Honorius's successors were even weaker than he was, and they honored Germanic chieftains with impressive but meaningless titles. In 476, one of those chieftains, Odovacar, deposed the last Roman emperor, 12-year-old Romulus Augustus. The Western empire had collapsed, for reasons both internal and external.

In general, the literacy level of the Roman people declined. The invasions destroyed or desolated urban centers and eradicated cultural advantages. The ruling Germanic

A.D. 1	100	200	300	400	500

- c. 30 Crucifixion of Jesus
- 54–68 Nero
- 68–79 Vespasian
- 67 d. of Peter

Gradual development of the Christian Liturgy

- c. 150 Ptolemy: *Harmonics*
- 285 Oxyrhynchos fragment
- 306–337 Constantine I
- 313 Edict of Milan
- 379–395 Theodosius I
- 380 Edict of Thessalonica
- 325 Council of Nicaea
- 374 Ambrose, Bishop of Milan
- 340 *Vulgate*
- 413 Augustine: *Confessions*
- 425 Founding of U. of Constantinople
- 476 Fall of Rome

Monastic communities arose

500	600	700	800	900	1000

Boethius fl.
Cassiodorus fl.

- 590 Gregory I, elected Pope, d. 604
- 751 Pepin King of Franks
- 756 Donation of Pepin
- 800 Charlemagne crowned Holy Roman Emperor
- 987 Hugh Capet King of France

527 Benedictine Order founded   Rise of monasteries   Music cultivated in monasteries

- c. 612 Hermitage established at Saint Gall
- c. 622–632 Mohammed fl.

840   912
Notker Balbulus

c. 840 ← Hucbald → 930

- 527–565 Justinian I, Byzantium
- 778 Battle of Roncevaux (Roland)
- 848 Abbey founded, St. Martial

The Mass continues to develop   format settled c. 1014

Byzantine *kanōn*   Carolingian reform of Roman chant
John Damascene d. 760   Church modes

Troping ——→ Sequences ——→ Liturgical drama

- c. 850 { *Musica enchiriadis* / *Scolica enchiriadis* }

Various liturgies and chants in use, with ultimate dominance of "Gregorian" type

Ambrosian chant

- 601 See of Canterbury

Sarum chant

Mozarabic chant

chieftains, recognized by the Eastern emperor, favored Germanic customs. If any indigenous Roman secular music was extant at that time, it would have had difficulty surviving in its pristine state.

Perhaps the greatest of the Ostrogothic barbarian kings was Theodoric (r. 489–526), who encouraged arts and letters at Ravenna, his capital. Among the educated Romans at his court were Boethius and Cassiodorus. Both wrote about music.

Cassiodorus (c. 485–c. 580) held various offices at the courts of Theodoric and Athalaric. After retiring (c. 540), he wrote *De artibus ac disciplinis liberalium litterarum* (The liberal arts), which contains a section entitled *Institutiones musicae* (Principles of music) based on ancient Greek writings. Cassiodorus knew Augustine's *De musica* and the works of Euclid, Ptolemy, and Alypius.

Anicius Boethius (480–524), philosopher and mathematician, became Consul in 510 and served as counselor to Theodoric until accused of treason and executed. Boethius's treatise *De institutione musica* (Principles of music) was considered the most authoritative source on music in the Middle Ages and was used as a text in universities for centuries. Boethius analyzed, discussed, and sought to explain the theories of Pythagoras, Nicomachus, Aristoxenus, and Ptolemy. In discussing Ptolemy's explanation of the Greek tonal system, Boethius used the Latin term *modus* as translation for the Greek word *tonos* (key). This error led medieval musicians into designating the modal scale patterns by the names of the Greek keys. Boethius stressed the importance of music in shaping morals and character (ethos), in the education of youth, and as a basis for philosophical studies. Moreover, he regarded the philosopher-critic, rather than the performer, as the true musician.

As did the ancient Greek theorists, Boethius emphasized the mathematical side of music and the macrocosmic-microcosmic relationship between the universe and music. Music was divided into three categories: (1) *musica mundana,* the macrocosm, the inaudible music of the spheres discernible in the orderly movement of the planets and the stars; (2) *musica humana,* the inaudible harmonious relationship between soul and body influenced by the order of the cosmos and comparable with musical consonance; and

(3) *musica instrumentalis,* the microcosm, the audible sounds called "music" that are produced by instruments (including voice) by means of the orderly application of acoustical principles. Nor would the idea be lost in the twentieth century—Paul Hindemith's *Die Harmonie der Welt* (The harmony of the world) expressed it symphonically in three movements whose titles were derived from classifications of music in Boethius's treatise.

The medieval educational system comprised studies in the seven liberal arts. Because of music's relationship with mathematics and the cosmos, it was grouped with arithmetic, geometry, and astronomy in the *quadrivium* of higher studies. The *trivium* of lower studies consisted of grammar, rhetoric, and logic.

THE ESTABLISHED CHRISTIAN CHURCH

During the second century, the New Testament was assembled, a body of dogma established, and the central organization of the church expanded. The spiritual and physical welfare of a Christian community was supervised by a bishop (*episkopos*) who had authority superior to that of the teaching elders and deacons. By the fourth century, a definite hierarchy existed within the church: The bishop of the leading city in each political province was a *metropolitan* with jurisdiction over his colleagues. The metropolitans of the most important cities—Rome, Constantinople, Antioch, Alexandria, and Jerusalem—were called *patriarchs*. Both the patriarch of Alexandria and the patriarch of Rome were entitled *pope*. The bishop of Rome was the only patriarch in the Western provinces; his prestige was increased by his location in the ancient capital of the empire and the belief that his authority was a legacy from St. Peter, who was considered the first bishop of Rome. However, not until the reign of Pope Gregory I (590–604) did the four Eastern patriarchs acknowledge the supremacy of their Roman colleague (Insight: "Pope Gregory I, 'the Great'").

The First Ecumenical Council, held at Nicaea in 325, was a gathering of all the bishops to resolve a doctrinal controversy. The decision of the council resulted in the formulation and adoption of a creed that, as modified by the Council of Constantinople (381) and

Pope Gregory I, "the Great"

Whether the ecclesiastical chant used in the Roman church was named for Pope Gregory I (b. 540; r. 590–604) is debatable, as is the precise extent of Gregory's involvement with church music. The official use of the term *Gregorian chant* stems from the ninth century, when Pope Leo IV (r. 847–55) declared use of *Gregoriana carmina* (Gregorian melodies) in the Roman liturgy compulsory on penalty of excommunication from Rome. Probably, the basis for some of the legends that attributed much of musical activity to Gregory I is the biography *Vita Gregorii magni* that was compiled by order of Pope John VIII (r. 872–82).

Undoubtedly, Gregory was a great pope. He was a Roman nobleman trained for a political career, serving for six years as papal ambassador to the imperial court at Constantinople. When he became pope, he assumed a position of effective leadership that was temporal as well as spiritual. He managed his papal court efficiently and authoritatively. He asserted and maintained the supremacy of the Western papacy and consolidated the church under his leadership. An important facet of that consolidation was reuniting the church at Milan with Rome.

Gregory was concerned with the spread of Christianity through missionary activity. In 596 Augustine (now known as Augustine of Canterbury) was sent to England, where Christianity was established among the Anglo-Saxons; centuries later, Anglo-Saxons were missionaries to the Franks. Aethelbert, King of Kent, was converted and baptized by Augustine, and in 601 the See of Canterbury was founded. On the Continent, conversions of rulers included the king of the Visigoths in Spain and the heir to the Lombard throne.

Gregory was interested in music as an adjunct to worship. We do not know whether he composed any chants, but he desired that they be standardized and codified. A papal choir had been in existence for more than a century, and Gregory realized the choir's importance in relieving officiating priests and deacons of the responsibility of much musical performance. He instructed Roman seminaries to train choir singers, and he founded orphanages with a similar aim. He helped standardize the liturgy somewhat by assigning certain antiphons and other chants to designated worship services and feast days, thus continuing the distribution of specific chants throughout the church year—a distribution that had been begun by his predecessors and was completed by his immediate successors in the papacy.

---

the Council of Chalcedon (451), ultimately became the so-called Nicene Creed, used as *Credo* of the Mass. The Council of Nicaea was called by Constantine I and was presided over by him, for Constantine considered himself Christ's representative on earth and God's vice-regent as well as head of the Roman empire. This idea survived, and for at least the next five centuries the emperors maintained authority over the church. Although Christianity divided mankind's allegiance between the political and heavenly kingdoms, there was cooperation between church and state.

THE CHURCH FATHERS AND MUSIC

It was indicated previously that the lack of extant primary source material for Roman music was presumed to be in some measure due to the activities of the early Christian church's zeal to exterminate all that it considered pagan. But to state that the early Christians were against music would be giving a false impression. Certainly, the church fathers appreciated music; they wished merely to channel its use in the proper direction and to guard the Christian church against the intrusion of any semblance of the orgiastic rites and music of the pagan cults. The writings of theologians such as St. Basil of Caesarea (c. 330–78), St. John Chrysostom (345–407), and Aurelius Augustinus (St. Augustine, 354–430; bishop of Hippo) reveal that they assigned to music a special place in the life of the church. Like Pythagoras and other ancient Greeks, these church fathers expressed a belief in the existence of a music of the universe that was created by the Holy Spirit and imbued with supernatural powers that enabled it to rout demons, summon angelic aid, heal the sick, strengthen moral character, and in numerous other ways contribute to the harmonious order of the world.

Psalms were especially favored, for they were inspired by God and singing them provided pleasure and help. Religious chant uplifted the mind and offered praise to God. St. John Chrysostom, patriarch of Constantinople, wrote that he considered as churches those assemblies at which there were prayers, psalms, dances of prophets, and singers with pious intentions. St. Jerome (340–420) advocated singing psalms, for they affected "the seat of the *ethos*" and determined a person's moral conscience. The Latin version of the Bible (*Vulgate*), prepared by St. Jerome in the fourth century, became the authorized version of the Scriptures used in the Roman Catholic Church.

Nor did these saints reject all musical instruments. According to St. Basil, the psaltery (a plucked stringed instrument with a resonator at the top) was particularly acceptable because it has the source of its sound above. This, he wrote, was an indication that persons should seek those things that are on high and not be led by pleasant melody to pursue carnal passions.

St. Augustine confessed that he so enjoyed church music that he sometimes felt he sinned and that occasionally he wished music would be banished from the church. However, he affirmed the usefulness of music in the worship service. Realizing that he was moved by the sung words and not by the music itself, he stated that he approved of the use of singing in the church as a means of strengthening weak minds and developing greater religious devotion. Augustine's treatise *De Musica* (c. 391), which was widely disseminated during the Middle Ages, concerns music as a liberal art. Five books are devoted to a detailed discussion of rhythm and meter; book six presents theological and philosophical views of music, including aesthetics and musical cosmology.

MONASTICISM

The influence of monastic regulations and work is still seen in religious practices and cultural life in the twentieth century. Monasticism existed in the third century in Egypt and the Syrian desert, where hermits lived in solitude. By the fourth century, more regulated monastic communities had arisen. The most important monastic system was the one established by Benedict of Nursia (480–543), who founded the monastery at Monte Cassino, south of Rome, in 529. This monastery's code of regulations (Rule of St. Benedict) spread throughout western Europe. Requirements of the Benedictine Order included prayer, meditation, and physical and intellectual work. Much of that intellectual work was done in the *scriptoria* (writing rooms), where monks copied and prepared books and manuscripts. Monasteries became depositories of knowledge, and the schools connected with them became the salvation of learning in times of sacking and burning, war and famine. Because materials for books and manuscripts were costly, only the most important and valuable items were copied. Certainly, where music was concerned, the secular and vernacular would have had the lowest priority.

ESTABLISHMENT OF PAPAL STATES

For the territory known as the Papal States, the Roman Catholic Church was indebted to the Franks, a confederation of northern tribes that gradually gained strength and power during the fourth century. Under their chieftain, Meroveus, the Franks allied with the Romans in their fight against Attila. Meroveus's grandson, Clovis (r. 481–511), extended the Franks' kingdom until almost all of Gaul had been gained, but after Clovis's death the Merovingian dynasty weakened. Strength lay in the hands of the king's chief minister, the mayor of the palace. In the early eighth century, the mayor, Charles Martel, earned considerable prestige through military prowess and was the real power behind the Frankish throne. Charles's son Pepin inherited the mayoralty in 741 but desired the title of king, for which he petitioned Pope Zacharias (r. 741–51). The request was granted. The Merovingian heir was placed in a monastery, and Pepin was anointed king (r. 751–68).

In 754 Pope Stephen III (r. 752–57) reanointed Pepin, along with his sons Carloman and Charles. Thus the Carolingian dynasty was established. In return for this, Pepin agreed to defend the pope against the Lombards, who were threatening. All the Lombard territories that Pepin conquered—the city of Rome and most of the lands of Ravenna—were given to the pope. This "Donation of Pepin" was the basis of the Papal States. Moreover, by the agreement and gift an alliance was formed whereby the Carolingians became the pope's temporal protectors.

Charles and Carloman jointly inherited the throne at Pepin's death. Carloman soon died, and Charles I

(Charlemagne) ruled alone. In 774 he confirmed the Donation of Pepin and went to Italy to battle the Lombards on the pope's behalf. While there, Charlemagne acquired the Lombard crown.

In 778 an army commanded by Charlemagne's nephew Roland was annihilated at Roncevaux in the Pyrenees. This disaster was memorialized in the medieval epic *Le Chanson de Roland* (The song of Roland). By 796 Charlemagne's kingdom extended from the Atlantic Ocean and the Pyrenees Mountains to the Elbe and Danube Rivers down to the center of Italy (fig. 2.1). In 800 Charlemagne went to Rome to help Pope Leo III (r. 795–816) quell a disturbance. There, at Mass on Christmas Day, the pope crowned him "Emperor of the Romans."

THE BYZANTINE CHURCH

As Rome's power faded, Constantinople grew to urban splendor and developed a brilliant cultural life. The University of Constantinople (founded in 425) prospered, and during the reign of Justinian I (r. 527–65) it supported chairs of philosophy, law, and Greek and Latin grammar and rhetoric. In many ways, Constantinople maintained the cosmopolitan tradition Rome had once acquired from the Hellenes.

Justinian sought to strengthen religious life throughout his extensive Byzantine Empire (fig. 2.2) and wanted Constantinople to be recognized as an ecclesiastical center. With that in mind, he ordered the construction of Hagia Sophia, which was dedicated on 27 December 537 (plate 2). St. Sophia and other churches were decorated richly with icons and mosaics; their leather-bound, jewel-encrusted liturgical books contain beautifully illumined pages.

The Church of San Vitale, in Ravenna, Italy, dedicated in 547, typifies Byzantine art and architecture. A pair of mosaic murals in the apse of the church depict the Offertory procession of the Mass and convey the view then prevalent that the emperor was God's vice-regent on earth (plate 3).

BYZANTINE HYMNS

In the Byzantine church, hymn singing was an important part of the liturgy. Byzantine hymns are of three

FIGURE 2.1 The extent of Charlemagne's empire and the Byzantine Empire in A.D. 814.

THE EARLY CHRISTIAN ERA

FIGURE 2.2 The extent of the Byzantine Empire during the reign of Justinian I (r. 527–65).

types: *troparia, kontakia,* and *kanōnes.* The *troparion,* used in the fourth and fifth centuries, developed from responses sung between psalm verses; *troparia* were poetic interpolations sung between the last several verses of a psalm. *Kontakia* flourished during the sixth and seventh centuries. At Matins, the daily morning service, there was no homily (sermon). Instead, the reading of the Gospel for the day was followed by the singing of the appropriate *kontakion,* a musical homily explaining or interpreting that Gospel. A *kontakion* consisted of from 24 to 30 poetic stanzas sung to the same melody.

The *kanōn* came into existence when the Council of Trullo decreed in 692 that daily preaching of the Word was obligatory for the higher clergy. To use both a *kontakion* and a homily would be duplication, so the *kontakion* was deleted and the *kanōn* created to serve as meditative commentary on the Scripture passages and the coordinating sermon. Originally, a *kanōn* consisted of nine main sections called *odes,* each with its own melody and each normally with nine stanzas. The text of each ode corresponded with one of the nine biblical **canticles** used in the liturgy. (A canticle is a special lyrical passage from a book of the Bible other than the Psalms.) Later, the second ode, based on the

Song of Moses (Deut. 32), was considered too somber and was omitted except during Lent. At first, *kanōnes* melodies were simple syllabic settings of the text. Gradually, the melodies became longer and more complex; when a *kanōn* was sung in slow tempo, much time was consumed by the singing of eight odes. This was especially problematic during Lent and Holy Week, when the services were longer. The remedy was to shorten the *kanōn;* the number of stanzas per ode was reduced to three.

During the second quarter of the eighth century, an important school of *kanōn* poet-composers flourished at the monastery of Mar Saba near the Dead Sea (fig. 2.2, St. Sabas). The most notable of these men were John of Damascus (c. 700–c. 760) and his foster brother Kosmas of Jerusalem (died c. 760). Among surviving hymns by Kosmas are nineteen *kanōnes* for the great feasts of the church year, including the penitential "Great Kanōn" based on Psalm 51, sung at Lauds on Thursday of Passion Week.

John of Damascus (John Damascene) is credited with introducing into the Byzantine liturgy the *oktoēchos*—eight-week cycles of hymns, each week's hymns composed in a different *echos,* or "mode." These *echoi* were not scale patterns but collections of melody patterns. The cycle of *echoi* began at Easter, the most important festival of the church year. On Easter and during the following week, a group of hymns in the First Mode (First Echos) was sung. The next week a group of hymns in the Second Mode was used, and so on. John played a significant role in the development of *kanōn* literature. In manuscripts containing model stanzas for *kanōnes*, the first melody in each group is attributed to him. Among extant hymns by John is the Easter *kanōn*, *Anastaseos imera*, known as the Golden Kanōn or Queen of Kanōnes. J. M. Neale's English translation of that hymn text, "The Day of Resurrection," is sung in many churches on Easter Sunday.

THE JEWISH SYNAGOGUE

The Jewish synagogue was an institution for the layperson. In the first century A.D., three daily prayer services were observed in the synagogue: in the morning sometime between 7 and 10 A.M., in the afternoon between 3 and 4 P.M., and in the evening "at dusk." At these services, there were prayers of praise, thanksgiving, supplication and personal petition, and benediction as well as professions of faith through doxology and the *Sh'ma'*, the creed prayer commencing "Hear, O Israel, The Lord our God, The Lord is one." The two doxologies in use were the *Kaddish*, whose opening phrases have much in common with Christians' The Lord's Prayer, and the *Kedusha*, or Thrice-Holy.

The weekday morning and evening services were similar in content, opening with an exhortation to prayer in praise of the Lord. The services include praise prayers, the *Kedusha*, the *Sh'ma'*, a required set of silent prayers offered standing, and conclude with the *Kaddish*. The afternoon service was simpler: one or two psalms were chanted, followed by the *Kaddish*. Observation of the Sabbath began with the service at dusk on Friday and continued through service at sunset on Saturday. The morning worship was more elaborate than that on weekdays and included the chanting of more than a dozen psalms (including the Hallelujah Psalms 146–50) and Miriam's Song (Exod. 15:1–19). Central to the service were readings from the Scriptures, one Lesson from the Pentateuch and one from the Prophetic Books, followed by appropriate prayers. The afternoon service, too, was expanded by additional psalms and portions of the Song of Songs. The evening service was characterized by prayers and psalms and concluded with the ceremony of *Habdala* (Separation).

Many of the practices in synagogue services became part of the worship services of the early Christians and carried over into the **liturgy** of the Catholic Church. (The liturgy is the prescribed ritual or format for worship in the church.) Common elements of the services of both faiths included the recitation or musical intonation of passages from Scriptures, the singing of psalms and hymns, the affirmation of a creed, praise through doxologies and a Thrice-Holy, congregational and priestly prayers, the giving of offerings, and the benediction. Grace and blessing over bread and wine, together with psalm singing, were ancient Jewish customs observed in worship in the home. Both Jewish and Christian faiths established liturgical calendars with similar organizational details.

As used around the first century A.D., the term **psalmody** referred to the musical intonation or chanting of any scriptural or liturgical texts. Passages from Scriptures were recited or chanted by one person in a kind of musical intonation that could be termed "speech-song." Such a rendition, done from beginning to end by one person, is **direct psalmody.** Not all scriptural texts were chanted or intoned in the same manner. The type of musical inflection varied with the text, the season of the liturgical year, and the specific occasion. The belief was prevalent among the Jews, as it was among the Greeks, that each type of music had a special character to which listeners (in this case, worshipers) reacted in a certain way.

The Book of Psalms was especially important in both Jewish and Christian services. Much scriptural poetry is structured in bipartite verses, designed for or conducive to **antiphonal rendition,** or performance in alternation: The first half of the verse is chanted by one group or choir of singers and the second half by another group or choir. Another form of antiphonal rendition is the chanting of psalm verses in alternation by two choirs, each choir chanting a complete verse of the psalm.

Responsorial psalmody was used also. The cantor or precentor sang a verse of psalm or Scripture, and the congregation answered with a certain response.

Psalm 136 provides an example, for the second half of each of its 26 verses is "For his loving kindness endureth for ever."

SUMMARY

Christianity survived various degrees of persecution before Constantine I advocated religious toleration in 313 and Theodosius I formally established it as the state religion in 380. Imperial espousal of Christianity brought also imperial guardianship that at times amounted to control. The church fathers supported music as an adjunct to worship; music's function was to enhance the service.

After the death of Theodosius, the Roman empire split apart. For reasons both internal and external, the Western segment declined and ultimately collapsed in 476. Theodoric was the greatest of the barbarians who ruled the Western kingdom, and at Ravenna, his capital, arts and letters were encouraged. There, in the early sixth century, Cassiodorus and Boethius wrote treatises on music. Boethius's *De institutione musica,* considered the most authoritative source on music in the Middle Ages, explained the macrocosmic-microcosmic relationship between the universe and music and divided music into three categories: cosmic, human, and instrumental. Boethius stressed the ethical and mathematical aspects of music.

Monasticism began in the third century as desert hermitages, and flourished. Monasteries were depositories of culture and learning in the darkest ages and housed copyists whose work made ancient treatises more available. In 529 Benedict of Nursia established at Monte Cassino the order that bears his name.

Gregory the Great elevated the papacy to a position of temporal and spiritual leadership. He reunited the Christian church, encouraged *scholae cantorum,* and continued the standardization and codification of liturgical chants that his immediate predecessors began and his successors continued.

In the middle of the fourth century, the Franks, under Merovius's leadership, strengthened considerably. After Clovis's death, the Merovingian dynasty weakened, and the real governing power lay in the hands of the mayor of the palace. In the middle of the eighth century, Mayor Pepin successfully petitioned Pope Zacharias for the title of king and, in return, donated to the pope the Italian lands that formed the basis of the Papal States. Charlemagne expanded the Frankish kingdom considerably and became so militarily valuable to the pope that on Christmas Day, 800, Pope Leo III crowned him Emperor of the Romans.

The Eastern empire, centered at Constantinople, enjoyed a brilliant cultural life and maintained the cosmopolitan tradition Rome had once inherited from the Hellenes. Justinian I (r. 527–65) fostered monasticism and strongly supported Christianity. By his decree in 528, daily singing of Matins, Lauds, and Vespers became compulsory. Hymn singing was an important part of the liturgy and included three types of Byzantine hymns: *troparia,* poetic interpolations used in the fourth and fifth centuries; *kontakia,* musical homilies that flourished in the fifth and sixth centuries; and *kanōnes,* meditative commentaries used after the Council of Trullo in 692. Notable composers of *kanōnes* were Kosmas of Jerusalem and John Damascene, who is credited with introducing the *oktōēchos* into the Byzantine liturgy.

The Jewish and Christian worship services and liturgical calendars are similar in several respects. Psalmody was an important feature of worship services of both faiths. Psalms were chanted in three ways: direct, antiphonally, and responsorially. Over the years, the expansion of antiphonal rendition led to the creation of new forms of Christian music.

ECCLESIASTICAL CHANT

3

The development of Western music is inseparably linked with the music of the Roman Catholic Church. The church not only was vital in preserving music through the so-called Dark Ages but also was the center of activity of the community. The music of the church was an integral part of lay life; church chants were sung outside its walls and frequently served as the basis for secular songs. From the ninth century on, composers have written music based on or incorporating chant melodies. In some centuries, settings of certain parts of the liturgy (specifically, motet and Mass) were the most significant forms of music. It is important, therefore, to understand the nature of ecclesiastical chant and the historically settled format of the Roman liturgy.

Ecclesiastical chant forms the largest body of monophonic music in existence, and most of that is Gregorian chant. Yet, opportunities to hear Gregorian chant performed in the traditional manner are rare. Until the early 1960s, one might have heard the liturgy sung in Latin in Gregorian chant in Roman Catholic churches throughout the world. However, in accordance with decisions and recommendations made by the Second Vatican Council (1962–65), services in the vernacular have superseded the Latin. Traditional Gregorian chant has been displaced by other music or supplied with vernacular translations of the text that the music does not accommodate. A considerable amount of new music, of all degrees of quality, has found its way into ecclesiastical use.

GREGORIAN CHANT

Gregorian chant is purely functional music designed to enhance the worship service and is objective and impersonal. It consists of a single unaccompanied melodic line constructed according to tonal patterns different from those forming the major and minor scales. Traditionally, it used Latin words and was originally intended to be sung by men and, from the fourth century, by women in cloistered religious communities. In other words, chant is monophonic and modal. It is usually sung in a flexible rhythm without regular accentuation or beat because, as written, no fixed temporal values are specified for the notes.

CHANT RHYTHM

To date, no manuscript or treatise has been located that gives explicit instructions for authentic performance of the rhythm of Gregorian chant, though there is evidence that some rhythmic variation in performance occurred. For instance, in some late-ninth-century manuscripts, the letters *t* and *c* appear above some note symbols. The *t* is interpreted as *trahere* (to prolong or lengthen) and the *c* as *celeriter* (quickly) (fig. 3.1). Sometimes a straight line is attached to a note symbol, and this is interpreted as a prolongation sign.

Treatises by eminent medieval theorists show disagreement concerning the rhythm of chant. In the twentieth century, several differing views exist. One group, known as mensuralists, believe that there were two note values, a long and a short, the long having twice the value of the short. Mensuralists have proposed several different systems by which these note values may have been arranged. Another group, called accentualists, contend that rhythm was governed by the accentuation (or stress) normally given the Latin words when spoken. In syllabic and neumatic chants (those with one syllable of text per note or neume), the primary accent of the Latin word is stressed. In melismatic chants (those with many neumes per syllable), the stress falls on the first note of each neume. Still another opinion is held by the Benedictine monks of Solesmes, France, who for well over a century have

been officially designated by the Vatican to edit and publish the liturgical books used in the Roman Catholic Church. They use a single indivisible beat or pulse as the fundamental rhythmic unit. Binary and ternary groupings of these pulses are freely interlaced and may form larger rhythmic units. The first note of the group, which they term the *ictus,* is most important rhythmically. In their rules for interpreting chant, the Solesmes editors state that the natural rhythm of Latin prose is the vital determinant of chant rhythm. They use three rhythmic indications: a vertical *episema* (') to indicate the *ictus,* a horizontal *episema* (−) to indicate a slight lengthening of a note, and a dot placed after a note (▪·) to double the value of that note.

MODERN NOTATION OF CHANT

In modern liturgical books, Gregorian chant music is printed on a four-line staff in plainsong ("square") notation that indicates relative rather than absolute pitches (fig. 3.2; DWMA4).

For each chant, one of two movable clefs is used: ⊏ or ⊏ , indicating, respectively, the position of

FIGURE 3.1 A portion of a late-ninth-century manuscript showing Gallican chant written in staffless heighted neumes. Notice the small letters *t* and *c* written above some notation symbols. The music is the Gradual *Liberasti nos* and the Verse *In Deo laudabimur* used in Mass on the twenty-third Sunday after Pentecost. (*Source: Ninth-century manuscript Codex 359, fol. 125, Stiftsbibliothek, St. Gall, Switzerland*)

c′ (middle c) or f (the f below middle c). Clef mobility keeps the chant notation on the staff and eliminates the necessity for ledger lines. Notation is by means of note symbols, which may appear as single square notes ▬▬ or in a grouping of two or more squares in a **neume** . Each square indicates one note. The notes are read from left to right, with one exception: in a *podatus*, or *pes* , the lower note is sung first. Compound neumes (groupings of more than three notes) may include oblique bars and diamond shapes, such as or . An oblique bar contains only two notes, one marked by each end of the bar; each diamond shape constitutes one note. The jagged note known as *quilisma* has the same value as other notes in a neume group but is sung lightly. The *quilisma* is always preceded and followed by one or several notes; it never begins or ends a neume. The small note in the neume is a liquescent neume and is sung lightly. A liquescent neume usually occurs on a diphthong, as the *au* in *lauda*, or where two consonants occur in succession, as the *ng* in *angelus*. Only one syllable is sung per neume, regardless of the number of notes involved. However, in melismatic chants many neumes may be notated to be vocalized to a single syllable of text. (For a guide to the correct pronunciation of ecclesiastical Latin, see the appendix.)

Only one chromatic alteration is used in Gregorian chant: B♭. Infrequently, the flat symbol appears immediately after the clef at the beginning of the chant, in which case it is in effect for the entire chant. More often, the flat indication occurs within a chant and is valid for only the word in which the symbol is involved or until the next phrase marking.

Chant music is not divided into measures by bar lines. Phrasing is indicated by vertical slashes intersecting one or more of the staff lines, depending on the importance of the phrase. A vertical slash through the top line of the staff (a quarter bar) marks the end of the smallest melodic division of the chant; a vertical line intersecting the center two lines of the staff (a half bar) marks the end of a section of a phrase; a full bar through all four staff lines marks the end of a complete phrase; and a double bar through all four lines indicates either the end of the chant or a change of chant performers. An asterisk (*) placed in the text of a chant marks the point at which the choir commences after a solo portion of chant, and vice versa. The letters *ij* and *iij* indicate, respectively, that the preceding phrase is to be repeated either once or twice.

The *custos* is a small guide symbol resembling half a note that is placed at the end of a line of music to designate the first pitch at the beginning of the next line. Such a guide was necessary in ages past when an entire choir might be required to read from a single huge page of vellum in a book chained to a lectern and when there might not be sufficient time for one's eye to travel back the width of the manuscript page to see the next neume and sing it without disrupting the rhythmic flow of the chant.

The symbol **℟** designates a Response. The symbol **℣** indicates that the words are a verse, as in a verse

FIGURE 3.2 *Kyrie* from Easter Mass (*a*) in Gregorian chant notation (*LU*, 16) and (*b*) transcribed in modern notation.

of Scripture; *Ps.* signifies that a portion of a psalm follows. The letters *e u o u a e* printed under neumes at the conclusion of a chant constitute an abbreviation derived from the last six vowels of the words *in saeculorum saeculorum Amen* ("through ages of ages. Amen" or "for ever. Amen") found at the conclusion of the *Gloria Patri,* the usual termination of a psalm or a canticle in the Roman rite. This abbreviation, known as the *evovae,* serves as a formula to indicate the particular variant ending of the psalm tone to be sung.

An arabic or roman numeral appearing at the beginning of a chant melody indicates the ecclesiastical mode of that chant. Each of the eight modes is designated by number, not by name. This labeling of the chants was a later addition and probably occurred sometime during codification when some person(s) analyzed the chants and classified them modally. Many of the chants, especially the early ones, give every indication of having been created by assembling melodic formulas, a process known as **centonization.** This process was common practice in the East, as evidenced by the use of melodic patterns called *maqām* by the Arabs, *rāga* by the Hindus, *ta'amim* by the Hebrews, and *echoi* by the Byzantines.

THE CHURCH MODES

The modes originally assigned to Gregorian chants are not identical with those used later in other medieval Western music. Rather, the church modes were a combination of Eastern practice and Western terminology.

In the Byzantine (Eastern) Christian church, chants were grouped according to the types of melodic motives they contained; these groups of melody types were divided into eight categories, arranged in four pairs, with finals on the pitches d, e, f, and g. Each category was an *echos* (pl., *echoi*); collectively, the eight categories formed the *oktōēchos.*

Sometime during the seventh or eighth century, the Carolingian (Frankish) clergy acquired a working knowledge of the Byzantine system. When Alcuin and his co-workers carried out Charlemagne's directive to write down the liturgy, they needed a method of organizing the melodies. They borrowed the Byzantine system and from it developed the system of eight church

modes and, concurrently, the system of eight psalm tones. Chant melodies were classified and grouped into basic categories that were arranged in numbered pairs, according to the **tessitura** (the average compass or general range) of the music. Antiphons and psalms were labeled with mode or psalm tone numbers. Conceivably, the Carolingian clergy assigned these classifications to chants to avoid pitch clashes when antiphons and psalm verses were combined for Introits, Offertories, and Communions. The first verified classification of chants according to a system of eight modal divisions is found in a fragment of a *tonary* in Charlemagne's *Psalter.* A **tonary** was a liturgical book that stated distinct preferences for using certain modes for specific types of chants. (Fig. 3.3.)

FIGURE 3.3 This page from a late-eleventh-century *Tonary* seems to contain an exercise for learning or identifying the modes. *(Fol. 128, MS Lat. 7211, Bibliothèque nationale, Paris)*

CLASSES AND FORMS OF CHANT

Ecclesiastical chant may be classified according to the source and literary nature of the text, the number of notes per syllable of text in the musical setting, and the manner in which it is performed. Texts may be biblical or nonbiblical, prose or poetry. For example, psalms and canticles are biblical poetry; Epistles are biblical prose. The *Te Deum laudamus* (We praise Thee, God) is nonbiblical prose; hymns are nonbiblical poetry.

Text settings may be **syllabic,** with one note of music per syllable of text; **neumatic** (now also called "semi-ornate"), with one neume per text syllable; or **melismatic,** with several neumes per syllable of text (fig. 3.4). Chants with lengthy texts were often given syllabic settings, as was Credo II (*LU*, 66). Alleluias, which are jubilant, usually exhibit melismatic settings (*LU*, 779). *Kyrie* (*clemens rector*) (*LU*, 79) is also melismatic. Examples of neumatic settings are the Easter Introit, *Resurrexi* (*LU*, 778), and the antiphon *Asperges me* (*LU*, 13).

In performance, some chants are **antiphonal,** with sections or phrases sung by alternating choirs; some are **responsorial,** sung by soloist with response by choir; and some are **direct,** sung from beginning to end without alternation. The Psalms provide examples of all three types.

PSALM TONES   In the liturgical services called Offices, the psalms are chanted antiphonally according to certain melodic patterns called **psalm tones.** Just as a psalm verse is constructed in two parts, so the psalm tone has a binary division. The major portion of each psalm verse is chanted in a kind of monotone on a pitch called variously the *tuba, tenor, dominant,* or *reciting note.* There are nine psalm tones: one for each of the eight ecclesiastical modes and the *Tonus Peregrinus* (migratory tone), which is distinctive in its use of two different reciting notes, one for each half of the psalm verse. The earliest verified use of the system of eight psalm tones is in the previously mentioned *Tonary of Charlemagne's Psalter.*

Psalms are sung as inflected recitative. The psalm tone commences with an *initio*—a two- or three-note *intonation* leading into the reciting note on which the verse is chanted. At the binary division of the psalm verse, a mediant cadence, the *mediatio,* occurs. The reciting note is resumed for the second half of the verse, which concludes with the *terminatio,* or final cadence (fig. 3.5). When the first part of the psalm verse is quite long, it is subdivided by a *flex*—a bending or lowering of the pitch by the interval of a second or a third for two notes; this is marked in the text by a small cross (†).

RECITING NOTES   Certain portions of the liturgy, such as prayers and readings from Scripture, are chanted in a kind of liturgical recitative that is very similar to but simpler than psalm tones. The chanting is done rather rapidly on a reciting note that usually approximates either pitch a or pitch c'. A

(a)

(c)

FIGURE 3.4 Chant text settings: (*a*) syllabic (*LU*, 780), (*b*) neumatic (*LU*, 13), and (*c*) melismatic (*LU*, 79).

1. Dóminus illuminá-*ti - o* **mé**-a, *et sá-lus mé-*a: quem ti-**mé**-bo?

FIGURE 3.5 A portion of Psalm 26 as intoned on Psalm Tone 4.

short intonation precedes the reciting note, and brief melodic cadences punctuate verse endings.

REGIONAL LITURGIES

Several different regional liturgies were in existence by the fourth century. All have basic similarities in text, format, and musical chant, yet each possesses unique features that probably resulted from regional peculiarities infiltrating the chants and liturgies that missionaries originally brought into the areas (fig. 3.6). The principal liturgies and chants were Byzantine in the East and Old Roman, Gregorian, Ambrosian, Gallican, Celtic, and Mozarabic in the West.

Mozarabic chant functioned in the liturgy in the Iberian Peninsula, where Christians living under Moslem rule were called "Mozarabs." In 1085 this liturgy was banned officially in favor of the Roman rite, but on petition of six churches in Toledo, permission was granted for continued use of Mozarabic in those specific places. Mozarabic liturgy is still used in a chapel of the Cathedral of Toledo. A sizable repertory of Mozarabic chant is extant, but the music has not been transcribed because much of the notation is illegible and undecipherable.

The Celtic liturgy and its chant originated in monastic communities in Ireland in the fifth century; it was used also in Scotland and some parts of England. Celtic communities produced significant illuminated manuscripts (e.g., *The Lindisfarne Gospels* and *The Book of Kells*). During the sixth and seventh centuries, Celtic monks migrated to Europe, where they established hermitages and monasteries. The most influential of these was located at St. Gall in what is now Switzerland but was then northern Italy. No pure Celtic chant seems to have survived.

Ambrosian chant is still used in the archdiocese of Milan. The chant was named for St. Ambrose, who was bishop of Milan from 374 to 397. A comparison of Gregorian and Ambrosian chants reveals that if the text was set simply, the Ambrosian chant is simpler than the Gregorian, and if the text was set ornately, the Ambrosian is more ornate than the Gregorian. According to St. Augustine, Ambrose brought into the Western church the Eastern customs of antiphonal psalmody and hymn singing. Many hymn texts have been

FIGURE 3.6 Location of principal monasteries, centers of the various chant types, centers of troping, and centers of early polyphony.

attributed to Ambrose, but only four are considered authentic.

Gallican chant and liturgy, used by the Franks, flourished as an oral tradition from the fifth to the eighth century. It was suppressed during the reigns of Pepin (r. 751–68) and Charlemagne (r. 768–814), who preferred the Roman rite and imported liturgical books from Rome. Probably, these rulers' desire to unify their Empire was more a factor in their liturgical reforms than was personal preference. The imported *Sacramentaries* were sketchy, at best, containing only the variable texts used for feasts that changed from day to day. In 786, Pope Hadrian I (r. 772–95) sent Charlemagne a Roman *Sacramentary,* which the king directed Alcuin to supplement and complete. (The **Sacramentary** is the liturgical book of the Western Christian Church for the use of the celebrant at Mass. It usually contains the Proper prayers, Collect, Secret, and other formulas and benedictions.) Undoubtedly, Alcuin incorporated local materials, and Gallican elements began to infiltrate the Roman liturgy. Because Alcuin had been head of York Cathedral school before Charlemagne brought him to Aix-la-Chapelle to direct the palace school, Celtic characteristics crept in, too. No examples of pure Gallican chant are known to exist, but some of the Gallican liturgy that was absorbed into the Roman can be identified, for example, the verse *Crux fidelis* (Faithful cross), which is sung antiphonally with stanzas of the Gallican hymn *Pange, lingua, gloriosi . . .* (Sing, tongue, the glorious . . . ; *LU,* 742; fig. 7.1) on Good Friday.

The term *Old Roman Chant* refers to a musical repertory that was definitely of Roman origin and that existed as an oral tradition in churches in Rome. According to the Benedictines of Solesmes, it was "put into notation in Rome and nowhere else" sometime after the eighth century and survived in Rome until the thirteenth century. Scholars believe the Old Roman Chant existed prior to c. 800, and it survives in two *Antiphoners* and three *Graduales* compiled after the ninth century. (Antiphoners and Graduales are specialized liturgical books containing chants; see p. 38.) However, the chants in these manuscripts differ from Gregorian only in specific minute details (plate 4).

Extensive modifications of the Old Roman Chant made by the Franks during the Carolingian era created the Romano-Frankish type that (with some further modification) ultimately became known as "Gregorian chant." Though the chant remained impersonal and objective, it became more expressive and less dependent on melodic formulas, and melodic intervals of thirds and fifths were included more often. The greater use of the third may have been a Celtic influence—the people of Britain seem always to have had a predilection for thirds and a "major" sound. Chants were further modified through the practice of troping (see p. 49), and new forms of chant were developed.

In many places, the basic Roman Catholic ritual was altered by the incorporation of local variations and customs that, after a time, became distinctive. Such variant rituals are referred to as the "Use" of that particular church or region. Sarum Use (fig. 3.7) was employed at Salisbury Cathedral from c. 1210 and throughout much of England in the Middle Ages and early Renaissance; it was formally abolished by royal decree in 1559. During the Renaissance, continental composers frequently based polyphonic compositions on Sarum chants.

FIGURE 3.7 A manuscript page from thirteenth-century Use of Sarum showing a portion of the liturgy used during Easter week. *(Source: Antiphonale Sarisburiense)*

SUMMARY

The development of Western music is inseparably linked with the music of the Roman Catholic Church. Ecclesiastical chant is the largest body of monophonic music in existence, and most of it is Gregorian chant. Chant is modal, functional music that is written in a distinctive notation. No manuscript or treatise has been located that gives explicit instructions for authentic performance of the rhythm of Gregorian chant, and several differing views exist concerning chant rhythm. The modes originally assigned to Gregorian chants were a combination of Eastern practice and Western terminology and are not identical with those used later in other medieval Western music. The first verified classification of chants according to a system of eight modal divisions is found in a fragment of a tonary in Charlemagne's *Psalter.*

Ecclesiastical chant may be classified according to the source and literary nature of the text (biblical or nonbiblical, poetry or prose), the number of notes per syllable of text in the musical setting (syllabic, neumatic, melismatic), and the manner in which it is performed (direct, responsorial, antiphonal). In the liturgical Offices, psalms are chanted as inflected recitative, according to psalm tone patterns. A simpler type of liturgical recitative, done on a reciting note, is used for prayers and readings from Scripture.

Several types of liturgies and chants were in existence: Byzantine in the East and Old Roman, Gregorian, Ambrosian, Gallican, Celtic, and Mozarabic in the West. Ambrosian chant is still used in Milan, but the Franko-Roman type known as Gregorian chant supplanted the other Western varieties in most places.

THE ROMAN LITURGY

4

From the earliest times, religious rites using music have been an important part of community life. The Roman liturgy and its chants were significant politically as well as within the church. Government and church leaders realized that a standardized liturgy (both texts and chants) was a way to unify and maintain cohesion within church and state. Moreover, the Roman liturgy and its chants have been a vital force in the development of Western music, inspiring hundreds of musical compositions and providing the impetus for new techniques and new forms. Until well into the sixteenth century, liturgical chants were the basis for much of the Western art music (secular as well as sacred) that was composed. Many of the finest composers of Western art music, including twentieth-century composers, have written Masses, Requiem Masses, and other liturgical music—music that may be heard in concert as well as in church services. Therefore, an understanding of the Roman liturgy and its development is essential to a study of music history.

Meetings of the early Christian communities commonly featured either reenactment of the Lord's Supper or psalm singing, Scripture reading, and prayer. These religious observances developed into the two principal services of the Roman Catholic Church, respectively, the Mass and the Offices. The prescribed ritual (liturgy) for the services developed gradually, and most of the essentials were settled by about the ninth century. Important changes occurred later: the Vatican's formal acceptance of the Credo into the Ordinary of the Mass in 1014, recommendations of the Council of Trent (1545–63) that caused the deletion of numerous Sequences from the Mass, and advocations and directives of the Second Vatican Council (1962–65; hereinafter Vatican II) that permitted use of the vernacular and that instigated reform of the liturgy and its music. Though Vatican II directed that congregations learn and be able to sing the Mass Ordinary in Latin, in many countries that directive has not been observed. The use of Latin in the service has almost become obsolete.

THE LITURGICAL YEAR

The calendar for the liturgical year, called the Proper of the Time, consists of the liturgical observance of all Sundays of the year and the commemoration of the principal events in Christ's life. Some of these events are fixed dates, as is Christmas; others are movable, as is Easter. The liturgical year may be outlined as follows:

Advent, a penitential season, commencing the fourth Sunday before Christmas

Christmas, the twelve days from Christmas Eve to Epiphany (6 January)

From 7 January until the Pre-Lenten season, the time called "after Epiphany"

Pre-Lent, a period of preparation, commencing nine weeks before Easter

Lent, a penitential season, from Ash Wednesday to Easter

Eastertide, from Easter to Pentecost (including Ascension Thursday)

Pentecost, or Whit Sunday, which is seven weeks after Easter

Trinity, from the first Sunday after Pentecost to the beginning of Advent

LITURGICAL BOOKS

The contents of the liturgical books are arranged according to the liturgical calendar. Early liturgical books contained only the texts for the great festival services as celebrated by the pope; those services were modified when used in smaller churches. The *Sacramentary,* used by a celebrant bishop or priest, contained only the texts that varied in accordance with the feast being celebrated. Presumably, invariable texts were memorized. The *Ordo* (pl., *Ordines*) was a book of directions detailing the procedural order of the ceremony and the actions accompanying the ritual.

Modern liturgical books containing the services of the Mass and the offices, both music and rubrics, have been edited by the Benedictine monks of the Abbey at Solesmes, France, and published since 1883. Texts for the Offices are in the *Brevarium* (Breviary) and texts for the Masses in the *Missale* (Missal). The *Antiphonale pro Diurnis Horis* (Antiphonal for the Daily Hours) holds text and music for the Offices; the *Kyriale* (Kyrial) contains music and texts for the Ordinary of the Mass, or that part of the Mass whose texts do not change; the *Graduale Romanum* (Roman Gradual) has in it the variable chants for the Proper of the Time and Proper of the Saints and includes in an appendix chants of the Ordinary and the Requiem Mass. The *Liber Usualis* (Common Book), published from 1896 to 1962, is a compilation of texts and chants for both Mass and Offices, as prescribed by the Roman Catholic Church between the Council of Trent and Vatican II.

In accordance with provisions of the Constitution *De sacra liturgia* (On sacred liturgy) adopted by Vatican II in November 1963, Pope Paul VI (r. 1963–78) directed that new editions of the liturgical books be prepared. The revised *Missale Romanum* was published in Rome in 1970, and revised editions of other liturgical books followed. *The Gregorian Missal for Sundays* (1990) and the *Graduale Romanum* (1974) have superseded the *Liber Usualis* and are intended to be used together. They present the "renewed" liturgical cycle, the various services approved by Vatican II, with directives for performance, and "put back into circulation certain authentic pieces not used for centuries while setting aside inauthentic neo-Gregorian compositions of the 19th or early 20th centuries." A volume containing Vespers and Compline is in preparation.

THE OFFICES

The Offices, or Canonical Hours, constitute the prescribed daily round of worship and prayer in monastic communities, whether recited privately or chanted in public. The Hours began as Vigils first held as night watches on Easter eve. Late in the fourth century, monastic services in Jerusalem included Vigils, Lauds, Terce, None, and Vespers. Early in the fifth century, the Offices observed were almost identical in all the church provinces, though the actual ritual differed in various areas.

The fixed order for the Offices was set by the Rule of St. Benedict in the sixth century: Matins, during the night but after midnight; Lauds, before dawn; Prime, 6 A.M.; Terce, 9 A.M.; Sext, noon; None, 3 P.M.; Vespers, at sunset; and Compline, before retiring. The Offices were intended to mark three-hour intervals, commencing with Matins just after midnight and concluding with Compline at 9 P.M., but practice altered this considerably. It was not unusual to find Matins, Lauds, and Prime being celebrated together, though in proper order, at about 6 A.M. or sunrise, and Compline, which grew out of the practice of saying prayers before retiring, occurring immediately after Vespers (see also p. 42).

Musically, the most important Offices are Vespers, Matins and Lauds, and Compline, in that order. All the Offices use: (a) chanting of Scripture passages (Lessons) with Responses, (b) singing of hymns, and (c) chanting of Psalms or Psalms verses with their **antiphons.** An antiphon is a liturgical chant performed as a refrain, usually before, after, and sometimes between individual verses of a psalm or canticle and its concluding doxology. Originally, this chanting was done from memory; for this reason, the early antiphons are simple syllabic or neumatic chants in a rather limited range, for example, *Lumen* (*LU*, 1357). Later, when soloists assumed responsibility for much of the liturgical singing, antiphons became more ornate. Antiphons are the most numerous type of chant.

Some Offices contain canticles, which, like psalms, are sung in alternation with antiphons. Figure 4.1 illustrates the procedure. Old Testament canticles are included in Matins and Lauds. New Testament canticles are sung in Lauds (*Benedictus Dominus Deus Israel*, "Blessed is the Lord God of Israel," the words of Zacharias, Luke 1:68–79); Vespers (*Magnificat anima mea Dominum*, "My soul doth magnify the Lord," the words of Mary, Luke 1:46–55); and Compline (*Nunc dimittis servum tuum Domine*, "Now lettest Thou Thy servant depart, Lord," the words of the aged Simeon, Luke 2:29–32). Polyphony was sung in Vespers from medieval times and was admitted in Matins and Lauds during *Tenebrae*, the last three days of Holy Week, but was excluded from the other Offices.

Compline uses also a **votive** antiphon to the Blessed Virgin Mary. (A votive chant or service is one honoring a particular saint.) There are four so-called Marian antiphons, one assigned to each of the principal divisions of the church year: *Alma Redemptorus Mater* (Gracious Mother of the Redeemer), used from the Saturday before Advent to and including 1 February; *Ave Regina caelorum* (Hail, Queen of Heaven), from 2 February through Wednesday of Holy Week; *Regina caeli laetare* (Rejoice, Queen of Heaven), from Easter Sunday to and including Friday after Pentecost (fig. 4.2); and *Salve, Regina* (Hail, Queen), from Trinity to the Saturday before Advent. These chants were eleventh- and twelfth-century additions to the Offices. They are not true antiphons and are not used with a psalm or canticle in the manner of antiphons (DWMA4).

FIGURE 4.1 The antiphon *Lumen* as sung traditionally with the canticle *Nunc dimittis*.

FIGURE 4.2 The Marian antiphon *Regina caeli laetare*.

THE MASS

EARLY HISTORY

The early Christians observed Jesus' directive to remember Him through symbolic commemoration of the Lord's Supper with the breaking of unleavened bread and sharing the wine cup. Prayers and singing of psalms figured prominently at these gatherings. As Christian communities increased in size, special religious services were held on Sabbath morning for this commemoration; later, in recognition of the first day of the week as "the Lord's Day," the service was moved to Sunday morning. By the second century, the commemorative rite had become known as the Eucharist, from the Greek word *eucharisto,* meaning "I give thanks." Portions of the synagogue service (e.g., reading Scripture passages and singing psalms) became part of the Christian ritual. In addition to recognized members of the Christian community, persons who had not yet embraced the Christian faith were present at the services. These persons, called catechumens, were not permitted to remain for the Eucharist.

During the first four centuries of the Christian church, the structured religious service commenced with a greeting and continued with what might be termed Liturgy of the Word: three Scripture readings (from the Old Testament, an Epistle, and a Gospel) interspersed with psalms singing; a homily, followed by a prayer. When this instructional liturgy was completed, the catechumens were dismissed. The second half of the service, the Eucharist or Communion observance, began with the offering of gifts, including the bread and wine, and their consecration. Special prayers were offered. Some of these prayers developed into the Preface and Canon and included the Sanctus (the Thrice-Holy, from Isaiah 6:3) but not the Benedictus that is now part of that chant. After the congregation partook of the bread and wine in the Communion ritual, another prayer was offered, and the congregation was dismissed.

Eventually, probably because the congregation consisted primarily of professed believers and few catechumens were in attendance, all present were permitted to remain for the Communion portion of the service. The early dismissal chant, no longer needed, was eliminated. A profession of faith was inserted when required. In the sixth century, the number of Scripture readings was reduced from three to two. Other changes occurred gradually.

By c. 375 the service was being called *Missa.* This name is derived from the chant with which the service concludes, *Ite, missa est,* signifying that the congregation is dismissed (*Ite,* Go) and that the message has been sent forth (*missa est,* it [the message] has been sent forth). Inherent is a directive in accordance with Matthew 28:19 and Mark 16:15: "Go into all the world and proclaim the gospel to all creation." The response *Deo gratias* (Thanks be to God) is, therefore, appropriate.

Greek was the language used in worship for about three hundred years. After Christianity was proclaimed the state religion of the Roman empire, vernacular replaced Greek in some areas, and Latin (which had been used in Christian churches in Africa for some time) became the official liturgical language of the Roman Catholic Church. (See also p. 42.)

THE MASS LITURGY

The Roman Catholic Mass liturgy attained its historically settled form by c. 1014. Numerous regional variations gradually infiltrated this basic format but were eradicated by the decrees of the Council of Trent in 1562 (discussed on p. 202), which mandated liturgical uniformity and the use of Latin (except for the Kyrie) throughout Catholic Christendom. The early division of the Mass into an instructional Liturgy of the Word and a commemorative Eucharistic Liturgy is apparent when the Mass is outlined as in figure 4.3. The numbering of the items in that outline indicates the order of performance and illustrates the interweaving of Proper and Ordinary (DWMA5). Recommendations and directives of Vatican II have effected some changes in the Mass liturgy since 1965 (Insight, "Reforms of Vatican II"; pp. 42–44).

The chants used in the Mass are classified as belonging to either the **Ordinary** or the **Proper** of the Mass according to whether their texts change. Chants of the Ordinary have texts that are invariable; the words remain the same for each rendition of the chant though the music to which they are set may differ. Chants of the Proper have variable texts that are appropriate to the season of the liturgical year

Ordinary of the Mass	Proper of the Mass	Proper / Ordinary (P) (O)
Text invariable	Text variable	
Sung in plainsong or composed music	Sung in plainsong; sometimes composed music used (e.g., motets)	Sung or recited in simple plainsong
Forms normal composed "Mass"		

Liturgy of the Word, for Instruction:

	1) Introit	
2) Kyrie eleison		
3) Gloria in excelsis Deo		
		4) Collect (P)
		5) Epistle (P)
	6) Gradual	
	7) Alleluia or Tract	
	8) Sequence used at Easter, Whit Sunday, Corpus Christi, Seven Dolours (and in Requiem Mass)	
		9) Gospel (P)

At this point, the Sermon (Homily) occurs, if one is presented.

10) Credo

Liturgy of the Eucharist:

	11) Offertory	
		12) Secret (P)
		13) Preface (P)
14) Sanctus, Benedictus		
		15) Canon (O) Pater noster
16) Agnus Dei		
	17) Communion	
		18) Postcommunion Prayer(s) (P)
		19) Ite, missa est or Benedicamus Domino Response (O)

FIGURE 4.3 Outline of the historically settled Mass liturgy used after c. 1014.

or the particular commemoration or feast being celebrated. Thus, the Ordinary, with its unchanging texts, forms a core of the Mass liturgy around which are placed the Scripture readings, psalm settings, and other texts (including the Homily) that are appropriate, or "Proper," to the specific religious occasion.

Mass may be sung or said at any hour from dawn until noon and on some evenings; on Christmas Eve, Mass is sung at midnight. A *Missa solemnis* (High Mass) includes chanting by a celebrant, a deacon, and a subdeacon and singing by choir with possibly soloist(s), the congregation, or both. In a *Missa lecta* (Low Mass), all texts are spoken or recited by one celebrant priest; no music is sung or chanted.

INTROIT The Introit (pronounced "in-tro-it") developed from the sixth-century custom of having processionals on important feast days, especially when the

(continued on page 44)

THE ROMAN LITURGY

Reforms of Vatican II

On 25 January 1959 Pope John XXIII (r. 1958–63) announced his plans to convoke the Twenty-First Ecumenical Council of the Roman Catholic Church. After nearly four years of preparation, that body, which became known as the Second Vatican Council (or Vatican II), began its deliberations. It met in four sessions: (1) 11 October to 8 December 1962, (2) 29 September to 4 December 1963, (3) 14 September to 21 November 1964, and (4) 14 September to 3 December 1965. The 16 documents prepared and approved by the Council were promulgated by Pope Paul VI (r. 1963–78), and an English translation of them was published in 1966 under the title *The Documents of Vatican II*. Of these documents, the Constitution *De sacra liturgia* ("On sacred liturgy") contains directives and recommendations that, either directly or indirectly, affect the liturgical music.

Vatican II sought to reform, simplify, and purify the liturgy and chant and, insofar as possible, to restore them to their original form and condition. To this end, it provided that research be done and that new editions of the liturgical books be prepared. Pope Paul VI carried out that directive, and the Benedictines of Abbaye Saint-Pierre, Solesmes, France, and the International Congress of Sacred Music prepared and published new editions of the liturgical books. In addition, they prepared a new book, *Liber cantualis* ("Book of chants"), containing a selected repertory of Gregorian chants, with Latin texts, suitable for international use. The *Liber cantualis* was specifically designed to comply with the Council's directive that, though it is permissible to celebrate the Mass in the vernacular, steps should be taken to ensure that the congregation is able to sing or to say together **in Latin** those parts of the Ordinary of the Mass that pertain to them (Art. 54, *De sacra liturgia*).

The liturgical calendar has been altered slightly with regard to nomenclature. The designation "Ordinary Time" has been assigned to the following periods: (1) from the Monday after the Sunday following 6 January, up to and including the Tuesday before Ash Wednesday, (2) from the Monday after Pentecost up to, but not including, the first evening prayer of the first Sunday of Advent.

Vatican II directed that the traditional sequence of the Canonical Hours (the Offices) be restored so that as far as possible they are again genuinely related to the time of day at which they are prayed. However, Prime is to be suppressed; Lauds and Vespers are to be considered the chief Hours and celebrated accordingly (Art. 89).

The Mass liturgy has been altered in several respects (fig. 4.4). The Council recommended that in the liturgy greater use be made of psalms and other Scripture passages and directed that "elements which have suffered injury through accidents of history are now to be restored to the earlier norm of the holy Fathers" (Art. 50). Therefore, the third Scripture reading has been restored to the Mass, and a new doxology has been added after the *Pater noster* (Lord's Prayer): "For the kingdom and the power and the glory are Yours for ever. Amen." In many churches, the psalms are being accorded more use; for example, several verses (instead of just one) are sung in the Introit.

Since 1965, *Benedicamus Domino*, once serving as an alternate dismissal chant, has fallen into disuse.

Some alterations have been made in the use and form of the Sequences. Before 1963, five Sequences were in use, and a particular one of them was incorporated in the Mass at certain specified feasts. By directive of Vatican II, "Except on Easter Sunday and Pentecost the Sequences are optional." Moreover, simplified versions of two of the Sequences have been provided: *Lauda Sion* and *Stabat Mater*. Rubrics in the *Graduale Romanum* of 1974 state that, if *Lauda Sion* is sung, either the complete or the abbreviated form may be used. The *Stabat Mater* appears as a Sequence in *Liber cantualis* in a strophic setting. However, the traditional setting of the *Stabat Mater* Sequence is printed in the *Graduale Romanum* of 1974.

The general atmosphere and structure of the Requiem Mass has changed. In accordance with the statement adopted by Vatican II that "the rite for the burial of the dead should evidence more clearly the paschal character of Christian death," the Requiem Mass has been altered to correspond with the twentieth-century view of death as a glorious home-going rather than a dreaded judgment. Most often, clergy wear white vestments for the rite. Three Scripture readings are used in the Service: Old Testament, New Testament other than Gospel, and Gospel; an Alleluia may be used before the Gospel reading. The Sequence is optional—the judgmental text of *Dies irae* is seldom chanted. A homily is presented, but no eulogy. The altered format of the Requiem Mass is given in figure 4.5. *(continued)*

THE MASS

Ordinary	Proper	Prayers and Lessons
	Introductory Rites:	
	1) Introit	
2) Kyrie eleison		
3) Gloria in excelsis Deo		
		4) Collect
	Liturgy of the Word:	
		5) First Reading: Old Testament
	6) Gradual	
		7) Second Reading: from Epistles, or Acts, or Revelation
	8) Alleluia or Tract	
	9) Sequence, used at Easter and Pentecost (optional at Corpus Christi, Seven Dolours, and Requiem)	
		10) Gospel
	11) Homily (Exegesis and Application of Scriptures)	
12) Credo		
		13) Intercessory Prayers
	Liturgy of the Eucharist:	
	14) Offertory	
		15) Secret
		16) Preface
17) Sanctus, Benedictus		
		18) Canon
	Communion Rite:	
		19) Pater noster Doxology Sign of Peace
20) Agnus Dei		
	21) Communion	
		22) Postcommunion Prayers
	Concluding Rite:	
		(Any brief announcements may be made)
		23) Benediction
24) Dismissal, Ite, missa est Response		

FIGURE 4.4 Outline of the Mass liturgy in use after Vatican II.

(continued)

REQUIEM MASS

Ordinary	Proper	Proper/Ordinary
	1) Introit: *Requiem aeternam dona eis Domine*	
2) Kyrie		
		3) Collect
		4) First Scripture Reading: from Old Testament
	5) Gradual (Responsorial Psalm)	
		6) Second Reading: Epistle
	7) Alleluia	
		8) Third Reading: Gospel
	9) Brief Homily	
	10) Offertory	
		11) Eucharistic Prayer: *Sursum corda*
		12) Preface for the Dead
13) Sanctus, Benedictus		
		14) Canon
		15) *Pater noster* Doxology Sign of Peace
16) Agnus Dei		
	17) Communion: *Lux aeterna*	
		18) Postcommunion Prayer(s)
		19) *Requiescant in pace.* *Amen*

FIGURE 4.5 Outline of the Requiem Mass in use after Vatican II.

pope visited a church in Rome. The music accompanying the procession from its entrance into the church and up to the altar had to be expandable or contractible, depending on the degree of pomp and the size of the procession. Originally, this music—the Introit—consisted of an antiphon, a complete psalm, the Lesser Doxology (*Gloria Patri*), and a repetition of the antiphon. The Introit could be shortened by eliminating psalm verses. In some churches the antiphon was chanted after each verse of the psalm and in the middle and at the end of the doxology and was performed antiphonally between two choirs or two half-choirs. At some time during the late eighth or early ninth century, the Introit was reduced to antiphon, one psalm verse, doxology, and antiphon and was performed after the celebrant reached the foot of the altar. Thus, the Introit became a prelude to the service rather than processional or entrance music. However, *The Gregorian Missal* directs that the Introit "be sung by the choir, and repeated after each psalm verse chanted by cantors, while the celebrant enters and venerates the altar."

An Introit is known by the first word of its antiphon's text. Some examples of Introits are *Resurrexi* (*LU,* 777) for Easter Mass, *Puer natus est nobis* (*LU,*

408) for Mass on Christmas Day, and *Requiem aeternam* (*LU*, 1807) for Requiem Mass. The antiphon *Resurrexi* (DWMA5) is mainly neumatic but contains some short melismas and thus contrasts with the simple intonation of Psalm 139:1, 2 and the doxology.

KYRIE ELEISON   The *Kyrie eleison* and *Agnus Dei* were Eastern imports that entered the Mass by way of the litany, where each of them frames solemn supplications and responses addressed to God, to the Virgin Mary, or to a particular saint. The Kyrie appeared in the litany in Milan in the fourth century and was in use in Rome by the sixth century. To the phrase *Kyrie eleison* (Lord, have mercy), used in pagan rites, the Christian church added *Christe eleison* (Christ, have mercy). The Greek text was retained in the Roman liturgy. In medieval times, the words *Kyrie eleison* were frequently elided in performance to *Kyrieleison*.

The Kyrie consists of nine phrases: *Kyrie eleison* chanted three times, *Christe eleison* chanted three times, and *Kyrie eleison* chanted three times (DWMA5). The triple rendition of each phrase of text permits a variety of musical settings as well as a kind of musical cadence rhyme in which all cadences employ a common phrase as a unifying feature. This may be seen in *Kyrie Rex Genitor* (*LU*, 31).

The Kyrie of the Requiem Mass (*LU*, 1807) uses the same music for all but the final phrase, which is slightly varied: AAA,AAA,AAA'. This pattern is especially suitable for congregational singing; probably this Kyrie is one of the oldest chants. Other formal patterns include overall ABA with all exclamations of the same text having the same music (*LU*, 28); ABC, with all utterances within a section using basically the same music (*LU*, 25); or more sophisticated versions of those patterns, with the musical phrases being expanded on repetition or even with different music for some of the repeated texts (*LU*, 22).

GLORIA   The Gloria, whose opening lines are the song of the heavenly host on the night of the Nativity (Luke 2:14), is sometimes called the Song of the Angels or the Greater Doxology. At first, the Gloria was included in the Mass only on those special occasions when a bishop was celebrant. Gradually, its use was extended to other festal days and Sundays, but the Gloria is excluded on penitential days, during Advent

and Lent, and from ferial and Requiem Masses. (A ferial day is a weekday on which no Catholic feast occurs.)

In performance the opening phrase, *Gloria in excelsis Deo* (Glory to God in the highest), is always chanted by the bishop or celebrant priest. Originally, the remainder of the chant was sung by the congregation, but portions were gradually assumed by assisting clergy, and ultimately all but the opening phrase was assumed by the full choir who chanted the Gloria antiphonally. There are no textual repetitions in this chant, and no overall formal pattern is apparent. Frequently, the musical setting of the Gloria is neumatic (DWMA5).

GRADUAL   The Gradual is very melismatic psalmody. It followed the First Lesson (first Scripture reading), and in performance the soloist stood on the *gradus*, the step leading to the raised pulpit. From this performance practice came the name *Gradual*.

Many Graduals were created by centonization. In each mode there were a number of standard melodic motives and phrases that, with their extensions and variations, were combined to form a Gradual. Occasionally, newly composed phrases or motives were inserted. Until the thirteenth century, the Gradual had ternary (ABA) form: a choral respond, a solo verse, and repetition of the choral respond. Then the Gradual was reduced to a choral respond followed by a solo verse. In modern performance, the Gradual commences with a solo intonation, but the choir sings most of the respond; a soloist sings the verse as far as its last phrase, at which point the choir joins for conclusion of the chant.

Some historically significant Graduals are *Viderunt omnes* (*LU*, 409), used in Christmas Mass; *Haec dies* (*LU*, 778), the Easter Gradual (DWMA5); and *Sederunt principes* (*LU*, 416), sung in Mass on St. Stephen's Day, 26 December.

ALLELUIA   The Alleluia came to the Christian church from the Hebrew synagogue; the Hebrew words *Hallelu Jah* mean "Praise ye Jehovah." In earliest times, this chant was sung throughout the year in both Eastern and Western churches as responsorial psalmody, with a soloist singing a verse and the congregation (later, the choir) responding with "Alleluia."

However, certain Roman popes placed restrictions on its performance. For instance, Gregory I prohibited it during Lent.

In modern liturgical practice, from Easter to Pentecost the word *Alleluia* is sung at the end of every important chant of the Proper, in both Offices and Mass, but the Alleluia has been excluded from the service when its joyous text is deemed inappropriate to the occasion—during penitential seasons and, until c. 1965, the Requiem. At those times, a Tract is substituted. As a general rule, when a Mass contains no Gloria, it contains no Alleluia.

In performance, a soloist sings the first Alleluia, which is repeated by the choir and concludes with the textless melismatic coda known as the *jubilus;* most of the ensuing verse is sung by cantors, and the choir joins them for the last phrase. Finally, a soloist sings the Alleluia as at the beginning, and the choir performs the *jubilus* (DWMA5). The Alleluia is one of the most melodious and artistic chants of the Mass. It is considered a very melismatic chant in the Roman rite, and it is even more florid in Eastern, Mozarabic, and Ambrosian liturgies.

TRACT   Called *cantus tractus* because the chant was designed to be sung from beginning to end without interruption, the Tract consists of a series of psalm verses, all from the same psalm, performed by a soloist. Rarely is a complete psalm used. The Tract is the most ancient solo chant of the Mass, having its roots in Hebrew synagogue solo psalmody. The ornate melodies, created by centonization, were constructed in the second and eighth modes only. Although included in the Mass when the joyous Alleluia is prohibited, the Tract is not particularly sorrowful or solemn. Even the tract used in the Requiem Mass, *Absolve, Domine* (*LU,* 1809), is well supplied with melismas (DWMA6).

SEQUENCE   The Sequence, which came into existence during the ninth century as a result of the practice of troping (discussed on p. 49), was sung in the Mass immediately following the Alleluia, from whose *jubilus* it seems to have sprung. If two Alleluias are included in the Mass, the Sequence follows the second one. Thousands of Sequences were composed during the Middle Ages and early Renaissance. These chants var-

ied from region to region and diocese to diocese, according to the particular customs and requirements of the churches in which they were used. As a result of the deliberations of the Council of Trent (see p. 202), all but four Sequences were eliminated from liturgical use: *Dies irae* (Day of wrath), *Victimae paschali laudes* (Praises to the paschal Victim), *Lauda Sion* (Zion, praise), and *Veni Sancte Spiritus* (Come, Holy Spirit). From the thirteenth century on, these Sequences have inspired and/or become a part of many composers' creative works.

Until c. 1965, *Dies irae* (*LU,* 1810), was sung after the Tract in the Requiem Mass. The poetic text, which is attributed to Thomas of Celano (d. 1250), consists of 18 strophes and a short requiem prayer. Most of the strophes are paired in the musical setting. Analysis of *Dies irae* by strophes gives the following pattern: a a b b c c a a b b c c a a b b c d e f.

Victimae paschali laudes (*LU,* 780), whose text is ascribed to Wipo (d. 1048), is sung in the Easter Mass (DWMA5). The setting is syllabic, and the pairing of strophes typical of Sequences is apparent in the music: a b b c c d.

Lauda Sion (*LU,* 945), used in Mass at Corpus Christi, was composed in 1263 by St. Thomas Aquinas (1227–74). Its long poetic text (24 strophes) is set syllabically in paired strophes.

Veni Sancte Spiritus (*LU,* 880), written in the late twelfth century, is sung on Whit Sunday (Pentecost) and for six days thereafter. Its ten rhymed strophes are set neumatically and are paired.

In 1727, Pope Benedict XIII (r. 1724–30) readmitted to the liturgy the Sequence *Stabat Mater dolorosa* (The sorrowful Mother stood) for use at the Feast of the Seven Sorrows of the Blessed Virgin Mary, celebrated on 15 September. This Sequence (*LU,* 1634v) is attributed to Jacopone da Todi (d. 1306). The *Stabat Mater* text is used also in the Offices as a hymn at Vespers on Friday after Passion Sunday.

CREDO   The Credo was first used liturgically as an individual profession of faith made at baptism; this accounts for the singular verb *Credo* (I believe). The text is the "Nicene Creed" (see p. 22). In Eastern and Mozarabic churches, the Credo was used in the Mass liturgy in the sixth century, but not until 798 was it regularly included in the Mass in Gallic or Roman

PLATE 1 Wooden votive tablet, c. 540 B.C., found in cave of Pitsa near Corinth. Among the worshipers in this sacrificial scene are a lyra player and an aulos player wearing a *phorbeia*. *(National Archaeological Museum, Athens)*

(a)

PLATE 2 Hagia Sophia (Church of Holy Wisdom), Constantinople, c. 1850. (*a*) View of the church from the southwest. (*b*) Interior of the church. The church was built for Justinian I between 532 and 537. The dome, which dominates the edifice, is 108 feet in diameter and its crown is 180 feet above the ground. The huge buttresses were added to the building sometime later, and the four minarets were added after the Ottoman conquest in 1453, when the church became a mosque. In the twentieth century the building was secularized, and it is now a museum. Polychrome lithographs made by Gaspare Fossati, c. 1850.

(b)

(a)

(b)

PLATE 3 Mosaic murals in the apse of the Church of San Vitale, Ravenna, Italy, depicting the Offertory procession of Mass: (*a*) The left mural in the apse portrays Emperor Justinian I flanked by Bishop Maximianus and other clergy, court officials, and military. (*b*) The right mural pictures Empress Theodora and her attendants. The rulers are carrying the bread and the wine vessel.

AD MISSAM IN DIE

PLATE 4 *Resurrexi* Introit with Psalm verses 138/139; 1, 2, from Easter Mass, showing derivation of its modern square notation from two of the early manuscripts consulted in its preparation. The black neumes above the square notation are from the tenth-century MS Laon 230; the red neumes below the square notation are from the eleventh-century MS Einsiedeln 121. *(From Graduale Triplex, 1979, Abbaye Saint-Pierre de Solesmes, 72300 Solesmes, France)*

churches. Then, in conjunction with Charlemagne's reforms, the Council of Aix-la-Chapelle decreed that the Credo be sung at Mass between the Gospel reading and Communion. Charlemagne's adviser, Alcuin, advocated using a Latin translation instead of Greek. Though Pope Leo III sanctioned the use of the Credo in Frankish churches, that chant did not officially enter the Roman Mass until Pope Benedict VIII required it in 1014 at the insistence of Emperor Henry II (r. 1002–24).

Originally, the Credo was deemed appropriate for Sundays and important feasts only; it is not included in ferial or Requiem Masses. In modern performance, the celebrant priest chants the first phrase, *Credo in unum Deum* (I believe in one God), and the choir or congregation continues from *Patrem omnipotentem* (the Father Almighty). Credo I (*LU,* 64) is considered the oldest Credo; its setting is almost completely syllabic, and recurrent use of melodic formulas is apparent (DWMA5).

OFFERTORY   St. Augustine is credited with introducing into the liturgy at Carthage the custom of singing an Offertory chant while the gifts of bread and wine were brought forward to be consecrated. The earliest Offertory chants in existence are elaborate melodies for antiphons and verses, which would indicate solo performance. In these eighth- and ninth-century manuscripts, the Offertory consists of an antiphon, two or three verses, and a respond or refrain that most often is an exact repetition of the conclusion of the antiphon. In Gregorian liturgy, verses were gradually deleted until only the antiphon remained; perhaps the deletions were concurrent with changes in the character of the offering and the manner of its collection. In Ambrosian and Mozarabic liturgies, Offertory verses are still present.

In modern performance, the first phrase of the Offertory is sung by one or more cantor(s), and the remainder of the antiphon is performed by a choir (DWMA5). The Offertory is highly melismatic. Frequently, the expressive character of the melismas suggests an early use of text painting, for example, melismas rising in pitch on the word *ascendit* (ascends) and lowering in pitch on *descendit* (descends).

SANCTUS/BENEDICTUS   The text of this acclamation is a combination of portions of verses from both the Old and the New Testaments. The Sanctus is taken from Isaiah 6:3 and the Hosanna and Benedictus from Matthew 21:9. Both Scripture verses were modified slightly. The Sanctus was used in the Hebrew synagogue; Hosanna and Benedictus were Christian additions.

Originally, congregation and clergy together sang the Sanctus. This is obvious from the concluding words of the Preface, which suggest that the people join the heavenly host in singing a hymn of praise, saying *Sanctus, sanctus, sanctus* (Holy, holy, holy). Gradual transference of the chant from congregation to assisting clergy to trained choir began in the eighth century and occurred at different times in different areas. In most churches, by the end of the twelfth century the choir had assumed full responsibility for the Sanctus. Since Vatican II, the congregation and the clergy sing the Sanctus. In the service, there is a pause after the Sanctus, during which time Elevation of the Host occurs; then the Benedictus is sung (DWMA5).

No standard pattern is apparent in the musical settings of the Sanctus. Some are syllabic; others are neumatic, except for melismas on the first three words. Frequently, these three melismatic pronouncements of the word *Sanctus* are set musically as a b a; often the two Hosanna sections are given identical or very similar music. An example is Sanctus II (*LU,* 21). It would seem natural to assume that syllabic settings of the Sanctus are the oldest. Yet, if the dating in the *Liber Usualis* is accurate, the reverse might be true, for Sanctus XVII (*LU,* 63), from the thirteenth century, is much simpler than others with earlier dating.

AGNUS DEI   Introduction of the Agnus Dei into the Mass in the late seventh century is credited to the Greek Pope Sergius I (r. 687–701). Like the Kyrie, the Agnus Dei is an acclamation, a petition for mercy. Part of the text is a modification of the words of John the Baptist, recorded in John 1:29: "Behold the Lamb of God, who takes away the sin of the world." Originally, in the chant, only a single line of text was used: *Agnus Dei, qui tollis peccata mundi, miserere nobis* (Lamb of God, who takes away the sins of the world, have mercy on us). At first this was sung by the congregation, as were the other chants of the Ordinary, but by the end of the eighth century the Agnus Dei was being sung by the trained choir in many churches.

At the time of its introduction into the Mass, the Agnus Dei was sung during Fraction. Breaking the loaves of leavened bread consumed a considerable amount of time; therefore, the chant was repeated an indefinite number of times. During the tenth and eleventh centuries, it became customary to use small pieces of unleavened bread instead of leavened loaves, and actual fraction was no longer necessary. Fewer repetitions of the chant were required. From time to time, the Agnus Dei was assigned other functions but ultimately was used to fill the time between Consecration of the Host and distribution of the Communion elements. The number of acclamations in the chant was finalized at three, and the third petition was revised, substituting the words *dona nobis pacem* (give us peace) for *miserere nobis* (have mercy on us). This change of text caused no musical problems; each of the two phrases contains six syllables, and the grammatical accentuation is identical (DWMA5). At the same time, an adjustment was made in the Agnus Dei of the Requiem Mass (*LU*, 1815); the word *sempiternam* was added to the last phrase to make the chant conclude *dona eis requiem sempiternam* (give them eternal rest).

Various formal patterns are found in the musical settings of the Agnus Dei, such as ABA (Agnus Dei XV, *LU*, 58), AAA (Agnus Dei XVIII, *LU*, 63), and AA'A (Agnus Dei IX, *LU*, 42). Sometimes, within an overall ABA setting of the three petitions, the musical setting of the words *qui tollis* is identical (Agnus Dei X, *LU*, 45). Musical cadence rhyme occurs often, as in Agnus Dei II, IV, VIII, and others.

COMMUNION   From early Christian times, the singing of a psalm or a hymn during Communion was common practice. Use of a hymn may have derived from Gospel accounts of events at the Lord's Supper: "And having sung a hymn, they went forth to the Mount of Olives" (Matt. 26:30; Mark 14:26). Several of the Church Fathers cited the use of Psalm 33 (34, KJV), in which verse 8 was considered especially appropriate: "O taste and see that the Lord is good."

The use of psalms and hymns was not identical in all liturgies. In Byzantine and Celtic rites, both hymns and psalms were used during Communion on different occasions. In the Ambrosian rite, two antiphons (without psalms) were sung: one during fraction of the Host and the other during distribution of the elements. In the Roman ritual, Communion music consisted of an antiphon and a psalm, with embellished psalm tones used for the verses. Originally, in the Roman Mass, Introit and Communion were similar; frequently, both used the same psalm with different antiphons. Some eighth-century *Ordines* detail explicitly the manner of performance, instructing the choir to commence singing the antiphon as soon as the priest began administering the sacrament, and to follow the antiphon with the psalm. When all communicants had partaken of the elements, the priest signaled the choir to sing the *Gloria Patri,* followed by repetition of the antiphon.

During the eleventh century, psalm verses were gradually deleted from the Communion; a century later, only the antiphon remained. At that time, the congregation received Communion infrequently.

Communion settings are not uniform in style. Most communions are rather short; the music possesses a serenity appropriate to the sacrament. Though many Communions contain melismas, the floridity is restrained rather than exuberant (DWMA5).

DISMISSAL   The dismissal *Ite, missa est* has always been chanted by the celebrant priest or a deacon. Originally, the congregation responded with *Deo gratias* (Thanks be to God). Eventually, the choir assumed this response, and it became more elaborate. In the eleventh century, the alternate dismissal chant *Benedicamus Domino* (Let us bless the Lord) came into use as replacement for *Ite, missa est* when the Mass did not contain a Gloria. Both dismissal chants and the response are sung to the same music.

Although the Mass attained its settled liturgical format through a process of gradual growth and development, a remarkable symmetry is apparent, especially with regard to the Ordinary. The affirmation of faith, the Credo, is centrally located. The texts of both the Gloria and the Sanctus include songs of the heavenly host, and the Kyrie and Agnus Dei parallel each other in many respects: both were Eastern imports, both are textually tripartite, and both were used in the litany in a manner similar to their employment in the Mass—the Kyrie at or near the beginning and the Agnus Dei at or near the end. The location of these chants in the Mass was balanced by similar antiphonal psalmody:

the Introit preceding the Kyrie and the Communion following the Agnus Dei. Moreover, the texts of these two acclamations contain some of the same phrases: the Greek *eleison* and the Latin *miserere nobis* both mean "have mercy on us." Perhaps this was one reason the Kyrie remained in Greek when the other chants were translated into Latin.

REQUIEM MASS

The Requiem Mass (Mass for the Dead) received its name from the first word of the antiphon to its Introit and its Gradual, which commences *Requiem aeternam dona eis Domine* (Give them eternal rest, Lord). Though the Collect, Scripture reading, Secret, and Postcommunion may vary on certain occasions, the remainder of the Proper and the Ordinary texts are invariable. Neither the Gloria nor the Credo is used in the Requiem; the Tract *Absolve, Domine* (Lord, absolve) traditionally replaced the Alleluia and was followed by the Sequence

Dies irae (Day of wrath; DWMA7). On very solemn occasions, the Responsory *Libera me, Domine* (Free me, Lord) is sung after the Communion. The traditional Requiem Mass, in the format used prior to the reforms of Vatican II, is outlined in figure 4.6.

In the development of the Requiem Mass, the Sequence was the last item to be added; the essential features of the Mass were settled by the fourteenth century. Prior to the Council of Trent, the Gradual *Si ambulem in medio umbrae mortis* (If I walk in the midst of the shadow of death) and the Tract *Sicut cervus desiderat ad fontes aquarum* (As the hart longs for springs of water) might be used as alternatives; these derive from Sarum Use.

TROPES

Troping is the expansion of a chant by means of (a) words added to an existing chant melisma, (b) music added to extend an existing melisma or to create a

REQUIEM MASS

Ordinary	Proper	Proper / Ordinary
Text invariable	Text invariable	
Sung: Plainsong or composed music	Plainsong, sometimes composed	Plainsong
	1) Introit: *Requiem aeternam dona eis Domine*	
2) Kyrie		
		3) Collect
		4) Epistle: I Thess. 4:13–18
	5) Gradual: *Requiem aeternam* ℣. *In memoria aeterna erit*	
	6) Tract: *Absolve, Domine*	
	7) Sequence: *Dies irae, dies illa*	
		8) Gospel: John 11:21–27
	9) Offertory: *Domine Jesu Christe*	
		10) Secret
		11) Preface for the Dead
12) Sanctus, Benedictus		
13) Agnus Dei		
	14) Communion: *Lux aeterna* (Sometimes, Responsory *Libera me, Domine* is included)	
		15) Postcommunion
		16) *Requiescant in pace. Amen.*

FIGURE 4.6 Outline of the Requiem Mass as sung prior to Vatican II.

THE ROMAN LITURGY

new one, or (c) new music and text added before, within, or at the end of an existing chant (DWMA8, 9). Textual tropes are commentary. Usually, textual interpolations complement, elaborate, or clarify the original words of the chant; the interpolations themselves, when considered apart from the original text, are coherent. It is not known precisely when and where troping began, for tropes are present in the earliest extant manuscripts of liturgical chant music, which date from the late eighth or early ninth century, but it is believed that the practice started in Frankish lands. Troping did not originate at St. Gall, though that monastery and St. Martial at Limoges became important centers of troping. The practice—and its name—may stem from the Byzantine church, where, earlier, interpolations called *troparia* were performed (see p. 26).

The troping of chants flourished during the tenth through the twelfth centuries. Virtually every kind of chant except the Credo was troped, and the practice gave rise to new forms of liturgical music. In accordance with recommendations for reform made by the Council of Trent, textual tropes were deleted from liturgical chants. Vestiges of tropes remain, however, in some textless melismas and in the titles of Kyries, such as Kyrie *orbis factor* (Lord, creator of the world). Moreover, the practice of troping gave rise to several new forms of church music, including the Sequence, liturgical drama, and the motet (discussed on p. 82).

Notker Balbulus, "the Stammerer" (c. 840–912), poet and author of many tropes, related in the preface to his *Liber Ymnorum* (Book of Hymns) the circumstances that first acquainted him with textual tropes. As a youth, he experienced difficulty remembering long melismas and sought some device to help him retain them. About that time (c. 852), a priest came to St. Gall from Jumièges (near Rouen) because his monastery had been devastated by Normans. Notker noticed in the refugee's *Antiphoner* that words had been written beneath certain melismas called *sequentiae* (Sequences). The supplemental texts were distasteful to Notker, but the idea fascinated him. He troped an Alleluia, then showed the trope to his teacher, who emended it and instructed, "Each neume of the melody should have one syllable." Notker continued to write tropes and, following the suggestion of Marcellus, choirmaster at St. Gall, assembled these in

Liber Ymnorum (c. 880). Notker wrote in his preface that he showed his tropes to other monks and that Marcellus had his choirboys sing some of them.

Liber Ymnorum is significant for several reasons. Its preface establishes an approximate time when troping was introduced at St. Gall. The book contains only texts, and in the early repertory a certain text fits only one melody. Scholars have been able to match Notker's texts with specific chants, to place certain chants definitely in the ninth century, and to determine that the most important melodies in the West Frankish liturgy were used also at St. Gall.

SEQUENCES

As described by Amalar of Metz (c. 775–c. 850) in *Liber officialis*, written c. 823, the *sequentia* was an extensive melisma substituted for the *jubilus* at the repetition of the Alleluia section after the Verse. Thus, in the early ninth century a definite relationship existed between the *sequentia* and the Alleluia—a relationship that later undoubtedly influenced placement of the independent Sequence after the Alleluia in the Mass. In many manuscripts, the same *sequentiae* appear in different contexts: (a) melodies alone, grouped in a section titled *Sequentarium*; (b) melodies with syllabically set texts, grouped in a section called *Prosarium*; and (c) melodies with or without texts, notated with the chants for which they are interpolations. Often, in both *Sequentarium* and *Prosarium* sections, a melody is preceded by the designation *Alleluia I,* implying that the notated melody was used as Amalar stated.

Sequentiae soon became detached from Alleluias and were written as independent chants—Sequences— each complete in itself musically and textually. Many Sequences cannot be linked with known Alleluias and may have been created without reference to any particular Alleluia. Yet, when the Sequence entered the Mass, the early association of Sequence with Alleluia was reflected in the location of the two chants in the liturgy.

The earliest Sequences are prose; even when endrhyme is present, the lines cannot be scanned poetically. Most of the Sequences written after A.D. 1000 are poetry and have recognizable rhyme scheme and regular accentuation that permits poetic scansion. By the twelfth century, Sequences contain poetic stanzas. The mature Sequence may be defined as a syllabic setting of a Latin text written mainly as a series of couplets that are isosyllabic lines; both lines of a couplet are sung to the same melody, but successive couplets use different melodies and usually differ in length.

The manner of performance of early Sequences is not known. Probably, they were sung antiphonally. Notker's mention of an Antiphoner and the association of Sequence with Alleluia lend credence to this. Although some Sequence texts mention instruments, it does not necessarily follow that those instruments were used in the church service. Such references may be only symbolic. At least one eleventh-century manuscript containing Sequences is illustrated by miniatures of instrumentalists, and in some regions legislation prohibited performance on certain instruments during church services. Edict and practice do not always coincide, however. Probably, the only musical instrument authorized for church use was the organ, but whether its tones supported the singing of Sequences is not known.

LITURGICAL DRAMA

Introductions to chants form an important part of trope repertory. These introductions vary considerably. Some are quite short and serve merely to set the scene or to identify a character or characters whose words form the ensuing chant. Notker included in *Liber Ymnorum* a cycle of eleven four-line introductory tropes to Introits of the Mass for the most important commemorations in the liturgical year. Some authors constructed introductions as dialogues, the performance of which varied in accordance with the ingenuity of the performers and the artistic indulgence of the local church authorities. Dialogue tropes to the Introit of the Mass are the simplest forms of liturgical drama. Important centers of liturgical drama were Winchester Cathedral in England and the Abbeys of St. Gall and St. Martial. Tenth-century *Tropers* from these centers survive.

The most important and most numerous of the early liturgical dramas are the *Quem quaeritis* dialogue tropes to Introits of the Masses for Easter and Christmas (fig. 4.7). Some of these are quite simple, but more than 400 are expanded versions—even tropes were troped. In its simplest form, the Easter dialogue consists of three sentences:

Quem quaeritis in sepulchro, o Christicolae?
Jesum Nazarenum crucifixum, o caelicola.
Non est hic, surrexit sicut praedixerat;
  ite, nuntiate quia surrexit de sepulchro.

Whom seek ye in the tomb, O Christians?
The crucified Jesus of Nazareth, O heavenly one.
He is not here, he is risen as he predicted;
  go, announce that he is risen from the tomb.

This version is in tenth-century manuscripts from both St. Martial and St. Gall (DWMA9). Manuscripts from the tenth to the sixteenth century contain enlarged versions, called *Visitatio sepulchri,* which are assigned various liturgical locations, including the Offices. In Sarum Use, the Easter drama appears in two fourteenth-century *Processionals* used at the Church of St. John the Evangelist in Dublin, where the drama was performed after the last Respond at Easter Matins. In a fourteenth-century manuscript used at the collegiate church at Essen, where both canons and canonesses served, the rubrics for *Visitatio sepulchri* show that the lines of the three Marys were sung by women and those of the angels by men. The participants wore normal ecclesiastical robes and were permitted to sing from a book.

In addition to *Quem quaeritis* dialogues, surviving liturgical dramas include an early thirteenth-century *Play of Daniel* created by students at the cathedral school at Beauvais, the *Conversion of Saint Paul* and the *Raising of Lazarus* from Fleury, the *Play of Herod,* and several dramas honoring the Virgin Mary and other saints. All the plays were intended to convey a mood of joyful celebration. The primary purpose of the *Play of Daniel* is to celebrate Christmas—the drama presents the biblical story of Daniel, prophet of Christ's coming, but the play's conclusion leaps ahead in time when an angel cries out, "*Natus est Christus!*" ("Christ is born!").

SUMMARY

The Mass and the Offices, the two principal services of the Roman Catholic Church, evolved from the religious observances of the early Christian communities. Practices of the Hebrew synagogue figured prominently in these observances; as the Mass developed, synagogue practices were retained and some items

FIGURE 4.7 *Winchester Troper* manuscript book open to page showing *Quem quaeritis* trope. *(MS 473, Parker Library, Corpus Christi College, Cambridge, England)*

were transferred from the Byzantine church. The Mass liturgy attained its historically settled basic format in 1014, when Pope Benedict VIII formally added the Credo to the Ordinary. Troping was an innovation of the ninth century; the Abbeys at St. Gall and St. Martial became important centers of it. The production of tropes led to new liturgical forms, among them the Sequence, the liturgical drama, and later the motet.

Liturgical reforms advocated by the Council of Trent (1545–63) resulted in the deletion of trope texts from the liturgy; all but four Sequences were removed from the Mass repertory. However, the *Stabat Mater* was readmitted in 1727. Further reforms occurred after Vatican II. In addition to permitting the use of the vernacular in the Mass Service, Vatican II advocated reform that would restore the chant and the liturgy as nearly as possible to the old Roman type. New editions of the official liturgical books that have been prepared by the Benedictine monks of Abbaye Saint-Pierre, Solesmes, France, explicitly detail the liturgy and music.

EARLY MIDDLE AGES

5

From the ninth through the eleventh century, the political pattern in Europe became increasingly fragmented and complex. The Carolingian empire was divided and subdivided more than once as rulers died and kingdoms were partitioned to satisfy heirs. Marauders invaded Europe from north, south, and east, conquering and plundering but not always bringing only destruction. The Arabs, who had learned much from the populations they conquered, contributed greatly to Western culture. Eastern science and Greek philosophy had been absorbed into Arab culture. The writings of Aristotle and other ancients had been translated into Arabic and given back to the Western world in Latin; the decimal system was accepted as the basis of mathematics, and the first medical school established at Salerno, Italy, was in an area with Muslim associations.

The tenth and eleventh centuries witnessed the rise of the feudal system and the growth of a monarchial system that used the church to its own ends by replacing insubordinate vassals with clergy to achieve political stability. These centuries saw an increase in population, the growth of towns and a revival of urban life, and the rise of a middle-class populace. Commerce and trade, which were at a low ebb after the dissolution of the Carolingian empire, now began their comeback.

Feudalism, begun under the Merovingians, was widespread in Europe by the twelfth century. Feudalism was a system of land tenure and personal relationships in which a lord gave land to vassals in return for specific services and pledged loyalty. The system, which embraced both clergy and laity, filled the need for protection. Contractual agreements between lord and vassal created a hierarchy that extended from the king to the lowest peasant. Linked with feudalism was the manorial system, under which landlords exercised financial, judicial, and other rights over peasants who were bound to their land. The widespread belief that the king provided security contributed to the rise of monarchies. Those in England and France were well established by the end of the twelfth century.

In Byzantium, art and scholarship flourished, and free education was available at the University of Constantinople. In spite of the apparent well-being of the empire, strained relations existed between Eastern and Western branches of the church. Triggered by the incompatibility of the papal envoy and the Eastern patriarch, a complete break between Eastern and Western churches occurred in 1054. On the heels of that came the onslaught of the Seljuk Turks.

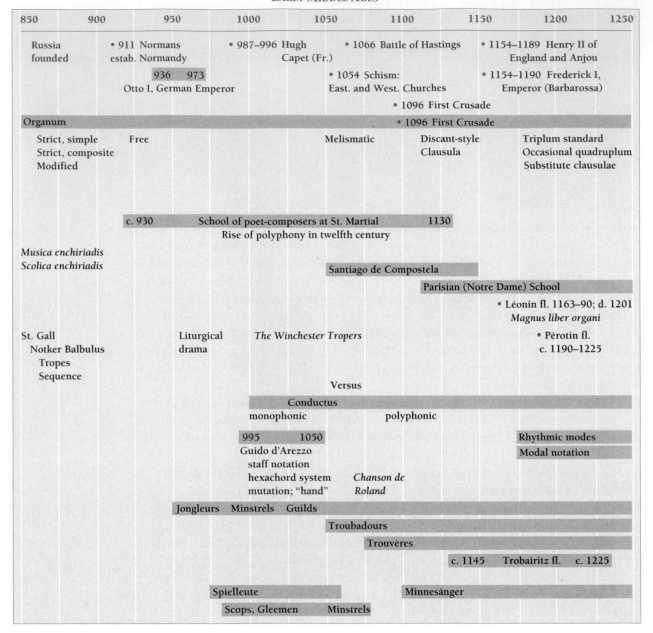

In 1095, Pope Urban II (r. 1088–99) called the First Crusade for the purpose of securing the Holy Land, particularly Jerusalem, from the Muslims. The Crusade was successful; Jerusalem was regained. Other Crusades ensued, until the middle of the fifteenth century. The Crusades had a significant effect on contemporary society. They strengthened the position of the papacy, stimulated commerce by creating a demand for luxury goods from the East, and invigorated intellectual activity through the making of new contacts.

During the ninth through the eleventh centuries, France, England, and several other nations of modern Europe emerged and began to develop (Insight, "Europe's National Beginnings"). Music flourished in churches and courts and undoubtedly had a place in secular life elsewhere. Part-music was improvised and

(continued on page 57)

Europe's National Beginnings

During the ninth through the eleventh centuries, several of Europe's nations emerged and began to develop. After the death of Louis I, the Pious (r. 814–40), the Carolingian empire was divided among his three sons. By the Treaty of Verdun (843), Lothar became emperor and received Italy and a middle portion of the empire called Lorraine, a territory that would be controversial even in the twentieth century; Charles II (the Bald) was given the western portion, which became "France"; the eastern part went to Louis I ("the German") and eventually became "Germany." The Treaty of Verdun was the first document written in the French and German languages; the use of both vernaculars indicates that eastern and western parts of the empire were already pulling apart. When Lothar I died (855), his empire was divided among his three sons: Louis II received Italy and the imperial crown, Charles was given Provence and southern Burgundy, and Lothar II received Lorraine. In 870 Lorraine was again partitioned, this time between Charles the Bald and Louis II.

In "Germany," the last Carolingian ruler, Louis the Child, died in 911. Thereafter, rulership became elective. King Conrad I (r. 911–19) had to withstand the dukes of Lorraine, Saxony, Franconia, Swabia, and Bavaria, as well as combat Magyar invasions. Otto I the Great (r. 936–73) dispensed with both problems (fig. 5.1). Conrad had created a monarchial administration excluding the dukes; Otto achieved political stability by choosing clergy as royal administrators. Otto's solution strengthened the power of the church as well as his own. Never-

theless, churchmen became the ruler's vassals.

Northmen came to Europe by sea in annual incursions that were especially disastrous to monasteries and churches. In 911 the Vikings captured a large district on the lower Seine River. This territory, called Normandy, served as a base for expeditions that, in the eleventh century, extended Viking rule considerably.

The Northmen moved across the English Channel, and after the Battle of Hastings (1066) England became Norman territory ruled by William I, the Conqueror. By this time, the Vikings were moving into southern Italy and Sicily. The last Arab base in Sicily was conquered by Normans in 1091. The Norman kingdom established there was not fused with the Germans until 1194, when Emperor

FIGURE 5.1 Territory ruled by Otto I the Great c. 937.

Europe's National Beginnings continued

Henry VI, husband of the Norman heiress, became King of Sicily, Apulia, and Calabria.

In France, Hugh Capet (r. 987–96) ruled only in Île de France, a small area between the Seine and Loire Rivers. Most of Hugh's successors in the eleventh century were deemed "helpless" rulers. Louis VI, the Fat (r. 1108–37), manipulated feudal law effectively, using it to suppress vassal uprisings by awarding churchmen governmental positions, a procedure that increased the support given him by the French church. Louis VII (r. 1137–80) was ineffectual. When Louis's marriage to Eleanor of Aquitaine ended in divorce, she wed Henry, Duke of Normandy and Count of Anjou and Maine, who became Henry II of England (r. 1154–89). England's control of territories on the Continent was one cause of the Hundred Years' War (fig. 5.2).

In southwestern Europe, the Franks had managed to keep invading Arabs south of the Pyrenees, but the Arab kingdom established at Cordova, Spain, in 756 survived until 1031.

FIGURE 5.2 Territories ruled by Henry II of England and Louis VII of France.

Europe's National Beginnings continued

Vikings invaded Eastern Europe and conquered the scattered Slavic tribes in Russia. In many areas, Slavic and Viking cultures merged. Gradually, a rather loosely organized confederacy of principalities came into being under leadership of the senior prince at Kiev. A strong Kievan state existed under the rule of Oleg (r. c. 880–912); he may be considered the real founder of that Russian state. The territory came within Constantinople's cultural sphere after Princess Anna, sister of Emperor Basil II, married Prince Vladimir of Kiev in 988.

The spread of Christianity into Slavic regions resulted also in creation of the Cyrillic Russian-Slavic languages. In the ninth century, the Slavs

established Great Moravia, a powerful principality in central Europe. In 863, at the request of Rotislav, ruler of Moravia, Pope Nicholas I sent St. Cyril and St. Methodius to them from Constantinople for purposes of conversion. These missionaries created the Slavic language, using Greek characters for the alphabet. Great Moravia succumbed to the Magyars at the beginning of the tenth century. The marauding Magyars were defeated by Emperor Otto I in 955 and were forced back to the Hungarian plains, where they settled. As time passed, this Slavic-Asiatic region in central Europe formed a barrier separating the two halves of Europe. The invasions of Asiatic tribes contributed to the

separation of East and West in Europe and strengthened the Slavic wedge between the two; constant invasions provided distraction, which increased the chaos.

In the eleventh century, the church supported rulers only to the extent that its own independence was not threatened. In 1059 the power that rulers exercised over the church was curbed somewhat when Pope Nicholas II (r. 1059–61) decreed that papal election would be by cardinals and expressly excluded secular intervention. Further rupturing of church-state relations occurred in 1073, when Pope Gregory VII (r. 1073–85) clearly outlined papal authority and declared papal supremacy.

eventually composed, principles were established governing the improvisation and composition of melodies, a system of music notation gradually developed, and theoretical treatises appeared.

MEDIEVAL MUSIC THEORY

MODAL SCALES

Medieval treatises concerning music were either philosophical and speculative, like Boethius's *De institutione musica,* or practical and theoretical, like *De harmonica institutione* (Harmonic principles) attributed to Hucbald (c. 840–930). Hucbald intended to provide a method for speedily and efficiently instructing the monastic choir at Tournai to sing chants accurately. He did not claim to have originated the system but merely explained it and illustrated each principle with a chant. The method is an extension of the system used by the Carolingians to classify chants according to melody types, and the presentation achieves a synthesis of Byzantine *oktoēchos,* liturgical (Gregorian) chant, and ancient Greek theory as interpreted by Boethius. What emerged was a system of eight diatonic scale patterns, arranged as four authentic-plagal pairs,

with **finals** on the pitches d, e, f, and g. These scale patterns were called **modes.**

Each pair of modes had the same pitch as **final** (ex. 5.1). An authentic modal scale began on its final, but a plagal scale began a perfect fourth below its final. The **reciting notes** (also called **dominants** or **tenors**) of paired modes differed, however. The dominant of an authentic mode was a perfect fifth above its final,

Example 5.1 The medieval modes.

unless that fifth was b; the dominant of a plagal mode was a third below the dominant of its related authentic mode, unless that pitch was b, in which case the pitch c became the dominant. Next in importance to the final, the dominant functioned at times as a secondary tonal center. The pitch b could not serve as dominant because two b pitches were in use: b-natural and b-flat. At that time, no other pitches were chromatically altered; b♭ is still the only chromatically altered pitch that appears in Gregorian chant. Moreover, the pitch b was unstable—in performance of nonliturgical music, to avoid the tritone f–b the performer(s) consistently lowered b to b♭.

The medieval modal scales were numbered individually from I to VIII. However, sometime during the late tenth century, the names of the ancient Greek *tonoi* became attached, fallaciously, to the medieval modes. This error was probably caused by Boethius's incorrect translation of the Greek word *tonos* (key) as "mode." Greek and medieval scale patterns that were assigned the same name differ in pitch content, direction, and internal intervallic structure (ex. 5.2). Modern liturgical books refer to modes by number, but most textbooks use the Greek names for the medieval modes.

Identification of a mode was by range, dominant, and final. Two scales comprising identical pitches were differentiated by their finals and dominants. (Compare the Dorian and Hypomixolydian patterns in ex. 5.1.) Modal classification of a melody is not always easy, because not all medieval melodies end on the final of a mode. Sometimes modal classification must be determined by tessitura and the frequency with which certain pitches occur. Usually, the dominant is prominent in a melody. Chants do not always use the entire octave range—some melodies have a range of only a fifth, whereas others use more than an octave. As notated, the modal scales contain no chromatically altered tones, but under certain circumstances b♭ might be used. Two things should be remembered: (1) in the Roman Catholic liturgical books the mode of each chant is stated, and (2) chant melodies were not notated as

absolute pitches; rather, in performance, melodies were transposed to fit vocal ranges.

NOTATION

The ancient Greeks notated pitches by letter names, and a kind of alphabetic letter notation was in use in some places in Europe as late as the eleventh century (fig. 3.3).

The earliest surviving manuscripts containing notated Western music that had practical use date from the ninth century. In these manuscripts, produced at St. Gall, the chant music is written in **accent neumes**—thinly drawn lines, hooks, and upward and downward curves intended to represent graphically the rise and fall of the melodic line. Use of the word *neume* for this kind of notation symbol may imply that the symbols were inspired by cheironomy, the ancient form of conducting through the use of hand signs, for the Greek word *neuma* means "gesture." In the Western church, hand movements were used to indicate melodic movements. In the Middle Ages, the word *neuma* denoted a short melodic passage, and a single written symbol was a *nota*. Infrequently, the word *neume* was used with its modern connotation; Guido used it that way.

In the ninth century, at some places in Frankish territory (e.g., in Aquitaine), **point neumes** were used to represent pitches. (Point neumes are heighted neumes that, for the most part, resemble dots and clearly indicate pitch differences. Accent neumes indicate the direction a melody moves but do not have placement that would indicate discernible pitch differences.) These dotlike neumes were placed above the words of the text without any point of reference to indicate a definite pitch. By the eleventh century, some scribes regularly drew a drypoint line across the page and heighted the neumes with reference to that line. Later, the line was inked, sometimes in color, and occasionally a letter was placed at the beginning of the line to designate a definite pitch. Such designation and coloration became customary; commonly, a red line was used for f and a yellow line for c′. These lines were forerunners of the staff.

EXAMPLE 5.2 Comparison of the ancient Greek Dorian mode with the medieval Dorian mode.

Ancient Greek Dorian Mode

T T S T T T S

Medieval Dorian Mode

T S T T T S T

In manuscripts compiled in the twelfth century, the notation indicates the pitches of the notes (fig. 5.3). Though the rhythm is not obviously indicated in the notation, a consensus of rhythmic knowledge must have existed at that time so that singers knew how to perform polyphonic music that was more complex than note-against-note. The manuscripts contain no instructional rubrics. There are three possibilities: (a) rhythm was free, (b) musical rhythm was based on the accentual or poetic rhythm of the text, or (c) musical rhythm was indicated in a way not obvious to musicians of later generations.

GUIDO D'AREZZO

Guido (c. 990–1050) seems to have been the first person to recognize the value of using a staff notation to designate definite pitches. He advocated learning chants by reading music rather than by rote and devised several aids for doing this.

At the Benedictine abbey at Pomposa, Italy, where he was educated, Guido acquired a reputation for teaching choirboys to learn new chants quickly. Bishop Theodaldus summoned him to Arezzo and assigned him to train singers at the cathedral school. Pope John XIX then invited him to Rome to explain his pedagogical system and the notation system used in an Antiphoner he had prepared. Because the hot, damp climate affected his health adversely, Guido stayed in Rome only briefly, then returned to Arezzo.

Guido's writings reveal his methods. In the prologue to his Antiphoner, he explained the notation system he used: specific pitches designated by neumes placed on the lines and spaces of a four-line staff with a yellow line for c′ and a red line for f. The colored lines identified the pitches associated with semitones. (In modern liturgical books, a four-line staff is still used for notation of Gregorian chant, with versions of the letters C and F identifying those pitch lines of the staff. The identification of certain staff lines by pitch letters became standard and survives in modern notation in the use of modified G and F letter shapes called **clefs.**)

In a letter to Brother Michael at Pomposa, Guido explained the method he used in teaching boys to learn quickly to sing chants previously unknown to them.

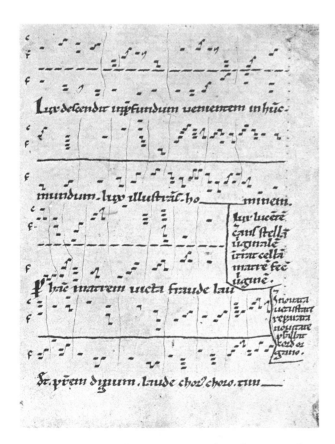

FIGURE 5.3 Portion of the organum *Lux descendit* as notated on folio 2 of British Museum MS Add. 36.881, a twelfth-century manuscript. The manuscript shown in figure 5.12 also dates from the twelfth century. (*Source: British Museum, London*)

FIGURE 5.4 Hymn *Ut queant laxis* (*a*) in chant notation (*LU*, 1504) and (*b*) in modern notation.

With the letter, Guido sent some music he had composed to aid in that teaching: (a) a chant (fig. 5.4) he required the boys to memorize to learn the scale steps and (b) a set of melodies designed to teach singers to sing at sight any neume they might encounter in any chant. Each of the first six phrases of Guido's chant *Ut queant laxis* begins with a different pitch and a different syllable of text; successively, the initial pitches of the six phrases form the C hexachord. The singers were expected to relate these six syllable-pitch combinations to the starting pitches of an unfamiliar chant and, in combination with the neumes memorized from the other set of melodies, to sing the new chant correctly.

The poem *Ut queant laxis,* written during the Carolingian era, entered the liturgy as a hymn to St. John the Baptist (DWMA10). Guido stated that he composed this chant melody to serve his specific pedagogical purposes. In the early eleventh century, the hymn was relatively unknown, except in northern Italy. As Guido's sight-singing method became known, use of his setting became widespread.

The pitch-syllable combinations Guido used for sight-singing have become standard but have been extended to include a seventh scale-step called *ti*. In the modern European fixed-*ut* system, *ut* always means C, *re* always means D, and so on. In America, the syllable *do* has replaced *ut*, and the system is movable (transposable). The term **solmization** is now applied to the practice of singing by syllables.

Guido's *Micrologus* (Short discourse) is the earliest extant comprehensive treatise that discusses both plainchant and polyphonic music. The treatise, addressed to singers, was designed primarily to improve skills in sight-singing and in using the new notation system. Guido stressed the importance of ear training and the value of letting the ear be the final judge when selecting melodic intervals, especially when forming cadences. (For Guido's views on organum, see p. 65.)

Guido recognized a scale of pitches covering the combined ranges of men's and boys' voices. The scale proceeded upward from G, which was written as Greek *gamma* (Γ), and included both b-natural and b-flat in its upper two octaves. The shape of the printed letter b indicated whether that pitch was *durum* (hard, harsh to the ear; b-natural) or *molle* (soft, pleasant; b-flat): the letter used for b-natural was a squared shape called *b quadrum* (♮), and that used for B-flat was a

rounded shape called *b rotundum* (♭). A few centuries later, scribal variants of these different shapes for b became the modern symbols used to indicate chromatic alterations: ♭, ♯, and ♮.

The scale was divided into seven overlapping hexachords (ex. 5.3) that do not coincide with medieval modes and that he did not in any way relate to modes. Hexachords that contain no b pitches were "natural"; those containing b-flat were *molle* (soft), and those containing b-natural were *durum* (hard). In other words, C hexachords were natural, G hexachords were hard, and F hexachords were soft. A syllable name was added to each pitch letter. That letter-syllable name located the pitch within the scale system and indicated the hexachord(s) in which the pitch resided. The lowest pitch in the scale system became *gamma ut* (from this came our word *gamut*); middle c (c′) was *c sol fa ut;* and e″, Guido's highest note, was *e la*.

When a singer encountered a melody whose range exceeded six notes, the requisite additional range was acquired through **mutation**—the singer selected a chant note that was resident in more than one hexachord and used that pitch as a pivot. The singer entered the pivot note by using its syllable name in one hexachord but exited the note by using its syllable name in another hexachord. This process, as applied to *Kyrie Summe Deus*, is illustrated in example 5.4. Mutation was not permitted where it would disrupt the *mi-fa* semitone but was usually accomplished at *re* of the new hexachord when ascending and at *la* of the new hexachord when descending. The process of moving from one hexachord to another by mutation is comparable with the modern process of modulating from one key to another by means of a pivot chord.

In classifying chants modally, Guido used the older system of four paired authentic-plagal modes rather than the eight individually numbered modes being used by some of his contemporaries. He regarded the last note of a chant melody as the final determinant of its modality.

Another pedagogical device was employed during the Middle Ages and Renaissance for teaching scales and intervals. Each of the pitches in the scale, from *gamma ut* to *e la*, was assigned to one of the joints of the left hand (fig. 5.5). The teacher pointed to a joint of his open hand, and the pupils were expected to respond by singing the proper pitch. Some twelfth-century music

EXAMPLE 5.3 The hexachord system.

EXAMPLE 5.4 Mutation is necessary when the eleventh-century chant *Kyrie Summe Deus* is sung by syllables. Using syllables, this chant would be vocalized as "re la la-re fa re ut re-la fa," moving from a C hexachord into a G hexachord temporarily and returning to the C hexachord.

manuscripts and most late medieval and Renaissance textbooks contained a sketch of the hand with the joints appropriately labeled. The device, known as the "Guidonian hand," was probably so-named because of

its use of Guido's terminology. There is no evidence that Guido invented it, nor is it present in any of his extant writings, but it was extremely significant. As late as the sixteenth century, strong objections to chromaticism were based on the fact that it was "not in the hand."

MEDIEVAL INSTRUMENTS

ORGAN

In the early Christian era, few organs seem to have been in use. Though the organ was known in Byzantium, it was not used liturgically; it was not a church instrument in western Europe until c. 900. There was an organ in the church of Cluain-Cremha, Ireland, in 814, perhaps the earliest date at which an organ is known to have been located in a church. There was neither organ builder nor organist available in Rome in 872, so Pope John VIII sent to Bavaria for a person with those talents. Customarily, organs came into western Europe from Byzantium or Greece by way of Bavaria or Hungary.

In *Schedula diversarum artium* (Treatise on various trades; c. 1100) by Theophilus, several chapters deal with practical organ building. At that time, pitch selection was by means of hand-operated slider keys, which formed the "keyboard"; a slider was pulled out, then pushed back manually (fig. 5.6).

Small positive organs were in use from the tenth to the seventeenth century (fig. 5.7). Keys might be either T-shaped or the slider variety; one person used both hands to operate the "keyboard" while another

FIGURE 5.5 A "Guidonian" hand, its joints labeled according to hexachord system solmization.

FIGURE 5.6 Miniature from MS 13096, folio 46, in Bibliothèque nationale, Paris, depicts musicians playing harps, vielle, slider organ, and psaltery.

FIGURE 5.7 A positive organ, placed on a table for use. *(Source: Michael Praetorius,* Theatrum Instrumentorum, *1620.)*

person worked the bellows. Early church organs were of this type. Even when larger organs became available in the thirteenth century, many churches retained positives.

Not until the twelfth century was the portative organ used (fig. 5.8). These small monophonic treble instruments usually had a range of about two octaves and were sometimes equipped with one or two drones. The single rank of pipes was sometimes arranged in two rows. The instrument, held at right angles to the body, was suspended from a strap placed across the back of the player's neck. In performance, the right hand operated buttonlike or T-shaped keys while the left hand worked the bellows.

STRINGS

The *organistrum* (hurdy-gurdy) was used in medieval churches from the tenth century. The instrument was five to six feet long and its fiddle-shaped body was equipped with three strings that sounded simultaneously when set in vibration by a hand-cranked rosined wooden wheel located at the lower end of the body. The strings were stopped by a set of rods in a short pegbox at the upper end of the body. The instrument had a one-octave range, including both B♮ and B♭. In performance, the instrument was placed across the laps of two persons, one of whom cranked the wheel

while the other operated the pitch rods (fig. 5.9). When large church organs came into use in the thirteenth century, the organistrum was employed less frequently; then, the instrument was made in a smaller size. The *vièle à roue* (vièle with a wheel) was a small hurdy-gurdy similar to the organistrum (fig. 5.10).

Vielle, fiedel, and *fiddle* are only a few of the names used to designate any medieval bowed stringed instrument having a **pegdisc.** (A pegdisc is the continuation of the neck of a stringed instrument into which tuning pegs are inserted from front or rear. If pegs are inserted from the sides, the extension is called a **pegbox.**) These instruments existed in a variety of shapes and sizes. Bowed stringed instruments were first used in the tenth century.

The Roman *lyre* survived, and by the year 1000 it was used in much of Europe. The *harp* was played in Ireland early in the Middle Ages and was introduced to continental Europe before the ninth century. Medieval harps were not standard in size or in number of strings. In epics such as *Beowulf,* harpers are referred to as historians, chroniclers, and entertainers. The *psaltery* was described by the Church Fathers and by Cassiodorus as a delta-shaped (Δ) instrument whose resonator was on top. In the late Middle Ages, the word *psaltery* meant a zitherlike instrument that existed in various shapes and that was plucked with either bare fingers or a plectrum.

The *lute,* brought to Spain by Islamic Arabs, was first used in France c. 1270.

FIGURE 5.8 A portative organ of Italian make, now in Conservatoire Royal de Musique, Brussels. The organ was carried by the performer, who operated the bellows (not visible in picture) with one hand and the keys with the other hand.

WINDS AND PERCUSSION

The transverse flute, or *cross-flute,* entered Europe from the East by way of Byzantium and the Slavic countries, and its use spread into Germanic lands. In the late Middle Ages this flute was primarily a military instrument. The vertical flute, or *flageolet,* was of Asiatic origin. Usually made from wood or reed, it seems to have been first used in Europe in the eleventh century. A beaked flute, sometimes played in pairs, was used in Europe from c. 1180 until the middle of the seventeenth century. This flute, played vertically, has its upper end shaped like a beak to facilitate blowing.

The *shawm,* a double-reed instrument introduced to western Europe from the Near East, was in use from the twelfth to the seventeenth century. The *musa* (bagpipe) was known to Romans in the first century but is not mentioned in other parts of Europe until the ninth century. The bagpipe may have been used a great deal as a folk instrument.

FIGURE 5.9 Portion of the carving on the Portico de la Gloria of the Cathedral of Santiago de Compostela, Spain. The two persons at the left are playing an organistrum.

FIGURE 5.10 Georges de La Tour (1593–1652): *Le joueur de vièle* ("The vièle player"). The man is playing a *vièle à roue,* or hurdy-gurdy. Note the crank that rotates the wheel, the keys, and the pegdisc with tuning pegs protruding from the top. (*Musée des Beaux-Arts, Nantes*)

FIGURE 5.11 A shofar. *(© Ted Spiegel)*

Early medieval *horns* made of wood or metal were used by Europeans for military purposes or by watchmen. From the eleventh century, carved ivory horns were used by nobility as hunting horns. One such horn was the *oliphant,* a short, thick, richly carved ivory horn that was end-blown. The Hebrew *shofar,* a ram's horn, is the only horn that has retained its original form from antiquity to the present (fig. 5.11).

The Church Fathers referred to the short straight trumpet by its Greek and Roman names: *salpinx* and *tuba,* respectively. After the fall of Rome, the trumpet seems to have fallen into disuse. It reappeared at the time of the Crusades—the long straight trumpet was war booty taken from the Saracens. The trumpet was used primarily as a signal instrument and by watchmen. The tones produced were in the low register. Performers puffed their cheeks when blowing the trumpet, and the sound generated was airy and tremulous.

Drums, which were introduced from Asia, were struck with sticks to beat time for dancing and singing.

EARLY POLYPHONY

Polyphony is the term given to the kind of music that results from simultaneously combining two or more independent melodic lines. Polyphony should not be confused with **heterophony,** which results from simultaneously performing two different versions of the same melody (e.g., performing a simple melody and an ornamented version of the same tune). Nor is polyphony identical with **magadizing,** or singing in octaves produced by simultaneously singing the same melody by changed (men's) and unchanged (boys') voices or by male and female voices.

ORGANUM

The polyphony used in liturgical music from the late ninth century to c. 1250 was called **organum,** meaning "organized" or "planned" music. The earliest surviving writings that clearly describe and give detailed directions for the production of organum are two anonymous treatises written c. 850–c. 900: *Musica enchiriadis* (Music manual) and *Scolica enchiriadis* (Commentary manual). (*Scolica* was that Latin term used to denote the marginal entries scholars penned in textbooks and treatises as explanatory comments on the subject matter presented.)

As explained and illustrated by music examples in *Musica enchiriadis* and *Scolica enchiriadis*, organum consisted of a chant melody, named *vox principalis* (principal voice), and one, two, or three additional voice parts derived by duplicating the chant melody in parallel motion at a specified harmonic interval that was regarded as a consonance. The duplicate voice was called *vox organalis* (organal, or planned, voice). The creation of an organal voice was permitted at three levels of consonance: the octave, the fifth, and the fourth. Three types of parallel organum are considered in these treatises: simple, composite, and modified.

Simple organum was produced by singing an exact duplicate of the chant melody in strict parallel motion at the interval of an octave, a fifth, or a fourth below the original chant. Strict simple organum at the fifth is shown in example 5.5 (DWMA11a). Actually, strict simple organum at the octave was contrived magadizing.

Composite organum was produced by doubling at the octave either or both of the voice parts of a simple organum (ex. 5.6; DWMA11b). Octave doubling of one or both melodic lines of a strict simple organum at the fifth, or a strict simple organum at the fourth, brought all three available consonant intervals into simultaneous use. There were two ways of doing this: (1) both lines of a strict simple organum might be duplicated at the octave, or (2) the principal voice could be duplicated an octave lower and the organal voice duplicated an octave higher.

Vox principalis
Vox organalis

Tu pa-tris sem-pi-ter-nus es fi-li-us
(You are the everlasting son of the Father.)

EXAMPLE 5.5 Example of strict simple organum.

Vox organalis
Vox principalis

etc.

Vox organalis
Vox principalis

Sit glo - ri - a Do - mi - ni in sae - cu - la
(Glory be to the Lord for ever.)

EXAMPLE 5.6 Example of strict composite organum. The two inner voices are the original *Vox principalis* and *Vox organalis*.

1. Rex coe - li do - mi - ne ma - ris un - di - so - ni
Ti - ta - nis ni - ti - di squa - li - di - que so - li.

2. Te hu - mi - les fa - mu - li mo - du - lis ve - ne-ran-do pi - is
Se ju - be - as fla-gi-tant va - ri - is li - be - ra - re ma - lis.

EXAMPLE 5.7 Transcription of the first two strophes of the Sequence *Rex coeli Domine*, an example of modified parallel organum. *Vox principalis* is the top voice; *vox organalis* is the bottom voice.

Parallel organum at the fourth was the only type of early organum modified, so the voices were not parallel throughout the chant. The necessity for modification seems to have been occasioned originally by the peculiar disjunct-tetrachord scale structure used in *Musica enchiriadis,* though it was implied that modification was desirable to avoid the tritone. In the examples presented, the *vox principalis* lies above the *vox organalis,* and most of the phrases begin and end on the unison. In one example (ex. 5.7; DWMA11c), the voices begin in unison, then diverge in oblique motion—the principal voice presents the chant melody while the organal voice reiterates its original pitch until the two voices are a fourth apart. From that point the voices sing in parallel fourths up to the penultimate interval; the last two intervals are unisons. This convergence on the unison at the end of a phrase was called **occursus** (meeting).

All early organum was improvised. It was based on chant and sung in a slow tempo, using the rhythm of the chant text.

Guido disliked strict parallel organum and preferred modified parallel organum at the fourth. He established rules for using oblique motion to avoid the tritone, which was considered *diabolus in musica* (the devil in music). In concluding a piece of modified parallel organum, Guido advocated achieving *occursus* by moving through the interval of a major third or a major second. His rules permitted *vox principalis* and *vox organalis* parts to cross for a brief time.

The significance of modified organum at the fourth is twofold: First, it was a forerunner of late eleventh-century free organum that admitted various intervals but placed restrictions on the kind of interval that could be used at the beginning and end of a phrase. Second, the care given the *occursus* foreshadowed the attention that would be focused on cadences and cadential preparation in future centuries.

When, where, and why was organum created? The definite date and place of origin and the reasons for its creation are not known. The earliest examples of Western polyphony are vocal part-music in which one voice is chant, so it might be conjectured that polyphony originated when men and choirboys, when singing together, could not find common pitches that were comfortable for singing chants in unison for a service, and duplication of the chant melody at a comfortable consonant interval was the solution for them. Or, perhaps choirboys and monks unintentionally magadized and, finding those octave sounds pleasant, consciously sought other harmonies. It is equally probable that this kind of parallelism existed in secular vocal or instrumental music that has not survived and that secular practices were borrowed for liturgical use. Still another conjecture is plausible: The creation of Western polyphony may have been a conscious endeavor as an extension of troping and the placement of the added (organal) voice determined logically by the application of Pythagorean proportional mathematics. *Scolica enchiriadis* contains a discussion of those Pythagorean principles. It is significant that organum flourished in abbeys that were centers of troping.

The practical use of organum is documented by a repertory of approximately 160 two-voice organa in a supplemental section of the later of two manuscripts known as *The Winchester Tropers* (fig. 5.12).

(a)

(b)

FIGURE 5.12 *The Winchester Troper* (MS 473), open to (*a*) folios 55v and 56r, showing monophonic troped chants, and (*b*) folios 135v and 136r, from the supplement at the back of the bound manuscript, showing the *vox organalis* part for those same chants. *(Corpus Christi College, Cambridge, England)*

As the title indicates, the manuscripts contain troped chants. The later manuscript, which was copied in the early eleventh century, is primarily a revised version of the early one. The manuscripts were copied in England, but the music they contain was probably used in western France. The music is notated in staffless neumes that are only partially heighted. (**Heighted neumes** are those written with vertical placement in staffless space on the page, thus making pitch differences discernible.) Two-thirds of the note-against-note organa in the supplement are Alleluias and Responds.

The anonymous treatise *Ad organum faciendum* (How to make organum; c. 1100) reveals that by the end of the eleventh century composition had begun to replace improvisation. The formation of organum was actually the creation of a new melodic line designed to enhance the chant rather than an improvised duplication of the chant melody. That choice was a factor in creating the *vox organalis* is indicated by music examples showing dissimilar organal lines constructed above the same chant melody. Parallel, oblique, and contrary motions were intermingled; a limited amount of voice crossing was permitted. The various consonant intervals—unison, octave, fifth, and fourth—were mixed freely. At times a dissonant third was included, followed by its appropriate resolution to the unison (DWMA12).

TWELFTH-CENTURY POLYPHONY

As news of organum reached other monastic communities, use of the technique spread. A few locales became centers, or "schools," of early polyphony: St. Martial de Limoges, Santiago de Compostela, and Notre Dame de Paris. The Limoges and Compostela centers flourished for a few decades, then waned and eventually were totally eclipsed by the Parisian school (discussed in chap. 6), whose works significantly influenced the development of Western music.

ST. MARTIAL (AQUITANIAN) SCHOOL   The Abbey of St. Martial de Limoges was founded in 848 at the site of the tomb of St. Martial, the first Bishop of Limoges. From c. 930 to 1130 a school of poets and composers flourished in Aquitaine, and the twelfth century was marked by the rise of Aquitanian polyphony. The Abbey became a repository of liturgical manuscripts that originated in southern France. These manuscripts form the richest surviving collection of west Frankish tropes, Sequences, and **versus** (verse-songs). Four of the manuscripts contain a total of 69 pieces of twelfth-century polyphony, along with other items (fig. 5.13).

The music from St. Martial Abbey exhibits two basic styles of polyphonic writing: **melismatic (florid) organum** and **discant**. Both styles are notated **in score**—the parts are arranged one below the other on different staves. The chant melody, placed in the bottom voice, is written on the lower of the two staves.

In **melismatic** (florid) organum, more notes than one—usually several or many notes—are written in the organal voice opposite one note of the original chant (fig. 5.14). Presumably, in performance each note of the chant melody was sustained by the choir (or a small group of singers) for a sufficient length of time to permit a soloist to sing the melisma written

FIGURE 5.13 The organum *Jubilemus exultemus*, a *Benedicamus* trope for the Nativity, notated in Aquitanian point neumes on folio 41 of MS Lat. 1139, the oldest of the extant St. Martial manuscripts. (*Bibliothèque nationale, Paris*)

FIGURE 5.14 *Benedicamus domino* in melismatic organum. *(MS Pluteus 29.1, folio 86v, Biblioteca Medicea-Laurenziana, Florence)*

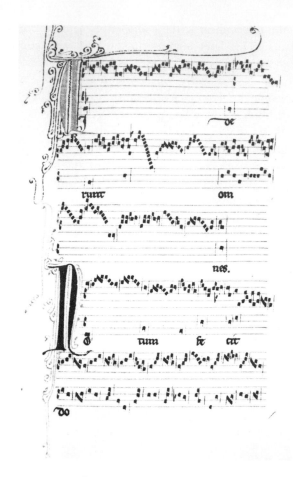

FIGURE 5.15 *Viderunt omnes* notated as organum duplum. *(MS W₂, fol. 53r, Wolfenbüttel, Herzog August-Bibliothek: Cod. Guelf, 628 Helmst)*

above that note of chant. It is believed that as polyphony developed, the improvised organal line gradually became more elaborate and the notes of the chant more sustained. Ultimately, the chant lost its melodic character and became a series of pedal points or drones, each of which supported a new melodic phrase. Eventually, this kind of organum was notated instead of being improvised in each performance. Because of the sustained character of the chant, melismatic organum is sometimes referred to as "sustained-note" style (DWMA13).

The voice parts were now given new names. This two-part polyphony was known as **organum duplum,** and the organal voice was called the **duplum** (fig. 5.15). The principal voice was renamed **tenor** (Latin *tenere,* "to hold"), probably because it held the original chant melody and sustained its tones. For several centuries, the melody on which a polyphonic composition was based (the *cantus firmus,* firm or fixed song) was

placed in the tenor voice. Until four-part polyphony became standard, the tenor was the lowest voice.

Text was indicated only for the chant (the tenor). Whether the soloist performed the duplum as textless vowel sound or sang the syllables of the chant words is not known. Vertical lines sketchily drawn through the staves at the ends of phrases aid in establishing congruence. Though phrases commence and end on the accepted consonances, dissonances occur as passing tones and sometimes produce interesting tonal clashes against the tenor pitches.

Discant is a style of writing in which a text was set syllabically in note-against-note polyphony. Lines of congruence seem to mark off measures in the music. Both voices use the same text, which is laid under the tenor. Later in the twelfth century, this style of polyphony admitted neume-against-neume writing, thus producing a text setting that was not purely syllabic

FIGURE 5.16 On folio 109r (old numbering cix) of MS Pluteus 29.1, in the verse *Pascha nostrum*, the word *Pascha* is notated as organum duplum, and the word *nostrum* is notated in discant-style organum. *(Biblioteca Medicea-Laurenziana, Florence)*

(fig. 5.16; DWMA14). Although one syllable of text was set per neume, each neume did not contain the same number of notes, so the two voices were not necessarily balanced note-against-note. Historians refer to this type of polyphony as "developed" discant. In some instances, discant style was further modified at important cadences to include a kind of neume-against-neume writing in which the syllables of text were set melismatically but the melismas of the two voice parts were balanced note-against-note.

A **versus** is a newly composed setting of a Latin sacred poem of scannable rhymed verse (DWMA15). This kind of song was used primarily as an extra-liturgical addition to a service on an important feast day. Most of the Aquitanian versus have texts that relate to the Incarnation and the Virgin birth. The musical setting of versus is discant, developed discant, or a mixture of those two styles. The two parts are in the same vocal range. All kinds of motion are used, but contrary motion predominates. When parallel motion occurs, the voices usually move in streams of parallel thirds or sixths. Phrases begin and end on accepted consonances: octaves, unisons, and fifths. Thirds and sixths are used freely; seconds and sevenths occur briefly as dissonant ornaments or passing tones. The lower part was probably composed first, and the upper line was written later to enhance the first melody. Ver-

sus and conductus seem to be the earliest polyphonic music not based on chant.

The oldest of the surviving manuscripts containing Aquitanian polyphony dates from the beginning of the twelfth century. Melismatic organum predominates in this manuscript. The other manuscripts date from the end of that century and show a preference for discant style. In the thirteenth century the Aquitanian school faded, and the center of activity shifted to Paris.

Santiago de Compostela   Santiago de Compostela is located in the northwest corner of Spain, in an area that has always been intensely Christian. Because the bones of St. James the Apostle (patron saint of Spain) were thought to be interred there, the Cathedral was a shrine of such importance in the Middle Ages that pilgrimages to it were comparable with those made to Rome and Canterbury. According to the *Liber Sancti Jacobi* (Book of Saint James), "choirs of pilgrims" from all parts of Europe kept perpetual vigil at the altar of the Cathedral; they brought with them and performed on all kinds of instruments: citterns, lyres, drums, flutes, flageolets, trumpets, harps, crwths, and others.

Liber Sancti Jacobi, housed in the Cathedral Library, contains in manuscript both texts and music for the complete services of the Vigil and Feast of St. James as they were performed early in the twelfth century. However, *Liber Sancti Jacobi* was not compiled at Santiago de Compostela, and the music it contains was not written by Spanish composers. Though the pieces were used in services honoring St. James, they may have been used at a church other than the Santiago de Compostela Cathedral. It is generally agreed that *Liber Sancti Jacobi* was written somewhere in France, perhaps at the Abbey at Cluny.

Liber Sancti Jacobi (Codex Calixtinus) contains both monophonic and polyphonic music and is an important source of performance practices of that time. The Codex, written c. 1137–39, shows that all sections of the Ordinary except the Credo were troped, as were portions of the Proper of the Mass and the Offices. The polyphonic settings of sacred rhymed Latin poems used for processionals and as introductions to the Offices were labeled *conductus*. The texts of the versus and conductus indicate clearly that these compositions are related to the religious celebrations.

All but 1 of the 21 polyphonic compositions are in a section at the end of the manuscript. These pieces comprise settings of (a) conductus and *Benedicamus Domino* tropes written in discant style and (b) untroped *Benedicamus* chants and Responsories written in melismatic (sustained-note) organum. Only those portions of the chants that were performed by soloists were given polyphonic settings; poetic texts were given discant-style settings. The polyphony is in score notation on four-line staves with vertical lines drawn through and connecting both staves to indicate textual or musical congruence either at harmonic consonances or at the beginning or end of a syllable.

One of the compositions on the first folio of the polyphonic section of the manuscript has three voice parts notated on two staves; two colors of ink (red and black) were used on the lower staff to differentiate the two parts notated there. Notating these two parts on the same staff was probably a space-saving device. This composition, *Congaudeant catholici* (Let Catholics rejoice together; fig. 5.17; DWMA16) is a *Benedicamus* trope with the refrain *Die ista* (This day). The seven two-line stanzas are set strophically. The two lower voices are in note-against-note counterpoint; the top voice was given from one to five notes to sing against each note in the lower voices. All parts move in the same vocal range, and voice crossing occurs. *Congaudeant catholici* seems to be the earliest three-part polyphonic composition that has survived.

FIGURE 5.17 The conductus *Congaudeant catholici* in manuscript.

SUMMARY

From the beginning of the ninth century through the twelfth century, the nations of modern Europe began to develop. Feudalism contributed to the rise of monarchies and was manipulated by governmental authorities to achieve political stability. Incompatibility between the papal envoy to Byzantium and the Eastern patriarch triggered a complete break between Eastern and Western churches in 1054. In reaction to invasions of the Seljuk Turks, Pope Urban II called the First Crusade in 1095; other Crusades followed.

Music flourished in churches, in courts, and undoubtedly in the secular life of the common people. Medieval treatises concern performance practices and detail theoretical principles by which chants and other melodies were to be classified or composed. Hucbald described a system of eight diatonic scale patterns that became known as modes. At some time during the late tenth century, the names of the ancient Greek *tonoi* were erroneously attached to these medieval modes.

Gradually, a system was developed for legibly and intelligibly notating music. Various kinds of letter notation systems were in use from the time of the ancient Greeks until the eleventh century. In ninth-century manuscripts written at St. Gall, music was written in accent neumes—symbols that graphically represented the rise and fall of the melodic line. In Aquitaine, point neumes were used to represent relative pitches. By the eleventh century, dry-point lines and heighted neumes were used; then colored lines labeled with pitch names appeared—forerunners of the staff. Guido d'Arezzo seems to have been the first person to recognize the value of using staff notation to designate definite pitches.

Guido developed a workable system of sight-singing by syllables that was based on his setting of *Ut queant laxis*. Also in use were a hexachord system with a process of mutating from one hexachord to another by means of a pivot tone and a pedagogical method that assigned the syllable names of pitches to the joints of a hand, later named the Guidonian hand. Guido's consistent use of a four-line staff, with the letters F and C identifying those pitch levels, certainly was influential in promoting that kind of staff notation.

Medieval instruments in use include organs, hurdy-gurdy types, bowed and plucked stringed instruments, flutes, double-reed wind instruments, horns, trumpets, and percussion instruments.

The polyphony used in liturgical music from the late ninth century to c. 1250 was called organum. Ninth-century treatises discuss three types of parallel organum: simple, composite, and modified. All early organum was improvised, based on chant, and sung in slow tempo using the rhythm of the chant text. Modified organum at the fourth was a forerunner of late eleventh-century free organum, and it foreshadowed the attention that would be focused on cadences and cadential preparation in future centuries. The definite date and place of origin and the reasons for the creation of organum are not known, but practical use of it is documented. By the end of the eleventh century, composition had begun to replace improvisation. Choice was a factor in creating the organal voice; parallel, oblique, and contrary motion were intermingled, and some voice crossing was permitted.

In manuscripts compiled in the twelfth century, the notation indicates the pitches of the notes, but the rhythm is not obvious. Important centers of polyphony were the Abbey of St. Martial de Limoges in Aquitaine and Santiago de Compostela in northwest Spain. St. Martial became a repository for liturgical manuscripts that originated in southern France, the richest surviving collection of west Frankish tropes, Sequences, and versus. The music from St. Martial Abbey exhibits two basic styles of polyphonic writing: melismatic (florid) organum and discant. In melismatic organum, many notes are written in the organal voice opposite one note of the original chant. As the organal line became more elaborate, the notes of the chant became more sustained; eventually, the chant became a series of pedal points, each serving as support for a new melodic phrase. This two-part polyphony was called organum duplum; the organal voice was called duplum, and the principal voice was renamed tenor. Discant is that style of writing in which a text was set syllabically in note-against-note polyphony, both voices using the same text. Later in the twelfth century, this style admitted neume-against-neume writing, known as "developed" discant. Versus were also written at St. Martial. The versus, a newly composed setting of a Latin sacred poem of scannable rhymed verse, was used primarily as an extra-liturgical addition to a service on an important feast day.

Santiago de Compostela Cathedral Library houses manuscripts of both text and music for the complete services of the Vigil and Feast of St. James as they were performed early in the twelfth century. Much of the liturgical music used there was troped. Texts of the polyphonic settings of sacred rhymed Latin poems used for processionals (labeled conductus) and versus indicate clearly that these compositions are related to religious celebrations. *Congaudeant catholici* seems to be the earliest three-part polyphonic composition that has survived.

Historians commonly refer to the period from c. 1160 to c. 1320 as the Age of *Ars Antiqua* (old art). Some historians perceive the era as being divided into two stages: Early Gothic, c. 1160 to c. 1250, and High Gothic, c. 1250 to c. 1320.

HISTORY OF PARIS

When Roman soldiers conquered Gaul c. 53 B.C., they established on one of the islands in the Seine River a settlement named Lutetia and developed it extensively. They built two wooden bridges to join the island to the mainland and constructed a stone-paved road across the island. The community church was a Gallo-Roman temple, Temple de Jupiter (fig. 6.1). By the fourth century, Lutetia had become "Paris." Occasionally, barbarians invaded, and between 845 and 885 Norman attacks brought hardship, followed by some years of famine, flood, and disease, with consequent decrease in population.

FIGURE 6.1 Paris in the third century.

In the twelfth century, Paris assumed intellectual and cultural leadership of Europe. The original island settlement, now Île de la Cité, was at the heart of the city. The Gallo-Roman temple had been replaced successively by a Christian basilica and a Romanesque church. The latter, constructed in Carolingian times, was a bishopric, the Cathedral of Notre Dame. The north or Right Bank of the Seine had become a trade center; the south or Left Bank was dominated by the newly formed university and was known as the Latin Quarter. Though vernacular tongues were in use in Europe, Latin was the official language of the church, the cathedral schools and universities, and the French government.

Religion and the supernatural dominated medieval life. Kings and prelates worked together to increase the prestige and wealth of church and state. A *universitas* had formed at Paris by c. 1200. Freedom of inquiry existed, but all learning was under the jurisdiction of the papacy; in 1215, Pope Innocent III formally authorized the corporation of the University of Paris. In the university, study of the seven liberal arts provided knowledge of the divine and the power to express that knowledge; many master teachers were theologians. The great cathedrals constructed in the twelfth and thirteenth centuries were considered physical representations of the heavenly kingdom on earth. The physical light admitted to the sanctuary through the windows was analogous to divine light; as stained glass helped create mysticism by transforming natural light, so polyphonic music was intended to intensify the aura of otherworldliness created by Gregorian chant.

When Maurice de Sully became Bishop of Paris in 1160, the cathedral chapter owned half of Île de la Cité and all the neighboring Île de Notre Dame. One of de Sully's first official acts as bishop was to arrange for replacement of the Carolingian church of Notre Dame with a great cathedral that would embody the new Gothic style of architecture, painting, and sculpture that had emerged in Île de France c. 1140 (Insight, "Notre Dame Cathedral").

Notre Dame Cathedral

Construction of the cathedral of Notre Dame de Paris, authorized by Maurice de Sully in 1160, was not completed during his 36 years as bishop; his five successors witnessed the continuing construction. Pope Alexander III laid the cornerstone of the cathedral in 1163. The Gothic structure rose in three stages: choir, constructed in 1162–82; transept and nave, completed in 1200; and façade, begun in 1190 and finished in 1250. As the cathedral was being built, the bishop ordered all buildings in the periphery demolished. On 4 December 1218, the relics were transferred from the neighboring church of St. Étienne to the new cathedral, and St. Étienne was torn down (fig. 6.2).

Notre Dame Cathedral was distinctive in many respects. The ribbed

FIGURE 6.2 Location of church of St. Étienne and the Cathedral of Notre Dame de Paris on the Île de la Cité c. 1217.

Notre Dame Cathedral continued

vault of the cathedral was exceptionally high—over 108 feet. The flying buttress was invented in the 1180s, and Notre Dame was the first structure to use true flying buttresses. A buttress is an architectural support built against and projecting from a wall to resist the thrusts from within (e.g., sidewise pressure and weight of the vaulting). A flying buttress arches away from the wall and consists basically of an inclined bar connected to an upper wall and grounded in a masonry mass some distance from that wall (fig. 6.3). Large stained glass

FIGURE 6.3 Apse of Notre Dame Cathedral, showing flying buttresses. *(© Robert Lamm)*

THE PARISIAN (NOTRE DAME) SCHOOL

When the Cathedral of Notre Dame was being constructed, a school of composers in and around Paris was producing polyphonic liturgical music. A treatise written c. 1275 by someone familiar with the music of England and France—possibly a student—provides tangible information concerning music at Paris during the century before his stay in Paris. That author, whose treatise is the fourth in a group of anonymous writings published by Coussemaker, is commonly referred to as Anonymous IV. He named two composers—Léonin and Pérotin—who made important contributions to the early polyphonic liturgical repertoire used there. Anonymous IV wrote, "And note that Master Leoninus, according to what was said, was the best composer (or singer) of organum [*optimus organista*], who made the great book of organum from the gradual and antiphonal for amplifying the divine service." This *Magnus liber organi* (Great book of Organum) was in use until the time of Pérotin the Great, who abbreviated it and composed many sections (called *clausulae*, discussed on p. 78) that were much better. Pérotin was considered the best composer (or singer) of discant (*optimus discantor*). He also composed three- and four-voice organa and monophonic and polyphonic conductus. Anonymous IV cited Péwindows were used to increase the amount of light admitted and to transform it. The interior of the edifice was cruciform, with double aisles but without chapels along the ambu-

latory. Portals were designed with three-dimensional jamb statues integrated with the architecture. The statues were painted and stood out against the golden background of the

façade. The rose window, 32 feet in diameter, appears as a gigantic halo for the sculpture of the Virgin and Child at its base (fig. 6.4).

FIGURE 6.4 West façade of Notre Dame Cathedral. *(Museum of Notre Dame de Paris)*

rotin's "excellent" four-voice settings of *Viderunt* (fig. 6.5) and *Sederunt* and his "renowned" three-voice settings of Alleluias with the verses *Posui adiutorium* and *Nativitas* (see fig. 6.8). Music composed by Pérotin was still in use at "the great Church of the Blessed Virgin" in Paris at the time Anonymous IV wrote his treatise.

One of the significant contributions made by the Parisian school of composers was the use of rhythm and meter—the employment of rhythmic modes

and modal notation—in the creation of polyphonic settings of chant.

RHYTHMIC MODES

Concerning rhythm, Anonymous IV wrote, "The notes . . . in the old books were excessively ambiguous, because the simple materials were all equal, . . ."

By the thirteenth century, the need for some means of notating rhythms had been met. In much the same

1160	1175	1200	1225	1250	1275	1300	1325

1163   Notre Dame Cathedral, Paris, constructed

Organum flourished   diminishes

Conductus   diminishes as composed piece, survives as style

Clausulae   Substitute clausulae

Substitute clausula troped, becomes Motet

Rise of Motet

Léonin fl.   Pérotin fl.   Franco of Cologne fl. c. 1250–80

Magnus liber   Organum triplum   *Ars cantus mensurabilis*

Organum duplum   and quadruplum

Petrus de Cruce
fl. c. 1270–1300

Mensural notation

Rhythmic modes: Modal notation

Some use of five-line staff

Hocket used

Technique of Voice Exchange (*Stimmtausch; Rondellus*) used

English rondellus motets

c. 1250 *Sumer is icumen in*

Troubadours ⎫
Trouvères   ⎬ ────────────────→ Adam de la Halle
       ⎭   b. 1245, d. 1288 or 1306

Le Jeu de Robin et Marion, 1285

Minnesänger

Trobairitz

Laude and   Cantigas de   c. 1325
Laude spirituali   Santa Maria   Robertsbridge
Codex

manner as musician-scribes of the late eighth century classified liturgical chants modally according to melodic patterns, thirteenth-century composers notated and classified rhythms according to patterns that they called **modes.** There were six rhythmic modes, identified by number. Modal rhythm was based on two values, long and short, arranged in stereotyped patterns markedly similar to the metrical patterns used for scansion of Latin and French poetry. For example, the long-short scheme of Mode I is the same as poetic *trochaic;* the short-long pattern of Mode II is identical with poetic *iambic* (ex. 6.1). Theorists called the threefold unit of measure for each mode a *perfectio* (perfection). In the medieval science of numbers, three was a perfect number—it was the smallest cardinal number to have a beginning, a middle, and an ending. Moreover, the perfection of the number three was related theologically to the Holy Trinity.

In the last quarter of the twelfth century, Aquitanian neumes were given more definite shapes and were written in square forms. The notation used for chant was adapted to meet the need for a notation that defined rhythms. Pitches and rhythmic pattern were united in specially devised neumes called **ligatures.** The form of the ligature—especially the first ligature of a phrase—indicated the rhythmic mode to be used (fig. 6.6). Modal notation was quantitative and was based on two note values: a *longa* (long), and a *brevis* (short), that might be altered. (The alterations and other complexities of the notational system need not concern us here.) Notational signs for rests were devised also. Mode V was usually written with a rest after each pattern, thus forming the equivalent of what is in modern music two complete measures. The rhythmic patterns were grouped in *ordines.*

FIGURE 6.5 Beginning of organum quadruplum *Viderunt* attributed to Pérotin, MS Pluteus 29.1, fol. 1r. *(Biblioteca Medicea-Laurenziana, Florence)*

EXAMPLE 6.1 The rhythmic modes with comparable poetic metric patterns.

EXAMPLE 6.2 Rhythmic Mode I in First, Second, and Third ordo patterns.

The number of times a pattern was repeated without interruption constituted its *ordo* (ex. 6.2).

Rhythmic modes were discussed in many thirteenth-century treatises. In *De musica mensurabili* (Concerning mensural music; c. 1240), Johannes de Garlandia introduced the use of strokes of different lengths to indicate rests of different durations. Garlandia seems to have been the first medieval theorist to give a thorough explanation of rhythmic notation; in general, he laid the groundwork for the system of mensural notation presented in treatises written by Franco of Cologne and others.

LÉONIN

Few twelfth-century polyphonic works can be attributed to specific persons. Léonin is one of those persons (Insight: "Léonin"). Léonin is credited with creating the *Magnus liber organi*—a significant achievement in the development of early polyphonic music.

The complete *Magnus liber organi* created by Léonin no longer exists in its original form. However, there survive three manuscripts that are considered the main sources of polyphonic settings of the Parisian school: MS Pluteus 29.1, in Florence; MS Wolfenbüttel 677 (W_1); and MS Wolfenbüttel 1206 (W_2). After studying these manuscripts, historians reconstructed the probable format of the original *Magnus liber organi* and determined that probably the repertoire was used in Notre Dame Cathedral.

Magnus liber organi was designed to be used by soloists. It contained two-part settings of the solo

FIGURE 6.6 Notation of rhythmic Mode I (*a*) in ligatures with (*b*) transcription. A phrase in rhythmic Mode I was notated as a three-note ligature that is followed by one or more two-note ligatures.

(a)

(b)

Léonin

A native of Paris, Léonin (c. 1135–1201) was educated at St. Benoît, a collegiate church subordinate to Notre Dame, and earned the *magister* degree. He served as canon and administrator at St. Benoît for over 20 years. By virtue of that position, he was a member of the Notre Dame clergy; by 1180 he had attained priesthood and became a canon at the cathedral. From the location of his signature on church documents, he ranked high in "clerical precedence." After 1190 his activity at Notre Dame diminished. His obituary is recorded at St. Victor Abbey, Paris, in 1201.

Léonin was an accomplished Latin poet. His surviving poetic writings are as follows: four moralizing poems, four letters that provide biographical data, and *Historia sacre gestas* (Acts of sacred history), his rendition of the first eight books of the Bible.

portions of responsorial chants for the great feast days of the liturgical year, commencing with Christmas Day—a cycle of the solo portions of Graduals and Alleluias for Mass and of the solo portions of the Great Responsories for Vespers. In the extant manuscript sources, the settings are arranged in two groups: (a) an Antiphonary section containing the Vespers Responsories, which were the most elaborate chants used for this Office during the Middle Ages, and (b) a Graduale section containing the chants for Mass.

Although the probable contents of the original *Magnus liber organi* have been determined, the *exact* nature of the music itself has not. It is presumed that the two-voice settings were melismatic organum, in which the tenor voice consisted of the solo portions of the original chant written in sustained note values, and that the duplum was a free-flowing melismatic line that incorporated some recurrent use of short melodic motifs. Léonin may have used modal rhythmic patterns in some portions of the duplum, for rhythmic modes and modal notation had limited use in northern France in his time. Possibly, Léonin was one of the composer-performers who were instrumental in creating modal rhythms and meters.

Because Anonymous IV referred to "better *clausulae*" created by Pérotin, it is presumed that Léonin's

Magnus liber organi contained *clausulae*. A **clausula** was a polyphonic section of chant in which both voices were written in discant-style counterpoint and proceeded at approximately the same rate. The clausula was a distinct section, with a final cadence; all kinds of motion were used, and the rules of consonance were respected. The basis of the section—the tenor voice—was a melismatic portion of solo chant. Both tenor and duplum were organized in measured modal rhythms (fig. 6.7). Where the original chant was syllabic, composers used sustained-note style and wrote "organum"; where the chant was melismatic, a setting in discant style (at first, note-against-note; later, with all voices rhythmically modal) was written. The solo portions of the great responsorial chants used at Notre Dame contained long melismas that were especially suitable for clausulae (DWMA14b).

In Pérotin's time, several different clausulae were constructed from the same chant melismas. These clausulae were of various lengths, and because the tenor melody was identical in all the settings, one clausula could be substituted for another without disturbing the basic structure of the service (DWMA17). **Substitute clausulae** were valuable because of their ability to alter the amount of time consumed by a service. The amount of time allotted to a chant varied according to the number of dignitaries present at the service and the amount of time required for the liturgical actions performed during the singing of that particular chant. If only a short amount of time was needed, a short clausula was used; if a longer period of time was required, a longer clausula was substituted.

Considerable variety was present in the music of a service in the churches of northern France in the late twelfth and early thirteenth centuries. Soloist(s) and choir alternated when monophonic chants were sung, and polyphony was used for some solo portions of the liturgy. Those polyphonic sections themselves provided variety, for melismatic organum (now called **organum purum,** or pure organum) could be alternated with sections in discant style, and clausulae could be used (DWMA14). Moreover, the substitution of different clausulae provided variety while fulfilling a liturgical function.

During the last decades of the twelfth century, composers began to write polyphony for more than two voices. Organum for three voices is called **organum**

FIGURE 6.7 MS Pluteus 29.1, fol. 87v–88r. The *Benedicamus domino* organum commencing at the end of the second pair of staves on folio 87v has the word *Benedicamus* set as melismatic organum (organum duplum) and the word *domino* set in discant style, as a clausula. The *Benedicamus domino* commencing at the top of folio 88r is a clausula. *(Biblioteca Medicea-Laurenziana, Florence)*

triplum (DWMA18) and that for four voices **organum quadruplum** (DWMA19). In the first quarter of the thirteenth century, use of organum triplum became standard in northern France; organum quadruplum was written for special occasions. Organum was notated in score. Commencing with the lowest voice, and reading from bottom of the score to the top, the parts are named tenor, duplum, triplum, and quadruplum. Theoretical treatises indicate that the parts were composed successively, in that order. The tenor held the section of the original chant on which the polyphony was based. The rhythm of the chant was altered; some portions were written in sustained-note style and others in modal rhythmic patterns (fig. 6.8). Some sections of organum triplum and quadruplum were in discant style. The upper voices were notated in

modal rhythms, with the first mode being the predominant choice. In the two or three upper voices of an organum, the composer might use a different rhythmic mode in each voice or might write all but one of three upper voices in the same modal rhythmic pattern. The measured discant style used in the upper voices of organum was not necessarily strict note-against-note counterpoint.

Each of the upper voice parts was written to be consonant with the tenor; agreement with all polyphonic voices was not expected. Contrary, oblique, and parallel motion were used. Although the unison, fourth, fifth, and octave were still considered perfect consonances, the fourth appeared less frequently, and sometimes the third was used within a phrase. At the beginnings and ends of phrases, the normal chord structure

FIGURE 6.8 Organum triplum *Alleluya Nativitas,* attributed to Pérotin. MS Helmstedt 1099 (W$_2$), fol. 16r. *(Herzog August-Bibliothek, Wolfenbüttel)*

Only the tenor had text—the word(s) of the chant on which the organum was based; the upper voices were textless. It is not known whether the singers sang the same syllable of text or voiced the same vowel sound as that being sung by the tenor or whether a single vowel sound, such as *ah,* was intoned throughout the piece. If changing vowel sounds were used rather than syllables, this would provide another element of contrast in performance. The vocal sound produced seems to have been a vibratoless intonation of pitches, which probably resounded effectively in the Gothic stone cathedrals and churches. Organum was intended to be sung by men in liturgical services; therefore, all the voice parts are at approximately the same pitch level. The melodies are narrow in range, and the voices frequently cross. In many passages, the modern listener is more aware of chord successions than of linear polyphonic melodies.

Many organa were quite long, and Parisian composers used various structural devices to organize their compositions. Melodic motives were unifying devices. Short motives were transferred from part to part, sometimes in reiteration, sometimes in inversion; at other times, motives appeared in melodic sequences or were repeated in the same voice part. Occasionally, composers wrote a few notes of incidental imitation at the beginning of a section or included a bit of canon. Voice exchange was employed frequently (ex. 6.3). The practice may have been imported from England, for the English used it extensively, referring to it as ***rondellus*** technique. The German term for voice exchange is **Stimmtausch.** The practice entails the exchange of motives or phrases between voices; sometimes all three of the upper voices of organum quadruplum might be involved in the interchange of material.

comprised an octave and a fifth above the tenor. Perfect consonances were expected at the beginning and end of each ordinal pattern of the rhythmic mode being used. In the chord successions that were created, harsh dissonances sometimes occurred, as did complete triads. However, stability lay in the hollow sound of the octave with the open fifth; for a conclusive cadence, the composer relied on a chord structure from which the third was absent.

EXAMPLE 6.3 One instance of Pérotin's use of *Stimmtausch* in the organum quadruplum *Sederunt.* Transcribed from MS Pluteus 29.1, fol. 6r.

PÉROTIN

That Pérotin (fl. 1190–c. 1225) worked in Paris during the last decade of the twelfth century is substantiated by Anonymous IV's citation of Pérotin's excellent four-voice polyphonic settings of *Viderunt omnes* and *Sederunt principes* and by decrees issued in 1198 and 1199 by the Bishop of Paris, Eudes de Sully, permitting the use of triple or quadruple organum in specified services in which those chants were sung. The Bishop's decrees were designed to eliminate frivolous and sometimes sacrilegious behavior of subdeacons, deacons, and priests when they took charge of the services celebrating the traditional medieval "Feasts of Fools" on several days after Christmas. At Christmas 1198, the Bishop's decree stated the format for celebration of First Vespers on the Vigil of the Feast of Circumcision (1 January) and permitted singing the Respond and the *Benedicamus Domino* in triple or quadruple organum by four subdeacons. (The specification of four subdeacons indicates that the bishop expected four-voice organum.) Also, at Matins the third and sixth Responds might be sung in triple or quadruple organum, and at Mass the Gradual and Alleluia might be sung in either triple or quadruple organum by "four men walking in procession." By a similar decree issued at Christmas 1199, Bishop de Sully established the format for the observance of the Feasts on St. Stephen's Day (26 December) and Circumcision, and permitted singing the Gradual or Alleluia of the Mass in triple or quadruple organum. Later, a similar decree was issued for St. John's Day (27 December). The Bishop's provision of additional money for those who sang polyphony on those days was an incentive to use quadruplum.

The Gradual used on 1 January was *Viderunt omnes*—the same one used at High Mass on Christmas Day; the Gradual used on St. Stephen's Day was *Sederunt principes*. Organum quadruplum settings of these chants survive, as does a quadruplum setting of *Mors*, a clausula from the Easter Alleluia verse *Christus resurgens* (DWMA19). Only these three quadrupla have been located. They have been attributed to Pérotin, though he did not sign his work.

Many of Pérotin's organa were quite long. In these organa, he used various unification devices, such as recurrent melodic motives, melodic sequences, voice exchange, and occasionally a few notes of incidental imitation at the beginning of a section or a bit of canon. A lengthy passage in canon was unusual, but Pérotin included a twelve-measure canon at the fifth in the quadruplum *Viderunt* (ex. 6.4). The performance of a lengthy organum quadruplum such as *Viderunt*, with the changing colors of the vowel sounds and chord successions and the patterns of the modal rhythms and melodic motives, must have had a kaleidoscopic effect that rivaled that of the light filtering through the large stained glass windows of Notre Dame Cathedral.

Composers of the Parisian school wrote organum until c. 1250; then their interest waned. Traces of organum that date from the fourteenth through the sixteenth centuries are found in some Germanic lands. In Iceland, strict parallel organum was used in the fourteenth century; in the twentieth century, Icelanders still sing *Tvisöngur*, two-part songs constructed in strict parallel fifths.

CONDUCTUS

The composers of the Parisian school did not confine their polyphonic writing to organum. The manuscripts previously mentioned (on p. 77) contain compositions that medieval theorists called *conductus*. Some texts received both monophonic and polyphonic settings. That Pérotin composed conductus is attested by Anonymous IV, who cited two of them.

EXAMPLE 6.4 Excerpt from organum quadruplum *Notum fecit dominus*, from *Viderunt*, showing canon between duplum and triplum. Transcribed from MS Pluteus 29.1, fol. 3v.

Conductus texts are metrical Latin poems dealing with a variety of subjects. Some texts are sacred but nonliturgical, some are devout and pious but not sacred, and others are serious and secular and often concern ethical or political and historical topics. Some conductus had quasi-liturgical use and probably found their way into services without official sanction. In such instances, a conductus might serve as a processional or an introduction to a liturgical chant. Some conductus may have been used for instruction, whereas others seem to have been designed purely for entertainment.

In the treatise *Ars cantus mensurabilis* (The Art of mensurable music; c. 1260), the theorist Franco of Cologne described the process of composing a "conduct." According to Franco, a conductus used for its tenor a newly composed melody. Against this melody, a duplum was written in discant style. If additional voices were desired, they were composed successively, and care was taken that any discordant notes in the triplum and quadruplum were concordant with one of the other voices. The English theorist Walter Odington disagreed slightly with Franco. In *Summa de speculatione musicae* (Comprehensive observations about music, c. 1300), Odington stated that conductus tenors might be either newly composed or preexistent melodies. In fact, some tenors were newly composed, but others exhibit a combination of newly composed and borrowed materials. The conductus and the versus (see p. 69) provide the earliest examples of completely original polyphonic compositions.

The conductus was less complex musically than organum. All voice parts moved within the same vocal range, which was rather narrow. Voice crossing occurred frequently; often the voices exchanged melodic fragments (*Stimmtausch*). The discant style of writing was organized to produce basically the harmonic intervals that were regarded as perfect consonances (octaves, fifths, and fourths). Thirds, though considered dissonant, occur frequently in some compositions. A triple division of the beat was used, and all voices moved in nearly the same rhythm. The music was in score notation, and the text was set syllabically or neumatically and was written under the tenor melody. The same music was used for each stanza of text; in other words, the setting was **strophic.**

A distinguishing feature of some conductus is the presence of *caudae*. **Caudae** are rather long, textless melismas that usually occur at the beginning, in the middle, and at the end of a conductus but may be present only at the end of one. The Latin word *cauda* (tail) is related to the Italian word **coda,** which is used to designate the passage or section that brings a composition to a satisfactory conclusion.

When performed, the conductus produced a sound that had, in effect, a chordal or pseudo-chordal texture. The kind of writing used for conductus was sometimes employed in other polyphonic compositions and is often referred to by historians as "conductus style."

It is generally presumed that the conductus was performed vocally, with all parts being sung and all voices singing the same text. However, it is possible that instrumentalists performed the upper parts or that vocal lines were doubled by instruments. If the parts were doubled, the caudae may have been performed instrumentally.

The conductus *Veri floris* (Of the true flower) exists in two- and three-voice polyphonic settings as well as in a monophonic version. This piece is a characteristic example of simple conductus (DWMA20). An example of a two-voice conductus with caudae interspersed throughout is *Roma gaudens iubila* (Rome rejoicing; fig. 6.9). The only cauda in the three-voice conductus *Hac in anni ianua* (In this new year) occurs at the end of the piece (DWMA21).

As was the case with organum, after 1250 composers gradually ceased writing conductus and turned their attention to the **motet.**

MOTET

When a single textual trope was sung by all the discant-style upper voices of organum triplum or organum quadruplum, the sound produced by the upper voices was similar to that of conductus. Pérotin's quadrupla *Viderunt* and *Sederunt* were supplied with tropes of this kind. This style of writing survived in the **conductus motet** (see p. 85).

The motet as an independent form of music originated when a text—a literary trope—was added to the duplum of an independent or substitute clausula. The texted duplum was called *motetus,* a Latinized noun formed from the French word *mot* (word). The independent clausula with added words and the entire species it generated became known as *motetus* (**motet**). A motet might have two, three, or four voice parts. As in organum, the third part was called the triplum and the fourth part the quadruplum. A motet with two additional texts is called a **double motet** and one with three additional texts a **triple motet.** Motets were not given titles. Rather, they are identified by the opening word(s)—the **incipit**—of each line of text, commencing with the highest voice, for example, *En non diu—Quant voi—Eius in Oriente* (Now in truth—When I see—His [star] in the East; fig. 6.10).

Because some independent clausulae with troped Latin texts in the duplum are found in Wolfenbüttel MS 677 (W_1), the date of origin of the motet is usually given as c. 1200. The most important extant manuscripts containing thirteenth-century motets are Montpellier Codex, Bamberg Codex, and Las Huelgas Codex.

Most of the extant motets are anonymous. Many motets exist in several versions, with variant versions appearing in different manuscripts. The same duplum or triplum melody may have sacred words in one manuscript and secular words in another, yet the tenor melody and its incipit remained constant. Music was used and reused. It was common for the same tenor to

FIGURE 6.9 Conductus with caudae: *Roma gaudens iubila*, MS W_1, fol. 107r. *(Herzog August-Bibliothek, Wolfenbüttel)*

FIGURE 6.10 Portion of motet *En non Diu—Quant voi—Eius in Oriente* transcribed from Montpellier MS H196, fol. 145v–146r.

be used with different melodies and texts in the upper voices. Nor was it unusual for a two-voice motet to be supplied with a triplum and appear in another manuscript as a double motet.

A motet was written in layers. A preexistent melody was selected to serve as the tenor, the foundation of the composition—the *cantus firmus*. The tenor melody was organized rhythmically, and another melody was composed to serve as its duplum. If a chant melisma chosen to serve as tenor was not long enough to balance the melody written as duplum, the chant melody was repeated until the proper length was attained. A third melody became the triplum.

Most thirteenth-century motets were based on sacred Latin tenors derived from chant. The portion of chant used was clearly identified by its text incipit. Until c. 1250, composers most often selected their motet tenors from the Latin clausulae tenors in *Magnus liber organi*. After c. 1250, composers began to use portions of other liturgical chants—kyries, alleluias, antiphons, and verses of the latter two—as tenors. When used for a motet, the borrowed tenor was written in a regular pattern in one of the rhythmic modes. Only the incipit of the Latin tenor text was written in the motet music, perhaps because the composer believed that performers would (or should) know the chant melody and its text. Possibly, the tenor melody was performed instrumentally. As the century progressed, motet tenors—and motets in general— became increasingly more secular. Melodies of monophonic secular songs sometimes served as motet tenors. Even street cries of vendors were used, as in *On parole—À Paris—Frèse nouvele* (They say—In Paris— Fresh strawberries).

In the earliest motets, the duplum was supplied with Latin words; by c. 1250, however, words for the upper voice(s) might be in Latin or French. Usually, duplum and triplum were in the same language. All texts were related in meaning, though sometimes the relationship was remote and tenuous. When the texts of the upper voices were in French, the poetry usually concerned love. Combining sacred and secular texts and music was not considered sacrilegious, for the church was at the center of secular life.

During the second half of the thirteenth century, the three-voice polytextual motet became standard. Composers made no attempt to achieve a homogeneous

sound; the voices enjoyed linear independence. Texts for the upper voices were set syllabically, and phrases of different lengths were used. Because of this, musical phrase endings overlapped, and often all voices did not cadence simultaneously until the end of the motet. At the final cadence, all voices were in perfect consonance, forming a final chord that consisted of either (a) an octave with an open fifth (and thus included a perfect fourth also), (b) an octave, (c) a fifth, or (d) a unison.

During the last half of the thirteenth century, three basic cadence patterns evolved (ex. 6.5). These became standard, forming the basis for cadences that were used during the next two centuries. In forming these cadences, each of the voices moved by step from the penultimate to the final note of its melody, the tenor proceeding down and the duplum and triplum moving up. This produced a final consonance that was the summation of three perfect consonances: the octave, the fifth, and the fourth.

EXAMPLE 6.5 Cadence patterns.

Each melodic line was consonant with the tenor; all voices were not necessarily consonant with one another. The upper voice(s) formed perfect consonances with the tenor at the beginning and end of each rhythmic pattern (and sometimes in between), and dissonances occurred as passing tones. Each melodic line lay within the scope of an octave. Because all voices moved within the same narrow range, voice crossing was common.

En non diu—Quant voi—Eius in Oriente may be considered a typical thirteenth-century motet of the Notre Dame school (DWMA22). The tenor was derived from the chant *Vidimus stellam eius in Oriente* (We have seen His star in the East), the verse of the Alleluia for Epiphany. The pitches of the chant were retained in the motet tenor, but the rhythm was restructured in the pattern of the first ordo of rhythmic mode I (fig. 6.11). Duplum and triplum employ a basically similar rhythm. The melodies create perfect consonances on the first and last notes of each rhythmic pattern of the tenor. The motet concludes on the consonance of a perfect fifth. Voice crossing occurs frequently; the two upper voices exchange texts and some melodic fragments in measures 1 to 4 and 21 to 24. The opening words of the triplum, sung by the duplum at the end of the motet, were borrowed from the refrain of a trouvère song. Such quotations were common in thirteenth-century motet texts. Canon occurs briefly in measures 5 and 6. The secular French texts of the two upper voices speak of love, but they have a tenuous relationship with the chant text through their reference to the budding rose, which symbolizes the Christ child. The tenor melody is repeated, commencing with the second note of measure 7. This treatment of the tenor foreshadows the fourteenth-century technique of isorhythm (see p. 110).

One type of motet was strongly influenced by conductus and is known as **conductus motet,** or **conductus-style motet** (fig. 6.12). In this type, the two or three upper voices strongly resemble the conductus. They move in basically the same rhythm and sing the same text simultaneously. The tenor is derived from chant and uses one of the rhythmic modes. The upper voices of conductus motets were notated in score, with the text written beneath the duplum. The conductus motet differs from conductus in that the motet tenor is a preexistent melody, has a different text incipit, and is notated in a rhythm different from that used by the upper voices. Although the production of conductus decreased considerably in the last half of

(a)

(b)

(c)

FIGURE 6.11 Melisma on *eius* in Alleluia verse *Vidimus stellam eius in Oriente, LU,* 460: (*a*) in Gregorian chant notation; (*b*) transcription of pitches; (*c*) rhythmic organization of those pitches for use as tenor of motet (cf. fig. 6.10).

the thirteenth century, some conductus-style motets were still composed.

In the early motets, the rhythm of the upper voices is structured similarly; no doubt the practice of writing the upper voices of clausulae in discant style influenced this. As more motets were produced, greater rhythmic variety was employed; it was not uncommon for a different rhythmic mode to be used for each voice. Before the century ended, composers were writing motets that were bilingual (if the tenor text was sung), polytextual, polyphonic, and polyrhythmic.

The earliest motets appear in manuscripts in score notation. It soon became evident that valuable manuscript space was wasted when the voice parts

FIGURE 6.12 Conductus-style motet based on chant melisma *Regnat.* MS Helmstedt 1099 (W$_2$), fol. 128v–129r. *(Herzog August-Bibliothek, Wolfenbüttel)*

were aligned, for the rhythmic modal notation of the tenor required much less space than the upper voices. Scribes began to place the voice parts successively on the manuscript page(s): the triplum first, the duplum next, and the tenor last (fig. 6.13). Later, motets appear in manuscripts with the triplum and duplum notation in parallel columns and the tenor ligatures written beneath these columns on a staff the width of the page (fig. 6.14). This latter kind of notation is called **choirbook notation.**

The original function of motets is not known. A motet whose duplum troped the text of the chant-based tenor may have had liturgical use. Possibly, the earliest motets were substituted, as were clausulae, in the performance of a complete organum; thus, they functioned liturgically. If all texts of a motet were sacred and in Latin, perhaps the motet occupied a special place as an independent piece used quasi-liturgically in celebration of a certain feast. Certainly, with the increased use of French vernacular in the upper voices, the concentration of the poetry on love, and the secularization of the tenor, the motet moved out of the realm of the church and into secular entertainment.

Thirteenth-century motets in which triplum, duplum, and tenor are distinctive rhythmically and melodically have come to be known as "Franconian" motets after Franco of Cologne (fl. c. 1250–after 1280). In those motets, the triplum was given the longest text, which was set in shorter note values than those used for duplum and tenor. Frequently, each melodic line was written in a different rhythmic mode. An oft-cited example of this is the motet *Pucelete—Je languis—Domino* (Maiden—I languish—Lord; DWMA23), in which the triplum uses Mode VI, the duplum Mode II, and the tenor Mode V. Typically, musical phrases in the triplum were short, or appeared to be short, because the text was set syllabically to fast-moving notes. Phrase endings in the two lower voices might coincide, or the duplum might have longer phrases than those of the tenor. Sometimes the chant-based tenor was cast in a rigid rhythmic pattern; at other times, phrases of varying lengths were used.

FIGURE 6.13 The motet *Ave Maria gratia plena—Ave lux luminum—Neuma* in Franconian notation with successive notation of voice parts. Triplum is at the top of the page; duplum follows; tenor commences in the middle of the bottom staff. MS H196, fol. 94r. *(Bibliothèque Interuniversitaire, Section Medecine, Montpellier)*

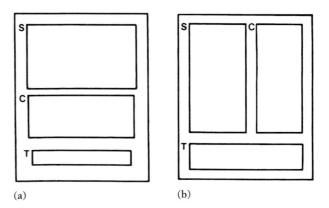

(a) (b)

FIGURE 6.14 Diagrams of manuscript pages written in (*a*) successive notation and (*b*) choirbook notation. The manuscript page shown in figure 6.16 is in choirbook notation.

Thirteenth-Century Music Theory

Franco of Cologne

The theorist Franco of Cologne may have been a composer, but no compositions have been located that can be definitely attributed to him. Anonymous IV wrote that Franco "notated some things differently in his books." Franco explained his notation system in his treatise *Ars cantus mensurabilis* (The art of mensurable music). The principles he established formed the basis of the system of notation that, with some modification and amplification, was used for two centuries.

Franco believed different note shapes should be used to signify the various note values. However, he did not introduce new note shapes. By formulating a set of rules for the correct notation of rhythms, he created a system that freed the existing symbols from ambiguity. He recognized four single-note shapes: *double long* ◗, *long* ◗, *breve* ■, and *semibreve* ◆. The relationship between these notes was founded on the principle of ternary grouping. The basic unit of time, the *tempus* (pl., *tempora*), was the breve.

The value of the double long remained constant; as its name implies, it always had the value of two longs. The long and the breve might be either perfect or imperfect, depending on whether they were subdivided into three or two smaller note values. A perfect long contained three *tempora,* an imperfect long had two. Although a breve normally had the value of one *tempus,* certain circumstances might cause it to be worth two *tempora,* in which case it was called an *altered breve.* In Franco's system, a breve normally comprised three semibreves; this was an innovation. Under certain conditions, however, a breve might have only two semibreves, one of which was worth twice as much as the other. Note that, with the exception of the double long, equal binary division of a note could not be notated. The durational value of the long, the breve, and the semibreve was determined not only by the shape of the note itself but also by the kinds of notes placed within a *perfectio* (perfection). A perfection was the equivalent of the modern "measure" or "bar" and contained three *tempora* (i.e., three lengths of time or three beats). Franco emphasized that the same rules that governed the relation between the long and the breve governed the relation between the breve and the semibreve. The equivalence between note values in the Franconian system and those used in modern notation is shown in figure 6.15.

Bar lines were not used. When clarification was needed, Franco placed a small stroke between notes to indicate a division between two perfections.

Notes might be grouped and written as ligatures. Directions were given so that notes in ligatures would be recognized as semibreves, breves, or longs. The following signs were used for rests:

Perfect long	Imperfect long	Perfect breve	Major semibreve	Minor semibreve	
= 3	2	1	2/3	1/3	Breve(s)

Petrus de Cruce (Pierre de la Croix)

The smallest note value in the Franconian system was the semibreve, and the breve could be divided into no more than three semibreves. By c. 1280, the need had arisen for a reliable way to notate the division of the breve into four or more semibreves or, preferably, for note values shorter than a semibreve. Composers were writing motets in which the triplum moved rapidly, in a speechlike rhythm, above a much slower duplum; usually, the chant-based tenor was written in a strict rhythmic pattern and was probably performed instrumentally. Triple meter prevailed. Motets exhibiting these stylistic traits are often referred to as "Petronian," regardless of whether Petrus de Cruce (fl. c. 1270–1300) composed them. The triplum of the motet *Aucuns vont souvent—Amor qui cor—Kyrie* (Some often go—Love that [wounds] the [human] heart—Lord have mercy; fig. 6.16 [see p. 89]; DWMA24) exhibits Petronian features.

Petrus de Cruce wrote motets whose tripla contained groups of from four to seven semibreves per breve. This was no whim—he used the number of semibreves required to set the syllables of the text. Sometimes Petrus placed dots in the music to group semibreves. These **dots of division** were his innovation. In Petronian motets, the style of the triplum differed considerably from that of the lower voice parts; often, the triplum assumed the character of a solo.

FIGURE 6.15 Portion of Franconian motet *Ave mundi—Ave salus—Aptatur* (*a*) in manuscript (Montpellier Codex, MS H196, fol. 379r) and (*b*) in modern transcription. The tenor, *Aptatur,* is based on a chant melisma. *(Bibliothèque Interuniversitaire, Section Medecine, Montpellier)*

By c. 1300, composers were writing tripla that contained as many as nine semibreves per breve. This liberal use of semibreves caused a deceleration of the beat, for it was impossible to achieve rhythmic uniformity of the semibreve. In performance, the breve received twice its previous temporal value, and the duration of the semibreve equaled that of the Franconian breve. In other words, the semibreve actually became the unit of the beat.

POLYPHONY IN BRITAIN

The amount of British polyphonic music that has survived from the twelfth and thirteenth centuries is meager, but significant pieces of English polyphony are extant in fragments of manuscripts and in collections of continental music. The polyphonic contents of the second *Winchester Troper* have been mentioned (p. 65). In Britain, the most active centers of polyphony were the important Benedictine abbeys: Reading Abbey, Bury St. Edmunds, and Worcester. The thirteenth-century English polyphony that has survived consists mainly of chant settings; troped chant settings; sequences, conductus, and *rondelli* (sing., *rondellus*); and motets. No large collection of purely English motets is extant, but traces of collections are found in incomplete manuscripts. The purely secular motet seems not to have been used in England.

The Old Saint Andrews Manuscript, known as Wolfenbüttel 677, or W_1, was compiled for and used in the Augustinian priory of St. Andrews, Scotland. The last fascicle of the manuscript contains a repertory of Ordinary and Proper sections for a cycle of votive Masses of the Blessed Virgin Mary (Lady Masses). The music is principally two-part polyphony in discant style, often note-against-note. In some of the Alleluias, a third (middle) voice part appears in some cadences. The manuscript contains no complete motets. However, at least six compositions that appear to be conductus have been identified as the upper voices of

FIGURE 6.16 Beginning of bilingual motet *Aucuns vont souvent—Amor qui cor—Kyrie eleyson.* MS H196, fol. 290v.

(Bibliothèque Interuniversitaire, Section Medecine, Montpellier)

conductus-style motets whose tenors were omitted from the manuscript.

The performance of polyphonic music in the liturgy is specifically detailed in some of the Customaries of the Use of Sarum (books of Rules and Regulations for practice of Sarum liturgy). For example, on Christmas Day and the following four days—the days of the feasts of St. Stephen, St. John the Apostle, the Holy Innocents, and St. Thomas—the *Benedicamus* was to be sung in two-part polyphony. At Westminster Abbey and St. Augustine's in Canterbury, the Benedictus, Magnificat, Sequences, and some processionals were sung in two-part polyphony on all principal feast days, and the soloists who performed polyphonic music received extra pay. In the Exeter Ordinal, the words *discantare, organizare,* and *jubilare* designated the type of polyphony that was to be performed.

Hocket is a polyphonic technique described by Walter Odington (fl. 1298–1316) in *Summa de specula-*

tione musicae. By using hocket, a composer created two voice parts from one melodic line in this way: The melody was truncated, and individual notes or small groups of notes were parceled out in alternation with rests to two voices so that, in performance, one voice was always silent when the other was singing. The sound effect produced was jerky, in keeping with the meaning of the Latin word *oquetus* (hiccup). Passages in hocket appear in some late thirteenth- and fourteenth-century motets; Petrus de Cruce used hocket occasionally. A composition in which hocket technique was used consistently was called a hocket.

Motets constitute the major portion of the music in the manuscript pages known as The Worcester Fragments. Some of these motets are conductus style. In others, the tenor is in a rigid rhythmic pattern, and the two upper voices have basically note-against-note counterpoint. Phrases of varying lengths create overlapping cadences. In some of the pieces, the lowest voice part is labeled *Pes* (foot or foundation) instead of Tenor.

The Verses of several Alleluias in The Worcester Fragments are supplied with tropes designed to be sung simultaneously with the liturgical text. Motetlike settings were written for these Verses. Some Alleluias were equipped with prelude tropes—motetlike settings of tropes intended to be sung as prelude to the soloistic beginning of the Alleluia. The rondellus *Alleluia psallat* (Alleluia, sings) is a prelude trope. Most prelude tropes exhibit *rondellus* technique.

As defined by Odington, **rondellus** is duple or triple voice exchange (i.e., phrase exchange). The word *rondellus* denotes either the compositional technique or a piece of music written entirely by means of that technique. Thirteenth-century English composers used rondellus extensively.

Manuscript Harley 978 in the British Museum contains, among other items, the index to a lost collection of 164 polyphonic pieces thought to have been used at Reading Abbey. The manuscript contains the Reading rota, *Sumer is icumen in* (plate 5; DWMA25). A **rota** is a canon, or round. *Sumer is icumen in* is a four-voice rota, superimposed on a duplex *Pes.* Rubrics provide instructions for performance. The *Pes* is a two-measure rondellus that is repeated until the piece concludes. This cantus firmus was derived from the first five notes of the Marian antiphon *Regina caeli* *laetare*; English secular words were substituted for the Latin sacred text. Two texts appear under the rota melody. Beneath the original rota text, which is in English, a later hand printed a Latin poem that commences *Perspice christicola que dignacio* (Observe, Christian, what an honor). The relationship between texts and music is intricate: (1) The melody of the *Pes* is the Easter-season Marian antiphon and the Latin text of the rota paraphrases a verse of a Sarum chant Sequence used on Easter Day—*Perspice christicolas, qualiter laeti.* (2) The English text of the rota speaks of the approach of summer and of events of nature occurring around Eastertime; the Latin concerns Christ's sacrifice and refers to the "heavenly husband-man" by the word *agricola* (farmer). (3) "Sing cuccu" in the *Pes* is echoed in the English "Lhude sing cuccu."

Sumer is icumen in is an ingenious composition. The independent character of its two melodies is apparent when one realizes that, in performance, no voice part forms parallel octaves or unisons with the lower voice of the *Pes.* It is conjectured that the composition dates from c. 1250. *Sumer is icumen in* is the only known six-voice composition prior to the fifteenth century and the only known composition that combines rondellus and rota techniques. Moreover, the composition is a motet because it is polyphonic, based on liturgical chant, and bitextual. And it is one of those rare motets in which duplum and triplum texts are in different languages.

MUSICA FICTA

The term **musica ficta** (literally, feigned music) refers to notes that were chromatically altered in performance to produce pitches not found in Guido's hexachord system and that were outside the gamut of Gregorian chant. Johannes de Garlandia seems to have been first to use and define *musica ficta* as being "when a tone is made into a semitone and vice versa." He stated that *musica ficta* was used to avoid "the error of the third sound" (i.e., the tritone). Magister Lambertus (fl. c. 1270) used the symbol ♮ to create an F♯. With the exception of Marchetto of Padua, who first used the ♯ symbol c. 1318, the only chromatic symbols admitted by thirteenth- and fourteenth-century theorists were ♭ and ♮.

SUMMARY

During the Age of *Ars Antiqua*, the Parisian school dominated Western music. Organum and conductus were developed to their fullest extent but began to wane c. 1250, when composers focused their attention on motets. Three-voice writing became standard, and occasionally four-part compositions were written. The motet, which began c. 1200 as a literarily troped clausula, became the dominant form of composition. This new form of music stimulated codification of the rhythmic modes and the production of a system of mensural notation. Triple meter was favored. Sound was confined within a narrow vocal range. Most compositions were based on liturgical chant; melodic lines, composed successively, were superimposed on a rhythmically structured liturgical cantus firmus. As was chant, the music was objective in spirit. Few chromatic alterations other than B♭ were notated; after c. 1260, some were created in performance as *musica ficta*.

A survey of the extant polyphonic music from the Age of *Ars Antiqua* indicates that at the beginning of the Age composed music was primarily sacred. As time passed, composers combined sacred and secular, Latin and vernacular, texts in their works; by the end of the thirteenth century, purely secular motets were being composed. A new "art" of composition was encroaching on the old; in the fourteenth century, *ars antiqua* would be superseded by *ars nova*.

MEDIEVAL MONOPHONY

7

Although attention has been focused on the development of polyphony, it must be remembered that throughout the Middle Ages monophonic music was being created and performed. It is possible to identify by name many of the composers of that monophony.

LATIN SONGS

Venantius Fortunatus (c. 530–609), the oldest known medieval poet of France, wrote both secular and sacred Latin poetry. Several of his hymns are used liturgically during Holy Week and Easter: (a) *Vexilla Regis prodeunt* (The banners of the King go forth), used at Vespers on Passion Sunday (*LU*, 545); (b) *Crux fidelis* (Faithful cross; fig. 7.1) and *Pange, lingua, gloriosi praelium* (Sing, tongue, the glorious battle), on Good Friday (*Graduale Romanum*, 182); and (c) *Salve, festa dies* (Hail, festive day), at Easter. *Vexilla Regis* and *Pange, lingua* were written in 569.

Isolated examples of the **epitaphium** (Greek, *epitaphion*, epitaph) and **planctus,** written in staffless neumes, survive in manuscripts from the seventh to eleventh centuries. An *epitaphium* is a poem or song performed at a funeral. A *planctus* is a lament. *Planctus Karoli* (Lament for Charlemagne) was probably written in 814; *Planctus cygni* (Lament of the swan) melody was in existence in the late ninth century. Laments contain valuable historical data; later, they became a significant type of music.

THE CAMBRIDGE SONGS

An eleventh-century manuscript at Cambridge University Library contains a collection of 47 Latin songs on a variety of sacred and secular subjects. The collection appears to be a repertory from which a wandering entertainer might select a program. One of the poems is a portion of Venantius's *Salve, festa dies*. Two of the "Cambridge Songs" have staffless neumes written above two stanzas of their poetry (fig. 7.2). One of these poems is *O admirabile Veneris idolum* (O lovely image of Venus), a love song. The same melody appears in letter notation in another manuscript for the pilgrim song *O Roma nobilis* (O noble Rome).

Even after polyphony was cultivated, most liturgical music was still monophonic chant. In medieval times, composers selected from Franko-Roman (Gregorian) and Sarum chant repertoires the melodies they used as cantus firmus bases for polyphonic works. New chants were still being composed for both Ordinary and Proper of the Mass and for the Offices. Hildegard von Bingen wrote some of these.

FIGURE 7.1 The chant *Crux fidelis* as used with *Pange, lingua.* (*From Graduale Romanum, copyright © 1974, Abbaye S. Pierre de Solesmes, F-72300 Sablé-Sur-Sarthe, Solesmes France. Reprinted by permission*)

FIGURE 7.2 The staffless neumes written above the first strophe of poetry for *O admirabile Veneris* in MS Gg.5.35 (The Cambridge Songs), fol. 441v. (*By permission of the Syndics of Cambridge University Library*)

HILDEGARD VON BINGEN

Hildegard (1098–1179), who became Abbess of Rupertsberg, is known for her diplomatic activities, her writings, and her musical compositions. She began writing musical settings of lyrical poetry in the 1140s. Ten years later, she assembled some of her works under the title *Symphonie armonie celestium revelationum* (Harmonic symphonies of heavenly revelation). Two extant manuscripts contain 77 poems with music: antiphons, responds, sequences, hymns, the Kyrie, the Alleluia, and three miscellaneous items. The compositions form a liturgical cycle; most of the works have designations that link them with feasts or classes of feasts. The texts are visionary with brilliant imagery. The music notation is in early German neumes, written on four-line staves with f and/or c letter-clef identification (fig. 7.3).

Hildegard's music is original composition, not based on chant formulas. The music relies on melodic patterns or formulas she composed, but her music is not patchwork or centonization. Her compositions vary from syllabic settings to ones that are highly melismatic. Sometimes the range is very wide and the melody verges on being improvisatory in its freedom. For example, the antiphon *In Evangelium,* for use in Vespers before Benedictus or Magnificat on the feast day honoring St. Ursula, has a range from c to f'; the respond *O vos, felices radices* covers a range from A to g'.

Hildegard's play, *Ordo virtutum,* is considered the earliest morality play (DWMA26). The plot concerns the battle for the Soul (*Anima*) waged between the Sixteen Virtues and the Devil (*Diabolus*). The play is written in dramatic verse and contains 82 melodies that are neumatic (or nearly so) settings of the text. *Diabolus* has no music; his lines are spoken.

ANONYMOUS LATIN SONGS

Many of the Latin songs of the late Middle Ages are anonymous. Some of them were written by wandering clerics who had no permanent positions but worked at whatever jobs they could obtain. Others were written and performed by persons known as *goliards,* who were

FIGURE 7.3 Hildegard von Bingen's antiphon *O gloriosissimi* in manuscript, Cod. 9, fol. 159r. *(Benedictine Abbey of St. Peter and St. Paul, Dendermonde, Belgium)*

rejects or dropouts from religious life. The "Bishop Golias" who was their mentor and the Order of Goliards, to which they supposedly belonged, never existed. Goliards had low social status. Their songs were of the "eat, drink, and be merry" type, appropriate to the wanton kind of life the goliards lived.

The largest surviving manuscript of secular Latin songs is in the Bavarian State Library in Munich. Until 1803 this manuscript was at the Benedictine monastery at Benediktbeuren. The manuscript contains more than 200 poems. Some are supplied with melodies written in staffless neumes; space was provided for notation for others. In 1847, J. A. Schmelker edited and published the poems as *Carmina Burana* (Benediktbeuren Songs). In 1937, Carl Orff composed musical settings for 25 of the poems, using the same title. Most of the poems in the manuscript are love songs and are notorious for their obscenity. Others parody religious

songs and services, irreverently and sometimes blasphemously. Included are some gambling and drinking songs, a few serious satirical poems, and six liturgical plays. Not all the poems are in Latin; approximately one-fourth of them are in a Bavarian dialect.

Monophonic *conductus* were written in the eleventh to thirteenth centuries. These nonliturgical, metrical Latin songs were probably used, originally, as processionals or background music when a person was being conducted from one place to another in a service. A conductus melody was newly composed. By the end of the twelfth century, the term *conductus* might be applied to any nonliturgical serious song with a metrical Latin text.

VERNACULAR SONGS

An early type of French vernacular song was the *chanson de geste* (song of heroic deeds). Long narrative epics of this kind were intended to be sung but were not supplied with music notation in manuscripts. The national epic of France, *Le Chanson de Roland* (Song of Roland), narrates the heroism of Charlemagne's nephew, Roland, who lost his life when ambushed by Basques at Saragosse in 778. The poem can be traced to the first half of the eleventh century and may be much older. Probably, *Le Chanson de Roland* was performed by a *jongleur*, who improvised the melody as he sang the words and accompanied his singing by strumming a stringed instrument, perhaps a harp. This kind of recounting of heroic deeds is described in the English epic *Beowulf*, which originated in the eighth century.

Jongleurs (jugglers) and *ménestrels* (minstrels) were at the bottom of the social scale. They were social outcasts personally but were acceptable as entertainers who were capable of providing all kinds of amusements. They were performers, not creators of music, and are important historically because their wanderings contributed to the spread and survival of medieval monophonic song. Names of some early jongleurs are known; Taillefer was jongleur to William the Conqueror. Sometime around 1120, Parisian jongleurs formed a guild, which remained active until abolished by law in the eighteenth century. Statutes enacted by the Paris guild in 1321 specify that the regulations applied to "*jougleurs et jougleuresses, menestreus et menestrelles.*" Moreover, 8 of the 37 signers of those statutes were women, among them Marie la Chartaine, Alipson Guerin, and Adeline Langois.

TROUBADOURS, TROUVÈRES

During the eleventh through thirteenth centuries, the poet-composers working in the south and north of France were known, respectively, as *troubadours* and *trouvères*. Both names translate literally as "finders" or "inventors." In southern France, the poets used the Provençal vernacular—*langue d'oc*; in northern France, *langue d'oïl* was used. In the respective dialects, *oc* and *d'oïl* mean "yes." Medieval *langue d'oïl* evolved into modern French.

Many of the troubadours and trouvères were from the nobility; however, a nonaristocrat might enjoy high social status because of exceptional talent. Marcabru (fl. 1128–50), Bernart de Ventadorn (c. 1130–90), and Guiraut de Bornelh (c. 1140–c. 1200) did. Many troubadours and trouvères sang their own songs. Minstrels also performed them and, as they traveled from place to place, taught them by rote to other performers. In the process, variant versions arose. Thus, some extant manuscripts contain different versions of some songs. The manuscript collections of French songs are called *chansonniers* (songbooks), from the French word *chanson* (song).

Not all troubadour and trouvère songs were written down, and of those that were notated many have been lost. Extant poems by troubadours number approximately 2,600; those by trouvères about 4,000. Surviving melodies are fewer: about 265 by troubadours and 1,400 by trouvères. Generally, the poetry is not profound, and the music may be quite simple. The poems cover a variety of subjects; the musical and poetical forms are equally varied. Most texts are set syllabically, with an occasional short melisma near the end of a poetic line. The melismas in any one song are similar, if not identical, which seems to indicate that they were standard melodic formulas. Phrases are short; melodies are modal and narrow in range, sometimes as narrow as a fifth and seldom greater than an octave. The rhythm is conjectural because the notation is nonmensural, and relative note values are not indicated. Modern transcription in triple meter seems suitable for many of the songs, but the rhythm used may have been at the discretion of the performer, and regular rhythmic patterns may not have been followed.

In the first part of the eleventh century, the troubadours called their sung poems *vers*. Later, distinctive terms were applied to specific types of sung poems. Several of the poetic and musical forms employed by the troubadours were paralleled by those of the trouvères and had similar names. The troubadour *canso* (trouvère *chanson*) was a song about courtly or chivalric love (Insight, "Courtly Love"). The troubadour *pastorela* (trouvère *pastourelle*), a narrative poem, depicts a pastoral scene in which a knight meets a shepherdess whom he seeks to seduce. Sometimes he succeeds, but more often the shepherdess's lover or a relative appears at the appropriate "saving" moment.

The troubadour *alba* (trouvère *aube*), a morning or dawn song, usually concerns either the parting of lovers at daybreak or a warning given to lovers that dawn is approaching. Some albas express concern for a companion who has been gone through the night, as does *Reis glorios* (Glorious King) by Guiraut de Bornelh (DWMA27).

Songs written in dialogue include the troubadour *tenso* (dispute) and *joc parti* (debate), comparable respectively to the trouvère *descort* and *jeu parti* (pl., *jeux partis*). Participants in the debates were addressed by name, and usually the poet-composer participated.

The *sirventes* was originally a song of service. The word service had a dual meaning: A borrowed secular melody served as music for a poem that a troubadour wrote for the lord he served. Sirventes were not necessarily complimentary; frequently, they were moral or political satires. Bertran de Born (c. 1145–c. 1215) was famous for his satirical sirventes.

The trouvère *chanson de toile* (picture song) has a narrative text related by a lady who commences by describing the scene in which she finds herself at the moment. Generally, the song continues with a tale of the lady's woes and the reasons therefor. (The French word *toile* was used to refer to either a piece of woven cloth or a picture such as that woven into the tapestries for which Arras was famous.)

The *lai* (lay), of Celtic origin, was a long narrative poem in the vernacular, written in rhymed couplets. One of the first French poets to write *lais* was Marie de France, who spent some time at the court of Henry II and Eleanor of Aquitaine; her *lais* were on historical or legendary subjects and were not intended for singing. Later, trouvères used the same kind of

Courtly Love

The term *amour courtois* (courtly love), rarely used during the Middle Ages, became popular after Gaston Paris used it in 1883 to designate the complex expression underlying the poetico-musical art of troubadours and their counterparts in France, Germanic lands, and Britain. Troubadours spoke of their works as expressing *fin' amors*—refined or courteous love; the Minnesinger termed it *Minnedienst* (servitude to love), and Chaucer called it "gentil lovyng" (genteel loving). That art, which flourished from the late eleventh through the fourteenth century, was the combination of poetry and music to serve a courtly ideal. The poetry was as important as the music—sometimes more so. In fact, some poet-musicians were members of literary guilds.

The specific date and place of origin of *fin' amors* is not known. The use of *langue d'oc* in early works tends to place its genesis in southern France, but it is apparent also in works that Chrétien de Troyes (b. 1144; fl. 1170–90) created at the court of Marie de Champagne, daughter of Eleanor of Aquitaine.

Fin' amors presented a doctrine of moral and mental discipline that encompassed a number of paradoxes. It had both sensual and spiritual aspects. The "love" it described could be both human and transcendental; though illicit, it should be morally elevating; it was passionate but disciplined and could be simultaneously humiliating and exalting. Themes frequently used were these: a knight's longing for an unattainable lady; a lover's lament over the social gulf separating him from his adored one; and the moral uplift and character-building resulting from a lover's disciplined service to a lady, with minimal reward. For instance, a knight might express feelings of love for a lady he adored but who was unattainable because she was his superior and belonged to the lord whom he served. Supposedly, the impossibility inherent in the situation strengthened the knight's character.

To some degree, *fin' amors* reflects the interdependency present in the structure of the feudal system. Just as a vassal (who might be a noble or a knight) was of lower social rank than the lord to whom he had sworn allegiance, so the professional musician who performed the song was socially inferior to the poet-musician who created it and to the lord and lady at whose court they both served.

---

couplet format for *lais* that were intended for singing, but their lyrics concerned love.

The troubadour *balada* or *dansa*, a dance song, usually has a text that mentions spring or a spring festival and refers to love. *Kalenda Maya* (The first of May festival), by Raimbaut de Vaqueiras (d. 1207), is a love poem set to music that has the character of an *estampie*, a stomping dance (DWMA28). However, *Kalenda Maya* uses aab structure rather than the typical *estampie* form (see p. 102).

The trouvères composed dance songs called *carole, ronde, rondel, rondelet,* and other diminutives of *ronde.* These were performed with round dances. Musically, dance songs were strophic with refrain; a soloist—perhaps the leader of the dance—sang the strophe, and the entire group sang the refrain.

MUSICAL FORMS Typically, the troubadour-trouvère songs are strophic, and many of them have refrains. Sometimes the refrain is a repetition of the opening phrase of the piece; at other times, only the closing strain of the first strophe recurs as refrain in the ensuing stanzas. The refrain may belong solely to the song in which it appears or may have been borrowed from another song; use of quotations as refrains was common practice in the late Middle Ages. The dance songs previously mentioned were forerunners of late thirteenth-century literary forms that became known as the **formes fixes** (fixed forms) of French poetry: *ballade, rondeau,* and *virelai.* In the fourteenth and fifteenth centuries, these three poetic forms dominated, and they directly affected the musical form of most of the secular music that was composed.

Both capital and lowercase letters are used in the analysis of formal structures of vocal music. Each distinctive melody is identified by a letter, alphabetically. For example, in the formal pattern AbbaA, two different melodies occur: a music and b music. A capital letter is used to indicate that a phrase of text set to a particular musical phrase recurs. Thus, the capital A in the formal pattern given indicates that the composition commences and concludes with the same words and the same music. In this particular formal pattern, the A music and words constitute a refrain. Use of the lowercase letter *b* twice indicates that the b music is used two times but the words differ. Similarly, the lowercase *a* indicates use of the same melody as A but with different words (ex. 7.1).

The trouvère *ronde* or *rondel* eventually came to be known by the name **rondeau** (pl., *rondeaux*). As a *forme fixe,* the literary *rondeau,* which incorporates a refrain, consists of a single eight-line stanza with only two rhymes; the musical setting comprises only two melodic phrases. All poetic lines having the same rhyme are sung to the same melodic phrase. The poetic and musical forms of the *rondeau* may be indicated by the same pattern of letters: ABaAabAB. However, some thirteenth-century *rondeaux* consist of only six lines; they do not commence with a refrain but follow the formal pattern aAabAB. The anonymous *C'est la jus* (It is the right) is a six-line rondeau, and *Prendés i garde* (Take care) by Guillaume d'Amiens has eight lines (ex. 7.2; DWMA29). Most thirteenth-century monophonic rondeaux appear without musical notation in literary works, such as *romans* (long narrative poems in the vernacular). The music for some of these rondeaux can be reconstructed because their refrains have been quoted in motets.

From the troubadour *balada* came the French **ballade** and **virelai** and the Italian **ballata.** Virelai and ballata use AbbaA form. Virelais having more than one stanza use the refrain only once between stanzas: AbbaA bbaA bbaA. An example of the virelai is *Or la truix* (Now I find . . . ; ex. 7.1; DWMA32).

Originally, both ballade and virelai commenced and concluded with a refrain; soon, however, the opening refrain was omitted from the ballade, with a resultant difference in formal structure. Adam de la Halle's *Dieus soit* (The gods be . . .) is a ballade with a refrain at both the beginning and the end of the stanzas (DWMA30).

The late thirteenth-century **ballade** text has three short stanzas that use the same meter and rhyme scheme and end with the same refrain. The musical setting for each stanza forms the pattern aab. Only a few Provençal dance songs using this form are extant. One is the anonymous *A l'entrada del tens clar* (At the coming of spring; ex. 7.3 [see p. 98]; DWMA31). As the musical setting of a *forme fixe,* the ballade frequently followed the pattern aabC, with C being the refrain. In other words, three sections of music were used, with the first section being repeated. The court poet-composer Machaut used this formal structure for the musical setting of some of his ballades (see p. 115).

Translation: I find her much too difficult, indeed!
Because she is so simple.
Much too presumptuous did I act,
Though I felt positively sure
Of what I shall not have for months, alas!
'Tis that which hurts me most of all.
I find her much too difficult, indeed!
Because she is so simple.

EXAMPLE 7.1 Transcription of *Or la truix,* a *virelai,* with formal pattern AbbaA marked.

The first troubadours whose names are known are Eblon (or Ebles), Viscount of Ventadour, and his contemporary Guillaume IX (1071–1127), Count of Poitiers and Duke of Aquitaine. Guillaume IX is the only known troubadour in the first quarter of the twelfth century whose poems have survived and are documented. His son, Guillaume X, supported but did not participate in the troubadour art; Marcabru worked at his court. The granddaughter of Guillaume IX, Eleanor of Aquitaine (1122–1202), was both patroness of troubadours and ancestress of trouvères. In 1137, Eleanor married King Louis VII of France (r. 1137–80); they had two daughters, Marie and Alix. Eleanor and Louis were divorced in 1152; soon thereafter Eleanor married Henry, Duke of Normandy and Count of Anjou and Maine, who became Henry II of England (r. 1154–89). One of their children was Richard Coeur-de-Lion (1157–99), a talented trouvère. The best known of Richard's songs is *Ja nus hons pris* (Indeed, no prisoner), written when he was captured and held for ransom by the Germanic emperor, Henry VI, during the Crusades. Richard's lyrics are set to aab-type music. According to legend, Richard's friend, the trouvère Blondel de Nesle (fl. 1180–1200), located the imprisoned Richard by means of a song they had coauthored.

Marie and Alix, in their respective positions as Countesses of Champagne and Chartres, actively supported poets and composers. Poesy and music flourished at the court at Champagne during the last 30 years of the twelfth century. Among those whom Marie encouraged were Chrétien de Troyes, Gace Brulé, and Conon de Béthune. Marie's grandson, Count Thibaut of Champagne (1201–53), who later became King Thibaut IV of Navarre, was one of the best trouvères.

The troubadours and trouvères flourished from c. 1086 to c. 1300. Among those active during the time of Léonin and Pérotin were troubadours Bernart de Ventadorn, Guiraut de Bornelh, Bertran de Born, Raimbaut de Vaqueiras, and trouvères Richard Coeur-de-Lion and Blondel de Nesle.

Translation: *Take care that no one looks at me! If anyone looks at me,*
tell me. It is all down there in those woods. *Take care*
that no one looks at me! The country girl tends the cows:
Pretty brunette, I am yours. *Take care that no one looks at me!*
If anyone looks at me, tell me.

EXAMPLE 7.2 *Prendés i garde*, a *rondeau*, by Guillaume d'Amiens, with formal pattern ABaAabAB marked. Transcribed from MS Reg. Christ. 1490, Biblioteca Vaticana, Rome.

a Solo: Chorus:

A l'en - tra - da del tens clar, E - y - a,

Solo: Chorus:

Pir joi - e re - co - men - çar E - y - a,

a Solo: Chorus:

E pir ja - lous ir - ri - tar, E - y - a,

Solo:

Vol la re - gi - ne mo - strar K'ele est si a - mo - rou - se.

b Chorus:

A - la - vi', A - la - vi - e, Ja - lous, las - saz

nos, las - saz nos bal - lar en - tre nos en - tre nos.

Translation: When the good weather comes, Eya, to bring back joy, Eya,
and to annoy jealous ones, Eya, I wish to show the queen
for she is so much in love. On your way, on your way, jealous ones,
leave us, leave us to dance among ourselves, among ourselves.

EXAMPLE 7.3 *A l'entrada del tens clar,* with aab formal pattern marked. Transcribed from MS *fr.*20050, fol. 82v, Bibliothèque nationale, Paris.

ADAM DE LA HALLE   Adam de la Halle (c. 1245–after 1306), who is considered greatest of the trouvères, was born at Arras in Picardie. He left Arras c. 1277, spent some time in Paris, and served Robert II, Count of Artois, in Italy. Adam wrote literary and musical works in almost every genre used in the late thirteenth century; he is one of the few medieval composers to have both monophonic and polyphonic compositions to his credit. His compositions survive in more than two dozen manuscripts, one of which contains all his known works. Included are 36 monophonic chansons, 18 monophonic *jeux-partis,* 16 three-voice *rondeaux* (songs with refrains), 5 three-voice motets, and 3 plays that contain some music. The *rondeaux* are some of the earliest polyphonic settings of dance songs. The most famous of his plays, and the one containing the most music, is *Le Jeu de Robin et de Marion* (The Play about Robin and Marion), a dramatic *pastourelle* in which spoken dialogue is interspersed with songs. The music is monophonic, but specified instruments accompany the singing. The play was first performed at the Naples court where Adam was working in 1285 (DWMA33).

TROBAIRITZ

Trobairitz (women troubadours) were active in southern France from c. 1145 to c. 1225. Their poems (*trobar*), written in Provençal, survive in several manuscripts. At least 18 trobairitz are known by name, but *vidas* (biographies in manuscripts) exist for less than half of them.

The trobairitz held a unique social position. They were aristocratic ladies—the *Midons* (Miladies) and the "adored things" to and about whom troubadours wrote poems of courtly love. Several trobairitz were patrons of troubadours, yet as poets these ladies and men met as equals. The trobairitz, too, produced love poems, but their lines discussed love realistically and candidly. Trobairitz verses were not visionary but were intimate in expression; at times the ladies frankly stated their feelings about physical love, both pro and con. In their poetry, the trobairitz expressed pride, joy, admiration, love, rejection, hurt, distaste, and injury; sometimes the verses question, doubt, or inquire. Some poems divest the knight of his chivalric armor and reveal the human character of the man. Trobairitz poems vary in rhyme scheme, number of strophes, and number of lines per strophe.

The trobairitz also wrote *tensos* in which the participants were clearly identified. In the poem *Gui d'Ussel, be.m pesa de vos* (Gui d'Ussel, I am distraught because of you), Maria de Ventadorn was distressed because Gui had given up composing. In 1209 a papal legate had directed Gui to cease writing poems about courtly love. Maria urged Gui to resume composition, then discussed with him the matter of the true social status of a man and a woman in love. Who outranked whom? Or were they equal? This *tenso* is one of the few trobairitz poems for which a **razo** survives. A *razo* is a prose paraphrase of a song, used by a *joglar* as an introduction to his performance of the song.

Maria de Ventadorn (1165–after 1221) was the daughter of Raimon II, Viscount of Turenne, in Limousin. She and her two sisters were praised in poetry by Bertran de Born, c. 1182. In 1183 Maria married Ebles V of Poitou, whose great-grandfather was troubadour Eblon. Maria was a patron of troubadours, including Gui. (She was not related to Bernart de Ventadorn.)

The trobairitz were aristocrats; *joglars* would have been available to perform their songs. The musical setting of only one trobairitz poem has been located— *A chantar mes al cor que n̄ deurie* (My heart must sing . . . ; DWMA34) by Beatritz, Countess of Dia. Another version of the poem begins *A chantar m'er de so qu'ieu non volria.* Three other poems by the Countess (born c. 1140) are extant. Beatritz married Guillem of Poitiers; their son was Count of Dia, and Beatritz chose to be known as Countess of Dia. The Countess was a friend of troubadour Raimbaut d'Orange (c. 1146–73), whose older sister, Tibors (c. 1130–82), was one of the trobairitz. According to her *vida,* Tibors wrote many *trobar,* but only a fragment of one of them survives.

Garsenda de Forcalquier (c. 1170–after 1257), wife of Alphonse II of Provence, held the highest social rank of all the trobairitz. She was regent of Provence in 1209–c. 1220. Among other known trobairitz are Almucs de Castelnau, Iseut de Capio, Guillelma de Rosers, Clara d'Anduza, and Bieiris de Romans.

SPANISH MONOPHONY

French and Provençal rulers and nobles frequently visited Spanish and Portuguese shrines and courts and took their musicians and poets with them. The Chris-

tian kings of Spain made similar visits to France and Provence. Troubadours and jongleurs traveled independently, too. Spanish musicians and rulers were quite aware of cultural developments north of the Pyrenees, and until the thirteenth century much of the poetry created in Iberia was in the Provençal language. After c. 1225, however, the Galician dialect of Portugal and the Spanish vernacular were used more frequently.

The most extensive and most important manuscript of Galician-Portuguese medieval music that has survived is the *Cantigas de Santa Maria* (Ballads about Saint Mary; fig. 7.4). The manuscript was prepared c. 1250–80 at the direction of Alfonso X the Wise, King of Castile and Léon (r. 1252–84). The parchment leaves contain a Prologue (intended to be sung; DWMA35a) and 400 songs honoring the Virgin Mary. Most of these 400 *cantigas* recount miracles attributed to the Virgin, but every tenth *cantiga* is a song praising her (DWMA35b). (The Galician word *cantiga* is pronounced with stress on the first syllable: *cántiga.*) The manuscript is beautifully illuminated with miniatures that provide valuable information concerning medieval instruments and musical performance (fig. 7.5). The Galician poems are set to music written in mensural notation on five-line staves. Both duple and triple meter were used. The songs have refrains and use AbbaA form.

FIGURE 7.4 First *cantiga de loor* from MS j.b.2 (MS b.I.2), fol. **29.** *(El Escorial, Madrid)*

FIGURE 7.5 Several of the many illuminations in MS b.I.2 depicting instrumentalists performing. *(El Escorial, Madrid)*

ITALIAN MONOPHONY

The proximity of northern Italy to Provence tended to promote the use of Provençal as well as Italian for poetry. The southern third of Italy, which with the island of Sicily formed the Kingdom of Sicily, was ruled from 1197 to 1250 by Holy Roman Emperor Frederick II, a respected statesman and a patron of arts and learning. Refugees from the cruelties of the "Albigensian Crusade" and the Spanish Inquisition sought and found protection at his Sicilian court.

Extant manuscripts contain little Italian secular monophony that was produced during the Middle Ages. No doubt a great deal of the monophonic music that was composed was never notated but was transmitted orally. There survive less than 200 thirteenth-century Italian nonliturgical religious songs called **laude** (praises; sing., *lauda*) or **laude spirituali** (spiritual praises). These are songs of wandering penitents who sought atonement for their sins by self-inflicted whippings and by singing songs of praise at wayside shrines. *Laude* are strophic and commence with a *ripresa* (refrain) that recurs after each strophe

(DWMA36). The music reflects the influence of Gregorian chant, folk song, and troubadour songs. In their turn, *laude* and the Italian flagellants influenced German penitents who created similar vernacular sacred songs called *Geisslerlieder.*

GERMAN MONOPHONY

The Germanic counterparts of the jongleurs were called *Spielleute* (entertainers). No *Spielleute* repertory has survived. Presumably, these wandering entertainers recited or sang epics and other poetry, told folk tales, and performed Latin and vernacular songs.

The art of the troubadours and trouvères strongly influenced the development of lyric poetry and song among the Germans. Frederick I Barbarossa, who was Holy Roman Emperor from 1154 to 1190, married Beatrice of Upper Burgundy. Frederick and Beatrice are credited with promoting French and Provençal song in the lands they ruled.

MINNESÄNGER   The twelfth- and thirteenth-century poet-musicians called *Minnesänger* (sing., *Minnesinger,* one who sings about courtly love) were the German counterparts of troubadours and trouvères. The types of songs created by the *Minnesänger* are similar to those produced by the troubadours and trouvères: (a) *Frauenstrophe* (ladies' songs) parallel the chanson de toile. (b) The *Tagelied* (song of day) heralds approaching dawn, as do alba and aube; and (c) the *Wächterlied* (watcher's song) is closely akin to these. (d) The *Streitgedicht* (dispute poem) is comparable to the jeu parti and tenso. (e) The *Minnelied* (pl., *Minnelieder,* love song) concerns courtly love (*Minne*), as do the canzo and early French chanson. (f) The *Kreuzlied* (song of the cross) finds its counterpart in the Crusaders' songs composed by trouvères. (g) The *Leich* is similar to the lai sung by the trouvères. (h) The German *Sprüche* (proverbs) are moralistic songs but are not satirical as are the troubadour sirventes. *Sprüche* texts may be religious or political and may express social criticism.

The Germanic poet-composers used a variety of formal patterns for their song settings. It is difficult to transcribe the music because, in extant manuscripts, the notation does not indicate relative note values or ends of phrases. Moreover, some scribes wrote the music above the poem, and, to save manuscript space, music that was used for a repeated section was written down only once.

Though the *Minnesänger* were active from c. 1150 to c. 1320, the period between c. 1180 and 1230 is considered their "golden age." Among the best of the German poet-composers were Wolfram von Eschenbach (c. 1170–1220) of Bavaria, Walther von der Vogelweide (c. 1170–1228), Neidhart von Reuental (c. 1190–c. 1237), Der Tannhäuser (c. 1205–70), and Heinrich von Meissen (c. 1250–1318).

Walther von der Vogelweide is credited with perfecting the Minnelied and Spruch and making them original compositions rather than relying on melodic formulas. One of the few of his poems for which the complete melody is extant is *Palästinalied* (Palestine Song; DWMA37).

Neidhart von Reuental tended to use realism and satirical wit in his poetry and particularly directed the satire toward rustic life and manners. Most of his lyrics commence with a description of either the winter or the summer season; hence, his poems are sometimes classified as being either "summer" or "winter" songs.

Der Tannhäuser was considered by later German poet-composers as one of the twelve *alte Meister* (old masters). His surviving poems—six Leich and ten Lieder—are important for the autobiographical data they provide. Tannhäuser and Wolfram von Eschenbach participated in a song contest held at the Wartburg in 1207, an event Richard Wagner depicted in his opera *Tannhäuser.* Wagner based his music drama *Parsifal* on Wolfram's epic *Parzival.*

Heinrich von Meissen is better known as Frauenlob (praise of ladies), a name he acquired because he regarded women highly and preferred use of the word *frouwe* (*Frau,* lady) rather than *wip* (*Weib,* woman). So strong were his feelings on the matter that he publicly debated the issue with a colleague. One of Frauenlob's songs begins: *"Ey ich sach in dem trone / Ein jungfraw"* (I saw on the throne / A virgin). Frauenlob was also an *alte Meister.*

MEISTERSINGER   The *Meistersinger* were citizens of German cities who belonged to guilds that regulated and promoted the composition and performance of songs (*Meisterlieder*). Meistersinger came primarily from lower and middle classes of society, but talented upper-class citizens were not excluded from the guilds. In contrast with the Minnesinger, who was a professional poet-composer, the Meistersinger regarded composing and singing as a serious avocation. Exactly when or where the first Meistersinger guild was formed is not known. The guilds were most active from the fourteenth through the seventeenth century, though a few still existed in the nineteenth. The last Meistersinger died in 1922. One of the most important of the Meistersinger guilds, and the only one about which specific information is available, was that at Nuremberg. Hans Vogel (died c. 1550) and the shoemaker Hans Sachs (1494–1576) were influential members of that guild, which Richard Wagner depicted in his opera *Die Meistersinger von Nürnberg.* (However, Wagner treated medieval stories, ideas, and forms of music in a nineteenth-century manner.)

Surviving manuscripts of Meisterlieder date from the fifteenth century; they contain words and music for approximately 16,000 monophonic songs. These songs, which the Meistersinger called *Bare* (sing., *Bar*), are constructed in three or more stanzas, each using the aab pattern now known as **Bar form** (DWMA37). The a sections were called *Stollen* and the b section *Abgesang.* Often the *Abgesang* was considerably longer than the *Stollen;* frequently, the last two lines of *Abgesang* melody were identical with the last two lines of the *Stollen* music. It is believed that Meistersinger melodies were intended to be performed as unaccompanied vocal monody, sung by soloists or, rarely, by a chorus.

ENGLISH MONOPHONY

In medieval England before the Norman Conquest, the professional musician was either a *scop,* who enjoyed a more or less permanent position as resident entertainer at the hall of a petty king, or a *gleeman,* who traveled from place to place and performed wherever and whenever he could find work. After the Norman Conquest, both scops and gleemen vanished, though their functions did not. *Minstrels* appeared and assumed the functions of both scop and gleeman, entertaining by singing songs or by reciting long narrative poems while strumming a harp. No examples of scop or gleeman music are extant.

The paucity of English music in surviving manuscripts may be attributed to the use of Norman-French at British courts after the Norman Conquest. French was the official language of the English court until the latter part of the fourteenth century, and Henry II was never willing to learn the English language. The greater part of the territory he controlled was on the European continent, and he and his wife, Eleanor of Aquitaine, spent little time in England. Though troubadours and trouvères visited the English court, and Richard I was a trouvère, the French poet-musicians never established a "school" in Britain. Moreover, there was no wholesale imitation of troubadour-trouvère style by English musicians.

The earliest surviving vernacular English songs are those by a Saxon hermit, St. Godric (died c. 1170). One of his nonliturgical religious songs, "Crist and Sainte Marie," uses portions of a Kyrie, both words and music, as framework at the beginning and end of the English lyrics. This seems to be an English *farse*—a liturgical chant with a single long vernacular trope inserted between the opening phrase and the remainder of the chant. Only three songs by St. Godric are extant; the other two are prayers.

Among the few thirteenth-century English secular songs that exist today are *Worldes blis ne last* (The world's bliss does not last); *Man mei longe him lives wene* (Long may man want his life to be); *Mirie it is while sumer ilast* (Merry it is while summer lasts), written c. 1225; and *Byrd one brere* (Bird on a briar), a love song.

INSTRUMENTAL MUSIC

Only a few pieces of purely instrumental music from the Middle Ages have survived. Yet literary writers and authors of theoretical and practical treatises mentioned instruments and instrumental performances. Miniatures illuminating manuscripts picture instrumentalists performing, and church and cathedral sculptures depict musical instruments. Each jongleur and minstrel was required to be proficient on a number of instruments. After guilds were formed, these professional musicians were subjected to proficiency examinations regularly. But the instrumental music that was performed has not survived. Perhaps it was never written down. Undoubtedly, melodies were passed on by rote. Musicians may have improvised on basic tunes or used the melodies of vocal music in their performances.

In the Middle Ages, some leisure time was occupied by dancing, and the presence of dance songs in surviving manuscripts indicates that singing accompanied dancing. The oldest form of choral dance is the circle or round dance, accompanied by the playing and singing of *dansas, baladas,* and other dance songs. Wolfram wrote in *Parzival* about knights and ladies dancing, and Neidhart mentioned *Tanz* (dance) and instrumentalists in several of his lyrics. Some of Neidhart's descriptions are quite informative; in one of his poems, he wrote that for the Tanz "three must fiddle in front and the fourth [person] pipe." The thirteenth-century poet Meier Helmbrecht also mentioned fiddling in connection with *Tanz*. Poet-historian Jean Froissart (c. 1333–1400) wrote of minstrels playing pipes while youths and maidens danced: First came the *estampies;* then, with scarcely a pause, the dancers joined hands and began a *carole* (round dance).

The estampie existed as both a poetic and a musical form. Only one of the medieval poems designated as estampies has music notation with it. This, the earliest extant musical composition called an estampie, is *Kalenda Maya* (p. 95). According to Raimbaut, the music was based on a melody he heard two "fiddlers" play.

Similar terms in different languages—French *estampie,* Provençal *estampida,* Italian *istampida*—indicate that this dance was widely known. Music for an estampie is constructed in sections, or periods, called *puncta.* Each *punctum* is repeated and is equipped with open and closed (first and second) endings. Although each punctum begins with new music, after the first few "measures" the melody is much the same as that in all the other puncta. Most of the extant estampies have from four to six puncta; a dance with only two or three is referred to as a *ductia.*

The manuscript of trouvère songs known as *Le Chansonnier du Roy* (The king's songbook) contains monophonic music in mensural notation for 11 instrumental dances. These are the earliest known instrumental estampies.

Thirteenth-century English manuscripts contain a total of four instrumental dances. All the dances are sectional, but none conforms completely to estampie form. The earliest known notated music for a keyboard instrument, probably an organ, is in the Robertsbridge Codex, fragments of a British manuscript written c. 1325–50. Three of the six keyboard pieces in that manuscript are transcriptions of vocal

FIGURE 7.6 An estampie, one of six pieces of keyboard music in the Robertsbridge Codex. MS Brit. Mus. Add. 28850, fol. 43v. *(The British Museum)*

motets (one incomplete), and three are estampies (one incomplete) (fig. 7.6; DWMA38).

An Italian manuscript of fourteenth-century polyphonic music contains also 15 medieval monophonic dances, 8 of them estampies. These 8 are structurally similar to other estampies but with much longer, more complex puncta, a fact that seems to indicate that they were performed for listeners rather than for dancers. The other 7 dance pieces include 1 *trotto,* 4 *saltarelli,* and 2 compositions entitled *Lamento di Tristano* and *La Manfredina,* respectively. *Lamento di Tristano* and *La Manfredina* are not single dances but contain pairs of related dances. Although paired dances are referred to in some trouvère poems, these two Italian instrumental pieces are the earliest surviving paired dance music.

SUMMARY

Throughout the Middle Ages, monophonic music of all kinds was created: instrumental and vocal, secular and sacred, liturgical and nonliturgical. Much of what was produced was never notated and was eventually lost; medieval monophony in extant manuscripts was inscribed decades and sometimes a century or two after it originated, and the variant versions that survive attest to years of oral transmission, alteration, and rote learning of the melodies. Traveling professional entertainers—jongleurs, minstrels, *Spielleute,* and others, most of whom remain anonymous—are significant historically because they widely disseminated vernacular monophony. Court patronage and the merging of lands and customs through marriages of nobility contributed also to the spread of secular songs.

Members of early twelfth-century Provençal nobility are the first known poet-composers of secular vernacular songs. Women were both patrons and *trobairitz.* The art of the Provençal *troubadours* was paralleled and surpassed by the French *trouvères* who, in their turn, influenced the Germanic *Minnesänger.* Songs created by French, German, and Provençal poet-composers were counterparts in subject matter and type. French and Provençal dance songs with refrains followed formal patterns that later became the three *formes fixes* of French court poetry and song. Instrumentalists accompanied the dance songs and performed independent dance music such as the estampie.

Trouvères and their songs were known in England but engendered no school there. Extant English monophony is sparse but provides the earliest surviving keyboard music. Surviving Italian medieval monophony consists mainly of *laude* sung by flagellants, and the extant Galician-Portuguese songs are primarily *cantigas* honoring the Virgin Mary.

LATE MEDIEVAL MUSIC

Before the end of the thirteenth century, Britain had been consolidated into a well-defined realm under a limited monarchy. Edward I (r. 1272–1307) conquered Wales but was unsuccessful in his attempts to gain Scotland. Perhaps his greatest achievement was the establishment of Parliament (1295). Both Lords and Commons were represented, but clear distinction between them and separation into House of Lords and House of Commons came in the fourteenth century. France had had a *Parlement,* and in 1302 Philip IV called a parliamentary assembly with middle-class representation—an *Estates General,* composed of the Nobility, the Clergy, and the Third Estate (middle class). This expansion of middle-class power was accompanied by a decline in feudal aristocracy. Chivalry degenerated into ceremonial display and a code of manners.

Feudalism never had a firm grip in Italy. Though France and England were developing as monarchies, Italy was a decentralized aggregation of rival states that were competitors in commerce, trade, and crafts. The leading states were known by their principal cities—Florence, Milan, Naples, and Venice—with central Italy comprising the Papal States (fig. 8.1). Heads of courts in these states were patrons of the arts.

Shortly before 1300, Pope Boniface VIII (r. 1294–1303) became involved in a heated dispute with Philip IV (r. 1285–1314) of France concerning Philip's taxation of clergy. A war of words culminated in Philip taking legal action against the pope; the shock hastened Boniface's death. His successor, Benedict XI (r. 1303–4), let Philip have his way. The French bishop of Bordeaux became Pope Clement V (r. 1305–13), and in 1309 he decided to move the papal residency from Rome to Avignon, in Provence, where it remained until 1377. The poet Petrarch (1304–74) called those years the "Babylonian captivity of the church," equating the period of the Avignon papacy with the Israelites' years of captivity in Babylon. The French popes who ruled at Avignon were able administrators of that opulent court and were liberal patrons of the arts. In 1377, Gregory XI (r. 1370–78) conceded to heavy Italian pressure and moved the papal residency back to Rome. After his death, the college of cardinals split into two factions; each elected a pope. One ruled at Avignon, the other at Rome. Thus began the Great Schism that lasted until 1417. During that time there were two and ultimately three rival claimants to the papal throne.

From 1338 to 1453, England and France were intermittently at war, and at times the fighting was fierce. The immediate cause of the Hundred Years' War was the claim of England's Edward III (r. 1327–77) to the French throne when Charles IV (r. 1322–28) died without a male heir. Underlying causes were more complex. Britain's control of important trade centers on the Continent—especially the wine-producing district around Bordeaux and the wool cloth and tapestry weaving industries at Ghent and Bruges in Flanders (fig. 8.2)—had long been a thorn in the flesh to the French, who sought to drive the "foreigner" out of those areas and eventually succeeded. In 1453 the only territory England held on the Continent was the port of Calais.

The war was still young when the Pestilence came. Trading ships from the East that docked at Italian ports late in 1347 left not only cargo but rats infected with fleas that carried bubonic plague, for which there was no known cure. The epidemic spread through Italy, then through Germany and France and outward to England in 1348, and into Spain in 1350. During 1347–51, the Black Death killed approximately 75 million people in Europe; one-third of the population of England died of it. The disease ravaged Europe again in the mid 1360s and still again around 1375. Characteristics of the disease, and its effect, engendered dance and song:

> *Ring around the rosies,*
> *Pocket full of posies,*
> *Atchoo! Atchoo!*
> *All fall down.*

There were also urban revolts, peasant insurrections, and heresies to be dealt with from time to time, such as the uprisings of the *Jacquerie* in France, the Lollards in England, the Hussites in Moravia, and the citizens of Anagni in Italy.

The Hundred Years' War was barely over when England was torn by the Wars of the Roses (1455–85) between the House of Lancaster and the House of York, rival claimants to the throne. Rivalry ceased when Henry VII (Tudor), a descendant of the House of Lancaster, became ruler in 1485; his wife was Elizabeth of York.

As cities and towns grew and the middle-class populace became larger and more influential, secular interests increased and vernacular languages became more important. Increased use of the vernacular in literature reflects this. Several literary masterpieces written in the vernacular contain references to music; Dante's *Divine Comedy* (1307); Boccaccio's *Decameron* (1353), which relates how several persons spent their days of isolation while trying to avoid the plague; and Chaucer's *Canterbury Tales* (1386). In 1362, legislation was enacted in

FIGURE 8.1 Italy c. 1365.

England requiring the use of the English language instead of Latin in law courts. Around 1380, the followers of John Wycliffe (c. 1328–84) translated the Bible into English and distributed copies. Morality plays became popular.

There was renewed interest in Greek and Latin classical literature. The beginnings of *humanism* were apparent, with its emphasis on human beings, their practical ethics and moral virtues, and their potentials in their earthly lives. Humanism was an intellectual movement in that it emphasized study of the classics and sought answers to questions in treatises of the ancient writers. In fourteenth-century philosophical thinking, divine revelation and human reason operated in separate spheres, as should church and state and religion and science. Petrarch is considered the first important Italian humanist.

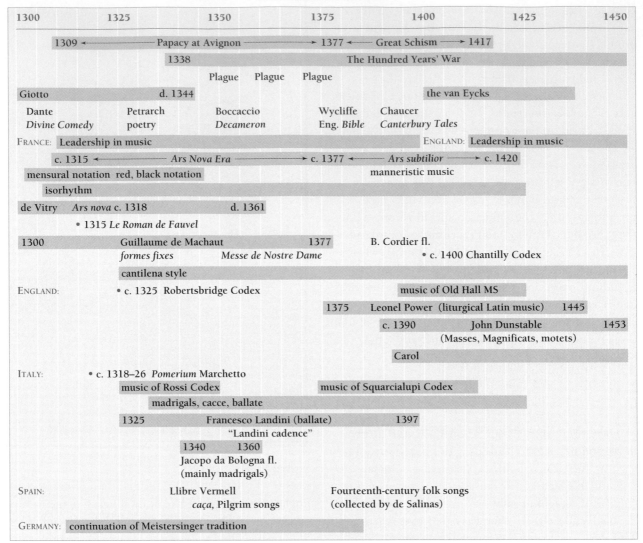

1300	1325	1350	1375	1400	1425	1450

1309 ◄———————— Papacy at Avignon ————————► 1377 ◄——— Great Schism ———► 1417

1338   The Hundred Years' War

Plague   Plague   Plague

Giotto   d. 1344   the van Eycks

Dante   Petrarch   Boccaccio   Wycliffe   Chaucer
Divine Comedy   poetry   *Decameron*   Eng. *Bible*   *Canterbury Tales*

FRANCE: Leadership in music   ENGLAND: Leadership in music

c. 1315 ◄——————— *Ars Nova Era* ———————► c. 1377 ◄——— *Ars subtilior* ———► c. 1420

mensural notation   red, black notation   manneristic music

isorhythm

de Vitry   *Ars nova* c. 1318   d. 1361

• 1315 *Le Roman de Fauvel*

1300   Guillaume de Machaut   1377   B. Cordier fl.

formes fixes   *Messe de Nostre Dame*   • c. 1400 Chantilly Codex

cantilena style

ENGLAND: • c. 1325   Robertsbridge Codex   music of Old Hall MS

1375   Leonel Power   (liturgical Latin music)   1445

c. 1390   John Dunstable   1453
(Masses, Magnificats, motets)

Carol

ITALY: • c. 1318–26   *Pomerium* Marchetto

music of Rossi Codex   music of Squarcialupi Codex

madrigals, cacce, ballate

1325   Francesco Landini (ballate)   1397

"Landini cadence"

1340   1360
Jacopo da Bologna fl.
(mainly madrigals)

SPAIN: Llibre Vermell   Fourteenth-century folk songs
caça, Pilgrim songs   (collected by de Salinas)

GERMANY: continuation of Meistersinger tradition

Medieval scholars, artists, authors, and composers hid essential meanings behind layers of secondary meanings and clothed thought in allegory so that truth lay behind natural appearances. This is exemplified in du Bus's *Roman de Fauvel,* Machaut's motets, and, more visibly, in the van Eycks' large *Ghent Altarpiece,* which, when unfolded, reveals new subjects depicted in sequence (plate 6, fig. 8.3, p. 108).

Changes were occurring in architecture, art, and sculpture. Sculpture was no longer viewed as part of the architecture of a building; individual pieces of free-standing sculpture were created for individual patrons. Artists often identified themselves by signing their creations. The work of Giotto di Bondone (1267–1337) is representative of some changes taking place in art. His paintings express naturalness and convey a feeling of solid three-dimensionality (plate 7). Perspective is apparent—sometimes created by haziness and variation of color, at other times by line—in the paintings of Huybrecht van Eyck (d. 1426) and Jan van Eyck (d. 1441) and the three Limbourg brothers who worked at the court of Jean, Duke of Berry.

FIGURE 8.2 France c. 1367. Shaded areas in Gascony, Aquitaine, Artois, and Flanders are territories owned by England.

The word *chapel* was used during the reigns of Pepin and Charlemagne to designate a reliquary, a repository for relics of saints and articles associated with the life of Christ. The most revered relic was the cape (*cappa*) of St. Martin. Persons who guarded the cape were *cappelani* (chaplains). Periodically, the *cappelani* sang *laudes* (praises) in honor of the relics and sometimes for high church officials and royalty. Gradually, the *cappella* (chapel) developed into a special staff of chaplains and clerics who officiated at services at a specified location. Kings kept royal chapels; princes and nobles had household chapels. Having a personal chapel was a symbol of prestige. In the fourteenth century, chapels of royalty and nobility came into prominence musically. By this time the chapel included a salaried group of vocalists and some instrumentalists. In 1334, Pope Benedict XII had at Avignon a Grand Chapelle of 30 to 40 members, plus a private chapel of 16 singers. In performance, singers clustered about a lectern that held a single huge choirbook of manuscript music. No more than 20 persons were able to see the music (plate 8).

FRANCE—*ARS NOVA*

The period of French *Ars nova* (New Art) extends from c. 1315 to c. 1375. During those years the production of secular music far exceeded that of sacred. Perhaps it only seems that way because more secular music was written down and has survived, but even that fact reflects the general increase in secular interests in the fourteenth century. Music was written in accord with new notational practices, some of which were codified c. 1322 by Philippe de Vitry in his *Ars nova*. The name given the era derives from the title of that treatise.

FIGURE 8.3 Detail from The Ghent Altarpiece. *(Cathedral of St. Bavo, Ghent)*

PHILIPPE DE VITRY

Philippe de Vitry (1291–1361), poet, theorist, and composer, spent much of his life in and around Paris. Although he received income from several **prebends** that he held simultaneously, he worked mainly at the French court as secretary and adviser to Charles IV (r. 1314–28), Philippe VI (r. 1328–50), and Jean II (r. 1350–64). (A prebend is an endowment or monetary allowance provided by a cathedral or large church as living expenses for a clergyman, though the recipient may not actually work at that church.) De Vitry was sent on several diplomatic missions to the papal court at Avignon, where he and Petrarch became friends. In 1351 de Vitry was appointed Bishop of Meaux, a position he held until his death.

De Vitry's complete *Ars nova* has not been located, but the variant versions of its last ten chapters (chaps. 15–24) that are extant contain his theoretical principles. In *Ars nova*, de Vitry codified the new aspects of rhythm and notation, especially with regard to imperfect mensuration and the minim. He recognized five note values: duplex long ▜ , long ▐ , breve ▪ , semibreve ◆ , and minim. ↓ The term *minim* did not originate with de Vitry; it was used earlier in Navarre.

Mensuration is the term that was given to the system governing the relationship between the long, the breve, and the semibreve. The Franconian system of notation was based on perfect mensuration (i.e., triple division of note values). De Vitry extended that system to include equal duple division of all note values down to and including the semibreve. The division of the long into breves was called *modus* (mood), the division of the breve into semibreves was *tempus* (time), and the division of the semibreve into minims produced *prolationis species* (prolation). Precise symbols designated the various **mensurations.** The mensuration signs can be related to modern time signatures (fig. 8.4).

The dot placed within the complete or broken circle as indication of perfection became known as *punctum perfectionis* (point or "prick" of perfection). The broken circle has been retained in modern notation where it represents $\frac{4}{4}$ meter, often referred to as "common time." (The symbol ₵ , with its designation "alla breve," which has also survived in modern notation, was not used by de Vitry but was an early Renaissance notation symbol used to shift the beat from the semibreve to the breve.)

In de Vitry's system, the semibreve might be subdivided in three ways: (a) *tempus perfect maius* (perfect major time) resulted when three semibreves were divided into three minims each, (b) *tempus perfectum medium* resulted when three semibreves were divided into two minims each, and (c) *tempus perfectum minimum* resulted when each semibreve contained three minims but minims followed one another so closely that further subdivision was impossible. This might be

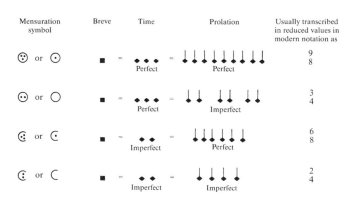

FIGURE 8.4 Interpretation of the mensuration symbols used by de Vitry to indicate the four prolations.

interpreted to mean that the tempo was quite rapid or that many minims were used in succession.

De Vitry is credited with the invention of red notes, which functioned (a) to temporarily alter note values from perfect (ternary) to imperfect (binary) or vice versa, (b) to designate any deviations from the original in a melody used as cantus firmus, and (c) to indicate transposition an octave higher. The earliest known motet with mensural red notation is *Garrit gallus—In nova fert—N[euma]* (The cock babbles—Changed into new—N; DWMA39; plate 9); de Vitry cited it as an example of that technique, called **coloration.** Red notes designate certain deviations from normal values, which were then written as solid black notes. For example, when written in red ink instead of black, a perfect note loses one-third of its value; therefore, it becomes imperfect.

Thirteenth-century music was written mainly in perfect mood (i.e., in longs and triple groupings of breves). In the fourteenth century, mood and time were used primarily in the lower voice(s) of motets. With the availability of shorter note values, the upper voice(s) usually were written in one or more of the prolations. The chief characteristic of French fourteenth-century music is its rhythmic organization, which was truly a "new art." Composers used with considerable freedom and ingenuity the variety of rhythmic possibilities at their disposal.

Much of de Vitry's music has been lost, and only 12 of his motets have survived. Of the extant motets only one has a French text; all others use Latin. The tenor is patterned (isorhythmic; discussed on p. 110) and proceeds in longer note values than the two upper voices, which are written primarily in semibreves and minims. Phrases in the upper voices are constructed to bridge rather than coincide with the rhythmic patterns of the tenor. In structure, each of de Vitry's motets is individualistic, poetically and musically.

OTHER THEORISTS

Johannes de Muris (c. 1300–c. 1350), in *Ars nove musice* (The Art of the new music; c. 1321), agreed with the principles of notation and mensuration set forth by de Vitry. There were those, however, who did not accept the changes without protest. Jacobus de Liège (c. 1260–c. 1331), in *Speculum musice* (Mirror of

music), championed the traditional music notation. Jacobus reported the division of the breve into as many as nine semibreves. His statement that the Franconian semibreve equaled the minim of the "moderns" confirms that the tempo of music had slowed.

The term *contrapunctus* (**counterpoint**) was first used and explained in anonymous treatises c. 1350, but throughout the fourteenth century the word *contrapunctus* meant note-against-note style of writing.

LE ROMAN DE FAUVEL

The earliest and one of the most important fourteenth-century French manuscripts containing music is MS fr.146 at Bibliothèque nationale, Paris. The major portion of this illuminated document is *Le Roman de Fauvel* (Narrative about Fauvel), a long satirical poem written by Gervais du Bus, who was a notary at the French royal chancery c. 1313–36 (fig. 8.5). According

FIGURE 8.5 Folio from *Le Roman de Fauvel* manuscript, MS *fr.146*. (*Bibliothèque nationale, Paris*)

to the poem, du Bus completed the *roman* on 6 December 1314. This poem is included in eleven other manuscripts. The copy in MS fr.146 is unique, however, because it contains musical interpolations that were added to the *roman* shortly after the poem was completed. The music enhances the moralistic satire of the narrative—an allegory on the social corruption then rampant in both church and state. In the manuscript, the music is anonymous.

The name of the main character, *Fauvel*, has several hidden meanings: (a) *fauve* denotes an unlovely brownish-yellow color or an animal that color; (b) *fauve* may also mean horse or ass; (c) *fau + vel* = veiled falsehood, or hypocrisy; and (d) the six letters of the name *Fauvel* represent six vices: *Flaterie, Avarice, Vilanie, Variété, Envie,* and *Lascheté* (flattery, greed, villainy, inconstancy, envy, and lasciviousness). In the allegory, persons of all social strata come to rub down or curry the ass, Fauvel (fig. 8.6). This action gave rise to the French expression *étriller Fauvel* (to curry Fauvel, or to flatter deceitfully); in modern English, the saying is "to curry favor."

The music comprises more than 50 monophonic pieces and 34 motets. The monophony includes types of liturgical chant and conductus in Latin, as well as lais, ballades, rondeaux, and virelais. The motets form a collection that exemplifies the various stages of motet development up to c. 1315. Early thirteenth-century, Franconian, Petronian, and early fourteenth-century motets are represented. One motet is four-voice; 10 are two-voice; and 23 are three-voice. Five motets have been identified as de Vitry's.

The mensural notation often conveys duple rhythm. A mixture of prolations was employed within a motet so that in modern transcription bar lines do not always coincide in all voices. The lack of physical alignment of notated parts was of no concern to fourteenth-century French musicians, whose music used neither bar lines nor score notation. Coloration was used in some motets. Another feature of the motets is **isorhythm.**

ISORHYTHM

The word *isorhythm* (same rhythm) is not found in late medieval treatises, nor is the compositional procedure described in detail in those writings, though the Latin terms *talea* and *color* (pronounced cōlor) were used. Isorhythm is a twentieth-century term coined by musicologist Friedrich Ludwig to indicate a special kind of structural organization frequently used by fourteenth-century composers in the tenors (and sometimes other voices) of their motets. The procedure involves the establishment of a rhythmic pattern, called **talea** (cutting; pl., *taleae*), that is reiterated one or more times in the tenor (the cantus firmus) of a composition. The melody of the isorhythmic voice part is called **color** (pl., *colores,* color or hue). The *color* may consist of a melodic segment that is repeated one or more times, or the entire tenor line may consist of only one statement of the melody. If melodic segments are used, their length may or may not match that of the *talea,* and their presentation may or may not coincide with statements of the *talea.* Isorhythm may appear in more than one voice of a polyphonic composition and may be combined with other compositional techniques, such as voice exchange or hocket.

In the isorhythmic motet *Detractor est—Qui secuntur—Verbum iniquum* (A disparager is—Those who follow—Iniquitous words; DWMA40) from *Roman de Fauvel,* the *talea* comprises six modern measures and is stated seven times in the tenor, whose text and melody are chant (fig. 8.7). Actually, a *talea* is a rhythmic ostinato pattern. The tenor of *Garrit gallus—In nova fert—N* is more complex: Three *taleae* form one *color;* each *talea* is symmetrical, with coloration in its center (plate 9, DWMA39).

FIGURE 8.6 Miniature in *Le Roman de Fauvel*, MS *fr.*146, depicts persons rubbing Fauvel, i.e., currying favor. *(Bibliothèque nationale, Paris)*

PLATE 5 *Sumer is icumen in,* English rota, c. 1250. Both rondellus and rota techniques were used in this motet. *(MS Harley 978, folio 11v. British Library, Reference Division, London)*

PLATE 6 H. and J. van Eyck. The Ghent Altarpiece, completed 1432. (*a*) Altarpiece closed, approx. 11'3″ × 7'3″; (*b*) altarpiece open, approx. 11'3″ × 14'6″. *(Original in St. Bavo Cathedral, Ghent)*

(a)

(b)

PLATE 7 Giotto di Bondone, *Lamentation*, fresco, 7'7" × 7'9", painted c. 1305. This mural is one of more than 40 frescoes that Enrico Scrovegni commissioned Giotto to paint in the Arena Chapel, Padua, Italy. *(© Fratelli Alinari/Art Resource)*

PLATE 8 Miniature depicting Johannes Ockeghem (wearing glasses) with his chapel singers. Note the storage space in the lectern for music, and in the table for liturgical books. *(MS fr. 1537, folio 58v, in Bibliothèque nationale, Paris)*

PLATE 9 Philippe de Vitry's isorhythmic motet *Garrit gallus–In nova fert–Neuma* as it appears in Le Roman de Fauvel. The three taleae of the notated Tenor form one *color*. (MS fr. 146, folio 44v, Bibliothèque nationale, Paris)

PLATE 10 Folio 122v of the Squarcialupi Codex (MS Med. Palat. 87) portrays Landini playing a portative organ. The composition is his madrigal *Musica son*. Various musical instruments are depicted in gold leaf in the border illumination. *(Biblioteca Medicea-Laurenziana, Florence)*

PLATE 11 Baude Cordier's rondeau *Belle Bonne*. (MS 564, folio 11v, Musée Condé, Chantilly)

PLATE 12 Jacob Senleches's virelai *La harpe de melodie*. A poetic rondeau written on the ribbon wrapped around the curved portion of the harp explains the virelai and gives instructions for its performance. *(MS 54.1, folio 10. Courtesy of The Newberry Library, Chicago)*

Isorhythm did not occur as the result of any one composer's sudden inspiration. Rather, its roots can be traced to thirteenth-century motet tenors structured in rhythmic modes and notated in a series of identical ligatures. The next stage in the development of isorhythm involved couching a liturgical cantus firmus in a certain *ordo* as a kind of rhythmic ostinato punctuated by rests and then combining repetition of the melody with that ostinato. This occurs in the thirteenth-century motet *En non diu—Quant voi—Eius in Oriente* (fig. 6.10; DWMA22). Full-fledged isorhythm emerged when composers devised tenors that reiterated individually designed rhythmic schemes (*taleae*). Melodic repetition was combined with this kind of rhythmic pattern also, most often in a manner that was not obvious. These procedures indicate that, though composers still based compositions on chant, they were constructing their works according to purely musical considerations rather than liturgical or textual ones. As the fourteenth century advanced, *taleae* became longer and more involved, and isorhythm invaded all voices of the motet and entered the Mass.

Composers organized tenors isorhythmically in three basic ways: (a) using several reiterations of *talea* but no melodic repetition, (b) combining one or more repetitions of *color* with reiterations of *talea,* and (c) using (b) plus a final statement of *talea* (with or without *color*) in diminution. All three of these plans were used by de Vitry and Machaut.

GUILLAUME DE MACHAUT

Guillaume de Machaut (c. 1300–77), renowned poet and leading French composer of the fourteenth century, held responsible positions at various royal courts and several important churches (Insight, "Guillaume de Machaut"). He spent much time at court, which probably accounts for the fact that most of his music is secular. However, in his few sacred compositions he made significant contributions to the development of music. Machaut composed monophonic and polyphonic pieces and used both conservative and avant-garde forms, styles, and techniques. His versatility and the high quality of his music were unparalleled in his time.

(a)

Translation:
Triplum: The slanderer is the most worthless fox.
By his slander he harms others and himself worse.
Duplum: [Those] who follow camps are wretched because
poorly [are their services rewarded].
Tenor: The Lord will despise an unjust and painful word.

(b)

FIGURE 8.7 (*a*) The isorhythmic motet *Detractor est—Qui secuntur—Verbum iniquum* in manuscript, MS *fr.*146; (*b*) transcription of the first two phrases of that motet. The first six measures of the tenor state the talea. (*Bibliothèque nationale, Paris*)

Guillaume de Machaut

Guillaume de Machaut was born in the province of Champagne in the diocese of Reims. Little is known of his early life and education except that he took holy orders. Sometime around 1323, he obtained a clerical position at the court of John of Luxembourg, who was King of Bohemia (r. 1310–46); various promotions elevated Guillaume to the position of king's secretary. King John traveled widely, and Guillaume was included in the king's large retinue. With King John's assistance, Machaut received from Pope John XXII (r. 1316–34) grants that provided income from Verdun, Arras, and Reims Cathedrals. When Pope Benedict XII (r. 1334–42) confirmed the Reims appointment in 1335, Machaut relinquished the others. He served King John until 1346, then became a canon at Reims. He had a house of his own and was at liberty to work at the court of John's daughter Bonne, wife of Jean, Duke of Normandy (who became Jean II of France, r. 1350–64). After Bonne's death in

1349, Machaut's patrons included Charles of Navarre; Jean, Duc de Berry; and Charles V of France (r. 1364–80).

In his poetry Guillaume recorded important historical data and interesting particulars of his personal life but said very little about his church work. He revealed that he was short of stature, blind in one eye, and suffered from gout. He enjoyed horseback riding and falconry and appreciated the beauty of nature. He related his experiences during the great plague that ravaged Europe (1348–50) and the siege of Reims (1359–60) during The Hundred Years' War. And, in *Livre du Voir Dit* (Book of the true story; c. 1365) he revealed "the true story" of his involvement with teenaged Péronne d'Armentières—a series of platonic episodes that generated a good deal of correspondence and inspired some romantic love poetry and songs.

During the last years of his life, Machaut prepared his own catalogue of his works. However, five extant

works are not included in that listing. The catalogue begins with a poetic prologue, then lists seventeen items of poetry, followed by seven categories of musical compositions: Lais, Motets, Mass, Hocket, Ballades, Rondeaux, and Virelais. Two works catalogued as poetry contain music: No. 5, *Remède de Fortune* (Fortune's remedy), in which seven songs are incorporated, and No. 15, *Livre du Voir Dit*, which has eight. In *Remède de Fortune*, Guillaume recounted the events of an entire day at a court. Musical performances are described, and, in connection with the minstrels' entrance into the great hall, more than 30 instruments are listed. *La Prise d'Alexandrie* (The Capture of Alexandria) contains a longer list of musical instruments.

Machaut was interred in Reims's Cathedral of Notre Dame. Evidence of his devotion to Our Lady is his endowment of a weekly performance of a Mass of the Virgin, a commemoration that was still observed in the eighteenth century.

MOTETS   The motet was an established form of secular music, but Machaut's treatment of that form was avant-garde in many respects. Of his 23 motets, 4 are for four voices; the remainder are for three. Three motets use French secular tenors; incipits of the Latin tenors of the others imply chant derivation. Six of the motets have Latin texts; two are furnished with Latin duplum and French triplum, and upper voices of the rest are in French. In the four-voice motets the contratenor is textless. Tenors and textless contratenors were probably performed instrumentally.

In the fourteenth century, the voice parts above the tenor were usually named **motetus** and **triplum.** In four-voice polyphony, the additional part was placed below the tenor and was called **contratenor** or **con-**

tratenor bassus (low [voice] opposite the tenor). Contratenor bassus was the predecessor of the modern **bass** voice part.

The Latin motets exhibit some of Machaut's finest work. They may have been used liturgically in the Offices. The motet *Felix virgo—Inviolata—Ad te suspiramus* (No. 23; Fortunate virgin—Inviolate—To you we breathe) is clearly a Marian motet. The tenor is derived from the Marian antiphon *Salve, Regina,* and the words of the two upper parts are addressed to the Virgin. Possibly, choirboys sang these upper parts while instrumentalists played tenor and contratenor on organs or sackbuts (ancestors of the trombone).

Machaut's notation employs the fourteenth-century mensurations explained by de Vitry. In the upper voices of 15 motets, Machaut used imperfect tempus with major prolation—the equivalent of modern $\frac{6}{8}$ meter; this is typical of French fourteenth-century polyphony. Most of the tenors use perfect mood.

With Machaut, the isorhythmic motet became an established form—one that interested composers through the fifteenth century. All Machaut's motets with Latin tenors are isorhythmic. In some motets, isorhythmic passages occur in the upper voices as well as in the tenor, along with one or more other techniques, such as hocket and syncopation. Machaut's *taleae* are remarkable for their symmetry and balance. Sometimes voice parts exchange *taleae*, and occasionally a *talea* is retrograde, thus creating a **rhythmic palindrome.** A palindrome reads the same backward and forward, as do the word "madam" and the rhythm in example 8.1. Frequently, Machaut alternated units of three breves and six breves in devising his patterns. In approximately half of his motets, he wrote the concluding statement of *talea* in diminution, sometimes one-half and sometimes one-third of the original note values. His isorhythmic tenors do not always contain melodic repetition. In those that do, most often *talea* and *color* do not coincide. Machaut imposed a high degree of structural rigidity on his isorhythmic compositions; however, he manipulated the intricate details of his music so skillfully that the restrictions are not apparent to the listener. Machaut required his music to please the ear.

Even his nonisorhythmic motets have tenors that are strictly structured. For example, the French motet *Trop plus—Biauté—Je ne suis* (Too much more—Beauty—I am not) is not isorhythmic, but its tenor is a rondeau pattern (abaaabab) formed from two very similar melodies with rhythms that are almost identical.

MASS *La Messe de Nostre Dame* (Our Lady's Mass) may be the longest single medieval composition extant. The work is significant historically because it is the earliest known unified polyphonic setting of the complete Mass Ordinary by one identified composer (Insight, "Other Mass Compositions," p. 117). The Mass is modal. The first three movements are in Dorian and the last three in Lydian. The music is four-voice polyphony, which was seldom written in that era. Machaut's setting includes the dismissal *Ite, missa est* and its Response, *Deo gratias.* Composers of polyphonic Masses rarely set the dismissal.

In writing the Mass, Machaut was no doubt influenced to some extent by the papal bulls that admonished composers of liturgical polyphony that the musical setting not obscure the text. He seems to have paid particular attention to correct declamation and to ensuring that the words of the text would be heard clearly. Also, he must have been aware of the fact that Pope John XXII had expressly forbidden the use of hocket in liturgical music, and he did not use much of it. Instead, he achieved the effect of hocket in some phrases by judiciously placing rests and using syncopation.

Those sections of the Ordinary with the longest texts, the Gloria and the Credo, were given nearly syllabic settings in note-against-note counterpoint so that the four voices almost always pronounce the text syllables simultaneously. Melismas occur in the Amen sections of these movements, however, and the Amen of the Credo is isorhythmic. The Gloria and Credo settings appear sectional, almost strophic, and in the Gloria very short textless passages occur between some phrases. These episodes may have been performed instrumentally; perhaps instruments doubled all voices. For emphasis, Machaut set certain words—*Et in terra pax* and *Jesu Christe* in the Gloria and *ex Maria Virgine* in the Credo—in duplex longs; in performance, the note-against-note counterpoint produced sustained chordal harmony. Many later composers gave these words similar emphasis. Machaut further emphasized the words *ex Maria Virgine* by preceding them with a general pause (ex. 8.2).

(a)

(b)

EXAMPLE 8.1 Rhythmic palindromes.

EXAMPLE 8.2 Machaut's setting of the words *ex Maria virgine* in the Credo of his *Messe de Nostre Dame* (mm. 69–78 in modern notation). Notice the general pause before this phrase begins, then the longer note values and change of mensuration used for this phrase.

The entire Mass exhibits profound rhythmic complexity, especially in those movements that are wholly or partly isorhythmic: Kyrie, Sanctus, Agnus Dei, and *Ite, missa est*. Some of the rhythmic intricacies involve interlocking and overlapping *taleae* and exchanging *taleae* among voices. Rhythmic symmetry pervades each movement—as a whole, in sections, and in individual *taleae*. For example, each section of the Kyrie is organized symmetrically, as is each acclamation within each section.

The tenors of the isorhythmic movements use chant melodies. The Kyrie is based on the tenth-century *Kyrie cunctipotens genitor Deus* from Gregorian Mass IV (*LU*, 25); Sanctus and Agnus Dei use eleventh- and thirteenth-century versions of those respective chants from Gregorian Mass XVII (*LU*, 61); the dismissal is based on the Sanctus from Gregorian Mass VIII (*LU*, 38). The isorhythmic sections are balanced and move outward from the center in rhythmic symmetry. In other words, they are palindromic. In the Agnus Dei, only the *qui tollis* sections are isorhythmic; isorhythm appears in all four voices of that section of Agnus Dei II.

Analysis of the *qui tollis* section of Agnus Dei II (DWMA41) gives some idea of the restrictions and rhythmic complexities involved in Machaut's isorhythmic compositions. Each voice has a *talea* that is rhythmically distinctive. Tenor and contratenor each present six statements of *talea*, arranged so that the rhythmic attack points in the two voices do not coincide. Combination of tenor and contratenor produce, in performance, a hocket effect. The composition becomes more intriguing if one analyzes the contratenor *taleae* as commencing one modern measure later than the tenor *taleae*. The two top voices each state a *talea* six times; the rhythmic patterns do not coincide—presentation of the *talea* in the motetus commences one measure later than in the triplum. Combination of these two voices produces syncopation. The section is 19 modern measures long; the fourth measure, and every third measure thereafter, constitutes a single sustained chord containing medieval perfect consonances. The melody of the top voice is constructed of alternating groups of three and six breves, which create the following symmetrical pattern:

Some sections of the Mass movements are much more complicated rhythmically than Agnus Dei II. Transcription into modern notation does injustice to Machaut's compositional genius, for bar lines impose artificial restraints on the music and often split ligatures, thus obscuring the full import of the rhythmic patterns Machaut created. It must be remembered that these complexities are not audibly perceived and that the quality of the music in no way suffers because of them.

In his compositions, Machaut sometimes used small melodic motives. Two motives appear frequently in the Mass:

Whether these motives were intended as unifying devices is not known, but the fact that they recur frequently is significant. They may be standard figures in Machaut's repertoire—they appear frequently in his other compositions.

HOCKET Like the Mass and Motet 23, *Hoquetus David* is Marian-related. Its isorhythmic tenor is derived from the long melisma on the word *David* that concludes the Alleluia Verse *Nativitas gloriosae virginis* (Nativity of the glorious Virgin). *Hoquetus David* is unique in fourteenth-century music. Machaut's reason for composing it, and the intended place and manner of its performance, are unknown. Because the *Hoquetus* is textless, instrumental rendition is presumed. Pérotin composed organal settings of part of the *Nativitas* verse, but the *David* melisma was performed as chant. Perhaps Machaut composed this hocket for use with Pérotin's organum as a substitute for the monophonic chant melisma. Pérotin, too, used hocket. The means of unification in this piece is, of course, the isorhythmic tenor, which is written in two sections, each with its own *taleae.*

LAIS In writing *lais,* Machaut was following in trouvère footsteps. Moreover, 15 of his 19 lais are monophonic. No musical lais have been located after Machaut, though poetic ones exist. Machaut usually constructed his lai texts in 12 stanzas that collectively use a musical pattern abcdefghijka. Each stanza is divided into halves, both set to the same melody. The modal melodies move mainly by step, with rests punctuating the musical phrases; the text setting is almost syllabic. Though the first and twelfth stanzas use the same melody, Machaut usually transposed it up a fifth (or down a fourth) for the final strophe. Lais 11, 12, 17, and 18 are polyphonic, and 11 and 12 are canonic.

BALLADES Machaut referred to the voice parts of his three-voice secular songs as *cantus* (melody), *tenor,* and *contratenor.* He stated that he composed the *cantus* first, then added the remainder of the music. His polyphonic settings place the lyrical melody of the cantus in a soloistic position, supported by textless tenor and contratenor designed for instrumental performance. This kind of musical setting is known as **cantilena style.**

Many of Machaut's secular songs are in the *formes fixes* of fourteenth-century court poetry: ballade, rondeau, and virelai. In his hands, these types of music became informal entertainment to be enjoyed by a nonparticipating court audience. The social function of music was changing. It was still a utilitarian art, serving primarily as an adjunct to worship and other activities and occupations, but one of those activities was court entertainment.

Machaut wrote 42 ballades with music: 1 monophonic, 16 two-voice, and 25 three-voice. Two of the latter are triple ballades: Number 17 is a three-voice canon with a different text in each voice, and in Number 29 the three voices have individual melodies and texts. Only ballade Number 1, *S' amours ne fait* (If love does not), is isorhythmic. He did not use isorhythm in any other secular songs.

The texts of the ballades resemble trouvère poetry and are constructed in three strophes with a refrain. Musically, the formal pattern of most of them is aabC. The a sections are provided with open and closed endings. Machaut often used musical rhyme, making the end of the second section of a piece musically identical with or a transposition of that of the first. In some early works only the cadences are alike (**cadence rhyme**), but gradually the rhyme was extended backward, and eventually six or even eight measures rhyme musically (ex. 8.3).

Syncopation, a prominent feature of many of Machaut's songs, sometimes creates harsh dissonances that are suitably resolved. At cadences, syncopation is frequently combined with an escape note, thus forming a **"Landini" cadence**—a cadence pattern named for Machaut's Italian contemporary, Francesco Landini (ex. 8.4).

RONDEAUX Machaut composed 21 musical rondeaux using the standard ABaAabAB pattern: 7 two-voice,

EXAMPLE 8.3 Machaut's use of cadence rhyme (musical rhyme) in the ballade *Biauté qui toutes autre*.

(a) (b)

(c)

EXAMPLE 8.4 The "Landini" cadence pattern. Note that (b) is a Phrygian cadence.

12 three-voice, and 2 four-voice. All of them are cantilena style, and only the cantus has text. Machaut's most unusual rondeau, *Ma fin est mon commencement* (DWMA42), is the one most widely known. Machaut's penchant for symmetry and balance is well demonstrated in this piece. The music interprets the text: "My end is my beginning and my beginning my end." The composition is symmetrical; a and b sections each consist of 20 modern measures. Machaut constructed the music in this fashion: (1) Cantus and tenor are the

reverse of each other. Moreover, the b music of the tenor is the retrograde of the a melody of the cantus, and the b melody of the cantus is the retrograde of the a music of the tenor. (2) The contratenor melody is half as long as the other voice parts, and the a music is used retrograde to form the b section. Machaut seems to have been the first composer to use the word **retrograde** in connection with a musical composition.

	A Section	B Section
Cantus:	Cantus **a** melody	Tenor **a** melody retrograde
Tenor:	Tenor **a** melody	Cantus **a** melody retrograde
Contratenor:	Contratenor **a** melody	Contratenor **a** melody retrograde

A more typical three-voice rondeau is *Se vous n'estes* (If you are not). Its first section concludes with a complete triad on the final of the mode, but the final chord of the second section is the traditional open-sounding octave and fifth.

VIRELAIS Machaut preferred to call his songs in this form *chansons balladées*; perhaps his pieces were in some way still associated with dancing. All of them use AbbaA form. There are 33 of them: 25 monophonic, 7 two-voice, and 1 three-voice. Each of them has three stanzas. In general, the musical style of these pieces is

Other Mass Compositions

In the fourteenth century, composers began to think of the *Mass* as being the five sections of the Ordinary that were sung: Kyrie, Gloria in excelsis Deo, Credo, Sanctus, and Agnus Dei. Machaut was not the only composer to set those texts. Nor did the papal bulls condemning certain kinds of polyphony and the state of polyphonic singing in the liturgy deter composers from writing liturgical polyphony. Apparently, they preferred setting individual Mass movements rather than the complete Ordinary. A good many independent movements survive, grouped together in manuscripts according to text (i.e., Kyries in one section, Glorias in another, etc.). Unless a composer signed his work (and many did not) or some unifying feature is obvious in several movements, there is no way of knowing which movements, if any, were intended to form a certain complete Mass Ordinary.

Movements of Masses were written in four styles of polyphony: (a) motet style, with the same text in two upper voices and a textless tenor; (b) cantilena style, with text in the top voice only; (c) conductus style, with all voices texted and simultaneous (or nearly so) pronunciation of text indicated; and (d) hybrid settings involving all the foregoing styles. A word of caution: Absence of a text in a manuscript does not mean that a text never existed for that voice part. A scribe may have inadvertently omitted the text. The music was sectional, corresponding with the sections of text in the movement being set; usually, the voices cadenced simultaneously at the ends of sections.

Several complete, or almost complete, fourteenth-century Mass settings are extant:

1. The Mass of Tournai, a three-voice Mass, is considered oldest of the surviving settings. It consists of conductus-style setting of the five movements of the Ordinary and motet-style setting of *Ite, missa est.* Probably all movements were not written by the same composer.
2. The Mass of Toulouse has no Gloria, and only a small portion of the Credo exists. Kyrie, Sanctus, and Agnus Dei are cantilena style, for three voices; *Ite, missa est* is a motet.
3. The Mass of Barcelona has five movements in miscellaneous styles. Some movements are for three and others are for four voices.
4. The Sorbonne Mass lacks a Credo, and Gloria and Sanctus are incomplete.

quite simple, with some use of melodic motives and musical rhyme. In more than half the virelais, Machaut supplied the b section with open and closed endings, a feature that would become standard with later composers.

Machaut was a transitional composer. Some of his works are linked to the past, some demonstrate clearly the advanced techniques and styles of his own day, and others predict future trends. Like Adam de la Halle, Machaut was a poet-composer. In some respects Machaut, too, was a trouvère. In his monophonic pieces, he followed trouvère tradition, but his cantilena settings of polyphonic ballades and rondeaux moved these forms out of the dance-song category and into the realm of art song. These pieces are accompanied vocal solos. Machaut broadened the thirteenth-century motet by the intricacies of his isorhythm and the new prolations. His four-voice Latin motets point toward the Latin sacred motets of Renaissance composers, in musical style, number of voices, and liturgical purpose. Their texts are entirely sacred, and each is related to a specific feast, event, or person. Machaut was writing four-part polyphony when most composers were writing for three voices. His greatest single achievement, *La Messe de Nostre Dame,* was the first of many unified polyphonic settings of the complete Mass Ordinary. Customarily, isolated movements were assembled to form a polyphonic Mass Ordinary (see Insight, "Other Mass Compositions"). However, in the late fourteenth century the situation began to change. The next generation of composers would regard Mass composition as a proving ground for their talents.

ITALY

In Italy, a gradual development of polyphonic music cannot be traced through compositions in manuscripts. In *Micrologus,* Guido discussed organum and referred to it as being practiced. A half-dozen thirteenth-century liturgical dramas containing some music for two equal voices have been located, and thirteenth-century *Ordines* of churches at Siena and Lucca designate organal singing of many melodies. Liturgical polyphony seems to have been improvised, even as late as the fourteenth century. If organum and motets were composed and notated, they have not survived. Seemingly, Italian secular polyphony appeared suddenly in the fourteenth century and flourished. Its roots may be in solo song with improvised polyphonic accompaniment. When French troubadours, jongleurs, and minstrels fled to Italy and Spain during the Albigensian Crusade (1209–29), undoubtedly they brought with them information concerning polyphonic music in southern France, especially at St. Martial. Italian *trovatori* (troubadours) were active to some extent in the thirteenth century, but only monophonic *laude* survive in manuscripts.

The earliest Italian treatise dealing with polyphony is *Pomerium artis musicae mensuratae* (Orchard of the art of measured music; c. 1318–26) by Marchetto da Padua (c. 1274–after 1326). Marchetto knew the French notation system and cited parts of it, but the Italian system included mensural combinations not used in the French one. These combinations produced a distinct rhythmic style different from that of the French. The *dot of division,* an essential feature of the Italian system, was used to separate groupings of notes and had a definitive and restrictive function similar to that of modern bar lines. By c. 1360, use of the Italian notational procedures had begun to decline. More and more, composers favored the French system.

MANUSCRIPT SOURCES

The oldest surviving manuscript containing Italian polyphony is the fragmentary Rossi Codex. Prepared before c. 1350, it provides the earliest notated examples of the three most-used forms of Italian *trecento* secular polyphony: madrigal, *caccia,* and ballata.

The most abundant manuscript source of fourteenth-century Italian secular polyphony is the Squarcialupi Codex, named for its former owner, Antonio Squarcialupi (1416–80), the most famous Italian organist of his time. In Florence, he served as organist at Cathedral S. Maria del Fiore (1432–80). He worked closely with both Lorenzo de' Medici (the Magnificent) and Guillaume Du Fay.

The Squarcialupi Codex, copied sometime between 1415 and 1440, contains 115 madrigals, 12 *cacce,* and 227 ballatas. The music is arranged in sections according to composer and in chronological order. The first folio of each section is beautifully illumined with floral, instrumental, or scenic borders and a miniature portrait of the composer (plate 10). Included are works by Giovanni da Cascia, Jacopo da Bologna, Gherardello da Firenze, Vincenzo da Rimini, Lorenzo da Firenze, Donato da Cascia, Niccolò da Perugia, Bartolino da Padova, Franciscus da Florentia (Francesco Landini), and others. The manuscript was never completed; 39 folios headed with composers' names have blank staves. Landini is represented by 146 compositions, Bartolino by 37, and Jacopo da Bologna by 28.

MADRIGAL

The **madrigal** was one of the earliest forms of Italian secular polyphony. Probably, the name *madrigal* derives from the composition's use of poetry in the vernacular or mother tongue (*matricalis,* belonging to the womb). Madrigal poems were constructed in two or three three-line stanzas with an additional two-line *ritornello* (refrain). The subject matter is amatory, idyllic, or pastoral; sometimes the tone is satirical. Most fourteenth-century madrigals were composed for two voices. The musical setting is strophic, with different music for the ritornello. Both voices sing the same text but do not always sing the words simultaneously.

Jacopo da Bologna's (fl. 1340–60) setting of Petrarch's *Non al suo amante* (Not to her lover; DWMA43) is typical. Written c. 1350, it is the only known contemporary setting of a Petrarch poem. The upper voice is more florid than the lower, with long melismas occurring on (or immediately after) the first and last accented syllables of each poetic line. The melismas resemble the *caudae* of conductus; composers probably were influenced by that form. Both voices sing the same text, but the lower voice enters three measures later than the upper voice. Music for the stanzas is in duple meter, and that for the ritornello is triple. A feature of Italian music is the sequential use of short melodic figures.

Jacopo's madrigals are fully texted in all voices, and there is no voice crossing. He seems to have been the first to write three-voice noncanonic madrigals. For him, the essence of music was a smooth, sweet melody. That he planned the modality of his pieces is apparent; over half his madrigals begin and end on the same pitch. In his madrigals, change of meter occurs only at the ritornello. His best-known madrigal is *Fenice fu'* (I was a phoenix), written c. 1360 (DWMA44).

CACCIA

The ***caccia*** (pl., *cacce*, chase, hunt), a three-voice composition, flourished c. 1345–70. It comprises a canon at the unison for two equal voices supported harmonically by an untexted (instrumental) lower line that commences when the first voice begins the melody. Frequently, a *caccia* concludes with a ritornello that may or may not be canonic. The *caccia* is a kind of pun, for one voice (*dux*, leader) is "chased" by another (*comes*, companion, fellow traveler) in strict imitation. The poetic text may describe a hunt or some sort of outdoor activity; hunting calls, bird songs, or other appropriate sounds usually appear in the music.

One of the *cacce* in the Squarcialupi Codex is *Tosto che l'alba* (As soon as the dawn; DWMA45) by Gherardello da Firenze. The two upper voices form a canon at the unison at the distance of ten measures, with a free supporting line commencing at the same time the first upper voice enters. The *dux* sings a long melisma on the last syllable of text while the *comes* completes the last phrase of text. The ritornello is canonic.

BALLATA

Undoubtedly, composers of the Italian ***ballata*** were influenced by the French *virelai*—the ballata uses a more elaborate version of virelai form. A two-line *ripresa* (refrain) frames a six-line poetic stanza containing three pairs of lines in bba rhyme scheme. The formal structure created is, therefore, AbbaA. The musical setting matches the poetic form. When the poetic text has more than one stanza, the form becomes Abba Abba A, and so on.

FRANCESCO LANDINI

Like de Vitry and Machaut, Francesco Landini (1325–97) was a poet-composer. He was the most important fourteenth-century Italian composer and the

leading composer of Italian *ballate*. His compositions represent approximately one-fourth of the entire extant Italian fourteenth-century secular repertoire.

In no music manuscript is Francesco named "Landini," nor does that name appear on his tombstone in the church of San Lorenzo. The name Landini was probably derived from his grandfather, Landino de Manno. Francesco's father, Jacopo del Casentino, was a painter of the Giotto school and cofounder of the Florentine guild of painters. Francesco, who was blind from early childhood as a result of smallpox, mastered several instruments and worked as organ builder, tuner, and instrument maker as well as church organist, singer, and composer.

Of the compositions definitely known to be Landini's, 90 are two-voice and 42 are three-voice ballatas. In addition, he composed 10 madrigals, 1 caccia, and 1 French virelai. If he composed any sacred music, it has not survived. Landini possessed a gift for expressive melody. His style varies from pure Italian to a synthesis of French and Italian. His three-voice madrigals indicate his knowledge of French techniques: *Si dolce non sonò* (Did not [Orpheus] sound so sweetly; DWMA46) uses isorhythmic tenor—9 seven-measure *taleae* in the stanzas and 2 ten-measure *taleae* in the ritornello.

Landini was a pioneer in composition of ballatas. In 82 of his two-voice ballatas, both voices have text. Many of the three-voice pieces are late works and use only one text, which is placed in the top voice (DWMA47). In the late works, he paid more attention to modality (beginning and ending a section on the same pitch), and at times phrases rhyme musically. Some syncopations are present. Frequently, phrases end with a 7–6–8 melodic succession, forming the ornament of the "Landini" cadence (ex. 8.5). Sometimes Landini (and other composers)

EXAMPLE 8.5 Example of Landini's use of 7–6–8 melodic succession in *Avrà tu pietà*, mm. 24–26 (final cadence of Ritornello).

119

(a)   (b)

EXAMPLE 8.6 Double leading-tone cadences, as used by Landini. Example (b) has the 7–6–8 progression of the "Landini" cadence.

wrote a cadence in which two voices move by a semitone into the final cadence chord, one voice rising to the mode final and the other rising to the fourth below (or its octave). Such a cadence is known as a **double leading-tone cadence.** Frequently, Landini used the 7–6–8 melodic succession in the top voice of such a cadence (ex. 8.6).

An overall survey of Landini's compositions seems to indicate that he used the older Italian style until c. 1370; from c. 1370 to 1385 there is infiltration of French stylistic characteristics, and from c. 1385 to 1397 a synthesis of French and Italian is apparent, with greater consideration for vertical harmony.

ARS SUBTILIOR

Ars subtilior (more subtle art) is the twentieth-century name given to the **manneristic style** of music composed c. 1375–c. 1420, a period almost coinciding with the Great Schism. Music written in this style is characterized by extremely complex rhythms and notation, drawn from both French and Italian practices. Principal centers of *Ars subtilior* were in southern France and northern Spain—at the courts of the French popes at Avignon, the Count of Béarn and Foix, and the King of Aragon. The chief manuscript sources of *Ars subtilior* music contain both sacred and secular polyphonic compositions: Credos, Glorias, motets, ballades, rondeaux, and virelais. Almost 50 composers are represented, including Baude Cordier (Baude Fresnel), Solage, Philippe de Caserta, Jacob Senleches, and Machaut.

The three-voice secular songs written in manneristic style use a newly composed tenor with rhythmic stability designed to support the upper voices. The basic intervals of the contrapuntal lines are consonances, but embellishments and rhythmic irregularities in the upper voice(s) often produce a highly dissonant effect. The *cantus* (top voice) appears to have been created for a professional singer of virtuoso caliber. Cohesion is achieved by the convergence of all contrapuntal lines for cadences at the ends of phrases.

Manneristic music developed gradually from the cantilena style of Machaut's ballades. The tenor became more independent and supportive, and the solo line was made more intriguing by minim displacements and melodic and rhythmic sequences. At the height of its development, manneristic music was characterized by extreme rhythmic flexibility and intricacy that included elaborate rhythmic subdivisions, displacement syncopation, alternate proportions, and split or half colorations. The notes may be black, red, or white (hollow notes with black outlines). *Ars subtilior* music attained a degree of rhythmic complexity that was not matched until the twentieth century.

Displacement syncopation was achieved when the notes comprising a perfection were separated, and the unity of that perfection was disrupted by the insertion of one or more complete perfections. A simple example in modern notation without bar lines is shown in example 8.7:

EXAMPLE 8.7 Displacement syncopation is created when the notes (marked with *) comprising a perfection are separated by the insertion of other perfections.

The notes marked with asterisks (*) form the disrupted perfection; the last note completes the perfection begun by the first note. Bar lines were not used when this music was written, nor were notated parts aligned in the manuscript. Syncopation is enhanced visibly by the presence of bar lines of modern notation. When bar lines are inserted, the modern notation becomes:

EXAMPLE 8.8 The displacement syncopation of example 8.6 in modern notation with bar lines.

In some modern transcriptions, the displacement syncopation is avoided on paper by changing the meter signature, using alternative barring, and then readjusting the meter signature so that bar lines coincide at cadence points (ex. 8.9).

EXAMPLE 8.9 Displacement syncopation is avoided (or disregarded) if the rhythm presented in example 8.7 is notated with several changes of meter signature.

This kind of modern notation does not accurately convey what the composer intended, but it probably does reflect the reaction of the performer, who, seeing only one line of the music, adjusted the rhythm after encountering an incomplete perfection.

Alternation of proportions provided another rhythmic variable. A simple example of this technique is the consistent alternation of a measure in $\frac{3}{4}$ with a measure in $\frac{6}{8}$ time while keeping the basic beat constant.

Another innovation of manneristic composition was clothing the musical composition in an appropriate artistic shape. Examples of this follow:

1. *Belle Bonne* (Beautiful Bonne, wise . . .), by Baude Cordier, is a rondeau notated on staves shaped and arranged to form a heart. In the text, the red outline of a heart is substituted for the word *coeur* (heart). (plate 11)
2. Jacob Senleches notated *La harpe de melodie* (The harp of melody) on staff lines that form the harp's

strings. Rubrics are encoded in a rondeau printed on the ribbon wound around part of the harp frame. (plate 12)

SPAIN

Music flourished at the fourteenth-century court of Catalonia-Aragon in northern Spain. Court records reveal the names of approximately 600 singers, minstrels, and *joglars* (jongleurs) who served there between c. 1290 and 1400. King John I of Aragon (r. 1350–96) was an enthusiastic patron of music and an avid collector of musical instruments, and he actively sought fine musicians for his court. The king wrote poetry and composed lais, virelais, and rondeaux, with French texts. Reportedly, the Aragon court resembled the papal court at Avignon in personnel and musical repertoire. Musicians employed at the court are represented in the *Ars subtilior* Chantilly Manuscript.

The *Llibre Vermell* (Red Book), a fourteenth-century manuscript, contains three *caças* and some short polyphonic *Cants dels Romeus* (Pilgrim Songs). The caça resembles the French *chace* in having no free instrumental tenor; directions indicate that these caças may be performed as either two- or three-voice canons. Melodies of several Pilgrim Songs are folk songs; some tunes remained popular for more than a century after *Llibre Vermell* was compiled.

ENGLAND

English medieval polyphony in extant manuscripts is almost exclusively liturgical and Latin. Undoubtedly, secular English music existed, but the constant wandering of many professional performers and their want of permanent patronage at some court prevented the inscription of their songs in manuscripts. Much music has been lost. Monastic communities and cathedral chapters with *scriptoria* placed priority on copying liturgical music. French music of all kinds, and especially the Notre Dame repertoire, was used in England. Organum and conductus were used in Britain well into the fourteenth century, after those forms had disappeared from continental service.

Surviving music indicates an English predilection for troping, rondellus technique, an emphasis on thirds and sixths, and some use of streams of parallel intervals. This parallelism sometimes produced discant-style two-voice pieces called **gymel** (twin voices).

Exactly what is meant by the term **English discant** is debatable. The term is frequently used in reference to the homorhythmic passages of smooth successions of $\frac{6}{3}$ chords (sounding like first-inversion triads) that appear in English music. According to some late medieval theorists, the English practiced improvising *around* a notated cantus firmus melody (called the *meane,* middle) to produce a parallel line a fourth above the cantus firmus and another a third below it, thus producing a stream of $\frac{6}{3}$ chords.

Other medieval English theorists describe discanting as singing an unnotated part against a notated chant or cantus firmus in note-against-note counterpoint. In this practice of discanting, consecutive perfect fifths and consecutive octaves were forbidden, and contrary motion was preferred, but occasionally passages of parallel thirds and sixths might be sung. The passages of parallel $\frac{6}{3}$ chord successions that appear quite often in notated English music of the late fourteenth and fifteenth centuries reflect the English predilection for thirds and sixths; the harmonious blend of these intervals contributes to the "sweet sound" of English music (ex. 8.10).

EXAMPLE 8.10 Burden II from the carol *Salve, sancta parents* contains streams of parallel $\frac{6}{3}$ chords. (*Source:* Salve, sancta parens, *mm. 17–19, in John Stevens,* Musica Brittanica, *Vol. 4,* Mediaeval Carols, *Stainer & Bell, Ltd., London, England*)

ENGLISH CAROL

In the late Middle Ages, the English *carol* was no longer associated with dancing—it was a polyphonic song with Latin, English, or mixed Latin-English text. However, the carol retained the form of a dance song. It was composed of uniform stanzas and had a **bur-**den (a kind of refrain) that was sung at the beginning and end of each stanza—a structure closely resembling the French virelai. Carols deal with all kinds of sacred and secular subjects; some praise the Virgin or celebrate the birth of Christ (DWMA48). Occasionally, a carol was used as an optional part of the liturgy at certain festivals. Often carols served as processional songs in civic, court, and church functions.

OLD HALL MANUSCRIPT

The Old Hall Manuscript is an important collection of English sacred music composed in the late fourteenth and early fifteenth centuries. Unfortunately, the manuscript is incomplete. The main part of the manuscript was copied c. 1410; additional pieces were entered c. 1420. The original compilation includes compositions by Leonel (Power), Pycard, Typp, Byttering, Chirbury, Excetre, Roy Henry, and others. Presumably, Roy Henry is King Henry V; his two works are a Gloria and a Sanctus. Persons represented by the added pieces include Damett and Dunstable. (Dunstable, a transitional composer, is discussed in chap. 9.)

Compositions are arranged by liturgical category, with movements of the Mass grouped in sections in the order of their appearance in the service. There is no Kyrie in the Old Hall Manuscript. Customarily, in England the Kyrie of the Mass was sung in chant and most often was troped. Polyphonic Kyries by English late medieval composers are almost nonexistent. Even later, some English composers wrote "complete" Mass settings without a Kyrie. Also, in English settings of the Credo, certain clauses were consistently omitted or phrases telescoped.

The mensural notation used for some of the compositions is highly sophisticated. Colorations are indicated by black, red, blue, and half-colored notes, and reversed and colored signatures appear. In most of the pieces, the tenor or *cantus firmus* is placed just above the bottom voice. In some of the Mass movements, specific instructions are given for certain passages to be performed by a chorus (not an ensemble of soloists). This does not necessarily imply that the chorus was large. At times, passages of duets alternate with passages for chorus; centuries later, that procedure characterizes post-Reformation Anglican verse anthems.

Various musical styles and techniques are represented:

1. Some three-voice pieces notated in score display English discant; the chant cantus firmus is in the middle voice, labeled *meane*.
2. More than 30 works are treble-dominated musically. In most of these, the text is shared by all voices. The top voice moves in a range slightly higher than the tenor and contratenor, which are in the same range and frequently cross.
3. The isorhythmic compositions display that technique in various stages of its development.
4. Seven compositions are canonic. None of them are structurally alike. A five-voice Gloria by Pycard may be the earliest extant example of a double canon. One of the anonymous Credos is for five voices, with the three upper voices written as a mensuration canon. (The three voices sing the same melody in different mensurations.)
5. Leonel sometimes placed a paraphrase of the chant cantus firmus in the top voice. Later, this paraphrase technique is used increasingly on the Continent.

The Old Hall Manuscript is historically significant for several reasons. It is one of few extant manuscripts containing an extensive repertory of English medieval music. That repertory confirms the existence and character of specifically English musical traits. It also reveals the extent of the development of English music and the influence of continental practices in that development, and it suggests influences that English composers may have had on continental music.

LEONEL POWER

Old Hall Manuscript contains 23 compositions by Leonel Power (c. 1375–1445). Little is known about Power's early life. In 1423, he became associated with the fraternity of Christ Church, Canterbury. By 1439 he had become master of the choir that sang services in the Lady Chapel.

Extant works known to be Power's number 40. All are liturgical—either settings of Marian texts or Mass movements. Like Machaut and Dunstable, Power was a pioneer in composing Mass cycles. He was interested in creating paired movements of the Ordinary; four

pairs are in Old Hall Manuscript. He achieved unification by means of (a) motives, including **head-motive** technique (using the identical motive at the opening of each movement or each section of a movement); (b) the same or related chants as tenor cantus firmus or placed in the top voice; and (c) parallel style and structure. He used some isorhythm.

Only one complete Mass has been definitely ascribed to him—Mass *Alma redemptoris mater.* In its four movements (there is no Kyrie) the tenor presents the first half of the *Alma redemptoris mater* chant unornamented so that it is clearly identifiable. Attribution of Mass *Rex seculorum* and Mass *Sine Nomine* wavers between Leonel and Dunstable. Power and Dunstable composed the earliest complete Masses based on a single cantus firmus, a practice that became standard procedure for the next generation of composers.

Power's compositions in Old Hall Manuscript far outnumber those of any other composer, and the variety of styles represented by those compositions indicates that by c. 1410 he had mastered all the compositional techniques and styles of his generation. He demonstrated capably his knowledge of French *Ars nova* and *Ars subtilior;* he combined with that a gift for creating melody and for using the full sonorities of English music. He composed skillfully for as many as five voices and was original and even daring in his combination of conflicting rhythms, yet he constructed contrapuntal lines so that each was basically consonant with all the others. His high level of musical craftsmanship is marred only by some lack of attention to correct declamation of text. (That may be scribal error.)

PERFORMANCE PRACTICE— *MUSICA FICTA*

Chromatic alterations other than B♭ were still considered *musica ficta*. Though the ♯ symbol was used more frequently before an f or a c pitch, especially by Italian composers, there were many instances where the application of a chromatic alteration was left to the performer. Unnotated chromatic alterations were applied to music for various reasons, all of which could be reduced to either *causa necessitatis* (necessity) or *causa pulchritudinis* (beauty). A set of rules was gradually formulated to regulate the chromatic alteration of pitches under certain specified conditions. For example, b between two a's was "soft" (♭), but b between two c's was "hard" (♮). Similarly, c between two d's was chromatically raised, as was f between two g's.

Chromatic alteration commonly occurred at cadences to reduce the whole step between the seventh degree of the modal scale and its final. Rules applicable here follow: (a) When the interval of a sixth proceeds to an octave, the sixth must be major (ex. 8.11a). (b) When the interval of a third proceeds to a fifth, the third must be major. (c) When the interval of a third moves to a unison, the third must be minor (ex. 8.11b). Application of these rules created cadences wherein the penultimate chord contained either a single or a double leading tone. No chromatic alteration was used at cadences with a final on e because normal use of the Phrygian modal scale provided the proper intervals (ex. 8.11c).

The tritone (f–b♮) was to be avoided both melodically and harmonically. In general, any augmented fourth or diminished fifth interval was chromatically

altered in performance. Occasionally, chromatic alterations were made simply because the adjusted musical sound was more pleasant.

In some late fourteenth-century music, **partial signatures** were used. For example, a ♭ might be placed at the beginning of the tenor line of a piece as a kind of "key signature," but this did not appear at the beginning of the music for the other voice parts. Presumably, the singer(s) would apply the appropriate chromatic alteration(s) where needed in the upper part(s). In many instances, the tenor is the only part needing the chromaticism.

The application of *musica ficta* was not a problem for persons living in the Middle Ages and Renaissance. For them, it was common practice. The music they created was practical—to meet the needs of their own age; they cared not whether it would be preserved for use after their lifetimes. They probably never gave that any thought. It is only for later generations who wish to perform this early music properly that problems arise because of unwritten or inconsistently notated chromatic alterations. In music written after 1450, the absence of chromatic alterations is even more apparent—they virtually disappear from the notation! Conscientious modern editors of early music do not add chromatic alterations to the music found in original sources; instead, they indicate in small symbols either above or below the staff the chromatic alterations that most likely were applied when the music was originally performed. In this way, modern performers may benefit from editorial advice and still see the music as it originally existed.

INSTRUMENTS

Most music manuscripts do not indicate the medium of performance for the music they contain. The presence or absence of text is not a reliable indication that the music is vocal or instrumental. Literary and pictorial sources indicate that in the fourteenth and early fifteenth centuries music was most often performed by small vocal and instrumental ensembles, usually with one musician per part. No doubt they used whatever was available that produced the desired result, a procedure this writer calls "the theory of availability." Some-

(a)

(b)

(c)

EXAMPLE 8.11 Chromatic alteration by application of *musica ficta* at cadences to comply with rules governing (*a*) a sixth (here, in outer voices) progressing to an octave, (*b*) a third moving to a unison, and (*c*) Phrygian cadences.

times instrumentalists doubled vocal lines or substituted for voices. In cantilena-style music the cantus was often performed by both a vocal soloist and an instrumentalist either or both of whom might appropriately embellish the line. Isorhythmic and textless tenors were probably intended for instruments.

Literary sources mention a great variety of instruments and cite specific uses of them. John Lydgate (c. 1373–c. 1450), in *Reson and Sensuallyte,* wrote of "Instrumentys high and lowe / Wel mo than I koude knowe" and of "lowde" instruments being used for dancing. French authors mentioned *haut* and *bas* instruments. The words "high" (*haut*) and "low" (*bas*) refer to volume, not pitch. High instruments were loud; low ones, soft. Loud instruments and larger ensembles were used on festive occasions, for especially solemn ceremonies, and outdoors; small ensembles of loud instruments provided music for dancing. There is no indication of crescendo and/or diminuendo in the music or that instruments were capable of any appreciable amount of variation in the volume of the sound they produced. Literary descriptions and artists' depictions indicate that ensembles grouped instruments of heterogeneous rather than homogeneous timbre. In general, the tones produced were clear and bright, even shrill and strained. Artists' and sculptors' portrayal of singers indicate this was true of vocal music, also. Observe carefully the head position, the formation of the mouth and lips, and the strained throat muscles of singers in paintings and sculpture (fig. 8.3). Some instructions for use of vibrato in specified instances indicate that, ordinarily, tone production was straight line, without vibrato.

Low instruments included recorder, flute, harp, lute, psaltery, portative organ, and vielle. High instruments included chalumeau or shawm, various kinds of horns, sackbut (ancestor of the trombone), and trumpet. Percussion instruments, depending on their size, might fit into either category.

Three types of organs were in use: portative, positive, and the large organs installed in large churches. By the late fourteenth century some organs (e.g., Rouen Cathedral, 1386) had a small second (or tenor) keyboard. This eventually became the organ's pedal keyboard. Most organ keyboards had C as the lowest note; both b♭ and b♮ were "white" keys. Keyboard instruments of the clavichord-harpsichord type appeared in the fourteenth century.

Summary

Literary accounts and pictorial representations indicate that in the fourteenth century music was enjoyed by all classes of society on all kinds of occasions. Undoubtedly, folk music was created, and instrumental and vocal music were improvised. Much of the extant music seems to have been composed for aristocratic patrons or inscribed in manuscripts compiled for them.

Traces of trouvère tradition are found in the monophonic songs of late medieval poet-composers and in the poetic forms used for their verses. However, fourteenth-century composers concentrated on three-voice polyphonic settings of secular vernacular texts. Most of the *chansons* followed the formal patterns of the *formes fixes* of court poetry; Italian madrigals seem to exhibit closer ties with the common people. The presence of refrains in many secular vocal forms is to some extent a vestige of thirteenth-century dance songs.

Rhythmic diversity, freedom, and intricacy constituted perhaps the most outstanding feature of fourteenth-century music, especially in France. Rhythmic freedom was aided by recodification and extension of notational principles to recognize equal binary as well as equal ternary division of notes and to introduce smaller note values. During the *Ars nova* era, the highly structured patterns of isorhythm provided an unobtrusive unifying device, but they became more complex as they were designed to express nonmusical as well as musical dimensions. Motets were written to mark special events and were deemed especially appropriate for ceremonial or political occasions. For this reason, motets were suitable vehicles for isorhythm and symbolism. In France, most motets were secular and vernacular; the tenors were derived from either sacred or secular sources. Late in the century, composers used sacred Latin texts for some of their motets. In England, the motet retained its Latin liturgical character; many motets were votive. Increased rhythmic freedom generated additional intricacies, many of which appeared in

Ars subtilior works. The degree of rhythmic complexity attained by composers of *Ars subtilior* music was unparalleled until the twentieth century.

Latin was used for settings of movements of the Mass Ordinary, some of which were composed as musically related pairs. Several complete, or almost complete, fourteenth-century settings of the Mass Ordinary are extant. However, Machaut's four-voice, unified, polyphonic setting of the complete Mass Ordinary is the earliest known such composition by one identified composer. Its four-voice structure was exceptional for that time, yet it was not long before English composers were producing four-voice polyphonic settings of complete Masses, Mass movements, and sacred Latin motets, in which the tenor was the next-to-bottom voice. Some English liturgical compositions call for choral singing of certain phrases of composed polyphonic service music.

As the fourteenth century advanced, more attention was paid to modality and its organization, both melodic and harmonic. Linear polyphony was still being written with melodic lines of equal interest, but now the melodic lines were constructed so that all of them were in agreement. In addition, cantilena-style settings were composed, with the lower polyphonic voice(s) providing harmonic support for the solo melody. As this treble-dominated polyphony grew in favor, a corresponding proficiency in organizing harmonies around modal centers is apparent. Rules governed the progression or succession of intervals (not chords), especially at cadence points, where the application of *musica ficta* created in the penultimate chord the equivalent of a leading tone. The concluding chord of principal cadences, and especially the final chord of a piece, comprised only perfect consonances (unison, octave, fifth). The sound of the music was important; chromatic alterations might be applied according to the rules of *musica ficta* for no other reason than to create a lovelier and more flexible melodic line. Thirds and sixths, considered imperfect consonances, appeared more frequently on strong beats, and short strings of parallel $\frac{6}{3}$ chord successions added sweetness to English music.

When the fourteenth century opened, French composers held musical leadership. During the first half of the century, French and Italian composers used differing notational systems and produced different styles of music, but by 1400 many Italian composers were notating their songs according to French principles, and the styles were beginning to coalesce. French domination of the musical scene lasted for most of the fourteenth century, but c. 1400 leadership passed to the English for a few decades. Through British composers who visited or worked in continental Europe, English musical practices were transmitted to continental composers, and the way was partially paved for the eventual emergence of a single international style of music.

TRANSITION TO THE RENAISSANCE

9

The fifteenth century was characterized by disputes. Within the Roman Catholic Church, the Great Schism was closed when the Council of Constance (1414–18) elected Pope Martin V (1417–31). However, the Council of Bishops claimed to have spiritual and temporal authority superior to that of the pope and the cardinals. This Conciliar Conflict (c. 1409–60) interfered with the reigns of Popes Eugene IV (r. 1431–47) and Nicholas V (r. 1447–55)—and the career of Du Fay—and was not settled until Pope Pius II (r. 1458–64) firmly reestablished papal authority.

The Holy Roman Empire was largely Germanic and was weakened by the increasing power of the states within it. Germanic lands had been parceled out to princes, and some free cities existed; all owed allegiance to the Holy Roman Emperor. Politico-religious battles were fought in Bohemia, where the Holy Roman Emperor sought to quell Hussite uprisings (1419–36). Jan Hus (1369–1415), a forerunner of the Protestant Reformation, inspired religious uprisings strongly colored by Bohemian patriotism. Hus was tried as a heretic, was condemned, and was burned at the stake. In 1436, the Hussites made peace with the church and acknowledged Emperor Sigismund (r. 1411–37) as King of Bohemia.

The Hundred Years' War between England and France continued intermittently. An English victory at Agincourt (1415) was celebrated on the battlefield by improvisation of the Agincourt Carol, *Deo gracias Anglia*. The French rallied under leadership of Jeanne d'Arc (1412–31). She was captured by the Burgundians in 1430, was tried, and was burned at the stake at Rouen in 1431. Until 1435, the powerful Burgundian dukes sided with England; Burgundian allegiance was transferred to France by the Peace of Arras (1435). The Hundred Years' War ended in 1453, and England gave up all its continental lands except Calais. England did not enjoy lasting peace. Civil war erupted in 1455 (see p. 105). During the reign of Henry VII (1485–1509), the English monarchy was secure.

By the end of the fifteenth century, the French monarchy was firmly reestablished. France had increased territorially, for Louis XI (r. 1461–83) regained lands through inheritance default—a fief reverted to the crown when no male heir survived.

In 1453 the Turks invaded the Byzantine Empire, captured Constantinople, killed Emperor Constantine XI (r. 1448–53), and subsequently converted Hagia Sophia into a mosque. Many Greek and Byzantine scholars sought refuge in Italy, where their presence contributed to the humanist movement and further stimulated interest in classical antiquity.

Five great states dominated the land we now call "Italy": Venice, Florence, Naples, Milan, and the Papal States (fig. 9.1). The government of each differed, but all the rulers were enthusiastic patrons of the arts. Smaller states had no political influence, but the rulers of many of them fostered the arts (e.g., the duke of Mantua and Este dukes of Modena and Ferrara).

Venice was a constitutional republic nominally headed by *Il Doge* but with actual power in the hands of the Senate and the Secret Ten. Upper-middle-class Venetian citizens had created a closed society with a government designed to promote the international trade that provided their wealth. By 1500 Venice had become the strongest state and had a small colonial empire in Dalmatia and the Greek Islands.

The republic of Florence was ruled for 60 years by de' Medici: Cosimo (1434–64), Piero (1464–69), Lorenzo "the Magnificent" (1469–92), and Piero II (1492–94). Lorenzo, a brilliant diplomat, made Florence the most influential (though not the most powerful) state. He subsidized some of the world's finest artists and writers; during his reign, Florence became the cultural center of Europe. Piero II was an ineffectual ruler whom the French forced into exile in 1494. Florence then came under the influence of Savonarola (1452–98), a fanatical Dominican monk, whose bonfires burning evil "vanities" destroyed much that was cultural and beautiful.

Milan was a dictatorship under the Visconti (until 1447) and Sforza dukes. Lodovico Sforza (1479–1500) was patron of some of the greatest artists and writers of all time (e.g., Leonardo da Vinci).

The centrally located Papal States had a unique elective monarchy, with power that supposedly transcended that of all other rulers. The fifteenth-century popes participated in political maneuvers and intrigues, maintained brilliant courts, and extravagantly patronized art and literature.

The Kingdom of Naples was relatively unimportant culturally. Politically, it was frequently between the pincers of Anjou and Aragon and was fraught with internal strife caused by the landed nobility. Nevertheless, talented musicians found employment at the Neapolitan court.

FIGURE 9.1 "Italy" in the fifteenth century.

1400	1425	1450	1475	1500

Schism ends 1417; Conciliar Conflict

Hundred Years' War 1453; 1455 Wars of the Roses 1485

Sea Exploration: Columbus; Vespucci

1412 Jeanne d'Arc 1431

• 1453 Turks capture Constantinople

Hus d. 1415; Hussite uprisings 1436

• c. 1453 Printing from movable metal type

1434 de' Medicis rule Florence 1494–97
Savonarola

1447 Sforzas rule Milan

ENGLAND: Leadership in music   FRANCE: Leadership in music

Leonel Power 1445

John Dunstable 1453

c. 1430 R. Morton 1478

c. 1450 W. Frye fl. 1475

Mass mvts.; Motets; Antiphons; Carols

FRANCE:

Ars subtilior 1420

c. 1400 G. Du Fay 1474

Faux bourdon

Isorhythm

Chansons and Motets; Cyclic Masses

Polyphonic Requiem Mass

BURGUNDY:

Chansons, Motets, Masses, Magnificats and Liturgical settings; *Basse danse*

c. 1400 Binchois 1460

c. 1430 Busnois c. 1492

c. 1435 Tinctoris (1511)

c. 1446 A. Agricola (1506)

SPAIN:

fl. 1455 Cornago 1485
Masses; polyphonic *canción*; Lamentations

GERMANY:

c. 1410 Paumann 1473
Organ playing   *Glogauer Liederbuch*   MS partbooks
    Lochamer Liederbuch

In Spain, Aragon and Castile were united in 1479 when Ferdinand, husband of Queen Isabella of Castile (r. 1474–1504), became King of Aragon. Both monarchs were interested in navigation and overseas expansion; so were the Portuguese. Under Portuguese sponsorship, Bartholomew Diaz sailed down the coast of Africa and discovered the Cape of Good Hope (1488), and Vasco da Gama sailed around Africa to India (1497–99). Spanish explorations commenced in 1492, when Ferdinand and Isabella financed the first of Christopher Columbus's four voyages to the New World, and he reached the West Indies. In 1497 the Cabots, representing Britain, reached Newfoundland, and Amerigo Vespucci began a series of voyages to Central and northern South America.

Many rulers commissioned literary and music manuscripts and employed renowned artists to illuminate them. The prayer book known as *The Book of Hours* was especially favored. It originated from a daily devotional service, the "Little Office of Our Lady," which was detached from the *Breviary* and became a separate prayer book called *The Book of Hours.* As popularity of *The Book of Hours* increased, other items were included: the Psalms, Gospel chapters, and calendars. The pages were beautifully illuminated with detailed scenes and intricately designed borders painted in all the available colors, including gold. Some of the most magnificent *Book of Hours* manuscripts are those created for Jean, Duke of Berry (plate 13).

Frequently, artists and musicians found employment in churches or courts outside their homeland. As members of a royal or ducal retinue, composers accompanied their employer on business or pleasure trips to foreign courts. Such was the case with John Dunstable, England's leading composer, whose music strongly influenced the work of continental composers.

JOHN DUNSTABLE

Dunstable (c. 1390–1453) was employed as a chapel singer by the Duke of Bedford, a brother of King Henry V. Bedford was Regent of France (1422–29) and Governor of Normandy (1429–35), and probably Dunstable was a member of Bedford's continental retinue. Dunstable was aware of musical developments at the Burgundian court; he may have known Du Fay and Binchois personally. Dunstable's work was well known in continental Europe. His influence on later French composers, especially Du Fay and Binchois, was attested by Martin le Franc, who wrote in *Le Champion des dames* (c. 1441) that Du Fay and Binchois were superior to their French predecessors because they were influenced by Dunstable and the *contenance angloise,* the English style of music.

The *contenance angloise* to which le Franc referred is audibly sweeter and fuller than the continental music of the era. Technical features producing that sound are (a) chords that regularly include the third (except final cadence chords), (b) passages in block chords or of lightly ornamented homorhythmic texture, and (c) polyphonic lines primarily consonant with all other lines, constructed with carefully prepared and resolved dissonances placed on weak beats. Textural contrast was provided by duets strategically placed in three-, four-, or five-voice compositions.

Approximately 51 compositions have been definitely credited to Dunstable. Authorship of 7 others has been attributed to either Dunstable or Power. Most of Dunstable's works are sacred, with Latin texts: Masses and Mass movements, antiphons, Sequences, hymns, Magnificats and other music for Offices. Much of Dunstable's sacred music is votive. Seven of Dunstable's works are for three voices, 7 are four-voice, and the carol *I pray you all* is for two. Only 5 secular works by Dunstable survive: the carol, 2 rondeaux, a ballade, and the modified ballata *O rosa bella* (O lovely rose).

Dunstable's compositions are of various styles: (1) isorhythmic; (2) nonisorhythmic, with chant cantus firmus in the tenor; (3) with melody (either freely composed or a paraphrase of a chant) in the top voice and two supporting lower voices moving at a slower pace; or (4) freely composed, without cantus firmus. Dunstable's melodies are typically English in their use of short note values in basically conjunct motion; any melodic skips present are usually thirds. There is no rhythmic redundancy or unnecessary repetition. Often the melody begins with a rising triad or an ornamented one.

In two isorhythmic motets written for Whit Sunday, Dunstable combined hymn and Sequence texts for Pentecost. Most of Dunstable's 14 isorhythmic motets exhibit a subtle propulsion (a drive) toward the cadence. In the tenor, the *color* is presented three times in note values that become proportionally progressively smaller, in the ratio of 3:2:1. A drive to the cadence is a regular feature of much Renaissance music.

The nonisorhythmic motet *Quam pulchra es* (How fair thou art; DWMA49) is the most carefully set of all Dunstable's works. It is freely composed, without cantus firmus. Several verses from *Song of Solomon,* as used in an antiphon in Sarum Rite, form the text. The conductus-style setting has a short string of parallel $^6_3$ chords in measures 12 to 14. Cadences are the standard medieval types or a slightly ornamented version of such. The closing Alleluia exhibits a drive to the cadence as well as the English preference for closing a motet with a long melisma.

GUILLAUME DU FAY

In his maturity, Guillaume Du Fay (c. 1400–74) was the most famous composer in Europe (Insight "Guillaume Du Fay"). He was respected not only because of his musical talents but also because he was highly intelligent, very well educated, and articulate. Among his associates and friends were persons of high ecclesiastical and political rank as well as composers. He knew Binchois, Busnois, and Ockeghem, all of whom held important court positions (fig. 9.2). When Du Fay decided to work at Cambrai Cathedral in 1439, musical leadership returned to northwestern Europe. During the course of his work there, his style gradually changed from medieval (Gothic) to the early Renaissance style of his mature Masses and motets—a purely choral style.

Du Fay's works are included in more than 70 fifteenth-century manuscripts inscribed in all countries where polyphony was practiced. His extant works include 7 complete Masses, 28 individual Mass movements, 15 settings of chants used in Mass Propers, 3 Magnificats, 2 Benedicamus Domino settings, 15 antiphon settings (6 are Marian antiphons), 27 hymns, 22 motets (13 are isorhythmic), and 87 chansons and chansonlike secular pieces. Some of Du Fay's works have been lost, including the *Missa de Requiem* mentioned in his will. Other lost works are known by name because they were mentioned in correspondence, in literary writings and treatises of others, or in records of performances or financial accounts listing payments to copyists.

SECULAR SONGS

Du Fay wrote most of his secular pieces when he was associated with a court or while he lived in Italy. Very few of his songs have Italian texts, however; French was the only language accorded international prestige. Six Italian songs appear in MS Canonici misc. 213 (fig. 9.3). Du Fay's setting of the first strophe of Petrarch's *Vergene bella* (Lovely virgin) is the earliest known musical setting of a portion of that poem, for which many others wrote music.

Du Fay's ballades are early works; four very late works are virelais. Most of his chansons are rondeaux, on subjects similar to those used by trouvères. Love, especially melancholy love, was a favorite topic but not the only one. Many of the secular pieces contain some religious symbolism; frequently, texts express

FIGURE 9.2 Miniature depicting Du Fay standing near portative organ and conversing with Binchois, who is holding a harp. Miniature from Martin Le Franc's poem *Le Champion des Dames* (1440–42), MS *fr.*12476. *(Bibliothèque nationale, Paris)*

FIGURE 9.3 Du Fay's *Dona i ardenti ray* and *Quel fronte signorille* as notated on fol. 73r, MS Canonici misc. 213. *(Bodleian Library, Oxford, England)*

Guillaume Du Fay

Guillaume Du Fay was born near Cambrai, in Hainaut. He was a choirboy at Cambrai Cathedral of Notre-Dame in 1409–12, and in 1413–14 he served as clerk there. In cathedral records his name is spelled "G. du Fay," and on music manuscripts it frequently was written as a notated fa between "du" and "y":

This same rebus appears in the four corners of his tombstone. That the name is pronounced in three syllables (du-Fah´-ee) is confirmed by the composer's musical settings of it and by Martin le Franc's poetic use of the name.

As part of the large retinue of Cardinal Pierre d'Ailly of Cambrai, Du Fay attended sessions of the Council of Constance (1414–18) and probably became acquainted with Carlo and Pandolfo Malatesta there. From c. 1420 to 1426 Du Fay served the Malatestas in northern Italy. Part of that time he resided at Bologna, where he studied at the university and obtained a baccalaureate degree in canon law. By May 1428 Du Fay had attained priesthood. From autumn 1428 to mid-1433, he was a singer in the papal choir of Martin V (r. 1417–31) and Eugene IV (r. 1431–47) at Rome. In 1434 Du Fay was employed at the Savoy court of Duke Amadeus VIII; later that year, Du Fay visited his mother at Cambrai. He returned to Savoy and served as *magister capellae* until June 1435, then reentered the papal chapel. During the winter of 1438–39, he worked at the court of Louis of Savoy.

Du Fay's career was affected by Conciliar Conflict. After the Council of Basle declared Pope Eugene IV deposed (June 1439), Amadeus VIII of Savoy was elected and became (anti)Pope Felix V (November 1439). Philip the Good of Burgundy staunchly supported Eugene, whereas Louis of Savoy favored his own father. The ecclesiastical see of Cambrai lay within Burgundian political jurisdiction. When Philip the Good confiscated the ecclesiastical benefices of persons favoring Felix, and each pope threatened those on the opposite side from himself with excommunication, Du Fay was forced to make a choice. Over the years, he had held benefices at various European churches simultaneously, including Cambrai Cathedral (fig. 9.4). To continue receiving stipends from Cambrai Cathedral and St. Donatien, he could not remain at the Savoy court. His loyalty to Cambrai was strong; he resigned at court,

---

Du Fay's personal feelings, as in *Adieu ces bons vins de Lannoys* (Farewell to these good Laon wines). Only eight of Du Fay's secular works are for four voices; all others are for three. Most of the early pieces are treble dominated, with music clearly intended for performance by a vocalist and at least two instrumentalists. In many of the pieces, untexted phrases for instrumental performance appear between vocal phrases; an instrumentalist may have doubled the vocal line throughout. *Vergene bella* (DWMA50) has this kind of setting.

Other pieces were written with two vocal lines and an instrumental contratenor; in such works, bits of canon and imitation occur in the two vocal lines. *Se la face ay pale* (If my face is pale) exemplifies this type of song. *Se la face ay pale* (DWMA51) is a *ballade equivocée*—that is, rather than following ballade rhyme scheme, the final syllables of lines of text are repeated in a different sense (*amer, la mer*). Only a few of Du Fay's chansons have all three voices texted. *Ce jour de l'an* (Today) is one; in it all voices enjoy some imitation and canon. Du Fay was one of the first composers to write noncanonic imitation.

Du Fay's secular style changed very little over the years. In his later works, there are fewer wide leaps in the lower voices, and rhythms seem a little more flexible with some intensification at the approach to final cadences. In his songs he used all kinds of final cadences: simple medieval ones, embellished cadences with and without the "Landini" figure, those in which the lowest voice moves up a fourth or down a fifth, and those in which the contratenor leaps up an octave (ex. 9.1, p. 134). He carried the vocal range upward, above Guido's gamut, to include f″ and g″.

FIGURE 9.4 Cathedral of Notre-Dame, Cambrai, as it existed early in the seventeenth century. The cathedral was sold and dismantled c. 1796. *(Revue de l'art chrétien, XLVII [1904], p. 107)*

months of 1450 and the years 1452–58 at Savoy, where court records indicate that in 1455 he was *maître de la chapelle.* In 1458 he returned to Cambrai and worked at the cathedral until his death.

Du Fay's duties at the cathedral were not solely musical, though music occupied much of his time. For five years he was master of the singers selected to perform polyphony in the cathedral. For several years he had general administrative responsibility for the entire cathedral choir—approximately 35 singers, 25 of whom sang polyphony. Du Fay was charged with buying robes, appraising talents, arranging for and evaluating the choirboys' musical and scholastic education, and paying singers. He supervised the copying of new music manuscripts and the renovation and augmentation of old books of liturgical music—this was more important to the church than his creation of new music. His house

was within a block of the cathedral and just across the street from the bakehouse, which he supervised for a while. At times he served as witness, procurator, and executor of wills; he represented the church at Council meetings, installed new chaplains, kept accounts and registries, traveled to Laon to buy wine, supervised woodcutting, and performed numerous other tasks necessary for smooth operation of the cathedral. And he composed.

In his will, Du Fay directed that certain liturgical works be performed at his deathbed and his funeral. Because other responsibilities that Sunday evening prevented his colleagues from singing at his deathbed, all the music he requested was performed at his funeral, including his *Ave Regina celorum* and *Missa de Requiem.* As he had requested, Du Fay was interred in St. Étienne Chapel at Cambrai Cathedral.

relinquished his benefices at Versoix and Lausanne, and returned to Cambrai. After Felix abdicated in 1449 and was reconciled with Pope Nicholas V (r. 1447–55), Du Fay could return to Savoy. He spent nine

MOTETS

The evolution of Du Fay's musical style from late Medieval to early Renaissance may be seen most clearly in his motets and Masses. Some motets seem to have served as patterns, in miniature, for Masses. Head motives, delayed entrance of lower voices, homorhythmic passages in sustained tones to draw attention to certain words, and cantus firmus technique are features of both motet and Mass. Some of Du Fay's motets follow fourteenth-century practice by being treble dominated, as is *Flos florum* (Flower of flowers). Some motets are isorhythmic, polytextual, secular polyphony based on a sacred cantus firmus. Others point toward sixteenth-century style by being purely sacred music, with a single text to be sung by all participating voices. The isorhythmic motets were written for special political, religious, or social occasions.

Du Fay is credited with being the first to use **faux bourdon** technique in a motet; he had used *faux bourdon* previously in Mass movements (see p. 134). In *faux bourdon,* two notated voices form a framework of basically parallel sixths with some octaves. A middle part is improvised by duplicating the top voice a fourth lower. Thus, the added improvised part creates a chain of parallel $\frac{6}{3}$ chords (ex. 9.2 p. 135). Audibly, *faux bourdon* resembles English discant and may have been a continental attempt to imitate the *contenance angloise.* However, in *faux bourdon* the main melody is in the top voice; in English discant, the main melody is in a lower voice, often the *meane.* The term *faux bourdon* is usually interpreted to mean "false bass" but may not have been so intended. One meaning of the French word *bourdon* is "omission"—originally, a scribal omission. Thus, the words *faux bourdon* might have been

EXAMPLE 9.1 Various cadences used by Du Fay.

written in a manuscript to indicate an *intentional* scribal omission of a part that was to be supplied through improvisation.

Faux bourdon technique was used to create an additional vocal line between the triplum and motetus for four passages in the basically three-voice isorhythmic motet *Supremum est mortalibus bonum* (The highest good for mortals is [peace]; ex. 9.2). However, each time *faux bourdon* is indicated, the tenor is silent; no more than three vocal lines sound at any time. Du Fay composed the motet in April 1433 in celebration of the peace treaty ending a conflict between King Sigismund (later Holy Roman Emperor) and Pope

Eugene IV. The exclamation *Eugenius et rex Sigismundus!* is set homorhythmically in sustained chords.

Symbolism is a characteristic of Du Fay's motets. Sometimes the symbolism is subtle and quite complex. The isorhythmic motet *Nuper rosarum flores—Terribilis est locus iste* (Recently roses—Awesome is this place; DWMA52) provides an example. See Insight, "*Nuper rosarum flores,*" p. 136. This motet is especially significant, for it seems to be the earliest of Du Fay's works to display (albeit in miniature) the style and form of his mature Masses: written for four voices, one serving as a firm bass; having metrically contrasted sections; using introductory duos; containing both canonic and noncanonic imitation; and juxtaposing linear counterpoint and four-voice vertical sonorities.

All of Du Fay's surviving isorhythmic motets were written before 1447. Later he composed some motet-like settings of chants for which the liturgical antiphon serves as cantus firmus. That he wrote the four-voice motet *Ave Regina celorum* (in 1464) in anticipation of his death is apparent from the interpolation *Miserere tui labentis du Fay* (Have mercy on Thy dying du Fay), troping the Marian antiphon text. The motet served as model for his *Missa Ave Regina celorum*.

MASSES

Eight complete Masses by Du Fay are extant: *Sine nomine* (unnamed); *Ave Regina celorum* (Hail, Queen of heaven); *Caput* (Head); *Ecce ancilla Domini* (Behold the handmaid of the Lord); *L'Homme armé* (The Armed man [i.e., soldier]); *S. Jacobi* (Saint James); *Se la face ay pale* (If my face is pale), and *Missa St. Antonii Viennensis. Missa sine nomine* and *Missa St. Antonii* are for three voices; the others are for four, with tenor as the next-to-the-bottom voice.

Missa Sancti Jacobi (c. 1425–28) uses *faux bourdon* in the Communion and may represent the earliest use of that technique. In one manuscript, rubrics direct the performer(s) to improvise the middle part by singing a fourth below the top voice.

Du Fay's authorship of *Missa Caput* has been questioned and the supposition advanced that this work is by an as-yet-unidentified English composer. If the Mass is Du Fay's, it is the oldest of his cantus firmus Tenor Masses. Cantus firmus technique had been used in Masses by English composers, but Du Fay may have been the first continental composer to employ it in a

EXAMPLE 9.2 Excerpt (mm. 110–14) from Du Fay's motet *Supremum est mortalibus bonum,* showing use of *faux bourdon* in mm. 110–13. The altus is the added part. *(© 1966 by American Institute of Musicology/Hänssler-Verlag, Neuhausen-Stuttgart, Germany) From Du Fay's* Supremus est Mortalibus Bonum, OPERA OMNIA Guglielmi Dufay, Vol. 1.

EXAMPLE 9.3 Head motive used in all five movements of *Missa Caput* attributed to Du Fay. In each movement, the two lower voices are *tacet* at the beginning. As in the original notation, this excerpt is presented without bar lines.

EXAMPLE 9.4 *Missa Caput,* Kyrie, final cadence. Notice the dominant-to-tonic progression in the bass, the complete triadic harmony with leading-tone effect of penultimate chord, and the absence of the third in the final chord.

complete Mass. These Tenor Masses are **cyclic**; that is, the same cantus firmus melody appears in all movements of the Mass. In *Missa Caput* the cantus firmus, placed in the tenor, derives from the long melisma on the word *caput* in the Sarum chant *Venit ad Petrum* sung during the foot-washing ceremony on Maundy Thursday. In Du Fay's Mass, the *caput* melody is written in long note values and the entrance of the tenor considerably delayed. This procedure would indicate that the cantus firmus melody was meant to be recognized; yet, placement in an inner voice somewhat covers it. Though the cantus firmus unifies the Mass and is its basis, the bottom voice is the foundation of the harmony. Each of the Mass's five movements is constructed in two sections—the first section in ternary meter; the second in binary. Superius and contra (alto) are paired much of the time and open each movement with a head motive (ex. 9.3). This unifying device was first used in Mass movements by English composers. A Mass in which a head motive is used consistently is sometimes called a **motto Mass.** In each movement, a

drive to the final cadence is apparent; the superius becomes more active, and the seventh degree of the modal scale appears frequently. Application of *musica ficta* establishes a "leading-tone" sound. The last two cadential pitches in the bottom voice are d and g, and the modal chords built upon them are comparable to the dominant-tonic cadential progression of key tonality (ex. 9.4).

Possibly, Du Fay composed *Missa Se la face ay pale* for the wedding of Charlotte of Savoy and Dauphin Louis (who became Louis XI) at Chambéry in 1451. Du Fay may have been the first to use secular music as cantus firmus for a cyclic Mass. The tenor of his chanson *Se la face ay pale* serves, virtually unchanged, as cantus firmus for the Mass. The complete tenor of the chanson appears at least once in each movement.

(continued on page 138)

Nuper rosarum flores

Du Fay composed his four-voice isorhythmic motet *Nuper rosarum flores* for performance in the Mass at which Pope Eugenius IV consecrated Santa Maria del Fiore Cathedral in Florence on 25 March 1436—New Year's Day according to the Incarnation calendar that Florence used then (fig. 9.5). The text's opening phrases refer to the pope's presentation, on Mid-Lent Sunday, of a Golden Rose award to the cathedral and, by inference, to Florence. This award, a golden branch of roses and leaves with a principal jeweled rose of red-tinted gold at the top, was presented annually to a republic, ruler, city, or Catholic person as a symbol of papal recognition of some outstanding service—usually, service to the church. Not all Golden Rose awards were identical; the number and size of the jewels varied considerably. Du Fay seldom used word painting, but when he referred to Eugene as successor to

St. Peter, the word *successor* is set imitatively. Noncanonic imitation was rare at that time.

The theme—the symbolic message—of this motet has been interpreted as "the divine unity of the Temple and the Virgin Mary." The poetic text and its musical setting reflect medieval religious numerology and the symbolism of the number 7, which represents the church and has many references to the Virgin Mary. Each stanza of text has 7 seven-syllable lines; the music is notated in multiples of 7 breves or phrases of 7 longs. There are two textless tenors, both based on the chant *Terribilis est locus iste,* the Introit used for dedication of a church. In the Florentine Graduale used at that time, that chant phrase had 14 notes.

Biblical reference and sacred geometry were factors in the construction of many cathedrals and are apparent in Santa Maria del Fiore and

Du Fay's motet. The large octagonal dome of the cathedral, designed by Filippo Brunelleschi (c. 1377–1446), reflects the octagon below it within the cathedral and the shape of the baptistery and symbolizes the eight persons whom God saved during the Great Flood (Gen. 6:18). The large size of the dome required extra support, and Brunelleschi used double vaulting, an architectural innovation. The two tenors presenting the cantus firmus—the foundation of the motet—represent the double vaulting of the dome, its architectural support (fig. 9.6). The tenor parts may have been performed instrumentally; instrumentalists may have doubled the vocal lines. At least one account of the ceremony mentions brass instruments.

A free canon is produced when each tenor presents the cantus firmus in a different mensuration at pitches a

FIGURE 9.5 Cathedral of Santa Maria del Fiore, Florence, constructed 1296–1436. View from the southeast. The campanile, designed by Giotto in 1334, was completed after his death; Brunelleschi designed the dome.

FIGURE 9.6 Sketch showing architectural details of dome of Cathedral of Santa Maria del Fiore, some of which inspired structural details of Du Fay's motet *Nuper rosarum flores.*

fifth apart. The cantus firmus is presented four times—once for each stanza of the poem—with rhythms proportionately altered 6:4:2:3. For each stanza, the two upper voices sing the same basic melodic material but with different elaborations. This type of variation is termed *isomelic.* In the manuscript, the cantus firmus is notated once for each tenor line, with the different mensurations specified (fig. 9.7).

The proportions Du Fay used for this motet reflect those pre-scribed in the Bible for the interior dimensions of Solomon's temple: 20 cubits wide, with the outer room 40 cubits in length, the Holy of Holies extending the length beyond the veil of the temple another 20 cubits, and the height of the structure being 30 cubits, thus giving 6:4:2:3 proportions. (It is generally agreed that the "royal" cubit, 20.9 inches long, was used in constructing Solomon's temple; an "original" cubit was shorter.)

Santa Maria del Fiore's baptistery doors present another relationship between the cathedral and Solomon. At the bottom of one door, Lorenzo Ghiberti designed a panel showing Solomon shaking hands with the Queen of Sheba. They are standing in front of a cathedral—the cathedral depicted is Santa Maria del Fiore.

FIGURE 9.7 Portion of the motet *Nuper rosarum flores* in manuscript MS α.X.1.11, fol. 67v–68r. *(Biblioteca Estense, Modena, Italy)*

Variety is achieved by not using all voices in all sections of the Mass. During the Renaissance, it became standard procedure for composers to use fewer than the full complement of voice parts for the *Christe eleison* section of the Kyrie, the *Pleni sunt coeli* and *Benedictus* sections of the Sanctus, and Agnus Dei II of polyphonic Mass settings.

Du Fay's use of the *L'Homme armé* melody as cantus firmus was an even bolder choice. He may have been the first composer to base a Mass on this secular song; for the next 150 years the melody was a favorite cantus firmus for polyphonic Mass settings (ex. 9.5). The origin of the *L'Homme armé* melody is unknown. Possibly, the tune emanated from a canonical house situated near Du Fay's home in Cambrai that was frequented by Du Fay and other priests and composers. In the early sixteenth century, a church-owned house known as *Maison l'homme armé* existed there. Perhaps it was there in Du Fay's time.

In this Mass, Du Fay permitted the cantus firmus melody to penetrate other voices from time to time. Sometimes portions of the melody appear imitatively in two voices; one voice may present a fragment of the melody in diminution (e.g., in Agnus Dei II). In Agnus Dei III, the tenor rubric reads, *Cancer eat plenus et redeat medius* (Let the crab proceed full and let it return half), thus directing the vocalist(s) to first sing the cantus firmus melody retrograde, giving the notes full value, and then sing it from beginning to end with note values halved (DWMA53).

It is regrettable that Du Fay's *Missa de Requiem* has been lost. It was one of his late compositions—Cathe-dral records indicate that it was "newly compiled" in 1470. Du Fay's is the first composed polyphonic Requiem Mass of record; previously, the Requiem Mass had been sung in plainchant.

Missa Ave Regina celorum is based on the same chant melody Du Fay used for his four-voice motet setting of that Marian antiphon. In fact, portions of the motet music are quoted note-for-note in the Mass. Construction of the Cathedral of Notre-Dame at Cambrai was completed in 1472, and the edifice was formally consecrated to the Virgin Mary on July 4. Probably, Du Fay composed his *Missa Ave Regina celorum* for that solemn ceremony, at which the Bishop of Arras officiated.

Masses *L'Homme armé* and *Ave Regina celorum* exhibit late fifteenth-century polyphonic techniques. The four voices are treated with more equality, and all participate actively in the polyphony. In his Masses, Du Fay was neither reactionary nor avant-garde. He employed a variety of techniques. He absorbed the techniques used by English composers and built on them, continually evolving toward the style of the later fifteenth-century "Netherlands" composers. For the next century, most of the polyphonic cyclic settings of the Mass were Tenor Masses.

The liturgical compositions Du Fay wrote for Cambrai Cathedral are unaccompanied vocal music. All music performed in that church was *a cappella*. Cambrai Cathedral had no organ, and all musical instruments except bells were excluded, even for processionals and on special feast days. The Cathedral owned 34 bells that were considered very important. According to historian Honoré Houdoy, services at Cambrai Cathedral were performed more solemnly and with more beautiful singing and "sweet carilloning" than anywhere else in Europe. The Cathedral's emphasis on *a cappella* polyphony, even after Cambrai became part of Burgundy, was due at least in part to circumstances that existed between the Cathedral and the papal chapel at Rome. To maintain the excellence of its choirs, the Cathedral sought the finest voices in the north; for the same reason, the papal chapel recruited heavily from Cambrai diocese. Later, many of the Cambrai singers in the papal chapel obtained benefices in Cambrai and eventually returned to the Cathedral to supervise the music, as did Du Fay. Thus, Cambrai Cathedral continued to use only *a cappella* choral music.

EXAMPLE 9.5 *L'homme armé* melody.

BURGUNDY

In 1364 Charles V (r. 1364–80) gave his brother Philip the small duchy of Burgundy bordering east-central France. Philip the Bold (r. 1364–1404) and succeeding dukes of the House of Valois gradually acquired additional territories and wealth (fig. 9.8). John the Fearless (r. 1404–19) retained territory and strengthened the duchy when France was being torn apart by the Hundred Years' War. During the reign of Philip the Good (r. 1419–67), Burgundy became the most powerful political entity in western Europe. Charles the Bold (r. 1467–77) was attempting to acquire additional territories when he was killed at the battle of Nancy. At the height of their power, the dukes of Burgundy controlled territory extending from the Rhône River to the North Sea. Charles died without a male heir; therefore, most of Burgundy reverted to and was annexed by France, but Charles's daughter, Marie (r. 1477–82),

FIGURE 9.8 The expansion of Burgundy and the extent of its possessions in 1477.

TRANSITION TO THE RENAISSANCE

inherited the Low Countries. After her death, these lands were governed by her son, Philip the Handsome (1482–1506). Marie's husband was Maximilian, son of Habsburg ruler Frederick III. The quality of the music at the Burgundian court so strongly impressed Maximilian that, in anticipation of the time when he would become Holy Roman Emperor, he assembled his own chapel; when he was crowned (1496), a sizeable body of musicians formed his Imperial *Kapelle*.

Although the designated capital of Burgundy was Dijon, the dukes maintained a traveling court and resided at Bruges, Brussels, Ghent, and other northern cities much of the time. No court in Europe was comparable with that of Burgundy. Philip the Good and Charles the Bold were patrons of the arts and employed some of Europe's most famous artists and musicians. Sculptor Claus Sluter and artists Huybrecht and Jan van Eyck worked for Philip; Jean Tapissier, Gilles de Binche (Binchois), Robert Morton, Hayne van Ghizeghem, Antoine de Busne (Busnois), Pierre de la Rue, and Alexander Agricola were among the composers who worked at the ducal chapel at various times. Though Du Fay is sometimes referred to as a Burgundian composer, he was not employed at the Burgundian court.

The court was a center of musical activity. By 1404 the chapel had increased to 28 singers, and in 1506 there were 33. The liturgy was sung in plainchant except on major feast days, when the service was resplendent with polyphony. Some sacred music was written by Burgundian composers. However, the court was worldly and luxury loving, and court composers were encouraged to write **chansons** (French secular songs). In addition to the chapel, the dukes maintained a large number of minstrels, who performed regularly. The quality and style of Burgundian court music were internationally famous. The fact that court musicians and composers traveled with their employers was one factor in the internationalization of the Burgundian style. Another factor was the expansion of the Burgundian style into the Habsburg court and ultimately into the Imperial court, both of which were quite mobile. Moreover, quite a few singers trained in Franco-Flemish cathedrals became members of the papal choir, and Italian rulers sought musical talent from the north to enhance their courts.

BURGUNDIAN MUSIC

Compositions by Burgundian composers survive in numerous manuscripts, most important of which are the seven Trent Codices and MS Canonici misc. 213. The Trent manuscripts contain music of non-Burgundian composers also. MS Canonici miscellany 213 reflects clearly the changes that occurred in notational practices. The music was written on paper in three different styles of notation: white notes almost 0-shaped, white notes similar to half-diamonds, and diamond-shaped black notes. Partial signatures were employed. After 1400, paper was used increasingly for music manuscripts. Parchment was reserved for liturgical books; paper, which was less expensive and easier to procure than parchment, was used for secular music. However, the concentration of ink in filled-in note heads was detrimental; it ate through the paper. Commencing c. 1430, manuscripts copied in Italy were written in white (hollow) notation; the change is apparent in French manuscripts of slightly later date and still later in English ones.

Besides chansons, Burgundian composers wrote motets, Magnificats, Masses, and other liturgical music. During the fifteenth century, the character of the motet changed considerably. Gradually, in the first half of the century, the motet's medieval characteristics—polytextuality (often in two different languages), secularity, and reliance on a cantus firmus tenor—were abandoned; then, isorhythm was forsaken. There was a marked return to creating motets for religious events, ceremonies, or liturgical purposes and setting Latin texts, with musical form treated freely. By the end of the century, the motet had become a polyphonic setting of a Latin religious text other than the Mass Ordinary. (Settings of the Ordinary would, of course, be Mass movements.)

Among Burgundian composers, treble-dominated three-voice polyphony predominated; imitation was used sparingly. *Faux bourdon* was sometimes employed in sacred music. Most compositions were in triple meter; in long, sectional works, duple meter provided contrast. Cross-rhythms, principally three against two, occurred in the lower voices. Lyrical simplicity characterized the principal polyphonic melody; melismas were included near cadences. The vocal range a composer used for a composition was determined by that of the singer(s) available to perform the work. In most compositions, vocal range remained within Guido's gamut; occasionally, it extended beyond (ex. 9.6). Cadential formulas were those shown in example 9.7 and ornamented versions of them. Though the music was modal, a sense of dominant-tonic relationship was becoming apparent, primarily at cadences.

EXAMPLE 9.6 Vocal ranges for which Burgundian composers usually wrote.

BASSE DANSE

The *basse danse* was the favorite court dance in the fifteenth and early sixteenth centuries. It was at its height at the Burgundian court during the reigns of Philip the Good and Charles the Bold. When performing the *basse danse,* couples moved quietly and gracefully with a gliding or walking movement of the feet. Costumes worn at court would have favored a slow dance. Gentlemen wore short doublets and tight-fitting hose; shoes were extremely pointed, the tips often projecting as much as two feet beyond the wearer's toes. Swords and hats were worn during dancing. Women's gowns, fashioned of heavy fabric, had full skirts with long trains. Women's hats (called *hennins*) were very tall, often heart-shaped or pointed with long veils extending down the back as far as a lady's knees or even to the floor.

Primary sources of *basse danse* music are MS 9085 in Brussels, a beautiful manuscript with gold and silver notation (plate 14), and *L'art et instruction de bien dancer,* printed by Michel de Toulouze c. 1496. *Basse*

EXAMPLE 9.7 Types of cadences written by Burgundian composers.

TRANSITION TO THE RENAISSANCE

danse music appears to be monophonic and is notated in uniform breves, which are augmented to longs when performed. The notation is merely a tenor cantus firmus the length of the choreography, with each note corresponding to a complete dance step. A letter symbolizing the dance step to be performed is below the appropriate note of the cantus firmus. In performance, three or four instrumentalists—usually a slide trumpet and two or three shawms—improvised polyphony based on the cantus firmus. *Basse danse* tenors were derived from tenors of favorite chansons, for example, Binchois's *Tristre plaisir* (Sad pleasure), *Mon doulx espoir* (My sweet hope), and *La merchi* (Pity).

GILLES DE BINCHE (BINCHOIS)

Gilles de Binche (Binchois; c. 1400–60) was born in Hainaut province near Mons. He probably grew up at court, for his father was court councillor, but nothing definite is known about Gilles's early life or education. There is no proof that he was an ordained priest. Priesthood was not required for chaplaincy at the Burgundian court, where he served from c. 1427 until February 1453. Nor was priesthood requisite for obtaining benefices; for much of his lifetime, Binchois received income from benefices he held *in absentia* at five churches. He did not have a university degree yet in 1452 was appointed provost of the collegiate church of St. Vincent at Soignies. At the time of his death, he was eulogized in laments by Du Fay, Ockeghem, and others.

Binchois is ranked third (after Dunstable and Du Fay) among the great masters of the first half of the fifteenth century. Though the major portion of his music is secular and courtly, in accordance with his position at the Burgundian court, Binchois composed a considerable amount of sacred music. His music was included in more than 50 manuscripts compiled in the fifteenth century. His surviving works comprise 12 single and 8 pairs of Mass Ordinary movements; 6 Magnificats; a *Te Deum; In exitu Israel* (When Israel left [Egypt], Ps. 113; KJV, 114); 28 short motets and settings of various hymns, antiphons, and a Sequence; 60 three-voice chansons (7 are ballades); and the four-voice chanson *Filles à marier* (Girls to be married, [never marry]).

CHANSONS   For chanson lyrics, Binchois chose writings of favorite court poets, such as Christine de Pisan's *Dueil angoisseux* (Anguished mourning) and Charles d'Orléans's *Mon cuer chante* (My heart sings). In the fifteenth century, rondeau was the dominant form of chanson; the favorite subject was courtly love.

All but one of Binchois's chansons are for three voices, with the principal melody usually placed in the top voice. The music is modal. Meter is usually ternary; the two lower voices move more slowly than the superius. In most of the chansons, only the superius has text. However, some chansons have words in two voices; in a few songs all voices are texted (e.g., the May song *Vostre alée* [Your journey]). That chanson provides an early example of **pervading imitation** (imitation in all voices). *Filles à marier* contains a good deal of imitation, but it is confined to the two upper voices. The untexted lines were intended for instrumental performance, and the presence of textless interludes between phrases of text in some songs suggests that an instrumentalist may have doubled the vocal line.

Binchois's melodies tend to be simple, graceful, and without rhythmic intricacies. His music has a kind of joyous melancholy, in keeping with the *Tristre plaisir et douloureuse joie* (Sad pleasure and dolorous joy) about which he wrote. He used musical material economically. Each phrase rises to a high point, then proceeds to a cadence. In many songs, the final cadence employs the octave leap to avoid successive parallel fifths (which actually are audible); the final chord is an octave with an open fifth. Occasionally, Binchois used an extremely wide range or an unusual range. In *De plus en plus* (DWMA54), the superius range is low, extending from g to c″. In *Jamais tant que je vous revoye*, the pitch f″, used twice, is marked with a ♭ each time to indicate that it is *fa ficta*—outside the Guidonian hand.

SACRED WORKS   Binchois seems to have been the only major composer in the fifteenth century who did not write a cyclic Mass, though he wrote individual and/or paired settings of all movements of the Ordinary. In his sacred music, he was conservative. Sections within Mass movements are contrasted in texture, range, and mensuration. Compositions based on liturgical chant present the chant elaborated and paraphrased rather than as tenor cantus firmus in long note values. The chant is meant to be recognized and often is placed in the top voice. That is the case in *Gloria, laus et honor* (Glory, praise and honor), based on a Sarum chant and set for three low voices. The lowest voice frequently descends to D, a fourth below Guido's lowest pitch.

The Kyrie based on Gregorian Kyrie VIII (*De Angelis; LU,* 37) presents the chant, slightly paraphrased, in both superius and contratenor. As seen in example 9.8, the original pitches of the chant were retained for the superius paraphrase but placed an octave higher. For the contratenor the chant was transposed and set a fourth below the superius. From time to time, successions of $\frac{6}{3}$ chords appear in the harmonic structure and usually are preceded or followed by $\frac{8}{3}$ chords. The influence of English discant is apparent. Some of Binchois's sacred works in Italian manuscripts have sections that are clearly marked to be sung by chorus (cf. English Mass movements in Old Hall manuscript).

Binchois used *faux bourdon* in his sacred music only. It is found in the Magnificats and *Te Deum laudamus.* Only one of his motets is isorhythmic.

Two of Binchois's sacred works are **contrafacta,** vocal pieces in which the original secular texts have been replaced by sacred ones (e.g., *Virgo rosa venustatis* [Virgin, lovely rose] is a *contrafactum* of the rondeau *C'est assez* [It is enough]).

Binchois is the foremost representative of the Burgundian style of musical composition. Theorists cited portions of his works as examples; he was consistently included in lists of the ten most skillful composers of polyphonic music. His chansons supplied material for major works by other composers; six of his songs were intabulated for keyboard and included in the *Buxheimer Orgelbuch.* His *Te Deum* was copied into choirbooks used in Milan and in Spain.

ANTOINE DE BUSNE (BUSNOIS)

Another significant Burgundian composer was Antoine de Busne (Busnois; c. 1430–92). From c. 1460 to 1465 he was at St. Martin de Tours; then he joined the court of Charles, Count of Chaulois. In 1467 Charles (the Bold) became Duke of Burgundy; Busnois was a singer in the ducal chapel. During 1477–83 he worked in the court chapel of Marie of Burgundy and the household chapel of Maximilian I of Austria. At the time of Busnois's death, he was *rector cantoriae* at St. Sauveur, Bruges.

Busnois was poet, musician, and composer; his chanson texts appear in contemporary collections of

EXAMPLE 9.8 Excerpt from the Kyrie Binchois based on Gregorian chant Kyrie VIII (*De Angelis*).

poetry. His secular songs were very popular, and his capable handling of Burgundian style caused his contemporaries to regard him second only to Ockeghem c. 1465–92. In addition to 64 secular polyphonic songs, Busnois's surviving compositions comprise 2 Masses, 6 motets, and settings of 2 hymns, 2 Marian antiphons, the Easter Sequence, and the Magnificat. Among the many manuscripts containing his chansons is the heart-shaped Chansonnier Cordiforme (plate 15). Most of the chansons are rondeaux; 13 are **bergerettes** (one-stanza virelais).

Busnois excelled in composing small forms. His chansons are typical of Burgundian style in the third quarter of the fifteenth century. Most of them are for three voices, with melodies characterized by simplicity and clear phrasing. Often all voices cadence simultaneously, thus establishing a feeling for the modality of the piece. Superius and tenor have smooth melodic lines with some bits of imitation; much of the time the contratenor is instrumental filler, but sometimes all three voices partake of motives imitatively. Busnois used a good deal of imitation, most often at the octave, unison, or fifth scale degree.

As Busnois's imitative use of small motives increased, the vocal range he covered in his three-voice writing expanded. The pitch F occurs frequently; sometimes a vocal line descends to D. Nor are these low pitches confined to the bottom part; they appear in the middle voice also, and sometimes the voices cross. He tended to avoid the harmonic interval of a fourth but frequently used parallel thirds, sixths, and tenths. This was a firm departure from late medieval harmonic practice.

Si placet (optional) parts for a fourth voice exist for some of the chansons; their presence indicates a growing demand for four-voice secular polyphony in the late fifteenth century. When a fourth voice was added, it was usually another contratenor, which necessitated clear differentiation of the two contratenor parts. This was accomplished by labeling one *contratenor altus* (high contratenor) and the other *contratenor bassus* (low contratenor). Eventually, the word "contratenor" was dropped, and the parts became simply "contraltus" or "altus" and "bassus." Often, the top voice was not labeled; sometimes it was identified as either *cantus* or *superius*. From this terminology came the modern designation of voice parts:

Name	Meaning	Became
Superius	"uppermost" or "top"	Soprano
Contratenor altus	"high against tenor" or "above tenor"	Contralto and Alto
Tenor	"holds melody"	Tenor
Contratenor bassus	"low against tenor" or "below tenor"	Bassus or Bass

Busnois's two extant Masses—*Missa O crux lignum* (O wooden cross) and *Missa L'Homme armé*—are four-voice cantus firmus Tenor Masses. The cantus firmus is unornamented and serves as skeletal framework for the Mass structure. Busnois was probably the second composer to write a Mass based on the *L'Homme armé*

tune. His Mass served as model for that by Obrecht. Thereafter, almost every well-known composer up to and including Palestrina wrote a *L'Homme armé* Mass.

Busnois used orderly procedures to achieve desired goals. For him, imitation was an integrative device, but it could also provide contrast or direct attention to either the climax of a piece or the beginning of a phrase. At times, he created rhythmic interplay between voices by commencing the imitation of a motive on the third beat of a ternary rhythm but retaining the previous rhythmic accent (i.e., on the first beat). Textual imitation adds subtlety. The interplay is more noticeable in modern transcriptions because bar lines are present. Short sequences and repeated rhythmic patterns serve as organizational devices.

Busnois occupies an important place in the development of contrapuntal music from Du Fay to Josquin. Busnois's style is a mixture of the old and the new. In his chansons he epitomizes the Burgundian style but includes more motivic imitation; in his sacred works, the sense of form, sense of harmony, and greater homogeneity of contrapuntal lines point ahead to the achievements of Obrecht and Josquin.

FRANCO-NETHERLANDS COMPOSERS

The term *Franco-Netherlands school* was invented by Gustave Reese (1899–1977) to encompass those composers working in countries known today as Belgium, the Netherlands, northern France down to Cambrai, and lands owned by the French king. Many talented Franco-Netherlands composers were employed at courts of Italian rulers, as was Alexander Agricola (c. 1446–1506). A native of Flanders, Agricola was employed at G. M. Sforza's Milan court in 1471–74, worked at Cambrai Cathedral in 1476, and c. 1490–93 was a member of the French royal chapel. His musical style is closely allied with that of late medieval Franco-Netherlands composers.

Johannes Tinctoris (c. 1435–1511) was esteemed in his own time as a writer and music theorist. His surviving compositions include 9 chansons, 6 Masses (one based on *L'Homme armé*) and a few motets and hymns. His compositional style is eclectic and transitional, reflecting elements of late medieval and early Renaissance music.

In his writings, Tinctoris considered all aspects of music from antiquity to his own time. His *Terminorum musicae diffinitorium* (Dictionary of musical terms, printed in 1495) is the earliest *printed* music dictionary. In *Liber de arte contrapuncti* (Book on the art of counterpoint; 1477), Tinctoris set down rules for correct and effective improvisation and cited music examples from Du Fay, Busnois, Ockeghem, and Caron. The emphasis Tinctoris placed on improvisation indicates its importance in the fifteenth century.

In *De inventione et usu musicae,* printed c. 1486, Tinctoris discussed, among other matters, the qualifications for being a good singer and singled out Ockeghem as the finest bass he knew. Several chapters of the treatise are devoted to instruments and instrumental performance practices. Instruments discussed include shawm, cromorne, bombarda, brass *tuba,* Italian *trompone* and French *sacque-boute* (early trombone types), lyra or *leute* (lute), viol, rebec, guitar, citole, and *tambura* (an oriental lute). In range, the shawm, cromorne, and bombarda were comparable with soprano, tenor, and contratenor voices; a low contratenor part might be played on the brass *tuba.* Wind instruments were played at church festivals, at weddings, at banquets, in processions, and on various civic occasions as well as for private entertainments at court. Invention of the guitar was credited to the Catalans; in Catalonia, women played guitar accompaniments when they sang love songs.

SPAIN

Johannes Cornago (fl. 1455–85) worked primarily at the Neapolitan courts of Alfonso I (r. 1442–58) and Ferdinand I (r. 1458–94). Only a few of Cornago's works are extant: 11 secular songs (5 with Italian texts, the rest Spanish); 2 Masses; and the four-voice *Patres nostri peccaverunt* (Our fathers sinned), one of the earliest polyphonic settings of a passage from Lamentations. Ockeghem made a four-voice setting of Cornago's three-voice chanson *Qu'es mi vida preguntays* (What is my life, you ask). Cornago is credited with developing a distinctly Spanish style of polyphonic courtly love song. His solo songs follow the form of the *canción* (contemporary Spanish lyric poetry), set musically as abba. His secular songs are three-part polyphony, with expressive melancholy melodies and long textless passages designed for instrumental performance.

ENGLAND

Only partial manuscripts of English music from the middle and late fifteenth century are extant. The Eton College Choirbook holds polyphonic votive antiphons honoring the Virgin Mary and Magnificat settings. The two sections of the Egerton manuscript contain a repertory of Sarum liturgical music for Holy Week and some carols. In the liturgical section are the earliest surviving examples of polyphonic settings of the Passion. Stylistically, the liturgical settings resemble the antiphons and hymns of Binchois and some early works of Du Fay. The harmonies reflect the English preference for sixth chords and continental use of *faux bourdon,* but the directive *a faux bourdon* never appears in the Egerton manuscript. In other words, there was a transformation of *faux bourdon* from improvisation to stylistic polyphonic writing.

Among the English composers active in continental Europe were Robert Morton and Walter Frye. Morton (c. 1430–c. 1478) served as clerk and chaplain at the Burgundian court from 1457 to 1476. Only 8 of his secular works survive; all are for three voices. Two of his songs, *Le souvenir de vous* (The memory of you) and *N'aray je jamais mieulx que j'ay* (Shall I never have better than I have), appear in at least 14 European manuscripts and served as bases for works by other composers, including Josquin.

Frye (fl. c. 1450–75) worked for almost a decade at Ely Cathedral and c. 1453 went to London as a cantor; he may have been in Burgundy for a time. His extant works comprise 3 Masses, the rondeau *Tout a par moy* (Everything has through me), the English ballade *Alas, alas,* 5 motets, and a few secular pieces also attributed to others. Josquin based his *Missa Faisans regres* (Having regrets) on this four-note motive from the second section of Frye's rondeau:

Frye's Masses are *Missa Summe Trinitati* (Highly, to the Trinity) and *Missa Nobilis et pulchra* (Noble and beautiful), both for three voices, and *Missa Flos regalis* (Royal flower), for four voices. All are cyclic, with unornamented cantus firmus placed in the tenor. Motto beginnings appear consistently, and duos provide

Music Printing (I)

During the fifteenth century, much of the music circulated in manuscript copies. It was possible to print music by means of woodblocks, but carving the blocks took infinite pains, and the inking had to be done very carefully to avoid fuzzing and blobs at the junctures of notes and stems and at staff intersections. Hollow note heads with a staff line through them were particularly troublesome. Woodblock printing was used for the first music printed in America, in the ninth edition of the so-called *Bay Psalm Book* (1698), and for some small books printed in the nineteenth century.

At some time during the 1440s, Johann Gutenberg (c. 1396–1468)

invented the technique of printing from movable type. Using that technique, c. 1450 he printed a book of liturgical texts for use at Constance, and in 1453–55 he printed a copy of the Bible. Until c. 1473 the printing of books containing music was makeshift—usually, the texts were printed and space was left for insertion of the notation and illuminated letters by hand. There survive a Constance *Graduale* with text and chant music printed by two typographical impressions somewhere in southern Germany c. 1473 (fig. 9.9), and a *Missale* with text and music printed typographically in red and black ink in Rome in October 1476. Both books are of excellent quality. In

1476–1500, at least 65 craftsmen were typographically printing liturgical books containing music. The principal centers of such printing were Augsburg, Bamberg, Basle, and Venice. Not until 1500 was a *Missale* with music printed in London. When music was printed typographically, the double impression method was used (i.e., separate printing of text and of notation).

In 1480, mensural music was first printed from type; it consisted of a few lines of notes, properly spaced, but without staff lines. The next extant examples were printed c. 1496 by Michel de Toulouze, in Paris. One of the books is *L'art et instruction de bien dancer* (see p. 141), which con-

---

contrast; the duo sections exhibit the English characteristic of commencing with a short simultaneous rest. Harmonies are primarily consonant, with many complete triads; most of the dissonances are suspensions, which are properly resolved. In accordance with English custom, *Missa Summe Trinitati* and *Missa Flos regalis* have no composed Kyries; a troped Kyrie was chanted. However, *Missa Nobilis et pulchra* is provided with a polyphonic setting of the troped *Kyrie (Deus creator)* text; the Kyrie is the longest movement of that Mass.

Three of Frye's motets are without cantus firmus: *Ave Regina* (Hail, Queen), *O florens rosa* (O flowering rose), and *Trinitatis dies* (Day of Trinity). The motet *Salve virgo mater* (Hail, Virgin Mother) exhibits parody relationship with *Missa Summe Trinitati*—the motet music parodies the Mass, which is unusual.

GERMANY

In Germany, middle-class citizens of the towns were interested in all kinds of music. Instrumental music was accorded a special place. *Stadtpfeiferei* (town pipers) were professional musicians who had their own guilds, as did the *Meistersinger.* The *Meistergesang* tra-

dition was strong and tended to exclude polyphonic song. However, in the last half of the fifteenth century, the **Tenorlied** was developing among the middle classes as a distinctly German type of polyphonic song. The *Tenorlied,* a solo song, used the melody of a preexistent *Lied* as "tenor" or cantus firmus, with two or three contrapuntal lines accompanying it. The accompaniment is more active rhythmically than the solo voice. In manuscripts, only the cantus firmus has the complete text underlaid. The *Tenorlied* became the principal type of German polyphonic *Lied* between c. 1450 and c. 1550.

Several important German manuscript collections survive, including the *Lochamer Liederbuch* (Locham Songbook, copied 1452–60) and the *Glogauer Liederbuch* (Glogau Songbook, copied c. 1480). The *Glogauer Liederbuch* comprises three paper partbooks; this is the earliest known example of partbook notation. This book holds 294 items including liturgical music for Mass and Offices, 120 motets, 63 German secular songs, and 59 textless pieces. In the manuscript all items are anonymous; some of the motets are *contrafacta* of French secular songs, and a few of the textless pieces have been identified as chansons.

Bound with the *Lochamer Liederbuch* is a manuscript of Conrad Paumann's *Fundamentum organisandi*

Music Printing (I) *continued*

FIGURE 9.9 Folio 1r from the Constance *Graduale*, the earliest known typographically printed music, c. 1473. Notation is Germanic style often referred to as *Hufnagelschrift* (horseshoe nail writing). The music, used on the first Sunday of Advent, is the Introit *Ad te levavi animam meam* (Unto Thee do I lift up my soul; Ps. 25:1–3) and the Verse *Vias tuas domine demonstra mihi* (Show me Thy ways, Lord; Ps. 25:4). (*British Library, London*)

tains 18 pages of music. Two pages are in mensural notation; the other pages have chant notation, with black notes printed on red four-line staves.

Around 1490, Ottaviano dei Petrucci went to Venice to study printing techniques so that he could print polyphonic music from movable type. His endeavors bore fruit early in the sixteenth century (see p. 170). Though he used a triple impression method, Petrucci consistently produced printed music and lute tablatures that were accurate, cleanly printed, and well spaced.

(Fundamentals of Organ-playing). Paumann's treatise appears also in the *Buxheimer Orgelbuch* (Buxheim Organ Book, copied c. 1470), which contains a large collection of organ pieces of the Paumann school. Paumann (c. 1410–73) was born blind. Despite heavy handicaps, he became Germany's foremost organist and was a lutenist and composer as well. He became famous internationally as organist and composer. Presumably, he improvised most of his works.

SUMMARY

The work of some fifteenth-century composers may be classified as late medieval and that of others as transitional, exhibiting some late-medieval traits but with features that pointed toward or became characteristic of Renaissance music. Until about mid-century, musical leadership was held by the English, many of whom worked in continental Europe. Dunstable was highly respected and was influential. After Dunstable's death, French composers were the recognized leaders, particularly Du Fay, Binchois, Busnois, and others who worked in northern France and the Low Countries. The mobility of Franco-Netherlands composers and the fame of the Burgundian court did much to promote an international musical style; Maximilian I's fascination with the music he experienced

at Marie of Burgundy's court helped disseminate that style within the Holy Roman Empire. However, English influence was apparent in the work of continental composers—in the increased use of thirds and sixths, the sixth-chord sound produced by *faux bourdon,* the use of a head motive (motto), the drive to the cadence, the paraphrasing of a cantus firmus, and cyclic settings of the Mass Ordinary. Probably, the drive to the cadence was influenced equally by concluding melismas in English works and by conductus *caudae.*

Composition of a cyclic polyphonic Mass—the first large-scale multimovement form in music history—was a challenge accepted by almost all important fifteenth-century composers. Continental composers set all five movements of the Ordinary, whereas English composers normally set only the last four. Most of the Masses were written for four voices—four-voice writing first became standard in polyphonic settings of the Ordinary. Most polyphonic Mass settings were unified by a cantus firmus, placed in the tenor; both sacred and secular melodies were borrowed for that purpose. By the last third of the century, canon, head motive, and imitation also served as integrative devices; at times, the cantus firmus permeated the other voices.

By c. 1450, the isorhythmic motet had virtually disappeared. The rigid structural basis isorhythm had provided was supplanted by a cantus firmus usually chosen from chant and placed in the tenor voice. The character of the motet gradually changed—usually a single Latin poetic text was set, and most often that text was sacred or was associated with a religious occasion. At times, a motet resembled a Mass movement in miniature; in fact, some motets were parodied in Masses. In both motets and Masses there was an increased tendency toward greater equality of voices.

Burgundian composers wrote motets, Masses, and settings of other liturgical texts but were encouraged to concentrate on chansons for court entertainment. Most chansons were three-voice cantilena-style polyphony in rondeau, virelai, or bergerette form; by c. 1470 the ballade had become obsolete. Some chansons were supplied with optional parts for a fourth voice. Tenors of popular chansons provided cantus firmi for Masses and *basse danses*.

The range of most compositions remained within the limitations of Guido's gamut; occasionally a superius extended upward to g'' and a contratenor bassus descended as low as E. Music was modal; an increased awareness of harmonies and harmonic successions was evident. Sonorities were predominantly consonant, with dissonance carefully controlled. Sixth chords resulted from the application of *faux bourdon* as well as being notated. The drive to the final cadence usually included the seventh degree of the modal scale; chromatic raising of this pitch through the application of *musica ficta* created a "leading tone" tendency. Rarely did the final chord of a piece contain the third, but the last two cadential chords frequently formed a modal harmonic succession suggesting the dominant-to-tonic progression in key tonality.

Instruments were available in wide variety. Instrumentalists provided music for dancing, performed chansons with vocal soloists, and probably doubled vocal lines of motets and Masses, especially on highly festive occasions. Not all churches had organs; a few cathedrals banned instrumental music. In Germanic lands, town musicians performed at the town halls regularly and participated in civic ceremonies. Some popular chansons and *Lieder* were arranged for keyboard.

The first music manuscripts in partbook format were copied in Germany c. 1450. At about the same time, Johann Gutenberg invented a method of printing with movable metal type. By the end of the century, a few books containing music had been printed by multiple impression.

THE RENAISSANCE: FRANCO-NETHERLANDS COMPOSERS

The *Renaissance* (French, rebirth) was an age of innovation and invention, an era that witnessed expansion through sea and land explorations and through astronomical, medical, and other scientific discoveries. The period was colored by *humanism,* which placed a high value on the individual. Many authors, artists, and scholars evidenced great interest in the classicism of ancient Greece and Rome. Artists drew on those ancient cultures for subject matter and patterned their works after classical models; scholars were interested in Greek and Roman literature. Both secular and religious topics provided themes for creative endeavors in all the arts.

A spirit of optimism prevailed—an attitude that it was the best of times and that the quality of the masterworks being produced would never be surpassed. In a sense, that was true. The Renaissance in art and literature began in the fourteenth century with the frescoes of Giotto and the poetry of Petrarch. Over the next two centuries, many persons created masterpieces, including visual artists Botticelli, Michelangelo, Cellini, Raphael, and Leonardo da Vinci; authors Dante, Boccaccio, Castiglione, Erasmus, Machiavelli, Thomas More, and Shakespeare; and composers Johannes Ockeghem, Jacob Obrecht, Josquin Desprez, Claudio Monteverdi, and Giovanni Pierluigi da Palestrina.

During the Renaissance it was common for a person to evidence interest and talent in many arts and sciences, not in just one. Many artists were sculptors and/or architects as well as painters; a number of musicians wrote the texts for their compositions. Leonardo da Vinci was not unusual in being poet, musician, inventor, and scientist as well as master of several visual arts. Renaissance authors voiced clear admiration for their contemporaries' talents. Boccaccio wrote in *Decameron* that Giotto had brought art out of the shadows; Tinctoris believed that no music written more than 40 years before his own time was worth hearing. To Glareanus, Josquin was the greatest of all composers. According to Castiglione, in *Il Libro del cortegiano* (The Book of the courtier; written 1508–16), a courtier required the ability to sing, to read and understand music notation, and to play diverse instruments; though the ability to sing polyphony was good, to be able to sing solos with lute accompaniment was much better.

In music history, the era known as the Renaissance is generally considered to encompass the years c. 1450–1600. Where music was concerned, there was no true rebirth or literal revival of ancient Greek and Roman classicism, for musicians and composers had no ancient music to use as models. It was not until c. 1564 that Girolamo Mei (1519–94) found the Greek hymns attributed to Mesomedes (see p. 8).

1400	1425	1450	1475	1500	1525	1550	1575

Hundred Years' War   1453

Greek treatises available in W. Europe
Mei located Greek hymns • c. 1564

• 1501 Petrucci: *Odhecaton*

• 1547 Loris: *Dodecachordon*

• 1504 Michelangelo: *David*

• 1511 Raphael: *School of Athens*

• 1514 Machiavelli: *The Prince*

• 1516 More: *Utopia*

Diffusion of Franco-Netherlands polyphonic style   Rise of Venetian School

c. 1410   Johannes Ockeghem   1497

c. 1450   Jacob Obrecht   1505

c. 1440   Josquin Desprez   1521

c. 1450   Heinrich Isaac   1517

c. 1459   Jean Mouton   1522

c. 1460   Pierre de La Rue   1518

c. 1490   Adrian Willaert   c. 1562

c. 1495   Nicolas Gombert   c. 1560

c. 1515   Jacob Clement   c. 1556

c. 1465   Pedro de Escobar   c. 1536

c. 1470   F. de Peñalosa   1528

c. 1500   Cristóbal de Morales   1553

Greek treatises and philosophic writings had been virtually inaccessible to Europeans for centuries, though they were known to Byzantine scholars. When Turkish invaders captured Constantinople in 1453, many scholars who fled Byzantium sought refuge in Italy. Among the valuable possessions they brought with them were manuscript copies of writings of Plato, Aristotle, Aristoxenus, and other authors in Greek and in Arabic translations. In Italy these writings were translated into Latin, and most of them were available to Europeans by c. 1500. Mei, who worked at the Vatican, read Greek plays and prepared editions of some of them, thoroughly studied the writings of Greek philosophers and theorists, and in his *de modis* (written 1567–73) comprehensively discussed the principles of Greek music theory, music education, and ethos. Mei's work was of fundamental importance in the development of monody and early opera in Florence in the late sixteenth century.

Heinrich Loris (known also as Glareanus) investigated Greek tonoi and medieval modes, then wrote *Dodecachordon* (1547; see fig. 10.6), in which he recognized 12 modes—the 8 medieval modes plus Aeolian and Ionian and their plagal modes. Aeolian and Ionian correspond, respectively, to modern A minor and C major scales.

Gutenberg's invention of printing from movable metal type in the 1440s, and Petrucci's adaptation of that process to the printing of polyphonic music (1501), made the preservation of music more practical and notated music more accessible. The fact that more music survives from the Renaissance than from previous eras may not indicate that more music was composed but, rather, that more copies were available and more secular music was preserved.

The major composers of the early Renaissance wrote Masses, motets, and chansons, with the amount of sacred music produced considerably outweighing that of secular. Most major composers wrote at least one unified Mass cycle. During the sixteenth century, the production of motets increased considerably. Also, there was growing interest in the composition of secular songs reflecting regional or national interests and customs; the texts of such songs were, of course, in the vernacular.

Some three-voice, treble-dominated polyphony was still being produced, but most of the music composed during the Renaissance was written in from four to six polyphonic lines of generally equal importance for voices homogeneous in timbre. The presentation of musical phrases in imitative counterpoint shared by all voice parts contributed to a feeling of linear equivalence, especially in those instances where a paraphrased cantus firmus was entrusted to the superius or a bassus clearly defined the modal harmonies. Though the music is modal and pitch and chord successions were determined by contrapuntal rules governing linear melodic movement and harmonic consonance among the lines, often the modal chords produced resemble triads or first-inversion triads of key tonality.

Only a small minority of Renaissance vocal music is polytextual. Composers became increasingly aware of the importance of setting texts so that listeners could clearly understand the words and comprehend their meaning. A single text set imitatively was more comprehensible than multiple texts set homorhythmically. Even more comprehensible was a homorhythmic syllabic setting of a single text, all voices singing the same syllable at the same time. The sixteenth-century term for such homorhythmic syllabic writing is **familiar style.** Composers used it to emphasize certain portions of a text and to provide contrast within a movement or section of a work. Some secular songs are almost entirely homorhythmic. Not only were composers concerned with textual clarity, they became increasingly interested in word (or text) painting. The total vocal range encompassed was gradually expanded. By c. 1500, it extended from B♭' to g''.

Instrumental pieces intended for dancing have recognizable rhythmic patterns that are strongly marked. Other instrumental works were written in rhythms designed to sound improvisatory.

Compositions were notated in the old mensural symbols, but the tempo had accelerated to the extent that the minim was now the unit of the beat. The notated music appears to be for unaccompanied voices, and some of the sacred music may have been performed in that manner. It is highly probable, however, that in performance instruments supported or substituted for one or more of the voice parts. Any chromatic alterations not notated but deemed necessary were made by the performers through the application of *musica ficta,* rules for which were printed in many theoretical treatises. For the most part, these regulations concern adjustments to be made to ensure the proper size of melodic and harmonic intervals. For example, a third included in the final chord of a composition must be major—a rule that often produces the type of concluding chord modern theorists term **Picardian.**

The prevailing style of music internationally during the early Renaissance was that of the Franco-Netherlands composers, many of whom were employed in important courts throughout Europe. Acknowledged masters of that style were Ockeghem, Obrecht, and Josquin.

Compositions by early Renaissance conservative composers are characterized by nonimitative (free) linear counterpoint with overlapping phrases and without internal cadences to interrupt the polyphonic flow; final cadences follow the forms favored by Du Fay and his contemporaries. The work of Ockeghem may be considered representative of the conservative early Renaissance composers. Progressive composers, such as Obrecht and Josquin, consistently used imitative counterpoint structured in **points of imitation,** and they used new cadential patterns that forecast the authentic and plagal cadences of key tonality and frequently included the third in the final chord of a work. The term *point of imitation* denotes a portion of a polyphonic composition in which a single musical subject, used to set a phrase (sometimes less) of text, is treated imitatively. The beginning of one point of imitation overlaps the conclusion of another so that, in analysis, a diagonal rather than a vertical aspect of the composition becomes apparent (ex. 10.1).

JOHANNES OCKEGHEM

It is presumed that Ockeghem (c. 1410–97) spent his early life in East Flanders. For a year (June 1443 to June 1444), he was a singer at the Cathedral of Notre Dame in Antwerp; from 1446 until c. 1450 he was a

EXAMPLE 10.1 Beginning of Josquin's motet *Ave Maria* shows phrases set as points of imitation.

(*Source:* Josquin Desprez: Werken, *edited by A. Smijers et al., 1921*)

member of the chapel of Charles, Duke of Bourbon, at Moulins. From 1451 until his death, Ockeghem served as singer, composer, first chaplain, and ultimately (from 1465) *maître de chapelle* to the kings of France: Charles VII (r. 1422–61), Louis XI (r. 1461–83), and Charles VIII (r. 1483–98).

The king of France was nominal abbot of St. Martin de Tours monastery, and in 1459 Charles VII appointed Ockeghem treasurer of that abbey, an office the composer held until his death. Being treasurer of St. Martin's was one of the most lucrative and responsible positions in the country. No doubt Ockeghem had some responsibility for music at the abbey. Religious ceremonies there were magnificent. Documents record expenditures in 1465 for a long robe of scarlet with grey fur so that Ockeghem would be better attired for services (plate 8).

Ockeghem enjoyed as benefices a canonicate at Notre Dame Cathedral, Paris (1463–70), and a chaplaincy at St. Benoît. In addition to journeys made as part of the king's retinue, he traveled within France on ecclesiastical business and went on a diplomatic mission to Spain. He visited Cambrai several times and enjoyed Du Fay's hospitality there.

Ockeghem was widely known and highly respected as a person as well as a composer and musician. His death was lamented by many distinguished poets and composers. In 1476 Tinctoris considered Ockeghem the leading composer at that time. Other authors commented on Ockeghem's contrapuntal achievements and included excerpts from his compositions in their treatises, but wrote nothing concerning the musicality

of his works. For centuries he was remembered primarily for his contrapuntal mastery and ingenuity rather than for the high artistic quality of his music. Only in the twentieth century has he been acclaimed on both counts.

The most important manuscript sources of Ockeghem's Masses is Chigi Codex C.VIII.234 at Rome. This manuscript, beautifully illuminated and bound in red velvet, contains 40 compositions of sacred music notated in choirbook format; 15 of those pieces were composed by Ockeghem. The music was copied on fine parchment in the white notation (black-outlined hollow notes) then in use (plate 16). Although most of the clef signs are in medieval shapes, occasionally the scribe used the modern bass clef sign (𝄢) (fig. 10.1).

Ockeghem's surviving works comprise 10 complete Masses, several Mass movements and incomplete Masses, a Requiem Mass, 9 motets, a Lament for Binchois, 21 chansons, and arrangements of 2 chansons (of Bedyngham and Cornago). To arrange Ockeghem's works in chronological order is impossible; he dated none of his works, and only one piece—the Lament—can be associated with a particular event.

SECULAR MUSIC

Ockeghem's chansons, like those of Du Fay and Binchois, are three-voice, treble-dominated polyphony but with the range expanded downward; thus, there was less necessity for voice crossing. Occasionally, imitation was used. In most of the chansons, only the superius has text. Undoubtedly, these songs were performed as vocal solos with instrumental accompaniment.

FIGURE 10.1 On these manuscript pages of Ockeghem's *Missa Fors seulement* Kyrie, the modern bass clef symbol appears at the beginning of the last staff on the left-hand page, but the Gamma clef sign was used on the first staff of that Bassus part to keep the notation on the staff. MS Chigi C.VIII.234. *(Biblioteca Vaticana, Rome)*

The chansons *Ma bouche rit* (My mouth laughs) and *Ma maistresse* (My mistress) were popular favorites. Both are virelais. In both chansons, the only simultaneous cadences occur at the ends of sections.

Prenez sur moi vostre exemple (Clothe me with your example) was a favorite of Isabella d'Este, who had it worked in marquetry in her study at Mantua. Marquetry, decorative inlaid work of wood and other materials, was frequently used in the Renaissance on walls and in corners of rooms to create an illusion of cabinetry and shelving (fig. 10.2). For *Prenez sur moi* Ockeghem notated a single melodic line that, when performed in accordance with directions, generates a three-voice canon at the fourth above. The piece is a **catholicon,** which means "universal"; in music, a catholicon is a composition that can be sung in more than one mode.

SACRED MUSIC

Ockeghem's style of writing secular music differed in several respects from that used for his sacred works. It is in the sacred works, particularly the Masses, that his contrapuntal genius, his ingenuity, and the development of his style may be seen to best advantage. Ockeghem's music is modally diatonic—chromatic alteration seldom appears. Melodies were constructed in long, flowing polyphonic lines in long-breathed phrases with seemingly infrequent cadences. Cadences

FIGURE 10.2 One of the many marquetry panels in the studiolo of the Duke of Urbino. Detail from the north wall.

within a movement were handled so skillfully that they never interfere with the onward flow of the linear polyphony. Downward expansion of the gamut produced a true bass range (ex. 10.2); in five-voice compositions the two lowest parts were labeled *Bassus*. It

(a)

(b)

EXAMPLE 10.2 (*a*) Total range encompassed and (*b*) ranges of voice parts in Ockeghem's music.

was not unusual for Ockeghem to include C in those vocal lines. Occasionally, the two *Bassus* lines were written in the same range, and some voice crossing occurred. When a bass part remained in a very low register for some time, Ockeghem used the Gamma clef ≣ to keep the notation on the staff.

In Ockeghem's writing, all voice parts are very nearly equivalent, and no voice part can be singled out as being the sole determinant of both phrase structure and harmonization; no vocal line can be eliminated without impairing the whole. It is evident that although Ockeghem was writing linear polyphony, he conceived all voices simultaneously. He was keenly aware of vocal timbres and used them effectively. Frequently, he enhanced one pitch in a chord by doubling it and blending timbres. He achieved contrast by (a) pairing voices and setting one pair against another, (b) writing sections of a movement as duos or trios and other sections with the full complement of voices, and (c) writing homorhythmic, chordal-sounding passages to emphasize certain portions of a text, a technique Machaut used in his Mass. Occasionally, Ockeghem added extra notes to the final chord of a movement by writing *divisi* parts in some voices; usually these parts double or sound the octave of pitches sung by other voices. At times, the final chord contains the third.

Ockeghem's treatment of melody and harmony is sometimes unpredictable but always purposeful. He seemed to delight in doing the unexpected, but he did not violate rules or disregard accepted procedures. In an era when imitation was being used increasingly, he

preferred to use canon, yet he never allowed the stricter device to impede the spontaneity or the melodic flow of the music. He did not shun imitation but used it incidentally.

A drive to the cadence is an important feature of Ockeghem's compositions. In cadential approaches, the rhythmic pace of all voices was accelerated, and dotted rhythms were included. Tension was increased by the presence of the tritone, and the seventh degree of the modal scale was used prominently. Probably, in performance, tritones in a cadential drive were not chromatically altered, and *musica ficta* was applied only where it would create a "leading tone" effect—just before the final chord (ex. 10.3).

MASSES Ockeghem based most of his Masses on melodies borrowed from secular songs or from chant, but the cantus firmus melodies are not always easily identified because he usually altered and adapted the original source material to serve the purposes of his composition. Moreover, his treatment of the cantus firmus varied considerably in each of those Masses. He did not always adhere strictly to the cantus firmus melody, nor did he always place that melody in the tenor voice to serve as scaffolding for the composition. Sometimes he (a) used a migrant cantus firmus, (b) changed the order of the phrases of the original melody, (c) placed the cantus firmus in two voices at the same time but without using canon or imitation or doubling the melody, (d) simplified the original melody, (e) freely paraphrased the cantus firmus, or (f) concluded a statement of the cantus firmus with newly composed material. For example, in *Missa Ecce ancilla Domini* (Behold the handmaid of the Lord; plate 16), whose cantus firmus was derived from the antiphon *Missus est Gabriel Angelus* (The angel Gabriel was sent), Ockeghem freely paraphrased the borrowed melody, sometimes changed the order of the chant's musical phrases, and in the Credo transposed the melody a fifth lower. But in *Missa L'Homme armé,* the secular melody is clearly recognizable in the tenor, handled with traditional cantus firmus technique.

Ockeghem seems to have patterned his *Missa Caput* after that attributed to Du Fay. The cantus firmus is not disguised; however, Ockeghem placed it in the lowest voice part rather than within the polyphonic texture—perhaps he was making symbolic reference to the word

EXAMPLE 10.3 In *Agnus Dei* III of Ockeghem's *Missa Caput,* the drive to the final cadence commences as the cantus firmus is concluding; note the increased use of smaller note values, dotted rhythms, and the abundance of tritones and seventh scale steps. *Musica ficta* would have been applied to only the penultimate pitches in superius and contratenor altus—pitches pointed up by suspensions—to create a double leading-tone cadence. *(From* **Missae Caput**, *edited by Alejandro Enrique Planchart. Copyright © 1964 Yale University, New Haven, CT. Reprinted by permission.)*

"feet" in the text of the Sarum chant from which the melisma was borrowed. All movements but the Kyrie commence with the two upper voices presenting a paired head motive. Another unifying device is Ockeghem's systematic conclusion of each movement (and some sections within movements)—the cantus firmus melody ends while the drive to the cadence is beginning or while it is still gaining momentum; the lowest voice is given an extended rest and then reenters with one or two statements of the final of the mode (d) at the very end of the cadence. The conclusion of the Agnus Dei of *Missa Caput* is shown in example 10.3. Note the increased use of smaller note values, the frequent occurrences of the tritone, the dotted rhythms,

the extended rest following conclusion of the statement of the cantus firmus, and the single utterance of the mode final by the lowest voice in the last chord. In setting the Credo of *Missa Caput,* Ockeghem followed the English custom of telescoping portions of the text.

Some of Ockeghem's Masses are unified by means other than cantus firmus (e.g., *Missa Quinti toni* [Mass in Mode V], written in the fifth mode). *Missa Mi-mi* has two unifying features, one of which probably explains its name. The movements are unified by a head motive—the pitches e-A-A-e or e-A-e—stated in the Bass voice (ex. 10.4). According to the hexachord system, the pitch e is labeled *e-la-mi*—it bears the syllable *mi* in the natural hexachord—but the pitch A, which is in the hard hexachord, is given *only* the syllable *re*. Therefore, the e-A descending fifth in the head motive of the Mass represents the syllables *mi-re* and does not explain the title. The other unifying feature of the Mass does. In every movement each of the four voices commences on a pitch that may be sung to the syllable *mi,* but, because two of the four voice parts commence on the same pitch, only three different *mi* pitches are sounded in each opening chord (see ex. 10.4). Also, all five movements end on *mi* chords. *Mi* pitches seem to be featured in the Mass; notice especially the contratenor at the beginning of the Gloria.

The Masses for which Ockeghem was most acclaimed by succeeding generations are *Missa Cuiusvis toni* (Mass in any mode) and *Missa Prolationum* (Prolation Mass). Both compositions have structural features that demonstrate Ockeghem's contrapuntal genius, and both are excellent music. *Missa Cuiusvis toni* is an extended catholicon that, with appropriate alteration by the performers, may be sung in any of the four authentic modes: I, III, V, or VII. The music is notated without clefs; instead, Ockeghem placed the symbol

on each staff in the position of the final of the mode. Singers must supply the clefs appropriate to the desired mode and apply *musica ficta* in the proper places. This Mass could have been used to test the ability of singers to transpose music. *Missa Cuiusvis toni* is unified by a head motive that appears frequently within the body of the composition also.

The unification of a Mass by an abstract idea involving a constructional procedure was a new technique. In Ockeghem's hands techniques enhance rather than

EXAMPLE 10.4 Beginnings of the five movements of Ockeghem's *Missa Mi Mi*. Note use of head motive and many "mi" pitches.

detract from the musical artistry. *Missa Prolationum* is proof of this. This Mass has neither cantus firmus nor head motive. It is unified by the fact that the movements form a cycle of double canons, proceeding from double canon at the unison through double canon at the octave (Kyrie through Osanna) and concluding with two double canons at the fourth (Benedictus and Agnus Dei I) and two at the fifth (Agnus Dei II and III). Double canon occurs when two canons are performed simultaneously. *Missa Prolationum* seems to be the earliest composition written as a cycle of canons. Later composers wrote works unified by this principle, for example, Palestrina's *Missa Repleatur os meum* and J. S. Bach's *"Goldberg" Variations*.

The name *Missa Prolationum* derives from Ockeghem's use of the four prolation signs to indicate both the mensurations of the various voice parts and the intervals of the canons. For each section of the Mass, only two lines of music were notated. Whenever possible, prolation signs were vertically aligned on the staff to indicate the interval of the canon; when this could not be done, verbal directions were supplied. Sometimes clefs were vertically aligned, too, and for a few sections all these informational devices were used. In

manuscript, one notated part bears the mensuration signs O and C ; the other part, labeled *Contra*, bears the mensuration signs ⊙ and ₡ (fig. 10.3). In the canon performed by the upper two voices, both parts use minor prolation, but one voice is in perfect time and the other in imperfect. Though both voices commence together, one proceeds in longer note values than the other, thus producing the canonic imitation. A similar situation occurs in the lower two voices; both use major prolation, but one is in perfect time and lags behind the other, which uses imperfect time (ex. 10.5; DWMA55).

For *Missa Fors seulement*, Ockeghem borrowed the superius and tenor lines of his chanson *Fors seulement l'attente* (Except for waiting). Material from both borrowed voices was used simultaneously but was placed in lower voice parts in the Mass; occasionally, small bits of all the chanson voices appear. This foreshadows true **parody** technique, which involves extensive borrowing from the total substance of a preexistent composition, such as a chanson or motet, as the basis for a Mass or Magnificat.

The *Requiem Mass* composed by Ockeghem is the earliest extant polyphonic setting of the Requiem. The

FIGURE 10.3 Credo of Ockeghem's *Missa Prolationum.* The aligned clef and mensuration symbols indicate that two voice parts are derived from each notated part. *(MS Chigi C.VIII.234, Biblioteca Vaticana, Rome)*

EXAMPLE 10.5 Beginning of Kyrie I of Ockeghem's *Missa Prolationum* in modern notation, showing double canon created in performance. *(From Johannes Ockeghem, Complete Works, 2d ed, Vol. 2. Copyright © 1947, 1966 American Musicological Society, Philadelphia, PA. Reprinted by permission of the American Musicological Society.)*

order of the liturgy in Ockeghem's *Requiem* differs in several respects from that of the modern Requiem. In the fifteenth century, local practices influenced which chants of the Proper were included in the Mass for the Dead. In Franco-Netherlands churches, it was customary to use the chant *Si ambulem* (If I walk; Ps. 24/KJV, 23) in place of the Gradual; Ockeghem observed that custom. In several sections allowance was made for the appropriate plainchant intonation to be sung by the officiating priest; then polyphony was furnished. For reasons unknown to us, Ockeghem's setting concludes with the Offertory; the remainder of the Requiem was sung in chant. The tessitura used for the entire Requiem is rather low and the tone color of each movement is distinctive. Contrast was achieved by varying the number of vocal lines—some sections are for two voices, others are for three or four. There is some text painting.

MOTETS   Ockeghem's motets follow no standard pattern, though most of them are Marian-related. Five motets are for four voices, and three are for five voices. In general, the tessitura is low, but that in *Alma redemptoris mater* (Kind mother of the Redeemer) is unusually high. The motets *Intemerata Dei mater* (Undefiled mother of God) and *Ave Maria* (Hail, Mary) were written in free counterpoint. *Intemerata Dei mater* closely resembles a Mass movement in miniature, with sections written in different mensurations and with duos and trios interspersed with full five-voice sonority. Ockeghem's other motets were based on chant, and the cantus firmus was usually ornamented or paraphrased.

JACOB OBRECHT

Jacob Obrecht (c. 1450–1505) was probably born in Bergen op Zoom, in Brabant (now part of Belgium). Nothing is known concerning his early life, his general education, or his musical training. He was a priest and c. 1476–78 was singing master at Utrecht. In 1479 he became choirmaster at St. Gertrude in Bergen op Zoom. He remained there five years, then spent a year at Cambrai as singing master to the choirboys. He served less than a year at St. Donatien, in Bruges, before requesting a year's leave to visit Ferrara. After returning to Bruges, he seems to have changed jobs annually, moving to Antwerp, to Bergen op Zoom, back to Antwerp, then to Bruges. He retired in 1500 because of poor health. In 1504 he returned to the ducal court at Ferrara, and in Italy contracted plague and died.

Obrecht was highly respected as a composer. Both manuscripts and printed books from the Renaissance preserve his compositions. Petrucci included some of Obrecht's chansons in *Harmonice musices odhecaton A* (One hundred polyphonic pieces, [Volume] A; 1501; fig. 10.4) and *Canti B* (Songs, [Volume] B; 1501); printed some of his motets in *Motetti a cinque, Libro primo* (Five-voice motets, Book One; 1505); and published *Messe Obreht* [sic] (Obrecht Masses; 1503), which contains five four-voice Masses.

Obrecht's surviving works include 26 Masses, 26 motets, and 27 chansons. The almost equal number of compositions in each category is deceptive, for some motets are quite long, and the chansons are generally rather short. The preponderance of sacred works is an indication of the interests of early Renaissance composers.

SECULAR MUSIC

Most of Obrecht's chansons are for four voices; only six are three-voice. Obrecht's use of Dutch for most of his secular pieces is very unusual. Three of the chansons are textless. More than half the chansons are supplied with only an incipit of the text. The absence of text does not always imply that a work was intended for instrumental performance; the piece may have been so well known that the publisher or scribe considered it unnecessary to underlay the text. Because of the absence of texts, specific statements cannot be made concerning formal structure of many of the chansons. However, it appears that Obrecht, like his progressive contemporaries, was abandoning the *formes fixes*. In general, the texture of Obrecht's four-voice chansons approximates that of his motets; the voices are more nearly equal rather than being treble-dominated, and sometimes phrases commence imitatively. These features may be seen in *T'saat een meskin* (There sat a maiden), a textless piece that seems to be instrumental. Obrecht's secular pieces are colored by melodic sequences and by frequent use of parallel thirds or tenths; both traits are characteristic of the secular works of Busnois, too. Some chansons survive under two titles and in both three- and four-voice versions, as does *Meskin es hu* (You are a maiden, fig. 10.4; also *Adiu, adiu*, Goodbye).

SACRED MUSIC

The characteristics of Obrecht's style are clearly visible in his sacred music. For the most part, melodies are constructed in smooth, singable phrases of moderate length, gently curved, or slightly arched. It is apparent that Obrecht envisioned and composed each of his works as a complete harmonic entity rather than building line on line. Often, the polyphonic lines blend in modal harmonies that produce what modern theorists term "root-position" chords. Internal cadences are unobtrusive and often are elided; final cadences frequently end with modal chord successions resembling the dominant-tonic chord progressions of key tonality. Imitation is used sparingly; sections of a work may commence with points of imitation, but an entire sec-

FIGURE 10.4 Obrecht's *Meskin es hu*, from *Harmonice musices odhecaton A*, published in 1501 by Ottaviano dei Petrucci, Venice, Italy.

tion or movement is not constructed by means of that technique. None of Obrecht's compositions is integrated by continuous imitation, a further step that was left for Josquin to take.

MASSES   Most of Obrecht's Masses are for four voices, and all were based on borrowed melodies. He did not abandon the idea of using a single borrowed melody as scaffolding, but frequently he used some of the cantus firmus material in more than one voice; often he borrowed from more than one vocal line of a chanson and, on occasion, used some of the quoted material simultaneously. Usually, he placed the main cantus firmus in the tenor. The borrowed material might be paraphrased, segmented, or combined with one or more other borrowed melodies. Schematic manipulation of the cantus firmus is an important feature of Obrecht's Masses. Obrecht was rational in his procedures—he selected the cantus firmus material, planned in detail the treatment of it, and adhered to his plan.

Obrecht did not write a true parody Mass. He used parody technique often but not as the prime constructional basis for a Mass.

Most of the major fifteenth- and sixteenth-century composers wrote *Caput* and *L'Homme armé* Masses. Obrecht modeled his *Missa L'Homme armé* on that composed by Busnois. He borrowed Busnois's cantus firmus but changed the mode. At times, Obrecht subjected the melody to augmentation and retrograde inversion, and he gave each voice an opportunity to sing the borrowed melody. Despite Obrecht's manipulations, the direct relationship between his Mass and its model is apparent—in overall length, similarity of sections and of movements, manner of polyphonic treatment of material, and location of modal transpositions. One way in which Obrecht's *Missa Caput* differs from those composed by his predecessors and contemporaries is that Obrecht relocated the cantus firmus in each movement.

Obrecht's contrapuntal genius rivaled—perhaps surpassed—that of Ockeghem. The measure of Obrecht's talent becomes apparent through analysis of a group of Masses in which the cantus firmus material is segmented (e.g., *Missa Maria zart* [Mass Mary tender] and *Missa Sub tuum praesidium* [Mass Under Thy protection]). These Masses have both an intellectual and an aesthetic basis. Obrecht created them according

to a threefold rational schematic: (a) segmented cantus firmus, placed in the tenor, as scaffolding; (b) subsidiary use of borrowed material in those sections of movements where the tenor is silent; and (c) cabalistic numerological symbolism carefully concealed in the mensuration notation and overall plan. Subsidiary use of borrowed material in Masses, unified by segmented cantus firmus scaffolding, is the direct quotation of an entire vocal line from the original source; this is presented in a section of the Mass not supported by a segment of the cantus firmus. Cabalistic numerological symbolism means that through a code of numbers hidden in the musical notation—the kinds of notes, their arrangement, the manner of their subdivision, the number of temporal units used, and so on—the composer made symbolic reference(s) to specific persons, places, things, and/or events in some way associated with the composition. Only through analysis of the music in the original mensural notation can this symbolism be interpreted; it is completely obliterated by transcription into modern notation.

Before notating the music for a Mass employing a segmented cantus firmus, Obrecht precisely computed the number of *taktus* (temporal units) to be used per section, per movement, and per Mass to incorporate the desired numerological symbolism. For example, the number of *taktus* Obrecht notated for *Missa Sub tuum praesidium* totals 888, the cabalistic number representing Christ. Obrecht's use of symbolism was not unique. Many scholars were expressing in their work the principles of Pythagorean proportions; the philosophies of Plato, Aristotle, and Boethius; mystic numerology; and *Gematrian* cabalism. (*Gematria* was a branch of cabala that interpreted Scripture by interchanging words whose letters have the same numerical value when added.) This kind of scholarly thinking and planning is inherent in many literary works, in theoretical diagrams and treatises (such as those by Gaffurius), and in works of art, such as Raphael's *School of Athens* (plate 17). To analyze in detail Obrecht's compositional procedures is beyond the scope of this book. A discussion of the principles and philosophies involved and an analysis of Obrecht's use of cabalistic symbology are included in musicologist Van Crevel's editions of *Missa Sub tuum praesidium* and *Missa Maria zart*.

Obrecht selected a melody to serve as cantus firmus, segmented it, and organized the segments with a rigidity comparable with that of isorhythm. Usually, a segment was used several times per movement, first appearing in long note values, then with values proportionately reduced. The segments are separated by rests; each segment is stated several times before the next segment is presented. The mensural notation is economical; directives to the singers are given by means of prolation signs placed on several lines of a single staff, repeat signs after the rests at the end of a segment of cantus firmus, and verbal canons (fig. 10.5). When segmenting the borrowed material for cantus firmus use, Obrecht disregarded the original phrasing of the melody.

In *Missa Si dedero* (Mass If I give up), there are sufficient segments to support all movements of the Mass, but this is not always the case. When all segments of the cantus firmus had been used prior to conclusion of the Mass, Obrecht presented the borrowed melody in a subsidiary manner in the remaining section(s) of the Mass. *Missa Si didero* is based on Agricola's three-voice song motet; to base a Mass on preexistent sacred polyphony was rare.

It must be strongly emphasized that all these machinations were skillfully concealed in the music. In no way did they detract from the serious function of the Mass, its aesthetic intent and content, or the overall effectiveness and beauty of the music when performed.

MOTETS Fourteen of Obrecht's motets are for four voices; seven are five-voice; six, three-voice; and one, six-voice. *Salve regina misericordiae* (Hail, merciful queen) exists in three- and six-voice versions; the upper three voices of the latter version are designated *puer* (boys). Many of the motets are large works constructed in two or more sections. Nearly all the motets are based on one or more borrowed melodies, with the cantus firmus manipulated in various ways. In many of the motets, the cantus firmus is in the tenor, and portions of the borrowed material appear in other voices.

Some motets are polytextual. *Factor orbis* (Creator of the world) is somewhat like a *quodlibet*—it incorporates texted musical phrases from several antiphons. A **quodlibet** (Latin, whatsoever you please) is a composition formed by combining phrases of well-known melodies and/or texts either successively or simultaneously.

Parce, Domine (Have mercy, Lord) was used by Glareanus in *Dodecachordon* to illustrate use of Aeolian mode (fig. 10.6; DWMA56). In this three-voice motet, the sustained notes of the cantus firmus appear in the tenor in rather short segments separated by rests, in contrast with the flowing, expressive counterpoint of the two upper voices. Several passages of parallel sixths

FIGURE 10.5 Page from the Tenor partbook of Petrucci's printed volume of Obrecht's Masses showing Tenor of Kyrie and Gloria of *Missa Je ne demande*. Petrucci printed the *Resolutio* of the Tenor beneath Obrecht's abbreviated notation.

FIGURE 10.6 Portion of Obrecht's *Parce, Domine* printed in Glareanus: *Dodecachordon*, 1547.

occur. Dissonance was carefully controlled; suspensions were used frequently, especially at cadence points. The final cadence illustrates Obrecht's use of parallel sixths interspersed with suspensions, and the descent of a fifth in the sustained pitches in the tenor create modal harmonies resembling the V–I chord progressions of key tonality.

JOSQUIN DESPREZ

Josquin (c. 1440–1521) was the foremost composer of secular music of his time and an acknowledged master of Mass and motet composition. Several of his compositions were cited as examples in theoretical treatises and were used as models by other composers. While Josquin was still living, Petrucci devoted three volumes solely to his Masses and included some of his motets, Mass movements, and secular songs in several books containing those specific types of music. Many literary and musical tributes to Josquin were written at the time of his death. Glareanus considered Josquin the greatest composer, Castiglione praised him, and Martin Luther said Josquin was "Master of the notes" whereas other composers were mastered by them.

Josquin Desprez. (*Woodcut from Petrus Opmeer:* Opus chronographicum, *1611*)

Data concerning Josquin's early life are not available. It is believed that he was born somewhere in northern France. In July 1459 he was employed as an adult singer at Milan Cathedral. At some time in 1473 he received a benefice from Galeazzo Sforza and was a singer in Sforza's chapel from July 1474 to December 1476. Then he transferred to the chapel of Cardinal Ascanio Sforza. Josquin entered the papal chapel in 1486; how long he remained there is not known. In 1501–3 Josquin was in France, where, reportedly, he was foremost among the singers at the court of Louis XII. In April 1503, Josquin became *maestro da cappella* at the court of Ercole I d'Este at Ferrara, a position he occupied for only one year. He went directly from Ferrara to Condé-sur-l'Escaut, in Hainaut, where he was one of four canons admitted to the Cathedral of Notre Dame. He remained there for the rest of his life.

Divergent features of the styles of Ockeghem and Obrecht appear in the work of Josquin and were used compatibly by him. Josquin's style is related to that of Ockeghem in the extensive use of canon, the paraphrasing or embellishment of borrowed melodies, the drive to the final cadence, and the unification of some multisectional or multimovement works purely by compositional procedures. Josquin's style is an extension of Obrecht's in the use of imitation, the singable nature of the melodies and their phrasing, the literal quotation of material as cantus firmus, and the rational schematic manipulation of basic material. A feature of Josquin's late motets is **pervading imitation,** a technique the next generation of composers would use often. He wrote a new musical phrase for each phrase of text and treated each phrase as a point of imitation, skillfully overlapping the definitive cadences at the conclusion of each phrase so that melodic flow was uninterrupted. Careful attention to correct declamation is characteristic of all of Josquin's writing.

Josquin's extant works include 18 Masses, 6 independent Mass movements, 95 motets, and 68 secular songs. None of Josquin's compositions are dated, and few contain references to events or persons so that dates can be assigned to them. It is believed that most of the works by which Josquin is best known were written after he became 50. Undoubtedly, many of his early works have been lost.

The distribution of works in a list of Josquin's compositions indicates not only his personal interests and the nature of his employment but also the general trend of musical composition in the late fifteenth and the sixteenth centuries. The overwhelming majority of Josquin's extant compositions are sacred music, and most of those works are motets. His personal interest in Marian music is apparent.

In the early Renaissance, the successful composition of a Mass was the accepted mark of a master composer. To apply some measure of originality to the traditional ways of unifying the five movements presented a decided challenge, for the unvarying text of the Ordinary and the liturgical conventions and objective nature of the service were in themselves restrictive. Room for experimentation was extremely limited. On the other hand, motet composition offered almost unlimited opportunity for experimentation. There were many texts from which to choose, length was not restricted, few precedents had been set, and, because motets were sung on special occasions, there was greater opportunity for expression and originality. More and more, in the early sixteenth century, composers chose to compose motets. As the century progressed, the motet became the vehicle for new ideas and the most progressive form of sacred composition.

SECULAR MUSIC

Most of Josquin's secular works are chansons, but he wrote a few *frottole*, e.g., *El grillo è buon cantore* (The cricket is a good singer). Possibly *El grillo* refers to Carlo Grillo, a singer Josquin knew at the Sforza court; however, the chirp of the cricket is imitated in the song. Approximately two-thirds of Josquin's chansons are for three or four voices; the remainder are for five or six. The chansons exhibit a variety of forms. Only a few follow the *formes fixes;* those are early works. Often, Josquin set long poems strophically; some of his songs are quite short and are through-composed. He soon abandoned cantilena style in favor of polyphonic settings in which the voices are of equal importance, or nearly so, with all parts meant to be sung. Frequently, in his four-voice settings, the voices are paired and are used imitatively, in dialogue fashion. Canon figures prominently in Josquin's chanson writing; imitation and repetition are characteristic. Canon and imitation intermingle in the five-voice *Faulte d'argent* (Lack of money), which is basically ternary in form. Quite often Josquin based chansons on preexis-

tent material, especially popular tunes, which he elaborated or paraphrased. A few of his chansons are light in texture and in a style that anticipates the one used by Janequin (see p. 184). Josquin's chanson *Comment peult haver joye* (How can I have joy) became the Lutheran motet *O Jesu fili David* (Oh, Jesus, son of David), a *contrafactum*. Some chansons survive without texts and may have been written for instruments.

SACRED MUSIC

MASSES   All but two of Josquin's 18 Masses (*De beata Virgine* and *Pange lingua*) were composed before 1505. He based most of his Masses on borrowed material: five on chansons by other composers, four on popular songs, four on chant melodies, and one on a motet. Of the remaining four, two are canonic, and two are unified by motives created from solmization syllables. All but one of the Masses were written basically for four voices; in some sections of some Masses one or two additional voices are generated by canon. In his Masses, Josquin was his most conservative. He demonstrated his ability to handle all the methods used by his predecessors and contemporaries as well as some advanced procedures.

Josquin used canon extensively, as did Ockeghem. *Missa ad fugam* (Canon Mass) is unified by a head motive, canon (usually between superius and tenor), and a melody that, if borrowed, has not been identified. Canon is present also in *Missa Hercules Dux Ferrarie* (Mass Hercules Duke of Ferrara). The contrived motive unifying this Mass was described by Zarlino as *soggetto cavato dalle vocali di queste parole* (subject carved from the vowels of the words). From the words "Hercules Dux Ferrarie," Josquin extracted the vowels and translated them into solmization syllables and pitches: *re-ut-re-ut-re-fa-mi-re* became the pitches *d-c-d-c-d-f-e-d:*

re ut re ut re fa mi re
Her- cu- les dux Fer-ra - ri - e

The motive thus created was treated as cantus firmus and was used in the superius as well as in the tenor. In Agnus Dei III, the number of vocal lines was increased from four to six; three pairs of voices present melodies in canon.

Josquin based two Masses on the *L'Homme armé* tune. In *Missa L'Homme armé super voces musicales* (Mass The soldier, on the musical syllables) he carried out a rational plan and achieved variety by schematic manipulation. The cantus firmus is presented successively on each pitch of the natural hexachord, commencing with c in the tenor of the Kyrie and ascending one pitch per movement until the Agnus Dei, where the borrowed melody is stated on g in Agnus Dei I and on a in Agnus Dei III. Despite the transposition, there is modal unity, for all movements end on d; in Agnus Dei III, the modal a concluding the transposed melody becomes the consonant fifth of the final d chord. In addition to straightforward presentation, the secular tune appears in retrograde, in diminution, in augmentation, and with all rests deleted (according to the directive *clama ne cesses,* cry aloud without stopping). When the cantus firmus is stated in small note values, it blends into the fabric. Sections of the Mass in which the cantus firmus does not appear were organized in other ways. In most sections of the Mass, the voice bearing the cantus firmus ends before the conclusion of the section—a procedure used by Ockeghem.

Missa L'Homme armé sexti toni (Mass The soldier, in sixth mode) was rationally planned and reflects Josquin's knowledge of compositional techniques used by Machaut, Du Fay, Ockeghem, and Obrecht. Sometimes the cantus firmus is treated as scaffolding; at other times it blends into the texture. Statement of the cantus firmus is not restricted to the tenor. The *Et resurrexit* section of the Credo is isorhythmic. In Agnus Dei III, the superius and contratenor altus voices, both *divisi,* sing a complex double canon. The movement concludes on a well-balanced F-f-a-c' chord.

Missa Pange lingua (Mass Sing, tongue) is based on the plainsong hymn of Fortunatus (see p. 91). The chant, slightly embellished, is woven into the contrapuntal fabric. For *Missa Fortuna desperata,* Josquin borrowed all three voices of the chanson *Fortuna desperata* and began his Mass as a parody of the chanson (ex. 10.6). Portions of the chanson are quoted in block elsewhere in the Mass, and each of the chanson voices served as cantus firmus in some Mass section. Josquin used parody technique to some extent in other Masses. He may have been the first composer to unify a Mass by means of parody; his *Missa Mater patris* seems to be the earliest Mass unified by parodying a motet.

Missa D'ung aultre amer (Mass To love another), based on the tenor of Ockeghem's chanson, is a *Missa brevis* (Short Mass). The Sanctus and Agnus Dei use the corresponding chants from Gregorian Mass XVIII. Josquin did not compose a Benedictus for *Missa D'ung aultre amer,* but he indicated that the *Prima Pars* of his motet *Tu solus qui facis mirabilia* (You alone who do miracles) was to substitute for the Benedictus of the Mass. (The *Secunda Pars* of that four-voice motet—the part not included in the substitution—quotes from both superius and tenor of Ockeghem's chanson.) Substitution of motets for sections of the Mass was common practice at Milan cathedral in the late fifteenth century.

EXAMPLE 10.6 (*a*) Opening of Busnois's chanson *Fortuna desperata* compared with opening of (*b*) Kyrie of Josquin's *Missa Fortuna desperata.*
(*Source:* Josquin Desprez: Werken, *edited by A. Smijers et al., 1921*)

(a)

(b)

MOTETS   Josquin's finest compositions are his motets. They are principally of two types: (1) four-voice settings of biblical texts, mainly psalms, and (2) large-scale five- or six-voice cantus firmus type compositions, usually based on melodies borrowed from chant. Many of the motets are Marian-related. In composing motets, he applied the same techniques used in Masses but used paraphrase and points of imitation more frequently.

Josquin seems to have been the first to compose motet-style psalm settings. The four-voice motet *Dominus regnavit* (The Lord reigneth; Ps. 92/KJV, 93) was freely composed. Paired voices were set antiphonally in keeping with the ancient manner of performing psalms; homorhythmic passages were used for emphasis.

Josquin's mastery of pervading imitation is apparent in his late motets. The polyphony is presented in a continuous flow in phrases structured as points of imitation, each point concluding with a clear cadence but the cadencing concealed by the overlapping of the points of imitation. The music is expressive of the text not only through Josquin's choices of melody and harmony but also through his manipulation of both to depict the meaning of the words. For example, a rising scale might be used for "ascend" and a descending scale for "descend"; as "heaven" is higher than "earth" and "hell" is still lower, so might their representative pitches be. Terms commonly used to indicate this kind of musical depiction are **word painting** and **text painting.** One aspect of text painting is *Augenmusik* (eye music), music in which the depiction is visible to the singers but not necessarily audible. Josquin's Lament on the death of Ockeghem is an extreme example of *Augenmusik*—the piece was written entirely in black notes.

Ave Maria . . . virgo serena (Hail, Mary . . . serene Virgin) exists in two settings: *Discantus secundus* and *tenor secundus* parts were inserted in the four-voice motet to form the six-voice version. The structure of the motet was designed to interpret and enhance the text being set. Basically, the music is in duple meter. In the four-voice version (DWMA57), the first four phrases are in points of imitation, with the first two points structured so the voices enter successively in canon at the octave or unison. The rhymed couplets of

the chant (a Sequence) that follows are also set imitatively as duets or trios interspersed with a point of imitation shared by all four voices. Triple rhythm is used for the two rhymed couplets forming the fourth strophe of the liturgical text, commencing with the words *Ave vera virginitas* (Hail, true virginity); all voices participate, the tenor entering one semibreve later than the others and in canon at the fifth below the superius, which creates some interesting syncopation. Duple meter resumes with the last notes of this strophe. After several points of imitation, all voices rest for the space of a full modern measure. Chordal declamation of the line *O Mater Dei, memento mei* (Oh, Mother of God, remember me) concludes with *Amen* sung as a sustained c-c′-g′-c″ chord. All the main cadences in this motet are on c.

The four-voice *Ave Maria, . . . benedicta tu* (Hail, Mary, . . . blessed art Thou) is based on the *Ave Maria* from a Gregorian votive Mass (*LU*, 1861). Josquin transposed the chant up a fourth, paraphrased it, and treated it imitatively much of the time. The cantus firmus permeates all voices of the motet. The last phrase is an Ockeghem-like drive to the cadence, filled with tritones and dotted rhythms and concluding on a g-g-d′-g′ chord. Though this work exhibits mature Renaissance style of motet composition, Josquin wrote an ornamented Landini cadence at the words *gratia plena* (full of grace), and he concluded the motet with a chord that lacks the third.

The lament of David for his son, Absalom, *Absalon fili mi* (Absalom, my son; II Sam. 18:33) may have been composed at the time of death of either the son of Pope Alexander VI (1497) or the son of Maximilian I (1506). The tessitura of the motet is low—the bass descends to B♭′ at the conclusion of the words *sed descendam in infernum plorans* (but weeping, descend into hell). In setting those words, Josquin wrote in all four voices melodies whose pitches spell out descending triads and also produce chord successions whose harmonies might be analyzed in modern terminology as harmonic progressions along the circle of fifths. The final chord is a hollow-sounding B♭′–B♭–f–b♭. (DWMA58).

Analysis of Josquin's works reveals that he applied the compositional techniques of all who preceded him—from anonymous thirteenth-century composers to Obrecht—as well as those used by his contemporaries. He dared to try new procedures and succeeded, and in several instances he charted paths other Renaissance composers would travel.

Josquin's Contemporaries

Perhaps the two most illustrious Franco-Netherlands contemporaries of Obrecht and Josquin were Heinrich Isaac and Pierre de La Rue.

Heinrich Isaac

In both quantity and quality, Isaac's music compares favorably with that of Josquin. Isaac's importance in music history is based equally on the uniformly high quality of his music and the fact that he was the first Franco-Netherlands master to disseminate that style in Germanic lands.

Isaac (c. 1450–1517) was born in Flanders; biographical data are not available concerning his activities prior to autumn 1484, when he visited Innsbruck. He was employed by Lorenzo de' Medici from 1485 to 1492; he set some of Lorenzo's carnival songs and his religious drama *San Giovanni e San Paolo* (St. John and St. Paul). During Savonarola's period of influence in Florence, Isaac had no court position but remained in Italy. In 1497 he became court composer to Emperor Maximilian I. The Church at Constance commissioned Isaac to compose some liturgical settings appropriate to their Use; in 1508–9 he wrote the cycles of Mass Propers that form the second volume of *Choralis constantinus*. Isaac spent most of his remaining years in Italy.

Three distinct compositional styles, and a mixture of those styles, are apparent in Isaac's works. His chansons, motets, and some of his Masses exhibit traditional Netherlands techniques; the *frottole* are Italian; and settings of Mass Propers, some of the Mass Ordinary cycles, and *Lieder* are German. When Isaac worked in Germanic lands, he adopted the performance practices and liturgical customs of the Germans; in Isaac's hands, technical elements of Franco-Netherlands style infiltrated Germanic forms. His secular pieces exhibit a variety of styles, from late Burgundian cantilena type to a kind of chanson approximating those by Josquin, with four almost-equal voices and some imitation.

Isaac composed approximately 40 settings of the Mass Ordinary, about half of which are Germanic and are based on appropriate liturgical chants; the others are in Netherlands style and use as cantus firmi nonrelated chants or secular melodies. Some of the Germanic Masses are **alternatim** settings based on chant Ordinaries; *alternatim* settings have polyphonic sections interspersed with sections in chant or with sections to be performed on organ. Most of the Masses are for four voices; some of the Germanic settings are five- or six-voice. The Mass cycles were unified by various traditional means.

In the late fifteenth and early sixteenth centuries, it was customary in Germanic lands to sing composed polyphonic settings of Propers in the service. Isaac composed approximately 100 cycles of Mass Propers; he is credited with writing the first polyphonic settings of Propers for the entire church year that can be attributed to a single composer. Of the three volumes of liturgical music entitled *Choralis constantinus*, only volume 2 was composed for Constance; the other two volumes were for the Habsburg Hofkapelle. All volumes were published posthumously; the third, unfinished at the time of Isaac's death, was completed by his pupil, Ludwig Senfl. In addition, Isaac wrote more than 50 motets that are unrelated to his Ordinary or Proper settings. At that time, many Germanic Mass settings contained no polyphonic Credo. Isaac composed 13 independent Credos suitable for insertion in that kind of Mass.

Isaac made significant contributions to the German Tenorlied. In his songs, the principal melody lies in the tenor, but the superius melody is only slightly less significant. The tenor and superius lines of *Isbruck, ich muss dich lassen* (Innsbruck, I must leave thee) are both so melodious that for some time there was a dispute about which voice bore the main melody. This song became the *contrafactum O welt, ich muss dich lassen* (O world, I must leave thee); Isaac's melody, harmonized by J. S. Bach, appears in several twentieth-century hymnals. Isaac handled canon capably and frequently combined two canonic voices with two imitative voices. This may be seen in *Zwischen Perg und tieffem Tal* (Between mountain and deep valley; DWMA59).

PIERRE DE LA RUE

Little information is available concerning the life of Flemish composer Pierre de La Rue (c. 1460–1518). His extant works include approximately 30 complete Masses, 2 Kyries, 5 Credos, about 30 motets, around 30 chansons, a cycle of Magnificats, and Lamentations of Jeremiah. The numerous two- and three-voice Lutheran motets attributed to La Rue are *contrafacta;* they are sections of his Masses supplied with new texts.

La Rue wrote canon and pervading imitation skillfully and used a variety of techniques to unify Masses. He preferred chants as cantus firmi for Masses and motets, liked to write passages for pairs of voices, and had a predilection for canon. Several of his Masses are completely canonic. La Rue used parody technique infrequently. *Missa Ave sanctissima Maria* (Mass Hail, most holy Mary) is a parody Mass based on a three-voice motet with the same title; in the Mass, three polyphonic lines yield six voice parts, through canon at the fourth above. The melodic flow of La Rue's polyphonic lines is in no way impeded by the rigidity of canonic technique. Some of his chansons are typically Burgundian in style—treble dominated, with only the superius texted, and using one of the *formes fixes.* In other chansons, the polyphonic lines are more nearly equal, with some imitation and with passages for paired voices. In this type of chanson and in some of the motets, La Rue's writing displays some similarity to Josquin's style.

JEAN MOUTON

Another excellent composer was Jean Mouton (c. 1459–1522). His compositions include 15 Masses, about 20 chansons, and more than 100 motets. In his Masses may be seen clearly the transition from cantus firmus technique to paraphrase and parody. Paraphrase is the free elaboration of an existing melody, with original and added notes subtly blended to form a seemingly new melody. **Parody** involves borrowing all lines of another polyphonic composition and supplementing and modifying them to create a new work. During the sixteenth century, parody supplanted the use of a single borrowed melody as cantus firmus and became the favored technique for Mass composition. Mouton is best known historically as the teacher of Adrian Willaert (see p. 167).

THE NEXT GENERATION OF FRANCO-NETHERLANDS COMPOSERS

The three most important Franco-Netherlands composers in the generation after Josquin were Nicolas Gombert, Jacob Clement, and Adrian Willaert.

JACOB CLEMENT

Jacob Clement (c. 1515–c. 1556) was known after 1545 as Clement non Papa, perhaps for clear identification from Netherlands composer Jacob Papa. Clement was a prolific composer; it is believed his surviving works were created within about 12 years. His sacred works include 14 Masses, a four-voice Requiem, 2 four-voice Magnificat cycles, 230 motets, and 159 *Souterliedekens* (little Psalter songs) and *Lofzangen* (praise songs). His surviving secular compositions comprise 79 chansons, 8 Dutch songs, 2 instrumental arrangements of chansons, 8 textless pieces, and 3 secular motets. Most of the secular pieces are four-voice.

Clement's polyphony is, for the most part, note-against-note, with texts set syllabically. Sometimes he wrote short melismas on the penultimate or antepenultimate syllable of a phrase (e.g., *Vox in Rama audita est* [A voice was heard in Rama]). His melodies were skillfully shaped, with careful attention to phrasing; canon was used sparingly but imitation persistently. The notation contains very few chromatic alterations. Musicologist Edward Lowinsky (1908–85) advanced the controversial theory that in their motets Netherlands composers relied on a "secret chromatic art" whereby numerous requisite unnotated chromatic alterations were supplied in performance through application of *musica ficta.* The theory is complicated but, in short, amounts to this: When a singer chromatically altered a pitch to avoid a tritone, the alteration created another tritone that required alteration, which in its turn created another; this kind of chain reaction filled a motet with unnotated chromaticisms (ex. 10.7).

The *Souterliedekens* and *Lofzangen* were printed by T. Susato in 1556–57 in four volumes, each comprising three partbooks: superius, tenor, and bassus. These were the first polyphonic settings of the 150 psalms in the Dutch language. The metrical texts, prepared by Willem van Zuylen van Nijevelt, were first published in Antwerp in 1540 and were set monophonically to melodies borrowed from popular songs. Clement, assisted by Susato, made simple three-voice polyphonic settings of those melodies, with the borrowed tune placed in either the tenor or superius. (Susato's settings are clearly identified.) Each voice is supplied with text, set syllabically. The *Souterliedekens* are strophic and predominantly homorhythmic; they were intended for use in home devotions.

NICOLAS GOMBERT

Nicolas Gombert (c. 1495–c. 1560) may have been a pupil of Josquin; he knew Josquin and lamented his death in the motet *Musae Jovis* (Muses of Jove). Surviving music by Gombert includes 11 Masses, a Magnificat cycle, more than 160 motets, and over 70 chansons. His compositional style is seen at its best in his motets, about 40 of which are Marian-related. The motets are for four, five, or six voices that are generally equal in importance, although at cadences the bass assumes a harmonic function. When writing for five or six voices, Gombert favored low tessitura. He consistently used pervading points of imitation; thus, clear phrase divisions and simultaneous cadencing were avoided. Frequently, final cadences are characterized by plagal extensions and pedal notes in the superius. Usually, dissonances were carefully prepared and resolved. At times, however, the polyphony seems to require the application of *musica ficta* to the extent that true modality is strained. One of Gombert's best-known motets is *Super flumina Babilonis* (By the waters of Babylon; DWMA60).

Most of Gombert's chansons are similar in texture and style to Netherlands motets but are more animated. Some chansons are lighter in texture, with syllabic text settings and marked rhythm. Gombert seldom used text painting; however, he composed two very descriptive chansons: *Resveillez vous* (Awaken), containing many bird calls, and *Or escoutez* (Now listen), which depicts the chase of a hare. Chansons of this type, filled with text painting, often are called *program chansons* though they are not true program music.

Many of Gombert's compositions served as the basis for instrumental works by other composers. His consistent use of pervading points of imitation was thus transferred to instrumental composition and became a factor in the evolution of the **ricercar** and basically

EXAMPLE 10.7 Measures 56 to 63 of Clement's motet *Vox in Rama* showing how the "secret chromatic art" could create a chain of tritones requiring chromatic alteration through application of *musica ficta* in performance.

imitative instrumental forms. (A *ricercar* is the instrumental counterpart of the motet.)

ADRIAN WILLAERT

Adrian Willaert (c. 1490–1562) was the first major Netherlands composer to obtain a permanent position in Venice. Willaert was influential in the formation of the "Venetian school" of composers and a major figure in the development of polyphonic music in Italy. He was studying law in Paris when he decided on a career in music and became a pupil of Jean Mouton. In 1515, Willaert entered the service of Ippolito I d'Este at Ferrara as singer. After Ippolito's death, Alfonso d'Este became Willaert's patron. In December 1527, Willaert was appointed *maestro da cappella* at the church of San Marco (St. Mark's), Venice, a position he held until his death.

Under Willaert's leadership, St. Mark's became the most prestigious chapel in Europe, and Venice became an important center for music. He maintained high standards, set texts according to correct declamation,

Adrian Willaert. *(Woodcut from his* Musica nova, *1559)*

FIGURE 10.7 Plan of St. Mark's, Venice. The original structure (outlined in solid black), dating from the eleventh century, reflects Byzantine architecture—the Greek cross with central dome and four domed bays. later additions (outlined in shaded grey) are Romanesque and Gothic.

and insisted that printers underlay texts accurately. Willaert was one of the most important composers and teachers in the sixteenth century. Among his pupils were Cipriano de Rore, Nicolo Vicentino, Andrea Gabrieli, and Gioseffo Zarlino.

St. Mark's had two fine organs, and excellent composers were employed as organists. The acoustical and physical properties of St. Mark's, which was structured with two opposing choir lofts and with many alcoves and balconies, were conducive to ***cori spezzati*** ("broken" or divided choirs)—small choral ensembles spatially separated for antiphonal singing and physically positioned for special effects (fig. 10.7). Later in the century, these features were used to full advantage by Giovanni Gabrieli. Antiphonal choral singing of polyphony had been done in Italy for at least a century. The polyphonic settings of hymns and psalms that Willaert composed for use at important liturgical festivals included ***salmi spezzati,*** settings of psalm verses for antiphonal singing by a divided choir; psalm verses with their responses; and

psalm verses without responses. In the *salmi spezzati*, two four-voice choirs sang alternate verses of psalms, then sang the concluding doxology together in eight-voice polyphony.

Willaert composed Masses, motets, Magnificats, hymns, settings of psalms, chansons, madrigals, other Italian secular vocal pieces, and three-voice *ricercars*. His sacred music—the major portion of his writing— was published in collections devoted solely to his works; most of his secular pieces appeared in anthologies with works by other composers. Three collections of motets were published in 1539; these are among the earliest published collections of motets by a single composer.

The 173 motets are some of Willaert's finest works. In them, the polyphony is designed to accommodate and complement the text in every respect. Textual phrases determine musical ones; rests do not interrupt words, phrases, or thoughts; and the rhythm enhances the correct Latin accentuation. Willaert skillfully evaded frequent complete cadences; often he wrote vocal lines as if leading into a complete cadence, then by a turn of phrase continued the polyphony. Complete cadences were deferred until the conclusion of a section.

Five of the motets are for seven voices, 38 for six, 51 for five, 78 for four, and 1 for three. The four-voice motets set a variety of Latin texts; a few are secular, and the sacred ones are both liturgical and quasi-liturgical. One of Willaert's important secular motets is Queen Dido's lament, *Dulces exuviae* (Sweet mementos), from Vergil's *Aeneid*.

Most of the five-voice motets were written for special occasions or to honor patrons. This type of motet is frequently bitextual; Willaert selected an appropriate cantus firmus and usually retained its text in one voice. Many of the six-voice motets are purely contrapuntal (without cantus firmus). In *Victimae paschali laudes* (DWMA61), the cantus firmus is shared by Sextus and Quintus voices. Triads are an important feature of the harmony, and the major third is included in the final chord.

Musica nova (New music; publ. 1559), a collection of four- to seven-voice motets and serious madrigals, is one of the few sixteenth-century publications to contain both sacred and secular works. The volume contains 25 secular Italian pieces, most of them settings of Petrarch's sonnets, and 33 large motets. *Musica nova* is especially significant because Willaert's sonnet settings, as madrigal cycle, are among the earliest large-scale vocal compositions.

Willaert is counted among the first generation of madrigal composers and was closely associated with Verdelot, who was one of the originators of the madrigal. (Madrigals are discussed on p. 175.) A number of Willaert's Italian secular songs are **villanesche,** light, pastoral, strophic songs with refrain. Willaert's chansons were relatively unknown in France but circulated widely in Italy. Many of them were written for the Ferrara court.

Spain and Spanish America

From time to time, Ockeghem and other Franco-Netherlands composers visited the Iberian peninsula, and Franco-Netherlands polyphony was known there. Spain became politically linked with the House of Habsburg when Philip the Handsome, son of Marie of Burgundy and Maximilian, married Juana la Loca, daughter of Isabella and Ferdinand of Spain. Chapels of Spanish Habsburg rulers were led or influenced by Netherlanders until well into the seventeenth century, and throughout the sixteenth century Spain's musical achievement increased. It is not surprising to find that works of Spanish composers were sometimes thought to be by Josquin. The years 1559–1659 are regarded by the Spanish as the *siglo de oro* (the golden century) of Spanish literature, art, and music. During the first half of that golden century, Spain was the political leader of Europe.

Pedro de Escobar (c. 1465–c. 1536), a Portuguese composer and singer, was for several years *maestro de capilla* of Seville Cathedral. His Masses and motets indicate that he was a skilled contrapuntist.

Francisco de Peñalosa (c. 1470–1528) was regarded as the finest Spanish composer of his time. The fact that his motet *Sancta Mater, istud agas* (vs. 11 of *Stabat Mater*) was attributed to Josquin attests his contrapuntal skill and describes his compositional style. Peñalosa's surviving sacred works comprise 7 Masses, 10 motets, 4 hymns, several Magnificat settings, and 10 secular pieces.

Cristóbal de Morales (c. 1500–53) was the first major Spanish composer of early sixteenth-century sacred music. He knew and possibly studied with Escobar and Peñalosa at Seville Cathedral. Morales served as *maestro de capilla* at Avila Cathedral (1526–28), worked at Plasencia Cathedral (1529–30), then moved to Italy, where, from 1535 to 1545, he sang baritone in the papal choir. Then he returned to Spain, where he worked as *maestro de capilla:* at Toledo Cathedral (1545–47), at Marchena for the Duke of Alva (1548–51), and at Málaga Cathedral (1551–53). The sacred music composed for performance at these Spanish churches appears to be *a cappella;* however, at Toledo Cathedral two organs were used at most services.

Only 5 of Morales's surviving works are secular. Extant are more than 20 Masses, 2 Requiem Masses, 2 Magnificat cycles, over 100 motets, and several Lamentations settings. Morales's style is comparable with that of Josquin and Willaert and evidences a firm foundation in Franco-Netherlands techniques. Morales set texts expressively with due regard for correct

Music Printing (II)

By 1498 Ottaviano dei Petrucci (1466–1539) had devised a workable method of printing polyphonic music from movable metal type. (See p. 147). He obtained from the Venetian government the exclusive privilege of printing lute and organ tablatures and polyphonic music in Venice for a period of 20 years. No other printer published music in Venetian territory until 1520.

The first book of music Petrucci printed under that privilege was issued in May 1501. Although it was entitled *Harmonice musices odhecaton A* (One hundred polyphonic songs, [vol.] A), the volume contained 96 three- and four-voice secular songs by well-known composers (fig. 10.4). *Canti B* (1501) and *Canti C* (1503)

continued the series. Petrucci printed by a triple-impression process: the staff lines first, then the notation symbols, and finally any words. The compositions in *Odhecaton* and its sequels were supplied with text incipits only. All volumes of music issued by Petrucci had oblong shape: □ . His first three publications (*Odhecaton A*, *Canti B*, and *Motetti A*) were in choirbook format; commencing with *Josquin Desprez: Misse* (1502), part-book format was used for volumes of Masses and motets (fig. 10.5).

Petrucci was the first to print tablatures of any kind. In 1507, he issued a book of lute tablatures by Francesco Spinacino. Between 1501 and 1509, Petrucci printed the 3 *Odhecaton* books, 5 books of *Motetti*, 16

volumes of Masses, 6 lutebooks, and 11 collections of frottolas. Early in 1511, Petrucci left his Venetian business in charge of a partner and returned to Fossombrone, where he printed Masses, motets, and secular songs until c. 1521.

The 61 editions of music issued by Petrucci were carefully prepared and clearly printed. His publications form the most important body of printed music issued during the first 20 years of the sixteenth century. More important, his development of a successful method of printing polyphonic music from movable metal type by multiple impression was a vital factor in the dissemination of polyphonic music during the early sixteenth century.

---

declamation. His motets were usually based on fragments of liturgical melodies; frequently, a chant fragment was used as ostinato in one voice of a motet. Important words of a text were set homorhythmically, sometimes in longer note values, for emphasis. Many of Morales's motets are bitextual, with one voice having a text different from that set for the other voices. An example of this is *Emendemus in melius* (Let us make amends), in which the middle voice (of five) sings *Memento, homo, quia pulvis es* (Remember, man, that you are dust; Gen. 3:19; DWMA62). Compositional techniques used in the Masses include cantus firmus (*Missa L'Homme armé*), canon (*Missa Caça*), ostinato, paraphrase, and parody. Six Masses are based on motets or chansons by Josquin, Févin, Gombert, Mouton, Richefort, and Verdelot; several Masses are Marian-related.

Morales was accorded international reputation. For almost a century after his death, his works were cited as models in theoretical treatises. He composed two books of Masses especially for the papal choir to which he belonged; they were published in Rome in 1544. In the same year, a manuscript copy of *Missarum liber*

primus (First book of Masses) arrived at Puebla Cathedral in Mexico, and in 1553 a printed copy of that book was in use at Cuzco Cathedral in Peru. Morales's music was performed at the memorial services for Charles V that were held at Mexico City Cathedral in 1559. Ecclesiastical appointments to Spanish and Portuguese cathedrals and missions in the New World were the province of the crown, and appointees enjoyed royal patronage. Cathedrals at Mexico City, Puebla, Cuzco, and other principal settlements were modeled after those in Europe. In 1553, Cuzco Cathedral had two organs situated at opposite sides of the choir. Iberian musicians were appointed to the positions of chapelmaster and organist(s) in these cathedrals; through these musicians, European sacred polyphony quickly found its way to the New World.

SUMMARY

The reliance on ancient Greek and Roman models that characterized literature and the visual arts during the Renaissance was not a prime factor in Renaissance musical developments; no examples of ancient Greek and

Roman music were discovered until after 1560. However, theoretical and philosophical treatises on ancient Greek music were available in western Europe c. 1500. The rise of printed music began c. 1500, when Petrucci adapted Gutenberg's method of printing from movable metal type to the printing of polyphonic music.

In the early Renaissance, Ockeghem, Obrecht, Isaac, and Josquin were the acknowledged masters of the Franco-Netherlands polyphonic style that prevailed internationally. Isaac helped diffuse that style in Germanic lands; it was the foundation of the music of Peñalosa and Morales in Spain, and Iberian musicians transmitted it to Central and South America. The most prestigious positions in European secular and ecclesiastical courts were awarded to Netherlanders until after c. 1555; then the Venetian school, led by Willaert, began its rise to prominence.

Masses, motets, and chansons were the principal types of compositions. Composers demonstrated their capabilities by writing Mass cycles, but motet texts offered greater opportunity for experimentation and attracted interest increasingly; by the beginning of the sixteenth century the motet was the favored form of sacred music. Both sacred and secular works provided source material for Masses. A melody chosen for use as cantus firmus might be set in the tenor or be migrant; often, borrowed material was embellished and paraphrased. Occasionally, a Mass parodied a chanson. Parody and paraphrase became the leading kinds of Masses written in the sixteenth century. Masses were unified by abstract ideas, numerological symbolism, canon, and other technical devices. Canon, preferred by Ockeghem,

was gradually superseded (but never eradicated) by less rigid imitation; early in the sixteenth century points of imitation began to pervade the musical fabric.

Contrast was achieved within a composition by voice pairings, by setting some phrases homorhythmically, or by writing some sections of a Mass movement as duos or trios. In sacred music, four-voice writing was common, five voices were used frequently, and compositions for six or more voices were written occasionally. All vocal lines were equivalent, or nearly so. Vocal range was expanded downward considerably, producing a true bass sound, but was extended upward only slightly; by c. 1500, the range extended from B♭' to g''.

Much of the secular music was three-voice, treble-dominated polyphony, performed by a soloist with instrumental accompaniment. By the beginning of the sixteenth century, four-voice chansons were being written, with vocal equivalency strengthened by the incorporation of imitative counterpoint.

A drive to the final cadence is an important feature of Masses and motets. Though Renaissance music is modal, the last chord successions of many compositions approximate the dominant-to-tonic progressions of key tonality. Obrecht's frequent use of Aeolian mode and careful attention to modal chord successions often created harmonies closely akin to those of key tonality, especially at final cadences, where chromatic alterations made through application of *musica ficta* produced a leading tone or a Picardian chord. Recodification of the modal system to include Aeolian and Ionian and their plagal counterparts signaled the approach of key tonality.

THE RISE OF REGIONAL STYLES

Franco-Netherlands counterpoint was an international musical language during the fifteenth and sixteenth centuries. Composers from the Franco-Netherlands worked in churches and courts throughout Europe. Yet in every region there was some vernacular vocal music with regional characteristics. During the sixteenth century regional styles achieved greater prominence. The styles were national in the sense that each was representative of a people with common culture and language, but they were not national in the sense that each represented a people united under a single government; for example, the regions now known as Italy and Germany did not become unified nations until 1871.

ITALY

LAUDA

Monophonic *laude* were sung throughout the fifteenth century; polyphonic *laude* were composed also. From c. 1480 to 1530, laude were very popular, especially in Florence; they form the largest body of Italian sacred music written c. 1500. These nonliturgical hymns of praise and devotion were intended for performance by laypersons and by semiprofessional companies of *lauda* singers who met regularly for devotions, especially for singing praises to the Virgin Mary. In some Italian churches and cathedrals, professional members of the choir were instructed to sing laude in certain chapels at specific times. Laude were sung by monks and nuns in monasteries and convents and were included in some religious plays. Savonarola, who condemned all polyphonic music except laude, wrote some laude texts.

Most polyphonic laude are two- or three-voice pieces; a few four-voice laude survive. The vast majority of laude have Italian texts, but a few are in Latin. The text is usually underlaid for the main melody only, which is in the top voice. For the most part, settings are simple, syllabic, and basically homorhythmic. The bass line may have been performed instrumentally. Each poetic line is given its own melodic phrase, and all voices begin and conclude phrases together.

Petrucci published two books of laude (1507, 1508). *Laude, libro primo* consists entirely of pieces by Innocentius Dammonis. *Laude, libro secondo* contains works by Cara, Tromboncino, Josquin, and others who composed *frottole* also.

After the Council of Trent, there was a surge of laude production. Among principal contributors to laude repertory in the last half of the sixteenth century were

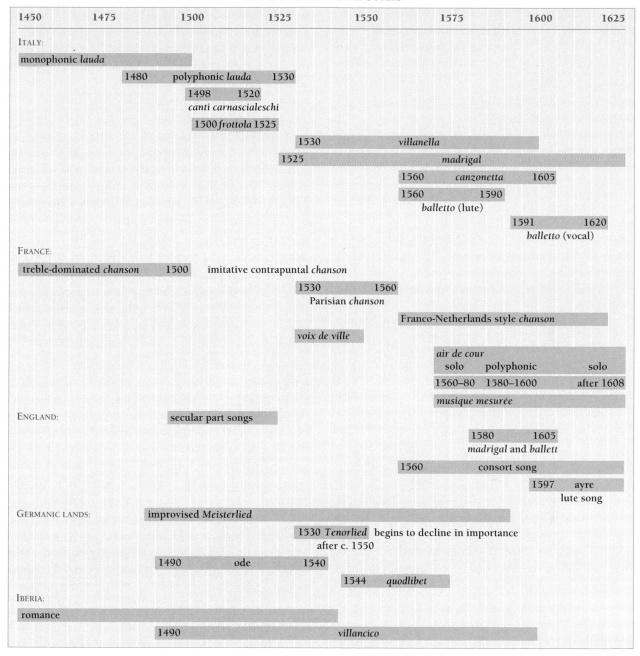

Giovanni Razzi (1531–1611), who assembled six collections of them, and Giovanni Animuccia (c. 1500–71), whose 12 books of laude were written primarily for Filippo Neri's Congregazione dell'Oratorio in Rome (see p. 261).

CANTI CARNASCIALESCHI

Canti carnascialeschi (carnival songs) are uniquely Florentine. During the late fifteenth and early sixteenth centuries festivals were held in Florence in conjunction with the pre-Lenten Carnival and Calendimaggio (a celebration of spring observed from May 1 to June 24). A feature of these festivals was the singing of several kinds of Italian part songs, known generically as *canti carnascialeschi*. *Mascherate* (masquerades) were performed by groups of masked men and boys on foot; *trionfi* (triumph songs) were performed by costumed singers on carts. Song texts were written by both aristocrats and commoners and were set to music by well-known composers such as Alexander Agricola and Isaac. Carnival songs reached a high level of artistic quality during the time of Lorenzo de' Medici, who wrote some texts. More than 300 texts and approximately 70 complete settings of carnival songs survive. Most of the songs are strophic with a refrain, similar in formal structure to the *ballata*. Musically, the songs are three- or four-part homorhythmic settings, usually in duple meter, with concern for correct declamation. Harmonic progressions are apparent. In many of the songs, each line of a strophe's text has a new musical phrase; each musical phrase has a clearly defined cadence, often on tonic or dominant. Presumably, the songs were performed with instrumental accompaniment, but only one manuscript specifies a lute. While Savonarola held sway (1494–97), all secular aspects of festivals were supplanted by religious processions, and laude replaced *canti carnascialeschi*. The collections of laude compiled by Razzi are important in the history of *canti carnascialeschi* for they preserve settings that might otherwise have been lost (e.g., Lorenzo de' Medici's *Trionfo di Bacco e d'Arianna* [Triumph of Bacchus and Ariadne]). After Savonarola's death, secularity again colored the festivals; carnival songs flourished between 1498 and 1520. Thereafter, carnival songs merged with other types of Italian secular music; for example, the *mascherata* became a type of *villanella* (p. 175).

FROTTOLA

In 1504 Petrucci printed a book of Italian secular songs entitled *Frottole* (Frottolas). Additional volumes ensued, and by 1514 he had issued 11 collections of them. Between 1510 and 1531, other Italian printers issued 15 collections of *frottole*.

The word **frottola** is a generic term covering various types of Italian secular song current in the late fifteenth and early sixteenth centuries. *Frottola* is used also to denote a specific type of Italian secular song, the *barzelletta*, sometimes called the "frottola proper." In general, frottole are three- or four-part polyphonic songs that are predominantly homorhythmic, with simple harmonies and the main melody in the top voice. Duple meter prevails. In four-voice frottole, usually all members of a triad are present in a chord; frequently the tenor sings in thirds with the superius. Movement in the bass line is principally by the interval of a fourth or a fifth, and at times a succession of modal harmonies approximates chord progressions of key tonality. For the most part, the text is set syllabically, each poetic line having its own melodic phrase. Frottole seem to fall into two compositional types: those in which all voices begin and conclude all phrases together, and those in which one voice enters one note later than the other voices but all voices conclude the phrase together (ex. 11.1). Settings are strophic or strophic with a refrain, those with refrain bearing formal resemblance to the fourteenth-century *ballata*. In many publications all voices have text for the refrain but only the top voice is supplied with text for the verse(s), which implies that a soloist sang the verses to lute (or possibly harpsichord) accompaniment, and other vocalists joined in the refrain.

(a)   (b)

EXAMPLE 11.1 Examples of *frottole* in which (*a*) all voices start together and (*b*) one voice enters later than the others. *(Source: Ottaviano Petrucci, Frottole, libro primo, edited by Rudolf Schwartz, Georg Olms, Hildesheim, and Breitkopf & Härtel Wiesbaden, 1967)*

PLATE 20 Henri Fuseli. *The Nightmare*, c. 1791, oil on canvas, 30¼" × 25". *(Goethe Museum, Frankfurt-am-Main)*

PLATE 19 Two pages of J. S. Bach's manuscript of *The Passion according to St. Matthew.* Bach wrote Scripture passages in red ink. The "Choral" is the Passion Choral as presented in No. 72 of Bach's *Passion*; it is followed by the recitative "*And siehe da, der Vorhang*" and the chorus "*Wahrlich.*" (See DWMA115.) Note Bach's use of C clef. *(MS P 25, Deutsche Staatsbibliothek, Berlin)*

PLATE 18 The Master of Female Half-Lengths. *Three Musicians*, also known as *The Concert*. The trio of voice, lute, and transverse unkeyed flute are performing Sermisy's chanson *Joyssance vous donneray* from partbooks. *(The Harrach Collection, Schloss Rohrau, Vienna)*

PLATE 17 Raphael Sanzio. *The School of Athens*, 1509–11, fresco, approx. 26′ × 18′. In Stanza della Segnatura, Vatican Palace, Rome. (© *Scala Art Resource*)

PLATE 16 Kyrie of Ockeghem's *Missa Ecce ancilla Domini.* (*MS Chigi C.VIII.234, folios 19v–20r, Biblioteca Apostolica Vaticana, Rome*)

PLATE 15 The chanson *Comme ung homme desconforte*. The heart-shaped *Chansonnier Cordiforme* manuscript is bound in red velvet covers. *(MS Rothschild 2973, folios 19v–20r, Bibliothèque nationale, Paris)*

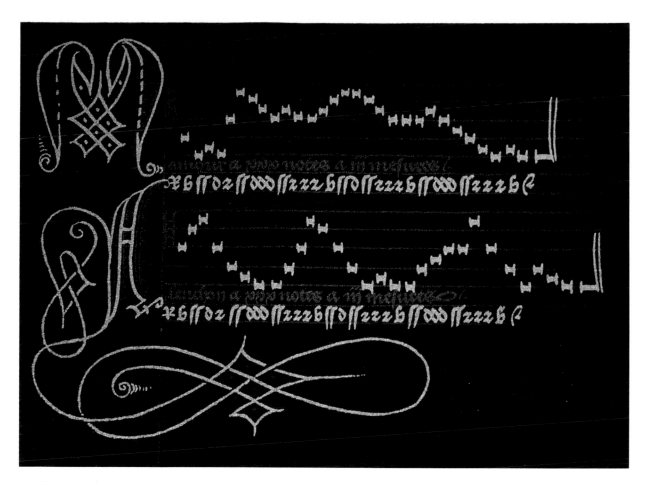

PLATE 14 Two *basse danses*, notated in gold and silver on black page. (MS 9085, Bibliothèque de Bourgogne, Brussels)

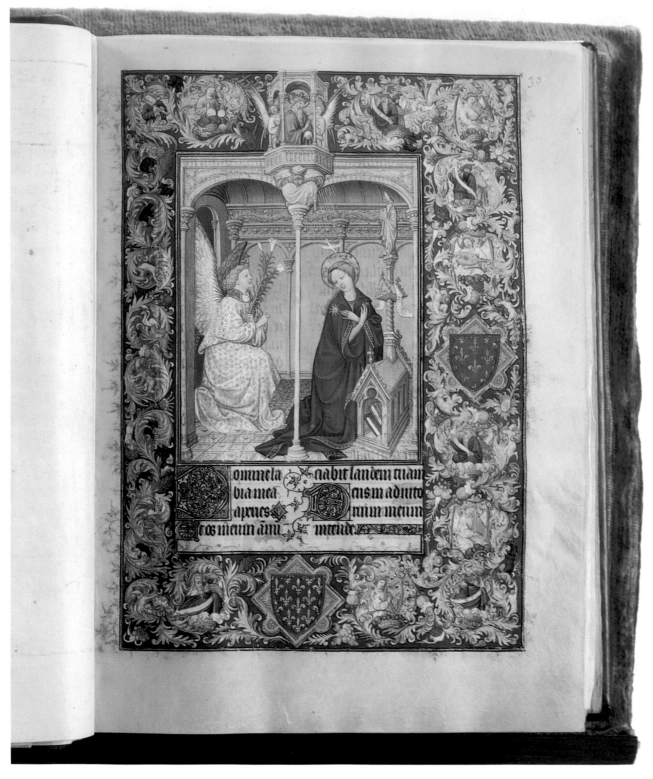

PLATE 13 Pol de Limbourg. Miniature depicting *The Annunciation*, folio 30r, *The Belles Heures of Jean, Duke of Berry*. Tempera and gold leaf on parchment. This full–page miniature is 5⅜″ × 8″ in size, on a folio 6⅛″ × 9⅜″. *(Original manuscript in The Cloisters Collection 1954. Metropolitan Museum of Art, New York)*

The frottola is rooted in the custom of reciting poetry to musical accompaniment, a practice that was widespread during the fifteenth century. The courts of the Este family provided fertile ground for the frottola; it flourished at Ferrara, Urbino, and especially at Mantua, where Isabella d'Este (1474–1539) and her husband, Francesco Gonzaga, maintained an especially fine musical establishment. Isabella had studied music; she was an accomplished performer on several instruments and understood the technical aspects of musical composition. Two of the leading composers of frottole were at Mantua: Marchetto Cara (c. 1470–c. 1525) and Bartolomeo Tromboncino (c. 1470–c. 1535). Both gentlemen were from Verona. Cara was *maestro di cappella* at Mantua in 1511–25. He composed music for more than 100 frottole in addition to setting odes, sonnets, and other types of Italian poetry. A characteristic of his frottole is subtle variation of the repetition scheme within the stereotyped *ballata* pattern (DWMA63).

Tromboncino's name appears in documents of the Gonzaga court from 1494 to 1501. In February 1502, he sang at the wedding of Lucrezia Borgia and Alfonso d'Este at Ferrara and served at their court from 1502 to 1513. He petitioned for repatriation as a Venetian citizen in 1521 and can be traced in that republic until his death. Tromboncino was one of the most prolific of the early frottolists. His known works include a cycle of Lamentations, the motet *Benedictus Dominus Deus,* 17 laude, and 168 frottole. He is especially important for his choice of more serious and better quality poetry early in the century, when most composers of frottole were setting mediocre or trivial verses. Many of the texts have been identified as the work of "classical" and Renaissance poets—Petrarch, Castiglione, and others. For his settings, Tromboncino preferred nonimitative polyphony rather than the usual simple homorhythmic style used by many of his contemporaries.

The frottola spread throughout Italy from north to south, eventually reaching Naples, and is historically significant in three respects: (1) Its chordal style and simple harmonies probably had some bearing on the homorhythmic counterpoint written by contemporary Franco-Netherlands composers working in Italy. (2) The frottola setting more serious poetry, especially the type that Petrarch termed *canzona,* was forerunner of the madrigal. (3) In Naples the lighter variety of frottola influenced the development of the *villanella,* which flourished from the 1530s to the early seventeenth century.

VILLANELLA

Villanella is a generic term used to denote a type of light music, often witty and sophisticated, designed for aristocratic audiences. Many *villanelle* satirize peasant life or the madrigal. Features of the villanella are simple chordal texture, melody in the top voice, and regular rhythms with some syncopation. Subtypes of villanella are differentiated by dialect, type of text, or social function. The *mascherata* was used for masked entertainments and carnival activities, *moresca* texts concern Moors; and the *giustiniana* usually relate amorous fantasies of old men. A harmonic device frequently appearing in villanelle is a chord stream of triads containing a series of parallel fifths—progressions forbidden by contrapuntal (and harmonic) rules.

MADRIGAL

The madrigal became the most significant type of Italian secular song during the Renaissance. Around 1530 the word **madrigal** was used generically in Italy to denote musical setting of various types of Italian verse—sonnets, *canzoni, ballate,* and others, one of which was called *madrigale.* Actually, the poetic *madrigale* is a single-stanza *canzone.* The sixteenth- and fourteenth-century (see p. 118) madrigals have only the name in common. The fourteenth-century madrigal is strophic with a **ritornello** (refrain). The sixteenth-century madrigal comprises a single stanza with a varying number of 7- and 11-syllable lines in a free rhyme scheme. The number of lines in a madrigal varies from 6 to 16; most madrigals contain 10. The sixteenth-century madrigal has no refrain, but often the last line is repeated. Some madrigals are moralistic (e.g., Arcadelt's four-voice *Il bianco e dolce cigno* [The white and gentle swan]).

Musically, the **sixteenth-century madrigal** is a through-composed setting of a one-stanza poem or a single stanza from a multistanza poem treated phrase by phrase. The music is usually quasi-sectional, constructed as a series of overlapping or interlocking phrases, some in imitative counterpoint, some in familiar style. In this respect, a madrigal setting resembles that of a motet or the *canzona*-type frottola. However, in performance the three varieties of vocal music differ: the frottola is soloist music, presumably instrumentally accompanied; the motet is polyphonic choral music; and the madrigal is ensemble polyphony for from 3 to 12 voices, one person per part (vocal chamber music).

The musical setting of a madrigal was designed to enhance the poetry. Composers of early madrigals seemed content to express the mood of a poem or to convey the meaning of its most significant lines. As the madrigal developed, considerable word painting was used. Sometimes composers included depictions for the visual enjoyment of the performers (e.g., black notation to portray blindness, darkness, death, sorrow, or moonless night).

Madrigal development can be viewed in three phases: (1) early madrigals, written c. 1525–c. 1545; (2) mature, or "classical," madrigals, composed c. 1545–80; and (3) late madrigals, produced c. 1580–1620.

EARLY MADRIGALS   Centers of early madrigal production were Rome and Florence. Some madrigals by Bernardo Pisano (1490–1548) are in a collection of his *canzoni* issued by Petrucci in 1520. Philippe Verdelot (c. 1475–c. 1535), a Franco-Netherlander working in Florence and Rome in the 1520s, was another pioneer madrigal composer; two publications issued in Rome c. 1526 contain individual madrigals by him. However, the first collection of pieces published as madrigals is *Madrigali de diversi musici: libro primo* (Madrigals by various composers: book I; 1530). The collection contains eight madrigals by Verdelot, two by Costanzo Festa, two by Sebastiano Festa, one by Maistre Jhan of Ferrara, some light Italian songs, and some chansons.

Verdelot, Costanzo Festa (c. 1480–1545), and Jacob Arcadelt (c. 1505–68) were the leading early composers of madrigals. Pisano may have influenced all of them, for he worked with each of them at some time. Two books of Verdelot's four-voice madrigals were published c. 1533; *Madrigali a cinque voci, libro primo* (5 vc.) appeared in 1535.

In the early madrigals, which are for three or four voices, some imitation is present, but the music is predominantly chordal, with clear cadences separating poetic phrases; expression is rather subdued. Frequent skips of a fourth or a fifth in the bass line create an interesting mixture of modality and key tonality. Festa's *Quando ritrova la mia pastorella* (When I find my shepherdess; DWMA64) is an example.

In the 1540s madrigals became quite popular; almost all composers working in Italy wrote some. They were sung regularly at court and were commissioned by aristocrats for special celebrations, by noblemen to honor their ladies, and by literary academies for their own entertainment. Sometimes madrigals served as incidental music or *intermedi* for plays.

More than 200 of Arcadelt's madrigals survive, most of them published in 1539–44. They contain a considerable amount of imitative counterpoint, with declamatory chordal writing reserved for important phrases. This may be seen in *Quando col dolce suono* (When with sweet sound).

CLASSICAL MADRIGALS   In the 1540s, the center of madrigal composition shifted to Venice. Adrian Willaert occupies an intermediate position as a composer writing in both early and classical madrigal styles. Although he wrote madrigals, canzoni, and *villanesche* in the 1540s, his madrigals were not printed as collections until after mid-century. *Musica nova* appeared in 1559. All but 1 of the 25 madrigals in that volume are settings of Petrarch's sonnets (see p. 169). Willaert's mature madrigals display a subtle mixture of imitative and chordal texture and precise declamation of text.

After 1540 some composers began to write some of their pieces in smaller note values (i.e., note heads filled in or black) with a C mensuration sign rather than in the usual white notation (i.e., note heads unfilled) with an *alla breve* ($\mathcal{C}$) signature. Madrigals written in this newer notation are referred to variously as *madrigali a nota nere* (madrigals in black notes), *madrigali a misura di breve* (madrigals in *breve* measure), or *madrigali cromatici* (madrigals in colored, that is, black, notation and using *crome* or flagged semi-minims). Cipriano de Rore (1516–65), a Netherlander working in Italy, used some of this newly fashionable notation in *I madrigali*, a book of five-voice madrigals (1542).

Though Rore composed Masses, motets, and chansons, he is remembered chiefly for his madrigals, approximately 120 of which survive. He was the leading madrigalist of his generation. Like Willaert, Rore preferred to set serious poetry of high literary quality, especially that of Petrarch. Rore's *Il terzo libro di madrigali a cinque voci* (1548) opens with a cycle of 11 **madrigali spirituali** (madrigals setting devotional texts)—a setting of stanzas of invocation to the Virgin Mary that conclude Petrarch's *Canzoniere, o Rime in vita e morte di Madonna Laura* (Songs, or Poems on the Life and Death of Madonna Laura). Other composers writing *madrigali spirituali* include Palestrina and Willaert.

All of Rore's madrigals are four- or five-voice settings. His writing is firmly rooted in traditional Franco-Flemish counterpoint; his five-voice madrigals are polyphonic, motetlike, and serious in tone. There is a good deal of imitation, and the bass line provides harmonic support while supplying a melodic contrapuntal line. Rore exercised concern for expressing the meaning of the poetry and used chromatic alterations and text painting effectively. *Da le belle contrade d'oriente* (From the fair regions of the east; DWMA65) is representative of his five-voice madrigals. His four-voice madrigals have a more transparent texture, and some are comparatively simple, though contrapuntal (e.g., *Anchor che col partire* [Even while departing], which is probably his most famous madrigal).

The usual publication format for madrigals was partbooks. Yet, in 1577 an edition of Rore's collected four-voice madrigals was printed in score, which indicates that the collection was prepared for study purposes and that Rore's four-voice madrigals were considered models of the form. This is one of the earliest books of printed scores in existence.

Other composers producing madrigals of the classical type were Andrea Gabrieli, Lassus, Palestrina, Giaches de Wert, and Philippe de Monte. Monte (1521–1603), Flemish by birth, went to Italy at an early age, and as Filippo di Monte he worked as singer, teacher, and composer. After 1553 he worked in various places in Europe for short periods of time; he served as Kapellmeister to Habsburg rulers from 1568 until his death.

Monte wrote 40 Masses, about 260 other sacred works, approximately 50 chansons, 5 books of *madrigali spirituali*, and more than 1,100 madrigals published in 34 books issued between 1554 and 1603. Most of the madrigals Monte composed before 1576 set texts by Petrarch or sixteenth-century poets writing in the style of Petrarch; for later madrigals Monte chose contemporary pastoral poetry, especially Guarini's *Il pastor fido* (The faithful shepherd).

Monte's madrigals, most of which are five- and six-voice pieces, demonstrate his mastery of counterpoint. However, he was not averse to violating contrapuntal rules to achieve an expressive effect. Characteristics of his style include frequent use of cross-relations, melismas in connection with text painting, and grouping of voices for special effects.

Flemish composer Giaches de Wert (1535–96), wrote both classical and late madrigal types. Little is known concerning his early life. His permanent employment at the Gonzaga ducal establishment in Mantua began in 1565. As *maestro di cappella,* he was in charge of music at the palatine basilica of Santa Barbara and at court. After Margherita Gonzaga's marriage to Alfonso II d'Este in 1579 (see p. 182), Wert received commissions from Ferrara and visited there frequently. Some of his madrigals appear in *Il lauro secco* (The dry laurel; 1582) and *Il lauro verde* (The green laurel; 1583), two compilations of madrigals honoring Laura Peverara, of the Ferrarese *concerto delle donne* (ensemble of ladies; see p. 182). The pieces in Wert's *L'ottavo libro de madrigali* (Eighth book of madrigals; 5 vc.; 1586) may have been performed by that small ensemble at Ferrara. From c. 1584 to 1589 Wert had a secret liaison with Tarquinia Molza, accomplished poet, conductor, and musician, who was a member of the second Ferrarese *concerto delle donne.* When Alfonso II learned of the affair, Tarquinia was dismissed, and Wert returned to Mantua.

Fourteen books of Wert's madrigals were published between 1558 and 1595, one for four voices (1561) and the rest for five. A book of his madrigals for five to seven voices was published posthumously in 1608. A volume of *villanelle* appeared in 1589. For his madrigals he selected poetry of high literary quality; he set 60 poems of Petrarch, and Ariosto, Tansillo, Tasso, and Guarini are each represented by a dozen or more settings. The first three books of madrigals are stylistically much like those of Rore—basically note-against-note counterpoint, in which textually rather than structurally induced imitation contrasts with chordal writing. Wert used unconventional melodic intervals (e.g., augmented second, leap of a seventh) more frequently than Rore or Willaert.

In Books IV–VI, there is a tendency toward more homophonic writing and more lyricism. Book VII contains the earliest-known settings of Tasso's *Gerusalemme liberata* (Jerusalem delivered). Book VIII includes settings of 12 stanzas from *Gerusalemme liberata* grouped according to textual dramatic content. In several places, the three high voices are definitely the main voices, with the lower voices having accompaniment status. **Concertante** structure is apparent in dialogues between upper and lower voices, a type of writing that is rooted in but goes beyond Josquin's method of contrasting vocal groups. (The term *concertante* signifies music that is, in a sense, soloistic but that contrasts with other music in the same piece—e.g., chamber music with contrasting sections used in dialogue fashion.) Some vocal lines in the madrigals in Book VIII exhibit very wide vocal range (ex. 11.2). Wert used chromatic alterations and text painting effectively but usually not to extremes. At times, through his skillful application of chromatic alterations, modality approaches key tonality. Wert's late madrigals evidence stylistic characteristics found also in works by his contemporaries and foreshadow some musical developments of the seventeenth century.

LATE MADRIGALS   In the late sixteenth century, native Italians resumed leadership in madrigal composition, the principal composers being Luca Marenzio (c. 1553–99), Carlo Gesualdo (c. 1561–1613), and Claudio Monteverdi (1567–1643). Luzzascho Luzzaschi (c. 1545–1607) also made some important contributions.

Marenzio's reputation as a composer is based on his secular compositions, particularly his madrigals. More

EXAMPLE 11.2 Measures 1 to 12 of Wert's *Solo e pensoso* illustrate the wide range encompassed by the vocal lines in some of his madrigals. From *Il settimo libro de madrigali*, 1581. (*Source:* G. de Wert: Collected Works, *edited by C. MacClintock and M. Bernstein*)

than 450 of his secular works survive. Marenzio grew up near Brescia. From c. 1574 to 1578 he was employed by Cardinal Madruzzo (d. 1578) in Rome; then Cardinal Luigi d'Este became his patron. In 1587 Ferdinando de' Medici employed Marenzio at Florence. Late in 1589 Marenzio returned to Rome, and in 1593 he entered the service of Cardinal Aldobrandini, papal secretary of state. Marenzio spent 1596–97 in Poland; he returned to Rome in 1599.

Marenzio's immediate success in Rome was partly because his early madrigals filled society's need for new music that could be sung by talented amateurs. Most of his pieces are for five voices. Characteristic of his writing are his setting of the poetry in short, concise musical phrases and his musically symbolic depiction of the text whenever possible. In addition, many of his pieces exhibit continuous polyphony (e.g., *S'io parto, i' moro* [If I leave, I shall die]). The madrigals in Marenzio's last six books (1591–99) are more serious than the early pieces, and the settings display more unusual harmonic treatment; however, he used chromatic alterations in moderation and only to achieve expressive effects. His setting of Petrarch's *Solo e pensoso* (Alone and thoughtful) appears to be a five-part instrumentally accompanied solo madrigal (DWMA66). The opening lines of the poem—"Alone and thoughtful I walk through the deserted fields with measured, slow, and dragging steps"—are presented in long note values as a quasi-cantus firmus by means of a passage that ascends chromatically from g' to a'', then descends chromatically to a sustained d''. Seventh and ninth chords are spelled out in the other voices.

Carlo Gesualdo, Prince of Venosa, was afflicted with melomania (a mad passion for music) that became increasingly obsessive and was complicated by melancholia as he grew older. He managed to keep his mania semisecret until the notoriety occasioned by his murder of his wife and her lover in 1590. In 1594 Gesualdo visited the Este court at Ferrara for two reasons: he was fascinated by reports of the musical establishment there, and he married Leonora d'Este (1561–1637), niece of Duke Alfonso II.

Gesualdo remained at Ferrara for several years. In 1594 his *Madrigali libro primo* (Madrigals, book I)—actually, his second book of madrigals—was published there. His first book of madrigals, originally published under the *nom de plume* Gioseppe Pilonij, was reissued in 1594 as *Madrigali libro secondo* (Madrigals, book II). Gesualdo found conditions at Ferrara conducive to composition; his third and fourth books of madrigals were published there in 1595 and 1596, respectively. He composed some madrigals for the *concerto delle donne* (see p. 180). At Ferrara, Gesualdo could maintain his aristocratic status and still work professionally with Luzzaschi and the virtuoso court musicians. Gesualdo admired Luzzaschi and was influenced by his use of chromaticism.

In 1597 Gesualdo returned to his castle at Gesualdo in Naples. His fifth and sixth books of madrigals were published there in 1611.

In his madrigal settings Gesualdo was primarily interested in conveying emotional expression, and he used chromaticism both harmonically and melodically for that purpose. He employed chromaticism wisely, restricting its abundant use to passages that are not complicated rhythmically. An example is *Moro lasso al mio duolo* (I die from my pain; DWMA67). Usually, Gesualdo confirmed audacious strident harmonies and unconventional chord progressions by immediately repeating them either exactly or in sequence.

Luzzascho Luzzaschi, a pupil of Rore, entered d'Este service in 1561 as a singer; in 1564 he was appointed first organist. Gradually, his duties were expanded to include directing a court orchestra, training some of the court musicians, composing for the court, and performing at the keyboard. By 1570 he was in charge of Alfonso II's private *musica da camera,* including the *concerto delle donne* (see p. 180). Eight books of Luzzaschi's madrigals were published during 1571–1604. *Madrigali per cantare, et sonare a uno, e doi, e tre soprani* (Madrigals to be sung and played by one, two, and three sopranos; 1601) contains madrigals composed for the repertoire of the *concerto delle donne.* The pieces, which were written before 1597—some perhaps as early as 1590—are supplied with keyboard accompaniment. This is the earliest extant publication containing written-out keyboard accompaniments.

Claudio Monteverdi occupies a transitional position between the Renaissance and Baroque eras. His first four books of madrigals are purely Renaissance compositions; the pieces in his next two books are transitional, and the madrigals in his seventh book are clearly Baroque. Discussion of Monteverdi commences on p. 243.

CANZONETTA

The **canzonetta** (little song), an Italian light, secular song, appeared in southern Italy c. 1560 and spread northward. The texts, usually strophic, treat subjects that are amorous, erotic, pastoral, or satirical. Early *canzonette* were treble-dominated, rhythmically varied homophony for three to five voices; three-voice *canzonette* became very popular in the early 1580s. By the end of that decade, four- and six-voice textures were preferred, and more contrapuntal elements were included. Those *canzonette* satirizing madrigals exhibit contrived simplicity and combine textural clarity with madrigalian devices such as word painting. *Canzonette* by Orazio Vecchi (1550–1605) and Marenzio were popular both in Italy and north of the Alps. By the end of the century, *canzonette* were sung in translation in Germany and England, and composers in those areas were writing pieces in *canzonetta* style.

BALLETTO

The **balletto** developed in connection with a specific Italian dance called *balletto*. Traditionally, *balletti* were performed in association with dancing. The Italian instrumental *balletto* (principally for lute) flourished from c. 1560 to 1590; the vocal *balletto* appeared c. 1591 and flourished for about three decades. After c. 1620 the instrumental chamber ensemble *balletto* became popular.

Giovanni Gastoldi (c. 1552–c. 1622), who worked for the Gonzagas at Mantua in 1572–1608, is credited with writing the earliest vocal *balletti*. His *Balletti a cinque voci con li suoi versi per cantare, sonare, e ballare* (*Balletti* for five voices, with music for singing, playing, and dancing) was published in Venice in 1591 and was reprinted a dozen times in two decades. *Balletti* are characterized as strophic and as homophonic in texture, with regular rhythmic patterns, clearly delineated phrases, and diatonic harmonies of key tonality. Modality is virtually nonexistent in *balletti*. Nonsense syllables, such as *fa-la-la* or *li-rum*, are interpolated at the ends of lines, or of couplets, or as a refrain. (The modern Christmas carol *Deck the Halls* is in essence a *balletto*.)

Balletti became popular outside of Italy. Many were written in Germany, and in England, where they were called *balletts*, those by Thomas Morley were very popular. Morley's *Balletts to Five Voyces* was published in both English and Italian (1595); the book mimics Gastoldi's collection—each piece is a parody of an Italian work. For example, Morley's *Sing wee and chaunt it* (DWMA68) is a parody of Gastoldi's *A lieta vita* (For merry life). Morley was aware that *balletti* were dance songs, for he mentioned that in his *A Plaine and Easie Introduction to Practicall Musick*. However, English *balletti* evidence greater attention to musical detail and text setting than Italian ones, and it is generally presumed that English *balletti* were not intended for use with dancing.

MUSIC AT NORTHERN ITALIAN COURTS

Marital ties linked the Este, Gonzaga, and Medici families, and personal visits between courts occurred frequently (fig. 11.1). These ruling families patronized the arts lavishly, and activities at their courts played an important role in the development of music in Italy during the sixteenth century. Innovative cultural events at one court soon were taken up at one or more of the others.

In the last half of the sixteenth century, the excellence of the musical establishment at the Este court at Ferrara was well known. Several ensembles were permanently maintained there. The *concerto grande* (large ensemble) performed at all large entertainments; in the 1570s this group comprised about 60 vocalists and instrumentalists. Court records indicate that the last male sopranos employed at the Ferrara court came in the late 1550s; thereafter, female sopranos were recruited. In the 1570s there were at court several aristocratic ladies who sang well: Lucrezia and Isabella Bendidio and Leonora Sanvitale di Scandiano (d. 1582). These talented amateurs sang solos and performed together as a *concerto delle donne* (ladies ensemble). These were prestigious noblewomen who would have been at court even if they had not been able to sing; they were not recompensed specifically for their singing. In 1577 they were joined by Signora Vittoria Cybò Bentivoglio. The four ladies performed together regularly in private concerts for a small select audience in the personal apartments of Lucrezia d'Este. Isabella and Lucrezia Bendidio sang solos and duets with harpsichord accompaniment and performed in the ensemble; sometimes Giulio Cesare Brancaccio (c. 1520–d. after 1585), a professional bass, sang with Lucrezia, Leonora, and Vittoria. Court composer Luzzaschi rehearsed the

FIGURE 11.1 Northern Italy in the sixteenth century.

small ensemble and played harpsichord accompaniments for the singers. Reportedly, this ensemble had a secret repertoire for their private concerts. In contemporary accounts, these private concerts of the *concerto delle donne* were referred to as **musica reservata** and **musica secreta** (plate 18).

In 1579 Alfonso II d'Este married Margherita Gonzaga of Mantua, whose lively interest in music, dancing, and the theatre had been fostered by the atmosphere of her father's court. Soon Alfonso added to the Ferrara court singers a female soprano whose singing Margherita had enjoyed at Mantua. Other semiprofessional women singers were attracted to the court, and gradually the original members of the *concerto delle donne* were replaced by semiprofessional singers—the new *concerto delle donne* was a virtuoso ensemble whose members were at court only because they possessed excellent singing voices. (The ladies were paid for singing and spent considerable time cultivating their musical talents, but they had not been trained from childhood for a musical career. That was not possible for a woman in the late sixteenth century.) The original "singing ladies" remained at court but no longer performed in the select ensemble.

In 1582, the *concerto delle donne* comprised Laura Peverara (c. 1545–1601), Anna Guarini (b. after 1561–d. 1598), and Livia d'Arco (d. 1611). Tarquinia Molza (1542–1617) joined the ensemble in 1583. The vocal talent of Laura Peverara was well known in Italy; renowned poets praised her in verses that famous composers set as madrigals. Two anthologies honor her: *Il lauro secco* (1582) and *Il lauro verde* (1583). Often Brancaccio and a tenor sang with three of the ladies in the *musica secreta* performances given in the chambers of Duchess Margherita. Giaches de Wert had in mind the talents of the *musica secreta* quintet at Ferrara when he composed his *L' ottavo libro de madrigali*.

The change in performance practices at Ferrara is significant—no longer were noble amateurs performing for their peers; semiprofessionals were performing before an audience. The virtuosi added diminutions to their solos; ornaments such as *passaggi* (passage work), *tiradi* (runs), *cadenze* (cadential ornaments), *trilli* (trills), *gruppi* (turns), and *messe di voce* (small crescendo-diminuendo on a sustained pitch) were planned and rehearsed before they were performed.

Solo madrigals so ornamented became known as **madrigali ariosi.** Wert notated ornaments of these kinds in more than one vocal line in several of the pieces in *L' ottavo libro de madrigali* (ex. 11.3). From the solo singing, a new style of polyphony arose in which some characteristics of the serious madrigal and the lighter forms of Italian song were intermingled: concentration of the main melody in the top voice, supported by uncomplicated harmonies, with little imitation. Several of the madrigals in Wert's *Eighth Book* are *concertato* type, with the three upper (female) voices clearly grouped and contrasted against the two lower (male) voices yet in agreement (in concert) with them (e.g., *Non è sì denso velo* [There is no veil so thick; DWMA69).

At Ferrara there was a strong tradition of singing associated with dramatic productions—**intermedi** (interludes between acts of a play) were presented by soloists in a vocal style midway between recitation and singing. That kind of performance may have promoted the establishment of a group of semiprofessional madrigal singers and the separation between performers and audience associated with the concerts given by such a group.

Margherita Gonzaga d'Este's interest in dancing led to the formation of a *balletto delle donne* (ensemble of dancing ladies) at Ferrara. Presentations by the ladies did not interpret a story through dance but consisted of a series of dances by costumed performers. There was, of course, instrumental accompaniment, and at times madrigals were interpolated. Both *balletto delle donne* and *concerto delle donne* seem to have existed at Ferrara until that duchy reverted to the papacy. G. B. Guarini's experiences at Ferrara are reflected in his inclusion of dancing and madrigals in *Il pastor fido*. At Ferrara that play was performed with music by Luzzaschi; at Mantua, new music was supplied by Wert.

At Mantua, Guglielmo Gonzaga (1538–87) was genuinely interested in the arts and was musically literate. A competent composer with published works, he could (and did) specify precisely in technical terms the style and content of the music he wanted composed. He maintained a permanent musical establishment with professional singers and music teachers. Outstanding composers, performers, artists, and authors were attracted to and found employment at

EXAMPLE 11.3 Excerpt from *Si com'ai freschi matutini rai,* No. 3 in *L'ottavo libro de madrigali* (1586), illustrates Wert's notation of ornaments in more than one vocal line. The ornaments are written out, not indicated by symbols. *(Source: G. de Wert: Collected Works, edited by C. MacClintock and M. Bernstein)*

Mantua. Madrigals were sung; dramatic presentations were enjoyed. Wert was the first madrigalist permanently employed at Mantua, where madrigals flourished after his arrival.

Vincenzo Gonzaga, brother of Margherita, spent considerable time at the Ferrara court in the early 1580s. After he inherited the duchy of Mantua, he attempted to copy at Mantua the musical establishment and performances he had witnessed at Ferrara. The regular musical establishment was enlarged, and a small ensemble of skilled professional female singers was assembled. Lucia and Isabella Pellizzari were employed by 1592 and were joined later by Lucrezia Urbana and

Caterina Romana (Caterina Martinelli). By 1600 Mantua was one of the leading musical centers in Italy.

A similar ensemble of "singing ladies" was formed at the Medici court in Florence in the early 1580s. Laura Bovia joined the court singers in 1581. In 1583 Giulio Caccini (c. 1545–1618) directed an ensemble of three sopranos at the Medici court; in 1584, Vittoria Archilei and a Bolognese lady (probably Laura Bovia) performed with other musicians at the festivities celebrating the marriage of Vincenzo Gonzaga and Leonora de' Medici. When the Florentine *concerto delle donne* was disbanded in 1589, Laura Bovia found employment in the ensemble at Mantua.

Several features of *concerto delle donne* and *balletto delle donne* performances at Italian courts in the late sixteenth century are historically significant: (1) women were featured as performers, (2) performances were rehearsed, (3) performers and audience were separated, (4) chamber music concerts were reserved for selected court personnel or important visitors (*musica reservata*), (5) vocal music was incorporated into dance scenes, and (6) both music and dance were integrated with drama.

FRANCE

CHANSON

Pierre Attaingnant (c. 1494–c. 1552) was active in Paris as printer and publisher of music from 1525 until his death. He invented a method of printing music notation in a single impression, a process that soon replaced the double- and triple-impression techniques used by other printers. This became the first international method of music printing. Single-impression printing reduced production time and costs considerably; more music could be printed, and it was available at affordable prices. In April 1528, Attaingnant published *Chansons nouvelles* (New songs). (Attaingnant's publication bears date 1527, but at that time the annual calendar commenced with Easter eve.) By 1552 he had published over 50 collections of chansons—approximately 1,500 songs. Those songs were distinctly French in character, and most had been written by composers living in and around Paris.

Chansons had always used the French language. In mid-fifteenth century, most chansons were written in the Burgundian treble-dominated style and followed one of the *formes fixes* of courtly poetry. During the late fifteenth century, the chanson was characterized by continuous polyphony with more equality among the voices, and it contained melodic figures, turns of phrase, and cadential formulae common to the musical vocabulary of most Franco-Netherlands composers. In chansons written c. 1500, the several polyphonic lines are equal in importance but independent. The gradual increase in this style of writing in the late fifteenth and early sixteenth centuries coincides with the gradual abandonment of formal patterns of the poetic *formes fixes*. It should be remembered that, although the imitative chanson used the same contrapuntal techniques as the motet, the two types of vocal music differed in purpose and text and in the fact that the chanson always used quicker and more decisive rhythms than the motet. Many chansons characteristically commenced with repeated pitches in the rhythm ♩ ♪ ♪, a feature that carried over into the instrumental canzona (see p. 219).

Among sixteenth-century Franco-Flemish composers writing imitative contrapuntal chansons were Gombert, Clement, Thomas Crecquillon (c. 1490–c. 1557), and Pierre de Manchicourt (c. 1510–64). Crecquillon's *Pour ung plaisir* (For a pleasure) was quite popular in Italy; Andrea Gabrieli made a keyboard arrangement of it.

The musical style of the chansons published in Paris by Attaingnant was markedly different. They were light in texture, strongly rhythmic, and usually in duple meter. Texts were set syllabically for four voices. Though the songs are predominantly homorhythmic and homophonic, with the main melody in the highest voice, short points of imitation were sometimes included. Frequently, the chansons are characterized by passages containing many repeated notes. The structure of each musical phrase corresponds with that of the poetry, but formally they were constructed in distinct short sections, some of which were repeated: aba, aabc, aba′ca″, and others. In many respects, this style of chanson—sometimes called the **Parisian chanson**—resembles the frottola. This type of chanson was especially popular during the 1530s and 1540s. Its principal composers were Claudin de Sermisy (c. 1490–1562), Clément Janequin (c. 1485–1558), and

Pierre Certon (d. 1572). All are well represented in Attaingnant's publications. Typical examples are Sermisy's *Tant que vivray* (As long as I live), *Jouyssance vous donneray* (Delight I will give you; plate 18), and *Vivray je tousjours en soucy* (Shall I live always in anxiety). (See ex. 11.4.) In *À ce ioly moys* (In this pretty month; DWMA70), a four-voice chanson in abba form, Janequin combined imitative polyphony and repeated notes in a kind of light patter. Many of Janequin's chansons are descriptive, containing bird calls, street cries, fanfares, and other realistic text painting. His most famous descriptive chanson is *La guerre*.

Almost all composers of chansons also wrote motets and Masses. Many chansons served as models for parody Masses or provided thematic material for Masses and motets.

During the last half of the sixteenth century, some composers, especially those working in northern France and the Netherlands, wrote chansons in the traditional Franco-Netherlands style. Parisian composers Claude Le Jeune, Jacques Mauduit, and others who wrote *airs de cour* and *musique mesurée* also composed serious polyphonic chansons. (*Airs de cour* and *musique mesurée* are discussed below.)

At the hands of versatile composers such as Arcadelt and Lassus, expressive madrigalian devices infiltrated chansons. Arcadelt wrote 126 chansons, most of them for four voices. Lassus composed some of the finest chansons written during the last half of the sixteenth century. Between 1550 and c. 1585 he wrote approximately 150 of them. Most of the poems he set were authored by French writers—Ronsard, Baïf, Villon, Marot, and others. The texts are of all kinds, from bawdy (*Il estoit une religeuse,* There was a nun) to serious; some have a moral or religious theme (*Susanne un jour,* One day Susanna; Dan., ch. 13, apocryphal). Lassus's musical settings vary accordingly: there are dialogues, Parisian patter-type chansons, serious motet-like pieces, and witty, light-hearted songs. Popular chansons such as *Bon jour, mon coeur* (Good day, my love) were arranged for keyboard.

VOIX DE VILLE, AIR DE COUR

Around the middle of the sixteenth century, a type of courtly poetry was written that was known as **voix de ville** (city voice). Occasionally, the alternate spelling

EXAMPLE 11.4 Sermisy's Parisian chansons contain features typical of the genre: (*a*) the opening three-note figure and the homorhythmic, syllabic style of *Tant que vivray;* (*b*) the repeated notes in *Vivray je tousjours en soucy* (mm. 1, 4–5). *(Source: Claudin de Sermisy,* Collected Works, *vol. 3, p. 138; vol. 4, p. 99.* Corpus mensurabilis musicae 52, *American Institute of Musicology)*

vau de ville was used; by c. 1580, the single word *vaudeville* was common. A *voix de ville* poem has several short stanzas that are set strophically to music in a homophonic chordal style with the melody in the top voice. In many respects, a *voix de ville* setting resembles that used for the Parisian chanson. Adrien Le Roy's publication *Le second livre de guiterre, contenant plusieurs chansons en forme de voix de ville* (The second book for guitar, containing several songs in *voix de ville* form; 1555) presents the complete text of each *voix de ville* together with its melody and tablature for guitar accompaniment.

Le Roy stated in the Preface to *Livre d'air de cours miz sur le luth* (Book of court airs set for lute; 1571) that the kind of song contained in this book was formerly called *voix de ville.* The volume contains 22 solo songs with lute accompaniment; the vocal and instrumental parts are on facing pages. The vocal part is in ordinary notation without bar lines, and the accompaniment is in lute tablature with bar lines. A solo song with lute accompaniment is known also as **lute song.**

During 1571–c. 1650, the term **air de cour,** or simply **air,** was used to denote a secular, strophic song sung at court for entertainment. *Airs de cour* were written for four or five unaccompanied voices or for solo voice with instrumental (usually lute) accompaniment. Nearly all the *airs de cour* composed between 1580 and 1600 are polyphonic; solo *airs de cour* with lute accompaniment flourished again after 1608.

MUSIQUE MESURÉE

In the last third of the sixteenth century, a group of French poets known as the *Pléiade,* chief of whom was Jean-Antoine de Baïf (1532–89), wrote **vers mesurée**—verses in which they attempted to apply to the French language an accentual version of the quantitative principles of Greek and Latin verse. Long was equated with accented syllables and short with unaccented syllables.

Baïf believed that music and poetry should be united as they were—or as he thought they were—in ancient times. To this end, he and some of his musical colleagues devised a system whereby *vers mesurée* could be set to music. Quantitative scansion of the poetry determined the musical note values—a long syllable was set to a note double the value of that used for a short syllable. The musical settings, called **musique mesurée,** were homophonic and almost totally homorhythmic so that the words could be heard clearly. The artificiality of the procedure prohibited true expression of the text; as a result, *musique mesurée* was short-lived. Its principal composers were Jacques Mauduit (1557–1627) and Claude Le Jeune (c. 1530–1600). At times, Le Jeune included short melismas in his settings of *vers mesurée* (e.g., in *Revecy venir du printans* [ex. 11.5; DWMA71]). *Airs de cour* written during the last quarter of the sixteenth century were influenced significantly by the asymmetrical rhythms and homophonic character of *musique mesurée.*

ENGLAND

Music flourished in England during the sixteenth century. Henry VIII (r. 1509–47) played organ, lute, and virginals and was a composer. Among his 34 surviving compositions are 13 instrumental pieces, the three-voice motet *Quam pulchra es,* and numerous three- and four-voice part songs. Music played an important part in court life during Henry VIII's reign. Edward VI (r. 1547–53) and Mary (r. 1553–58) also supported music. Elizabeth I (r. 1558–1603) was a competent virginalist. During her reign, music attained a high level of excellence rarely equaled thereafter.

In the early sixteenth century, secular part-songs flourished. Essentially, these were English-language chansons presumably intended for choral singing. One of the earliest music books printed in England is a collection of such songs: *In this boke ar cōteynyd xx sōges, ix of iiii ptes and xi of thre ptes* (In this book are contained 20 songs, 9 of 4 parts and 11 of 3 parts; 1530).

ENGLISH MADRIGAL

The influence of the Italian madrigal was felt strongly in England in the last two decades of the sixteenth century. Manuscript copies of Italian madrigals, some of them in English translation, were circulating in England by mid-century. Increased interest of the English in madrigals c. 1580 inspired Nicholas Yonge (d. 1619) to edit and publish *Musica transalpina* (Music across the Alps; London, 1588), a collection of 57 Italian madrigals with texts translated into English. Before 1598, four other collections appeared, including Yonge's second anthology, also entitled *Musica transalpina* (1597).

During the 1590s nearly all English composers wrote some madrigals. Even William Byrd, who favored other song forms, composed two madrigals. Thomas Morley (c. 1557–1602) was the leading composer and provided the stylistic model for the Elizabethan light madrigal that enjoyed great popularity for about a decade. Morley's first two books are entitled *Canzonets or Little Short Songs to Three Voyces* (1593) and *Madrigalls to Foure Voyces* (1594). The pieces in these books are relatively simple and are clearly harmonic but contain more counterpoint than Italian light madrigals of the time. Both *The First Book of Balletts to Five Voyces* (1595) and *The First Book of Canzonetts to Two Voyces* (1595) were printed in English

EXAMPLE 11.5 Opening of Le Jeune's *Revecy venir du printans* set as musique mesurée. *(© 1951/1959 by American Institute of Musicology/ Hänssler-Verlag, Neuhausen-Stuttgart, West Germany. From: Claude Le Jeune, AIRS, [1608] edited by D. P. Walker/Miscellanea I, vol. I)*

and Italian editions issued simultaneously; these books consist principally of free transcriptions of works by Gastoldi and Felice Anerio (c. 1560–1614) and are even lighter music than Morley's earlier madrigals. The strophic settings are homophonic and dancelike, often with a refrain that incorporates *fa-la* syllables. Morley's madrigals are markedly lacking in chromaticism, word painting, and dramatic effects—features found in the madrigals of his English and Italian contemporaries. Among his best-known works is *Aprill is in my mistris face* (4 vc.; 1594; DWMA72).

Morley's anthology *The Triumphes of Oriana to 5. and 6. Voices* (1601) is modeled after the Italian anthology *Il trionfo di Dori* (The Triumphs of Dori; 1592). The English publication was designed to honor Queen Elizabeth I, who was frequently referred to in contemporary pastoral poetry as "Oriana." Each of the madrigals in the anthology concludes with the lines: "Then sang the shepherds and nymphs of Diana, / 'Long live fair Oriana'!" or a slight variant thereof.

Thomas Weelkes (1576–1623), John Wilbye (1574–1638), and John Bennet (fl. 1599–1614) also contributed to English madrigal repertory. Bennet's writing is in many respects similar to that of Morley, but his pieces are replete with word painting and other madrigalisms (e.g., the pastoral *Thyrsis, Sleepest Thou?*). Weelkes's and Wilbye's settings are more serious than those of Morley and their music less Italianate than his. In general, English composers gave greater attention to the purely musical features of their madrigal settings than to the depiction or dramatization of textual elements. Word painting is present but is assigned a role subservient to the overall musical structure of the piece.

The various types of English madrigals were intended primarily for performance by unaccompanied solo voices; however, title pages of many publications state that the pieces are "apt for voices and viols," and doubtless the pieces were performed by any available combination of voices and viols. The pieces were printed in partbooks in notation devoid of bar lines. English composers paid particular attention to correct declamation of text. Although vocal performance of all lines might evoke a fascinating accentual counterpoint, this never interfered with the musical phraseology.

Consort Song

The consort song is an exclusively English type of vocal music that flourished in the late sixteenth and early seventeenth centuries. Around the middle of the sixteenth century the consort of viols became increasingly popular as a performing ensemble in England. Some English composers wrote songs for one or more solo voices with an *obbligato* (required) instrumental accompaniment that was usually intended for a consort of viols. Songs of this kind are known as **consort songs.** The compositional style of the consort song was not affected by either the Italian madrigal or the French air. Consort songs were being written in the early 1560s, but the stature of the consort song was enhanced considerably in the 1570s, when William Byrd adopted it in preference to the madrigal; his earliest settings of English poems are strophic songs for one solo voice and a consort of viols. All of Byrd's consort songs are strophic settings in which the text is set syllabically, and the lines of text are clearly differentiated; frequently, there is a melisma on the penultimate syllable of a line of text.

Sometimes the consort song was expanded by the addition of a chorus. When an ecclesiastical text was set and the accompaniment was suitable for performance on organ, the consort song became a **verse anthem,** a form that Byrd is credited with inventing (see p. 200). Byrd and Orlando Gibbons (1583–1625) were the leading composers of consort songs. More than half of Gibbons's verse anthems have fully written-out accompaniments for viols and alternative accompaniments for organ.

Lute Song or Ayre

The **lute song** and the solo song with viol accompaniment became popular in France early in the sixteenth century but did not flourish in England until the late 1590s. Its rise in popularity in England coincided with the decline of the English madrigal. In England the solo song with lute accompaniment was commonly known as **ayre.** Its leading composers were John Dowland (1563–1626) and Thomas Campion (1567–1620).

Dowland's *The First Booke of Songes or Ayres of Foure Partes with Tableture for the Lute* (1597) contains 21 songs written for performance either by solo voice with lute accompaniment or as four-part songs

FIGURE 11.2 Dowland's ayre *Fine knacks for ladies*, as printed in the original edition.

with or without lute. *The Second Booke of Songs or Ayres* was published in 1600; *The Third and Last Booke of Songs or Aires* appeared in 1603. In these publications the solo ayres have the vocal and lute music printed on the same page, no doubt for the convenience of the vocalist who wanted to play his own accompaniment (fig. 11.2, left side). Most of Dowland's songs, including the well-known "What if I never speede," from *The Third and Last Booke of Songs or Aires,* are printed in two versions: for vocal ensemble and as vocal solo with lute accompaniment. In the original publications, the music is printed so that all the performers could sit around a table and read the music from the same book (fig. 11.2).

Other well-known ayres by Dowland are "Flow my tears" from *The Seconde Booke of Ayres,* "Go crystall teares" (1597), "Fine knacks for ladies" (1600), "Sweet stay a while, why will you rise?" (1612), and "In dark-

ness let mee dwell" (1610; DWMA73). Many of Dowland's works are characterized by melancholy; the tragic and emotionally intense "In darkness let mee dwell" is accompanied by piercing discords.

GERMANIC LANDS

MEISTERLIEDER

The composition and performance of music was an avocation for the *Meistersinger,* each of whom worked at another trade. **Meisterlieder,** the monophonic German songs created and performed by members of the Meistersinger guilds, flourished especially during the sixteenth century, yet relatively few *Meisterlieder* melodies have been preserved, for the art of the Meistersinger was an almost exclusively oral tradition. After 1540, guild regulations expressly forbade the performance of printed music at the public concerts given by

Meistersinger. Sources relative to the Meistersinger and their music include records of guild meetings, posters announcing guild activities, artwork, and historical accounts written by Meistersinger, such as Cyriac Spangenberg (1528–1604). J. C. Wagenseil (1633–1703) included some *Meisterlieder* in his treatise (1697) on the Meistersinger of Nuremberg, one of the most important sixteenth-century guilds and that to which the shoemaker Hans Sachs belonged. Wagenseil's treatise was Wagner's prime source of information for the opera *Die Meistersinger von Nürnberg,* in which Sachs is a character.

Meisterlieder were performed unaccompanied, usually by a vocal soloist and occasionally by a chorus. A *Meisterlied* comprises an odd number of stanzas—a minimum of three—constructed poetically and set musically in aab form (bar form). The extant melodies are narrow in range and are notated without any rhythmic indications; presumably, the rhythm is determined by the text.

POLYPHONIC *LIED*

In the second decade of the sixteenth century several German printers published collections of anonymous polyphonic **Lieder** (Ger., songs; sing., *Lied*). In later editions, some of the pieces are identified as the work of Adam von Fulda (c. 1445–1505), Heinrich Finck (c. 1445–1527), Paul Hofhaimer (1459–1537), and Heinrich Isaac. Finck and Isaac are considered masters of the polyphonic *Lied.*

Both fifteenth- and early sixteenth-century polyphonic *Lieder* may properly be termed *Tenorlieder* because the main melody lies in the tenor voice. In the fifteenth century the tenor was often the highest voice of the song; in the sixteenth-century pieces the tenor is the highest male voice and is surrounded by other voices whose music is more disjunct and has livelier rhythm. Isaac's Lieder do not always follow this pattern, however. *Isbruck, ich muss dich lassen* exists in two versions, one of which has the main melody in the superius. In *Zwischen Perg und tieffem Tal* (DWMA59), bass and tenor present the main melody in canon at the octave. Elements of Netherlands counterpoint frequently infiltrate Isaac's Lieder. This is a more outstanding characteristic of the Lieder written by Isaac's pupil Ludwig Senfl (c. 1486–1543), who brought the polyphonic Lied to artistic perfection.

From c. 1530 to c. 1555, many published collections of polyphonic Lieder contained pieces in from two to eight parts, with the performance instruction that the music might be performed by any suitable combination of voices and instruments. No doubt publications of this kind were an attempt to supply the demand for Lieder for home and communal music making.

After the middle of the sixteenth century, the secular *Tenorlied* decreased in importance, though sacred music in Tenorlied style was still composed for use in Lutheran churches. The polyphonic Lied is preserved in some sacred songs by Michael Praetorius (c. 1570–1621). Hans Leo Hassler (1562–1612) wrote almost 60 polyphonic Lieder setting his own texts. *Ach, süsse Seel'* (Ah, sweet soul; 6 vc.) and *Mein G'müt ist mir verwirret* (see p. 195; DWMA74a) exemplify his Lieder style. Many of the Lieder composed by Lassus (p. 210) after c. 1570 resemble motets or chansons (e.g., *Ich armer Mann* [I, poor man]).

ODE

Poetic odes created in classical antiquity were intended to be sung; the word *ode* derives from the Greek word meaning "I sing." Usually, the music was improvised; however, a few medieval settings of odes by Sappho and Horace survive.

In the 1490s academic interest in the classical ode was extended to musical composition when the German humanist Conradus Celtes commissioned his pupil Petrus Tritonius to compose four-voice settings illustrating the poetic meters in Horace's odes. Tritonius's settings, in Tenorlied style, were sung by students at the end of lectures; in 1507 those settings were published. In 1534 Senfl made new settings of the odes, in cantional style, with Tritonius's tenor melodies as the superius, and new harmonizations. During the sixteenth century, choral odes were included at the ends of acts in Latin plays written by German schoolmasters. These plays were on sacred or allegorical subjects and were performed by students.

QUODLIBET

The *quodlibet* (lit., whatsoever you please) is a piece in which well-known melodies or fragments of melodies (with or without their original texts) are combined successively or simultaneously. Composers wrote *quodlibets* for humorous parody or to display technical virtuosity. Though a few pieces of this kind were created in medieval times, the term *quodlibet* was first used in connection with music in 1544, when Walter Schmetzl published a collection of 25 such songs. Songs of similar structure appeared in other countries during the Renaissance: the *fricassée* in France, *messanza* or *misticanza* in Italy, *medley* in England, and *ensalada* in Spain.

IBERIA

The principal types of Spanish sixteenth-century secular vocal music are the *romance* and the *villancico*. The **romance** is a ballad (i.e., its text is strophic and narrative). Musical settings of romances are for three or four voices and are strophic and homophonic, with the main melody in the top voice. The exact manner in which a *romance* was performed is not known. In manuscripts, the text is underlaid for the first strophe only, and only under the principal melody. These songs may have been performed by a soloist with instrumental accompaniment; however, it is generally believed that until c. 1550 these romantic ballads were sung at court chorally.

The term **villancico** is a diminutive of *villano*, meaning "peasant." The *villancico* originated in a medieval Spanish dance lyric with a refrain; its formal construction resembles that of the *ballata* and *virelai*: a prefatory refrain, followed by several strophes separated by the refrain, and a concluding refrain. The refrain is called *estribillo;* the strophe, *copla.*

Early *villancicos* are for three or four voices. The music is contrapuntal, with the main melody in the superius; the other voices provide accompaniment. Usually, the text is underlaid for the superius only and is set syllabically. Duple mensuration prevails. Important composers of the early *villancico* are Juan del Encina, Pedro de Escobar, and Francesco Peñalosa.

Juan del Encina (1468–1530), Spanish poet, dramatist, and composer, was one of the first to write dramatic works specifically for performance, with instructions that specify singing and dancing. The earliest of these are religious plays associated with festivals such as Christmas and Easter and resemble medieval mystery plays; his later plays are secular and pastoral.

Music and dancing are included in all of Encina's plays and are an integral part of the action. Encina placed a *villancico* either midway through or at the conclusion of the play; sometimes *villancicos* were sung and danced in both places in the play. Texts of the *villancicos* concern the preceding dramatic events. Some of Encina's *villancicos* are intended for solo or duet vocal performance with instrumental accompaniment; in others, all parts are to be sung. His melodies are expressive and flowing but are concise, with syllabic settings of text; the final cadence of the verse is slightly ornamented. The pieces are homorhythmic polyphony, but the rhythm, influenced by the accents of the poetry, is flexible and varied (DWMA75).

Six *romances* by Encina are extant. These are simple syllabic settings, cast in four phrases; they are homorhythmic, chorale-like, and serious.

The next generation of sixteenth-century Spanish composers wrote polyphonic *villancicos* in which all voices share text and melody. Imitative counterpoint predominates, but homorhythmic counterpoint appears frequently. Often the text comprises the *estribillo* and one *copla.*

Villancicos composed around the middle of the sixteenth century reflect the influence of the Italian madrigal. Typical *villancicos* of this time appear in published collections of works by Juan Vasquez (c. 1510–c. 1560): *Villancicos y canciones* (*Villancicos* and canzonas; 1551) and *Recopilación de sonetos y villancicos* (Collection of sonnets and *villancicos*; 1560). The *estribillo* is expanded and often leads directly (i.e., without pause) into the single *copla,* which is through-composed; a varied form of the *estribillo* concludes the piece.

In the last quarter of the sixteenth century some devotional and liturgical *villancicos* were produced. Some of these were secular pieces with modified texts, whereas others were new compositions.

SUMMARY

A great amount of secular music was produced during the sixteenth century, by the end of which the center of interest in musical composition was secular song. Much secular music was written for use at court. However, the emergence of a large bourgeois public for whom music was primarily a form of recreation created a body of performing amateurs who provided a ready market for printed anthologies of secular music. In Germanic lands, tradesmen for whom music was an avocation composed and performed their own secular music and maintained high standards through guild regulations.

Though some monophonic music was produced, most of the sixteenth-century secular songs were polyphonic, with the main melody in the highest voice. Both ensemble music and instrumentally accompanied vocal solos were composed. Except for the presence of a lute tablature, or the statement on a title page that a collection was suitable for singing or playing, printed music appeared to be unaccompanied vocal music. Instrumentally accompanied solo song was not new, but the prominence, in the late sixteenth century, of the vocal solo with simple harmonic accompaniment was an important factor in musical developments in the seventeenth century.

Each region had distinctive types of vernacular vocal music, but the Italian madrigal, with its expressive musical language, was the most influential. Not only did it influence the style of secular music in England, Spain, and other countries, but the manner in which madrigals were performed at several Italian courts during the last two decades of the sixteenth century (performers before an audience, planned and rehearsed performances, and the inclusion of solo and ensemble madrigals in dramatic productions) was an indication of the direction of musical developments in the seventeenth century.

REFORMATION AND COUNTER-REFORMATION

From time to time over the centuries there had been agitation for various kinds of reform—administrative, doctrinal, political, musical—within the Roman Catholic Church. Periodically, papal complaints had been registered against polyphony, but composers and performers had managed to circumvent most papal anti-polyphonic directives or recommendations.

In the main, the church had weathered all storms. It had survived the exile in Avignon and the Great Schism, Wycliffe and the Lollards had been suppressed, and Hus had been burned at the stake, but his followers had been granted small doctrinal concessions. Musically, the Hussites preferred simple, monophonic hymns; they exiled polyphony and musical instruments from their churches. Around the mid-sixteenth century, their austerity began to soften, and some note-against-note part-music crept in.

A new religious sect arose in Bohemia and Moravia c. 1450. The group, known as Bohemian Brethren, eventually established an independent church with lay priesthood. Certain of their beliefs (e.g., the equality of all persons in a society without class distinctions) brought the Brethren persecution, imprisonment, execution, and, in 1618, expulsion from Bohemia and Moravia. Remnants of the sect survived in Saxony; in 1722 the brotherhood was reestablished in Herrnhut as Moravian Brethren. Shortly thereafter, some Brethren emigrated to America, where they made significant musical contributions (see p. 396). Brethren settlements in Pennsylvania, especially at Bethlehem, were important centers of music.

For the Brethren, singing was an integral part of everyday life—at home, in school, and in the church. In the sixteenth century, they rarely used polyphony, though children were taught part-singing in school. The Brethren's preference for monophony was probably a reflection of their belief in the equality of all things. Their interest in hymns is reflected in the compilation and publication of extensive hymnbooks, the first of which appeared in 1505. Jan Blahoslav's compilation (1561) contained about 750 hymns. The melodies are relatively simple, with close affinity between the vernacular words and the music.

The Reformation

MARTIN LUTHER

Martin Luther (1483–1546) unintentionally created the rift that caused the Protestant Reformation. When he posted his 95 theses on the Schlosskirche door, which served as the community bulletin board at Wittenberg, he was merely announcing that he wanted to debate those controversial points with an interested party. The incident was the opening wedge that split the Catholic Church. The reforms Luther advocated were primarily doctrinal. His theological beliefs were based on Scripture, not church traditions; practices such as the sale of indulgences were repugnant and sacrilegious to him. When the church could not subdue Luther, he was excommunicated; when called before the Diet of Worms, he refused to recant and was condemned as a state outlaw. Nevertheless, he continued to teach and preach, and virtually all sixteenth-century Protestant reformers were influenced to some extent by his activities.

Luther considered music a gift of God, second only to theology; the place of music in the sixteenth-century Lutheran church mirrored this view. Luther stated his position clearly in the Preface to Walter's *Geystliches gesangk Buchleyn* (Little book of sacred songs; see p. 196): "It is not my view that the Gospel should cause all the arts to be struck down and disappear; on the contrary, I should like to see all the arts, and especially music, used in the service of Him who gave and created them." Luther's attitude toward instrumental music is inherent in the Preface to his *German Mass*: "Whenever it was helpful I would have all the bells peal, all the organs thunder, and everything sound that could sound." Yet, in many sixteenth-century Lutheran churches the organ was used only for intonations before and interludes between unaccompanied vocal music.

Luther had received musical training in school; as a youngster, he sang in the *Kurrende,* a boys' choir that went about singing from door to door to obtain alms. As an adult, he had a fine tenor voice, was an accomplished performer on flute and lute, understood music theory, and was a skilled composer. He enjoyed Franco-Netherlands polyphony, especially that of Josquin. Two four-voice motets by Luther are extant: *Höre Gott meine Stimm' in meiner Klage* (God, hear my voice in my complaint) and *Non moriar, sed vivam* (I shall not die, but live; Ps. 118, vs. 17). Luther believed that music had educational value and ethical power; he advocated *Kantorei* and choir schools and congregational participation in the service music. (A *Kantorei* was a choir of professional singers employed by a church.)

Luther had no desire to abolish Latin. His *Formula missae* (Order of the Mass; 1523) was intended for use by cathedrals, collegiate churches, and other congregations that knew Latin. It consisted primarily of the Ordinary in chant; hymns might be added after the Sanctus and Agnus Dei. The *Deudsche Messe* (German Mass; 1526; fig. 12.1) was designed for churches with congregations of "unlearned lay folk."

DEUDSCHE MESSE (1526)

Introit   (A hymn or psalm, in 1st mode)
Kyrie   (troped)
Collect
Epistle   (on 8th tone)
Nun bitten wir den Heiligen Geist   (Now let us pray
        to the Holy Spirit)   replacing the Gradual
Gospel   (on 6th tone)
Sermon   (based on the Gospel text)
Lord's Prayer
Communion sacrament, in condensed form
Communion hymn: *Jesus Christus, unser Heiland*
        (Jesus Christ, our Savior)
Jesaja dem Propheten des geschah (Isaiah the prophet
        saw) = the German Sanctus
Optional: *Christe, du Lamm Gottes* (Christ, Lamb of God
        = the German Agnus Dei

FIGURE 12.1 Outline of Luther's German Mass.

The *Deudsche Messe* was an altered version of the Roman Catholic Mass. The Gloria was omitted, German hymns were substituted for some sections, and other sections were omitted or shortened. The portions retained were not merely textual translations from

Martin Luther.

paring materials for the church, Luther sought the advice of composers whose music he admired and musicians whose opinions he trusted: Ludwig Senfl, Conrad Rupsch, Georg Rhau, Johann Walter, Sixtus Dietrich, and others.

The Lutheran church made some use of **Leisen** (sing. *Leise*), German folk hymns in which the refrain *Kyrieleison* or *Kyrieleise* (Lord, have mercy) concluded every stanza. Luther expanded some of the older *Leisen* and wrote some new hymns in *Leise* style.

CHORALE

At the heart of Lutheran music is the German *Choral*, or *Kirchenlied* (church song), called in English a **chorale.** A chorale is a German hymn comprising a text and a melody and was originally sung *a cappella;* thus, a chorale is comparable to a monophonic chant. In the early Lutheran church, chorales were intended for congregational singing; most chorales are strophic. Some sixteenth-century chorales were newly composed melodies, and others were *contrafacta*—chants, nonliturgical spiritual songs, secular melodies, or folk songs fitted with German sacred texts. For example,

Latin into German but adaptations, for Luther realized that in a vernacular Mass the musical and textual rhythms and accents must be compatible. Luther's was not the first vernacular German Mass, nor was it intended as a definitive format for the Lutheran vernacular service; many variants were used. When pre-

REFORMATION—COUNTER-REFORMATION

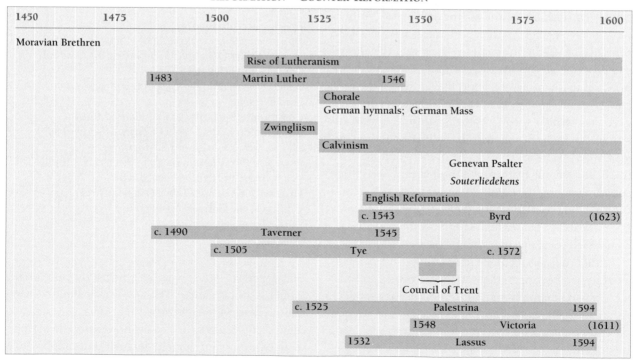

1450	1475	1500	1525	1550	1575	1600
Moravian Brethren						
		Rise of Lutheranism				
	1483	Martin Luther	1546			
			Chorale			
			German hymnals; German Mass			
		Zwingliism				
			Calvinism			
				Genevan Psalter		
				Souterliedekens		
			English Reformation			
			c. 1543	Byrd	(1623)	
	c. 1490	Taverner	1545			
	c. 1505	Tye		c. 1572		
			Council of Trent			
		c. 1525	Palestrina	1594		
			1548	Victoria	(1611)	
		1532	Lassus	1594		

the chant *Veni Redemptor gentium* (Come, Redeemer of the people) became *Nun komm' der Heiden Heiland* (Come, Savior of the nations); the folk song *Es hat ein Meidlin sein Schuh verlorn* (A maiden has lost her shoe) was transformed to *Gottes Huld hab ich verlorn* (I have lost God's grace). To provide a sufficient number of suitable chorales for the church, Luther urged his composer friends and music advisers to write chorales and make *contrafacta*. Luther wrote numerous chorale texts and is credited with composing and/or arranging the music for them. His best-known chorale is *Ein' feste Burg ist unser Gott* (A mighty fortress is our God; fig. 12.2). Luther's hymns were intended to convey a message, not create a mood. He wrote the music in mensural notation, with the semibreve as the basic unit of the beat. In terms of modern metronome markings, the hymns were probably sung at a tempo of approximately M.M. ♩ = 60.

In early January 1524 the first Lutheran hymnal appeared, entitled *Etlich Christlich lider* (Some Christian songs) but commonly referred to as *Das Achtliederbuch* (The Book of eight songs). The volume contained four chorale melodies and eight texts: one anonymous, three by Paul Speratus (1484–1551), and four by Luther. Four other collections of chorales appeared in 1524. In succeeding years, several similar publications ensued.

FIGURE 12.2 Luther's chorale *Ein' feste Burg ist unser Gott* in manuscript.

Chorales were set polyphonically for choir use. Various compositional styles were employed: (1) the melody treated as cantus firmus, written in long note values and placed in the tenor; (2) each melodic phrase written as a point of imitation, in Netherlands-motet style; (3) the melody in the tenor voice, with the other voice(s) in pseudo-chordal counterpoint; and occasionally (4) in *cantional* style, with the chorale in the top voice. As the sixteenth century advanced, use of treble-dominated style increased. In 1586 Lucas Osiander (1534–1604) published *Fünfftzig geistliche Lieder und Psalmen* (Fifty sacred songs and psalms), the first collection of chorales in four-part cantional-style settings. Frequently thereafter, chorales were set as simple chordal harmonizations of a soprano melody. Probably, in performance the chorale melody was sung, and the organ (or possibly other instruments) doubled the melody and provided the harmony.

Chorales served as basic material for motets in much the same manner as chant was used. Polyphonic pieces of this kind, known as **chorale motets,** were composed for two or more voices. A chorale-based **bicinium** or **tricinium** (a two- or three-voice composition) resembles a twelfth-century organal motet in that the principal melody appears in the tenor (the bottom voice) and is supplemented and enhanced by the polyphony of the other voice(s) (ex. 12.1). In other chorale motets, the chorale melody might be treated imitatively, or it might be retained in one voice while other voices supplemented it with imitative counterpoint. Near the end of the sixteenth century, chorale motets were written increasingly. Hans Leo Hassler and Michael Praetorius wrote some of the finest Lutheran motets of that era. Hassler's 52 four-voice *Psalmen und christliche Gesänge* (Psalms and Christian songs; 1607) are stylistically conservative and are written in imitative linear counterpoint with some canon and other techniques typical of mid-sixteenth century style. Hassler also composed many secular songs. The melody of his Lied *Mein G'müt ist mir verwirret* (My peace of mind is disturbed, [this has a maiden done]; 1601; DWMA74) was used by Johann Crüger with Paul Gerhardt's words *O Haupt voll Blut und Wunden* (O bloody and wounded head); that combination of text and tune was reharmonized by J. S. Bach and used five times in the *Passion according to St. Matthew.*

EXAMPLE 12.1 Opening phrases of Johann Walter's *bicinium* chorale setting of Luther's *Ein feste Burg*. *(From Georg Rhau: Musikdrucke VI, Bicinia gallica, latina, germanica. Bärenreiter Kassel, Basel, London/Concordia Publ. House, St. Louis/London)*

Bach's setting appears in modern hymnals as the Passion hymn *O sacred head, now wounded*.

JOHANN WALTER

Walter (1496–1570) became personally acquainted with Luther at some time prior to 1524. In autumn 1525, when Luther was drafting the *German Mass*, Walter and Conrad Rupsch served as his advisers. Walter wrote Magnificat and Psalm settings, motets, many Tenorlieder and hymns, and two Passions. His *Passion according to St. Matthew* (1550) uses German text and sets the words of the *turba* (the crowd) in polyphony and the solo portions in chant.

Walter's significance in music history rests primarily on his *Geystliches gesangk Buchleyn* (Little book of sacred songs; 1524), preparation of which Luther supervised and for which he wrote the preface. This, the earliest published collection of Lutheran choral music, was intended for use by young persons. The first edition contained 5 Latin motets and 38 Lieder; texts for 23 of the German settings were by Luther. The Lieder are cantus firmus works: 36 are Tenorlieder, and 2 are treble dominated. Walter's collection served as model for other collections, many of which included some of the same material.

GEORG RHAU

On several occasions, Luther consulted Georg Rhau (1488–1548) about liturgical music. Rhau became one of the most important sixteenth-century publishers of music for Reformation churches. His extant publications provide a representative repertory of music used in early Protestant worship and pedagogy. Church school curricula included both secular and sacred music.

From his childhood, Rhau was involved in music. He earned a baccalaureate degree at the University of Wittenberg; undoubtedly, he became acquainted with Luther while studying there. Rhau composed Magnificat and Psalm settings, Latin motets, German hymns, and at least one Mass; these works are not extant. In 1518–20 he served as Kantor of the Thomasschule and Thomaskirche at Leipzig and was a member of the music theory faculty at Leipzig University. From 1523 until his death, he operated a publishing business in Wittenberg.

Between 1538 and 1545 Rhau issued 15 major collections of polyphonic music. One of these was *Newe deudsche geistliche Gesenge CXXIII . . . für die gemeinen Schulen* (123 New sacred songs in German . . . for community schools; 1544). This compilation of motets and polyphonic arrangements of chorales include compositions by leading Germanic composers of the early sixteenth century. Stylistically, the chorale settings vary considerably; thus, the book presents an overview of early Protestant styles. Some pieces are similar to Tenorlieder, some resemble Franco-Flemish motets, and others are homorhythmic, with the chorale melody in the superius. As the century progressed, use of treble-dominated pseudo-chordal style increased.

SCANDINAVIA

Denmark governed Norway and Sweden from 1379 until 1522, when Sweden achieved independence. Finland remained a Swedish province. Swedish rulers actively supported music, and sacred music was an important subject in the school curriculum. In the sixteenth century, Lutheranism coexisted with traditional Latin Gregorian services. In 1531 Olaus Petri prepared the Swedish vernacular Mass, using Luther's *Formula missae* as the basis. Polyphony was seldom used. Chorales occupied a central position in worship, and many German chorales were adapted for Scandinavian use, but until 1586 hymnbooks contained only texts.

A young Finnish student at the University of Rostock, Theodoricus Nylandensis (c. 1560–c. 1616), compiled a song anthology that was published in 1582 as *Piae cantiones . . .* (Sacred songs . . .). Twelve of the 74 songs in the collection are polyphonic, for from two to four voices; the other 62 are monophonic melodies. Gustav Holst (1874–1934), Jean Sibelius (1865–1957), and John M. Neale (1818–66) made settings of some of these melodies; several of Neale's harmonizations have become familiar carols (e.g., "Good King Wenceslas looked out").

FRANCE, SWITZERLAND, AND HOLLAND

In those parts of France and Switzerland affected by the Reformation, church music was restricted drastically. Ulrich Zwingli (1484–1531) and his followers regarded art and music as powers to distract the faithful rather than as beneficial adjuncts to worship. Zwingli was educated in music and considered pursuing a career in music. After ordination to priesthood (1506), he entered a monastery but continued his musical activities. In 1518 he was appointed people's priest at Grossmünster in Zurich. Within three years, he began a radical reformation that reduced ritual and ceremony to a minimum and ultimately excluded music. In 1527 the organs in Grossmünster were dismantled; no organ music was performed in that church for almost 350 years. Though Zwingli came to be regarded as an enemy of music, he never completely relinquished his personal use of it; he composed several settings of sacred vocal texts c. 1520–29. Zwingli's reform spread through the northern cantons of Switzerland; the southern cantons remained Catholic. Eventually, civil war erupted, and Zwingli lost his life in the second Cappel War.

Jean Calvin (1509–64) studied theology in Paris and law in Orléans and Bourges. In Paris in the early 1530s he became interested in reformed doctrines. When the court proscribed Lutheranism there, Calvin fled to Switzerland. In 1536 he visited Ferrara, where he met Clément Marot (c. 1496–1544), who had made metrical translations of some of the Psalms to be sung to popular French secular melodies for the enjoyment of persons at the court of François I. Calvin was interested in Marot's texts.

Calvin spent 1537–38 in Geneva, then went to Strasbourg, where he was influenced by Martin Butzer's (1491–1551) limitation of service music to monophonic congregational singing. Calvin supervised preparation of *Aulcuns pseaulmes et cantiques mys en chant* (Some psalms and canticles set to music; 1539), an anthology of 9 of his own and 13 of Marot's translations, with some melodies from Strasbourg hymnals. In Geneva in 1541 Calvin worked to establish an order of service that included congregational unison singing of psalms and canticles in the vernacular. In 1542 he published an anthology of psalms that became the nucleus of Calvinist music. Théodore de Bèze (1519–1605) completed the metrical translation of the Psalms begun by Marot. The complete Psalter—the Genevan, or Huguenot, Psalter—was published in 1562 simultaneously in Geneva, Paris, and Lyons. It contained 125 melodies, many by Loys Bourgeois (c. 1510–60). His melody for Psalm 134, used in English-language Psalters for Psalm 100, is commonly called "Old Hundredth." It is still used as both hymn and doxology in many Protestant churches (fig. 12.3).

Polyphonic settings of psalms were used in home devotions. The earliest polyphonic settings were published in 1546 by Pierre Certon (d. 1572). Bourgeois's *Pseaulmes cinquante de David* (Fifty Psalms of David; Lyons, 1547) had wider circulation. Claude Goudimel (c. 1515–72) began publishing small books of *Pseaumes . . . en forme de motetz* in Paris in 1551; by 1564 he had completed setting the 150 Psalms. Claude Le Jeune wrote predominantly chordal four- and five-voice polyphonic settings of the entire Genevan Psalter; his Psalter was translated into several languages and circulated widely.

In Holland a Dutch metrical version of Psalms made by Willem van Nyevelt was in use c. 1540. In the seventeenth century this was gradually superseded by Dutch translations of the Genevan Psalter. Three-voice polyphonic settings of *Souterliedekens* made by

FIGURE 12.3 (*a*) Loys Bourgeois's melody for Psalm 134 in *Le Psautier Huguenot*; (*b*) modern use of the same melody, harmonized by Bourgeois c. 1551, for a Doxology. (*Source: Figure b text by Bishop Thomas Ken, 1692, Old Hundredth [original rhythm] "Genevan Psalter," arr. by Louis Bourgeois, 1551, English version of last phrase*)

(b)

Clement and Susato were published in partbooks in 1556–57 (see p. 166). Jan Sweelinck (1562–1621) wrote a polyphonic setting of the entire Genevan Psalter, using the melodies as the basis for pieces in various styles for four to eight voices. Sweelinck's settings were intended for private devotions in the homes of wealthy amateurs. The collection is considered a monument of Netherlands sacred polyphony.

ENGLAND

Much of the extant polyphonic English sacred music from the late fifteenth and early sixteenth centuries consists of votive antiphons, Magnificats, and Masses. Most of this music is for five or six voices, displaying typical English full sonority. A characteristic of English music is the use of a long melisma in the concluding phrase or word of a piece, (e.g., on the final *Alleluia* or *Amen* of a motet or anthem [ex. 12.2]).

TAVERNER, TYE, AND TALLIS

John Taverner (c. 1490–1545) was the most important English composer during the first part of the sixteenth century. He was the first instructor of choristers at Cardinal College (now Christ Church, Oxford), which opened in 1526. His most significant works are festal Masses, Magnificats, and votive antiphons. These display the traits typical of English music at this time. His Masses contain no Kyrie, and some phrases are omitted from the Credo. Often Taverner used a melodic fragment sequentially as a kind of ostinato in a melismatic passage or developed a melodic fragment through imitation or canon.

Taverner, Tye, and John Sheppard (c. 1515–c. 1559) each composed a four-voice Mass based on the secular tune *The Western Wynde* (ex. 12.3). All three men treated the cantus firmus as the basis for variations, which suggests that they knew one another and may have been working in the same vicinity or that there

EXAMPLE 12.2 The long melisma on "Amen" concluding Byrd's *Christ Is Risen.* (*Source: Wm. Byrd,* Songs of Sundry Natures, *originally published 1589*)

EXAMPLE 12.3 *The Western Wynde melody.*

was a specific reason for their composing this Mass in that manner. Other Masses by these three composers have similarities. Taverner's Mass is a set of 36 contrapuntal variations, systematically arranged with 9 variations per movement. The arrangement of variations within the Gloria parallels that of the Credo, and the plan of the Sanctus corresponds with that of the Agnus Dei.

Taverner based his six-voice *Missa Gloria tibi Trinitas* on the first antiphon sung at Vespers on Trinity Sunday in Sarum rite. He placed the cantus firmus in the alto voice and used the melody as the basis for both solo and full sections. This Mass is significant historically for its generation of numerous instrumental *In nomine* pieces (see p. 219).

Christopher Tye (c. 1505–c. 1572) and Thomas Tallis were recognized as leading English composers around the middle of the sixteenth century. Tye composed Latin and English sacred music and instrumental works, including 21 *In nomine* consort pieces. (See DWMA85.) He was a keyboard player, but his numerous works for viol consort suggest that he was also an accomplished viol player.

The first recorded information concerning Tallis (c. 1505–85) is his appointment as organist at the Benedictine Priory, Dover, in 1532. From c. 1545 until his death he was a member of the Chapel Royal. In 1575 Tallis and William Byrd were granted a 21-year monopoly for printing music and manufacturing music paper. These Letters Patent were the first of their kind in England. Tallis and Byrd jointly produced *Cantiones . . . sacrae,* an anthology of Latin motets; each contributed 17 works, perhaps commemorating the seventeenth year of Elizabeth's reign. After Tallis's death, Byrd leased the monopoly to a printer; when it expired in 1596, the Queen granted Thomas Morley a monopoly.

A list of Tallis's music reflects ecclesiastical changes in England. He composed Masses and votive antiphons during Henry VIII's reign, Anglican Services and anthems while Edward VI ruled, Latin hymns and a Mass when Mary was Queen, and both Latin and English music after Elizabeth I was crowned. His motet *Gaude gloriosa* praises Queen Mary for restoring Catholicism. Among his finest vocal compositions are two sets of *Lamentations.* Tallis composed numerous keyboard works and several pieces for viol consort.

THE ENGLISH REFORMATION

England's break with the Roman Catholic Church resulted from political conditions and the personal desires of Henry VIII. The formal separation occurred in 1534. In 1535 the Act of Supremacy named Henry "Supreme Head on earth of the Church of England." Through Thomas Cromwell (1485–1540), the king effected dissolution of Britain's monasteries and confiscated their wealth. Many valuable manuscripts were lost or destroyed. The English church retained a form of Catholicism without the pope. Music was not appreciably affected until Archbishop Cranmer indicated in 1544 that votive antiphons and votive Masses were no longer to be used and that syllabic settings of liturgical texts were preferable. Under Edward VI (r. 1547–53), Calvinism and Lutheranism were tolerated, and the Church of England became Protestant. In 1548 the Dean and Chapter of Lincoln Minster were ordered to sing anthems in English, using syllabic settings; the Act of Uniformity (1549) directed that the only liturgy to be used for public worship was that in the English Book of Common Prayer.

Thus, the English Reformation consisted of six principal changes: (1) subordination of church to state, (2) separation from the papacy, (3) abolition of monasteries, (4) adoption of English for Bible readings and services, (5) simplification of church ceremonies, and (6) adoption of Protestant doctrines.

Queen Mary (r. 1553–58) was a devout Catholic; during her brief reign Catholicism returned. The pendulum swung the other way again with the accession of Elizabeth I (r. 1558–1603), who opposed Catholicism. By the Act of Settlement (1559), she abolished Sarum rite and restored Anglican but permitted the use of Latin in specified collegiate chapels and certain churches whose congregations preferred it.

English Protestantism brought changes in liturgical terminology and a new body of English church music. The principal form of Anglican music is the **Service.** As in the Catholic Mass, a Service contains sections that vary in accordance with the church calendar. A complete Service comprises music for the unvarying sections of Morning Prayer, Evening Prayer, and Communion; these correspond to Matins, Vespers, and Mass in Catholic liturgy. The Communion music comprises the Decalogue (Responses after the Commandments) and/or Kyrie, the Creed, Sanctus, Benedictus, Agnus Dei, and Gloria; often, only Kyrie and Creed were composed. In the sixteenth and seventeenth centuries, a Service using contrapuntal, melismatic music was termed a **Great Service;** one using syllabic, homorhythmic music was a **Short Service.** There was no difference in the number of musical items Short and Great Services contained. Christopher Tye and Thomas Tallis were the first to compose Services in accord with Cranmer's recommendation for syllabic settings.

The Anglican version of the motet is the **anthem.** A **full anthem** is choral throughout and is usually contrapuntal. Many appear to be *a cappella* but may actually have been accompanied when performed. A **verse anthem** alternates accompanied solo verses with choral ones; solo verses may be for one or more soloists. William Byrd (c. 1543–1623) is credited with writing the first verse anthems.

In the sixteenth century, the fluctuation between Catholic and Anglican worship necessitated a certain amount of adaptability on the part of English composers. Some of them produced both Catholic and Anglican music of high quality.

Gradually, an English Psalter developed. Myles Coverdale's *Goostly psalmes and spirituall songs* (c. 1539) contained the earliest metrical psalms in English that were printed with tunes. However, the book was banned because some of the melodies were Lutheran chorales. *Certayne Psalmes* (c. 1548) by court poet Thomas Sternhold (d. 1549) contained 19 psalms in metrical English verse, without music. In 1549 an enlarged Psalter was published, containing 37 of Sternhold's metrical psalms, plus 7 by John Hopkins; there was no music. Protestants who fled England during Queen Mary's reign took the Sternhold and Hopkins Psalter with them to Geneva, Frankfurt, and Holland. By 1562 the entire Psalter had been versified; this Sternhold and Hopkins Psalter was the most important English Psalter of the sixteenth century.

English Protestants who went to Holland were influenced by practices there. Eventually, a Psalter was produced that combined English and French-Dutch elements: *The Book of Psalmes: Englished both in Prose and Metre,* published by Henry Ainsworth in 1612. This was brought to America by the Pilgrims in 1620.

WILLIAM BYRD

William Byrd brought English virginal music to a high level of excellence. He composed some of the finest Latin church music produced in England during the latter part of the sixteenth century, as well as very fine Anglican church music. Byrd's Anglican music continued to be used after his death. During the revival of Tudor and Jacobean music in the 1880s, his music attracted attention; in the twentieth century there has been renewed interest in his motets.

Nothing is known about Byrd's ancestry or his early life. Probably, he studied with Tallis at some time. Three motets written for Sarum liturgy indicate that Byrd was composing by the age of 16. From 1563 to 1572 he was Organist and Master of the Choristers at Lincoln Cathedral, where he began to compose English virginal music. His keyboard *Fantasia in A minor* and some *In nomine* settings for viol consort date from this period. In 1570 Byrd was admitted to the Chapel Royal, and c. 1572 he held a joint appointment with Tallis as organist.

Byrd's earliest settings of English poems are consort songs. Some of them are settings of English metrical psalms. Those psalm settings with simple choruses at the ends of stanzas lie at the root of the verse anthem. When he was at Lincoln Minster, there was considerable need for new Anglican music. With the exception of Byrd's *Great Service,* his English liturgical music became a staple of the cathedral repertory.

During the 1580s Byrd renewed his commitment to Catholicism. He composed a number of motets relating to the Babylonian captivity; in these he used word painting extensively. In 1583–84 he and Philippe de Monte (1521–1603) exchanged Latin motets on verses from Psalm 137, *Super flumina Babilonis.* At this same time, Byrd composed music for the Anglican church (e.g., *Rejoice unto the Lord,* written for Accession Day 1586). At some time during the 1580s he composed the *Great Service* for the Anglican church.

In 1588 Byrd published *Psalmes, Sonets and Songs,* a collection of part-songs adapted from consort songs. This was only the third book of English songs that had been published. Two books of *Cantiones sacrae* (Sacred songs) were issued: Book I for five voices (1589) and Book II for five and six voices (1591). From Book I comes the verse anthem *Christ rising again,* in which Byrd effectively applied chromatic alterations to bring about cross-relations (ex. 12.4).

After 1590, Byrd resumed composition of Roman Catholic church music. In 1593–95, he composed and published three Masses for three, four, and five voices. The four- and five-voice Masses are considered the finest Mass settings written by an English composer up to that time.

Byrd composed two books of *Gradualia* (publ. 1605, 1607). They contain pieces that are motet sections rather than motets, for many can serve more than one liturgical function. Complete Mass Propers are provided—Introit, Gradual, Tract/Alleluia, Offertory, Communion—for the major feasts of the church year, plus Marian feasts and Masses. The high quality of Byrd's contrapuntal writing and his use of Netherlands techniques may be seen in *Ego sum panis vivus* (I am the living bread; DWMA76) from *Gradualia,* Book II. Byrd seems to have been the first English composer to use Franco-Flemish imitative contrapuntal techniques easily, effectively, and expressively.

Byrd's last collection of *Psalmes, Songs and Sonnets* (1611) contains full anthems (English choral motets), verse anthems, six-part consort songs, and two fantasias for consort. The keyboard music Byrd composed after 1590 consists primarily of pavans and galliards, but he wrote three important variations: *Go from my window, John come kiss me now,* and *O mistress mine, I must.* Some of his pavans, galliards, and preludes were included with keyboard music by Bull and Gibbons in *Parthenia* (publ. c. 1612).

EXAMPLE 12.4 Measures 1 to 13 of Byrd's verse anthem *Christ rising again.* Note the cross relations between f♯ and f′ in measures 4, 8, and 13. *(From Historical Anthology of Music, Vol. II, edited by Archibald T. Davison and Willi Apel. © 1950 by The President and Fellows of Harvard College; renewed 1978 by Alice D. Humez and Willi Apel. Reprinted by permission of Harvard University Press, Cambridge, MA.)*

The Counter-Reformation

Pope Paul III (r. 1534–49) comprehended the problems caused by Protestantism and approached them through conciliation. He appointed commissions and councils to assess the condition of the Roman Catholic Church and to recommend corrective measures. At first, he sought reconciliation with the Protestants. A conference in 1541 between some Catholic and Protestant leaders came to nought. Pope Paul then turned to reformation within the Catholic Church—in effect, a *Counter*-Reformation. He planned a conference of Catholic leaders—a conference that has become known as "the Council of Trent."

One of the Catholic leaders was Cardinal Caraffa, who became Pope Paul IV in 1555. Another leader was Don Iñigo Lopez de Loyola (1491–1556), who became a soldier of the church when his military career was cut short by an injury in 1521. He went to Paris to study, accepted orthodox Catholicism unquestioningly, and was imbued with religious fervor. He was convinced that he could best serve God by preaching, teaching, and supporting the Pope. Loyola and his followers formed a brotherhood that they called *Societas Jesu* (Company of Jesus), headed by a General. Members took four vows: poverty, chastity, obedience, and allegiance to the Pope. Loyola sought to propagate the beliefs of the Company and the Catholic Church through education. By 1556 the *Societas Jesu* had more than 1,000 members, and 30 Jesuit colleges and secondary schools were operating throughout Europe. Jesuits were influential politically, serving as councillors and confessors to rulers and securing appointments on important commissions. Jesuits attended meetings of the Council of Trent.

In May 1542 Pope Paul III issued the *bulla* convoking the first meeting of the Council of Trent. The Council deliberated in three sessions: December 1545–March 1547, April 1551–April 1552, and January 1562–December 1563. During the course of the sessions four popes reigned. On 26 January 1564 Pope Pius IV (r. 1559–65) issued the bull *Benedictus Deus*, proclaiming as law the Council's decrees. Church music was only a small part of the Council's work. Concerns in that area included (1) the intrusion of secularism, evidenced in Masses parodying chansons or using secular cantus firmi; (2) extensive multivoiced imitative polyphony that obscured texts and made their meaning incomprehensible; (3) wide variances in liturgical music, such as innumerable different Sequences in use in various locales; (4) widespread use of musical instruments, especially "noisy" ones, in church; and (5) the irreverent attitude, carelessness, and bad habits of singers (incorrect pronunciation, poor enunciation). The last point was the subject of a reprimand given by Pope Marcellus II to the papal singers on Good Friday 1555, the third day of his reign (see p. 205). The only music known to have been composed especially for performance at a session of the Council was *Preces speciales* (Special prayers), which Jacobus de Kerle (c. 1531–91) composed in 1561. The conservative style and devotional spirit of Kerle's music convinced the Council that polyphony need not be abolished from church music.

Where music was concerned, the only direct action taken by the Council of Trent was liturgical: Textual tropes were eliminated, and the number of Sequences was reduced to four, specifically, *Victimae paschali laudes* (Easter); *Veni, Sancte Spiritus* (Whit Sunday); *Lauda Sion* (Corpus Christi); and *Dies irae* (Requiem). The Sequence *Stabat Mater dolorosa* (The sorrowful Mother was standing) was readmitted to the liturgy in 1727. The Council directed that impurity and lasciviousness, secularity and "unedifying language," were to be avoided so that "the House of God may truly be called a house of prayer." Actual reform was left to local authorities; in the Holy See and the Curia it was the pope's responsibility. The approved format for the Mass (later referred to as the Tridentine Mass format) remained in effect until Vatican II (see fig. 4.3). The deliberations of the Council were effective in making composers conscious of the fact that church authorities were aware of their use of secular materials; for a time, Masses with a secular relationship were named

Missa sine nomine (Untitled Mass). Several composers, including Palestrina, stated or implied in prefaces to published works that the music had been composed in accordance with the reforms of the Council of Trent. Many composers aimed at a musical style that incorporated a melodic line moving primarily by step in smoothly curved phrases that were easily sung; counterpoint that was rather transparent, having imitative sections interspersed with homorhythmic passages; avoidance of chromaticism other than that occasioned by normal application of *musica ficta;* uncomplicated, regular rhythms; and intelligibility of text setting. Emphasis was placed on the function of music as an adjunct to worship rather than as an aesthetic enhancement of a service. The music of Giovanni P. da Palestrina (c. 1525–94) and several of his contemporaries conforms to those standards.

GIOVANNI PIERLUIGI DA PALESTRINA

To some extent, the Counter-Reformation and the deliberations of the Council of Trent influenced Palestrina's work, but legends exaggerate his participation in those events. When the Council of Trent first convened, his career was beginning; when the meetings concluded, his career was well established (Insight, "Giovanni Pierluigi da Palestrina"). He did not appear before the Council, nor was any of his music per-

formed at the meetings. In October 1577 Pope Gregory XIII (r. 1572–85) appointed Palestrina and Annibale Zoilo (1537–92) to prepare a new edition of the Roman *Graduale* in accordance with the recommendations of the Council. The project had not been completed at the time of Palestrina's death. Others continued the work; the *Editio Medicaea* (Medici Edition) was published in 1614 and was used until the Vatican Edition was published in 1908.

Palestrina has occupied a unique position in the history of music. Legends that proclaimed him the "savior of church music" contributed greatly to this. Since the early seventeenth century, Palestrina has been upheld as chief exponent of the strict style of diatonic modal counterpoint used in the sixteenth century. Though other composers were writing in that style, Palestrina's music provided the models to be followed. He is the first composer to be so consciously imitated by later generations. Pietro Cerone (1566–1625) cited his work in *El melopeo y maestro* (Melopoeia and the master; 1613). In 1725 Johann J. Fux (1660–1741) published *Gradus ad Parnassum* (Steps to Parnassus), a pedagogical treatise that explains Renaissance counterpoint through a dialogue between Master Aloysius (Palestrina) and pupil Joseph (Fux). Each succeeding generation of theorists has produced a pedagogical treatise based on Palestrina's style.

Almost all of Palestrina's life was spent in association with the Roman Catholic Church, and his music reflects that. The aura of the Roman Catholic Church emanates from it, as it does from Gregorian chant. His sacred music is conservative, serious, and objective and thus most appropriate for liturgical use. His compositional style may be seen clearly in his Masses. There is little secularity, and most of that is confined to his madrigals. Careful attention was paid to correct declamation; the texture of the musical fabric does not obscure intelligibility of the text. The basis of Palestrina's style is Franco-Flemish imitative counterpoint, with which he was thoroughly familiar. In some Mass movements, pervading imitation occurs, each phrase of text having its own melodic motive and being set imitatively. In other movements, imitative sections are interspersed effectively with homorhythmic passages. There is almost no chromaticism;

Giovanni P. da Palestrina

Giovanni Pierluigi da Palestrina

Giovanni Pierluigi was born in the town of Palestrina near Rome. He received his early education and musical training in Rome, where he served as choirboy at Santa Maria Maggiore. From 1544 to 1551 he was organist and choirmaster at St. Agapito Cathedral in his home town. Presumably, he composed Masses and other sacred music while there, but none survives. In 1547 he married Lucrezia Gori. They had three sons, all musically talented; Rodolfo (1549–72), Angelo (1551–75), and Iginio (1557–1610).

Cardinal Giovanni M. del Monte, Bishop of Palestrina, was Palestrina's first patron. Shortly after the Cardinal became Pope Julius III (r. 1550–55), he appointed Palestrina *maestro* of Cappella Giulia, the musical chapel at St. Peter's (Rome). In January 1555 Palestrina was admitted to the pope's Cappella Sistina, without examination, without consent of the other singers, and in spite of the fact that he was married. Julius died in March 1555; his successor, Pope Marcellus II, reigned only three weeks (d. April 30) and was succeeded by Pope Paul IV (r. 1555–59). In September 1555 Pope Paul enforced the Sistine Chapel's rule of celibacy and dismissed Palestrina and two other married

singers. Palestrina's successor was Giovanni Animuccia (1500–71).

In October 1555 Palestrina became *maestro di cappella* at the church of St. John Lateran; he left there suddenly in July 1560 after a dispute relative to funds for the musicians and took with him his son Rodolfo, a choirboy. In March 1561 Palestrina was appointed choirmaster at Santa Maria Maggiore, where he worked for five years. In 1564 he accepted summer employment at Villa d'Este, at Tivoli. In 1566–71 he taught music at the Jesuit Seminario Romano, where his three sons were enrolled; from August 1567 to March 1571 he again served Ippolite II d'Este.

In 1568 Emperor Maximilian II offered Palestrina the choirmaster position at Vienna, but he declined. Guglielmo Gonzaga also offered Palestrina employment but withdrew the offer because he could not afford to pay the high salary Palestrina requested. For Gonzaga's chapel at Mantua, Palestrina composed 11 Masses based on chants peculiar to the Mantua liturgy.

After the death of Animuccia, Palestrina returned to Cappella Giulia as choirmaster and worked there for the remainder of his life. At times he considered and declined other positions. Between 1572 and 1580

epidemics of plague struck Rome; Palestrina was seriously ill, and his wife and sons Rodolfo and Angelo died. (Rodolfo had just been appointed organist at the Mantua court.)

In 1581 Palestrina married Virginia Dormoli, widow of a prosperous Roman fur merchant; for the next decade Palestrina participated actively in the fur business and in real estate. He continued to compose and to have his works published. In 1584 he was instrumental in establishing an association of professional musicians, the Vertuosa Compagnia dei Musici di Roma, that had concern for the welfare of its members and was active in arranging for publication of their works.

Palestrina's fame spread beyond Italy; some of his sacred music was performed in Munich, and four of his madrigals were included in *Musica Transalpina* (see p. 186). Late in 1593 Palestrina contemplated retirement. As he was preparing to leave Rome in January 1594, he became ill; he died on February 2. Crowds attended his funeral services at St. Peter's; he was interred there under the pavement of Capella Nuova. That chapel was destroyed during subsequent remodeling of St. Peter's, and Palestrina's remains were lost.

---

of course, rules of *musica ficta* were applied. Although Palestrina wrote modal linear polyphony, the melodic lines often converge to form triadic chords. His harmonic awareness is apparent in his resolution of some tensions seemingly according to harmonic rather than purely intervallic laws. Frequently, the bass line moves by leaping a fourth or a fifth. Palestrina was writing modal counterpoint, and his music cannot be analyzed

according to principles of key tonality. In many respects, Palestrina's style does not differ appreciably from that used by others of the Roman school in their sacred music.

Palestrina was the first sixteenth-century composer for whom nineteenth-century musicologists prepared an *Opera omnia*. His known compositions include 104 Masses, more than 375 motets, a cycle of

68 offertories, a cycle of 65 hymns, 35 Magnificats, 5 sets of Lamentations, and more than 140 secular and spiritual madrigals. He seems to have composed only *a cappella* vocal music; the organ works once attributed to him are spurious.

SECULAR MUSIC

At various times Palestrina composed madrigals; they are his least important compositions. One of his first published works was a madrigal in an anthology (1554); a book of his four-voice madrigals was published in 1555, and another book appeared in 1586, though the pieces were probably composed earlier. Generally, Palestrina's madrigals are quite conservative in style. Two of them, *Io son ferito* (I am wounded; 1561) and the sonnet *Vestiva i colli* (The hills are clothed; 1566), became very popular. Palestrina wrote 8 five-voice *madrigali spirituali,* settings of 8 stanzas of Petrarch's *Vergini.* Palestrina rued having composed madrigals, and he expressed this regret in the dedication to *Motettorum liber quartus ex Canticis canticorum* (Fourth book of motets from Song of Songs; 1584). However, madrigalesque word painting is a feature of those motets.

SACRED MUSIC

Palestrina composed Masses of every type being written during the sixteenth century. His *Missarum liber primus* (First book of Masses; 1554) was the first book of Masses published in Rome. Some of Palestrina's Masses are freely composed, as is *Missa Papae Marcelli* (1567 or earlier). The reason for its composition is unknown; possibly, it reflects Good Friday 1555, when Pope Marcellus admonished his chapel singers concerning their performance of Holy Week music and advised that sacred music be sung clearly, in a suitable manner, so that the words could be heard and understood. That Palestrina's Mass was designed for intelligibility of the words is apparent.

Approximately 80 percent of Palestrina's Masses are chant based; this percentage takes into consideration the fact that many of the motets serving as basis for parody Masses are themselves chant based. There are 53 parody Masses, 22 of them derived from his own works (e.g., *Missa Hodie Christus natus est* [Mass Christ is born today]). In 35 Masses, chants or secular mel-odies are paraphrased. In accordance with tradition, Palestrina retained Gregorian chant for the Introit, Gradual, Tract, and Communion of his *Missa pro defunctis* (Requiem Mass) and paraphrased the appropriate chants in the other movements. Fifteen other Masses are based on plainsong Mass cycles.

There are seven cantus firmus Masses, including a five-voice *Missa L'homme armé,* the four-voice *Missa Ecce sacerdos magnus* (Mass Behold the great priest) in his first publication, and a six-voice *Missa Ave Maria.* These reflect the Flemish tradition, as do the canonic Masses. *Missa Ad fugam* (Canon Mass; 4 vc.) is in double canon throughout. In *Missa Repleatur os meum* (Mass My mouth shall be filled; 5 vc.; 1570), Palestrina's systematic application of canon is just the reverse of Ockeghem's procedure in *Missa prolationum.* From Kyrie through Agnus Dei I, Palestrina wrote canons in decreasing intervals of imitation from octave to unison, then constructed a double canon in the final Agnus Dei—one at the octave, the other at the fourth. In each canon the interval and distance of imitation correspond; for example, in canon at the octave the *comes* enters eight semibreves after the *dux* commences. The three-voice Crucifixus and Benedictus sections have no canon.

Canons appear within Masses that are basically constructed according to other techniques. The hard hexachord serves as cantus firmus for the six-voice *Missa Ut re mi fa sol la* (Hexachord Mass). A seventh voice is added in the final Agnus Dei to sing the cantus firmus in canon at the fifth below Superius II.

The six books of motets Palestrina published in 1563–84 contain 177 of his motets and three by others: his sons Rodolfo and Angelo and his half brother Silla. More than one-third of Palestrina's approximately 375 motets are for 4 voices; almost as many are for 5. Of the remainder, 60 are for 8 voices, and 10 are for 12. Most of his motets are based on antiphons and responsory texts.

The early four-voice motets are models of Renaissance polyphonic composition, displaying correct voice leading and intervallic construction, carefully controlled dissonance, and equilibrium of part writing. Texts are set with correct declamation, usually by complete phrases. These features may be seen in the motet *Lauda Sion* (1563), based on the Sequence for the feast of Corpus Christi (DWMA77). The motet is basically in duple meter. It commences imitatively, the four voices entering in turn from superius down to bass; each phrase of text is given its own melody, with slight overlapping of phrases at cadence points. Phrases are smoothly curved and of suitable length to be sung easily. Short melismas occur near the ends of phrases. The words of supplication, commencing *Bone pastor, panis vere* (Good shepherd, true bread), are set homorhythmically in triple (perfect) meter. There is a return to duple meter for the final phrase and *Amen.* The *Missa Lauda Sion* (DWMA78) was derived from the motet.

The four-voice motet *Sicut cervus* (As the hart) exhibits typical "Palestrina curves" within its phrase structure—a gradual rise of the melodic line balanced by a gradual decline (ex. 12.5). Typical construction of a bass line is displayed in the eight-voice *Alma Redemptoris Mater,* written for double choir.

Between 1588 and 1593, Palestrina published two books of Litanies and four important collections of other liturgical compositions: settings of Lamentations, hymns, Magnificats, and offertories. The fact that he had previously written other cycles in some of these categories implies that in some Italian churches polyphony had replaced Gregorian chant for these portions of the services.

Palestrina wrote several cycles of liturgical works, including *Hymni totius anni* (Hymns for the entire year; 1589), a cycle of 45 hymns, and *Magnificat octo tonum liber primus* (Magnificats in 8 Tones, Book I; 1589), two series of Magnificats in the eight Tones. The cycle of 68 Offertories for the entire church year, *Offertoria totius anni* (1593), is historically important. It is one of the first settings to be freely composed, in motet style, without any reference to chants. A shorter set by Lassus is similar in style.

TOMÁS LUIS DE VICTORIA

One of Palestrina's contemporaries in Rome was Tomás Luis de Victoria (1548–1611). Victoria was the greatest Spanish composer in the Renaissance and wrote some of the finest church music produced in Europe during his time. He received his early musical training at Avila Cathedral, where he served as choirboy. When his voice changed c. 1565, he was sent to Jesuit Collegio Germanico, Rome. He enrolled as a singer. At that time, Palestrina was teaching at the Jesuit Seminario Romano; Victoria may have gone to him for some lessons. Certainly, Victoria was well acquainted with Palestrina's compositional style.

From 1569 to 1574, Victoria was singer and organist at Santa Maria di Montserrato, Rome. Also, in 1571 he was engaged to teach music at Collegio Germanico and ultimately served as *maestro di cappella* there (1573–77). In 1575 he attained priesthood and joined the newly formed community of lay priests led by Filippo Neri (discussed on p. 261). Victoria was a chaplain at St. Girolamo from 1578 to 1585 but derived most of his income from five benefices he held at Spanish churches. Five volumes of his music were published during those years: hymns, Masses, motets, Magnificat settings, and Offices for Holy Week.

In the dedication of *Missarum libri duo* (Masses, Book II; 1583) Victoria expressed his desire to return to Spain as a priest. King Philip II appointed him chaplain to Dowager Empress Maria, at Monasterio de las Descalzas de Santa Clara, Madrid. Victoria was *maestro* of the convent choir from 1587 to 1604, then served as organist until his death. That choir comprised 12 priests (3 per part) and 4 boys; instrumentalists were hired for Easter and the octave of Corpus Christi. Instrumental doubling of vocal lines was widely practiced in Spain.

EXAMPLE 12.5 Palestrina's setting of the first phrase of Vulgate Psalm 43 (KJV, 42) in the superius of his motet *Sicut cervus* shows the balanced rise and fall typical of his melodic lines.

Victoria wrote only sacred music, and most of it was published during his lifetime. His works comprise 20 Masses, 52 motets, 8 psalm settings (7 for 2 four-voice choirs, 1 for 3 four-voice choirs), 38 hymns, 2 Magnificat settings (with polyphony for alternate verses only), the Offices for Holy Week, and other liturgical works including Responsories, Sequences, and the Office for the Dead.

Twelve of Victoria's Masses parody his own works: eight are based on motets, three on Marian antiphons, and one on a psalm setting. Four of the Masses parody works by Guerrero, Morales, Palestrina, and Janequin. Victoria's nine-voice *Missa pro victoria* (Mass for victory), based on Janequin's chanson *La guerre,* was popular in Spain. *Missa quarti toni* (Mass in fourth mode) is freely composed; the other four Masses are paraphrase type.

Victoria was one of the first composers to base a Mass on one of his own motets; the first Mass in which he did so is *Missa Dum complerentur* (Mass When [the day of Pentecost] had fully come; 1576). Palestrina and Guerrero did this later. Victoria's *Missa Ave Regina coelorum* and *Missa Alma Redemptoris Mater,* both eight-voice Masses for double choir, were performed frequently in Bogotá, Colombia, and Mexico City in the early seventeenth century. These two Masses parody Marian antiphon settings by Victoria. A characteristic of Victoria's Masses is tonal fluctuation, seen in such melodic successions as e–f–e♭ and f–g–f♯. Basically, Victoria wrote modal counterpoint. However, in the Masses his treatment of Dorian mode often becomes minor key tonality.

The motets *O magnum mysterium* (O great mystery) and *O vos omnes* (O, all ye [who pass]; DWMA79) are among his best-known compositions. *O vos omnes* is a four-voice setting of Lamentations 1:12. In it Victoria combined imitative counterpoint with dramatic, attention-getting repeated notes. The command *attendite et videte* (behold and see) is emphasized by general rests. Minor seconds are plentiful. The expressive quality characteristic of Victoria's style is felt in his setting of the words *sicut dolor meus* (like unto my sorrow; ex. 12.6).

Whereas Palestrina's music is coolly impersonal, Victoria's is expressive within the bounds of decorum. Quite a few of Victoria's compositions convey a sense of joy and well-being that may be a reflection of his optimistic attitude and joyful nature. On the other hand, sorrowful texts elicited from Victoria dolorous music, as evidenced by his settings of Lamentations. Some of Victoria's music is mystical and intense; the Lamentations contain some definite Spanish elements.

ORLANDE DE LASSUS

Lassus (1532–94) was one of the great composers of sacred music in the last half of the sixteenth century (Insight, "Orlande de Lassus"). Unlike Palestrina, Lassus was not ashamed of writing secular music and composed quite a lot of it. Moreover, secular works figured prominently as bases for his sacred works. Lassus wrote more than 2,000 compositions, in all genres used during his era: Masses, motets, Magnificat settings, Passions, hymns, psalm settings, other liturgical

EXAMPLE 12.6 Victoria's expressive setting of the words "*sicut dolor meus*" concluding his motet *O vos omnes.* *(From* Historical Anthology of Music, *Vol. I, edited by Archibald T. Davison and Willi Apel. © 1946, 1949 by The President and Fellows of Harvard College; renewed 1974 by Alice D. Humez and Willi Apel. Reprinted by permission of Harvard University Press, Cambridge, MA.)*

Orlande de Lassus

Orlande de Lassus was born in Mons, in Hainaut. Nothing definite is known about him prior to the summer of 1544, when he was noticed by Ferrante Gonzaga, who took him to Sicily. Lassus spent 1547–49 in Milan. He next obtained employment as a singer in the Torza household in Naples and may have begun to compose at that time. Then he went to Rome, where he was a singer in the household of Archbishop Altoviti.

In the spring of 1553, when he was 21, Lassus succeeded Animuccia as *maestro di cappella* at St. John Lateran. Lassus must have had an excellent reputation as a musician to secure such an important post. In 1554 he returned to Mons to visit his parents; when he arrived, he learned they had died.

Early in 1555, Lassus traveled to Antwerp, where he met printers Susato and Laet, and some publications resulted: a collection of four-voice madrigals, *villanesche*, chansons, and motets (Susato, 1555) and a volume of five- and six-voice motets (Laet, 1556). In Venice, Gardane published Lassus's *First book of madrigals* (1556) for five and six voices. Apparently, Lassus delayed publishing his works until several collections had accumulated.

In 1556 Duke Albrecht V of Bavaria decided to revitalize his Munich court chapel by employing Franco-Flemish singers. He engaged Lassus as *tenor secundus* and hired six more Netherlanders; in 1560 he sent Lassus to Flanders to recruit chapel singers. In 1562 Andrea Gabrieli was in the retinue accompanying Albrecht V and his chapel on a state visit to Frankfurt am Main; Lassus and Gabrieli became friends. Years later, Giovanni Gabrieli joined

the Munich chapel; he may have studied with Lassus.

Ludwig Daser was *maestro di cappella* when Lassus joined the chapel. When Daser was pensioned in 1563, Lassus was appointed chapelmaster; he retained that position until he died. Lassus's responsibilities at the Munich court included supplying requisite music for services and all special religious feasts, political ceremonies, and private celebrations. For Morning Service, polyphonic Masses and motets were needed. Vespers required Magnificats and motets. He supervised the education of choirboys, arranged for copying of manuscripts, and secured printed music for the ducal library.

In 1558 Lassus married Regina Wäckinger. They had six children; three of their four sons became musicians: Ferdinand (c. 1560–1609), Rudolf (c. 1563–1625), and Ernst (b. after 1565–d. after 1594).

Lassus's reputation as composer spread throughout Europe. Volumes of his music were published by the most reputable printers. He received honors rarely given to musicians: In 1570 Emperor Maximilian II (r. 1564–76) bestowed on him a patent of nobility; in 1574 Pope Gregory XIII named him Knight of the Golden Spur; on three occasions he was invited to the French court of Charles IX (r. 1560–74). In 1575 Lassus's Caecilian motet was awarded the prize at Evreux.

Duke Albrecht died in 1579. Wilhelm reduced the size of the ducal chapel considerably, but Lassus declined an invitation to work at Dresden. Albrecht had provided that Lassus would receive his salary for life, and Lassus did not want to leave Munich. He complained that he felt

Portrait of Lassus. Original painting at the Erziehungsinstitut, Munich, Germany.

old, but he continued to compose, and in 1581–85 many of his works were published. Around 1590, his son Ferdinand joined the Munich court to assist him; Rudolf was then court organist and music instructor to the younger members of the choir, and Ernst was a singer in the court chapel.

Orlande de Lassus was in poor health during the last decade of his life and frequently consulted the court physician about feelings of depression. However, he still accompanied Duke Wilhelm on official journeys. Lassus composed intermittently; his last volume of works (1594) comprises a cycle of 20 spiritual madrigals entitled *Lagrime di San Pietro* (Tears of St. Peter) and the seven-voice motet *Vide homo quae pro te patior* (See, man, how I suffer for you).

Lassus died in Munich on 14 June 1594, and was interred in the Franciscan cemetery there. When the Franciscan establishment was secularized, the monument that marked his grave was moved to the garden of the National Museum in Munich.

music, chansons, madrigals, and Lieder. More than 100 volumes of Lassus's compositions were published between 1555 and 1619.

SACRED MUSIC

Lassus's musical style is as versatile as his compositional output. He is best known for his motets. *Magnum opus musicum* (Great book of music; 1604) contains 516 of his 525 motets, edited by his sons Ferdinand and Rudolf. Lassus's motets are varied in style, but in all of them—in fact, in all of Lassus's compositions—the words generate the music and are master of it. His music is expressive and at times moody and dramatic. Harmonic clarity is apparent in all his motets; even when much chromaticism is present, the contrapuntal lines often form triadic chords within the modal harmony. This may be seen in the first nine measures of *Carmina chromatico* (Chromatic songs), the introductory motet of the *Prophetiae Sibyllarum* (Prophecies of the Sibyls) cycle (ex. 12.7). *Prophetiae Sibyllarum* comprises 13 motets, one as introduction and one invoking each of the 12 Sibyls who prophesied the coming of Christ. These motets indicate Lassus's awareness of avant-garde practices and may reflect some influence of Vicentino and Rore. Lassus *chose* to write in a conservative style; he was well aware of contemporary developments.

Stylistically, Lassus's early motets exhibit a combination of Franco-Netherlands and Italian practices. Imitation is important, and voice pairing occurs frequently; both techniques appear in *Tristis est anima mea* (My soul is sorrowful; 1565; DWMA80). The five voices enter imitatively, but bass and middle voice are paired, and the top voice enters at a pitch widely separated from the others. The use of antiquated chord structure

(no third) in the simultaneous cadence on *mortem* (death; m. 14) effectively emphasizes that word. *Circumdabit me* (surround me) is depicted musically.

Canon is used in *Creator omnium Deus* (God, Creator of all), based on a setting by Willaert; *Fremuit spiritu Jesu* (Jesus's spirit groaned) is unified by an ostinato. In some motets Lassus employed cantus firmus or *soggetto cavato* techniques. In others, he alluded to a chant but did not present it complete in any one voice. Chordal declamation appears in motets written between c. 1555 and 1570. Text painting is used but does not disrupt the balance or fluidity of the contrapuntal lines. The chromaticism of *Carmina chromatico* includes (in modern notation) all the semitones of the tempered C chromatic scale. In Lassus's time, these pitches may have been sung in *just* intonation.

Most of Lassus's motets are sacred. Probably, at one time he considered writing a cycle of motets for the entire church year, for among the motets in *Magnum opus musicum* are sections that fit the liturgical calendar. There are motets based on the Marian antiphons, Gospel motets, and Epistle motets (e.g., *Cum essem parvulus* [When I was little; I Cor. xiii:11]).

German and French as well as Latin are used in secular motets (e.g., for drinking songs). Some of the humorous motets are macaronic. (Macaronic texts use a mixture of languages.) Some of the two- and three-voice motets seem to have been written for didactic purposes (e.g., the 24 *bicinia* [1577]).

Lassus composed approximately 60 Masses, two of which are Requiem Masses. He used parody technique in most of his Masses, basing them primarily on motets but using secular songs as models also. In these parodies, Lassus usually made direct quotation from his model in the Kyrie, then alluded to the model at

EXAMPLE 12.7 Lassus's chromaticism forms triadic chords in the modal harmony at many places in *Carmina chromatico*, the short introductory motet of *Prophetiae Sibyllarum*, composed c. 1560.

significant places in the other movements. His handling of parody technique is considerably varied; his Masses are instructive in the various ways of using that technique. Three of Lassus's best Masses are *Missa Dixit Joseph* (Mass, Joseph said; 6 vc.); *Missa In te Domine speravi* (Mass, In Thee, Lord, I will hope; 6 vc.), both based on his own music, and *Missa Io son ferito* (Mass, I am wounded; 5 vc.), based on Palestrina's madrigal. *Missa Jesus ist ein süsser Nam'* (Mass, Jesus is a sweet name; 6 vc.) is one of two Masses based on German music. The fact that Lassus parodied secular works in his Masses indicates that in Germanic lands there was less strict compliance with the recommendations of the Council of Trent than in Italy. Also, Lassus stubbornly resisted some of those recommendations.

Court customs caused him to write several syllabic *Missae breves* (Short Masses). For example, *Missa Venatorum* (Hunt Mass; 4 vc.) was designed for a brief service on days the court went hunting.

Approximately half of Lassus's 101 Magnificat settings are based on Gregorian chant; the remainder parody chansons, madrigals, and motets. Lassus was the first composer to use parody technique in Magnificat settings. For most of these parodies he used his own motets and chansons. He composed five Magnificat cycles, each comprising a six-verse setting for all eight Tones.

Lassus composed at least four Passions, one according to each of the Gospel Evangelists. The *Passion according to St. Matthew* was still performed in 1743; during the Baroque era it was supplied with *basso continuo* accompaniment. (*Basso continuo* is discussed on p. 229.)

SECULAR MUSIC

Lassus composed some of the finest chansons written during the last half of the sixteenth century. Between 1550 and c. 1585 he wrote approximately 150 of them (see p. 189). He wrote no Lieder until 1567, by which time he was sufficiently familiar with the German language to set it properly. He was wise to wait, for Senfl had worked at the Munich court, and his excellent Lieder were well known. Lassus used both sacred and secular poems for his 93 Lieder and set texts in various ways: some are Tenorlieder; others are motetlike or madrigalian. *Ich armer Mann* (I, poor man; 1576) is humorously satirical.

Lassus wrote approximately 176 Italian secular pieces: madrigals, villanellas, and morescas. *Libro de villanelle, moresche, et altre canzoni* (Book of villanellas, morescas, and other songs; Paris, 1581), contains some of his most popular Italian songs; for example, *Matona mia cara* (Matona, my dear), which is witty and slightly suggestive. Many of his later madrigals are more serious, especially the poetry Petrarch wrote after the death of his beloved Laura.

SUMMARY

Several times over the centuries there had been agitation for various kinds of reforms within the Roman Catholic Church. Until the first quarter of the sixteenth century all activities that papal authorities deemed heretical had been suppressed. In 1517 Martin Luther unintentionally caused the rift that created the Protestant Reformation. Luther suggested few changes in the Mass liturgy but proposed a possible format for a German Mass. He favored the arts, especially music; congregational singing held an important place in Lutheran services. In northern Germanic lands, where both Latin and German Masses were in use, Lutheranism enriched liturgical music by the chorale, chorale motet and other polyphonic chorale settings, and contrafacta. At the heart of Lutheran music is the chorale. Under Luther's supervision new chorales were composed and preexistent melodies adapted as chorales. Among composers working with Luther in the creation of a body of Lutheran church music were Walter and Rhau. Lutheranism spread through northern Germanic lands and into Scandinavian countries, where it coexisted with Catholicism. In southern Germanic lands, Roman Catholicism was affected only by the Counter-Reformation.

In those parts of France and Switzerland affected by the Reformation, music was restricted drastically. Zwingli ultimately excluded all music from services, and Calvin restricted church music to singing the Psalms. Marot's and de Bèze's metrical French translations of the Psalms were set to melodies by Bourgeois and others; these formed the Genevan (Huguenot) Psalter published in 1562. In Holland, Dutch translations of that Psalter gradually superseded the *Souterliedekens*. Polyphonic settings of the Psalms were used in home devotions.

England's break with the Roman Catholic Church in 1534 resulted from political conditions and the personal desires of Henry VIII. During much of the remainder of the sixteenth century, the pendulum swung between Catholicism and Anglicanism, with ultimate supremacy given the latter. The Anglican Service replaced the Mass; full and verse anthems replaced motets. In addition to writing Anglican Services, Byrd composed some of the finest Latin church music produced in England during the latter part of the sixteenth century.

Within the Catholic Church, a Counter-Reformation occurred. Where music was concerned, the Council of Trent eliminated textual tropes, reduced the number of liturgical sequences to four, and directed that impurity, lasciviousness, secularity, and improper language be avoided; actual reform was left in the hands of local authorities. The approved Tridentine Mass format remained in effect until Vatican II. Many composers aimed at a musical style that incorporated smoothly curved melodic phrases, with little or no chromaticism, and regular rhythms; counterpoint was rather transparent, imitative counterpoint being interspersed with homorhythmic sections. Intelligibility of text was a major consideration. The Masses and motets of Palestrina and Lassus exemplify this style. The sacred music of Victoria is more expressive than that of Palestrina and is some of the finest produced during the sixteenth century. Lassus was very versatile. In addition to sacred works, he wrote German, Italian, and French secular music and composed some of the finest chansons of his era.

RENAISSANCE INSTRUMENTAL MUSIC

13

The Renaissance is generally thought of as an age of vocal music, and most of the surviving music from the Renaissance is vocal polyphony. However, a wide variety of musical instruments existed, and an important musical development during the sixteenth century was the creation of a body of music literature designed especially for instruments—music that (a) had its own styles and forms, (b) was idiomatic to the specific instruments sounding it, and (c) was coherent and meaningful without relying on words. Moreover, didactic literature—both treatises and music—was written.

INSTRUMENTS

Most Renaissance instruments were built in families or sets incorporating graduated sizes; a set of a particular type of instrument provided coverage of the entire vocal range then in use, in homogeneous instrumental timbre. An ensemble in which all instruments belonged to the same family was called a **whole consort;** an ensemble including various kinds of instruments was a **broken consort** (fig. 13.1). Instrumental ensemble music published before c. 1597 did not specify instrumentation. One of the earliest pieces to specify exact instrumentation—trombones, cornetto, and *violino*—is Giovanni Gabrieli's *Sonata pian e forte* (Sonata soft and loud; c. 1597 DWMA81). Music for keyboard or lute was identifiable by the peculiarities of its **tablature,** which is the general term used for notational systems in which pitches are indicated by letters, numbers, or symbols other than notes on a staff (fig. 13.2). Title pages of some printed music stated that it was *per cantare e sonare* (for singing and playing), *convenable tant à la voix comme aux instruments* (suitable for voice and/or instruments), or "apt for voyces or vyols." The actual instrumentation was determined by the musician in charge of a performance, who selected appropriate instruments from those available at his place of employment.

Instruments were still classified as loud (*haut*) or soft (*bas*); in general, the sounds they produced had less volume and less intense tonal colors than those of modern instruments. However, a blanket comparative judgment should not be made to the detriment of Renaissance instrumental sonorities. Environmental effect must be considered—the effect of such factors as the acoustical properties of the constructional materials of the chambers in which the music was performed, the presence or absence of tapestries or other draperies in the rooms, the degree to which the auditors' ears were (or were not) bombarded by noises created by daily living conditions, and the resultant auditory sensitivity (or lack of it) to musical nuances. Re-

FIGURE 13.1 This woodcut illustrates a broken consort performing. Instruments represented include viola da gamba, cornetto, lute, transverse flute, and virginal. *(Source: Adam Berg: Patrocinium musices, 1589)*

(a)

(b)

FIGURE 13.2 (a) Italian and (b) French lute tablatures. Each line represents a course. The figure 0 or the letter *a* indicates an open string, and subsequent numbers or letters (in numerical or alphabetical order) represent frets. Each number or letter on a line indicates the point on the course (i.e., the fret) at which the finger must stop the string to produce the required pitch. *(Source: Figure a—Petrucci, Intabolatura de lauto. Libro primo. Venice, 1507, p. 39. Figure b—Denis Gaultier, La Rhétorique des dieux, Berlin, Kupferstichkabinett MS. 142, ca. 1650, p. 25)*

naissance audiences may have enjoyed finer musical subtleties than many modern listeners can comprehend.

Also, tuning and temperament must be considered. Voices are capable of producing at will pure fifths and thirds (**just intonation**) in any mode, but Renaissance instruments could not do this. The **mean-tone** system in use c. 1500 is based on a fifth slightly smaller than the perfect fifth. This tuning is fairly satisfactory melodically and harmonically when only one or two flats or sharps are involved, but noticeable pitch discrepancies result when more chromatics occur because flatted notes are higher than sharped ones (e.g., a♭ is higher than g♯). Some sixteenth-century organs were constructed with divided keys so that flatted and sharped notes could be played more accurately in tune; however, this proved inadequate for the needs of increased chromaticism, more fully developed harmonies, and modulations. Experiments with **equal temperament**—the division of the octave into 12

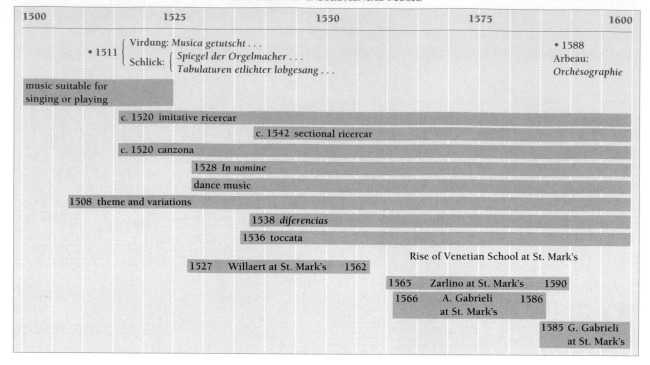

1500	1525	1550	1575	1600

• 1511 {
Virdung: *Musica getutsch* . . .
Schlick: {
Spiegel der Orgelmacher . . .
Tabulaturen etlichter lobgesang . . .

• 1588
Arbeau:
Orchésographie

music suitable for singing or playing

c. 1520 imitative ricercar

c. 1542 sectional ricercar

c. 1520 canzona

1528 *In nomine*

dance music

1508 theme and variations

1538 *diferencias*

1536 toccata

Rise of Venetian School at St. Mark's

1527   Willaert at St. Mark's   1562

1565   Zarlino at St. Mark's   1590

1566   A. Gabrieli   1586
at St. Mark's

1585 G. Gabrieli
at St. Mark's

equal semitones—began c. 1518, but the system was not clearly expounded until c. 1600 and not widely accepted until c. 1740–80.

For performance of the extremely chromatic madrigals he was interested in composing, Nicola Vicentino (1511–c. 1576) designed and had built c. 1560 two keyboard instruments—an *arcicembalo* and an *arci-organo*—that would sound all the various intervals contained in the diatonic, chromatic, and enharmonic *genera* used by the ancient Greeks.

The earliest printed treatise describing musical instruments is Sebastian Virdung's *Musica getutsch* (Music, [written] in German; 1511). The writing, structured as dialogue, is illustrated by woodcuts of instruments and tablature notation (fig. 13.3). Treatises by other authors ensued. One of the most notable Renaissance treatises on musical instruments is *De organographia* (Concerning instruments), which is volume 2 of Michael Praetorius's *Syntagma musicum* (Treatise on music; 1618). An appendix in that volume is entitled *Theatrum instrumentorum* (Theater of instruments); it contains 42 woodcuts of scale drawings illustrating the various instruments discussed (fig. 13.4).

WIND INSTRUMENTS

The principal types of wind instruments were recorder, *cromorne*, shawm, cornetto, trumpet, and trombone. The recorder was intended for use as an ensemble instrument; usually, recorder sets comprised a trio or a quartet of instruments. The first recorder method was published in Venice in 1535; dance music was printed by Moderne (Lyons), Attaignant (Paris), Susato (Antwerp), and others.

The *cromorne* (French, crooked horn; German, *Krummhorn*) is a J-shaped woodwind whose double reed is enclosed in a cap. A set of cromornes contained six instruments. Though used sporadically in the early fifteenth century, the cromorne was in vogue as an ensemble instrument c. 1475–c. 1600.

The shawm, a woodwind with an exposed double reed, was considered a loud instrument for ensemble use. Shawms were constructed in families of six, with sizes ranging from high treble to great bass.

The cornetto (little horn), a wooden instrument with a cup-shaped mouthpiece of ivory or bone, was made in both straight and curved models and in three sizes. Mainly, the cornetto was used with trombone

FIGURE 13.3 Description of clavichord and virginal, with
illustrations, printed in Virdung's *Musica getutscht* (1511).

1. Nicolo Bassett 2. Krummhorns 3. Soft Cornets 4. Bagpipe with Bellows.

FIGURE 13.4 Woodcut illustration of wind instruments. *(Source:
Plate XIII in M. Praetorius's* Syntagma musicum, *Volume II, De Organographia, 1620)*

and organ as support for choral music. The cornetto
was the nucleus of the instrumental ensembles formed
by Andrea and Giovanni Gabrieli at Venice c. 1600.

The straight trumpet existed from antiquity; the
trumpet with looped tubing appeared c. 1400. During
most of the fifteenth century, trumpeters were employed as town musicians, principally as tower watchmen. After c. 1480, however, five-part trumpet consorts
performed at many courts; ownership of a trumpet
ensemble was a symbol of a ruler's importance. In 1482,
there were 18 trumpeters at the Sforza court. The social
prestige of trumpeters mounted considerably in 1548,
when, by decree, Charles V placed them directly under
the jurisdiction of the emperor.

Trombones were used at the Burgundian and
Franco-Flemish courts by the mid-fifteenth century. In
addition to ensemble performance with cornetto and
organ to double voices singing choral music in church
services, trombonists played in town and court bands.

STRINGED INSTRUMENTS

The viol, a bowed stringed instrument with a fretted
fingerboard, first appeared in Spain in the last third of
the fifteenth century and quickly became known in
other European countries; it flourished as both solo
and ensemble instrument until c. 1750. Viols were
built in six sizes: treble, alto, small tenor, tenor, bass,
and contrabass (*violone*). A viol consort usually consisted of treble, tenor, and bass viols; a chest of viols

contained two of each of those sizes. The viol is characterized by a wide neck, sloping shoulders, and deep
ribs. Seven gut frets gird the neck and fingerboard at
semitone intervals. The six strings are tuned in fourths
around a central major third: bass *viola da gamba* tuning is D–G–c–e–a–d′; the treble viol is tuned an octave
higher. In the sixteenth century, the tenor viol was
sometimes tuned a fifth below the treble and sometimes a fifth above the bass. All viols are played in an
upright, almost vertical position, with the instrument
resting on the player's lap or calves. Thus, the viol was
properly named *viola da gamba* (leg viol). Unlike the
modern 'cello and string bass, the instrument had no
end pin for support. (The term *viola da braccio*, meaning "arm viol," was used in the sixteenth century to
designate instruments of the violin family.) To stop a
string, the viol player's finger firmly depresses a string
directly behind a fret, thus bringing that string into
tight contact with the fret; when the string is bowed,

the timbre of the sound produced is that of an unstopped (open) string. The viol bow stick is convex and is gripped underhand with the palm upward; tension of the bow hair is controlled by pressure of the middle finger directly on the hair. The bow is glided over the strings without pressure. Heavy accents cannot be produced on a viol; therefore, the instrument is ineffective for dance music. However, the viol is very responsive and resonant; its tone is quiet, with a distinctive reedy or nasal quality—characteristics ideal for the clarity of texture vital to effective performance of polyphonic music.

Instruments of the violin family—violin, viola, violoncello—were in existence in the second quarter of the sixteenth century. Jambe de Fer described them and discussed their use in his treatise *Epitome musicale des tons, . . . violes et violons* (Music treatise on tones, . . . viols and violins; Lyon, 1556). The violin differs from the viol in having four strings tuned in fifths, an unfretted fingerboard, an arched back and belly, and rounded and less-sloping shoulders. The violin bow stick is grasped primarily between the player's thumb and middle finger, with the hand held palm downward; the bow is drawn across the strings with varying degrees of pressure. Because of its capability to accent rhythmically, the violin is suitable for performing dance music—one of its principal functions in the Renaissance. No one knows who invented the violin; it seems to have originated in the Milan-Brescia-Cremona area of Italy. Founder of the Cremonese

school of violin making was Andrea Amati (c. 1510 or earlier–c. 1580); his descendants crafted superb instruments until after 1675. Amati instruments were imported to the French court by Catherine de' Medici, Charles IX, and Henri IV. Accounts of the performance of the dramatic ballet *Circé* at court in 1581 relate that two of the five-voice dances were played by ten violins. In the first three-quarters of the sixteenth century, violins were used primarily to double vocal lines and to supply music for dancing. Prior to 1600, violinists generally held lower social status than violists—viols were played by aristocratic amateurs as an avocation as well as by professionals, but violinists were professional musicians hired to perform at court, for municipal or church festivities, or for special celebrations at a wealthy household.

The lute was one of the most popular Renaissance instruments; most households owned at least one. Training in playing the lute was considered an essential part of the education of a cultured lady. Lutes were constructed in several sizes; performance of most of the surviving music requires treble, tenor, and bass instruments. The Spanish lute (*vihuela*) resembles a guitar; the standard lute used in other European countries is characterized by a body shaped like a halved avocado, a wide neck with a fretted fingerboard, and a pegbox bent backward at right angles to the neck of the instrument (fig. 13.5). The sixteenth-century lute had eleven strings arranged in six **courses,** two strings for all but the highest course. (A course is a group of strings

(a)

(b)

FIGURE 13.5 Illustrations of (*a*) lute and other string instruments and (*b*) lute neck with frets lettered on the courses. (*Source: Virdung: Musica getutscht, 1511*) tuned in unison or as an octave and sounded simultaneously to obtain increased volume.) The tenor lute was tuned either G–c–f–a–d′–g′ or A–d–g–b–e′–a′. The strings of the two lowest courses might be tuned in unison or in octaves, for example, G–g c–c′; those of the next three courses were always tuned in unison. Tones are produced from the six courses of strings by plucking them with the fingertips. Chords as well as single notes can be played, and rapid runs and ornaments are not especially problematic. Lute tones are rather soft, being more suitable for a chamber than a concert hall. The lute was used as a solo instrument, in ensembles, and to accompany singers.

KEYBOARD INSTRUMENTS

The generic term *clavier* (French, keyboard; German, *Klavier*) was used for keyboard instruments other than the organ. Two types of claviers existed: clavichord and harpsichord. In outward appearance, the fifteenth-century clavichord was a rectangular box with a keyboard set into one of its long sides (see fig. 13.3). Depressing a key causes a brass tangent to strike, from below, a pair of strings within the box and remain in contact with the strings until the key is released. A pair of strings can sound only one pitch at a time. Increased or decreased pressure on the key can slightly alter a pitch once it has begun sounding or create a vibrato. In the fifteenth century all strings in a clavichord were the same length and were tuned in unison; differences in the sounding length of each string (i.e., the portion of the string activated by a tangent) created the different pitches. By the mid-sixteenth century, the clavichord had a four-octave range, from F to f′′′ but lacked F♯ and G♯. (In other words, the lowest octave was a "short" octave—short two pitches.)

The harpsichord was invented c. 1400. During the Renaissance, instruments of the harpsichord type were built in various shapes and sizes and were known by different names, such as *clavicembalo, clavecin, spinet,* and *virginal*. When a harpsichord key is depressed, a jack is activated and a plectrum plucks a string, thus sounding a pitch. The harpsichord was both a solo and ensemble instrument. In the late Renaissance, many harpsichord cases were lavishly decorated with beautiful paintings.

The portative organ disappeared from use early in the sixteenth century; positive organs remained in use until the early seventeenth century. The *regal* was a small positive organ with reed pipes only. Early in the sixteenth century, it was incorporated into the large church organ as a rank of pipes, although some independent regals were still being used in the seventeenth century. The Renaissance church organ could cover the entire gamut in a uniform sonority, or, by means of a variety of stops, different tone colors could be produced. The slider-chest, built into the organ c. 1500, could easily isolate or combine separate ranks of pipes. Pedal keyboards, with solo pipes and with couplers to manuals, first appeared in Germanic and Franco-Netherlands territories, then were introduced in other countries. Organ-playing techniques improved during the sixteenth century; if desired, harmonies could be played on the pedals alone. However, thumbs were almost never used in playing. Renaissance organ cases were richly ornamented and often had side cases whose doors sheltered beautiful paintings.

Spiegel der Orgelmacher und Organisten (Mirror of the organmaker and organ player; 1511) by Arnolt Schlick (c. 1460–c. 1522) is the first German publication dealing comprehensively with organ building and playing; the book contains some organ music. Schlick's *Tabulaturen etlicher lobgesang und lidlein uff die orgeln un lauten* (Tablatures of some praise songs and little songs for organ and lute; 1511) contains the earliest printed organ tablatures. The advanced state of some German organs and Schlick's talents as organist may be seen in his *Ascendo ad Patrem meum* (I ascend unto my Father), a ten-voice organ work that, according to Schlick, could be played on the organ with four parts on the pedals and six parts on the manuals. The chorale-like cantus firmus, set in long notes in an inner voice, is surrounded by contrapuntal melodies.

The church organ was used both as a supportive and a solo instrument. Verses of some liturgical music, such as the Magnificat and various sections of the Proper of the Mass, were often performed alternately by singer(s) and organ. Similarly, certain sections of Kyrie or Gloria might be performed by organ in alternation with singers. In the sixteenth century, some complete settings of the Mass Ordinary were written according to this alternation principle—organ polyphony alternating with vocal music. Such a setting is known as an **Organ Mass.** An example is Cavazzoni: *Missa Apostolorum*. Sometimes short organ solos, called **versets** or **verses,** were substituted for chant in some portions of the Proper of both Mass and Offices. Organ pieces written in the style of motets served a like purpose. Schlick composed eight canonic versets, in from three to five voices, on the Sequence *Gaude Dei genitrix* (Rejoice, mother of God; DWMA82).

PERCUSSION

Various percussion instruments were used during the Renaissance: anvil and hammer, bells and chimes, small cymbals, side drum, dulcimer (psaltery), tabor, tambourine, trapezoid-shaped triangle with jingling rings at its angles, nakers (like six- to ten-inch kettledrums), kettledrums (timpani), and xylophone. Percussion instruments were used mainly for religious ceremonies, civic processions, military signals and encouragement, and dancing. If notated music was used, it has not survived; presumably, percussionists learned rudiments by rote and improvised music appropriate to the occasion. In *Orchésographie* (1588), Arbeau clearly described percussion instruments; stated that the side drum—a type of snare drum—was used as a pacemaker to organize military marches; and notated the various rhythms used by French drummers. Percussion instruments had been described and depicted previously in treatises by several authors, including Virdung (1511), Schlick (1511), and Martin Agricola (1528), and in an anonymous encyclopedic manuscript prepared c. 1585 for Henry III of France. The *Strohfiedel,* or xylophone, was first mentioned by Schlick as "wooden percussion." Dulcimers were popular and were played by hitting the wire strings with sticks. True kettledrums—large copper timpani—were introduced to western Europe from Russia early in the fifteenth century. These were cavalry instruments, carried by horses, that were associated with war, pomp, and ceremony. In 1511, Virdung wrote disparagingly about timpani, called them *Rumpelfesser* (rumbling tubs), and said they had been created by the devil. But royalty desired them and added them to their instrument collections. Almost invariably timpani were played along with trumpets; players of both kinds of instruments were highly esteemed. In Germany, the Imperial Guild of Trumpeters and Kettledrummers was established by decree in 1528; its members guarded their craft and transmitted their performance secrets by rote from generation to generation. No doubt this kind of professional secrecy was partially responsible for the lack of notated music for percussion instruments.

INSTRUMENT COLLECTIONS

Many churches and courts owned rather large collections of instruments. This was necessary so that complete sets of instruments were available for performance of ensemble music or to support voices with instruments of homogeneous timbre. Rosters of permanent employees at these institutions include names of instrumentalists. In the sixteenth century, it became fashionable to collect instruments; some wealthy households owned hundreds of them. Surviving inventories indicate that 70 to 80 percent of the instruments in most collections were winds. Instruments in private collections were not treated as art objects to be admired but were used and might be loaned to professional musicians. Valuable decorated harpsichords usually were considered part of the decor of their respective chambers and were used only in those rooms. In most court residences and private palatial homes, a keyboard instrument was kept in every room in which music was performed. Persons who could not amass as many instruments as they desired might simulate collections by means of *marquetry.*

INSTRUMENTAL MUSIC

Instruments were used to double vocal lines or substitute for them, to provide accompaniment for vocal solos, to work in alternation with vocalists, and to perform ensemble and solo music. Some pieces were written especially for instrumental performance. This music was of four main types: (1) pieces modeled on or derived from vocal compositions, (2) dance music, (3) variations, and (4) improvisatory works.

MUSIC FROM VOCAL MODELS

Instrumental performance of vocal music soon led to the composition of purely instrumental pieces of similar character. Motet and chanson served, respectively, as prototypes for the imitative ***ricercar*** (Ital., *ricercare,* to seek, to try out) and *canzona* (Ital., chanson). The contrapuntal ricercar is characterized by imitative treatment of one or more themes that usually are not melodically or rhythmically individualistic; stylistically, the ricercar is very similar to the motet. Terminology was not explicit; this kind of composition might be labeled *ricercare, capriccio, fuga, verset, fantasia,* or some other name.

The precise origin of the imitative ricercar is not known. The keyboard ricercars in Marc Antonio Cavazzoni's (c. 1490–c. 1560) *Recerchari, motetti, canzoni . . . libro primo* (Ricercars, motets, canzonas . . . book 1; 1523) and those of his son Girolamo (c. 1525–c. 1578) in *Intavolatura cioè recercari canzoni himni magnificati . . . libro primo* (Intabulations of ricercars, canzonas, hymns, Magnificats . . . book 1; 1543) resemble the imitative motet. Likewise, the 18 pieces named *ricercari* that are in *Musica nova* (New music; 1540) are in motet style, with pervading imitation. Most ricercars are of short to moderate length.

Imitative ricercars were written for instrumental ensembles and for organ. Some ensemble ricercars were labeled *da cantare et sonare* (to be sung and played); presumably, they were vocalized on solmization syllables. The imitative ricercar for organ might be monothematic or might have several themes each treated rather extensively in a separate section of the piece. Some of the earliest sectional ricercars were written c. 1542 by Girolamo Cavazzoni (DWMA83). The organ monothematic ricercar and the organ canzona are ancestors of the fugue (see p. 276). An imitative ricercar by Antonio de Cabezón is entitled *Fuga al contrario* (Fugue in contrary motion).

Some nonimitative instrumental pieces of improvisatory nature were written for lute, organ, and viols and were also entitled *ricercare.* These are more properly classified with the toccata and free prelude.

The term **canzona** originally denoted an instrumental arrangement of a polyphonic chanson; frequently, such an arrangement was labeled *canzon francese* (French chanson) or, if for an ensemble, *canzon da sonar* (instrumental chanson). Early canzonas closely resemble the chanson. In fact, the Italian word *canzona* and the French word *chanson* have the same meaning—"song." Most canzonas commence with the ♩ ♩ ♩ (or ♩ ♩ ♩) rhythmic figure that typically opens a chanson (ex. 13.1). Lute transcriptions of polyphonic chansons were in existence early in the sixteenth century. The earliest examples of keyboard arrangements of polyphonic chansons—called *canzoni*—appear in M.

A. Cavazzoni's *Recerchari motetti canzoni . . . libro primo.* In G. Cavazzoni's *Intavolatura cioè recercari canzoni,* one canzona is a condensation and complete reworking of Josquin's *Faulte d'argent* (ex. 13.1). However, by 1540, original compositions entitled *canzoni* were being written for keyboard and for instrumental ensembles. Around midcentury, ensemble canzonas were written with distinct sections that had contrasting themes both melodically and rhythmically. As the canzona developed, the sections increased in length and diversity. An example is Tarquinio Merula's canzona *La Strada* for two violins, violoncello, and organ (1637; DWMA84). At this time, the terms *canzona* and *sonata* were used interchangeably. In the seventeenth century, the longer sections split apart into independent "movements," and the **sonata da chiesa** (church sonata) emerged. In it, the fugal second movement is a vestige of the canzona. Title is not always clear indication of the character of a piece. Andrea Gabrieli's *Ricercare del 12° tono* (Ricercar on the 12th tone) exhibits characteristics of a canzona; it is clearly sectional and employs the unifying principles of repetition and contrast, as does Merula's *La Strada.*

Among instrumental ensemble music derived from vocal models is a unique type that is exclusively English—the **In nomine** (In the name). This type had a single model: that section of the Benedictus of John Taverner's six-voice Mass *Gloria tibi Trinitas* setting the words *In nomine Domini* (In the name of the Lord). The cantus firmus for that Mass is the Sarum antiphon *Gloria tibi trinitas aequalis* (Glory to thee, equal trinity). In the *In nomine* portion of the Benedictus of the Mass, the entire antiphon appears in long note values in the second-highest voice, which is labeled *Mean.* That section of the Benedictus was used as an independent composition for voices and in various arrangements: for voice(s) with instruments and as a purely instrumental piece for keyboard or for consort. Taverner made the first instrumental arrangement (for viols) of his Mass section; his contemporaries soon followed his lead (DWMA85). Approximately 65 *In nomine* pieces written in the sixteenth and seventeenth centuries are extant.

In addition to canzonas and ricercars, liturgical vocal music provided models for organ compositions. There were organ Masses and versets, settings of Lutheran chorales, and pieces based on plainchant.

EXAMPLE 13.1 Comparison of the opening of (*a*) Josquin's chanson *Faulte d'argent* and (*b*) Cavazzoni's organ canzona based on that chanson.

DANCE MUSIC

From the mid-sixteenth to the mid-seventeenth century, dancing was popular both as a social art and in the theater. A wealth of dance music appeared in print, and the strong rhythmic patterns of dance music permeated secular vocal music of the era. Dancing-masters abounded; both nobility and middle-class citizens sought to acquire dancing skills. Three basic kinds of dances were performed at social gatherings: stately processional types, such as the *pavane*; circular dances, such as the *branle*; and progressive "long-line" dances, such as the *allemande*. Dance music was written for performance by ensemble, keyboard, or lute. Usually, two or three contrasting dances were grouped together. Favorite combinations paired a slow, stately dance such as *pavane* (*pavan, padovana*) with a leaping dance such as the *gaillarde* (Italian, *gagliarda*, English, *galliard*) or a *passamezzo* (or *pass' e mezzo*, lit., a step

and a half) with a *saltarello*. Both *pavane* and *passamezzo* are slow, stately, processional-type dances in duple meter; *gaillarde* and *saltarello* are rollicking, leaping dances in compound duple ($^6_8$) meter interspersed with hemiola ($^3_4$) passages. The *pavane* uses a gliding step that produces an undulating movement reminiscent of a peacock's strut; the *gaillarde* is more vigorous with higher leaps than the *saltarello*, whose steps are more like skipping. The *gaillarde* was one of the few dances men performed with their heads uncovered; when dancing the *gaillarde*, a man held his hat in his hand. In Germanic lands, a slow dance in duple meter might be followed by a *Proportz* or a *Tripla*, a fast dance in triple meter. It is not uncommon for paired dances to use the same melody or variants of it.

Other paired sixteenth-century dances include the *allemande* and *courante*, which became standard movements of the seventeenth-century suite. The *allemande*

(French, German dance; English, *alman* or *almain*; Italian, *allemanda*) may have originated as a German version of the *basse danse*. By the mid-sixteenth century, however, the *allemande* was a distinct genre. It is a couple dance in which a man and a woman proceed side by side, in a stately procession of couples moving to duple-meter music in moderate tempo, from one end of the hall to the other; the line then reverses, and the couples return to their original starting point. The allemande is followed by a *courante* (French, running; Italian, *corrente*), a contrasting dance in triple meter. The *courante* was a kind of pantomimic wooing dance performed by couples moving in a zigzag pattern from one end of the room to the other. The *Bergomasca*, also a wooing dance, was a round dance.

Not all Renaissance dances were paired. The *jig*, which originated in the British Isles, was danced in Scotland, Ireland, and England. It existed as a male solo dance and a couple dance. Both types are characterized by vigorous movement up and down. During the reign of Elizabeth I, the jig became a popular couple dance at the English court and spread across the English Channel into France.

Printed dance manuals were available for purchase. Such books contained descriptions of the dances, instructions for performing them, dance music, and sometimes comments about the musical structure. Many fifteenth-century dance manuals are anonymous; a typical sixteenth-century book is *Orchésographie* by Thoinot Arbeau. Morley included a section on dances and dance music in *A Plaine and Easie Introduction to Practicall Musicke*.

Dances are significant in the development of music not only because music is an integral part of their performance but also because the pairing of contrasting dances led to larger groupings and because their music generated stylized versions that, in the seventeenth century, became the Baroque suite and **sonata da camera** (chamber sonata).

Ballet de cour (court ballet) was popular at the Burgundian and French courts. The earliest ballet in which poetry, music, scenery, and dance were combined in support of drama was *Circé ou le Balet comique de la Royne* (Circé or The Queen's dramatic ballet; performed 15 October 1581). Not until 1609 was another dramatic ballet of comparable quality performed in France.

VARIATIONS

Sets of variations on a theme were written principally in Spain and England. However, the earliest surviving examples appear in Petrucci's *Intabolatura de Lauto,* Vol. 4 (Lute tablatures; 1508). Dance pieces were especially favored as bases for variation sets. In Spain, variation technique was highly developed by Luys de Narváez (fl. 1530–50) and Antonio de Cabezón (1510–66). Narváez's book *Los seys libros del delphin* (The six books of the dauphin) is believed to be the earliest publication to contain pieces clearly identified as *diferencias* (sets of variations). Narváez's variations are of two types: (1) those in which the cantus firmus is present in each variation (e.g., variations on the hymn melody *O gloriosa domina*) and (2) variations on ostinato harmonies (e.g., *Diferencias sobre Guárdame las vacas* [Variations on *Watch my cattle*]). Cabezón, blind from childhood, was one of the greatest keyboard performers of his time. In his *diferencias*, the cantus firmus is placed in a different voice in successive variations; individual variations are not sectioned off but flow into one another. (*Diferencias sobre Caballero* Variations on *The Cowboy*; DWMA86) Cabezón was avant-garde in advocating use of the thumbs when playing organ.

An early sixteenth-century English example of continuous variation on a short *pes* (or ground) is *My Lady Carey's Dompe* (c. 1530). This three-voice work, the oldest of 16 extant *domps,* is a series of variations written above ostinato tonic and dominant harmonies.

One of the most important manuscript sources of English sixteenth-century keyboard music is *The Mulliner Book,* compiled c. 1550–c. 1575 by Thomas Mulliner. It contains dance pieces, transcriptions of secular and sacred vocal works, organ versets, and cantus firmus–type variations on hymn and chant melodies. A school of English virginalist composers flourished in the late sixteenth century. (The **virginal** was a type of small harpsichord with only one set of strings and one keyboard.) Chief among this school was William Byrd; others of importance were John Bull, Giles Farnaby, Orlando Gibbons, and Thomas Tomkins. At their hands, all known variation types attained artistic and technical maturity. Bull, Byrd, Farnaby, and Gibbons are the most important composers represented in *The Fitzwilliam Virginal Book,* a manuscript copied c. 1609–19. More than two-thirds of the approximately 300 pieces in that manuscript use some form of variation technique; most of the types of variation used in the sixteenth century are represented. Works by English virginalists exerted an important influence on northern European composers of keyboard music, such as Jan Sweelinck.

IMPROVISATORY WORKS

Improvisation was widely practiced during the Renaissance. Performers usually improvised by (1) adding one or more new polyphonic lines to an existing melody selected as cantus firmus, (2) embellishing or paraphrasing an existing melody, or (3) freely improvising without reference to a preexistent melody or harmony or predetermined formal pattern. The extemporization of one or more additional polyphonic lines was an extension of the practices of English discant and continental *faux bourdon*. Fleshing a composition from a skeletal musical line was practiced wherever and whenever the *basse danse* was performed. Extemporaneous embellishment or paraphrasing of a melodic line was an outgrowth of compositional practice—composers embellished and paraphrased preexistent melodies when writing Masses and motets.

Freely improvised compositions were given various titles, such as *fantasia* or *fancy, preambulum* or other designations for *prelude, ricercar,* and *toccata* (from the Italian verb *toccare,* to touch). Vihuelists and lutenists improvised introductions to popular court airs to establish the mode and create the mood of the piece.

Many compositions in improvisatory style are included in *El Maestro* (The Master; 1536) by Luys de Milán (c. 1500–c. 1561 or later). *El Maestro* is the earliest printed collection of guitar (vihuela) music and the earliest source of music with verbal tempo indications. The treatise is an instruction manual with music for performance and performance instructions (fig. 13.6). It contains both vocal and instrumental music and includes *pavans, tentos,* and 40 fantasias composed in idiomatic vihuela style. *Fantasia no. 17* is an example (DWMA87).

The earliest surviving pieces of freely composed keyboard music appear in tablature in fifteenth-century German manuscripts such as the *Buxheimer Orgelbuch* (see p. 147). Two rhapsodic *ricercari* are among the keyboard music in *Recerchari, motetti, canzoni* by M. A. Cavazzoni; these rambling pseudo-improvisatory pieces were intended as introductions to motet transcriptions.

FIGURE 13.6 Folio VI verso of Luys de Milán's *El Maestro* (1536). The last four staves of notation contain a *pavane.*

The first pieces designated as *toccatas* appeared in the sixteenth century. A *Tochata* by Francesco Canova da Milano is one of three toccatas in Casteliono's *Intabolatura de leuto* (Lute tablatures; 1536). More important is *Il transilvano dialogo sopra il vero modo di sonar organi, et istromenti da penna* (The Transylvanian dialogue concerning the true method of playing organs and harpsichords; Part I, 1593), the first comprehensive treatise on organ playing, by Girolamo Diruta (c. 1554–c. 1611). The treatise, written as dialogue between the inquiring Transylvanian and Diruta, summarizes keyboard practice of the time. The discussion includes rudiments of music and music notation, basics of organ playing and harpsichord playing, transposition and modulation, and performance practices such as when and how to properly ornament a melody. Diruta provided music examples to clarify the principles; complete compositions illustrate various

FIGURE 13.7 Examples of correct manner of performing *tremolo* given by Diruta in *Il Transilvano dialogo* (1593), Part I, p. 18.

problems encountered in performance. Examples of *tremolo* and *groppi*—ornaments like the modern *trill* and *turn*—show clearly that in music of Diruta's time these ornaments are measured and are begun after the notated pitch is sounded (fig. 13.7). The compass of the keyboard is from A to a''.

Diruta, a pupil of Claudio Merulo (1533–1604), included in the *Prima parte* of his treatise toccatas by himself, Merulo, Andrea and Giovanni Gabrieli, Luzzaschi, and several others. Diruta's toccatas consistently use passage work in one hand against chords in the other (DWMA88); toccatas by some of his contemporaries alternate passage work with chordal and imitative phrases. Merulo's toccatas, published in *Toccate d'intavolatura d'organo* (Toccatas in organ tablature; 2 vols.; 1598, 1604), contain brilliant passage work alternated between hands, sustained chordal passages, and ricercar-like sections.

THE VENETIAN SCHOOL

Venice was an independent city-state whose public officials were elected to office; political prominence and authority did not reside in any one noble family. The city had no tradition of artistic patronage, though ceremonial music had been composed and performed when special occasions had warranted it. There is no record of any kind of formal musical establishment at the church of San Marco (St. Mark's) until the early fourteenth century, when Zuccheto was appointed organist. Not until 1408 was a *schola cantorum* founded at St. Mark's to provide trained singers for the choir. In 1420 the cathedral was San Pietro di Castello. (A cathedral is the principal church in a bishop's see and contains the bishop's throne, the *cathedra*.) San Marco did not become a cathedral until 1807. The church was located next door to the ruler's palace and was in essence Il Doge's private chapel; the clergy, *magister cantus,* and musicians at San Marco were primarily responsible to Il Doge and his administration and secondarily responsible to ecclesiastical authority.

Musical activity in Venice increased during the last quarter of the fifteenth century: various religious confraternities began to employ four or six vocalists and an equal number of instrumentalists on a permanent basis; a new organ was built at St. Mark's, and in 1490 Francesco d'Ana (c. 1460–c. 1503), one of the earliest of the important *frottola* composers, was appointed second organist there. Also in the 1490s Petrucci set up his print shop in Venice and soon began publishing music. In 1520 San Marco was elevated to basilica status. (A basilica is the designated church at which the pope worships or conducts services when he is in the city.) A *maestro di cappella* was appointed who, with the assistance of the two organists, was responsible for teaching the boys and young priests and for directing all of the music at the church. Adrian Willaert was *maestro di cappella* from 1527 to 1562.

Under Willaert's supervision the musical establishment at St. Mark's was enlarged and strengthened. High standards of musical excellence were established and maintained; Willaert selected new musicians carefully and insisted that they be excellent performers, well versed in counterpoint and musical style. Auditions for the organist positions were highly competitive, and candidates were subjected to stringent examination.

The sixteenth-century organists at St. Mark's were excellent composers as well as renowned performers. By 1562 the *maestro di cappella* position at St. Mark's was the most desired one in Italy. Willaert's successor was one of his pupils, Cipriano de Rore, another Netherlander. Rore left in 1564 and was succeeded by Zarlino, who expanded the musical establishment. In 1568 a permanent instrumental ensemble (three players) was appointed; a dozen or more additional instrumentalists might be hired for special occasions. After 1575, the combined talents of choirmaster Zarlino, organists Andrea and/or Giovanni Gabrieli, 30 choir singers, and about 20 instrumentalists brought music at St. Mark's to unprecedented heights of excellence. Musical resources there were ample for division into **cori spezzati,** with small groups of performers—often ensembles producing contrasting sonorities—placed in the various choir galleries (see fig. 10.7). Performances by spatially separated choirs, both vocal and instrumental, were a prominent feature of Venetian church music between c. 1575 and c. 1610 (DWMA89).

During the last quarter of the sixteenth century, as knowledge of musical events in Italy—particularly developments at San Marco—spread abroad, musical leadership was assumed by the Italians. Musicians from European regions north of the Alps traveled to Italy to study and to work. Some came to Venice especially to study with Andrea or Giovanni Gabrieli, and the Venetian school, headed by native Venetians, flourished.

Andrea Gabrieli

Andrea Gabrieli (c. 1510–86) came to the church of San Marco as a singer in 1536. In 1557 he was employed as organist at San Geremia and was an unsuccessful competitor for the position of first organist at San Marco. In 1562 Gabrieli traveled to Frankfurt as a member of Duke Albrecht V's retinue. While there, Andrea and Lassus became friends. The five-voice motets Gabrieli published as *Sacrae cantiones* (1565) reflect many aspects of Lassus's style. When the second organist position at San Marco was open in 1566, Gabrieli competed and received the appointment. He advanced to first organist in 1585.

Andrea Gabrieli made significant contributions to many musical genres. As organist, composer, and teacher, he was highly respected; through his pupils, especially Giovanni Gabrieli and H. L. Hassler, Andrea was influential in Italy and Germanic lands.

Andrea Gabrieli's extant vocal works include 6 Masses, over 100 motets, almost 200 madrigals, and some secular choral compositions; his instrumental pieces comprise keyboard canzonas, organ *intonationi* and toccatas, keyboard and ensemble ricercars, and 3 organ Masses. The *intonationi* are short preludes, in improvisatory style, with chords for one hand and figuration for the other. Some of the ricercars are contrapuntal and nonsectional and closely approach being monothematic fugues; others are actually canzonas.

For his madrigals, Gabrieli chose light pastoral verses; he tended to set texts syllabically for verbal clarity and sometimes used word painting. Many of his motets, published posthumously in *Concerti* (1587), are for eight or more voices, all texted. In writing for divided choirs, Gabrieli effected a quickly moving dialogue in phrases of varying lengths, using simple harmonies and homophonic texture. Vocal lines may have been doubled by instruments, especially those in which the tessitura is quite low. With the expanded instrumental resources at St. Mark's during the 1580s, Gabrieli was able to write vocal music wherein he reinforced the lower voices with trombones and the upper voices with cornetts, thereby achieving timbral contrasts. He was well aware of the effectiveness of such contrasts and seems to have deliberately exploited them in some of his ceremonial works for more than one choir.

Giovanni Gabrieli

Giovanni Gabrieli (c. 1553–1612) received his musical training from his uncle. For a time, Giovanni worked at the court of Albrecht V in Munich. In 1584 he served as temporary organist at San Marco, where, after participating in the competition held in January 1585, he received a permanent appointment. After the death of Andrea Gabrieli in 1586, Giovanni edited many of Andrea's compositions and published them along with some of his own.

Giovanni's early music shows the influence of Andrea and Lassus. The works most characteristic of Giovanni's style are those for divided choirs. The earliest of these works were published, with some works by

Andrea, in *Concerti*. That volume is an important source of ceremonial music performed in Venice. Compositions by uncle and nephew are similar in style—contrasting groups of different sonorities, high voices against low ones, and in performance supplying instrumental support for some or all voices, especially those in which the tessitura is low or quite high. This style is more refined in Giovanni's *Sacrae symphoniae* (Sacred symphonies; 1597) with thematic material developed and with dialogue between choral groups structured in a more irregular manner. Giovanni's interest in writing for divided choirs lessened after 1605, when he became interested in more modern (i.e., Baroque) techniques.

There is no indication that Giovanni Gabrieli composed any complete Masses or organ Masses. A catalogue of his works includes 6 twelve-voice Mass movements, 7 Magnificats, more than 100 motets and liturgical settings, about 30 madrigals, and many instrumental compositions: canzonas, sonatas, *intonationi*, ricercars, fugues, and fantasias. He was the most prolific composer of instrumental ensemble works during his era. Many of his instrumental works are innovative, as are the 14 *canzoni* and 2 *sonate* in *Sacrae symphoniae* published in 1597. The term *sonata* indicates merely that the composition is instrumental. *Sonata pian e forte* (DWMA81) is one of the first compositions in which specific instrumentation is designated; it is the earliest known ensemble work in which dynamic contrasts are indicated. The eight-voice composition is for two choirs: *Coro I*, a cornetto and three trombones, and *Coro II*, a *violino* and three trombones. The low tessitura of the *violino* part indicates that probably it was intended for a *viola da braccio*. In his instrumental works Gabrieli used only cornetto, trombone, and *violino*; his preference for these instruments may have been conditioned by the fact that skilled performers on them were readily available at St. Mark's. Gabrieli applied the principle of repetition after contrast in several of the *canzoni* included in *Canzoni et sonate* (publ. 1615), a collection of instrumental ensemble works in from 3 to 22 voices. Some of these pieces were supplied with *basso continuo* (a continuous fundamental bass line), a fact indicating that Gabrieli was writing in the new Baroque style (see p. 229).

SUMMARY

Significant developments in instrumental music occurred during the Renaissance. A variety of instruments existed, with winds predominating; most types of instruments were built in families or sets containing graduated sizes. Instrumental music might be performed by a whole consort to produce a homogeneous timbre or by a broken consort to enhance one or more of the polyphonic lines. In the late sixteenth century, spatially separated choirs or groups, frequently combining voices and instruments, performed in *concertato* style.

Some instruments, such as the portative organ, disappeared from use; many Italian churches had two permanently installed organs, one large and one small. New instruments appeared, including harpsichord, large copper timpani, and the violin family. The lute was the most popular household instrument. Most churches and courts, many rulers, and wealthy citizens amassed large collections of instruments. Treatises were published that described and depicted instruments and discussed matters of technique and performance practice. Some contained music for performance.

Although instruments continued to be used to double, support, or substitute for voices, composers began to write music specifically for instruments; by 1600 a small but significant body of idiomatic instrumental music existed. This music was of four main types: (1) pieces modeled on or derived from vocal compositions, (2) dance music, (3) variations, and (4) freely composed and quasi-improvisatory works. Some types of instrumental music engendered Baroque forms: The organ monothematic ricercar and the organ canzona were predecessors of the fugue, the ensemble canzona influenced the Baroque *sonata da chiesa*, and paired dances were nuclei of the Baroque *suite*.

Adrian Willaert brought international prestige to the *maestro di cappella* position at the church of San Marco, Venice. Musicians from all over Europe came to St. Mark's to study, and a Venetian school developed. Through Willaert's pupils, colleagues, and successors working at St. Mark's as chapelmasters and organists, musical leadership was transferred from Franco-Netherlanders to native Italians. Italy retained that leadership for more than a century.

THE BAROQUE ERA

14

The historical period between c. 1600 and c. 1750 and the style of the music composed during that era are generally known as **Baroque.** The French word *baroque,* a derivative of Portuguese *barroco* (an irregularly shaped pearl), was first applied to music in a derogatory sense in 1746 by Noel Pluche, who contrasted *musique chantante* (smoothly flowing, songlike music) and *musique baroque* (fast, pulsating, noisy music with surprising, audacious sounds). J. J. Rousseau, in his *Dictionnaire de musique* (1768), wrote: "A baroque music is that in which the harmony is confused, charged with modulations and dissonances, the melody is harsh and little natural, the intonation difficult, and the movement constrained." Around 1755, the word *baroque* was used in adverse criticism of architecture. In 1839, historian Jacob Burckhardt applied the word *Barockstyl* to the kind of art produced in the decadent phase of the Renaissance. Gradually, art historians discontinued using *baroque* as connoting the bizarre, extravagant, and irregular and advanced the idea of *Baroque* style as a legitimate expression of a historical period. Music historians were reluctant to accept this concept and preferred such designations as Thorough-bass Period, Figured-bass Era, *Concertato*-style Period, or Third Style Period. Not until c. 1940 was *Baroque* generally (though not universally) accepted as the name for this musical style period.

Changes in musical style were noticeable in Venice in the 1560s (though some of the music then being published had been composed a decade or two earlier). By 1580 elements of the new style were widespread in northern Italy; they gradually permeated continental Europe and by the third decade of the seventeenth century had infiltrated Britain. By midcentury, the new musical language had been firmly established, and composers could use it expressively and freely.

At the outset, as composers sought more extensive and intensive means of expressing thoughts and emotions musically, they altered existing forms of Renaissance music, such as madrigals and motets. Some of the new stylistic elements appear in Willaert's *Musica nova* (compiled in 1540s, published in 1559), Giovanni Gabrieli's motets, the accompanied and concerted madrigals Luzzaschi and Wert composed for the *concerti delle donne,* and the musical entertainments staged at Estense and Gonzaga courts.

THE BAROQUE ERA

1575	1600	1625	1650	1675	1700

ENGLAND:

Elizabeth I ——→ 1603 ←— James I ——→ 1628 ←Charles I→1648 · · · 1660 ←——→ 1685–88 ←William III

Charles II James II and Mary

• 1649 Commonwealth

• 1588 defeat of Spanish Armada

1608 · · · John Milton · · · 1674

• 1667 *Paradise Lost*

1590 · · · 1616
Shakespeare fl.
• 1602 *The Merry Wives of Windsor*
• 1604 *Othello*

1652 · · · astronomer Edmund Halley · · · (d. 1742)

1642 · · · Isaac Newton · · · (d. 1727)

(1573) · · · architect Inigo Jones · · · 1652

• 1611 King James Version, *The Bible*, published

• 1672 Banister's first public concert, London

1675 · · · 1710
St. Paul's Cathedral built—
Christopher Wren

FRANCE:

Henri III →1589 ←— Henri IV ——→ 1610 ←— Louis XIII ——→ 1643 ←— Louis XIV ——→ (1715)

• 1600 m. Maria de' Medici

1622 · · · 1642 · · 1652
Richelieu · · · Mazarin

Paris, Europe's cultural center

1622 · · · Molière · · · 1673

1606 · · · Corneille · · · 1684

1639 · · · Racine · · · 1699

• 1682 LaSalle claims Louisiana for France

SPAIN:

Philip II ——→ 1598 ←— Philip III ——→ 1621 ←— Philip IV ——→ 1665 ←— Charles II ——→ 1700

Netherlands revolt
• 1583 Netherlands independence from Spain
El Greco fl. in Spain

HOLY ROMAN EMPIRE:

1576 ←— Rudolf II ——→ 1612 ←→1619 Ferdinand II 1637 Ferdinand III 1657 ←— Leopold I ——→ (1705)

Matthias

1618 Thirty Years' War 1648

RUSSIA:

1584 · · · 1605
Boris Godunov
1584 ←——→ 1598 ←—→
regent · · · Tsar'

227

THE BAROQUE ERA

TWO PRACTICES, THREE STYLES

The new music did not supplant the Renaissance style of music but coexisted with it. Throughout the Baroque era—for the first time in music history—two distinct styles of music were purposely cultivated. Authors and composers used various terms to differentiate these styles, including *stile antico* (old style) and *stile moderno* (modern style), *stylus gravis* (severe [strict] style) and *stylus luxurians* (luxuriant [ornamented] style). Claudio Monteverdi used the terms *prima prattica* (first practice) and *seconda prattica* (second practice)—in fact, he may have invented those terms. In the preface to *Il quinto libro de madrigali* (The fifth book of madrigals; 1605), Monteverdi differentiated the two "practices" thus: *Prima prattica* is the style of vocal polyphony written according to the accepted rules governing Franco-Netherlands counterpoint, as codified in Gioseffo Zarlino's (1517–90) *Le istituzioni harmoniche* (The harmonic institutions; 1558). In *prima prattica,* the composer's main concern is the beauty of the contrapuntal writing; in other words, the music dominates the text. *Seconda prattica* is the new style of vocal polyphony in which the text dominates the music, in accordance with Plato's statement (in the *Republic*) that melody, relationship of sounds, and rhythm should follow the words or thought of the text. In *seconda prattica,* effective expression of the text justifies deviation from contrapuntal rules and legitimizes such things as unprepared dissonances, unorthodox resolutions, and melodic crudities. According to Monteverdi, *prima prattica* attained perfection with Willaert; *seconda prattica* was used by Rore, Gesualdo, Luzzaschi, Wert, Caccini, Monteverdi, and numerous others.

Some theorists prepared detailed and comprehensive classifications of the types of musical styles existing within each of the two basic practices. In *Breve discorso sopra la musica moderna* (Short discourse on modern music; 1649) Marco Scacchi (c. 1600–c. 1685) stated that Renaissance composers had only one practice and one style in which to write music, but composers of his time had the advantage of two practices and three styles. The two practices are those that Monteverdi defined though Scacchi named them differently. Scacchi used these oft-quoted phrases: in the first practice "harmony is mistress of the text," and in the second practice "the text is mistress of the harmony." As models for *prima prattica* he chose Josquin, Lassus, and Palestrina; eventually, that type of music became known as "Palestrina style." Scacchi's three styles reflect the intended use of the music: *ecclesiasticus* (church), *cubicularis* (chamber), and *scenicus seu theatralis* (scenic or theater). Within each of these three styles were many subdivisions. Scacchi's classification had wide acceptance. It was expanded by later seventeenth-century theorists and formed a basis for the divisions of musical genres in J. J. Fux's counterpoint text, *Gradus ad Parnassum* (Steps to Parnassus; 1725), and the classification of styles in Johann Mattheson's *Der vollkemmene Kapellmeister* (The perfect Chapelmaster; 1739).

IDIOMATIC COMPOSITION

In the Baroque era, the mainstream of musical development divided. One branch continued developing vocal music, with concentration on dramatic or quasi-dramatic music, both sacred and secular. The other branch developed idiomatic instrumental music. When emancipated from almost total dependence on vocal forms, instrumental music flourished, and by the end of the era it was well on its way to a position of dominance. Idiomatic instrumental styles were developed, such as those for violin and for harpsichord. Composers began to write for specific instruments, and idiomatic instrumental repertoires accumulated. In ensemble music, instruments were selected for their specific tone colors, either to blend or to contrast. Members of the violin family became favored instruments in Italy and eventually supplanted viols in France; harpsichord and organ music began to be differentiated, and the fortepiano was invented. Composers used a larger variety of words as tempo markings and began to indicate dynamics in the musical notation.

THE AFFECTIONS

Widespread interest in the writings of the ancient Greeks (especially Aristotle) resulted in a preoccupation with and a concern for the **affections**—rationalized emotional states, or passions—described by those authors. The fact that ancient Greek and Roman rhetoricians considered it the duty of orators to arouse the passions in their listeners engendered in composers the same sense of obligation to portray musically the emotional states expressed by the text being set. Throughout the Baroque era, composers endeavored to represent musically the various affections. This may well have been the feature of the music that first caused it to be called *baroque,* in the original sense of that word. Composers depicted anger, fear, and other affections boldly, even violently, for passions were no longer viewed as human weaknesses, and the ability to feel emotions deeply was appreciated. Critics unaware of a composer's motivation and intention could have considered a composition of this kind grotesque or bizarre.

Composers endeavored to express in their vocal music the basic affections related to the texts, not their own feelings. Musical interpretation of a text might cause some rapid shifts between radically different emotional states, expressed in the extreme. However, during much of the Baroque era, a composition—or a movement of a multimovement work—expressed only one affection, and its representation served as a means of unifying the composition. In portraying the affections, composers did not rely on their own ingenuity but drew on a common repertoire of musical devices or *figures.* A figure might be as simple and obvious as a rapid scale passage or an undulating serpentine melodic line, or it might be a complex and unobtrusive combination of melody, rhythm, harmony, and texture. Many Baroque composers—especially those working in Germanic lands—used special musical figures to depict and reinforce literal and implied meanings of texts. Commencing around the middle of the seventeenth century, many theorists devoted portions of their treatises to defining, describing, and categorizing types of the affections and presenting ways in which the passions could be expressed musically. Representation of the affections was not limited to vocal music; composers used the same musical devices in their instrumental works.

Writers drew other analogies between rhetoric and music. One of these compares the creation of a musical composition with the preparation of an oration or a piece of writing. (The terminology was, of course, borrowed from Latin writings on rhetoric.) The creative process involved three steps: *inventio* (Latin, the inventive faculty), finding the subject; *dispositio* (Latin, a regular arrangement, order), planning or outlining the work; and *elaboratio* (Latin, worked out, elaborated), fleshing out the skeletal outline by composing the music, writing the treatise, or preparing the actual wording of the oration.

TEXTURE: *BASSO CONTINUO*

In some of the *musica secreta* performances at the Ferrara court in the 1580s, the *concerto delle donne* and a professional bass sang madrigals, accompanied at the keyboard by Luzzaschi. Sometimes one soprano and the bass sang with harpsichord accompaniment. Contemporary accounts of some of those performances describe in detail the embellishments embroidering the treble. Accompanied solo singing was not new—the *cantilena*-style polyphony of Machaut bears witness to that. The novelty was the texture—a polarity of florid treble and firm bass with unobtrusive accompaniment. These features became characteristic of Baroque music and were displayed prominently in the trio sonata (see p. 285).

During the last decades of the sixteenth century, some church music printed in Italy included a *bassus pro organo* (organ bass) part. Such a bass, later called **basso seguente** (following bass), was formed by notating the lowest pitch to be sung at each successive point throughout the piece. Using these pitches as foundation, the organist played above them the chordal harmonies of the piece and usually reinforced the imitative entries of the voices also. The earliest known *basso seguente* survives in manuscript copies of *Ecce beatam lucem* (Behold the blessed light), the 40-part polychoral motet (for four choirs of 8, 10, 16, and 6 voices) that the Florentine court composer Alessandro Striggio (c. 1540–92) composed for the wedding of Duke Albrecht IV of Bavaria in 1568. (Striggio's son, also named Alessandro, was librettist for Monteverdi at Mantua.)

By 1600, composers had begun to write independent bass lines rather than slavishly following the vocal pitches. Some of these basses not only provided the foundation for improvised harmonies but were melodic lines integrated with the vocal polyphony. Because the bass line was continuous throughout the composition, it came to be known as **basso continuo** (continuous bass) or *thoroughbass* (bass [played] throughout). Most often, the basso continuo was a **figured bass;** that is, composers placed Arabic numerals or symbols for chromatic alterations above or below some of the basso continuo notes to convey their intentions with regard to the harmony (ex. 14.1). The numbers indicate the intervals at which pitches are to be supplied above the bass note. However, in the early Baroque, many basso continuo lines were unfigured.

The process of improvising the accompaniment outlined by the basso continuo line is called **realization.** When basso continuo was first used, a keyboard player provided the accompaniment. Soon, however, it became customary for two instrumentalists to perform this task—the continuous notated bass line was played on a bass instrument capable of sustaining tones (e.g., violoncello, viola da gamba, bassoon), and the harmonies were improvised on an instrument capable of producing chords (e.g., keyboard, lute). A specialization of functions—accompanist and soloist—resulted, a division of labor wherein those instruments (and their players) realizing the basso continuo for accompaniment were classified as *fundamental,* and those providing the melody (and embellishing it) were *ornamental.* This division of labor was a factor in the creation of the instrumental concerto.

No individual composer invented basso continuo, though Ludovico Grossi da Viadana (c. 1560–1627) claimed in the preface to *Cento concerti ecclesiastici* (One hundred church concertos; Venice, 1602) that he had done so. Three works with figured basses were published in Florence and Rome in 1600; Emilio de' Cavalieri's (c. 1550–1602) *Rappresentatione di Anima, et di Corpo* (The play about Soul, and Body; Rome, February 1600) was the first of these. However, Viadana seems to have been the first to use the term *basso continuo* in print and the first to compose a basso continuo with the dual function of participating in the melodic, imitative polyphony and providing the foundation for the nonnotated chordal accompaniment.

The transition from *basso seguente* to basso continuo can be traced by examining several works by the same composer. For example, in Viadana's *Cento concerti ecclesiastici, Salve regina* (Hail, queen) uses *basso seguente* in all but a very few measures; *Exaudi me, Domine* (Hear me, Lord) has basso continuo. Monteverdi's fifth, sixth, and seventh books of madrigals also show the transition (see p. 247–8). Some of the pieces in Book 5 appear to be *a cappella,* others have *basso seguente.* In Book 6, some madrigals are supplied sporadically with measures of basso continuo, interspersed with the directive *"basso seguente"* and no notated bass notes. Book 7, named *Concerto,* has basso continuo throughout.

The use of basso continuo did not cease when the Baroque era came to an end but continued to a diminishing extent until c. 1800.

In addition to works that exhibited a polarized texture of firm bass and florid treble, composers wrote music in *stile antico.* The homogeneous blend of equal voices in linear counterpoint was still present in *a cappella* motets and madrigals. Some instrumental ensemble music did not include basso continuo; solo keyboard and lute music did not need it. In those contrapuntal pieces equipped with a basso continuo, the flow and blend of the linear melodies was regulated by the harmonic framework the basso continuo defined. In other words, instead of being intervallically determined and regulated, as it was during the Renaissance, the linear counterpoint was harmonically based and controlled. Polyphony not only persisted throughout the Baroque era, it attained perfection in the music of J. S. Bach.

Harmonic control permitted the increased use of dissonance. In the early seventeenth century, both chromaticism and dissonance were experimental and

EXAMPLE 14.1 A few measures of figured bass.

were sometimes used to an extreme. Around the middle of the century, use of dissonance was modified and controlled, its main employment being in quasi-improvisatory instrumental pieces, such as fantasias and toccatas. Ultimately, by the last part of the Baroque, when the system of major-minor key tonality had been perfected, chromaticism and dissonance were used freely but within the boundaries of the harmonic system.

During the Renaissance, counterpoint was modal; melody was diatonic and in a rather narrow range; and harmony, created as a by-product of the partwriting, through the interaction of intervallically regulated melodic lines, amounted to a series of chordal successions. In the Baroque era, counterpoint was harmonically based; melody might be either diatonic or chromatic, and its range was rather wide; and harmony was planned and deliberately created by means of chords that progressed according to principles of key tonality.

KEY TONALITY

Key tonality may be defined as a system of chordal relationships based on the attraction of a tonal center, the tonic chord, whose root gives the key its pitch name. Though each of the chords within the system is a self-contained entity, each chord has a functional relationship to the others and, more especially, to the tonic chord.

The evolution of the system of major-minor key tonality was a slow process that began in the Renaissance and was not completed until late in the Baroque era. A vital step in that process was the recognition of the triad as a harmonic unit. The Ionian scale on C and the Aeolian scale on A, recognized by Glareanus (in *Dodecachordon;* 1547) as part of the modal system, remain modal as long as they are considered in terms of melodic patterns and intervals. They do not become C major and A natural minor scales until their pitches are viewed as roots of chordal harmonies with the functions and relationships of key tonality. Once the functions and relationships were established, the scale patterns could be transferred from modality to key tonality.

The change from *basso seguente* to *basso continuo* and the use of figured bass indicated that composers were thinking chordally (and performers whose employment required them to realize *basso continuo* parts were forced to do so). However, many *basso continuo* lines were melodic, and their harmonies were regulated by a melodic principle. The presence of certain sequences of chords in modulations or at cadence points did evidence some planned harmonic progressions. In many instances, the conflict between modality and key tonality within a composition enhanced that work. Not until composers conceived their compositions in terms of chordal-harmonic functional relationships was the evolution completed. The earliest surviving music that fully realizes key tonality with no trace of modality—the music of Corelli—was published after 1680. No theoretical explanation of the system was advanced until Rameau's *Traité de l'harmonie* (Treatise on harmony) was published in Paris in 1722.

RHYTHM

At the beginning of the seventeenth century, composers writing sacred music in *stile antico* continued to use the even rhythmic flow of the *tactus* (the beat) that characterized Renaissance counterpoint. (The tactus remained constant, its regularity and rate of speed being comparable with that of a healthy human pulse.)

However, two other types of rhythmic organization prevailed: (a) a regular metrical rhythm derived from the definite patterns of strong and weak beats that were vital to dance music and (b) a flexible unmetrical rhythm that was founded on speech. Frequently, for variety and contrast in multisection or multimovement works, composers used these two kinds of rhythm successively (e.g., following a quasi-improvisatory section with a rhythmically precise one).

NOTATION

With changes in rhythm came changes in notational practices. Near the end of the sixteenth century, when publishers were beginning to print compositions in score form, bar lines were used as a matter of convenience in coordinating the various parts. In the seventeenth century, composers used bar lines to mark off—or *measure*—the definite patterns of strong and weak beats used in their music. At first the use of bar lines was not consistent, for the patterns did not regularly recur. Not until the middle of the seventeenth century were bar lines used systematically to mark off **measures** of regularly recurring rhythmic patterns of strong and weak beats. By this time, most of the old proportion signs had been supplanted by modern **time signatures,** such as $\frac{4}{4}$, $\frac{3}{4}$, and $\frac{2}{4}$. Two proportion signs remained in use: C and ₵. The broken circle C retained its Renaissance connotation—one breve per tactus imperfectly subdivided—and in Baroque terminology denoted one measure divided into two groups of two, or $\frac{4}{4}$. The ₵, referred to in the twentieth century as "cut time," proportioned the breve to half-tactus—a tempo twice as fast as C—and is comparable to a $\frac{2}{4}$ time signature. During the seventeenth century, it became customary for the composer to place a single time signature at the beginning of a composition (or movement) to indicate the basic rhythmic pattern used in that work.

Three movable clef signs were in use, as they had been since the fifteenth century, representing f, c′, and g′ pitches. By the Baroque era, their shapes had been stylized and somewhat resembled those in modern use. Composers placed individual or grouped flat or sharp symbols at the beginning of a composition as a kind of key signature, but it was not until the late eighteenth century that a specific signature was definitely associated with a certain key. It was not unusual for a signature to have sharps placed on both the line and the space for f♯ or flats on both the space and the line for e♭ (fig. 14.1a). Often, Baroque composers wrote signatures with one less flat or one less sharp than the corresponding modern signature (fig. 14.1b). Moreover, during much of the Baroque era, a chromatic alteration of a

FIGURE 14.1 Examples of early key signatures: (*a*) with octave doubling of sharps or flats, and (*b*) with one less flat than in the modern signature. *(Figure a source: F. Geminiani. The Art of Playing on the Violin, 1750. Figure b source: J. S. Bach, autograph manuscript, 1720. University of Tübingen Library)*

(a)

(b)

pitch did not affect an entire measure but was valid for only the note it immediately preceded, unless that note was repeated or the musical figure in which the alteration appeared was immediately and exactly repeated one or more times (an intervening bar line notwithstanding). In other words, the presence of the bar line was of no importance where chromatic alterations were concerned. (See Insight, "Music Printing [III].")

Music Printing (III)

In Venice, Nuremberg, Paris, and Antwerp, music publishing reached a peak shortly before 1580. Many of the volumes of music printed in Venice after that date show a decline in quality—the music is less spacious on the page, and a general lack of craftsmanship is apparent in many books. Printing by means of incised copper plates had been invented but was still experimental in the early sixteenth century. There were sporadic attempts to apply the process to music—often it was used for music notation in art prints. The earliest known practical music printed from engraved copper plates is a volume of lute tablatures by Francesco da Milano issued sometime before 1540.

The first publisher to be successful in printing books of music *entirely* from incised copper plates was Simone Verovio (fl. 1575–1608). In 1586, he engraved and printed two volumes of music, one of them being *Diletto spirituale* (Spiritual delights), a collection of three- and four-voice canzonettas with accompaniment for keyboard and lute. Either because the process was too time consuming or because it was too expensive—certainly not because of inferior workmanship—Verovio issued only about 20 editions between 1586 and 1608.

During the seventeenth century, engraved music seems to have been largely a luxury enjoyed by distinguished patrons. For example, in England in 1613, engraved plates were used for printing *Parthenia,* an anthology of virginal music by Byrd, Bull, and Orlando Gibbons that was a royal wedding gift. Later in the century, John Walsh in London and Estienne Roger in Amsterdam realized the commercial advantages of engraving music. Some composers (e.g., Telemann and J. S. Bach) engraved some of their own music.

Letterpress printing and manuscript copying of music were still used extensively until c. 1700. In fact, letterpress printing was the most feasible method when most of the book consisted of text. Some publishers issued some music in manuscript instead of in printed copies. Publishing in manuscript was favored by many eighteenth-century Italian opera companies because it gave them a greater measure of control over the production of certain works and because manuscript notation could be altered more easily than printed music. Undoubtedly, controlled publication in manuscript form is the reason some music is not extant.

Pear- or teardrop-shaped notes appear in some manuscripts in the early sixteenth century. Around 1530, Étienne Briard, a type designer working in Avignon, designed and cut music type with rounded note heads (fig. 14.2). His type was first used by Jean de Channey for printing Carpentras's (c. 1470–1548) *Liber primus missarum* (First book of Masses; 1532). However, Verovio's engraved notes more nearly approximate the oval note heads of modern printed music.

Until well into the seventeenth century, many printers used note heads cut as lozenges, squares, or diamonds, with stems centered. The innovator of type with oval or roundish note heads with stems placed either to the left or to the right was John Heptinstall, a London printer, who first used it in 1687. Oval or rounded note heads became standard in the eighteenth century.

FIGURE 14.2 Excerpt from the Kyrie of a Mass by Carpentras that Jean de Channey printed in 1532 from music type designed by Briard. (*Source: Carpentras: Liber primus missarum. Avignon, 1532*)

SUMMARY

Music in the Baroque era was characterized by two practices—old-style Renaissance counterpoint in which music dominated the text and modern music in which the text was of prime import—and three styles (church, chamber, and theater). As composers began to write idiomatically for instruments, regard for instrumental music heightened, purely instrumental forms evolved, and instrumental repertoires (both solo and ensemble) accumulated. Composers attempted to portray musically the affections expressed in the texts. In texture, the new music exhibited a polarity of florid treble and firm bass; filler harmonies, not notated, were improvised as the accompanists realized the *basso continuo* line. Modality persisted through much of the seventeenth century; the system of major-minor key tonality slowly evolved. Two types of rhythmic organization prevailed: (a) the regular metrical rhythm vital to dance music and (b) a flexible unmetrical rhythm founded on speech. Notational practices reflected changes in the music: figured bass, bar lines, meter, and key signatures came into use. New printing methods were developed, and by the eighteenth century rounded note heads appeared.

BAROQUE VOCAL MUSIC

15

MONODY

Monody is the modern term for the kind of Italian accompanied solo song, especially secular song, that was in use c. 1600–40. Giulio Caccini (c. 1545–1618), who is credited with inventing this kind of song, first wrote them as solo madrigals with continuo accompaniment and set the same kind of poetry as that used for polyphonic madrigals. The composition of works of this kind indicates a desire on the part of composers that the words be heard clearly and seems to presuppose an audience of some sort. Most monodies were written for high voice and had a figured bass that usually was realized by a keyboard player only; however, Caccini suggested that, for his monodies, a chitarrone or other suitable stringed instrument (e.g., theorbo or lute) be used. Around 1620, strophic arias began to supplant solo madrigals and by c. 1630 had done so. Composition of monody was centered in northern Italy, principally in Florence before 1620. More than 100 composers wrote monodies; Caccini, Alessandro Grandi (c. 1575–1630), Jacopo Peri (1561–1633), and Sigismondo d'India (c. 1582–1629) made significant contributions. Monody was an important forerunner of Italian aria and chamber cantata.

The first publication containing solo madrigals, Caccini's *Le nuove musiche* (The new music; Florence, 1601–2), was influential in establishing the popularity of monody in Italy. *Le nuove musiche* contains 12 solo madrigals and 10 arias, the latter being either strophic songs or strophic variations. In **strophic variation,** the bass line remains constant (or very nearly so) while the melody for each strophe varies. In Caccini's monodies, an expressive vocal line is projected against a harmonic background conceived as support for the voice. He sought to reflect the structure of the poem through a setting that was rather declamatory, with a flexible rhythm. In *Le nuove musiche,* Caccini included advice on how to elaborate a song. Perhaps the best-known song in the collection is *Amarilli mia bella* (Amarillis, my sweetheart; fig. 15.1; DWMA90).

For much of his career Caccini was employed by the Medici in Florence. From 1570 to the mid-1580s, he participated in meetings of an informal academy, the "Camerata," which met at the home of Count Giovanni de' Bardi (1534–1612). There he was exposed to the humanistic ideals of Girolamo Mei (1519–94), Vincenzo Galilei, and Bardi. Under that influence, Caccini developed monody and a style of singing that he described as being closely related to speaking in tones. That style became known as ***stile recitativo*** (recited style).

Mei was mentor to the Camerata. In 1572 Galilei learned of Mei's research into Greek music, contacted him, and conveyed his ideas concerning monody to the Camerata.

FIGURE 15.1 The opening portion of Caccini's *Amarilli mia bella*, whose figured-bass line indicates that harmonies include a number of dissonant 11ths resolving to 10ths and 7ths resolving to 6ths. *(Source: Caccini: Le nuove musiche, 1601/2)*

Mei and Galilei affirmed that the correct way to set a text was through a solo melody that approximated the natural speech inflections of a fine orator. Caccini, who was in Rome in 1592, may have received those same views from Mei personally.

During his lifetime, Caccini's greatest renown was as singer and singing teacher. His daughters, Francesca (1587–1640) and Settimia (1591–c. 1638), composed and were employed as singers at Medici courts; Francesca was one of the highest-paid musicians at the Florentine court. Her *Il primo libro delle musiche* (First book of music; 1618) is an important contribution to monody repertoire. In her solo songs, which no doubt were composed for her personal use, she exploited the brilliance of the human voice. Her *La liberazione di Ruggiero* (The liberation of Ruggiero; 1625) was the first Italian opera performed outside of Italy—in Warsaw in 1628.

OPERA

One of the most important new musical developments in the seventeenth century was the origin, growth, and dissemination of opera. **Opera** (Italian, work) is drama presented musically, with all or most of the text being sung and with appropriate instrumental music, as required by the plot or for accompaniment. It is a combined-art form, an amalgamation of various aspects of art (scenery, costumes), literature (poetic or prose lines of plot), theatre (acting), and dance, with vocal and instrumental music.

PRECURSORS OF OPERA

The association of music with drama was not new. It can be traced back to the ancient Greeks—to the prize-winning drama of Thespis (534 B.C.), which had one actor and a chorus, and the tragedies of Aeschylus, Sophocles, and Euripides (fifth century B.C.), which used three actors and a citizens chorus of 12 to 15 men. Mei believed that Greek dramas were sung throughout.

Medieval liturgical dramas, such as *Quem quaeritis, christicolae?* and *The Play of Daniel*, were sung and dramatized in church. In Hildegard von Bingen's morality play, *Ordo virtutum*, every character but the devil sings. Religious mystery plays, produced by medieval trade guilds, used music only incidentally; the same is true of miracle plays dramatizing events in the lives of saints and performed on their feast days. Some trouvère compositions may have been acted; certainly, Adam de la Halle's *Le jeu de Robin et de Marion* is suitable for dramatization.

Some Renaissance authors placed choral music at the beginning or conclusion of the acts of their plays. For Juan del Encina, music was an integral part of the action, and he included villancicos in his plays.

It became customary during the sixteenth century to present allegorical, mythological, or pastoral interludes between the acts of a comedy. Such an interlude was called an **intermedio.** *Intermedi* served a practical purpose—they divided the play into acts, for the curtain, once opened, remained open until the play concluded. Some attempts were made to correlate the subject of *intermedi* with that of the drama or to unify the *intermedi* used with a drama so that collectively they presented another plot. All *intermedi* contained music—some were elaborate musical productions.

Descriptions of *intermedi* abound, but few complete *intermedi* are extant. Surviving are two sets performed at nuptial festivities at the Medici court in Florence: those composed by G. B. Strozzi for the wedding of Cosimo I de' Medici to Eleonora of Toledo in 1539 and those performed for the wedding of Ferdinando de' Medici and Christine of Lorraine in 1589. For the

THE DEVELOPMENT OF OPERA

1575	1600	1625	1650	1675	1700

ITALY:

madrigals   pastorales   madrigal comedies

monody

• 1602 Caccini: *Le Nuove musiche*

• 1581 Galilei: *Dialogo*

intermedi   opera

FLORENCE:

Bardi's Camerata   Corsi's Academy

• 1598 *Dafne*

• 1600 Peri: *Euridice*

ROME:

• 1600 Cavalieri: *Rappresentatione di Anima, . . .*

• 1632 Landi: *Il Sant' Alessio*

MANTUA:

• 1607   *L'Orfeo*

Monteverdi:

• 1608   *Arianna*

VENICE:

• 1637 First public opera house

• 1640   *Il ritorno d'Ulisse . . .*

Monteverdi:

• 1642   *L'incoronazione di Poppea*

Venice becomes the operatic capital

NAPLES:

• 1684

A. Scarlatti

GERMANIC LANDS:

• 1627 Schütz: *Dafne*   • 1668 Cesti: *Il pomo d'oro*

• 1644 Staden: *Seeleweg*

Singspiel

FRANCE:

• 1581 *Circé*

dramatic ballet   ballet du cour   (1632   )   Lully   1687

from 1652 in France   • 1674 *Alceste*

tragédies lyriques

ENGLAND:

masque

plays with music

• 1656 *The Siege of Rhodes*

• 1684 Blow:

Venus and Adonis

• 1689

Purcell:

Dido and

Aeneas

SPAIN:

• 1629 Vega: *La selva sin amor*

• 1660 Calderón: *La púrpura de la rose*

latter, texts by Giovanni de' Bardi, Ottavio Rinuccini (1562–1621), and Laura Guidiccioni (1550–99) were set to music by Marenzio, Peri, Caccini, Cavalieri, and others. Bardi chose as the theme for the musical stories the power of ancient music. One *intermedio,* depicting Apollo's victory over the serpent Python, is a direct ancestor of the first opera, *Dafne.* Much of the music in these *intermedi* consisted of lavishly embellished solos with simple harmonic accompaniment. Vittoria Archilei (1550–c. 1620), Italian soprano and lutenist, had a

1575	1600	1625	1650	1675	1700

Oratorio

Rome: Neri's Oratory Congregation sings *laude*

• 1619 Anerio—*volgare* oratorios for Neri

oratorio latino

Carissimi: *Jephte*

Charpentier in France

Cantata

L. Rossi, M. Marazolli

c. 1650   Carissimi

• 1670 Stradella, Steffani

A. Scarlatti

Passion

motet passion

• 1641 Selle: oratorio passion

• 1645 Schütz: *Die sieben Worte* . . .

• Schütz: 5 *Historiae*

major part in the performance; for some of her solos she played her own chitarrone accompaniment.

The ***pastorale*** (pastoral) is a genre in literature, drama, and music that depicts characters and scenes of rural life. Poets had written about shepherds and shepherdesses, rural deities, and rustic scenes for centuries. By the end of the sixteenth century, the predominant type of Italian poetry produced was the pastorale. Cavalieri composed settings for several of Laura Guidiccioni's pastorales, including *Il satiro* (The satyr) and *La disperazione di Fileno* (Fileno's despair), both performed at Carnival in Florence in 1590, and *Il giuoco della cieca* (The game of blindman's buff), performed at the Pitti Palace, Florence, in 1595 and 1599. These settings are lost.

Madrigal settings that were made of dramatic scenes from lengthy poems, such as Tasso's *Gerusalemme liberata* and Guarini's *Il pastor fido,* may have contributed to the emergence of opera. Such settings did lead to the creation of **madrigal cycles,** series of madrigals presenting an uncomplicated plot through descriptive music and (sometimes) dialogue. Orazio Vecchi's (1550–1605) *L'Amfiparnaso* (The slopes of Parnassus; 1597) comprises a prologue and 13 scenes grouped into 3 acts. Vecchi's designations of this work as *comedia harmonica* and *comedia musicale* generated the twentieth-century term *madrigal comedy* for

the genre. Adriano Banchieri (1568–1634) also composed madrigal cycles.

THE FIRST OPERAS

During the years the Camerata met at Bardi's home, another group of artists and literati gathered at the home of Jacopo Corsi (1561–1602), composer and patron of the arts. After Bardi moved to Rome in 1592, Corsi was the recognized leader of the principal cultural group in Florence. Among the frequent guests at Corsi's home in the 1590s were Peri and Rinuccini. Occasionally, Monteverdi visited there. Corsi and those who met at his home sought an effective way to set stage music—a ***stile rappresentativo*** (theatrical style)—a manner of singing that was more expressive than ordinary speech but less melodious than song. They arrived at a style in which a declamatory melody, in flexible rhythm, with irregular phrasing, is presented over a static bass. However, they did not use that style exclusively; in dramatic productions, both dialogue and soliloquy occur, and their presentation differs.

DAFNE   Late in 1594, Corsi, who had begun a setting of Rinuccini's pastorale *Dafne,* requested Peri to complete the music in *stile rappresentativo. Dafne,* which is considered the first opera, was performed at Corsi's home during Carnival 1598 and in revised form several times during the next decade. Rinuccini's **libretto** (the text that is set to music) is extant, and six of the songs have been located—single strophes of music with additional stanzas of text. The style of the vocal line differs in some of the songs, but this cannot be ascribed to the fact that two of the songs are by Corsi and the others attributed to Peri. In some the metric pulse is regular; in others, rhythm is flexible and measuring irregular. Only *Qual nova meraviglia!* (What amazing news!), the messenger's song, has nonstrophic text and music that could be considered declamatory recitative (ex. 15.1). **Recitative** is the term ultimately given to the style of vocal music designed to imitate natural speech inflections. As opera developed, recitative became the style used for narrative prose and rapid passages of dialogue to carry the action between soliloquy-type songs.

Dafne comprises a prologue and six scenes. The thesis of the plot—to demonstrate the dangers that await those who scorn Love's power—is presented by Ovid, who sings the prologue, *Da' fortunati campi* (From the fortunate fields). For scene 1, Rinuccini reworked material he had written for an *intermedio* in 1589 (see p. 237). In the *Dafne* scene, a chorus of nymphs and shepherds complain about a monster that has been destroying their flocks. Apollo appears and slays Python. After Apollo tells the nymphs and shepherds that they are safe, the chorus sings in praise and gratitude: *Almo Dio, ch'il carr' ardente* (Almighty God, who in the fiery chariot). Scene 2 is dialogue: Apollo taunts Cupid, belittling his prowess in shooting love's arrows. Cupid vows vengeance; he plans to gain control over Apollo by darting him. In scene 3, Apollo becomes enamored of the nymph Dafne, who spurns him. Cupid, in scene 4, brags to Venus about his victory over Apollo. The fifth scene is the climax. *"Qual' nova meraviglia!"* (What amazing news!) the messenger sings. He tells the people (the chorus) that Dafne, to escape Apollo's relentless pursuit, prayed for divine intervention and was transformed into a laurel tree. The messenger describes Apollo's grief; there are responses from the chorus. In the final scene, Apollo stands before the tree, declares his love for Dafne, and vows to wear laurel leaves in his hair always. The scene concludes with choral commentary addressed to Dafne, *Bella ninfa fuggitiva* (Beautiful fugitive nymph; DWMA91).

EXAMPLE 15.1 Beginning of *"Qual nova meraviglia!"* from *Dafne.* (From William V. Porter, *"Peri and Corsi's* Dafne: *Some New Discoveries and Observations"* in Journal of the American Musicological Society, Vol. XVIII, No. 2, p. 180, Summer 1965. Copyright © 1965 American Musicological Society, Philadelphia, PA. Reprinted by permission of the American Musicological Society)

In many respects, *Dafne* established a pattern that was followed by other composers of early opera. Some structural features of *Dafne* were used consistently for more than a century: (1) The opera commences with a prologue in which a character not otherwise involved in the story apprises the audience of the central theme of the opera. (2) The text is poetry, and the plot is based on classic mythology. (3) Pastoral characters and scenes are incorporated. (4) An emotional appeal or moving prayer is sung by the main character, and the difficulty is resolved at the crucial moment by divine intervention. (Later, this kind of resolution is referred to as *deus ex machina*.) (5) The music is mainly accompanied solo song, though some use is made of chorus. (6) Choral singing concludes the opera.

Though composers stated that they were seeking to approximate the manner in which the ancient Greeks presented their dramas, the humanists' interest in ancient Roman culture is apparent in Rinuccini's libretto. The plot is constructed and developed along lines used by the Roman poet Ovid (43 B.C.–A.D. 18) in his dramas. Therefore, Rinuccini's choice of Ovid to present the prologue of *Dafne* is appropriate.

EURIDICE   Corsi was responsible, too, for the production on 6 October 1600 of the Peri-Caccini setting of Rinuccini's *Euridice* at the wedding festivities for Maria de' Medici and Henri IV of France (r. 1589–1610). Peri, who was acclaimed for his beautiful tenor voice, sang the role of Orpheus; Corsi played harpsichord accompaniments behind the scenes. Caccini, out of jealousy, would not permit any of his court singers to perform Peri's music and rewrote their songs: Euridice's music, three choral pieces, and a few solo lines of nymphs and shepherds. In the preface to his published *Euridice,* Peri credited Caccini with these.

Rinuccini's libretto has a prologue and five scenes. He modified the mythological tale to give the traditional tragedy a happy ending—one more appropriate for a royal wedding. This is indicated in the prologue, sung by Tragedy (fig. 15.2). Briefly, the story is this: Euridice, Orpheus's beloved, is gathering flowers in the meadow with nymphs and shepherds. She is bitten by a snake and dies. The nymph Dafne carries the tragic news to Orpheus. Grieving, he consults Venus, who, promising him triumph over death, leads him to Hades. There, Orpheus pleads with Pluto, obtains Euridice's release, and takes her back to earth.

Each scene concludes with a strophic chorus summarizing the scene's events. Peri's music is appropriate to each happening; he had sufficient mastery of *stile rappresentativo* to regulate the degree of emotional intensity expressed. Orpheus's deeply emotional monologues are colored by unexpected harmonic progressions, unprepared dissonances, suspensions, and frequent rests, as in *Non piango e non sospiro* (I do not weep and I do not sigh; scene 2), sung after Dafne tells him of Euridice's death, and the lament *Funeste piagge* (Funereal shores; scene 4), sung when he stands on the shores of the underworld. How different are the joyous harmonies and small graces in Orpheus's songs about love at the beginning of scene 2! Dafne's recounting of her message is true recitative, commencing calmly, gaining momentum as she becomes more emotional; this increased agitation Peri accomplished through smaller note values, suspensions, and flexible rhythm above static harmony. (The role of Dafne was sung by a boy soprano, Jacopo Giusti.)

The prologue music in *Euridice* resembles that of *Dafne* in several respects. The prologues are in the same key, and there is marked similarity in both treble and bass in the opening measures. Peri may have left composition of the prologue until last and, pressed for time, borrowed and remodeled. There are indications that composers relied on some standard melodic patterns when composing strophic monodies and arias.

In performance, the solos were appropriately ornamented; Peri and Caccini would have seen that this was done correctly. In Peri's published *Euridice,* he included an *Avvertimento* (Notice) concerning the proper realization of his figured-bass lines:

AVVERTIMENTO.

S Opra la parte del basso, il diesis congiunto col 6. dimostra sesta maggiore, e la minor: senza 'l diesis; Il quale quando è solo, è contrassegno della terza, ò della decima maggiore: Et il b. molle, della terza, ò decima minore; e non si ponga mai, se non a quella sola nota, doue è segnato, quantunque piu ne fussero in vna medesima Corda.

Above the bass line, a sharp in conjunction with a 6 denotes a major sixth, and a 6 without a sharp is a minor sixth. When a sharp is alone [above a note], it signifies a major third or tenth; and a flat alone, a minor third or tenth. And a chromatic alteration is never to be played except with the one note on which it is marked, although there may be several notes of the same pitch denomination.

It was a peculiarity of Baroque music notation that a chromatic alteration placed above or before a note affected the pitch of *only* that note, unless the note was immediately repeated, a bar line notwithstanding. In the Baroque era, the bar line did not have the same connotation with regard to chromatic alterations as it does in modern notation.

Caccini prepared a complete setting of *Euridice* (1601), which he claimed he had written earlier. His music is more melodious than Peri's, more in the style of the monodies in *Le nuove musiche*. It should be noted that Caccini's spectacle, *Il rapimento di Cefalo* (The abduction of Cefalo), was part of the wedding festivities and was performed three nights after Peri's *Euridice.* Peri sang in Caccini's production.

Peri composed other dramatic works in the ensuing years; unfortunately, all of those that he referred to as operas or oratorios are lost. An **oratorio** resembles an opera but places greater emphasis on chorus, usually has a narrator, and is presented without stage action,

FIGURE 15.2 First page of original printed score of Peri's *Euridice* (1600/1601).

scenery, or costumes (see p. 260). Most oratorios are on religious subjects; however, oratorios and operas may be sacred or secular.

EMILIO DE' CAVALIERI

Cavalieri served Cardinal Ferdinando de' Medici in Rome, and when the cardinal became Grand Duke of Tuscany in 1587, Cavalieri was appointed overseer of all artistic and musical activities and supervisor of all artists, craftsmen, and musicians at the Florentine court. Cavalieri's music for the final *ballo* in the sixth *intermedio,* with Laura Guidiccioni's text *O che nuovo miracolo* (O, that new miracle), was performed at the nuptial festivities there in 1589.

Cavalieri was in charge of the wedding festivities honoring Maria de' Medici and Henri IV and composed for the banquet on 5 October 1600 a setting of Guarini's *La contesa fra Giunone e Minerva* (The contest between Juno and Minerva). But somehow Caccini gained control over the production of the main nuptial spectacle to the exclusion of Cavalieri. The latter, disappointed, disgruntled, and disillusioned over what he considered the poor quality of all the nuptial spectacles except those presented at the banquet, left for Rome and never returned to Florence. When Caccini and Peri engaged in a controversy over which of them invented *stile rappresentativo,* Cavalieri asserted that he had. Peri, in the preface to his published *Euridice,* stated that he first heard the style in Cavalieri's music but claimed to be the first to use that style in opera.

From time to time during the 1590s, Cavalieri had supervised musical productions in Rome. In February 1600, his *Rappresentatione di Anima, et di Corpo* was presented in Rome twice, in the Oratory of Chiesa Nuova. This is the earliest known performance in an oratory of a large-scale musical dramatic work containing monodies. *Rappresentatione di Anima, et di Corpo,* according to its dedication, was prepared for publication in September 1600 and is the earliest printed score using figured bass.

Rappresentatione di Anima, et di Corpo is in three acts, each containing several short scenes. The play opens with a lengthy spoken dialogue between Avveduto (Wisdom) and Prudentio (Prudence); the music commences with a short prologue, sung by Tempo (Time), and concludes with two choruses. Once the music begins, there is no further spoken dialogue; Avveduto and Prudentio have no singing roles. *Rappresentatione di Anima, et di Corpo* contains strophic songs, madrigals, speechlike recitative, and choral songs (labeled *ballo*) with dancelike rhythms and meters. Undoubtedly, dancing accompanied the singing of those *balli.* Instrumental *ritornelli* serve as interludes between strophes and unify the work. (A **ritornello** is a short passage of music that recurs several times as a kind of refrain.) A five-part instrumental *Sinfonia* is performed between chorus Nos. 15 and 16 and between chorus Nos. 54 and 55. *Ritornelli* and *sinfonie* were used later by composers of early opera. The recitatives in *Rappresentatione . . .* contain false relations and sudden changes of harmony but lack the rhythmic flexibility and variety found in Peri's recitatives.

Rappresentatione di Anima, et di Corpo is variously referred to as opera and oratorio. It was first performed in the Oratory of a church, and Avveduto and Prudentio are sometimes considered narrators. However, when *Rappresentatione . . .* was presented in Rome, it was staged as a musical dramatic production. Cavalieri's *Rappresentatione di Anima, et di Corpo* is an allegorical opera.

LIBRETTISTS

Music alone does not make an opera; an appropriate libretto is vital. Thus, Laura Guidiccioni and Ottavio Rinuccini were shaping forces in the development of early opera—Guidiccioni wrote expressive poetic texts in lines with an irregular number of syllables to be set to music in *pastorales* and *intermedi*. Rinuccini couched his Ovidian plots in lines of similar construction. Cavalieri set many of Guidiccioni's lines. Rinuccini provided texts for Corsi, Peri, Caccini, Monteverdi, and others.

Laura Guidiccioni, daughter of Nicolò Guidiccioni and Caterina de' Benedetti, was born in Lucca. It is not known when she married Orazio Lucchesini. She was persuaded by Ippolito Santini, priest at the cathedral, to pursue her literary talents. He urged Orazio to take Laura to Florence, where cultural activities, especially at the Medici court, might provide an outlet for her poetry. There her talent flourished. She met Tasso, Guarini, and Rinuccini and was well acquainted with Corsi, Peri, Caccini.

Ottavio Rinuccini's literary service at the Medici court began in 1579. His historical significance, musically, lies in his ability to write verse suitable for setting in *recitativo* style and in his construction of an Ovidian plot that was tragicomic. A prologue and a happy ending resulting from divine intervention are characteristic of his libretti. From time to time between 1600 and 1604, Rinuccini visited the French court. There he observed court ballet, and its influence can be seen in some of his later works (e.g., *Il ballo delle ingrate* [The ingrates' dance]). He furnished the libretto for Monteverdi's opera *L'Arianna* and poetry for sonnets, canzoni, and madrigals.

Alessandro Striggio (1573–1630) served the Mantua court as diplomat. His father (also named Alessandro) was a madrigalist, and the son edited and pub-lished several volumes of his father's works. However, the younger Alessandro's main contribution to the development of music is literary—he prepared several libretti for Monteverdi, including the opera *L'Orfeo*, the ballet *Tirsi e Clori*, and *Lamento d'Apollo* (lost).

MANTUA

At Mantua, the chapel singers and instrumental ensemble employed by Duke Vincenzo I Gonzaga were of virtuoso caliber. Court singers included Lucrezia Urbana, Caterina Martinelli, Adriana Basile, and Francesco Razi. In 1589, when Monteverdi joined the court musicians as violist, Wert was court *maestro di cappella,* and G. P. Gastoldi (c. 1551–c. 1622) was chapelmaster at the basilica of Santa Barbara, where high-quality church music was performed. Vincenzo presented weekly Friday evening concerts at the palace and promoted theatrical entertainments. Reportedly, the court singers performed madrigals in "a theatrical manner."

A number of persons at Mantua were aware of opera's existence. Members of the Gonzaga family had attended opera performances in Florence, Alessandro Striggio had performed in them, and undoubtedly Monteverdi had discussed them with Corsi and others. In 1607, when Francesco Gonzaga and the Accademia degli Invaghiti requested Monteverdi to compose an opera for Carnival, Striggio provided the libretto for *L'Orfeo* (Orpheus). Though *Euridice* and *L'Orfeo* are based on the same fable, and Striggio's model was Rinuccini's *Euridice,* the operas differ considerably. *L'Orfeo* is more advanced musically and is more effective theater, for Monteverdi thought in terms of human drama, though Striggio adhered more closely to the traditional myth. In the first performance, *L'Orfeo* did not have a happy ending—Apollo did not descend from heaven to console Orpheus, as in the revised version. However, the choice of conclusion may have been made from necessity. *L'Orfeo* was first performed in a "small room of apartments the duchess used," and probably that room could not accommodate the requisite machinery for a god's descent from heaven. Some solo roles were sung by castrati (Insight, "Castrati"); one of the *concerto delle donne* may have sung the Messenger role. There was a major difference in the performance of Monteverdi's later operas—though castrati performed in some of them, women sang the leading

Castrati

Castrati, male singers who had been castrated before puberty to preserve the high treble voice range (either soprano or alto), figured prominently in the music of the seventeenth and eighteenth centuries. The operation itself was never sanctioned by church authorities, but the castrato voice was almost universally admired. Most of the castrati were Italian, though some were Spanish and a few English.

The reason for the increased number of castrati in the late Renaissance and throughout the Baroque is not known. Undoubtedly, one factor was the belief prevalent in many lands that women were to be silent in church. Another factor may have been the multiplicity of parts in contrapuntal vocal music. Male soprano and alto voices were much more powerful than female ones, and seldom was a boy's voice strong enough to hold up a treble part in an ensemble. Falsettists and castrati were admitted to the Sistine Choir in the second half of the sixteenth century; Lassus had six castrati in his chapel choir at Munich in the 1570s.

Castrati played important roles in opera from the time of its inception. In the Papal States, from the time of Pope Sixtus V (r. 1585–90), there was a ban on women appearing on the stage, but the extent to which this was enforced varied considerably. In view of the relationship between the Medici, the College of Cardinals, and the papacy, it is not surprising that the role of Euridice in Peri's opera *Euridice* (1600) was sung by a castrato and the role of Dafne by a boy soprano. Monteverdi's *L'Orfeo* had castrati in the cast; many other instances can be cited. Moreover, composers wrote heroic male roles for high voices that could be sung by either tenors or castrati. There were no castrato parts in French opera, and French control in some parts of Italy at the beginning of the nineteenth century prevented employment of castrati to some extent.

Castrati were at the height of their popularity between 1650 and 1750. Operatic roles were written for them after that time (e.g., by Mozart, Gluck, and Meyerbeer). Among the most famous eighteenth-century castrati were Caffarelli, Farinelli, and Tosi. They were treated as celebrities and enjoyed the adulation accorded them. Although Pope Pius X (r. 1903–14) formally banned castrati from the papal chapel in 1903, there were castrati in the Sistine Choir until 1913.

female roles. There were excellent female sopranos at Mantua, and Monteverdi considered their talents when he composed.

Late in 1607, Marco da Gagliano (1582–1643) set Rinuccini's revised *Dafne;* when it was performed at Mantua in 1608, Caterina Martinelli sang the leading role. The success of that opera prompted Vincenzo to commission another from Monteverdi. He composed *L'Arianna* (Ariadne; 1608), but its performance was postponed because of the death of Caterina Martinelli, who was to have sung the title role. Only fragments of *L'Arianna* survive. Virginia Andreini, who was employed at court after Caterina died, did not have talent comparable to that of Caterina; this is reflected in the simpler melodic style Monteverdi used in *Il ballo delle ingrate.*

Musical activities at Mantua declined after Vincenzo's death in 1612. Later that year, Monteverdi moved to Venice, where he became *maestro di cappella* at St. Mark's church. Occasionally, he composed pieces for the Gonzaga court, but only the ballet *Tirsi e Clori* (Thyrsis and Chloris; 1616) survives.

CLAUDIO MONTEVERDI

The transition from Renaissance to Baroque may be seen in the work of Monteverdi (1567–1643; Insight, "Claudio Monteverdi," p. 244). Though he composed much sacred music, he is best known for his secular works, many of which embody Baroque characteristics. In his first several books of madrigals and in much of his sacred music, he employed the principles of Netherlands counterpoint, which he termed *prima prattica* or *stile antico* (first practice or old style). In some of his works, he applied the affective principles of the *seconda prattica* or *stile moderno* (second practice, or modern style) to music that was basically in Renaissance style. Some of his other works are clearly in Baroque style.

Claudio Monteverdi

Claudio Monteverdi (1567–1643) was born in Cremona, Italy. His father, a physician, sent him to Marc' Antonio Ingegneri (1547–92), *maestro di cappella* at Cremona Cathedral, for music training, but he was not a choirboy. By the age of 16, Clau-

Claudio Monteverdi. Portrait by Bernardo Strozzi (1582–1644). *(Trioler Landesmuseum Ferdinandeum, Innsbruck, Austria)*

dio had published three books of music: three-voice motets (1582), four-voice *Madrigali spirituali* (1583), and three-voice *Canzonette* (1583). Next, two books of his five-voice madrigals appeared (1587, 1590).

Monteverdi had no permanent position until 1589, when he was hired as violinist and viol player at the Mantua court of Duke Vincenzo I Gonzaga. When Giaches de Wert died, Monteverdi hoped to succeed him as *maestro di cappella*, but Pallavicino was chosen. Not until 1601 was Monteverdi elevated to *maestro di cappella* at the Gonzaga court. By that time, his reputation was firmly established in Italy.

In 1599 Monteverdi married Claudia de Cattaneis, a court singer. They had three children, the eldest of whom, Francesco (1601–c. 1679), worked as singer and composer at St. Mark's, Venice, from 1623 to 1679.

Undoubtedly, Claudio Monteverdi performed in the ensemble accompanying theatrical productions at court; in 1604 he wrote some ballet music. In February 1607 his first opera, *L'Orfeo*, was presented at Man-

tua. Then Claudia became ill; her death in September was a crushing blow. Monteverdi was disinclined to remain at Mantua, but his opera *L'Arianna* (Ariadne) was scheduled for production at court, and he needed to attend rehearsals. The production was not ready for Carnival season and was rescheduled to coincide with nuptial festivities honoring Francesco Gonzaga and Margaret of Savoy in May 1608. Caterina Martinelli, who was to sing the Ariadne role, was stricken with smallpox and died; Virginia Andreini, a member of a traveling troupe, sang the role on short notice. Monteverdi wrote other music for the celebration, including *Il ballo delle ingrate*.

After Claudia's and Caterina's deaths, Monteverdi suffered from severe depression. He asked to be released from court responsibilities, but his petition was denied. In 1610, when he was granted a pension but still was not released, he actively sought a new position and went to Rome to arrange for publication of a volume of sacred music. When he returned to Mantua, he began another

Monteverdi's musical style is rooted in his understanding of Plato's ideas concerning music. He interpreted literally Plato's statement that music is composed of text, the combination of sounds, and rhythm—because Plato listed text first, it was of prime import; the music was secondary and was subservient to the text. Closely related to this is the concept of *ethos* as expressed by ancient Greek philosophers—the ability of music to move the affections and to affect the entire person. Plato stated that all aspects of music had this power, rhythm as well as melody and *tonos;* just as there was direct correlation between certain *tonoi* and certain character traits, so there was direct correlation between certain rhythmic patterns and certain emo-

tional states. It was Monteverdi's aim to compose music in which the text was presented clearly and in a manner that expressed its affective nature accurately. To this extent, his ideas and those of the Florentine Camerata were in accord. However, Monteverdi believed his aims could be realized in polyphonic music; the Camerata turned to homophony and accompanied monody. This does not imply that Monteverdi rejected homophony; he wrote some homophonic music, but he sought to achieve new ends through traditional means. For example, he continued to compose madrigals after others had discarded the genre.

In his application of the principles of ethos through rhythm, Monteverdi created **stile concitato,** the excited book of madrigals. After the death of Vincenzo I (1612), the duchy experienced financial difficulties; Francesco Gonzaga reduced the size of the court's musical body, and Monteverdi was dismissed.

After almost a year of idleness, Monteverdi auditioned for and obtained the *maestro di cappella* position at St. Mark's church in Venice. He retained that position until his death. The quality of musical performances at St. Mark's had declined considerably, and music was at a low ebb there when Monteverdi assumed his duties. Under his leadership, conditions improved, but music at St. Mark's never regained the heights to which it had soared during the Gabrielis' tenure. Transference of some of the compositional workload at St. Mark's to younger composers enabled Monteverdi to accept commissions from other sources: secular academies, religious confraternities, wealthy Venetian families, and Italian courts. For Mantua he composed several works, but in 1620 he declined an offer to return to the Gonzaga court. He still felt some bitterness over some of the conditions at his previous employment there. His full-length opera *La finta pazza Licori* (1627) was intended as part of the succession festivities for Vincenzo II. When Vincenzo II died (1628) without an heir, the Gonzaga line ended, and Monteverdi's connection with Mantua was severed.

In 1628 Monteverdi was granted leave of absence from St. Mark's to visit Parma and fulfill a commission for several items for the Farnese court. *Gli Amori di Diana e d'Endimione* (The Love of Diana and Endymion) was produced there in 1628; that music is lost. From time to time, Monteverdi composed stage works for performance at the Mocenigo home in Venice. Two such works were *Combatimento di Tancredi et Clorinda* (1624) and *Proserpina rapita* (Proserpina abducted; 1630).

During the 1630s, Monteverdi seems to have written little music—a Mass of thanksgiving for deliverance from the epidemic of plague that swept through Venice in 1630–31 and *Scherzi musicali* (1632), a small collection of arias and madrigals for one and two voices with basso continuo. *Madrigali guerrieri et amorosi* (Madrigals of war and love), published in 1638, had been written earlier. A collection of sacred music appeared in 1641.

Monteverdi's *L'Arianna* was revived in 1640; thereafter, he resumed composition of opera. *Il ritorno d'Ulisse in patria* (Ulysses's return to his homeland) was produced at Teatro San Cassiano in 1640 and in 1641; Venetian singers performed it in Bologna in 1640, also. *Le nozze d'Enea con Lavinia* (The marriage of Aeneas and Lavinia) was presented at Teatro SS Giovanni e Paolo in 1641; only the scenario and libretto survive. Monteverdi's last opera, *L'incoronazione di Poppea* (The coronation of Poppea), was produced at SS Giovanni e Paolo in 1642.

In 1643 Monteverdi obtained leave to visit Cremona. He died shortly after he returned to Venice. His remains were interred in the chapel of St. Ambrosius in the church of Santa Maria dei Frari; a commemorative plaque marks the place.

style. His use of measured tremolo in *Non schivar, non parar* (Not to dodge, not to parry) from *Combatimento di Tancredi et Clorinda* (The fight between Tancred and Clorinda) is an example of this (ex. 15.2). *Non schivar, non parar* contains printed instructions for playing *pizzicato* on bowed string instruments.

Monteverdi advanced the idea of two practices: *prima prattica,* Renaissance polyphony and with emphasis on the music, and *seconda prattica,* the presentation of the text through music expressing its affections. Baroque composers used Monteverdi's terminology but altered the meaning of *seconda prattica.* Monteverdi believed that the Renaissance modal system was antiquated and advocated a wider and more expressive use of dissonance. In his madrigals, he achieved this by (1) using melodic intervals expressly forbidden by Renaissance contrapuntal principles (e.g., a downward leap of a minor sixth); (2) notating embellishments commonly improvised, thereby making their dissonances visible instead of fleetingly audible; (3) writing unprepared dissonances; and (4) resolving suspensions irregularly. His harmonic innovations did not go without criticism. Theorist G. M. Artusi (1540–1613) singled out for attack certain dissonant passages in *Anima mia perdona* and *Cruda Amarilli* (ex. 15.3; DWMA92). Monteverdi responded in the Foreword to his fifth book of madrigals by referring to a "Second Practice" of modern music, and saying, "concerning consonances

EXAMPLE 15.2 Excerpt from Monteverdi's *Non schivar, non parar* (mm. 30ff.) containing the measured tremolo of *stile concitato* and printed instructions for playing *pizzicato*. *(Source: Madrigals of War and Love)*

and dissonances, there is another way of considering them, different from the established way, which . . . defends the modern method of composing." Two years later, a declaration in Claudio's defense asserted that harmony must be servant of the text and not its master, a principle that underlies all of Monteverdi's music. Such criticism and discussion of Monteverdi's works kept his name before the public and heightened circulation of his music.

MONTEVERDI'S WORKS   Much of Monteverdi's music has been lost. His works that survive intact include 3 operas, a ballet, 12 volumes containing approximately 250 madrigals and other secular songs, 5 volumes of sacred music, and approximately 20 sacred pieces published in anthologies.

Sacred Music   For the greater part of his career, Monteverdi was in the service of the church, yet the amount of his sacred music that survives is minimal. There is no evidence that he had any responsibility for church music prior to 1601, and his position as *maestro di cappella* at Mantua did not include furnishing music for Santa Barbara. Possibly, he wrote *Sacrae cantiunculae* (Enticing sacred songs; 1582) in connection with his counterpoint lessons from Ingegneri.

The volume published in 1610, containing a Mass for the Virgin, Vespers with two Magnificat settings, and motets, was dedicated to the pope, which suggests that Monteverdi wanted church employment. In contrast to the Renaissance style of the Mass, the Vesper psalms display a mixture of styles. Some psalm settings are madrigalesque. In others, walking bass lines, ostinato or ground bass, and basso continuo are present. The chant-based melodies are subjected to various techniques, including **falsobordone,** cantus firmus, and strophic variation. *Falsobordone,* a type of chordal recitation used in Italy and Iberia in the sixteenth and seventeenth centuries, is *a cappella* four-voice homophonic chant notated as root-position triads and using the form and melody of a Gregorian-chant psalm tone. This technique was used principally in setting Vesper psalms, Magnificats, and Lamentations. In the Vespers, the tenor motet *Nigra sum* (I am black) incorporates material from the Lament in *L'Arianna*. The Magnificats, for voices and instruments, are among the earliest *concertato* settings of that canticle.

Monteverdi's Venetian sacred music was published in two collections (1641; posth. 1651). Though the collections are large, they cannot possibly contain all the music he composed for St. Mark's during his 30 years of service there. Three compositional styles are represented: strict Renaissance counterpoint, *seconda prattica*, and mixed.

Monteverdi's church music is unusual in its inclusion of many secular elements, especially operatic ones. During the first half of the seventeenth century, most Italian churches adhered to Renaissance-style music; composers in church positions had little or no opportunity to write opera. The fact that Monteverdi was permitted to engage in secular theatrical productions while employed by a major Italian church evidences his employers' and contemporaries' high regard for his talent. In essence, he pursued two careers

EXAMPLE 15.3 *Cruda Amarilli*, measures 9–14. Artusi objected to the dissonances between soprano and bass in measure 13 and the notated ornaments in measures 12–13.

simultaneously. He may have deliberately delayed publication of some of his church music because of its avant-garde character—the inclusion of operatic elements would have precluded its use in other Italian churches at that time. Many of Monteverdi's compositions foreshadow the merging of sacred and secular elements that became common practice a century later.

Madrigals Monteverdi's madrigals are among the finest composed during the late Renaissance and early Baroque era. His philosophy, *prima le parole, poi la musica* (first the words, then the music), is borne out in his settings. Most of his madrigals were written for professional singers, both women and men. Many of the poems he set were by Tasso and Guarini.

The first six books of madrigals are for five voices. The presence of three linked madrigals in the first book (1587) hints at Monteverdi's later interest in madrigal cycles. Most of the poems in Book II (1590) are pastoral, and the settings reveal Monteverdi's talent for imaginative imagery as well as his mastery of conventional word-painting devices. In a few madrigals two sopranos and an alto form an ensemble; perhaps the *concerto delle donne* from Ferrara had performed in Mantua, or Monteverdi was writing for a similar trio at the Gonzaga court.

Two cycles by Tasso and poems by Guarini dominate Monteverdi's third book of madrigals (1592). Par-

ticular attention was paid to setting the words expressively; dissonance plays a large role in this. Madrigals in cycles are linked by inconclusive endings.

The fourth and fifth books (1603, 1605) contain some of Monteverdi's best madrigals. In Book IV the words are emphasized through homophonic texture and natural accentuation and declamation; melismas are reserved for expressive purposes. Chromaticism is rare; dissonance is minimal, but when present it is intense. In declamatory passages, only the chord is written; the rhythm is left to the singers who must perform with ensemble precision. More than half the poems in Book V are from Guarini's *Il pastor fido* (see DWMA92). Where Monteverdi desired specific embellishments he notated them. Several of the madrigals in Book V are furnished with a *basso seguente* line that, at first glance, seems unnecessary in performance. Undoubtedly, Monteverdi notated that line because he wanted to reinforce the bass line and the instrumental sonority. The last six madrigals have a basso continuo that supplies pitches not present in the vocal harmonies; often it forms the third part in a trio. Frequently, an embellished solo voice supported by an instrumental bass effectively contrasts with the full ensemble.

Book VI (1614) is the product of a bereaved man grieving deeply. Approximately half the volume is taken up by two madrigal cycles: an arrangement of the *Lamento d'Arianna* and the threnody *Incenerite spoglie*.

In the latter, Monteverdi integrated recitative in the madrigal structure, used highly expressive harmonies, and reserved extreme dissonance for important climaxes. This cycle is ranked among the finest of his madrigals. Most of the single pieces in Book VI are *continuo* madrigals.

Monteverdi titled Book VII *Concerto* (1619). Each piece has a basso continuo line, and most of the madrigals are instrumentally accompanied duets of these types: (1) comparable in style with solo continuo madrigal, (2) arias, and (3) a series of continuous variations above a ground bass such as romanesca or passacaglia.

In the Foreword to Book VIII, *Madrigals of War and Love* (1638), Monteverdi explained that the volume contains music depicting the three humors of man: (1) "stillness," reflected in calmness; (2) "agitation," reflected in war; and (2) "supplication," reflected in love or passion. Music, Monteverdi wrote, must depict these humors and inspire these states in listeners. "Agitation" is depicted in the battle cycle *Combatimento di Tancredi et Clorinda,* where *stile concitato* and *pizzicatto* are introduced. Three singers form the cast: the Crusader Tancred and the Muslim girl Clorinda, who sing in arioso dialogue, and a narrator. Descriptive accompaniment is provided by string orchestra, with basso continuo.

Book IX (1651) contains madrigals previously published.

Stage Works Throughout his career, Monteverdi wrote ballets. The most significant of them are *Il ballo delle ingrate* and *Tirsi e Clori.* When writing a ballet, Monteverdi studied the choreography before composing any music; similarly, he became thoroughly familiar with a poem or an opera libretto before setting the text.

The earliest surviving stage production by Monteverdi is the revised score of *L'Orfeo* produced at Mantua in 1607. Striggio's libretto encompasses five scenes, requiring two scene changes: scenes 1, 2, and 5 are set in the Thracian fields, scenes 3 and 4 in Hades. The prologue is sung by Music, who pays homage to the Gonzagas, tells of the power of music, mentions the music of the spheres, and describes the scenery. Only a small portion of *L'Orfeo* is recitative; Monteverdi included madrigal, monody, arioso, and all kinds of in-

strumental music. The overture is a short toccata; orchestral *ritornelli* and *sinfonie* appear throughout the opera. The orchestra comprised 40 instruments that were used in small ensembles for affective purposes, programmatic effects, and dramatic functions, such as covering scenery changes and dividing the opera into "acts." For scenes set in Hades, trombones, chitarrone, and regal are used, pastoral scenes are accompanied by recorders and harpsichord, and harp and violins or viols simulate heavenly music and the sound of the lyre. Short sinfonias between scenes effect a change of mood or place. Strophic variation is used for the prologue and for *Possente spirto* (Powerful spirit), Orfeo's appeal to Charon for aid in crossing the river Styx.

Monteverdi's insight into human nature and his ability to characterize through music are apparent. Charon, the underworld ferryman who transports souls across the Styx into Hades, is cast as a bass; his indifference to Orfeo's plea is conveyed by the unchanged melody of his reply. Hope, who travels with Orfeo to Hades's gates, is a soprano. *L'Orfeo* is Renaissance in its presentation of characters as allegorical representations; however, Monteverdi reveals through his music the human side of those characters. Orfeo, son of Apollo and Calliope, has both a human and a godly nature; allegorically, he represents the power of music, yet in the final strophe of *Possente spirto* his humanity is revealed. *Possente spirto* (DWMA93) requires vocal virtuosity; for this piece Monteverdi wrote two solo lines, one unornamented and the other with all embellishments notated, thus indicating to the singer the manner in which he wanted the solo performed (ex. 15.4). Monteverdi's notation of ornaments provides a valuable guide to vocal performance practices in Italy in the first decade of the seventeenth century. Monteverdi and Striggio seem to have been aware of the medieval mathemati-

EXAMPLE 15.4 Opening measures of Orfeo's *Possente spirto* for which Monteverdi notated the solo line twice, once unornamented and once with the appropriate embellishments.

Fibonacci

Leonardo Pisano (c. 1170–d. after 1240), Italian mathematician known as Fibonacci, studied the various numerical systems available for use in calculation and found Hindu-Arabic numerals the most satisfactory. His treatise *Liber abaci* (Book of the abacus; 1202) appeared when very few people knew those numerals and how they could be used in arithmetical operations. Copies of *Liber abaci* circulated widely. Fibonacci's *Practica geometria* (Practice of geometry) appeared in 1220; it was followed by *Liber quadratorum* (Book of square numbers; 1225), an exposition of equations containing squares. Though *Liber quadratorum* is considered Fibonacci's masterpiece, *Liber abaci* was more influential.

Leonardo is remembered by modern mathematicians and musicians principally for the "Fibonacci numbers" sequence—[1], 1, 2, 3, 5, 8, 13, 21, 34, 55, and so on. This, the first recursive number sequence known in Europe, was derived from a problem in *Liber abaci*:

A pair of rabbits is placed in a walled enclosure. How many pairs of rabbits will be produced from this pair in a year if it is presumed that every month each pair of rabbits produces a new pair that becomes productive in the second month? (Answer: 377 pairs.)

As the numbers in that recursive series increase in magnitude, the ratio between succeeding numbers approaches the "Golden Section" (*phi*, or $\frac{1+\sqrt{5}}{2}$), the ancient mean and extreme ratio, whose value is .6180.... Scientists have observed that the numbers (and the ratio) are present in nature, for example, in pine cones, in spirals in animal horns and shells, and in flowers. This special proportional relationship (known as the "Golden Proportion" or "Golden Ratio") appears to be a natural phenomenon that can be expressed in arithmetical, algebraic, and geometric terms: the lesser is to the greater as the greater is to their sum. It is encountered in geometry quite often and is present in figure 15.3, where A + B is to A as A is to B (or xy:A :: A:B).

From ancient times, architects and artists knew and used Golden Proportion in their works, and many composers, from the Middle Ages to the present have incorporated Fibonacci numbers and Golden Proportion in their musical designs. Analysis of a number of important works by outstanding composers reveals a structural relationship to recursive numbers and a structural or dynamic climax or some other highly significant event positioned 61.8 percent of the way through a composition.

FIGURE 15.3 Diagram of the Golden Proportion.

cian Fibonacci's theory of the Golden Section—*Possente spirto*, the climax of the opera, is positioned in Act III in accord with that ratio (Insight, "Fibonacci").

Contemporary accounts indicate that Monteverdi's *L'Arianna* was dramatically superior to *L'Orfeo* and was more popular, but from *L'Arianna* only the libretto and *Lamento* survive. This Lament was the first of many written by Monteverdi and was greatly admired. Soon operatic laments became quite popular.

The music for *La finta pazza Licori* (Licoris's pretended insanity; 1627) has been lost. Extant correspondence indicates this was a full-length comic opera, which was unusual at that time. The characters are humans, without allegorical association.

Two of Monteverdi's last three operas are extant; *Le nozze d'Enea con Lavinia* (The marriage of Aeneas and Lavinia; 1641) is lost. In both *Il ritorno d'Ulisse in patria* (Ulysses's return to his native land; 1640) and *L'incoronazione di Poppea* (The coronation of Poppea; 1642) the portrayal of the characters and their emotions is excellent. Penelope, Ulysses's wife, was given much expressive recitative. In *L'incoronazione...*, Nero's neurotic sudden changes of mood are depicted by contrasting single phrases; that role was written for a high castrato. Nero acts predictably in every situation—cruel with Drusilla, generous with Poppea, and angry with Seneca. There are fine arioso laments for Otho (Poppea's husband) and Octavia (the deposed empress). Another realistic depiction is the trio (act II, scene 3), in which Seneca's three friends try to dissuade him from suicide. The inclusion of a trio in an opera was unusual at that time.

Comic interludes appear in these operas, often given to nonessential characters. Particularly effective is the disguise scene, where Ottone, wearing Drusilla's clothes, sneaks into Poppea's garden. Scenes like this were made easier by the fact that some of the male roles were sung by castrati. The *buffo* duet between Valletto and Damezella (act II, scene 5) seems to foreshadow some written by Mozart.

These last two operas reflect a general trend in Venetian opera in the 1640s and the fact that they were written for performance in commercial rather than court theater: They are constructed with a prologue and three acts (instead of five), require less lavish scenery, and fewer and less variety of instruments. The chorus is less crucial to the drama. Arias are in closed forms, and there is a clear distinction between recitative and aria, though there are instances in which recitative flows through arioso into aria.

ROME

The presentation of Cavalieri's *Rappresentatione di Anima, et di Corpo* in Rome did not inspire immediate sequels. There, opera composition was sporadic until almost 1630. In 1606, Agostino Agazzari (1578–1640) composed the pastoral opera *Eumelio* for performance at Seminario Romano. A prologue sung by Poetry is followed by three short acts, each concluding with a chorus. *Eumelio* consists mainly of recitatives and strophic arias for solo voice accompanied by basso continuo. Agazzari's music is very similar to that of Cavalieri.

Stefano Landi (c. 1586–1639) was a student at Seminario Romano when *Eumelio* was performed there. By 1618 he was *maestro di cappella* to the Bishop of Padua. Landi's first opera, *La morte d'Orfeo* (The death of Orpheus; 1619), was performed in Rome and is considered Rome's first secular opera. Its musical style resembles Monteverdi's *L'Orfeo*. Landi was admitted to the papal choir in 1629 as an alto; he did not write another opera until 1631. Meantime, Filippo Vittali's *Aretusa* was performed at Ottavio Corsini's home in 1620, and Domenico Mazzochi's *La catena d' Adone* (The chain of Adonis) was presented at Marquis Evandro Conti's house in 1626.

Rome had no central secular formal court; opera developed mainly through the interest and patronage of wealthy churchmen. Theaters were constructed in homes; private presentations of operas helped circumvent papal opposition to female singers and women appearing on stage. During 1631–44 the Barberini nephews of Pope Urban VIII (r. 1623–44) regularly presented operas in their residences. On two occasions in 1632 Landi's sacred opera *Il Sant' Alessio* (Saint Alexis) was performed at Palazzo Barberini. The libretto was by Giulio Rospigliosi (1600–69), who became Pope Clement IX (r. 1667–69). Rospigliosi is credited with originating, through his libretti, both sacred opera (nonallegorical) and comic opera. Many of his serious opera libretti contain comic roles. His poetry is excellent, and he was well versed in the demands of staging and music. His plots have more characters than the very early operas, and some have subplots. Composers reacted to these features by creating a kind of recitative that was less melodious, with many repeated notes over static insignificant harmonies, to quicken the delivery.

Il Sant' Alessio is Landi's most important work. It is the first opera on a historical subject and the first on the inner life of a human character. The opera comprises a prologue and three acts. The prologue and acts II and III are each preceded by a *sinfonia*; acts I and III commence with a chorus, and every act concludes with a chorus and dancing. The *sinfonie* are the earliest opera overtures that are not mere fanfares. The opening *sinfonia* is in four sections and foreshadows *sonata da chiesa* in form. The *sinfonie* preceding acts II and III are canzonalike; each is in three sections, fast-slow-fast in tempo. That structure anticipates the **Italian overture** used later in the seventeenth century (p. 255). The third section of the *sinfonia* to act II is itself sectional, commencing chordally and continuing in imitative counterpoint; it suggests the form that has become known as **French overture** (p. 258).

Within the next decade, Roman opera changed considerably. The creators of the first operas viewed them as *dramma per musica*—drama through music—with drama being of first importance. But by c. 1642, the quality of the music and the production of an entertaining spectacle had become the main concern; the integrity of the drama was minor. The mythological stories that formed the basis for most of the operas were altered considerably.

The extent to which Roman opera changed may be seen in the work of Luigi Rossi (c. 1597–1653), who composed only two operas. For Carnival, 1642, Rossi wrote for Cardinal Antonio Barberini *Il palazzo incantato* (The enchanted palace; libretto, Rospigliosi). The opera has numerous characters in addition to chorus and dancers; the plot and subplots are filled with intrigue and lightened by comedy. Its performance was an extravagant spectacle lasting seven hours. In 1646, when the French court wanted to produce an opera similar to those presented by Barberini, Cardinal Mazarin (1602–61) contacted Rossi. Rossi's *Orfeo* is the first Italian opera written specifically for Paris. The librettist buried the mythological tale in intrigue and comedy that required many additional characters and scenes and much music for solos, choruses, and dancing. Rossi was one of the leading Roman composers of vocal music—his chamber cantatas are excellent—and *Orfeo* contains many beautiful arias and ensembles. Its performance at the French court in 1647 lasted six hours.

VENICE

In Venice during Grimani's reign (1597–1605) it was customary to perform a pastoral fable in the courtyard of the palace three times a year. Those pastoral presentations cannot be considered early operas. Monteverdi's madrigal cycle *Combatimento di Tancredi et Clorinda* was performed at the Mocenigo home in 1624, and his (lost) opera *Proserpina rapita* was presented there in 1630. There is no indication that other operas were performed in Venice at that time.

In fact, little dramatic music was performed in Venice until the first public opera house, Teatro San Cassiano, was established there in 1637. The venture was largely supported by subscription sales of boxes, but single admission tickets were available. When Teatro San Cassiano proved successful, several more opera houses were constructed, including Teatro SS Giovanni e Paolo (1639). A Venetian theater was usually named for the parish in which it was located; a theater was built and owned by a noble family but was managed by an impresario. Monteverdi's last operas were produced at San Cassiano and SS Giovanni e Paolo.

After Monteverdi's death, Pietro Francesco Cavalli (1602–76) was the leading composer of operas in Venice. In 1616, as a boy soprano, Cavalli entered St. Mark's *cappella;* his voice matured to tenor, and he remained in the *cappella.* In 1639, he was appointed second organist at St. Mark's. Almost simultaneously, he invested in Teatro San Cassiano and began to write operas. Four of his 33 operas—*Egisto* (1643), *Giasone* (Jason; 1649), *Xerse* (Xerxes; 1655), and *Erismena* (1656)—became part of standard opera repertoire in Italy during the 1660s and 1670s. *Giasone* was his most popular opera.

After much hesitation, Cavalli accepted Mazarin's commission to compose an opera for the marriage of Louis XIV to Maria Teresia of Spain in 1660. *Ercole amante* (Hercules in love; 1662) was not completed in time for the festivities, and a revised version of *Xerse* was substituted. Alterations included transposing Xerxes's role down to bass-baritone range and inserting ballet scenes by Lully.

For the 24 years that Cavalli composed operas, his style remained fairly stable. Free verse is usually set as recitative accompanied only by basso continuo; in almost all the rare instances when strings provide recitative accompaniment, viols are used. Cavalli's arias are strophic, usually in triple meter, with text set syllabically except for occasional small flourishes to beautify the vocal line. Most of his operas contain at least one lament; these are either modeled on Monteverdi's *Lament d'Arianna* or use an ostinato bass based on a descending tetrachord (sometimes labeled "passacaglia"). Cavalli wrote orchestral *sinfonie* and *ritornelli* and used some *stile concitato.*

Cavalli's main competitor was Antonio Cesti (1623–69), whose opera *Orontea* (1656) enjoyed popularity in Italy equal to that of Cavalli's *Giasone.* When Cesti became a Franciscan monk, he chose to use the name "Antonio." His given name was Pietro. He has often been referred to, erroneously, as "Marc' Antonio." In 1659 he secured release from his monastic vows but remained a secular priest. Cesti spent considerable time at the imperial court in Innsbruck, where 5 of his 15 operas were produced; 5 of the others were written for Vienna. He wrote at least 68 secular cantatas and 5 sacred vocal pieces.

Orontea is typical of Cesti's operatic writing. Usually, his arias are strophic. Most of them have only basso continuo accompaniment; for *ritornelli* he used two violins with basso continuo. In general, his music is not as vigorous and forceful as that of Cavalli.

Il pomo d'oro (The golden apple; perf. Vienna, 1668) is more spectacular than most of Cesti's operas because it was created for the wedding festivities of Emperor Leopold I (r. 1657–1705) and Princess Margherita of Spain. Leopold was a major patron of music and also a composer. Some of the arias in *Il pomo d'oro* are by him. That opera, a lavish court production, has a cast and orchestra larger than those in most of Cesti's operas.

Between the time of its inception and the time of Cesti's death, opera changed considerably. After 1650, music was no longer the accessory vehicle through which drama was effectively presented, in the manner of the ancient Greeks, but had become the prime factor in opera, and drama was accessory to the presentation of music, which was concentrated in solo singing. Recitative and aria were two distinct types of solo song, and **arioso** was midway between the two. Vocal ensembles were seldom used, and instrumental music consisted of overtures, introductions, and *ritornelli*. The view of opera prevalent in the late 1660s and the general formal outline then in use remained fairly constant for approximately the next two centuries.

Venetian opera was spread through Italy by itinerant opera troupes that obtained patronage in cities they visited, employed local musicians when necessary, and gave performances for paid admission. Opera was disseminated also by aristocratic patrons (e.g., Barberini) who, for various reasons, went into exile in other countries; by foreign rulers or officials (e.g., Mazarin) who experienced opera at other courts and commissioned similar works for special occasions at their own; by Italian composers (e.g., Cesti) who secured appointments in other countries; and by foreign composers (e.g., Schütz) who studied or worked in Italy for a time and then returned to their own lands. Opera, which originated in the experiments of a handful of humanists, literati, and musicians in Florence in 1600, was to be one of the major forms of Western music.

During the second half of the seventeenth century, Venice remained the principal Italian center of opera. Among the successful composers there in the 1660s and 1670s were Antonio Sartorio (1630–80), Giovanni Legrenzi (1626–90), and Carlo Pallavicino (d. 1688).

Sartorio's *L'Adelaide* (Adelaide; 1672) seems to be the first of many Venetian operas specifying trumpets in the orchestration, mentioning trumpets in the texts, and incorporating trumpetlike figures in the vocal line. Sartorio's operas are on heroic subjects, both mythological and historical. He was especially adept at expressing deep passions musically and juxtaposing the heroic and the banal for comic relief.

Legrenzi's operas are heroic-comic, with complicated plots requiring large casts and much machinery (fig. 15.4). Often in arias he combined two or more formal aspects; for example, **motto,** ostinato bass, and da capo (ABA) form may appear in the same aria. A **motto aria** is one in which the opening phrase of the vocal solo is presented, is followed by a rest or two, and then is restated and the aria proceeds. In the aria *Vanne ingrata crudel e spietata* from *Il Giustino* (1683), Legrenzi used a motto beginning and a bass line of constantly moving eighth and sixteenth notes; both features were used frequently in the late seventeenth and early eighteenth centuries (ex. 15.5).

NAPLES

Opera was introduced in Naples c. 1652 when a traveling troupe, Febi Armonici, presented some Venetian operas there. A Neapolitan, Francesco Provenzale (c. 1626–1704), became associated with that troupe; in 1653 Febi Armonici presented his first opera, *Il Ciro* (Cyrus), at Teatro SS. Giovanni e Paolo.

In 1676 Filippo Coppola, court *maestro di cappella* established the custom of chapel musicians producing operas for royal name days and anniversaries. On other occasions, itinerant companies performed operas at the palace. Coppola was succeeded as chapelmaster by P. A. Ziani; after his death (1684), Alessandro Scarlatti was appointed to the post (see p. 254). When the Duke of Medinacelli ruled (1695–1702), Neapolitan opera rose to unprecedented heights of splendor.

By the end of the seventeenth century, operas composed at Naples exhibited features that became standard in eighteenth-century Italian opera. Two distinct types of recitative emerged: (1) *recitativo semplice* (simple recitative), later called *recitativo secco* (dry recitative), in which the solo voice was accompanied by basso continuo only (harpsichord and sustaining bass instrument) and used for lengthy dialogue and monologue to proceed quickly through the narrative,

FIGURE 15.4 (*a*) Machinery used for (*b*) cloud scene in Legrenzi's opera *Germanico sul Reno* (Venice, 1676). *(From the Appendix of Diderot and d'Alembert's Encyclopédie (10), Paris, 1772)*

(a)   (b)

and (2) **recitativo accompagnato** (accompanied recitative), in which the solo voice was orchestrally accompanied and used for extremely emotional or dramatically tense situations. *Recitativo accompagnato* was not always orchestrally accompanied throughout; short portions of it might be sung unaccompanied or with basso continuo and the orchestra used to reinforce the high points or to punctuate emotional outbursts in the solo line.

Commentary and soliloquy were set as aria, for which a variety of forms were used. Simple ternary form (ABA) was lengthened considerably. Often composers (or scribes) did not write out the repeat of the A section but simply indicated it by the words **da capo** (from the beginning) placed at the end of the B section, and designated the conclusion of the aria by the word **Fine** (end) placed at the end of the A section. If the aria begins with an orchestral introduction that is not to be repeated when the A section is returned, the words **dal segno al fine** (from the sign to *fine*) appear at the end of the B section of the aria, and the appropriate sign of congruence indicates the place to which the performers return.

Composers continued to use the term *arioso* (arialike) to denote that a melody is neither as rhythmically free as in recitative nor as regular and lyrical as in aria.

EXAMPLE 15.3 Beginning of aria *Vanne ingrata crudel e spietata* from Legrenzi's opera *Il Giustino*. Note the motto opening and the running bass line.

Actually, *arioso* was in use before speechlike *recitativo secco* came into existence.

The transition from the style of Baroque opera prevalent in the last decades of the seventeenth century to the newer style used in the eighteenth century is evident in the operas of Alessandro Scarlatti, who is no longer considered the founder of the Neapolitan school but the composer who brought it into prominence.

BAROQUE VOCAL MUSIC

ALESSANDRO SCARLATTI

Alessandro Scarlatti (1660–1725) was born in Palermo. At the age of 12, he was sent to Rome with his two sisters, Anna Maria (1661–1703) and Melchiorra (1663–1736), who were singers. Nothing further is recorded concerning Alessandro until April 1678, when he married Antonia Anzalone. Two of their ten children, Pietro (1679–1750) and Domenico (1685–1757), had careers in music.

Anna Maria Scarlatti enjoyed a singing career. She appeared in Pietro Agostini's (c. 1635–80) *Il ratto delle sabine* (The rape of the Sabines; Venice, 1680). She married twice; her second husband, shipowner Nicolo Barbapiccola, became impresario of Teatro San Bartolomeo in Naples in 1703, and he staged Domenico Scarlatti's first operas. Melchiorra eventually settled in Naples. Allegedly, she was influential in 1684 in securing Alessandro's appointment as *maestro di cappella* at the Viceroy's chapel there.

In 1679, Alessandro Scarlatti's first oratorio and first opera were performed in Rome. Queen Christina of Sweden and Cardinals Pamphili and Ottoboni became his patrons. All of them maintained theaters in their palaces, and Scarlatti composed at least four more operas, six more oratorios, and many cantatas under their auspices (see p. 267). At that time there was no activity in public theaters in Rome because of the opposition of Pope Innocent XI (r. 1676–89).

That Naples became a center of opera is largely due to Scarlatti's endeavors—he composed over half the new operas presented in Naples between 1684 and 1702. More than 40 of his operas from those years survive, and many of his works are lost if, as he claimed, *Lucio Manlio* (1705) is his eighty-eighth stage work. The main patrons of opera were the viceroys, who had theaters in the palace and summer residence and promoted the public theaters. The principal public theater, San Bartolomeo, had a permanent opera company, and Scarlatti became its director. Customarily, in Naples the first performance of a cantata or opera was at the palace; then the production was transferred to Teatro San Bartolomeo.

In 1702 Scarlatti visited the Medici court in Florence but failed to secure a position. Next, he went to Rome (1703), where he found that public theaters had been closed since 1700, and there were few performances of opera in private theaters. Therefore, he composed cantatas, serenatas, and oratorios. In 1707, for Venice, he wrote *Il Mitridate Eupatore,* one of his best operas.

In 1708 Scarlatti resumed his position as chapelmaster at Naples. Under Grimani's patronage, he composed 11 operas, including *Il Tigrane* (1715). Around 1706, Neapolitans had become interested in comic opera in vernacular dialect with popular style music, and works of that kind flourished in small theaters there. Scarlatti wrote comic *intermezzi* for three of his operas and composed one comic opera, *Il trionfo dell' onore* (The triumph of honor; 1718).

From 1718 to 1722 Scarlatti lived in Rome, where he composed the operas *Telemaco* (1718), *Marco Attilio Regolo* (1719), and *La Griselda* (1721). The latter is his last surviving opera. With the exception of a minor part for tenor, all roles in *La Griselda* were for castrati. Its performance marked the professional debut of Giovanni Carestini (c. 1705–59), one of the most talented sopranos of his day, as Griselda. In 1722 Scarlatti returned to Naples and spent his remaining years in comparative retirement.

Scarlatti labeled most of his operas *dramma per musica.* He preferred serious plots with happy endings and historical or imaginary personages, stylized, with

Alessandro Scarlatti. Artist is unknown. *(Civico Museo Bibliografico Musicale, Bologna)*

no inner life revealed. Usually, the characters are rulers, their confidants, and their servants and most often are presented in pairs. His operas contain many arias, usually quite short, set off by recitatives in which the musical interest is minimal. Recitative-aria pairing became standard. However, he wrote many scenes in which no aria occurs. Act II, scene 4 of *La Griselda* (DWMA94) consists of a long *secco* recitative dialogue between Griselda and Ottone, followed by Griselda's *da capo* aria *Figlio! Tiranno!* (Son! Tyrant!). The *stile concitato* of the string orchestra mirrors Griselda's agitation. In Scarlatti's early operas, arias in ABA form are common; after c. 1698, full *da capo* arias predominate. Rarely do his aria melodies exceed a tenth in range. Most of the arias in his early operas have only basso continuo accompaniment; for the longer *da capo* arias, orchestral accompaniment is provided. Customarily, he concluded an act with an important aria sung by a major character.

Because *La Griselda* concerns the King and Queen of Sicily, it was natural for Scarlatti to include some **siciliana** arias. Derived from folk song, a *siciliana* melody is simple, *cantabile*, in slow $\frac{6}{8}$ or $\frac{12}{8}$ meter (ex. 15.6). Usually associated with pastoral scenes, it sometimes is rather melancholy. Frequently, Scarlatti used the Neapolitan sixth chord in the sicilianas and placed the flat supertonic in the upper part.

The orchestral *sinfonie* Scarlatti composed for overtures to his operas usually have no musical connection with the operas they introduce. The *sinfonia* that opens *La griselda* is an **Italian overture,** having three distinct sections, in Presto-Adagio-Presto order of tempo.

Near the end of Scarlatti's career, his contemporaries considered his music out of date. Nevertheless, the era of Italian Baroque opera composition that began with Monteverdi and proceeded through Cavalli and Cesti attained consummation with Scarlatti.

EXAMPLE 15.6 Measures 1–6 of the *siciliana* aria *Colomba innamorata* sung by Ottone in act II, scene 2 of *La Griselda.* Note that "solo" in the continuo line means that the keyboard player is not to fill in harmonies. *(From The Operas of Alessandro Scarlatti, edited by Donald Grout and Joscelyn Godwin. [copyright] 1975 by The President and Fellows of Harvard College. Reprinted by permission of Harvard University Press, Cambridge, MA)*

FRANCE

It was some time before opera caught a foothold in France. There were several reasons for its failure to do so: a long-standing tradition of theater in Paris, the French love of staged dance (ballet), and the fact that the French language is difficult to sing. Professional theater was strong in Paris. In 1608 one prestigious troupe was permitted to call itself The King's Players, and it was not long before a theater was constructed in the palace. In the early seventeenth century, the principal French playwright was Alexandre Hardy (c. 1575– c. 1630), who supplied The King's Players with several hundred tragicomedies. He was followed by three outstanding dramatists: Pierre Corneille (1606–84) and Jean Racine (1639–99), noted for their tragedies, and J.-B. Molière (1622–73), acclaimed for his comedies.

Ballet de cour (court ballet) had been a featured form of entertainment at the French court since the performance of *Circé* in 1581. In *Circé*, poetry, music, decor, and dance were combined to support a central dramatic action—destruction of the power of the enchantress Circé and the reestablishment of order and harmony. *Circé* is musical drama and as such is precursor to opera in France.

After Henri IV was assassinated (1610), Maria de' Medici served as regent for her son, Louis XIII (b. 1601; r. 1610–43), but soon sought political power for herself. For a time, Richelieu (1585–1642), minister at court, was able to reconcile mother, son, and the French nobility. In 1622 Richelieu was created cardinal. Eventually, Louis believed that Richelieu alone could maintain order in France and in 1624 named him first minister; Richelieu gained almost complete control of the government. After Richelieu's death, Cardinal Mazarin became principal minister of France. He had experienced opera in Italy and saw it as a means of political intrigue in France—it could divert attention from his own political maneuvers. To that end, he introduced Italian opera at court and invited Italian opera companies and composers to Paris. Because of the French penchant for ballet, the Italian operas that Mazarin brought to Paris were adapted to include ballet scenes.

Louis XIII was succeeded by his five-year-old son, Louis XIV (r. 1643–1715), with Anne of Austria as matriarchal regent and Mazarin as minister. When plans were made for Louis XIV's marriage to Maria Teresia of Spain in 1660, Mazarin invited Cavalli to compose an opera for the festivities (see p. 251). (A Spanish opera was also written for that wedding; see p. 260.)

When Mazarin died, Louis XIV determined to assume complete personal control of the government. *Privilèges* (permits) to establish theaters and to print music and books had to be obtained from the office of the minister of finance, J. B. Colbert. Louis XIV was interested in music, dance, and the theater. At the age of 13, he danced on stage for the first time in *Ballet de Casandre*. Two years later, in *Ballet de la nuit* (Ballet of the night), a young Florentine named Giovanni Battista Lulli danced on stage alongside the king.

JEAN-BAPTISTE LULLY

Lulli (1632–87) was brought to France in 1646 by Roger de Lorraine to help his niece learn the Italian language. Lulli became an accomplished dancer, learned to play guitar and violin, and heard *airs* and dialogues. He retained the Italian spelling of his name until 1661, when he became a naturalized French citizen.

In 1652 Lully went to Paris. In February 1653 he and the king danced in the *Ballet de la nuit,* and in March Lully was appointed composer of instrumental music to the king. He was responsible for composing instrumental music for court ballets, and he performed in some of them. By 1656 he had permission to conduct the 16 *petits violons,* whose performance practices he disciplined; by 1666 the *petits violons* and the *24 violons du Roi* were combined under his direction for court ballet performances. From 1664 to 1670 Lully collaborated with Molière in writing *comédies-ballets.*

Pierre Perrin (c. 1620–75), a librettist of mediocre talent, convinced Colbert that France should have its own opera and obtained a 12-year *privilège* to establish academies for the performance of opera anywhere in the realm. Perrin collaborated with composer Robert Cambert (c. 1627–77). In March 1671 the academy in Paris opened with their opera *Pomone;* it had 146 performances. Perrin had hired business managers whose methods were unscrupulous, as a result, he found himself in debtors prison. Lully purchased Perrin's *privilège* and settled the debts. Then Lully constructed an opera theater and selected Philippe Quinault (1635–88) as librettist. During 1673–83 Lully composed a new opera each year except 1681. Quinault provided the libretti for 11 of them.

Lully's principal contribution to the development of music was in opera. However, he composed a considerable amount of religious music for the royal chapel. On 8 January 1687, to celebrate the king's recovery from an operation, Lully conducted more than 150 musicians in a performance of his *Te Deum* (written in 1677). It was Lully's custom to beat time by striking the floor with a cane—in French, a *baton* (stick). During his performance, he inadvertently hit one of his toes with the sharp point of that cane. Despite medical treatment, gangrene set in. Lully refused to permit amputation of the toe, and his condition deteriorated. He died on 22 March.

Jean-Baptiste Lully

LULLY'S WORKS   Lully's stage works may be grouped by genres into three temporal periods: (1) 1653–63, *ballets de cour*; (2) 1663–72, *pastorales, comédies-ballets,* and *tragédies-ballets*; and (3) 1672–87, large stage works. The latter group includes the pastorale *Les fêtes de l'Amour et de Bacchus* (The festivals of Love and of Bacchus; 1672), the 13 operas termed *tragédies lyriques,* the 2 ballets *Le triomphe de l'amour* (Love's triumph; 1681) and *Le temple de la paix* (The temple of peace; 1685), and *Acis et Galatée,* a *pastorale héroïque* (1686).

During his first decade at the French royal court, Lully learned to differentiate between Italian and French musical styles. Until 1661 most of his music for court ballets was Italianate. Then he distinguished clearly between French and Italian styles and reserved songs in the Italian language for comic scenes or laments. He became adept at setting comedy and used comic scenes to inject social satire. Gradually, he transformed *ballet de cour* from a collection of dances and autonomous scenes into a dramatic spectacle with a prologue and choral finales.

In the *comédies-ballets* composed during 1663–72, Lully began to write passages of recitative and wrote short *airs* with words set syllabically in short phrases. *Les amants magnifiques* (The magnificent lovers; 1670) contains some features of the operas Lully composed later: a prologue sung throughout, *ritournelles* for winds, and use of the orchestra to dramatize entrances. In *comédie-ballet,* part of the text is sung and part of it spoken. In some of the Lully-Molière *comédies-ballets* (e.g., *Le bourgeois gentilhomme* [The middle-class gentleman; 1670]), there is a merging of music, dance, and

poetry that foreshadows *opéra comique. Psyché* (1671), originally a *tragédie-ballet,* was transformed into a *tragédie lyrique* (i.e., an opera) in 1678 when Lully and Thomas Corneille added recitatives and made minor alterations.

The *tragédies lyriques* are on a larger scale than Lully's earlier works and have continuous music. Their subjects are drawn from Greek mythology or Latin and Spanish chivalric romances. In most of Lully's operas, the drama deals with the conflict between glory and duty or between glory and love. The main plot concerns a pair of lovers and one or more rivals; in the subplot, persons of lesser importance are implicated in parallel intrigue. Lully's *tragédies lyriques* have a prologue and five acts; this became standard in French opera.

In composing *tragédie lyrique,* Lully considered the poetry of prime importance and wrote music appropriate for correct declamation of the text. The drama was developed through simple recitative, which Lully insisted be sung exactly as he notated it—with no alteration in the rhythm other than the fluctuations specifically notated and with only the embellishments he notated or approved.

In many recitative-air combinations, Lully used orchestra for introductory *ritournelle* and to accompany the air but used only basso continuo for the recitative. After 1679 he used accompanied recitative more often. In *Amadis* (1684) and *Roland* (1685), the leading roles are written principally in accompanied recitative. In French opera in Lully's time, the distinction between accompanied recitative and air is not as great as that between recitative and aria in Italian opera. Lully's favorite small ensemble was the duo. Often, he involved the chorus in the action by writing short choral utterances of encouragement or supplication. The chorus was used also in **divertissements.** A divertissement is a section (or scene) within an act of a large stage work, such as opera, that consists of dances, vocal solos, and ensembles and may or may not be essential to the plot.

Lully's basic orchestration was five-part strings, with occasional doubling by oboes and bassoons, plus basso continuo. When other instruments, such as trumpets or drums, were required for special effects, he added them. The precision of Lully's orchestra was much admired, especially by foreign visitors at court. Georg Muffat (1653–1704) explained Lully's style and orchestral techniques in the forewords to his publications (see p. 297).

Lully used **French overtures** in his *ballets de cour* and *tragédies lyriques.* A French overture is in two sections, each marked to be repeated. The overture commences with a slow section that is homophonic and that features dotted rhythms. The second section, in a fast tempo, is fugal or quasi-fugal and concludes with a brief return to the slow tempo and dotted rhythms of the beginning (see overture to *Alceste,* DWMA95). The overall mood of a French overture is serious, dignified, and festive.

Lully's *tragédies lyriques* set the standard for French opera for the eighteenth century. Succeeding composers made few alterations in his basic plan other than to expand the *divertissements* containing ballets and choruses. Increased emphasis on ballet is reflected also in the creation of **opéra-ballet** by André Campra (1660–1774). In *opéra-ballet* there is an overall idea, but each act is independent and contains a divertissement. Campra's first *opéra-ballet* was *L'Europe galante* (1697).

ENGLAND

During the seventeenth century, there flourished in England an aristocratic entertainment known as **masque,** so-named because in some portions of the performance participants wore masks. Based on an allegorical or mythological theme, a masque is a blend of lyric and dramatic poetry, song, dance, and instrumental music presented in elaborate settings.

Some of the finest court masques were written between 1605 and 1631 by poet laureate Ben Jonson (1573–1637) and were presented in settings created by stage architect Inigo Jones (1573–1652). Jonson's *Masque of Blackness* (1605) was the first masque to use a stage and curtain (instead of dispersed scenery in a room); at this point, masque moved out of the realm of court entertainment and into that of theater. *Masque of Blackness* is the first masque from which specific music survives—one song by Alfonso Ferrabosco (1578–1628). Jonson structured the masque in five or six "entries" (the word "act" was not used) commencing with a prologue. Dance was considered the most important element in a masque; next came the staging, with machinery and sets; and then the text, with music as a mere accessory to the total presentation. Usually, the plot was developed in spoken dialogue. An exception is Jonson's *Lovers Made Men* (1617), which, according to its preface, was sung throughout "after the Italian manner, *stylo recitativo,* [composed] by master Nicholas Lanier." None of that music survives. Lanier (1588–1666) is credited with being the first to set English words in the style of Italian recitative in "Bring away this sacred tree," from *The Masque of Squires* (1617). That song is extant.

Masques were given privately during the Civil War (1642–49), the Commonwealth (1649–60), and the Restoration of Charles II (c. 1660–85). In 1653, Christopher Gibbons (1615–76) and Matthew Locke composed the music for James Shirley's (1596–1666) *Cupid and Death:* recitatives, airs, choruses, dances, and other instrumental pieces.

William Davenant's (1606–68) *The Siege of Rhodes* (1656), often referred to as the first English opera, was sung throughout. Five composers supplied the music, the most significant being Henry Lawes and Matthew Locke. *The Siege of Rhodes* differs from masque in having a unified dramatic plot; moreover, it concerns a contemporary heroic subject.

John Blow's (1649–1708) setting of *Venus and Adonis* (1684) is variously considered masque and miniature opera. The work is sung throughout and contains elements of opera, but it is not of the same stature as Purcell's *Dido and Aeneas.*

During the Commonwealth period, Oliver Cromwell banned theater productions but permitted concerts, stage performances of plays with music, and "moral representations" that included music and dance. Henry Purcell (1659–95) expanded plays by inserting incidental music and lengthy *divertissements;* usually, a French overture preceded the play. The plays contained so much music that they virtually became semioperas.

Purcell's only true opera is *Dido and Aeneas* (1689), composed for performance at dancing master Josias Priest's School for Young Ladies, in Chelsea. The libretto is by Nahum Tate. *Dido and Aeneas* is based on the tragedy of Dido, Queen of Carthage, as related in Vergil's *Aeneid.* The three-act opera has four principal roles and takes a little over an hour to perform. The orchestra consists of strings and basso continuo. A French overture opens the opera; there are recitatives, arias, choruses, and dances. Dido's lament ("When I am laid in earth") and the recitative preceding it ("Thy hand, Belinda") constitute one of the finest recitative-aria combinations in opera literature (DWMA96). Purcell cast Dido's lament in binary form with a bass line that is an extended chromatic passacaglia ground. The aria concludes with an orchestral passage in which melodic sighs lead directly into the final chorus, "With drooping wings."

During the eighteenth century, no English composer achieved lasting success in the field of opera.

GERMANIC LANDS

Attempts to establish German (i.e., vernacular) opera met with limited success in many places. Italian and French opera fared better. In 1627 Martin Opitz adapted Rinuccini's libretto *Dafne* for Heinrich Schütz to set to music. This, the first opera created in Germany, was performed at Hartenfels castle in Torgau as part of the nuptial festivities for the Elector's daughter Sophia Eleonora and Landgrave Georg II of Hessen-Darmstadt. Unfortunately, all of Schütz's stage works are lost (see also p. 264).

Emperor Leopold I was interested in music and composed some operas, oratorios, arias, Masses, and other vocal works. His music is Venetian in style, but the language of the texts varies. During his reign, the Hofkapelle was expanded considerably, and many Italian composers and musicians were employed.

Agostino Steffani (1654–1728) worked at the Munich court as a singer, organist, and composer for 21 years. While there, he composed six operas. Disap-

pointed at not being named imperial Kapellmeister in 1688, Steffani sought employment at Hanover. The Duke had built a new theater, and in 1688–98 a permanent Italian opera company was maintained. Steffani was appointed Kapellmeister and supervised the theater. For a few years he had ample time for music; he composed many chamber duets and at least six operas. Then his diplomatic talents were recognized, and his various political and ecclesiastical assignments left little time for composing.

Steffani's finest compositions are his chamber duets; these secular pieces are typical of the Italian solo cantatas of that time. J. G. Conradi (d. 1699) introduced French operatic style into Germanic lands c. 1690, and Steffani incorporated in his operas elements of French music (e.g., ballet, French overture, and arias in minuet and gavotte rhythms). Most of his arias are in *da capo* form; some use motto. Two of his operas are based on German history: *Alarico* (Munich, 1687) and *Henrico Leone* (Hanover, 1689). The operas Steffani composed for Hanover provided stimulus for opera composition in northern Germany, and in the late 1690s they were translated into German and staged in Hamburg.

German opera was slow in getting started. Among its influential predecessors are church and secular school plays that contained songs, traveling troupes whose dramatic presentations contained vocal and instrumental pieces, musico-dramatic performances presented by religious orders, and various forms of court entertainment. In 1644 German poet Georg Harsdörffer published in the journal *Frauenzimmer Gesprächspiele* (Women's Dialogues) the sacred play *Seeleweg;* it is designated *Singspiel* (play with music). The pastoral poem is by Harsdörffer, and its through-composed musical setting by Sigmund Staden (1607–55) contains recitatives and strophic songs. Many historians consider *Seelewig* the earliest surviving German opera.

Singspiel became the usual German term for opera in the late seventeenth century. The term was appropriate, for many of the early operas in German consist of spoken dialogue and strophic songs.

In Hamburg, despite violent opposition from church authorities, a group of musicians founded a German opera company in 1678, and German-language operas were performed at the Theater am Gänsemarkt until

c. 1750. At the outset, local poets provided the librettos. No outstanding virtuoso singers were employed, and castrati were not used. The most important composer of German operas for Hamburg was Reinhard Keiser (1674–1739), who wrote approximately 75 stage works for performance there between 1696 and 1734. Keiser seems to have been the first to write German comic operas. The subjects of Keiser's operas are varied and cosmopolitan. He used accompanied recitative, with effective harmonic changes to highlight emotion; aria forms include binary, strophic variation, *basso ostinato,* and *da capo.* His dramatic use of arioso foreshadows Bach's treatment of it in his Passions. A notable feature of Keiser's operas is his inventive instrumentation; folk as well as traditional instruments were used to achieve proper sound effect.

RUSSIA AND BOHEMIA

While Bohemia and Moravia were under Habsburg rule, Italian opera flourished at their courts, but Russia was relatively isolated from western European musical developments. Not until Anne's reign (r. 1730–40) was an Italian opera company permanently established at the Russian court.

The earliest opera based on a Bohemian subject is *Primislao, primó re di Boemia* (Primislao, first king of Bohemia; anonymous; 1698). Bartolomeo Bernardi's (c. 1660–1732) *Libussa,* on the same legend, was performed at Prague in 1703. When Emperor Charles VI decided in 1723 to establish his court permanently at Vienna, the importance of Prague declined considerably, and there were few lavish musical entertainments in Bohemian castles.

SPAIN

The earliest Spanish drama completely set to music was Lope de Vega's *La selva sin amor* (The forest without love; 1629). When it was performed, the instrumentalists were hidden from the spectators' view, as was the case in early Italian opera.

Pedro Calderón de la Barca (1600–81) wrote plays for secular public theater until he became a priest in 1651; thereafter, he became Spain's leading exponent of Christian drama. He wrote short allegorical sacred plays, and spectacular court plays and used music in them increasingly. Through his use of a semispoken style of recitative, Calderón was instrumental in bring-ing opera to the Spanish court. Juan Hidalgo (c. 1613–85) and Calderón created *La púrpura de la rosa* (The purple of the rose; 1660) to celebrate the marriage of Louis XIV and Spanish Infanta Maria Teresia. That music is lost. Hidalgo's *Celos aun del aire matan* (Jealousy, even of the air, kills; 1660), on a libretto by Calderón concerning the jealousy of Diana's nymphs, is the earliest Spanish opera whose music survives. It consists of recitatives, strophic arias, and choruses. When these operas were performed, women sang most of the male roles.

Calderón is credited with inventing the **zarzuela,** a Spanish dramatic form that combines singing and dancing with spoken dialogue. He wrote his first *zarzuela* in 1648. That he patterned the mature *zarzuela* after Italian opera is apparent in *El laurel de Apolo* (Apollo's laurel; 1657). In the late seventeenth century, Spanish composers wrote *zarzuela* rather than serious opera.

In Spanish colonies in America, opera was composed early in the eighteenth century. In 1701 the Viceroy of Peru commissioned Tomás de Torrejón y Velasco (1644–1728) to write an opera to honor Philip V (r. 1700–46) on his eighteenth birthday and the first year of his reign. Torrejón set *La púrpura de la rosa,* and it was performed at the palace, Lima, in October. Torrejón, born in Spain, went to Peru c. 1658; from 1676 until his death, he was *maestro di capilla* of Lima Cathedral. *Le púrpura de la rosa* is his only opera. It has been performed, in Baroque manner, several times in the 1990s.

The second opera produced in the New World was composed by Mexican-born Manuel de Zumaya (c. 1678–1756), chapelmaster at Mexico City Cathedral. His *La Parténope* ([Queen] Partenope)—the first full-length opera composed in North America—was performed at the palace, Mexico City, on 1 May 1711.

ORATORIO

An **oratorio** is a large-scale composition that resembles an opera but places greater emphasis on chorus; is presented without stage action, scenery, or costumes; and most often has a narrator. Usually, the narration is sung. The chorus may be used for narrative and dramatic purposes as well as for commentary or summation of the plot. Although an oratorio may be secular, most have sacred subjects. The name "oratorio" derives from the place in which this kind of composition was first performed, the Oratorio (prayer room) of a church. Forerunners of oratorio include liturgical drama, certain Offices for special saints' feasts, early presentations of Passion liturgy in dialogue, and dialogue laude. Immediate antecedents of oratorio are motets with narrative texts (such as Lassus's settings of Bible stories), dramatic renditions of the Passion, and *laude spirituale.*

NERI'S ORATORY CONGREGATION

Filippo Neri (1515–95) devoted his life to charitable works and prayer. In 1551 a small group of laymen met regularly in his living quarters in Rome for prayer and religious discussions. Neri included the singing of *laude spirituale* in the spiritual exercises. Within three years, the group increased to such an extent that meetings were held in a special prayer room (Oratorio) of the church. In 1575 Pope Gregory XIII (r. 1572–85) recognized Neri's group as a religious order, Congregazione dell' Oratorio (Oratory Congregation) and assigned them a new building, Chiesa Nova (New Church). Neri's significance in music history lies in his emphasis on congregational singing of laude, his use of music to attract people to the Oratory services, and his association with composers who wrote music specifically for those services.

Giovanni Animuccia composed two books of laude for Neri's Congregazione: *Il primo libro delle laudi* (4 vc.; 1565) and *Il secondo libro delle laude* (2–8 vc.; 1570). The first volume holds simple, chordal settings of Latin and vernacular devotional texts; the second book is slightly more elaborate musically, with increased harmony and voicing and without complex polyphony so that the words might be clearly understood. Some of Animuccia's laude had narrative or dramatic texts; thus, they were influential in the beginnings of the vernacular oratorios presented by Neri's Congregation c. 1600.

Giovanni Anerio's (c. 1567–1630) *Teatro armonico* (Harmonic theatre; 1619), written for Neri's Oratory Congregation, contains 94 works with vernacular texts based on biblical subjects or lives of saints. Seven of the pieces are considered oratorios. With them Anerio inaugurated the **oratorio volgare** (vernacular oratorio). The longest and most dramatic composition in the volume is *La conversione di S. Paolo* (The conversion of St.

Paul), for four soloists and double eight-part chorus. By the middle of the seventeenth century, both *oratorio latino* and *oratorio volgare* were written. Musically, the types are similar, the only difference being in the language used for the texts.

Among the most advanced oratorios c. 1650 are Giacomo Carissimi's *Daniele* (Daniel) and the anonymous *Giuseppe: oratorio per la Settimana Santa* (Joseph: oratorio for Holy Week), the earliest known oratorio based on the Passion. These works have solo lines for a *Testo* (narrator). Each oratorio is divided into two *Partes,* each *Parte* concluding with a chorus. When an oratorio was performed in an Oratory, a sermon was delivered between the *Partes.* The music contains recitative, arioso, and aria types; all forms commonly used for opera arias are represented. Most of these oratorios use only basso continuo for accompaniment; some add two violins for interludes, for *ritornelli,* and for doubling choral voices.

GIACOMO CARISSIMI

Carissimi (1605–74) is the first important composer of oratorios and was well known for his cantatas, of which at least 200 survive. He composed several Masses and numerous motets, in which he never ventured beyond the traditions of the forms. Carissimi wrote both Latin and vernacular oratorios. For Latin oratorios he chose biblical subjects from the Vulgate, usually from the Old Testament. Sometimes Scripture is used literally, and sometimes it is paraphrased or supplemented. Presumably, he prepared the texts himself. He termed the narrator *Historicus* (Storyteller) and often used chorus for part of the narration. He did not shun experimentation.

On the surface, Carissimi's music seems remarkably simple. However, when writing musical speech he considered correct verbal accentuation and accurate and expressive articulation of phrases and sentences so that each word or phrase fits into the whole with the appropriate expression of its emotional content. To achieve this, he used dissonance, ornaments, word painting, or whatever technical device seemed suitable; his compositional approach was similar to that of Monteverdi. *Judicium Salomonis* (The Judgment of Solomon) exemplifies this.

The best known of Carissimi's 14 extant oratorios is *Jephte* (Jephtha; composed before 1650), based on Judges xi: 19–40 (excerpt, DWMA97). Historicus sings the introduction. In monodic recitative, Jephtha (tenor) vows, If the Lord will give the Israelites victory in battle, Jephtha will sacrifice the first being that comes to greet him when he returns home. In solo arias, duets, and choruses, the story of Jephtha's victory is told. Historicus opens the next scene in *recitativo* narration, relating Jephtha's triumphant return home. His only daughter comes to greet him. In dialogue recitative, Jephtha explains the circumstances to her; she acknowledges that she must be sacrificed. She spends two months in the mountains with her companions bewailing her fate. A brief chorus introduces the daughter's song, *Plorate, plorate colles* (Weep, weep hills), an affective recitative in which the cadences of her phrases are echoed by two of her companions (sopranos). The oratorio concludes with a six-voice choral lament, *Plorate filii Israel* (Weep, daughters of Israel), a madrigalesque piece with imitation and polychoric echo effects.

The only composer after Carissimi to write Latin oratorios in quantity was his pupil Marc-Antoine Charpentier (c. 1645–1704), who composed about 50 of them and who transmitted the Latin oratorio to France. Carissimi's influence is apparent in the form and style of Charpentier's oratorios. Among Carissimi's Italian contemporaries, the most important composer of Latin oratorios was Domenico Mazzochi (1592–65), who wrote seven, most of them called dialogues.

During the reigns of Emperors Leopold I, Joseph I (1705–11), and Charles VI (1711–40), the Viennese court was an important center of sacred dramatic music in the Italian language. Leopold I composed at least nine sacred dramatic compositions. His *Il sagrifizio d'Abramo* (Abram's sacrifice; perf. 1660) is the earliest oratorio known to have been performed in Vienna. (Also see Insight, "Women Composers of Dramatic Works".)

PASSION

A **Passion** is the story of the Crucifixion as recorded in the Gospels. The oldest Passion story included in the liturgy is that according to St. Matthew, which, by

---

INSIGHT

Women Composers of Dramatic Works

Between 1670 and 1725, several women were active in northern Italy and Austria as composers of opera and oratorio. Angiola Scannabecchi of Bologna (1662–1708) was painter and composer. Printed libretti for four of her oratorios survive; the music is lost. Three of those works were performed in the Oratory of St. Filippo Neri, Rome: *Il martirio di S. Colomba* (The martyrdom of St. Colomba; 1694), *Li Giochi di Sansone* (Samson's trick; 1694), and *L'Esterre* (The Stranger; 1695). *Cristo morto* (The dead Christ) was performed for the Confraternity of Santa Maria della Morte on Good Friday evening, 1696.

Libretti survive for two operas and two oratorios by Maria Anna von Rachenau (c. 1651–c. 1710), Chor-meisterin at St. Jakob auf der Hülben. *Le sacre visione di S. Teresia* (The sacred vision of St. Teresia; 1703) is dedicated to Leopold I.

Manuscript scores and libretti are extant for four oratorios by Camilla de Rossi that were performed at the Viennese court during the reign of Joseph I: *S. Beatrice d'Este* (1705; libretto, Cardinal Pamphili), *Il Sagrifizio di Abramo* (Abram's sacrifice; 1708), *Il Figliuol Prodigo* (The prodigal son; 1709), and *S. Alessio* (St. Alexis; 1710).

Caterina Grazianini's *S. Geminiano vescovo e protettore di Modena* (St. Geminiano, bishop and protector of Modena) was performed in Modena, then given in Vienna in 1705 and 1715. The music survives in manuscript.

Maria Grimani (fl. 1713–18) may have worked in Italy as well as in Vienna. The dedication of *Pallade e Marte* was dated 4 April 1713 at Bologna, and the work was performed 4 November 1713 in celebration of Emperor Charles VI's name day. This was the first opera by a woman composer to be performed in the imperial court theater. Grimani's oratorio *La visitazione di Elisabetha* (Elisabeth's visitation) was performed immediately after *Pallade e Marte* in 1713 and was given again in 1718; *Le decollazione di S. Giovanni Battista* (The beheading of St. John the Baptist) was presented in 1715. In Grimani's works, almost all recitatives are *secco,* and most of the arias are *da capo* form with basso continuo accompaniment.

---

decree of Pope Leo I (r. 440–61), was to be chanted on Palm Sunday and on Wednesday of Holy Week. Two centuries later, the St. Luke Passion displaced the St. Matthew on Wednesday; from the tenth century, the St. Mark Passion was sung also, on Tuesday of Holy Week. The text was chanted by one singer, but some ninth-century manuscripts suggest a dramatic approach to the presentation by indicating different manners of reciting or different pitch levels for the words of Christ, the *turba* (crowd), and the narrator. After c. 1250, the liturgical presentation approximated the early liturgical drama, for it became customary to have the story chanted by three priests using contrasting ranges and tempos to represent Christ, the *turba*, and the narrator. Division of the Passion presentation among three singers became almost universal by the fifteenth century. (In some churches it is still chanted in that manner.) The first monophonic choral presentation of the *turba* occurred c. 1350.

Polyphonic settings of the Passion date from the fifteenth century. A passion play in which motet-style polyphony was used for only those portions of text representing *turba* participation in the Passion is known as **responsorial Passion.** At first, three reciting tones of three priests were combined to create the polyphony of the *turba*. As the century advanced, two kinds of responsorial Passion settings were written: (1) the **choral** or **dramatic** Passion, in which portions of the text, including the *turba* and the words of Christ, are set polyphonically, and the remainder is monophonic, and (2) the **through-composed** or **motet** Passion, in which the complete text receives polyphonic setting.

In the sixteenth century, Passions composed for use in Italy and in Catholic churches in Germanic lands were the responsorial type, but the words of Christ were not set polyphonically. The Passions Lassus composed for the Bavarian court chapel are responsorial.

In Protestant Germany, Luther opposed "acting out the Passion in words and pretence," though he did not object to simple responsorial presentation of it. Nevertheless, both monophonic and polyphonic settings of Passion texts were sung in service on the four Sundays before Easter and during Holy Week through Good Friday. The Passion settings Johann Walter made c. 1550 became models for responsorial Passions in the Lutheran church. Antoine de Longueval's (fl. 1507–22) motet Passion is the earliest known setting

to incorporate portions of text from all four Gospels—termed a **summa Passion.** Thus it included all seven words of Christ on the cross.

A model for motet Passions was *Die deutsche Passion . . . nach . . . Sancte Johanne in Figural-Gesang bracht* (The German Passion, according to St. John, in polyphonic song; 1568) by Joachim à Burck (1546–1610). Johann Machold's (d. 1595) inclusion of the strophe *O Jesu Christe, Gottes Sohn* (O Jesus Christ, God's Son) in his *St. Matthew Passion* (1593) inspired the practice of inserting strophic hymns into the Passion.

With the rise of concerted music and the emergence of sacred opera came the **oratorio Passion,** which uses recitative, arioso, aria, ensembles, chorus, and a few purely instrumental pieces as well as instrumental accompaniment. The earliest oratorio Passions were those by Thomas Selle (1599–1663), whose *Johannespassion* (St. John Passion; 1641) was the first to include instrumental interludes.

In the second half of the seventeenth century, it became customary to insert poetic meditations (solo arias, or recitative-aria combinations) as the Passion story progressed and chorales associated with the Passion (for choir or congregational singing). The presentation usually commenced and concluded with a chorale. By adhering to a text taken from only one Gospel, a composer met the requirements of orthodox Lutheranism. Some writers prepared completely original Passion texts. C. F. Hunold's *Der blutige und sterbende Jesus* (The bleeding and dying Jesus) as set by Keiser in 1704 is a free paraphrase replete with graphic details. B. A. Brockes' libretto *Der für die Sünden der Welt gemarterte und sterbende Jesus* (Jesus, martyred and dying for the sins of the world), though an expressive free paraphrase, is less graphic. It attracted Keiser (1712), Telemann (1716), Handel (1717), Mattheson (1718), and others. Settings of completely paraphrased libretti had little use in worship but were influential in the development of the cantata.

LUTHERAN CHORALE

Between c. 1570 and c. 1630 many new chorale melodies appeared, among them contrafacta and settings of Paul Gerhart's poems. During most of the sixteenth century, composers set chorales as primarily note-against-note harmonizations with the melody in the tenor.

In 1586, in an endeavor to encourage congregational singing and to ensure audibility of a chorale melody and understanding of its text, theologian-composer Lucas Osiander (1534–1604) published *Fünffzig geistliche Lieder und Psalmen* (Fifty sacred songs and psalms)—settings that he termed *Kantionalsatz*. These are homophonic, chordal settings of traditional Lutheran chorales, with the melody in the superius and with a fermata marking the end of each phrase. (The fermata was not intended to prolong the value of a note. It should be remembered that the congregation did not have hymnals and that congregational singing of chorales was led by a cantor who "lined-out" the melody, phrase by phrase, each phrase being repeated by congregation and choir.) Some influence of Italian *falsobordone* and *villanella* may be seen in cantional settings. For the next fifty years *Kantionalsatz* were produced in Lutheran Germanic lands. Among the significant composers writing them were H. L. Hassler, Melchior Franck, Johannes Eccard, J. H. Schein, and Michael Praetorius.

Various types of polyphonic chorale motets were written also. In some, the chorale melody was retained as cantus firmus in one voice, either tenor or superius; in others, the chorale was presented systematically, phrase by phrase, in points of imitation; in still others, the chorale cantus firmus was migrant. The influence of the Italian madrigal is visible in some polyphonic chorale settings.

Praetorius's *Musae Sioniae* (9 vols.; 1605–10), which contains over 1,200 compositions, is considered a comprehensive survey of all types of chorale composition produced during the first 80 years of the Reformation.

As the seventeenth century advanced, composers wrote chorales with basso continuo lines and included other instrumental combinations, thus producing a type of sacred vocal concerto, or chorale concerto. Heinrich Schütz composed some music of this kind but did not use chorale melodies.

HEINRICH SCHÜTZ

Heinrich Schütz (1585–1672; Insight, "Heinrich Schütz"), considered the greatest German composer of the seventeenth century, is the first German composer to have international renown. His use of German texts

Heinrich Schütz. From a portrait by Christoph Spetner (1617–99). *(Original in Karl Marx Universität, Leipzig)*

and the fusion of German and Italian styles present in his music form the foundation of the German music composed during the remainder of the Baroque era. Apparently, he did not compose any independent instrumental music, and all his stage works are lost. Some secular and a considerable amount of sacred music—over 500 works in all—survives, presenting a panorama of Schütz's compositions. In one important respect, Schütz's music differs from that of other major composers of sacred music of that time: few traces of chant or Lutheran chorale melodies are present.

At first Schütz wrote Italianate music with Italian texts; he composed only two volumes with Latin texts. His *Il primo libro de madrigali* (First book of madrigals; 1611) comprises 19 unaccompanied five-voice Italian madrigals stylistically similar to those in Monteverdi's Book V. The motets and concerto settings in *Psalmen Davids* (Psalms of David; 1619) reflect Schütz's study with Gabrieli at St. Mark's—Venetian *concertato* style is apparent. Next Schütz wrote a *summa* Passion setting, *Historia der . . . Aufferstehung . . . Jesu Christi* (Story of the . . . Resurrection . . . of Jesus Christ; 1623) and published a volume of Latin motets, *Cantiones sacrae* (Sacred songs; 1625), in which madrigalesque word painting colors basically conservative counterpoint (ex. 15.7, p. 266). In 1626–27 Schütz prepared the

Heinrich Schütz

Heinrich Schütz's early childhood was spent at Weissenfels, where he received music instruction from the local Kantor. Late in 1599 he became a choirboy at the court of Landgrave Moritz at Kassel. When Schütz's voice changed in 1608, he entered the University of Marburg to study law, but soon Moritz sent him to Venice to study with Giovanni Gabrieli. In 1613 Schütz returned to Moritz's court as organist. However, Elector Johann Georg I of Saxony wanted Schütz at Dresden and, in 1617 named him electoral Kapellmeister, a position he held to the end of his life, though he spent several years at the royal court of Denmark.

Schütz married Magdalena Wildeck on 1 June 1619. He included copies of his *Psalmen Davids* (Psalms of David) with the wedding invitations he sent to church and city councils throughout Saxony. Magdalena died on 6 September 1625. Schütz placed their two daughters in Magdalena's mother's care. He never remarried.

During an extended visit to Italy in 1628–29, Schütz discussed various aspects of music with Monteverdi, secured some instruments and in-strumentalists for the Dresden court, and published some sacred music. In autumn 1631 Saxony entered the Thirty Years' War in alliance with Sweden. Economic pressures at the Dresden court were heavy; music resources at the chapel declined drastically. When Crown Prince Christian of Denmark invited Schütz to Copenhagen to direct the music at a royal wedding celebration, he accepted, but months elapsed before he could leave Dresden. In December, he was appointed Kapellmeister to King Christian IV (r. 1588–1648) but retained his Dresden post. Schütz was in Copenhagen until mid-1635. When he returned to Dresden, he sent copies of many of his works, both printed and manuscript, to Copenhagen; over the years, he continued to do this. The Dresden Kapelle library and the Danish royal chapel at Copenhagen were both destroyed by fire, and Schütz's works in those archives were lost. Economic hardship compelled Schütz to leave many of his works unpublished. The war dragged on. There were no funds for training new personnel, and by 1639 the Dresden court chapel had dwindled to fewer than ten singers.

Schütz spent most of 1642–44 in Denmark as court Kapellmeister, then visited various German cities before returning to Dresden. He had been connected with the court at Brunswick-Lüneburg since 1638 and had encouraged the Duchess to compose. He was a frequent guest at Brunswick and Wolfenbüttel, and in 1655 was appointed senior Kapellmeister at Wolfenbüttel. He placed copies of many of his works in the Wolfenbüttel library. Those works survive, as do his manuscripts, in the Hessische Landesbibliothek, Kassel.

In 1645, Schütz requested permission to retire from his position at Dresden. This was the first of many petitions that either were ignored or brought him only a few months away from court. Not until George II became Elector (1657) was Schütz given a pension and permitted to retire. He retained the title of Chief Kapellmeister, however, and continued to compose. Some of his finest works—the Passions and *Christmas Story*—date from his retirement years. After 1670 Schütz made his home in Dresden. He died there, peacefully, in November 1672.

---

so-called Becker Psalter (SWV 97a–256a; 1628. SWV = *Schütz-Werke-Verzeichnis*, the catalog of Schütz's works). The Psalter is a series of simple settings, in four-part harmony, of theologian Cornelius Becker's German paraphrases of Psalms.

Many of the occasional works Schütz wrote have disappeared, including the opera *Dafne* (see p. 259) and several ballets. Among his published occasional music is *Musicalische Exequien* (Funeral music; SWV 279–81; 1635), commissioned for the funeral of Prince Heinrich Posthumus of Reuss.

While visiting Italy in 1628–29, Schütz published *Symphoniae sacrae* (Sacred symphonies; SWV 257–76), a book of Latin motets. In all of them, the accompanying instruments are those that became standard trio sonata ensemble: two violins, violone, and keyboard (organ). But Schütz's choice of solo and duet voicing varies considerably. In five instances, two *symphoniae* pair to form a long motet. *Symphoniae IX* and *X,* respectively, *Prima Pars* (DWMA98) and *Secunda Pars* of the same motet, set selected verses from Song of Solomon (chap. iv). The instrumental *sinfonia* that commences

EXAMPLE 15.7 Schütz's setting of *toto corpore extensum* (whole body stretched out), measures 16–18, Motet XXIII, is typical of the madrigalesque word painting he used in the Latin motets in *Cantiones sacrae* (1625).

(Source: Heinrich Schütz: Neue Ausgabe sämtlicher Werke, Band 9, p. 16)

Symphonia X provides contrast when the two *partes* are performed as a single large motet.

Schütz published *Symphoniarum sacrarum secunda pars* (Sacred symphonies, part 2) in 1649 and *tertia pars* (part 3) in 1650. In both volumes, German texts are set for solo voices accompanied by two violins, violone, and organ; a few pieces in part 3 have parts for chorus with those lines doubled by additional stringed instruments. Many of the works in part 3 are cantatas. In *Saul, was verfolgst du mich* (Saul, why persecutest thou me?) Schütz used *concertato* in a manner that anticipates *concerto grosso*.

Two volumes of *Kleiner geistlichen Concerten* (Little sacred concertos, 1636; 1639) contain motets for one to five solo voices, with basso continuo for organ.

Schütz's next major work was *Historia der . . . Geburth Gottes und Marien Sohnes, Jesu Christi* (Story of the birth of God's and Mary's Son, Jesus Christ; SWV 435; 1660), the "Christmas Oratorio." This is the earliest German setting of the Nativity story to have the evangelist's words sung in recitative instead of monophonic chant. Five years later, he composed three Passions: *Historia . . . nach . . . St. Johannem* (Story . . . according to . . . St. John; SWV 481a, 1665; rev. SWV 481, 1666); . . . *St. Matheum* (SWV 479, 1666); and . . . *St. Lucam* (SWV 480, 1666). These modal works are similar in style, with narrative and dialogue in unaccompanied recitative that is reminiscent of chant and the chorus having *a cappella* contrapuntal settings resembling motets.

Nothing is known concerning the origin of Schütz's *Die sieben Wortte unsers lieben Erlösers und Seeligmachers Jesu Christi* (The seven words of our beloved Savior Jesus Christ; composed 1645, publ. 1873). There is no record of its performance during his lifetime, though parts in manuscript are extant. It is one of Schütz's finest compositions. *Die sieben Wortte . . .* is for five soloists (Christ and four evangelists) and chorus, with strings and basso continuo (organ) accompaniment. The quiet, deeply devotional nature of the modal music (DWMA99), the absence of performance data, and the small dimensions of the work lead one to believe that it was composed for highly personal reasons. Schütz's *Historiae* and *Die sieben Wortte . . .* are the most significant Lutheran music in these semidramatic forms before J. S. Bach.

During his lifetime, Schütz was accorded unparalleled recognition as a composer. He was a master teacher, and his pupils were a credit to his teaching. With the exception of the Becker Psalter, Schütz's works fell into oblivion after his death and were not rediscovered until c. 1830. Arnold Mendelssohn (1855–1933), Philipp Spitta (1841–94), and Johannes Brahms were influential in promoting a renaissance of Schütz's music, but the biblical cantatas of the *Symphoniarum sacrarum* volumes and the larger semidramatic works received the most attention. Not until after 1920 was there general recognition of his works and of his stature as a composer.

Cantata and Song

The precise meaning of the term **cantata** (lit., a piece to be sung) varied during the seventeenth century. The term seems to have been used first by Alessandro Grandi (c. 1575–1630) in *Cantade ed arie* (Cantatas and arias, c. 1619), a collection of 42 pieces for solo voice with basso continuo accompaniment. The pieces labeled "cantata" are strophic variations. However, for about a decade the term *cantata* was applied rather indiscriminately to continuo-accompanied vocal solos in various forms.

From c. 1625 to c. 1750, cantata, opera, and oratorio were the three principal forms of vocal composition. The principal center of cantata composition in Italy was Rome, where the homes of the leading patrons of music provided fertile ground for the cultivation of vocal chamber music. Between 1630 and 1670 two main types of cantatas were composed: short works containing a single aria and longer compositions with a number of sections written as recitative, arioso, or aria, as the text dictated. The subject matter of cantatas varies considerably and includes amorous, didactic, or occasional material that is lyrical or quasi-dramatic in character.

The two most prolific cantata composers in Rome in the second quarter of the seventeenth century were Luigi Rossi and Marco Marazzoli (c. 1605–62). Marazzoli's extant cantatas number 379; about 300 of Rossi's survive. They wrote cantatas in a variety of forms, styles, and textures and sometimes set the same texts. In the works of both composers, formal structures are clearly defined—strophic songs, strophic variations, binary, ternary, *da capo* arias, and songs with ostinato bass lines for the simpler cantatas and for sections in the longer ones and recitative, arioso, and aria in the multisection ones. Rossi was especially skilled at moving smoothly from recitative to aria.

At mid-seventeenth century the two leading Italian composers of cantatas were Carissimi and Cesti. Most of Carissimi's cantatas are multisectional or multimovement, with clear distinction between recitative, arioso, and aria.

By 1670 the strophic-variation aria had been supplanted by the aria on an ostinato bass, and the cantata was almost totally patterned in clearly differenti-ated recitatives and arias, with the arias usually in *da capo* form. Alessandro Stradella (1644–82) and Agostino Steffani wrote cantatas of this kind. Stradella made a special contribution to the development of instrumental music by using instrumental ensemble accompaniment in many of his cantatas. He clearly distinguished between recitative and aria but moved easily from one to the other.

The greatest composer of cantatas was Alessandro Scarlatti. Of his approximately 600 extant cantatas, more than 500 are for solo voice (usually soprano) and basso continuo. Many of these pieces were composed for aristocratic patrons in Rome. Cantatas Scarlatti composed during his first stay in Rome (1672–84) reflect the influence of the older composers then working there. Most of the cantatas he wrote in 1703–4 consist of two *da capo* arias, each preceded by a recitative. This became a more or less standard pattern for secular cantatas composed during the eighteenth century, except in France.

In Bologna, Maurizio Cazzatti composed at least nine books of vocal music, most of them containing some solo cantatas and arias. Giovanni M. Bononcini, of Modena, who published two volumes of cantatas (1677–78), seems to have been the first to use the term *cantata per camera* (chamber cantata). His son Giovanni (1670–1747) wrote 12 duet cantatas and more than 300 solo cantatas, about a third of them with two violins and basso continuo.

Barbara Strozzi (1619–64), a pupil of Cavalli, composed at least six volumes of arias, madrigals, and cantatas in 1644–64. Several of her cantatas are very large works with a wide variety of writing (e.g., *Lagrime mie* from *Diporti di Euterpe*, Op. 7 [My tears, from pastimes of Euterpe; 1659]). One of Strozzi's works is a multisection wedding cantata. Some of her compositions have instrumental ensemble *ritornelli* and accompaniment.

Duchess Sophie Elisabeth (1613–76) of Brunswick-Lüneburg was trained at her father's court, Mecklenburg-Güstrow, where outstanding English instrumentalists were orchestra personnel. To escape war in 1629, she moved to the Kassel court, another active music center. In 1635, she married Duke August of Brunswick-Luneburg, founder of the Wolfenbüttel library, which became and has remained one of the most important repositories for music. Sophie was responsible for the establishment (in 1638) and continual upgrading of the Brunswick court orchestra; Schütz was her musical adviser and, after 1655, her composition teacher. Most of her surviving works are sacred songs. She was instrumental in establishing the tradition of performing ballets and theatrical works with music at birthday celebrations and composed for them. Representative of her festival cantatas is *Glück-wünschende Freudensdarstellung* (Congratulatory presentation; 1652) for four soloists, four-part chorus, four strings, and basso continuo.

In France, interest was concentrated on the *ballet de cour* and *tragédie lyrique* until c. 1700. Jean-Baptiste Morin (1657–1744), who served Philippe III, Duke of Orléans, was a pioneer in cantata composition in France. His first book of cantatas appeared in 1706; a second followed in 1707. The works combine French lyrical melody with its delicate ornamentation and elements of Italian arias, such as motto beginning, ostinato bass and accompaniment figures, *da capo* form, and trio sonata ensemble accompaniment. Morin's works set the musical style for *cantate françoise,* and J.-B. Rousseau (1671–1741) set the style for its lyrics. Soon other French composers were writing cantatas, and the genre flourished during the first quarter of the eighteenth century. Louis-Nicolas Clérambault (1676–1749) effected a real blend of Italian and French styles, as in his masterpiece, *Orphée* (1710).

English composers wrote songs with basso continuo accompaniment, but the term *cantata* was not used until 1710, when Walsh published Johann Pepusch's (1667–1752) *Six English Cantatas*, Book 1. *Six English Cantatas*, Book 2, and *12 Cantatas in English* appeared in 1720. In structure, the works are Italianate—two *da capo* arias preceded and separated by recitatives, accompanied by basso continuo and one or two obbligato instruments. The harmony exhibits the English penchant for major tonality, and the melody displays typical English tunefulness.

The outstanding composer of English songs was Henry Purcell. *Orpheus Britannicus* (London, 1698) is a large collection of his vocal solos, duets, and trios; John Blow published a similar collection, *Amphion Anglicus* (London, 1700). For ceremonial celebrations or state occasions, large works for soloists, chorus, and orchestra were commissioned, and Purcell wrote a number of these, including a setting of N. Brady's *Hail, bright Cecilia* for St. Caecilia's Day, 1692.

Secular songs and cantatas were composed in Germany, but the cantata attained its highest development after 1700 as sacred music associated with the Lutheran church service. In the last half of the seventeenth century, music printing was at a low ebb in Germany, and repertoires were amassed in manuscript. Among the few collections of solo songs published were Adam Krieger's (1634–66) *Arien* (Arias; Leipzig, 1656) and *Neue Arien* (New Arias; Dresden, 1667), each collection containing 50 songs. In the second edition (1676) of *Neue Arien,* 10 songs were added. Texts of the songs vary from pastoral and mythological love poems to bawdy drinking songs. Most of the songs are for solo voice with basso continuo; 20 of them are for from two to five voices, and all are supplied with instrumental *ritornelli*. The *Neue Arien* are strophic songs, with each strophe in binary or bar (aab) form and five-part instrumental *ritornelli* between strophes. Seemingly, composers wrote few independent songs during the last decades of the seventeenth century, but possibly because of printing difficulties many songs did not survive. Also, song was absorbed into the composite forms then current—opera, cantata, and oratorio.

SUMMARY

Monteverdi was a principal figure in the transition from Renaissance to Baroque in music. He realized that two styles of music could coexist and originated the idea and the terminology of two practices: *prima prattica* or *stile antico,* denoting Renaissance polyphony in which music took precedence over words, and *seconda prattica* or *stile moderno,* in which the text dominated the music. Baroque composers adopted the concept of two practices but with somewhat different connotations. For them, *seconda prattica* denoted accompanied monody. Monteverdi believed either practice could be used in polyphonic music. He wrote ensemble madrigals long after other composers abandoned them. Some of his church music is traditional Netherlands-based polyphony; in other sacred music, outdated compositional techniques (e.g., cantus firmus) mingle with operatic elements.

Monteverdi's interpretation of Platonic precepts convinced him of music's power to move human affections. He used dissonance expressively, for affective purposes, and associated certain rhythmic patterns with certain human emotions. His affective use of rhythmic figures resulted in his creation of *stile concitato,* the excited style, featuring measured tremolo.

In Florence, the interests of the humanists and literati led to the creation of accompanied monody and then to an approximation of dramatic presentations in the manner of the ancient Greeks and Romans. Opera resulted. Opera, and the similarly structured forms known as oratorio and cantata, were the main forms of vocal music composed during the Baroque era. Opera had many precursors: ancient Greek dramas, medieval liturgical dramas, religious mystery and morality plays, some trouvère plays, *intermedi,* dramatic madrigals, and pastorale. Madrigal cycles were being composed during the years that composers were beginning to write opera.

Dafne, the first opera, a Florentine court presentation in 1598, was followed by several operas on the Euridice-Orpheus myth, produced at Florence and Mantua. Florentine composers relied heavily on recitative-type monody; Monteverdi included strophic variations, arioso, and madrigals and used ostinato figures and longer ground bass melodies. Monteverdi was interested in psychology, knew human nature, and was adept at characterization. His composition of a full-length comic opera was unusual, as was his choice of subject matter for his last opera—historical events with human characters.

By the early 1630s, the operatic center was Venice, where the first public opera house opened in 1637. Venetian opera was spread throughout Italy by traveling opera companies and was extended to other lands by enthusiastic patrons who moved to other countries, by foreigners who experienced opera while visiting Italian courts, by Italian composers who secured appointments in other countries, and by foreign composers who studied and worked in Italy and carried opera back to their own lands. Italian-born Lully was primarily responsible for the creation of French opera, with its emphasis on *divertissements* and ballets. No national school of opera formed in England. Opera was slow getting started in Germany, where it was rooted in *Singspiel* and school drama. A German opera company was established in Hamburg in 1678, and German opera was enjoyed there for about 50 years. In Spain, Calderón invented the *zarzuela,* modeled after Italian opera but using spoken dialogue. Very early in the eighteenth century, operas were composed in Peru and Mexico.

Allegorical opera, bordering on being sacred, began in Rome in 1600, with the staging of *Rappresentatione di Anima, et di Corpo* in the Oratory of Chiesa Nuova. True sacred opera originated in Rome c. 1630 with the operas of Landi and the libretti of Rospigliosi.

Oratorio was an outgrowth of Neri's religious meetings in Rome, where it evolved from the musical dialogues of Anerio. Later oratorios resembled opera in musical design but were not staged and were usually on religious subjects. By the mid-seventeenth century, both Latin and vernacular oratorios were written.

The Passion, a liturgical presentation for centuries, assumed the character of oratorio in the seventeenth century, using recitative, arioso, aria, ensembles, chorus, and a few purely instrumental pieces. The Passions of Schütz are the most significant Lutheran music in this form prior to J. S. Bach. Composers of Lutheran church music wrote numerous chorale settings, both homophonic and polyphonic.

In 1600, the term cantata denoted a piece of vocal music. As the seventeenth century advanced, features of opera were absorbed by cantata. By 1650, cantata was structured as a series of recitative-aria combinations. In the Lutheran church, the cantata was given an instructive function and placed in the liturgy in proximity to the homily. The Lutheran cantata reached its height at the hands of J. S. Bach.

BAROQUE INSTRUMENTAL MUSIC

*D*uring the seventeenth century the production of instrumental music increased steadily, and by the end of the century it was on a par with vocal music in both quality and quantity. Four principal types of instrumental works were written: (1) dance music, either for dancing or stylized and intended for listening; (2) quasi-improvisatory works; (3) variations; and (4) pieces in imitative counterpoint, either nonsectional works such as the *ricercar* or sectional pieces of the *canzona* type, written for the most part in imitative counterpoint but sometimes including sections stylistically different. These categories are not mutually exclusive; for example, quasi-improvisatory style or variation technique might appear in any of the types. Moreover, the title given a piece does not always indicate its true character—a piece entitled *fantasia* might be a ricercar or might be in improvisatory style.

INSTRUMENTAL MUSIC TYPES

PIECES IN IMITATIVE COUNTERPOINT

Most ricercars are nonsectional compositions of motetlike character with thematic material treated in continuous imitation. Generally, the pieces are of short to moderate length. Most ricercars are monothematic, but some polythematic ricercars exist. Terminology was not precise; this kind of composition might be labeled *ricercar, capriccio, fuga, verset, fantasia,* or some other name. Eventually, the monothematic nonsectional ricercar merged into the fugue.

The term *fantasia* (imagination, whim) was frequently applied to a ricercar-type composition that was of considerable length and had a rather complex formal organization. An example is Sweelinck's *Fantasia chromatica* (Chromatic fantasia), in Dorian mode (DWMA100). In this imitative piece, the subject, a chromatically descending tetrachord, is introduced in the alto part and is restated immediately in the superius, accompanied by countersubject in the alto. Essentially, the subject remains unchanged throughout the work. Many of the technical devices common to fugue are present. Compositions of this kind are difficult to classify, for they are monothematic, imitative, and contrapuntal, as is a ricercar; they contain many elements of fugue, and they are quasi-improvisatory.

In the seventeenth century, English composers wrote contrapuntal *fancies* or *fantasias* for chamber ensembles of strings. Short fugal sections characteristic of the

1600	1625	1650	1675	1700	1725	1750

ricercar

monothematic nonsectional
ricercar and canzona } merge into fugue

canzona

sectional canzona becomes *sonata da chiesa*

contrapuntal fancy; fantasia

dance music stylized

collections of dance music

• 1649 Froberger: suites of dances

• 1620s—grouping of   • c. 1650 gigue included in suite
allemande-courante-sarabande

• 1693 order of movements in suite standardized

French lute *style brisé* transferred to keyboard by Froberger and Chambonnières

keyboard toccata   with fugato sections   with alternating free-fantasia and fugal sections   toccata and fugue

various well-tempered tunings   equal temperament c. 1735

fugue

chorale-based organ compositions

keyboard sonata
• 1692 Kuhnau Sonatas

variation: theme and variation

continuous variation over ostinato bass

English *fancy* are present in Matthew Locke's *Fantazia* for a consort of four viols. Works that John Jenkins (1592–1678) labeled *fancy* exhibit characteristics of both ricercar and canzona; some of his *fancies* for two violins and bass resemble Italian trio sonatas.

During the seventeenth century, the canzona might be structured in one of these ways: (1) in several contrasting sections, each having its own theme treated imitatively, in a manner resembling the points of imitation of a chanson and with the final cadence prefaced by a cadenzalike passage (e.g., the anonymous *Canzona per l'epistola* [Epistle Canzona; DWMA101]); (2) as a *variation canzona,* in which variations or transformations of a single theme serve as subject matter for the several sections (e.g., G. M. Trabaci's *Canzona francese* [French canzona]); or (3) in several contrasting sections that are unrelated thematically and that vary considerably in length and musical style (e.g., Frescobaldi's *Canzona*). Many canzonas commence with the rhythmic figure 𝅗𝅥 ♩ ♩ or a variant thereof.

As the seventeenth century advanced, composers gradually altered the canzona by writing fewer sections but increasing their length; contrasting meters and tempos were designated. In some canzoni, homophonic sections alternated with contrapuntal ones. Eventually, the multisectional canzona was supplanted by the multimovement *sonata da chiesa,* in which one movement, usually the second, was fugal.

VARIATION

Variation technique was used in much seventeenth-century instrumental music. The principal types of variation are rooted in Renaissance compositional procedures. These types are cantus firmus variation, melodic paraphrase variation, and variation over an ostinato bass or chordal framework. Also, composers wrote sets of variations on secular songs; song variations were favored by composers of harpsichord music late in the seventeenth century and became known later as **theme and variation.**

271

In **cantus firmus variation,** the melody remained virtually unchanged through all repetitions but usually was not retained in the same part in all variations. In each variation the melody was surrounded or supported by different counterpoint. Cantus firmus variation had considerable use in organ music, especially in chorale variations. Examples abound in Samuel Scheidt's *Tabulatura nova* (New Tabulature; 3 vols.; 1624), the first German publication of keyboard music notated in score. The first two volumes contain mainly sets of variations, including eight sets of cantus firmus variations based on Lutheran chorales. Volume 3 contains a repertory of liturgical music for the church year. The hymn settings are variation sets.

In **paraphrase variation,** the contrapuntal harmonies remain constant, and in each variation the melody is given different embellishments. The melody is always apparent and is usually retained in the uppermost part. J. A. Reincken's (1623–1722) *Partite diverse sopra l'Aria "Schweiget mir von Weiber nehmen"* (Diverse variations on the song "Say nothing to me about getting married") is an example.

In the late Renaissance and early Baroque eras, repeated chordal schemes with bass lines that were fixed successions of root-position triads served as the basis for some dance music—*passamezzo, Romanesca, Ruggiero, La Folia,* and others. During the many repetitions of the bass line, or harmonic **ground,** as it became known, melodic and contrapuntal variation occurred within the chordal framework. Some of the bass lines were associated with treble melodies (e.g., *Romanesca*), but after their initial presentation in a piece those melodies were usually obscured by figuration. Each repetition of the harmonic pattern formed a **parte** or variation section; the entire composition was a **partita,** or set of variations. Frescobaldi's *Partite sopra l'aria della Romanesca* (Variations on the Romanesca song) is one.

The polarized concentration on bass line and melody during the Baroque era resulted in emphasis being placed on the bass line itself as a ground for variations, and shorter **basso ostinato** patterns such as *passacaglia* and *chaconne* received increased attention as foundation for continuous-variation pieces. Originally, there may have been a distinction between passacaglia and chaconne, but composers used the terms interchangeably to such an extent that attempts to definitively differentiate them have been futile.

Dance Music

A wealth of dance music was produced during the seventeenth century—music for dancing; incidental music for dance scenes in operas, plays, and other spectacles; and stylized dance pieces for listening pleasure. Elements of dance music infiltrated other music, for example, the clear metric organization of the rhythm, specific rhythmic patterns, standardized chordal schemes, and well-known ground bass and treble melodies. Most of the individual dance pieces were in binary form, but some use was made of alternating form (such as ABACADA) and continuous variation.

Dancing was cultivated by the nobility and by their middle-class emulators; there was an abundance of dancing-masters to assist in the pursuit of dancing skills, and some dance manuals were printed. Ballroom dancing was a daily pastime at court and an important part of state celebrations. The types of dances included stately processional dances, leaping dances, circle dances, and progressive long dances. Many dances popular during the Renaissance remained favorites in the seventeenth century, but gradually changes crept in. By the end of the century most of the dances had been transformed considerably, though they still retained their Renaissance names.

Dances   By 1600, the *basse danse* had disappeared; its position as an introductory dance was taken over by the *pavane.* Paired with the pavane was the *galliard,* a lively but not rapid dance. In Italy in the early seventeenth century, the pavane was rare, but the galliard was a favorite dance. Early in the century, the *passamezzo* and *saltarello* were still used, but by c. 1640 the passamezzo was no longer danced.

The *allemande* and *courante* were popular but were not always paired. By the mid-seventeenth century the tempo of the courante had become much slower. In the second half of the century it was the preferred dance for inaugurating a court ball, but after 1700 the courante was rarely danced. Early in the seventeenth century, English composers wrote stylized versions of the *alman* for keyboard; *The Fitzwilliam Virginal Book* contains several.

The *zarabanda* (*sarabande*) appeared in Spain in the 1580s and by the early 1620s was known in Italy. Presumably, the zarabanda originated in Latin America. The *chacona,* described as passionate, sensual, and wild, was sung and danced in Mexico in the 1590s; it reached Spain before 1605 and became the leading Spanish dance during the first quarter of the seventeenth century. The chacona became slower and more dignified as it spread through France and into Germany during the second quarter of that century. The danced passacaglia was similar to the chacona but less unbridled.

The *jig* was sung and danced as court entertainment during the reign of Elizabeth I. Jigs were a substantial part of farces called *jiggs* and appeared as incidental music in plays; stylized jigs were written for instrumental ensembles. A form of jig was introduced into France by Jacques Gaultier (died c. 1660). The French called the piece *gigue;* soon *gigues* appeared in French collections of harpsichord and lute music. For both English and French, the word jig or gigue signified a style as well as a specific dance. The words *en gigue* were sometimes appended to other pieces (e.g., *allemande en gigue*). The gigue became popular in Germany as a stylized dance form after 1650.

SUITE   Many collections of dance music were published, and dance music was included in collections of instrumental music intended for use by trained amateur musicians. Certain dances were printed as pairs, and in a few books sequences of dances were indicated. The earliest known use of the term *suytte* (lit., pieces following one another) for a group of dance pieces (groups of *bransles*) occurred in Estienne du Tertre's *Septième livre de danceries* (Seventh book of dance pieces; 1557).

During the first quarter of the seventeenth century, there was a great deal of mobility and interchange among musicians of all nationalities. Musicians worked at foreign courts, and many persons went to Italy to study. This internationalism is reflected in the grouping of dance pieces into the **suite.** English composers, especially those working in Germanic lands, seem to have been the first to group several dances that originated in different countries and to link the dances thematically. German composers soon took up the practice.

Grouping of pavane, galliard, courante, and allemande became common.

One of the most significant collections of grouped dances is J. H. Schein's *Banchetto musicale* (Musical banquet; 1617). The volume contains 20 numbered groups of dances for five unspecified instruments ("but preferably viols") without basso continuo. As stated in the preface, the dances "correspond with one another in both mode and invention." Each group—Schein did not call the groups suites—is the combination of two paired dances, *pavane-galliard* and *allemande-tripla,* separated by a courante. The *tripla* is a strict proportional reworking—a variation—of the allemande in triple time.

The suite for keyboard or lute became a multi-movement musical entity in three stages: (1) In the 1620s, three dances—allemande, courante, and sarabande—formed the core of the suite. (2) Around 1650, a *gigue* was often included with the other three dances, but the movements were presented in no established order. (3) By c. 1680 a standard pattern had been established for the order of the core movements. This may be illustrated by three collections of suites by Johann Jakob Froberger (1616–67). One autograph manuscript, dated 1649, holds five suites; four of them consist of allemande-courante-sarabande, and Suite No. 2 contains allemande-courante-sarabande-gigue. A second autograph manuscript, written before 1656, contains five suites, each having four movements arranged as allemande-gigue-courante-sarabande. Note that all suites but one conclude with a sarabande, a slow dance. In a book of Froberger's suites published in 1693, the *publisher* arranged the movements to conform with the pattern then standard: allemande-courante-sarabande-gigue. It is not known whether Froberger himself ever sanctioned that order. All Froberger's suite movements are in binary form, with each half repeated; all movements of a suite are in the same key (DWMA102). Usually the allemande and courante have limited thematic relationship.

Froberger wrote several pieces entitled *Tombeau, Lamentation,* or *Lamento;* each is in the style of an allemande and was used in lieu of the allemande in a suite. During his travels, Froberger observed and absorbed characteristic elements of French and Italian musical styles; he amalgamated them with German stylistic traits. Through his keyboard suites he helped transfer to Germany the French stylistic concept of the various dances.

The four dances German composers accepted as standard movements in the keyboard suite might be supplemented by an introductory movement (*intrada, praeludium*) and/or one or more optional movements placed before or after the sarabande or after the gigue. Such optional movements might be *gavotte, bourrée, minuet, chaconne,* or other stylized dances. Sometimes a dance—especially a courante or a sarabande—was followed by an ornamented version of that dance, called a **double.** The number of movements in a Baroque suite varies considerably—there may be as few as 3 or as many as 24 (in some French suites); most of the Baroque suites contain 4 to 6 rather short movements. The addition of optional dance movements reflects French influence—the French considered a suite more an anthology of dances than a strict sequence of movements in a multimovement work. The French are credited also with establishing the characteristic style and idiom of each of the dance movements.

The movements of a suite contrast in meter and tempo, but all movements are in the same key, and most are in binary form. The **allemande** is in moderate tempo and duple meter and usually is polyphonic in texture, with all parts sharing in a continuous flow of music written in small note values. Normally, the allemande commences with an **anacrusis** (upbeat).

The allemande is followed by a French **courante** (running) or an Italian **corrente.** Though the words are literal synonyms, their musical connotation is not identical. Composers were not always particular about which label they chose for this movement and sometimes attached an Italian name to a movement in French style or vice versa. At times, French and Italian styles were intermingled in a movement. The Italian *corrente,* in $\frac{3}{4}$ or $\frac{3}{8}$ meter, is filled with running notes and proceeds at a lively tempo. The French *courante* is in $\frac{3}{2}$ or $\frac{6}{4}$ meter but is more moderate in tempo; it is highly stylized, with subtle syncopations, and is somewhat more contrapuntal than the *corrente.* Typically, the courante uses dotted rhythms, such as ♩. ♫ | ♩ ♩ ♪ or ♩. ♫ | ♩. ♫ , which reflect the hopping character of the actual dance. Some use of hemiola is usually present, as in the combination of $\frac{3}{2}$ meter in one part with $\frac{6}{4}$ in another.

The **sarabande** is in a slow tempo and in triple meter, usually $\frac{3}{2}$. It commences on the beat. The rhythmic pattern ♩ ♩. ♩ | ♩ 𝅗𝅥 is typical; note the slight cessation of motion and consequent agogic accent created by dotting the second note.

The **gigue** (Italian, *giga*) is in quick tempo and in compound duple or triple meter ($\frac{6}{8}$, $\frac{9}{8}$, $\frac{12}{8}$); occasionally, $\frac{4}{4}$ meter and dotted rhythms were used. Features of the melody are triplets and frequent wide leaps; imitative counterpoint is common. Frequently, a gigue commences with an eighth-note anacrusis; often the second section of the binary-form movement starts with a mirror inversion of the opening motive.

QUASI-IMPROVISATORY COMPOSITIONS

Pieces in improvisatory style were written for solo keyboard or solo lute and were called **fantasia, toccata,** or **prelude.** The fantasia was aptly described by Mersenne, who wrote in *Harmonie universelle* (1636) that the musician might "employ whatever inspiration comes to him, without expressing the passion of any text." Fantasias vary considerably in length, form, and meter.

The composed *prelude* evolved from short improvisations made by lutenists checking the tuning or keyboard players testing the touch of their instruments. Church organists improvised short "preludes" to establish the mode and pitch of music to be sung during the liturgy. A composed prelude has no special form but usually is a self-contained piece.

Toccatas were composed in the late sixteenth century by Diruta, Gabrieli, and others; many toccatas were written in the seventeenth and early eighteenth centuries. Toccatas vary considerably in content and design. In Merulo's toccatas, one hand has brilliant runs and ornamental figuration to perform while the other hand plays predominantly chordal material. Both hands share in both types of material. Some of Frescobaldi's toccatas are reserved and mystical, without undue technical display, and are well suited to the portions of the Mass for which they were intended (e.g., the toccatas in *Fiori musicali* that are used at Elevation of the Host). Other toccatas by Frescobaldi are brilliant and rhapsodic, with figuration in two or three lines simultaneously (e.g., *Toccata IX* [DWMA103]).

Froberger transmitted Frescobaldi's toccata style to Austria. Some of Froberger's toccatas have many sections; continuity and systematic organization are apparent in the contrapuntal sections, in contrast with the rhapsodic figuration of sections in improvisatory style.

FRENCH LUTE MUSIC

The earliest known French suites with allemande-courante-sarabande nucleus are François Chancy's (d. 1656) six short suites for mandore (a small, lutelike instrument) published in *Tablature de mandure* (1629). Lute music flourished in France in the early seventeenth century and is highly significant historically, for lutenists cultivated a musical style that was transferred to harpsichord and that influenced the entire French style of composition for more than a century.

Lute and harpsichord are incapable of sustaining tones. Lutenists dealt with this problem by breaking the chords into arpeggiations and figurations, sounding the tones of melody, harmony, and bass individually and distributing them through the various registers of the instrument in a more or less continuous flow of small note values. It was left to the listener to assimilate the component parts and complete the musical picture from the lutenist-composer's sketch. This presents no difficulty, for usually the melody is unclouded, phrases are clearly defined, and all basic elements of the music—melody, harmony, rhythm, and texture—are coordinated. If seventeenth-century lutenists had a special name for this style, it has not survived; on the twentieth century, the term **style brisé** (broken style) was coined to describe it. In conjunction with their special style, lutenist-composers developed a system of **agréments** (graces, i.e., little ornaments) some of which they indicated in the notation by small symbols; other graces were improvised at the discretion of the performer. Composers of keyboard music adapted the lutenists' style to the harpsichord, along with the system of *agréments*. Some composers used the word *luthée* (luted) in connection with keyboard music written in this style. Foreign musicians who visited France became acquainted with these techniques and introduced them in their countries.

Significant contributions to seventeenth-century lute repertoire were made by Denis and Ennemond Gaultier. Ennemond (1575–1651) achieved fame at court as performer and lute teacher; though his lute solos were widely known, very few of them were printed during his lifetime. Denis Gaultier (1603–72)

played his lute in the salons of Paris; he had no court position. Compositions by Ennemond and Denis are similar in style, and some confusion exists with regard to the authorship of some works. A number of pieces are signed only "Gaultier." There survive in manuscripts approximately 75 dance pieces, mainly courantes and allemandes and several harpsichord transcriptions of some lute compositions.

Livre de tablature (Tablature book; 1672) contains an equal number of pieces by Denis and Ennemond; the attributions are clear. Ennemond is represented by a lute suite in the collection *Suittes facile* (Easy suites; 1703). Both *Pièces de luth sur trois differens modes nouveaux* (Lute pieces in three different new modes; c. 1672) and *La rhétorique des dieux* (The rhetoric of the gods; c. 1652; fig. 13.2b), which the title pages state are by Denis, contain some pieces attributed to Ennemond in other sources. *La rhétorique des dieux* contains 56 stylized dances, grouped into 12 sets, one in each of the 12 modes. Each set comprises allemande, courante, sarabande, and a varied number of other dances in random order.

La rhétorique des dieux concludes with a program suite—a *tombeau* (lament) for lutenist Henri L'Enclos (c. 1593–1649). The Gaultiers were pioneers of the *tombeau* for lute. The instrumental *tombeau* follows the tradition of the *déplorátions* that Medieval and Renaissance poets and composers wrote in commemoration of an esteemed colleague at the time of his death.

ORGAN MUSIC

Most of the composers who made significant contributions to the development of organ music during the seventeenth and early eighteenth centuries worked in the northern and central parts of Germany, in Lutheran areas. In the southern territories, where Catholicism prevailed, the organ functioned mainly to supply accompaniment for the services, including cantus firmus–type liturgical compositions.

At the beginning of the seventeenth century, the chief composers of organ music were Jan Sweelinck of Amsterdam and Samuel Scheidt of Halle. Scheidt's principal contribution to organ literature is *Tabulatura nova* (see p. 272). Sweelinck was one of the most respected organists of his time. Among his pupils were the founders of the north German school of organists, which culminated in J. S. Bach. All Sweelinck's instrumental music is for keyboard. He wrote in the established forms of the time and incorporated quasi-improvisational and variation techniques in many of his compositions. In most of his toccatas, homophonic or imitative sections are interspersed with sections of extended passage work. His monothematic fantasias, with imitation on tonic and dominant levels, are important forerunners of the monothematic *fugue*.

German organists and composers influential later in the century include Franz Tunder (1614–67) and Dietrich Buxtehude (c. 1637–1707) at Lübeck; F. W. Zachow (1663–1712) at Halle, who was Handel's teacher; Johann Kuhnau (1660–1772), J. S. Bach's predecessor at Leipzig; Johann Christoph Bach (1642–1703) of Eisenach, the most important Bach musician prior to Johann Sebastian; and Johann Pachelbel (1653–1706) of Nuremberg and Erfurt. All of them composed vocal as well as instrumental music.

Three principal types of organ music were written: quasi-improvisatory compositions usually termed *toccata* but sometimes named *prelude* or *fantasia; fugue;* and chorale-based compositions. To a lesser extent, passacaglias and chaconnes were produced.

TOCCATA

The toccata retained its quasi-improvisational character and became a vehicle for virtuosic display. Toccatas by German composers are distinctive in having passages featuring pedal work. The rhapsodic nature of the toccata was somewhat disciplined by the use of sequences and by the inclusion of sections of imitative counterpoint. Occasionally, a brief homophonic section was included. Pachelbel used sequences effectively in his short *Toccata in e minor.* The contrast between freedom and discipline may be seen in toccatas that commence quasi-improvisationally and include one lengthy fugal section; often, compositions of this type were entitled *Praeludium cum fuga* (Prelude *with* fugue). One *Praeludium cum fuga* by Buxtehude is a toccata-type piece with several well-defined sections that contrast in tempo, meter, and style, including a fugal Allegro.

The imitative contrapuntal (i.e., fugal) section of the toccata gradually was accorded increased importance and ultimately became an independent piece—a fugue—which often was coupled with and introduced by a quasi-improvisatory, virtuosic toccata, fantasia, or prelude (e.g., Johann Christoph Bach's *Praeludium und fuge* [Prelude *and* fugue]).

FUGUE

The term *fuga* (flight) was applied variously over the centuries to imitative works now known as **canons** and to pieces with imitative entries. The motetlike ricercar or fantasia, and those organ *canzoni* that are monothematic and nonsectional, were important forerunners of the independent **fugue.** Sweelinck might have named his *Chromatic fantasia* a *fuga* (DWMA100); in it he used many technical devices that became standard in fugue: augmentation, diminution, the crowding of entries termed *stretto,* and variation of the subject. Frescobaldi's *Ricercare dopo il Credo* and some of G. Gabrieli's canzoni also represent early stages in the development of fugue.

The fugue did not attain perfection until the major-minor system of key tonality had been fully developed. The viability of the fugue as a keyboard work was dependent on tempered tuning of keyboard instruments. The culmination of these developments resulted in J. S. Bach's production of *The Well-Tempered Clavier* [vol. I] in 1722—a series of 24 preludes and fugues, one in each major and minor key, all suitable for performance on the same keyboard instrument, which had been tuned according to one of the well-tempered methods then current.

In its perfected form, the independent fugue is an imitative contrapuntal composition characterized by two types of sections that are not clearly marked off: (1) **expositions,** in which the subject is stated and is imitated on tonic and dominant tonal levels, and (2) **episodes,** which are usually modulatory and in which the subject does not appear in its entirety. Within the fugue there is a definite tonic-dominant tonal organization, and there is a sense that the musical material is being propelled energetically toward a climax that is ultimately resolved by the concluding measures of tonic key tonality. In contrast, the ricercar is modal (or more closely related to modality than to key tonality) and tends to move serenely and steadily toward its close without varietal disruption or effective climax.

Chorale-Based Compositions

During the late seventeenth and early eighteenth centuries, composers used the chorale as the basis for several kinds of instrumental compositions: (1) chorale fugue; (2) chorale prelude; (3) chorale partita, also known as chorale variations; and (4) chorale fantasia.

The **chorale fugue** is a short work in which the first line of a chorale is treated as the subject of a fugue. An organist might perform a chorale fugue in the Lutheran service as preparation for congregational singing of the chorale; Pachelbel, J. C. Bach, and other organists in central Germany were the principal composers of chorale fugues.

The **chorale prelude** is a rather short polyphonic setting of an entire chorale melody. The individual phrases of the chorale are not separated by interludes. Composers treated the chorale melody in various ways: (1) the entire melody might be presented in long note values and be retained in the uppermost part throughout the composition; (2) the entire melody might be written in long note values but the individual phrases be distributed successively among the several polyphonic lines; (3) the entire melody might be ornamented or paraphrased and retained in the superius; or (4) each phrase of the chorale melody might be treated as a point of imitation, as in a *chorale motet* or *chorale ricercar*. Buxtehude frequently paraphrased or embellished the chorale melody, as he did in his chorale prelude on *Nun komm, der Heiden Heiland* (Now come, Savior of the heathen). Chorale preludes by Scheidt, Buxtehude, Pachelbel, and J. S. Bach on the melody *Vater unser im Himmelreich* (Our Father in heaven) are presented in DWMA104. The chorale prelude attained culmination in J. S. Bach's *Orgel-Büchlein* (see DWMA117).

The **chorale partita**, or **chorale variations**, is a set of variations based on a chorale melody. Scheidt made extensive use of chorale variation in *Tabulatura nova*. Pachelbel and J. S. Bach composed several chorale partitas in which the original proportions and often some other features of the preexisting melody were retained in each variation. An example is Bach's chorale partita on *O Gott, du frommer Gott* (O God, thou good God). The exact liturgical function of the chorale partita is not known; perhaps works of this kind substituted for motets at times when a choir was not available.

The **chorale fantasia** is a large composition in which the chorale melody is freely and elaborately developed; usually each phrase appears several times with different treatment. Tunder and Buxtehude composed impressive chorale fantasias. Presumably, these works were designed for the Lübeck *Abendmusik* concerts (see below). A basic structural plan was to present each line of the chorale melody twice, once unadorned as a cantus firmus in long note values and once highly ornamented. An example is Buxtehude's chorale fantasia on *Ich ruf zu dir* (I call to Thee). Chorale fantasias by Sweelinck and Scheidt are conservative in comparison with those produced later in the century. Two chorale fantasias by Reincken are large-scale, virtuosic works, incorporating much ornamentation and passage work, echo effects, and frequent hand crossing (one of his specialties).

German Composers

Dietrich Buxtehude   At the time of Buxtehude's birth, the town of Buxtehude was controlled by Denmark; Dietrich always considered Denmark his native country. In 1668 Buxtehude succeeded Tunder as organist at the Marienkirche, Lübeck. Buxtehude became a citizen of Lübeck on 23 July and on 3 August married Anna Tunder. Presumably, marriage to Tunder's daughter was one condition of Buxtehude's appointment. For almost 40 years Buxtehude was Marienkirche's organist.

In addition to playing for services and supplying requisite music therefor, Buxtehude reinstated the *Abendmusik* church concerts and scheduled them at 4 P.M. on the last two Sundays of Trinity and the last three Sundays of Advent. These concerts included oratorios or cantatas, vocal concertos, arias, and organ works. A large part of Buxtehude's fame derived from the *Abendmusiken*, which were attended by musicians from all over Germany.

All but eight of Buxtehude's surviving vocal works have sacred texts. His secular works are wedding music; his 120 sacred compositions include cantatas, vocal concertos, chorale settings, and strophic arias.

Buxtehude wrote his organ music for the typical north-German organ with three manuals and an independent pedalboard, all capable of producing contrasting tonal colors. (See Insight, "Keyboard Instruments.") In Buxtehude's organ works the pedals participate fully, even in the virtuosic display. His organ compositions are of three types: continuous variation over an ostinato, freely composed, and chorale based. His three ostinato pieces—*Ciaconne in c minor, Ciaconne in e minor*, and *Passacaglia in d minor*—are among his best-known works.

All Buxtehude's freely composed works contain fugal sections. Typically, he began with a prelude, then alternated fugal sections with quasi-improvisatory ones containing virtuosic passage work.

Buxtehude's chorale-based works are mainly short chorale preludes, with the chorale melody highly ornamented and in the top voice; the other three voices provide contrapuntal (usually nonimitative) accompaniment. These pieces use two manuals and pedals. His chorale fantasias are virtuosic pieces in which each phrase of the chorale melody is treated separately and is developed extensively (e.g., *Ich ruf zu dir*). He wrote a few chorale variations. His settings have three or four verses and usually are for manuals only; some verses are *bicinia*.

Buxtehude's extant harpsichord music consists of 19 suites and 6 sets of secular variations. Almost all the suites comprise allemande-courante-sarabande-gigue; occasionally, a *double* is inserted.

ITALIAN COMPOSERS

GIROLAMO FRESCOBALDI Girolamo Frescobaldi (1583–1643), the leading Italian composer of keyboard music in the first half of the seventeenth century, wrote keyboard works in all the forms then current. He lived in Ferrara until 1597. Some of his compositions reflect his awareness of musical developments at court—the embellishments Luzzaschi notated in the madrigals composed for the *concerto delle donne*, the extreme chromaticism used by Gesualdo, and the polyphonic madrigal with harmonies and texture not far removed from the *seconda prattica* of which Monteverdi wrote.

In July 1608 Frescobaldi was named organist at St. Peter's, Rome. From time to time he played organ in other churches and played harpsichord at musical gatherings in apartments of several cardinals. In 1628–34 he served as court organist in Florence and then returned to St. Peter's, where he worked until his death.

Although Frescobaldi composed both sacred and secular vocal music, his reputation rests primarily on his instrumental works. Almost all his compositions are notated in *partitura* (i.e., in open score), each voice of the music notated on a separate staff. His published instrumental works include a book of fantasias (1608); two books of toccatas (1615, 1627); four books of ricercars, canzonas, and capriccios (1615, 1624, 1626, posth. 1645); *Fiori musicali* (Musical flowers; 1635); and some partitas.

Frescobaldi's stated aim was to raise the quality of organ music and organ playing. The prefaces of his published works contain didactic information concerning the proper execution of ornaments and tempos. He used tempo markings liberally and advised the performer to commence a piece slowly so that succeeding phrases might seem livelier.

Frescobaldi's toccatas were designed for virtuosic display; they are structured in numerous sections that contrast sharply in character. Present in them are complicated cross-rhythms, proportional changes, imitative counterpoint, considerable chromaticism, and much figuration, especially in the approach to the final cadence, which Frescobaldi sometimes marked *Non senza fatiga si giunge al fine* (Not without effort does one reach the end). These features are present in Toccata IX, from *Il secondo libro di toccate, canzone, . . .* (1627; DWMA103).

Since the mid-eighteenth century, *Fiori musicali* has been Frescobaldi's most famous publication. Most of the music in the volume is arranged as three organ Masses: *Messa della Dominca, Messa delli Apostoli*, and *Messa della Madonna*. An **organ Mass** is a series of polyphonic compositions designed to replace movements of the Ordinary and Proper of the sung Mass; each organ movement is based on a Gregorian chant corresponding with that movement of the Mass. For the Ordinary of these Masses, Frescobaldi composed only the Kyrie; each Kyrie is a cantus firmus setting based on a chant that he identified. Toccatas, ricercars, and canzonas serve as substitutes for sections of the Proper: Introit, Gradual, Offertory, and Communion. Each Mass contains toccatas to be played before the Kyrie, before some ricercars, and during Elevation of the Host; ricercars for use after the Credo and in some instances after the Communion; and canzonas for use after the reading of the Epistle and after the Communion. Introductory toccatas are quite short. Those designed to precede ricercars create a kind of prelude-and-fugue structure; there are few examples of this kind of pairing in Italian organ music. Toccatas to be used during Elevation of the Host are longer and more complex. Typical of the ricercars is *Ricercare dopo il Credo* (Ricercar after the Credo) from *Messa della Madonna* (DWMA105). The canzonas are considerably longer than the ricercars and are sectional, with contrasting tempo markings indicated; canzona subjects are less chromatic than those used for ricercars. Some are variation canzonas (e.g., *Canzona dopo l'Epistola*).

Among Frescobaldi's works are some individual dance pieces and some *partitas* that are sectional compositions and are related to dance music and to variations (e.g., *Partite sopra l'aria della Romanesca*).

BERNARDO PASQUINI Only recently has Bernardo Pasquini (1637–1710) been recognized as the most important Italian composer of keyboard music between Frescobaldi and Domenico Scarlatti (see p. 336). Pa-

squini's talent was comparable with that of Frescobaldi and equal to that of Corelli (see p. 290ff.). As a composer, Pasquini made significant contributions to vocal as well as to keyboard music. Many of his operas, oratorios, cantatas, and motets have been lost. Surviving compositions indicate that in the development of Roman opera, Pasquini stands between Cesti and Alessandro Scarlatti.

Little of Pasquini's music was published. His surviving keyboard works include 15 sets of variations, 4 passacaglias, 17 suites of dances, numerous individual dances, 34 toccatas, 11 imitative contrapuntal compositions (canzonas, ricercars, capriccios, a fantasia, and a *Fuga*), 4 sonatas for organ, and the figured-bass part only for 28 three-movement harpsichord sonatas.

Pasquini is credited with establishing the keyboard suite in Italy. His suites are basically *allemanda-corrente-giga* grouping; the number and type of any additional dances vary. The sets of variations are dance related and include variations on *Bergamasca* and *La Folia*.

Keyboard Instruments

INSIGHT

BAROQUE ORGAN

The most important German organ builders were members of the Schnitger and Silbermann families. Arp Schnitger (1648–1719) constructed more than 150 organs of all sizes. Many of his organs had three or four manuals and a pedalboard of 26 or 27 keys. The "natural" keys of the manuals were covered with ebony, beech, or strips of glazed pottery; the "sharps" had bone or ivory covering. Schnitger's organs had a four-octave compass, from C to c''', the lowest octave being a short one. Most Schnitger organs were in mean-tone temperament (i.e., octaves and ascending thirds tuned true, fifths narrowed) and were tuned about three-fourths of a tone higher in pitch than the standard a' = 440 now in use. Schnitger preferred metal pipes, probably because they were easier

to make and to voice than wooden ones. J. S. Bach considered the Schnitger organ in Jakobikirche, Hamburg, one of the finest organs he ever played; that organ was still extant in 1987.

In Alsace, Saxony, and Dresden, Andreas (1678–1734) and Gottfried (1683–1753) Silbermann were famous for building fine organs. From 1706 to 1710 Gottfried worked in partnership with Andreas in Strasbourg, then established his own shop in Freiberg. Later, Gottfried enjoyed the patronage of Frederick the Great. Several of Gottfried's organs are extant, including one built for Freiberg Cathedral in 1710–14 and one made in 1721–22 for St. Marien Church, Rotha.

Baroque organs were designed so that the performer could achieve a homogeneous blend of sound yet

could enhance and bring into prominence clearly and brilliantly any one of the polyphonic lines. Thus, the instrument was admirably suited for performance of both polyphonic and homophonic music. In the twentieth century, there has been great interest in accuracy of performance practices, and many organs have been built simulating Baroque specifications, especially along the lines of Silbermann instruments. Silbermann organs are heard at their best in performance of Bach's fantasias, toccatas, and fugues, but Schnitger organs render chorale preludes with finer subtleties.

During the Baroque era, testing and proving organs was very important. When a new organ was completed, experts were invited (and were paid handsomely) to come from other cities to examine and test every detail of that organ's construction. J. S. Bach was in great demand as an organ prover. He praised the work of Johann Scheibe (c. 1680–1748), who in the 1720s enlarged the organs at Thomaskirche and Nicholaikirche (both three-manual instruments, with 36 stops) and in 1742–44 constructed a two-manual organ at Johanniskirche, Leipzig.

CLAVIER

The term *clavier* (French, keyboard; German, *Klavier*) is generally interpreted to mean harpsichord or clavichord. However, composers used the word *clavier* indiscriminately for keyboard music, and at times music

designated for "clavier" may have been intended for performance on an organ. In the seventeenth and eighteenth centuries, the most famous builders of harpsichords were Flemish, especially members of the Ruckers family in Antwerp. Other builders include members of the Hass and Fleischer families in Germany; Tabel, Shudi, and Kirckman in England; Zenti and Cristofori in Italy; and the Blanchets, the Jacquets, and Taskin in France. In the 1630s, Jehan Jacquet (d. after 1658), of Paris, was considered one of the best harpsichord makers of that time. His son Claude (c. 1605–1674) was equally talented.

Many harpsichord builders constructed clavichords also. A few clavichords built by J. C. Fleischer and H. A. Hass in the 1720s are extant. Gottfried Silbermann was renowned for his clavichords; C. P. E. Bach used one of them for almost half a century. In the early 1730s, Silbermann began to construct fortepianos with action similar to that used by Cristofori. J. S. Bach's adverse criticism of Silbermann's fortepianos resulted in lighter action and stronger treble register. The fortepiano was not widely used until the second half of the eighteenth century.

CLAVIER MUSIC

The types of music written for clavier (harpsichord, clavichord) during the late seventeenth and early eighteenth centuries include quasi-improvisational pieces (such as toccata, fantasia, and prelude); fugues; variations (such as chaconne, passacaglia, and theme and variations); suites; and, after c. 1690, sonatas. The two most important types were suite and theme and variations.

THEME AND VARIATIONS

During the last half of the seventeenth century, many composers wrote original themes for their sets of variations. Such a theme was a short songlike piece, called *aria, air,* or simply *thema* (theme). The theme was stated, then followed by a series of sections (often numbered), each a variation of the theme. Composers did not completely abandon the use of borrowed thematic material, however. In the eighteenth century, theme and variations was used increasingly not only as a separate composition but as a movement—often the second—of a multimovement form.

SUITE

Many harpsichord suites were composed during the late seventeenth and early eighteenth centuries. Froberger's contributions to the suite have been mentioned (see p. 273). In most of the suites published after 1690, the movements appear in allemande-courante-sarabande-gigue order, with optional dance(s) placed between sarabande and gigue. In Kuhnau's *Neue Clavier-Übung* (New Clavier-pieces; Part I, 1689; Part II, 1692), each volume contains seven suites.

SONATA

Before c. 1690 the term *sonata* was associated primarily with instrumental ensemble music. A few composers entitled isolated pieces for solo harpsichord *Sonata,* but these compositions had nothing in common with the ensemble sonatas of the time.

The solo harpsichord *Sonata in B♭* that Johann Kuhnau (1660–1722) included as the final piece in Part II of *Neue Clavier-Übung* (1692) contains five short sections, in slow-fast-slow-fast-slow order of tempo, the last slow section being a repetition of the first. The internal structure and style of the sections closely resembles that of the Italian trio sonata. Two published collections of Kuhnau's harpsichord works consist entirely of solo sonatas: *Frische Klavier Früchte* (Fresh Keyboard Fruits; 1696), containing seven sonatas, and *Musicalische Vorstellung einiger Biblischer Historien* (Musical representations of some Biblical stories; 1700), containing six. Each sonata in *Frische Klavier Früchte* has from three to six movements that contrast in tempo, key, thematic material, and style. The *Musical representations*, better known as "Biblical Sonatas," are multimovement programmatic compositions, each prefaced by a prose description of the Old Testament incident musically represented. Each section has an Italian subtitle that designates the particular action or emotional state represented by that portion of the music. The sonatas are *The fight between David and Goliath; Saul cured by David through music; Jacob's wedding; Hezekiah, sick unto death and restored to health; Gideon, savior of Israel;* and *Jacob's death and burial.* The religious element is present also in Kuhnau's symbolic use of chorale melodies. For example, Hezekiah's complaint is depicted through the choral melody *Ach, Herr, mein arme Sünder* (Oh, Lord, my poor sins; fig. 16.1), the melody J. S. Bach used for the chorale text *O Haupt voll Blut und wunden.*

Kuhnau is credited with transferring the instrumental ensemble sonata to clavier and introducing that type of composition in Germany.

FRENCH COMPOSERS

JACQUES CHAMPION DE CHAMBONNIÈRES Jacques Champion, Sieur de Chambonnières (1602–72), is considered the founder of the French school of harpsichord playing in the Baroque era and is credited with being the earliest important French composer of harpsichord works written in the new *style brisé* idiom. He transmitted the *style brisé* to his pupils and to foreign musicians who heard him perform or who, like Froberger, had manuscript copies of some of his works.

A brilliant harpsichordist, Chambonnières was at the height of his career at court by 1650 and was sought after as a teacher. Among his pupils were Louis Couperin (1626–61), Nicolas-Antoine Lebègue (c. 1631–1702), and Jean d'Anglebert (1635–91). In 1657 Chambonnières was replaced as royal harpsichord teacher, and late in 1662 he resigned the remainder of his court duties in favor of d'Anglebert. To obtain needed income, he published *Les pièces de clavessin* (Harpsichord pieces; 2 vols.; 1670), comprising 60 individual pieces arranged into groups or suites. At least 142 of Chambonnières's harpsichord works survive in manuscript; all are dance pieces, mainly allemandes, courantes, sarabandes, and gigues.

ELISABETH JACQUET DE LA GUERRE By the time Elisabeth-Claude Jacquet (c. 1666–1729) was 10 years old, she had a reputation for remarkable ability to sight-sing difficult music, play harpsichord, accompany, improvise, transpose, and compose. She attracted the attention of Louis XIV, who encouraged her career. By 1684 she had married organist Marin de la Guerre (d. 1704).

Elisabeth retired from public performance in 1717 but continued to compose. Her surviving works include the five-act opera *Cephale et Procris* (1694), a comic scene written for Théâtre de la Foire (1715), three volumes of cantatas (1708, 1711, and one undated), *Pièces de clavecin* (Harpsichord pieces; 1687), six sonatas for violin with basso continuo (1707), two violin sonatas with basso continuo for viola da gamba

FIGURE 16.1 Excerpt from Kuhnau: (Biblical) *Sonata 4*, with the chorale melody (pitches marked x) placed uppermost. *(Biblischer Historien, Leipzig, 1700)*

BAROQUE INSTRUMENTAL MUSIC

and organ (MS), four trio sonatas (MS), and some songs printed in various early eighteenth-century anthologies. A ballet and a *Te Deum* that she composed have not been located. The *Pièces de clavecin qui peuvent se jouer sur le viollon* ([14] Harpsichord pieces which may be played on the violin; 1707) comprise two suites (DWMA106). Included in the volume is a table of *agréments* showing correct interpretation of the symbols she used in her notation.

FRANÇOIS COUPERIN *LE GRAND*   François Couperin *le grand* (1668–1733), composer, harpsichordist, and organist, is considered the most important French musician between Lully and Rameau. Several Couperins served as organists at St. Gervais, Paris, including Louis Couperin (François's uncle), from 1653 until his death in 1661, and Charles (François's father), from 1661 until his death (1679). François was given the position when he became 18, but he served as deputy organist long before then. After his father's death, François became the protegé and pupil of royal organist Jacques-Denis Thomelin (c. 1640–93) and in 1693 succeeded him. There were four royal organists; a different one attended the royal chapel each quarter of the year. By c. 1700 Couperin was recognized as the leading French composer; however, he did not receive another royal appointment until 1717, when he succeeded d'Anglebert as royal harpsichordist.

Two of François's children were talented: Marie-Madeleine (1690–1742) was organist at Maubisson, and Marguerite-Antoinette (1705–c. 1778) was court harpsichordist in 1730–41. She was the first woman to hold that position.

François Couperin published only one volume of organ works, *Pièces d'orgue* (Organ pieces; 1690). The two organ Masses that comprise this volume are comparable in quality with those composed and published by the noted organist Nicolas de Grigny (1672–1703) in his *Livre d'orgue* (1699). Couperin's organ pieces are not small works—the offertories, especially, are extensive and impressive. The *Pièces d'orgue* reveal Couperin's melodic gift, contrapuntal skill, and ability to handle current formal structures with ease. In the seventeenth century, the organ Mass was cultivated primarily in France and Italy.

Couperin composed some excellent instrumental chamber music (see p. 295), some secular songs and

François Couperin *le grand.* Engraving (dated 1735) by Jean J. Flipart.

cantatas, and a considerable amount of sacred vocal music, but his more than 235 harpsichord pieces are his greatest compositional achievement. Most of them were published as *Pièces de clavecin* (Harpsichord pieces; 1713, 1717, 1722, 1730). In each volume the pieces are grouped into what Couperin called *ordres;* the four volumes contain a total of 27 *ordres* (DWMA 107). An **ordre** contains as few as 4 or as many as 24 small pieces, and most have from 8 to 15. All pieces in an *ordre* are in the same or parallel tonality (e.g., the *Second ordre* contains d tonality pieces, both major and minor). A few pieces bear the names of standard suite movements (allemande, courante, sarabande, gigue). Most of the pieces have fanciful titles, such as *Le Rossignol en amour* (The nightingale in love), *La reine des coeurs* (The queen of hearts), and *La mysterieuse* (The mysterious lady). It was not Couperin's intention that an *ordre* be considered a unified multimovement work to be performed as an entity. Rather, a performer was expected to select from an *ordre* several pieces to be played.

Couperin used three formal structures for his harpsichord pieces: binary, rondeau, and chaconne. In his rondeaux, the theme (labeled *rondeau*) is usually four or eight measures long; the episodes (termed *couplets*)

FIGURE 16.2 Excerpt from Explanation of Ornaments that Couperin published in *Premier livre de pièces de clavecin* (1713).

vary in length and design. Some pieces labeled chaconne or *passacaille* are in rondeau form. This was not unusual; Elisabeth Jacquet de la Guerre, Louis Couperin, and Chambonnières wrote chaconnes in rondeau form.

In some pieces, especially those of allemande type, Couperin used the *style brisé* favored by lutenists. He was extremely careful to notate ornament symbols accurately, and he included in his publications a table explaining the meaning of the *agrément* symbols he used (fig. 16.2). In 1733 François d'Agincourt (1684–1758) credited Couperin with standardizing the system of *agréments* (and the symbols representing the ornaments) then in use in France.

Couperin was an excellent harpsichord teacher. His theoretical writings provide insight into his didactic methods and beliefs and constitute valuable sources concerning performance practices in the early eighteenth century. In *L'art de toucher le clavecin* (The art of playing the harpsichord; 1716, rev. 1717), Couperin considered various aspects of a pupil's early training in playing harpsichord; discussed fingering, *agrément* symbols and ornamentation (with specific examples), and other matters of performance practice; and suggested fingerings for difficult passages in the pieces published in *Pièces de clavecin*.

IBERIAN COMPOSERS

The earliest surviving keyboard music printed in Portugal is *Flores de musica pero o instrumento de tecla & harpa* (Musical flowers for keyboard and harp; 1620), a collection of works by Manuel Rodrigues Coelho (c. 1555–1635). *Flores de musica* is his only known work. The volume contains 24 *tientos* (imitative contrapuntal works similar to the Italian ricercar), approximately 100 versets for liturgical use, and 4 intabulations of Lassus's chanson *Susanne ung jour.*

Francisco Correa de Araujo (c. 1577–1654) was born in Portugal but worked in Spain. His only surviving music is in his *Facultad organica* (Organ School; 1626), a theoretical treatise with a repertory of didactic organ music illustrating the points presented. *Facultad organica* contains 62 *tientos,* 3 sets of variations, 2 cantus firmus settings of sacred melodies, and 2 intabulations of chansons.

Juan Bautista José Cabanilles (1644–1712) brought to culmination the Iberian tradition of organ music that began with Cabezón and was continued by Coelho and Correa. Cabanilles's knowledge of *concertato* style is apparent in the eight sacred choral works that were discovered in the early 1970s; some of these pieces are for 12 voices, divided into two or three choirs. The vast majority of Cabanilles's music is for organ: at least 200 *tientos,* approximately 170 versets for liturgical use, several sets of variations, some toccatas, and some dance pieces. His contrapuntal mastery is apparent in the *tientos,* most of which are polythematic. His excellent short monothematic *tientos* are filled with sharp dissonances, surprising harmonic progressions, and unusual melodic intervals. He wrote many of the *tientos* for broken keyboard registration (*medio registro*)—that is, he assigned independent registrations to the upper and lower parts of the organ manual so that one hand could be soloistic.

Carlos de Seixas (1704–42), organist and harpsichordist, was the most important Portuguese composer during the first half of the eighteenth century.

Although contemporary accounts indicate that he composed 700 keyboard works, only 88 have been located. Seixas used the terms *toccata* and *sonata* interchangeably. Some pieces are single-movement works that are typical Baroque toccatas; others are sonatas containing from one to five movements, each in binary form. Viewed overall, Seixas's sonatas portray the transition between Baroque and Classic styles.

SPANISH AND PORTUGUESE AMERICA

Missionaries to America considered music an essential part of the religious teaching of native populations and used it in connection with religious observances and in conversion of the natives. By the end of the seventeenth century, every village and small town had from two to three dozen native musicians performing in choirs and small orchestras. Choirmasters and organists in the cathedrals were from Iberia or had been trained there. Most of the instrumentalists listed in church account books were Indians—violinists, oboists, bassoonists, trumpeters, and harpists. The earliest Brazilian art music that has been located was composed in 1759.

ENSEMBLE MUSIC

TERMINOLOGY

As early as the thirteenth century the Provençal word *sonada* was used in literature to denote a piece of instrumental music; in succeeding centuries, authors of literary works referred to instrumental pieces as *sonnade, sonada,* or *sennet.* The term was used by composers in the sixteenth century—Milán's *El maestro* contains *villancicos y sonadas.* Near the end of the sixteenth century, several terms were used interchangeably and imprecisely in connection with ensemble music; those used most frequently are *sonata, sinfonia,* and *concerto.* Sometimes the words *sonata* and *canzona* were used together in titles or subtitles—*canzon da sonar,* instrumental song—or interchangeably, *canzoni overo sonate,* canzonas or sonatas. Originally, the term *canzona* was used to denote an instrumental arrangement of a polyphonic song, usually a chanson; gradually, the term was used for a polyphonic instrumental work that was based on a chanson and was imitative in character. The earliest works termed canzonas that were independent of vocal models were written for instrumental ensemble and were imitative, quasi-fugal pieces. As the canzona became longer and more individualistic in style, fewer sections were used per piece. Eventually, the canzona was supplanted by the sonata and survived as the fugal or quasi-fugal Allegro movement(s) of the sonata later known as **sonata da chiesa** (church sonata).

The Italian word *sonata* meant merely a piece of instrumental music, in contrast with *cantata,* a vocal composition. In the early seventeenth century, *sonata* and *sinfonia* were used interchangeably to label instrumental interludes in vocal works, introductory sections of vocal compositions, or (rarely) a separate movement serving as prelude to a vocal composition. Later in the century, *sinfonia* was used to label a movement preceding a group of dances.

Not until around the middle of the seventeenth century was the designation **sonata** used with any degree of uniformity in meaning. Most of the instrumental works termed *sonata* were **absolute** (i.e., nonreferential, nonprogrammatic) music, were sectional or multimovement pieces of chamber music performed by one person per part, and had no connection with vocal music. Exceptions to these generalities did occur and do exist.

Around 1660, composers applied two technical designations to distinguish types of sonatas: Works designated *sonata* or *sonata da chiesa* were intended for performance in church, as part of the Proper of the Mass, as filler between Mass movements, or as Postlude (or very rarely as Prelude) to the service. Pieces designated **sonata da camera** (chamber sonata) were intended for performance at court for diversion or in private concerts for a patron, at private concerts that were part of *Accademia* meetings, or at private or public concerts given in homes. A *sonata da camera* comprised a group of stylized dances, each movement properly identified (e.g., allemande, corrente), but might commence with a nondance movement as introduction or prelude. In other words, a *sonata da camera* was really a kind of suite. In a *sonata da chiesa* the individual movements were labeled with tempo markings only, though some of the individual movements might actually be dances or dancelike in character.

Most of the sonatas composed in the last third of the seventeenth century were written for two treble instruments (usually violins) with basso continuo. The notation—three lines of music—gave rise to the term **trio sonata** for this kind of composition. Four performers were required for performance because the basso continuo line was played on an instrument capable of sustaining the notated pitches their full written value (usually a violoncello, a viola da gamba, or violone) and was doubled on an instrument capable of supplying the implied supporting harmonies, which the performer improvised (usually harpsichord or organ). The *accompanied solo sonata* gained popularity after 1700. Three instrumentalists were needed for its performance: the soloist (usually a violinist, flutist, or bass violist) and two performers for the basso continuo accompaniment. Less frequent were *unaccompanied solo sonatas* and *ensemble sonatas,* usually written for two to six stringed instruments, one per part. Many *sinfonie* and ensemble sonatas are stylistically indistinguishable from one another.

The word ***concerto*** was commonly used in Italy in the first half of the seventeenth century to denote vocal music accompanied by instrumentalists, especially church music. At times the term was used synonymously with *concertato* to mean vocalists and/or instrumentalists performing in opposition to, yet in agreement with, one another. The word was applied similarly to purely instrumental music during the Baroque era.

The first compositions that gave identity to the instrumental concerto were sonatas written for an orchestra divided into a small ensemble of soloists, called the ***concertino*** (little ensemble), and a larger instrumental ensemble, known as the ***concerto grosso*** (large ensemble). In several instrumental works composed c. 1675 Stradella contrasted a concertino of trio sonata texture (two treble instruments playing in the same range plus basso continuo) with a concerto grosso of stringed instruments plus basso continuo. This kind of instrumentation was not standard but was the type most used by succeeding generations. It is not known exactly when or by whom the term *concerto grosso* was first applied to a composition of this kind, but the terminology was in use by around 1700. Corelli's *Concerti grossi,* Op. 6, became the most famous models of the form; they were well known before their publication in 1714. Concertos written for a soloist with orchestral accompaniment were composed by Torelli, Albinoni, and Jacchini c. 1700.

ITALY

In the seventeenth century, northern Italy was the leader in the production and performance of instrumental chamber music. This kind of music flourished especially at Venice, Modena, and Bologna, sites of the main development of the sonata.

VENICE At St. Mark's, Giovanni Gabrieli adapted *cori spezzati* methods to the canzona and created an instrumental chamber music idiom. The talents of the cornettists, trombonists, and violinists working there inspired the composition of *concertante* music. After Gabrieli's death, the musical chapel at St. Mark's sank to a low ebb. It improved considerably during Monteverdi's tenure, but Monteverdi's only instrumental music was associated with his vocal works. The composition of canzonas and canzonalike sonatas was taken up by violin virtuosi such as Fontana and Marini, who were the leading figures in the early development of the sonata, especially the solo sonata.

Giovanni Battista Fontana (died c. 1630) was a native of Brescia; he worked there and in Rome, Venice, and Padua. His only surviving compositions are sonatas preserved in a posthumous memorial publication: *Sonate a 1. 2. 3. per il violino, o cornetto, fagotto, chitarone, violoncino o simile altro istromento* (Sonatas in 1, 2, 3 parts for violin, or cornett, bassoon, chitarrone, 'cello, or other similar instruments; 1641). Of these pieces, 6 are for solo violin with basso continuo, and 12 are for two violins with basso continuo; some of the latter are supplied with a *concertante* part for violoncello or bassoon. All the sonatas have numerous short sections contrasting in tempo, meter, and style. Some sections are homophonic, others contrapuntal with canzonalike imitation. In general, the writing is quite conservative. No strong tonal relationships are present; often the bass line is melodic and serves as another contrapuntal line rather than true accompaniment.

Biagio Marini (c. 1587–1663) was employed as a violinist at St. Mark's, Venice, from 1615 to 1620. In 1623–49 he served at the court at Neuburg an die Donau, then worked intermittently at Milan, Ferrara, and Vincenza. After 1656 he lived alternately in Brescia and Venice. His compositions were published in at least 22 volumes. An overview of several volumes gives a sampling of the kinds of instrumental music he wrote. *Affetti musicali,* Op. 1 (Musical affects; 1617), contains dance pieces, canzonas, sinfonias, and sonatas for one to three violins or cornetts with basso continuo. In this volume Marini used the words *sinfonia* and *sonata* interchangeably. Some of the sinfonie for one violin have basso continuo lines that are truly accompaniment; these seem to be the earliest datable examples of solo violin sonatas with basso continuo **accompaniment.** The three solo sinfonie in Marini's *Madrigali e symfonie,* Op. 2 (Madrigals and sinfonias; 1618) are more violinistic and require double stopping. In them the performance directive *affetti* (supply appropriate ornaments) appears for the first time in Marini's music (ex. 16.1).

In *Sonate, symphonie . . . e retornelli,* Op. 8 (1629), sonatas and sinfonias are clearly differentiated—sonatas are longer, with more varied structure, than sinfonias. One solo sonata contains a section in **scor-**

datura (instrument tuned unconventionally); a *Capriccio* has triple-stops throughout; and there is an echo sonata for three violins. Works with these kinds of special effects reflect Marini's contact with German virtuosi.

Marini's *Per ogni sorte di strumento musicale diversi generi di sonate, da chiesa, e da camera,* Op. 22 (Sonatas, *da chiesa* and *da camera,* for all sorts of musical instruments of various kinds; 2–4 instruments with basso continuo; 1655), comprises six sonatas, four of them divided into separate sections. Though these are not movements per se, the pieces indicate clearly that composers were beginning to think of the sonata as a multimovement work.

MODENA   When Cesare d'Este moved the family seat to Modena in 1598, the center of musical activity shifted from the cathedral to the court. Este patronage and the reputation of the court chapel attracted outstanding musicians from all over Italy. During 1647–65 Marco Uccellini (c. 1630–80) attracted many to the court and the cathedral. He initiated at Modena a tradition of violinist-composers that antedated the Bologna school by more than a decade. Seven of Uccellini's printed volumes of instrumental music are extant; Opp. 2–5 are mainly sonatas. He wrote triadic themes and modulated through the circle of fifths by means of sequences; his excursions into the keys of B major and E♭ minor were unusual in music for stringed instruments at that time. In his music, the range used for violin extended to g'''. The solo violin sonatas in Opp. 4

EXAMPLE 16.1 Marini's designation *Affetti* directed the performer to embellish this passage in his *Sonata per il violino per sonar con due corde,* Op. 8 (1629).

and 5 contain *scordatura* passages, double-stops, wide leaps, and brilliant figuration. Uccellini's use of instrumental puzzle canons was characteristic of the Modena school.

French influences invaded music at Modena after Alfonso IV d'Este married Laura Martinozzi, niece of Cardinal Mazarin, in 1665. Elements of French musical style appeared in the *sonata da camera,* in sets of dances, and in pieces labeled "in the French style." This can be seen in some of the music composed by Giovanni M. Bononcini (1642–78). In 1666–75 Bononcini published eight volumes of sonatas and dance music (Opp. 1–7 and 9). His predilection for counterpoint is discernible in even his earliest works. Instrumental canons, known as *artificii musicali,* are a feature of his work. Bononcini's *sonate da chiesa* in Opp. 1–6 are clearly related to the canzona; in the sonatas of Op. 9, slow homophonic movements alternate with fast contrapuntal ones. His writing for violin is refined, never exceeding third position in range. Though traces of modality are found in his works, his music reveals his knowledge of major-minor key tonality. Bononcini's sonatas for stringed instruments are considered the highest achievement of the late seventeenth-century Modena school of instrumental music.

The reign of Francesco II d'Este (1674–94) marked the most brilliant phase of music at the Modena court. Francesco commissioned compositions, stimulated musical performances at court, amassed an excellent library, and helped establish the university. The music library at his court was the core of the music collection of Biblioteca Estense, Modena.

BOLOGNA Bologna was an important commercial, cultural, and educational center and was second in importance only to Rome within the Papal States. In 1450 Pope Nicolò V sanctioned the establishment of a chair of music at the University of Bologna. Several academies stimulated, regulated, and consolidated all musical activities and strove to ensure a high level of performance. The Accademia Filarmonica, founded in 1666, held weekly meetings to discuss theoretical works and to perform and analyze members' new compositions. Thus, the academy could exercise control over its members, determine musical taste, and ensure an acceptable musical style.

Bologna's public musical life was centered in the chapels of its numerous churches, especially San Petronio. The number of excellent performers permanently employed in San Petronio's musical chapel was

FIGURE 16.3 Interior of San Petronio, Bologna, with view of the two opposing organs, as seen from the corretto and looking toward the east.

fairly large. In 1661, 33 musicians were on the regular roster; on special occasions, the performing ensemble numbered more than a hundred. Although instrumentalists participated in performances at San Petronio as early as the fifteenth century, they were first added to the chapel as regularly paid members in the late sixteenth century. Acoustics in the church are superb. On either side of the high altar are choir stalls with musicians' galleries, each with an organ—an ideal antiphonal arrangement (fig. 16.3).

The famed Bologna school had its inception with the appointment of Maurizio Cazzati (1620–77) as *maestro di cappella* at San Petronio in 1657. Cazzati remained there until 1671, then moved to Mantua to serve as court *maestro di cappella*. At San Petronio, Cazzati increased the number of instrumentalists employed. Excellent violinists were attracted, and within a short time the city became the recognized center for violin playing. Cazzati contributed significantly to the repertoire of instrumental music, especially that for trumpet and strings. Ten of his 66 extant volumes of published music contain instrumental works; 5 of the collections contain a total of 54 sonatas. Manuscripts in the San Petronio archives contain many of his sonatas for one or two trumpets and strings; multiple string parts indicate that these pieces were performed orchestrally. Cazzati's trumpet sonatas are important precursors of Torelli's sonatas and concertos.

Cazzati's *Sonate a due, tre, quattro, e cinque, con alcune per Tromba*, Op. 35 (Sonatas for 2, 3, 4, and 5 [instruments], with some for trumpet; 1665), includes three sonatas for trumpet, violin, alto and tenor viols, and violone. Cazzati stated that a violin might be substituted if a trumpet player of sufficient capability was not available.

Cazzati's *12 Sonate a due istromenti cioè violino, e violone* (12 Sonatas for 2 instruments, namely, violin and violone; 1670) are considered the first published *solo* violin music of the Bologna school because almost all the violone line is identical with the basso continuo part for organ. The cornetto is specified as an alternative for violin; the solo part, which is neither virtuosic nor lyrical, is as idiomatic for cornetto as for violin. Range is limited to two octaves, c' to c'''. Each sonata is in four movements, with some thematic resemblance among movements of a sonata. The soloist was expected to ornament the slow second movements. Cazzati's restrained and serious approach to violin music is characteristic of the Bologna school; perhaps this reflects the religious atmosphere at San Petronio.

Cazzati is historically important because (1) under his leadership the musical chapel of San Petronio attracted excellent instrumentalists and composers to Bologna, (2) he composed and encouraged others to contribute to repertories for accompanied solo violin and for trumpet and strings, and (3) he included instrumental works of this kind in services at San Petronio.

G. B. Vitali Giovanni Battista Vitali (1632–92) joined the musical chapel at San Petronio in 1658 as singer and *violone da brazzo* player; in 1671 he was appointed *maestro di cappella*. In 1673, he moved to Modena to serve as *vicemaestro di cappella* at the Este court. While working at Modena, Vitali was a connecting link between the court and San Petronio.

Although Vitali composed numerous vocal works, he is known mainly for his instrumental music; he contributed significantly to the development of the trio sonata. He specifically designated as *da chiesa* the trio sonatas of his *Sonate a 2 violini col suo basso continuo per l'organo*, Op. 2 (1667).

Vitali's *Artificii musicali*, Op. 13 (1689), a pedagogical work, systematically presents 60 instrumental canons in order of increasing difficulty. *Artificii musicali* seems to be the earliest collection of its kind in the Baroque era and is an important precursor of Bach's *Musikalisches Opfer* (p. 311).

Pietro degli Antonii Pietro degli Antonii (1648–1720) spent his entire life in Bologna but was *maestro di cappella* at churches other than San Petronio. His compositions comprise operas and secular pieces, Masses, motets, and organ works. He was one of the first to write solo violin sonatas with a melodic line so lyrical and rhapsodic that the basso continuo is reduced to purely harmonic support. His Sonata No. 5, a trio sonata, is in *Scielta della Suonate* (1680), the earliest known anthology of sonatas.

Degli Antonii was the only composer of the Bologna school to make the solo sonata his principal field of activity. In *Sonate a violino solo*, Op. 5, he employed the Neapolitan sixth (lowered supertonic), unprepared sevenths, deceptive cadences in which the leading tone is suspended but not resolved, and changed from minor to major tonality over the same root. Occasionally, the keyboard accompaniment enjoys modulatory excursions around the circle of fifths while the solo violin is assigned sequential passages (e.g., in Op. 5, No. 6, *Grave*).

Domenico Gabrielli   Noted 'cellists at San Petronio include Petronio Franceschini (1650–81) and Domenico Gabrielli (1651–90). Gabrielli composed some of the earliest music for violoncello. His advanced performing technique is reflected in the florid passage work and the double-, triple-, and quadruple-stops included in his sonatas and ricercars for unaccompanied 'cello. His *Balletti, gighe, correnti, alemande, e sarabande*, Op. 1, comprises 12 paired dances, each pair in a different key, ranging from E♭ to A major and from C minor to B minor. There are extant six of Gabrielli's sonatas for one or two trumpets with orchestra, written for performance at San Petronio. He included the 'cello as an obbligato instrument in the trumpet sonatas and constructed a movement in one of the sonatas as a concertante duet for trumpet and 'cello with basso continuo—a trio sonata.

Giuseppe Torelli   Giuseppe Torelli (1658–1709), virtuoso violinist, contributed greatly to the development of concerto grosso and solo concerto and to the repertoire for trumpet and strings at Bologna. A native of Verona, Torelli moved to Bologna in 1682. During 1686–89 and again in 1701 he was a member of the San Petronio musical chapel.

More than 100 of Torelli's works exist only in manuscript. Most of them are for trumpet(s) in D, violin(s), and/or oboe(s). Four volumes of his chamber music for strings were published in Bologna in 1686–88:

Sonate à tre, Op. 1, ten trio sonatas for violins and basso continuo. Seven of these *sonate da chiesa* each have four movements arranged in slow-fast order, with the second movement usually in a related key. Generally, first movements are chordal, second movements imitative, and fourth movements dancelike.

Concerto da camera à due violini e basso, Op. 2, 12 *sonate da camera* for two violins with basso con-

tinuo. Dances in the individual suites vary, but allemande, corrente, balletto, and gigue are represented, and each suite concludes with a gavotte, minuet, or sarabande.

Sinfonie à 2. 3. e 4., Op. 3, 12 sonatas of which 6 are trio sonatas.

Concertino per camera, Op. 4, 12 sets of dance pieces for violin and violoncello, without basso continuo. These may be the earliest violin-'cello duos by a Bolognese composer.

In 1679 Torelli became interested in composing for trumpet. No doubt he was inspired by Giovanni Pellegrino Brandi, an excellent trumpet player, who, in 1679–99, participated in the annual celebrations whereby San Petronio honored its patron saint. For these declarations, Torelli and other Bolognese composers wrote sonatas and sinfonias for solo trumpet and strings; a work of this kind was performed to begin the Mass and was followed by the Kyrie.

Torelli's Op. 5, *Sinfonie à tre e concerti à quattro* (1692), comprises six trio sonatas and six concertos. The concertos are orchestral works; Torelli's specifications that multiple instruments be used per part seem to be the earliest printed instructions for orchestral performance. Similarly, Torelli indicated in the preface to *Concerti musicali*, Op. 6 (1692), that passages marked "solo" are for one violin; on all other parts three or four instruments are to be used. Two of the 12 concertos contain short solo episodes; these pieces foreshadow the approach of the solo violin concerto.

Torelli's Op. 8, *Concerti grossi con una pastorale per il Santissimo Natale* (Concerti grossi with a pastorale for the most holy birthday [i.e., Christmas]), was published posthumously. Actually, only six of the pieces are concerti grossi; the other six are solo concertos. Because Torelli dated very few of his compositions, it cannot be determined whether any of his solo concertos antedate those written by Albinoni in 1700 and Jacchini in 1701.

Some features of the fully developed Baroque solo concerto are apparent in Torelli's concertos. Most of them have three movements, arranged in fast-slow-fast tempo pattern. Concerto No. 7 of Op. 8 is a representative example. In the Allegros, imitative *ritornelli* alternate with soloist episodes using idiomatic figuration;

in contrapuntal passages the top voice clearly dominates. (In a concerto movement, the term **ritornello** signifies the recurring passage performed by the orchestra or *tutti*.) The last *ritornello* is a recapitulation of the first. Torelli's Allegro themes are rhythmically vigorous and are colored by sequences and suspensions. The concerto's middle movement, an Adagio in a related key, is for soloist accompanied by the basso continuo duo.

ARCANGELO CORELLI

Arcangelo Corelli (1653–1713; Insight, "Arcangelo Corelli") was esteemed in Italy as violinist, composer, and teacher, and he is still highly regarded by musicians everywhere. He was adept at directing both instrumental and vocal music, and occasionally he assisted other composers by writing portions of their works. Twice in March 1689, Corelli led very large ensembles of singers and instrumentalists in performance of Masses. Reportedly, he composed a "sinfonia with trumpets" for one of those services. This lends credence to the attribution to him of the Sonata in D for trumpet, two violins, and basso continuo; however, there is the possibility of a scribal error in the manuscript, and that trumpet piece may belong to Torelli.

Corelli prepared for publication six sets of compositions for stringed instruments, each set containing 12 works:

Sonate a tre, Op. 1 (Rome, 1681): 12 trio *sonate da chiesa* for two violins, violone or archlute, with bass for organ.

Sonate da camera a tre, Op. 2 (Rome, 1685): 11 *sonate da camera* and a chaconne, for two violins, and violone or harpsichord.

Sonate a tre, Op. 3 (Rome, 1689): 12 *sonate da chiesa* for two violins, violone or archlute, with bass for organ.

Sonate a tre, Op. 4 (Rome, 1694): 12 *sonate da camera* for two violins and violone.

Sonate a Violino e Violone o Cimbalo, Op. 5 (Rome, 1700): *six sonate da chiesa,* five *sonate da camera,* and theme and variations on *La folia,* for solo violin with violone or harpsichord.

Concerti grossi, Op. 6 (Amsterdam, 1714): 12 concerti grossi for obbligato soloist ensemble of two violins and violoncello and optional large ensemble of two violins, viola, and bass. Eight of these concerti are *da chiesa.*

In addition, Estienne Roger of Amsterdam published (c. 1715) six *Sonate a tre* for two violins with basso continuo, as *Ouvrage posthume* of Corelli.

Two subsequent editions of the Op. 5 Sonatas are significant. The first reprint of that volume was made by Pierre Mortier of Amsterdam. To the fourth edition of that reprint, Mortier added Corelli's own ornaments for the slow movements of the six *sonate da chiesa* (see DWMA109). John Walsh of London immediately pirated and published that ornamented edition. No other eighteenth-century editions contain those graces.

It is interesting to note that (1) most of Corelli's compositions are trio sonatas, the most fashionable ensemble music of the time; (2) the four volumes of trio sonatas were published first; and (3) in assembling his compositions, he observed the distinction between *da chiesa* and *da camera* sonata types and grouped pieces of similar character together. Moreover, he specified for *da chiesa* trio sonatas the full sound of both violone and organ continuo; *da camera* trio sonatas use *either* violone or harpsichord. According to the title page, the concerti grossi may be performed as trio sonatas; both concertino 'cello part and *ripieno* bass are supplied with figures for keyboard realization. This can be interpreted in two ways: (1) that the figures supplied with the concertino 'cello part are to be realized by a keyboard player when the pieces are performed as trio sonatas; or (2) that two continuo keyboard instruments are to be used when the compositions are performed as concerti grossi. When each group has its own keyboard instrument, the small and large ensembles can be separated spatially, as they probably were when a concerto grosso was performed in Corelli's time.

CORELLI'S STYLE   Corelli wrote almost exclusively for bowed stringed instruments and wrote idiomatically for them. Rarely does the violin part extend beyond third position. The first three positions are the area of greatest comfort in playing the violin, especially on the Baroque violin, for the instrument's neck and fingerboard were considerably shorter and had a slightly different slant than that of modern stringed instruments. Also, the first three positions match in compass the range of the most gifted sopranos at a time when *bel canto* was considered the highest type of vocal art.

Arcangelo Corelli

Arcangelo Corelli (1653–1713) was born a month after his father's death. The Corellis were prosperous landowners in Fusignano, a small town near Bologna, and Signora Corelli was able to provide her children (four sons and a daughter) with education befitting the family's elevated social status. As a child, Arcangelo received music lessons. At the age of 13, he went to Bologna to pursue classical studies, but on hearing the musicians at San Petronio he determined to study violin seriously and studied in Bologna at least four years. In 1670 he was admitted to the Accademia Filarmonica. Though he worked primarily in Rome from 1675 until his death, he considered himself a member of the Bologna school. The title pages of his first three published works name him *Arcangelo Corelli da Fusignano, detto il Bolognese* (Arcangelo Corelli of Fusignano, called the Bolognese).

In Rome, Corelli was soon recognized as one of the leading violinists

Arcangelo Corelli. *(The Bettmann Archive)*

and an outstanding director of instrumental ensembles. The list of his performances is impressive. For a short time, he worked as chamber musician to Queen Christina of Sweden, who, after her abdication, resided in Rome. Account books at the church of San Luigi list Corelli as leader of ten violins there in 1682.

In 1684 Corelli began to take responsibility for and to perform in musical functions at the palace of Cardinal Pamphili; in July 1687 Pamphili employed him as music master. Corelli and his pupil Matteo Fornari resided at the palace. Frequently they performed trio sonatas and concertino parts in concerti grossi with Spanish 'cellist G. L. Lulier (c. 1650– after 1708), who was also employed by Pamphili. Another who frequently performed with Corelli was Bernardo Pasquini (see p. 279). Pasquini and Corelli were friends and had some of the same patrons. Corelli led the orchestra for performances of several of Pasquini's works, including opera, and for at least one oratorio by Lulier. (Leading the orchestra meant conducting while serving as concertmaster of the orchestra.) In the Accademia di S Cecilia (the musicians' guild), Pasquini became head of the organists, and Corelli was head of the other instrumentalists.

When Pamphili moved to Bologna in 1690, Cardinal Ottoboni became Corelli's patron. Ottoboni held regular Monday evening concerts at the palace and invited all visiting dignitaries and famous composers and musicians in Rome. Corelli directed those concerts and also the performances of operas at the palace and at Teatro Tor di Nona. Account books indicate that he contributed concerti and sinfonie for several special per-

formances, but the compositions are not identified. The overture that Corelli composed for Lulier's oratorio *S Beatrice d'Este* (1689) still exists.

In April 1706, Corelli, Pasquini, and Alessandro Scarlatti were admitted to the Arcadian Academy. All members of the academy used pseudonyms—Corelli's was Arcomelo Erimanteo.

After 1708 Corelli no longer performed in public. Late in 1712, his health deteriorated considerably, and he moved from the palace to his brother Giacinto's apartment, taking with him the vast treasure of paintings he had accumulated. Corelli died on 8 January 1713; he was interred in the Pantheon in the chapel of St. Joseph. Though interment in that chapel was restricted to architects, painters, and sculptors who were members of the Artistica Congregazione dei Virtuosi al Pantheon, Corelli was placed there by special indulgence of Pope Clement XI. For several years, some of Corelli's concerti grossi were performed in the Pantheon on the anniversary of his death. At Ottoboni's suggestion, the Elector honored Corelli posthumously with the Marquisate of Landenburg.

By his will, Corelli left one painting of his choice to Cardinal Ottoboni and a Breughel canvas to Cardinal Colonna; Corelli's brothers received the remaining 134 pieces in his art collection, which included landscapes by Poussin, a Madonna by Sassoferrato, and several canvases by Trevisani. Corelli bequeathed to Fornari his musical instruments, manuscripts, the plates of Op. 4, and the plates prepared for the unpublished Op. 6. Fornari arranged with Estienne Roger, Amsterdam, for publication of Op. 6.

Corelli's music is characterized by clear key tonality; he seems to be the earliest composer to write exclusively in major-minor key tonalities. Basically, Corelli's music is diatonic. He employed sequences systematically, using harmonic sequences to effect modulations and melodic sequences to extend a melodic line or as imitative dialogue. Composers of the Bologna school experimented with sequences that moved the tonality around the circle of fifths, and Corelli was no exception. Both homophony and polyphony are included in each of Corelli's compositions; at least one of the fast movements—usually the second movement—is fugal or contains fugato passages. Corelli's linear counterpoint is harmonically based and is governed by key tonality. He wrote chains of suspensions frequently. Except in the trio sonatas of Op. 2, he seldom notated the so-called Corelli clash—the harmony created by delayed introduction of a cadential leading tone so that it coincides with the anticipation of the tonic in an upper voice (ex. 16.2). However, in some cadences, improvised ornamentation could create that dissonance. Some of Corelli's cadences are of the type favored a century later by Mozart and his contemporaries: a trill on the supertonic above a dominant-seventh chord, resolving to the tonic (ex. 16.3). In the approach to the final cadence of a movement in triple meter, Corelli frequently used hemiola, for example, by notating the penultimate measure of a $\frac{3}{4}$ movement as implied $\frac{3}{2}$ meter (ex. 16.4).

In some sonatas there is thematic relationship between movements; however, most movements are monothematic. Many of the slow movements appear to be very sustained and bare; the performer was (and is) expected to ornament the written notes lavishly. When Corelli did not want such ornamentation he indicated that fact by the words *Arcate sostenuto e come stà* (sustained bowing and as it stands) or simply *come stà*. That directive appears in the first Grave of *Concerto Grosso*, Op. 6, No. 8 ("Christmas" concerto); in that short movement the parts, continually intertwining, move from beginning to end without arriving at a single intermediate cadence, and Corelli did not want his notation ornamented.

TRIO SONATAS In Corelli's trio sonatas, the two coequal upper parts move in the same range and are always in proximity but are separated from the bass by a wide interval. When the basso continuo includes a keyboard instrument, the harmonies of the realized bass line fill the space; however, a gap still remains between violins and 'cello. The violin parts often cross, especially in imitative passages; in their moments of homophony they frequently move in parallel thirds. In many of the slow movements, chain suspensions create exciting harmonies. The tessitura within which the violins move is limited, usually about two octaves. There is no evidence of virtuoso display. Several of the trios could be played entirely in first position; third

EXAMPLE 16.4 Hemiola cadence concluding movement 3 of Corelli's Sonata Op. 5, No. 3.

EXAMPLE 16.2 Example of the so-called Corelli clash.

EXAMPLE 16.3 This cadence from Corelli's Sonata Op. 5, No. 1, movement 2, with its cadenza and the cadential trill on supertonic over dominant seventh, is a direct precursor to the type of cadenza frequently used by Mozart. The + is the symbol used for a trill.

position is not exceeded. The writing for 'cello is idiomatic and easily playable in the lower positions, and the tessitura is kept below violin range.

Many of Corelli's *da chiesa* trio sonatas comprise four movements arranged in slow-fast-slow-fast order of tempo; in most of the trio sonatas all movements are in the same key. The *da chiesa* sonatas usually commence with a Grave or other dignified movement suitable for church. The second movement is fast and fugal, and the bass is an integral part of the imitation. Corelli's fugal and canonic themes are well conceived; J. S. Bach borrowed the subject and countersubject of Corelli's *Vivace*, Op. 3, No. 4, and used them note for note in an organ fugue (BWV 579). Corelli subjects his canonic themes to inversion, augmentation, diminution, and other contrapuntal devices. The *da camera* trio sonatas begin with a *Preludio*, followed by rather sedate dance-related movements, and conclude with a lively dance, such as a gigue or gavotte (see DWMA108).

CONCERTI GROSSI   The concerto grosso was still relatively new in Corelli's time, and the number and kind of instruments placed in the opposing ensembles varied. The instrumentation that Corelli used became standard. The concertino is a string trio, possibly with its own continuo keyboard instrument; thus, the idiom of the trio sonata is projected against an orchestral background of strings with keyboard. The *ripieno* group never plays alone but is used to reinforce the concertino, the more difficult parts are reserved for the soloists. Orchestral parts are easy; the viola enjoys a real part and is not merely filler. In each concerto, one slow movement is in a contrasting key. The most famous concerto grosso is No. 8, called the "Christmas Concerto" because of Corelli's notation on the *Pastorale,* which he included as an optional final (6th) movement: *Fatto per la Notte di Nativitata* (Written for Christmas Eve).

SOLO SONATAS   Each of Corelli's Op. 5 solo sonatas commences with a slow movement and concludes with a fast one. Each of the six *sonate da chiesa* in that volume has five movements; the first three *sonate da camera* have four movements, the next two sonatas have five. Eight of the sonatas are in major keys and have one slow movement in the relative minor. Some of the sonatas appear deceptively simple on the printed page.

They are technically demanding, however, and require command of both bowing and fingerboard techniques. *Moto perpetuo* movements, arpeggiations, rapid runs, double- and multiple-stops, and cadenzas appear in these pieces. Nothing is included merely for virtuoso display; every technical aspect is justified by the musical content of the movement as a whole. Many passages can be performed easily in second position; proper execution of others requires sequential shifting through three positions. There is no evidence that Corelli indicated any fingerings to be used; he did designate specific bowings. No dynamics are indicated—the flow and momentum of the music inspires the performer to apply them appropriately. Fortunately, copies of Mortier's and Walsh's editions containing the ornaments "composed by Corelli" are extant.

Many characteristics of Corelli's style can be seen in *Sonata da chiesa*, Op. 5, No. 1 (DWMA109). The sonata comprises five movements unlabeled except for tempo indications. The first movement, in D major, is essentially in binary form. It opens with a Grave introduction, followed by an interlude of arpeggiated chords that modulate to A major for another brief Adagio; these three sections are repeated at the dominant level, with an extension of the final Adagio to close the movement in D. All Grave and Adagio sections are to be embellished by the soloist. The Allegro second movement, in D major, is polyphonic. A vestige of trio sonata texture remains in the solo sonata in the fugal fast movements, for the violinist is required to handle polyphonic presentation of the imitative thematic material through double- and multiple-stopping. In the penultimate measure of this movement, Corelli notated a short cadenza that concludes with a trill on the supertonic over a dominant-seventh chord, then resolves to tonic (ex. 16.3). The third movement, an Allegro in D major, is a *moto perpetuo* of broken-chord figurations. The Adagio fourth movement is in B minor. As notated, the melody is lyrical and expressive; it becomes even more beautiful when properly embellished. The movement concludes with a hemiola Phrygian cadence that moves through F♯ minor in a descending tetrachord to end on a Picardian F♯ major chord (ex. 16.5). The final Allegro is fugal, with the violin presenting imitative polyphony through double-stopping. The thematic material is related to that of the second movement, as is the formal plan.

EXAMPLE 16.5 A Phrygian cadence with hemiola and a Picardian final chord concludes movement 4 of Corelli's Sonata Op. 5, No. 1.

One of the most difficult compositions in Op. 5 is Sonata No. 12, *La Folia* theme and 23 variations. In the late seventeenth century, the *folia* was a stately solo dance. In France it was called *Folies d'Espagne* (Spanish lunacy); in England it was known as *Farinelli's Ground*. Corelli used both melody and bass line of *La Folia* as theme and created variations with a triple role: variations of a melody, variations on a ground bass, and variations in bowing techniques.

CORELLI'S INFLUENCE   Corelli's published music was reprinted many times and was disseminated widely. Numerous "Christmas concertos" were modeled after his; the sinfonia for strings in Handel's *Messiah* is stylistically similar to the last movement of Corelli's "Christmas concerto." Corelli's solo violin sonatas, Op. 5, were his most popular compositions; by 1800, 45 editions of the volume had been printed. Many composers imitated his compositional style; several composers patterned works after the *ciaconne* of Op. 2 and the variations on *La Folia*. Tartini (see p. 345) used the *Gavotte* from solo sonata No. 10 as the theme of his *L'Arte dell' arco* (The Art of bowing), 50 variations for the study of bowing techniques.

As a conductor, Corelli was a stern disciplinarian, demanding that string players in an orchestral section use uniform bowings. He was the most influential violin teacher of his century. Many of his pupils became outstanding concert artists and teachers who transmitted his principles of violin playing to future generations. Among those pupils were G. B. Somis (1686–1763) and Francesco Geminiani (1687–1762). Geminiani, who worked principally in England, wrote numerous compositions and several treatises, including the very popular *The Art of Playing on the Violin* (1750), which was based on Corelli's teachings.

Henry Purcell. Portrait by John Closterman, 1695.
(Original in National Portrait Gallery, London)

ENGLAND

HENRY PURCELL   Purcell (1659–95) was one of England's greatest composers. As a boy, he was a chorister in the Chapel Royal. He is represented in Playford's *Catch that Catch Can* (1667) by the three-part song *Sweet tyranness*. In 1677 he succeeded Matthew Locke as composer-in-ordinary for violins and in 1679 succeeded John Blow as organist at Westminster Abbey. From 1682 to 1695 Purcell was one of three organists attached to the Chapel Royal; the others were John Blow and William Child. Purcell was active as composer at court, also. He died in November 1695; his funeral was held in Westminster Abbey, where he was interred.

Most of Purcell's surviving music dates from after 1679. He made important contributions in several areas: the opera *Dido and Aeneas* (1689); "incidental" music for plays (e.g., Dryden's *The Indian Queen* [1695] and *King Arthur* [1691]) to an extent that makes those plays semioperas; welcome songs and odes, the most significant being the *Ode for St. Cecilia's Day* (1692), an important forerunner of Handel's English oratorios; anthems, both verse and full, for service and for special occasions such as coronations; more than 100 secular songs, some of which were included in the collection *Orpheus Brittanicus;* keyboard works, including eight harpsichord suites, some dances, and a few organ voluntaries; and a considerable body of instrumental ensemble music. A Purcell autograph manuscript of harpsichord music discovered in London late in 1993 contains the Suite in A minor (Z663) with a previously unknown Jig, the Suite in C major (Z665/666) with a previously unknown Prelude, and 12 miscellaneous pieces, three of which were previously unknown.

Purcell's genius is especially apparent in his instrumental works. Available to him at court were recorders, oboes, trumpets, timpani, and strings. For *Dido and Aeneas* he used only strings; in *The Tempest* he added one oboe; for the other semioperas and plays he used all available resources. The ensemble "Sonata" played "while the Sun rises" in Act IV of *The Fairy Queen* is one of the earliest instrumental compositions to commence with a timpani solo. Purcell was a master of canon and ground bass. He handled winds effectively, writing obbligato lines for them in vocal solos and treating winds and strings antiphonally in ensemble music.

Purcell's independent ensemble music fits into two categories: works for viol consort, a medium virtually obsolete at that time, and sonatas for violins with basso continuo for bass viol and keyboard. The *Sonnata's of III Parts* (composed c. 1680, publ. 1683) are 12 trio sonatas. His fantasias for viols and several of his *Ten Sonata's in Four Parts* (publ. posth., 1697) were composed c. 1680. The chaconne in that publication is one of Purcell's finest instrumental compositions. Modality is present in the viol fantasias, but Purcell's knowledge of major-minor keys is evident. The two *In nomine* pieces (for viols) are traditionally English, with counterpoint enveloping the cantus firmus *Gloria tibi Trinitas* plainsong melody.

FRANCE

The French were slow to accept or write sonatas and concertos for stringed instruments. The first concertos written by a resident of France and published there were the four concerti grossi in Michele Mascitti's Op. 7 (1727). Mascitti (c. 1663–1760), an Italian-born violinist, settled in Paris in 1704 and became immensely popular. All his printed works are for strings. Issued in nine collections between 1704 and 1738, they comprise 100 solo sonatas (mainly *da camera*), 12 trio sonatas, and 4 concerti grossi. His works are patterned after Corelli's, but he adapted Corelli's style to suit French taste.

During the late seventeenth and early eighteenth centuries, when the violin and 'cello were becoming increasingly important, there flourished in Paris a school of bass viol (gamba) players and composers. At the center of that school was Marin Marais (1656–1728), who wrote more than 550 compositions for one, two, or three bass viols (gambas), with basso continuo. His *Pièces en trio pour les flûtes, violon, et dessus de viol* (Trios for flutes, violin, and treble viol; 1692) are considered the first trio sonatas published in France. Marais's works mark the full flowering of bass viol (i.e., gamba) music in France.

FRANÇOIS COUPERIN *LE GRAND*   François Couperin *le grand* (see p. 282) also composed *Pièces de violes* (Paris, 1728) for bass viol and basso continuo. Couperin may have written trio sonatas as early as 1692, but they were not printed until decades later. In France there was controversy concerning the merits of French and Italian musical styles. Couperin admired the music of both Corelli and Lully and attempted to remain neutral in the controversy by including in his music elements of both styles. *Les nations: sonades et suites de simphonies en trio* (The nations: sonatas and sets of instrumental trios; 1726) contains four works, each comprising a sonata *da chiesa* and a suite, for two violins with basso continuo. In each composition, Italy is represented by the sonata and France by the suite.

In other chamber music works, too, Couperin aimed to reconcile or to show the compatibility of French and Italian musical styles. In the preface to *Les goûts-réunis* (The styles reconciled; 1724) he expressed his high regard for the Italian sonata, his belief that his composition of Italianate music was not disrespectful to his French heritage or to Lully, and his neutral position in the controversy. *Les goûts-réunis* contains (1) *Le Parnasse, ou L'apothéose de Corelli, grande sonade en trio* (Parnassus, or The apotheosis of Corelli, large trio sonata), a *sonata da chiesa* for two violins and basso continuo, and (2) a series of eight *Nouveaux concerts* (New ensemble music), suites for unspecified instrumentation.

Reconciliation of French and Italian styles is represented programmatically in *L'apothéose composé à la mémoire immortelle de l'incomparable Monsieur de Lully* (Apotheosis composed for eternal memory of the incomparable M. de Lully; 1725): Lully and Corelli meet on Parnassus; their respective styles are juxtaposed. Then Apollo convinces them that musical perfection will result from the union of French and Italian styles, and they perform together, playing the two treble parts of a trio sonata.

JEAN-MARIE LECLAIR Jean-Marie Leclair (1697–1764), the founder and first great violinist of the French school, achieved a modification of Corelli's style that suited French taste. To effect this synthesis, he combined elements of Lullian dance and French harpsichord and bass viol pieces with Italian sonata style. Leclair was well grounded in the French style and was well acquainted with Corelli's style, for he had studied with Somis.

Leclair's earliest known works are 10 sonatas for violin and basso continuo in a manuscript anthology compiled c. 1721 that contains 69 violin sonatas by French and Italian composers. He composed several volumes of solo sonatas, at least one book of trio sonatas, and a dozen concerti grossi. His music is technically difficult, with double- and multiple-stops, difficult figurations, excursions into high positions, and double trills. He wrote some entire movements in multiple-stops, occasionally writing a chord so extended in range that the thumb had to be used on the G-string to stop the lowest note of the chord. Leclair used a slightly longer violin bow than did Corelli, and the bowing techniques specified in his compositions reflect this advantage. Leclair's melodies are constructed in relatively short phrases, with ornaments in moderation but completely written out. The harmonies are tonal with some surprising chromatic progressions and occasional enharmonic modulations.

GERMANIC LANDS

In Germanic territories the Thirty Years' War had a disastrous effect on all the arts. Courts and towns, impoverished by war, had little money for patronage and reduced the size of Hofkapelle, Kantorei, and Stadtpfeiferei; more and more, composers wrote for small ensembles. Music printing almost completely halted; few volumes of music were printed during the last half of the seventeenth-century, and most of those were issued in Nuremberg. It was expensive and time consuming to produce music manuscripts in multiple copies; therefore, most of the music that was composed was designed for local use rather than for general circulation.

SONATAS   The outstanding violinist-composers working in German and Austrian courts were Heinrich von Biber (1644–1704) and Johann Walther (c. 1650–1717). Biber, a native of Bohemia, was Kapellmeister at Salzburg in 1684–1704. His compositions include works for solo violin, instrumental ensemble, 3 operas (only 1 survives), at least 15 school dramas, and a good deal of sacred music.

The instrumental ensemble compositions consist of dance pieces and sonatas in four, five, six, or eight parts. Among the sonatas are works for solo trumpet with strings and basso continuo, for trumpets and timpani, for recorders with strings and basso continuo, and for strings with and without basso continuo. Biber was a formidable virtuoso on the violin. His sonatas for solo violin reflect his own capabilities. To play them, the violinist needed technical facility over the entire length of the violin fingerboard—seven positions at that time. The eight *Sonatae violino solo* (1681) contain polyphonic passages filled with multiple-stops and brilliant figuration above ostinato bass lines; some movements include passages requiring *scordatura*, which was used to achieve richer sonorities and special tone colors and to make obtainable multiple-stops not ordinarily possible on the violin (ex. 16.6).

All but two of Biber's so-called *Mystery* (or *Rosary*) *Sonatas* require *scordatura*, different for each sonata. The designation *Mystery* or *Rosary* derives from the fact that in one manuscript each of the first 15 sonatas

EXAMPLE 16.6 Some of the *scordatura* tunings specified by Biber for his *Mystery Sonatas*

is prefixed by a depiction of one of the 15 mysteries of the rosary. The sixteenth sonata, a polyphonic *Passacaglia* for unaccompanied violin, is the most important precursor of J. S. Bach's D-minor *Chaconne*.

SUITES, DANCE MUSIC   Early in the seventeenth century, English violists working in Europe familiarized continental musicians with ensemble dance music for four or five viols; Netherlands, Danish, and German composers began to write similar pieces for groups of wind or stringed instruments. Pieces of this kind appear in Hassler's *Lustgarten neuer teutscher Gesäng, Balletti, Gaillarden und Intraden* (Pleasure garden of new songs in German, *balletti*, galliards, and *intrade*; 1601) for four to eight parts, and in Scheidt's four-volume *Ludorum musicorum* (Musical pastimes; 1621–22), also for four to eight parts. Pavane and galliard were paired, with related thematic material; allemande, courante, and other pieces were individual dances. Customarily, German musicians performed a dance that was written in duple meter and then, by improvising, they transformed it to a second dance in triple meter, a *Tripla* or *Proporz*.

German composers expanded a suite by progressive variation, all dances being thematically related; such a group is known as a **variation suite.** Frequently, the dances in a variation suite were unified by a head motive. The variation suite reached a peak with Schein's *Banchetto musicale* (see p. 273).

Gradually, in the middle Baroque era, the paired pavane-galliard with which an ensemble suite usually began was replaced by paired allemande-courante. Johann Rosenmüller's (c. 1619–84) surviving instrumental works include a collection of dances for three instruments with basso continuo (1645) and two volumes of ensemble *sonate da camera* (1667; 1682). The 1682 collection displays Rosenmüller's assimilation of the Italian style of sonata composition, which he helped transmit to the north.

The French musical style and the standards of ensemble playing imposed by Lully were transmitted to Germany by Georg Muffat and others. The multilingual prefaces to Muffat's published works are especially significant, for in them he presented detailed information concerning Corelli's and Lully's performance practices, including bowing technique and proper ornamentation. *Florilegium primum* (1695) contains seven orchestral suites; *Florilegium secundum* (1698) contains eight. Muffat's suites commence with a French overture, and the five-part string texture reflects Lully's instrumentation.

Excellent orchestral suites are in J. K. F. Fischer's *Journal du Printemps* (Spring Journal; 1695) and J. S. Kusser's *Composition de musique suivant la méthode françoise* (Musical composition according to French style; 1682). Kusser seems to have been the first to add the French overture to the German orchestral suite.

SUMMARY

Throughout the seventeenth century, the composition of idiomatic instrumental music increased steadily; by 1700 it equaled vocal music in quality and quantity. Four principal types of instrumental music were written: dance music, quasi-improvisatory pieces, variations, and contrapuntal works of ricercar or canzona type. Stylized dance music evolved into the suite, in a basic format of allemande-courante-sarabande-gigue with additional movements optional. Fugue grew out of organ ricercar, and the ensemble canzona eventually was supplanted by *sonata da chiesa*.

The idiomatic style (*style brisé*) developed by French lutenists was transferred to harpsichord, along with systematized symbols for ornaments. French lutenists pioneered in composition of the *tombeau* (lament), related to the *déplorations* of medieval and Renaissance poets and composers.

Three principal types of organ music were written: quasi-improvisatory pieces (usually named toccata), fugue, and chorale-based compositions. The latter category includes chorale fugue, chorale fantasia, chorale partita, and chorale prelude. Among important composers of organ works were Frescobaldi, Pasquini, and Buxtehude.

Types of clavier music include quasi-improvisational pieces, fugues, variations, suites, and, after c. 1690, sonatas. The two most important types were suite and theme and variations. Significant contributions to the development of clavier music were made by Kuhnau in Germany and Chambonnières, Elisabeth Jacquet, and François Couperin in France. Couperin's *L'art de toucher le clavecin* is an important source of information concerning performance practices. In Iberia, important organist-composers were Coelho,

Correa, Cabanilles, and Seixas. Spanish missionaries considered music an important part of religious teaching, and choirmasters and organists in Spanish-American colonies were trained in Europe.

The principal types of compositions for instrumental ensembles were sonata (*sonata da chiesa*) and related forms, suite (*sonata da camera*) and related forms, and concerto. Most of the sonatas composed during the last third of the seventeenth century were trio sonatas. Some sonatas were written for solo instrument with basso continuo; a few sonatas were written for unaccompanied solo violin.

The word *concerto* was commonly used in Italy during the first half of the seventeenth century to denote vocal music accompanied by instrumental ensemble. Around 1675, composers began to write instrumental ensemble concertos—concerto grosso.

Northern Italy led in the production and performance of instrumental chamber music, with Venice, Modena, and Bologna being sites of the main development of the sonata. At Bologna instrumental music flourished. Torelli contributed greatly to the development of concerto grosso and to the repertoire for trumpet and strings. Corelli wrote almost exclusively for bowed stringed instruments. He seems to have been the first composer to write exclusively in major-minor key tonalities. He made systematic use of melodic and harmonic sequences and was equally skilled in writing polyphony and homophony; his linear counterpoint is harmonically based. Corelli was the most influential violin teacher of the era; his pupils carried his didactic principles throughout Europe. Public regard for violin playing was raised to the extent that, in the eighteenth century, violins supplanted viols.

Purcell, one of the greatest English composers of all time, composed opera, music for plays, occasional songs and odes, anthems, and instrumental pieces.

The French were slow to write sonatas and concertos. Couperin, in addition to composing for keyboard, contributed to the repertoire of chamber music for strings. Leclair is considered the founder and first outstanding violinist of the French violin school. The French musical style and the standards imposed by Lully were transmitted to Germany by Georg Muffat and others. Orchestral suites by German composers were important forerunners of similar works by Telemann and Bach. Biber's *Passacaglia* for unaccompanied violin is an important precursor of Bach's *Chaconne*.

Great strides were made in the advancement of instrumental music during the seventeenth century. Even greater accomplishments were made by master composers in the first half of the eighteenth century.

PREEMINENT COMPOSERS OF THE EARLY EIGHTEENTH CENTURY

17

Several musical styles are apparent in the first half of the eighteenth century. The Baroque, with all grandeur, reached its height. In France the light-textured *style galant* (or *rococo*) came into vogue and passed through two stages; in northern Germany *empfindsamer Stil* (expressive style) flourished. After 1730, Preclassic elements predicted the trend music would take in the last half of the century. (These styles are discussed in Chapter 18.) Some composers worked entirely within one style, others incorporated two or more styles in their compositions. Composers were concerned with the music of their own time and wrote music that met the needs of their employers. Music was practical—didactic works were written for a composer's current pupils, not for future generations; theoretical treatises and performance manuals were written to explain current practices to contemporaries. Preservation of the historical past did not enter into consideration. All of these facts are visible in the lives and works of five preeminent composers: Antonio Vivaldi, Georg Philipp Telemann, Jean-Philippe Rameau, Johann Sebastian Bach, and George Frideric Handel.

ANTONIO VIVALDI

Vivaldi (1678–1741) was born in Venice. He had music lessons, but he was educated for the priesthood and was ordained early in 1703. However, asthma, angina pectoris, or a combination of those diseases rendered him incapable of officiating at services. Instead, he worked as *maestro di violino* at Pio Ospedale della Pietà, one of four charitable institutions in Venice whose main purpose was to care for the sick or to supervise the education of indigent, illegitimate, or orphaned children. *Ospedali* provided for hundreds of girls, and music was an important part of the curriculum. By 1700 each *ospedale* employed a full-time *maestro di cappella* and two or more specialists to teach various instruments. Each *ospedale* had its own choir and orchestra and gave concerts regularly and frequently in their chapels. An ensemble of approximately 40 girls—selected from all four *ospedali*—performed on special occasions. The instrumentation varied depending on the talent available. New music was programmed for each concert, much of it written by *ospedali* music teachers and other Venetian composers. The performances attracted large crowds and prompted donations to the institutions.

Vivaldi was associated with the Pietà until 1740 but was away from the *ospedale* intermittently for various reasons: poor economic conditions affecting the institution's budget or travels to perform or to arrange for opera productions in other cities. However, during his lifetime no other violin *maestro* was ever appointed at the Pietà.

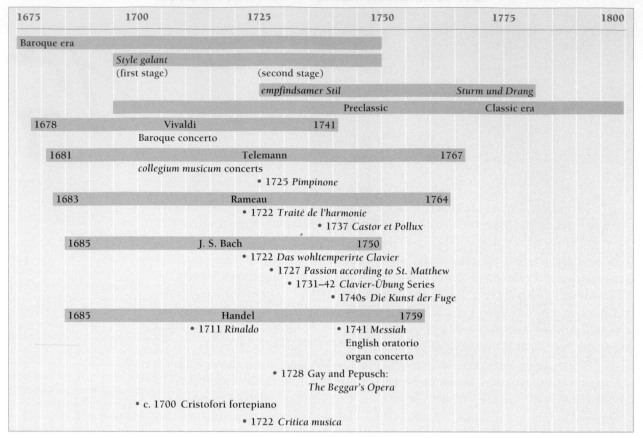

By 1704 Vivaldi was composing. When a dozen compositions of the same genre had accumulated, they were published. His Op. 1, comprising 12 trio sonatas, was printed in 1705; a set of 12 sonatas for violin with basso continuo was issued as Op. 2 in 1709. Twelve concertos—four each for one, two, and four solo violins with string orchestra—form his *L'estro armonico,* Op. 3 (Harmonic whim), published in 1711 by Étienne Roger of Amsterdam, one of the finest music publishers of the time. *La stravaganza,* Op. 4 (Eccentricity), 12 concertos featuring solo violin, appeared in 1714. Concertos poured from his pen—he composed hundreds of them, and they constitute the vast majority of his works.

After 1710 Vivaldi pursued a career as opera composer and impresario. Though he wrote at least 49 operas, only 21 are extant, and some of those are incomplete. He considered himself primarily an opera composer, but his contemporaries regarded him as a violinist.

After his death, he was virtually forgotten for several decades. Not until c. 1905 were Vivaldi's significant contributions to the development of the concerto recognized. In the 1920s many of his autograph scores—presumably, his personal collection—were located. Since then, one of his Glorias and some of his concertos, especially *The Seasons,* have been performed frequently.

VIVALDI'S MUSIC

In addition to operas, Vivaldi's vocal music includes motets, psalm settings, Magnificats, Vespers, Masses, Mass movements, oratorios, cantatas, and serenatas. Most of the cantatas are for soprano or alto soloist with basso continuo and consist of recitatives and arias in regular alternation.

Vivaldi's surviving instrumental compositions include approximately 90 sonatas (trio and solo), 16 sinfonias, and more than 500 concertos with diverse solo

Antonio Vivaldi. **Engraving by La Cave.** *(The Bettmann Archive)*

instrumentation. About 350 of the concertos are for one solo instrument with string orchestra and basso continuo; approximately two-thirds of those 350 are for solo violin. More than 40 concertos are for two soloists, usually two identical instruments, and most often two violins. Unusual combinations, such as viola d'amore and lute, indicate the variety of talent possessed by the young women at the Pietà. About 30 concertos require more than two soloists; 60 are orchestral concertos (no individual soloists); and in 20 concertos the individual soloists combine to form the ensemble playing the *tutti* parts.

Vivaldi gave many of his concertos special titles alluding to the person for whom the piece was written, the soloist, the overall mood of the composition, an unusual technical feature of the work, or the program depicted. For example, 7 of the 12 concertos in *Il cimento dell'armonia e dell'inventione,* Op. 8 (The contest between harmony and invention; publ. c. 1725), are programmatic: Nos. 1–4, individually entitled *La primavera* (Spring), *L'estate* (Summer), *L'autunno* (Autumn), *L'inverno* (Winter)—collectively called *La stagione* (The seasons); No. 5, *La tempesta di mare* (Storm at sea); No. 6, *Il piacere* (Pleasure); and No. 10, *La caccia* (The hunt).

Vivaldi's most important contributions were made to the concerto. He strengthened and expanded the elements of Baroque concerto style and formal structure used by Torelli, but Vivaldi's themes are more concise and his rhythms more driving than those of Torelli. Moreover, Vivaldi transferred to his concertos the techniques he employed in writing opera arias: opposing soloist and ensemble, balancing tension with release, and concluding a movement with a synthesis of the musical ideas presented.

Most of Vivaldi's concertos have three movements, in fast-slow-fast order of tempo, with the middle movement usually in a contrasting key closely related to that of the two Allegros. Though all movements are not of the same length and character, they are of equal importance. The final Allegro is usually shorter and more animated than the first; the slow movement is lyrical, expressive, and sometimes passionate, and for it the orchestral instrumentation is reduced. In the two outer movements, orchestral *ritornelli* in the tonic key begin and conclude the movement, and ritornelli in other keys alternate with solo episodes. Though the soloist clearly dominates the ensemble and the composition, it is apparent that the orchestral and soloist music were conceived as a unit, for the orchestra does not merely accompany. The ritornelli are highly organized and function as consolidating and stabilizing factors between the passages of idiomatic, brilliant figuration by which the soloist advances the musical plan. The concerto's opening measures precisely indicate the tonality of the work, for example, by spelling out the tonic triad or arpeggiating the tonic chord, by iterating the key note vigorously several times, or by a scale (ex. 17.1; DWMA110).

Though Vivaldi frequently borrowed from himself, reworking themes and entire movements and reusing them, his musical style is not static or stereotyped; he was aware of contemporary trends and kept pace with the changing times in which he lived. His instrumental music is primarily homophonic, with counterpoint used incidentally. His early solo and trio sonatas display Corellian traits; his sinfonias, orchestral concertos, and some solo concertos composed after c. 1726 exhibit characteristic features of Preclassic style (e.g., balanced phrases, homophonic texture, triplet sixteenths, melodic sighs, and carefully placed ornaments). Some movements of the concertos in *La cetra,* Op. 9 (The

(a)

(b)

(c)

EXAMPLE 17.1 The opening measures of Vivaldi's concerti emphasize the tonic key: (*a*) Op. XI, No. 2, mm. 1–2; (*b*) Op. III, No. 6; (*c*) Op. III, No. 5.

Lyre; 1727), are in Preclassic style (e.g., No. 2, mvt. 2 [DWMA110]).

Vivaldi's concertos and sinfonias were models for other composers. The overall plan of the Baroque concerto and the concept of solo-tutti contrast developed by Vivaldi were transmitted to later eighteenth-century composers and still survive in concertos and other forms of instrumental music.

GEORG PHILIPP TELEMANN

In the early and middle eighteenth century, Telemann (1681–1767) was considered the leading German composer. He was extremely prolific—more than 4,000 of his compositions are extant—and wrote French, Italian, and German music in Baroque, Rococo, and Preclassic styles. Besides adding considerable music to most categories of the repertoire, he made significant contributions in the areas of music theory, music education, and concert organization.

Telemann was the youngest of two sons in an upper-middle-class Magdeburg family. None of his ancestors were musicians. Most of the men, including his father (d. 1685) and brother, were clergymen. At the Magdeburg Gymnasium and Domschule, Georg received no special training in instrumental music, but by the age of 10 he had learned to play several instruments. He studied the pieces written by the school's Kantor and tried to compose. When, at age 12, he attempted to compose an opera, his mother forbade any further involvement with music and sent him to school at Zellerfeld. There,

Georg Philipp Telemann. Artist is unknown.

in addition to academic studies, he learned of the association between music and mathematics. He taught himself more about composition and wrote some pieces that the local *Stadtpfeiferei* performed. In 1697, Telemann went to Hildesheim to study at the Gymnasium. He wrote incidental music for several school dramas and, with other Protestant students, performed cantatas in the Catholic Church. On visits to Hanover and Grunswich he first encountered French and Italian instrumental music and Italian opera. He studied the compositional styles of Corelli and Steffani and tried to write similarly.

In 1701 Telemann entered Leipzig University to study law. (The university law curriculum provided the best education available; many persons not intending to practice law followed that course of study.) Although he concealed his compositional endeavors, his roommate discovered one of the pieces and arranged for its performance at Thomaskirche. That performance was the turning point in Telemann's life. The mayor of Leipzig commissioned Telemann to compose a cantata every two weeks for Thomaskirche. From then on, music was Telemann's lifework. During his student days at Leipzig, Telemann met Handel, who had already attracted attention in the musical world. They became good friends, frequently exchanged ideas about music, and shared an interest in rare plants.

In Leipzig, Telemann quickly became involved in many musical activities. In 1702 he founded a **collegium musicum,** a group of students who met to perform all kinds of music, much of it newly composed. He arranged for the collegium to give public concerts regularly and programmed sacred and secular music indiscriminately. That year, he became music director of the Leipzig Opera. He composed several operas for performance there and employed student musicians as well as professionals. From time to time over the next 20 years, Telemann wrote operas for performance at Leipzig.

Telemann was appointed organist at Neukirche in 1704. He served also as church music director, without additional salary, and arranged for his collegium to present sacred music concerts at the church regularly. Johann Kuhnau (1660–1722), Leipzig city music director and Kantor at Thomaskirche, became indignant at Telemann's involvement in so many activities, primarily because Telemann was encroaching on Kuhnau's "territory" and achieved results that Kuhnau considered impossible without additional city funds. Students whom Kuhnau thought should be singing at Thomaskirche were performing at Neukirche, in collegium, and at the Opera. The city fathers heeded Kuhnau's complaints—they forbade Telemann to work at the Opera.

In 1705 Telemann was appointed court Kapellmeister at Sorau (now in Poland). There, he and Erdmann Neumeister (1671–1756), the court chaplain, became friends. Neumeister made a significant contribution to music history through his religious poetry. Between 1650 and 1750 there was conflict within the Lutheran church between Orthodoxy and Pietism. Whereas Orthodox believers advocated strict adherence to dogma and the established ritual of the Lutheran Mass with its formal music sung by a trained choir, Pietists sought a less formal, more personal relationship with God and Christ and favored private devotions of laypersons and worship services that included music with more personal lyrics and congregational singing. Neumeister published a number of polemic writings against Pietism

but was not a strict adherent of Orthodoxy. Some of his poetic texts have the less formal, personal element that Pietists sought. Between 1695 and 1742, Neumeister wrote nine cycles of cantata texts, each cycle containing texts for all Sundays of the church year and extra texts for special feasts. The cycles were of three types: biblical verses and poetic aria texts, and an occasional chorale, to be set to music for soloists and chorus; madrigalesque poetry, suitable for musical setting as recitative and aria, in the manner of Italian secular solo cantata; and a combination of the foregoing two types, which became the standard cantata in the eighteenth century. Telemann set two of the cycles for the Eisenach court, and J. S. Bach used portions of Neumeister's cycles in several of his works.

Telemann was appointed Kapellmeister at the Eisenach court in 1708, where he composed chamber music, overtures, and concertos for the orchestra. There he met J. S. Bach, and another lasting friendship began. In 1709 Telemann married Louise Eberlin of Sorau. She died two years later, shortly after the birth of their daughter.

In 1712 Telemann became Frankfurt city music director and Kapellmeister at Barfüsskirche. For the church he composed at least five cycles of cantatas for the liturgical year, and for the city he wrote whatever music was needed. Though he had no teaching assignment, he trained the schoolboys for choir singing. He directed the collegium musicum and organized weekly public concerts. Telemann acquired citizenship in Frankfurt in 1714 through marriage to Maria Textor.

On Neumeister's recommendation, in 1721 the city of Hamburg invited Telemann to be Kantor of the Johanneum and music director for five churches. There the demand for new music was immense: two cantatas for each Sunday, a passion annually, and additional music for church and civic ceremonies and special events. Yet, he found time to participate in opera, direct the collegium, and present public concerts. The most famous collegia musica in Germany were at Leipzig (founded by Telemann) and Hamburg (founded in 1660 by Matthias Weckman). Telemann established public concerts in Hamburg; after 1722, both aristocracy and middle-class citizens attended them.

When the city council objected to Telemann's unassigned activities with public concerts and opera and forbade his participation in theatrical and operatic performances, he retaliated by applying for the position of Kantor at Leipzig's Thomaskirche. Six men applied for that position; one was J. S. Bach. Telemann received the appointment, but the Hamburg council refused to release him. Instead, they raised his salary and ceased objecting to his involvement with public concerts and opera. In 1722–38 Telemann was music director of the Hamburg Opera. He composed light opera as well as *opera seria*. Perhaps his greatest operatic success was *Der geduldige Socrates* (The patient Socrates; 1721). Telemann's comic opera *Pimpinone* (1725) was first performed as an intermezzo; it antedated Pergolesi's *La serva padrona* by about eight years. Both *Socrates* and *Pimpinone* contain elements of *opera buffa* style, such as **patter** (rapid singing of many syllables on one note) and ensembles.

Telemann began publishing his works while he was in Frankfurt. He wanted to get printed music into the hands of middle- and lower-class citizens and wanted that music suitable for home use, as many sizable families had their own instrumental and/or vocal ensembles. He made simplified arrangements of some of his works and indicated alternate or optional instrumentation for others. Parts and instrumentation designated *obbligato* are required; *ad libitum* parts and instrumentation are optional.

Between 1725 and 1740 Telemann published at least 44 items, including (1) an untitled cycle of 72 cantatas for the church year; (2) *Harmonischer Gottes-Dienst* (1725–26), a cycle of 72 sacred cantatas for general use; (3) *Musique de table* (Dinner music; 1733), three sets of chamber music compositions for various instruments (DWMA111); (4) *Fantaisies pour le Clavecin: 3 Douzaines* (36 harpsichord fantasies; 1733), the first and third dozens Italianate, the second dozen in French Preclassic style; and (5) *Singe-, Spiel-, und Generalbassübungen* (Vocal, instrumental, and thoroughbass studies; 1733), which includes, among other music, a collection of 48 strophic secular songs for home use.

The earliest music periodicals appeared in the third decade of the eighteenth century in Germany. They were of two kinds: critical journals such as Johann Mattheson's (1681–1764) *Critica musica,* the first music journal (1722); and periodicals containing music, such as *Der getreue Musikmeister* (The faithful music master). The latter seems to have been the first music periodical to be issued regularly, once every two weeks. It contained both vocal and instrumental music; some of Telemann's sonatas appeared first in that periodical.

After 1740 Telemann's creative activity decreased considerably. He continued to compose Passions and oratorios; perhaps his attraction to oratorio resulted from his correspondence with Handel. Some of the music in Haydn's *Die Jahreszeiten* (The Seasons) resembles portions of Telemann's oratorio *Die Tageszeiten* (The Times of Day; 1734).

TELEMANN'S MUSIC

From Telemann's voluminous compositional output, works in the following categories survive: (1) sacred cantatas (5 published cycles, each containing 72 cantatas; at least 1,100 individual cantatas); (2) festal church music for funerals, inaugurations, special thanksgiving, and other ceremonial events; (3) Masses, oratorios, Passions and Passion oratorios, psalm settings, and motets; (4) occasional vocal music for weddings, academic, political, or civic military ceremonies; (5) operas—7 complete operas and portions of a dozen others; (6) secular cantatas (56 complete) and serenades; (7) Lieder; (8) a lute suite; (9) keyboard pieces (mostly harpsichord), including suites, fantasies, chorale preludes, fugues and fughettas; and (10) instrumental solo and ensemble works, including concertos, sonatas, overtures, sinfonias, divertimentos, and various other chamber music. He wrote much more music that has been lost. Also, he edited and published some music and treatises by others.

Telemann's oratorios are transitional between the Baroque and Classic eras. His operatic experience infiltrated his sacred music to the extent that he used musical imagery to express the text and its meaning. Much of his music displays Preclassic elements. The songs in *Singe-, Spiel-, und Generalbassübungen* conform to Telemann's belief that a melody should be comfortable to sing and that a strophic poem should be set to a single stanza of music that is suitable for every poetic strophe and yet adequately conveys the meaning of each individual verse. The songs have no extremes of register or virtuosic ornamentation.

Much of Telemann's instrumental music is not technically demanding. Some pieces are written in Baroque counterpoint; in others he combined Preclassic and Baroque characteristics. For many of his keyboard and chamber music pieces he favored *galant,* using uncomplicated melodies cast in clear, periodic phrases, with accompaniment subordinate to melody. Some of his quartets (none of which use classic string quartet instrumentation) are conversational in style, and some of his harpsichord fantasies exhibit incipient sonata form.

TELEMANN'S INFLUENCE

In the eighteenth century, a patron or employer controlled the amount and kind of music a composer produced, and an employee's sphere of activity was defined by the nature of his position. Telemann refused to be bound by such limitations. He disregarded and ultimately broke down barriers between sacred and secular. He violated the conventions of his time by writing operas and being involved with the theater when he held the post of Kantor, by including sacred and secular music on the same concert program, and by promoting and directing public concerts that were not associated with any institution. He was influential in bringing all kinds of music to the people, by encouraging student musicians to perform in collegia musica and opera as well as in church, by establishing public concerts at which a variety of sacred and secular selections were performed, and by publishing editions of music suitable for performance by amateurs. He ensured reasonably correct performance of some of his music by including instructional material in the publication.

Telemann's music was forgotten for many decades, and other persons were credited with contributions that he made to the development of music. Not until the twentieth century was his true stature realized.

JEAN-PHILIPPE RAMEAU

Rameau (1683–1764) was the most important French musician in the eighteenth century. He received his early musical training from his father, who was organist at St. Étienne Church in Dijon. Rameau's parents intended that his career be in law; not until he was

Jean-Philippe Rameau. Portrait by A. J. Aved. *(Original painting in Musée des Beaux-Arts, Dijon)*

18 did they agree, reluctantly, that music should be his profession.

Rameau visited Italy in 1701. In January 1702 he was temporary organist at Avignon Cathedral, and in May he became organist at Clermont Cathedral in Auvergne. He resigned in 1706 and went to Paris, where he served as organist to the Jesuits and Mercredians and published *Premier livre de pièces de clavecin* (First book of harpsichord pieces; 1706). When his father became ill in 1709, Rameau returned to Dijon and assumed his father's duties at the cathedral. In 1713–15 he worked as organist to the Jacobins in Lyons, then returned to Clermont Cathedral, where he remained until c. 1722. Then he moved to Paris. He seems to have had no regular employment during the next nine years.

At Lyons and Clermont, Rameau composed some psalm settings and secular cantatas and wrote *Traité de l'harmonie reduite à ses principes naturels* (Treatise on harmony reduced to its natural principles; Paris, 1722) and *Nouveau système de musique théorique* (New system of music theory; 1726). These publications made Rameau famous as a theorist. However, he wanted to write opera. For several years, his endeavors to interest a librettist were unsuccessful. Meantime, some secular cantatas and two more books of his harpsichord pieces were published: *Pièces de clavecin avec une méthode sur le mécanique des doigts* (Harpsichord pieces, with a fingering method; 1724) and *Nouvelles suites de pièces de clavecin* (New sets of harpsichord pieces; c. 1728).

In 1726 Rameau married Marie-Louise Mangot, a talented singer. He earned a living by teaching harpsichord lessons and by composing incidental music for musical comedies performed in the popular Fair Theaters. In 1732 he became organist at Ste. Croix-de-la-Bretonnerie, and from 1736 to 1738 he held a similar position at the Jesuit Novitiate Church.

At some time before 1731, Rameau was introduced to Alexandre-Jean-Joseph Le Riche de la Pouplinière (1693–1762), a wealthy patron of the arts. For 22 years (1731–53) La Pouplinière employed Rameau as organist, clavecinist, orchestra conductor (conducting from the keyboard), composer-in-residence, and clavecin teacher to Mme Pouplinière. At La Pouplinière's, Rameau met poet-playwright Abbé Simon-Joseph Pellegrin (1663–1745) and realized his ambition to write operas. Pellegrin provided the libretto for *Hippolyte et Aricie* (Hippolytus and Aricia). Rameau's *tragédie lyrique* was performed in 1733, first at La Pouplinière's, then at L'Opéra. Pellegrin was 70; Rameau was 50.

Performance of *Hippolyte et Aricie* at L'Opéra touched off one of the pamphlet wars for which the French are noted. Supporters of Rameau (*Ramistes*) praised his accomplishment; others (*Lullistes*) deemed his writing too Italianate and declared him a traitor to Lully and the French opera tradition. In the preface to his opera-ballet *Les Indes galantes* (The gallant Indies; 1735), Rameau expressed his admiration for Lully and his loyalty to traditional French opera, but the Lullistes were not placated. Disputes arose after each successful performance of an opera by Rameau.

Les Indes galantes comprises a prologue and four self-contained *entrées* (acts), each entitled and set in a different remote locale: *Le Turc généreux* (The generous Turk), on an island in the Indian Ocean; *Les Incas du Pérou* (The Incas of Peru); *Les fleurs* (Flowers), a Persian festival; and *Les sauvages* (The savages), in an American forest.

Many persons consider the opera *Castor et Pollux* (Castor and Pollux; 1737) Rameau's masterpiece. In 1739 the opera *Dardanus* and the opera-ballet *Les fêtes d'Hébé* (Festivals of Hebe) appeared. Two *comédie-ballets, La Princesse de Navarre* (The Princess of Navarre) and *Platée,* were composed in 1745 for the nuptial festivities for the Dauphin and Infanta Maria Teresia of Spain. Rameau wrote almost two dozen more stage works, many of them commissioned for special occasions. The most important of those works is the *tragédie en musique Zoroastre* (1749).

In 1753 Rameau ceased working for La Pouplinière. He composed, conducted scientific investigations into music theory, and wrote about his findings. From time to time, he became involved in polemics. He was drawn into the dispute over the respective merits of French and Italian music, the *Querelle des bouffons* (see p. 352), and he engaged in heated arguments with Rousseau and d'Alembert over erroneous statements made in *Encyclopédie* articles about music. In May 1764 Rameau was ennobled. He died in Paris less than two weeks before his eighty-first birthday.

RAMEAU'S MUSIC

Rameau's extant music includes 4 books of clavecin solos, 1 clavecin solo published separately, 1 volume of chamber music, 4 nonliturgical motets or psalm settings, 6 secular cantatas, and about 30 stage works. The cantatas and motets are the least important.

STAGE WORKS   *Hippolyte et Aricie* and other operas by Rameau correspond with the general plan followed by Lully and Quinault. Each act includes a long *divertissement* of singing and dancing. The drama is advanced mainly by recitative, usually accompanied and quite melodic; Rameau's recitatives are more melodic than those of Lully. Often, there is no distinct stylistic contrast between recitative and aria. Rameau used three basic forms for his arias: binary (AB), ternary (ABA, or da capo), and rondeau (more than one repetition after contrast, as in ABACA or longer). Choruses and action dances are closely associated with the drama and sometimes contribute to the action (e.g., the chorus of demons guarding Hell in Act III of *Castor et Pollux*).

Rameau's music shows his understanding of the characters in his operas and the situations in which they are involved. The tomb scene of *Castor et Pollux* is an excellent combination of intense grief and ritual. A contrasting mood—blissful tranquility—is depicted when Castor, having been redeemed through the sacrificial act of his twin, views the Elysian fields and sings *Séjour de l'éternelle paix* (Abode of eternal peace; DWMA112).

The overtures to Rameau's early operas follow the basic French overture form used by Lully, but the fast sections are less contrapuntal than those of Lully. Many of Rameau's overtures (e.g., that of *Hippolyte et Aricie*) contain thematic material that is heard later in the operas. Overtures to later operas are more varied; some are programmatic, such as that of *Zoroastre;* some are tripartite like an Italian overture.

KEYBOARD MUSIC No organ music by Rameau has been located. His extant keyboard music comprises 53 clavecin solos and a volume of chamber music—*Pièces de clavecin en concerts*—that contains five suites for harpsichord, violin or flute, and viol or another violin. All the solos except his harpsichord transcriptions of five concerted pieces and *La Dauphine* were composed before he began writing opera. He extemporized *La Dauphine* at royal wedding festivities in 1747.

The imitative linear counterpoint or lutelike arpeggiated harmonies in a few of the keyboard pieces are reminiscent of the late Renaissance or very early Baroque. Some pieces are clearly Baroque; others exhibit features of Preclassic style (e.g., triplet sixteenths and melodic sighs). *L'Enharmonique,* with its numerous chromatic alterations, thirty-second notes, some quintuplets, and frequent abrupt changes of expression, seems to anticipate Rococo or *Sturm und Drang* (storm and stress) pieces by C. P. E. Bach (DWMA113). At times, it seems that Rameau wanted more than the harpsichord was capable of giving—he wrote arpeggiations covering the entire compass of the keyboard and long tied notes that the instrument could not sustain.

Prefatory material in Rameau's books provides notated examples designating precisely how the embellishment symbols he used are to be interpreted and, in Book II, instructions and exercises for fingering that specify use of the thumbs—though standard practice today, this fingering was relatively new in Rameau's time. Hand crossing is designated; long roulades in sixty-fourth notes and rapid arpeggiations spanning more than three octaves require hand-over-hand technique, as in *Les trois mains* (Three hands; ex. 17.2).

EXAMPLE 17.2 Rameau: *Les trois mains,* mm. 40–44, presents a 16th-note arpeggiation over four octaves, followed by 64th-note *roulade* and cadence. *(Source: Pièces de clavecin, revised edition, 1731)*

The ten compositions in Rameau's *First book of clavecin pieces* might be considered a suite, though he did not call them that. Two are in A major, the remainder in A minor. The *Prelude* commences with a lutelike quasi-improvisatory section, written without bar lines. The other nine pieces are in binary form.

Book II contains 21 genre pieces and stylized dances; Book III contains two suites of intermingled dance and genre pieces. Rameau orchestrated at least 13 of his clavecin solos and incorporated them in his stage works (e.g., *Tambourin* from Book II, used in *Les fêtes d'Hébé.* Rameau's clavecin pieces reveal his mastery of the instrument; collectively, they present a panorama of past styles, contemporary practices, and future developments in harpsichord music.

TREATISES

Rameau applied in his compositions the principles set forth in his theoretical treatises. He regarded music as a science and sought to establish that its universal harmonic principles derive from natural causes. His most important and most influential treatise was *Traité de l'harmonie.* The principles he formulated clarified the compositional practices of his own time, served as a springboard for investigations by succeeding generations of theorists, and have been basic to and influential in the understanding of harmony for two centuries.

Rameau believed that harmony is the foundation of all music; melody is derived from harmony. He began by investigating the physical nature of a fundamental sound, then considered harmonic generation, harmonic inversion, and the fundamental bass. These are his conclusions:

1. A vibrating body generates a fundamental tone whose component parts (partials) form what is

called the overtone series. The first, second, and fourth partials produce the primary consonances—octave, perfect fifth, and major third; when combined, they form the perfect chord. The octave is considered a replica of the fundamental sound; therefore, the major triad derives from the overtone series. (The third partial produces the perfect fourth, which was discounted because it is the inversion of the fifth and forms an octave with the octave.) Rameau experienced difficulty when he tried to explain the derivation of the minor triad through natural principles; he did establish the melodic minor scale, however.

2. The chord is the most important element in music. Chords are built of thirds, and a triad may be expanded by the addition of one or more thirds, provided two major thirds are not stacked successively; in this manner chords of the seventh and ninth are created.

3. The identity of a chord is determined by its root; inversion does not change the chord's identity but merely weakens the chord. In a series of harmonies, the important factor is the root-progression of the chords (the *fundamental bass*), not the notated bass notes.

4. The primary chords, in order of importance, are the tonic, dominant, and subdominant; other chords are related to and are secondary to these. This is the concept of functional harmony.

5. Modulation may be effected by a change in function of a chord—the principle of modulation by pivot-chord. (Essentially, Rameau was applying to harmony and key tonality the pivot-pitch principle used by Guido in mutation from one hexachord to another; see p. 60.)

Rameau sought to explain the derivation of the diatonic scale by proceeding upward through a series of fifths (c–g–d′–a′, etc.) and reducing the pitches to close proximity; however, the fourth scale degree was missing. A satisfactory explanation for the derivation of that pitch eluded him for some time. Ultimately, he explained it through the triple geometric progression 1:3:9, placing the tonic in the center and flanking it by fifths (F:c:g). This accounts for his naming the fourth the **sub**dominant—the fifth below the tonic.

JOHANN SEBASTIAN BACH

The ancestry of J. S. Bach (1685–1750) can be traced to Veit Bach (d. 1577), baker and cittern player in Thuringia. Most of Veit's descendants possessed some musical talent, which they used in positions under municipal government and/or church patronage. The Bachs were proud of their musical heritage. Children received musical training from parents or other relatives; when a son was born, it was presumed that his vocation would be music. Most of the Bachs were instrumentalists, usually keyboard players, and some made instruments; a few wrote music. J. S. Bach copied 20 of their compositions into an *Alt-Bachisches Archiv* (Bach Ancestral Record) that he maintained. In the last quarter of the seventeenth century, several Bachs held important positions in Thuringia. Johann Ambrosius (1645–95) was court trumpeter and town music director at Eisenach; his twin brother, Johann Christoph (1645–93), was a court violinist and town musician at Erfurt. Their cousin Johann Christoph (1642–1703) was organist at the Eisenach court chapel; his brother Johann Michael (1648–94) was an instrument maker and composer.

Johann Sebastian Bach, born at Eisenach on 21 March 1685, was the youngest of the eight children of Johann Ambrosius Bach and Maria E. Lämmerhirt (1644–94). At the local Latin School Sebastian received a general humanistic-theological education that included singing; his father taught him to play violin. When his mother died, his father remarried. After Ambrosius died, Sebastian's stepmother was financially unable to maintain the household, so Sebastian and his brother Jacob went to live with their brother Johann Christoph (1671–1721), organist at Ohrdruf. At the Lyceum, Sebastian received a broad, enlightened education that included religion and singing; Christoph gave him keyboard lessons and probably trained him to assist with organ repairs.

Sebastian moved to Lüneburg in April 1700. There he studied at St. Michael's School and sang treble in the *Mettenchor* (Matins choir) until his voice changed. On 4 March 1703 he obtained a position as orchestral violinist at the Weimar court of Duke Johann Ernst. Bach's stay there was short. In June he was invited to examine and play the new organ at Neukirche, in Arnstadt. As a result of that performance, he was appointed organist there in August. His duties at Neukirche were light; he had ample time for organ playing, and his primary interest was performing. He requested four weeks' leave to visit Lübeck to hear Buxtehude perform but stayed away almost four months and thereby jeopardized his job. While at Arnstadt, Bach began to compose organ music, and he accepted some organ pupils. For the remainder of his life he attracted pupils.

At Easter 1707, Bach successfully auditioned for the post of organist at Mühlhausen; the first version of his *Cantata No. 4, Christ lag in Todes Banden* (Christ lay in bonds of death), was probably performed as part of that hearing. His duties for the city and St. Blasius Church began in July. In October he married Maria Barbara Bach, a distant cousin.

Bach resigned at Mühlhausen in July 1708 to become court organist for Duke Wilhelm at Weimar; there, Bach wrote many of his organ pieces. In March 1714 he was named Konzertmeister, also. During those Weimar years he became acquainted with Telemann, who worked in Eisenach, and a lasting friendship developed. Six of Bach's children were born at Weimar, including Wilhelm Friedemann and Carl Philipp Emanuel; Telemann was Emanuel's godfather.

J. S. Bach was appointed Kapellmeister at the Cöthen court of Prince Leopold in August 1717. Frequently, Bach was sent to other cities to examine and/or purchase keyboard instruments. In 1719, he was near Halle and tried in vain to contact Handel, who was visiting there. Bach made several attempts to contact Handel, but they never met; perhaps the difference in their musical interests was a factor.

It was customary for the prince to take musicians with him when he traveled; on several occasions Bach accompanied him to the Carlsbad spa. On returning from such a trip in July 1720, Bach learned that Maria Barbara had died and that her funeral had already been held. After Maria's death, he considered taking a church organist position. Yet, when offered the position at Jakobikirche, Hamburg, he declined. In 1721 he became acquainted with courtsinger Anna Magdalena Wilcke (1701–60); they married on 3 December. She was a competent musician and made many of the fair copies of Bach's works.

Johann Sebastian Bach. Painted by Elias Gottlieb Haussmann in 1746. *(Original in Town Hall, Leipzig)*

At Cöthen Bach had no church responsibilities. Most of the pieces he composed there are for clavier or are instrumental chamber music. Among the latter are the *6 Suites a Violoncello Solo senza Basso* (6 Suites for unaccompanied violoncello; c. 1720); six violin and harpsichord sonatas (1717–23); and *Sei Solo à violino senza Basso accompagnato* (Six solos for unaccompanied violin; 1720). Also, he completed the "Brandenburg" Concertos (1711–21). Several didactic volumes were produced: *Clavier-Büchlein vor Wilhelm Friedemann Bach* (Little book of keyboard pieces for Wilhelm Friedemann Bach; 1720; see p. 316), some of *Das wohltemperirte Clavier* (The well-tempered clavier; 1722), and much of the first *Clavier-Büchlein für Anna Magdalena Bach,* which contains the first five French suites and other pieces.

In 1722 there was a vacancy at Leipzig, and Bach was among the six who applied. Though the position was prestigious and employment by the city of Leipzig offered greater economic security for his family and educational advantages for his sons, Bach considered it a social step down from his court post. Telemann was the committee's first choice, but he declined the offer; Graupner, too, rejected the invitation. The Leipzig officials then hired Bach, though they deemed his talents mediocre.

In mid-1723 Bach moved to Leipzig and was employed there as Kantor at Thomasschule and Music Director of Leipzig—not as organist—for the rest of his life. He was responsible for the music at Leipzig's four principal churches, for the musical training of Thomasschule pupils, and for supplying whatever music the town council required. The Thomasschule pupils formed the four church choirs; choirboys, university students, and professional town musicians performed together at civic ceremonies. Thomasschule was a boarding school for boys, and pupils there ranged in age from 12 to 23. Medical data indicate that in the seventeenth and eighteenth centuries puberty occurred later than it does in the twentieth century. Some of Bach's older pupils at Thomasschule had soprano and alto voices of solo quality and several years of practical experience. For any performance Bach had at his disposal at least 16 singers and an equal number of instrumentalists. On special occasions or for performance of a Passion, 40 singers could be assembled. Kuhnau had introduced the performance of Passions in Leipzig in 1721; Bach continued the practice but alternated the annual Passion presentation between Thomaskirche and Nicolaikirche.

Bach personally directed at St. Thomas and St. Nicholas on alternate Sundays; he assigned to others the duties at St. Peter and St. Matthew. As Introits, sixteenth-century Latin motets were sung, accompanied only by harpsichord, and the congregation sang well-known hymns, but new organ music (e.g., chorale preludes) was needed. In the Lutheran service, the cantata served a liturgical function. On Sundays and feast days, a cantata was performed between the Gospel reading and the homily; if the cantata was in two parts, the first part was sung after the Gospel reading and the remainder after the homily. Bach was required to provide a cantata for each Sunday and each church feast, Passion music for Good Friday, and Magnificats for Vespers for three feasts. For Leipzig he planned five complete cycles of cantatas for the church year (i.e., about 60 cantatas annually). Two cycles were completed; composition of the third was interrupted, and

only portions of the others have survived. The *Passion according to St. Matthew* was probably composed in conjunction with the fourth cycle of cantatas and was performed as early as 1727, then revised for use in 1729 and 1736.

Bach received extra compensation for music for weddings and funerals. He taught music lessons, gave concerts in other towns, and examined and tested new and rebuilt organs. In 1725 he began a second *Büchlein* for Anna Magdalena, and in 1726 he published some keyboard music. Six *Partitas* BWV 825–30 (BWV = *Bach-Werke-Verzeichnis*, Bach Works Catalog) were first printed singly (1726–31); later, they were assembled as *Clavier-Übung* (Keyboard-practice), Volume I. (The catalog of J. S. Bach's works was prepared by Wolfgang Schmieder c. 1950. Sometimes S, for Schmieder, is used instead of BWV.)

Bach became director of the Leipzig collegium musicum in April 1729. Perhaps he assumed the additional responsibility because he needed extra money to support his expanding family—beginning in 1723, a child was added to the family annually. Or he may have wanted opportunities to compose and perform more secular music. Possibly, this extracurricular activity served as release from tensions caused by controversies with the headmaster at Thomasschule. Under Bach's direction, the collegium presented concerts regularly on Wednesdays. After 1733, the collegium performed some secular cantatas by Bach that in style and dramatic character approximate opera. In fact, he called this kind of cantata *dramma per musica*.

In 1733 Bach composed the Kyrie and Gloria of the *Mass in B minor* and sent them to the Elector of Saxony at Dresden with an application for the title of court composer. However, Bach was not accorded that title until 1736.

Bach continued to publish his music. In 1735–39 Volumes II and III of *Clavier-Übung* were prepared and printed, and between 1738 and c. 1742 he compiled the 24 preludes and fugues that constitute the book now known as *Das wohltemperirte Clavier*, Volume II. In 1741 he went to Berlin to visit Carl Philipp Emanuel, harpsichordist to King Frederick the Great of Prussia (r. 1740–86), and traveled to Dresden to visit Count von Keyserlingk. Bach's "Goldberg Variations" were a result of that visit (see p. 316).

EXAMPLE 17.3 King Frederick the Great's theme, used by Bach for the pieces in *Musikalisches Opfer*.

In August 1742 Bach composed the "Peasant" Cantata. Its style reveals that Bach was aware of Preclassic developments and could incorporate elements of that style in his music.

Between 1742 and 1745 Bach composed the *Symbolum Niceum* (Credo) and c. 1748 assembled the *Mass in B minor*. Around 1745 he revised some of the organ chorales written at Weimar, then prepared the six organ transcriptions of cantata movements that Schübler published c. 1749—the "Schübler" Chorales.

In 1747 the king invited Bach to visit the royal court. Frederick, a flautist, was seriously interested in music and asked Bach's opinion of the Silbermann fortepianos at court. Bach pointed out their faults and later supplied Silbermann with suggestions for improving the instrument. Frederick provided a theme and requested Bach to extemporize canons and fugues on it (ex. 17.3). Bach obliged but thought he had not done his best. When he returned to Leipzig, he composed *Musikalisches Opfer* (Musical Offering)—two ricercars, a trio sonata, and ten canons, all based on the king's theme—and sent them to the king, with this Latin acrostic: **R**egis **I**ussu **C**antio **E**t **C**anonica **A**rte **R**esoluta (At the king's command, the melody and additions were worked out in canonic style). In deference to the king, Bach included flute in the instrumentation.

In the mid-1740s Bach wrote a compendium of fugal composition—*Die Kunst der Fuge* (The Art of Fugue), In his last years he began revising it and preparing it for publication. He died before the revision was completed, and one of his sons, presumably Emanuel, published the incomplete revision in 1751. The organ chorale *Vor deinen Thron* (Before Thy throne; BWV 668) was included to complete the publication.

In June 1747 Bach joined the Correspondirende Societät der Musikalischen Wissenschaften (Society of Musical Sciences). As a scientific work, he submitted to the society canonic variations on *Vom Himmel hoch* (From heaven on high; BWV 769) and a six-voice triplex canon—three simultaneous two-voice canons—(BWV 1076). This is the music Bach is holding in the portraits painted by Elias G. Haussman in 1746 and 1748 (see p. 309). Shortly before 1745, Bach began experiencing eye problems. He had cataracts, and, in 1750, when he was almost totally blind, he underwent surgery. Complications ensued; he never regained his eyesight, and his physique was weakened. On 28 July 1750 he suffered a stroke and died a few hours later. His body was interred in St. John's cemetery.

Bach's modest estate, consisting principally of his manuscripts and numerous harpsichords and string instruments, was divided among his widow and surviving children. Wilhelm Friedemann received most of the manuscripts and sold them to individual purchasers. Anna Magdalena gave the cycle of chorale cantatas to Thomasschule. Most of C. P. E. Bach's share was ultimately acquired by Preussische Staatsbibliothek. These holdings, which constitute the most important collection of Bach's surviving works, were divided in time of war so that a single disaster could not destroy all of them. Very few of the items owned by Johann Christian have survived; the location of material received by the other children is unknown. From time to time, compositions have been located; in 1984, 38 organ chorales were found in manuscripts at Yale University.

INFLUENCES

Many factors influenced Bach's career: a working knowledge of Renaissance and Baroque contrapuntal techniques; an awareness of the techniques, styles, and forms used by his contemporaries and assimilation of the best of their stylistic characteristics into his work; a thorough understanding of voices and instruments and of virtuosity; craftsmanship, perseverance, and planning, coupled with family pride, talent, and personal genius; the patronage system, by means of which an employer dictated, controlled, and stimulated an individual's artistic production; and a religious conviction that the primary purpose of his life and his work was to glorify God. Bach was well-educated in theology and interpreted the biblical and liturgical texts he set to music from a theologian's viewpoint. His religious conviction is expressed overtly in dedications and by inscriptions such as the letters J. J. (*Jesu, juva,* Jesus, help) and S. D. G. (*soli Deo gloria,* To God alone be glory) that appear at the beginning and end of his cantatas or the letters I. N. J. (*in nomine Jesu,* in Jesus's name) above the first piece of music in Wilhelm Friedemann's *Clavier-Büchlein.*

BACH'S MUSIC

Bach wrote effectively in almost all genres used during the late Baroque era. Though he composed no operas per se, the secular cantatas designated *dramma per musica* and the *Passion according to St. Matthew* demonstrate his ability to write expressive dramatic music in operatic style. He wrote few single compositions; he planned cycles or sets, volumes, and series of volumes methodically. When he composed, he followed rhetorical principles, as did many of his German contemporaries. Invention—finding the musical idea, melody, or theme—was the first step; next came outlining and planning the composition and then elaborating on the idea and notating the finished product. For example, to a chorale melody he added the bass, then the middle parts; when writing a fugue, he invented the subject, sketched out the entries, planned the harmonies, then wrote the piece. When Bach transcribed, adapted, or arranged works of others, he improved on the original. Unlike Telemann, who wrote music for dissemination to the general public, Bach composed for the capabilities of performers he knew. Symbolism pervades Bach's music. In addition to the Baroque *Figurenlehre* used to denote the affections, he included alphabetical and other types of numerology and chiasma—the symbological relationship between the Greek letter *chi* (χ), Christ, and the cross.

VOCAL MUSIC

Cantatas Most of Bach's secular cantatas and more than one-third of his sacred ones have been lost. The sacred cantatas are of various types. Bach used texts from the Lutheran Bible and from chorales and combined biblical and chorale texts and wrote some himself. A chorale might be used as final movement of a cantata; to open and conclude a cantata; at the beginning, middle, and ending; or alternately with another text. Bach's earliest extant cantatas date from Mühlhausen and are mainly settings of biblical or chorale texts. (The cantata numbers are the BWV numbers of the works; i.e., Cantata No. 4 is BWV 4.)

Cantata No. 4, *Christ lag in Todes Banden* (comp. c. 1707; rev. 1724), is based on seven stanzas of Luther's Easter hymn, published with the chorale tune in 1524. Using Luther's terminology, Bach called the stanza-movements of his cantata *Versus.* The cantata opens with a 14-measure Sinfonia that Bach may have designed as his alphabetical numerological signature: BACH = 2 + 1 + 3 + 8 = 14. (Other symbolism present in Bach's setting is too detailed for analysis here.) The complete Lutheran chorale melody in its original tonality forms the cantus firmus, recognizable in each Versus; the seven Versus, treated as chorale variations, are arranged symmetrically (fig. 17.1). The central movement, *Es war ein wunderlicher Krieg* (It was a wonderful battle), is a chorale motet.

Cantata No. 80, *Ein' feste Burg ist unser Gott* (A mighty fortress is our God), was composed in 1715 and revised c. 1724 for performance at Leipzig on the Feast of the Reformation. The cantata commences by presenting the first stanza of the chorale as a chorale fantasia for all performing forces (DWMA114). The voices, doubled by stringed instruments, present each phrase of text fugally. In Bach's original scoring, two oboes (as *dux*) and violone with organ (as *comes*) present the chorale melody as cantus firmus in canon at the distance of one measure. These were the two outer parts, written on the top and bottom staves of the score. Was Bach thus symbolizing the all-encompassing nature of God

FIGURE 17.1 Diagram of the symmetrical structural plan of Cantata No. 4.

Sinfonia	Versus						
	I	II	III	IV	V	VI	VII
	Chorus	Duet	Solo	Quartet	Solo	Duet	Chorus
	SATB	SA	T	SATB	B	ST	SATB

as mighty fortress? After Sebastian died, someone, presumably Wilhelm Friedemann Bach, added timpani and three trumpets to the instrumentation. However, Bach's enclosure of the entire performing ensemble within the chorale melody was not disturbed, for the first trumpet, in *clarino* register, doubles the oboe an octave higher.

The second stanza of Luther's chorale is presented as a soprano-bass duet in D major; their accompaniment is structured as a trio sonata. Bach used nonchorale poetic texts in movements 3 and 4. The third movement, for solo bass with continuo, is a pathos-filled recitative supported by unstable chromatic harmonies, followed by an arioso in F♯ minor; the fourth is an aria in B minor for solo soprano with continuo. In the fifth movement (D major) the chorale melody returns, sung in unison by the choir, with a flowing yet energetic orchestral accompaniment. Nonchorale poetic texts are inserted for movements 6 and 7, which are, respectively, a recitative (B minor) and arioso (D major) for solo tenor with continuo and a duet for tenor and alto with accompaniment in trio-sonata texture. The cantata concludes with the fourth stanza of the chorale (D major) in simple four-part harmony suitable for performance by all present in the sanctuary; instruments double vocal lines in the appropriate registers.

In Leipzig, secular cantatas were performed on various special occasions and at Thomasschule, the university, collegium musicum concerts, or private homes of persons being honored. Plots of secular cantatas were usually rather simple, with mythological, allegorical, or pastoral characters. The best-known of Bach's secular cantatas are the *Kaffee Kantata* (Coffee Cantata; BWV 211; perf. c. 1734) and the "Peasant" Cantata (BWV 212; perf. August 1742).

Motets Because Bach wrote motets for special occasions only, there is no reason to believe that he composed more than the six that survive. The occasion for his creation of *Lobet den Herrn alle Heiden* (Praise the Lord, all nations; Ps. 117) is not known; *Singet dem Herrn ein neues Lied* (Sing unto the Lord a new song) was written for the birthday of Friedrich August, King of Poland and Elector of Saxony; the other four motets were first sung at funeral or memorial services.

Jesu, meine Freude (Jesus, my joy; 1723) comprises 11 movements symmetrically arranged (fig. 17.2). The music is based on Johann Crüger's chorale tune, *Jesu, meine Freude* (1653); for text, Bach used six chorale verses and Romans 8:1–10. Motet verses 1 and 11 are musically identical, setting hymn stanzas 1 and 6 to four-part (SATB) harmonization of the chorale melody. The second movement (SSATB) is in binary form with the text (Rom. 8:1) set twice, the first presentation commencing in E minor and cadencing in B minor, the second progressing from B minor to tonic E minor. In each presentation, the last half of the Bible verse is treated fugally. Bach frequently concealed fugues within the musical fabric. All five voices are singing when the tenor introduces the subject, which is gradually woven into the counterpoint at two-measure intervals as it is assumed by each of the other voices. Bach set the text expressively, with appropriate word painting; for example, sinning by "walking according to the flesh" (*nach dem Fleische wandeln*) is depicted by the melodic descent of a diminished fifth and a long melisma (mm. 37–44).

Movement 3 sets the second hymn stanza as a five-voice chorale. In movement 4 (SSA trio or semichorus), the meaning of the biblical text (Rom. 8:2) is musically depicted by the divergent counterpoint of the alto part. The movement ends on an open octave, b–b′. The fifth movement is a chorale variation in which the music at times soars, rages, and is serenely

FIGURE 17.2 Diagram of the symmetrical structural plan of the motet *Jesu, meine Freude*.

sustained, as the text dictates. Movement 6 is a five-voice choral fugue in G major, concluded by an Adagio in B minor. The hymn text returns in the seventh movement (E minor; SATB), with the unadorned chorale melody in soprano. Movement 8 is an alto-tenor-bass trio (or semichorus) setting of Romans 8:10, in C major, characterized by extensive melismas on the words *Geist* (Spirit), *Leben* (life), and *Gerechtigkeit* (righteousness). The movement concludes with a Phrygian cadence on an E-major chord as a dominant preparation for the A-minor tonality of the next section. In movement 9 (SSAT), a chorale variation, altos sing the chorale melody in four-measure phrases widely separated by rests. The other contrapuntal lines form an independent musical entity that effectively sets the text. Musically, movement 10 is a condensation of movement 2.

Oratorios, Passions In 1734–35 Bach wrote three multimovement works that he called oratorios. All are parodies of earlier cantatas supplemented by new material. In their use of Gospel texts, they form a link with the Lutheran *historia* and Passion. For *Oratorium tempore Nativitatis Christi* (Christmas Oratorio; BWV 248) Bach borrowed from four cantatas. From reworked and new material he formed six cantatas, with differing instrumentation and voicing; they were performed individually on 25, 26, and 27 December 1734 and 1, 2, and 6 January 1735. *Kommt, eilet und laufet* became the Easter Oratorio (BWV 249); Cantata No. 11, *Lobet Gott in seinen Reichen* (Praise God in His Kingdom), is the Ascension Oratorio.

Bach composed five Passions. Two have survived complete: the *Passion according to St. Matthew* (BWV 244) and the *Passion according to St. John* (BWV 245). The text and portions of an early version of the *Passion according to St. Mark* (BWV 247) are extant. Two of the Passions are lost. Bach's Passions contain several four-part harmonizations of chorale melodies. The melody of the chorale *O Haupt voll Blut und Wunden,* which appears five times in the *St. Matthew Passion,* was originally a Lied (see p. 195).

The *Passion according to St. Matthew* is for double chorus, soloists, double (duplicate instrumentation) orchestra, and two organs. The Gospel text, from Matthew 26 and 27, is narrated by tenor (as Evangelist) in solo recitatives and by chorus. Often the chorus has dialogue and thus participates in the action. Interspersed with the narration are chorales, arias, and some recitatives (actually, ariosos). The words of the added recitatives and arias are by Picander (C. F. Henrici; 1700–64), who supplied texts for many of Bach's cantatas. This Passion is a massive work—its performance takes approximately four hours. Bach divided it so that in the service half of it could be performed before the homily and the remainder after it. Part I opens and closes with great chorale fantasias. The alto solo that commences Part II is taken up by chorus; the Passion concludes with a chorale-based movement whose words of mourning balance those of the opening chorale fantasia.

The *St. Matthew Passion* music is expressive, dramatic, and closely akin to opera in many instances, for example, Nos. 69–70, the alto recitative (actually an arioso) *Ach, Golgotha!* (Oh, Golgotha!), and aria *Sehet, sehet, Jesus hat die Händ* (See, see, Jesus' hands [outstretched]). The last presentation of the Passion Chorale is followed by the Evangelist's recitative relating, with descriptive accompaniment, the rending of the Temple veil. The ensuing passage, *Wahrlich, dieser ist Gottes Sohn* (Truly, this is the Son of God), is one of the most effective short choruses ever written (DWMA115; plate 19).

Other Vocal Music In the Lutheran church, Magnificats were sung at Vespers. Bach's Magnificat in D (BWV 243) is suitable for use at Vespers on any major feast day. In Bach's time, Latin *Missa brevis* (Kyrie and Gloria, with Lutheran additions) was used in some Leipzig churches, including Thomaskirche. Bach composed four *Missae breves;* all are for soloists, choir, and orchestra.

Bach's *Mass in B minor* has a liturgical text but is not suitable as a service, primarily because of its vastness. The Mass is a compilation Bach made c. 1747–49 of sections written at various times, some of them containing parodies of movements of other Bach works; performing resources vary considerably from movement to movement. The Credo is remarkable in many respects: its overall structural symmetry, the use of Gregorian chants as cantus firmi in the *Credo in unum Deum* and *Confiteor* sections, the symbolic central location of the

Crucifixus, the latter's ostinato bass, and the representation within this movement (as well as throughout the Mass) of various styles of composition.

Approximately 375 of Bach's chorales survive. His chorale collections were probably used in teaching students to realize figured bass. The only extant source of individual arias and songs by Bach is the *Notenbüchlein für Anna Magdalena Bach* (Little music-book for Anna Magdalena Bach; 1725).

KEYBOARD MUSIC   Bach composed keyboard works in an almost unbroken succession throughout his career. The earliest datable work is the *Capriccio in B♭* (BWV 992), composed c. 1703.

Bach wrote specifically for organ *or* clavier (harpsichord or clavichord). In most of his organ works

pedalboard is obligatory. The clavichord has only one manual; though its tone is small, it is a very sensitive instrument capable of producing some delicate shadings. The two-manual harpsichord, with octave strings and stops, can double sounds in three octaves, change tone quality, and produce broad contrasts; its sound carries farther than that of the clavichord. Clavichord music can be played on harpsichord, but the reverse is not possible. Bach did not write for the fortepiano, though he probably knew of its existence by 1722, when Mattheson wrote about it (Insight, "The Fortepiano").

Clavier-Übung Series   Bach published four volumes of keyboard music under the title *Clavier-Übung* (Keyboard-practice). The word *practice* in Bach's title does not denote that the volumes contain exercise or study

The Fortepiano

The fortepiano was invented by Bartolomeo Cristofori (1655–1731), keyboard instrument maker and custodian of musical instruments at the court of Ferdinand de' Medici, in Florence. Cristofori began making an *arpicembalo che fa il piano e il forte* (harpsichord that can play soft and loud) in 1698. By 1700 he had completed at least one of the new keyboard instruments whose strings were activated by hammer strokes instead of by plectra. Cristofori's early fortepianos were in wing-shaped outer cases patterned after Italian harpsichords. Three wing-shaped instruments had been built by 1709. Cristofori's basic principles of fortepiano construction were sufficient for the demands made on the instrument throughout the eighteenth century. Three instruments built by Cristofori in the 1720s survive; the one at the Metropolitan Museum of Art, New York City, has a range of four and a half octaves (fig. 17.3). Gottfried Silbermann learned

of Cristofori's fortepiano through an article in Mattheson's *Critica musica* and began his experimental fortepiano construction in the 1730s.

Early Silbermann fortepianos had action identical with that Cristofori used.

FIGURE 17.3 Fortepiano made by Cristofori in Italy c. 1720. The three legs are part of a separate stand on which the instrument is placed. *(Crosby Brown Collection of Musical Instruments, 1889. Metropolitan Museum of Art, New York City)*

material but should be interpreted in the sense of performance practice—the works illustrate various styles, forms, and performance practices of Bach's day.

Clavier-Übung I (1731) contains the six partitas (BWV 825–30) that Bach had published singly. Each partita has the four standard suite movements and one or more extra pieces known as *galanteries;* prelude, aria, menuet, gavotte, rondeau, *burlesca,* scherzo, and so on. These partitas are the finest representations of the mature Baroque suite.

In *Clavier-Übung* II (1735) Bach published *Concerto nach italiänische Gusto* (Italian Concerto; BWV 971) and *Ouvertüre nach französicher Art* (Overture in French style; BWV 831), a large partita for two-manual harpsichord. The Italian Concerto exemplifies the transcription to harpsichord of a concerto for solo instrument and orchestra; the solo is played on one manual, and the orchestral *tutti* is played on the other.

Clavier-Übung III (1739) contains organ works. The first piece in the volume is a Prelude in E♭; the last piece is a Fugue in E♭, a triple fugue, commonly referred to as the "St. Anne Fugue" because one of the three fugue subjects is derived from the St. Anne hymn tune (ex. 17.4a). The key of E♭, the three themes in the Prelude, and the three Fugue subjects (ex. 17.4b) symbolically represent the Trinity. Moreover, the Prelude and the Fugue each have three main sections. The Prelude and Fugue are usually performed together as though they were a single work. Placed between them in the volume are 21 chorale arrangements and 4 duets. Bach included three arrangements of the chorale *Allein Gott in der Höh' sei Ehr* (Only God in Heaven is Lord) and two arrangements of each of nine other chorale melodies, one arrangement designed for a two-manual organ with pedalboard, and a smaller-scale arrangement for manuals only. This is liturgical music; the central doctrines of the Lutheran Church are represented by the chorale themes.

Clavier-Übung IV (1742), *Aria mit verschiedenen Veraenderungen* (Aria with diverse variations), is one of the finest sets of variations ever written. Count Keyserlingk may have commissioned the work for his harpsichordist, J. T. Goldberg; from this comes the popular title "Goldberg Variations." The Aria is a sarabande, a symmetrical binary in G major in $\frac{3}{4}$ meter; both halves are to be repeated. The bass line of the Aria is the basis for 30 variations in various forms, meters, moods, and

EXAMPLE 17.4 (*a*) First phrase of hymn with "St. Anne" melody in soprano; (*b*) the subjects of Bach's triple fugue, BWV 552.

styles. Logically, to mark the beginning of the second half of the variation set, Bach wrote Variation 16 as a French overture. He composed a series of nine canons, from unison through ninth, arranged them in ascending intervallic order, and spaced them evenly throughout the work as Variations 3, 6, 9, 12, and so on. The thirtieth variation is labeled *quodlibet.* Bach included in it two German tunes that were popular in his day: *Ich bin so lang bei dir nicht g'west* (It's been so long since I've been at your house) and *Kraut und Rüben haben mich vertrieben* (Cabbage and turnips have driven me away). After Variation 30 appears the directive *Aria da capo e Fine* (Repeat the Aria). Thus, the variations are framed. The unified structure of the composition indicates that Bach intended it to be played in its entirety. Yet, he wrote sectional variations so that if the insomniac Count fell asleep while his harpsichordist was playing the piece, there was a convenient stopping place at the end of each variation.

Didactic Works The *Clavier-Büchlein* for Wilhelm Friedemann contains some instructional theoretical data, some music by other composers, Bach's 15 two-part *Inventions* (BWV 772–86), the 15 three-part *Fantasias* later published as *Sinfonias* (BWV 787–801), several of the pieces known as *Twelve Little Preludes,* and some of the preludes used in *Das wohltemperirte Clavier* (fig. 17.4).

FIGURE 17.4 This manuscript page from Bach's *Clavier-Büchlein vor Wilhelm Friedemann* holds part of an early version of the Prelude in C major published in *Das wohltemperirte Clavier.*

Das wohltemperirte Clavier (1722) contains 24 preludes and fugues, presented in ascending chromatic order of key tonality, commencing with C major. All pieces could be played on a single clavier with well-tempered tuning, but whether Bach meant **equal temperament**—the division of the octave into 12 equal semitones—is debatable. Several kinds of well-tempered tunings were in use at that time. The first person to openly advocate equal temperament seems to have been Rameau, in *Génération harmonique* in 1737. Bach modeled *Das wohltemperirte Clavier* after *Ariadne musica* (Musical Ariadne; 1715) by J. K. F. Fischer (c. 1670–1746). *Ariadne musica*, for organ, contains 20 miniature preludes and fugues in 19 major and minor keys and in Phrygian mode on E; the pieces are arranged in ascending order of key tonality, commencing with C major. Bach's preludes in *WTC* are actually *études*, for each is concerned with and concentrates on at least one technical problem in a musical context. The two- to five-voice fugues in Bach's volume summarize concisely the various aspects of monothematic fugal writing (DWMA116).

Between 1738 and c. 1742, Bach compiled another volume of 24 *Preludes and Fugues,* arranged in the same manner as *Das wohltemperirte Clavier.* The compilation is commonly referred to as *Das wohltemperirte Clavier,* Volume II, but Bach did not give it that title.

Bach planned the *Orgel-Büchlein* for instructional purposes. Its title page reads "Little Organ Book, wherein a beginning organist is given instruction in diverse ways of developing a chorale, and for improving pedal technique also, since in these chorales the pedal is considered essential." A couplet follows: "To honor the Most High God alone, To instruct my fellow-men." Bach had planned to write a series of 164 miniature chorale preludes for the entire liturgical year. Only 46 were completed (BWV 599–644). In them, the chorale melody is recognizable and is most often in the top voice. Some of the chorale preludes contain word painting and symbolism, for example, *Durch Adams fall ist ganz verderbt* (Through Adam's fall everything was spoiled; BWV 637; DWMA117).

Harpsichord Suites   In addition to the Partitas in *Clavier-Übung* I, Bach composed two sets of six suites each. These are commonly known as the *French Suites* (BWV 812–17) and the *English Suites* (BWV 806–11), though Bach did not so designate them. Nor do the titles describe the styles of the music—some dances in the *English Suites* are more French than English, and in the *French Suites* there are some Italian correntes. Each suite contains the standard stylized dances and additional short movements. Each *English Suite* commences with a prelude. In some suites, a movement is followed by a *double*. In the first *English Suite* two *doubles* follow Courante II; in performance, if the harpsichordist does not wish to add embellishments to that Courante, either *double* may be substituted. There are two Gavottes in *English Suite No. 3*; the second dance serves as Trio to the first, and a *da capo* is required to conclude the movement.

Other Keyboard Works   Among Bach's surviving clavier works there are numerous miscellaneous suite movements, preludes and fugues, fantasias, and toccatas. The most significant of these are the *Chromatic Fantasia and Fugue* in D minor (BWV 903) and the toccatas in F♯ minor (BWV 910) and C minor (BWV 911). Also, there survive 16 keyboard concertos that are transcriptions or arrangements of concertos by other composers.

Early in Bach's career, he seems to have concentrated on composing organ works—chorale preludes, chorale partitas (chorale variations), fantasias, toccatas, preludes, and fugues. In some of these compositions, pedal work figures prominently. The *Fantasia and Fugue in G minor* (BWV 542) combines quasi-improvisational sections with contrapuntal interludes. The *Passacaglia in C minor* (BWV 582) is prelude to a large double fugue; for one of the fugue subjects Bach used the first half of the passacaglia theme. Bach's fugue subjects vary considerably, from chorale types to Italianate figuration.

The chorale partitas are in four groups. The first two sets and a portion of the third were written c. 1700–7; the fourth set, canonic variations on the Christmas chorale *Vom Himmel hoch da komm' ich her,* was composed c. 1747. The "Schübler" Chorales (BWV 645–50) are organ transcriptions of cantata movements. Perhaps the best known is *Wachet auf* (BWV 645), from Cantata No. 140, movement 4.

Among Bach's last works are *Musikalisches Opfer* (BWV 1079) and *Die Kunst der Fugue* (BWV 1080). Bach did not specify instrumentation for *The Art of Fugue*. Presumably, he intended the work for keyboard but notated the music in open score so that the individuality of each voice would not be obscured. *The Art of Fugue* illustrates all kinds of fugal devices and various types of monothematic fugues from the simplest to the most complex. All the fugues are based on the same subject, though countersubjects vary. In the published version, the last *Contrapunctus* breaks off after Bach entered, as countersubject, the musical spelling of his name:

B A C H

The Art of Fugue may be considered the third compendium in Bach's series on the composition of monothematic fugues—a series begun in 1722 with *Das wohltemperirte Clavier.*

ORCHESTRAL WORKS   Much of the orchestral music Bach wrote at Cöthen and for the Leipzig collegium musicum has been lost. Among the surviving works are the "Brandenburg" Concertos (BWV 1046–1051). These concertos are significant because they use a variety of instrumental combinations rather than the stan-

dard Italian concerto grosso instrumentation. The third and sixth are orchestral concertos; the other four feature soloists.

There survive several concertos for solo harpsichord(s) with string orchestra. Most of these concertos are arrangements of violin or oboe concertos by Bach or other composers. Bach composed two concertos for solo violin and string orchestra, in E major (BWV 1042) and A minor (BWV 1041); a concerto in D minor (BWV 1043) for two violins with string orchestra; and a concerto for flute, violin, and harpsichord, with strings (BWV 1044).

The four *Ouvertures* (BWV 1066–69) are orchestral suites. The slow movement of the third *Ouverture* has been arranged for violin and keyboard as *Air for the G String*.

CHAMBER MUSIC   Ensemble chamber music by Bach includes six sonatas for violin and harpsichord (BWV 1014–19), three sonatas for viola da gamba and harpsichord (BWV 1027–29), and six sonatas for transverse flute and harpsichord (BWV 1030–35). Most of these are *sonata da chiesa* type. In several of them the harpsichord has the dual rule of melody instrument and continuo accompanist; thus, a trio sonata texture is projected.

Bach composed a *Partita* in A minor (BWV 1013; c. 1720) for unaccompanied flute, seven large works for lute, and two sets of works for solo violin and solo 'cello. The *Six Solos for unaccompanied violin* (BWV 1001–6; 1720) comprise three sonatas and three partitas, arranged so that every four-movement sonata is followed by a partita of five or more movements. The sonatas are constructed according to the formal pattern of the Italian *sonata da chiesa*; the partitas are sets of stylized dances. This set is a landmark in violin literature (see fig. 17.5).

The *Six Suites for unaccompanied violoncello* (BWV 1007–12; c. 1720) mark a high point in literature for that instrument. The Fifth Suite calls for *scordatura* tuning of the 'cello; the Sixth Suite was written for a five-string instrument.

The violins, violas, and violoncellos of Bach's day and those in use in the twentieth century differ structurally in several respects; surviving instruments of the violin family that were built before c. 1750—instruments by

Amati, Guarneri, Stradivari, and other luthiers—have been adapted for modern use. A few of the differences follow: at mid-eighteenth century, the violin fingerboard was about two-and-one-half inches shorter than it now is, the neck of the instrument was approximately one-half inch shorter and was not as flat as it now is, and the bridge was slightly shorter and was flatter (less arched), which may have facilitated the rendition of chords and polyphonic music. The violin and viola chinrest had not yet been invented. In performance, the instrument rested on the player's collarbone and was supported by the upper chest (fig. 17.6). The bow was shorter, with a higher arch; there was no uniform way of regulating tension of bow hair, and most violinists controlled that tension with the right thumb (fig. 17.7).

GEORGE FRIDERIC HANDEL

Handel was born in Halle on 23 February 1685. At an early age, he showed an interest in music, but his father denied him an instrument, partly because he wanted him to have a career in law. Somehow, Handel gained

FIGURE 17.6 Some of the alterations made in violin and bow construction during the last half of the eighteenth century are apparent when the instrument Leopold Mozart is playing in this portrait, printed in his treatise in 1756, is compared with the instrument pictured at the right, which was used by his grandchildren in the 1790s. *(Portrait from Leopold Mozart: Versuch einer gründlichen Violinschule; 1756)*

FIGURE 17.5 Bach's manuscript for unaccompanied violin Sonata No. 1, mvt. 1. *(Source: J. S. Bach autograph manuscript, 1720. University of Tübingen Library)*

FIGURE 17.7 Violin bows used by seventeenth- and eighteenth-century virtuosi who were master teachers are representative of the changes that were being made in bow construction. *(From H. Abele, The Violin and its Story, 1905)*

access to a clavier and practiced diligently. On a family visit to the court of Saxe-Weissenfels, he astonished everyone by playing the organ. At the Duke's urging, arrangements were made for George to study music with F. W. Zachow at Halle.

In February 1702 Handel entered the University of Halle, and in March he (though Lutheran) became organist at the Calvinist Domkirche. A year later, he moved to Hamburg, obtained a position as an orchestral violinist—later, as harpsichordist—at the Opera and taught private music lessons. Reinhard Keiser was opera director at that time. At Hamburg, Handel and Mattheson became friends; together, they visited Dietrich Buxtehude at Lübeck to investigate the possibility of one of them succeeding him as organist, but when they learned that marriage to Buxtehude's daughter was requisite for the position, they lost interest. (J. S. Bach also declined, for the same reason.)

While in Hamburg, Handel composed three operas. *Almira* and *Nero* were performed early in 1705. *Nero* is lost. The third opera was divided and produced at Hamburg in 1708 as *Der beglückte Florindo* (Happy Florindo) and *Die verwandelte Daphne* (Transformed Daphne). Probably, Handel wrote a number of his instrumental pieces at Hamburg and revised them later.

From autumn 1706 to February 1710 Handel was in Italy. (See figures 17.8a and 17.8b for comparison of Bach's and Handel's travels.) Handel visited Florence, Venice, and Naples and spent several months of each year in Rome, where Francesco Ruspoli employed him as a household musician. Handel received no regular salary but was expected to compose secular cantatas for performance at weekly concerts. In April 1708 his *Oratorio per la Resurrezione di Nostro Signor Gesù Christo* (Oratorio for the resurrection of our Lord Jesus Christ) was presented at Ruspoli's palace. Stylistically, the oratorio is operatic, and those performances were spectacular. The 45-piece orchestra was led by Corelli. At the first performance, soprano Margherita Durastanti sang the role of Maddalena. For the next performance Durastanti was replaced by a castrato because Pope Clement XI (r. 1700–21), who attended, objected

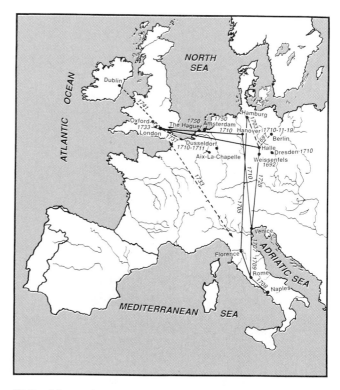

FIGURE 17.8 (*a*) All of Bach's journeys were made to cities in Germanic lands.

(*b*) Handel's travels were much more extensive than Bach's.

to women singing in opera. Papal decree forbade opera in Rome, but composers dodged the prohibition by writing cantatas and oratorios in operatic style.

Handel wrote other music while in Italy, including three large-scale Latin motets and the operas *Aci, Galatea e Polifemo* (Acis, Galatea, and Polyphemus; 1708) and *Agrippina* (1709).

Handel's visit to Italy was a shaping force in his career. His mobility permitted him to meet the leading composers, attend performances of their works, and observe their styles. He learned about the composition of opera, oratorio, chamber cantata, concerto, and solo and trio sonatas in the places those forms originated. From Alessandro Scarlatti, Handel learned to write long-breathed melodies in *bel canto* style. In performance, he demonstrated his organ-playing talent, and he proved his equality with Domenico Scarlatti at the harpsichord. At Ruspoli's, he made advantageous professional contacts; several persons who performed his works in Rome joined him in London later.

While in Italy, Handel received invitations to visit Hanover and England. In June 1710 he was appointed Kapellmeister to George, Elector of Hanover, but was granted a year's leave of absence to visit London. Handel stayed in London eight months; he was received

George Frideric Handel, Portrait in oils, made c. 1748 by Philippe Mercier. *(Archiv für Kunst und Geschichte, Berlin)*

at court, concertized, visited Queen's Theatre (the opera house), and composed *Rinaldo,* which was performed there in 1711. Then he returned to Hanover. In 1712 he obtained permission to visit London again. In 1713–16, he lived at Lord Burlington's home, where he became acquainted with the Arnes, Pepusch, and other English composers. Queen Anne commissioned him to compose works commemorating the Peace of Utrecht; he composed an Ode for the Queen's birthday; and his *Te Deum* and *Jubilate* were performed in St. Paul's Cathedral in 1713.

Queen Anne died in 1714, and the Elector of Hanover became George I, King of Great Britain (r. 1714–27). The story that Handel had incurred the Elector's disfavor by overstaying his London leave and that he placated George I through performance of the *Water Music* is probably untrue. However, Handel did compose special music—presumably, the *Water Music*—for performance on a barge during a royal procession on the Thames River 17 July 1717.

In 1716 Handel visited his relatives in Halle and may have gone to Hamburg. During that visit, he acquired Brockes's Passion oratorio poetry and set it later. Late in 1716 Handel returned to London and revised some of his operas for performance that season. At the end of June 1718 the opera house closed permanently. That summer James Brydges, who became Duke of Chandos, employed Handel as resident composer. For Chandos, Handel composed 11 anthems, a *Te Deum* in B♭, and two masques in English: *Acis and Galatea* and *Esther.*

In 1719–28 Handel was a salaried employee of the Royal Academy of Music, a promotional organization formed for the purpose of firmly establishing Italian opera in London. Some of his finest *opere serie* were written and performed in 1723–25: *Giulio Cesare in Egitto* (Julius Caesar in Egypt), *Tamerlano,* and *Rodelinda.* *Admeto* (1727), in which Handel had to balance the roles played by rival singers Faustina Bordoni and Francesca Cuzzoni, was a success in spite of the fact that the singers' rivalry incited obnoxious comments from opposing factions in the audience.

A number of factors contributed to the collapse of the Royal Academy—temperamental singers, rivalry among composers, public factions supporting opposite sides of the internal squabbles, plus the fact that Londoners were weary of an art form in a foreign language most of them did not understand. Pepusch and Gay were aware of the language problem and wrote in English *The Beggar's Opera*, a ballad opera in which sections of spoken dialogue alternate with songs set to the tunes of popular ballads (see p. 353). *The Beggar's Opera* was performed 29 January 1728 at Lincoln Fields and was repeated 61 times. Its success cut into Handel's profits, but his popularity did not suffer.

In 1721, Handel was appointed composer to the Chapel Royal. Special events required new music, such as the four anthems performed in Westminster Abbey at the coronation of George II (r. 1727–60). One or more of those anthems has been performed at every subsequent British coronation. Early in 1727 Handel became a naturalized British citizen.

In 1729, Handel and Johann Heidegger (1666–1749), an impresario, leased King's Theatre for five years and planned a subscription series of operas to be produced there. The venture had little success at first. In 1732, the children of the Chapel Royal performed Handel's oratorio *Esther* (a revision of the masque) at the Crown and Anchor Tavern; the choruses were sung by the Westminster choirs. That was the first performance of oratorio in London. Costumed singers (most of them boys) acted the drama; the choirs were placed between the stage and the orchestra "after the manner of the Ancients." A problem arose when Princess Anne requested Handel to transfer the performances to King's Theatre—the Bishop of London forbade stage presentation of a sacred subject in the opera house. But Handel revised and enlarged the score, and *Esther* was performed "in the manner of the Coronation Service," without action, and with books in the choirboys' hands.

Then began serious rivalry with the Opera of the Nobility, a company headed by the Arnes, who included in their production series pirated performances of Handel's works. Handel retaliated in various ways—with revisions, enlargements, pasticcios, macaronic English-Italian texts, dances, and ballet—but drew small audiences.

In April 1735 Handel produced several oratorios. Gradually, oratorio performances were moved closer to the Lenten season, and by 1745 it had become standard practice in England to perform oratorios during Lent. In 1735, when seeking something new to attract large audiences to his productions, Handel decided to perform organ concertos between acts of his oratorios. To meet his need, Handel created the concerto for organ and orchestra. He composed (and partially improvised) at least four organ concertos that spring; they became a regular feature of the oratorio season. Handel's virtuosity at the organ should not be compared with that of J. S. Bach, for the instruments they used and composed for differed considerably. At that time, organs equipped with pedals were rare in England.

Handel continued to compose operas until January 1741, though his own company and that of his rivals closed in June 1737. He lost money but was never bankrupt. His last operatic success was *Alcina* (1735); even the excellent operas *Serse* (Xerxes; 1738) and *Deidamia* (1741) met with public indifference.

On 13 April 1737 Handel suffered a stroke that caused slight mental impairment and temporarily paralyzed his right arm so that playing and conducting were impossible. Within six months he recovered sufficiently to continue his musical activities, but for the next four years his health was somewhat impaired. In 1738 he wrote *Saul*; in 1739 he composed *Exodus* (renamed *Israel in Egypt*), set Dryden's *Ode for St. Cecilia's Day*, and wrote the 12 *Grand Concertos* for strings.

Throughout his life, Handel assisted charitable organizations. His reputation for generosity brought him a joint invitation from the Duke of Devonshire and the governors of three charitable institutions in Ireland to aid their causes by giving a series of concerts in Dublin. Between 22 August and 14 September 1741, Handel prepared the English oratorio *Messiah*; some of the music was newly composed, but much of it was borrowed from earlier works. The libretto, prepared by Charles Jennens, uses words taken exclusively from the Bible. The oratorio was performed in Neale's Music Hall on 13 April 1742. Most of the soloists came from London; in Dublin Handel engaged Susanna Arne Cibber (1714–66) as an alto soloist. The audience was deeply moved by her singing of "He was despised." Handel's oratorio *Saul* was given on 25 May, and *Messiah* was repeated on 3 June. At all the oratorio performances Handel played organ concertos. Crowds attended the concerts, the works were received with enthusiasm, and a considerable sum was raised for the charities. However, when *Messiah* was performed in London, it was a failure, primarily because many persons considered presentation of biblical words in a playhouse blasphemous. *Messiah* was not accepted by London audiences until it was presented at Foundling Hospital Chapel in 1750.

In April 1743 Handel suffered another slight stroke from which he soon recovered. When the Prince of Wales requested a new opera, Handel composed *Semele*. Next he wrote the Dettingen *Te Deum* and anthem (*The king shall rejoice*), the oratorios *Joseph and his Brethren* and *Belshazzar,* and the musical drama *Hercules*. He then composed the oratorio *Judas Maccabeus*. When the king commissioned martial music "with no fiddles" for the fireworks display at Green Park to celebrate the Treaty of Aix-la-Chapelle (1749), Handel wrote *Music for the Royal Fireworks*.

He began composing the oratorio *Jephtha* in 1751. Then glaucoma and cataract caused loss of sight in his left eye and weakened the other. Treatment by specialists and surgeries were unsuccessful, but blindness did not deter Handel. He performed from memory or improvised, and he dictated his compositions to J. C. Smith. In September 1758 Handel became ill; he died at home on 14 April 1759. In accordance with his wishes, his body was interred in Westminster Abbey.

Handel had no close friends among composers except Telemann. Handel respected Rameau and admired Purcell's music but openly voiced dislike of the work of contemporary English composers. Handel never married; the bulk of his estate was inherited by a niece in Germany. He willed his harpsichord, scores, and music books to Smith; they are now in the British Museum.

Handel composed music rapidly. Comments made by his contemporaries indicate that ideas came to him at the keyboard or as he read through a libretto, and he planned the music mentally, then notated his mental image. His talent for improvising is apparent in the ways he worked out an initial motive. Occasionally, he made sketches, and often he revised works. He borrowed from himself and from others, sometimes reworking the borrowed material and at other times using it verbatim. His mature style is eclectic, with the various elements he selected smoothly woven into his musical fabric. Basically, Handel's style is Italianate, with added French, German, and English elements. He learned from Keiser how to orchestrate for woodwinds and from Corelli how to write for stringed instruments; the influence of Alessandro Scarlatti is apparent in his vocal works. Handel's odes indicate that he knew Purcell's. Handel was trained to write stage music; his orchestration is suited to the subject matter and to the talents of those he wanted to sing the roles. He wrote a good deal for high male voices; if good alto castrati were not available, he assigned male roles to female singers. If the vocal range and quality were suitable, it made no difference whether male or female was cast in a role.

VOCAL MUSIC

Handel is best known as the composer of *Messiah*. However, his career was principally in the field of opera—from 1705 to 1741 he composed and conducted operas; he wrote almost 40 of them. His 3 masterpieces of 1723–25—*Giulio Cesare, Rodelinda,* and *Tamerlano*—surpass operas written by his contemporaries. In *Tamerlano* he first used clarinets in the opera orchestra. During his lifetime, his operas were performed in London, Hamburg, and Rome, but there is no record of any Handel opera being performed anywhere between 1755 and 1920. A revival of Baroque opera began in Germany in the 1920s and gradually spread to other countries; some of Handel's best operas are being performed again.

Twentieth-century producers of Baroque operas must decide whether to give authentic performances or to adjust the operas to fit modern ideas of staging. When Handel's operas were performed in the eighteenth century, the curtain rose at the beginning of the opera, after the overture, and did not descend until the end of the last act. Pairs of panels (back flats) meeting in center stage were fit into grooves and could be pulled apart by the operation of a single machine to "open" a new scene (fig. 17.9). Intermediate curtains were not used until c. 1750. Scene changes were made quickly in view of the audience; the musical structure was designed with this in mind. The music was designed to cover or to point up the changes. In most scenes there is a gradual tapering off of characters in view. Almost all acts conclude with one person remaining on stage; thus, most acts end with a soloist singing a large aria.

Stage lighting was by tallow candles and oil lamps. In England, the house lights—candles in chandeliers—remained on throughout the performance. The audience received programs containing the Italian words and their English translation.

In his operas Handel used three basic types of subject matter: historical, as in *Giulio Cesare*; mythological, as in *Admeto*; and romantic, as in *Orlando*. The supernatural element—sorcery, witchcraft, magic transformation—figures in five operas (e.g., in *Orlando*); for Handel's special effects, the full complement of Baroque theatre machinery was required.

The operas Handel composed in Hamburg show his indebtedness to Keiser; those he wrote in Italy and during his first years in London reflect the influence of Alessandro Scarlatti. Except for its final number, *Rinaldo* consists entirely of recitative-aria pairs. As his operatic style matured, Handel became more inventive and manipulated recitatives and arias to suit his musical purposes. At times, he built up to an aria by approaching it through recitative and arioso. Some accompanied recitatives are intensely emotional; arias exhibit numerous different designs. Recitative is not always followed by aria; two recitatives or two arias may occur in succession, or one aria might interrupt another (DWMA118). Sometimes two arias are combined to form an extended duet; occasionally, for humor or irony, an aria is trans-

posed and given to another character to sing back to its original interpreter. Occasionally, a **cavatina** (aria without *da capo*) is tucked in. Handel understood human nature, could characterize well, and was able to translate comic situations as well as serious emotions into effective music; he did so in *Agrippina* and in *Serse*. In some operas Handel associated certain keys with particular characters (e.g., in *Admeto*); later, this procedure would be favored by Richard Wagner.

The English oratorio was Handel's innovation. Its most significant feature—highly contributory to its success—is that it is in English. Handel could never speak English without an accent, but he made accurate and masterful musical settings of that language as it was used in his time.

Contributory to Handel's invention of the English oratorio was the fact that the middle-class English appreciated familiar Bible stories but the Bishop of London intervened against stage performance of them. Handel realized that middle-class English people had turned against Italian opera, yet he was reluctant to abandon writing for the theater. He described many of

FIGURE 17.9 Plan of interior of King's Theater.
(*Source: G. Dumont, Parallèle de Plans des plus belles salles de Spectacle, published 1764*)

his oratorios as "sacred dramas," and he included in their music many operatic structural devices. Handel recognized that oratorio had several advantages: without costumes and scenery, it was less expensive to produce; because there were no scene changes and no entrances and exits, fewer changes of key were needed; virtuoso singers were unnecessary; and a small professional chorus, such as the Westminster choir and the Chapel Royal choirboys, could be used. Note that Handel used an all-male chorus and that it was small. Handel's oratorios deal with human experiences, and a moral is apparent, but the presentations were intended to be historical and dramatic rather than religious. They are for performance in the concert hall, not in church. Their plots have a double connotation—the personal plights of the characters and the fate of the nation or humanity. *Semele,* with its moral "Don't tempt the gods," is variously considered opera, oratorio, or opera-oratorio. Although *Semele* and *Hercules* are performed in the manner of oratorio, Handel considered them musical drama, and in style they are closer to opera than to oratorio. On the other hand, *Messiah* is clearly an oratorio, and in it Handel effected a fusion of German Passion, Anglican anthem, and Italian opera, plus an expression of his own faith.

Handel was a master of choral writing. This is seen in his oratorios and in his anthems. In the oratorios, the chorus narrates, comments on the action, and participates in it; often, the chorus becomes alive and personal rather than aloof and impersonal. In his great choral fugues, Handel balances polyphonic sections with blocks of homophony. The voice leading is smooth, and the parts lie within the most effective part of their vocal ranges. Where maximum fullness is desired, the chord pitches are in close position (the four parts brought close together) with upper voices in middle register and tenors and basses rather high. Rests are used most effectively, with general pauses like open windows between massive blocks of sound, especially just before final cadences (e.g., *And the Glory of the Lord* [DWMA119c], and *Hallelujah* choruses). Affective and pictorial symbolism is present in the oratorios, as in much Baroque music; examples in *Messiah* include "Every valley," where the mountain and hill are brought low, and the crooked made straight (DWMA119b), and the twisting figure depicting straying in "All we like sheep."

Handel's church music includes Latin psalm settings for use in a Roman Catholic Church; the Brockes *Passion,* which is Lutheran; and Anglican music composed for performance in royal ceremonies or private chapels. Though Handel was Lutheran, chorales seldom appear in his music.

It is estimated the Handel composed 150 cantatas during his stay in Rome. More than 100 survive. Approximately 75 have basso continuo accompaniment; the remainder use various instruments. Some of the longer cantatas for more than one voice (e.g., *Apollo e Dafne*) are, in essence, one-act operas.

More than 40 songs by Handel are extant. Approximately 2 dozen of them are English; 8 are Italian, 9 are French, and 1 is Spanish.

INSTRUMENTAL MUSIC

Most of Handel's orchestral writing was done in connection with his stage works; the *Water Music* and *Music for the Royal Fireworks* were commissioned. The *Water Music* comprises three suites for different instrumental groups. *Music for the Royal Fireworks* is on a larger scale, written for 37 woodwinds, 18 brass instruments, and 3 timpani; Handel added string parts (doubling winds) for a later performance.

The 6 *Concerti Grossi,* Op. 3 (publ. 1734), are often erroneously called "oboe concertos," probably because two oboes are in the instrumentation. The 12 *Grand Concertos,* Op. 6 (1739), for strings, are on a par with Bach's *Brandenburg Concertos.* Handel expanded *sonata da chiesa* structure by adding one or two movements, usually in dance rhythms, to the standard slow-fast-slow-fast pattern. In each concerto, one Allegro is fugal. The concertos exhibit a variety of moods, and Handel's improvisational talent and inventiveness are reflected in the varied treatment given the thematic material. There exist also 3 *Concerti a due cori* (1747–48) for two groups of winds with string orchestra.

Handel invented the organ concerto. Each of his concertos can be related to the oratorio for which it was created. Three sets, each containing six concertos, were written between 1735 and 1751. Two more concertos were published in 1797. These pieces are most effective when played on a small organ with a small orchestra; a continuo harpsichord is required.

During Handel's lifetime, four sets of his sonatas were published: Op. 1, 12 sonatas for transverse flute, recorder, violin or oboe, with basso continuo; Op. 2, 6 trio sonatas for two flutes, oboes, or violins, with basso continuo; 3 sonatas for flute and basso continuo; and Op. 5, 7 trio sonatas for violins or flutes, with basso continuo. Autographs of all the sonatas of Op. 1 are not extant, and Handel's intended instrumentation for each sonata is not known. The Op. 1 sonatas are mainly *sonata da camera* type and show Corelli's influence. The Sonata in D major, No. 13, for violin and basso continuo, survives in autograph; it was not in the original Op. 1 and is the finest of the solo sonatas.

Each of the two volumes entitled *Suites de pièces pour le clavecin* (Keyboard suites; pub. 1720, 1733) contains eight suites. From the first book come the *Passacaille* in G minor and the set of variations known as *The Harmonious Blacksmith*. The *Aria* in B♭ from the first suite in the second book was used by Brahms as the theme for his *Variations on a Theme by G. F. Handel*, Op. 24. In 1735 Walsh published six *Fugues or Voluntarys for the Organ or Harpsichord*. There survive also a *Klavier-Buch aus der Jugendzeit* (Clavier book from youth) and isolated keyboard works that cannot be dated. In general, Handel's harpsichord works are inferior to those of J. S. Bach and Domenico Scarlatti.

SUMMARY

Bach, Handel, Rameau, Telemann, and Vivaldi were craftsmen who achieved success and eminence in their own time. Their works demonstrate their competence in traditional composition, their awareness of current trends, and their ability to reconcile the conflict between contrapuntal and homophonic styles. They achieved the ultimate with the established forms and styles of the late Baroque and, when those forms would not suffice, created some new forms. Each was aware of what the others were doing, though they seldom (if ever) had personal contact with one another. During the early and middle eighteenth century Telemann was the leading German composer, and Handel was accorded international acclaim. In the twentieth century, Bach is regarded as one of the most important composers of all time.

Bach studied the music of other composers, absorbed the best features into his own musical style, and infused that blend with his originality and genius. In many forms, his music attained a degree of excellence that has never been surpassed (e.g., fugue, theme and variations, organ chorale and chorale prelude, harpsichord partita, sonatas and suites for unaccompanied violin and unaccompanied violoncello, and Passion). Though he wrote no operas, he used operatic style in some cantatas and Passions. The didactic keyboard works he created have become staple educational repertoire. As organist, technician, and acoustician, he frequently counseled instrument builders.

Telemann brought music to the middle classes by editing and publishing music suitable for amateurs to use at home, by organizing collegia musica, and by establishing a regular series of public concerts. He broke down barriers between sacred and secular music by programming both types on the same public concert and by composing and directing operas while employed as Kantor in a Lutheran church.

Vivaldi, Handel, and Rameau excelled at writing opera. In addition, Vivaldi broadened and perfected the Italian Baroque solo concerto. When opera proved unprofitable financially, Handel created the English oratorio and, as an adjunct to it, the organ concerto. As a composer of choral music, Handel is peerless; his masterful choral fugues have never been equaled.

Rameau built on the operatic foundations laid by Lully and carried French opera to greater heights. He scientifically investigated and clearly explained in his treatises the principles of harmony and key tonality underlying the music of his time—principles that remained valid for music composed in succeeding centuries.

Each of these men composed music to meet immediate needs—to fulfill the requirements of his own employment and to benefit and enrich the lives of his own generation. That much of their music has become standard repertoire and continues to provide enrichment is in itself a tribute to their greatness.

EIGHTEENTH-CENTURY PRECLASSIC MUSIC

18

During the eighteenth century, the political and cultural complexion of Europe changed considerably. Russia, "Westernized" under Tsar' Peter the Great (r. 1689–1725), became a European power. The central-European Germanic provinces remained disunited, each under its own ruler, and collectively governed (nominally) by a Holy Roman Emperor who almost always was chosen from the Austrian Habsburg dynasty. Within the empire, there were frequent boundary disputes caused by envious neighbors with territorial ambitions. Perhaps the most envious was King Frederick II ("the Great") of Prussia (r. 1740–86), who seized Silesia from Maria Theresa (r. Austria 1740–80) and coveted other territory. Though Maria Theresa directly inherited the Habsburg lands of her father, Emperor Charles VI, a woman was ineligible for the imperial throne. Only gradually was Maria Theresa acknowledged as ruler—by Austria in 1740, Hungary in 1741, and Bohemia in 1743. In 1745 Maria's husband, Francis I, was named Holy Roman Emperor; he was succeeded by their son, Joseph II (r. 1765–90). Italy was an aggregation of states rather than a true nation and lacked even nominal central leadership. Britain was a colonial and sea power, with strong Germanic ties acquired when the Elector of Hanover became King George I of England (r. 1714–27). France was an absolute monarchy; under Louis XIV (r. 1643–1715) it became the most powerful nation in Europe. Louis XIV was an avid patron of the arts, especially music, and his Versailles court with its many cultural activities was the model for other European courts. The reigns of Louis XV (1715–74) and Louis XVI (1774–89) became increasingly corrupt, inefficient, and seemingly directionless; ultimately, the Old Régime (i.e., the absolute monarchy) collapsed during the French Revolution.

THE ENLIGHTENMENT

The historical period variously referred to as "the Enlightenment" or "the Age of Reason" began c. 1685, gathered momentum during the next 50 years, and continued until the outbreak of the French Revolution. The movement was humanitarian and secular, against superstition and the supernatural, and skeptical about religious authority and dogma. Its leaders believed in the "dignity of man," sought the betterment of humanity through proper education, and placed emphasis on reason and on knowledge gained through experience (empiricism) and scientific experiments. Knowledge, acquired through education, provided power to achieve liberation from the evils that beset humanity. Humanitarian ideals were embodied in the American colonies' Declaration of Independence and in the United States Constitution.

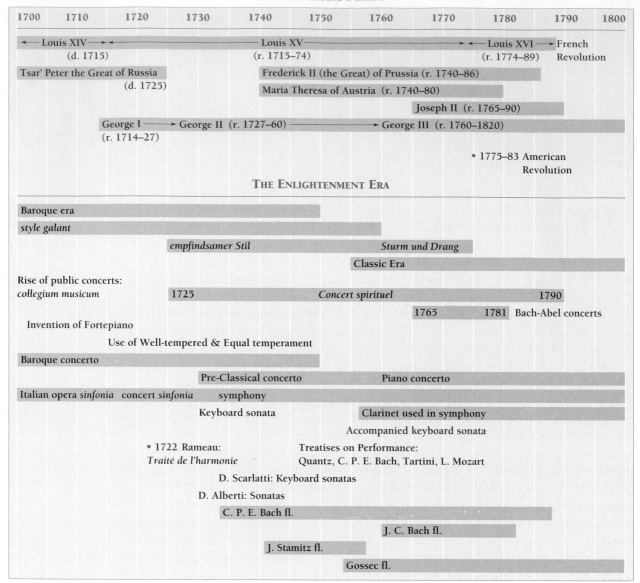

1700	1710	1720	1730	1740	1750	1760	1770	1780	1790	1800

◄—Louis XIV—►◄————————————Louis XV————————————►◄—Louis XVI—►French
(d. 1715)   (r. 1715–74)   (r. 1774–89) Revolution

Tsar' Peter the Great of Russia   Frederick II (the Great) of Prussia (r. 1740–86)
(d. 1725)   Maria Theresa of Austria (r. 1740–80)
                                          Joseph II (r. 1765–90)

George I ——► George II (r. 1727–60) ——————————► George III (r. 1760–1820)
(r. 1714–27)

• 1775–83 American
Revolution

THE ENLIGHTENMENT ERA

Baroque era

style galant

empfindsamer Stil   Sturm und Drang

Classic Era

Rise of public concerts:
collegium musicum   1725   Concert spirituel   1790
                                 1765   1781   Bach-Abel concerts

Invention of Fortepiano

Use of Well-tempered & Equal temperament

Baroque concerto

Pre-Classical concerto   Piano concerto

Italian opera sinfonia   concert sinfonia   symphony

Keyboard sonata   Clarinet used in symphony

Accompanied keyboard sonata

• 1722 Rameau: Treatises on Performance:
Traité de l'harmonie   Quantz, C. P. E. Bach, Tartini, L. Mozart

D. Scarlatti: Keyboard sonatas

D. Alberti: Sonatas

C. P. E. Bach fl.

J. C. Bach fl.

J. Stamitz fl.

Gossec fl.

During the Enlightenment, science, rationalism, and freedom advanced considerably. One expression of the ideas of tolerance and brotherly love was the formation of fraternal organizations such as the Freemasons. Formally founded as a fraternal Lodge in England in 1717, Freemasonry spread throughout Europe and to America; among its members were rulers (Frederick the Great, Joseph II of Austria), statesmen (Benjamin Franklin, George Washington), philosophers (Lessing), authors (Swift), poets and dramatists (Klopstock, Schiller, Goethe, Beaumarchais), composers (Mozart,

Haydn), and talented upper- and middle-class persons. Some rulers were "enlightened" despots—Frederick the Great, Catherine II of Russia (r. 1762–96), and Emperor Joseph II (r. 1765–90); others were merely despots. Louis XVI, in the early years of his reign, was enlightened but gradually became purely despotic.

The roots of the Enlightenment extend back to medieval times, to reaction against church authorities who sought to dominate every phase of life. However, the obvious beginnings of the eighteenth-century movement were in England in the writings and

FIGURE 18.1 Europe in 1715.

scientific experiments of such men as John Locke (1632–1704), Isaac Newton (1642–1727), and David Hume (1711– 76). On the Continent, impetus was provided by articulate Frenchmen who were acquainted with those Englishmen's ideas: Montesquieu (1689–1755), Voltaire (1694–1778), and Denis Diderot (1713–84), and by Swiss-born Jean-Jacques Rousseau (1712–78), who worked in France. These men called themselves *philosophes* (philosophers), though all were not philosophers in the true sense.

Diderot planned and organized the production of the *Encyclopédie* (1751–76), whose articles stirred up enough controversy to make them a causal factor in the French Revolution. The *Encyclopédie* was not a reference work as is a modern encyclopedia; rather, each volume was intended to be read from cover to cover.

Rousseau wrote the articles on music for the *Encyclopédie*. Also, he expressed his ideas on education and politics in two books meant to be read in conjunction: *Émile* and *Social Contract* (1762). Voltaire's bold writings brought him imprisonment in the Bastille and later, from time to time, self-imposed exile in countries tolerant of his beliefs. At the Prussian court, Voltaire's influence was extensive. He reached, among others, the critic Lessing (1729–81) and philosophers Moses Mendelssohn (1729–86) and Immanuel Kant (1724–1804). In *Was ist Aufklärung?* (What is Enlightenment?; 1784), Kant revealed his own philosophy, a synthesis of empiricism and rationalism, and answered his essay's question with *Sapere aude!* (Dare to know!). Voltaire's influence is apparent in the writings of Francesco Algarotti (1712–64) and Cesare Beccaria (1738–94).

By the mid-1780s, most of the *philosophes* had died. Just as living conditions had prompted and influenced their thinking, so had their ideas affected living conditions. The issue of individual rights versus state rights (and its resolution) shows this.

ASPECTS OF MUSICAL LIFE

The rise of a more or less independent spirit, leading from the accordance of divine right to kings to a belief in human rights and brotherhood, is exemplified in France and North America in revolution and is reflected in activities of the musical world. The rise of the middle class to an influential position brought with it the popularization of art and learning, treatises written in the vernacular, novels and plays depicting ordinary people with everyday emotions, literature in prose, and public concerts. As music printing increased, instructional materials were placed on the market and developed from mere statements of principles to methods containing exercises and études for practice. Around mid century, numerous "do-it-yourself" instruction books, especially for learning to play the violin, were marketed. The manufacturer of keyboard instruments increased considerably. Books of songs and keyboard music designed for use by amateurs in their homes were readily available; title pages with pictures of ladies playing instruments imply that some publications were intended for women. Music journals were issued more or less regularly, containing all sorts of music news—reviews, criticism, lists of newly published music, announcements of concerts, and even, so far as space would permit, some printed music. When space ran out, the piece was broken off (sometimes in mid measure) and was continued from that point in the next issue.

PUBLIC CONCERTS

The term **concert,** used for a public nontheatrical performance of music, came into existence in England in the late seventeenth century. During the Commonwealth era, when court activities were nonexistent, music patronage was in the hands of upper-middle-class citizens, and performances of music were presented in private homes and businesses. In 1672 John Banister (1625–79) set aside a room of his house for public subscription concerts; his series lasted six years. However, it was decades before a systematically organized public concert series was established in England—the Bach-Abel concerts, which presented 10 to 15 concerts annually, from January 1765 to May 1781.

Public opera houses were operated in various continental European cities in the seventeenth century, but there was no great interest in public concerts of nontheatrical music until the 1720s. Private performances at courts and in the homes of wealthy patrons entertained aristocrats and nobility; middle- and lower-class citizens heard music at church and participated in family amateur music making. Commencing in the 1720s and continuing through the century, the public concert developed significantly. Telemann made collegium musicum concerts a feature of civic musical life by scheduling regular public concerts at Frankfurt in 1712–21 and at Hamburg in 1722–23. Musicians in other German cities followed his lead. J. A. Hiller (1728–1804) mounted a series of subscription concerts in Leipzig in 1762 that led to the establishment of the *Gewandhaus Konzerte* in 1781.

In France in 1725 oboist Anne Danican Philidor (1681–1728) founded the *Concert spirituel.* He negotiated a contract with the government for a series of public performances during those seasons when theaters were closed by ecclesiastical regulations. The *Concert spirituel* was in existence in Paris until 1790. Many wealthy patrons in and around Paris entertained invited guests at weekly concerts in their homes. La Pouplinière maintained an orchestra and presented concerts regularly in his home in 1731–62.

In North America, concerts "in an English manner" were presented by visiting companies in Boston in 1731 and in Philadelphia from 1734. The first concert of record in New York was organized by Charles Pachelbel (1690–1750) in 1736. Pachelbel became organist at St. Philip's Church, Charleston, South Carolina, in 1737 and sponsored concerts in his home in Charleston. Soon prominent citizens in other colonial cities did likewise.

PRECLASSIC STYLES

The term *Preclassic* is generally applied to those styles of eighteenth-century music that led to and were absorbed into the *Classic* style exhibited in the mature works of Mozart and Haydn. The term *Preclassic* most appropriately encompasses the French *style galant* and

Italian *galante* style, the north-German *empfindsamer Stil* (sensitive style), and the latter's extension into *Sturm und Drang* (storm and stress). The Preclassic grew out of the Baroque and coexisted with it but was in some respects a reaction to it. Many composers wrote in both Baroque and Preclassic styles.

STYLE GALANT

As the center of cultural activity shifted from the church to the salon, *style galant* emerged in aristocratic and courtly circles. *Galant* music is light and graceful, elegant, sometimes witty, and pleasing to the ear on first hearing. It is thin-textured homophony, characterized by simple melodies in short phrases, uncomplicated harmonies, and a slower harmonic rhythm than that used by Baroque composers. Major key tonalities were preferred. Notated music began to take on a different appearance, for instead of notating only treble and bass lines and relying on the harpsichordist to supply the inner parts, as was customary in Baroque music, some composers of Preclassic music notated the complete harmony. Figured bass was not discarded; it had some use throughout the eighteenth century. However, the bass line lost the independence and leadership it had enjoyed (especially in Baroque counterpoint) and functioned as support for and accompaniment to the melody. The inner voices merely supplied filler harmonies. Lest the slower harmonic rhythm with static harmonies become boring, broken chord figurations were used: **murky bass** and, after c. 1735, **Alberti bass.** A murky bass is an accompaniment in broken octaves (ex. 18.1a). More popular was Alberti bass, named for Domenico Alberti (c. 1710–40), who was the first composer to make frequent use of it. The technique consists of a broken triad figuration, created by playing the notes in this order: lowest, highest, middle, highest (ex. 18.1b). Alberti composed (after 1736) more than 36 harpsichord sonatas in which Alberti bass appears often.

Style galant retained the decorativeness of Baroque music but dispensed with grandeur. In its maturity, *style galant* employed explicitly designated ornaments, appoggiatura sighs, Lombardic rhythm (♪ ; sometimes called the "Scottish snap"), feminine cadences (final cadence chord on weak beat of measure), melodic triplet sixteenth notes, and fussy dynamic contrasts. Representative examples of *style galant* may be found

(a)

(b)

EXAMPLE 18.1 (a) Murky bass. (b) Alberti bass. *(Example b source: Domenico Alberti: Sonata 3 in E♭ major, mvt. 2. MS 35973, Biblioteca del Conservatorio di Musica, Naples, Italy)*

in François Couperin's keyboard works, Leclair's violin sonatas, Tartini's violin concerti, and eighteenth-century suite movements known as *galanteries* (e.g., menuet, bourrée).

EMPFINDSAMER STIL

After 1750, German music was dominated by a form of *style galant.* J. G. Harrer (1703–55), Bach's successor at Leipzig, advocated it. In northern Germany, the style was given new expressiveness and became *empfindsamer Stil* (the sensitive style). In that style, the Baroque idea of an entire composition expressing only one basic affect was supplanted by the belief that, within a piece, there should be a continual change of expression or affection, together with appropriate changes in dynamics. J. J. Quantz (see also p. 340) advocated using all levels of dynamic shading, from *ppp* to *fff*, and stressed the necessity of avoiding the alternation of *piano* and *forte*, which produced the terraced dynamics of Baroque music. Expressive nuances were of utmost importance. They were a feature of C. P. E. Bach's keyboard playing; the clavichord, his preferred instrument, could respond to his subtle shadings. In the works of C. P. E. Bach, *empfindsamer Stil* reached a high point. His music is finely nuanced, with periodic melody constructed in short phrases and supported by light-textured accompaniment. He stated that the human singing voice provided the model for good instrumental melodic writing; melodies should be free of excessive ornamentation and should be simple enough so that beautiful tone quality and expressive nuances could be appreciated. At times, Bach's melodies border on operatic recitative. Never did he write melody merely to tickle the ear; his music was designed to touch and move the listener.

STURM UND DRANG

Sturm und Drang was a movement in German literature c. 1760–85 with the artistic aim of frightening, shocking, stunning, or overcoming with emotion. Adherents of the movement believed strongly in personal freedom, especially freedom from conventions that shackled artistic creativity. The most representative form of *Sturm und Drang* was drama, but parallel movements arose in all the arts. Authors penned "Gothic" novels such as Horace Walpole's *The Castle of Otranto* (1764). Artists sought to convey terror by painting storms, shipwrecks, macabre scenes, and nightmarish visions (e.g., Henry Fuseli's *The Nightmare* [plate 20]).

In instrumental music by German composers, the emotional expressions and contrasts of *empfindsamer Stil* sharpened and intensified to become passionate outbursts characteristic of *Sturm und Drang*. Some of C. P. E. Bach's "Prussian" Sonatas and symphonies, and the dark, stormy moods portrayed in some of Joseph Haydn's minor-key symphonies written c. 1770 (e.g., Nos. 44 and 49), are *Sturm und Drang* expressions.

Opera librettists created frightening situations that composers and set designers intensified with music, costumes, and staging. Examples may be found in the works of Jommelli and Traetta. Classical composers produced some magnificent, terrifying scenes: Gluck's scene with the Furies in *Orfeo ed Euridice,* the tomb scene in Mozart's *Lucio Silla,* and the conclusion of *Il Don Giovanni.* In *Sturm und Drang* scenes like these, the seeds of nineteenth-century German Romantic opera were sown.

FORMAL STRUCTURE

Some formal patterns preferred by Baroque composers remained in favor. Most Lieder and other art songs were strophic. In opera, the *da capo* (ABA) aria reigned supreme. Occasionally, some German composers carved away the *da capo* section and wrote cavatinas.

For most of their instrumental pieces, Preclassic composers used binary form but enriched, modified, and expanded that pattern. As a result of this modification and expansion, a new form emerged, albeit in an embryonic or incipient stage—a form that would be established by Haydn, Mozart, and other Classic composers and that nineteenth-century theorists would call **sonata form.** (There is no record that eighteenth-century composers ever gave this kind of formal structure that special name.) Sonata form was the most important structural design principle in instrumental music from the Classic period to the twentieth century.

The evolution of sonata form from simple binary may be summarized and diagrammed as in example 18.2. A simple binary form consists of two complementary main sections, A and B, each of which is usually marked to be repeated. (With repeats, the pattern is AABB.) The piece opens in the tonic key and modulates to a closely related key, where it cadences; the second section begins in that key and modulates to the tonic key in sufficient time to clearly establish the tonic before cadencing (ex. 18.2a). If the piece is in a major key, modulation is usually made to the dominant; if the piece is minor, modulation is to relative major. Often, the musical material commencing the B section is a transposition of the opening measures of the piece (ex. 18.2b); occasionally, eighteenth-century composers inverted the melodic motive when using it to begin the B section (ex. 18.2c). **Cadence rhyme** was common; that is, the cadence at the end of the A section was transposed to the tonic for the final cadence (ex. 18.2d). Sometimes the rhyming termination was extended backward by including the approach to the cadence in the transposition (ex. 18.2e).

It was not unusual for Preclassic composers to duplicate the opening measure(s) of the piece when returning to the tonic key near the conclusion of the B section (ex. 18.2f). Sometimes all the A section was restated in its original key as conclusion to the B section—of course, making the necessary harmonic adjustment to ensure cadencing in the tonic key (ex. 18.2g). A binary form in which the first section is substantially returned, in its original key, in the final portion of the second section, is called a **rounded binary.** With repeats, the formal pattern of such a binary is AABABA. Rounding a binary could

(a) Simple binary form.

||: A :||: B :|| (= A A B B)

||: Tonic → Related .. Cadence :||: Related ... → Tonic .. Cadence :||
          key   key

Major: I   →   V   Dominant   Dominant → Tonic   I
Minor: i   → Relative   I   Relative → Minor   i
                   major   major   tonic

(b) Transposition of beginning of A section used to begin B section.

(c) Inversion of beginning of A section used to begin B section.

(d) Binary form with cadence rhyme.

||: Tonic → Dominant .. Cadence :||: Dominant → Tonic .. Cadence :||
                                                              Rhyme

(e) Binary form with cadence rhyme and approach to cadence also transposed.

||: Tonic → Dominant .. Cadence :||: Dominant → Tonic .. Cadence :||
                                                              Rhyme
                                                     with approach to
                                                     cadence transposed

EXAMPLE 18.2 The evolution from simple binary form toward sonata form. (continued on p. 334)

lengthen its second section considerably and make the form asymmetrical.

When composers began to manipulate the thematic material in the B section of a rounded binary form—to fragment and develop the thematic material and to venture into keys beyond the dominant—**sonata form** came into existence. J. G. Harrer composed movements in sonata form, with respectable developments,

EIGHTEENTH-CENTURY PRECLASSIC MUSIC

(f) Binary form with cadence rhyme, approach to cadence transposed, and opening measures of A section returned simultaneously with return to tonic key.

||: Tonic → Dominant .. Cadence :||: Dominant → Tonic ..... Cadence :||
                                                  with   Rhyme
                                                  Beg. of A   with
                                                  Section   approach
                                                               transposed

Return
to

(g) Rounded binary. ||: A :||: B A :|| (= A A BA BA)

||: Tonic → Dominant .. Cadence :||: Dominant → → Double Return: .... Cadence :||
                                                  of Tonic & of (Tonic Key) Rhyme
                                                  all or most of
                                                  A Section

EXAMPLE 18.2 *continued from p. 333*

in the 1730s. Movements in incipient sonata form—that is, with B sections exhibiting some manipulation of thematic material but without true development sections—appear in the keyboard works of Domenico Scarlatti and C. P. E. Bach.

Sonata Form

The term *sonata form* refers to the constructional principle of a movement, not the form of the multimovement work called *sonata.* (The terms *sonata-allegro* and *first-movement form* are limiting misnomers. Sonata form does not require any specific tempo, neither is its use limited to the first movement of a multimovement work.)

Sonata form was not described by theorists before the 1790s, though it had been in use for about 50 years. H. C. Koch (1749–1816) seems to have been the first to describe it adequately, in his *Versuch einer Anleitung zur Composition* (Treatise on Composition, 3 vols.; 1782–93). Koch's treatise is an extensive treatment of composition; his descriptions of forms, with "formal models" (music examples), make his essay a major contribution. Koch did not use the term *sonata form* but described that kind of formal structure as binary, written in two distinct units, each unit usually marked to be repeated. He explained that this kind of binary contains a two-part tonal structure (i.e., tonic-to-dominant and dominant-to-tonic) expressed in three main sections (statement of material, manipulation of material, restatement of material).

From the viewpoint of the Preclassic composer and the eighteenth-century theorist, sonata form was a monothematic rounded binary form in which (a) the first section established the tonic key, then modulated to dominant (or relative major), where it cadenced; (b) the second section commenced in dominant (or relative major), developed (i.e., manipulated) previously stated material, and increased tension by modulating into keys more remote than dominant; then (c) made a strong, clear return to the tonic key and, simultaneously, began a restatement of the material of the first section in the tonic; and (d) on completion of the restatement, cadenced in the tonic (fig. 18.2). Composers did not always follow that pattern strictly. Rarely, in the first section of a composition in minor, a composer modulated to the dominant minor key. Moreover, the theme stated at the outset might generate subsidiary thematic material, but the most important factor in the formal pattern was *tonality*—statement of key, digression to a closely related key and then to more remote keys, and return to the original key.

Though eighteenth-century composers made frequent use of sonata form, they never referred to it by that name. Perhaps the frequent use of the form in works entitled "Sonata" prompted a nineteenth-century theorist to term it "sonata form." By the mid-nineteenth century the term was in use, and theorists analyzing this form called the first section *exposition,* the first part of the second section *development,* and the restatement *recapitulation.*

The Baroque *sonata da chiesa* gradually disappeared and was supplanted by a different kind of multimovement composition called **sonata.** Though most Preclassic sonatas were for solo keyboard, some were written for other instruments (e.g., flute or violin). The Baroque trio *sonata da chiesa* existed into the Classic period—Gluck and Haydn wrote some. Eventually, it was supplanted by true trios: the piano trio (violin, 'cello, piano) and the string trio (2 violins, 'cello). The trio sonata was forerunner of the piano quartet and the string quartet.

The first real flowering of the Preclassic sonata for solo keyboard came after 1735, with the works of Domenico Scarlatti (though he called them *essercizi,* or studies), Domenico Alberti, C. P. E. Bach, and many lesser-known Italian and German composers.

FIGURE 18.2 Diagram of monothematic sonata form.

Alberti wrote two-movement works, whereas most of Bach's have three. After 1740, a three-movement fast-slow-fast structural plan resembling that of the Italian opera overture (sinfonia) was used increasingly. It comprised an Allegro, a lyrical Andante that was usually quite short, and a Finale with dancelike rhythm, often a *gigue* or *menuetto*. That the Preclassic sonata bears little resemblance to Baroque *sonata da chiesa* is due primarily to cultural interests of the time. Few sonatas were written expressly for use in church. Rather, they were intended for performance at court, in concerts, and by amateurs at home. Some sonatas were designed for teaching purposes (e.g., Scarlatti's *Essercizi* and Arne's *Lessons*).

Domenico Scarlatti. Painted c. 1740 by Domingo Antonio de Velasco. *(Instituticao José Relvas, Alpiarça)*

DOMENICO SCARLATTI

Domenico Scarlatti (1685–1757), composer, teacher, and performer, was born in Naples. Presumably, he received his musical training from his father, Alessandro Scarlatti. Commencing in September 1701, Domenico worked at the royal court at Naples; he composed two operas for performance there in 1703. The following spring Alessandro ordered Domenico to make a journey to Venice. Nothing is known concerning the next four years of his life. From 1709 to 1713 he was employed as composer at the private court of exiled Polish queen Maria Casimira, in Rome. For performance there he composed a cantata, an oratorio, and six operas. He attended the weekly chamber music recitals at the palace of Cardinal Ottoboni, became acquainted with Corelli, and met Handel. Late in 1713 Domenico became *maestro di cappella* of the Basilica Giulia, and early in 1714 he secured an additional appointment as *maestro di cappella* to the Portuguese ambassador to the Vatican. Thus, Scarlatti was composing music for both sacred and secular use. In 1719 he moved to Lisbon, where he was *mestre* of the patriarchal chapel until 1728. Scarlatti returned to Italy three times. In 1724 he visited Rome, in 1725 he spent some time with his ailing father in Naples, and in 1728 he returned to Rome to marry Maria Caterina Gentili. He never again left Iberia.

In Lisbon, Scarlatti's responsibilities included the music education of King John V's daughter, Maria Barbara. For her he created many if not all the approxi-

mately 555 keyboard "sonatas" that are his most significant work. In 1728, when Maria Barbara married Spanish Crown Prince Fernando, Scarlatti was among those who accompanied her to Madrid. The last 28 years of his life were spent there.

Until 1719 Scarlatti had a career in opera without much success. In Iberia he had opportunities to develop his capabilities as teacher, to provide keyboard music that would interest his royal pupil yet challenge and develop her talents, and to incorporate in that music the characteristic sounds and customs of Iberia. He could experiment with a new compositional style and test the viability of new ideas. For 35 years he wrote keyboard pieces—the "sonatas" for which he is acclaimed.

Scarlatti was influential principally in Iberia and in England. His influence can be seen in the work of Antonio Soler (1729–83) and Sebastián de Albero (1722–56), both of whom he knew.

SCARLATTI'S MUSIC

Scarlatti's sonatas bearing L. numbers were catalogued by Alessandro Longo, those with K. numbers by Ralph Kirkpatrick, those with P. numbers by Giorgio Pestolli, and those with G. numbers by Kenneth Gilbert. In the principal manuscript sources, many of the pieces seem to have been grouped by pairs; there is no proof that Scarlatti composed them in pairs, though he may have arranged some of them that way later.

Each piece (sonata, or sonata movement) is an *essercizo*—an étude; each presents at least one consistently

The Étude

The **étude** emerged during the late eighteenth century and by 1800 had become an important teaching tool. An étude is a complete musical composition featuring at least one consistently recurring problem of physiological, technical, or musical difficulty that requires of the player not only mechanical application but proper study and correct interpretation as well. In contrast, an **exercise** is a chiefly mechanical note pattern of undetermined length, designed for the player's drill on a specific technical aspect of his instrument. An exercise is never, strictly speaking, a complete *musical* composition.

When, around 1700, persons began to write and publish method books and tutors for learning to play the violin, they included for practice small dance pieces, usually in binary form. As the violin increased in popularity, more methods were published; these became more comprehensive verbally and musically. Not only was more music included, the compositions were longer and were designed to cope with technical difficulties. Usually, such pieces were entitled "Caprice" or "Lesson for . . . ," and the didactic purpose of each study was clearly indicated. Études were not confined to technical problems; equally important was the matter of taste (style) or expression. The étude had no form that could be considered exclusively its own. However, many of the early études were in binary form.

Books composed solely of compositions that were designated as études began to appear in Paris after 1785. Detel's *Étude* for flute is listed in Sieber's catalog for 1786. Antonio Bartolomeo Bruni's (1757–1821) *Caprices & Airs variés en forme d'études pour un violon seul* (Caprices & varied airs in the form of études for one unaccompanied violin; 1787) seems to have been the first publication for the violin to use the word *étude* in the title and to indicate in print that caprices and varied airs could be études. His *Cinquante études* (Fifty études) appeared c. 1795. Similar volumes published by violinists working in Paris, for example, Fiorillo (1788), Kreutzer (c. 1800), and Gaviniès (1800), have become standard instructional repertoire.

Books of études for piano appeared early in the nineteenth century. The most important of these were prepared by pianists of the London school, for example, Cramer's *Studio per il pianoforte* (Studies for piano; 1804–10) and Clementi's *Gradus ad Parnassum* (Steps to Parnassus; 1817–26).

---

recurring problem that requires of the player both mechanical application and musical interpretation (Insight, "The Étude"). Included are hand crossing, rapid reiteration of notes, arpeggio figurations extending the full length of the keyboard, and patterns requiring use of the thumb. Scarlatti's sonatas differ considerably from the typical Baroque binary, though outwardly they follow that form (fig. 18.3). Frequently, there is cadence rhyme, and sometimes it is quite extensive. There is no recapitulation, but often the binary is rounded. In several sonatas the first part of the second section is developmental, evidencing that Classic sonata form is incipient.

Characteristics of Scarlatti's sonatas include: (1) frequent use of the *acciaccatura* (lit., crushed grace note), a lower auxiliary note briefly sounded simultaneously with its resolution (ex. 18.3a and b; also, Sonata L. 429, mm. 2–6); (2) blurred or obscured resolutions; (3)

FIGURE 18.3 Diagram of typical binary structure of a Domenico Scarlatti sonata movement.

vamping; (4) phrase elision; (5) bold modulations achieved by means of chromatic alteration; and (6) a rather plain sequential pattern enhanced or surrounded by an auxiliary line of chromatic filigree. The term *vamp* describes a section of indeterminate length that conveys the impression of stalling or waiting for the entrance of important musical material (ex. 18.3c). At times Scarlatti wrote a phrase several measures long and brought it to cadence, then repeated it but replaced the cadential measure(s) with the initial measures of a new phrase; thus, in repetition, the phrase was elided, and the retained portion served as impetus or booster to the new material.

Among areas of special concern in performance practice are the correct interpretation of Scarlatti's ornaments and Scarlatti's manner of drawing long curved lines above or below the final measures of the first half of a sonata to indicate the omission of those measures when repeating the section; often, the measure beginning the second section is identical with one of those omitted (ex. 18.3d).

Ornamentation symbols used in Iberia in the eighteenth century do not always correspond with those used elsewhere in Europe; no treatise has been located that definitively explains all the markings used by Iberian composers. The very small notes Scarlatti wrote as graces can be interpreted as appoggiaturas, and the trill symbols are clear. The directive *Tremulo nell' A la mi re*—note the use of Guido's nomencla-

ture—in measures 56–58 of Sonata in D Major (K. 119; DWMA120) can be interpreted as an inner trill. In those sonatas intended for performance on clavichord, the word *tremulo* may indicate an ornamental vibrato. Not all Scarlatti's keyboard sonatas were written for harpsichord: K. 287, K. 288, K. 328 were for organ, and Maria Barbara owned clavichords and fortepianos.

PRECLASSIC CONCERTO

The formal structure of the concerto for solo instrument and orchestra that Vivaldi established was followed by Preclassic composers and was infused with *galant* characteristics. Preclassic composers wrote solo concerti for violin, 'cello, flute, oboe, or bassoon, with an orchestra of strings and basso continuo. Quantz wrote more than 300 flute concerti and more than 200 flute sonatas for Frederick the Great. J. S. Bach created the concerto for solo keyboard and string orchestra when he transcribed and adapted for harpsichord

EXAMPLE 18.3 (a) An acciaccatura as notated; (b) an acciaccatura as performed, all notes being sounded together initially but the crushed notes being released immediately; (c) vamping, as used in Scarlatti's Sonata in A minor, K. 175 (L. 429), mm. 27–32; (d) Scarlatti's use of long curved lines above and/or below the final measures of the first half of a sonata indicates the omission of those measures when the section is repeated. *(Source: Sonata in D major, K.535)*

(a)

(b)

(c)

(d)

some of Vivaldi's concerti. Bach's sons contributed a great deal to the development of the solo keyboard concerto: Wilhelm Friedemann (1710–84) composed 6 of them, Johann Christoph Friedrich (1732–95) wrote at least 6, Johann Christian wrote more than 30, and C. P. E. (1714–88) wrote more than 50. Joseph Haydn was influenced by C. P. E. Bach's keyboard concerti; those by J. C. Bach influenced Mozart, who perfected Classic concerto form.

Many of C. P. E. Bach's concerti are in minor keys. Most of his concerti have three movements, but a few have four. The opening movements follow the ritornello form used by Vivaldi. Bach's writing, especially in the slow movements, is in *empfindsamer Stil*—the soloist's part is brilliant as well as expressive.

J. C. Bach was the first to adopt the piano for public performance. He encouraged its use as solo instrument by stating that certain works were suitable for piano, for example, *Sei concerti per il cembalo o piano e forte,* Op. 7 (Six concertos for harpsichord or pianoforte; 1770). Bach balanced the small tone of the piano with trio-sonata orchestral instrumentation. Some of Bach's concerti have three movements, but most have only two. Stylistically, they are infused with *galant* elements. Themes are well defined, and melodies are Italianate. In the fast first movements of his concerti, Bach merged ritornello and sonata form, opening the movement with an orchestral section, entirely in tonic key, that resembles the first section (the exposition) of a sonata-form movement. At the conclusion of the recapitulation, the soloist improvised a cadenza; a coda brought the movement to conclusion. Slow movements of Bach's concerti resemble arias. Bach wrote his concerti for himself; he was both soloist and keyboard continuo player. This meant that the harpsichordist (or pianist, as the case might be) performed throughout the composition. At that time the composer-keyboard player usually was the conductor.

CARL PHILIPP EMANUEL BACH

C. P. E. Bach was the chief representative of north German *empfindsamer Stil* and one of the four principal composers active during the last half of the eighteenth century. The others were Gluck, Haydn, and Mozart, who are considered Classic composers. Bach produced some works that are in Classic style.

Besides being a prolific composer, Bach was a theorist, keyboard teacher, and virtuoso performer. His fame surpassed that of his father in the decades immediately following Sebastian's death. Sebastian was the only music teacher Emanuel ever had. His instrumental study was confined to keyboard, and he was exposed to a wealth of material from his father's works. Emanuel's musical experience was broad, covering sacred and secular instrumental and vocal music of many styles and nationalities and in all genres except opera.

While attending Leipzig University (1731–34), Emanuel lived at home and was musical assistant to his father. After transferring to the University of Frankfurt-an-der-Oder in 1734, he taught keyboard lessons and composed music for public concerts or special occasions. Before moving to Frankfurt, Emanuel had written five keyboard sonatas, six keyboard sonatinas, a keyboard suite, seven trios, a flute solo, an oboe solo, two harpsichord concertos, and some chamber music. During the next four years he enlarged that list by at least a dozen more instrumental works.

In 1738 Crown Prince Frederick of Prussia employed Emanuel to perform chamber music (Fig. 18.4). Bach was not the only accompanist among the court

FIGURE 18.4 Adolf Menzel's painting *Frederick's Flute Concert at Sans Souci* depicts Frederick the Great playing the flute accompanied by his chamber orchestra, with C. P. E. Bach at the harpsichord. Quantz is standing at the extreme right, almost out of the picture. The music room at *Sans Souci,* in Potsdam, is small, with yellow walls, white woodwork, and gilt accents; the flooring is parquet hardwood. *(Neue Nationalgalerie, Berlin.)*

EIGHTEENTH-CENTURY PRECLASSIC MUSIC

musicians; his compositions were seldom performed at court, and his salary was very low. On the other hand, he had ample time to teach, compose, and write. In 1742 he witnessed the establishment of the Berlin Opera and learned about dramatic music from performances there. However, he never composed an opera. The most influential compositions Emanuel wrote while at court were solo keyboard pieces, including the six "Prussian" Sonatas (1743) and six "Württemburg" Sonatas (1744).

Publication of Part 1 of *Versuch über die wahre Art das Clavier zu spielen* (Essay on the true art of playing keyboard instruments; 1753) established Emanuel Bach's reputation as the leading keyboard teacher of that time. Part 2 of Bach's *Essay* appeared in 1762. In the late twentieth century, Bach's *Essay* is considered one of the most important practical treatises on music written in the eighteenth century—a standard guide to all aspects of keyboard performance practices. Emanuel stated rules clearly and illustrated them with examples.

Bach may have felt compelled to write his *Essay* because he knew Quantz was preparing a treatise. Quantz's *Versuch einer Anweisung die Flöte traversiere zu spielen* (Instructional essay on playing the transverse flute; 1752) contains only five chapters on flute playing; the remainder concerns almost all phases of musical performance. Quantz's treatise is the most comprehensive and reliable source of information about the eighteenth-century flute and its playing technique. Quantz and Bach wrote for the one-keyed (D♭ key) conical transverse flute developed by Hotteterre, the standard model during the first half of the eighteenth century.

When J. S. Bach died, Emanuel took into his home his young half-brother, Johann Christian. Emanuel maintained close contact with Telemann, who became almost a second father to him. When Telemann died (1767), Emanuel was named his successor at Hamburg. However, Bach's association with the Prussian court was not completely severed. When he left the king's employ, Frederick's sister, Princess Anna Amalia (1723–87; Insight, "Princess Anna Amalia") named him her nonresident chapelmaster.

Bach was Kantor of the Lateinschule at Hamburg for 20 years. In many respects, his position paralleled that his father had held at the Tomasschule. Emanuel's

Princess Anna Amalia

Anna Amalia was an accomplished keyboard player, a capable violinist and flautist, and a composer. Her first music lessons were from her brother; then she studied with Berlin organist Gottlieb Hayne and J. P. Kirnberger. Anna Amalia's oratorio *Der Tod Jesu* (The Death of Jesus) preceded that by K. H. Graun. Kirnberger used an excerpt from it as a model in his composition treatise *Die Kunst des reinen Satzes in der Musik*. Anna Amalia composed arias, chorales, songs, marches, and sonatas. Several of her works have been published, including a *Sonata for Flute* (F major) and a *Trio Sonata*. She amassed a library of several thousand books and more than 650 musical items, including autograph scores by J. S. and C. P. E. Bach, Handel, Hasse, Kirnberger, and Telemann. She bequeathed that library to the Berlin Joachimsthalschen Gymnasium. In 1914 the music portion was transferred to the Royal Library and is now in German government libraries in Berlin.

duties included providing music for approximately 200 performances annually for five churches, plus music for the school and for special civic, political, and religious ceremonies and occasions of all kinds. He taught keyboard lessons, and performed and published music. Also, he edited a serial, *Musikalisches Vierley* (Musical Quarterly; 1770), a compilation of keyboard pieces, chamber music, and songs with keyboard accompaniment, by various composers, for general popular use.

For Gottfried van Swieten, Austrian ambassador to Prussia, Emanuel composed six symphonies (W182 = H657–62; 1773) and dedicated to him the third collection of *Sonaten für Kenner und Liebhaber* (Sonatas for connoisseurs and amateurs; 1781). When van Swieten returned to Vienna, he actively championed the music of J. S. and C. P. E. Bach and Handel by arranging for performances of their works at weekly concerts. Through van Swieten, Mozart became acquainted with this "old" music. Awareness of Emanuel Bach spread. Haydn played some of his keyboard sonatas; C. G. Neefe (1748–98), who taught Beethoven, knew Emanuel's keyboard music and Sebastian's *The Well-Tempered Clavier.*

During the last 20 years of his life. C. P. E. Bach was required to be primarily a composer of church music. Among his extant sacred works are psalm settings, chorales, cantatas, Passions, and the oratorios *Die Israeliten in der Wüste* (The Israelites in the wilderness; 1769) and *Auferstehung und Himmelfahrt Jesu* (Jesus's resurrection and ascension; c. 1777). Emanuel's oratorios are the best written in Germany during that era. Bach's employment demanded a vast amount of choral music, but at that time Lutheran church music was declining. The place of choral music in the life of the congregation was changing; use of the traditional chorale in the service had diminished. Although it was Emanuel's job to supply requisite music for the churches, this choral music became of secondary importance to him, and many times he adapted works of others.

C. P. E. BACH'S MUSIC

Bach created music on two levels: to meet his own high standards and to please his patron and/or appeal to the public. His finest compositions are 6 collections of keyboard pieces for connoisseurs and amateurs (W55–59, W61); next in importance are 12 keyboard concertos (W41–47) and 10 symphonies (H657–66). ("W" numbers are those in Wotquenne's thematic catalogue; "H" numbers are from Helm's catalog.)

Emanuel's first composition was for keyboard, and he composed keyboard works all his life. The harpsichord was the preferred keyboard instrument in Emanuel's time. He performed on it and composed for it; however, he preferred the clavichord, which was capable of producing subtle and expressive shadings. On the clavichord he could produce the *Bebung* (vibrato) because the metal tangent remained in contact with the string until the player's finger released the key. Emanuel's fantasias, rondos, and some of his sonatas sound best when played on clavichord. Present in them are abrupt changes of mood, remote modulations, and the characteristics of *empfindsamer Stil*—melodic sighs, triplet sixteenths, sudden dynamic changes, Lombardic rhythmic figures, chromaticism, and various kinds of ornaments indicated by symbols and miniature notes. His last five sets of keyboard sonatas (1780–87) are for fortepiano.

Many of Bach's keyboard sonatas are rather conservative. Some were written for popular consumption (e.g., the sonatas *für Liebhaberinnen* [for lady amateurs; W54; c. 1765–66]).

Bach's sonatas are usually in three movements, in fast-slow-fast order of tempo. The outer movements are in binary form, with a kind of development and a recapitulation in the second half. Bach tended to develop themes as soon as he stated them; consequently, the development section immediately after the double bar is rather short. Usually, the slow movements are through-composed. His choice of key for some of his sonatas was unusual (e.g., F minor). Haydn and Beethoven were influenced by Bach's Sonata in F minor.

Bach's concertos for harpsichord and orchestra are virtuosic keyboard works, designed for his own use. Basically, he followed Vivaldi's formal plan; however, the outer movements are a blend of ritornello and sonata form.

Bach wrote 12 "sonatinas" for solo harpsichord and orchestra. In these concertato-type works the solo harpsichord music is often quite virtuosic; for this reason the sonatinas are sometimes classified as miniature concertos. The sonatinas resemble suites, however, for they contain from 2 to 10 short movements in binary or miniature sonata form, and all movements are in the same key.

C. P. E. Bach was one of the principal symphonists of the north German school. Some of his 20 symphonies are in *empfindsamer Stil*; the four *Orchester-Sinfonien mit 12 obligaten Stimmen* (Orchestral symphonies with 12 required parts; W183 = H663–66; 1776) exhibit the fire and energy of *Sturm und Drang*. Symphony No. 3 (H665; F major) has three movements: Allegro di molto (DWMA121), Larghetto, and Presto. The general tone of the first movement foreshadows Beethoven; in fact, Beethoven borrowed the first theme (see p. 415, 417).

Emanuel's chamber music includes solo sonatas with basso continuo; trio sonatas; harpsichord/violin and harpsichord/flute duets; chamber sonatas that are true trios for two instruments and harpsichord; and three quartets for flute, viola, violoncello, and harpsichord, written in Classic style, with balance of parts, thus foreshadowing the piano quartet. Bach was one of the first composers to elevate the keyboard from its accompanist/continuo status and make it an equal partner in chamber music or give it a leading role in ensemble music.

C. P. E. Bach composed approximately 300 songs with keyboard accompaniment. These are strophic settings in which the poetry is more important than the music. For this reason, the harmony is intentionally thin. The settings are simple but effective.

Emanuel seldom wrote fugues or used Baroque counterpoint. They did not fit the style of music he espoused. The *Magnificat* (1749) contains a rare instance of his use of fugue, in the *Sicut erat in principio* section.

THE SYMPHONY

The symphony took its name from and was a direct outgrowth of the Italian opera overture (sinfonia) in use during the last two decades of the seventeenth century. However, the Preclassic symphony is indebted to several other forms—especially trio sonata and Baroque concerto (solo, concerto grosso, and orchestral)—for certain internal details of structure, texture, style, and instrumentation.

Usually, the overture to an early eighteenth-century Italian opera served merely to advise the audience that the opera was about to commence; it bore no thematic relationship to the opera it prefaced. Consequently, an opera overture could be performed as an independent piece on other occasions. Many opera overtures were published as sinfonie without reference to the operas for which they had been written.

Around 1730, composers began to write concert sinfonie, following the tempo plan Alessandro Scarlatti devised in 1681 for his opera overtures: three movements, in fast-slow-fast order, with the finale dancelike in character and usually in triple meter ($\frac{3}{8}$ or $\frac{3}{4}$). The instrumentation used most often was strings, two oboes, two horns, and basso continuo; this became the standard Preclassic orchestra. Occasionally, a piece would call for flutes instead of oboes, but not for oboes *and* flutes because it was common for the same persons to play both instruments. Of course, composers wrote for whatever combination of instruments was at their disposal; this might be only strings with basso continuo, and the number of strings might be as few as three or four.

The number of independent symphonies known to have been written in 1730–40 is quite small. Among the few composers making substantial contributions to the repertoire during that decade were G. B. Sammartini (1701–75) in Milan and J. G. Harrer, who was then working in Dresden. Harrer wrote at least 27 symphonies.

Sammartini is credited with the earliest datable concert symphony using rudimentary but recognizable sonata form. That sinfonia was originally the overture to his opera *Memet* (1732). He usually constructed his symphonies in three movements: the first movement in sonata form or an approximation thereof; a slow, lyrical second movement characterized by expressive chromaticism and *galant* ornamentation; and the third movement either in concise sonata form or a minuet. Sammartini recognized the functional difference between an opera overture (which prefaces a larger work) and a concert sinfonia (complete in itself), and he designed the symphony Finale so that it would bring the multimovement work to an impressive conclusion. His early symphonies are scored for strings and basso continuo and are thin-textured (DWMA122). Some of them might be called orchestral trio sonatas, or trio symphonies. Most of the 37 symphonies he wrote c. 1740–58 include either two trumpets or two horns. His 12 late symphonies (c. 1759–74) are Classic in style, with independent parts for two oboes, and with 'cello and bass often independent (instead of doubling each other).

Though sonata form eventually became the accepted (and expected) structural pattern for the first movement of a symphony, many of the early sinfonie used other forms, such as binary, rounded binary, or exposition-recapitulation (no development). In fact, pure sonata form rarely occurs. Rather, within the basic outlines of that form, there were many variants.

Composition of Italianate concert symphonies spread into other areas of Europe by Italians working outside Italy and by northern European composers who returned to their native lands after studying or working in Italy. Occasionally, composers wrote four-movement symphonies, with a minuet or gigue-like finale. After 1740, the symphony gradually supplanted the Baroque concerto as the leading form of concerted instrumental music. It has retained that status in the succeeding centuries.

Other composers whose works were important in the early history of the symphony include Nicolò Jommelli at Stuttgart and Baldassare Galuppi, Johann

Stamitz at Mannheim, J. G. Graun and C. P. E. Bach at the Prussian court and later at Hamburg, Georg Monn and G. C. Wagenseil at Vienna, and L. G. Guillemain and F.-J. Gossec at Paris (see map, fig. 18.5).

MANNHEIM

Mannheim supported virtually no musical life until 1720, when Karl Philip, Elector Palatine (r. 1718–42), moved his entire court there. Music at Karl Philip's court consisted of concerts and church music; there was no opera until 1742. Karl Philip died on the last day of 1742 and was succeeded by his granddaughter's husband, Prince Karl Theodor (b. 1724; r. 1743–99).

Several factors contributed to Mannheim's rise to prominence as a center of music: The Palatinate was at peace while its court was at Mannheim. Karl Theodor was a performing musician. During his tenure, the size of the court chapel increased considerably. Johann Stamitz was a strict disciplinarian who insisted that every instrumentalist be properly trained and perform with the utmost precision. His successor, Christian Cannabich (1731–98), was even more pedantic. Most of the musicians were exceptional in being virtuoso soloists as well as superb ensemble players; many were excellent composers.

The orchestra at Mannheim became the largest and finest in Europe. In 1756 Stamitz had at his disposal 56 instrumentalists. The ensemble was famous for precision of attack, uniform bowing in the string sections, and the ability to produce the slightest dynamic nuances. Among the effective special effects that brought acclaim to the orchestra were (a) extended crescendos and diminuendos, ranging from softest *pianissimo* to loudest *fortissimo;* (b) unexpected general pauses that created great windows of silence; (c) measured tremolo; (d) the "roll," scale passages in measured tremolo, coupled with crescendo (ex. 18.4a); and (e) the "Mannheim rocket," the rapid upward arpeggiation of a chord over a wide range (ex. 18.4b). Discipline lay at the heart of the orchestra's fine performances. Stamitz controlled the ensemble with slight movements of his bow, a nod of his head, or a glance.

JOHANN VÁCLAV ANTON STAMITZ   Stamitz (1717–57) received his early musical training from his father and attended the Jesuit Gymnasium in Jihlava, Bohemia. The Bohemian Jesuit schools produced some of the foremost musicians in Europe at that time. In 1741 Stamitz joined the Mannheim court orchestra as a violinist, soon became Konzertmeister, and by 1750 was Director of Instrumental Music. In 1754–55 he worked for La Pouplinière in France; then he returned to Mannheim and worked at court until his death, at age 39.

Stamitz composed chamber music, concertos, symphonies, orchestral trios, cantatas, and liturgical music, including at least one Mass. His symphonies and 10 orchestral trios are his most important works; approximately 60 symphonies are extant. His early symphonies are scored for strings with basso continuo;

FIGURE 18.5 The principal centers of symphony composition in the eighteenth century.

EXAMPLE 18.4 (a) The "Mannheim roll." (b) the "Mannheim rocket."

occasionally, he included 2 horns. In later works he used 2 horns, 2 oboes *or* 2 flutes, and in 5 of the symphonies, 2 trumpets and timpani. He included 2 clarinets in some of the symphonies he wrote in Paris.

For the most part, Stamitz reinforced what the Italians were doing in the transference of sinfonia as opera overture to sinfonia as concert symphony. His principal innovation in symphonic writing is his adoption of the four-movement structural plan: a fast first movement in sonata form, a slow second movement, minuet and trio third, and a Presto or Prestissimo finale. He seems to have been the first composer to use that formal design consistently; it occurs in more than half his extant symphonies and in nine of his orchestral trios. Often, the first movements have two themes, with presentation of the second theme assigned to winds. Because there were excellent wind-instrument players at Mannheim, Stamitz treated winds independently much of the time rather than have them double string parts. His symphonies contain all the Mannheim mannerisms—dynamic surprises and nuances, melodic sighs, the "roll," and the "rocket." Representative of Stamitz's symphonic writing is *Sinfonia a 8* in D major (*La Melodia Germanica,* No. 1; written c. 1755; DWMA123).

VIENNA

In the eighteenth century, Vienna lay at the crossroads of European civilization. As the seat of the Holy Roman Empire, it exerted widespread cultural influence. The *Hofkapelle* was maintained, and excellent composers and musicians were employed there. More important was the patronage of numerous aristocratic families, such as the Esterházy, Lobkowitz, and Lichnowsky, whose establishments provided a favorable climate for musical talent. Viennese attention, during the Preclassic era, seems to have been directed primarily toward Italian opera and chamber music, though a few composers produced symphonies in profusion. One who did was Georg C. Wagenseil (1715–77); 82 symphonies by him are extant. His symphonies were performed frequently and were disseminated internationally. He used a three-movement scheme: fast-minuet-fast or fast-slow-minuet. In general, the symphonies have small dimensions and three-voice texture. First movements are *galant* in style and, viewed chronologically,

reflect Wagenseil's increasing command of the principles of sonata form. The slow movements of his early symphonies contain many Baroque elements, but gradually the writing becomes lighter, more delicate, more *galant*. Likewise, the finales gradually become more substantial; in the late symphonies, frequently the finale is a rondo.

Georg Monn (1717–50) is considered a leading Viennese composer of symphonies. His symphonic style is conservative. All his symphonies have small proportions; he seldom included horns, and many of his themes are motivic.

Among František X. Dušek's (1731–99) extant works are 20 string quartets and 40 symphonies that vary stylistically from *galant* to Classic. In his three-movement symphonies, the order of movements is fast-slow-fast; in the four-movement ones, and in most of the string quartets, a fast-slow-minuet-fast pattern is followed. First movements are bithematic, in sonata form, with brief development sections; a few finales are extensive rondos.

PARIS

In Paris c. 1723–89 music was dominated by opera. When religious regulations forbade theatrical presentations, public concerts were scheduled by the *Concert spirituel.* In addition, concerts were given almost every day somewhere in or near Paris at some patron's home. The *Concert spirituel* was one of the central institutions in Parisian nonoperatic life. Important local musicians and visiting artists often performed their own compositions there. The journey from Mannheim to Paris could be made with relative ease, and composers from Mannheim frequently appeared at *Concert spirituel.*

Louis-Gabriel Guillemain (1705–70) seems to have been the first Parisian to compose symphonies. His 12 symphonies are extant. Written for two violins and basso continuo, they are Italianate and *galant* in style.

The most important symphonist working in Paris after 1756 was François-Joseph Gossec (1734–1829). He came to Paris from the Netherlands in 1751, with a letter of introduction to Rameau. A vacancy in La Pouplinière's orchestra had just occurred, and Gossec was hired immediately to play violin and bass. He worked for La Pouplinière until 1762.

Gossec wrote approximately 50 symphonies, of which 47 survive. His *Symphonie in D* (1761) is one of the first orchestral works in France to use clarinets. Gossec favored the clarinet and did a great deal to promote its use. Most of his symphonies are four-movement works, with Menuet. The sonata-form fast movements are bithematic and contain Mannheim mannerisms. It is surprising that Gossec did not include trombones in any of his symphonies, especially because he used trombones in his operas and liturgical music.

Gossec made major contributions to the development of music in France by promoting use of the clarinet, providing a vast repertoire of military wind ensemble music, helping establish the Paris Conservatoire and creating instructional materials for its curriculum, and composing symphonies. Beethoven and Berlioz were influenced by Gossec's works.

TREATISES

Around the middle of the eighteenth century, several important treatises concerning performance practices were written by men who were recognized as outstanding performers, teachers, and composers. Quantz's *Versuch einer Anweisung die Flöte traversiere zu spielen* (see p. 340) was translated into French and published simultaneously in Berlin and Paris in 1752. The following year, C. P. E. Bach's *Versuch über die wahre Art das Clavier zu spielen* was published in Berlin. Leopold Mozart's *Versuch einer gründlichen Violinschule* (Essay on the fundamental principles of violin playing) appeared in Augsburg in 1756; and in Paris in 1771 P. Denis published Giuseppe Tartini's *Traité des Agrémens de la Musique* (Treatise on ornaments in music). These writings provide valuable information not only about playing flute, keyboard, and violin but also about the proper performance of all kinds of eighteenth-century music. All these treatises are available in English translation as well as in their original languages.

Tartini (1692–1770) was the most renowned Italian violinist in the mid-eighteenth century. Violinists from all over Europe were attracted to his "School of the Nations" at Padua. Among his pupils were Pietro Nardini (1722–93), Signora Maddalena Lombardini-Sirmen (1735–c. 1786), Pierre de la Houssaye (1735–1818), and Giovanni F. Nicolai (leading violinist in Rome in 1770). Sirmen, who had a brilliant career in Paris, continued her studies by correspondence; a lesson-letter Tartini wrote to her in March 1760 has been published many times.

Several of Tartini's students copied his *Regole per arrivare a saper ben suonar il Violino* (Rules for learning to play the violin well); French and Italian manuscript copies are extant. A modern multilingual edition entitled *Traité des Agréments de la Musique* was published in 1961. The treatise, whose rules for ornamentation are applicable to both vocal and instrumental music, was in existence before 1756; Leopold Mozart pirated large portions from it for his essay on violin playing.

Tartini's violin sonatas and virtuosic violin concertos—approximately 135 of each—and numerous sinfonie considerably enriched the repertoire. Tartini blended elements of *style galant* and *empfindsamer Stil* with northern Italian characteristics; his works are predominantly Preclassic.

MUSIC IN AMERICA

In New Spain (Mexico) the principal centers of musical activity were the large cathedrals at Mexico City, Puebla, and Valladolid (now Morelia). Almost all the music that has survived from the eighteenth century is vocal and sacred, much of it with instrumental accompaniment, which indicates that, in composed music, sacred music predominated. A number of instrumentalists—more strings than winds—are listed on cathedral rosters.

Some secular and some purely instrumental music was written, however. The second opera known to have been composed in the New World, *La Parténope* ([Queen] Partenope), by Manuel de Zumaya (c. 1678–1756), was performed at the viceroyal palace on 1 May 1711. Only the libretto survives.

At Valladolid, the *Colégio de Santa Rosa*, a convent for orphan girls, was founded in 1738. In connection with the *Colégio*, a school of music was founded c. 1740. In the *Colégio* archives are two sinfonie in Preclassic style. There must have been a local orchestra (at either the school or the church) capable of performing them.

Vocal Music

ITALIAN OPERA

The Arcadian neoclassical reform that occurred in Italian literature in the late seventeenth century effected some changes in the structure of the Italian opera libretto. Literary neoclassicists were concerned primarily with the purity of dramatic types, the purposes of drama, the concepts of decorum and verisimilitude, and the observation of the three unities of time, place, and action. Neoclassicists recognized only two kinds of drama as legitimate forms—tragedy and comedy—and insisted that there be no mixing of tragic and comic elements in a drama; each form had its own rules with regard to type of plot, characters, and style. However, literary reformers were only partially successful in their attempts to subject opera libretti to such strict regulation, for the amorous intrigues common to opera plots often involved a mixture of character types.

When the libretto was purged of comic elements, **opera seria** (serious opera) resulted. Usually, opera seria plots were based on heroic stories dealing with affairs of state, the downfall of rulers, or similar events and included a conflict of passions. Almost always, by the end of the opera the main characters had been extricated from their dilemmas. The poetic style was lofty. Apostolo Zeno (1668–1750) and contemporary poets observed the three unities, decreased the number of arias in an opera, and considered carefully the function of those arias and their placement within the opera. In 1718 Zeno became court poet to Emperor Charles VI but accepted that appointment under the condition that he not be required to write comedy or occasional poetry. When Zeno retired in 1729, Pietro Metastasio (1698–1782) succeeded him.

METASTASIO

Metastasio became the greatest Italian dramatist and poet of his era. Because he encountered no serious rivals, he was able to shape and dominate opera seria. During the eighteenth and early nineteenth centuries, his 27 three-act heroic opera libretti were set more than 800 times. In the late 1720s, Metastasio standardized opera seria format. Actually, he was aided by circumstances. Economic conditions at Italian opera houses could not support large expenditures for spectacle, so extravagant *divertissements* were out of the question. Casts were smaller, and there were only three acts, with fewer scene changes. Generally, Metastasio's cast numbered six or seven characters, the principals being *primo uomo* (leading man, a castrato), *prima donna* (leading lady, a soprano), and a tenor (as father, king, mentor, or similar role); secondary characters included *secondo uomo* (castrato), *seconda donna,* and whoever else was requisite to the plot. Often, a "magnanimous tyrant" was included.

Though Metastasio considered music an accessory to his dramas, the fact that his poetry was set to music exercised considerable influence on the structure and style he used. The libretto settled into an alternation of unrhymed recitative (to propel the narrative) and strophic aria (for commentary, reaction, and reflection). Occasionally, a duet was inserted; larger ensembles were rare. After playing the overture, the orchestra had little to do except accompany the singers. Most recitatives were *secco,* with minimal harmonic support supplied by basso continuo; only at points of heightened dramatic action was *recitativo accompagnato* used. Musical interest was centered in the arias. Italian singers were the finest in Europe. Certain singers attracted the public to attend opera performances repeatedly. Thus, both librettist and composer were encouraged to concentrate on arias.

Judiciously, Metastasio distributed the arias within the opera in accordance with the importance of the characters and positioned an aria at the end of a scene, usually culminating in the singer's exit. It was the composer's task to ascertain that successive arias differed to some degree in musical style. Almost invariably, composers set arias in *da capo* form, but within that basic ABA outline considerable variance was possible. The A and B sections might be of equal length, or the B section might be quite short. Tonally and melodically, an aria might resemble a rounded binary, or the orchestral introduction might be treated as a ritornello, recurring between phrases or couplets of the text. By c. 1760, some composers were writing arias with a tonal plan approximating sonata form. The *da capo* pattern provided ample opportunity for a singer to improvise ornaments on the return of the A section and permitted the insertion of a virtuosic cadenza just prior to the final cadence.

Concentration of musical interest in the aria gave rise to numerous abuses. Many singers, capitalizing on personal popularity, demanded that poets and composers include additional arias and alter others to provide greater opportunity for virtuosic display. If their demands were not met, singers substituted arias for which they were famous, regardless of the musical and dramatic unsuitability and the ethical impropriety of such action. Sometimes the *da capo* section of an aria was embellished to extremes. Critics and some composers decried the rampant abuses, but their words of condemnation had no immediate effect. Joseph Addison's (1672–1719) essays in *The Spectator* (London, c. 1711–12) and Benedetto Marcello's (1686–1739) satire *Il teatro alla moda* (The fashionable theater; Venice, c. 1720; fig. 18.6) point out specific abuses. Important reforms were not forthcoming until the mid-1740s.

In the late 1720s and early 1730s, opera composers began using *galante* style. Leonardo Vinci (c. 1690–1730) seems to have been the first to do so. Other composers working in Italy at this time who used *galante* style in operas include Nicola Porpora (1686–1768), Johann Adolph Hasse (1699–1783), and Giovanni Battista Pergolesi (1710–36).

PERGOLESI

Both *galante* and the older style of opera are present in the work of Pergolesi. Though Pergolesi is best known for *La serva padrona*, one of his finest operas is *L'Olimpiade* (1735), which contains intensely expressive, lyrical melodies structured in periodic phrases. In *L'Olimpiade,* the aria is assigned a new function—to bring the action in a scene to climax rather than summarize it. For stanzas that increase the tension *da capo* form is inappropriate. Pergolesi's treatment of *Se cerca, se dice* (If searching, asking) was a model for others setting that text.

Tragedy and comedy were combined when the acts of an opera seria were interlaced with and separated by

FIGURE 18.6 Title page of the composer Benedetto Marcello's satire *Il teatro alla moda.* The gondolier represents Vivaldi.

the acts of a comic *intermezzo* (see also p. 349). Sometimes the intermezzo was accorded greater acclaim than the opera seria. Such was the case with *La serva padrona* (The maid as mistress; 1733), Pergolesi's intermezzo for his opera *Il prigionier superbo* (The proud prisoner; 1733). *La serva padrona,* for three characters—a soprano, a bass, and a mute—accompanied by strings and basso continuo, clearly displays Pergolesi's genius for setting comic scenes and character depiction. The story concerns a clever girl who, through intrigue, rises in social status from servant to mistress in the home of a wealthy old bachelor. Eight years earlier, Telemann had used a similar plot for *Pimpinone,* which had only two singing roles and was popular as an independent comic opera.

Because *La serva padrona* originated as an intermezzo, it has no overture. The work opens with a short aria sung by the irascible Uberto as he waits for the maid to answer his summons. Serpina's first aria reveals her wit and determination and her scorn for Uberto.

Most of the music is in major; that sung by Uberto is almost always in flat keys, whereas Serpina's is in sharps. Not all the arias are *da capo*. Much of the time, the melodic line is disjunct, and, though there is much repetition of short motives, the music is never monotonous. Unexpected accents on off-beats produce comic effects. Each act concludes with a duet (DWMA124).

Almost immediately after its première, *La serva padrona* was staged independently. It became a favorite with traveling opera troupes and was performed throughout Europe, reaching Paris in 1746 and again in 1752 (see p. 352).

HASSE

Hasse joined the Hamburg Opera Company in 1718 as a tenor. Late in 1721 he visited Italy. He studied with Alessandro Scarlatti, assimilated the Italian operatic style, and became one of the most successful opera and intermezzo composers in Naples. His *Artaserse* was produced in Venice in 1730; *Dalisa* and *Arminio* soon followed, with mezzo-soprano Faustina Bordoni (1700–81) as prima donna.

Faustina and her celebrated rival, soprano Francesca Cuzzoni (c. 1698–1770), were the first *prime donne* to achieve international acclaim and were among the finest singers of the era. Under the guidance of Benedetto Marcello, Faustina studied singing with Gasparini. In addition to her remarkable singing voice, she was endowed with acting ability, beauty, and a charming personality. In the 1720s, she sang leading roles in many of Handel's operas in London; in

Faustina Bordoni. Painted by Rosalba Carriera in 1757. *(Ca'* *Rezzonico, Venice)*

1728–31, she sang in various cities in northern Italy. Faustina married Hasse in 1730 and for the remainder of her life her career was linked with his.

Early in 1730, Hasse was appointed Kapellmeister to the Elector of Saxony. By 1750, Hasse was Europe's most successful opera composer. Approximately 75 of his operas are extant. Hasse became Metastasio's favorite composer, justifiably, for he complied with the librettist's requests, heeded his suggestions, and composed music that complemented the poetry perfectly. Hasse set 24 of Metastasio's libretti, some more than once.

In Hasse's opere serie, the orchestral accompaniment was (at Metastasio's suggestion) minimal and transparent. Attention was focused on the lyricism and fluidity of the vocal line. He constructed beautiful melodies that are elegant and smoothly flowing and supported them with simple harmonies. Gradually, *da capo* aria was displaced by abridged *da capo* or *dal segno* types; by 1771 he was writing some through-composed arias, and he decreased the number of arias per opera by about 50 percent. *Il Ruggiero,* his last opera, contains 16 arias, only 6 of them *da capo.*

As Hasse carried the Italian *galante*-style setting of neoclassical opera seria to Dresden in the 1730s, other Italian-trained opera composers transmitted that style to other courts. Nicolò Jommelli (1714–74) went to Vienna and later to Stuttgart; Tommaso Traetta (1727–79) went to Vienna and on to Mannheim; J. C. Bach composed *galante* style operas in London.

JOMMELLI

Hasse, Leo, and other composers working in Naples during Jommelli's student years shaped his compositional style. His career as a composer of stage works was launched with two comic operas performed in Naples in 1737; by 1745 he was enjoying a successful career as an opera and oratorio composer. In his operas Jommelli used orchestral resources advantageously. He frequently treated first and second violins as separate textural lines, sometimes scored an independent part for viola, and used dynamic markings abundantly, especially crescendo. Orchestral innovations that often are credited (erroneously) to Stamitz and the Mannheim school—the use of a contrasting second theme in the dominant key, contrasting passages (or sections) for pairs of instruments, and the

"Mannheim rocket"—really originated with Jommelli in sinfonie composed in the 1740s. His sinfonie were heard in Germany before 1750 and in Paris soon thereafter.

Jommelli was at the height of his career in 1753. His liturgical music was sung at the Vatican, his opere serie were performed throughout Europe, and traveling troupes included his comic operas in their repertoires. The performances that provoked the notorious *Querelle des Bouffons* in Paris included Jommelli's *Il paratajo* (The tapestry). As Kapellmeister at Stuttgart he had almost unlimited resources and absolute control over every aspect of opera production except choice of subject matter. He composed operas that were cosmopolitan in style, used orchestral resources to the fullest, and elevated the orchestra from accompanist to equal partner with the singer.

JOHANN CHRISTIAN BACH

Johann Christian, youngest son of J. S. Bach, served for a short time as second organist at Milan Cathedral—he converted to Catholicism in 1757—before turning to opera composition. After successful performances of several operas, including settings of Metastasio's *Artaserse* (1760), *Catone in Utica* (Cato in Utica; 1761), and *Alessandro nell' Indie* (Alexander in India; 1762), Bach moved to London to write operas for King's Theater. Twelve of his operas survive, all Italianate in style.

In 1766 Bach met soprano Cecilia Grassi (c. 1740–82), who was prima donna in serious operas at King's Theater that season. At some time after 1776, they married. Grassi's theatrical talent was modest; reportedly, her voice was sweet, and she sang with perfect intonation. Bach composed several cantatas for her, and during 1773–76 she performed regularly in Bach-Abel concerts.

TRAETTA

Tommaso Traetta wrote both comic and serious operas. In 1758 he was appointed to the court at Parma with the assignment of combining elements of French *tragédie lyrique* with Italian elements in opera. As his fame spread, he received commissions from Vienna, Turin, and Mannheim. Traetta relied heavily on orchestral color for expressive effect, wrote many accompanied recitatives, and structured arias in forms other than *da capo*. In Vienna, he was influenced considerably by Gluck's operas. In 1768 Traetta became musical director of opera at the court of Catherine II (r. 1762–96) at St. Petersburg. There he produced his operatic masterpiece, *Antigone* (1772), in which he repeatedly used a few easily identified motifs (e.g., a figure depicting sobbing). Such motivic repetition may have been commonplace at the time, but until that is proven it must be assumed that Traetta used techniques of later importance in opera.

INTERMEZZO

In the eighteenth century, the term intermezzo (pl., *intermezzi*) was used to denote a comic interlude sung between the acts of an opera seria. The intermezzo can be traced back to entertainments presented between the acts of plays during the early Renaissance. Intermezzi—then termed *intermedi*—covered gaps in the dramatic performance when no one was on stage. The earliest *intermedi* consisted of music played behind the scenery and functioned to mark off the acts in the drama. Gradually, visible interludes were used; mimed, dance, and sung entertainments were presented between acts. At the Medici court in Florence in the early sixteenth century, costumed entertainers appeared between acts, and each interlude was designed to point up the passage of time between the action in the segments of the drama it separated. As *intermedi* became longer and more spectacular, the time element disappeared.

In the early seventeenth-century monodic operas, *intermedi* were used as divisions between acts. Moreover, some sixteenth-century *intermedi* provided subject matter for operas. By the end of the seventeenth century, the scenic spectacles presented between acts often included the comic servants of the opera cast. Sometimes the *intermedi* were of greater interest than the drama itself.

Occasionally, in the eighteenth century, short ballets served as intermezzi, but more often comic scenes were presented. At Naples, until c. 1720, intermezzi related to the subject and cast of the opera seria were incorporated into almost every new opera. Elsewhere in Italy, particularly in Venice, dramatically independent comic intermezzi were prepared by the composers of the serious operas with which they were first performed. The intermezzi used with an opera followed a continuous plot; thus, in performance the acts of a serious opera and a short comic one were interlaced.

The *commedia dell'arte* (comedy of artisans), centuries old, was a model for librettists writing intermezzi. Borrowings from it include stock characters with traditional names, comic antics, disguises, tricks, and regional dialects (Insight *"Commedia dell'arte"*). As early as 1716, itinerant troupes included intermezzi in their repertoire.

In the second quarter of the eighteenth century, the intermezzo entered its golden age, especially in Naples. Almost all composers working there composed some of them. One of the most common plots concerns a cunning woman, cast as maidservant, widow, or shepherdess, who plays a trick on her male partner or traps him into matrimony—or both. Frequently, the lady's name matches her character (e.g., Vespetta [little wasp] in *Pimpinone* and Serpina [little snake] in *La serva padrona*).

In its maturity, the intermezzo assumed a rather rigid format. The libretto, usually in two acts, was designed for two singing roles and often included one or two mute characters. Each act contained two or three *da capo* arias, separated by *secco* recitatives, and concluded with a duet. The music was homophonic, with melodies in short phrases supported by simple harmonies. Often, local dialects were used for part or all of the texts. Only when an intermezzo was performed independently of the drama for which it was created did it require an overture.

OPERA BUFFA

Opera buffa and intermezzo developed contemporaneously in the eighteenth century. Opera buffa is full-length comic opera with a comparatively large cast of characters with singing roles. Usually, the cast included a pair of young lovers whose plans for marriage were hindered by some misunderstanding or

---

INSIGHT

Commedia dell'arte

The *commedia dell'arte* was an actor-centered, improvised form of comic drama that appeared in Italy in the 1540s and flourished for about two centuries. The actors were professionals—skilled improvisators, endowed with imagination and ready wit and adaptable to almost any kind of audience and playing condition. Equipped with only skeletal scripts that sketched out the main turns of event in a few basic plots, they relied on their ingenuity to flesh out comic drama suited to current conditions and the locale in which they found themselves. Use of local dialect(s) was an important feature of the presentation. Because no parts were written, the dialogue was always new and fresh.

There was a set of stock characters, most of them wearing standard costumes (now regarded as "tradi-tional") and masks. Included were two elderly men (parent, guardian, or professionals), two *zanni* ("madcap" male servants), a maidservant, a pair of lovers, and one or two other persons, as needed. In Italy, the two lovers played unmasked and spoke in elegant Tuscan; most of the others used dialect(s). Standard guardian types were Pantalone, a miserly old merchant, usually Venetian; *il Dottore* (the doctor), a boring and pedantic Bolognese lawyer whose lengthy speeches led one to question his learning; and Capitano—later Scaramuccio—a military adventurer or cowardly soldier who boasted of his conquests in war and love. Typical *zanni* were Pulcinella, hunchbacked and with a large nose, and Arlecchino, a nimble, witty servant but a capricious and heartless lover. Two *zanni* were characterized as witty fool and comic rustic. Columbine (dove-like, gentle), a maid, was Arlecchino's female counterpart. Once assigned a certain role, a performer always played that role and acted consistently and realistically. Female roles were played by women.

Itinerant troupes spread the *commedia dell'arte* throughout Europe. Everywhere it remained essentially the same, though slight modifications were made. Between 1750 and 1800, the *commedia dell'arte* gradually died out. However, its use of regional dialect and its stock characters and style influenced and left their marks on ballet, intermezzo and comic opera, the dramas of Shakespeare and Molière, and some poetry and novels. From time to time, traces of *commedia dell'arte* have appeared in some twentieth-century works.

ban; generally, the lovers exploited their elders' foolishness to their own advantage. Other characters included professional persons whose foibles were deliberately exaggerated—a rich merchant, an unscrupulous lawyer, a bungling doctor, a clumsy servant—for, according to belief then current, comedy should instruct the audience through caricature. Often, these professional portrayals reflect the stock characters of *commedia dell'arte*. Other features of comic opera were exploitation of the bass voice, use of ensemble finale, and regional dialects. In opere buffe containing both serious and comic characters, the serious characters spoke in Tuscan and the comic characters in dialect.

The earliest known full-length opera buffa produced in the eighteenth century was Antonio Orefice's (fl. 1708–34) *Patrò Calienno de la Costa* (Father Calienno of Costa; Naples, 1709). Soon Naples became a center for comic opera. At Rome, after c. 1736, comic operas were given during Carnival; in Venice they were presented regularly in the 1740s. Most of the early comic operas were written by composers trained or born in Naples, such as Leonardo Vinci, Leonardo Leo (1694–1744), and Nicola Logroscino (1698–c. 1765).

Baldassare Galuppi (1706–85), of Venice, was the first composer of opera buffa to receive international acclaim. He did so with *Il filosofo di campagna* (The country philosopher; 1754). The comic operas Galuppi composed after 1749, especially those setting the satiric fantasy libretti of Carlo Goldoni (1707–93), are especially fine. Leo and Logroscino used the ensemble finale, but Galuppi closed the acts of his comic operas with a kind of chain finale—a series of short sections linked together and culminating in the ensemble finale. This effect may be credited to Goldoni, who enlarged the finale in length, number of participants, and density of plot. Goldoni increased the importance of the stage setting by creating libretti that demanded beautiful scenery. By accelerating the action and simplifying the plot, he reduced considerably the amount of recitative required and increased the ensemble effects. This stimulated the composer to use a greater variety of musical forms. One of these was the **arietta,** a short, through-composed solo that was not followed by the singer's exit from stage.

At this time, in Venice and in Vienna, the librettist regulated and controlled the form of the drama and in general, the form of the music. The poet distributed the musical numbers according to the requirements of the drama and the specifications of the opera director and company that was to produce the work. Rarely was a composer consulted when a libretto was being written. However, an opera director might make drastic changes in a work because of available facilities or to suit his singers.

Commencing c. 1750, poets began to create some comic opera plots that differ in character from the traditional ones—sentimental or pathetic plots that sometimes contain an element of tragedy while being basically humorous. This kind of comic opera was called **dramma giocoso** (jocular drama). Goldoni wrote a libretto of this type for *La buona figliuola* (The good girl). In its 1760 setting by Niccolò Piccini (1728–1800), *La buona figliuola* became the most popular comic opera of the decade.

Another important work of this type is Giovanni Paisiello's *Il barbiere di Siviglia* (The Barber of Seville; 1782). *Dramma giocoso* reached its peak with Mozart's *Il Don Giovanni* (1787).

LIGHT OPERA OUTSIDE ITALY

In all light opera other than Italian, spoken dialogue was used instead of recitative, and in each country light opera was given its own distinctive name.

OPÉRA COMIQUE

The French form of light opera was called *opéra comique*. The earliest known play that interspersed spoken French dialogue with solos and duets is Adam de la Halle's pastourelle *Le jeu de Robin et de Marion*, written c. 1285. About 450 years later, entertainments of similar construction, known as *comédies mêlées d'ariettes* (plays mixed with little songs), were popular in Paris; however, in those *comédies* the dialogue was considerably expanded by bawdy jokes inserted extemporaneously by the entertainers.

From late medieval times, a type of entertainment called *sotie* (farce) was given at the two Paris *Théâtres de la Foire* during the pre-Easter and summer seasons. Stock characters in these farces included a pretty maiden named Columbine, her lover Arlequin, the old father Cassandre, and the greedy servant Paillasse or the rascal Scaramouche. In the mid-seventeenth century, farces made extensive use of instrumental accompaniment, but after 1670 the use of music was severely restricted by Lully's royal patents.

In 1697 the Comédie-Italienne was suppressed in France, and the Fair Theaters acquired that repertoire. Included were comedies with considerable musical content—overtures, dances, parodies of Lully's operas, and **vaudevilles.** During the reign of Louis XIV, vaudeville texts satirized court and political happenings. Popular melodies were often reused, with many different sets of words. The tunes resemble folk songs—rather short, in a narrow range, with a persistent rhythmic pattern and text set syllabically.

In 1707, when theatrical monopolies prevented the Fair Theaters from presenting spoken dialogues, they mimed scenes and displayed the actors' lines on large placards. Words of the vaudevilles were similarly presented for group singing by the audience. Many songs were structured as couplets with a refrain. In 1715, publicity notices referred to these entertainments as *opéra-comique.* A year later, the Fair Theaters secured permission to present "spectacles mixed with music, dances, and *symphonies* under the name Opéra-Comique."

As opéra comique developed, more original music was added. The entertainment gradually expanded, and each act concluded with a **vaudeville final**—all the important characters were assembled on stage, where each sang one or two verses of a vaudeville. The ensemble finale remained an important feature of opéra comique, and its influence was felt in opera seria (e.g., Gluck's *Orfeo ed Euridice*).

QUERELLE DES BOUFFONS For decades the relative merits of French and Italian music had been debated, though for a time attention had been diverted by comparison of Rameau's and Lully's operas. In August 1752, Bambini's Italian troupe performed Pergolesi's *La serva padrona* in Paris, between the acts of Lully's *Acis et Galatée*. This touched off the *Querelle des Bouffons*—a partisan exchange of pamphlets, letters, and articles that involved more than three dozen writers and lasted about two years. The controversy stimulated production of opéras comiques. Even Rousseau, who had

praised French librettos but declared Italian music superior, composed an opéra comique, *Le devin du village* (The village soothsayer; 1752; DWMA125). Modeled after the Italian intermezzo, with only three characters and no spoken dialogue, the work exhibits folklike simplicity and blends French and Italian styles.

GRÉTRY André-Ernest-Modeste Grétry (1741–1813) dominated the field of opéra comique during the last half of the eighteenth century and contributed to the development of serious opera as well. Of his more than 60 stage works two-thirds are opéras comiques. One of the finest eighteenth-century opéras comiques and one of Grétry's greatest successes is *Les fausses apparences, ou L'amant jaloux* (False appearances, or The jealous lover; 1778).

Grétry was a master of ensemble writing and was adept at characterization. He used orchestral resources economically but effectively and wrote accompaniments that supported and emphasized the text without detracting from it. Dances are included in all of his stage works. All these features appear in *Richard Coeur-de-lion* (Richard the Lion-hearted; 1784), which is noteworthy in several respects: (1) There is rudimentary use of **Leitmotif** (a kind of musical label for a character, place, thing, or idea). (2) It is an early example of **rescue opera,** a forerunner of Cherubini's *Les deux journées* (The two days; 1800) and Beethoven's *Fidelio* (1805). In rescue opera, a person in peril of death is saved through the heroic endeavors of a devoted friend. Richard is rescued by the trouvère Blondel. (3) Some of the airs and dialogues reflect the new romanticism entering music, (e.g., the romance *Une fièvre brûlante* [A burning fever]). Beethoven knew *Richard Coeur-de-lion*—he wrote a set of variations for piano on *Une fièvre brûlante*.

During the Revolutionary period, many opéras comiques dealt with political and social issues. (See also Insight, "Concerts and Counterrevolution in France.") Opéra comique flourished well into the nineteenth century.

BALLAD OPERA
A *ballad opera* is a play, usually comic, in which spoken prose dialogue is interspersed with verses set to traditional tunes or popular melodies. In England in

Concerts and Counterrevolution in France

The period termed the Thermidorean Reaction (from the collapse of the Reign of Terror on 27 July 1794 through spring 1797) was a time when musicotheatrical productions and audience reaction to them strongly influenced political and cultural affairs. The Terrorist government encouraged performance of dramas with political plots to generate and stimulate republican enthusiasm. For several years after the Terror collapsed, the government was unstable, swinging between royalist and revolutionary extremes. Such instability fostered political dissent in which dramas, operas, and concerts played a significant role. In addition to presenting politically oriented entertainment, theater provided a convenient venue for dissenting factions to publicly express their opinions, and the government could not suppress the various counterrevolutionary activities.

When *Concert spirituel* performances ceased in May 1790, the Théâtre Feydeau began presenting concerts (as well as operas) and also dramas performed by a troupe of actors who had been imprisoned for their royalist views. Concerts were associated with activities of the *ancien régime*, many of the dramas presented were politically oriented, and audience reaction often was violent. The concert music programmed was itself a form of demonstration—instrumental music was especially suitable for audience reaction because they were not hampered by lyrics or narrative.

One counterrevolutionary group, known as *jeunesse dorée* (gilded youth) because they emulated the wealthy in their clothing and habits, expressed anti-Jacobin and antiegalitarian views vociferously and chose the reactionary popular song *Réveil du peuple* as their anthem. When the Directoire ordered theaters to begin every evening performance with *La Marseillaise* or another officially approved song, audience reaction was divided. Some persons responded by applauding; others sang *Réveil du peuple* or demanded performance of it. Many reactionary and antigovernment popular songs were written. The *guerre des chansons* (chanson war) that ensued inflamed the 1795–96 concert season and enabled reactionaries to advance their political position considerably. Only the affluent could afford theater/concert tickets; gradually that selective audience became more interested in cultural affairs than politics. By 1797 the *guerre des chansons* had subsided, political music virtually disappeared from concert programs, and overtures, symphonies, concerti, and vocal selections returned. Audiences still had political preferences and antirepublican sentiment still existed; such views were expressed more subtly and overt interest in fashion and cultural affairs was evidenced.

the eighteenth century the melodies were derived from a variety of sources, not the least of which were "dancing-master" books then being published.

John Gay was the first English librettist to insert familiar melodies into spoken dialogue; he placed 69 such tunes within *The Beggar's Opera,* which was performed with great success in London in 1728. For this, the first English ballad opera, Johann Pepusch composed an overture and the bass lines for the tunes. The story concerns the depravity of many lower-class persons then living in London and parallels such evils as robbery and prostitution with political wiles and professional abuses. The music itself is not without political satire (e.g., the tune *Walpole* is included). Some of the roles are caricatures of politicians then active and criminals who had been executed for their crimes.

The success of *The Beggar's Opera* provided incentive for a multitude of similar works by English authors. The subjects were political, social, historical, patriotic, or mythological, usually with a satirical twist. Rarely were the composers identified. Ballad operas were performed throughout Britain and were enjoyed by all social classes, whereas Italianate opera was available only in London and only to the wealthy. The popularity of *The Beggar's Opera* was renewed when a twentieth-century version, *Die Dreigroschenoper* (The Threepenny Opera; 1928), was created by Bertolt Brecht (1898–1956), with music by Kurt Weill (1900–50).

One of the most significant ballad operas was Coffey's (d. 1745) *The Devil to Pay* (1731), which was translated into German. In 1766, at the hands of C. F. Weisse and J. A. Hiller, it became a *Singspiel*.

English ballad operas were produced in America, commencing with John Hippisley's (1696–1748) *Flora, or The Hob in the Well* (1729), presented in Charleston, South Carolina, in 1735. Some Americans attempted to write ballad operas c. 1770 but had little success.

SINGSPIEL

The form of light opera that arose in north and central Germanic lands was known as **Singspiel.** In 1598 the designation *Singspiel* was applied to plays containing some music, and during the seventeenth century the term was commonly used to connote stage works containing vocal music. Singspiel had a variety of predecessors, including medieval mystery plays and all kinds of secular plays with music performed by traveling troupes. The latter presentations usually included a comic character whose name changed according to the area in which the performance occurred; in Germany he was called Pickelhäring or Hanswurst. Italian itinerant *commedia dell'arte* companies affected the development of Singspiel directly through their presentations in Austria and southern Germany and indirectly through the influence of the Comédie-Italienne on the repertoire of the Paris Fair Theatres. The immediate sources of north German Singspiel were the French *comédies mêlée d'ariettes* and English ballad opera. Germans were aware of the popularity of ballad operas in London, and it was not long before translations and adaptations of them were on the boards in Germany.

After the Hamburg opera failed in 1738, the only permanent troupe performing Singspiel was the Hanswurst company in Vienna. They were the first to present true Singspiel and had done so from c. 1710. Their plays, given in the vernacular, contained scenes featuring peasants or servants (who used regional dialect) and included music. The members of that company were actors and actresses who could also sing; music was accessory to the comedy.

The persons most significant in the rise of Singspiel in northern Germany in the eighteenth century were dramatist-poet C. F. Weisse (1726–1804) and composer J. A. Hiller, who collaborated on a dozen of them. The dialogue was spoken in vernacular prose, with music occurring at emotional peaks. Hiller's vocal solos were simple strophic songs; rarely, he inserted some recitative and an aria. Dances and marches were included, and frequently a *vaudeville final* was used.

The best eighteenth-century composer of Singspiel was Mozart. Excellent Singspiel music was written by Georg Benda (1722–95), Karl Ditters von Dittersdorf (1739–99), and Johann R. Zumsteeg (1760–1802).

In northern Germany, the Singspiel gradually acquired Romantic characteristics and eventually merged with early nineteenth-century German Romantic opera. By the beginning of that century, only slight differences remained between opera with spoken dialogue and true Singspiel, and the distinction is not always readily perceived. In southern Germany and Austria, farces and lighter music was preferred.

SECULAR SONG

Many of the songs written during the first half of the eighteenth century exhibit extreme simplicity. For the most part, this can be attributed to the *galant* ideals and the general high regard for sincerity, lack of affectation, and even sentimentality. Undoubtedly, much more secular song was composed than has survived.

In France, in the first half of the eighteenth century, the term **romance** was used to denote a strophic song usually recounting an ancient love story but occasionally concerning an historical event of gallantry. The melody was simple and lyrical and in a rather narrow range, the harmony thin, and the mood sentimental. Around mid century, composers began to incorporate romances in opéras comiques; Rousseau was one of the earliest to do so, in *Le devin du village.* For romances included in opéra comique, minimal orchestral accompaniment was provided; for solo romances only the melody and basso continuo were notated. Printed collections of romances were available before 1770.

Near the end of the seventeenth century, some French poets texted (or parodied) preexistent instrumental pieces, especially dance music, thereby creating solo songs. The practice spread to Germany, where it was taken up by university students. Albrecht Kammerer's manuscript book, dated 1715, contains dance music for keyboard, with texts added. Two decades later, such manuscript books were direct models for published collections of similar songs.

In Germany, in the last quarter of the seventeenth century, selections from Italian cantatas and operas filled the published song collections. At the beginning of the eighteenth century, there was a dearth of secular

Lieder publications. Because of this, the first three decades of the eighteenth century have been dubbed *Die Liederlose Zeit* (The Songless Era).

In the 1730s collections of parody Lieder—piano music with incidental texts—appeared. One of the most significant of these was assembled by Johann Scholze (1705–50), who used the pseudonym Sperontes. His anthology, *Die singende Muse an der Pleisse* (The muse of song on the Pleisse [River]; 1736), contains 68 musical selections and 100 poems. The keyboard pieces Sperontes used are minuets, polonaises, and marches written in *style galant*. Only melody and basso continuo were notated; Sperontes did not underlay the text but printed the poem at the end of the keyboard music.

The fact that some pieces in Sperontes's and similar parody collections were decidedly unvocal, and others caused unnatural declamation of the text, prompted some critical essays establishing rules for proper composition of Lieder. In *Von der musikalischen Poesie* (Concerning musical poetry; 1752), Christian Krause (1719–70) stated that a Lied should be relatively short; should have a melody resembling a folk song, easily singable by an amateur; should express the mood and meaning of the text; and should have a simple accompaniment sufficiently independent that the melody could be sung without it. Of equal significance is the fact that Sperontes's anthology instigated the publication of collections of newly composed Lieder.

After 1750, Berlin was the principal center of Lieder composition, with Franz Benda, C. P. E. Bach, and K. H. Graun the leading figures. Their songs are strophic, with text set syllabically to expressive melodies resembling folk song and with very simple keyboard accompaniment.

A second Berlin school of Lieder composition arose c. 1770, with J. A. P. Schultz (1747–1800), J. F. Reichardt (1752–1814), and C. F. Zelter (1748–1832) the chief composers. During the second half of the eighteenth century, there was a surge in Lieder composition—more than 750 collections of Lieder were published in Germany, whereas during the first half of the century only 40 collections were issued. Music journals included Lieder in their issues. The increase in production of Lieder continued steadily, well into the nineteenth century.

MASSES AND MOTETS

During the first half of the eighteenth century, most composers of opera wrote Masses also. Though some persons continued to write Masses in *stile antico,* the operatic style invaded much of the church music. Thus, a *stylus mixtus* (mixed style) was created, in which solos were quite florid and resembled operatic arias; some choral sections were provided with independent orchestral accompaniment and instrumental interludes, whereas others were in *stile antico* with instrumental doubling of the vocal lines. Choruses with independent orchestral accompaniment were homophonic, with text set syllabically, and sometimes were structured in forms usually associated with instrumental music. It was customary for the *Amen* endings of the Gloria and Credo to be written as fugues, and often *empfindsamer Stil* was used for the *Cruxifixus*. In Lutheran areas of Germany, composers wrote chorale motets with texts from the German Bible.

Local conditions and traditions played an important part in determining the style used for church music. In Italy and in Catholic areas of south Germany and Austria, Masses and motets were affected by Italian opera. At Dresden, Hasse used a mixture of styles for choral sections and wrote solos as florid and operatic as arias. At the imperial court in Vienna, J. J. Fux composed about 80 Masses. He recognized and used three distinct styles: strict *stylus a cappella* (unaccompanied traditional counterpoint); a *stile antico* that was not quite as strict, with vocal parts doubled by violins, trombones, and organ; and *stylus mixtus*. He described all three in his treatise *Gradus ad Parnassum* (see p. 203).

In France, the kings preferred Low Mass and favored motets. Customarily, Mass in the royal chapel included three motets: a choral *grand motet* (large motet), a *petit motet* (small motet) sung at Elevation, and a motet setting of Psalm 19:10 (French Prot. 20:10), *Domine salvum fac regem* (Lord, save the king), which served as a salutation to the king and closed all Masses. A *grand motet* consisted of a psalm setting for solo voice(s), ensemble, and five-part chorus, with a five-part orchestra doubling the choral lines and providing interludes and independent accompaniment for ensembles and soloist(s). Michel-Richard de Lalande (1657–1726) wrote more than 70 grands motets and 7 settings of *Domine salvum fac regem* for the royal chapel. In style, a grand motet by Lalande closely resembles a German cantata—it contains solos (arias) and ensembles interspersed with polyphonic choruses. French composers wrote motets (both grand and petit) for the Versailles chapel until c. 1789.

After 1750, no continuous line of motet development can be traced. The motet never regained the prominent position it held during the Middle Ages and Renaissance.

Summary

During the eighteenth century, the political and cultural complexion of Europe changed considerably. The Enlightenment, a humanitarian movement, placed emphasis on reason and on knowledge gained through proper empirical education. Science, rationalism, and freedom advanced considerably. Freemasonry spread throughout Europe and to America. The rise of a more or less independent spirit, leading from accordance of divine right to kings to a belief in human rights and brotherhood, culminated in revolution in France and in North America.

The general rise of the middle class to an influential position brought changes in musical activities. As music printing increased, music for amateurs flooded the market, especially tutors for learning to play an instrument, books of songs, and keyboard music. Music journals containing all kinds of music news (and some music) were issued more or less regularly. After 1720, public concerts of nontheatrical music were performed frequently in many of the larger European cities; in the 1730s some European musicians concertized in the American colonies.

The term *Preclassic* comprises those styles of eighteenth-century music that led to and were absorbed into the Classic style of Mozart and Haydn: *style galant, empfindsamer Stil,* and *Sturm und Drang. Galant* music is light, graceful, elegant homophonic music characterized by simple melodies, short phrases, uncomplicated harmonies, and a slower harmonic rhythm than that used in the Baroque era. Lest static harmonies become boring, murky and Alberti basses were used. At its peak, *style galant* employed ornaments in moderation, an abundance of appoggiatura sighs,

Lombardic rhythms, melodic triplet sixteenth notes, and fussy dynamic contrasts. In northern Germany after c. 1750, the *galant* was given new expressiveness and became *empfindsamer Stil.* Its principal exponent was C. P. E. Bach, whose music is finely nuanced, with periodic melodies constructed in short phrases and supported by light-textured harmonic accompaniment. *Sturm und Drang* resulted when the emotional expressions and contrasts of *Empfindsamkeit* were intensified to become passionate outbursts and dark, stormy moods. *Sturm und Drang* was most effective in opera.

Some formal patterns preferred by Baroque composers remained in favor: strophic songs, *da capo* arias, ritornello concerto movements, and binary form. New forms emerged: cavatina and sonata form. Sonata form evolved as composers expanded and modified binary form. Gradually, the Baroque *sonata da chiesa* was supplanted by the multimovement sonata, which at first was written principally for solo keyboard. The first real flowering of the Preclassic sonata for keyboard came after c. 1735, with the works of Domenico Scarlatti, Alberti, C. P. E. Bach, and others. Some early sonatas had two movements, but after 1740 most sonatas followed a three-movement scheme: Allegro, lyrical Andante, and dancelike Finale. As used by Preclassic composers, sonata form, the constructional principle of a single movement, was an expanded and modified rounded binary form. Usually, the first movement of a multimovement sonata was in sonata form.

The formal structure of the concerto for solo instrument and orchestra that Vivaldi established was followed by Preclassic composers. J. S. Bach created the concerto for solo harpsichord and string orchestra when he adapted for harpsichord some of Vivaldi's concerti. Bach's sons contributed much to the development of the solo keyboard concerto—Emanuel Bach's concerti influenced Haydn, and J. C. Bach's influenced Mozart. J. C. Bach was the first to adopt the piano for public performance and to publish piano concerti. C. P. E. Bach composed many keyboard sonatas and concerti; he was one of the principal symphonists of the north German school.

The concert symphony was a direct outgrowth of the Italian opera overture. Significant contributions to the development of the independent symphony were made during 1730–40. Sammartini is credited with the earliest datable concert symphony using rudimentary but recognizable sonata form. He usually constructed symphonies in three movements: a fast first movement in sonata form; a slow, lyrical second movement characterized by expressive chromaticism and *galante* ornamentation; and a finale designed to bring the multimovement composition to an effective close.

The cosmopolitan atmosphere of the age fostered spread of the Italian concert sinfonia northward into Europe. The centers of symphony composition were Mannheim, Vienna, Paris, and Potsdam; composers contributing to the development of the concert symphony include J. Stamitz, C. P. E. Bach, Monn, Wagenseil, and Gossec. Most Preclassic symphonies have three movements; occasionally, four movements were written, with the last movement usually a minuet or a gigue. Under Stamitz's direction, the Mannheim court orchestra became the finest in Europe.

Music was an important influence in Spanish colonies in the New World and was included in the curriculum in cathedral and convent schools. Though most of the composed music was sacred and vocal, orchestral instruments were used in concerted works as well as for accompaniment, and some purely instrumental music was written.

Several treatises by Preclassic composers provide valuable information concerning performance practices of the time: Quantz's essay on flute playing, C. P. E. Bach's essay on playing keyboard instruments, Leopold Mozart's book on violin playing, and Tartini's treatise on ornaments.

Books of didactic pieces termed études appeared in Paris after 1785. The earliest of these publications were for flute and for violin; London pianist-composers published books of piano études early in the nineteenth century.

The reform of Italian literature that effected separation of tragic and comic elements in drama caused dramatists to purge the opera libretto of comic elements, thus creating opera seria. Metastasio shaped and dominated opera seria. The standard libretto required an alternation of recitative and *da capo* aria, with an occasional small ensemble and very little work for the orchestra. Concentration of musical interest in the arias gave virtuoso singers a measure of power that they were quick to grasp and abuse. Critics agitated for reforms that were slow in coming.

Tragedy and comedy were combined in a stage presentation when comic *intermedi* were performed between the acts of a serious opera. Sometimes an intermezzo achieved greater notoriety than the opera seria, as did Pergolesi's *La serva padrona*. Composers trained in Naples transmitted *galante*-style opera seria to other lands.

Opera buffa and intermezzo developed contemporaneously in the eighteenth century. Most of the early comic operas were written by composers trained or born in Naples. Features of comic opera were the ensemble or chain finale, exploitation of the bass voice, and the inclusion of regional dialect(s). Poets prepared comic opera libretti that contain elements of tragedy or that are pathetic or sentimental while being basically humorous—opera called *dramma giocoso*.

In France, light opera, known as opéra comique, evolved from farces and vaudevilles given at the Fair Theaters. During 1735–50 opéra comique was refined considerably, but the rustic element was retained, and the vaudeville final remained an important feature. Performances of Italian intermezzi in Paris in the 1752–54 seasons ignited and fueled the *Querelle des Bouffons* and stimulated the production of French light opera. Later, political and social issues were subjects of opéras comiques. Grétry contributed to the development of both opéra comique and serious opera; his *Richard Coeur-de-lion* is an early example of rescue opera.

Italian opera in London was not a profitable business. The success of *The Beggar's Opera* stimulated production of ballad operas on a variety of subjects, usually mingled with satire. English ballad operas and French *comédies mêlée d'ariettes* were the immediate sources of north German Singspiel. Eventually, Singspiel merged with early nineteenth-century German Romantic opera.

A considerable amount of secular song was produced. In France, the romance appeared; at mid century romances were incorporated in opéras comiques. Some French poets created solo songs by texting pre-existent keyboard pieces; the practice spread to Germany. Sperontes's *Der singende Muse* and similar publications instigated the production of collections of newly composed Lieder and put an end to the "Song-less Era." After 1750 Berlin was the principal center of Lieder composition. Hundreds of collections of Lieder were printed during the second half of the eighteenth century, and the production of Lieder continued well into the nineteenth century.

Most composers of opera also wrote church music. Some used *stile antico,* but operatic style infiltrated much of the church music and created a mixed style. Local conditions and traditions determined the style used. In Italy, both *stile antico* and *stylus mixtus* were used. Catholic areas of south Germany and Austria were affected by Italian opera. In France, the grand motet flourished. In Lutheran areas of Germany, some chorale motets were composed. After 1750, no continuous line of motet development can be traced.

THE CLASSIC ERA

19

During the last half of the eighteenth century, Austria, through the Habsburg dynasty, governed much of Europe, for the Emperor and Empress of the Holy Roman Empire were also the elected heads of several other countries. As the ideas of tolerance, brotherly love, and consideration for the worth and dignity of the individual regardless of rank spread, Emperor Joseph II attempted to rectify injustices, to improve literacy by educating the people, and to promote religious tolerance. German became the official language of the empire. However, Leopold II (r. 1790–92) revoked much that Joseph had decreed.

Within the Holy Roman Empire, there were numerous church states, such as Salzburg, closely allied with Rome. Archbishop Colloredo (r. 1771–1803) endeavored to institute reforms that were in accord with enlightened ideas, but he met with opposition because those reforms would have eliminated deeply rooted traditions. The Archbishop fled Salzburg a few hours before Napoleon's troops entered the city on 10 December 1800. On Colloredo's formal abdication in 1803, Salzburg ceased being an ecclesiastical state. Napoleon entered Vienna in 1805 but did not set up his establishment at Schönbrunn castle until 1809.

Gradually, middle-class citizens achieved greater importance politically, economically, and culturally. Interest in the arts increased. Musical amateurs obtained instruction from professional musicians or published tutors; family and neighborhood music making was an essential part of life. Near the end of the century, there were many traveling virtuosi. Listeners paid admission to attend public concerts, and those who could afford it sometimes commissioned works. A great deal of music was composed, but much of it was lost because it was never published. "Publication" did not necessarily mean printing; publishing houses sold manuscript copies of music, too. Copyright protection was virtually nonexistent.

The church remained an important patron of music. At monasteries music was copied and preserved in their libraries. Secular court and aristocratic patronage began to wane; musicians could not rely on that for total support. For most of his life, Haydn had the patronage of the Esterházy family and accepted the measure of servitude attached to it. Mozart found such obeisance obnoxious and left the Salzburg court, but in Vienna, as an independent musician, he struggled to provide a living for his family. Beethoven was accepted as an independent artist-composer and was more successful financially.

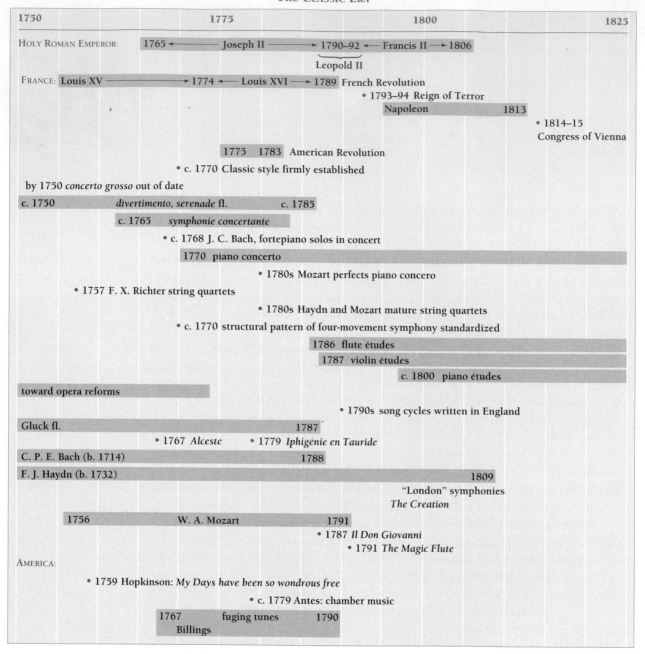

| 1750 | 1775 | 1800 | 1825 |

HOLY ROMAN EMPEROR: 1765 ← ———— Joseph II ————→ 1790–92 ← ——— Francis II ——→ 1806

Leopold II

FRANCE: Louis XV ————————→ 1774 ← —— Louis XVI ——→ 1789 French Revolution

• 1793–94 Reign of Terror

Napoleon 1813

• 1814–15 Congress of Vienna

1775 1783 American Revolution

• c. 1770 Classic style firmly established

by 1750 *concerto grosso* out of date

c. 1750 *divertimento, serenade* fl. c. 1785

c. 1765 *symphonie concertante*

• c. 1768 J. C. Bach, fortepiano solos in concert

1770 piano concerto

• 1780s Mozart perfects piano concero

• 1757 F. X. Richter string quartets

• 1780s Haydn and Mozart mature string quartets

• c. 1770 structural pattern of four-movement symphony standardized

1786 flute études

1787 violin études

c. 1800 piano études

toward opera reforms

• 1790s song cycles written in England

Gluck fl. 1787

• 1767 *Alceste* • 1779 *Iphigénie en Tauride*

C. P. E. Bach (b. 1714) 1788

F. J. Haydn (b. 1732) 1809

"London" symphonies
The Creation

1756 W. A. Mozart 1791

• 1787 *Il Don Giovanni*

• 1791 *The Magic Flute*

AMERICA:

• 1759 Hopkinson: *My Days have been so wondrous free*

• c. 1779 Antes: chamber music

1767 fuging tunes 1790
Billings

Customarily, the chronological boundaries of the Classic era in music have been set as c. 1750–c. 1825. Indeed, the roots of Classicism do extend back to 1750 (and even earlier) and tap the resources of both Preclassic and late Baroque styles. However, the Viennese idiom that exemplifies and distinguishes the music of the Classic era emerged c. 1770 as a distillation of elements of the *galant* and *empfindsamer* styles synthesized with elements of the learned (contrapuntal) style. This synthesis was achieved by Joseph Haydn more fully than by his contemporaries, and the Viennese Classic style was firmly established in the instrumental works he created in the 1770s. Haydn's works were widely disseminated in Europe in the 1780s, and a more or less universal cosmopolitan musical language resulted. That language is seen to best advantage in the middle and late works of Haydn, the late works of Mozart, and the early works of Beethoven and Schubert. By c. 1820 musical Romanticism was well under way.

The Classic style is characterized by clarity, balance, and restraint. Composers attempted to pursue a middle ground between the too easy and the too difficult. They sought to create music that had universal appeal, with a degree of simplicity that prevented it from becoming mentally taxing to listeners, music that was refined without being stiff. Form was important; most of the music was constructed in regular phrases and periods. A basically homophonic texture prevailed, with counterpoint used for contrast or for developmental purposes. Instrumental melodies, especially those in slow movements of multimovement works, frequently resemble operatic arias (e.g., the slow movements of Mozart's *concerti* K. 191, 595). Folk or folklike elements—melodies resembling or based on folk song, folk dance rhythms, and drones—were incorporated in multimovement works (ex. 19.5). Instrumental color became a significant factor in defining a theme. Harmony and rhythm were as important as melody. No new harmonic materials were introduced, but harmonies were treated differently and were used functionally in a wider sense, with concern for chordal relationships between keys as well as within a key. Major tonalities predominate. Harmonic rhythm, which had slowed during the Preclassic era, was a significant factor in articulating large-scale forms as well as in sustaining individual phrases. Harmonic clarity was important; when moving from one key to another, the tonality was established clearly at the beginning and end of the modulation. The functional tonic-to-dominant (and its reverse) was gradually expanded by employing secondary dominants, and within a modulation pivot chords might function subtly. Methods of development changed from being the restatement of a portion of a phrase in several different keys to being fragmentation and working out of thematic material. As the era progressed, composers selected themes with more regard for developmental possibilities than for melody.

Principal Genres and Forms

The principal genres of music composed during the Classic era were sonata, symphony, concerto, chamber music, and opera. All are multimovement forms, and each has its roots in types of music written in the Baroque and Preclassic eras. To each genre the prominent Classic era composers gave new dimensions. Opera reforms begun by Jommelli, Traetta, Gluck, and others are in evidence in Mozart's mature works; with Mozart, opera rose to unprecedented heights. Haydn's experimentation, inventive imagination, and productivity contributed more to the development of the symphony than any other single composer. He and Mozart developed a characteristic style for the string quartet. In Mozart's works, the Classic solo concerto—especially that for keyboard—attained perfection. Haydn and Mozart wrote some excellent piano sonatas, but it was Beethoven who brought that genre to a peak.

The structural principle most often used for a movement was sonata form (or a variant thereof). Next in frequency of use was theme and variations, a favorite form for improvisation; many compositions of this type were never written down.

Sonata

In the 1770s, hundreds of composers wrote solo keyboard sonatas, frequently with titles conveying the option *cembalo o fortepiano* (harpsichord or fortepiano). Not until c. 1785 did the word *cembalo* begin to disappear from titles. During the last decades of the eighteenth century, the accompanied keyboard sonata—usually with violin as accompanist—became popular. Most of the piano/violin sonatas by Mozart and Haydn fall into or are not far removed from this category. In Beethoven's piano/violin and piano/'cello sonatas, the performers are equal participants in chamber music.

Symphony

By the late 1780s, many symphonists had adopted a four-movement structural scheme that has come to be considered the standard pattern of the Classic symphony. Haydn's and Mozart's last symphonies are excellent examples of this scheme (fig. 19.1).

From time to time, composers altered the internal structure of a movement. The most significant modification was the addition of a slow introduction to the sonata-form first movement. Leopold Hofmann

Movement	Tempo	Key	Form
First	Fast	Tonic	Sonata form
Second	Slow	Related key	Ternary, sonata form, abridged sonata form, theme and variations, or rondo
Third	Moderately fast	Tonic *	Compound ternary
Fourth	Fastest	Tonic	Sonata form, rondo, or sonata-rondo

*Trio is almost always in a related key.

FIGURE 19.1 Outline of structural scheme of four-movement Classic symphony.

(1738–93) of Vienna, a prolific composer of symphonies, seems to have been the first to do this consistently, commencing as early as 1761. Many slow introductions are characterized by dotted rhythms, which indicates that the concept of a slow section as introduc-

tion to a fast sonata-form movement was probably derived from French overture. Commencing a symphony with a slow introduction became common practice in the late 1780s but was not done invariably. Mozart wrote slow introductions for only Symphonies Nos. 36, 38, and 39; 11 of Haydn's "London" symphonies have slow introductions. On the other hand, Mozart's decision not to repeat the development-recapitulation section of the sonata-form first movement of Symphony No. 31 was exceptional at the time.

CONCERTO

Johann Christian Bach played a major role in the development of the Classic concerto for piano and orchestra (Insight, "The Piano [I]"). Though Bach was one of the chief masters of *style galant*, several of his *Six Concertos*, Op. 1 (1763), *Sei concerti per il cembalo o piano e forte*, Op. 7 (Six concerti for harpsichord or pianoforte; 1770), and *A Third Sett of Six*

The Piano (I)

On 2 June 1768, in London, for the first time the fortepiano was used in concert as a solo instrument; J. C. Bach, the soloist, used a "square" (actually rectangular) piano made in England by J. C. Zumpe (1735–83) (see fig. 19.2).

During the last half of the eighteenth century, Johann A. Stein (1728–92) of Augsburg was one of the greatest German makers of keyboard instruments. Mozart, according to his letters, preferred Stein fortepianos because the action (individual escapement) was better. The Stein fortepiano of Mozart's time had a compass of five octaves, from F' to f'''. Normally, the naturals on the keyboard were covered with ebony, and the sharps were covered with bone or ivory. Inside the piano, the narrow hammers were covered with leather. In the upper register, Stein fortepianos produced clear, very bright tones; pitches in the bass regis-

FIGURE 19.2 In Johann Zoffany's painting *The Cowper and Gore Families* (1775), the lady is playing a Zumpe-style square piano.
(*Yale Center for British Art, New Haven, Conn.*)

ter were round and full, and, because strings were very thin, bass tones sounded clearly. Many eighteenth-century pianos were equipped with right and left knee-levers that served the same function as the sustaining pedal on the modern piano (to lift the

dampers); this allowed a richer tone. Dynamic gradations from *pp* to *ff* were possible. Though the fortepiano had limited tonal volume, it could hold its own against the small orchestra used at that time.

Concertos, Op. 13 (1777) are stylistically more Classic than *galant* and often are described as sounding "Mozartean." In reality, Mozart is indebted to Bach for some stylistic traits.

Bach commenced each of the concerti in those sets with a fast movement, as did Vivaldi, but modified Vivaldi's first-movement structural pattern by combining elements of Baroque concerto-ritornello and sonata form. Such a movement can properly be termed **sonata-concerto form.** In fact, in 1793 H. C. Koch described it as such: "The concerto's first *Allegro* contains three principal periods which the soloist performs, and which are enclosed by [i.e., are alternated with] four secondary periods played by the orchestra as ritornelli" (*Treatise on Composition,* III, p. 333). This ritornello-solo alternation is the Baroque concerto aspect. Koch then stated that the three principal solo sections followed the same basic structural scheme and harmonic pattern as the first movement of a symphony. (At that time, the term "sonata form" was not used.) Koch considered the first solo section the exposition of the movement, with the responsibility for laying out the main themes in the proper tonalities; the first ritornello opened and closed in the tonic and served as introduction.

As written by Bach, the concerto's first movement consists of four distinct sections: orchestral ritornello, *concertante* exposition, modulatory fantasia, and recapitulation (fig. 19.3a). Detailed internal construction of the first movement is as follows: (1) an orchestral ritornello that usually remains in the tonic key and contains the principal theme (and sometimes a second theme), a transition, and closing (cadential) material; (2) a *concertante* section resembling the exposition (i.e., the first section) of a sonata-form movement, in which the soloist presents the first theme in the tonic key and new thematic material in the dominant, interspersed with portions of the orchestral ritornello and concluding with the orchestral ritornello closing material in the dominant key; (3) a modulating section more like a free (but controlled) fantasia than a true development, moving into more distant keys before returning to the dominant key and usually concluding with the soloist playing a long trill on the dominant and a short cadenza; and (4) full recapitulation of all thematic and ritornello material, now presented in the tonic key, concluding with a long cadenza improvised by the soloist and followed by the orchestral ritornello closing material as coda (fig. 19.3b; DWMA126).

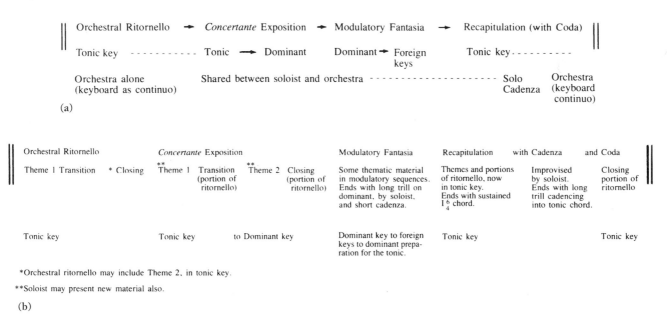

FIGURE 19.3 (*a*) Outline of structure of first movement of concerto for keyboard and orchestra used by J. C. Bach; (*b*) detailed outline of internal structure of first movement of concerto for keyboard and orchestra used by J. C. Bach.

Some of Bach's keyboard concerti have only two movements. In his three-movement concerti, the second movement is arialike. Usually, the finale is a minuet or a rondo or may contain elements of both.

Mozart began writing concerti by making arrangements of isolated movements from sonatas by other composers, including J. C. Bach. Bach's concerti were Mozart's models when he composed his first original piano concerto (K. 175; 1773). For his concerti, Mozart adopted the three-movement fast-slow-fast overall scheme favored by Vivaldi. Mozart constructed a concerto's first movement according to the sonata-concerto form used by Bach but gradually modified and refined that pattern, retaining its basic ritornello and adding full-scale sonata-form features (fig. 19.4a). Gradually, Mozart changed the modulatory free fantasia section into true development and ultimately gave the concerto, as a whole, symphonic dimensions. Strings remained the core of the orchestra, but instrumentation was augmented to include flute, two oboes, two bassoons, and sometimes two clarinets, two trumpets, and timpani. Mozart's last piano concerto, K. 595, exemplifies his symphonic treatment of the form (DWMA127). The second movement of a Mozart concerto is an instrumental aria; usually, the third movement is a kind of rondo.

Though no two of Mozart's sonata-concerto movements are exactly alike, he did follow a basic structural pattern. The opening orchestral ritornello normally includes both first and second themes, plus *tutti* closing (cadential) material, and remains in the tonic key. Most often, the *concertante* exposition commences with the soloist stating the first theme; after appropriate transitional material, the second theme is stated in the dominant, followed by a portion of the orchestral ritornello in the dominant. The third section resembles a sonata-form development, with tensions achieved through wide modulations, thematic fragmentation and manipulation, and occasionally the addition of some new material. This section concludes with a dominant preparation—and usually the soloist plays a long trill over a dominant chord—leading into the next section, full recapitulation of thematic and ritornello material, now in the tonic key. The recapitulation concludes with a sustained orchestral I$^6_4$ chord. Next, the soloist improvises a cadenza, concluding it with a trill on the super-

tonic over a V$_7$ chord; the trill terminates with a small figure termed *Nachschlag:*

This trilled chord is a signal to the orchestra that the cadenza has concluded and that the next chord, resolving the dominant-seventh to the tonic, will commence the coda. The closing orchestral ritornello constitutes the coda (fig. 19.4b; DWMA127).

SYMPHONIE CONCERTANTE

The **symphonie concertante,** an orchestral form featuring two or more soloists, appeared in the late 1760s, became very popular during the 1770s, flourished until c. 1830, and then almost disappeared. The rise of symphonie concertante was influenced primarily by social conditions: expansion of the public concert, an audience of middle-class citizens who enjoyed virtuosic display, the use of larger orchestras (though small in comparison with twentieth-century ones), and improved social status of musicians. Usually, local musicians were the soloists in a symphonie concertante.

Most of the extant symphonies concertantes are three-movement works that, in structure and style, closely resemble the Classic concerto for soloist and orchestra. The remainder have two movements or, rarely, four.

The earliest composers of symphonies concertantes worked in Paris or at Mannheim. Paris publishers printed their works, and Paris became the principal center of symphonie concertante composition. Among the numerous composers contributing to the genre there were F.-J. Gossec and Ignace Pleyel (1757–1831). G. M. Cambini (1746–1825) wrote about 80, J. C. Bach composed 15, and Karl Stamitz (1745–1801) wrote more than 30. Haydn wrote only one full-fledged work of this kind—the *Symphonie concertante* in B♭, Op. 84. Mozart composed at least six. His first, *Concertone,* K. 190 (1773; C major), features two violins, oboe, and 'cello and is *galant* in style. The *Sinfonia concertante* in E♭, K. 364 (1779), for violin and

Orchestral Ritornello comparable to exposition	→	*Concertante* Exposition featuring soloist	→	Development	→	Recapitulation	(with Coda)
Tonic key - - - - - - - - - - - - - - -		Tonic → Dominant		Dominant to foreign keys		Tonic key - - - - - - - Cadenza	Tonic
Orchestra alone (keyboard continuo)		Shared between solo and orchestra - Solo					Orchestra (keyboard continuo)

(a)

Orchestral Ritornello	*Concertante* Exposition (featuring solo)	Development	Recapitulation	with Cadenza	and Coda
Theme 1 Transition Theme 2 Closing	Theme 1 Transition Theme 2 Closing (portion of (portion of ritornello) ritornello)	Thematic development. Some new material may be added.	Themes and portions of transitions, now in tonic key. Ends with sustained I$^6_4$ chord.	Improvised by soloist. Ends with long trill over V$_7$ and cadences to I.	Closing portion of ritornello
Tonic key	Tonic key to Dominant key	Dominant key to foreign keys to dominant preparation for tonic.	Tonic key		Tonic key

(b)

FIGURE 19.4 (*a*) Outline of structure of concerto-sonata form used for first movement of a concerto for piano and orchestra by Wolfgang Mozart; (*b*) detailed outline of internal structure of concerto-sonata form used by Mozart.

viola soloists and orchestra, is Classic in design but calls for *scordatura* viola.

The symphonie concertante never completely disappeared. Isolated examples exist among the works of nineteenth- and twentieth-century composers.

DIVERTIMENTO

By 1750, the concerto grosso was out of date. The concertato principle found expression in light, entertaining types of ensemble music—*divertimento, serenade, cassation, notturno,* and, after 1765, *symphonie concertante*. Almost all court composers in south Germany, Austria, and Bohemia wrote divertimento-type music. Much of it was created for special occasions, for it was music suitable as background for social events, and the instrumentation varied according to the performing forces available. Generally, the music was intended for a small ensemble and was performed by one person per part; some pieces were written for small orchestra. A divertimento might have from two to nine movements, most of them in binary form, arranged so that tempi contrast. In the 1760s, a five-movement structural plan was common: Allegro-Minuet-Andante-Minuet-Allegro. The eventual omission of the first Minuet produced the multimovement plan that ultimately became standard for the Classic string quartet.

Joseph and Michael Haydn and Leopold and Wolfgang Mozart were among the many composers writing numerous compositions of divertimento type. Wolfgang Mozart's serenade, *Eine kleine Nachtmusik*, K. 525 (A little nightmusic; 1787), for string quintet, originally contained five movements; the second movement, presumably a Minuet, is lost. In the twentieth century *Eine kleine Nachtmusik* is usually performed by string orchestra.

The greatest significance of the divertimento-type composition is the exclusion of basso continuo from the ensemble. The absence of harpsichord accompaniment paved the way for Classic chamber music and for the disappearance of keyboard from the orchestra. Not until the end of the eighteenth century was the harpsichord completely eliminated as a requisite member of the orchestral ensemble. Haydn did not include basso continuo in the scores of his London symphonies, but when the works were first performed he was at the keyboard supporting the harmonies.

STRING QUARTET

The string quartet came into being c. 1745 when viola was added to the trio sonata ensemble and keyboard deleted. For a time, either 'cello or bass might be used as the lowest instrument; sometimes the part was marked simply "Bass." Isolated examples of true quartet writing appeared earlier, for example, Alessandro Scarlatti's *Quattro sonate a quattro per due violini, violetta e violoncello senza cembalo* (Four quartet sonatas for two violins, viola, and violoncello without keyboard; 1720). Genuine string quartet literature seems to have evolved from *divertimenti* and from quartet-symphonies (quartets that are transcriptions of symphony movements), such as those written in the 1740s by Johann Stamitz at Mannheim and by Georg Monn at Vienna.

Franz X. Richter (1709–89) wrote more than 40 pieces of chamber music. His 6 string quartets, Op. 5 (written c. 1757; publ. 1768), are the most significant. In some ways, these quartets are conservative: each has three movements, most of them in binary form, and there is considerable use of imitative counterpoint. The finale of No. 2 is labeled *Fugato presto*. In other respects, Richter was considerably in advance of his contemporaries in the use of minuet as finale (Nos. 3 and 4), a real development section in some movements, and responsibilities given to viola and 'cello, producing balance among parts (e.g., No. 3, mvt. 1 [ex. 19.1]). In the Op. 5 quartets, Richter anticipated the genuine quartet style of later Classic composers.

CHAMBER MUSIC WITH PIANO

True chamber music that included piano developed slowly. Before c. 1760, the keyboard played an essential but supporting role in ensemble music: fleshing out the skeletal treble-bass notation by supplying the harmonies, augmenting the musical texture, and maintaining the rhythmic flow. As the Baroque trio sonata waned, and basso continuo was gradually phased out, the 'cello found a place in the string quartet. There was increased interest in the piano, but it was still a relatively new instrument and did not blend easily with other instruments. Composers writing for small instrumental ensembles that included piano either allowed the keyboard to dominate the ensemble or relegated the piano to accompaniment status. Not until the 1780s did composers achieve tonal balance and genuine dialogue among the instruments of a chamber music ensemble that included piano. In piano trios, Mozart solved the problem by writing a good deal of the piano part between the 'cello and violin lines.

CHRISTOPH WILLIBALD GLUCK

Although Gluck (1714–87) composed 8 trio sonatas, 18 symphonies, 5 ballets, and numerous sacred and secular vocal pieces, he is remembered primarily for

EXAMPLE 19.1 Richter: String Quartet, Op. 5, No. 3, mvt. 1, mm. 19–38. *(Source: Denkmäler der Tonkunst in Bayern, Vol. XXVII/Jg. 15 of orig. ed., pp. 22–23)*

his operas. As a musician and composer, Gluck was largely self-taught. From 1727 to c. 1735 he was in Prague, where he earned his living by making music as best he could—performing with church choirs or at neighborhood fairs and, for a short time, serving as organist at Tyn Church. He spent two years (1735–37) in Vienna, then secured an orchestral position in Milan, where he became acquainted with the works of Italian symphonists and opera composers. The success of his first opera, *Artaserse* (Milan, 1741), brought commissions for seven more operas. After the production of *Ippolito* early in 1745, Gluck went to London, where he wrote two operas for the Haymarket Theater. Neither was well received.

In 1746–52 Gluck visited Hamburg, Dresden, Copenhagen, and Vienna. For Vienna's Burgtheater he composed *Semiramide* (1748). While in Copenhagen in 1749, he consulted with music critic Johann Scheibe (1708–76), whose theories on opera, published in 1749, include the following: (1) the orchestral overture or prelude should lead directly into the first scene of the opera, (2) even recitative can express the passions, and (3) various ascending levels of recitative (e.g., *secco* to *accompagnato* to *arioso*) can be used to lead into aria, which in turn rises to emotional heights. In *La contesa de' numi* (The strife of the gods;

Christoph Willibald Gluck. Portrait by J. S. Duplessis, painted in Paris in 1776. *(Oesterreichische Nationalbibliothek, Portraitsammlung, Vienna)*

1749), Gluck caused the orchestral introduction to Act I to lead directly into Jupiter's accompanied recitative, which links the prelude with the ensuing drama. This did not make Gluck a "reformer"—it was but a very small step in that direction.

From 1753 to 1761 Gluck served first as Konzertmeister and then as Kapellmeister in the household of the imperial field marshal. Meantime, Gluck's interests had taken a different turn. In 1752, Count Giacomo Durazzo (1717–94) began to direct theatrical affairs at Vienna and by 1754 had responsibility for the Burgtheater and the Kärntnertor. Each of those theaters had its own actors, ballet troupe, and orchestra. A French drama company was brought to court to perform drama, ballet, and opéra comique. Durazzo imported opéras comiques from Paris and engaged Gluck to adapt them to Viennese taste. Gradually, Gluck replaced the French music with pieces of his own; eventually, he composed complete opéras comiques. His first was *La fausse esclave* (The false slave; 1758); he wrote seven more before 1762.

When given the opportunity, Gluck wrote opera seria. In 1755 he composed *L'innocenza giustificata* (Innocence justified) for the emperor's birthday; for Carnival season in Rome in 1756, he set Metastasio's *Antigono*. In adherence to operatic conventions in Rome, all solo roles were sung by men. Their brilliant performance obtained for Gluck the patronage of Cardinal Albani (1692–1779) and the Cavalier of the Golden Spur award from Pope Benedict XIV (r. 1740–58).

Gluck worked in Vienna until the end of 1762. In 1761 Raniero de Calzabigi (1714–95) arrived in Vienna and met Durazzo, choreographer Gasparo Angiolini (1731–1803), and Gluck. Calzabigi was well-acquainted with ballet, opera, and Metastasio's ideals. He was aware of the problems plaguing opera production, had a critical attitude toward Metastasio, and had definite views concerning opera esthetics. Calzabigi, Angiolini, and Gluck shared ideas and created the dramatic ballet *Don Juan* (perf. October 1761), a coalescence of dance, music, and pantomime. Gluck borrowed several items from that ballet for operas, including *Orfeo ed Euridice*. A repertoire of more than 150 ballets in the Schwartzenberg Archive at Český Krumlov indicates that Gluck was considerably involved with pantomime and dance drama at Vienna.

GLUCK'S "REFORM" OPERAS

The most important collaboration of Gluck, Angiolini, and Calzabigi in 1762 was *Orfeo ed Euridice*. Traces of Baroque opera remain in that work—the mythological tragic ending is averted by the god Amore, and the opera concludes with a ballet and a jubilant chorus.

The drama is in three acts, each containing two scenes. When the curtain opens, Orpheus is standing at Euridice's grave; the music is a simple but rich choral *tombeau* (lament). The *ballo* that follows is functional, providing exit music for the chorus and bringing consolation to the bereaved husband. Thus, at the very beginning of the opera, drama, music, and ballet are unified. The usual *secco* recitative-exit aria combination found in Italian opera is not present here. Instead, there is a sense of dramatic continuity, to which Gluck's choice of tonalities contributed considerably.

In Act II, serene pastoral and threatening infernal scenes and moods are juxtaposed. Orpheus descends into Hades, where he seeks Euridice's release. At first, his simple song is met with terrifying "NO!" responses chorused by the Furies (DWMA128). Finally, he wears down their resistance and obtains permission to lead Euridice out of the Underworld, provided he does not look back to ascertain that she is following him. Act II is a masterpiece.

In Act III, Orpheus responds to Euridice's appeals and embraces her, then realizes that by so doing he has lost her forever. *Che farò senza Euridice?* (What shall I do without Euridice?) he sings. Amore, pitying him, restores Euridice to life. The opera concludes with an ensemble finale reminiscent of vaudeville final. *Che farò senza Euridice?* (DWMA129) became one of the most famous opera arias of the eighteenth century. Its lyric simplicity, balanced phrases, the melodic sighs in the vocal line, and broken chord figurations in the accompaniment typify the emerging Classic style.

Orfeo ed Euridice contains no *secco* recitative. From the outset, chorus and ballet participate functionally in the action. In this opera, French and Italian elements were blended; music, drama, and dance merged and became fused, thus creating a unified theatrical production.

During the next five years, Gluck wrote several stage works. *Alceste* (1767) exhibits his mature style and his fusion of Italian, French, and German operatic elements. When *Alceste* was published (1769), Gluck stated his reform aims in the dedication: (1) to compose music devoid of superfluous ornamentation, expressive of the text, and appropriate to the circumstances in the drama; (2) to construct each aria in a form suited to the situation, rather than relying on traditional *da capo;* (3) to remove the sharp contrast between recitative and aria by using more *accompagnato* recitative and *arioso,* and avoiding *secco* recitative; and (4) to relate the overture to the ensuing drama.

Gluck's objectives are directly related to the principles advanced by Scheibe. Others had agitated for similar reforms. Actually, Gluck did not accomplish all of his stated aims in *Alceste,* but the objectives that were realized did much to equalize the balance between music and drama. The overture, which leads into the first scene, is truly a tragic introduction to the opera. The arias are not all structured with *da capo.* Though much of the recitative is *accompagnato,* there is some *recitativo secco.* The chorus participates effectively in the action. The tragic mood persists almost to the end; then comes Amore, *deus ex machina,* to effect a happy ending.

Gluck's next reform opera, *Paride ed Elena* (Paris and Helen; 1770), was not a success. Part of the problem was Calzabigi's drastic alteration of the mythological story; he blamed himself completely. Noteworthy in *Paride ed Elena* is Gluck's incorporation of themes from the opera in the overture, as Handel had done in *Deidamia.*

Influential in Gluck's career was his move to Paris late in 1773. For performance there in 1774 he prepared a French version of *Orfeo ed Euridice,* using no castrati, and casting Orfeo as a tenor. Also, *Iphigénie en Aulide* premiered in Paris in 1774. Gluck revised that opera (perf. 1775), then went to Vienna to be court chapelmaster.

In May 1777 he returned to Paris; in September, *Armide* was produced. When Gluck and Piccinni (1728–1800) both began setting Quinault's *Roland,* a heated controversy developed. Gluck abandoned his project. Both Piccinni and Gluck set *Iphigénie en Tauride* (Iphigenia in Tauris), and this time Gluck persisted; his opera is a masterpiece. In it he successfully blended traditional Lully-Rameau *tragédie lyrique* with Italian opera seria and eliminated several problems that had plagued Italian opera. The drama is developed by musical means, ballet and chorus are integrated with the action, and resolution of the dramatic situation is effected by human means. Gluck used instruments effectively—especially trombones—to support the action and characterization. At times he interrupted an aria by recitative, as he had done in *Orfeo ed Euridice* and *Iphigénie en Aulide*.

Iphigénie en Tauride marks the summit of Gluck's operatic writing. It is a four-act opera of large proportions, employing soloists, chorus, orchestra, and ballet in a manner that balanced drama and music. With it, he evidenced his mastery of opera in Classic style. A German version of *Iphigénie en Tauride* was produced in Vienna in 1781; Mozart learned much by attending the rehearsals. Others influenced by *Iphigénie en Tauride* include Hector Berlioz and Richard Wagner.

Gluck's *Echo et Narcisse* (Echo and Narcissus; 1779) was a failure; he contemplated writing another opera but was prevented from doing so by a series of strokes that were temporarily paralytic. Near the end of his life, he composed a dark-toned *De profundis* (Out of the depths; chor., orch.). It was performed at his funeral.

Gluck's historical significance lies principally in his ability to establish an equilibrium between music and drama, to effect some reforms of opera seria, to revitalize opéra comique, and to blend elements of French *tragédie lyrique*, Italian opera seria, and German opera into a cosmopolitan Classic opera style. The balance he achieved between music and drama was a step toward the music dramas of Wagner. Gluck's influence was felt by generations of opera composers. Simplicity is a prime factor in his style. A master of characterization and the portrayal of human emotions, he was keenly aware of the importance of timing and adeptly positioned details in exact relationship to the total effect of the drama. He employed dramatic irony skillfully, frequently using the audience's foreknowledge of the mythological story for this purpose (e.g., Agamemnon's ruse to kill Iphigenia). Later, Berlioz used audience foreknowledge similarly in *Les Troyens*.

FRANZ JOSEPH HAYDN

Although Franz Joseph Haydn (1732–1809) is recognized as having composed music that clearly exemplifies the perfected Classic style, he lived through, experienced, and participated in many musical style

Franz Joseph Haydn. Painted by Rössler. Original is in the Faculty of Music, Oxford University.

changes, all of which are reflected to some extent in his music—the last stages of the Baroque, the Preclassic *galant,* rococo, and *empfindsamer* styles, the time of *Sturm und Drang,* the development and maturation of Classic style, and the encroachment of early Romanticism. Haydn and Mozart are jointly credited with developing and perfecting the Classic symphony and string quartet.

HIS LIFE

Joseph Haydn was born in Rohrau, Lower Austria (fig. 19.5). He was the second of the 12 children of Mathias and Anna Koller Haydn; 2 of his brothers, Michael (1737–1806) and Johann Evangelist (1743–1805), had careers in music. Music was part of Haydn's home life; all of the children participated in family music making and neighborhood concerts. At the age of six, Joseph was sent to Hainburg to live with a distant relative, a schoolmaster. In 1740, Haydn was accepted as a choirboy at St. Stephen's Cathedral, Vienna, where he served as a chorister and soloist until his voice changed c. 1750. The cathedral choir school concentrated on preparing the choirboys for singing the church music; there was some training in instrumental music but no music theory or composition lessons. Yet, before Haydn left St. Stephen's, he had begun to compose church music. A *Missa brevis* in F (c. 1749) is extant.

Haydn was sufficiently skilled on harpsichord, organ, and violin to earn a meager living in Vienna in 1750–60 by giving keyboard lessons, playing in orchestras and for church services, and in general accepting

FIGURE 19.5 Most of Haydn's life was spent a short distance from his birthplace, Rohrau. Eszterháza stands between the present towns of Fertöd and Süttör.

whatever musical jobs came his way. He lived in a small attic room in the Michaelerhaus, where Princess Maria Esterházy (mother of Paul Anton and Nikolaus) occupied the first floor and Metastasio lived on the third floor. Through Metastasio, Haydn met Nicola Porpora (1686–1768), composer and singing teacher, who employed him as accompanist. Working for Porpora profited Haydn greatly; besides learning a good deal about singing, he came in contact with prominent musicians such as Gluck. However, as a composer, Haydn seems to have been largely self-taught.

In 1758 or 1759, Haydn was appointed music director to Count Karl Morzin. For Morzin, he composed some divertimenti for wind instruments and his first symphony. In 1760 Haydn married. He had hoped to wed Josepha Keller, but when she entered a convent, he agreed to marry her elder sister, Maria Anna Aloysia (1729–1800). The marriage was not a happy one.

On 1 May 1761 Haydn contracted to serve Prince Paul Anton Esterházy (b. 1711; r. 1734–62) as House Officer and Vice-Kapellmeister in Eisenstadt. Haydn

was subordinate to Gregor Werner (1693–1766), Ober-Kapellmeister, in the area of choral music only. The contract spelled out Haydn's responsibilities as well as regulations pertaining to his personal behavior and dress. He was responsible for the care of the music and instruments belonging to the estate and for the training and supervision of the instrumentalists. He was required to compose whatever music the prince required, was forbidden to give away or sell copies of that music, and was not to compose any music for any other persons without special permission. (Later, he was permitted to accept commissions and to arrange for publication and distribution of his works.) Though the terms of the contract seem quite restrictive, they were not unusual at that time. Frequently, patrons assigned musicians other household tasks and required them to wear special clothing. The beneficial aspects of patronage far outweighed the restrictions. In addition to providing regular income for composers plus lodging for themselves and their families, it assured performance of their works. Composers were constantly prodded to produce new works, for the emphasis was on new music, not repeat performances of works written previously. Haydn, in the comparative isolation of the Esterházy estate after 1766, was forced to rely on his ingenuity and was free to experiment. By his own admission, composition was difficult for him; many times he prayed for ideas. He regarded his talent as a gift from God. At the beginning of a composition, Haydn inscribed the words *In nomine Domini* (In the name of the Lord) and at the conclusion of the work *Laus Deo* (Praise God). Sometimes he added *et B. V. Mā. et omī S^{tis}* (and Blessed Virgin Mary and all the Saints). Situations at court sometimes provided inspiration for a composition (e.g., Symphony No. 45, the so-called Farewell Symphony; see p. 377).

The Esterházy orchestra was small but excellent; in 1761, it had 10 to 12 members. Haydn increased its size, but it never numbered more than 25. Among its members were violinist Luigi Tomasini, 'cellists Joseph Weigl and Anton Kraft, and horn players Thaddeus Steinmüller and Karl Franz. The works Haydn composed during his first years at Eisenstadt reflect the measure of their talents and the high standard of music at the Esterházy court. A number of those compositions have become standard repertoire (e.g., Symphonies Nos. 6, 7, and 8, entitled *Le matin, Le midi,* and *Le Soir* [Morning, Noon, and Evening]).

Prince Paul Anton was succeeded by his brother Nikolaus (b. 1713; r. 1762–90). Before his accession, Nikolaus had spent considerable time at his hunting lodge near Süttör, south of the Neusiedler See (fig. 19.5). He had the lodge enlarged to a palace, which he named "Eszterháza." Commencing in 1766, Nikolaus moved his court there for most of the year but kept the chapel choir at Eisenstadt. At Eszterháza, there were two large music rooms and two theaters, one for opera and one for marionette plays. Haydn wrote at least five puppet operas; only *Philemon und Baucis* is extant. Customarily, two operas were produced per week; these were mainly light operas, some of them written by Haydn but most of them imported. Haydn wrote much *Tafelmusik* as well as music for the two concerts that were given each week. Additional concerts were given when dignitaries visited court. Chamber music was performed almost daily in the prince's private chambers. Nikolaus played 'cello, viola da gamba, and baryton (fig. 19.6), a large instrument similar to the bass viola da gamba but equipped with two sets of strings. The set passing over the fretted fingerboard was bowed; the set alongside the fingerboard vibrated sympathetically with those bowed or might be plucked. Among Haydn's extant works are 126 trios for baryton, viola, and violoncello; 12 divertimenti for 2 barytons and bass or 'cello; and a duet for 2 barytons. The baryton became obsolete early in the nineteenth century.

In 1766 Ober-Kapellmeister Werner died, and Haydn was appointed to that post. This meant he could compose church music, which had always interested him. While in Esterházy employ, Haydn began a personal catalog of his works that he maintained, in a somewhat unorganized manner, throughout his life. In 1776 he prepared an autobiographical sketch for publication. He considered himself primarily a composer of vocal music; perhaps, because he was a singer, it was natural for him to do so. Also, at that time, few of his instrumental works were known outside Eszterháza.

At some time during the early 1780s, Haydn and Mozart became acquainted. They were never close friends, but their association was mutually beneficial, especially in symphony and string quartet composi-

FIGURE 19.6 This baryton was made in Austria in 1779. *(The Crosby Brown Collection of Musical Instruments, 1889, The Metropolitan Museum of Art, New York City)*

tion. Also, Haydn met Gottfried van Swieten, at whose home in Vienna some musicians gathered weekly to study the music of Bach and Handel.

Haydn remained in the employ of the Esterházy family until Prince Nikolaus died. Prince Anton (b. 1738; r. 1790–94) did not share Nikolaus's love for music and disbanded the orchestra. Because there was little work for Haydn at court, he moved to Vienna. Shortly thereafter, he was commissioned to compose some symphonies for the London orchestra. Under management of impresario J. P. Salomon (1745–1815), Haydn worked in London from January 1791 to July 1792 and from February 1794 to August 1795. In England, he composed a number of works, including the 12 "London" symphonies; conducted numerous concerts; performed at court; and became interested in collecting and arranging British folk songs (see p. 373).

On 8 July 1791 Oxford University honored Haydn with a Doctor of Music degree. The "exercise" he submitted was a *canon cancrizans a tre* setting the text "Thy voice, O Harmony, is divine." At this Oxford event, his Symphony No. 92 was performed, thus its name, "Oxford" Symphony. On his travels between London and Vienna in 1792, Haydn visited Bonn, where he heard Beethoven play, examined some of his music, and encouraged him to come to Vienna.

Late in 1795 Haydn resumed limited service as Kapellmeister for the Esterházy family. Prince Nikolaus II (b. 1765; r. 1794–1835) annually commissioned a new Mass to celebrate his wife's name day; Haydn wrote six of them. There was time now for Haydn to compose works of his own choice. He wrote a few string quartets and some sacred music, including a *Te Deum* in C, a vocal version of his orchestral (1785) *Die Sieben letzten Worte* (The Seven last words; 1795–96), and six English psalm settings.

While in England, Haydn had been particularly impressed by the British national anthem and wanted a hymnlike anthem for his country. In 1797 he composed *Gott! erhalte Franz den Kaiser* (God! protect Franz the Emperor) as a birthday gift for the emperor (ex. 19.2). For many years the song, known as the *Emperor's Hymn,* was Austria's national anthem. In 1922, Haydn's music was supplied with new words, commencing "*Deutschland, Deutschland, über alles*"—an adaptation of a poem by the Minnesinger Walther von der Vogelweide. During Hitler's regime, Haydn's music was used for the Nazi party song. In the 1980s, the same music, with still another text, served as national anthem for the German Federal Republic. In the 1990s it is unified Germany's anthem. The music is in some Protestant hymnals with the text "Glorious things of thee are spoken, Zion, city of our God."

Haydn spent his last years in Vienna. Occasionally, he attended concerts, the last one being a performance of *Die Schöpfung* (The Creation), which Salieri conducted at the university on 27 March 1808. The choir consisted of boys and men, and the orchestra was very small.

Haydn, in weakened condition, was at his home in the suburb of Gumpendorf when Napoleon entered Vienna in mid-May 1809. After the city surrendered, the general ordered a guard of honor before Haydn's home. Haydn died quietly at home on 31 May. His remains were interred in Hundsturm Cemetery; years later, they were moved to the Bergkirche in Eisenstadt.

HAYDN'S MUSIC

The exact number of compositions Haydn wrote is not known. The only catalog made during his lifetime was compiled by Haydn himself, with some later entries by some of his students; it is incomplete and unreliable. In 1919 Anthony van Hoboken (1887–1983) prepared the first thematic catalog of Haydn's works. Later, musicologists cataloged specific genres. In the following discussion, the opus numbers of the string quartets and the numbers of the symphonies and keyboard sonatas are those in Hoboken's catalog.

VOCAL WORKS   It is natural that Haydn, trained as a choirboy, commenced his career as a composer by writing sacred vocal music. His youthful products are works of a talented, noninnovative composer. Between 1759 and 1765 Haydn wrote no church music; only after succeeding Werner did he resume composition of liturgical music. His Masses are sincere expressions of faith and devotion. The *Cäcilienmesse* (Caecilia Mass; 1766) is cantata type, constructed as a succession of self-contained arias and choruses. *Missa Sancti Josephi* (St. Joseph Mass; c. 1769) conveys a greater sense of continuity, for solos lead into and blend with the choruses. (This work is known also as the *Great Organ Mass.*) The *Mariazeller Messe* (Mass for Mariazell; 1782) was commissioned for Mariazell monastery in Styria. As in late Baroque Masses, fugues conclude the Gloria, Credo, and Agnus Dei.

Haydn composed no more church music for 14 years. This hiatus was probably caused by an imperial decree restricting the use of orchestrally accompanied music in church in 1783–92, but he did not immediately resume composition of church music when the ban was listed. Between 1796 and 1802, he composed six Masses (SATB soloists, 4-vc. choir, orch., organ) for Prince Nikolaus II Esterházy. In them, Haydn's symphonic style is apparent not only in the orchestral music but in the manner in which symphonic formal principles infiltrate the vocal music without negating the traditional structure of the Mass.

EXAMPLE 19.2 First phrase of the melody of Haydn's "Emperor" hymn. Translation: God! protect Franz the Emperor.

Two of the Masses are directly related to conditions in Europe: *Missa in tempore belli* (In time of war, known as *Paukenmesse*, or Kettledrum Mass; 1796), and *Missa in angustiis* (Lord Nelson Mass, or *Imperial Mass*; 1798).

Missa Sancti Bernardi von Offida (Mass for St. Bernard of Offida; 1796) is known as *Heiligmesse* because Haydn used the hymn *Heilig, heilig* (Holy, holy) in the Sanctus. The *Schöpfungsmesse* (Creation Mass; 1801) uses a theme from the oratorio in two sections. The *Harmoniemesse* is also called the *Wind-band Mass* (1802). Presumably, the *Theresienmesse* (Theresia Mass; 1799) was named for the Empress.

Haydn composed three true oratorios. *Il ritorno di Tobia* (The Return of Tobias; 1774–75) consists mainly of Italianate arias. Haydn's other oratorios reflect his knowledge of Handel's *Messiah* and *Israel in Egypt.* Salomon gave Haydn a copy of John Milton's *Paradise Lost,* and Haydn requested van Swieten to consider it for an oratorio. Van Swieten not only prepared the libretto for *Die Schöpfung,* basing it on material from *Genesis* and *Paradise Lost,* he also supplied Haydn with detailed instructions for setting it.

Die Schöpfung (1796–98) is scored for SATB soloists, four-part chorus, and full orchestra, with basso continuo for harpsichord. The instrumental preludes, introductions, and interludes are descriptive music. Symbolism is evident throughout the oratorio in the choice of keys and instrumentation and in word painting. Storms and the crashing sea are presented in D minor, a key Haydn had used for other "storm" works. Flashes of lightning are depicted by flute, and *divisi* lower strings portray great whales and other sea creatures being created and multiplying. *Die Schöpfung* commences in C minor and, after touching on several transient tonalities, settles into C major as God makes order out of chaos. C major—the key associated with glory, power, majesty, and heaven—is used for God's creation of mankind, but the oratorio concludes in B♭, tonally depicting the fall of Adam and Eve. Especially impressive is the opening "Representation of Chaos," with its Romantic harmonic coloring, followed by recitative and chorus, and the choral proclamation, "And there was LIGHT!" climaxing on a great C-major chord. Other choruses (e.g., "The Heavens are telling") are almost as masterful. Into the composition of *Die Schöpfung* Haydn poured the wealth of his knowledge of composition—blended the styles and forms associated with symphony, Mass, opera, and traditional oratorio—to create a masterpiece that is a worthy successor to Handel's *Messiah.*

The libretto for *Die Jahreszeiten* (The Seasons) was also prepared by van Swieten. The music includes powerful choruses, excellent accompanied recitatives and arias, and pleasant rural depictions of the changing seasons.

Many of the secular cantatas and stage works that Haydn composed for the Esterházy court have been lost or survive only in fragments. Most of his 15 Italian operas were opera buffa or *dramma giocoso* types. Of his three serious operas, *Armida* (1783) and *Orlando paladino* (1782) were well received. Haydn openly acknowledged Mozart's superiority in the field of opera.

Haydn wrote approximately 50 solo songs with keyboard accompaniment. At least 9 of the 14 songs with English texts (1794–95) are settings of poems by Anne Hunter (1742–1821). Among Haydn's fine, small vocal works are 13 part-songs with keyboard accompaniment. Moreover, folk-song repertoire was considerably enriched by the more than 400 arrangements of British folk songs that Haydn and his pupils prepared for English publishers.

KEYBOARD WORKS Keyboard works occupy a relatively minor place among Haydn's compositions. There are approximately 50 sonatas, a handful of concertos, several sets of *Tema con variazioni* (Theme with variations), and a few miscellaneous pieces such as the *Fantasia* in C (publ. 1789).

The early sonatas (1750–67) are in major keys and are closely related to divertimento. In fact, Haydn labeled many of them that. Most of the extant early piano sonatas have three movements—Nos. 6 and 8 have four—with all movements of a work in the same key. The second or third movement is usually a minuet with trio. The first movement (and also the last movement when it is not minuet/trio) is a rounded binary (fig. 19.7). The second movement, when not a minuet, has a *cantabile* melody in *galant* style with accompaniment that incorporates "Alberti bass" figuration.

The sonatas written c. 1770–80 (Nos. 20–39) reflect the influence of C. P. E. Bach, a debt Haydn acknowledged. Four of them are in minor keys: No. 20, C minor; No. 32, A minor; No. 34, E minor; and No. 36, C♯ minor. The music is expressive and intense. In

```
     ‖: A :‖: B A :‖     (= A A BA BA)


‖: Tonic ──▶ Dominant .. Cadence :‖: Dominant ──▶──▶ Double Return    ... ... ...   Cadence :‖
                                                     of Tonic and    (Tonic key)   rhyme
                                                     of beginning,
                                                     most, or all
                                                     of A section
```

FIGURE 19.7 Diagram of rounded binary form: (a) overall structural scheme; (b) detail of key tonality within the structural scheme.

Sonata No. 25 (E♭), the minuet is canonic; in No. 26 (A), it is *al rovescio* (i.e., the second half is the retrograde of the first half.

Haydn's mature Classic style is present in some of the sonatas of the last group. Sonatas Nos. 49 (E♭), 51 (D), and 52 (E♭) were written after Haydn visited London, where Dussek loaned him one of the latest English pianos. Sonata No. 52 is a large three-movement work whose first movement (Allegro) is in sonata form. Extremes of range, rapid scale passages, and figuration are important features of the movement. The second movement (Adagio) is *galant* in style. The Presto final movement is virtuosic. In stature, Sonata No. 52 is comparable with Haydn's mature string quartets.

CHAMBER MUSIC   In the last half of the eighteenth century, a prince's chambers were often the setting for concerts that included orchestral works as well as compositions for smaller ensembles and soloists. The works programmed on such concerts, and the concerts themselves, were frequently referred to as **chamber music.** Very early in the nineteenth century, the term *chamber music* took on a different connotation—ensemble music performed by one person per part. Haydn composed chamber music of both types: duos, trios, quartets, quintets, and sextets for strings; sonatas for violin and keyboard; piano trios; and trios, quartets, sextets, octets, and nonets for various combinations of string and wind instruments. In developing the string quartet, Haydn made his greatest contribution to chamber music. But Haydn did not originate the string quartet.

Haydn's early quartets (1762) are divertimento and transcription types. His experience writing 40 symphonies is reflected in the six quartets of Op. 9 (1768–70)—four-movement works in which the first-violin part is brilliant. Occasionally, the other instruments share in the thematic material, and viola and 'cello are accorded some independence.

In the Op. 17 (1771) and Op. 20 (1772) quartets, the first-violin part is virtuosic at times, but there is more equality in the distribution of thematic material among the instruments. To some degree, this equality results from the increased use of imitative and invertible counterpoint. Half the Op. 20 quartets conclude with a *Fuga* employing more than one subject. In these movements, fugue is used as a compositional technique to enrich the homophonic texture rather than as a polyphonic form. Each quartet has four movements, but placement of the Minuet vacillates from second to third movement. In Haydn's string quartets the position of the Minuet was never firmly established. Whether he placed it second or third seems to have depended on where he thought it would exert the most influence in stabilizing the overall tonic key tonality of the quartet.

Some of the *Sturm und Drang* expressive elements that color the symphonies written in the early 1770s appear also in the Op. 17 and Op. 20 quartets. All the Op. 20 quartets have marked individual differences. In some of the sonata-form first movements, Haydn employed a device used frequently in his symphonies—the ***fausse reprise*** (false recapitulation; see p. 377). One instance occurs in Op. 20, No. 4, mvt. 1 (ex. 19.3).

Haydn wrote no more string quartets until 1781; then the six Op. 33 quartets appeared. With them, he began using the designation "string quartet"; previously, he called his pieces in this genre "divertimenti." The Op. 33 quartets are variously called "Russian" because Haydn wrote them for Grand Duke Paul of Russia, and "*Gli Scherzi,*" supposedly because in each quartet a movement labeled *Scherzo* replaced the Minuet. Basically, these *scherzi* are still minuets but are lighter in mood and have faster tempo indications than usual. "*Gli scherzi*" literally means "Jokes," and when these movements are played too fast, Haydn's humor is lost. Humor occurs in other movements and is conveyed through melodic character, false starts, pizzicato, half-cadences where full ones are expected, and, in the Finale of No. 2, an abrupt, unexpected conclusion.

Haydn stated that the Op. 33 quartets were written "in an entirely new, special way." In general, they are light, happy music, with some folklike themes, and the slow movements seem especially expressive and emotional. However, some of the melodies are more elaborate rhythmically and contain more distinctive intervals. Haydn broke down those melodies and developed some of the motivic fragments contrapuntally. Haydn's "new, special way" of writing is thematic development using contrapuntal devices in a homophonic relationship. The development section of Op. 33, No. 2, mvt. 1, is an example (DWMA130). The most popular of the Op. 33 quartets was No. 3 (in C), filled with graces that have given it the nickname "The Bird."

A single quartet in D minor constitutes Op. 42 (c. 1783–85). During the remainder of the decade, Haydn wrote 18 string quartets. The 6 *Prussian* quartets, Op. 50 (1787), dedicated to King Friedrich Wilhelm II (r. 1786–97), reflect the fact that the king was an accomplished 'cellist. The other 12 quartets were written for and dedicated to Johann Tost, who published them in three sets: Op. 54 (3 quartets, 1788), Op. 55 (3 quartets, 1788), and Op. 64 (6 quartets, 1790). In general, these four sets of chamber works parallel in quality and stylistic traits the symphonies composed during the late 1780s. However, the first movements of Haydn's quartets do not have the slow introductions that characterize his symphonies. This is not a lack but an advantage—such introductions would have impaired the intimacy of the quartets. There is a noticeable increase in chromatic passages in the Op. 50 and Op. 64 quartets. Doubtless, this is directly related to Haydn's awareness of the chromaticism in Mozart's music and the association between the two composers when Haydn wrote these quartets.

Haydn's late quartets include Op. 71 (3 quartets, 1793), Op. 74 (3 quartets, 1793), Op. 76 (6 quartets, 1797), Op. 77 (2 quartets, 1799), and Op. 103 (1803), which he abandoned after completing only the slow

(a)

(b)

(c)

EXAMPLE 19.3 Haydn's String Quartet, Op. 20, No. 4, mvt. 1: (*a*) mm. 1–6; (*b*) mm. 132–40, a *fausse reprise* near the beginning of the development section; (*c*) mm. 206–24, return of the opening measures in the subdominant key, followed by actual recapitulation at m. 217.

movement (B♭) and the Menuetto. Op. 103 is usually referred to as being in B♭ major, yet the Menuetto—normally constructed in the tonic key of the composition—is in D minor. In the Op. 71 and Op. 74 quartets, written after Haydn visited London, the first movements have introductions varying in length from two or three chords to several Adagio measures. This resulted from Haydn's observance that, in London, chamber music was often performed in concert rooms as entertainment for listeners and not primarily for the performer's enjoyment. The introductions are not solely prefatory material; usually, that music was woven into the fabric of the entire movement. Tendencies toward romanticism characterize these works, especially Op. 74—an expanded harmonic palette, sudden shifts of tonality to remote keys, far-ranging modulations, and formal liberties such as development within recapitulation or telescoping development and recapitulation.

The Op. 76 quartets are intensely expressive. They abound in passages illustrative of Haydn's continual experimentation, his development and enrichment of forms through new uses of compositional techniques, the expansion of his harmonic vocabulary, and his exploration of remote key tonalities. In these quartets, the slow movement is second and the Menuetto third. All the minuets have the character of *scherzi* and bear Italian tempo markings denoting that they are to be played quickly. This same kind of Menuetto appears in the "London" symphonies.

Haydn's Op. 77, Nos. 1 (G) and 2 (F), his last completed large-scale instrumental works, composed in 1799, mark the summit of Haydn's string quartet writing. They exhibit the subtle wit and the other stylistic traits that characterize Haydn's other late quartets and symphonies.

SYMPHONIES When considering Haydn's 104 symphonies, it must be remembered that he wrote for a patron, that the instrumentation of a composition was determined by that of the orchestra at his disposal, and that the degree of difficulty of the work was geared to the capabilities of the members of the patron's performing ensemble. A keyboard instrument is required for all Haydn's first 50 symphonies; though he seldom specified it thereafter, he continued to use it, even for the "London" symphonies.

Haydn's first five symphonies were written for Count Morzin; symphonies Nos. 6–81 were designed for the Esterházy orchestra. Most of the early symphonies are scored for two oboes, two horns, and strings, with basso continuo. Commencing with No. 20, other wind instruments were occasionally included. Not until 1779, beginning with No. 70, was flute added consistently.

For his early symphonies, Haydn maintained no standard structural plan. Many of them have the three-movement fast-slow-fast formal structure derived from expansion of the Preclassic sinfonia: an Allegro in tonic key; an Andante in contrasting tonality, usually parallel minor or subdominant; and a Minuet or an Allegro with gigue characteristics (e.g., No. 19), in tonic. A few of the early symphonies are in four movements. Some of these (e.g., Nos. 21 and 22) resemble Baroque *sonata da chiesa*: Andante-Allegro-Minuet-Presto, with all movements in the same key and each movement in binary form. Yet, No. 3 (1762) exhibits the overall scheme that became standard in the Classic symphony: Allegro (G major), Andante moderato (G minor), Minuet/Trio (G major), and Allegro (G major).

Symphonies Nos. 6, 7, and 8 have the four-movement structure of the Classic symphony. All three feature violin and 'cello soloists and are to some degree programmatic. Symphony No. 7 resembles Baroque concerto grosso in the writing for a concertante trio of two violins and violoncello, and there is a suggestion of opera in the *recitativo* passages for solo violin in the Adagio (ex. 19.4).

Symphony No. 31 (D major), the "Hornsignal" Symphony, was originally designated symphonie concertante. The work has several distinctive features: It is scored for four horns instead of the usual two, and the first movement commences with the solo horn-call that gave the symphony its nickname. The Adagio, featuring solo violin, uses a melody whose opening phrase closely resembles an old Netherlands song of thanksgiving. The fourth movement, constructed as theme with variations, concludes with a Presto unrelated to the theme.

Haydn wrote few symphonies in minor keys, but in 1768–73 he composed five of them: Nos. 26, 39, 49, 44, and 52 (in that order). Symphonies Nos. 44 and 52 exhibit a degree of expression closely akin to *Sturm und Drang.* The *Trauer* (Mourning) Symphony, No. 44, commences Allegro con brio with a monothematic sonata-form movement in which Haydn begins to develop the theme in the exposition; further development occurs in the middle section of the movement. The Minuet (in tonic E minor), a canon at the octave, is placed second; its Trio is in parallel major. The third movement, an Adagio (E major), is one of the loveliest slow movements Haydn ever composed. The Presto finale is monothematic, in sonata form with abbreviated recapitulation.

In 1771–74, Haydn composed Symphonies Nos. 42–48, 50–52, 54–56, 64, and 65. These works are on a larger scale than earlier symphonies, with greater harmonic richness, with modulatory excursions farther afield in the development sections, and with greater intensity of expression. For several of these symphonies Haydn chose keys that were exceptional in the eighteenth century: No. 45 is in F♯ minor, No. 46 in B major, and No. 49 in F minor. The inner tonal scheme of No. 45, the "Farewell" Symphony, is also exceptional. The opening Allegro is in F♯ minor, the slow second movement in A major, the third movement in F♯ major, and the finale commences Presto in F♯ minor, then moves into an Adagio section that begins in A major and ends in F♯ major. Extramusical reasons occasioned the Adagio conclusion—in it Haydn gradually reduced the instrumentation, and when a musician finished playing his part, he packed up his instrument, blew out the candles on his music stand, and departed. Only two performers remained to conclude the work. (Haydn's hint was effective—

the prince permitted the musicians to say a temporary "Farewell" to Eszterháza and return to the city.) Another feature contributes to the individuality of Symphony No. 45—Haydn introduced a new theme in the development section of the first movement. This is the only symphony in which he did so.

Often in the sonata-form movements of symphonies written in the 1770s, Haydn used a *false reprise*—in the development section, after some development has occurred, the first theme returns as though commencing the recapitulation but is abandoned in favor of continued development before actual recapitulation occurs. The surprise element is important and is seen in harmonies, key relationships, and deviations from traditional structural patterns.

In the symphonies composed during the 1780s, Haydn sometimes used **sonata-rondo form** in the last movement. Basically, this construction resembles a seven-part rondo (ABACABA), with the first ABA treated as exposition, the C section being developmental, and the last ABA section being recapitulation (the B music presented in the tonic key; fig. 19.8). Haydn first used sonata-rondo for the finale of Symphony No. 77. He did not introduce the form—Mozart had used it previously.

Also in the 1780s, Haydn changed the kind of principal theme he used for the opening movement of a symphony. Instead of writing a triadic or scalar type of theme that emphasized the tonic, as Baroque and Pre-classic composers had done, he constructed simple, pliant themes suitable for fragmentation and development and distributed the thematic material more

EXAMPLE 19.4 Haydn: Symphony No. 7, mvt. 2, mm. 16–20, one of several recitative-like violin solo passages in the movement.

(a) Seven-part Rondo:	Rondo theme	First digression	Rondo theme	Second digression	Rondo theme	First digression repeated	Rondo theme
	A	B	A	C	A	B	A
Keys:	Tonic	Dominant	Tonic	Related	Tonic	Tonic	Tonic
(b) Sonata-rondo:	Theme 1	Theme 2	Closing based on Theme 1	Development of themes	Theme 1	Theme 2	Closing based on Theme 1
	A	B	A	C	A	B	A
Keys:	Tonic	Dominant	Dominant	Various	Tonic	Tonic	Tonic

‖⟵————— Exposition —————⟶‖ Development   Recapitulation —————⟶‖

FIGURE 19.8 Comparison of seven-part rondo form and sonata-rondo form.

widely among the instruments instead of assigning it to only one or two sections of the orchestra.

In 1785–86, Haydn composed Symphonies Nos. 82–87 for performance in Paris. Symphonies Nos. 88–91 (1787–88) were commissioned by private individuals; No. 92 is the "Oxford" Symphony.

Haydn's symphonic writing culminates in the two sets of "London" symphonies, Nos. 93–98 (1791–92) and Nos. 99–104 (1793–95). These are large works for a large orchestra and exhibit Haydn's mastery of symphonic writing. In most of them, the first movement commences with a long, slow introduction, featuring the dotted rhythms commonly associated with the first section of a French overture. Not always does the introduction begin in the designated key of the symphony; for example, Symphony No. 104, in D major, opens in D minor (DWMA131). Nor are developmental features reserved for the middle section of the form; they may infiltrate the entire move-

ment. In only one of these symphonies (No. 101) does the development section commence in the dominant key; instead, Haydn used mediant, submediant, or a plagal key (subdominant or supertonic). The long introduction is balanced by increased length of the coda, which often is developmental. Haydn's fondness for folk songs is apparent in his choice of thematic material—the first and the fourth movements of No. 104 provide examples of folk-song-*like* themes (ex. 19.5). In Symphonies Nos. 99, 100, 103, and 104, the melody used as first theme is restated in the dominant as the second theme; this substantiates current belief that change of key tonality rather than melodic content defines the secondary theme in a sonata-form movement. As if to prove the point, in some works Haydn stated the thematic material twice in the tonic key in the recapitulation (e.g., No. 104, mvt. 1). The movement's closing theme is clearly defined.

EXAMPLE 19.5 Some themes in Haydn's Symphony No. 104 resemble folk-song melodies: (*a*) mvt. 1, theme 1; (*b*) mvt. 4, theme 1.

In the "London" symphonies, most of the second movements are theme and variations. The third movements are structured as Minuet/Trio, but the tempo is much faster than that of the courtly dance. In accordance with tradition, instrumentation is reduced for the Trio. (Incidentally, the Trio was so-named because originally that section was often performed by an instrumental trio.) Customarily, the Trio is in a related key. In some of the Minuets and the Trios, the second section of the music is developmental. Finales are very fast, in sonata form or sonata-rondo; all are in duple meter. Humorous touches color several of the Finales.

Two trumpets and timpani are included in all the "London" symphonies; in No. 100, the "Military" symphony, triangle, cymbals, and bass drum are added in the second and fourth movements. Sometimes the trumpets are given independent parts instead of doubling horns; similarly, 'cellos frequently have music different from that of the string basses. In the last set of six symphonies, only No. 102 does not require two clarinets.

Several of these symphonies acquired nicknames from unusual features of their second movements, for example, the steady ticking rhythm in No. 101, the "Clock," and the crashing *forte* chord concluding the subdued presentation of the theme in the Andante of No. 94, the "Surprise."

An overview of Haydn's symphonies shows a variety of formal patterns and a diversification of inner structural schemes that prevented the symphonies from becoming stereotyped. In developing thematic material, he adeptly balanced counterpoint with homophony. All movements were increased in length and complexity. Haydn's imagination, inventiveness, and constant experimentation brought the symphony to Classic proportions and to a level of development that fostered the masterworks of Beethoven.

CONCERTI Haydn did not concertize; his concerti were written for others to perform. His concerti written before 1765 are Preclassic in style. The Concerto in D for harpsichord or piano and orchestra (publ. 1784) used Classic three-movement format; contrary to custom, orchestral forces are not reduced for the slow movement. Of the surviving violin concerti, that in G major is the finest. The 'cello concerti were written

for Eisenstadt 'cellists, the C-major work (c. 1765) for Weigl, and the D-major work (1783) for Kraft. The D-major concerto contains brilliant and virtuosic technical effects: harmonics, octaves, passages labeled *sul G* (on the G string) and *sul D*.

Haydn created his *Concerto per il clarino* in E♭ (Trumpet Concerto; 1796) for Anton Weidlinger (1767–1852), the trumpet player who, c. 1793, invented the keyed E♭ trumpet (Insight, "Trumpet"). In Haydn's concerto, the trumpet is treated not only as a military/martial instrument but also as one capable of virtuosity, lyricism, and chromaticism. Weidlinger's trumpet had five keys that were played by the left hand while the performer held the instrument with his right hand. All chromatic tones between concert b♭ and c''' were available on the E♭ keyed trumpet, and Haydn's music displays the extremes of the range. Weidlinger performed Haydn's concerto in 1800. Shortly thereafter, the work fell into obscurity and was not brought to light until 1929. It has risen in popularity since 1950 and has been performed frequently.

WOLFGANG MOZART

Joannes Chrysostomus Wolfgangus Theophilus Mozart (1756–91), born in Salzburg, Bavaria (Austria), was the seventh and last child of Leopold and Anna Pertl

Wolfgang Mozart. Detail from Joseph Lange's unfinished oil painting of Mozart at the piano (c. 1783). Original is in the Mozart Museum, Salzburg, Austria.

Maria Anna Mozart

As a child, Maria Anna Mozart, called "Nannerl," evidenced exceptional talent as a keyboard performer. She received her first lessons from her father and experienced her first success in public performance when the Mozarts made a musical tour to Munich in 1762. Nannerl participated in the family's musical tours until c. 1769; thereafter, she was permitted to perform only at home. She then turned to musical composition, which pleased Wolfgang, who examined her work and commented favorably. None of her music survives. In 1784, she married J. B. von Berchtold zu Sonnenburg (1736–1801), a councillor at St. Gilgen. After her husband's death, Nannerl moved to Salzburg, where, until she became blind c. 1825, she taught piano lessons. Her diaries and letters provide important information concerning the Mozart family.

Mozart. Only two of their children survived infancy: Wolfgang and Maria Anna (1751–1829; Insight, "Maria Anna Mozart"). Instead of Theophilus ("love of God"), Mozart sometimes used the German name Gottlieb but preferred the translation Amadé or Amadeo; he rarely used Amadeus, except in jest.

Wolfgang demonstrated extraordinary musical talent by the time he was 4. Before he was 6 he was composing music. He never received any formal schooling; most of his musical training came from his father. At the age of 6, Wolfgang was a harpsichord virtuoso; soon he became an excellent organist and violinist also. When Leopold realized that his children were unusually gifted, he decided to promote and exhibit their talents. In January 1762, he took them to Munich, where they played harpsichord for the Elector of Bavaria. It was the first of many journeys that filled most of the next decade of Wolfgang's life. Eventually, his talents were displayed in all the principal cities and courts of Germany and Austria as well as in France, England, Holland, and Italy. Frequently, he was subjected to tests to prove he was truly a prodigy. His memory was astounding—he could accurately reproduce a work after hearing it only once, a capability he retained throughout his life. The tours during his impressionable years were beneficial; he met important composers and performers and was exposed to different musical styles. Elements of those styles appeared in his own compositions; some were used

for a time and then rejected, others were absorbed into his musical style.

In Paris, early in 1764, Wolfgang's first published compositions appeared—two pairs of sonatas for keyboard and violin, Op. 1 (K. 6, 7) and Op. 2 (K. 8, 9). Six sonatas of the same type (K. 10–15) were issued in London in 1765; six more (K. 26–31) were printed at The Hague in 1766. In these sonatas, the keyboard part is self-sufficient; the violin provides accompaniment. Harpsichord sonatas with violin ad libitum were especially favored by Johann Schobert (c. 1735–67), a German composer active in Paris in the 1760s. The influence of Schobert's sonatas is apparent in these early Mozart works. Schobert's music made a lasting impression on Mozart; borrowings from Schobert's keyboard sonatas appear in some of Mozart's piano concertos and later keyboard sonatas (e.g., Sonata in A minor K. 310).

During the 15 months the Mozarts spent in England, Wolfgang became acquainted with the sonatas and symphonies of J. C. Bach and C. F. Abel. In Chelsea, near London, Wolfgang composed his first symphonies.

In autumn 1767 the Mozarts visited Vienna and Bohemia, then spent about a year in Vienna. By that time, Wolfgang had composed arias and scenes for voice and orchestra; now, he wrote a full-length opera buffa, *La finta semplice* (The feigned simpleton) which was produced in May 1769 at Salzburg. However, some compositions by Wolfgang were performed in Vienna in 1768: a one-act *Singspiel, Bastien und Bastienne,* and a festal Mass, K. 139. Most of 1769 was spent in Salzburg, where Wolfgang composed another Mass and several other sacred works, some minuets, and three serenades. Late in October, he was appointed honorary Konzertmeister at the Salzburg court of Archbishop Colloredo.

Between mid-December 1769 and March 1773, Leopold and Wolfgang made three extensive journeys to various Italian cities. In addition to performing and sight-seeing, Wolfgang had some counterpoint lessons from G. B. Martini (1706–84) at Bologna and, at Florence, formed a friendship with the precocious English violinist-composer Thomas Linley (1756–78), whose talents closely paralleled his own. That friendship was good for Mozart, for it made him realize that he was not unique.

The influence of G. B. Sammartini of Milan is apparent in several symphonies Mozart wrote at this time. In general, Sammartini's symphonies are characterized by a texture similar to that of chamber music, with frequent passages of dialogue between instruments, intense rhythmic drive, varied treatment of sonata form, and structural continuity achieved by frequent elision of themes and/or sections. Slow movements are rich in lyricism and in imitative passages. Some portions of Sammartini's late symphonies have been described as "Mozartean"; in reality, Mozart assimilated characteristics from Sammartini. In Italy, Mozart composed his first seven string quartets: K. 80 (1770) and K. 155–60 (1772–73); they also reflect Sammartini's influence.

Most significant of the compositions Mozart wrote during these years are two opere serie: *Mitridate rè di Ponto* (Mithridates, King of Pontus; 1770) and *Lucio Silla* (1772). For the famed castrato Venanzio Rauzzini, Mozart wrote the motet *Exsultate, jubilate* (Rejoice greatly, jubilantly; K. 165; soprano, orch.), a three-movement work that concludes with a brilliant *Alleluia.*

In 1773 Leopold took Wolfgang to Vienna, where they heard Haydn's Opp. 17 and 20 string quartets. Those quartets inspired Wolfgang to compose the set K. 168–73, in which some of Haydn's characteristics took root. Back in Salzburg, in December 1773, Mozart wrote his first original piano concerto, K. 175 (D major), and his first string quintet, K. 174 (B♭ major).

SALZBURG, 1773–81

In Salzburg's provincial atmosphere, Wolfgang was discontent, but his applications for court positions elsewhere were fruitless. In 1773–74 he composed the earliest of his works to find a place in concert repertoire—Symphonies K. 183 (G minor) and K. 201 (A major) and the Concerto for Bassoon and Orchestra (K. 191)—works that attest his maturity. From this time forward, his compositions reveal an increase in his musical stature, and his individuality comes to the fore. Elements of styles experienced on his travels are visible in his writing and blend in varying degrees to produce a cosmopolitan, "Mozartean" flavor. Present are Italian lyricism (e.g., lyrical second themes, arialike slow movements), *style galant* (melodic sighs, triplet sixteenths, measured tremolo), Germanic seriousness with emphasis on counterpoint and greater formal complexity, and the expressive intensity of *Sturm and Drang*. Symphony No. 25 (K. 183), often referred to as "the little G minor," is Mozart's second minor-key symphony and indicates his awareness of his contemporaries' use of minor keys in works whose musical intensity is comparable with the depth of feeling expressed in *Sturm und Drang* literature.

A commission Mozart received in 1774 for an opera buffa for the Carnival season in Munich resulted in *La finta giardiniera* (The feigned gardener). Mozart's earliest surviving piano sonatas date from that Munich visit: Sonatas K. 279–83 (in C, F, B♭, E♭, and G, respectively), which were written as a group, and K. 284 (D major). His other significant works in 1775 are five concerti for violin and orchestra that show his steady development in the genre (see p. 391). Though he continued to write concerti, he never composed another for solo violin. (The "Adelaide" Concerto is spurious.)

When, in 1777, the Archbishop denied the Mozarts' several requests for permission to travel so that Wolfgang could perform at other courts, Wolfgang requested his release. In response, the Archbishop dismissed both father and son but soon reinstated

Leopold. Wolfgang was delighted to be released. He hoped a tour would bring fame and a lucrative position. He and his mother traveled to Munich, Augsburg, Mannheim, and Paris. In each city, Mozart's endeavors to obtain a Kapellmeister position failed, partly because of his lack of experience in that capacity and partly because prospective employers believed that employing Wolfgang meant hiring Leopold also. Wolfgang was offered an organist post at the Versailles court but rejected it.

In some respects, the tour was productive. At Mannheim, Mozart observed orchestral practices and was fascinated by the clarinet. He renewed acquaintance with Cannabich, met Holzbauer and flautist J. B. Wendling, and fell in love with soprano Aloysia Weber (c. 1761–1839). Mozart received a commission for three flute concerti and four flute quartets. He completed only two concerti (K. 313 in G, K. 314 in D) and two quartets (K. 285 in D, K. 285a in G). Two keyboard sonatas composed at Mannheim, K. 309 (C major) and K. 311 (D major), together with K. 310 (A minor) written in Paris, were published later as Op. 4. A sonata for piano and violin, K. 296 (C major), engendered another set, K. 301–6. In most of these sonatas, the violin plays a subordinate role. In Paris, Mozart composed several theme-and-variations keyboard pieces, some ballet music, at least one sinfonia concertante for winds and orchestra, and his Symphony No. 31 (K. 297), which was performed at the *Concert spirituel* on Corpus Christi (June 1778). In that symphony he combined Mannheim and Paris styles.

In July Mozart's mother contracted fever and died. When Wolfgang belatedly broke the news to his father, Leopold urged him to return to Salzburg. He did so, by a circuitous route, through Strasbourg, Mannheim, and Munich. In Munich, he found Aloysia Weber more interested in her career than in him. Mozart was always enthusiastic about her singing. He created the role of Madame Herz in *Der Schauspieldirektor* (The Impresario; 1786) for her, and she was Donna Anna in the first Vienna performance of *Il Don Giovanni* (1788). For Aloysia's older sister, Josepha (c. 1759–1819), Mozart wrote the part of Queen of the Night in *Die Zauberflöte* (The magic flute).

In mid-January 1779 Wolfgang returned to Salzburg. He was dejected, and with good reason: He had found no suitable position and knew he could not earn his living concertizing; his expenditures had hurt family finances, relations with his father were strained, his mother had died, and he had fallen in love and had been rejected. Now, he willingly accepted an appointment as organist to the Archbishop. His duties included teaching the choirboys and composing whatever music was required. During the next two years, he wrote some Masses and Psalms settings, and several symphonies, concerti, and serenades. He also began a Singspiel that he never completed. The most significant of these works are the "Coronation" Mass (K. 317), considered his finest Salzburg Mass, and the *Sinfonia concertante* in E♭ (K. 364).

In the summer of 1780 Mozart was commissioned to compose an opera for Munich and wrote *Idomeneo*. While in Munich in 1781, he composed several short vocal pieces, the Oboe quartet, and three piano sonatas (K. 330–332).

Meantime, the Archbishop and his retinue had gone to Vienna for festivities celebrating the imperial accession of Joseph II, and in mid-March Wolfgang was summoned there. When the Archbishop denied him several opportunities to perform before the emperor, Mozart again rankled at the conditions of his servitude and requested release. At first, his request was denied, but, in June, after a stormy interview with the Archbishop, Mozart was dismissed and was literally kicked out of the Archbishop's service. From that time on, Mozart was virtually disinherited by the court and city of Salzburg and was literally disinherited by his father. Where Salzburg was concerned, it was as though Mozart no longer existed.

VIENNA, 1781–91

Mozart decided to remain in Vienna and took a room at the Webers. Aloysia had married Joseph Lange, and Mozart became interested in her younger sister, Constanze (1762–1849). On 4 August 1782 Constanze and Wolfgang were married. To fulfill a vow made then, Mozart began to write the Mass in C minor (K. 427) but completed only Kyrie and Gloria. Most of the Sanctus and Benedictus were notated, and the Credo was begun, but they were abandoned. On 26 October 1783 the Kyrie and Gloria, supplemented by Mass movements previously composed by Mozart, were performed at St. Peter's Abbey Church, Salzburg. Constanze sang the soprano solo.

Mozart's first few years in Vienna were prosperous. He had several pupils, and he was in demand as pianist and composer. His first Vienna publication was a set of piano/violin sonatas (K. 296, K. 376–80; 1781). Composition of *Die Entführung aus dem Serail* (The abduction from the harem) occupied much of his time during the spring of 1782. Many of Mozart's finest compositions—most of the works responsible for his being considered a great composer—were written during the Vienna years. During this decade, his compositions were influenced principally by works of J. S. Bach and Joseph Haydn. For several years Mozart attended the weekly gatherings at Baron van Swieten's home that were devoted to studying the music of Handel and Bach. In those sessions, Mozart was introduced to *Das wohltemperirte Clavier* and other Bach works. After 1783, Mozart used counterpoint increasingly.

In 1781, poet Lorenzo da Ponte (1748–1838) came to Vienna; he achieved his first success as opera librettist working with Mozart. Their collaboration produced the operas *Le nozze di Figaro* (The marriage of Figaro; 1786), *Il Don Giovanni;* 1787), and *Così fan tutte* (Thus do they all; 1790).

Between December 1782 and January 1785, Mozart composed his finest string quartets: K. 387, 421, 428, 458, 464, and 465. Published as a set in 1785, they were dedicated to Haydn. In 1782, Symphony No. 35 was created for a Haffner family celebration; Symphony No. 36 was dashed off for a concert at Linz in 1783. (The symphony catalogued as No. 37 is not by Mozart.) Symphony No. 38 (1786) was written for performance at Prague. In approximately six weeks in summer 1788, Mozart composed his finest symphonies, Nos. 39–41. In 1785–86, he wrote six piano concerti, including K. 466 (D minor) and K. 467 (C major); the former became his most popular piano concerto in the nineteenth century. Between 1787 and 1791, he wrote the string quintets K. 515–16, 593, and 614 and created the excellent Clarinet Quintet, K. 581 (A major; 1789) for clarinetist Anton Stadler (1753–1812).

After Gluck died (1787), Mozart was named Imperial Chamber Music Composer at a small fraction of Gluck's former salary.

Mozart became a member of a Vienna Lodge of the Order of Freemasons in 1784 and was active in Freemasonry for the remainder of his life. The ideals of Freemasonry meant a great deal to him. He translated some elements of Masonic ritual into musical symbols and incorporated them in some of his works (e.g., *Die Zauberflöte*). He wrote a number of compositions for Masonic occasions, including *Mauerische Trauermusik* (Masonic Funeral Music, K. 477; 1785); the Adagio in B♭, K. 411 (1785); and the Cantata, K. 623 (1791), his last completed composition. During the last years of his life, when he experienced financial difficulties, his fellow Masons assisted him. Neither Wolfgang nor Constanze could manage money very well, but they never experienced abject poverty. They had six children, only two of whom survived to adulthood: Carl Thomas (1785–1858) and Franz Xaver (1791–1844). Both sons were talented musically; Franz played piano and composed.

In 1791 Wolfgang was appointed assistant Kapellmeister at St. Stephen's Cathedral, Vienna. That year he completed *Die Zauberflöte,* a Singspiel; *La clemenza di Tito* (The clemency of Titus), an opera seria; Piano Concerto in B♭, K. 595; Clarinet Concerto in A, K. 622; the motet *Ave verum corpus* (Hail, true body; K. 618; D major; SATB, strings, organ); and began the *Requiem* (K. 626). The *Requiem* was commissioned anonymously by Count Franz Walsegg, who intended to use it as a memorial service for his deceased wife. The Mass was unfinished at the time of Mozart's death and was completed by his pupil and close friend, Franz Xaver Süssmayr (1766–1803). Undoubtedly, Mozart and Süssmayr had discussed the composition.

Mozart died on 5 December 1791. He was buried in a mass grave at St. Marx cemetery outside the city limits (Insight, "Mozart's Death and Burial").

MOZART'S WORKS

Mozart seldom used opus numbers or dated his works. No extensive catalog of his music was available until Ludwig von Köchel (1800–77) published his *Chronologisch-thematisches Verzeichnis* (Chronological-thematic catalog; 1862) of Mozart's known works, a chronological listing with **incipits** (the first few measures) of the theme of each movement and some documentary data pertinent to each work. Subsequent discoveries have altered some of Köchel's findings, and his *Verzeichnis* has undergone some revisions; however, Mozart's works are still referred to by K. numbers.

Mozart's Death and Burial

Drs. Closset and Sallaba, the physicians who attended Mozart, registered his fatal illness as "severe miliary fever." However, their treatment, which included bleeding the patient and inducing vomiting, fosters the assumption that Mozart succumbed to acute inflammatory rheumatic fever. No autopsy was performed. Mozart's body was interred in conformity with imperial regulations then in force; therefore, there was no body to exhume for later examination. Mozart's medical history indicates that for at least 10 years he had suffered intermittent attacks of rheumatic fever. Constanze Mozart wrote that Wolfgang's final illness commenced with swelling of his feet, ankles, hands, and wrists, to the extent that soon he was unable to turn over in bed without assistance. Fever caused him to sweat profusely. No doubt the prescribed treatment aggravated his condition and hastened his death.

Official regulations stipulated precisely the funeral and burial procedures to be followed. By decree, in 1784 Emperor Joseph II ordered that all vaults, churchyards, and "God's acres" be closed; only large plots of ground located a suitable distance outside city limits, and without exposure to any water source, could be used as cemeteries. Funerals, with music and prayers, would be conducted at church, but no graveside services or ceremonies were permitted. Preferably, only one priest would accompany the body to the cemetery, where the gravedigger and his assistants would perform their prescribed duties. Graves were to be communal, each occupied by five adults, layered one on top of another. Two children occupied one adult space. Rapid decomposition of remains was desirable; no embalming or preservation measures were permitted. Cremation was costly and was not advocated. Survivors were permitted to erect a memorial to the deceased, but the marker must be placed along cemetery walls, not within the cemetery.

Unless an epidemic was rampant, a corpse could not be buried until 48 hours after death, and not after 6 P.M. in winter or 9 P.M. in summer. The corpse, unclothed, was to be sewn into a linen sack and placed in a parish-owned wooden coffin for transportation to the cemetery. There, the linen-shrouded body was transferred from the coffin to the assigned layer in the communal grave and was strewn with a thick layer of unslaked lime, then covered with earth. The coffin was returned to the church for reuse. In 1785, under societal pressure, Joseph II amended his decree and permitted burial in a coffin, but he strongly recommended using only a linen sack. It was assumed that total decomposition occurred in 8 years; therefore, burial plots were emptied and reused after 8 years.

Mozart's funeral was held at St. Stephen's Cathedral, Vienna, the afternoon of 7 December. He was not given "a pauper's funeral" but was accorded the same respect any non-aristocratic Viennese citizen would have had at that time—every person was entitled to at least a third-class burial. If the deceased's estate was insufficient and the survivors could not pay the fees, no monetary amount was entered in the ledger, and the item was marked "gratis." Records at St. Stephen's indicate an assessment of "8 fl. 56 kr." for Mozart's funeral and interment—an amount in excess of minimum—plus "wagon, 3 fl." The account is marked "Paid." The charge of 3 florins for a hearse indicates that Mozart had a new coffin and may have been buried in it. No charge was made for a hearse for a sack burial.

Mozart was interred in St. Marx Cemetery, located about 3 miles from St. Stephen's Cathedral, and approached by a narrow unpaved lane. Reliable sources report inclement weather the evening of 7 December 1791. The lane would have become muddy, and it is reasonable to believe that no mourners accompanied the body to the grave. Possibly, the body was not actually interred until dawn of 8 December. Imperial regulations required that there be a small building, kept unlocked, at each cemetery to shelter a body overnight in case severe weather prohibited evening burial. By the time anyone sought out Mozart's burial place, it could not be located. The gravedigger's records indicated the row but not the exact grave. Periodically, until c. 1808 Constanze and several friends tried to locate Mozart's grave without success. By 1808 that row of graves would have been plowed and reused.

No description of Mozart's funeral service has been located. The itemized account in the Cathedral ledger does not show a payment to musicians. It is difficult to imagine Mozart's funeral without music. There was music at the Lodge of Sorrows that his Masonic lodge held in his memory in 1791, and some of his own works were performed at the memorial service in Prague, which more than 4,000 persons attended.

CHURCH MUSIC   Mozart began writing church music in 1766 and wrote Masses, motets, and other sacred music fairly regularly until c. 1781. With the exception of *Missa in honorem sanctissimae Trinitatis* (Mass in honor of the most holy Trinity; K. 167; 1773), the Masses and other sacred works Mozart composed for Salzburg are concise and somewhat austere. Archbishop Colloredo's insistence that a complete Mass, with an Epistle Sonata, should last only three-quarters of an hour restricted the music to *Missa brevis* proportions. The "Coronation" Mass (C major), written for the ceremonial crowning of a statue of the Virgin in a church near Salzburg, is less condensed. Like the other Masses, it is scored for SATB soloists, four-part choir, and orchestra. Though Mozart never completed the Mass in C minor, it is considered one of his finest Masses.

The Requiem is a major work. Mozart finished the Introit and Kyrie and wrote out in draft score (i.e., voice parts, figured bass, indications for instrumentation) the sections from *Dies irae* through *Hostias*. Süssmayr composed Sanctus and Benedictus, Agnus Dei, and *Lux aeterna* to complete the Mass.

The motet *Ave verum corpus* is a small masterpiece, basically homophonic, with perfect voice leading and with polyphony introduced where it is most effective.

OPERAS   It is not odd that, at an early age, Mozart was attracted to opera; it would have been stranger had he not been. The eighteenth century was dominated by Italian opera; in addition to its obvious presence in performances, its influence was felt in other vocal forms, both sacred and secular, and in the structure of some instrumental forms. Yet, with all his talent for the dramatic, Mozart did not specialize in opera. He regarded opera as primarily a multimovement *musical* composition rather than a dramatic production in which music was an auxiliary, and he incorporated within his operas a variety of musical forms that he adapted to dramatic means.

Bastien und Bastienne, La finta semplice, Mitridate, rè di Ponto, and *Lucio Silla* are works by a talented young composer who did not yet fully understand characterization and musical depiction of drama. Nor is there anything exceptional about *Il rè pastore* (The shepherd king; 1775). The autograph score for Act I of *La finta giardiniera,* a conventional opera buffa, was lost, but a copy of the original Italian score was located in 1965.

Idomeneo, rè di Creta (Idomeneus, King of Crete) marks the beginning of Mozart's maturity as an opera composer. Basically, *Idomeneo* is a conventional opera seria of the old Metastasian type—recitatives regularly alternating with arias, few ensembles, brilliant coloratura arias requiring improvised cadenzas, and a principal role for a male soprano. Most of the recitatives are accompanied, and there are large choral scenes, some of which are reminiscent of scenes by Rameau or Gluck. Mozart's acquaintance with French opera is apparent in his inclusion of ballet. He consistently associated certain motives with individual characters and their emotions (e.g., Electra's jealousy) and used tonalities for special effect. Electra's disorientation is depicted not only through her actions and words but also musically by a C-minor recapitulation in a D-minor aria!

Die Entführung aus dem Serail has a Turkish setting—use of Turkish background was popular in the eighteenth century—and the orchestra includes characteristic instruments of the Janissary, the military bodyguard of Turkish sovereigns. The action is carried by spoken dialogue, but this opera contains more music than the usual Singspiel. Mozart made some concessions to the singers, notably, the coloratura arias designed to display the virtuosity of soprano Catarina Cavalieri (1760–1801), who created the role of Constanze. (Catarina, considered one of the finest singers in Vienna in 1777–93, sang principal roles in several Mozart operas, e.g., Donna Elvira in *Il Don Giovanni* and the Countess in *Le nozze di Figaro.*) Mozart used coloratura to delineate drama inherent in the text. In this opera he notated every grace and cadenza, thereby eliminating the possibility of improvisation by the singers. The opera concludes with a vaudeville final. With *Die Entführung aus dem Serail* Mozart elevated Singspiel from comparatively amateur status to an artistic level; therein lies the work's significance.

For *Le nozze di Figaro* Lorenzo da Ponte adapted P.-A. Beaumarchais's (1732–99) *Le mariage de Figaro* (written 1781, perf. 1784), diminishing the subversive aspects but retaining the basic clash between aristocracy and lower classes. Central to the opera are love and class conflict; present in abundance are irony and satire. The solution of the conflict was some ground gained by the underprivileged class. Often, the term *absolute musicality* is used to describe Mozart's music, meaning that his music does not reflect events in his personal life or the world about him. Such a blanket statement is inaccurate. Mozart, da Ponte, and Beaumarchais were well aware of social inequalities and oppression and had experienced them to some extent, for all three men had lower-class backgrounds. Because of their respective talents, they had gained a degree of acceptance in the highest social circles. In several operas, Mozart censured and ridiculed the aristocracy; his personal experiences sharpened his psychological insight so that he could aptly delineate character and use musical satire effectively. In all Mozart's Singspiele, opera buffa, and *dramma giocoso* works, from *Zaide* (1780) on, there is increased evidence of his concern about moral injustice, presented as a background of menace, threat of seduction, or rape, often with double meaning of both lyrics and music. Two examples are "*Se vuol ballare*" in *The Marriage of Figaro* and the "Catalog" aria in *Don Giovanni*. Unfortunately, audiences too often comprehend only the humorous aspect.

Mozart termed *Le nozze di Figaro* a *commedia per musica* (comedy through music); actually, it is a *dramma giocoso*, for both tragedy and comedy are present. The humor is not that of situation comedy but is dramatic and often is underlined with irony. There is some delightful text painting, for example, the melodic intervals matching Figaro's measuring and Susanna's fainting with a declining scale. Mozart's opera is a well-coordinated multimovement composition, and for some of those movements he adeptly used symphonic formal structures. For example, in Act II, the strong wills of the Count and Countess conflict with regard to Susanna, who is present but hiding; tensions increase before the conflict is resolved. Ingeniously, to fit the dramatic situation, Mozart wrote the trio "*Susanna, or via sortite*" in miniature sonata form (DWMA132). The form and the three singers take the dramatic situation seriously; only for the audience is it comic. Through Mozart's excellent writing, the singers transform stock figures into real persons participating in and reacting to actual happenings. Mozart's ability to characterize is particularly effective in his ensemble writing, especially in the ensemble finales where, gradually, all the characters are assembled on stage and all threads of plot and subplot are gathered together and cumulatively woven into the fabric to effect either a climax or the final solution. In *Le nozze di Figaro* ensembles play a more important role than in Mozart's previous dramatic works. The opera commences with a duet between Figaro and Susanna; subtly, this advises the audience that the emphasis is not on Figaro as hero but on the *marriage*, an ensemble (French *ensemble*, together). Mozart's point is lost when the opera is referred to as "Figaro."

Il dissoluto punito, ossia: Il Don Giovanni (The libertine punished, or Don Juan), a two-act *dramma giocoso*, concerns divine retribution rendered a libertine and blasphemer. The Don Juan legend had been presented in drama since c. 1615 and in opera since 1713, but in Mozart's work the Don appears for the first time as a real person—a romantic rebel who is charming, ruthless, and unrepentant. Mozart's music portrays him superbly.

The opera is a synthesis of comedy and tragedy—the comedy of the Don's continual conquests and the situations in which he finds himself because of his amorous desires and the tragedy of murder, divine vengeance, and punishment by death. Moments of comedy occur in many serious scenes. Donna Elvira constantly complains about the Don jilting her; her plight is pathetic, but she is subjected to ridicule in "asides" that evoke audience laughter. When Leporello, the Don's valet, endeavors to console her by giving a detailed account of his master's amorous conquests, his rendition of the catalog aria is humorous. For a time, the listener takes him seriously, then realizes that he is exaggerating. Occasionally, the orchestra adds its musical laughter as Leporello tallies the victims in *Madamina, Il catalogo è questo* (Young lady, this is the catalog . . . ; DWMA133).

As in traditional, pre-reform Italian opera, much of the action in *Il Don Giovanni* is conveyed through *secco recitative*. However, Mozart rarely used *da capo* aria. The arias and duets are not always static or reflective; at times they represent dramatic developments. The overture, a sonata-form movement in D major, opens with a dignified introduction in D minor that, except for the absence of trombones, uses the same instrumentation, key, and musical material associated with the awesome appearance of the Commandant's statue at the climax of the opera. In the last half of the eighteenth century, trombones were still associated primarily with church music, and in this opera Mozart restricted their use to those times when the statue and the demons associated with it appear on stage. Elements of nineteenth-century German Romantic opera are present in those scenes.

Così fan tutte, ossia La Scuola degli Amanti (Thus do they all, or The school for lovers), on an original libretto by da Ponte, is a melodious, lighthearted work in the tradition of old Italian opera buffa. *La clemenza di Tito* is in many respects a conventional serious opera. The restrained style Mozart used for the music is well suited to the topic and to the modified Metastasio libretto.

Die Zauberflöte was successful immediately and has remained so. The libretto, by Emanuel Schikaneder (1751–1812), runs the gamut from simple buffoonery to impressive solemnity, from childlike belief in magic to the sublime. Considerable machinery is required for the many magic effects. Some characters are enigmatic, appearing to be evil but ultimately revealed as being good. Papageno is a comic of the "Hanswurst" type (p. 354). The opera's connections with Freemasonry were neither accidental nor secret. Also, the mystical, perfect number three figures prominently in the opera.

Die Zauberflöte is a Singspiel in the sense that it uses spoken dialogue and contains humorous scenes. However, Mozart's label for it—*grosse Oper* (great, or grand, opera)—is more appropriate; it is probably the first and is certainly one of the great modern German operas. The music is Germanic in character, even to the use of a Lutheran chorale as basis for the duet of the Men in Armor (Act II), which is constructed as a kind of Baroque chorale prelude. The mood of much of the music is solemn. Mozart included some recitatives and wrote appropriate musical declamation. His music fits perfectly the accents and rhythm of the German language and is sufficiently flexible to move from declamatory to arioso passages without disturbing the musical flow.

Mozart's use of keys hints at procedures that would be followed to a greater extent in the nineteenth century, especially by Wagner. The key of *Die Zauberflöte* as a whole is E♭ major; certain keys are consistently associated with specific kinds of persons or situations: G major for comic characters, G minor in painful situations, F major for the priests, and C minor for the otherworldly. Several themes are recurrent.

Manuscripts located in 1996 indicate that in 1790–91 Mozart collaborated with others in the composition of the fairy-tale operas *Der Stein der Weisen* (The Philosopher's Stone) and *Der Wohltätige Derwisch* (The Beneficent Dervish). Both fairy-tale operas were commissioned and produced (as was Mozart's *Die Zauberflöte*) by Emanuel Schikaneder, director, at Theater auf der Wieden, Vienna.

With *Il Don Giovanni* and *Die Zauberflöte* Mozart brought opera to heights never before scaled. In his hands Singspiel became an art form, and the first steps were taken in the establishment of a national German opera. Through his psychological insight and skillful characterization, attention is focused on the individual person and that person's relationship to and interaction with others. No longer is expression of an abstract emotion—an affect—central to the composition. Symphonic styles were adapted to operatic writing. In the operas written with da Ponte, Mozart dealt with serious social issues of his time, using instrumentation, tonality, and sharp differentiation of musical styles to illustrate the chasm between social classes. It was not Mozart's intention to institute operatic reforms, nor did he make great changes in the theatrical forms of his day. His fusion of the comic and the serious, his ability to maintain the action on both levels, and the depth of characterization he brought to opera were important factors in its development.

SYMPHONIES In Mozart's time, symphonies were regarded as "curtain-raisers" and filler material for concerts. Mozart wrote approximately 50 symphonies, some of which are now lost. The development of his compositional skills and the changes in his musical style may be seen clearly in his symphonies—their composition was spread over almost all his career. His symphonic style evolved as his models changed: from J. C. Bach (1764); to the Viennese school of Monn, Wagenseil, and Holzbauer (1767); to Sammartini and other Italian masters of the sinfonia (1770); to Stamitz and others of the Mannheim school; and to Haydn (after 1772). In Mozart's last 3 symphonies, elements of these various influences coalesce with his individual characteristics and produce the symphonic style that is "Mozartean."

In England, 8-year-old Wolfgang copied two symphonies—one was C. F. Abel's Op. 7, No. 6—and composed four others. Two of Mozart's symphonies were preserved from the time of their composition. Two others, K. 16a in A minor and K. 19a in F major, were located in 1980 and 1983, respectively. Symphony No. 1 in E♭, K. 16, for two oboes, two horns, strings, and basso continuo, is a short three-movement work in Preclassic sinfonia style and reflects Mozart's acquaintance with works of J. C. Bach. The first movement (Allegro molto, ¾ meter) approximates sonata form, with three themes, the first of them outlining the tonic triad (ex. 19.6). The short development section consists of repetitions of the first theme in different keys; that theme does not appear in the recapitulation. The slow movement (Andante, C minor, ²⁄₄) is in binary form; the finale (Presto, E♭, ³⁄₈) is a rondo. Mozart's orchestral treatment of all the instruments is idiomatic, with sensitivity to tone colors and use of the winds to reinforce harmonies, to provide accents, and, about half the time, to double the strings.

For the symphonies he wrote in Vienna in 1767 (K. 43, 45, 148) Mozart used the four-movement plan favored by Viennese symphonists, but he reverted to three-movement sinfonia pattern for some of the Italianate works he created in 1770 (K. 74, 81). In 1772–74, Mozart composed 17 symphonies, almost evenly divided between three- and four-movement structure. Haydn's influence is apparent in some of the four-movement works, notably Symphonies No. 20, K. 133 (D major), and No. 25, K. 183 (G minor). Mozart wrote only three minor-key symphonies, two of them in G minor and both filled with intense emotion.

Symphony No. 29, K. 201 (1774), uses the same instrumentation as Mozart's first symphony. First, second, and fourth movements of K. 201 are in sonata form with exposition and development-recapitulation sections repeated, then followed by the coda. Menuetto with Trio constitutes the third movement. Symphony No. 31, a three-movement work in D major, is Mozart's first symphony with clarinets.

Mozart's last six symphonies are standard orchestral repertoire. Symphony No. 35, K. 385 (D major; 1782), the "Haffner" Symphony, originated as a six-movement serenade (but *not* the "Haffner" Serenade, K. 250) written for a Haffner family celebration. Mozart created the four-movement symphony by deleting the serenade's opening march and second minuet. In the "Linz" (No. 36, K. 425) and the "Prague" (No. 38, K. 504) Symphonies, the first movement commences with a slow introduction, something Mozart used in only one other symphony, No. 39.

Mozart's mastery of developmental techniques, and of symphonic structure, is apparent in his last three symphonies. In comparison with his other symphonies, these compositions have more extended forms and more complex development sections and exhibit greater use of counterpoint, chromaticism, and unifying motives among the movements of a work. Each of these symphonies has four movements, arranged in the same order, with the slow movement in a related key. The wind instrumentation of the symphonies differ slightly; No. 39, K. 543 (E♭ major), has no oboes; No. 41, K. 551 (C major; "Jupiter"), has no clarinets; and No. 40, K. 550 (G minor), has neither trumpets nor timpani and in its first version had no clarinets. The symphonies differ vastly in mood. The E♭-major symphony is the most cheerful of the three, the C-major sounds majestic and victorious, and the G-minor is filled with intense emotion and passion, at various times conveying grief, pain, or joy.

Outstanding features of Symphony No. 40 are its concentration on the second, especially the minor second, its chromaticism, and Mozart's skillful use of counterpoint. The minor second appears at the outset, in the reiterated "melodic sigh" motif that forms much of the first theme—a theme whose melody hovers around the dominant pitch and mentions the tonic g only slightly (in m. 4; ex. 19.7a). In the slow movement, the imitative entry of second violins creates a hammering harmonic second and is accompanied by chromaticism (minor seconds) in the bass (ex. 19.7b). Minor seconds occur in the second measure of the Menuetto theme (ex. 19.7c). In the Finale's first theme, the "melodic sigh" atop the "Mannheim rocket" and the chromaticism in the winds' response provide more minor seconds (ex. 19.7d). The violin melody of the second theme, presented *piano* (mm. 70–85), is filled with

EXAMPLE 19.6 Mozart: Symphony No. 1, K. 16, mvt. 1, theme 1.

EXAMPLE 19.7 Mozart: Symphony No. 40, K. 550: (*a*) mvt. 1, mm. 1–5; (*b*) mvt. 2, mm. 1–6; (*c*) mvt. 3, mm. 1–3; (*d*) mvt. 4, mm. 1–4; (*e*) mvt. 4, theme 2.

minor seconds (ex. 19.7e). In every movement of this symphony, the first theme commences on an upbeat.

The first movement (Molto Allegro, G minor) is in sonata form. A general pause (m. 43) calls attention to its chromatic, lyrical second theme, which is divided between strings and winds. Counterpoint plays a large role in the sonata-form second movement (Andante, E♭). In measures 44–46, the *forte* E♭-minor seventh chord and the ensuing chromatic dissonances probably were an aural shock in the 1780s. Tonality returns to G minor for the last two movements. Themes of the Menuetto and Trio (in parallel major) suggest Austrian folk music. In the Allegro assai finale, in sonata form, constant alternation of *piano* and *forte* adds to the agitation. Tension is created almost immediately in the development section by unison utterance, *forte,* of an altered version of the "rocket," followed by stabbing downward leaps of a diminished seventh—the sevenths marked by wedges to indicate sharp staccato articulation and punctuated by rests. The development section concludes *forte* on an F♯ diminished-seventh chord; after a general pause, the double return (to tonic key and opening measures of the movement) for recapitulation commences *piano.*

SOLO KEYBOARD WORKS Mozart's surviving solo keyboard works consist primarily of 17 independent sets of variations, 18 sonatas, and some fantasias. The theme-and-variations sets are charming but not distinctive. Theme-and-variations compositions were popular in Paris, and in general Mozart's sets of variations follow the Parisian pattern: If the theme is in a major key, one variation is in minor; if the theme is in duple meter, one variation is in triple time; one variation is an Adagio. The 12 variations on the old French nursery rhyme *Ah, vous dirai-je maman* (Ah, shall I tell you, mama; K. 265) are a representative example. That melody is better known in America as "Twinkle, twinkle, little star."

The solo sonatas are usually constructed according to the following scheme: first movement in sonata form with contrasting themes; second movement, either Adagio or Andante, exhibiting expressive lyricism; and third movement, a lively rondo that in two instances (K. 311, 333) includes a cadenza.

In the sonatas composed in 1775, the K. 279–83 group and K. 284, *style galant* is apparent, as is the influence of Haydn and C. P. E. and J. C. Bach. Mozart ranked K. 309 and K. 311, written in 1777, among his most difficult sonatas. By then, he was using a Stein fortepiano. The small, light hammers of Stein fortepianos with individual escapement levers contributed to ease of performance of rapid passages, especially those containing repeated notes.

Sonata K. 331 (A major) has become a favorite, though it is not typical of Mozart's sonata writing. The Andante grazioso first movement presents an 18-measure rounded binary theme, followed by 6 highly expressive, difficult variations. The middle movement is an A-major Menuetto with Trio in D major. The finale reflects the interest in Turkish Janissary music. Labeled *Alla Turca* (in Turkish style), it is a rondo in A minor with an A-major refrain.

When published in Vienna in 1785, Sonata K. 457 was prefaced by the *Fantasia* K. 475, both in C minor. This implies that continuous performance was intended. Both compositions are indebted to similar works by C. P. E. Bach. The *Fantasia* has six distinct sections, the last being a return to *Tempo primo* and the initial material, as a kind of recapitulation. Its concluding measure is a dashing three-octave C-minor scale that ends on a C-minor chord spanning the same distance. The Sonata commences *forte* with a staccato arpeggiation of the tonic chord, played in octaves, and the sonata-form first movement gathers strength as it proceeds. This, Mozart's most forceful sonata, presages the development of the sonata in Beethoven's hands. In fact, it exerted considerable influence on Beethoven. The second movement, in E♭ major, is a lovely Adagio whose main theme, in its successive presentations, is furnished with increasingly elaborate embellishments. Then, the same driving force that propels the first movement of the sonata is present in the syncopated triadic theme that begins the finale. However, in the finale, general pauses diminish the power and permit the intrusion of an element of despair, the *pathétique* character of C-minor tonality. (DWMA134.)

The Sonata in D major, K. 576 (1789), Mozart's last piano sonata, is his most difficult one. In its three movements there is no trace of the Alberti bass that characterizes many of his piano works; other kinds of broken-chord figurations are used. The first movement contains much skillfully written counterpoint. The A-major Adagio middle movement is filled with elaborate figuration; this movement also was a model for Beethoven. The strength of the Allegretto rondo finale is not weakened by the fact that it contains much that is *galant*.

CONCERTI   Mozart's chief contributions to the historical development of instrumental music are his treatment of the concerto and his defining of Classic concerto structure. The composition of concerti occupied him throughout his career. Moreover, his choice of fortepiano (rather than harpsichord or clavichord) as his solo keyboard instrument did much to promote the use of that instrument.

Mozart's earliest concerti for keyboard and orchestra (K. 37, 39, 41) are arrangements of sonata movements by other composers, including J. C. Bach. The influence of J. C. Bach on Mozart's career should not be minimized.

The *original* concerti Mozart composed for piano and orchestra may be divided into four groups: (1) those written in Salzburg, 1773–79 (K. 175, 238, 246, 271; the three-piano concerto K. 242; and the two-piano concerto K. 365); (2) those written in Vienna, 1782–83 (K. 413, 414, 415); (3) those written in 1784 (K. 449, 450, 451, 453, 456, 459); and (4) those written in 1785–91 (K. 466, 467, 482, 488, 491, 503, 537, 595). Fourteen of the 17 concerti composed during the Vienna years were created for Mozart's own performances. The sharp decline in his soloist appearances after 1786 is reflected in the fact that he wrote no piano concerto in 1787, one in 1788 (K. 537), and no more until 1791 (K. 595).

For his first *original* piano concerto, K. 175, Mozart added two trumpets and timpani to the standard orchestral instrumentation. The work is longer and somewhat more complex than J. C. Bach's concerti, and the finale exhibits both *galant* and contrapuntal elements.

Mozart next composed the bassoon concerto and his five violin concerti: K. 207 (B♭ major) and K. 211 (D major), which display some Baroque characteristics; K. 216 (G major), which begins with a theme from an aria ritornello in *Il rè pastore*; K. 218 (D

major), whose first movement is a blend of concerto-ritornello and sonata form; and K. 219 (A major), which concludes with a Menuetto. Of the five, the last three are richer and of greater depth and are excellent examples of his mature style.

Mozart resumed composition of piano concerti in January 1776. Within 12 months, he produced K. 238 for himself, the triple concerto K. 242 for three lady amateurs, K. 246 for Countess Lützow, and K. 271 for Mlle Jeunehomme. Of these, K. 271 is the most substantial.

Mozart's next two concerti were for flute—K. 313 in G, K. 314 in D (1778). They are idiomatic, pleasing, nonvirtuosic works. He composed K. 299 for flute and harp in 1778 and the *Sinfonia concertante* in E♭, K. 364, for violin and viola, in 1779. Early in 1779, for his sister and himself, he wrote K. 365 (E major; two pnos., orch.), which may be considered a companion piece to (but not quite equal to) K. 364. Mozart aimed at moderation in the three piano concerti composed for his own use in Vienna during fall and winter 1782–83: K. 413, 414, and 415.

Two of the concerti (K. 449 in E♭, K. 453 in G) that Mozart composed in the spring of 1784 were intended for his pupil, Barbara Ployer; the other two, K. 450 in B♭ and K. 451 in D, were for himself. Later that year, he composed K. 456 (B♭) for Viennese virtuosa Maria Theresia von Paradis (1759–1824) to perform on an extended concert tour in Paris and London. Paradis, daughter of the imperial court secretary, was also a composer; most of her works are lost.

Mozart's D-minor concerto, K. 466 (1785), his first concerto in a minor key, is a dramatic work filled with pathos and passion. The solo and orchestral parts are sharply contrasted. Some of the themes in the first movement are introduced by and belong exclusively to the soloist. Mozart's choice of key for the Andante is unusual—B♭, the subdominant of the relative major—a shift in tonality that might be expected from Beethoven 15 years later. Mozart's next concerto, K. 467 in C major, is symphonic in sound. Its Andante, in F, is an expressive aria (in ABA form) presented by the piano against a background of muted strings; the C-major finale is a sonata-rondo.

During winter 1785–86, Mozart wrote three piano concerti—K. 482 in E♭, K. 488 in A, and K. 491 in C minor. The first two are lighter than those written earlier in the year, as though Mozart sensed that his popularity was slipping and wished to regain the favor of Viennese audiences. Certainly, he did so with K. 482. When he performed it, the audience so appreciated the slow movement, an Andante in C minor, constructed as theme and variations, that he had to repeat it immediately. This seems to indicate that in the late eighteenth-century applause was rendered after each movement of a multimovement work instead of being reserved until the end of the last movement. Or, possibly, Mozart did not play all three movements of the concerto as a unit; in that era, it was not unusual for the movements of a multimovement work to be performed individually and interspersed with other items on a concert program.

For K. 491 Mozart used the richest orchestration he ever employed in a piano concerto; one flute, pairs of oboes, clarinets, bassoons, horns, and trumpets, plus timpani and strings. Piano concerto K. 503 (C major; 1786) is a grandiose work, conveying a triumphant, victorious mood. Often considered the counterpart of K. 491, it may be regarded also as an intensification of K. 467.

Mozart completed his last piano concerto, K. 595, in Bb, on 5 January 1791 and performed it on 4 March in Vienna. Mozart's complete mastery of concerto composition is evident; the first movement is a textbook example of concerto-sonata form (DWMA127).

In the Concerto in A for clarinet and orchestra, K. 622 (October 1791), Mozart exploited all registers of the clarinet without undue exhibition of virtuosity and provided no opportunity for the soloist to improvise cadenzas. The apparent simplicity of the concerto is at times deceptive; that apparent simplicity is what makes this work so effective.

CHAMBER MUSIC: QUARTETS   Mozart's 26 string quartets may be divided into two basic groups: the 16 quartets written in 1770–73, works numbered K. 80, 136–38, 155–60, and 168–73, and the 10 quartets composed in 1782–90, consisting of the 6 dedicated to Haydn (K. 387, 421, 428, 458, 464, 465); one dedicated to F. A. Hoffmeister (K. 499); and the "Prussian" quartets (K. 575, 589, 590).

Mozart's first quartet, K. 80, reflects the influence of the north Italian trio sonata: second violin has many passages in thirds, sixths, and tenths with first violin; viola and 'cello provide accompaniment. His next nine quartets have three movements each. The quartets written in Salzburg in 1772 (K. 136–38) are structured alike, with principal interest in the violin parts, opening themes built on tonic chord figures, and, in sonata-form movements, sectional developments in which only one theme is used at a time. Quartets K. 155–60 (1772–73) are in concertante style—upper against lower strings, or solo violin against second violin and viola, with 'cello continuo. Strong, sudden dynamic contrasts indicate Mannheim influence.

Quartets K. 168–73 (1773) are Viennese in style and reflect Mozart's acquaintance with Haydn's Op. 17 and Op. 20. Each of these Mozart works has four movements, with Minuet included; there is considerable use of counterpoint, resulting in greater

EXAMPLE 19.8 Mozart: String Quartet in C major, K. 465 ("Dissonance" Quartet), mvt. 1, mm. 1–11.

independence of parts and more importance accorded the three lower instruments.

Mozart seldom composed without having either a commission or a professional need for a particular work. Yet, between December 1782 and January 1785, he wrote six string quartets for purely personal reasons. Inspired by Haydn's Op. 33 quartets and stimulated by a desire to show his esteem for the older composer, Mozart honored him with this series of quartets. They are Mozart's finest string quartets. They surpassed any that Haydn had composed up to this time and influenced Haydn's later string quartets, especially with regard to chromaticism. These "Haydn" quartets are a heterogeneous set, each quartet being to some extent individualistic yet all having some traits in common. Mozart's only use of a slow introduction in a string quartet occurs in the first movement of K. 465 (C major), a contrapuntal introduction replete with cross-relations, seconds, and other dissonances that belie the movement's G-major tonality and cause the composition to be known as "Dissonance" Quartet (ex. 19.8). Though these six quartets elicited praise from Haydn, they brought Mozart much criticism (especially concerning the dissonant C-major K. 465). In the Hoffmeister quartet, the sonata form movements are colored by unusual modulations and unexpected occurrences of developmental passages.

The quartets Mozart wrote during the last decade of his life exhibit the characteristic of his mature style: instrumental themes of a vocal nature, short chromatic lines, a good deal of harmonic freedom, pervading thematic development, and considerable use of counterpoint, forming a closely knit texture.

CHAMBER MUSIC: QUINTETS Mozart composed nine quintets: six for strings, two for one wind instrument and the string quartet complement, and one for piano and winds. His first string quintet (K. 174) was written in 1773, shortly after he became acquainted with Sammartini's string quintets in Italy; 14 years elapsed before he wrote another. By then, he knew the quintets of Michael Haydn and Luigi Boccherini, but, instead of using two 'celli as they did, Mozart employed two violas to widen the tonal expanse without great gaps in texture. The string quintets he composed in 1787, K. 515 in C major and K. 516 in G minor, are masterpieces. They are direct antitheses in mood and charac-

ter, the C-major quintet exhibiting classical serenity and the G-minor work depicting depths of emotion and a style more romantic in nature. In this respect, as well as in keys, they are comparable with his last two symphonies.

Mozart's genius as a composer of chamber music is fully revealed in the Clarinet Quintet. He wrote idiomatically for clarinet, with due regard for its timbre, registers, agility, and finer subtleties. In this work, he did not allow the clarinet to become the soloist, nor did he so embed it within the ensemble that its distinctive characteristics were overshadowed. Rather, he created a texture in which there is perfect tonal balance. Leadership in introducing themes is divided between clarinet and first violin, but all the instruments share in later presentation of the thematic material. In the Finale, a set of variations, Mozart's treatment of the various instruments is especially remarkable.

CHAMBER MUSIC WITH PIANO The change in the role of the keyboard from soloistic domination to equal partnership in the ensemble may be seen in Mozart's piano trios, piano quartets, and especially in his 33 sonatas for violin and keyboard. In the 16 early sonatas (K. 6, 7; K. 8, 9; K. 10–15; K. 26–31), the keyboard part is self-sufficient; if the violin part were deleted, a keyboard solo sonata would remain. To some degree, duetting, dialogue, and sharing of thematic material occur in Sonatas K. 301–306. However, in many passages the musical sense would not be damaged if the violin line were omitted. Not until 1781, in Sonatas K. 376–380, did Mozart achieve genuine violin-piano partnership. The Sonata in B♭, K. 481 (1785), which he wrote for and performed with Regina Strinasacchi (1764–1839), is a masterpiece, as is the Sonata in A, K. 526 (1787).

Among Mozart's chamber music with piano are other masterpieces: the Piano Quartets K. 478 in G minor (1785) and K. 493 in E♭ major (1786) and the Piano Trios K. 502 in B♭ major (1786) and K. 542 in E major (1788).

OTHER COMPOSERS

Though Mozart and Haydn are considered the outstanding Classic Era composers, dozens of excellent composers were active in Europe in the late eighteenth century. Vienna attracted many, at least transitorily; some remained there, but most moved on to other Austrian and German cities, to Italy, and to France. Leopold Gassmann (1729–1774) and Antonio Salieri (1750–1825) obtained posts at the imperial court and remained in Vienna.

Salieri received his early musical training in Italy. When in Venice in 1766, Gassmann noticed him, brought him to Vienna, and guided his further education. At the imperial court Salieri learned much about opera composition from Metastasio and Gluck. The performance of Salieri's *Armida* at the Burgtheater in 1771 marked the beginning of his career as an opera composer. He composed more than three dozen operas, and during 1778–1804 he enjoyed operatic successes in Italy and Paris as well as in Vienna. In 1774 Salieri succeeded Gassmann as imperial court composer and Italian opera conductor and in 1788 was also appointed court Kapellmeister. Thus, while still in his twenties, Salieri held one of Europe's most important musical posts. He served at the imperial court for over half a century. In addition to operas, Salieri composed cantatas and other secular pieces, oratorios, Masses and other sacred works, and orchestral and chamber music. He exerted considerable influence as a teacher. Among his outstanding pupils were Beethoven, Czerny, Liszt, Schubert, and Weigl.

Salieri acquired a reputation for intrigue, justifiably, but the widespread rumor that he poisoned Mozart is not true. There is no record that Salieri ever did anything to harm Mozart.

Johann Zumsteeg held several important posts at the Stuttgart court. His numerous compositions include Masses, sacred and secular cantatas, operas, 'cello concerti and other instrumental works, and almost 300 Lieder and ballads. Zumsteeg's long ballads were published singly; his shorter songs were issued in collections (e.g., the seven volumes entitled *Kleine Balladen und Lieder* [Little ballads and songs; 1800–1805]). The songs he composed after 1791 are historically significant because they lie midway between the works of the second Berlin school and the songs of Franz Schubert. Zumsteeg set most of the well-known ballad texts of his time, and his settings were models for works by later composers. Schubert patterned his early ballads (1811–16) after Zumsteeg's and set some of the same texts, sometimes using the same key tonality and meter,

as in *Die Erwartung* (Expectation) and *Ritter Toggenburg* (Knight Toggenburg). Zumsteeg was one of the earliest composers to use recitative effectively in lyric song. In his ballads, he made extensive use of descriptive figurations; his ability to depict mood was excellent. Some of his ballads are Romantic (e.g., his through-composed setting of Bürger's *Lenore* [1798]). Two of his finest Lieder are his settings of Kosegarten's *Nachtgesang* (Nightsong; 1800) and von Salis's *Das Grab* (The Grave; 1802). The brief strophic setting of *Das Grab* (F minor) is a masterpiece of solemn emotional depth.

MUSIC IN NORTH AMERICA

In the British colonies in North America, subscription and benefit concerts of instrumental and vocal music written by European composers date from the 1730s. However, the first music by native-born North American composers did not appear until the second half of the century. Those composers include Francis Hopkinson (1737–91), James Lyon (1735–94), William Billings (1746–1800), and John Antes (1740–1811).

Early in the eighteenth century, singing schools resulted from a desire among ministers to improve the quality of singing in their churches. These schools were instructional sessions devoted to teaching singing and note reading. The publication of tune books with instructional introductions commenced in the 1720s. Some tune books contained only melodies and were designed to be used with metrical versions of Psalms texts; in other tune books, texts were included.

James Lyon's tune book (*Urania or A Choice Collection of Psalm-Tunes, Anthems, and Hymns* (1761) is a compilation of 96 pieces, most of them for four voices. It was the first publication to identify works by native American composers and contains the first printed compositions by Lyon, Hopkinson, and William Tuckey (1708–81). Lyon is represented by three psalm tunes and two anthems; his "Let the Shrill Trumpet's Warlike Voice" is one of the earliest anthems by an American composer. *Urania* was the first American tune book to include English **fuging-tunes,** a type of composition that soon became an American favorite. A typical fuging-tune has two sections, the second of them marked to be repeated. The piece begins as a simple four-part chordal harmonization of a psalm tune— the tune is in the tenor—which is brought to cadence,

EXAMPLE 19.9 Beginning of the *fuge* section of a *fuging-tune*.

usually on the tonic. The second section commences with the **fuge**—successive contrapuntal entrances of the four voices, with a semblance of imitation; after all voices have entered, chordal harmonization is resumed and continues to the end of the section (ex. 19.9). In some fuging-tunes, the fuging section incorporates more than one imitative passage.

In 1770, William Billings, a tanner and self-taught musician, published his first tune book, *The New-England Psalm-Singer.* This, the earliest tune book to contain only American music, was the first printed collection of sacred music by a single American composer. In the volume are psalm and hymn tunes, anthems, canons, and fuging-tunes. Perhaps the most famous of the pieces are the four-voice canon *When Jesus Wept* (DWMA135) and *Chester,* which, equipped with additional stanzas, became a popular Revolutionary War song. Billings published six volumes of vocal music, the last of them in 1794.

Francis Hopkinson, a Philadelphia native, was an attorney by profession and had many avocations. A staunch American patriot, he was a member of the Continental Congress, signed the Declaration of Independence, designed government seals and the nation's first flag, and served as a judge from 1779 until his death. He was a skilled draftsman, an excellent literary satirist, and a talented amateur musician who performed as harpsichordist and organist, composed, designed an improved type of harpsichord plectrum, and invented a new instrument—the bellarmonic. The bellarmonic was similar to Franklin's glass harmonica (fig. 19.9) but had metal instead of glass bowls. Hopkinson is the first known native American composer of

FIGURE 19.9 Benjamin Franklin's glass harmonica. The glasses, impaled on a spindle operated by a treadle, revolved through water. The player, seated, touched the moistened edges with fingertips.

vocal music. His secular song *My days have been so wondrous free* (1759), a setting of a poem by Thomas Parnell (1679–1718), is one of several original compositions that Hopkinson copied into his personal music book in 1759–60. Included in that oblong manuscript book is *An Anthem from the 114th Psalm* (dated 1760), which may antedate any anthem composed by James Lyon.

Late in 1788, Hopkinson's *Seven Songs* appeared, the first printed collection of secular songs by a single American composer. Actually, the collection contains eight songs. "My gen'rous heart disdains" is a delightful rondo (DWMA136). Stylistically, Hopkinson's melodies are Preclassic, but his music is notated in the Baroque manner, as melody fitted only with figured (or unfigured) bass.

Several American diplomats were knowledgeable about music. Benjamin Franklin (1706–90) played guitar and sticcado-pastorale (a kind of miniature xylophone with glass bars); after hearing music played on tuned glasses, he invented the glass harmonica. The glass harmonica became popular in Europe during the last quarter of the eighteenth century; at least a dozen composers wrote music for it, including Mozart and Beethoven.

Thomas Jefferson (1743–1826) was a fine violinist. Frequently, he invited friends to his home to make music; he owned sufficient music to accommodate requests for either vocal or instrumental selections, solo or ensemble. After the federal library was burned during the War of 1812, Jefferson sold the books in his personal library to the government. Included were nine writings about music; these formed a nucleus for the Music Division of the Library of Congress.

Benjamin Carr (1768–1831) was born in London, where he studied music and learned the music publishing trade. In 1793 he emigrated to Philadelphia, where he was influential as publisher, editor, concert promoter, teacher, conductor, organist, and singer. His compositions in 1794–1800 include a ballet, two ballad operas, several piano sonatas, and *Federal Overture* (1794). After 1800, Carr composed about 60 songs and much sacred music; of the latter, the most significant is the collection *Masses, Vespers, Litanies, Psalms, Anthems, & Motets* (1805). His songs are settings of substantial poetry (e.g., by Shakespeare and Sir Walter Scott). Carr's **song cycle,** *Six Ballads from the Poem of the Lady of the Lake,* Op. 7 (1810), appeared shortly after Scott's work was published. A song cycle consists of a group of songs, each complete in itself, that have something in common; for example, all the texts concern the same topic, relate a series of events, or are by the same poet. Several English composers wrote song cycles in the 1790s, but the practice was not imported to continental Europe until after 1813. Carr's

songs, intended for professional singers, are sensitive, through-composed settings, with good balance between voice and accompaniment. In this respect, they antedate the style of Schubert's and Schumann's art songs.

John Antes is considered the first American-born composer to have written chamber music. Born in Frederick, Pennsylvania, he was educated by the Moravian Brethren at Bethlehem, where music occupied an important place in communal living. There, he learned to make harpsichords and stringed instruments and crafted the first violins, violas, 'cellos, and string basses built in America. Several of Antes's instruments are extant and in playable condition. In 1764, Antes emigrated to England, then to Germany, where he was ordained into the ministry by the United Brethren (Moravians); late in 1769 he was assigned to their missionary post in Cairo. While in Egypt, Antes composed a set of six quartets, which, in 1779, he sent to Benjamin Franklin, who was then at Passy, France. Those quartets are lost. Antes was recalled to Europe in 1781 and subsequently was assigned to work in England. His *Tre Trii, per due Violini e Violoncello,* Op. 3 (Three Trios, for two violins and violoncello) were published in London c. 1790 (DWMA137). Each trio has three movements whose tempi differ, with the middle movement in a related key. Stylistically, the music is Classic and sounds quite Haydnesque. In addition to the Trios, Antes's extant music consists of 35 concerted anthems and solo songs and about 55 hymns. His finest concerted work—in fact, one of the finest in the entire Moravian repertory is *Go, Congregation, Go—Surely He has borne our griefs,* for soprano, four-part chorus, and strings (DWMA138).

Antes, though American-born, composed music after he left America. However, his music—especially his hymns and sacred concerted compositions—was known and was used by Moravians living in America. During the last half of the eighteenth-century, European-born Moravians living in America composed a large amount of music for use by Moravians in Moravian communities in eastern Pennsylvania and at Salem (now Winston-Salem), North Carolina. The Moravian Church placed strong emphasis on music, both congregational (hymns) and concerted (anthems, sacred duets and solos, instrumental pieces);

much music was written by composers within the Moravian Church itself. However, that music was intended for use exclusively by Moravians and had little or no direct influence on the mainstream of American music.

Most of the secular music performed in Canada from the time its first settlements were founded until the middle of the nineteenth century was folk music brought there by French and British immigrants. Catholic and Jesuit missionaries from France established settlements in Canada early in the seventeenth century and, using hymns and adaptations of folk songs, began to teach religion to the Indians. For this purpose Jean de Brébeuf (martyred by Iroquois, 1649) wrote the Huron carol *Jesous Ahatonhia* (Jesus is born; 1642). Some anonymous sacred music in the seventeenth-century manuscripts in the Ursuline archives in Quebec—music used during the tenure of Mother Marie de St. Joseph at the Ursuline convent (1639–52)—may have been written by clergy living in Quebec. Some instrumental music was used in church; there was a church organ in Quebec in 1661.

British settlers came to Canada in the eighteenth century and vied with the French for control of the land. Gradually, Britain gained territory through treaties and battles until it had complete control of Canada. James Lyon, who served as a minister in Nova Scotia in 1765–71, may have used *Urania* there. Military bands stationed at the forts provided music lessons and concerts of music by European composers. Musical composition was an avocation. Joseph Quesnel (1746–1809) composed two ballad operas, *Colas et Colinette* and *Lucas et Cécile,* for which the vocal parts survive.

SUMMARY

The Viennese Classic idiom is a synthesis of elements of *galant, empfindsamer,* and learned styles. This synthesis was achieved by Haydn more fully than by his contemporaries, and the Viennese Classic style was firmly established in the instrumental works he created in the 1770s. Haydn's works, widely disseminated in the 1780s, influenced other composers to the extent that a more or less universal cosmopolitan musical language resulted. This musical language, which is characterized by clarity, balance, and restraint, may be seen to best advantage in the middle and late works of Haydn, the late works of Mozart, and the early works of Beethoven and Schubert.

Though composers wrote Masses and operas, most of the music written in the Classic era was instrumental. The principal genres composed c. 1770–c. 1820 were symphony, sonata, solo concerto, chamber music, and opera. The structural principle most often used for a movement was sonata form or a variant thereof (sonata-rondo, sonata-concerto, abridged sonata). Next in frequency of use was theme and variations.

Haydn contributed more to the development of the symphony than any other single composer. His symphonies provide excellent examples of the various stages of that development. By the late 1780s, a four-movement structural scheme became standard, with sonata form used for first and last movements and Minuet/Trio for third. Some sonata-form movements had slow introductions. Gradually, the orchestra was increased in size; by 1800 the instrumentation for symphonies included trumpets, clarinets, and timpani.

Haydn and Mozart developed a characteristic style for the string quartet and composed quartets that are basic to the repertoire. J. C. Bach introduced the concerto for piano and orchestra, with first movement containing features of both ritornello and sonata form. In Mozart's hands, the structure of the solo piano concerto was defined. He retained the three-movement overall scheme favored by Vivaldi and modified Bach's first-movement pattern by adding full-scale sonata-form features. Usually, the second movement of a Mozart concerto is an instrumental aria; the third movement is a kind of rondo. Ultimately, Mozart gave the concerto, as a whole, symphonic dimensions. The symphonie concertante, featuring two or more soloists with orchestra, flourished c. 1780–c. 1830, then almost disappeared. Divertimenti and similar works (*cassation, notturno, serenade*) for small ensemble provided background music for social events.

Though Haydn considered himself primarily a composer of vocal music, and wrote operas, Masses, and other sacred and secular vocal works, his most significant contributions were made in the instrumental realm. His oratorios are his most important contribution to vocal repertoire.

Gluck was one of several composers who worked to reform opera. The reforms that he advocated and the equilibrium between drama and music that he achieved in his operas were highly significant to the development of that genre. Mozart brought opera seria and Singspiel to unprecedented heights. In several respects, *Die Zauberflöte,* a Singspiel, foreshadows nineteenth-century German Romantic opera; *Il Don Giovanni* is a *dramma giocoso* masterpiece. But in these and in his other late operas Mozart had a secondary aim—he was voicing his concern about social injustices and violent crimes and was seeking reforms.

Haydn and Mozart composed some excellent piano sonatas, but it was Beethoven who brought that genre to a peak. Several innovations barely perceptible in Haydn's instrumental works (e.g., commencing a symphony in a key other than its tonic, and modulation to a key a third removed) were brought to fruition by Beethoven. Zumsteeg's Lieder and ballads lie midway between the works of the second Berlin school and the songs of Schubert.

In America, singing schools resulted from a desire to improve the quality of singing in church and led to the publication of instructional tune books. The first music by native-born North American composers—Francis Hopkinson, James Lyon, William Billings, and John Antes—appeared in the second half of the eighteenth century. Hopkinson was the first native-born American to compose a secular song; Antes was the first American to write chamber music. Benjamin Franklin and Thomas Jefferson were competent performers. Franklin invented the glass harmonica. When Jefferson shared his personal library with the federal government, he provided the nucleus of the Music Division of the Library of Congress. Benjamin Carr, an Englishman active in Philadelphia, composed one of the earliest song cycles.

Most of the secular music performed in Canada from the time of its first settlements until the middle of the nineteenth century was folk music brought to Canada by French and British immigrants. Canada was controlled by Britain after 1763, and concerts of European music, as well as music lessons, were provided by members of military bands stationed at forts. Late in the century, ballad operas were popular; vocal parts from two ballad operas by Quesnel survive.

FROM CLASSICISM TO ROMANTICISM

20

*I*n the last decades of the eighteenth century, the humanitarian ideals and theories of the philosophers of the Enlightenment became realities of life, engendering powerful emotions and actions. The search for liberty, equality, and fraternity led to revolution in America and France. The American colonies' Declaration of Independence, formulated in 1776, asserts that all men are created equal. The United States, the first new nation to free itself from imperial domination, established a constitutional federation based on a Bill of Rights and representative government that is still in existence and that has had a major impact on civic ideals throughout the world. The French, through their revolution, experienced constitutional representative government, a revolutionary dictatorship based on mass terror, and Napoleon Buonaparte's military leadership, with his European conquests and his imperialistic seizure of power. The French presented a powerful example—perhaps the first complete one—of popular mass nationalism and a national army. The Holy Roman Empire came to its end in 1806. Throughout Europe political attitudes changed, new standards of social equality gradually appeared, and codes of law were altered. At the Congress of Vienna (1814–15) national boundaries were established as the map of Europe was redrafted for the purpose of stabilizing Europe and establishing a reasonable balance of power.

In France, in 1792 C.-J. Rouget de Lisle (1760–1836) wrote the *Chant de guerre pour l'armée du Rhin* (War song for the Rhine Army). That song, frequently sung by the Marseilles Volunteer Battalion, became known as *La Marseillaise* when it was adopted in 1795 as the French national anthem.

Through appointed Commissions, France's postrevolutionary government appropriated for preservation in national archives all important music manuscripts and valuable musical instruments. In August 1795 the government legally established the Conservatoire National de Musique (Paris Conservatory) to provide free or almost free tuition in music for all talented pupils, without distinction as to rank or social position. This was the first step toward the gradual establishment, commencing in 1822, of 56 national music schools throughout France. Music commissioned to commemorate military victories and governmental successes was performed at celebrations held regularly for decades following the French Revolution. This created a vast repertoire of music for wind band, massed choruses, and orchestra. The effect of such celebrations was felt in other countries, in creative works centered around heroism. In opera, the strong feelings, suspense,

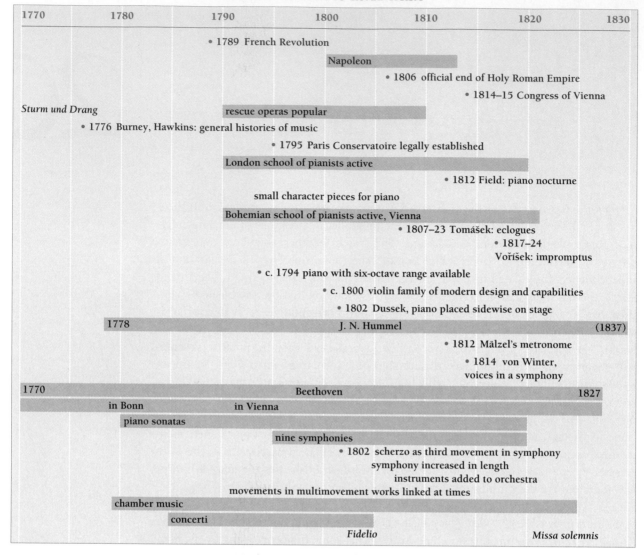

1770   1780   1790   1800   1810   1820   1830

- 1789 French Revolution

Napoleon

- 1806 official end of Holy Roman Empire
- 1814–15 Congress of Vienna

Sturm und Drang

rescue operas popular

- 1776 Burney, Hawkins: general histories of music
- 1795 Paris Conservatoire legally established

London school of pianists active

- 1812 Field: piano nocturne

small character pieces for piano

Bohemian school of pianists active, Vienna

- 1807–23 Tomášek: eclogues
- 1817–24 Voříšek: impromptus
- c. 1794 piano with six-octave range available
- c. 1800 violin family of modern design and capabilities
- 1802 Dussek, piano placed sidewise on stage

1778   J. N. Hummel   (1837)

- 1812 Mälzel's metronome
- 1814 von Winter, voices in a symphony

1770   Beethoven   1827

in Bonn   in Vienna

piano sonatas

nine symphonies

- 1802 scherzo as third movement in symphony
symphony increased in length
instruments added to orchestra
movements in multimovement works linked at times

chamber music

concerti

Fidelio   Missa solemnis

and dramatic tension of revolutionary and postrevolutionary times found expression in libretti based on actual revolutionary events and on rescue plots and included crowd scenes.

Many composers became interested in folk music. Hundreds of settings of folk songs were published, and folk-song melodies were used as themes in sonatas and symphonies. Interest in early music increased. In 1776 two general histories of music were published: Charles Burney's (1726–1814) *A General History of Music from the Earliest Ages to the Present Period* and Sir John Hawkins's (1719–89) *A General History of the Science and Practice of Music*. Those histories are more valuable for contemporary views of music than for historical accuracy.

THE LONDON SCHOOL OF PIANISTS

London, because of its rich concert life, active publishing houses, and a prosperous piano industry that produced instruments of superior quality and efficiency, attracted foreign musicians, especially pianists. In the 1790s, the pianists working in London included

Muzio Clementi (1752–1832; Italian), J. B. Cramer (1771–1858; German), Jan L. Dussek (1760–1812; Bohemian), and John Field (1782–1837; Irish). By 1800, George Pinto (1785–1806; English) had joined them.

After moving to London in 1785, Clementi manufactured pianos and published music. His firm issued the first editions of several of Beethoven's major works. Clementi's influence on succeeding generations of pianists and composers of piano music was tremendous. Among his pupils were Cramer, Field, Dussek, and Meyerbeer. Beethoven used Clementi's piano sonatas in his teaching; they directly influenced some of Beethoven's piano sonatas. Clementi's most important didactic works are *Introduction to the Art of Playing on the Piano Forte,* Op. 42 (1801), and *Gradus ad Parnassum* (Steps to Parnassus; 3 vols.: 1817–26), a collection of 100 keyboard pieces that is a compendium of Clementi's works covering approximately 45 years.

As a performer, Cramer was noted for his expressive legato touch, which became a stylistic norm in the nineteenth century. Although Cramer wrote many compositions for piano, his only work that is widely known in the twentieth century is *Studio per il pianoforte* ([84] Studies for piano; 2 vols.: 1804, 1810). Beethoven and other nineteenth-century pianists used those studies in their teaching.

Dussek had a brilliant career as a pianist. After moving to London c. 1788, he frequently performed at Salomon's concerts. In 1799 Dussek returned to continental Europe to concertize and became Kapellmeister to his former pupil, Prince Louis Ferdinand of Prussia (1772–1806), an excellent pianist. In 1807–12 Dussek worked for Talleyrand in Paris. Dussek's late works (c. 1793–1812) are characterized by frequent modulations to remote keys, altered chords, nonharmonic notes, and much chromaticism. Except for the chromaticism, Beethoven assimilated into his sonatas all that Dussek had to offer. The influence of Dussek's Op. 35 and Op. 39 sonatas on Beethoven's sonatas is particularly noticeable. One similarity is shown in example 20.1. Stylistic elements present in Dussek's Sonata XIII (Op. 35, No. 3; C minor; 1797) appear in sonatas Beethoven and Chopin composed later. Dussek's influence is apparent in compositions by Schubert, Liszt, and other Romantic composers.

(a)

(b)

EXAMPLE 20.1 (*a*) Dussek: Sonata, Op. 39, mvt. 1, mm. 1–4; (*b*) Beethoven: Sonata, Op. 10, No. 1, mm. 1–5.

Dussek was one of the few composers of that era who wrote idiomatically for harp. His wife, *née* Sophia Corri (1775–1847), concertized as harpist and pianist and composed music for both instruments.

Field was one of the first to write small **character pieces** for piano—nonprogrammatic pieces that evoke a mood, or a scene, or an idea suggested by the title. In England, the rapidly rising middle class participated actively in music making and favored short works over multimovement compositions and large works with long-range emotional effects. In 1812, Field invented the *nocturne* for piano and used it not only as an independent piece (DWMA139) but as a movement of a multimovement work. Field had an expressive, delicate touch and cultivated a style of piano playing characterized by singing melodies and a quasi-improvisatory air. His compositions were designed to exploit the piano's capabilities—percussive, harmonic, melodic, sustaining—without becoming mere technical display. Field greatly influenced Chopin's playing style and the compositions of Chopin, Liszt, and others.

Pinto was the most daring composer of the London school. His *Grand Sonatas* (Op. 3; 1803) exhibit romanticism comparable with that of Chopin and Liszt. The Sonata in E♭ minor, Op. 3, No. 1, contains passages that are striking parallels with some in the first movement of Beethoven's Sonata No. 31, Op. 110. Pinto was influential in the English revival of J. S. Bach's music c. 1800.

BOHEMIAN PIANISTS

Several Bohemian pianist-composers active in Vienna made significant contributions to piano literature: Václav Jan Tomášek (1774–1850), Jan Václav Voříšek (1791–1825), and Johann Nepomuk Hummel (1778–1837).

Tomášek, an excellent teacher, counted among his outstanding pupils Voříšek and Eduard Hanslick. Though Tomášek venerated Mozart, he did not limit himself to Mozart's style. Tomášek wrote operas and other stage works, sacred and secular choral compositions, orchestral and chamber music, as well as piano pieces. In addition to 7 sonatas and 5 sets of variations, his piano solos include 15 rhapsodies, 3 dithyrambs, 6 caprices, and 42 pastoral pieces that he called **eclogues.** The eclogues (1807–23) are light, lyrical pieces with uncomplicated textures and are not technically demanding. Schubert knew Tomášek's eclogues; many of Schubert's works and the eclogues have common features (e.g., the sudden reappearance of a major-tonality theme in the minor, or vice versa, and doubling in thirds and sixths). Among Tomášek's hundreds of songs are settings of many poems by Schiller and Goethe, including *Erlkönig* (Erlking). Two of his best songs are *Nähe des Geliebten* (Near the beloved; Op. 53, No. 2), a through-composed setting, and *Mignons Sehnsucht* (Mignon's longing; Op. 54, No. 1).

Voříšek received his early musical training from his father. While still a child, Voříšek toured in Bohemia as a keyboard virtuoso. He studied composition with Tomášek, who stressed the importance of counterpoint and of Bach's *Das wohltemperirte Clavier.* Because of his enthusiasm for Beethoven, Voříšek moved to Vienna, for, musically, Prague favored the Classicism of Mozart, an attitude Voříšek considered reactionary. Rhythmically and thematically, Voříšek's music reflects his knowledge of Beethoven's piano works; both composers frequently used rhythmic displacement to effect a climax. However, Voříšek's use of diminished chords and chromatic progressions is more like that of Schubert and Chopin. Voříšek and Schubert were friends. Their compositions reflect this to some extent—Voříšek's vocal music shows Schubert's influence, and Schubert's piano music was influenced by Voříšek. Voříšek pioneered the piano character piece, Romantic in style, usually ternary in form, which he entitled rhapsody, eclogue, or impromptu. His *Impromptus,* Op. 7 (1822), *Impromptu* in B♭ (1817), and *Impromptu* in F (1824) preceded and strongly influenced Schubert's impromptus.

Hummel, too, was a child prodigy. When he was eight, the family moved from Pressburg to Vienna. In 1786–88 the boy studied with Mozart, then studied with Clementi, and during the 1790s had lessons from Albrechtsberger, Salieri, and Haydn—the persons with whom Beethoven studied. From 1804 to 1811, Hummel was deputy Kapellmeister at the Esterházy court; thereafter, he held similar positions at Stuttgart and Weimar.

Beethoven's quick success in Vienna was somewhat traumatic for Hummel. The playing styles of the two men distinctly differed, and their pupils and admirers took sides and quibbled, thus creating two schools of piano playing in Vienna c. 1800. Hummel limited his performance repertoire almost exclusively to his own music and that of Mozart, and his style was Mozartean—a restrained Classicism, neat and delicate, with emphasis on fluent technique and textural clarity; he could create an illusion of speed without actually taking a rapid tempo. Beethoven produced a full tone and stressed technical power and dramatic execution; his music incorporated orchestral effects and a wide range of dynamics. Hummel formed the link between the style of Mozart and Clementi and that of Schubert, Mendelssohn, and Chopin, a chain of piano playing that bypassed Beethoven. Professionally, Hummel was Beethoven's greatest rival in Vienna, yet they were friends.

Hummel wrote music for all performing media then current and in all genres except the symphony, in which he felt intimidated by Beethoven's genius. Hummel's compositional style is basically Classic, though works written after 1814 are tinged with Romanticism and contain chromatic passing tones, secondary dominants, and modulations by thirds. Hummel stands as one of the foremost representatives of late Classicism, whereas Beethoven points toward Romanticism. Beethoven was a dominating figure on Vienna's musical scene in the early nineteenth century. When he moved there in 1792, music lovers were still recovering from Mozart's death, and Haydn was interested in composing symphonies for the London orchestra. The atmosphere in Vienna was conducive to Beethoven's quick acceptance and rise to fame.

LUDWIG VAN BEETHOVEN

Ludwig van Beethoven (1770–1827) was born in Bonn and grew up in court surroundings. At the time of Ludwig's birth his father, Johann van Beethoven (c. 1740–92), was a tenor at the Electoral court, and his grandfather, Ludwig (Louis) van Beethoven (1712–73), was Kapellmeister there. Ludwig was the second of Johann's seven children, only three of whom survived infancy; his brothers, Kaspar Anton Karl (1774–1815) and Nikolaus Johann (1776–1848), played important roles in his life.

When Ludwig was very young, his father taught him to play piano and violin; after the age of eight, Ludwig had lessons from local organists, and a relative taught him viola and violin. Beethoven had no formal education beyond elementary school. In 1779 Christian Neefe came to court; from him Beethoven received organ, counterpoint, and composition lessons and learned Bach's *Das wohltemperirte Clavier.* At that time Beethoven's hands were still small and his fingers stubby, but he was determined and mastered the preludes and fugues. By 1782 he served as deputy organist when Neefe was away from court. By then, Beethoven was composing music. His early works were issued without opus number (WoO): [9] *Variations on a March by Dressler* (1782) and three piano sonatas dedicated to Elector Maximilian (1783).

In 1783 Neefe hired Beethoven as orchestral harpsichordist at court, a responsible position that exposed him to all musical genres and styles then current. Beethoven's duties at court were light. He taught piano lessons, studied violin with Franz Ries (1755–1846), and in 1785 composed three piano quartets (pub. 1828). In 1787 he visited Vienna and, while there, met Mozart. The Vienna visit was cut short by Beethoven's mother's illness and subsequent death. Then, his father began drinking heavily and was dismissed at court. Ludwig realized the gravity of the situation, petitioned for and received half his father's salary to help support his brothers, and, at age 18,

Ludwig van Beethoven. Oil painting by Willibord J. Mähler, 1815. *(Gesellschaft der Musikfreunde, Vienna)*

assumed responsibilities as head of the family. For four years he played viola in the court chapel and theater orchestras. Twice he was commissioned to compose cantatas for special occasions, but the works were not performed. He composed (anonymously) the music for the *Ritterballett* (perf. 1791). His 24 variations (for piano) on Righini's *Venni amore* were published in 1791.

When Haydn visited the Bonn court in 1792, Beethoven showed him the funeral cantata he had written to honor Emperor Joseph II. Haydn invited Beethoven to Vienna, and in November Beethoven moved there. For approximately a year, he studied with Haydn, then Haydn returned to London. Meantime, Beethoven had become disillusioned with Haydn's teaching and had gone to Johann Schenk (1753–1836) for counterpoint and composition lessons. In 1794–95 Beethoven studied counterpoint with J. G. Albrechtsberger (1736–1809) and in 1801–2 took lessons in setting Italian texts from Salieri.

The Piano (II)

John Broadwood (1732–1812) began manufacturing "square" pianos in England c. 1767 and by c. 1785 had made many improvements in the mechanics and design of the instrument. He improved the escapement, attempted to equalize string tension, and continually sought to produce an instrument capable of greater volume of sound and increased dynamic flexibility. By 1800, piano keyboards had been changed from black naturals and light or white-topped chromatics to the white naturals and black chromatics of the modern keyboard. Broadwood preferred the wing-shaped piano, with three unison strings per note throughout the instrument and with three pedals. Thus, a composer could specify and expect true *una corda, due corde,* and *tutte le corde* responses. Haydn, Clementi, Dussek, Field, and Beethoven were among the first composers to write pedaling instructions in their music. For Field's and for Beethoven's music, pedaling is crucial. From c. 1791 until well into the nineteenth century, the leading pianists used Broadwood instruments. Beethoven's last piano sonatas would have been virtually impossible without the Broadwood piano he received in 1818.

Dussek was the first (in 1802) to have the piano placed sidewise on the stage so that the audience could view the performer's profile. He encouraged Broadwood to extend the compass of the piano from five to five-and-one-half octaves (F′–c″″) in 1791 and upwards to six octaves (F′–f″″) in 1794. Not all keyboards had the extended range, however. During the first quarter of the nineteenth century, range continued to be expanded. Beethoven, in his sonatas, often carried the bass to the piano's lowest note, but not until Op. 106 (*Hammerklavier Sonata;* 1817–18) was that pitch below F′. A bass passage written in octaves would, of necessity, become a single line when continued octave doubling would have required pitches lower than F′. The 88-key keyboard considered standard on modern pianos was not available until c. 1830.

In 1796, Érard *frères,* of Paris, began to manufacture grand pianos in the English style. In 1808 they patented a repetition action and in 1821 patented another that greatly improved the player's ability to repeat notes rapidly. Érard's repetition action became the basis of virtually all double-escapement actions in the twentieth century. The Austrian firm headed by Konrad Graf (1782–1851) began early in the nineteenth century to use quadruple stringing on pianos in an endeavor to increase volume and gave Beethoven one of their pianos (fig. 20.1).

FIGURE 20.1 Beethoven's last piano, a gift of the Viennese piano manufacturer Konrad Graf, has quadruple rather than the usual triple strings. The instrument is in Beethoven-Haus, Bonn.

In Vienna, as in Bonn, Beethoven acquired friends among the nobility. Some Viennese maintained private orchestras (Lobkowitz), opera companies (Esterházy), and chamber ensembles (Razumovsky); others (van Swieten) organized private concerts. Patronage was waning, and Beethoven had no patron and no steady job. How, then, did he earn his living? His principal resources during his first few years in Vienna were playing piano at gatherings in the halls and salons of aristocrats, appearing as assisting artist in concerts given by other musicians, teaching piano lessons to wealthy pupils, and publishing some compositions by subscription, that is, soliciting orders for printed copies of a work, paying for its publication, and selling the copies at his own price. After he had been in Vienna long enough to establish his reputation, he gave some concerts, received commissions for some compositions, sold performance rights to some of his works (usually for a six-month period), and was paid for some dedications. He received some monetary gifts from friends and benefitted from an annuity set up by three friends.

For the first few years in Vienna, all went well for Beethoven. Then he experienced difficulty hearing. The affliction worsened, and he sought medical aid. When he realized that ultimately he faced total deafness, he despaired. He was barely 30, yet the end of his career as virtuoso pianist was in sight. The struggle within himself was intense; more than once he contemplated suicide. Finally, at Heiligenstadt in 1802, he came to terms with his dilemma. With great strength of character, he determined that, despite encroaching deafness, he would pursue a career as composer. He wrote a letter to be read to his brothers after his death in which he described his trauma and explained his decision to mingle with society only when necessity demanded such contact. In that letter, known as "the Heiligenstadt Testament," he stated that he had already been "hopelessly afflicted" for six years.

After making his decision in Heiligenstadt, Beethoven returned to Vienna. Between 1802 and 1812, he wrote the majority of his symphonies, six piano sonatas, three piano concerti, three piano trios, the opera *Fidelio*, five string quartets, incidental music for three plays, and several other works. After 1808 he no longer performed in public as piano soloist, though he participated in chamber music. His last performance as pianist was 11 April 1814 when his "Archduke" Trio was first performed.

Occasionally, Beethoven attempted to meddle in his brother Johann's affairs but was rebuffed. Also, from time to time, Ludwig considered marriage but either was rejected or lost interest. The lady in whom he was most interested was never named in his correspondence; usually, she is referred to as "the immortal beloved." Probably, Beethoven composed the song cycle *An die ferne Geliebte* (To the distant beloved; Op. 98; 1816) with her in mind.

The death of Kaspar Beethoven in 1815 precipitated another crisis. Kaspar's will named his widow and Ludwig co-guardians of Kaspar's son, Karl, then nine years old. Ludwig disapproved of the boy's mother and doubted her capabilities as guardian. Litigation ensued; in July 1820, the final decision favored Beethoven. Meantime, Beethoven had been ill. By 1818 his deafness had deepened to the extent that communication with him had to be written. Extant conversation books are one-sided, indicating that he replied orally.

After the guardianship was settled, Beethoven's compositional activity increased. In 1820–26 he created a number of masterpieces, including Piano Sonatas Nos. 30–32; Symphony No. 9; the *Missa solemnis;* String Quartets Opp. 127, 130–32, and 135; and the *Grosse fuge,* Op. 133.

Beethoven received a crushing blow in July 1826, when Karl attempted suicide. After Karl recovered, Beethoven arranged for him to enter the army.

In late September 1826, Beethoven went with his brother Johann to Gneixendorf. When Beethoven returned to Vienna in December, he was seriously ill. His condition (cirrhosis resultant from hepatitis) worsened and was complicated by pneumonia. When he realized that the end was near, he prepared his will, leaving his entire estate to Karl. On 26 March 1827 Beethoven died.

PERSONAL CHARACTERISTICS

At age 30, Beethoven was attractive, dark complexioned, with dark brown deep-set eyes and black hair. Though he was not tall, he was stocky of build and of lofty bearing. There was about his countenance a look of determination. He had tremendous vitality, and his energy was seemingly boundless. His disposition was that of an autocrat. At times domineering, self-willed, and quick to anger, he was equally quick to remorse, and he could be wonderfully kind. Visible in his character are traces of self-sufficiency and arrogance. The sketchbooks in which he jotted down and revised his musical ideas provide a record of his creativity and work methods, document his constant striving for perfection of his musical ideas, and indicate his desire for continual self-improvement.

In many respects, Beethoven was a representative of the Enlightenment. His delight in nature, his interest in the brotherhood of man, and his belief in a personal God all found places in his music—and all concur with Enlightenment thinking.

In later life, deafness and serious illness wrought changes in Beethoven's character and disposition. His hair greyed, his complexion became florid, and often his appearance was unkempt. In direct contrast with his seeming lack of concern for his personal appearance is the high regard he maintained for himself as musician and composer and for his compositions. His esthetic doctrine was the same as that of Johann Schiller (1759–1805)—that it is the moral obligation of a work of art to uplift and ennoble an audience.

BEETHOVEN'S MUSIC IN GENERAL

Grouped according to genre, Beethoven's music includes the following completed works: 9 symphonies; *Wellington's Victory;* 2 independent orchestral concert overtures (e.g., *Coriolan Overture,* inspired by but never performed with Collin's tragedy *Coriolan*); incidental music for 6 dramas, including *Egmont* and *Die Ruinen von Athen* (The Ruins of Athens); 2 ballets, the most significant being *Die Geschöpfe des Prometheus* (The Creatures of Prometheus); the opera *Fidelio;* 2 Masses (in C and in D); the oratorio *Christus am Ölberge* (Christ on the Mount of Olives); the *Fantasia* ("Choral Fantasy"; piano, vcs., orch.); a violin concerto, 5 piano concerti, and a triple concerto (piano, violin, 'cello, and orch.); 9 piano trios; 32 large sonatas for piano; 10 sonatas for violin and piano and 5 for 'cello and piano; at least 20 sets of variations for solo piano; 2 *Romances* (violin, orch.); and 16 string quartets plus the *Grosse Fuge.* He wrote many songs, arias, *scenas,* several pieces for wind band, short piano pieces, almost 200 arrangements of folk songs with piano trio accompaniment, and numerous pieces of miscellaneous types.

Beethoven's personality and his beliefs are inherent in his music. His boundless energy is found in driving rhythms, in pressing fugues (String quartet, Op. 59, No. 3, mvt. 4), in the quiet murmuring of a brook (Symphony No. 6, mvt. 2), and in robust marches that serve also to provide relief from tension, to change the mood, or to engender humor (Symphonies Nos. 3 and 9). He expressed humor in a variety of other ways, such as the delayed entrance of an instrument (timpani, in Symphony No. 9, mvt. 2), pitch limitations imposed on an instrument (bassoon's "do" and "sol" in Symphony No. 6, mvt. 3), and general pauses that interrupt the rhythmic flow (Symphony No. 5, mvt. 1, recapitulation). The various moods that colored Beethoven's disposition—even his abrupt shifts between contrasting moods—are present in his music: tenderness, joy, exuberance, sadness, melancholy, and the serenity and peace that he found while walking down a country lane.

Many of Beethoven's themes are constructed from small motives. Motivic generation of thematic material and motivic development figure prominently in his style; he subjected motives to incredible degrees of modification. Frequently, he used a chromatically rising or falling passage coupled with a crescendo to herald a theme's arrival (e.g., Quartet, Op. 18, No. 3, mvt. 4, mm. 53–56). Often, in sonata-form movements of piano sonatas, he presented the first theme *piano* but recapitulated it *forte* (e.g., Op. 2, No. 1, mvt. 1, mm. 1–2, 101–2). Habitually, he directed attention to a new theme by prefacing it with a rest (as did Mozart) or a diametrically opposed dynamic (e.g., *sf* or *ff* prior to *pp* entrance of theme). General pauses served also to effect unexpected modulations to remote keys.

When composing, Beethoven disregarded the comfort or convenience of the performer. He considered only the pitches, timbres, and effect he desired; it mattered not at all to him whether the production of a passage was difficult or awkward. Probably, bassists and 'cellists suffered most because of this (e.g., *Serenade,* Op. 8, mvt. 5, mm. 52–55, 'cello part, or Symphony No. 5, mvt. 3, Trio, bass part).

Beethoven was an innovator. In some early works, he was already experimenting. After he mastered Classic forms and style, his harmonic language became more forceful and daring, his modulations bolder. He used augmented sixth chords (the so-called German, Italian, French, and mixed sixths) effectively. Sudden modulations, especially to keys a third away from the tonic—a striking departure from the modulations expected in that era—were a lifelong feature of his style. Nor was he more cautious where form was concerned. To Beethoven, form was not a mold into which music was to be poured—his music could not be so confined. Rather, form was an elastic band, expandable at any point, capable of containing all that needed to be expressed without ever becoming so distorted that its identity was lost or so extended that it snapped. Beethoven never shattered form; he stretched it. Through his experiments with form, modulations, developmental processes, and instrumentation, music's horizons broadened considerably.

STYLE PERIODS

Customarily, Beethoven's music is divided into three chronological periods based on stylistic differences exhibited in the music: (1) early works composed at Bonn and Vienna, 1782–c. 1802; (2) works composed in or near Vienna, c. 1803–c. 1815; and (3) late works, composed c. 1815–1827. However, the first style period must be subdivided and the youthful works he wrote at Bonn (1782–92) considered separately from the early works he composed in Vienna (1793–c. 1802). Divisions such as these are not clear-cut; works produced near the end of one period may exhibit characteristics of the next and vice versa.

BONN, 1782–1792   From the Bonn period, approximately 40 works survive. A dozen of them were written in 1782–85: four piano sonatas, three piano quartets, two rondos for piano, *Variations on a March by Dressler* (C minor), and two songs. That most of these works were published is significant.

The most substantial of these early works are the three piano quartets and the three "Elector's" Sonatas (see p. 403) in Eb, F minor, and D. These are three-movement sonatas, in a style combining early Classic and *empfindsamer Stil*. The passionate mood of the F-minor sonata links it with Beethoven's later piano sonatas in that key (Op. 2, No. 1, and Op. 57). The use of F minor was not common then, though C. P. E. Bach composed three keyboard sonatas in F minor; Beethoven knew Bach's works. Beethoven began the sonata-form Allegro assai first movement of his F-minor sonata with a Larghetto maestoso introduction, a few measures of which return in the development section; he used this feature in several later sonatas. Each of the piano quartets (Eb, D, C) was modeled after a specific piano/violin sonata by Mozart (K. 380, 379, 296). The significance of these sonatas and quartets lies in Beethoven's awareness of and interest in Viennese Classic style and in his high regard for the multimovement sonata.

During the next few years Beethoven wrote very little music. After 1789 he completed several sets of variations for piano based on themes by others, some Lieder, concert arias with orchestral accompaniment, a funeral cantata for Emperor Joseph II (d. 1790), a cantata for the accession of Leopold II, and an Octet in Eb for winds (1792; revised, pub. as Op. 103, 1830). In addition, there survive some sketches and many fragments of movements. The best of the late works from the Bonn period are the sets of variations and the cantatas, all of which contain seeds of later works. The funeral cantata (SATB, 4-vc. chorus, orch.) opens and closes with an excellent, expressive chorus in C minor. In the eighteenth century, C minor was regarded as the *pathétique* key; Beethoven would use it often in later works.

VIENNA, 1793–C. 1802   During his first years in Vienna, Beethoven composed primarily for piano. It was as an improviser that he first impressed Vienna. Very few of those variations were notated. As his horizons expanded, he branched out into many genres. In addition to 20 piano sonatas, during his first decade in Vienna he created concert arias, Lieder (e.g., *Adelaide*, Op. 46), two piano concerti, three violin/piano sonatas (Op. 12), two 'cello/piano sonatas (Op. 5), three string trios (Op. 9), six string quartets (Op.18), the ballet *Die Geschöpfe des Prometheus* (Op. 43), two symphonies, many pieces for Viennese social life (e.g., ballroom dances, marches, and sets of variations), and some pieces for mechanical clock.

He revised some of his Bonn works, used some sketches made at Bonn in new compositions, and mastered Viennese Classic style and sonata form. His 3 Piano Trios, Op. 1 (in Eb, G, and C minor) appeared in 1795. Beethoven frequently chose minor keys, especially C minor, as the main tonality of his large works or for movements within them. Three piano sonatas composed in 1793–95 were published as Op. 2 in 1796; the first of these, in F minor, was modeled after C. P. E. Bach's F-minor Sonata No. 3.

In multimovement forms, Beethoven experimented with the balance of the movements and varied their character. Of significance is his view of the sonata as an expansive form in which all movements work toward a climax in the finale.

As the 1790s drew to a close, Beethoven began to write string quartets, concerti, and symphonies. Also, he was more innovative. His harmonic language became more forceful and daring, his modulations bolder. Often, he commenced a composition on a chord other than the tonic or in a tonality other than the main key of the piece (e.g., Symphony No. 1).

VIENNA, C. 1803–C. 1815 In this period Beethoven's compositions reflect the greater maturity and depth of character he attained through his personal battle at Heiligenstadt—the strength emanating from the inner conflict, mental anguish, and physical pain caused by the cruel blow fate had dealt him and his determination to rise above it. This is seen especially in the "heroic" works: *Sinfonia Eroica, Fidelio,* and the incidental music for Goethe's *Egmont.* Strength and a sense of power and/or victory are conveyed through the music of Piano Concerto No. 5 ("Emperor") and the "Waldstein" and "Appassionata" piano sonatas, also.

This period was dominated by orchestral works: Symphonies Nos. 3–8, the last three piano concerti, the violin concerto, and the *Fantasia,* Op. 80. Instruments were added to the orchestra as needed (e.g., piccolo, contrabassoon, and three trombones in Symphony No. 5 and four horns in the *Léonore* overtures). Instrumental parts became more demanding technically, and, as instruments were improved, Beethoven's demands became greater.

Increasingly, Beethoven expanded the dimensions of form. He blurred dividing lines by disguising or varying material in the recapitulation or by connecting movements of a multimovement work. Development sections grew long and complex; codas were expanded to become virtually second developments concluding with quasi-recapitulatory reference to the first theme. Often, he used theme groups or a multitude of themes and motives, all conceived for their developmental possibilities. Frequently, an introductory motive or theme was designed with regard to later incorporation of all or part of it into the form as a whole (e.g., the introductory phrase of Sonata No. 17 [Op. 31, No. 2] or the cyclic motive of Symphony No. 5). This kind of thematic recurrence was not entirely new in Beethoven's works, but the treatment was more expansive.

Frequently, the first theme of a fast movement was constructed so that it needed completion (e.g., Symphony No. 3, mvt. 1 [ex. 20.8a]). It was not uncommon for a first theme to generate all others within a movement or a work.

Beethoven's innovations were bolder and his stylistic changes more radical in his string quartets and piano sonatas than in his symphonies. That made his contemporaries reluctant to accept works like the Op. 59 quartets. A sense of the dramatic pervaded many works of this period (e.g., *Quartet serioso,* Op. 95). He concluded several minor-key compositions with a movement or coda in the parallel major, almost as though paying homage to old rules governing the Picardian ending. Adverse criticism elicited from Beethoven words to the effect that posterity would understand his music— the first indication that a composer thought of his works being performed by later generations.

VIENNA, C. 1815–1827 After 1815, Beethoven produced his most abstract and most sublime music. His principal works from this period are *An die ferne Geliebte,* the last five piano sonatas, the *Diabelli Variations, Missa solemnis,* Symphony No. 9, and the last six string quartets.

Outstanding characteristics of Beethoven's last style period are (1) the meditative quality of the works, (2) development of thematic material to the seeming exhaustion of all its potentialities, (3) increased use of counterpoint, and (4) the blurring of demarcations between theme groups, between sections of a movement, and even between movements of works. He expanded transitions and bridge passages and wrote a kind of merging bridge passage in which he gradually shifted from one musical area to another without pinpointing the exact moment of transition. His predilection for the flatted submediant key and for modulations by thirds is apparent to a much greater degree. He included passages of instrumental recitative and arioso in many works and showed a deeper concern for lyricism within sonata form.

Beethoven studied the works of Bach, Handel, Palestrina, and earlier composers and incorporated some of their techniques in his works. Handel's choral fugues were models for those in Beethoven's *Missa solemnis.* Beethoven researched Zarlino's *Istitutione harmoniche* and used the correct modes for the *Et incarnatus* of the *Missa solemnis* and in the Quartet, Op. 132, mvt. 3. He was aware of the new genres being used in England and touched on areas that received greater attention from later nineteenth-century composers, for example, the song cycle (*An die ferne Geliebte*) and small character pieces for piano, such as *Für Elise* (For Elise) and the *Bagatelles.*

Throughout his career, Beethoven's use of the principles of variation and fugue increased. Each of these compositional techniques can be, and were, used by Beethoven in several ways: (1) as an independent composition (*Variations in C minor,* WoO 80, variations on a harmonic ground; *Diabelli Variations,* theme and variations; and the *Grosse Fuge*); (2) as a movement of a multimovement composition (Symphony No. 5, mvt. 2, variations on two themes; Sonata No. 31, Op. 110, *Fuga* finale; and a fugue as Var. 32 of *Diabelli Variations*); and (3) as a technique within another formal plan for a single movement (the variations within the finale of Symphony No. 9, and the fugue within the sonata-form finale of String Quartet, Op. 59, No. 3). Beethoven skillfully embedded fugue and variation techniques in sonata form and in the complete sonata structure.

Piano Sonatas

The piano sonata occupies a central position in Beethoven's work. Because he composed piano sonatas throughout his life, each of his stylistic periods is represented in them. In this genre he introduced and experimented with new ideas, new procedures, and new interpretations that he incorporated in other works.

The sonatas Beethoven wrote in Bonn have been considered previously. Approximately two-thirds of his piano sonatas were composed between 1793 and 1802; stylistically, the 3 written in 1802 fit into his second Vienna period. In formal structure, Sonatas Nos. 1–20 vary considerably. Ten of them (Nos. 1–4, 7, 11–13, 15, 18) have four movements; 2 have two movements (Nos. 19, 20); the remainder have three. Sonata form was used for first movements in the first 13 sonatas composed (Nos. 1–11, 19, 20); finales are usually some type of rondo. The minuet, when included, is not the elegant Classic type; often, Beethoven replaced it with a livelier movement, such as scherzo (e.g., Op. 2, No. 2). Sometimes he omitted both minuet and scherzo (e.g., Op. 10, Nos. 1, 2, and Op. 13). However, the four-movement Sonata No. 18 (Op. 31, No. 3) contains a Scherzo as second movement and a Menuetto/Trio as third. Sonata 12 (Op. 26; Ab) contains no sonata-form movement; the work commences with an Andante con Variazioni (theme and variations), has a Scherzo/Trio second movement, has a *March funebre sulla morte d'un Eroe* (Funeral march on the death of a hero; Ab minor) as third movement, and concludes with an Allegro rondo.

Among those whose works influenced Beethoven's writing for piano were Clementi, Haydn, C. P. E. Bach, and Dussek. All of them used minor keys, especially C minor and F minor. The finale of Clementi's F-minor sonata, Op. 10, No. 6 (1784), in particular, exhibits characteristics found in Beethoven's works of the middle and late 1790s. Both Clementi and Dussek were fond of major-minor parallelism or dualism—moving from C major to C minor within a movement or using a passage in Eb minor to prepare for a section in Eb major. However, such parallelism was common procedure in compound ternary form (e.g., Menuetto in major, Trio in minor). Clementi's works were probably responsible, to a great extent, for the full texture, octave doublings, *moto perpetuo* sections, and active, middle-register accompaniments in Beethoven's sonatas as well as some harmonies then considered abrasive.

Beethoven absorbed a great deal that other pianist-composers had to offer. However, to imply that Beethoven's style of piano writing was derived principally from outside influences would be erroneous. Though outside influences are important and stylistic similarities and direct borrowings can be pointed out, Beethoven's talent and his originality—his invention of musical material and his ingenuity in treatment of it—must be acknowledged.

The three sonatas Beethoven published as Op. 2 were dedicated to Haydn and reflect his influence as well as that of C. P. E. Bach. Beethoven's F-minor sonata (Op. 2, No. 1) contains several *galant* characteristics. In Op. 2, No. 2 (A major), both second and fourth movements are rondos; the third movement is a scherzo with trio (A major/A minor). Of the Op. 2 sonatas, No. 3 (C major) is the most brilliant and the most difficult to perform.

Sonata No. 4 (Op. 7; Eb major; 1796–97) is Beethoven's first real masterpiece in this genre. The figure opening the sonata-form first movement (ex. 20.2) recurs throughout the movement as a unifying device, much needed because of the diversity of themes. The

EXAMPLE 20.2 Beethoven: Sonata No. 4, Op. 7, mvt. 1, mm. 1–4.

coda is the longest Beethoven had written up to this time. The second movement is a Largo in A major (ternary form, with coda). Though not so labeled, the Allegro third movement is a scherzo (E♭ major), whose trio (E♭ minor) is a *moto perpetuo* in triplets. Realizing that a fast finale would spoil the effectiveness of the previous movements, Beethoven concluded with a seven-part Rondo, Poco Allegretto e grazioso.

On the whole, the three sonatas of Op. 10 (1796–98) are representative of Beethoven's first Vienna period; yet, when they were published (1798), critics considered them too experimental. Sonata No. 8, Op. 13 (C minor; 1798) was named *Pathétique* (touching, moving) by Beethoven, perhaps because of the affect formerly associated with its key. Beethoven gave programmatic titles to only two piano sonatas; the other is No. 26, *Les Adieux*. The *Pathétique* Sonata has three movements: a sonata-form Allegro di molto e con brio introduced by a dramatic, solemn Grave whose first three measures recur, slightly altered, to commence the development and the coda; a lyrical Adagio cantabile (A♭ major) constructed as a five-part rondo; and a seven-part Rondo (Allegro; C minor), with coda, as finale.

Beethoven labeled each of the two sonatas of Op. 27 (1800–1) *quasi una fantasia*. Fantasia elements are present in the first movement of each work, and elements of sonata form appear in the finale of each sonata. The C♯-minor sonata Op. 27, No. 2, is popularly known as the "Moonlight" Sonata. The nickname derives from the sonata's first movement, which, when performed on a piano of the type Beethoven used in 1801, could very well make a listener think of moonlight.

The greater freedom of form, more audacious choice of keys, and more remote modulations that characterized the sonatas composed during the last years of Beethoven's first decade in Vienna are features of work written during his second Viennese style period. Of the 7 sonatas (Nos. 21–27) that he wrote in 1803–15, Nos. 21 and 23 are the most significant.

Sonata No. 21, Op. 53 (C major; 1803–4), was composed after Beethoven had come to terms with the reality of his increasing deafness. The work, dedicated to Count von Waldstein, is known as the "Waldstein" Sonata. Throughout the sonata, there is an abundance of many types of figuration, much of it thematic. Often, fast rhythmic motion offsets the fact that the harmonic rhythm is slow. Prolonged trills, sometimes placed between left-hand figuration and upper-voice melodic line, and extensive scale passages in octaves alternating between hands (and played *pp*) are features of the rondo finale. This sonata is a masterpiece that attests Beethoven's ability to tastefully control virtuosic elements rather than flaunt them flamboyantly.

Sonata No. 23, Op. 57 (F minor; 1804–5; DWMA140), named "Appassionata" by the publisher, is a dramatic three-movement work. A sense of tragedy and strength is apparent from the outset, conveyed in the dark tones of the F-minor first theme, with its dramatic dotted rhythms and its unharmonized first measures doubled two octaves lower. Basically, the theme is an extended tonic-to-dominant progression; however, its sequential repetition on the flatted supertonic (Neapolitan) moving to its dominant (VI) certainly must have shocked Beethoven's contemporaries. The second theme group commences in A♭, the relative major, then moves to A♭ minor. Just prior to the Più Allegro coda, the music dwells on a figure not unlike the cyclic motive of the Fifth Symphony (ex. 20.3). The Andante con moto (D♭ major), a theme with four variations, proceeds directly into the finale, an Allegro non troppo (F minor) in which a new theme is introduced in the development section. Only the development-recapitulation section of the finale is marked to be repeated; in the second ending, tempo is gradually but quickly increased to Presto for the coda.

Between 1817 and 1822 Beethoven composed Sonatas Nos. 28–32. All are characterized by exceptional developmental techniques, more frequent use of polyphony (especially fugal sections), still more daring harmonies and remote modulations, and thematic or motivic relationships between movements. Sometimes a passage of dramatic recitative interrupts the flow of a movement. Beethoven showed a decided preference for modulating to or writing movements in the flatted submediant key; at times he did this

EXAMPLE 20.3 Beethoven: "Appassionata" Sonata, mvt. 1, the four measures preceding the Coda.

subtly, enharmonically. Often, a remote modulation is prefaced by a general pause rather than by dominant preparation. Several of the last sonatas present the performer with tremendous technical difficulties (e.g., *Hammerklavier Sonata,* No. 29, Op. 106 [B♭; 1817–18]).

Beethoven's last three piano sonatas are his most introspective ones. In them he evidenced little concern for traditional formal patterns and the Classic overall structural scheme of the sonata—almost as if he deliberately tried to violate established conventions. Consistently, he displaced the slow movement; scherzo/trio were disguised, and sonata form, when used, was treated with considerable freedom.

In Sonata No. 31, Op. 110 (1821–22), the first theme is genesis of all the others. The lyrical first movement (Moderato, A♭ major), in free sonata form, contains rhapsodic passages and has a very short development section. In the Allegro molto middle movement (F minor), Beethoven used a Silesian folk melody. The movement's concluding Picardian chord is heard as dominant to the B♭-minor opening of the finale, which commences Adagio, ma non troppo with a tripartite modulatory introduction—lyrical Adagio, dramatic *Recitativo,* and *Arioso dolente* (A♭ minor)—then, without a break, moves into a three-voice *Fuga* (A♭ major), tragic in mood. Still with no break between sections, the *Arioso* returns, varied, in G minor. In the middle of its final measure, another *Fuga* (G major) begins. The many contrapuntal devices Beethoven used become complex and include stretto, augmentation, diminution, and stretto with double diminution. The sonata concludes triumphantly, *ff,* with a four-measure, rippling arpeggiation of the A♭-major chord.

Beethoven's last sonata, Op. 111 (C minor; 1822), has only two movements. These are unrelated yet complementary: an *appassionato* C-minor first movement with Maestoso introduction, and a C-major Adagio con-

sisting of *Arietta* theme with four variations (in $\frac{9}{16}$, $\frac{6}{16}$, and $\frac{12}{32}$ meters). A coda recapitulates the theme, and an impressive epilogue concludes with a great crescendo passage that suddenly drops from *f sf* to *p* and *pp* for the last measure.

VARIATIONS

The 21 sets of variations Beethoven wrote for piano are basically of two types: (1) those based on songs and arias that were popular at the time—pieces prepared for public performances or originating as improvisations created in public performances and later notated, and (2) those with original themes or with thematic material unrelated to popular music—more serious works comparable with the piano sonatas in degree of difficulty and mood. Compositions in the first category include variations based on arias from operas by Dittersdorf, Paisiello, Salieri, Süssmayr, von Winter, and Grétry. In the second category are the *"Eroica" Variations,* in E♭, Op. 35, and *Thirty-two Variations* in C minor, WoO 80.

More significant is *33 Veränderungen über einen Walzer* (33 Variations on a Waltz), Op. 120. In 1819, Anton Diabelli (1781–1858) wrote a waltz theme that he submitted to 50 composers with the request that each of them write a variation on it so that he might publish a composite set. All but Beethoven complied with the terms of the request. Beethoven considered Diabelli's theme inconsequential—he called it a "cobbler's patch"—yet made from it a set of variations that many critics consider comparable to J. S. Bach's "Goldberg Variations." None of Beethoven's variations is included in Diabelli's composite set; instead, in 1823 Diabelli issued Beethoven's work as a separate set. In Beethoven's variations, written in contrasting moods, styles, and *tempi,* the theme is transformed rather than merely varied. Beethoven's "Diabelli Variations" became a model for sets of variations by later composers.

One of the loveliest of Beethoven's sets of variations for chamber ensembles is that based on Mozart's *La ci darem la mano,* from *Il Don Giovanni* (2 oboes, Eng. horn; 1795). Beethoven incorporated variation technique in large multimovement compositions: in symphonies (Nos. 3 and 9, finale; No. 5, mvt. 2), in his late sonatas (Op. 109 and 111), and in string quartets (Op. 131, mvt. 4).

CHAMBER MUSIC

Throughout his life, Beethoven was interested in chamber music. Yet, in no single category of chamber music is there a complete panorama of his style changes.

TRIOS   In addition to the piano trios and piano quartets completed at Bonn, several works begun at Bonn were completed or rewritten in Vienna. Among the latter are the three Piano Trios (E♭, G, and C minor) published as Op. 1 (1795). Present in them are two devices that became characteristic of his style: themes constructed from repetitions of a short motive, and sudden modulations to keys a third above or below the tonic. Each trio follows the Classic four-movement structural scheme of the complete sonata, with the third movement either Menuetto/Trio or Scherzo/Trio. The third Piano Trio is the most significant of the three.

In 1808 Beethoven composed the two Piano Trios, Op. 70, in D and E♭. The D-major Trio is a closely knit, passionate, three-movement work constructed from a minimum of motivic materials. Its nickname, "Ghost Trio," derives from the mysterious and expressive character of the D-minor second movement.

The "Archduke" Trio in B♭, Op. 97 (1811), written for Archduke Rudolph of Austria (1788–1831), is magnificent. It comprises four movements: (1) Allegro moderato, B♭, in sonata form, with the second theme in the submediant; (2) Scherzo in E♭. whose Trio commences with a chromatic theme in B♭ minor; and (3) Andante cantabile, D major, theme with five variations and coda, which moves without a break into (4) an energetic Rondo finale. The Andante cantabile is one of Beethoven's loveliest movements.

Before composing string quartets, Beethoven wrote several string trios in complete sonata structure in which violin, viola, and 'cello are equal participants: Op. 3, in E♭, (before 1794), and the three trios of Op. 9, in G, D, and C minor (1797–98). Also for string trio is a multimovement *Serenade* in D (Op. 8; 1797) that opens and closes with a March. The *Serenade* is excellent, but it is not easy and is seldom performed.

STRING QUARTETS   Beethoven had available for rehearsals and first performances of his chamber music for strings an experienced quartet headed by first violinist Ignaz Schuppanzigh (1776–1830). That quartet performed weekly Friday morning concerts at the home of Prince Lichnowsky, where Beethoven lodged.

When Schuppanzigh's quartet complained about the strange harmonies of the Op. 59 quartets, Beethoven replied that later generations would understand them —an indication that Beethoven's thinking was revolutionary, too, in that he intended his music not only for his contemporaries but for future generations to enjoy. Beethoven was the first of the great composers to have at his disposal instruments of the violin family in their modern construction—with fingerboard and neck lengthened and their slope altered, bridge more highly arched, and longer bows with newly developed frog to control hair tension—and his writing for strings shows that he took full advantage of the increased range and the more advanced bowing techniques made possible by those structural changes.

Beethoven's quartets are considered the backbone of string quartet literature. The six quartets of Op. 18 (F, G, D, C minor, A, B♭; written 1798–1800) were grouped as a set for publication. The D-major quartet follows the Classic models of Haydn and Mozart with regard to general outline of form and tempo. Key relationships within and among movements are not conventional, however.

The Op. 59 quartets (1805–6) are representative of Beethoven's mature style of quartet writing. They were commissioned by Count Andrei Razumovsky (1752–1836), Russian statesmen and competent violinist. The quartets, in F, E minor, and C, respectively, are related by Beethoven's use of Russian folk-song melodies in the F-major and E-minor works and by an original melody resembling a Russian folk song in the slow movement of the C-major one. *Slava* (Russian, Glory; ex. 20.4), incorporated in the E-minor quartet, was used by Musorgsky in his opera *Boris Godunov* (see p. 534). The Op. 59 quartets differ radically from Beethoven's earlier quartets in many respects. The movements are of larger proportions than those of previous quartets, and Beethoven's ability to write long, complex developments is evident. Some of the codas resemble second developments. Beethoven was more daring with regard to tonal relationships and formal structure, blurring and disguising sectional divisions within movements and sometimes linking movements.

The C-major quartet (No. 3) is the finest of the set. The work opens with a diminished-seventh chord on f♯, proceeds with a slow introduction in which no key is established, then barely touches on a C-major

EXAMPLE 20.4 The Russian melody *Slava* (Glory), as presented by viola in the trio of Beethoven's String Quartet, Op. 59, No. 2, mvt. 3.

chord, *piano*—the first chord of the Allegro vivace— before embarking on an extensive modulatory section that eventually cadences into C major and establishes it as tonic. The movement is colored by dominant-seventh and augmented-sixth chords. Modified sonata form was used for the melancholy Andante con moto (A minor). The third movement is a Menuetto with Trio (C major/F major). After the Menuetto *da capo*, a coda brings the movement to a close on the dominant seventh of C, and the directive *attacca subito* moves the music immediately into the fourth movement. In the first three movements, Beethoven used counterpoint effectively, but his most brilliant contrapuntal writing occurs in the Allegro molto (C major) sonata-form finale. The first theme is presented as the subject of an energetic fugue. In the recapitulation, a counter-subject in staccato half notes provides harmony.

Total deafness, serious illness, and family problems made Beethoven increasingly introspective; this is reflected in his last quartets. When Prince Nikolai Galitzïn commissioned "some quartets," Beethoven composed Op. 127 (E♭; 1824), Op. 132 (A minor; 1824–25), Op. 130 (B♭; 1825–26), and, as part of Op. 130, the *Grosse Fugue* that later became Op. 133 (B♭).

Op. 132 has five movements. Composition of the quartet was interrupted by severe illness that influenced Beethoven to write as third movement *Heiliger Dankgesang eines Genesenen . . .* (A convalescent's sacred song of thanksgiving). The brief fourth movement is a march that has a recitative-like section rather than a trio. The recitative proceeds without pause into the A-minor Allegro appassionato fifth movement, which concludes in A major.

In its original completed form, Op. 130 was a six-movement quartet concluding with the *Grosse Fuge*. At the suggestion of publisher Matthias Artaria (1793–1835), Beethoven removed the *Grosse Fuge* from Op. 130, and Artaria published it as an independent string quartet, Op. 133. It commences with an *Overtura* (In-troduction; G major) that presents the first of the two principal themes on which the quartet is based. In the ensuing Allegro (B♭) that theme is stated in diminution. Then the word *Fuga* appears above a new theme, and a double fugue is begun. Both themes are used, separately and together, in the several fugal sections that make up the piece, and both themes are developed extensively. The fugue is sometimes strict and obvious, sometimes free, sometimes hidden. The movement concludes with a brief Allegro molto section that summarizes the subjects.

Beethoven delayed writing a new Finale for the Op. 130 quartet until late in 1826; it is the last movement he completed before his death. On the whole, Op. 130 is a bright quartet. Its first two movements, Adagio ma non troppo; Allegro (sonata form with slow introduction) and Presto (scherzo/trio), are in B♭ major. Placed third is the slow movement, a D♭-major Andante con moto, *poco scherzando*. The fourth movement, *Alla danza tedesca* (In the style of a German dance), is a minuet (G major) with a waltz-like trio, but rather than *da capo* Beethoven developed the thematic material. A slow, expressive *Cavatina* (E♭) forms the fifth movement; it closes with a diminuendo to *pianissimo*, at which dynamic level the viola states the murky pedal that begins the new Finale Allegro, a sonata-rondo in B♭.

The C♯-minor quartet, Op. 131, has seven movements designed to be performed without a break. The traditional complete sonata structural scheme appears as movements 2, 4, 5, and 7. The unity of the work lies in the uninterrupted succession of its movements, which may be outlined as shown in figure 20.2 (DWMA141, mvts. 1, 2). In the coda of the fifth movement all instruments play an 18-measure passage staccato, *pianissimo*, and *sul ponticello* (bowed near the bridge)—this is the earliest use of *sul ponticello* in string quartet music.

Quartets Opp. 132, 130, 133, and 131 form a cycle with melodic, motivic, and tonal relationships. The

Movement	1	2	3	4	5	6	7
Key	C# minor	D major	B minor to E major	A major	E major	G# minor	C# minor
Tonal Relationship	Tonic	Neapolitan, or as V/V (dominant of dominant)	Relative minor of D, to dominant of A	VI of C# minor, or subdominant of E	Relative major of C# minor	Dominant of C# minor	Tonic
Form	Free fugue	Modified sonata form	Recitative serving as introduction to mvt. 4	Theme and variation	Scherzo with Trio	Introduction to mvt. 7; in Rounded Bar form	Sonata form

FIGURE 20.2 Outline of Beethoven's String Quartet, Op. 131.

four-note motive that opens Op. 132, the first of the four quartets to be composed, appears within the initial theme presented in the *Overtura* of the *Grosse Fuge,* recurs at the beginning of the fugal Allegro, and is embedded in the thematic material of all quartets in the cycle. Moreover, the keys of the first four movements of Op. 131 form the motive, as stated in the first two measures of Op. 132 (ex. 20.5). Many other relationships could be pointed out. The entire cycle displays Beethoven's contrapuntal skill and his technical mastery of string quartet composition. (The F-major quartet, Op. 135, a short, four-movement work composed in 1826, is not part of the cycle.)

ENSEMBLE SONATAS   The title page of the two 'cello/piano sonatas, Op. 5 (F major, G minor; 1796), states that they are "For harpsichord or piano with violoncello *obligato*," indicating that the 'cello part is vital to the ensemble. These are the earliest sonatas written for 'cello and keyboard in which the keyboard is not considered a *continuo* instrument.

In the Sonata in A major, Op. 69 (1807–8), the musical material is shared equally by 'cello and piano.

Op. 131 mvt. 1 — C♯ minor · D major mvt. 2 · B minor mvt. 3 · A major mvt. 4

(a)

Op. 132, mm. 1-2.

(b)

EXAMPLE 20.5 (*a*) Keys of the first four movements of Op. 131; (*b*) motive stated in mm. 1–2 of Op. 132.

The two sonatas of Op. 105 (C major; D major; 1815) for 'cello/piano display increased use of counterpoint, more textural variety, and greater freedom of form.

Beethoven's violin/piano sonatas carried the genre far beyond the works of Haydn and Mozart. Nine sonatas were written in 1797–1803; the tenth was composed in 1812. Three sonatas (Nos. 5, 7, and 10) are structured with four movements, according to the complete sonata scheme; each of the others has three. No two sonatas—in fact, no two movements—are exactly alike.

When the Op. 12 sonatas (D, A, E♭; 1797–98; pub. 1799, ded. to Salieri) appeared, Beethoven's contemporaries were highly critical of his harmonies and modulations. In addition to contemporary Classic traits, the works exhibit traces of *style galant* and elements of emerging Romanticism and contain some difficult and highly sophisticated passages. Sonatas, Op. 23 (A minor; 1800) and Op. 24 (F major; 1800–1) probably were intended as a pair but were published separately. The "Spring" Sonata is a perfect complement for the tense outer movements of the A-minor work. Part of the charm of the "Spring" Sonata is its apparent simplicity, which is at times deceptive.

Beethoven's last five violin/piano sonatas are true duos. The Op. 30 sonatas (A, C minor, G; 1801–2) contain difficult cross-rhythms, trills and small cadenzas to be played as duets, chain passages, and long scales. Often the violin line is in the middle of three-voice writing. The C-minor sonata makes enormous demands on the performers.

Beethoven prepared the "Kreutzer" Sonata, Op. 47 (A major; 1802–3) for a concert he performed with the mulatto violinist George Bridgetower (c. 1779–1860) in May 1803. To have a new sonata ready in time, Beethoven quickly finished the first two movements of an A-major sonata on which he was working, stripped the fourth movement from Op. 30, No. 1 (not yet published), and appended it as Finale. At the concert, the audience demanded an encore of the middle movement, an Andante with four variations, some of them virtuosic. Before Op. 47 was published (1805), Beethoven and Bridgetower had a disagreement, and Beethoven dedicated the sonata to violinist Rodolphe Kreutzer (1766–1831). However, Kreutzer claimed he did not understand the work and refused to play it.

Beethoven designed his G-major sonata, Op. 96 (1812), for violinist Pierre Rode (1774–1830) but dedicated it to Archduke Rudolph, who, with Rode, first performed it. The sonata contains numerous difficult passages for both instruments.

SYMPHONIES

Beethoven's nine symphonies form the core of modern symphonic repertoire. They have influenced all symphonies written since they were composed. They attest Beethoven's mastery of Classic style and forms, show the development of his individualistic style as a composer of symphonic orchestral works—his innovative treatment of harmonies, keys, thematic material, and forms—and, in his last symphony, the introspective character of his last works. At the heart of this development is his view of the structure of a single movement as sonata *principle* rather than sonata *form.*

Symphony No. 1, Op. 21, in C major, has Classic proportions and form and uses as third movement the traditional Minuet/Trio (though it sounds much like a scherzo). The orchestral instrumentation is standard for the time; however, winds have more than the usual degree of prominence. The influence of Haydn's "London" symphonies is reflected in Beethoven's use of slow introductions to the first and fourth movements, and that of Mozart's Symphony No. 40 is apparent in the *fugato* opening of the sonata-form second movement. In other respects, the C-major symphony is the work of a talented, self-assured composer writing a *Grand Symphony* designed to please no one other than himself. The Adagio introduction to the sonata-form first movement provides a sample of Beethoven's harmonic audacity. Instead of the expected solid statement of the symphony's C-major tonality, the first chord is a dominant seventh in the key of F, and the

first measure presents a perfect authentic cadence in F major. This is followed by a deceptive cadence in C and a V_7–I progression in G (ex. 20.6a). For the next seven measures the ear debates the final outcome of tonality that seems to waver between G and C major. Then unison strings utter an ascending G-major scale harmonized with a dominant seventh of C; there is a rapid descent of a fifth, and the exposition commences, Allegro con brio, with a *piano* C-major chord. The marchlike first theme firmly proclaims C-major tonality (ex. 20.6b). The Adagio introduction to the Finale is humorous. After the *ff* pronouncement of a sustained G pitch, a C-major scale that commences on its dominant is timidly released in segments gradually increasing in length. There is a brief general pause. Then, Allegro molto e vivace and *piano*, the complete scale begins the vivacious first theme (ex. 20.6c). The entire finale is light and animated.

Symphony No. 2, Op. 36, in D major (1802), lies on the border between Beethoven's first and second Vienna style periods. It, too, opens with an Adagio introduction but proclaims D as tonic before exploring other tonalities. A trilled motive in the introduction (ex. 20.7a) recurs with an extension in the first measure of the Finale, where it is part of a larger interrogation (ex. 20.7b) that finds its answer in the coda of that movement (ex. 20.7c). The trilled motive is almost identical with the one that opens C. P. E. Bach's Symphony No. 3 (ex. 20.7d). The Second Symphony's outer movements have long, developmental codas, and a new theme is introduced in the coda of the Finale. In the sonata-form slow movement (Larghetto, A major), the first theme is in two eight-measure strains (a theme group), each repeated with different instrumentation; there are three other themes. The third movement, labeled *Scherzo,* is characterized by frequent sharp contrasts in dynamics, timbre, instrumentation, and tonality.

Symphony No. 3, *Eroica* (Heroic), in E♭ (1803), is one of Beethoven's most important works. In 1798 Beethoven and countless others regarded Napoleon as a representative of the common people working to advance the republican aims of liberty, equality, and fraternity. The idea of writing a symphony for such a hero appealed to Beethoven. He planned to title the work "Bonaparte." However, when he learned that Napoleon had had himself proclaimed emperor, Beethoven

(a)

became so incensed that he destroyed the original manuscript's title page. On the copy, "Bonaparte" was scratched out so violently that a hole was torn in the page. (Beethoven did not destroy or change any of the music.)

French revolutionary music—particularly the marches and grand symphonies of Gossec and his contemporaries—influenced Beethoven when he composed this symphony. The only introductory material consists of the two crisp, *forte,* E♭-major chords with which full orchestra commences the symphony (DWMA142). The first theme—based on the E♭ triad— is bass, befitting a hero, and is announced by 'cellos, then taken over by horns. (Beethoven added a third horn to the orchestra.) The simplicity of the theme is counteracted by the unexpected C♯, which hints at heroic daring deeds (ex. 20.8a, p. 418). Here, it resolves upward through D to E♭, but in the recapitulation it precipitates a modulation to the key of F (mm. 402–7).

(b)

(c)

EXAMPLE 20.6 Beethoven, Symphony No. 1: (*a*) mvt. 1, mm. 1–4; (*b*) mvt. 1, theme 1; (*c*) mvt. 4, mm. 1–14, introduction and beginning of theme 1. (Full orchestra plays first chord of mvt. 4.)

What seems to be a new theme in the development (m. 284ff.) is actually **thematic transformation,** the modification of a theme so that, in a new context, it appears to be different but actually constitutes the same elements (ex. 20.8b). Thematic transformation, an application of the principle of variation, was exploited by nineteenth-century composers (especially Liszt) for unification purposes. Near the end of the development section of the *Eroica*'s first movement, while violins play tremolo *ppp* in dominant-seventh harmony, the first horn enters with the first theme, in the tonic key. The effect was shocking—as if the horn player had

EXAMPLE 20.7 (*a*) Beethoven, Symphony No. 2, mvt. 1, motives, mm. 29–30; (*b*) Beethoven, Symphony No. 2, *Finale*, mvt. 4, mm. 1–3; (*c*) Beethoven, Symphony No. 2, mvt. 4, mm. 423–42, string parts; (*d*) C. P. E. Bach, Symphony No. 3, mvt. 1, mm. 1–6.

(a)

(b)

(c)

(d)

FROM CLASSICISM TO ROMANTICISM

(a)

(b)

EXAMPLE 20.8 Beethoven, *Sinfonia Eroica:* (*a*) mvt. 1, mm. 1–8, two introductory notes and first theme; (*b*) mvt. 1, mm. 284ff., theme transformed.

miscounted and had entered too soon! But dominant-seventh harmony persists, then resolves to E♭, and recapitulation begins. The first theme figures prominently in the coda, and the transformed theme introduced in the development is brought back in the coda—this was novel.

A solemn *Marche funebre* (Funeral march) in C minor constitutes the symphony's slow movement. The minor tonality of the *Marche,* its dotted rhythms and muffled drums (simulated by string bass also) are conventional; the Trio (C major) is a eulogy. The Scherzo (E♭) is exceedingly fast and is *sempre pianissimo* and staccato for its first 90 measures; in its Trio, the three horns, maintaining the heroic E♭ tonality, present the principal phrases alone, as a trio. Beethoven had used the theme of the Finale before—in the finale of *Prometheus,* as a *contredanse,* and for the piano variations, Op. 35. His use of the Prometheus theme here may be a symbolic reference to heroism—the courage of an individual striving for victory over hopeless odds. In the Allegro molto (E♭) Finale of the *Eroica,* it is again treated as theme with variations, but several other themes are introduced, one of them marchlike. The movement concludes Presto, its last two crisp E♭ chords matching those that began the symphony.

It was Beethoven's custom to work on several compositions at the same time. This was the case with his Fourth and Fifth—and possibly his Sixth—Symphonies, all composed between 1806 and 1808. Because the Fourth Symphony is lighter in weight and mood than the others, it usually receives little attention. It is an adventurous work, though conventional in overall form.

Undoubtedly, Symphony No. 5, Op. 67, in C minor (1807–8), is Beethoven's best-known symphony. It is a cyclic work whose opening motive

—the first notes of the yellowhammer's (a bird's) song—colors the entire work and is found, rhythmically or melodically, in every movement. To some persons, this symphony represents Beethoven's determination to achieve success in the field of music despite his deafness—the C-major finale of the C-minor symphony signifying ultimate victory. During World War II, the cyclic motive was likened to the letter V in Morse Code (...–) and was a symbol of victory.

The Allegro con brio first movement conforms with the general outlines of Classic sonata form. The movement commences in C minor by stating the principal motive as introduction (mm. 1–5) and then as first theme; second and third themes are in the relative major, in which key the first section ends. After the section is repeated, development occurs, followed by recapitulation, with some digression from expected procedure: the insertion of a small cadenza for oboe and return of the second theme in C major. The coda is long and developmental. Beethoven chose the submediant key, A♭, for the Andante con moto, a set of variations on two themes. The Allegro third movement, an irregular Scherzo with Trio, concludes with a transitional passage that leads directly into the Finale. The Scherzo opens in C minor with a "Mannheim

Violoncello

Basso

(a)

Allegro assai

(b)

EXAMPLE 20.9 (*a*) Beethoven, Symphony No. 5, mvt. 3, mm. 1–5, theme 1; (*b*) Mozart, Symphony No. 40, K. 550, mvt. 4, mm. 1–2. Both themes use the "Mannheim rocket" followed by a melodic sigh.

rocket" figure similar to that commencing the Finale of Mozart's Symphony No. 40 (ex. 20.9) and closes on a short, unharmonized, orchestral C. Imitative counterpoint is a feature of the C-major Trio. Only its first section is literally repeated; at the end of the second section, what seems to start a *da capo* of the Scherzo blends into a long bridge passage colored by the cyclic motive. Softly, timpani sound the motive, then, subtly altering the rhythm until the beats blur into a roll, make the transition to the quadruple meter of the triumphant C-major Finale. For the Finale, Beethoven added to the orchestra a piccolo, a contrabassoon, and three trombones; this seems to be the first use of these instruments in a symphony.

Beethoven's sketchbooks contain many remarks about his Symphony No. 6, Op. 68, in F major (1808). In addition to *Sinfonia pastorella* (Pastoral Symphony), he referred to the work as "recollections of country life," and stated in the score that the music is "more the expression of feeling than of tone-painting." Instrumental music that was inspired by or that attempted to describe a nonmusical idea, scene, story, or event was not new in the nineteenth century, though it became very popular then. It was well established by 1700 (see Kuhnau, p. 281) and can be traced intermittently in earlier centuries (see Sakadas, p. 11). Franz Liszt (1811–86) is credited with being the first to apply the term **program music** to descriptive or referential music.

The *Pastoral* Symphony's five movements have programmatic titles: (1) "Awakening of pleasant feelings

on arriving in the country," (2) "Scene by the brook," (3) "Happy gathering of country folk," (4) "Thunderstorm," and (5) "Shepherd's song: Happy and thankful feelings after the storm." Basically, Beethoven followed the structural scheme of the Classic symphony, but, when the peasants' merrymaking was interrupted by a sudden summer storm, what was more logical than to interrupt symphonic structure by inserting an additional movement to depict that storm? (This is an excellent example of *Sturm und Drang* characteristics.) To maintain continuity in the musical description, movements 3, 4, and 5 are played without a break.

As usual, Beethoven was very conscious of tone color. For the last two movements, two trombones and two trumpets were added to the orchestra, and the shrill tones of piccolo color the storm. For the murmuring of the brook in the Andante, Beethoven wrote harmony for second violins, violas, and two muted solo 'cellos; the other 'cellos duplicate the string bass line. In the coda of the Andante, flute, oboe, and clarinet imitate the calls of nightingale, quail, and cuckoo; earlier in the symphony, the yellowhammer's alternate call and the trilling of other birds are heard. The first theme of the third movement resembles and may actually be an Austrian folk song; the shepherd's song, in the last movement, parallels a melody in Haydn's Symphony No. 6.

Piccolo, trombones, and contrabassoon are not in the orchestra for Beethoven's next two symphonies. Symphony No. 7, Op. 92, in A major (1811–12), is Romantic, exhibiting contrasts and dualities. Throughout the symphony, there is an abundance of *ostinato* figures and scales.

Symphony No. 8, Op. 93 (F major; 1812), is traditional in overall form and tonal scheme. The second movement (abridged sonata form; B♭) is labeled Allegretto scherzando (in a playful mood). In the regularity of its rhythm Beethoven parodied the steady tapping of Mälzel's chronometer (Insight, "Mälzel") as it marked the time. The first theme is that of a canon Beethoven had jotted down for Mälzel.

Symphony No. 9, Op. 125, in D minor (comp. 1817–23), the "Choral" Symphony, is Beethoven's longest symphony. In it he incorporated ideas and sketches that covered a period of 30 years. As early as 1793, he wanted to compose a setting of Schiller's ode *An die Freude* (To Joy). Ultimately, Beethoven set only

Mälzel

Johann N. Mälzel (1772–1838) received musical training from his father but chose to become an inventor. Among his inventions was the Panharmonicon, a mechanical "instrument" (or automatophone) activated by bellows and pinned cylinders and capable of reproducing orchestral or wind ensemble music. Mozart, Haydn, and Beethoven were among those writing music for Panharmonicon use (e.g., Beethoven's *Wellington's Victory*). Mälzel also made ear trumpets, several of which Beethoven owned. Another of Mälzel's inventions was the chronometer, a pendulum device for determining the tempo for performance of a musical work. Using such a chrono-

meter, Beethoven placed tempo indications on many of his compositions. While in Amsterdam in 1815, Mälzel learned of a better chronometer designed c. 1812 by Dietrich Winkel (1780–1826). Mälzel recognized the possibilities in Winkel's double-pendulum design—using an oscillating rod weighted at both ends—and appropriated it but added a scale of tempo divisions. Mälzel named the apparatus "Metronome" and patented it as his own invention. Though Winkel sued Mälzel and won, the device is still known as Mälzel's Metronome (fig. 20.3).

FIGURE 20.3 One of Mälzel's metronomes. *(Gesellschaft der Musikfreunde, Vienna)*

those stanzas concerned with the universal brotherhood of man through joy and its basis in an eternal heavenly Father's love. Thematically, the symphony is related to the "Choral Fantasy." The symphony's first three movements are expansions of traditional forms: The D-minor sonata-form first movement opens with a slow introduction commencing on the dominant—the open fifth A–E, sustained and *pianissimo*—and concludes with a long, developmental coda. Structurally, the second movement is compound ternary incorporating elements of fugue, scherzo, and sonata form. Beethoven's humor is apparent in the tardy entrances of the timpani (tuned in octaves). This movement exemplifies Beethoven's ability to organize a movement around a single rhythmic motive. The slow movement, placed third, is an alternating form comprised of two contrasting themes with variations.

The fourth movement is unique, not in its inclusion of voices—that had been done previously, for example, in 1814 by Peter von Winter (1754–1825)—but in its formal structure. It is a cantata, though Beethoven referred to it as *Variationen*; it comprises variations on two themes. The movement opens with a *fortissimo* discord (which is striking when there is no long pause

after the third movement) and a clamorous fanfare in which all but strings participate. Representative portions of the three previous movements pass in review, each in appropriate key and tempo, as if auditioning; each is rejected by means of instrumental recitative. Winds suggest a new theme, which is accepted and is extended into the melody that has become the *Hymn to Joy*. The song is repeated four times, with different instrumentation; there is transition to D minor and recapitulation of the movement's stormy introductory measures. Then, baritone soloist remonstrates, "Oh, friends, not these strains! Instead let us sing more pleasant and more joyful ones!" Different combinations of solo and choral voices, with orchestra, present three stanzas of *To Joy,* with some variations in the music. A brief transition culminates with heightened joy in the words "with God!" At this point, to relieve the high dramatic tension, Beethoven inserted a brisk *alla marcia* variation in ⅛ meter (in B♭) for winds with piccolo and Turkish Janissary instrumentation added. Solo tenor and male chorus sing a portion of the fourth strophe of Schiller's ode; after an orchestral interlude—a double fugue, both subjects derived from the hymn melody—chorus and orchestra repeat the ode's first stanza. For the next section of the cantata three trombones are added to the orchestra. The music becomes majestic and the mood devotional. Chorus and orchestra introduce a new theme, and the tempo slows to Adagio when the chorus implores people to seek and adore their Maker. As the last words are sung softly against tremulous orchestral background, the movement reaches a high point of mysticism. Tonality returns to D major for the next variation, an energetic Allegro in $\frac{6}{4}$ meter; now the rhythmically altered hymn melody and the lyrics of the first stanza are combined with the theme and text the chorus has just presented. For years this section of the cantata was considered unsingable because of the high tessitura of the vocal parts. The movement's Prestissimo coda is a brilliant development of both themes, presented by chorus and full orchestra. The symphony concludes orchestrally; the final progression from A in the winds down to a quick unison D by the orchestra recalls the open fifths of the symphony's first sounds.

While working on the second movement of Symphony No. 9 in 1822, Beethoven made arrangements to write a symphony for the London Philharmonic Society. Certainly, as he worked intermittently on the Ninth Symphony, he had in mind the instrumentation and capabilities of the London orchestra. The London Philharmonic Society had performance rights to the work (in England only) for 18 months.

The première on 18 October 1988, in London, of an orchestral work purported to be a realization of Beethoven's sketches for the first movement of Symphony No. 10 in Eb elicited considerable comment from musicologists and composers. Reliable authorities examined the sketches and the realization and concluded that there is no basis for the assumption that Beethoven intended the sketches for a symphony and that the movement is essentially the work of Barry Cooper, who made the "realization."

WORKS FOR SOLO INSTRUMENT(S) AND ORCHESTRA

During his first decade in Vienna, Beethoven composed three piano concerti for his own use and two *Romances* for violin and orchestra (Op. 50, F major; Op. 40, G major). The first two concerti (No. 1, C; No. 2, Bb) are uncomplicated; No. 3 (C minor) is more difficult. Between 1803 and 1809, he composed three

more solo concerti, two for piano and one for violin; a triple concerto (for piano, violin, 'cello); and the *Fantasia,* Op. 80. The Violin Concerto, Op. 61, in D major (1806), is one of the finest ever written; solo and orchestral parts are ideally balanced.

The piano part of the triple concerto was written for Archduke Rudolph; the other piano works were for Beethoven's own use, and he gave Concerto No. 4, Op. 58 (G major), and the *Fantasia* their first performances. For all his concerti Beethoven used the overall fast-slow-fast structural scheme, with the middle movement in a related key and the finale a rondo. The G-major concerto commences with solo piano presenting the first theme, then the orchestra enters and continues the exposition.

In Concerto No. 5, Op. 73 (Eb major, "Emperor"), Beethoven again deviated from Classic sonata-concerto structure. In the first movement, he prefaced the orchestral exposition with quasi-improvisational dialogue between orchestra and soloist; when this material is reintroduced as transition from development to recapitulation, it is apparent that the "improvisation" was a calculated part of the design. Customarily, the soloist was given carte blanche to extemporize a lengthy cadenza at the conclusion of the recapitulation, but at this point Beethoven wrote, "Do not create a cadenza but immediately attack the following" and notated his own cadenza—the latter portion of it accompanied by the orchestra. The slow second movement is in the remote key of B major. Near the end of that movement, a modulation to the dominant key of Eb is achieved by a single semitone progression from B to Bb, and, as the soloist hints at the impetuous Rondo that is to come, second and third movements are linked and blended together without pause.

At some time between composition of Concertos Nos. 4 and 5 Beethoven acquired a new piano—a larger, more resonant instrument with a full six-octave keyboard (F'–f''''); he used the entire range in the "Emperor" Concerto. In that work the piano is equal partner with the orchestra; in a few places the orchestra plays a lesser role.

Karl Czerny (1791–1857), who performed the Eb concerto in public in 1812, may have been the first to do so. Czerny, who had studied with Beethoven, was particularly known for his authentic interpretation of Beethoven's works. For several years Czerny gave all-Beethoven programs weekly in his own home. Czerny was an excellent piano teacher; among his numerous pupils were child prodigies and *virtuosi,* including Anna von Belleville Oury (1808–80), Sigismond Thalberg (1812–71), and Franz Liszt. As a teacher, Czerny's most important contribution, historically, was transmitting Beethoven's ideas, techniques, and interpretations to Liszt. As a composer, Czerny is best known for his pedagogical works—his thousands of exercises and études reflect the changes in the mechanics of the piano and in the techniques of piano playing that occurred during his lifetime. Most significant among Czerny's published pedagogical works are his *Complete Theoretical and Practical Pianoforte School,* Op. 500 (1839), and the little-known treatise *School of Extemporaneous Performance* (Vol. I, Op. 200; Vol. II, Op. 300), important because of its information on nineteenth-century performance practices and improvisation techniques.

In 1814–15 Beethoven sketched out in full score the major portion of a movement in D major for piano and orchestra but abandoned the work. His autograph manuscript is extant. Some persons refer to this as his unfinished Concerto No. 6. The movement is in modified sonata-concerto form, but the music is basically symphonic in character, with piano assigned an obbligato rather than a soloistic role.

LARGE VOCAL WORKS WITH ORCHESTRA

Twice in 1790, the Elector of Cologne commissioned Beethoven to write cantatas (see p. 403; 407). Neither cantata was performed. Yet, in those works Haydn saw sufficient evidence of outstanding talent to invite Beethoven to Vienna to study with him.

In 1803 Beethoven began to set Schikaneder's libretto *Vestas Feuer* (The Vestal Fire) but soon abandoned it. At that time, French operas were in vogue in Vienna, especially those by Cherubini and Méhul (see p. 431–32). Beethoven knew Cherubini's operas *Les deux journées* (The two days) and *Lodoïska,* and they were to some extent the models for his setting of Bouilly's *Léonore ou L'Amour conjugal* (Léonore, or Married Love). Beethoven's *Léonore* was first performed on 20 November 1805, a few days after Napoleon's armies entered Vienna. The opera was not well received. Both music and libretto underwent

considerable revision, and the opera was renamed *Fidelio.* During the revision, Beethoven wrote four overtures. All four survive, but only the last is known as the "Overture to *Fidelio*"; the others are, respectively, "*Léonore* Overture" No. 1, No. 2, and No. 3.

Fidelio is a typical rescue opera, with a blend of suspense, personal loyalty, and the triumph of good over evil. That blend is apparent in the dungeon scene in which Fidelio saves Florestan's life. Present in *Fidelio* are elements that foreshadow German romantic opera. The work is a Singspiel, with spoken dialogue. Beethoven effectively used **melodrama** to open the horror-filled scene in which Rocco and Fidelio dig the grave of Pizarro's intended murder victim, Florestan. (A melodrama is a stage piece without singing but with action and speaking that is accompanied by or alternates with orchestral music.) Throughout the opera, tensions are relieved by elements of comic opera.

Beethoven's interest in dramatic works was expressed in incidental music for plays: 10 pieces for Goethe's *Egmont* (1809–10), 9 for Kotzebue's *Die Ruinen von Athen* (1811), 10 for Kotzebue's *König Stephan* (1811), and 4 for Duncker's *Leonore Prohaska* (1815). Also, he composed another cantata, *Meeres-stille und glückliche Fahrt* (Calm sea and prosperous voyage; 1814).

The Mass in C, Op. 86 (SATB soloists, 4-vc. choir, orch.; 1807), was commissioned by Prince Nikolaus Esterházy II. Undoubtedly, Beethoven regarded the commission as an honor and a challenge, for he realized he was following in Haydn's footsteps.

When Archduke Rudolph was appointed Archbishop of Olmütz, Beethoven decided to compose a *Missa solemnis* for his installation. The Mass in D, Op. 123 (SATB soloists, 4-vc. choir, organ, orch.), resulted. Beethoven intended the Mass as a statement of his personal faith. Certainly, it is a universal statement as well. The composition reveals Beethoven's acquaintance with and knowledge of liturgical and theological traditions as well as musical ones. For example, in the Agnus Dei he made three (instead of two) complete presentations of *Agnus Dei, qui tollis peccata mundi, miserere nobis*—the triple literal acclamation used in the ninth and tenth centuries (see Chap. 4)—before the *dona nobis pacem.* The orchestral episodes in this movement are treated much as tropes to a chant.

(a)

Ky-   ri-   e

(b)

EXAMPLE 20.10 (*a*) A typical Kyrie *topos* (traditional formula); (*b*) Beethoven, *Missa solemnis*, beginning of Kyrie.

Besides writing music appropriate to the text, Beethoven filled that music with historical and liturgical symbolism. In the *Et incarnatus est,* he composed a quasi-chant melody in Dorian mode. *Mortuos* (death) was depicted by a rest or by "dead" chords (those lacking the third). There is text painting and musical depiction of the celebrant's actions (e.g., a rising vocal line used for a line of text during which the celebrant raised his arms). The Kyrie commences with the traditional Kyrie text formula (*topos*) used for a *Missa solemnis* (ex. 20.10). Omnipotence is expressed powerfully, with trombones. Beethoven interpreted the text according to the German *Bible,* wherein the Latin word *tuba* was translated *Posaune* (trombone; cf. Exod. 19:16). To express the extremes of the Last Judgment, Beethoven caused trombones to play in A♭ minor. In accord with tradition, he concluded the Gloria and Credo with fugues. Additional examples can be cited.

Beethoven considered the *Missa solemnis* his greatest composition. In scope, excellence, and sincere expression of faith, it is comparable to J. S. Bach's *Mass in B minor.* Beethoven's *Missa solemnis* is too long and too elaborate for liturgical use. Moreover, he took some liberties with the liturgical text (e.g., repetition of some phrases in the Gloria and Agnus Dei). Nevertheless, the *Missa solemnis* is a symphonic depiction, pictorial and symbolic, of everything that the Mass was and is intended to represent.

SUMMARY

The French Revolution and its aftermath had cultural as well as political consequences. Creative works centered around heroism; dramas and operas used rescue plots, and dramatic tension was heightened by crowd scenes. Music was affected also through government appropriation of manuscripts and valuable instruments for preservation in national archives, the establishment of the Paris Conservatoire, and the creation of a vast number of commemorative works for massed ensembles. At the time of the Revolution, several important European musicians, particularly pianists, deserted Paris for London where they found a rich concert life, a rising middle class eager to participate in music making, active publishing houses, and piano manufacturers working to produce instruments capable of greater volume of sound and increased dynamic flexibility and technical facility and with wider compass. The London school of pianist-composers included Cramer, Clementi, Dussek, Field, and Pinto. Cramer and Clementi wrote didactic works still used by many piano teachers. Field, who invented the *nocturne* for piano, greatly influenced Chopin's playing style and the compositions of Chopin, Liszt, and others. Beethoven knew Dussek's works and absorbed all that he had to offer; some striking parallels are present in their sonatas.

The leading Bohemian composers in Vienna were Tomášek, Voříšek, and Hummel. Tomášek and Voříšek pioneered in the composition of Romantic character pieces for piano. Schubert was influenced by Tomášek's *eclogues* and Voříšek's *impromptus;* Voříšek's vocal music reflects Schubert's influence. Pianistically, Hummel was Beethoven's chief rival in Vienna. Hummel's style was Mozartean, with emphasis on fluent technique and textural clarity. Beethoven produced a full tone and stressed technical power and dramatic execution; his music exhibited orchestral effects and a wide range of dynamics. Hummel linked the style of Mozart and Clementi with that of Schubert, Mendelssohn, and Chopin; Czerny transmitted Beethoven's playing style to Liszt.

As a young man, Beethoven became thoroughly familiar with the Viennese Classic style of music and mastered, then extended, that style. At the height of his career as pianist, hearing problems hampered him;

as deafness encroached, he gradually withdrew from social contacts until he became almost a recluse. In seeking release from personal problems, he grew more and more introspective and explored the depths of music's possibilities. In Beethoven's works, one finds a synthesis of Viennese, Parisian, and English musical styles. In its turn, Beethoven's music became the source of many features of nineteenth-century Romantic music. Beethoven's music bridges Classic and Romantic styles and is, at the same time, individualistic.

Customarily, Beethoven's music is divided into three main chronological style periods: (1) youthful works written at Bonn, 1782–1792, and early works composed in Vienna, 1793–c. 1802, when he mastered Classic style and began to experiment within the general outlines of traditional sonata structure; (2) works composed in Vienna, c. 1803–c. 1815, a period dominated by orchestral and "heroic" compositions; and (3) late works, composed c. 1815–1827, in which boundaries are blurred, counterpoint is prominent, and themes and motives are developed to their utmost, often through fugal and variation techniques.

Beethoven composed in all the genres of music current during his lifetime. The *Mass in D* is comparable to Bach's *Mass in B minor,* and the "Diabelli Variations" are on a par with Bach's "Goldberg Variations." Beethoven's piano sonatas, string quartets, and symphonies form the backbone of standard repertoire in their respective categories.

The piano sonata occupies a central position in Beethoven's work. In sonatas he introduced and experimented with new ideas, procedures, and interpretations that he incorporated in other works. Sonata No. 4, Op. 7, is his first real masterpiece in this genre; the three sonatas of Op. 10 are stylistically representative of his first Vienna period. The "Waldstein" and "Appassionata" sonatas exhibit the greater freedom of form, more audacious choice of keys, and more remote modulations typical of his second Viennese style period. Sonatas Nos. 30–32 display characteristics of his last style period.

Beethoven's last five violin/piano sonatas are true duos. His Violin Concerto is one of the finest ever written; Piano Concertos Nos. 4 and 5 and the "Ghost" and "Archduke" Trios are frequently performed.

In Beethoven's early string quartets, experimentation is mingled with Classic tradition. The "Razumovsky" quartets are representative of his mature style of quartet writing; in them, he was more daring with regard to tonal relationships and formal structure, blurring and disguising sectional divisions within movements, and sometimes linking movements. The late quartets Opp. 132, 130, 133, and 131 form a cycle with melodic, motivic, and tonal relationships. The C♯-minor quartet, Op. 131, fully exhibits characteristics of his late style.

Beethoven's symphonies attest his mastery of Classic style and forms. They show the development of his individualistic style as composer of symphonic works—his innovative treatment of harmonies, tonalities, thematic material, and forms—and, in his last symphony, the introspective character of his last works. At the heart of the development of Beethoven's style is his view of the structure of a single movement as sonata *principle* rather than sonata *form.* His orchestral writing reveals his knowledge of improvements made to individual instruments and advancements in performing techniques. *Fidelio* and *Sinfonia Eroica* are typical of the "heroic" works Beethoven composed in the years following his Heiligenstadt decision. The *Eroica* is one of his most important works. Its length, formal structure, and general programmatic character and Beethoven's choice of thematic material and his developmental procedures (which include thematic transformation, fugue, and variation) make it a landmark in symphonic literature. Symphony No. 5 marks the first use of trombones in a symphony. It is a cyclic work of large proportions, with long developments and developmental codas. The *Pastoral* Symphony was a springboard for composition of numerous programmatic symphonies. Symphony No. 9, though not the first symphony to include voices, was unique in having a cantata with its finale.

Beethoven's compositions have affected all music since his time. Throughout the nineteenth century, his sonatas, symphonies, string quartets, violin concerto, and last piano concerto were viewed as standards for achievement and provided models to be emulated.

EARLY NINETEENTH-CENTURY MUSIC

*R*evolution did not bring peace or freedom to the French people. By a *coup d'état* in 1799 Napoleon Buonaparte seized the reins of the government. In his hands, the Republic became first the Consulate (1799–1804), then an empire. Through military conquests and puppet rulerships, Napoleon expanded his empire, extending his control over the Low Countries, western Germanic lands, a large part of Italy, and into Iberia. Thus, he upset—almost destroyed—the European "balance of power." Not only did his armies ravage the land, but in his desire for personal and national aggrandizement he looted the conquered territories, transported their art treasures to France, and established museums to house them. Napoleon's downfall came at the hands of Britain, Austria, Prussia, and Russia. After suffering military defeat, he abdicated in April 1814 and was exiled to Elba. Yet, *in absentia,* he assembled an army of 1500 and on 1 March 1815 returned to France, regained control of the government, and held power for a hundred days before being defeated at the Battle of Waterloo and being banished to St. Helena in the Atlantic.

The Congress of Vienna (1814–15) redesigned the map of Europe (fig. 21.1) and restored the European balance of power. Control of the French government was restored to the former royal dynasty and entrusted to Louis XVIII (r. 1814–24). The French government was required to pay a large indemnity and return the art treasures to their rightful owners.

Austria was ruled by Francis I (r. 1792–1835), with the aid of his powerful adviser, Prince Metternich (1773–1859). The prince's tenure as Austria's chancellor of state (1809–48) is known as "The Age of Metternich." In eastern Europe, and in parts of central Europe, the aristocratic political and social order still functioned.

In the New World, the idea of colonies acquiring independence, as the United States had done, spread to Latin and South America, and one by one Spanish and Portuguese colonies became small autonomous countries. The boundaries of the United States were extended westward through Jefferson's purchase of the vast Louisiana Territory from France in 1803, and by the time the French and Indian War ended (1815) Britain had secured control of Canada.

During the first quarter of the nineteenth century, the arts prospered in France. Napoleon commissioned many works, established competitions, and awarded prizes for various forms of art. Painting, sculpture, architecture, the manufacture of porcelain and glassware, figurines, tapestries, and needlepoint flourished. Several Arcs de Triomphe

EUROPE
IN 1815

FIGURE 21.1 Europe in 1815. The heavy boundary line marks the boundary of the German Confederation.

were erected. The Temple of Glory that Napoleon commissioned, which was completed after his downfall, became La Madeleine, a church. One of Napoleon's favorite artists was Jacques Louis David (1743–1825), painter of "Buonaparte Crossing the Alps." Napoleon and Josephine enjoyed music—concerts were given at the palace, in the Tuileries Gardens, and in Josephine's apartments—but Napoleon preferred the theater and opera and exercised considerable control over their subject matter and production. His code of regulations for the theater, drawn up in October 1812, is still in effect.

The age was colored by romanticism, with its subjectivity, its emphasis on the expression of personal feelings and emotions, and its interest in nature and in the spiritual and supernatural (both religious and demonic). These traits found expression in the novels of Sir Walter Scott, in the poetry of Wordsworth, Keats, Shelley, and Byron; in Goethe's *Faust;* and in many pieces of art. Women gained recognition as authors, though some published under male names— Mme de Staël, Aurore Dudevant (George Sand), and Mary Ann Evans (George Eliot). Anne-Louis Girodet's (1767–1824) painting *The Burial of Atala* (plate 21), based on Chateaubriand's novel *Atala,* simultaneously presents passionate love, death and burial, and pure religion. *Los Caprichos* (Caprices), a series of etchings and aquatints by Francesco Goya (1746–1828), is a commentary on various topics, including witchcraft, demons, fantasy, and social conditions. Goya's war

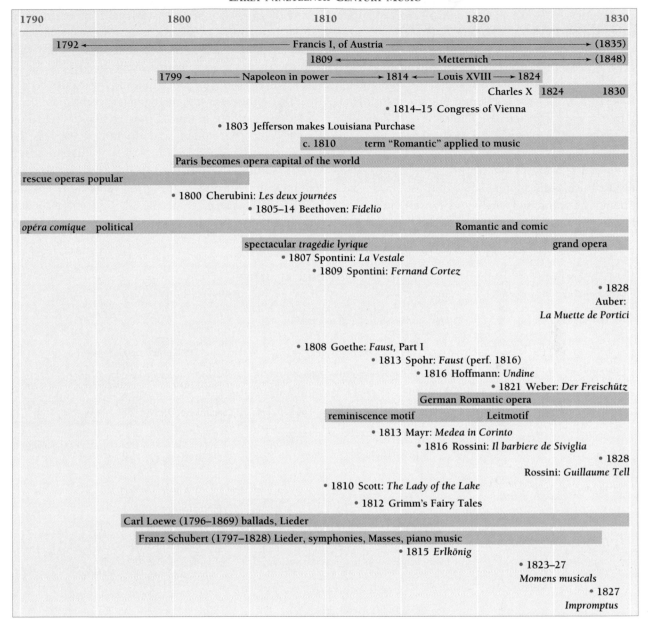

1790	1800	1810	1820	1830

1792 ◄──────────── Francis I, of Austria ──────────── ► (1835)

1809 ◄──────────── Metternich ──────────── ► (1848)

1799 ◄──────── Napoleon in power ──────── ► 1814 ◄──── Louis XVIII ──── ► 1824

Charles X 1824 1830

• 1814–15 Congress of Vienna

• 1803 Jefferson makes Louisiana Purchase

c. 1810 term "Romantic" applied to music

Paris becomes opera capital of the world

rescue operas popular

• 1800 Cherubini: *Les deux journées*

• 1805–14 Beethoven: *Fidelio*

opéra comique political Romantic and comic

spectacular *tragédie lyrique* grand opera

• 1807 Spontini: *La Vestale*

• 1809 Spontini: *Fernand Cortez*

• 1828
Auber:
La Muette de Portici

• 1808 Goethe: *Faust*, Part I

• 1813 Spohr: *Faust* (perf. 1816)

• 1816 Hoffmann: *Undine*

• 1821 Weber: *Der Freischütz*

German Romantic opera

reminiscence motif Leitmotif

• 1813 Mayr: *Medea in Corinto*

• 1816 Rossini: *Il barbiere de Siviglia*

• 1828
Rossini: *Guillaume Tell*

• 1810 Scott: *The Lady of the Lake*

• 1812 Grimm's Fairy Tales

Carl Loewe (1796–1869) ballads, Lieder

Franz Schubert (1797–1828) Lieder, symphonies, Masses, piano music

• 1815 *Erlkönig*

• 1823–27
Momens musicals

• 1827
Impromptus

paintings, particularly *The Third of May, 1808* (plate 22), depict the horror and brutality of Napoleon's invasion of Spain. Landscapes painted by England's John Constable (1776–1837) won gold medals when exhibited in France, and J. M. W. Turner's (1775–1851) treatment of light in his watercolors foreshadowed the work of French impressionists late in the century.

ROMANTIC MUSIC

The words "romance" and "romantic" stem from *lingua roman* (lit., Roman tongue)—the "Low" Latin tongue and the vernacular languages derived from it—and are related to the French noun *le roman* (romance, novel, or story), a long narrative poem written in the vernacular (e.g., the fourteenth-century *Le roman de la rose* and *Le roman de Fauvel* [see p. 109). The term "Romanticism" (German, *Romantik*) began to appear in essays on music c. 1810 and seems to have been used first in connection with Beethoven's music. However, nineteenth-century Romanticism in music had its roots deep in eighteenth-century Classicism—it was not a break with Classicism but an extension, alteration, and expansion of it. Romantic traits are visible in some of C. P. E. Bach's *Sturm und Drang* pieces, in some of Haydn's symphonies written c. 1768–74, and in several of Mozart's late works. Some musicologists debate the classification of some of those Haydn symphonies as *Sturm und Drang* and consider them early manifestations of Romanticism.

A basic characteristic of Romantic music is its boundlessness, its seeming disregard for or freedom from limitations. In an article in *Allgemeine musikalische Zeitung* in 1813, E. T. A. Hoffmann stated that music "is the most romantic of all the arts . . . for its sole subject is the infinite." Indeed, music does border on the infinite, for it is intangible, invisible, and fleeting, existing only in time. Often, composers relied on tone colors, harmonies, and rhythms to express the feelings and deeper meanings that words could not relate sufficiently. In the nineteenth century, there was a great outpouring of **program music**—referential music and instrumental music (and, occasionally, vocalized tones without words) that described, char-

TABLE 21.1 ROMANTIC DUALITIES		
CONTRADICTION: RELATIONSHIP BETWEEN	SOLUTION OR TREATMENT	REPRESENTATIVE EXAMPLES
Words and Music	Equal partnership of text and musical setting:	
	a. in Lied	Schubert: *Erlkönig* *Gretchen am Spinnrade* Schumann: *Der Nussbaum*
	b. in Opera and Music Drama	Wagner: *Tristan und Isolde* *Der Ring des Nibelungen*
	Composers as Authors:	
	a. of essays about music	Schumann: *Davidsbündlerblätter* *An Opus Two; New Paths* Weber: *Notices* (re: operas produced) Wagner: *Bayreuther Blätter* (re: his stage works)
	b. of poetry, libretti for setting	Wagner: stage works: *Tristan und Isolde; Die Meistersinger; Der Ring des Nibelungen;* others
	c. of stories, novels	Hoffmann: *Fantasiestücke* Weber: *Tonkunstlers Leben*
	Inclusion of vocal music in instrumental forms	Beethoven: *Symphony No. 9* ("Choral") Loewe: *Piano Sonata in E major* Liszt: *Eine Faust-Symphonie*
	Instrumental works based on vocal music	Schubert: Quintet, *Die Forelle* Quartet, *Der Tod und das Mädchen* *Wandererfantasie* for piano
	Program music (referential music)	Beethoven: *Symphony No. 6* ("Pastoral") Berlioz: *Symphonie fantastique* Liszt: *Les Préludes;* symphonic poems Loewe: *Mazeppa,* tone poem for piano
Composer and Audience	Composer writing for:	
	a. specific performer(s) both commissioned and noncommissioned	Schubert: for Vogl; duets for Esterházy pupils; for Slavík and von Bocklet
	b. performance before circle of friends	Schubert: for *Schubertiaden* (Vienna) Rossini: for *Samedi soirées* (Paris)
	c. unknown performers, unknown future audiences	Beethoven: Quartets, Op. 59; other works
	d. personal expression without regard for audience	Beethoven: Quartets, Op. 59; other works

acterized, presented, interpreted, or was inspired by a nonmusical subject or idea that the composer indicated by title, explanatory remarks, or prefatory material. An early nineteenth-century example is Beethoven's *Pastoral Symphony,* which he stated was an expression of *feelings* rather than a musical description of pastoral scenes and events.

Another feature of Romantic music is the presence of a blend of opposites within a work—contradictory factors woven into the musical fabric so skillfully that they appear as intriguing dualities rather than harsh contrasts or clashes of principle. These are detailed, with representative examples, in table 21.1.

Many of the traits that characterize Romantic art are manifest in Romantic music—subjectivity, the expression of personal feelings, sentimentality, a preoccupation with nature (especially in its wild state), an interest in the world of magic and fairy tale, an intrigue with all aspects of the supernatural (sacred, eerie, and demonic), and a desire for freedom from the limitations of conventional formal patterns and harmonic rules. The emphasis placed on individual characteristics varied from region to region, but the basic traits remained fairly constant. Underlying Romantic music was the desire to be original and forge into the future unrestrained by limitations of the past,

TABLE 21.1 **ROMANTIC DUALITIES,** *continued*		
CONTRADICTION: RELATIONSHIP BETWEEN	**SOLUTION OR TREATMENT**	**REPRESENTATIVE EXAMPLES**
Individual and Crowd (Masses)	Virtuoso composer-performer(s) with or without orchestra, accompaniment	Paganini, Liszt, Chopin, Weber, others
	Single performer in solo recital	Clara Schumann, Franz Liszt
	Conductor directing with baton, and standing between audience and performers	Spohr, Weber
	Composer(s) not recognized performer(s)	Wagner, Auber
Professional and Amateur	Composer showing concern for amateur music making in home, community, in addition to writing works for own use.	Schubert: works for family quartet, neighborhood orchestra, and brother's school groups
		Liszt: transcriptions of symphonies, stage works, etc. for piano
Religious (godly) and Irreligious (demonic) aspects of the Supernatural	Combining both aspects in the same work, juxtaposed or used separately	Berlioz: *Symphonie fantastique*
Sacred and Secular	Inclusion of liturgical texts in secular works	Liszt: *Dante Symphony*
		Mahler: *Symphony No. 8*
	Settings of liturgical texts not suitable for church Service:	
	a. too large, or with repetitive phrases	Beethoven: *Missa solemnis*
	b. intended for memorial to war dead or personal friends	Berlioz: *Grande Messe des morts* *Te Deum laudamus*
		Verdi: *Requiem Mass* (for Manzoni)
	c. text set is not standard one	Brahms: *Ein deutsches Requiem*
Urban and Rural	Composers living and working in urban centers, writing for urban audiences, preoccupied with Nature, especially in its "wild" state, and composing program music of landscapes, seascapes, etc.	Beethoven: *Symphony No. 6* ("Pastoral")
		Mendelssohn: *Hebrides Overture* ("Fingal's Cave")
		Schumann: *Symphony No. 1* ("Spring")
	The wilderness of Nature depicted in opera scenes, settings	Weber: *Der Freischütz*
National and Cosmopolitan or International	Inclusion of folk song and folk dance elements, of own and of other countries	Chopin: mazurkas, polonaises
		Beethoven: Quartets, Op. 59 (Russian)
	Expression of patriotism, national sentiment	France: Commemorative works Opéras comiques
	Interest in Eastern exoticism	*à la Turk* and *Janissary* movements; new orchestral colors; new harmonies

a yearning for expansion, and experimentation in the production of new harmonies and tone colors that resulted in the improvement of standard instruments and the invention of new ones.

The humanitarian emphasis on individual worth and the Enlightenment ideals of the "brotherhood of man" brought a new awareness of the individual, and in the search for individual identity there came not only a desire for originality and personal expression but also a search for one's roots. The value placed on one's personal and national ancestry was balanced by musicians' and artists' high regard for their artistic heritage. This led to increased interest in folk song and a search for, study of, and performance of works of great composers of the past, especially J. S. Bach, Handel, and Palestrina. At times, those works were seen through Romantic eyes, as in the piano accompaniments that Schumann and Mendelssohn provided for Bach's *Six Solos for Unaccompanied Violin,* works that are complete as Bach wrote them. Performances of masterpieces by Bach and Palestrina led to publication of their "Complete Works" later in the century, and the search for and location of those works brought into existence the science of historical musicology.

MUSIC IN FRANCE

In France during the first half of the nineteenth century musical interest centered on opera, and Paris became the opera capital of the world. Early in the century the focus was on *opéra comique.* It spread throughout Austro-Germanic lands, became popular, and dominated opera repertoire there. Italian opera composers were attracted to Paris and stayed to write French operas.

OPÉRA COMIQUE

During the Revolutionary period, the light, sentimental, mildly satirical kind of opéra comique was considerably overshadowed by a type that dealt seriously with political and social issues and aimed to edify rather than entertain. Spoken dialogue and melodrama were retained, comic elements were minimized, and plots included common folk (e.g., fishermen, peasants, or tradesmen) in key roles. Rescue operas were plentiful, many of them incorporating horror, violence, and highly spectacular scenes of natural catastrophes—fires, storms, earthquakes, or volcanic eruptions. A number of early opéras comiques were merely revolutionary propaganda and have little artistic value, but later works, by composers such as Cherubini and Méhul, have artistic merit.

For about a decade, serious all-sung opera was pushed far into the background by the successes of opéra comique. The main reasons for this were as follows: (1) The various governments encouraged the composition of works with themes that could stir up patriotism, and they viewed opéra comique as an appropriate vehicle for this. (2) In 1801 the two rival theaters in Paris failed. The surviving participants formed a single company, which opened a theater in 1802. Gradually, the public wearied of weighty subjects in opéra comique, and lighter types again came into vogue. Some are comic; others have Romantic plots. The music consists of simple, melodious **ariettes** (vocal solos, or airs) with light-textured orchestral accompaniment, ensembles, and usually some dance pieces. Among the most important opéra comiques of this type in the 1820s and early 1830s were Boieldieu's *La Dame blanche* (The white lady; 1825), Auber's *Fra Diavolo* (Brother devil; 1830), and Hérold's *Zampa* (1831) and *Le Pré aux clercs* (The field of honor; 1833).

French interest was attracted by Italian comic opera when Rossini's *L' Italiana in Algieri* (The Italian woman in Algiers; Venice, 1813) was performed in Paris early in 1817. Rossini (see p. 448) came to Paris late in 1824 as director of Théâtre-Italien and remained there five years. When he had command of the French language, he composed French operas for L'Opéra. His influence on French opera was all-pervasive.

LUIGI CHERUBINI Cherubini (1760–1842), a native of Florence, Italy, began his career as a composer of church music. Then he turned to opera. After successes in Italy and in London, he moved to Paris. For half a century, he was a dominating figure in French musical life. He made major contributions to opera, church music, and music education. From 1793 to 1842 he served the French government as an educator. In 1793, he was appointed Inspector of Instruction and also taught at the newly formed Institut National de Musique. When the Institut became the Paris Conservatoire, Cherubini was named one of its five inspectors, the others being Gossec, Grétry, Le Sueur, and Méhul. Cherubini worked with other faculty members to draw up acceptable curricula in harmony, *solfege,* and counterpoint. He published several pedagogical writings, including a textbook on counterpoint and fugue (1835).

In Paris, Cherubini achieved success with his operas. Several of them were excellent: *Lodoïska* (1791), *Médée* (1797), and *Les deux journées, ou Le porteur d'eau* (The two days, or The water carrier; 1800). *Les deux journées,* performed throughout Europe, was translated into German as *Der Wasserträger.* Never again did Cherubini achieve the measure of success with opera that *Les deux journées* brought him, though he composed operas until 1833. After 1803 his popularity declined for various reasons: poor libretti; a change in Parisian taste to favor the lighter, tuneful type of opéra comique written by Boieldieu; Napoleon's dislike of Cherubini's works; and the emergence of spectacular grand opera composed by Spontini and favored by Napoleon. Cherubini's importance in the history of opera lies in his expansion of opéra comique movements, his use of the genre to deal seriously with dramatic situations and contemporary issues, and his enriched orchestration. He was especially concerned with convincing dramatic portrayal, expressive recitative, and effective writing for ensembles.

Lodoïska, a *comédie heroique* (heroic comedy), is a rescue opera: Lodoïska, imprisoned in a castle, is rescued by her beloved, Floreski. Spoken dialogue is used; there are some comic scenes and some revolutionary music with triadic melodies and simple harmonies. Cherubini's operas and Masses were greatly admired by Beethoven, who had at hand copies of *Lodoïska* and *Les deux journées* when he composed *Fidelio.* Floreski and Lodoïska may have been Beethoven's models for the characters Florestan and Leonore in *Fidelio.*

Médée is concerned with psychological conflict. Through vocal tessitura, fluctuations of tempo, sudden extreme dynamic contrasts, unexpected pauses and interruptions of the melodic line, new orchestral colors, and other devices, Cherubini portrayed Medea's mental anguish and inner conflict.

Les deux journées deals with social injustice and its rectification: a Savoyard family of water carriers rescues unjustly persecuted aristocrats; the prisoner escapes hidden in a water cart. Spoken dialogue is used, and the melodrama in the last two acts is superb. Ensemble singing predominates (e.g., a chorus of soldiers [Act II] and a bridal chorus [Act III]). The only solos occur at the beginning of the opera; they contain motives that recur throughout the work.

After 1816 most of Cherubini's compositions were church music: seven Masses, two Requiem Masses, numerous motets, and many short sacred pieces. His best Masses are the Requiems; their *Dies irae* sections are among the finest ever composed. The C-minor Requiem (1816; SATB chor., orch.) was commissioned by the French government to commemorate the anniversary of the execution of Louis XVI. Cherubini created a setting sufficiently universal to honor any great person. Though the work won immediate acclaim and has continued to be regarded highly, it was not universally accepted in the nineteenth century. When the Archbishop of Paris objected to its performance at Boieldieu's funeral because women's voices were included, Cherubini determined to write a Requiem Mass that could not be barred from his own funeral for the same reason. He scored his D-minor Requiem Mass (1836) for TTB chorus and orchestra but wrote the first tenor part quite high. High tenor voices were fairly common in France. Cherubini's use of them had several advantages, including greater freedom in chord spacing and the tone color of the high tessitura in the male voice. Most tenors were trained to carry their voices into falsetto register with ease when a lyrical passage required them to do so.

ÉTIENNE-NICOLAS MÉHUL   Méhul (1763–1817) was educated at a Franciscan convent and probably was intended for priesthood. Reportedly, his chronic ill health prevented that. After publishing two volumes of keyboard sonatas (1783, 1788), he chose a career in composition. In 1793 he joined the faculty of the Institut National de Musique (later, Paris Conservatoire).

Méhul wrote numerous revolutionary and commemorative patriotic pieces. His symphonies, five of which survive, reveal his awareness of orchestral color and his experiments with timbres. Frequently, he wrote 'cello parts in the tenor register, subdivided the string sections, and required horns to play stopped notes, even at rapid tempos. Méhul was the most important French symphonist between Gossec and Berlioz.

Méhul's 40 stage works include operas, opéras comiques, and 4 ballets that were produced at L'Opéra. In his operas, he made considerable use of recurrent motives (e.g., the "motto theme" of guiding Love in *Mélidore et Phrosine* [1794]). His most important opéra comique is *Joseph* (1807). He treated the biblical story simply and used various types of music, including old hymns, dramatic ensembles, and simple tunes with uncomplicated harmonies. Méhul was concerned that the music for each stage work create an atmosphere appropriate to the setting of the plot. Some of his works require large performing resources; crowd scenes became a prominent feature of French operas. His overtures are especially noteworthy for their incorporation of musical materials that occur in the opera and for tone painting. German Romantic opera composers were influenced by Méhul's opéra comiques, especially in orchestral scoring and the use of recurrent or **"reminiscence"** motives. Weber's operas reflect his knowledge of Méhul's works.

ALL-SUNG OPERA

Between the Revolution and the 1820s there were very few great successes at L'Opéra. Under the Empire, Napoleon wanted productions at L'Opéra to portray the grandeur of France and to do so with Classic decorum but with spectacle that glorified him. He could control productions because he reinstituted the system of Privilège, which the revolutionary government had abolished in 1790. Under that system, which was begun in 1507, publishers and theaters were required to obtain a Royal Privilège (License) to print or perform a work. In 1797 the government imposed a tax on published music and required music publishers to have their publications stamped on payment of the fees. That law remained in effect until c. 1841.

Two of the earliest spectacular operas were *La Vestale* (The Vestal virgin; 1807) and *Fernand Cortez* (1809), both by Gaspare Spontini (1774–1851). They were significant forerunners of the monumental operas produced at L'Opéra in the second quarter of the century. Then, the term **grand opera** was used to refer specifically to the most monumental, spectacular operas produced at L'Opéra. The earliest successful

grand opera was Auber's *La muette de Portici* (The mute girl of Portici; 1828). Another was Rossini's *Guillaume Tell* (William Tell; 1829).

GASPARE SPONTINI   Spontini's first great success in Paris came in 1807 with *La Vestale,* which requires enormous performing resources for the pageantry of processions and ceremonies—there are massed choruses and long instrumental pieces. Dialogue is in recitative; arias are filled with Italianate lyricism, but the harmonies basically move between tonic and dominant. Doubtless, Spontini's ability to combine elements of French *tragédie lyrique* with Italian lyricism accounted for *La Vestale*'s success.

Napoleon may have suggested the subject for Spontini's next opera, *Fernand Cortez,* because of its political implications—the emperor saw in Cortez's conquest of Mexico a parallel with his own invasion of Spain. Spontini revised the opera in 1817; the new version entered standard repertoire at L'Opéra. Spontini composed only three more works for L'Opéra. The last of them, *Olimpie* (Olympia; 1819), a tragédie lyrique laden with spectacle, contains some of his finest music.

In the history of French opera, Spontini occupies a transitional position. His tragédies lyriques are a continuation of the traditional form of French opera with large choruses and huge spectacles; thus, he adds a vital link to the chain formed by Lully, Rameau, and Gluck—a link between Gluck and Hector Berlioz (see p. 486). At the same time, *La Vestale* and *Fernand Cortez* are important forerunners of grand opera, the spectacular works performed at L'Opéra during the period of its greatest magnificence.

DANIEL-FRANÇOIS-ESPRIT AUBER   Auber (2–1871), a pianist, did not decide on a career in music until 1803. In 1805 one of his short comedies attracted the attention of Cherubini, who accepted him as a pupil. Auber's most significant compositions are his operas, most of which set libretti by Eugène Scribe (1791–1861). Auber's first operas were failures, and, disheartened, he wrote no music for almost five years. For a time, in 1823, he imitated Rossini's vocal style; in 1824, he sought a purely French style. Then, wisely, he began combining the two, eventually achieving a synthesis and mingling humorous—sometimes mordant wit—and Romantic elements, as he did in *Fra Diavolo*.

In 1828 Auber and Scribe were commissioned to write a "*grand opéra*" for L'Opéra. *La muette de Portici* resulted. Based on the Neapolitan insurrection of 1647, the opera contains spectacular crowd scenes and colorful ballets. When performed in Brussels in 1830, *La muette de Portici* was instrumental in inciting the Belgians to revolt against the Dutch. Though Auber and Scribe collaborated on grand operas until 1851 and opéras comiques until 1861, in quality they never surpassed *La muette de Portici*. After 1840, Auber's style changed, and he wrote a more lyrical, more serious type of opéra comique, of which *Manon Lescaut* (1856) is the best example.

GRAND OPERA

The new style of opera—grand opera—was firmly established as a result of the joint endeavors of librettist Eugène Scribe, composer Giacomo Meyerbeer, and Louis Véron (see also p. 478). Standards for grand opera were set by several masterpieces—*Robert le diable* (Robert the devil; 1831) and *Les Huguenots* (The Huguenots; 1836) by Meyerbeer (1791–1864), *Gustave III* (1833) by Auber, and *La Juive* (The Jewess; 1835) by Jacques Halévy (1799–1862)—all on libretti by Scribe.

Scribe was primarily responsible for developing the grand opera libretto. Usually, his plots have historical settings that provide ample opportunity for crowd scenes and spectacle, including ballet. Central to the drama are passionate human relationships and the effect on them of conflicting forces—human, natural, or supernatural—over which the characters have no control. Often, that conflict had contemporary relevance. In writing a libretto, Scribe paid careful attention to the dramatic framework, delineated characters whose personalities and fortunes permitted effective musical contrasts, and adeptly created sequences of scenes that work up to a grand finale.

Meantime, important changes had occurred at L'Opéra. Coal gas lighting, first used in London in 1817, was safe and controllable. In 1822 it was used for the first time at L'Opéra to light the stage for *Aladin* (Aladdin), by Nicolas Isouard (1775–1818) and Angelo Benincori (1779–1821). For that production, scene designer Pierre Cicéri (1782–1868) and painter Louis Daguerre (1787–1851) created realistic sets in which they applied new techniques being used in popular Parisian theaters. In 1822, as a private enterprise, Cicéri founded a workshop that manufactured and sold reproductions of sets used at L'Opéra. Through shops of this kind, some of which sold costumes and properties also, a fairly uniform international style of opera staging was gradually established.

MUSIC IN AUSTRO-GERMANIC LANDS

In Austro-Germanic lands, the most significant contributions made during the first three decades of the nineteenth century were in the areas of solo song (*Lied*) and opera. The general tenor of musical and literary works created in France at the time of the Revolution struck a responsive note among authors and composers in Germanic lands, where the various political states had no overall unity as a nation. Authors, in their search for a national consciousness, used as subject matter folklore and legends as well as political themes and actual incidents; composers converted those poems into ballads and Lieder and those stories, dramas, and fairy tales into Singspiele and operas. In the nineteenth century, literary nationalism extended to historical novels and dramas with common folk as major characters.

The philosopher Johann Herder (1744–1803) considered music basic to all culture and education. He was interested in folk song and folk poetry and, in 1778–79, published two collections of *Volkslieder* (folk songs)—in fact, he coined the term **Volkslied.** Germany had no native opera tradition; Italian opera had flourished at German and Austrian courts, and in the late eighteenth century French opera was gaining a strong foothold. Joseph II's endeavor to establish a German opera company at the imperial court theater in 1777 was unsuccessful. Herder advocated a German national opera based on traditional materials. In one of his essays on music, he expressed his idea of opera becoming a unified theatrical work in which all of the arts merged—a kind of *Gesamtkunstwerk* (complete, collective artwork).

Among the leading Romantic poets was Clemens Brentano (1778–1842), whose importance to music is primarily as coeditor, with Joachim von Arnim (1781–1831), of the collection of folk poetry entitled *Des Knaben Wunderhorn* (The boy's magic horn; 1805–8).

Poems from that collection inspired settings by many composers. The most significant collection of fairy tales was *Kinder- und Hausmärchen* (Children's and family fairy tales, 2 vols.; 1812–15; known as "Grimm's Fairy Tales"), by Jakob (1785–1863) and Wilhelm (1786–1859) Grimm.

German nationalism found a place in opera gradually, as elements of magic and the supernatural were transferred to Singspiel and it became infused with Romantic components. One of the earliest of the "magic" Singspiele was Mozart's *Die Zauberflöte* (1791). Operas by Parisian composers were popular in Austro-Germanic lands early in the nineteenth century, and German composers incorporated some features of French rescue operas and opéras comiques in their works. Two German operas—E. T. A. Hoffmann's *Undine* (perf. Berlin, August 1816) and Ludwig Spohr's *Faust* (comp. 1813; perf. Prague, September 1816)—prepared the way for Carl Maria von Weber, who firmly established German Romantic opera in Singspiel with *Der Freischütz* (The free marksman; 1821) and in opera seria with *Euryanthe* (1823). Gradually, recitative supplanted spoken dialogue; melodrama was retained for special effects.

German Romantic opera was relatively short-lived; the last important one was Wagner's *Lohengrin* (perf. 1850). The significance of the genre lies not merely in its expression of German nationalism but also in the striving of German composers, especially Weber, to effect a synthesis of the various related arts collaborating in the production of an opera and thereby create a *Gesamtkunstwerk*. This prepared the way for Wagner, whose *Der Ring des Nibelungen* (The Nibelung's Ring) is the ultimate *Gesamtkunstwerk* and contains elements of German Romantic opera.

In its definitive form, German Romantic opera is characterized by (1) plots based on German legend, fairy tale, myth, or medieval history; (2) scenes of country life and nature in its wild state; (3) a cast of characters that includes supernatural beings, nobility, and common folk—the naive and pure, the evil, and the supernaturally possessed; (4) elements of magic and the supernatural treated as powerful forces capable of threatening, influencing, directing, or dominating the lives of humans; (5) the ultimate triumph of good over evil, as salvation or redemption, or even "rescue"; and (6) use of simple, folklike, Germanic melodies, with harmonies and orchestral timbres appropriate to the dramatic situation.

LUDWIG SPOHR

Spohr (1784–1859) was the most significant German minor composer in the first half of the nineteenth century. A virtuoso violinist, he concertized throughout Europe, at first singly, and in 1806–22 with his wife, harpist Dorette Scheidler (1787–1834). Spohr attracted violin pupils from all over Europe. In addition to contributing a vast amount of literature to violin and harp repertoire, he made a major contribution to violin playing when, c. 1820, he invented the "violin-holder" (i.e., the chin rest), which has become a standard addition to the instrument. Spohr's placement of the device directly over the tailpiece, in the middle of the base of the instrument (fig. 21.2), indicates the manner in which the violin was held then. Spohr was one of the earliest to conduct with a baton instead of using a roll of paper or a violin bow.

Spohr composed 13 operas, 10 symphonies, some concert overtures and other orchestral pieces, 4 clarinet concertos of mediocre quality, 34 string quartets, 4 double string quartets, about 2 dozen other pieces of chamber music of various kinds, more than 90 solo songs, some part songs, a Mass, at least 5 oratorios, and numerous other sacred and secular choral works. His finest oratorio is *Der Fall Babylons* (The fall of Babylon; 1840).

Spohr's first successful opera was *Faust*. An important feature of it is the systematic use of "reminiscence

FIGURE 21.2 Spohr's "violin-holder," now called a chin rest, was attached to the violin by the instrument's tailpin and extended over the tailpiece.

motives" and "harmonies of the then and now"—an associative system of melodies and harmonies woven into the fabric of the entire opera. In *Faust*, these motives and harmonies function as psychic symbols. Reminiscence motives are used to a greater extent in *Zemire und Azor* (1819), a two-act fairy-tale opera whose plot centers on redemption.

Much of Spohr's music is Classic in form, but his compositions reflect his knowledge of works by Méhul, Spontini, and Cherubini. The stylistic developments Spohr effected in his operas were of far-reaching significance and foreshadow Wagner's work in several respects: the associative use of recurrent themes, later called *Leitmotifs*; the writing of through-composed rather than number opera; and the choice of harmonies and orchestral timbres to create atmosphere.

E. T. A. HOFFMANN

Ernst Theodor Amadeus Hoffmann (1776–1822) originally enjoyed a career as lawyer and judge. He had received music training, and in 1804 he abandoned the legal profession for a career in music. From 1809 to 1815, he wrote essays on music and reviews of performances for *Allgemeine musikalische Zeitung*. Also, he authored *Fantasiestücke* (Fantastic tales; 1814–15) inspired by music. Wandering through many of those stories is the eccentric Kapellmeister Johannes Kreisler, a Romantic musician figment of Hoffmann's imagination. Many of Hoffmann's tales inspired music, for example, Tchaikovsky's ballet *The Nutcracker*, Schumann's *Kreisleriana*, and Offenbach's *Les Contes d'Hoffmann* (The Tales of Hoffmann). Hoffmann's most important contribution was probably literary—providing plots and referential material for other composers' works. However, he did compose. His most significant composition is *Undine*, a Romantic number opera based on a German fairy tale. Scenes of medieval splendor contrast with scenes of wild, unspoiled nature; there are choruses of earth and water spirits. Weber attended some performances of *Undine* in Berlin.

CARL MARIA VON WEBER

Weber (1786–1826), one of the leading German composers of his time, also effected much-needed reforms in the theater. From early childhood, he was at home in the theatrical world in which his parents worked.

Not until he was 9 years old did he have competent instruction in music. His best instruction came from Michael Haydn, under whose guidance Weber composed six fughettas for piano (pub. 1798). In Munich, Weber wrote a Mass (rev. 1802; pub. 1926) and his first opera, *Die Macht der Liebe und des Weins* (The power of love and of wine; 1800; lost). In Freiberg, he wrote the opera *Das Waldmädchen* (The forest maiden; perf. 1800; fragments extant), and in Salzburg he composed *Peter Schmoll und seine Nachbarn* (Peter Schmoll and his neighbors; 1801–2; perf. 1803; dialogue lost). Meantime, he had written a few songs, some choral canons, and several short piano pieces. Next Weber moved to Vienna, where he studied with Abt Vogler (1749–1814). On Vogler's recommendation, 17-year-old Weber was appointed Kapellmeister at Breslau.

In 1806–7 Weber worked at Carlsruhe, where he composed two C-major symphonies, some variations, and the Horn Concertino (rev. 1815). He next was employed at Stuttgart as secretary to the Duke of Württemberg. There he wrote six piano duets for teaching purposes, a dozen songs, a cantata, incidental music for a play, and the Romantic opera *Silvana* (1808–10). By then Weber had become a virtuoso pianist. For his own use he composed a set of variations on an original theme, *Momento capriccioso, Grande polonaise,* and the Piano Quartet in B♭. He wrote critical articles on music and began a novel, *Tonkunstlers Leben* (A composer's life). Weber's status at Stuttgart was jeopardized by his father, whose meddling created financial difficulties that resulted in the Webers' banishment from the area.

To earn funds to settle those debts, Weber concertized. He resumed studies with Vogler and composed Piano Concerto No. 1 (C major), six violin/piano sonatas, the Clarinet Concertino (E♭ major), and *Abu Hassan*, a Singspiel. At this time, he read the fairy tale *Der Freischütz* and decided to use it for an opera, but his librettist had other priorities.

When on concert tours, Weber composed few significant works: two clarinet concerti (No. 1, F minor; No. 2, E♭ major; 1811), a bassoon concerto (F major; 1811), and Piano Sonata No. 1 (C major; 1812). The waltz was becoming popular, and he wrote six sets of waltzes for piano and one set for wind ensemble.

In 1813, Weber became theater director and conductor at Prague. He completely reorganized the theater system, then produced Spontini's *Fernand Cortez* and other French operas. Weber's familiarity with those operas directly influenced his own opera composition—some of his characters have prototypes in them. At Prague, Weber had little time for composition for several reasons: The Prague public had not been receptive to some of the repertoire changes, and Weber decided to introduce unfamiliar works by publishing newspaper articles on them. Health problems plagued him—chest pains, sore throat, and aching hip. When he returned from treatment at a spa, or from vacation, he found standards at the theater deteriorating. Soprano Caroline Brandt joined the company in December 1813; Weber loved her but could not persuade her to marry him then. Weber's most important works from the Prague years are *Leyer und Schwert* (Lyre and Sword; Vols. 1 and 3, solo vc. with pno.; Vol. 2, *a cappella* male chorus), a clarinet quintet (B♭; 1815), the cantata *Kampf und Sieg* (Combat and Victory; 1816), and the *Grand duo concertant* (cl., pno.; 1816). The *Leyer und Schwert* part-songs are among the earliest of many such patriotic outpourings in Germanic lands in the nineteenth century.

Weber moved to Berlin in autumn 1816. At that time he wrote piano sonatas No. 2 (A♭ major) and No. 3 (D minor) and *Die Temperamente beim Verluste der Geliebten* (Emotions on the loss of the beloved; 4 songs), one of the earliest song cycles.

In 1817 Weber became *Musikdirektor* at Dresden and faced the task of developing German opera in a court and city atmosphere dominated by Italian music and musicians. He reformed every aspect of the theater, then introduced some French operas. He had time to compose only officially commissioned works (e.g., incidental music for the play *Der Weinberg an der Elbe* [Weinberg on the Elbe], in which Richard Wagner appeared as an angel).

Caroline and Carl married in November 1817. Weber continued his theater work, began *Der Freischütz,* and composed two offertories (1818) and two Masses (E♭, 1817–18; G, 1818–19). In the spring of 1819 he was ill with tuberculosis but by summer was well enough to write some piano pieces: *Aufforderung zum Tanze* (Invitation to the dance), *Rondo brillante,*

Polacca brillante, and part of Piano Sonata No. 4 (C minor; completed in 1823). In 1820 he wrote some incidental music and began but abandoned the comic opera *Der drei Pintos* (The three Pintos; completed by Gustav Mahler, 1888).

In 1821 Weber sketched an F-minor piano concerto that ultimately became *Konzertstück* (Concert piece), and he completed *Der Freischütz.* The opera was an outstanding success. For the 1822–23 season at Kärntnertor Theater Weber set *Euryanthe* by Wilhelmine von Chézy (1783–1856). *Euryanthe* was not really successful until sung by soprano Wilhelmine Schröder-Devrient (1804–60) in Dresden in 1824.

Tuberculosis was making inroads, and Weber knew he had only a few years to live, but he accepted a commission for an opera, composed *Oberon* (1825–26), and went to London to rehearse and conduct it. He died there on 5 June 1826 and was interred in Moorfields Chapel. In 1844 Richard Wagner arranged for transfer of Weber's remains to Dresden and composed two works for the interment services: *An Webers Grabe* (At Weber's grave; *a cappella* male chorus) and *Trauermusik* (Funeral music; band) on themes from *Euryanthe.*

WEBER'S MUSIC Weber contributed significantly to the development of opera: his theatrical reforms, his desire for unification of the arts involved in opera production, and his definitive establishment of German Romantic opera with *Der Freischütz.* Elements of German Romantic opera are present in *Peter Schmoll*—bourgeois characters in important roles, nature, fate, resolution of the situation through intervention of a holy man, and melody resembling folk song. They are exhibited to a greater extent in *Silvana,* the story of a knight wooing and winning a mute girl living in the woods. There are, of course, a villain (a bass) and a huntsmen's chorus. Because *Silvana* uses the revised libretto and some music from *Das Waldmädchen,* elements of German Romanticism in Weber's music probably extend back to 1800.

Der Freischütz mingles human and supernatural, good and evil: To win a shooting match and obtain the post of head ranger and the hand of Agathe, the hunter Max uses "free" bullets magically directed to their mark (thus he is the "free" marksman). At midnight, in Wolf's Glen, seven magic bullets are cast (DWMA143). In the competition, the seventh strikes Agathe, who is protected from death by a bridal wreath a hermit has blessed (benevolent supernatural power).

Much of *Der Freischütz* takes place at night, and effective lighting is important. Weber used Argand oil lamps, whose adjustable lighting could be made brighter than candlelight. *Der Freischütz* is a Singspiel, a number opera with spoken dialogue. Weber skillfully used dialogue to lead into singing, sometimes bridging them with melodrama, thus creating longer scenes and avoiding pure number opera.

Weber's use of recurrent motives and associative key tonalities and tone colors anticipated some of Wagner's techniques. In *Der Freischütz* the key of C major is associated with benevolent powers and D major with the natural, normal, healthy world. Samiel, being evil, never sings. He is represented musically by piccolo trills. The diminished-seventh chord f♯–a–c–e♭ is associated with him and with evil, and the notes of that chord provide the key scheme for the Wolf's Glen scene. In that scene, Weber freely used motives and phrases previously heard in the opera. In *Euryanthe,* he used the motive associated with Eglantine's deceit and a diminished-seventh chord similarly but more expansively. Weber's systematic use of recurrent themes extended beyond the technique of *Reminiszenzmotiv* then in use. Recognizing this, F. W. Jähns (1809–88), Weber's biographer and cataloger of his works, invented the term **Leitmotif** (leading motive) to describe Weber's practice. A Leitmotif is a kind of musical tag or label, a recurrent clearly defined theme or coherent musical idea that is intended to represent or symbolize a person, thing, place, idea, state of mind, or even a supernatural force. Obviously, a Leitmotif is a unifying device. In *Euryanthe,* Weber further weakened the set aria and took an important step toward the development of music drama. At the beginning of Act III of *Euryanthe* he used a series of highly chromatic chord progressions in which the "Tristan" chord (the first chord in Wagner's *Tristan und Isolde,* f–b–d♯–g♯') figures prominently.

All but one of Weber's chamber music works (the Clarinet Quintet) include piano. His solo piano music reflects his knowledge of the styles of Dussek and Cramer. Weber was one of the best pianists of his day, and the works he wrote for his concertizing are considered difficult by modern pianists. His most popular piano piece is *Aufforderung zum Tanze.* It was the first

Detail from John Hayter's lithograph (1826) depicting Weber conducting *Der Freischütz* at Covent Garden.

of many large concert works based on the waltz. In 1841 Berlioz orchestrated the piece (*L'invitation à la valse*).

Weber was one of the earliest conductors to stand at a podium and direct the orchestra with a thick baton that he grasped in the middle. His orchestrations are superb, but his purely orchestral works are unimportant.

Weber's writings include his unfinished novel, critical essays, poetry, and occasional pieces. In the "notice" that he published a few days before a performance, he made critical comments concerning the opera and its composer and frequently discussed technical and aesthetic details of the work and its production. Visible in his writings is constant concern for the advancement of German music and German musicians.

LESSER COMPOSERS OF OPERA

After Weber's death, the composition of German Romantic opera was carried on by a number of lesser composers, chief of whom was Heinrich Marschner (1795–1861). Marschner attracted attention as an opera composer in 1820, when his *Heinrich IV und d'Aubigné* (Henry IV and d'Aubigné; 1818) was produced by Weber at Dresden. The finest of Marschner's 13 operas is *Hans Heiling* (1833). Marschner wrote a sung, through-composed prologue but used spoken dialogue for the body of the work, with some melodrama. Stylistically, *Hans Heiling* stands midway between the work of Weber and that of Wagner.

In the area of German comic opera, Albert Lortzing (1801–51) made significant contributions. His aim was to provide entertainment, and he did so admirably. *Czaar und Zimmermann* (Czar and Carpenter; 1837) and *Der Wildschütz* (The poacher; 1842) are excellent examples. Lortzing wrote his own texts and set them as number opera. A characteristic of his style is the effective introduction of dialogue, as interjections, in musical numbers. His humor is delightful, as in the rehearsal scene in *Czaar und Zimmermann,* where the choir misunderstands the choirmaster's instructions and repeatedly bungles entrances. Lortzing excelled in writing comic bass roles.

Another composer of comic opera was Otto Nicolai, whose *Die lustige Weiber von Windsor* (The merry wives of Windsor; based on Shakespeare; 1849) is a mixture of Italian and German musical styles.

LIEDER

Many singers and composers working in Austro-Germanic lands were as interested in Lieder and secular choral music as they were in opera. Some composers had little success with opera (e.g., Franz Schubert). Others, like Anna Fröhlich and Luise Reichardt, were teachers and/or chorus directors. Carl Loewe concertized in addition to holding municipal and church positions; thus, he promoted the circulation of his Lieder and ballads.

CARL LOEWE

Loewe (1796–1869) received his first training in music from his schoolmaster father and was a choirboy in the church at Cöthen. By the age of 12, Loewe had some published songs and instrumental pieces. A devout Catholic, he studied theology at Halle University. From 1820 to 1865 he worked in Stettin, as professor and Kantor at the Gymnasium and seminary,

and from 1821 as municipal Musikdirektor and organist at St. Jacobus Cathedral. He composed sacred and secular music in all genres. By 1835 he was famous throughout Germanic lands as composer, conductor, and singer. Then he made international concert tours. Rarely did he sing songs by other composers; many of his ballads need vivid interpretation, and at this he excelled. In Vienna, he was acclaimed as "the north German Schubert."

Loewe's 6 operas and 17 oratorios are stylistically similar. Many of his piano sonatas are programmatic, and some are unusual, for example, Op. 16, in E major, whose slow movement is a song for tenor.

Loewe is remembered for his approximately 375 solo songs with piano accompaniment. Some of his finest songs are early works; the 31 *Hebräische Gesänge* (Hebrew Songs, Opp. 4, 5, 13, 14; comp. 1819–26, pub. 1825–27) and the 3 ballads of Op. 1 (pub. 1824): *Edward* (1818), *Der Wirthin Töchterlein* (The innkeeper's little daughter; 1823), and *Erlkönig* (Erlking; 1818). Frequently, Loewe chose texts by Herder, Uhland, and Goethe, the poets represented in Op. 1. Loewe had a predilection for ballads. In setting them, he often used modified strophic structure, and he contrasted (but did not necessarily alternate) arioso with dramatic accompanied recitative, as he did in *Der Wirthin Töchterlein* and *Archibald Douglas* (Op. 128, 1857). Though melodically different, Loewe's and Schubert's (comp. 1815, pub. 1821) settings of *Erlkönig* are similar in several respects—key, agitated piano accompaniment, a rise in pitch as the child becomes more frightened, the lilting words of the coaxing Erlking, and use of recitative in conclusion—but whether Loewe saw Schubert's work in manuscript is debatable. Loewe's setting of the old Scottish ballad *Edward* is his best-known song. It is filled with dark, brooding sonorities.

Many of Loewe's ballads are Romantic, with elements of horror, the supernatural, folklore, and fairy tale. In Loewe's songs, as in Schubert's, the piano does not merely accompany the singer but enters into partnership with the voice in interpreting the poetry. For Loewe, the poem was of prime import; he composed a vocal line suited to the poem, with secondary consideration for the style of narration and the descriptive effects. He rarely wrote introductions or postludes; when he did, they were brief.

FRANZ PETER SCHUBERT

Schubert (1797–1828), the only great native Viennese composer, was the eleventh child of schoolmaster Franz Theodor and Maria Schubert. Only 4 of their 12 children survived infancy: Ignaz, Ferdinand, Karl, and Franz Peter. Franz Theodor personally gave the children some musical training, and family music making was important; both Ferdinand and Franz Peter wrote music specifically for performance by family members. Ferdinand (1794–1859) became a respected educator in Vienna, held an organist-choirmaster position also, and composed vocal music.

Franz's violin and piano playing soon surpassed that of his father and brothers. When he was 9 years old, he was sent to the Liechtental parish church organist for piano, organ, violin, singing, and harmony lessons. In 1808 he was accepted as a choirboy in the imperial court chapel and admitted to the Stadtkonvikt, the principal Viennese boarding school, where he formed a lifelong friendship with Josef von Spaun. Schubert was an excellent student. Eventually, court Kapellmeister Antonio Salieri took over supervision of his musical training.

Schubert's earliest extant compositions include *Fantasie* in G major for piano duet (D. 1; 1810), six Minuets for winds (D. 2d; 1811, lost and located in 1969), and the songs *Hagars Klage* (Hagar's lament, D. 5; 1811), *Des Mädchens Klage* (The maiden's lament, D. 6; 1811), and *Eine Leichenfantasie* (A funeral fantasy, D. 7; 1811). During school vacations, Schubert played viola in the family string quartet. Only a few of the quartets he wrote in 1811–14 have survived. The best of them is that in E♭ major, D. 87 (1813). Schubert's works are generally known by their "D" numbers, according to the catalog prepared by Otto Erich Deutsch (1883–1967).

Of the many works Schubert composed in 1813, the finest is Symphony No. 1 (D major, D. 82). Near the end of 1813, he left the Stadtkonvikt, took a training course for elementary teachers, and in autumn 1814 began teaching in his father's school. He continued lessons with Salieri until the end of 1816. Schubert was rejected by military conscription authorities because his eyesight was defective, and he was too short (about five feet tall). In 1814, Schubert's Mass No. 1 (F major, D. 105) was performed twice. On 19

Franz P. Schubert. *(Courtesy of the Free Library of Philadelphia)*

October 1814 he created his first masterpiece—*Gretchen am Spinnrade* (Gretchen at the spinning wheel, D. 118). Later that year, Spaun encouraged him to set Johann Mayrhofer's (1787–1836) *Am See* (At the sea, D. 124) and arranged for them to meet. In 1815 Schubert set Mayrhofer's play *Die Freunde von Salamanka* (The friends of Salamanka, D. 326) as a Singspiel.

Schubert taught in 1815 but disliked the work. That year he composed more music than in any other single year of his life. Among those works are 2 symphonies (No. 2, B♭ major, D. 125; No. 3, D major, D. 200), 2 Masses (No. 2, G major, D. 167; No. 3, B♭ major, D. 324), 4 Singspiele, a piano sonata (C major, D. 279), numerous dances for piano solo, a string quartet (G minor, D. 173), a set of 10 Variations in F for piano solo (D. 156), much choral music (most of it for male voices), and about 145 songs—settings of poetry by Klopstock, Körner, Goethe, Mayrhofer, Schiller, and others. The songs vary from very short, (e.g., *Wandrers Nachtlied*; Traveler's night song, D. 224; 13 measures) to very long ballads (e.g., *Adelwold und Emma*; D. 211; 610 measures, not counting repeats). Twenty measures of music (repeated for the 4 strophes) suffice for *Die Mainacht* (May night, D. 194). Among the 30 settings of Goethe's poems are some of Schubert's finest and most famous songs, including *Heidenröslein* (Little heath rose, D. 257) and *Erlkönig* (D. 328). *Erlkönig* is probably Schubert's best-known song, and many critics consider it his greatest.

In 1816 Schubert decided to devote all his time to composition, but not until late October did he abandon teaching, and then the break was only temporary. A factor in that move may have been his first commission, which resulted in the cantata *Prometheus* (D. 451; lost), performed at Josef Witteczek's house. A few years later, that house was the setting for many *Schubertiaden,* evening concerts devoted to Schubert's music and attended by a circle of Schubert's friends and sometimes their families (fig. 21.3). For private social gatherings of this kind Schubert wrote many songs; they were not intended for public concerts. He was not a concert artist and preferred performing chamber music or accompanying his friends. Domestic evening concerts were not unique to Schubert's group of friends. As the educated middle class enjoyed and cultivated music, particularly piano and vocal music, those who could afford pianos purchased them, and friends gathered in their homes for concerts. This may be viewed as an expansion of the aristocrats' chamber music concerts for which eighteenth-century composers wrote serenades.

In 1816 Schubert wrote Symphonies No. 4, which he entitled *Tragic,* in C minor (D. 427), and No. 5, in B♭ major (D. 485); Mass No. 4 (C major, D. 452; pub. 1825); 3 violin/piano sonatas (D. 384, 385, 408; pub. 1836 by Diabelli as sonatinas); String Quartet in E major (D. 353); and more than 100 songs. One of those songs, *Der Wanderer* (The traveler, D. 489), became very popular.

In 1817 Schubert met baritone Johann Vogl (1768–1840), and a close friendship developed. Vogl, a member of the Vienna court opera, had sung the role of Pizarro in Beethoven's 1814 revision of *Fidelio* and was himself a composer of vocal music, but he is remembered as friend of Schubert and ideal interpreter of his songs.

During most of 1817, Schubert was without gainful employment. That year he wrote 55 songs, several piano sonatas and sonata movements, the violin/piano Sonata in A major (D. 574), String Trio in B♭ (D. 581), and 2 overtures "in Italian style." He also began Symphony No. 6 (C major, D. 589; 1817–18). The "Italian" overtures were inspired by Rossini's operas, which were extremely popular in Vienna at this time; in these overtures Schubert imitated Rossini's style. Of the songs, the most important are *Gruppe aus dem Tartarus* (Group from Tartarus, D. 583), *Der Tod und das Mädchen* (Death and the maiden, D. 531), and *Die Forelle* (The trout, D. 550).

In autumn 1817 Schubert resumed teaching in his father's school but resigned in July 1818 to become music teacher to Johann Esterházy's two daughters. In January 1818 his setting of Mayrhofer's *Am Erlafsee* (At Erlaf lake, D. 586; 1817) was printed in a periodical; it was his first published work. In March and in May his C-major "Italian" overture was performed in concert. In summer Schubert worked for the Esterházy in Hungary; in winter, the Esterházy and Schubert returned to Vienna, where he taught the daughters but

FIGURE 21.3 Moritz von Schwind's *Schubert Abend bei Josef von Spaun* (1826), a sepia drawing depicting a *Schubertiade* at Spaun's home. Schubert is at the piano; Vogl, at his right, is singing; Spaun is seated at Schubert's left, in the position of page turner. *(Historisches Museum, Vienna)*

resided with Mayrhofer. That those two pupils had comparable talent is reflected in his compositions for them—about a dozen piano duets, including the Sonata in B♭ (D. 617). In 1818 Schubert wrote 14 songs. That summer he composed a *Deutsches Requiem* (German Requiem, D. 621), which his brother Ferdinand appropriated. Not until 1880 was Franz's authorship revealed.

During the next two years Schubert enjoyed being with his widening circle of friends; he composed 22 songs in 1819 and 23 in 1820. Between February 1818 and November 1822 he made sketches for works that he never composed, began compositions that he never finished, and commenced others that he completed years later (e.g., Mass No. 5 [A♭ major, D. 678; 1819–22]). He finished only the first movement of a string quartet in C minor (D. 703). Known simply as *Quartettsatz* (Quartet movement), the work marks a new seriousness in Schubert's chamber music. It was not incompetence, lack of ideas, or neglect that caused Schubert to leave works unfinished but illness. He was experiencing the early stages of syphilis, whose increasingly serious attacks he would battle for the rest of his life.

Vogl took Schubert to Steyr for the summer of 1819. There, Sylvester Paumgartner commissioned the Quintet in A major (D. 667; pno., vln., vla., vcl., str. bass). The work has five movements. Schubert constructed the fourth movement as variations on *Die Forelle*; thus, the work's nickname, "The Trout Quintet."

Schubert was becoming more widely known as a composer, but publishers were not willing to issue his works. Perhaps they thought music by a nonconcertizing composer would not sell. In 1821 some of Schubert's friends had 20 of his songs published (as Opp. 1–8) by private subscription. Then the 36 waltzes for piano solo (D. 365; 1816–21) and a set of 8 variations for piano duet (D. 624; 1818) were published, and he was invited to write a variation on Diabelli's waltz theme for the collection.

Since c. 1812, Schubert had been writing choral pieces, many of them for male ensembles. One of his finest is *Gesang der Geister über den Wassern* (Song of the spirits over the waters, D. 714; 2d version, 1821). He continued to write solo Lieder, about a dozen in 1821 and 30 in 1822. In August 1821, he sketched and partly scored Symphony No. 7 (E major, D. 729)

but never finished it. (Schubert's sketches were edited or realized in 1883 and again in 1934 with less than satisfactory results.) Schubert abandoned the symphony when he and Franz von Schober collaborated on the opera *Alfonso und Estrella* (D. 732; 1821–22).

Schubert's most important compositions in 1822 are *Wandererfantasie* for piano (C major, D. 760; pub. 1823) and the "Unfinished" Symphony No. 8 (B minor, D. 759). It is conjectured that work on the symphony was interrupted by composition of the *Wandererfantasie;* then serious illness prevented him from working on it. For the rest of his life, Schubert would suffer increasingly from ever-deepening ravages of syphilis on his central nervous system. Schubert gave the autograph manuscript of the incomplete symphony to Josef Hüttenbrenner for transmission to his brother Anselm, apparently as a gift. The manuscript contained the completed score of the first two movements and the first nine measures of the third. The remaining leaves in the gathering were blank; one sheet had been cut out. That sheet, found by Christa Landon (1921–77) c. 1968, contains the score for measures 10 to 20 of the third movement. Schubert's piano sketches for that movement have been located and the entire Scherzo/Trio constructed. There is no indication that Schubert planned a fourth movement. The "Unfinished" Symphony lay submerged in Anselm Hüttenbrenner's collection of Schubert works until the 1860s. It was first performed, as a two-movement work, in 1865.

The only significant piano solo Schubert wrote in 1823 was a piece in F minor that eventually became No. 3 in a set of six works published collectively in 1828 as *Momens musicals* [sic] (Musical moments; see p. 444). He wrote another in 1824 and four more in 1825–27. In 1823 he wrote eight Lieder, including *Du bist die Ruh'* (You are rest, D. 776), and composed the song cycle *Die schöne Müllerin* (The fair maid of the mill, D. 795) on poems by Wilhelm Müller (1794–1827). Schubert was interested in composing stage works but had little success. In 1823 he composed the opera *Fierabras* (D. 796; first perf. 1897), which Kärntnertor Theater director Barbaia rejected on theatrical grounds. Schubert next wrote incidental music (but no overture) for Chézy's Romantic play *Rosamunde* (D. 797).

In 1824 Schubert created three important pieces of chamber music: the Octet (F major, D. 803) and the string quartets in A minor (D. 804) and D minor (D. 810). During the summer, he taught Esterházy's daughters and wrote some piano duets, including the Sonata in C major ("Grand Duo"; D. 812). In 1825 he composed the piano sonatas in A minor (D. 845) and D major (D. 850) and may have begun writing Symphony No. 9 (D. 944; c. 1825–28), known as the "Great C-Major."

Schubert's vocal works in 1824 comprise only 3 choral pieces and 8 Lieder, but in 1825 his output of Lieder increased by 23 songs. Among them are 5 songs from Scott's *The Lady of the Lake,* including *Ellens Gesang III* (Ellen's song III, D. 839), the well-known *Ave Maria* (cf. Carr, p. 396). In 1826, Schubert wrote two dozen Lieder, including 3 Shakespeare songs and 4 *Gesänge aus Wilhelm Meister* (Songs from *Wilhelm Meister;* D. 877). One of the latter, *Nur wer die Sehnsucht kennt* (Only he who knows loneliness, or None but the lonely heart) was set by many composers. Two of the Shakespeare songs are better known by their first lines: *Ständchen* (Serenade, D. 889), generally referred to as "Hark, hark, the lark," and *An Sylvia* (To Sylvia, D. 891), usually called "Who is Sylvia?"

The pieces Schubert wrote in 1826 include the String Quartet in G major (D. 887), the Piano Sonata in G major (D. 894), and *Rondo brillant* (B minor, D. 895; vln., pno.). The *Rondo* and the *Phantasie* (C major, D. 934; 1827) were written for Bohemian concert artists, violinist Josef Slavík (1806–33) and pianist Karl Maria von Bocklet (1801–81). The *Phantasie* indicates Schubert's knowledge of the structural and technical capabilities of the most advanced instruments of the time. The violinist needed an instrument of modern dimensions and the Tourte-improved bow, whose resiliency would produce cleanly and easily the rapid spiccato passages. The pitch range covered in the violin part extends from g to e''''; the pianist needed a six-octave keyboard (F'–f'''') and used all of it but the top note. Slavík, the first modern Bohemian violinist to achieve international acclaim, was also a composer. His sudden death at age 27 dashed hopes that he would become a second Paganini (see p. 487).

Schubert's major instrumental works in 1827 are the eight *Impromptus* for piano solo (D. 899, D. 935). No doubt his choice of title was influenced by Voříšek

Impromptus. In November and December Schubert wrote the Piano Trio in E♭ major (D. 929; perf. 26 March 1828). In 1827 or 1828 he wrote the Piano Trio in B♭ major (D. 898). Schubert composed much vocal music in 1827: a *Deutsche Messe* (German Mass; D. 872), several choral works including a setting of Grillparzer's *Ständchen* (Serenade, D. 920), 21 Lieder, and the song cycle *Die Winterreise* (Winter journey, D. 911). One of the Lieder is *Edward*, in Herder's translation (see Loewe, p. 438).

Schubert was not well in 1828, yet he composed, participated in *Schubertiaden,* and socialized with friends. At times he had mentioned arranging a public recital, but not until spring 1828 did he do so. An all-Schubert program was presented on 26 March, but the composer performed in it only as accompanist for five songs sung by Vogl.

The principal instrumental works Schubert composed in 1828 are 3 piano sonatas (C minor, D. 958; A major, D. 959; B♭ major, D. 960) and the String Quintet in C major (D. 956; 2 vln., vla., 2 vc.). He never wrote a piano concerto, nor did he make sketches for one. His vocal compositions that year include Mass No. 6 (E♭ major, D. 950), a few choral works, and 21 Lieder. Thirteen of the songs were published as *Schwanengesang* (Swan song, D. 957; comp. Aug. 1828; pub. 1829). *Schwanengesang* is not a song cycle. The publisher added to the collection a fourteenth song, *Der Taubenpost* (The carrier pigeon, D. 965a; comp. Oct. 1828).

Every summer Schubert had gone on vacation with a friend, but in 1828 he was too exhausted to go. In September he went to live with his brother Ferdinand. There he completed three piano sonatas and the C-major string quintet. In October he wrote for Anna Milder-Hauptmann (1785–1838), famed Berlin soprano, *Der Hirt auf den Felsen* (The shepherd on the rock, D. 965; October 1828; voice, pno., cl.). It was Schubert's last completed song and is one of his loveliest.

By mid-November Schubert was very ill. He died on November 19 and was interred in Währing cemetery, near Beethoven, whom he had greatly admired. Though Schubert and Beethoven lived near one another in Vienna, they met only once—when Beethoven lay dying, Schubert went to see him. Many persons wrote poems eulogizing Schubert, and friends financed a monument-sculpture to honor him. Part of those funds were proceeds from a memorial concert given by Anna Fröhlich (1793–1880), Viennese soprano and pianist; Schubert had composed music for her; for her sister Josefine (1803–78), who was an internationally known opera singer; and for their pupils. (Two other Fröhlich sisters were talented, and the Fröhlich home in Vienna was a center of musical activity.) Grillparzer, who had provided texts for several of Schubert's works, wrote his epitaph, which, in translation, reads, "Here the art of music entombed a rich possession, but even fairer hopes."

SCHUBERT'S MUSIC IN GENERAL   Schubert was, in many respects, a Classic composer. Many of his compositions were written to suit the talents of specific performers or ensembles. He wrote no program music; only one of his instrumental pieces bears a special title (Symphony No. 4, *Tragic*), and he left no clue to the reason for it. He used Classic formal structures, sometimes modifying them slightly, but making no radical changes. He did write a greatly expanded Scherzo with Trio for the third movement of the "Great C-Major" Symphony. In some early works, he began the recapitulation of a sonata-form movement in the subdominant, and in the finale of the "Great C-Major" Symphony the recapitulation commences in E♭ major.

Schubert used some counterpoint in his Masses, but in his instrumental music he rarely used counterpoint for long stretches. Exceptions occur in the finales of *Wandererfantasie* and the *Phantasie* (D. 934). Schubert used counterpoint skillfully (e.g., presenting portions of three themes simultaneously in Symphony No. 9). Schubert's violin/piano duos are filled with interesting, unobtrusive contrapuntal techniques, including rondellus and canon.

Schubert's characteristic techniques may be summarized as (1) presenting the initial material in unison or in octaves; (2) using the opening material prominently in the development but omitting it from the recapitulation; (3) concluding a movement with a citation of the material used at its commencement, either by using it to begin the coda or by making it the final statement; (4) stating the first theme of an instrumental work or the first melodic phrase of a song twice, perhaps with slight alteration the second time; (5) foreshadowing a section or a movement in the cadential motive that immediately precedes it; (6) preparing the ear to receive modulation to a certain key but abruptly shifting to a different one; (7) achieving modulation by a move of a third or via a Neapolitan progression; (8) abruptly shifting to the key of the second theme but modulating carefully in preparation for the recapitulation; (9) fostering tonal ambiguity by wavering between major and minor or by simultaneously voicing pedals that are dominants in different keys; and (10) writing out trill terminations rather than using symbols. Many of these traits appear in the "Unfinished" Symphony.

Schubert's skill at modulating cannot be overemphasized. At times, his modulations are extensive and complex; sometimes, they are concise and traditional; at other times, they are abrupt, effected by the intrusion of a single foreign note into a chord or by the insertion of a general pause and a leap into the new key. A surprising modulation is made after an unexpected measure of general pause (m. 62) in the first movement of the "Unfinished" Symphony, and an effective sudden modulation from G major to B major occurs crossing from measure 200 to measure 201 in the finale of the "Great C-Major" Symphony. Where key sequence was concerned, Schubert was often adventurous, and he used harmonies imaginatively—in this he was Romantic. One of his favorite devices was wavering, seemingly in tonal indecisiveness, between major and minor forms of a chord or a key, as in the familiar *Ständchen* (Serenade) or *Das Heimweh* (Homesickness).

VOCAL MUSIC   There was not a lot of great church music produced during the first half of the nineteenth century. Schubert wrote six Catholic Masses, and the last two of them—in A♭ and E♭—are among the finest of that time. Much of the writing is homophonic, but Schubert supplied the traditional fugal endings where expected. In Schubert's Masses, the apparent omission of portions of the standard liturgical text are not an indication of his personal beliefs. There was at that time some laxity with regard to the Mass text, and undoubtedly Schubert set the text with which he was familiar. It was not at all unusual to find slightly different versions of the liturgical text in use in the various parishes in Vienna in the early nineteenth century. Competent editors have carefully inserted the controversial "omitted" phrases of text without damaging the music. Therefore, musicological purists may perform the Mass as Schubert wrote it, and theological purists may perform it with the complete standard liturgical text. Two excellent choral works by Schubert are *Der 92. Psalm* (The 92d Psalm, D. 953; 5 soloists, mixed chorus, 1828) and *Gesang der Geister über den Wassern,* for two four-part choirs of tenors and basses and a choir formed of the three lower string instruments.

Schubert composed more than 600 Lieder. Formally, he used four basic types of text settings: (1) strophic, or strophic with a refrain, with each strophe (stanza) of text sung to the same music (e.g., *Heidenröslein* or *An Sylvia*); (2) modified strophic, in which some of the strophes use identical music but changes are made in the music for parts or all of other strophes (e.g., *Die Forelle*); (3) through-composed (German, *durchkomponiert*), in which the music for each strophe is different (e.g., *Erlkönig*), and (4) *scena*, which is sectional, with different episodes in varying *tempi* and moods (e.g., *Der Wanderer*).

Schubert's accompaniments vary considerably but are always suited to the text and melody of the song. The accompaniments range from very easy to very difficult (see ex. 21.1). The folk-song–like *Heidenröslein* has a very simple accompaniment (DWMA144). For *Meeresstille* (Calm sea, D. 216) Schubert wrote rolled chords in whole notes, to be played *pianissimo*. The piano part for *Der Doppelgänger* (The shadow, or The spectral self, D. 957, No. 13) is an ominous knell that forms a grand bass with an ever-present F♯ pedal. In *Gretchen am Spinnrade* the accompaniment represents Gretchen's restlessness and her thoughts as well as the whirring of the spinning wheel.

Schubert's *Erlkönig* resembles a miniature opera as the story dramatically unfolds (DWMA145). Besides the narrator, the characters are a father, a sick child, a horse, and the Erlking (specter of death). Schubert portrayed the roles as he would have treated operatic actor-singers with different personalities and different vocal ranges. Before the narrator begins the story, the piano establishes the tonality and the mood by fourfold statement of a G-minor motive that depicts the rhythm of the horse's hoofs and the father's anxiety as, with his ailing son in his arms, he rides homeward late at night. The boy becomes more and more frightened; with each

utterance his voice rises in pitch as he tells his father about the Erlking, who attempts to lure the child away. The father tries, unsuccessfully, to calm his son. When the text speaks of the groaning child, the piano rapidly reiterates a dissonant V_7 of C for a measure, then moves through C minor, *fortissimo*, forcefully and chromatically into A♭ major. The riders reach their destination—the horse's hoofs are silent. Then, in *secco* recitative, *pianissimo*, the narrator states, "In his arms, the child was dead." The vocal line ends in the dominant (D) but the piano punctuates the sentence *forte*, with a V_7–I cadence in G minor—the typical conclusion for an eighteenth-century operatic recitative.

Schubert's earliest Lieder show Zumsteeg's influence, especially in ballad settings. The two composers set some of the same poems in the same manner and even in the same keys. As Schubert grew older, he became more sensitive to the inner meaning as well as to the literal meaning and external pictorial details of the poetry he set. He became adept at translating poetry into music, thus effecting the synthesis of music and words that created masterpieces such as *Winterreise*. In his songs, piano and voice share the music in partnership. In this kind of Lieder writing, Schubert was a pioneer. It is understandable that publishers, seeing his music in manuscript but not hearing it performed, would regard it as unusual and hesitate to publish it.

If Schubert was not completely satisfied with a setting, or if he saw in a poem the possibilities for more than one musical interpretation, he wrote more than one setting. Schubert did not shy away from poems packed with emotion. He set texts by unknown and little-known writers as well as works by great authors. Schubert wrote some meaningful poetry but did not set it to music.

PIANO WORKS   Among Schubert's keyboard works are several sets of character pieces: six *Momens musicals* [sic] (D. 780, pub. 1828), eight *Impromptus* (D. 899, Nos. 1–2 pub. 1827, Nos. 3–4 pub. 1857; D. 935, pub. 1838), and three *Klavierstücke* (Piano pieces, D. 946; comp. 1828; pub. 1868). All these pieces owe something to the *Eclogues* of Tomášek and the *Impromptus* of Voříšek but are not imitations of their works. The *Impromptus* are larger works than the *Momens musicals*.

(a)

(b)

(c)

(d)

(e)

EXAMPLE 21.1 Excerpts from Schubert's Lieder illustrating various types of accompaniment he used: (a) *Heidenröslein*, mm. 1–4; (b) *Meeresstille*, mm. 1–4; (c) *Der Doppelgänger*, mm. 1–8; (d) *Gretchen am Spinnrade*, mm. 1–4; (e) *Der Abend*, mm. 1–4. *(Source: Franz Schuberts Werke: Kritisch durchgesehene Gesamtausgabe, ed. J. Brahms, E. Mandyczewski, et al. Leipzig: Breitkopf & Härtel, 1864–97)*

Schubert wrote all the *Impromptus* in flat keys, but the publisher transposed No. 3 from G♭ to G for the collection. No. 3 is typical of Schubert's writing—a *cantabile* melody is accompanied by an arpeggiated sextuplet figure over chordal Romantic harmonies (DWMA146).

Schubert wrote 21 piano sonatas, but some are incomplete. His finest are the last three: D. 958, C minor; D. 959, A major; and D. 960, B♭ major. Structurally, each has its first movement in sonata form; the second movement is a songlike Andante in either ternary or five-part alternating form; the third, either scherzo/trio or minuet/trio; and the fourth, rondo. Thus, Schubert favored the Classic structure Beethoven used in his early sonatas. However, Schubert's sonata-form movements are devoid of the extensive, exhaustive type of motivic development found in Beethoven's piano sonatas. In D. 958 and D. 959 Schubert introduced new themes in the development section instead of developing to the fullest the themes presented in the exposition. Stylistically, his songlike slow movements are akin to his Lieder; the third movements are light and dancelike.

Wandererfantasie is a cyclic work based on the line *Die Sonne dünkt mich hier so kalt* from Schubert's Lied, *Der Wanderer*. The fantasy comprises four movements designed to be played without a break. It commences with an Allegro con fuoco, in C major, that is episodic, then moves into an Adagio theme-and-variations second movement that presents the song theme in C♯ minor and concludes the last variation with a passage in E major. The Presto is a Scherzo (A♭) with two Trios (D♭); the finale, an allegro in C major, opens with a fugato.

Schubert's comments concerning piano playing, stated in a letter dated 25 July 1825, give some insight into the proper performance of his works: "Several people assured me that the keys become singing voices under my hands, which, if true, pleases me greatly, since I cannot endure the accursed thumping in which even distinguished pianoforte players indulge and which delights neither the ear nor the mind."

CHAMBER MUSIC   From 1811 until his death Schubert was interested in performing and composing chamber music. His early chamber music shows the influence of the orchestral works of Haydn and Mozart. Some movements in those early works follow traditional formal and harmonic patterns so strictly that they could serve as composition textbook examples. Not until 1816 did Schubert's own style begin to emerge in his chamber music.

Most of Schubert's chamber music was composed before the end of 1820—before he wrote *Quartettsatz*. It is an excellent example of his mature writing for string quartet and is one of the few works in which he used counterpoint to any extent. He completed only three more string quartets: D. 804 in A minor (comp. and pub. 1824), D. 810 in D minor (comp. 1824; pub. 1831), and D. 887 in G major (comp. 1826; pub. 1851). In the *Quartettsatz* and in some of the sonata-form first movements of these quartets, Schubert used three key centers in both exposition and recapitulation, sometimes adjusting the order in which he recapitulated the material so that the movement would conclude in its basic key and with the thematic material that began it.

The D-minor quartet has been called a musical essay on death. The second movement is based on Schu-bert's Lied, *Der Tod und das Mädchen,* and the chorale-like presentation of the theme records Death's steady approach toward the Maiden, as stated in the Lied. The Scherzo is very short; the Presto is a tarantelle.

Schubert's most important quintets are the Piano Quintet in A major, D. 667 (comp. 1819; pub. 1829; see p. 441), and the String Quintet in C major, D. 956 (comp. 1828; pub. 1850). The C-major Quintet (2 vln., vla., 2 vc.) is Schubert's chamber music masterpiece. The inclusion of a second 'cello allowed him to widen the range and group the instruments in various combinations of twos and threes. Present in the music are expressive, lyrical melodies, contrasting moods, and complex rhythms. This is one of the loveliest pieces of Romantic chamber music created in the first half of the nineteenth century.

Other significant chamber music by Schubert includes the Octet, the violin/piano works previously mentioned, and two Piano Trios, in B♭ major (D. 898; pub. 1836) and E♭ major (D. 929; pub. 1828). The Octet was commissioned by Count von Troyer, a clarinetist who knew Beethoven's Septet and wanted a similar work. Schubert added second violin to the instrumentation Beethoven used. There are some structural and motivic similarities between the Septet and the Octet, but there are definite stylistic differences.

ORCHESTRAL MUSIC   Schubert wrote only three works for solo instrument and orchestra, all featuring violin: *Concertstück* (Concert piece, D major, D. 345; 1816), *Rondo* (A major, D. 438, with strings; 1816), and *Polonaise* (B♭ major, D. 580; 1817).

His orchestral works consist of several overtures and nine symphonies. He modeled his first six symphonies after those of Mozart and Haydn. The Schubert symphonies most frequently performed in the twentieth century are the "Unfinished" in B minor (pub. 1867) and the "Great C-Major" (pub. 1840).

The "Great C-Major" Symphony is very long. Portions of it contain repetitious figuration that some performers consider boring, but the work has tremendous rhythmic drive and is filled with intense emotional expression and beautiful melodies. The interval of a third is prominent in melodies, rhythmic motifs, and tonalities throughout the composition. This symphony attests Schubert's ability to use counterpoint skillfully and unobtrusively and reveals his flair for orchestral color. Some of his characteristic techniques are handled in an unusual manner; for example, the opening theme is presented by two horns in unison *piano,* with a *pianissimo* echo, followed by a second statement of the theme by winds accompanied by strings. The first movement has three contrasting themes in addition to the thematic material presented in the introduction; all the themes, including the introduction, are fragmented and recombined in the development. In this work, Schubert used three trombones and frequently asked them to play *piano.*

SCHUBERT'S CONTRIBUTIONS Schubert made a vast and priceless contribution to music repertoire. He pioneered in writing Lieder in which words and music are so synthesized that the music is a translation of the poetry. In the last year of his life, he used some harmonies and tonal effects that were striking, but his work had little effect on the development of music during the first half of the nineteenth century. At the time of his death, Schubert was not a major composer; he was little known outside of Austria. Before 1825, publishers were reluctant to issue his work, and relatively few of his compositions had been published by 1828. After his death, his compositions lay submerged for decades. By the time they surfaced—some of his greatest compositions did not come to light until the 1860s—any harmonies, modulations, or tonal innovations in which he actually pioneered had become ordinary musical language.

LUISE REICHARDT

Luise (1779–1826), the daughter of Johann F. (1752–1814) and Juliane Benda (1752–83) Reichardt, inherited musical talent from both parents. Her mother, a singer, composed keyboard sonatas and Lieder; approximately 20 of her works survive. Luise's father, a violinist and pianist, was a prolific composer and authored many articles on music and musicians. The Reichardt home was a meeting place for musicians, artists, writers, and other intellectuals, and from time to time that circle was entertained by Luise's singing and piano playing.

By 1813 Luise had moved to Hamburg, where she taught singing, directed a women's chorus, and was influential in the formation of the Hamburg Sing-verein (Singing Society). Reichardt regarded the composition of music decidedly secondary to her pedagogical career. Yet, she composed more than 100 songs and choral pieces, and most of them were published. Her first Lieder were included in a collection with some by her father, issued in 1800. Two published collections of her songs were reviewed in *Allgemeine musikalische Zeitung* (1806, 1827). Many of her songs remained popular throughout the nineteenth century; some appear in many twentieth-century anthologies. One such song is *Hoffnung* (Hope; DWMA147), which is comparable in style and quality with Schubert's *Heidenröslein.* Reichardt's vocal lines are usually lyrical and the accompaniments quite simple, devoid of any special motivic interpretation of text.

MUSIC IN ITALY

By the end of the eighteenth century, Austrian and German composers had assumed leadership in instrumental music. During the first half of the nineteenth century, the only area of instrumental music in which Italians produced works of any consequence was opera overture. Many of these were written in sonata form or a variant thereof and have become a part of standard concert repertoire as independent pieces. Church music was a concern of Italian composers, but no outstanding works were created during the first half of the nineteenth century. Italy had a rich opera tradition, however, and early nineteenth-century Italian composers concentrated on musical theater. In Italy all opera was sung throughout. Revolutionary opera and that dealing with contemporary social problems had little following in Italy, which was still a land of separate states.

Italy was overshadowed by events in Paris, but Italian composers working in the French capital made significant contributions to the development of opera there. After beginning careers in Italy, the two greatest Italian-born composers of the time, Cherubini and Spontini, went to Paris and wrote French-language operas in the French manner.

The opera reforms advocated by Gluck and Jommelli had not been generally accepted in Italy;

performances of the operas of J. Simon Mayr throughout the land did much to promote that acceptance. Also, the popularity of Rossini's comic operas throughout the Italian states was instrumental in effecting a unification of styles.

JOHANNES SIMON MAYR

Mayr (1763–1845), a Bavarian, studied composition in Italy. In Venice, he composed church music, oratorios, and cantatas. Peter von Winter and Piccinni urged him to write opera, and in 1795–1800 he wrote almost two dozen operas and one-act farces for Venetian theaters. Commencing with *La Lodoïska* (2d version, 1799), he provided opere serie more or less regularly for Milan's La Scala. With the production of *Ginevra di Scozia* (Guinevere of Scotland; Trieste, 1801), he gained renown throughout Italy. From 1802 until his death, Mayr was *maestro di cappella* at the cathedral of Santa Maria Maggiore, Bergamo. He reorganized the cathedral choir school, and under his supervision that school provided its pupils, tuition free, a more complete course of study in music than was available in most Italian music schools at that time.

Mayr composed 60 operas in 1794–1814 and wrote 8 more in the next decade. His masterpieces are *La rosa bianca e la rosa rossa* (The white rose and the red rose; 1813) and *Medea in Corinto* (Medea in Corinth; 1813), modeled after Cherubini's *Médée*. Mayr put into practice many of the reforms advocated by Gluck. Consistently, instead of writing exit arias, Mayr had the *prima donna* or *primo uomo* sing a cavatina at the beginning of a scene and remain on stage for continuation of the action. He included a considerable number of ensembles in his operas. By using accompanied recitative, he constructed long dramatic segments in which several scenes were bridged; *Medea in Corinto* and *La rosa bianca* . . . provide excellent examples of this, a feature that later nineteenth-century composers incorporated in their operas. Mayr used a device that Rossini adopted—the so-called Rossini crescendo: short motivic figures repeated, over alternating tonic and dominant pedals, with gradually thickening orchestration to create a crescendo effect (see pp. 449, 451). Mayr combined Italianate melody with German harmonies and an orchestration characterized by independent writing for winds. Frequently, he included obbligato passages.

After 1815, Mayr devoted most of his time to church music. There exist in manuscript more than 600 works that he would not allow to be published.

GIOACHINO ROSSINI

Rossini (1792–1868) was the principal Italian composer working in Italy in the first quarter of the nineteenth century. His work marks the transition from eighteenth- to nineteenth-century styles in Italian opera. After a successful career in Italy, he moved to Paris, where he contributed significantly to the development of grand opera.

Rossini was born in Pesaro in the Papal States. His parents were musicians employed by a traveling opera company. Rossini's father taught him to play horn, and he had some music lessons from a local priest. In 1804 Rossini entered the Liceo Musicale in Bologna, where he studied composition, counterpoint, singing, 'cello, and piano. While there, he wrote a Mass, some other sacred music, some instrumental pieces, and a cantata. In 1805, he sang in Ferdinando Paer's (1771–1839) *Camilla.*

Rossini's career as opera composer began in 1810, when Teatro San Moïse in Venice commissioned *La cambiale di matrimonio* (The marriage contract). Five of his works were produced in 1812, among them the sacred opera *Ciro in Babilonia* (Cyrus in Babylon, sometimes called an oratorio), *La scala di seta* (The silken ladder), and *La pietra del paragone* (The touchstone). Because Rossini composed operas in quick succession, he did a considerable amount of self-borrowing.

Two operas that Rossini wrote in 1813 brought him international acclaim: *Tancredi* (Tancred; opera seria) and *L'Italiana in Algieri* (The Italian woman in Algiers; opera buffa). In *Tancredi*, formal numbers are separated by *secco* recitative, but within the numbers there are important dramatic events. As did Mayr, Rossini opened a scene with a **cavatina.** This might comprise two successive lyrical sections (*cantabile* solo and *cabaletta*), or it might consist of a short lyrical solo, a nonlyrical choral interruption in a contrasting key, and *cabaletta* in the same key as the opening solo. An example of the latter type of cavatina is Amenaide's prayer scene *Giusto Dio che umile adoro* (Just God whom I humbly worship), Act II, *Tancredi*. By writing this kind of scene, a composer prevents an aria from freezing the action. A **cabaletta** is a short aria that has a persistent rhythm and a repeat that permits the soloist to improvise embellishments. When used in the finale of an act, a *cabaletta* (there called the **stretta**) is usually in rapid tempo, and there is mounting excitement.

Though castrato singing was declining in fashion, Rossini wrote a few castrato roles. Usually, he wrote leading roles for the natural male voice. However, in several operas he wrote trousers roles (male roles sung by women); for example, in *Tancredi*, the hero role is for contralto.

Neapolitan opera was becoming stagnant. In an effort to revitalize it, impresario Domenico Barbaia employed Rossini to be musical and artistic director for his theaters and to compose operas for them; Rossini retained the right to travel and to compose for other theaters. From 1815 to 1822 Rossini worked under that contract. For Naples he composed principally opera seria. *Elisabetta, regina d'Inghilterra* (Elizabeth, queen of England; 1815) marks his first use of *recitativo accompagnato*. Accompanied recitative was not new to Naples—Mayr had used it in *Medea in Corinto* (1813). Isabella Colbran (1785–1845), who had been Medea in Mayr's opera, created the role of Elizabeth; that of Norfolk was sung by tenor Manuel García.

Colbran, the leading dramatic coloratura soprano of the early nineteenth century, sang opera in Barbaia's Teatro San Carlo in 1811–23; Rossini designed leading roles in several operas to display her talents. Colbran and Rossini married in 1822. She retired from the stage in 1824. Colbran was also a composer; she wrote four volumes of songs.

Rossini followed *Elisabetta* with two works for Rome: the rescue opera *Torvaldo e Dorliska* (1815) and the comedy *Almaviva, ossia L'inutile precauzione* (Almaviva, or The useless precaution; 1816), based on Beaumarchais's play, *Le barbier de Séville* (The barber of Seville). *Almaviva* was chosen as the title for Rossini's opera to distinguish it from Paisiello's (1740–1816) *Il barbiere di Siviglia* (1782). The only similarities between Paisiello's and Rossini's operas are the dramatic situations. Cesare Sterbini wrote new verse for Rossini's opera, added chorus, and created the old servant Berta.

Il barbiere di Siviglia is Rossini's masterpiece, his best-known work, and one of the great Italian comic operas. Yet, *Almaviva* was a failure on opening night.

Gioachino Rossini.

Why? Perhaps the Roman audience interpreted Rossini's changes and his new style as lack of respect for Paisiello, who was still living and whose *Il barbiere di Siviglia* was highly regarded in Rome. Perhaps any new opera on that plot would have been considered impertinent and would have been given similar reception. When the opera was produced in Bologna a few months later, only the title was new: *Il barbiere di Siviglia*. The *Almaviva* performed in Rome on 20 February 1816 was essentially the same *Il barbiere di Siviglia* known in the twentieth century. It was the first opera sung in Italian in New York, brought there in 1825 by Manuel García (Insight, "The Garcías").

In *Il barbiere di Siviglia* Rossini used *secco* recitative for much of the dialogue but wrote sectionalized arias and ensemble finales. The opera provides excellent examples of Rossini's style and musical wit. Basilio's *La calunnia* (Slander; DWMA148) displays the "Rossini crescendo" at its finest. The orchestral phrase basic to the crescendo is first presented by strings, playing *sul ponticello, pianissimo* (ex. 21.2). With each repetition of the passage its register ascends, and gradually orchestral forces are increased; strings return to normal bowing position, and articulation

The Garcías

Manuel García (1775–1832), tenor, was educated at Seville Cathedral's choir school. By the age of 18, he was well known in Spain as singer, composer, and conductor of opera. His *El seductor arrepentido* (The repentant seducer; 1802) was one of the earliest Spanish operettas. García worked in Paris in 1808–11, then went to Italy to sing opera. There he met Rossini, and for him created the roles of Norfolk in *Elisabetta* and Almaviva in *Il barbiere di Siviglia*. García was acclaimed internationally as singer. He sang Almaviva in the première of *Il barbiere di Siviglia* in Italian in London, Paris, and America.

García's opera company included his family and three other singers; in 1825 he brought Italian opera to America. The troupe performed 6 Rossini operas, Mozart's *Il Don Giovanni*, and some of García's more than 40 operas and operettas. Lorenzo da Ponte, librettist for *Il Don Giovanni*, was living in America and assisted with that production in New York. The García company remained in the New World until 1829, then returned to Paris. García was an excellent singing teacher. All his children had careers in music: Josefa Ruíz-García, Manuel Patricio García, Pauline Viardot (1821–1910), and Maria Malibran de Bériot (1808–36). Malibran, said to have one of the finest voices of all time, first appeared in opera in Naples in 1814 and sang leading operatic roles internationally.

Pauline Viardot excelled at singing highly dramatic roles. Her performances benefitted the careers of several opera composers, including Gounod, Massenet, and Fauré; she was one of the first to perform Brahms's *Alt-Rhapsodie*. Viardot composed some operettas, some of which are in the repertoire. *Cendrillon* (1904) was performed at Newport, Rhode Island, in 1971. Many of her songs have been published, some of them settings of Russian texts.

Manuel P. García (b. 17 March 1805, d. 1 July 1906), a baritone, sang opera professionally until 1829. After the García opera company returned to Paris, he taught singing and began to study the physiology of the voice. In 1840 he presented to the Académie des Sciences, Paris, his *Mémoire sur la voix humaine* (Report on the human voice), a treatise that formed the basis for all subsequent investigations into physiology of the voice. Also in 1840, his *Traité complet de l'art du chant* (Treatise on the art of singing) was published in Paris. García taught at Paris Conservatoire (1847–50) and at the Royal Academy of Music, London (1848–95). In 1855 he invented the laryngoscope; for this Königsberg University awarded him a Doctor of Philosophy degree.

---

becomes staccato—an excellent musical depiction of spreading rumor.

Rossini wrote two more operas for Naples, then composed *La Cenerentola* (Cinderella; 1817) for Rome and *La gazza ladra* (The thieving magpie; 1817) for Milan. The operas he wrote under his Neapolitan contract show a gradual decrease in the number and prominence of solo arias and an increase in the number and length of ensembles, more use of accompanied recitative and use of a more dramatic type of accompanied recitative, treatment of the chorus as an active participant in the drama, and a growing tendency to notate embellishments rather than allow soloists to improvise them at will.

Rossini's thirty-fourth opera, his last for an Italian theater, was *Semiramide* (1823), a tragedy. At the première, the role of Semiramide was sung by Isabella Colbran, for whom it had been designed; that of Arsace, a trousers role for contralto, was sung by Rosa Mariani.

While in Italy, Rossini composed a dozen cantatas, some incidental music, miscellaneous vocal pieces, and several sacred works, including a *Messa di gloria* (1820).

The Rossinis left Italy in autumn 1823, traveling first to Paris, then to London. In August 1824 Rossini contracted to become director of Théâtre-Italien in Paris and to write operas for that theater and L'Opéra. Under his direction, Théâtre-Italien attained its greatest glory. He produced not only his own works but also Italian operas by other composers, including Meyerbeer's *Il crociato in Egitto* (The crusader in Egypt).

The only new opera Rossini composed for Théâtre-Italien was an occasional work, *Il viaggio a Reims*,

EXAMPLE 21.2 Rossini, *Il barbiere di Siviglia*, "La Calunnia," mm. 18–24 of the Allegro. In measure 20 the strings present the basic figure that is repeated several times to produce the so-called Rossini crescendo.

ossia L'albergo del giglio d'oro (The journey to Reims, or The Golden Lily Inn; June 1825), a one-act *dramma giocoso* performed in conjunction with coronation festivities for Charles X. The score of *Il viaggio a Reims* disappeared for a time, resurfaced c. 1850, then was lost again. The autograph copy was found in the library of Santa Cecilia in Rome in the early 1980s, and the work was performed to open the Rossini Opera Festival in Pesaro in 1984. *Il viaggio a Reims* was given its American première on 12 June 1986 in St. Louis, Missouri.

Late in 1826 Rossini concentrated on composing for L'Opéra. First, he revised two of his Italian operas: *Maometto II* (Mohammed II; 1820) became *Le siège de Corinthe* (The siege of Corinth; 1826), a *tragédie lyrique*, and *Mosè in Egitto* (Moses in Egypt; 1818) became *Moïse et Pharaon*, (Moses and Pharaoh; 1827), an *opéra*. The revisions amounted to more than changing the language and adding ballet. New librettists altered the plots, the music was rewritten, and each opera was lengthened by one act.

Then, Rossini was ready to write new operas. Working with librettists Scribe and Delestre-Poirson, he composed *Le Comte Ory* (Count Ory; 1828), an *opéra comique*. For his next opera, Rossini used a historical, patriotic theme—the heroic ventures of William Tell during the Swiss struggle for freedom from oppression. *Guillaume Tell* (1829) was Rossini's last opera. Produced when the Revolution of 1830 was brewing, the opera stirred the sympathies of the French for their own cause. *Guillaume Tell* is one of the first important grand operas. Rossini integrated spectacular crowd scenes, processions, and ballets into the story, and the chorus is central to the drama. The Swiss freedom fighters' ceremonial vow is magnificent. Characterizations are excellent; reminiscence motives are used effectively. In *Guillaume Tell* Rossini skillfully united Italian lyricism with French declamation and spectacle.

For the remainder of his life Rossini lived in semiretirement. Various reasons for his failure to write another opera have been advanced: weariness, illness, marital problems, and differences of opinion with the new administration of Théâtre-Italien and L'Opéra. All have a few grains of truth in them; none have been proven. In 1829 he negotiated with Charles X and his government a contract that provided Rossini a lifetime annuity and stipulated that he would write four new operas, one every other year. Then came the Revolution of 1830. Charles X was dethroned, and Rossini's contract and annuity were canceled. He took legal action to get the annuity reinstated.

Rossini did not cease composing. He wrote cantatas and choral works for special religious and state occasions, other vocal music, and some instrumental pieces. Most significant of these works are the *Stabat mater* (2d version, 1841), *Petite messe solenelle* (Little solemn Mass; Paris, 1864), and *Péchés de vieillesse* (Sins of old age; 1857–68), 150 "album-leaves" that Rossini did not want published. He created these pieces of musical wit for his *samedi soirées*, Saturday evening gatherings held at his home. Some of the piano pieces were quite difficult, for example, *Prélude prétentieux* (Pretentious prelude), whose fugal subject and parodies of contrapuntal devices reveal Rossini's serious study of the works of J. S. Bach.

Isabella and Rossini legally separated in 1837; in 1845 he married Olympe Pellisier. Since 1840 Rossini had suffered from a chronic disease that slowly worsened; he became seriously ill in 1868 and died in November. He was buried in Paris until Olympe died in 1887; then his remains were moved to Florence. In his will, Rossini provided for the establishment of a Liceo Musicale in Pesaro and two annual prizes in composition to be awarded in Paris. His autograph music was left to Pesaro, and in the 1970s the Fondazione Rossini began work on a critical edition of his complete works.

Music in Iberia

At the beginning of the nineteenth century, music in Iberia was dominated by Italian opera. However, pianist-composer João Bomtempo (1775–1842) worked in other genres. He was the first Portuguese composer of symphonies. His works include two symphonies, six piano concerti, many piano pieces, some chamber music, and some sacred music. His finest work is the *Requiem Mass* (1819). Bomtempo founded the Conservatório Nacional de Musica (1835) and was influential in transforming music teaching in Portugal.

The most important Spanish composers left Spain to work in Paris, London, or Russia. For guitar virtuoso Fernando Sor (1778–1839), the move was obligatory. He fought against the French when they invaded but c. 1810 accepted an administrative post in the French government; after the French retreated (1813), Sor had to leave Spain. His earliest surviving work is the opera *Il Telemaco nell' isola de Calipso* (Telemachus on Calypso's isle; 1797). His symphonies, string quartets, cantata, motet, and Mass have disappeared. He was acclaimed as much for his 33 Italian ariettas and ballets as for his guitar playing. In the twentieth century, Sor is best known for his contribution to classical guitar repertoire: approximately 70 compositions and *Méthode pour la guitare* (Guitar method; 1830).

Music in America

Latin and South America
During 1810–30 Latin American colonies began to gain independence; Mexico did so in 1821. The principal Mexican composer was José Elizaga (1786–1842),

who composed mainly church music in Classic style. He was well acquainted with the music of Mozart and Beethoven and pioneered in promoting performances of their music in Mexico. Most of the performances in Mexico City were by European artists; a few comedies with music by native composers were presented. García's company was the first to sing Italian opera in Italian there in 1827. Commencing in 1831, an Italian opera season was an annual event at Teatro Principal, and until 1871 even native-born composers had to write their operas in Italian to get them performed there.

Before Brazil acquired independence (1822), most of the music making there was associated directly with church services. Around 1800, hundreds of native musicians and composers were active. Most of the music that has been located is liturgical. The only known work in the vernacular—portions of a Christmas oratorio (1789)—was found in 1967.

As a result of French invasion of Portugal in 1807, Queen Maria I (r. 1777–1816) and her son Dom João (regent for Maria I 1799–1816; King John VI, r. 1816–26) moved their court to Rio de Janeiro, where the royal chapel stimulated musical activities considerably. However, Marcos Portugal (1762–1830), court *mestre de capela,* remained in Lisbon until 1811. Then he resumed his court position, and for almost a decade he exercised musical dictatorship in Rio. He produced several Italian operas and composed a comic opera, *A saloia namorada* (A peasant girl in love; 1812), on a libretto by Brazilian poet Domingos Barbosa. The catalog of Marcos's works lists 35 Italian operas, 21 Portuguese comic operas, and more than 100 pieces of church music. He composed Brazil's *Hino da independência* (Hymn of independence; 1822).

From 1808 to 1811, José Mauricio Nunes García (1767–1830), *mestre de capela* at Rio de Janeiro Cathedral, served as *mestre de capela* at the Portuguese court. He was one of Brazil's finest composers. Of his extant compositions, 225 are liturgical, 5 are instrumental, and 5 are secular vocal works and include one opera. His masterpiece is the *Requiem Mass* (1816), commissioned for the funeral of Queen Maria.

In the La Plata River Viceroyalty, Buenos Aires was the most important city musically, with activity centered in the church and the theater. Plays with music (*tonadillas* and *zarzuelas*) were presented in the theaters in the late eighteenth century, and Italian operas were performed regularly after 1824.

North America

During the first quarter of the nineteenth century, European professional musicians came to the United States to concertize and to perform ballad operas and plays with incidental music. Some of those professionals settled in America (e.g., oboist Gottlieb Graupner [1767–1836], organist George K. Jackson [1745–1823], and librettist Lorenzo da Ponte). The music centers were Philadelphia, New York, and Boston. Polemic writings appeared debasing fuging tunes and other pieces by singing-school music masters and praising the works of Handel and Haydn. In 1815 a few musicians in Boston founded the Handel and Haydn Society for the performance of choral and instrumental music. Similar societies were established in other major cities. In 1825 García's opera company performed Italian operas in New York. Tune books were compiled and popular songs were written, but there were no outstanding American-born composers or performers during this quarter-century.

In Canada, cultural activities were local and depended to a great extent on talents of local residents. The centers of musical activity were the church, the coffeehouse, and, in larger communities, the military band. Touring companies performed ballad operas in Quebec, Montreal, and Halifax. In 1820 Thomas Linley's comic opera *The Duenna* was the first opera produced in Newfoundland.

Summary

In the first half of the nineteenth century, Paris became the opera capital of the world and attracted Italian opera composers who eventually wrote operas in the French style. For a time, opéra comique served as a vehicle for patriotism; then lighter types of opéra comique became the vogue. All-sung opera was pushed into the shadows until the 1820s.

Cherubini's rescue operas, particularly *Les deux journées*, were models for similar operas by composers throughout Europe. Use of recurrent themes, or reminiscence motives, a feature of the operas of Cherubini,

Méhul, and other composers working in Paris, led to a kind of Leitmotif used by Weber. Auber, in opéras comiques, achieved a blend of comic and Romantic elements, then turned to a more serious, more lyrical type. Parisian composers did not limit their writing to opera. Cherubini (and Schubert) wrote some of the finest Catholic Masses produced during the first half of the nineteenth century; Méhul composed symphonies. Many composers were concerned educators who helped formulate government educational policies, taught at the Paris Conservatoire, and determined its curricula.

Before 1820 very few all-sung operas were successful in Paris. Napoleon favored the spectacular, especially if it honored him and France; through Privilèges, he controlled what was staged. Spontini's *La Vestale* (1807) and *Fernand Cortez* (1809) were significant forerunners of the monumental grand operas produced at L'Opéra c. 1828. Spontini's tragédies lyriques were a continuation of the traditional French form of opera; thus, he forged another link in the chain—Lully, Rameau, Gluck, and Spontini—that led to Berlioz. The earliest successful grand operas were Auber's *La muette de Portici* (1828) and Rossini's *Guillaume Tell* (1829). Through the joint efforts of Scribe, Meyerbeer, and Véron in the early 1830s, grand opera masterpieces were produced and standards established. Changes in theatrical practices in the 1820s—new methods of lighting and scenic design—greatly affected opera production.

In Austro-Germanic lands, the most significant developments were in the areas of solo song and opera. Collections of folk poetry inspired many song settings. German nationalism entered opera gradually through legend and fairy tale; elements of magic and the supernatural appeared in Singspiele. In 1816 Hoffmann's *Undine* and Spohr's *Faust* prepared the way for Weber, who firmly established German Romantic opera in Singspiel with *Der Freischütz* (1821) and in opera seria with *Euryanthe* (1823). Gradually, recitative supplanted spoken dialogue in German operas. Melodrama was retained for special effects. Weber and other German composers strove toward *Gesamtkunstwerk,* a unification of all the arts through opera. Weber's efforts to effect theatrical reforms did a great deal to improve standards of opera production. Minor German composers who contributed to opera include Marschner and Lortzing. German composers did not limit themselves to opera. Spohr and Weber were competent conductors; Hoffmann was author, music critic, and painter. Weber, a virtuoso pianist, contributed to clarinet repertoire also; his works for *a cappella* male chorus in *Leyer und Schwert* were among the earliest of many such patriotic German songs in the nineteenth century. Weber's published critical essays foreshadowed the editorial writings of Schumann.

Most important among the many composers of Lieder and ballads were Loewe and Schubert. They wrote in many genres but are remembered chiefly for their solo songs with piano accompaniment. In his Lieder Schubert so synthesized words and music that his music is a translation of the poetry. His late string quartets and last two symphonies are important contributions to the repertoire. His works were not widely disseminated during his lifetime; many were disregarded, forgotten, or lost for some time after his death. As his works gradually came to light, they influenced the works of major composers.

Italy, which had held musical leadership, took a lesser role in the early nineteenth century. Many Italian composers were attracted to Paris. Italy's rich opera tradition was not lost, however, for in Italy composers concentrated on opera. Spoken dialogue made no inroads—all opera was sung throughout. Mayr, a Bavarian working in Italy, put into practice many of the operatic reforms advocated by Gluck and Jommelli and did much to promote acceptance of those reforms throughout nonunified Italy. Besides writing 60 operas, Mayr composed a vast amount of church music, taught, and greatly improved the quality of music education in his locale.

Rossini was the principal Italian composer working in Italy in the first quarter of the nineteenth century. His works show the transition from eighteenth- to nineteenth-century styles in Italian opera. Though he preferred to write for the natural male voice, he sometimes wrote for castrati and in several operas designed the hero's role to be sung by a woman. After successes in Italy and in Vienna, he moved to Paris, where he helped develop grand opera. After the Revolution of 1830, Rossini ceased writing opera and turned to other types of composition. His most important nonoperatic work is his *Stabat mater.*

Manuel García's opera company performed Rossini's works throughout Europe and was the first to perform opera in Italian in America. After a short career as singer, Manuel P. García worked as scientist and singing teacher; he invented the laryngoscope and wrote the treatise that formed the basis for all subsequent investigations into physiology of the voice.

At the beginning of the nineteenth century, music in Iberia was dominated by Italian opera. With Napoleon's invasions, conditions changed. The Portuguese royal court moved to Brazil, and several Iberian composers pursued careers elsewhere in Europe (e.g., Sor and Bomtempo). Later, some composers returned to Portugal, as did Bomtempo; he was the first Portuguese composer to write symphonies.

In 1810–30 Latin American colonies began acquiring independence. The principal nineteenth-century Mexican composer was Elizaga, who wrote mainly church music. He was influential in founding Mexico's first music conservatory.

In Brazil, hundreds of native musicians and composers were active; most of their known compositions are liturgical music. Marcos Portugal, court *mestre de capela,* composed Italian and Portuguese operas and church music; José Mauricio, one of Brazil's finest native composers, wrote mainly liturgical music. In the La Plata River Viceroyalty, Buenos Aires was the most important city musically, with activity centered in the church and in opera.

In North America, European musicians concertized and gave theatrical performances. The centers of music in United States were Boston, New York, and Philadelphia. Tune books were compiled and some popular songs written, but there were no outstanding American-born composers or performers during those years. In Canada the centers of musical activity were the local church, coffeehouse, and military band.

NINETEENTH-CENTURY MUSICAL EXPANSION

22

Between 1825 and 1870, the developments with the most significant social and political consequences were industrialization and the rise of nationalism. Industrialization brought increased urbanization. Great factories with powered machinery appeared throughout Europe, and wealthy industrialists and merchants sought to dominate politics. Among the new industrial procedures was the loom invented by J. M. Jacquard of Lyons, in which a series of rectangular punched cards controlled the complex patterns of the silk threads weaving the fabric. Inspired by the principle of the Jacquard loom, London inventor Charles Babbage (1792–1871) designed (but never built) an "Analytical Engine" operated by a kind of mechanized intelligence—a stored memory and programs encoded on spinning cylinders. Ada Lovelace (1815–52), in a published commentary (1842) on Babbage's engine, wrote that a machine of this type with pitches and harmonies encoded on spinning cylinders "might compose elaborate and scientific pieces of music of any degree of complexity or extent." Lovelace stated that the machine could not *originate* anything but could carry out whatever it was programmed to perform. Thus, before the middle of the nineteenth century Lovelace advanced the idea of computer-generated music.

Britain was the leading industrial power between 1825 and 1870 and was the most stable politically. France was, in many respects, the culturally dominant nation but was unsettled politically. In the 1830 Revolution, the monarchy of Charles X (r. 1824–30) was overthrown. Louis Philippe (r. 1830–48) was crowned "King of the French" but was deposed in 1848 as a result of working-class uprisings. Louis Napoleon was named president and soon approximated dictatorship as "Emperor Napoleon III." That régime collapsed during the Franco-Prussian War (1870).

There were numerous uprisings in other European countries. The doctrine of nationalism—the establishment of states according to nationality of peoples instead of on the basis of dynastic inheritance or intermarriage—gained strength. The Italian people, who for centuries had lived in separate kingdoms, duchies, and republics, were finally united in several steps (fig. 22.1) as a kingdom under Victor Emanuele I of Savoy. Unification of the German people as an empire under Kaiser Wilhelm I (and his minister Otto von Bismarck) occurred after Prussia successfully waged war with France in 1870. In America, the Civil War was fought (1861–65) to preserve the republic and national unity. The patriotism and nationalism rampant throughout the Western world found expression in the arts. In music, nationalism became increasingly apparent during the last half of the century.

FIGURE 22.1 The unification of Italy may be viewed as the expansion of Sardinia. The extent of Sardinia (*a*) in January 1859; (*b*) in August 1859; (*c*) in April 1860; (*d*) after October 1860. Notice how The Patrimony of St. Peter (The Papal States) has diminished.

The first stirrings of socialism and socialistic labor movements appeared. Among those producing thought-provoking publications on economic and social conditions were Friedrich Engels and Karl Marx, authors of *Communist Manifesto* (1848). Their ideas were welcomed not only by factory workers but by people experiencing crop failures. Those failures caused many persons to emigrate to America.

The arts were important. Philosophers discussed them and wrote about them. Georg F. W. Hegel (1770–1831) taught a course on esthetics; his *Lectures on Aesthetics* were published posthumously (1835–38). Some patronage of the arts still existed, but for the most part success for the musician meant concertizing and gaining public acclaim. The concert-going populace was no longer an elite group but consisted of persons from all walks of life. More and more, women were manifesting their talents in the arts—writing and publishing novels and poetry, composing and publishing music, directing choral ensembles, and concertizing. Schumann, in one of his essays, compared the musical populace of his time with politicians and divided them into "liberals, middlemen, and reactionaries, or romanticists, moderns, and classicists." In an era in which composers were confronted with making a choice of audience for whom to write, Schumann was a spokesman against the "philistines"—those who "catered to the crowd" by writing easily salable merchandise.

1800	1825	1850	1875

- Revolution of 1830
- Revolution of 1848
- 1861–65 Civil War in United States

1809 — Abraham Lincoln — 1865

- 1869 Suez Canal opened

- 1848 Marx-Engels: *Communist Manifesto*

Unification of Italy
Unification of Germany } • 1871

Cecilian movement

- c. 1825–70 Britain the leading industrial power: France culturally dominant

increase in amount of program music

character pieces for piano

- 1840 first complete solo recital

voices increasingly included in symphonies

concert overture

revival of J. S. Bach's works; Bach Gesellschaft founded

piano becomes the most important solo instrument

opéra comique

1875 •
Bizet: *Carmen*

lyric opera
- 1859 Gounod: *Faust*
- c. 1855 *opéra bouffe* fl.

grand opera — begins to diminish
- 1831 Meyerbeer: *Robert le diable*

- 1856–58 Berlioz: *Les Troyens*

opera semiseria

- 1831 Bellini: *Norma*

Mendelssohn
- 1836 *St. Paul*; 1846 *Elijah*

- 1840 Robert Schumann: Lieder

- 1830 Berlioz: *Symphonie fantastique*

- 1843 { Leipzig Conservatory founded; Clara and Robert Schumann on faculty

- 1842 New York Philharmonic Society founded

CECILIAN MOVEMENT

Commencing around 1825 and continuing through the century, there was increasing interest in the music of Palestrina and other composers who wrote liturgical *a cappella* polyphony. That interest generated a movement that fostered a return to use of *a cappella* choral music in the church, particularly music in the style of Palestrina. (Whether Palestrina's music actually was performed *a cappella* is debatable, but in the nineteenth century that was believed to have been the case.) As an offshoot of this, there arose c. 1848 a movement that advocated use of Gregorian chant in its purest form. In some regions, this meant strict adherence to the *Editio Medicaea* published in 1614. In other areas, particularly those in accord with the beliefs of the Solesmes school, there was a desire to go back further to the St. Gall Codex and the choral style of the late Middle Ages. The movement was in direct opposition to the views of the Enlightenment, which sought complete integration of instrumental and vocal music in liturgical services.

The reform movements had little effect on actual practice during the first half of the nineteenth century. In France the movement was strong; it established use of *a cappella* choral music and Gregorian chant in services. In Germany in 1869 the Allgemeine Cäcilien-Verein (General Cecilian Society) was formed for the purpose of eliminating integrated music from services; in 1870 Pope Pius IX officially sanctioned that Society and its stated purposes. The Cecilian movement—named for St. Cecilia, patron saint of music—spread rapidly, and in many regions there was strict demarcation between styles of church and secular music. Contemporary nineteenth-century musical developments were considered untenable where church music was concerned; sacred music that integrated instrumental/vocal and secular/sacred styles was unacceptable for performance in church.

One result of the Cecilian movement was the improvement of singing in the church. A provision of the 1903 *Moto Proprio* of Pope Pius X stressed the importance of this and made musical education of the clergy compulsory. Another result was the preparation and publication of new editions of liturgical chant books. The *Regensburg Edition*, based on the *Editio Medicaea* and advocated by the Society of St. Cecilia, appeared in 1875. Both it and the *Editio Medicaea* were supplanted by the *Editio Vaticana*, prepared in compliance with the 1903 *Moto Proprio*.

VOCAL MUSIC

Nineteenth-century composers wrote several kinds of vocal music: (1) accompanied solos (Lieder, ballads, romances, and other solo songs, including arrangements of folk songs); (2) part-songs and choruses, chiefly on secular texts, for male, female, or mixed ensembles; (3) sacred music intended for use in church services; (4) large works for chorus and orchestra, with or without vocal soloist(s), intended for concert performance (oratorios, cantatas, and single- or multi-movement independent pieces); and (5) operas. A number of symphonic works incorporated chorus and/or soloist(s) in one or more movements.

In Schubert's hands, German vernacular song was an art form in which the music expressed the emotion and meaning of the words, words and music became fused, and keyboard and vocalist were equal partners. As Schubert's Lieder became more widely known in mid-nineteenth century, many composers emulated his style, but few (e.g., Schumann) matched his genius. The embodiment of words into music that is present in Schubert's Lieder extended into piano music where, without lyrics, in such pieces as *Lieder ohne Worte*, the music alone paints the picture or tells the story.

Hundreds of part-songs were written in the nineteenth century. Many of them were patriotic and were engendered by the frequent political uprisings in European countries between 1825 and 1875. Other part-songs were written for performance at music festivals in Germany and in Britain or for use by the choral societies that existed in almost every German town. Only a few of the part-songs have had frequent performances in the twentieth century.

Most nineteenth-century composers wrote some church music. In the area of liturgical service music, the finest Catholic masses were composed by Cherubini, Schubert, and Liszt. Rossini's *Stabat mater* is excellent, though operatic in style. Liszt and Mendelssohn were among those writing settings of the Psalms; Samuel S. Wesley wrote 27 anthems for the Anglican church.

The terms *oratorio* and *cantata* were not clearly differentiated. Though a cantata might be either sacred or secular, most of them are secular; usually, a cantata is shorter and less dramatic than an oratorio. Among the excellent cantatas composed in the mid-nineteenth century are Mendelssohn's *Die erste Walpurgisnacht* (The first Walpurgis night) and R. Schumann's *Das Paradies und die Peri* (Paradise and the Peri).

Customarily, a composer labeled a work "oratorio" if it dealt with a sacred subject and there was a part for narrator; however, narration might be given to chorus. Some Romantic oratorios were based on religious legends (e.g., Liszt's *Die Legende von der heiligen Elisabeth* [The Legend of St. Elisabeth]); others concern the life and work of martyrs (e.g., Loewe's *Johann Hus*). The subject matter of an oratorio might be either contemplative or dramatic; however, an oratorio is not intended to be staged, nor are the singers specially costumed for its performance. Representative oratorios on contemplative subjects are Spohr's *Die letzten Dinge* (The last Judgment) and César Franck's *Les béatitudes* (The beatitudes). The finest nineteenth-century oratorios are Mendelssohn's *St. Paul* and *Elijah*. Excellent choral writing is vital to an oratorio, and Mendelssohn's expertise in this regard placed his works second only to Handel's in the eyes of the English.

Quite a few large works on sacred subjects were written for performance in church but were not intended for and were not appropriate for liturgical services. Representative of such works are Berlioz's *Grande Messe des morts* and *Te Deum laudamus,* conceived for military-political commemorations. Verdi's *Requiem* was written as a memorial to a specific individual, and Brahms's *Ein deutsches Requiem* (A German Requiem) does not follow a liturgical format. In the twentieth century, these works have been performed in concerts.

INSTRUMENTAL MUSIC

Instrumental music composed during the nineteenth century includes orchestral works, chamber music, compositions for solo instrument with orchestral or keyboard accompaniment, and solo piano pieces. Any of these instrumental types might be **program** (descriptive, or referential) music or **absolute** (nonreferential, or "pure") music. The orchestral works were principally symphonies, concert overtures, and stylized dance music. All the types of symphonies can be related to those of Beethoven. Programmatic works are related to his *Pastoral Symphony;* cyclic works, those with movements that are linked, and those that commence in one key and conclude in another are related to his Fifth Symphony. Symphonies that include voices stem from his Ninth Symphony. Unconventionality of formal structure may derive from his Sixth Symphony or from his Ninth. "Heroic" symphonies and those with thematic transformation have their roots in *Sinfonia Eroica.* Aside from an unconventional introduction, Beethoven's First Symphony is conventional absolute music, as are his Second, Fourth, Seventh, and Eighth Symphonies.

Almost all the chamber music written in the nineteenth century is absolute music of traditional types:

sonata, trio, quartet, quintet, and other ensemble music with one person per part.

Most of the solos with orchestral accompaniment are concerti. The principal solo instruments were piano and violin; a few solos were written for 'cello and for clarinet. Throughout the nineteenth century, the piano was the most important solo instrument and was considered indispensable in every middle- and upper-class home. Anyone aspiring to some degree of gentility learned to play the piano. For it composers wrote dance pieces (waltz, mazurka, polonaise, and others), character pieces (ballade, barcarolle, impromptu, and others), concert études, solo sonatas, variations, and fantasias.

PIANO PLAYING

After c. 1828, several styles of piano playing were evident. As piano construction improved, composers wrote music that was increasingly more demanding technically. In the 1830s Liszt composed some pieces that required the 88-key keyboard. Field and Hummel bridge the Classic style of Clementi and Mozart and the Romantic style of Chopin and Liszt. Field and Hummel played with clarity, brightness, and elegance, as did Chopin and Liszt, with never a suggestion of pounding or "thumping." Chopin and Schubert stated their dislike of forceful playing. Field was first to use the pedal as an integral part of the piano; in his music, as in Chopin's, proper pedaling is vital for the wide-spaced harmonies.

Successful pianists who aimed to impress with showmanship and audacity include Louis M. Gottschalk (1829–69), Sigismund Thalberg (1812–71), and Friedrich Kalkbrenner (1785–1849). Their compositions are of lesser quality than those of Chopin and Liszt. Kalkbrenner was admired by Chopin; both men were capable of power when needed but also achieved effects by means of delicacy, subtlety, and refinement.

The impressive, colorful pianists whose technical display did not detract from their effective interpretation of the music were Franz Liszt (1811–86), Anton Rubinstein (1829–94), and Hans von Bülow (1830–94). Von Bülow, pupil of Friedrich Wieck and later of Liszt, was well known as a conductor. Rubinstein's concert career began when he toured Europe in 1854. With the assistance of Duchess Elena Pavlovna, he founded the Russia Musical Society, whose concerts he conducted, and established St. Petersburg Conservatory (1862). He was director of the Conservatory until 1867, when he again concertized in Europe.

Liszt was considered the finest pianist of his time (see Chap. 23). In his compositions and performance style he exploited the piano's capabilities in a manner previously unknown. Liszt was the first to play a complete solo recital (London, 1840), unassisted by and not shared with other musicians. His recitals included works by his predecessors and contemporaries as well as his own compositions and transcriptions of orchestral overtures and symphonies.

The outstanding pianists with solid musicianship, concern for correct interpretation, and technical perfection without pretentious display or pointless bravura were Felix Mendelssohn-Bartholdy (1809–47), Clara Wieck Schumann (1819–96), and Johannes Brahms (1833–97).

Liszt preferred to teach master classes rather than private lessons. Czerny, his teacher, gave up a performance career to teach. In the second half of the nineteenth century, teaching became a career for many who considered performing of secondary importance.

MUSIC IN AUSTRO-GERMANIC LANDS

Though there was no Austro-German empire after 1806, close ties existed between Austria and the German states throughout the nineteenth century. After the Congress of Vienna, Germany was even more divided than it had been previously. The search for a national identity found expression in the music of German composers as well as in literature.

The most important music publishing houses were in Leipzig, but others existed in large German cities, and music printed in Vienna was readily available throughout Germany. As the century advanced, there was increased interest in the music of great composers of the past, particularly Bach, Handel, Palestrina, and Gabrieli. By midcentury, plans were made for preparation and publication of complete editions of the works of Palestrina and Gabrieli. Composers and scholars searched for old music, and many persons collected manuscripts. By 1850, music of the past had found a

place in concert repertoire. As the nineteenth century advanced, interest in early music increased, the search for it and study of it continued, and performance of it on concert programs became normal procedure.

Beethoven's achievements in symphony and string quartet were so highly regarded that, for a time, many composers hesitated to work in those genres. However, all kinds of music were composed, especially solos such as Lieder and character pieces. Romanticism flourished and was evident in subjects of operas, in program music, and in choral part-songs. Choral societies existed in almost all cities and towns. In Vienna, dancing was a popular pastime, and the waltz was the favorite dance. Composers wrote numerous sets of waltzes for concert performance.

The founding of Leipzig Conservatory (1843) and the Berlin Hochschule für Musik (1868) was followed by the establishment of conservatories in other major cities. Outstanding faculty provided excellent instruction in all areas of music. Considerable importance was attached to teaching, to serving as director of a conservatory, or to being conductor-director of an opera house or of a society that presented a regular season of concerts.

FRÉDÉRIC CHOPIN

Pure Romanticism is seen in most of the piano music of Frédéric Chopin (1810–49), a native of Warsaw. At the time of his birth, the Grand Duchy of Warsaw was part of the Kingdom of Saxony; technically, Chopin was a citizen of a Germanic land. Chopin's mother, who was Polish, had had sufficient musical training to be able to sing well and to teach piano; his father, who was French, taught French language and literature in a boarding school the couple operated. Frédéric had literary and musical talent: at age 7, he was writing poetry, could improvise, and composed several pieces, including a polonaise (published) and a march (lost). By 1818, when he made his first public appearance as a piano soloist in a concerto, Chopin knew that he wanted a career in music. During his high school years (1823–26), he studied music at Warsaw Conservatory and in 1825 composed a *Rondo* in C minor, his Op. 1 (pub. 1825). In 1826 he performed two benefit concerts, enrolled at Warsaw Conservatory, and composed music for his own use. His *La cì darem la mano varié*

Frédéric Chopin. Portrait by Eugène Delacroix (1838). *(The Louvre, Paris. © R.M.N.)*

(Variations on [Mozart's] *La cì darem la mano,* Op. 2; pno., orch.; pub. 1830) was followed by a Sonata in C minor (Op. 4), *Rondo à la Mazur* (Op. 5), and nine *Mazurkas* (Opp. 6, 7).

In 1829 Chopin went to Vienna, had some works published, and performed two successful concerts of his own music. He returned to Warsaw, composed two piano concerti and some études, and in the spring of 1830 played a concert at the National Theater. His virtuosic performance, coupled with the Polish character of his compositions, caused the public to view him as a national composer, but in a short time his glory diminished. In 1830 Schumann heard Chopin play the *La cì darem la mano* variations and wrote the article *Ein Opus II,* in which he made salient remarks about the music and proclaimed through one of his fictitious characters, "Hats off, gentlemen, a genius!"

A concert Chopin performed in Paris in February 1832 received excellent reviews, and his acceptance there was assured. He moved in the highest social circles, but he did not enjoy performing before large audiences. He limited his concert appearances to once or twice a year, and sometimes those were as second pianist to another artist. During his entire career, he performed only about 30 public concerts. No other performer achieved so great a reputation with so few concerts. In some respects, Chopin's temperament as a performing musician resembled that of Schubert—he preferred to perform in salons before small audiences or at gatherings of his friends. Chopin's style of playing, with its subtle nuances and his use of sustaining pedal to blur harmonies and blend tones, was more suited to a small audience.

To earn his living, Chopin taught. Though he enjoyed teaching, his real interest was composing, and it was not long before he was recognized in Paris as a composer and could earn his living that way.

In 1836 Chopin experienced bouts of serious illness, and his health declined; by 1838, his ailment had been definitely diagnosed as tuberculosis. As the illness progressed, his compositional output diminished; in 1844 he wrote only the B-minor Sonata.

Over the years, he had several love affairs. That of longest duration (1837–47) was with French novelist Aurore Dudevant (George Sand; 1803–76). After Chopin broke with her, his health deteriorated rapidly. Composition no longer interested him. In February 1848, almost on the eve of the Revolution, he performed in a concert in Paris, then went to Britain and gave several performances there. When he returned to Paris in 1849 he was quite ill. He died on October 17. As he had requested, Mozart's *Requiem Mass* was performed at his funeral, which was at La Madeleine; special permission had to be obtained for women to sing there.

INFLUENCES AND STYLE   The composer-performers most influential on Chopin's playing and composing were Field and Hummel. Polish national dances and melodies were shaping forces on Chopin's music; possibly, he knew the mazurkas, polonaises, and nocturnes of Polish pianist Maria Szymanowska (1789–1831). Another factor was the kind of piano available to him and its technical capabilities. Without the double-escapement action Érard patented in 1821, it would not have been possible for Chopin to articulate clearly the rapidly repeated notes that appear so often in his music. Also, leather-covered hammers contributed to the soft tone quality.

Chopin did not write program music. His music is graceful, sensitive, expressive, and Romantic, and proper performance of it demands of the player impeccable technique and touch. His melodies are lyrical;

usually, they are periodic, eight measures long, and basically diatonic. Chopin was skilled at improvisation and preferred thematic variation rather than fragmentation as a developmental tool. Chromaticism was used to vary and develop themes. Grace notes, passing tones, and ornaments are abundant. Repetition with variation and return after contrast were his basic formal procedures. Frequently, he used a kind of rondo, for example, *Nocturne,* Op. 9 No. 2, constructed as A–A'–B–A''–B'–A'''–Coda–Cadenza–Cadence. In Chopin's music strict counterpoint and polyphony are rare. In his harmonies, he used dissonance freely, daringly, and shockingly (ex. 22.1). Often, he modulated enharmonically; sometimes he simply assumed a new key. At times, his melodies seem to be generated by the harmonies he used, for he was adept at weaving melody into accompaniment figurations or weaving accompaniment figurations around melody. Frequently, the rhythms are those associated with dances. Chopin used the *sostenuto* pedal not only to sustain a melodic line or a harmony but, more importantly, to expand the compass of a chord and extend the harmony well beyond the normal octave span of a hand (ex. 22.2). Proper pedaling is vital when performing Chopin's music.

Tempo rubato is an important characteristic of Chopin's music. His own explanation of the term is as follows: The hand playing the accompaniment adheres to strict tempo; the hand playing the melody relaxes the tempo, then unobtrusively accelerates it in order to resume synchronization with the accompaniment.

CHOPIN'S WORKS   Chopin's piano solos include 26 preludes, 27 études, 21 nocturnes, 4 impromptus, 16 polonaises, 61 mazurkas, 20 waltzes, 3 sonatas, 4 bal-lades, 4 scherzi, fantasias, 4 variations, 4 rondos, marches, and numerous pieces bearing such titles as *Barcarolle* (Op. 57, Op. 60), *Bolero* (Op. 19), *Bourrée* (2 WoO, pub. 1968), and *Tarantelle* (Op. 43). He wrote 1 Fugue (A minor; 1841, pub. 1898) and 1 Canon (F minor; c. 1839). For piano and orchestra there are 2 concerti (F minor, E minor), *Variations on La cì darem la mano, Fantasia on Polish airs, Grand Polonaise in E♭,* and the concert rondo *Krakowiak* (Op. 14; 1828). Also, there are a piano trio, 3 chamber music works for 'cello and piano, a set of variations for flute and piano, and 19 songs in Polish texts.

There are two single *Preludes,* in A♭ major (WoO; 1834, pub. 1918) and C♯ minor (Op. 45; 1841), and a set of *24 Preludes* (Op. 28; 1836–39; pub. 1839). The Op. 28 *Preludes* are short independent pieces, one in each major and minor key. They are arranged in the volume in major-minor pairs, commencing with C major and A minor, and proceed first in ascending numbers of sharps and then in descending numbers of flats. *Prelude* in E minor, Op. 28 No. 4 (DWMA149), is a one-part form, 25 measures in length.

Each volume of *Études,* Op. 10 and Op. 25, contains 12 studies; in addition, Chopin wrote 3 études for Moscheles's *Méthode* (1839). There are études in most of the 24 keys. Chopin seems to have been the first pianist to write études with sufficient musicality to be performed in public without revealing their underlying pedagogical purpose. The E-major *Étude,* Op. 10 No. 3, was Chopin's favorite; its apparent simplicity is deceptive. Most of the Op. 25 études are very demanding. The "Winter Wind" *Étude,* Op. 25 No. 11, commences Lento with two statements of the dirgelike tolling figure on which the composition is based (ex. 22.3; DWMA150). The body of the study is an Allegro

EXAMPLE 22.1 Frequently Chopin's use of dissonance was daring: *Scherzo,* Op. 20, mm. 591–601. (*Source: F. F. Chopin: Dziela wszystkie [Complete Works] 1949–1961, edited by I. J. Paderewski, 1953 Instytut Fryderyka Chopina, Warsaw, Poland, Vol. V [Scherzos]*)

con fuoco in which one hand steadily reiterates harmonizations of the somber theme while the other hand is a whirlwind of activity.

Chopin's mazurkas and polonaises were some of the earliest nineteenth-century music based on national idioms. He composed *Rondo à la Mazur* and a *Mazurka* in G major in 1826; that year, Maria Szymanowska's *24 Mazurkas* appeared in Leipzig. Chopin made no direct quotations from Polish dances—he used their characteristic rhythms, melodies, and harmonies. The mazurka originated near Warsaw; the name of the dance derives from the folk who lived in that area, the Mazurs. There are three types or regional variations of mazurka; the *mazur,* the *obertas,* and the *kujawiak.* All use triple meter, with the second or third beat of the measure stressed. The raised fourth degree of the scale, a feature of the Lydian mode, is characteristic of Polish music and of Chopin's mazurkas. Many of his mazurkas are in some kind of rondo form.

The stately processional-type Polish dance that, sometime in the seventeenth century, the French named "polonaise" had existed for centuries. Stylized instrumental versions of it appeared in the seventeenth century, and in the eighteenth century some were written by Bach, Handel, Couperin, and others. In Chopin's hands, the polonaise became a symbol of Polish nationalism. The most popular and the finest of his polonaises is that in A♭ major, Op. 53 (1842).

Chopin's nocturnes are subjective, introspective, expressive pieces. Clearly, they were influenced by those of Field, though Chopin's harmonies are more complex. Chopin's skill at improvisation is apparent in his nocturnes; this, along with Romantic harmonies, enriched them considerably. Usually, each time the melody recurred Chopin embellished it increasingly, and occasionally he inserted small cadenzas. This may be seen in his *Nocturne* in E♭ major, Op. 9 No. 2. In several respects that work resembles Field's *Nocturne* in A major, No. 9. A greater similarity exists between Chopin's *Nocturne* in A♭ major, Op. 32, and Field's *Nocturne* No. 5, in B♭ major. Both convey a nostalgic atmosphere (DWMA151 and 139).

EXAMPLE 22.2 Chopin used the pedal to expand the compass of a chord and extend harmony beyond a normal handspan: (*a*) *Étude*, Op. 10, No. 11, mm. 1–3; (*b*) *Nocturne*, Op. 27, No. 1, mm. 1–4.

(a)

(b)

EXAMPLE 22.3 Chopin: *Étude*, Op. 25, No. 11, mm. 1–4. The dirge-like tolling figure that begins the *Étude* serves as basis for the piece. (*Source:* F. F. Chopin: Dziela wszystkie [Complete Works] Vol. II, edited by I. J. Paderewski, 1949 Instytut Fryderyka Chopina, Warsaw, Poland)

NINETEENTH-CENTURY MUSICAL EXPANSION

Chopin's C-minor Piano Sonata was unsatisfactory to both his teacher and himself. In 1837 he composed a *Marche funèbre* as an isolated composition; three years later, he wrote three movements to surround it and thus created his second Piano Sonata (B♭ minor; Op. 35). It is a Romantic work, with Scherzo/Trio placed second and the slow movement third, and with an unusual Finale. The sonata climaxes with a Presto filled with chromatic passages played by both hands an octave apart. Chopin's third and last Piano Sonata (B minor, Op. 58; 1844) is more conventional. Chopin was un-orthodox in writing recapitulations of sonata-form movements. Usually, he returned the second theme first; sometimes he omitted the first theme or returned it in a key other than the tonic.

In the composition of instrumental ballades, Chopin seems to have had no predecessors. His ballades are large one-movement works constructed according to the principle of repetition after contrast. A characteristic of the ballades is the consistent use of one of the themes varied or transformed each time it reappears.

Chopin's significance in the development of music lies in his ability to write music particularly suited to the piano, taking full advantage of its unique capabilities rather than attempting to draw from it orchestral sonorities. He thoroughly understood the piano of his day, viewed it as a solo instrument, and made the most of its distinctive, expressive qualities. His hands were small, and his fingerings were often unorthodox, yet his playing was virtuosic. His best compositions are those in which he was unhampered by traditional forms: ballades, nocturnes, preludes, and études.

FELIX MENDELSSOHN (BARTHOLDY)

Felix Mendelssohn (1809–47) grew up in a cultured environment provided by his parental home and by the city of Berlin, where there was some social equality for citizens who followed the Jewish faith. The Mendelssohns themselves provided their children's early education, including music lessons. All four children had talent: Rebekka sang, Paul played 'cello, and when Fanny and Felix showed exceptional pianistic talent, they had lessons from Ludwig Berger (1777–1839). Felix had violin lessons and painting/drawing lessons also. Later, he created some beautiful landscape watercolors (plate 23) and wrote poetry, some of which he set to music.

Felix Mendelssohn. Portrait by Edward Magnus (1845). Original in Mendelssohn-Archiv, Leipzig.

In 1816, the Mendelssohn family lived in Paris. There, Fanny and Felix received piano lessons from Marie Bigot (Insight, "Marie Kiéné Bigot"). That year Abraham Mendelssohn (1776–1835) had his children baptized as Christians; later, he converted to Christianity and adjusted the family name to Mendelssohn-Bartholdy. Christian and Enlightenment beliefs were important factors in Felix's career.

When the Mendelssohns returned to Berlin, Fanny and Felix had theory and composition lessons from C. F. Zelter (1758–1832), noted composer of Lieder, who was director of the Berlin Singakademie. Mendelssohn's great-aunt, Sara Levy (1763–1854), had recommended Zelter as their teacher. Levy had been a harpsichord pupil and patroness of W. F. Bach and had known C. P. E. Bach; she appeared as harpsichord soloist at the Singakademie on several occasions in 1806–8. Levy had a large library of music composed by members of the Bach family. Her library was available to Zelter, members of the family, and the Singakademie. Zelter taught J. S. Bach's works to his pupils and promoted the performance of Bach's works in Germany. Zelter and Bach's music were shaping forces in the careers of Fanny and Felix Mendelssohn.

Probably, Felix's earliest surviving composition is a small piano piece labeled *Recitativo*, dated 1820. His compositions in 1820–21 include seven sinfonie, four piano sonatas, a cantata, some Singspiele, about two dozen small piano pieces, and a few songs. Those works were performed in the Mendelssohn home, which after 1825 was an important cultural center in Berlin. Several times a week persons gathered there to

Marie Kiéné Bigot

Pianist Marie Kiéné (1786–1820) received her early musical training from her mother. In 1804 Marie married Paul Bigot, librarian to Count Razumovsky. She had access to all music in the Count's library. In Vienna, she performed in concert, often as partner of violinist Ignaz Schuppanzigh. She knew Salieri, Haydn, and Beethoven and played some of their music in their presence. Those composers highly praised her playing. The Bigots moved to Paris in 1809; there Mme Bigot moved in musical circles that included noted composers such as Cherubini. Bigot lost his life in the 1812 Russian campaign, and Mme Bigot earned her living by teaching. From time to time, she composed; some of her piano pieces were published in Vienna and Paris.

hear and discuss literature, to view and discuss art, or for a musicale.

In 1821 Felix met Goethe, who influenced his life and work significantly. In 1822 Mendelssohn began to write works in large forms. Representative of this stage in his development are the Piano Concerto in A minor and the Violin Concerto in D minor (both WoO), the latter Mozartean in style. In 1822 he wrote his first settings of Psalms, the Magnificat in D, some solo songs, some part-songs for male chorus, a piano quartet, and three fugues for piano. By 1825, his mature style was manifest; it is apparent in the Octet, Op. 20.

Regularly, on Friday mornings, Zelter held practices at his home for the purpose of singing music by "old masters." There, Mendelssohn first heard Bach's Passion music. He was overjoyed when his grandmother gave him a copy of Bach's *St. Matthew Passion*. Commencing in 1827, a small choir met weekly at the Mendelssohn home to sing some of that music. Early in 1829, Mendelssohn, actor Eduard Devrient (1801–77), and Zelter made plans for the Berlin Singakademie to perform Bach's *St. Matthew Passion*. The performance—the first in almost a century—took place on 11 March, with Mendelssohn conducting, and was repeated 10 days later and again on Good Friday.

The Mendelssohns were financially secure, and Felix spent several years traveling. In 1829 he visited London, where Ignaz Moscheles (1794–1870) intro-

duced him in musical circles. As composer or performer—sometimes both—Mendelssohn participated in four large concerts there. Britain became an important part of his life; he returned often to participate in music festivals, especially those at Birmingham. In 1829 he visited Scotland and considered composing a Scottish Symphony. A trip to the island of Staffa inspired an overture, *Die einsame Insel* (The solitary isle).

In 1830 Mendelssohn declined the offer to fill the chair of music at University of Berlin. During the next few years he traveled widely in Europe and England. He composed, performed, and conducted concerts—he was already recognized as an excellent conductor. Mendelssohn studied Handel's oratorios and conducted performances of them in Düsseldorf. In 1835 he was named conductor of the Leipzig Gewandhaus orchestra. He improved standards of orchestral performance, the quality of programs presented, and economic and social conditions for orchestral players. He programmed music by historically significant composers as well as works by his contemporaries. When Robert Schumann located Schubert's "Great C-major" Symphony, Mendelssohn gave the work its world première (21 March 1839). Often, he invited outstanding soloists to perform with the orchestra. He organized chamber music concerts, arranged for performances of cantatas and oratorios, occasionally appeared as soloist, and programmed some of his own compositions. There was increased interest in Bach's music, and in 1840 Mendelssohn conducted a performance of Bach's *St. Matthew Passion* at Thomaskirche. It is not surprising that the University of Leipzig conferred on Mendelssohn an honorary doctorate.

In 1840 Mendelssohn convinced King Friedrich August II of Saxony of the need for a music conservatory in Leipzig. When Leipzig Conservatory opened in 1843, Mendelssohn was director. He designed the curricula and assembled an outstanding faculty. He composed and performed, and each year he attended the Birmingham (Britain) Festival.

Though Mendelssohn did not feel well during 1846, he continued teaching, conducting, and other activities. The news of his sister Fanny's sudden death on 14 May 1847 was a blow from which he never fully recovered. His last completed work was the String Quartet in F minor, Op. 80, written as a Requiem for Fanny. It is somber. In October he suffered some slight strokes; he became seriously ill on 3 November and died the next day. His remains were interred in Trinity Cemetery in Berlin near Fanny's grave.

MENDELSSOHN'S STYLE Mendelssohn was essentially a Classic composer, albeit with some Romantic tendencies, particularly the ability to convey ideas or paint scenes musically. He wrote in traditional forms; when he altered them, his modifications did not obscure the traditional patterns. He studied and performed the works of Bach, Handel, and Mozart and applied in his own works many of the principles that governed theirs. He could write counterpoint without pedantry, included fugato passages in his large instrumental works, and in his oratorios wrote choruses with both homophonic and fugal sections. As a composer, he was not a pioneer. Chromaticism played a relatively small role in his music. His orchestrations are superb and show his thorough understanding of orchestral instruments and his ability to use their tone colors effectively.

ORCHESTRAL WORKS Mendelssohn's orchestral works comprise 13 sinfonie, 5 symphonies, and 6 overtures. The overtures are programmatic, most of them in sonata form. *Ein Sommernachtstraum* (A Midsummer Night's Dream; 1826), based on Shakespeare, takes the listener on a delightful excursion into a fairy-tale world; the music is often described as "elfin." (Mendelssohn's other incidental music for *A Midsummer Night's Dream* consists of *Scherzo, Intermezzo, Nocturne,* and *Wedding March.*) *Ruy Blas* (1839) served as overture to Victor Hugo's play; Mendelssohn also supplied a *Romance* for that play.

The other overtures were intended as concert pieces. *Meeresstille und Glückliche Fahrt* (Calm sea and Prosperous voyage; 1828), based on two poems by Goethe, is in two contrasting sections, matching the mood of the respective poems. *Die Hebriden* (The Hebrides, Op. 26; 1830) is an expanded version of *Die einsame Insel. Die schöne Melusine* (The lovely Melusine; 1833) portrays moods and events in the legend of that mermaid.

The 13 sinfonie came to light in 1960. All of them are for string orchestra; however, No. 8 exists in two versions, one with winds. The works show the influence of Bach and Handel as well as Viennese Classic style.

For his symphonies, Mendelssohn used a four-movement structural scheme but occasionally altered Classic formal patterns. Symphonies Nos. 3 and 4 ("Scottish" and "Italian") are the best known of his symphonies. The "Italian" and "Reformation" Symphonies were not published until the edition of Mendelssohn's complete works appeared in the 1870s.

Symphony No. 1 (C minor, Op. 11; 1824) is stylistically like the sinfonie. Symphony No. 5 (D major, Op. 107; 1832), the "Reformation" Symphony, was planned for celebrations commemorating the Lutheran Reformation and the Augsburg Confession, celebrations that did not take place. The sonata-form first movement contains the psalmodic formula that commences the *Magnificat in the Third Tone* (*LU,* 215) and the *Nunc dimittis* (*LU,* 271) and statements of the "Dresden Amen" (ex. 22.4). The Finale constitutes variations on Luther's chorale *Ein' feste Burg ist unser Gott.*

Symphony No. 4, "Italian" (A major, Op. 90; 1832–33), follows standard Classic form, with the finale being a Neapolitan *saltarello* in A minor. Symphony No. 2, *Lobgesang* (Hymn of Praise, B♭ major, Op. 52; 1840), was written to commemorate the four hundredth anniversary of the invention of printing. In some respects, this symphony resembles Beethoven's Ninth. The first three movements of the *Lobgesang* are

EXAMPLE 22.4 (*a*) The liturgical "Dresden Amen," J. G. Naumann's (1741–1801) harmonization of a traditional melody for use at the Royal Chapel, Dresden; (*b*) Mendelssohn's "Reformation" Symphony, mvt. 1: "Dresden Amen" as presented by strings in mm. 33–36, in mm. 38–41, and in the Andante preceding the recapitulation.

instrumental; the last is a 10-movement cantata for vocal soloists, chorus, and orchestra and concludes with a great choral fugue on the Lutheran chorale "*Nun danket wir.*"

Mendelssohn made sketches for a "Scottish" symphony in 1829, but that was the last symphony he completed. The movements of Symphony No. 3, "Scottish" (A minor, Op. 56; 1842), are to be played continuously. Though passages from the introduction to the first movement serve as introductions to the other three movements, this symphony is not a cyclic work.

CONCERTI   Mendelssohn wrote seven concerti for soloist(s) and orchestra: three for one piano (A minor, 1822; No. 1, G minor, 1831; No. 2, D minor, 1837), two for two pianos (E major, 1823; A♭ major, 1824), and two for violin (D minor, 1823; E minor, 1844). The E-minor Violin Concerto is comparable with those of Beethoven and Brahms. Mendelssohn was an excellent violinist, and in this work his writing for the instrument is demanding but idiomatic. He structured this concerto according to the traditional overall scheme but linked the movements to ensure that the work would be performed as a unit. The first movement begins with one and one-half measures of orchestral introduction rather than the customary orchestral exposition. The cadenza is written out and serves as transition between development and recapitulation. At the end of the first movement, a sustained B pitch voiced by bassoon as dominant of the E-major chord pivots to become leading tone of C major and link the first and second movements. In the C-major Andante, the soloist supplies a portion of the accompaniment to the melody line of the second theme. A modulatory Allegretto non troppo commencing in A minor links the second movement with the finale, an Allegro molto vivace in E major. Mendelssohn's humor comes to the fore in the opening of the finale, as the orchestra firmly pronounces the tonic chord *fortissimo* and the soloist replies *pianissimo* with a *scherzando* arpeggiation of the dominant-seventh chord. After a musical debate as to whether the melody should commence on tonic or dominant, the orchestra is victorious, and the soloist plays the first theme in the tonic. Soloist and orchestra share the coda. Structurally, this concerto goes a step beyond Beethoven's "Emperor" Concerto.

Mendelssohn, in using a brief introduction instead of an orchestral exposition, making the cadenza functional, and linking all movements, provided a model for other composers.

CHAMBER MUSIC   Mendelssohn's chamber music includes three piano trios, four piano quartets, seven string quartets, two string quintets, a sextet (D major, Op. 110; 1824; vln., 2 vlas., vc., bass, pno.), the Octet (E♭ major, Op. 20; strings; 1825), six sonatas, and some lesser works. There are two sonatas for violin/piano, two for 'cello/piano, one for viola/piano, and one for clarinet/piano.

His most important chamber music works are the Octet, the Piano Trios in D minor (Op. 49; 1839) and C minor (Op. 66; 1845), and the three String Quartets, Op. 44 (D major, E minor, E♭ major). Many persons consider the Piano Trios the most excellent examples of Mendelssohn's chamber music. Of the quartets, the E♭-major work is the finest. In it Mendelssohn placed the scherzo second and followed the slow movement with a brilliant finale. The Octet, considered the earliest of Mendelssohn's mature works, is not a double string quartet (though it has that instrumentation) but an eight-voice composition. Its four-movement structure follows the Classic pattern, except for tonality: the outer movements are in E♭, the Andante in C minor, and the Scherzo in G minor. The Scherzo is excellent. In it there are bits of humor and some of the "elfin" lightness that characterizes *Ein Sommernachtstraum.*

KEYBOARD SOLOS   Mendelssohn was a superb pianist and an excellent organist. For organ he composed *Three Preludes and Fugues* (Op. 37; 1837), *Six Sonatas* (Op. 65; 1845), several single fugues and single preludes, some chorale settings, and some lesser works. The preludes and fugues and the sonatas show Bach's influence. Sonatas Nos. 3 and 6 are frequently performed in church as prelude or postlude to a service.

Mendelssohn wrote numerous solo piano works, ranging in type from sonatas and large fantasias through preludes and fugues to caprices, *Lieder ohne Worte* (Songs without words), and small character pieces. There are 48 *Lieder ohne Worte* published in sets of six and a few individual ones. Most of the characteristic titles were supplied by publishers; Mendelssohn disapproved of such appellations. The name "Song without Words" is appropriate; most of the *Lieder ohne Worte* resemble untexted accompanied solo songs and are in ternary form, with the second A section an expansion of the first rather than exact repetition of it.

Mendelssohn's most noteworthy piano works are *Rondo capriccioso* (Op. 14; 1824); *Six Preludes and Fugues* (Op. 35; 1835–36): *Fantasia, Sonate écossaise* (Scottish sonata, F♯ minor, Op. 28; 1833); and *Variations sérieuses* (Serious variations, D minor, Op. 54; 1841). The Op. 35 preludes are actually études; Bach's influence is apparent in the fugues. Of the preludes and fugues, the first (E minor) is the finest. *Variations sérieuses* is brilliant, idiomatic, and difficult but not virtuosic. The *Fantasia,* in F♯ minor, has three movements, to be played without a break. Structurally, it is similar to Beethoven's Op. 27, No. 2 sonata.

STAGE WORKS   Early in his career, Mendelssohn was interested in stage works. In 1820–23 he wrote a *Lustspiel* (comedy), a Singspiel, and three comic operas. The dialogues for two of the comic operas and for his opera *Der Hochzeit des Camacho* (Camacho's Wedding; 1825) are lost. The one-act comic opera *Die Soldatenliebschaft* (The soldier's love affair; 1820) and *Die beiden Pädagogen* (The two pedagogues; 1821), a one-act Singspiel, were produced in Wittenberg and Berlin, respectively, in 1962. In 1829 Mendelssohn wrote a one-act Liederspiel. During the next 17 years he composed incidental music for a half-dozen plays, including *A Midsummer Night's Dream* and *Ruy Blas.* He began an opera, *Loreley,* in 1847.

VOCAL MUSIC   Mendelssohn's most significant large works for vocal soloists, chorus, and orchestra are his oratorios *St. Paul* (1836) and *Elijah* (1846). A third oratorio, *Christus* (Christ), was not completed. *St. Paul* and *Elijah* reveal Mendelssohn's mastery of choral writing and establish him as a worthy successor to Handel and Haydn in oratorio composition. In these works Mendelssohn included all the types of music Handel used, and, as Bach had done in the *St. Matthew Passion,* he inserted harmonized chorales. The overture to *St. Paul* is based on the chorale *Wachet auf,* and the chorale recurs within the oratorio. One of the lovely arias in *St. Paul* is "But the Lord is mindful of His own."

Elijah, written in English and performed at the Birmingham Festival in August 1846, was more popular in Britain than in continental Europe. (The work was published in German in 1847.) The oratorio, based on I Kings 17–19, opens with a short Prologue in which Elijah (bass soloist) prophesies no rain. Then comes the Overture, which proceeds directly into the first chorus, the plea of the people for help. The chorus is vital to *Elijah,* and Mendelssohn's choral writing is superb. The climax of Part I of the oratorio is the resolution of the confrontation between Elijah, prophet of Jehovah, and the people, worshipers of Baal—Elijah's recitatives interspersed with the crowd's choral pleas to Baal and, after Elijah's prayerful aria "Lord God of Abraham," and the quartet's advice to "Cast thy burden upon the Lord," the crowd's dramatic choral response to Jehovah's answer, "The fire descends from heav'n!" (DWMA152). For the large choral numbers, Mendelssohn used full orchestra, including three trombones, ophicleide, and organ. The distinctive tone quality of the ophicleide, a brass instrument now obsolete, cannot really be replaced by modern instruments (Insight, "Ophicleide").

Mendelssohn's church music includes works for Catholic, Lutheran, Anglican, and Jewish services. For the Anglican church, he composed a *Te Deum* (1832), *Nunc dimittis* (1847), *Jubilate* (1847), and *Magnificat* (1847), all with English texts. His Psalms settings are in a variety of forms. Some resemble cantatas, others are motets; some are *a cappella,* others have instrumental accompaniment, sometimes including instruments that raised theological objection. Some of the music on liturgical texts was written for the Berlin Singakademie, as were many short community songs. Mendelssohn wrote many part-songs—most of them for male chorus—for German and English music festivals.

Mendelssohn composed six secular cantatas, the finest being *Die erste Walpurgisnacht* (Op. 60; chorus, orch.; 1832). More than 110 solo songs and 13 duets by him survive.

INFLUENCE, CONTRIBUTIONS   Mendelssohn was the leading German composer during the second quarter of the nineteenth century and was highly regarded throughout Europe as conductor, performer, and com-

Ophicleide

The ophicleide was introduced c. 1817 by Halary, a French instrument maker, and patented by him in 1821. It is a keyed brass instrument with a strictly conical bore, a wide bell, and a cup-shaped mouthpiece. The instrument might be described as a very large, upright keyed bugle, and the quality of the tone it produces is comparable with that of a tenor cornet (obsolete). The ophicleide has a compass of three octaves. The first ophicleides were bass instruments built in C and Bb, but a "family" of ophicleides was soon developed. The Bb bass ophicleide was the size most widely used, and when played well its tone is full and resonant. Among the composers who wrote orchestral parts for ophicleide were Spontini, Mendelssohn, Schumann, Verdi, and Wagner. In the twentieth century, ophicleide parts are usually assigned to the orchestral tuba, but it cannot really replace the characteristic ophicleide tone.

The ophicleide was the immediate ancestor of the saxophone. Around 1850, Adolphe Sax was repairing an ophicleide and wanted to hear what its sound would be if he substituted a clarinet (reed) mouthpiece for the normal cup-shaped brass one. Thus, he conceived a new instrument—the saxophone.

Bass ophicleide, as pictured on the title page of V. Caussinus's *Solfege-Méthode pour l'Ophicleide Basse,* Paris, c. 1840.

poser. In those capacities, he participated in music festivals in Germany and Britain. He was in great demand as conductor and conducted at concerts in major cities of Germany and Britain. As a pianist, he promoted the concerti of Beethoven and Mozart.

Mendelssohn composed well over 250 pieces in nearly all genres and made especially valuable contributions to the repertoire in his oratorios and the E-minor Violin Concerto. He was instrumental in the revival of Bach's music through performance of the *St. Matthew Passion* and other works. He programmed Handel's oratorios, though often they were presented in altered and somewhat Romanticized versions. Mendelssohn was cognizant of the work of his contemporaries and promoted the careers of many symphonists (Schumann, Gade, and Berlioz) by programming their works in Leipzig. He assisted performers (e.g., Joseph Joachim [1831–1907] and Jenny Lind [1820–87]) by presenting them as soloists at Gewandhaus. As director/conductor of the Gewandhaus orchestra, Mendelssohn strove for higher standards of performance and for better conditions for instrumentalists. He planned programs that would acquaint audiences with works from various historical periods. He was instrumental in founding Leipzig Conservatory and, as its director, assembled an outstanding faculty that included Clara and Robert Schumann, Ferdinand David, and Carl F. Becker.

Shortly after Mendelssohn's death, his friends in Leipzig and in Britain founded scholarships in his honor. The Mendelssohn scholarship is one of the most highly valued prizes in Britain; its first recipient was Arthur Sullivan (1856). In 1878 the Mendelssohn Foundation was established in Germany, and scholarships were awarded annually from 1878 to 1934. Then the Nazi regime discredited Mendelssohn because of his Jewish background, and the Foundation was forced to cease operations. The awarding of Mendelssohn scholarships was resumed in Germany in 1963.

FANNY HENSEL

Fanny Mendelssohn (1804–47), sister of Felix, was a fine pianist and composer. Her earliest known composition is a Lied written in December 1819. Lieder comprise the bulk of her known works. Abraham Mendelssohn was strongly opposed to Fanny having a

Fanny Mendelssohn Hensel. Drawing by her husband, Wilhelm Hensel. *(Historical Pictures Collection/Stock Montage)*

career in music; he believed that the only career for a woman was that of housewife. However, Felix included some of Fanny's Lieder in two of his song collections. Three songs in his Op. 8 (1828) are Fanny's: *Das Heimweh* (Homesickness), *Italien,* and *Suleika und Hatem,* the latter for two voices and piano. Felix's Op. 9 (1830) includes Fanny's *Sehnsucht* (Longing), *Verlust* (Bereavement), and *Die Nonne* (The Nun).

In October 1829 Fanny married court artist Wilhelm Hensel (d. 1861), who urged her to publish her music. However, she published nothing under her own name while her father lived. Then, her Lieder *Die Schiffende* (The one sailing; 1837) and *Schloss Liebeneck* (Liebeneck castle; 1839) were printed in song collections. Fanny's first public appearance as piano soloist occurred in 1838 when she performed Felix's Piano Concerto No. 1.

Fanny, her husband, and their son (Sebastian) spent the winter of 1839–40 in Italy. There she composed a good deal and performed for their friends. When the Hensels returned to Berlin, Fanny occupied herself with housewifely duties but continued composing and participating in Sunday musicales at the Mendelssohn home. After her mother's death (1842), Fanny planned the musicales and sometimes performed in them as pianist and as director of a choral group that rehearsed regularly. Three volumes of her music were published in 1846: *6 Lieder für 1 Singstimme mit Pianoforte* (songs for 1 voice with piano, Op. 1), *4 Lieder ohne Worte für Pianoforte* (Op. 2), and *6 Gartenlieder* (*a cappella* part-

songs, SATB, Op. 3). In 1847 three books of her piano pieces and another volume of six Lieder were issued (Opp. 4, 5, 6, 7). Her Piano Trio, Op. 11, was first performed at a musicale in the family home in April 1847. Many persons consider this her finest work.

On 14 May 1847, Fanny became ill while rehearsing a group for a performance of Felix's *Walpurgisnacht;* she died that night. Several volumes of her works were published posthumously: *2 Bagatellen* (Bagatelles, piano; 1848), *4 Lieder ohne Worte* (Op. 8; 1850), two books of Lieder (Opp. 9, 10; 1850), the Piano Trio (1850), and *Pastorella* (piano; 1852). Her character pieces for piano indicate that she was aware of current trends.

Hensel composed more than 250 Lieder, and, in addition to the instrumental works mentioned, she is known to have composed one overture and five vocal works with orchestra. About 100 of her Lieder and other works are in private collections. Many of her early Lieder resemble folk songs and are strophic; those written after 1829 are more sophisticated and are in various formal structures—strophic, modified strophic, through-composed, and ternary—and the songs written during the 1840s contain bolder harmonies and enharmonic modulations. Viewed generally, Hensel's known songs exhibit stylistic variety. Occasionally, the piano doubles the vocal line, but usually there is independence of voice and keyboard. Sometimes the vocal melody is projected against reiterated pedal notes; sometimes chords are broken into figurations. Phrases are of irregular lengths (two, three, or four measures); often piano and voice share in melodic interplay. Some of her Lieder are comparable with works by Robert Schumann. Schubert may have been an influence in songs Hensel wrote after 1840, for she played some of his songs while in Italy that year. Of course, Felix was an influence—they customarily discussed each other's music.

Among Hensel's works are German, French, Italian, and English songs. Her choice of poets is comparable with that of Schubert and includes Goethe, Heine, Müller, Eichendorff, and little-known poets who were members of the Mendelssohn circle. It was not unusual for Fanny and Felix to set the same texts (e.g., Goethe's *Erster Verlust*). Fanny and Schubert set some of the same poems (e.g., Mignon's song, *Kennst du das*

Land [Do you know the land] from Goethe's *Wilhelm Meister*). Hensel's setting, written in 1822, differs from most of her early works in being through-composed.

In the 1980s, as a result of increased awareness of the role of women in music history, many of Hensel's compositions were published and recorded. Certainly, she was a significant composer in the second quarter of the nineteenth century.

ROBERT SCHUMANN

Robert Schumann (1810–56) was the youngest (fifth) child of August Schumann, an author, publisher, and bookseller in Zwickau, Saxony. Robert was educated in Zwickau schools and received music lessons from local musicians. In 1822 he composed a setting of Psalm 150 (SA soloists, pno., orch.), an overture, and a short chorus. Then his literary talent surfaced in poems and short prose articles, some of which his father printed. Throughout Robert's life, he maintained a dual interest in literary writing and musical composition and succeeded in both fields.

In 1826–27 Robert formed three habits: drinking champagne excessively, keeping a detailed and explicit diary, and womanizing. The first habit he eventually overcame, and the second supplies interesting biographical details, but the third was the most costly to him, for through it he contracted syphilis.

In 1828 Schumann entered Leipzig University as a law student. That year he heard Clara Wieck perform and arranged to study music with her father. Over the next few months, Schumann composed a group of songs, eight polonaises for piano (pub. 1933), a set of variations for piano duet, and a piano quartet in C minor. He abandoned university studies in 1830. He continued music lessons with Wieck but soon became dissatisfied with his teaching. Schumann studied thorough-bass and counterpoint with Heinrich Dorn (1804–92), but Schumann's attitude and work were lackadaisical, and Dorn discontinued the lessons. In 1830 Schumann composed *Thème sur le nom "Abegg" varié pour le pianoforte* (Theme on the name "Abegg" with variations, for piano; Op. 1)—influenced by Meta Abegg and by Moscheles's *Alexandre* variations. Throughout his life, Schumann translated names into musical motives for his works.

Robert Schumann. Lithograph by J. Kriehuber, 1839. Original in Robert-Schumann-Haus, Zwickau, Germany. *(Courtesy of the Free Library of Philadelphia)*

Meantime, Schumann turned to literary writing. He invented fictitious names for his friends, his associates, and himself—names that appeared in his writings for years. In 1830 Schumann heard Chopin play his *Variations on La ci darem la mano* and wrote the essay *Ein Opus II* (see p. 461). That article, published in *Allgemeine musikalische Zeitung,* was the first of Schumann's critical essays on music.

Piano playing was becoming difficult for Schumann. The fingers of his right hand were weakening. This was formerly attributed to his possible overuse of some kind of mechanical device to improve his technique. It is now believed that the weakness was a side effect of treatment Schumann received for syphilis. When he realized that a career as performer was out of the question, he concentrated on composing and writing. Wieck, Schumann, and some friends established the *Neue Leipziger Zeitschrift für Musik* (Leipzig New Journal for Music) and began publication in April 1834. In 1835 the journal was renamed *Neue Zeitschrift für Musik* (NZfM); Schumann was its editor for about a decade. His most significant article for *NZfM* that year was a long essay on Berlioz's *Symphonie fantastique,* in which he analyzed the work in detail, discussed its program, and praised Berlioz's mastery of instrumentation/orchestration.

Schumann became attracted to Clara Wieck. They fell in love and in 1837 decided to marry. For months

Wieck evaded a direct answer to Schumann's request for Clara's hand, then refused. Certainly, Wieck viewed Schumann's personality and financial prospects in the proper perspective; also, Wieck was motivated by his personal and financial interest in Clara's career. Undoubtedly, Wieck's objections fueled the romantic fires. Parental permission was required by law; Clara and Robert had to go through long, unpleasant legal proceedings before securing permission to marry in 1840.

During those years, Schumann composed piano music that was published, and the *NZfM* prospered. In 1839, when he located in Ferdinand Schubert's possession a number of Franz's unpublished works, including the "Great C-major" Symphony, he shared his discovery with Mendelssohn (see p. 465).

In 1840 Schumann wrote more than a hundred Lieder. Most are solos with piano accompaniment, and 6 are part-songs for male voices. Most of the songs were published in volumes containing from 3 to 26 songs. Sometimes a volume was devoted to settings of poetry by a single author, for example, Eichendorff (Op. 39) and the song cycles, *Frauenliebe und -leben* (Woman's love and life, Op. 42; von Chamisso's poems) and *Dichterliebe* (Poet's love, Op. 48; Heine's poems).

Clara encouraged Robert to write a symphony. In 1832, he had made sketches for a G-minor symphony but had completed only its first movement (pub. 1972). In January and February 1841, he composed his Symphony No. 1 (Op. 38). Mendelssohn conducted its first performance at Gewandhaus in March on a concert presented by Clara. This spurred Robert to more orchestral writing: *Overture, Scherzo, and Finale* (E minor/ E major; Op. 52); *Fantasie* (A minor; pno., orch.); and Symphony No. 2 (D minor), revised in 1851 and renumbered No. 4 (Op. 120). In 1845 two movements were added to the *Fantasie,* and it became the Piano Concerto in A minor (Op. 54).

Next, opera captured Robert's attention. He adapted Thomas Moore's (1779–1852) poem *Lalla Rookh* for text. Ultimately, Schumann's work became the cantata *Das Paradies und die Peri* (Op. 50; 1843).

In 1842 he turned to chamber music and created three string quartets (A minor, F major, A major), a piano quintet (E♭ major), and a piano quartet (E♭ major).

For five months in 1844, the Schumanns were on concert tour in Russia. Clara's success weighed heavily on Robert. He became melancholy and in August experienced a nervous breakdown. At the end of 1844, the Schumanns moved to Dresden. Robert wrote 10 pieces for pedal-piano (Opp. 56, 58) and *Six Fugues on B-A-C-H* (Op. 60), which he designated as suitable for either pedal-piano or organ. In December he drafted a C-major symphony; it became his Symphony No. 2. Sporadically, he worked on *Szenen aus Goethes "Faust"* (Scenes from Goethe's *Faust;* vocal soloists, chor., orch.). However, in 1846 a continual singing sensation in his ears inhibited his creativity for months.

In April 1847, after seeing Friedrich Hebbel's (1813–63) drama *Genoveva,* Schumann decided to use the medieval legend of Geneviève as basis for an opera. The libretto (his own) contains forest scenes, black magic, a ghost, and flames engulfing a witch, but the music lacks the dramatic power, strength, and excitement that could have produced an opera comparable with Weber's *Der Freischütz.* Nevertheless, *Genoveva* (Op. 81; 1847–49) *is* German romantic opera.

Schumann had spurts of activity during which he composed rapidly and produced several works; then he would be unproductive for months. After becoming director of the Dresden Liedertafel, a male singing society, he composed choral works, chamber music, instrumental solos with orchestra, songs, and piano pieces, including *Album für die Jugend* (Album for the young, Op. 68) and *Waldscenen* (Forest scenes, Op. 82). In 1849 he composed *Lieder und Gesänge aus Wilhelm Meister* (Lieder and songs from *Wilhelm Meister,* Op. 98a) and *Requiem für Mignon* (Requiem for Mignon, Op. 98b).

In 1850 Schumann became municipal music director of Düsseldorf. Things soon began to go amiss, and increasingly there was dissatisfaction with his work. His health and mental stability steadily deteriorated, and medical treatment had no appreciable effect. Clara did not realize the extent of his illness and his incompetency as director—she blamed his colleagues for his difficulties. Though there were periods of apathy, he wrote several large works for chorus and orchestra, including a Mass (Op. 147) and a Requiem Mass (Op. 149).

The many compositions Schumann created in 1853 include a Violin Concerto (D minor; pub. 1937) and *Fantasie* for violin and orchestra (C major, Op. 131) both for Joachim, whose playing excited Schumann. When Joachim introduced Johannes Brahms to the Schumanns, Brahms's playing of his own works inspired Schumann's essay *Neue Bahnen* (New Paths), in which Schumann predicted Brahms's talent in composing for "massed forces in the chorus and orchestra."

In February 1854 Schumann asked to be taken to an insane asylum; instead, his doctor advised bed rest. Only after Schumann attempted suicide by plunging into the Rhine River was he placed in a private mental institution near Bonn, where he remained for the rest of his life. Brahms and Joachim visited him from time to time, but because Clara's visits upset him considerably, she stayed away until just a few days before his death (29 July 1856).

CONTRIBUTIONS AND STYLE   Schumann was a Romantic composer. His main contributions were in the areas of vocal music (especially Lieder) and piano music. He usually composed at the keyboard, and he included piano in almost all his works. In fact, he thought pianistically. In many of his Lieder voice and piano are partners, with the vocal line adding another tone color to the piano music. *Der Nussbaum* (The walnut-tree; DWMA153) is an example. In no way does this lessen the quality of the Lieder—it enhances the quality.

Bach was an important influence in Schumann's music, particularly in the mature works. So was the music of Beethoven, Schubert, Chopin, Paganini, Weber, Hummel, and Clara Wieck. Often, Schumann quoted from the works of others; an undisguised instance is his use of *La Marseillaise* in *Die beiden Grenadiere* (The two grenadiers). From Clara he borrowed themes and motives, and works of hers inspired him to create similar ones. Clara's urging that he write in large forms influenced him to compose symphonies.

Much of Schumann's music is programmatic, but in many instances the program was not disclosed. Some of his piano pieces have programmatic titles that were assigned as afterthoughts and had no bearing on the composition of the music. Schumann concealed from the world a great deal of the intensely personal part of his music. Much of his music is introverted, associated with the private world of his thoughts and feelings and with events in his life. His fantasy world contributed,

too; from it came the "larvae" and "butterflies" and the descriptive names he assigned to his associates and himself: Florestan, Eusebius, and others in the illusory League of David, of which Schumann was the self-appointed leader. These characters appear in his critical writings and in his music, for example, *Davidsbündlertänze* (Dances of the League of David, Op. 6, 1837), *Carnaval* (Op. 9, 1834–35), and *Ein Opus II.* Literature of all kinds inspired Schumann, but the literary associations in his music are not always obvious (e.g., the relationship between *Papillons* and Jean Paul's *Flegeljahre* and between *Waldscenen* and Laube's *Jagdbrevier*).

In performing Schumann's piano pieces, correct pedaling is extremely important. Also, careful attention must be paid to rhythm, for Schumann often used cross-rhythms and syncopation.

PIANO MUSIC   Schumann's piano music varies from moderately easy pieces for children to difficult concert works. Character pieces make up most of the works and are his most important contribution to piano literature. Most of these pieces are grouped in sets or cycles. In some groups each individual piece is complete in itself. However, throughout *Davidsbündlertänze,* Schumann presents the two sides of his personality—Florestan (passionate and extrovert) and Eusebius (dreamy and introvert)—and some of the pieces are complementary. Some sets are composed of very short pieces: *Kinderscenen* (Scenes from Childhood), *Waldscenen, Papillons,* and *Davidsbündlertänze. Album für die Jugend* contains delightful little pieces for children. Large character pieces form the cycles *Phantasiestücke* (Fantasy pieces), *Kreisleriana* (Pieces about Kreisler), *Nachtstücke* (Night pieces), and *Noveletten* (Novelettes). E. T. A. Hoffmann's writings about the fictitious Kapellmeister Kreisler inspired *Phantasiestücke* and *Kreisleriana.*

Carnaval: scènes mignonnes sur quatre notes (Carnaval: miniature scenes on four notes) is a programmatic cycle of 21 short character pieces, most of them dancelike, with thematic variation. The four notes were derived from the letters ASCH, the name of the town in which Schumann's friend Ernestine von Fricken lived. The theme is stated in long note values in a section enigmatically titled *Sphinxes,* placed between the eighth and ninth pieces, a section not to be performed. Among the miniatures are *Florestan* and *Eusebius* (representing Schumann), *Chiarina* (Clara), *Estrella* (Ernestine), *Chopin*, and *Paganini* (DWMA154).

Schumann's most important large works for piano are the Concerto, *Phantasie in C* (Op. 17), and *Symphonische Etüden* (Symphonic études, Op. 13, C♯ minor). The Concerto's first movement reflects Schumann's knowledge of Beethoven's "Emperor" Concerto. The second movement, an *Intermezzo* in F, concludes, after a long general pause, with a rapid A-major scale that extends into the first measure of the Finale (Allegro vivace, A major). All movements bear some thematic relationship.

For *Symphonische Etüden* Schumann borrowed a theme from Herr von Fricken and constructed massive and diverse variations on it. Schumann wrote three other sets of études. Two sets, each containing six études, are based on Paganini's *Caprices for Unaccompanied Violin;* another set comprises free variations on a theme from the Allegretto of Beethoven's Symphony No. 7.

Schumann's three piano sonatas (F♯ minor, G minor, F minor) follow the traditional four-movement structural scheme. The sonata-form first movements are less than satisfactory because of Schumann's inability to develop the thematic material in the development section. The slow movement of the F-minor Sonata consists of four variations on a theme by Clara.

CHAMBER MUSIC   In 1842 Schumann composed six chamber music works: three string quartets (A minor, F major, A major, Op. 41), a piano quintet (E♭ major, Op. 44), a piano quartet (E♭ major, Op. 47), and *Phantasiestücke* for piano trio (Op. 88). Both sides of Schumann's personality, the dreamy and the passionate, are present in the quartets. The quintet is excellent and is frequently performed. Schumann composed three Piano Trios: Op. 63 in D minor (1847), Op. 80 in F major (1847), and Op. 110 in G minor (1851). The finest is Op. 63. In 1851 he wrote two sonatas: one in A minor (Op. 105) for piano and violin; one in D minor (Op. 121) for violin and piano. There *is* a difference in the musical emphasis.

SYMPHONIES   Schumann's symphonies are Romantic works, filled with lyricism, and often the internal structure of their movements is unorthodox. Originally, Schumann intended to label each movement of Symphony No. 1, the *Spring Symphony* (B♭ major), with a descriptive title related to spring; that would have been appropriate to the character of the music. The first movement, portraying spring's awakening, is in sonata form with introduction and coda, but the development section is minimal, and a new lyrical theme is introduced in the coda. The songlike Larghetto (E♭ major) that follows is a five-part rondo. The Scherzo (D minor) has two Trios, one in triple and one in duple meter, thus forming a five-part rondo (fig. 22.2); a coda follows the last return of the Scherzo. The development section of the Finale uses thematic variation rather than thematic development and is unusual in that all strings except basses play constant tremolo.

The numbering of Schumann's four symphonies does not reflect the order of their composition. He composed a second symphony (D minor) in 1841, but it was revised and published in 1851 as Symphony No. 4. Its four movements are to be played without a break; in them there is thematic interrelationship—the slow introduction to the first movement provides germinal motives for thematic material of all four movements. In both the first and the last movements Schumann introduced a new lyrical theme near the end of the movement. The significance of the D-minor symphony lies in the novelty of its structure and the fact that it is so closely woven.

Schumann began Symphony No. 2 (C major; comp. 1845–46; pub. 1847) with a slow introduction having a motto theme presented by brass and containing thematic material used in succeeding movements. In the Finale, he introduced a new lyrical theme near the end of the movement. At Düsseldorf, in five weeks, he

mvt.3   Scherzo with 2 Trios

‖: A :‖: B   A   :‖ C ‖ C Dev. ‖ A ‖ B   A   ‖: D :‖ : Dev. D : ‖ Transition ‖ A ‖ B ‖ C ‖ D ‖
   Scherzo   Trio I   Scherzo   Trio II   Scherzo   Coda

FIGURE 22.2 Diagram of formal structure of third movement of Schumann's Symphony No. 1, Op. 38, the "Spring" Symphony.

composed Symphony No. 3 (E♭ major; Op. 97; 1850), the "Rhenish" Symphony. The work has five movements, two of them slow.

VOCAL MUSIC   Schumann is the true successor to Schubert in composition of Lieder. Schumann's Lieder are not as spontaneous as those of Schubert, but they are filled with lyricism and Romantic harmonies. The settings vary from accompanied melody to works in which piano and voice enjoy true partnership, for example, *Der Nussbaum,* in which the voice begins a phrase and the piano completes it (DWMA153). In other songs, after the piano has taken over the melodic line, the vocalist enters with the same material.

Schumann and Schubert set some of the same poems, but their settings differ considerably. As did Schubert, Schumann used various formal types— strophic, modified strophic, and through-composed— depending on his sensitivity to the meaning of the poetry. In the same way, he selected the type of accompaniment for his melodies, and his Lieder exhibit a great variety of accompaniment types. Sometimes the accompaniment contains or hints at the presence of a countermelody. Schumann almost always wrote a piano prelude and postlude to his songs; sometimes the postlude spoils the overall effect. In *Die beiden Grenadiere,* the quiet concluding chords detract from the stirring majesty of the vocal line and *La Marseillaise.* *Die beiden Grenadiere* has modified strophic setting, as does *Mondnacht* (Moonlight night; DWMA155). The latter song exhibits extreme musical economy, eight measures of music recurring several times. Schumann set translations of foreign-language poems, as well as German ones, and works of his little-known contemporaries, as well as those of noted authors. The song cycles *Dichterliebe* and *Frauenliebe und -leben* are excellent.

In addition to solo songs, Schumann wrote many duets, trios, quartets, and part-songs. The best of his choral works are the large works for vocal soloists, chorus, and orchestra, such as *Das Paradies und die Peri,* *Szenen aus Goethes Faust,* and *Requiem für Mignon.* He completed one opera, *Genoveva,* and composed incidental music for Byron's *Manfred* (1848–49).

CRITICAL WRITINGS   Schumann's critical essays take the reader into the fantasy world in which he lived much of the time; the articles are interesting and infor-

mative. Some of them aided composers' careers. He made some excellent observations, but his judgments were subjective. This is apparent in the conversation of the fictional *League of David,* whose members advocated the kind of music he composed.

CLARA WIECK SCHUMANN

Clara (1819–96) was the daughter of Marianne Tromlitz (1797–1872) and Friedrich Wieck (1785–1873). Marianne sang the soprano solos in public performances of Mozart's Requiem (1816) and Beethoven's C-Major Mass (1817) and appeared as piano soloist at Gewandhaus on several occasions during 1821–24. Wieck was a self-taught musician who developed a philosophy of education and a system of teaching that was most effective, as evidenced by several of his pupils (e.g., his daughters, Clara and Marie, and Hans von Bülow). Wieck owned a business where he sold pianos, and he had a music-lending library in Leipzig. Marianne and Wieck were legally separated in 1824, and he obtained custody of all but the youngest child. Marianne and Wieck each remarried.

Clara's education in music was thorough and practical, but her general education was neglected. She did not speak until she was almost 5, and when she did

Clara Wieck Schumann. *(Archiv für Kunst und Geschichte)*

begin to talk it was rumored that her hearing was impaired. She had learned a little piano before her parents separated; thereafter, Wieck established a strict regimen of music study for her: piano, violin, singing, theory, harmony, counterpoint, and composition lessons. In addition, there were long daily walks, for physical exercise was essential. Social contacts were important, and Clara was present at cultural gatherings in the Wieck home. In 1828 Wieck took Clara to Dresden, where she gave a few private performances. On 20 October 1828, at Leipzig's Gewandhaus, Clara played in her first solo concert. Two years later she performed her first complete public recital in the same hall.

In 1828 Robert Schumann heard Clara perform and arranged for lessons with her father. Robert and Clara became friends, and the friendship deepened into love, but they were not permitted to marry until 1840 (see p. 471–72).

Customarily, concert artists included at least one of their own compositions on their programs. Clara had learned to improvise and could include music of that kind. By 1830 she was composing, and by 1840 her Opp. 1–11 had been published. Her Op. 7 is a Piano Concerto in A minor, with string orchestra (or quintet) accompaniment.

Clara concertized after she married, despite the fact that, over the next 14 years, she had eight children. Undoubtedly, it was necessary for her to work to help meet household expenses. Sometimes she and Robert toured together, leaving a maid in charge of the children; sometimes Clara went alone or with another woman. From time to time, Clara wrote some music, but she deferred to Robert's greater talent and usually submitted her compositions to him for criticism. Some of her works contributed to or inspired his compositions. She preferred to include his works on her recital programs rather than her own; sometimes she included both.

Clara was one of the first concert artists to present recitals alone. When appearing as a soloist, she played from memory. She enjoyed playing chamber music and sonata recitals. Clara was the first woman to have a successful international career as a concert pianist. She maintained a rigorous concert schedule until 1873; then she reduced her schedule somewhat, though she believed she should perform in 50 concerts per year. She concertized until she was past 70.

When Leipzig Conservatory was established, the Schumanns were on the faculty. Reportedly, Mendelssohn invited Wieck to teach there, but he declined. During Robert's illness and after his death, it was necessary for Clara to concertize in order to support the family. After 1855 she rarely composed. By then she had 23 published works with opus numbers and some without; an additional 15 or 16 works were unpublished.

In 1878, Clara joined the faculty of Hoch conservatory in Frankfort am Main as principal piano teacher. She was an excellent teacher. Though she considered students' individual differences, she insisted that her students master technique, play with seeming relaxation, pay attention to minute details, and interpret the music in conformity with the composer's era and style. She instructed, "Play what is written; play it *as it is* written."

In 1877, after being assured of Brahms's assistance, Clara contracted with Breitkopf & Härtel to prepare a critical edition of Robert's complete works. She relied heavily on Brahms for advice and for the actual editing of the orchestral, choral, and ensemble works. He prepared the supplementary volume.

Clara died at home on 20 May 1896 while listening to her grandson Ferdinand play some of Robert Schumann's music.

HER MUSIC   In addition to the Piano Concerto, a remarkable composition for a 15-year-old, Clara Schumann's works comprise a Piano Trio (G minor, Op. 17; 1846, pub. 1847), a Piano Concertino (F minor, 1847), *Drei Romanzen* (3 Romances, Op. 22; vln./pno.), about 40 piano pieces, 26 Lieder, a few part-songs, and cadenzas for concerti by Beethoven and Mozart. Many of her Lieder are excellent, for example, *Liebst du um Schönheit* (Lov'st thou for beauty; Op. 12, No. 2; DWMA156). The three settings of Rückert's poems that constitute Clara's Op. 12 were published with nine of Robert's as *Zwölfe Gedichte aus "Liebesfrühling"* (12 Poems from *Springtime of Love,* his Op. 37).

The piano pieces are chiefly character pieces, variations, and stylized dances (polonaises and waltzes). The *Soirées musicales* (Musical evenings, Op. 6; 1835–36) —Toccatina, Ballade, Nocturne, Polonaise, and 2 Mazurkas—indicate that Clara knew Chopin's compositions and perhaps those of Maria Szymanowska as well. Szymanowska concertized in Leipzig in 1823, and most of her approximately 60 piano pieces were published there in 1820–25.

Clara's finest composition is her Piano Trio. After it was published, Robert composed his Piano Trio, Op. 63. Clara compared her work with his and belittled her talent. Mendelssohn praised her work, and her Trio was frequently performed in the nineteenth century. Clara composed only two works according to the complete sonata scheme: an unpublished *Sonatine* (Allegro, Scherzo, Adagio, Rondo; 1841–42) and the Piano Trio (Allegro moderato, Scherzo, Andante, Allegretto). In the development section of the Trio's Finale, Clara skillfully wrote a fugato.

MUSIC IN DENMARK

Until the middle of the nineteenth century, very little music by Danish composers was known internationally. Music had flourished in Denmark, and several important European composers (e.g., Schütz) had worked at the Danish court. In the nineteenth century, plays (with and without music), operas, and Singspiele were performed at the Royal Theater, and the Royal Orchestra presented numerous concerts. Two Danish composers were significant in the nineteenth century: Johann Peter E. Hartmann (1805–1900) and Niels Gade (1817–90).

Hartmann was organist at Vor Frue Kirke, composed music, conducted concerts, and taught at Siboni conservatory. In 1829 he married Emma Zinn (1807–51), who composed and published songs under the pseudonym Frederik Palmer. Hartmann's masterpiece, the opera *Liden Kirsten* (Little Christine; 1846), was performed at Weimar in 1856. For the most part, however, Hartmann's music was known only in Denmark. Much of his music is quietly nationalistic, with elements of folk music, traditional hymns, national songs, and, in his operas, the atmosphere of medieval ballads. His surviving works include three operas, incidental music for several plays, two ballets, four concert overtures, two symphonies (G minor and E major), three violin/piano sonatas, other chamber music, numerous piano and organ pieces, and much vocal music.

Gade's first important compositions were the ballet *Faedrelandets muser* (The Fatherland's muses; 1839) and the concert overture *Efterklange af Ossian* (Echoes from Ossian, Op. 1, 1840). Gade's Symphony No. 1 (C minor, Op. 5; 1842) was performed at Gewandhaus in 1843, and Mendelssohn brought Gade to Leipzig, as assistant conductor of Gewandhaus Orchestra. In 1847 he succeeded Mendelssohn as conductor of that orchestra.

In 1848 Gade returned to Copenhagen. He established a permanent orchestra and choir and was director of Copenhagen Academy of Music in 1866–90. Some of his works reflect Mendelssohn's influence (e.g., the string Octet and the *Koncertstykke*), but mainly Gade's works have distinctly Danish character. He included material from Norse mythology in some vocal works. His extant compositions include nine symphonies, seven overtures, keyboard works, chamber music (mostly for strings), pieces for violin and orchestra, ballets, operas, incidental music to plays, cantatas, choral works, and songs.

Gade is historically significant because he introduced some elements of Romanticism into Danish music and helped initiate the national Romantic movement that influenced the next generation of Danish composers. After 1860, Gade was gradually overshadowed by younger Scandinavian composers, particularly Edvard Grieg (1843–1907).

MUSIC IN FRANCE

In France during the second quarter of the nineteenth century, music was dominated by opera, especially grand opera. The success of grand opera in the 1830s was due to the combined efforts of a half-dozen persons: Véron, the director of L'Opéra; Scribe, the librettist; Meyerbeer, the composer; Cicéri and Duponchel, the scene designers; and Auguste Levasseur, the claque leader.

GRAND OPERA

Opera and theater had succeeded in France because they were enjoyed by royalty and were government supported. Government control was broken temporarily during the French Revolution but was resumed under Napoleon. From 1811 until the 1830 July Revolution, the operation of theaters and opera houses in Paris was subsidized by the government. Immediately after the 1830 Revolution, government contracts with dramatists, librettists, and composers were canceled.

Government subsidy was gradually withdrawn from L'Opéra, and its operation was leased for six-year periods to a director-entrepreneur who was personally responsible for its financial success or failure. First to hold that lease was Dr. Louis Véron (1798–1867), who viewed L'Opéra as a business venture and operated it as such. He studied all aspects of opera production and employed the best talents available for everything connected with it. When Véron resigned in 1836, L'Opéra was secure musically and financially. Moreover, he had made a profit—only Lully had done so before him.

Véron began by having the auditorium remodeled. To gain the support of the bourgeoisie, he held opera balls that were financially profitable, and he removed the "No Admittance" sign from the stage door. He reviewed the personnel roster, culled out the deadwood, and reduced salaries, especially in orchestra, chorus, and ballet. Then he considered the choice of librettist, composer, set and costume designers, and even the leader of the claque. Véron was aware of the most successful productions in the late 1820s—Auber's *La muette de Portici* and Rossini's *Guillaume Tell*—and determined to produce works of that kind. Those works followed the traditional lines of Lully's tragédie lyrique and Gluck's *tragedia per musica.*

Véron chose Eugène Scribe (1791–1861) as librettist. Scribe had worked in vaudeville, had written libretti for opéra comique, and knew how to capture and retain audience attention. His libretti were original scripts based on or related to historical events. His boldest and most successful ones dealt with issues of political and religious freedom (e.g., *La muette de Portici, La Juive* [The Jewess] and *Les Huguenots*). Because Scribe was of the bourgeoisie, he could understand and express their attitudes. In his libretti, Scribe blended Romanticism with the conventional elements of opera. Throughout Véron's tenure at L'Opéra, Scribe was his preferred librettist. Just as Lully had relied on Quinault, and eighteenth-century composers of opera had turned to Metastasio, so Véron depended on Scribe to create effective libretti. Scribe never failed him.

Véron selected Scribe's *Robert le diable* as the first grand opera to be produced. Scribe originally intended *Robert le diable* as *opéra comique,* but in 1827 composer Giacomo Meyerbeer (1791–1864) rejected the idea. Meyerbeer (original name, Jakob Beer) had studied composition with Zelter, B. A. Weber, and Abt Vogler. Meyerbeer was a virtuoso pianist but chose not to concertize. Early in 1816 he went to Italy to collect folk songs, met the leading performers and librettists, and began to compose Italian operas. The musical climate seemed favorable, so he remained in Italy. During the next nine years he wrote five Italian operas and the semiserious melodrama *Margherita d'Anjou* (Marguerite of Anjou; 1820). His greatest success in Italy came with *Il crociato in Egitto* (The crusader in Egypt; Venice, 1824), which was equally successful when performed in London (1825) and in Paris (1826).

In 1831, when Véron and Scribe cast about for an experienced opera composer, they had few choices. Rossini had decided not to write any more operas, Auber was setting another of Scribe's libretti, Spontini was working in Germany, and Cherubini was considered too old. So Meyerbeer was approached. This time he was receptive. When performed in November 1831, *Robert le diable* brought Meyerbeer the greatest success he had ever known. In 1836 he and Scribe had similar success with *Les Huguenots. Robert le diable* and *Les Huguenots* are considered the definitive works that established the style of French grand opera.

Robert le diable concerns the contest between Good and Evil for a man's soul, a contest in which the devil uses all possible means but still loses. In composing the music, Meyerbeer drew on several models: the orchestration of Mayr, the choral writing of Spontini, and the vocal solos of Rossini. Meyerbeer's composition was excellent. He effectively realized the full dramatic and emotional potentials of a situation. The soloists, some of whom had been trained by Manuel García, used a blend of French and Italian singing styles.

The success or failure of an opera is determined by more than just the quality of its music and its libretto. Many contributing factors must be taken into account. Among these are stage setting, costumes, and properties. Véron and his scene designers, Edmond Duponchel (1795–1868) and Pierre Cicéri (1782–1868), knew this. In their productions, the scenery was not merely background but environment and was closely allied with the action. The designers made the stage setting as authentic and realistic as possible. They insisted on accuracy in costuming, used real objects (instead of imitation ones) as properties, and replaced flat backdrops with dimensional-effect scenery that extended the space considerably. Cicéri and Duponchel were well acquainted with the panoramic treatment of scenes in the tableaux of the popular *spectacles d'optiques* and the revolving floors used in connection with diorama, and they used as many of these devices and effects as they could. For example, in the cloister scene in Act III of *Robert le diable,* Duponchel based his setting on the cloister Montfort-l'Amaury. In that divertissement scene, long-dead nuns arise from their graves, cast off their musty habits, and dance in the moonlight (plate 24). Achieving the proper sepulchral effect of pale moonlight over a cemetery was no problem with the new, controllable gas lighting. House lights were lowered during the production, and stage lights were dimmed during scene changes. So effective were the sets for *Robert le diable* that sets for later works were measured by them. In view of the importance attached to stage settings and the popularity of tableaux entertainments in Paris, it is understandable that Hector Berlioz (see p. 485) wrote operas constructed in **episodes,** without dramatic continuity, placed in tableau-like settings.

Another important factor in the success of *Robert le diable* was the claque, which, firmly persuasive, guided audience taste. Auguste Levasseur, claque leader, studied the libretto, attended rehearsals, and knew the singers and dancers. His claque, well-trained and responsive to his signals, was scattered strategically among the audience. (The theatrical term for this is *papering the house.*)

The characteristics of the musical construction of French **grand opera,** as defined by the most successful productions in the early 1830s, particularly Meyerbeer's *Robert le diable* and *Les Huguenots,* are these: Grand opera is sung throughout, but there are relatively few arias and almost no pure recitative. Those arias that are included occur at the beginning rather than at the end of a scene, and the soloist remains on stage at the conclusion of the aria. In style, the solo songs are less elaborate and may be narrative; the lyricism of solo song is secondary to movement of the drama. Usually a solo is interrupted by choral or ensemble interjections that may occasion dialogue sections. Instead of dialogue by means of recitative, arioso is used. The language of the libretto does not interfere

with the music. Much of the action takes place in festive settings such as processions, mass meetings, and social gatherings. Ensembles of all sizes, from trios to full chorus, are an important part of the drama. Spectacular choral and ballet divertissements, in accord with historical events, are woven into the drama and the music so that they contribute to the continuity of the plot; they serve to relax audience attention briefly but do not permit it to stray from the story. For example, *La Juive* takes place in the fifteenth century at the time of the Great Schism, when there were three rival popes and when anti-Pope John XXIII and Emperor Sigismund arranged a meeting at Constance in an attempt to end the Schism. The pomp connected with the circumstances provided ample material for crowd scenes and ceremonial spectacles. The chorus participates in the action. There are excellent examples of this in *Les Huguenots,* for example, Act IV, scenes 22 and 23, including the romanza and continuing through the Benediction of Daggers (DWMA157). In 1831 L'Opéra had a superb chorus master in Jacques Halévy (1798–1862), who was also a composer.

The most important grand operas produced at L'Opéra in the 1830s—those that established the course of French opera—were on libretti by Scribe: Meyerbeer's *Robert le diable* (1831), Auber's *Gustave III* (1833), Halévy's *La Juive* (1835), and Meyerbeer's *Les Huguenots* (1836). All were new scripts with stories akin to the Gothic romances that were popular literary fare in Europe. Both common folk and aristocracy were included in the plots. Each plot involved a major decision related to historical and sometimes contemporary issues—a decision with which the audience could empathize. For example, Valentine, in *Les Huguenots,* must choose between life with Catholicism and death with her Huguenot lover.

French grand opera was produced throughout the nineteenth century, though to a lesser extent after 1850. Patriotic themes were popular during the Revolution of 1848. When Louis Napoleon came into power, he placed L'Opéra, then experiencing financial deficit, back under government control.

Grand opera, as a type, was not confined to Paris. Its influence is apparent in works by Italian and German composers: Bellini's *I Puritani* (The Puritans; Paris, 1835); Verdi's *Les vêpres siciliennes* (Sicilian vespers; comp. 1839, Scribe libretto; Paris, 1855) and *Aïda* (Cairo, 1871); and Wagner's *Rienzi* (1842). Touches of grand opera appear in some twentieth-century operas.

OPÉRA COMIQUE

Almost all composers of serious opera wrote opéras comiques also, and Scribe wrote both kinds of libretti. Operas were produced in two different theaters in Paris, L'Opéra admitting only large-scale works sung throughout and L'Opéra-Comique producing only works with spoken dialogue. When government subsidies were withdrawn after the Revolution of 1830, L'Opéra-Comique experienced financial difficulties and, a few months after the successful première of Hérold's *Zampa* (May 1831), was forced to close for a short time. Paris riots in 1832 caused another closing that lasted all summer. When L'Opéra-Comique reopened, *Zampa* was in the repertoire. Shortly after Hérold's *Le pré aux clercs* was produced (December 1832), he died and never realized its tremendous success. Both *Zampa* and *Le pré aux clercs* are the romantic type of opéra comique.

Scribe and Auber dominated opéra comique for about half a century. Between 1813 and 1869, Auber composed 34 opéras comiques, and all but 6 were on libretti by Scribe. Among their successes were *Leicester,* (1823), *Fra Diavolo* (1830), *Le domino noir* (The black domino; 1837), *Les diamants de la couronne* (The crown diamonds; 1841), and *Manon Lescaut* (1856). Auber's last opéra comique, *Rêve d'amour* (Love's dream; 1869), was in essentially the same style as his early works—dealing with amusing situations, witty and worldly without emotional depth, with uncomplicated music. Casts were comparatively small. The plots were either romantic or semiserious drama or comedy and sometimes a mixture of both. This indicates that, as far as style and content were concerned, music at L'Opéra-Comique was relatively stagnant during 1825–70.

GEORGES BIZET   Bizet (1838–75) worked as rehearsal accompanist at L'Opéra-Comique while he was studying composition at Paris Conservatoire. He could have been a concert pianist; instead, he became a composer. After winning the Prix de Rome (1857) and spending the required years in Italy, he returned to Paris and began to compose operas. In 1866 he contracted with Leon Carvalho (1825–97) to compose some works for Théâtre-Lyrique. After Carvalho became director of L'Opéra-Comique (1868), Bizet wrote opéras comiques for production there. His greatest work is *Carmen* (1873–74), produced at L'Opéra-Comique in March 1875.

Carmen was so different from the usual opéras comiques that it was a failure. The audience was shocked and puzzled by it; they considered some of the situations coarse and obscene. The plot was serious—a tragedy. The spoken dialogue was that typically used by the types of characters depicted at that time. The same can be said of the situations in the story. Bizet presented characters realistically, in true-to-life situations, with normal reactions. The dramatic mezzo soprano Célestine Galli-Marié (1840–1905), a petite lady with a vibrant personality, created the role of Carmen. Bizet used a folk song for Carmen's song *Coupe-moi, brûle-moi* (Cut me, burn me; Act I). The entr'acte to Act IV is based on a song by Manuel García. Bizet thought he was using a folk song for *Habanera,* but he learned later that it was *El arreglito* (A little arrangement) by Sebastién de Yradier (1809–65) and acknowledged that.

Carmen is a landmark in the history of opéra comique. With it Bizet brought opéra comique to a peak. More important, through use of a serious subject and presentation of a tragedy with spoken dialogue, Bizet destroyed the artificial line of demarcation between opéra comique and opéra. *Carmen* could not have been performed at L'Opéra because of its spoken dialogue, and Théâtre-Lyrique was no longer in existence. Technically, the subject was too serious for L'Opéra-Comique, but Carvalho decided to produce the opera. Bizet's realistic portrayal of characters and situations in *Carmen* had considerable influence on the composition of **verismo** (realism) operas at the end of the nineteenth century.

Before his death (June 1875), Bizet prepared the vocal score, without the spoken dialogue, for publication, and it was issued later that year. Later, Ernest Guiraud (1837–92) substituted recitatives for the spoken dialogue so that the work might be performed at L'Opéra, and he toned down some of the scenes. The recitatives spoil the opera. They remove from it the portions of melodrama that were so effective. Attempts have been made to restore the opera to its original state, but all the original spoken dialogue has not been located.

LYRIC OPERA

In France, c. 1845, three principal theaters were producing operas: L'Opéra, for large-scale serious works in French, such as grand opera, that were sung throughout; L'Opéra-Comique, for lighter, nontragic works in French with spoken dialogue; and Théâtre Italien, for Italian operas. Composers writing French operas that were sung throughout but were on a smaller scale than grand opera experienced difficulty getting their works produced. In 1847 Opéra National was founded with the express purpose of producing French operas that were rejected by L'Opéra-Comique because they were sung throughout and that could not be performed at L'Opéra because they were considered too small or too light. The new theatre, whose name was changed in 1852 to Théâtre-Lyrique, did not deny production to midscale works with spoken dialogue. Many composers writing operas for production at Théâtre-Lyrique designated their works *opéra lyrique* or simply *opéra;* if the opera had spoken dialogue, the composer might label it *opéra dialogué,* as did Charles Gounod (1818–93). The subject matter of many of the operas produced there was romantic drama or fantasy. Théâtre-Lyrique was at its height during 1856–68, while Carvalho was director. It closed in 1870 because of financial difficulties during the Franco-Prussian War.

Several operas by Bizet were produced at Théâtre-Lyrique, including *Les pêcheurs de perles* (The pearl fishers; 1863) and *La jolie fille de Perth* (The pretty girl from Perth; 1867). Among the most successful productions there were Gounod's *Le médecin malgré lui* (opéra comique; 1858), *Faust* (opéra dialogué; 1859), and *Roméo et Juliette* (opéra; 1867), and Ambroise Thomas's (1811–96) *Mignon* (1866).

Gounod's *Faust* concerns only that portion of the legend dealing with the love story of Faust and Marguerite and the lovers' destruction through Mephistopheles's treachery. The spectacular element is present but is reduced in importance; characters are more humanized than in many grand operas of the time. Marguerite's ballad *Il était un roi de Thulé* (There was a king of Thulé) has a tinge of modality and delightful conversational interruptions; the "Jewel Song" is excellent. Gounod's ability to write meaningful, expressive, lyric melody is apparent. *Faust* is almost never performed as originally written, for in 1860 Gounod converted it to grand opera and substituted recitatives for the spoken dialogue; later, he added a full-length ballet. Gounod was at his best in opéra comique.

OPÉRA BOUFFE; OPERETTA

Pure comic opera was almost nonexistent in Paris during the first half of the nineteenth century. In 1850 Jacques Offenbach (1819–80), a 'cello virtuoso, was appointed conductor at Théâtre Français, a theater producing spoken drama in Paris. Unable to get some of his stage music produced, he decided to produce his works himself. He rented a small theatre, and in July 1855 began presenting a series of short comic pieces. In 1856 he moved to a larger theater, and by 1858 Parisians were interested in *opéra bouffe* (comic opera). His first triumph came with *Orphée aux enfers* (Orpheus in the underworld; 1855), which satirized the Orpheus myth. *La chasse,* the music played while Orpheus and Euridice flee from Hades, is the Cancan. Other successes ensued, chief of which were *La belle Hélène* (Beautiful Helen; 1864), satirizing the story of Helen of Troy; *Barbe-bleu* (Bluebeard; 1866); and *La vie parisienne* (Parisian life; 1867). Frequently, Offenbach achieved humor by quoting music that was familiar to the audience and substituting satirical words or using the borrowed themes in incongruous situations. The music is always more or less subdued and never obscure the words. Offenbach composed approximately 90 comic operas and operettas. **Operettas** are musical theatrical works, light and sentimental in character, with spoken dialogue and some dancing. Offenbach also wrote some ballets and *Les contes d'Hoffmann,* depicting three stories by E. T. A. Hoffmann as episodes in Hoffmann's love life.

Operettas became popular in Vienna after 1860, in England during the last quarter of the century, and in the United States after 1900. The principal Viennese composers were Franz von Suppé (1819–95) and Johann Strauss II (1825–99). Many of Strauss's operettas are standard repertoire, especially *Die Fledermaus* (The Bat; 1874).

LOUIS-HECTOR BERLIOZ

Berlioz (1803–69) was the oldest of the six children of Dr. L.-J. Berlioz, a highly respected citizen of La Côte-St. André, France. Hector's mother was a devout, strict Catholic; his father's intellectual pursuits were wide and his views liberal. As a child, Hector was much interested in literature. He had flute and guitar lessons and, without a tutor, acquired a basic knowledge of harmony by studying Rameau's *Traité de l'harmonie* and other treatises. While in his early teens, he began to write music. In 1819 *Le dépit de la bergère* (The shepherdess's spite), a **romance,** was published. A romance is a lyrical, strophic song on an epic or amorous subject.

In 1821, to please his father, Berlioz entered medical school in Paris. He was attracted to opera and attended a performance of Gluck's *Iphigénie en Tauride.* Gluck's music strongly influenced Berlioz's style. In 1822 Berlioz arranged for composition lessons and in 1823 wrote an operatic setting of de Florian's *Estelle et*

Némorin. He continued medical studies until he obtained his baccalaureate (1824), then music occupied his time. When funds from home were cut off, he worked as a chorus singer and taught flute and guitar lessons. In 1826 he enrolled at the Conservatoire as a composition student and wrote the opera *Lénor, ou les derniers francs juges* (Lénor, or the last French judges), which was never performed.

In 1827–28 Berlioz had some experiences that greatly affected his life and work: He attended performances of Shakespeare's plays, including *Hamlet,* in which Harriet Smithson acted; he heard Beethoven's Symphonies Nos. 3 and 5 for the first time; and he read Gérard de Nerval's (1808–55) translation of Goethe's *Faust.* Beethoven's symphonies turned Berlioz's attention toward instrumental music; his infatuation for Smithson was translated into *Symphonie fantastique;* Shakespeare's plays and Goethe's *Faust* became the basis for several compositions. Berlioz's interest in literature never flagged; this is reflected in his compositions.

Berlioz was awarded the Prix de Rome for his cantata *La mort de Sardanapale* (The death of Sardanapale, 1830). Only a fragment of that work survives. The cantata he submitted for the 1828 competition, *Herminie* (Erminia), contains the melody he used for the *idée fixe* (obsession), the recurrent theme in *Symphonie fantastique.*

Winning the Prix de Rome was important to Berlioz, but he did not want to leave Paris. He was romantically involved with pianist Camille Moke (see p. 487), and he was in Rome only a short time when he became concerned because he had not heard from her. He started back to France to check on her, learned that she had married Camille Pleyel, and planned to shoot them both and to kill himself. Fortunately, he was deterred. He returned to Rome, composed *Le retour à la vie* (Return to life), later named *Lélio,* and wrote overtures based on Shakespeare's *King Lear* and Scott's *Rob Roy.*

Berlioz had been obsessed with Harriet Smithson (1800–1854) since he first saw her on stage. When he returned to Paris in 1832, he pursued her relentlessly. After a whirlwind courtship during the course of which he attempted suicide, they were married in 1833. The marriage was not the happy one Berlioz envisioned. At this time, he earned a living by writing

Hector Berlioz. A photograph made c. 1865.

critical articles for French journals and papers. He disliked the work but excelled at it and was better known as critic than as composer. In 1832–42 he participated as conductor in from two to five concerts per year in Paris—concerts shared by several artists and an orchestra. Because he strongly advocated strict adherence to composers' notated music and realized that many performers and conductors altered music freely, Berlioz did not want others to conduct his works. For the next two decades, he conducted performances of his music in Germany. Commencing in 1842, he toured frequently with mezzo-soprano Marie Recio (1814–62), for whom he composed *Les nuits d'été* (Summer nights; 1840–41) and other songs.

Frequently, Berlioz was chief conductor at French national commemorative celebrations and composed works for them, (e.g., *Grande messe des morts* [Requiem Mass; 1837] and *Te Deum laudamus* [1849]). In the early 1840s he worked on his *Grand traité d'instrumentation et d'orchestration modernes* (Treatise on modern instrumentation and orchestration, Op. 10; pub. 1843).

Harriet Berlioz was paralyzed for several years. After her death, Berlioz married Marie Recio. During the last six years of his life, Berlioz was in ill health and prepared his *Mémoires*. He died on 11 March 1869.

STYLE CHARACTERISTICS Characteristics of Berlioz's style are as follows: (1) effective and free use of counterpoint, including the combination of melodies or themes first presented separately, and fugato sections in which successive entries do not adhere to traditional tonic-dominant practice; (2) treatment of the bass line as a melody placed contrapuntally against another melody in an upper voice; (3) construction of melodies in irregular phrase lengths; (4) use of chromatic inflections (especially the flatted submediant pitch) in basically diatonic melodies for the purpose of characterization or expression of mood; (5) use of basically Classic harmonic vocabulary in nontraditional manner, with progressions chosen for expressive reasons rather than the expected functional ones; (6) frequent use of recurrent themes, theme transformation, and thematic variation (e.g., *Harold in Italy* and *Symphonie fantastique*); (7) orchestration centered on instrumental color, sometimes combining dissimilar instruments to achieve the desired coloristic blend and considering as standard orchestral instrumentation some instruments

formerly included only for special effects (e.g., English horn and harp); and (8) spatial distribution of voices and/or instruments (e.g., performers offstage) for special effects.

Berlioz was concerned not only about the sound of his music *per se* but about the suitability of the music to the size and acoustics of the hall in which it was to be performed. With Berlioz as with Gabrieli (see p. 224), the spatial distribution of sound was important. Berlioz's achievements in orchestration were remarkable. His orchestration treatise was the first textbook written on that subject.

Berlioz's significance for the development of music lies in his first three symphonies, his orchestration treatise, and *Les Troyens*, with which he brought the French style of opera to a peak. The nineteenth century knew only truncated versions of the opera, so it could not be appreciated as the masterpiece that it is. Berlioz was an individualist and a Romanticist and was relatively unaffected by the work of his contemporaries but was aware of and influenced by the music of Beethoven and Weber and to a lesser extent by Gluck, Spontini, and Méhul. The many grandiose works written to commemorate French military, patriotic, and political events also had an effect on Berlioz's works.

Berlioz had a penchant for program music. Just as Schubert was able to translate poetry into sound and create a miniature drama from a Lied (e.g., *Erlkönig*), so Berlioz could synthesize programmatic ideas with orchestral music to create drama without words (e.g., *Symphonie fantastique*).

INSTRUMENTAL MUSIC Berlioz's orchestral works comprise four symphonies, five overtures, and *Rêverie et caprice* for violin and orchestra (1841). Of the overtures, *Le carnaval romain* (Roman carnival; 1844), a brilliant orchestral piece based on material from his opera *Benvenuto Cellini*, is the one most frequently performed. The other overtures are *Waverly* (c. 1828) and *Intrada di Rob Roy Macgregor* (Overture on Rob Roy Macgregor; 1831), both based on novels by Scott; *Le roi Lear* (King Lear; 1831); and *Le corsaire* (The Corsican; 1844).

Symphonie fantastique: Episode de la vie d'un artiste (Fantastic symphony: Episode in an artist's life; 1830) was Berlioz's first symphony. In it he aimed to create (1) a large-scale orchestral composition that was a unified whole rather than a set of movements that could be performed individually and (2) a work that possessed dramatic and lyric significance. The work is unified through a recurrent theme (ex. 22.5) and through the unfolding of the drama. The printed program that Berlioz provided the audience outlines the events experienced by a young man in delirium after seeking release from the anguish of unrequited love by taking opium. In the translation of those experiences into music, the Beloved became an *idée fixe,* a recurrent theme (sometimes transformed or varied), a glittering thread woven into the fabric of the symphony. Berlioz was that lovesick lad; Harriet Smithson was the Beloved, whom, at that time, he had not even met.

Notwithstanding the authenticity of the program Berlioz provided, the symphony is autobiographical to a greater degree in that it reflects numerous shaping forces in Berlioz's life between the ages of 12 and 27: (1) his infatuation as a 12-year-old for 18-year-old Estelle Duboeuf; (2) his liking for Vergil's *Aeneid* and concern for the plights of mythological Dido and Phaedra; (3) his mother's devout religious beliefs and his professed atheism; (4) his proximity to French revolutionary ideas, the guillotine, and the execution of André Chénier; (5) his medical studies and the psychiatric term in vogue, *idée fixe;* (6) his reading of De Quincey's *Confessions of an English Opium Eater* and Chateaubriand's *Genius of Christianity;* (7) his intellectual experiences in Paris—Shakespeare, Hoffmann, Goethe's *Faust,* and Hugo's *Ronde du Sabbat;* (8) his study of Beethoven's music and Weber's *Der Freischütz;* and (9) musical themes designed for some of his own early compositions. Not even the *idée fixe* was new— Berlioz had used it in 1828 to represent the female warrior Erminia, ill-fated beloved of the Christian knight Tancred (in Tasso's *Gerusalemma liberata*).

Structurally, *Symphonie fantastique* reveals Berlioz's knowledge of Beethoven's symphonies in at least three ways: it is cyclic (Fifth Symphony), there are five movements (Sixth Symphony), and the slow movement is third instead of second (Ninth Symphony). The first movement of *Symphonie fantastique,* labeled "Reveries, passions," is in sonata form. Winds and muted strings create a mood of reverie, playing a C-minor melody originally used by Berlioz in *Estelle et Némorin.* The *idée fixe* is presented in C major by flute and violins. The second movement, "A ball," is a waltz; the middle portion of the movement is devoted to the *idée fixe.* The third movement is a pastorale, a "Scene in the Fields," in which English horn and oboe simulate the echoing and dialogue of Alpenhorns, using the Swiss cowherds' horn call that Berlioz enjoyed when visiting his grandparents. The Beloved's presence is felt when flute and oboe play the *idée fixe.* The pastoral mood is interrupted by timpani rumblings—thunder at first distant, then moving closer; the serene melody piped by shepherds continues to the end of the movement (cf. Beethoven's Sixth Symphony). In the fourth movement, "March to the Scaffold," the man dreams that because he has killed his Beloved, he is condemned, led to the guillotine, and executed. Timpani prelude the approach of the solemn processional march. A brilliant climax is achieved in the coda. Clarinet ponders the *idée fixe;* a great G-minor chord crashes (descent of the guillotine blade), and ominous G-major chords conclude. The finale is "A Witches' Sabbath," in which he envisions his funeral; his Requiem is a burlesque (DWMA158). It is an eerie scene, with C clarinet caricaturing the *idée fixe* to depict the witchly transformation of the Beloved and polyrhythmic orchestral parts signifying conclusion. E-flat clarinet more extensively mocks the Beloved. Solemn tolling of bells is heard in the distance. Violas and oboe timidly propose a dance tune but are effectively silenced (cf. Beethoven's Ninth Symphony, Finale). The *Dies irae* is heard. Low strings

EXAMPLE 22.5 The *idée fixe,* the recurrent theme in Berlioz's *Symphonie fantastique.*

commence the witches' round dance, presented fugally; ultimately, it is combined with the *Dies irae* (combination of melodies is another resemblance to the Finale of Beethoven's Ninth). Strings playing *col legno* (with the wood of the bow) add to the diabolic glee. This movement has been called "the first symphonic presentation of the macabre in the literature."

Verbally and financially, Niccolò Paganini encouraged Berlioz to write *Harold en Italie* (Harold in Italy; 1834), his second symphony. In this four-movement work, the solo viola represents Harold, who observes Italian scenes. Each movement has a descriptive title. The work is cyclic; the recurrent theme appears unchanged in all movements. In the finale, as in Beethoven's Ninth Symphony, themes of the preceding movements are recalled and new themes presented. Throughout the symphony Berlioz used counterpoint effectively (e.g., combining the viola melody contrapuntally with the other themes). The solo viola is not limited to its special theme but is given other melodies and accompanying figures as well. *Harold en Italie* is an important contribution to symphonic repertoire, especially because it features solo viola.

Berlioz called *Roméo et Juliette* a dramatic symphony. It has a choral introduction, three instrumental movements corresponding to the first three movements of a traditional symphony, and a choral finale. The purely instrumental movements are *Fête chez Capulet* (Festival at the Capulet home); *Scène d'amour* (Love scene), the slow movement; and *La reine Mab* (Queen Mab), a scherzo/trio. *La reine Mab* is played as a concert piece, usually programmed as "Queen Mab Scherzo." The scherzo is a whirlwind *moto perpetuo*. Berlioz depicted the fairy world with delicacy and lightness. Strings are muted, and players are asked to use techniques associated at that time with solo playing: spiccato and ricochet bowings and harmonics sustained for many measures. Berlioz was specific in his directives to performers and indicated precisely in the music how he wanted passages played.

The *Grande symphonie funèbre et triomphale* (Large funeral and triumphal symphony; 1840) was commissioned by the French government for a commemoration honoring participants in the July 1830 Revolution. Berlioz scored the work for large military band for the out-of-doors performance. Later, for an indoor performance, he added strings; still later, he added six-part chorus (SSTTBB) with a patriotic text.

All Berlioz's orchestral works are programmatic; his treatment of melodies and harmonies and his orchestrations are Romantic. Though he viewed form as flexible, he never completely discarded sonata form and the complete sonata structure. He seemed not to regard the various musical media as separate and distinct entities but merged vocal and instrumental, soloist(s), and large ensemble. He wrote no piano music. The few pieces of chamber music he wrote as a youth are lost.

OPERAS Berlioz composed six operas; four survive complete, and each is different. He destroyed *Estelle et Némorin*. Five numbers survive from *Lénor.*

Benvenuto Cellini (1834–37), an opera semi-seria, was not a success. Paris audiences preferred lighter, more entertaining subjects or works with great spectacles. *Benvenuto Cellini* has some crowd scenes, and both comic and serious elements are present in the opera, which concerns the goldsmith and sculptor Benvenuto Cellini (1500–71). The opera presents a chain of episodes rather than unfolding a plot, and audiences were not ready for that at L'Opéra. However, staged episodes were not new to Paris—entertainments of that kind were presented in the popular theaters in the tableaux of *spectacle d'optique* and diorama.

Around 1850 Berlioz planned an opera based on the second and fourth books of Vergil's *Aeneid;* in 1856 he commenced a libretto. By 1858 he had completed the music but made revisions during the next five years. *Les Troyens* (The Trojans) is a monumental five-act grand opera of epic proportions. To obtain a performance of part of the opera, Berlioz divided it: Acts I–II became Part I, *La Prise de Troie* (The Capture of Troy); Acts III–V became Part II, *Les Troyens à Carthage* (The Trojans at Carthage), and presents the story of Queen Dido of Carthage, Aeneas's sojourn there, and the fate of the Trojan people. Part II was performed at Théâtre-Lyrique in 1862 and was well-received, but Carvalho made drastic cuts after the first performance. Part I had its première at Karlsruhe in 1890. The first act is massive. It presents the armistice, the celebration outside the walls of Troy, and the entry of the wooden horse into the city. Act II is the shortest of the five, with two balanced scenes.

Les Troyens is a scene opera containing many large choral and ballet presentations, appropriately placed and never included merely for spectacle or theatrical effect. The large scene-complexes present only the essential stages of the action. Berlioz's characterization is superb. He restrained the use of chromaticism to instances where it would be most effective. The vocal lines are expressive, clean, and devoid of superficial opulence. The harmonies convey effectively the emotions appropriate to each scene. The final scene, Dido's death and funeral pyre, is magnificent.

Les Troyens is the most important French opera written in the nineteenth century, yet that century barely knew it. The opera was not performed in its entirety during Berlioz's lifetime. In fact, Berlioz never heard Part II performed completely. This opera, Berlioz's masterpiece, places him at the peak of a long tradition of opera in France, a tradition that begins with Lully and proceeds through Rameau, Gluck, Spontini, and Meyerbeer—to Berlioz.

Berlioz's last opera, *Beatrice et Benedict* (1860–62), is an opéra comique. He prepared his own libretto, based on Shakespeare's *Much Ado about Nothing*. The opera contains 15 numbers interspersed with spoken dialogue. Each of the 2 acts has 3 choruses and scenes for 1, 2, or 3 voices.

CHORAL WORKS   In 1828–29 Berlioz composed *Huit scènes de Faust* (Eight scenes from *Faust*) based on Nerval's translation of Goethe's *Faust*. Later, the eight scenes were expanded and combined with an arrangement of the *Rákóczy March* and other music to form *La damnation de Faust* (The damnation of Faust; 1845–46), which Berlioz called a dramatic legend. A blend of the symphonic and dramatic, it is intended for concert performance, not staging, though the score contains stage directions to explain the course of events. The music comprises 20 scenes, organized in four main sections. The work is for three soloists (Faust, Marguerite, and Mephistopheles), seven-part chorus (alto is not divided), and orchestra. Chorus is important, participating as penitents, students, soldiers, sylphs, carousers, and occupants of Heaven and Hell.

L'enfance du Christ (The infancy of Christ; 1850–54), a sacred trilogy, is a mixture of opera, oratorio, and symphony. The score is supplied with stage directions, but the work was not intended for staging.

La damnation de Faust and *L'enfance du Christ* represent a compromise between the stage works with which Berlioz desperately wanted to achieve success and the symphonic works for which he could more easily secure performance and which he believed would be accepted more readily.

Of Berlioz's works for national commemorative celebrations, the most important are *Grande messe des morts* and *Te Deum laudamus*—monumental and deeply religious works that require enormous performing resources. The Requiem Mass, in traditional liturgical format, was designed for performance in the church of Les Invalides, which could accommodate the huge ensembles. Spatial separation of performers is a feature of both compositions. This is a link with the distant as well as the immediate past, extending back to Gabrieli's use of *cori spezzati* at St. Mark's Church and also relating to the use of many ensembles that participated individually, in combination, and *en masse* in the postrevolutionary commemorative celebrations held in Paris.

The *Te Deum laudamus* was intended for a military celebration in 1832, but Berlioz did not finish it in time. The 1849 score of the work calls for orchestra, organ, tenor soloist, and two 100-voice choirs. In 1851 Berlioz added a third choir—600 children—to sing in unison and "to represent the people who, from time to time, add their voices to the ceremony of praise." Berlioz's knowledge of Bach's *St. Matthew Passion* is apparent not only because of the children's choir but also in the use of counterpoint. The organ is seldom used simultaneously with the rest of the performers, and its spatial separation from them is necessary. As principal conductor, Berlioz controlled tempo by means of a special metronome whose electrical pulsations were transmitted simultaneously to subconductors in the various locations.

Two movements of the *Te Deum* are purely instrumental: a *Prelude* (third movement) and a *March* designed as processional for visible pageantry, including presentation of the Colors. Berlioz instructed that these movements should be omitted when the *Te Deum* is performed on occasions that are neither for thanksgiving after a victory nor for a service of military character. Therefore, in an ordinary concert, these two movements should be omitted.

At various times in the *Te Deum,* the music appropriately conveys majesty, brilliance, and soft supplication. The final choral movement, *Judex crederis esse venturus* (We believe that Thou wilt come to be our judge), is some of the most powerful music ever written. Berlioz considered that movement "the most imposing thing" he had ever composed.

Among Berlioz's works are several choral compositions that are small in scope but monumental in style and that were designed for national commemorations. There are also serene, contemplative works and pieces of exquisite delicacy. Berlioz wrote numerous songs for solo voice(s) and orchestra. Among the finest of these are *Les nuits d'été.*

BERLIOZ AS AUTHOR Berlioz prepared some of his own libretti, wrote critical articles for Paris journals, and authored fiction and fantasy. His essays on music contain valuable information concerning compositions, performances, performers, and new instruments; he prepared short biographies of outstanding composers and his own *Mémoires.* He was one of the first to advocate firmly that music should be performed as written, in the style of the composer's era, not modernized in performance or published in editions that adapted the original notation to contemporary practices. His treatise on instrumentation and orchestration has been mentioned.

MINOR COMPOSERS

Among the minor composers in France in the mid-nineteenth century were Louise Dumont Farrenc (1804–75) and Camille Moke Pleyel (1811–75). Both were outstanding performers and excellent teachers—they were among the few women faculty members at significant music conservatories before 1850.

At the age of 14, Camille Moke performed concerti in public concerts; by 1830 she was on the music faculty of a girls' school in Paris. She was engaged briefly to Berlioz but in 1831 married Camille Pleyel (1788–1855). When they separated in 1835, she resumed concertizing. She appeared on some programs with Liszt and performed four-hand compositions with him. From 1848 to 1872, Mme Pleyel taught piano at Brussels Conservatory. She composed several piano pieces, including *Rondo parisien* (Parisian rondo, Op. 1), and some fantasias.

Mme Farrenc, a pianist of professional stature, was Professor of Piano at Paris Conservatoire from 1842 to 1873. In the nineteenth century, she was the only woman musician at the Conservatoire to hold a permanent position of that rank. Her first published compositions appeared in 1825. Among her works are 2 overtures, 3 symphonies, a nonet for winds and strings, a sextet for piano and winds, 2 piano quintets, a string quartet, 2 piano trios, 2 violin/piano sonatas, a 'cello/piano sonata, and numerous piano pieces. The *Nonet* (E♭, Op. 38; 1849) was especially acclaimed. Her pedagogical works include more than 80 études. She and her husband, Aristide Farrenc (1794–1865), compiled, edited, and published a collection of keyboard works by earlier composers, *Le trésor des pianistes* (Pianists' treasure, 23 vols.; Paris, 1861–74).

MUSIC IN ITALY

In Italy during the nineteenth century, musical interest was centered on opera. To many Italian composers, success in music meant success in opera. Most Italian composers wrote a good deal of church music, secular songs, and some instrumental works, but they either turned to composition in other genres after having a career in opera or considered other genres of lesser importance. A noteworthy exception was Niccolò Paganini.

NICCOLÒ PAGANINI

Virtuoso violinist Niccolò Paganini (1782–1840) dazzled the world with his exceptional technical skills and his effective musical interpretation and attracted the attention of other nineteenth-century composers and performers to the extent that several emulated his virtuosity in their own performances and compositions. Also, Paganini played mandolin and guitar exceptionally well. He composed solos for all three instruments, wrote some chamber music that included them, and created some music for orchestra and voice.

Paganini began concertizing at the age of 12 to earn money for music lessons. In 1805, he became solo violinist at the court of Napoleon's sister, Princess Elise Baciocchi, ruler of Lucca. Disappointed because he was never offered the *maestro di cappella* post, in 1809 he resumed concertizing. He had mastered the violin techniques of his time and had developed a few techniques with which other violinists were as yet unfamiliar (e.g., ricochet bowings, left-hand pizzicato, and double-stops in harmonics). His hands were large and his fingers long and slender, and by extension he could play in three positions without shifting. He had a predilection for playing an entire composition on one string. When gauged strings were available, he used thin gut strings so that the upper strings would break more easily and he would be forced to complete a piece on only one string. In 1810–28 he concertized throughout Italy, creating a furor wherever he played.

During part of 1822–23, Paganini was so ill that he could not concertize; it was the first of many bouts with catarrhal phthisis, a tubercular disease that in turn claimed his vocal cords, his violin playing, and his life. In 1824 he met singer Antonia Bianchi; their son Achille was born in July 1825. While Paganini's liaison with Bianchi lasted, she assisted in some of his concerts and performed his vocal compositions; when they separated in 1829 (they never married) Paganini obtained custody of Achille and by court action legitimized him.

In 1828–34 Paganini concertized internationally. In Vienna, he programmed orchestral works by Beethoven, Mozart, and Haydn as well as his own works. Those programs reveal an interesting practice—the performance of symphonies and concerti by movements rather than as complete entities. Though the movements were performed in their proper order, solos or movements of other works were performed between them. Paganini was an excellent quartet player and performed the quartets of Haydn, Mozart, and Beethoven.

In 1833 Paganini encouraged Berlioz to write an orchestral work featuring viola. Berlioz anonymously placed a notice in the *Gazette musicale* to the effect that he was to compose a "dramatic fantasy" for orchestra, chorus, and solo viola and that Paganini would play the viola part. By the time Berlioz completed *Harold in Italy*, Paganini was too ill to play concerts.

During 1835–37 he served on the administrative commission of the ducal theater at Parma; in 1837–38 he invested heavily in the Casino Paganini in Paris, which admitted illegal gambling. In October 1838 he was critically ill and completely lost his voice; thereafter, he communicated by writing. Before leaving Paris in December, he attended a Berlioz concert at which *Harold in Italy* was performed. Paganini indicated his appreciation of Berlioz's work by giving him 20,000 francs, sufficient to support him while he composed *Romeo et Juliette*.

Paganini's health deteriorated steadily. He visited Genoa in autumn 1839, then went to Nice to spend the winter. He died there on 27 May 1840.

Many musicians were influenced by Paganini's compositions as well as by his technical wizardry and his beautiful tone quality when playing Adagio melodies. Only the German school of violinists (e.g., Spohr and Joachim) was adamantly opposed to his style. Paganini's virtuosity was a shaping force in the style of Liszt (see p. 507–8). Several composers used Paganini's compositions as the basis of or models for their own works, among them, Chopin, Liszt, Schumann, Brahms, and Rachmaninov. Paganini's 24 *Caprices for Unaccompanied Violin* are standard study and performance repertoire. Tone quality was very important to Paganini. He owned two complete quartets of Stradivari instruments, for matched timbre in playing quartets. One set is owned by the Corcoran Gallery, which loans it to reputable performing quartets in the United States.

ITALIAN OPERA

In accordance with tradition, the clear separation between opera seria and opera buffa was preserved until almost midcentury. Only gradually did Romantic elements infiltrate Italian opera, and never did they permeate to the same extent as in Germany or France. There were two main reasons for this: the many independent states with their own traditions and restraint on the part of the librettists. Felice Romani (1788–1865) and Salvatore Cammarano (1801–52), who prepared libretti for Mayr, Donizetti, Bellini, and a few for Verdi, used only moderate amounts of Romanticism. They derived plots from literature and fairly recent history rather than from ancient history and mythology—British literature and English history were especially favored—but they modified the Romantic elements. Verdi worked closely with Piave and other librettists and firmly controlled every aspect of his operas. He was Romantic only in his concern for realistic portrayal and characterization. In other respects, he followed tradition. However, composers made some changes. As Rossini had gradually supplanted the castrato hero with a contralto, so later composers supplanted the contralto hero with a tenor. Bellini was the first Italian composer to write typically Romantic roles for tenor. Verdi included roles for baritone and for *basso cantante*, a firm singing bass.

Paris attracted and kept many Italian composers and fine performers. The principal Italian composers of opera during the second quarter of the nineteenth century were Gaetano Donizetti and Vincenzo Bellini. Donizetti, trained by Mayr, was the direct precursor of Giuseppe Verdi, who dominated the Italian opera scene from 1842 to 1893.

GAETANO DONIZETTI Donizetti (1797–1848) was the fifth of six children in an extremely impoverished family in Bergamo, Italy. In 1806 the Cathedral of Santa Maria Maggiore in Bergamo opened its free music school, with Mayr as director. Donizetti was accepted in the first class of students and received excellent, thorough training in music. Mayr arranged for Donizetti's further study with Padre Martini in Bologna. When Mayr was unable to fill a commission for an opera for Rome, he turned over his contract to Donizetti. Then Barbaia offered him a contract, and he went to Naples as successor to Rossini. In 1822–30 Donizetti composed 24 mediocre operas for Naples. With his thirty-first opera, *Anna Bolena* (Anne Boleyn; Milan, 1830), an opera seria, he experienced his first major success. Donizetti composed rapidly; he wrote several operas a year in addition to other works. He again achieved success with the comedy *L'elisir d'amore* (The elixir of love; 1832) and *Lucrezia Borgia* (1833).

A visit to Paris in 1835 revealed to Donizetti the caliber of musical and dramatic talent in opéra comique and provided his first exposure to French grand opera. He returned to Naples for production of *Lucia di Lam-*

Gaetano Donizetti.

mermoor and attempted to write opera in French style. Then he began to develop his own distinctive style. In Paris in 1840 he had success with *Les martyrs* at L'Opéra and *La fille du régiment* (The daughter of the regiment) at L'Opéra-Comique. *Don Pasquale* was produced at Théâtre-Italien in 1843.

Donizetti wrote more than 600 compositions, including 70 operas, over 100 songs, some vocal chamber music, numerous pieces of church music, 2 oratorios, more than 2 dozen cantatas, 19 string quartets, 3 string quintets, miscellaneous pieces of other instrumental chamber music, some piano solos and duets, about 15 sinfonie, and a few other orchestral works. Among the sacred music is a Requiem Mass written in memory of Bellini. Of Donizetti's operas, the most important are the opere serie *Anna Bolena, Lucrezia Borgia,* and *Lucia di Lammermoor;* the opéra comique *La fille du régiment;* the comica *L'elisir d'amore;* and the opera buffa *Don Pasquale.*

Don Pasquale is considered Donizetti's comic masterpiece, yet some of the most striking segments of it, and of the comedy *L'elisir d'amore,* are not at all comic. This signals a breaking down of the traditional distinction between opera seria and opera buffa. Donizetti's music is not as brilliant as Rossini's, nor does it have the sincerity and earnestness conveyed by Verdi's music. Yet, those works Donizetti composed after 1835 point directly to the early works of Verdi.

Donizetti was influenced in the composition of opera by the resources at hand—the types of voices in the particular opera company and the demands of the leading singers. Though his music is expressive and he could bring out the dramatic or the humorous in a given situation, he did not use daring or chromatic harmonies, and he seems to have always considered the vocal line(s) as being of greater significance than the orchestral accompaniment. Donizetti is seen at his best in his comic operas. *Don Pasquale* and *L'elisir d'amore* have been part of opera repertoire since they were first produced.

VINCENZO BELLINI Bellini (1801–35), a native of Sicily, received his musical training first from his father and then from his grandfather, who were composers and music teachers. In 1819 he entered Naples Conservatory. When he completed his study there, his opera semiseria, *Adelson e Salvini,* was performed by a cast of male students. As a result of that performance, Bellini received a commission from Teatro San Carlo for *Bianca e Fernando* (1826). During 1827–33 Bellini composed nine operas. *La straniera* (The foreign woman; 1829) was criticized for its lack of coloratura; in succeeding operas Bellini included more coloratura but carefully regulated its use. He succeeded again with the opere serie *I Capuleti e i Montecchi* (The Capulets and the Montagues; 1830) and *La sonnambula* (The sleepwalker; 1831). When *Norma* was performed at La Scala in December 1831, Bellini proclaimed it a fiasco. His judgment was faulty—he had created a masterpiece. *Norma* is the story of a Druid high priestess and her unfaithful lover, a Roman proconsul. Giuditta Pasta (1797–1865), Italian soprano, created the title role. By that time Bellini had established a lasting friendship with Pasta, who for at least a decade was acclaimed as the greatest soprano in Europe. Her voice was not perfect, but she had an extended range and could sing lyric and dramatic roles equally well. She created the title role in Donizetti's *Anna Bolena* and the leading role (Amina) in Bellini's *La sonnambula.* In 1833, in a performance of *I Capuleti e i Montecchi,* she sang the Romeo role. After Bellini met Pasta, he designed the leading soprano roles in most of his operas to suit her talents, and when his operas were performed under his direction in London and Paris in 1833, she sang those roles in most of them.

Bellini returned to Milan and spent several months resting. In 1834, for Théâtre-Italien, he composed *I Puritani* (The Puritans). After its successful performance (January 1835) he stayed in Paris. In mid-August he became seriously ill, and on 23 September he died. A few days later, Théâtre-Italien opened the season with *I Puritani.*

Bellini's music was influenced by Rossini, Zingarelli (his teacher at Naples Conservatory), working friendships with Romani and Pasta, and the folk music of Sicily, much of which had been absorbed into art music. The lyrical style of Bellini's early music was derived from Rossini; gradually, Bellini controlled and narrowed that lyricism and infiltrated it with emotion. He set text carefully, with regard for correct declamation and the proper mood of the phrases. He demanded of Romani an emotional libretto, filled with exciting situations. In composing music to fit those situations, Bellini sought a balance between *bel canto* lyricism and dramatic tension. He constructed melodies in broad curves built from small segments; this may be seen in *Casta diva,* the cavatina and prayer scene from Act II of *Norma* (DWMA159). That scene provides an example of the manner in which an aria was incorporated into a scene containing sections in different tempi and involving ensemble participation. This was not new—Mayr and others used it effectively. In *Casta diva,* the melodic climax comes at the end; Bellini used motives sequentially to build phrases and to build to that climax. When repeating phrases, he embellished them. Many of his melodies feature scale passages in semitones (*Casta diva,* m. 118ff, or mm. 150–53); he often wrote passages with ever-widening pitch intervals (mm. 154–60). He tended to select a rhythm and have it permeate an entire piece or a great section of it.

Besides opera, Bellini wrote numerous sacred and secular vocal works and pieces for keyboard and for orchestra. His "complete works" have not been issued.

MUSIC IN ENGLAND

Oratorios and part songs were an important part of the many music festivals in England. The provincial festivals promoted the formation of choral societies and the singing of part-songs and glees. Festivals were held throughout the land, but that at Birmingham was the most significant. Birmingham regularly commissioned choral works by continental composers. The affection of the English for oratorios influenced Mendelssohn to write them—*St. Paul* and *Elijah* were composed for and performed at Birmingham festivals. Other oratorios that had premières at English festivals were Spohr's *The Fall of Babylon* (1840), Gounod's *La rédemption* (1882), and Dvořák's *St. Ludmilla* (1886).

Since the time of Purcell, the only English composer whose work was known internationally was Thomas Linley, whose music was soon forgotten after his death in 1778. In the nineteenth century, Irish singer-composer Michael Balfe (1808–70) had international success with *The Bohemian Girl* (1843), which was translated into French, Italian, and German. Balfe composed 29 operas, a ballet, a few songs, a piano trio, and a piano/'cello sonata.

During the last quarter of the nineteenth century, Arthur S. Sullivan (1842–1900) attained fame with his operettas and comic operas, especially those setting libretti by W. S. Gilbert. *Trial by Jury, The Gondoliers, H.M.S. Pinafore, Yeomen of the Guard,* and *The Mikado* are still favorites. Behind the comedy in many Gilbert and Sullivan operettas is satire of specific political and cultural conditions in England at that time. Sullivan composed more serious works, including the oratorio *The Prodigal Son* (1869), Anglican anthems and other Service music, a *Te Deum* (1902), choral works with orchestra, orchestral and chamber music, and much vocal music.

In the area of English church music, Samuel S. Wesley's (1810–86) Services and 27 excellent anthems were an important contribution to Anglican church music. His music is specifically English, and his style is distinctive. In some of his long anthems, he incorporated recitative, arialike solos, and fugal sections. He composed some organ music for Services; secular and sacred songs, choruses, and part-songs; and some piano solos. Wesley was influential in promoting the performance of Bach's music in England.

MUSIC IN NORTH AMERICA

UNITED STATES

Between 1825 and 1875, many Europeans immigrated to the United States from Britain and Germany. Some came to join friends and relatives living here; others came because of unfavorable or revolutionary political conditions in their native lands or the crop failures in 1848. Among those who came to concertize in America in 1843–57 were Norwegian violinist Ole Bull (1810–80), soprano Jenny Lind (1820–87), German soprano Henriette Sontag (1806–54), and pianist Sigismond Thalberg (1812–71).

Music in the United States in the nineteenth century was of two basic kinds: so-called popular music, which was naive and untrained, and cultivated or art music based on European models. There were reasons for this duality. The United States was undergoing vast and rapid territorial expansion, and the settlements within the country's boundaries were of three types: pioneer settlements with little or no contact with cultural events outside one's own community, new towns with limited outside contact, and established urban centers such as New York, Philadelphia, and Boston. In general, the nineteenth-century view of music was that it belonged in the province of women, foreigners who came specifically to concertize or to teach music, and the effeminate.

Art music was of five general kinds: church music, songs, piano music, orchestral or ensemble music, and opera. In all categories except the first, individuality and subjectivity were highly esteemed. Church music was given priority because it was functional music; there was great concern for good singing in church services and meetings. Among those who taught in singing schools, composed hymns, and worked for the cause of music education were Lowell Mason and William Bradbury.

Lowell Mason (1792–1872) composed over 1,200 hymns with simple four-part harmony and adapted as hymns hundreds of melodies by other composers. He placed the melody in either the tenor or the soprano. Among Mason's best-known hymns are *Olivet* ("My faith looks up to Thee") and *Missionary Hymn* ("From Greenland's icy mountains"); these are in many Protestant hymnals. For a dozen years (1813–24) Mason taught in singing schools and compiled a collection of songs suitable for singing in Sunday school. He pioneered in music education by getting singing introduced in four public schools in Boston on an experimental basis in 1837, by setting standards for that teaching through doing it personally and without salary at first, and by composing and publishing collections of songs suitable for that teaching (fig. 22.3).

FIGURE 22.3 Lowell Mason: *The Song Garden*, Second Book, published by Oliver Ditson, Boston, in 1864.

Stephen Foster. Portrait in oils, c. 1859. Original is at Federal Hill, Bardstown, Kentucky.

William Bradbury (1816–68), a native of Maine, received music lessons at home. In the 1830s he attended some of Mason's classes in Boston, then served for more than a year as singing school teacher in Maine. After 1841 he worked in churches in New York, taught singing school classes there, and organized annual festivals in which hundreds of children sang. As a result of those festivals, singing was introduced into New York public schools. In addition to 28 anthems and more than 800 hymns, Bradbury wrote 78 secular songs, some patriotic male choruses, and other vocal music.

In the area of song, many persons set sentimental, nostalgic verses to music for voice with piano accompaniment. Many of these were used at home or in community concert programs. Some are of the "tear-jerker" variety (e.g., Bradbury's *The Lament of the Blind Orphan Girl*), simple tunes and harmonies in strophic settings of sad sentimental lyrics. Some texts were set as melodrama, and during the Civil War years many were patriotic. Part-songs for unaccompanied male voices were entertainment music at home or in concerts. **Männerchor** (male singing societies) were organized at Philadelphia in 1835 and in several other cities. **Glees** (part-songs for entertainment) were brought over from England and generated composition of similar songs by Americans.

America's principal song writer in the mid-nineteenth century was Stephen Foster (1826–64). Basically, he was self-taught in music, much of his knowledge of composition coming from his interest in and study of the works of Mozart, Beethoven, Weber, and other masters. Foster had a gift for melody and could harmonize melodies fairly well. His first published song was *Open Thy Lattice, Love* (1844). Foster was the first American-born composer to earn his living entirely from song writing; he did so for the last 14 years of his life. Foster wrote approximately 150 songs of all kinds, many of them love songs addressed to or about a lady who was unattainable. *Jeanie with the Light Brown Hair* is an example. Some songs use pentatonic scales and resemble Irish folk songs—Foster's ancestry was Irish. Other songs indicate that Foster knew Rossini's music. When minstrel shows became popular in the 1840s, Foster contributed some songs to the repertoire of the "Original Christy Minstrels." After 1850, he wrote some "plantation songs," nostalgic songs that reminisce on bygone days (e.g., *My Old Kentucky Home* and *Old Folks at Home*). His last songs were patriotic, related to the Civil War.

PIANO MUSIC   There were several prosperous piano manufacturing firms in the United States in the mid-nineteenth century. Chickering, in Boston, made both "square" and grand types. Heinrich Steinweg (Henry Steinway) established his firm in New York in 1850;

Mason & Hamlin began business in 1854. Hundreds of composers published piano solos in sheet music—musical trifles usually constructed as theme and variations or fantasias, related to the ability to improvise.

Louis Moreau Gottschalk (1829–69) was the first American musician to be acclaimed internationally as a virtuoso performer. From the age of 4, he had private music lessons. In 1842 he went to Paris for further study. When he returned to the United States in 1853, he was a seasoned concert artist of virtuoso caliber. For the remainder of his life, he was almost continually on concert tour.

Gottschalk composed piano solos, works for piano and orchestra, symphonies, marches, operas, and accompanied vocal solos. Some of his finest piano works stem from the years he spent in the Antilles (e.g., *Souvenir de Porto Rico* [1857]). Many of his piano pieces and some of his symphonies have programmatic titles (e.g., Symphony No. 1, *La nuit des tropiques* [Night in the tropics], 1858). In Latin and South America, Gottschalk organized festivals at which ensembles of 300 to 600 instrumentalists performed his works. In his use of large performing ensembles, he was like Berlioz.

One characteristic of Gottschalk's style is the frequent quotation from works by other composers. The piano solo *Le banjo* (1855) is an example of this. In his use of quotations as musical and psychological devices, Gottschalk presages Charles Ives. Wherever Gottschalk lived and worked, he absorbed all the Creole, Latin American, Spanish, and Negro rhythms that surrounded him, and these appear in his music. His treatment of some rhythms is closely akin to the ragtime and jazz that emerged at the end of the century.

ORCHESTRAL MUSIC; OPERA   The first permanent orchestra in the United States—the New York Philharmonic Symphony Society—was established in 1842. The Boston Symphony was founded in 1881. Comparatively little orchestral music was written by American composers at this time. The Moravians in Pennsylvania wrote their music primarily for their own communal use. An overture and two symphonies by Charles Hommann (c. 1800–c. 1840) are known, and William H. Fry (1813–64) wrote at least four programmatic symphonies.

Two of George F. Bristow's (1825–98) symphonies, composed for the New York Philharmonic in 1856 and 1859, sound similar to those of Mendelssohn. Bristow's *Niagara Symphony* (1893), modeled after Beethoven's Ninth, is for soloists, chorus, and orchestra. Bristow composed approximately 120 works, including overtures, string quartets, piano pieces, an oratorio, cantatas, a Mass in C (1885), and the opera *Rip van Winkle* (1855).

The least significant genre of music in America in the mid-nineteenth century was opera. Fry wrote three: *Aurelia the Vestal* (1841; never performed); *Leonora* (1845), the first opera by an American composer to be publicly performed; and *Notre Dame of Paris* (1864). The operas are in English and are not distinctive musically.

In the mid-nineteenth century, two American journalists concerned themselves with music. Fry, writing for the *New York Tribune,* championed the cause of American music and, with Bristow, instigated the inclusion of American works on programs of the New York Philharmonic. John S. Dwight (1813–93) published a weekly *Journal* devoted to music criticism and promotion of works by master European composers. Between 1852 and 1881, 41 volumes of that *Journal* were published. In them are critiques of concerts, discussions of new works, and significant writings by European authors concerning European composers.

CANADA

Marie Lajeunesse (1847–1930) was born near Montreal. She received her first music training from her father, then studied in Paris and Milan. While abroad, she adopted the name Emma Albani. In 1870 she made her operatic début as Amina in *La sonnambula* and soon became one of Europe's leading dramatic sopranos. She performed also at the Metropolitan Opera in New York. Emma Albani was the first Canadian-born musician to be accorded international acclaim as a performer.

Pianist-composer Calixa Lavallée (1842–91), a native of Verchères, Quebec, received his first music instruction from his father, a music teacher, violin maker, and bandmaster. Later, Calixa studied at Paris Conservatoire. When he returned to America, he settled in Boston. In 1880 he was asked to compose a Canadian national song for a festival in Quebec; *O Canada* resulted. In 1980 *O Canada* was officially declared Canada's national anthem. Among Lavallée's extant works are some cantatas, the operetta *The Widow* (1882), and some piano music. One of his best-known piano pieces is *Le papillon* (Butterfly).

SUMMARY

The middle quarters of the nineteenth century witnessed increased industrialization, urbanization, and political unrest. The ideology of nationalism gained strength and led to the unification of Italy and Germany. The first stirrings of socialism and socialistic labor movements appeared. The arts were important, but patronage was waning, and most musicians earned their living by teaching and by concertizing. Women published their compositions, taught, and concertized.

Composers wrote several kinds of vocal music: accompanied solos, part-songs and choruses, liturgical music, large choral works with orchestral accompaniment, and operas. A number of symphonic works incorporated chorus and/or soloists. Church music was affected to some extent by the Cecilian movement, which advocated the use of Gregorian chant in its purest form and sought to eliminate integrated music from church services in favor of Palestrina-style *a cappella* choral music. Results of that movement were the improvement of singing in the church and new editions of liturgical chant books.

Instrumental music includes orchestral works, chamber music, compositions for solo instrument with orchestral or keyboard accompaniment, and solo piano pieces. Any of these genres might be program music or absolute music. Most of the instrumental solos with orchestra are concerti. The piano was the most important solo instrument and was considered essential in the homes of all who aspired to some degree of gentility. For it composers wrote dance pieces, character pieces, études, sonatas, variations, and fantasias. Several styles of piano playing were evident, and, as piano construction improved, composers wrote music that was increasingly demanding technically and that took full advantage of the instrument's capabilities.

Music printed in Vienna and Leipzig was readily available throughout Germany. Plans were made for editions of the complete works of Palestrina and Bach. By 1850, music of the past had found a place in concert repertoire. A number of conservatories were established with outstanding musicians on their faculties.

In lands under Austro-Germanic rule, music seems to have been dominated by composers who were superb pianists. Chopin composed music particularly suited to the piano, taking complete advantage of its unique capabilities rather than attempting to draw from it orchestral sonorities. Characteristic of his music are the interweaving of melody and accompaniment figures, *tempo rubato,* and use of the sustaining pedal to expand the compass of a chord beyond a normal handspan. His best works are those in which he was unhampered by traditional forms: ballades, nocturnes, preludes, and études.

Mendelssohn contributed to the development of music in many ways: by promoting the revival of Bach's music, by establishing and serving as director of Leipzig Conservatory, by conducting the Gewandhaus Orchestra, and by programming works by historically significant composers and by contemporary composers. He composed in almost all genres and made valuable contributions to the repertoire with his E-minor Violin Concerto and oratorios. Fanny Mendelssohn Hensel was an accomplished pianist who composed a fine Piano Trio and excellent Lieder.

Robert Schumann's main musical contributions were Lieder and piano music. In many of his Lieder the voice and piano are partners, sharing in the musical presentation of the poetry. Through critical reviews of compositions and performances, he promoted the careers of several musicians. Clara Wieck Schumann was the first woman to have a successful international career as concert pianist. She was on the faculty of Leipzig Conservatory and was the principal piano teacher on the faculty of Hoch Conservatory. Her finest composition is her Piano Trio.

In France, music was dominated by opera, especially grand opera. Its success in the 1830s was due to the combined efforts of Véron, the director of L'Opéra; Scribe, the librettist; Meyerbeer, the composer; Cicéri and Duponchel, scene designers; and Auguste, leader of the claque. Grand opera is sung throughout, has few arias and almost no pure recitative, promotes much of the action through spectacular scenes strategically woven into the drama, and makes much use of ensembles of all sizes, particularly chorus. The most important grand operas produced at L'Opéra in the 1830s—those that established the course of opera in France—were Meyerbeer's *Robert le diable,* Auber's *Gustave III,*

Halévy's *La Juive,* and Meyerbeer's *Les Huguenots.* Almost all composers of serious opera wrote opéra comique also. In the history of opéra comique, Bizet's *Carmen* was a landmark. Not only did it bring the genre to a peak, but, through use of a serious subject and presentation of a tragedy with spoken dialogue, it destroyed the artificial line of demarcation between opéra comique and opéra. Bizet's realistic portrayal of characters and situations presaged *verismo* opera. Some operas could not be performed at L'Opéra because they were too small or their subject matter and music were too light; such an opera was termed opéra lyrique. Other types were opéra bouffe and operetta. Opéra bouffe was instigated and popularized by Offenbach, whose *Orphée aux enfers* satirizes the Orpheus-Euridice myth.

Opera in France attained new heights with Berlioz's *Les Troyens.* Berlioz contributed significantly to symphonic literature with *Symphonie fantastique,* a cyclic work exhibiting many of the characteristics and dualities of Romanticism. His most important contribution to composition and to music education was *Grand traité d'instrumentation,* the first textbook on orchestration. His critical writings contain valuable information concerning compositions, performances, performers, and new instruments. He was one of the first to advocate firmly that music should be performed as written, in the style of the composer's era, not modernized in performance or published in editions that adapted the original notation to contemporary practices.

Paganini, through virtuosic performances and exploitation of all bowing and fingering techniques then available, did much to advance violin playing. Outstanding pianists emulated his virtuosity, and his works inspired other composers' compositions.

Music in Italy was centered on opera. The traditional clear separation between opera seria and opera buffa (both sung throughout) was preserved until almost midcentury. Gradually Romantic elements infiltrated Italian opera but never permeated to the same extent as in Germany or France. The principal Italian composers of opera during the second quarter of the nineteenth century were Donizetti and Bellini. Donizetti, trained by Mayr, was the direct precursor of Verdi.

England favored the oratorio, and oratorios by many well-known composers were first performed at English festivals. The most significant English composers were Arthur Sullivan, in the field of operetta, and Samuel S. Wesley, who is considered successor to Purcell in the area of Anglican cathedral music.

Music in the United States was of two basic kinds: "popular" music and art music. Art music was of five general kinds: church music, songs, piano music, orchestral or ensemble music, and opera. Mason and Bradbury wrote numerous hymns. Both men taught in singing schools, and Mason pioneered in music education by getting singing introduced into Boston's public schools and by setting standards for that kind of teaching. America's principal song writer in midcentury was Stephen Foster. Gottschalk, whose talent paralleled that of Chopin, successfully concertized in Europe and throughout the Americas. In some of his works, his treatment of rhythm is closely akin to ragtime and jazz, and in his use of musical quotations he presaged the work of twentieth-century composer Charles Ives. In 1842 the first permanent symphony orchestra was established in the United States—the New York Philharmonic—but American composers wrote little music for its use. Operas composed by Americans were inconsequential. Dwight's weekly *Journal,* with its critical and informative articles on music, was a significant contribution.

Canadians active as professional musicians include singer Emma Albani, the first Canadian-born musician to win international acclaim as a performer, and pianist Lavallée, composer of Canada's national anthem.

PREEMINENT COMPOSERS OF THE LATE NINETEENTH CENTURY

In many European countries, much of the nineteenth century was filled with uprisings and revolutions of various kinds. In France, the Revolutions of 1830 and 1848 were followed in 1870 by the Franco-Prussian War. And for Germanic peoples and Italians, uprisings and warfare ultimately brought national unification—the nations of Germany and Italy were formally established by treaties in 1871. Many authors, artists, and musicians were actively involved in the struggles to achieve national identity. In Germany, Richard Wagner wrote controversial articles, joined a revolutionary organization, and took part in uprisings, but only covertly were his sentiments expressed in his music. Giuseppe Verdi lent his name to the Italian unification movement, served in parliament, and voiced his patriotic feelings through the mouths of characters in his operas. The revolution seems to have affected Franz Liszt only indirectly—through its effect on the lives of associates who fled from their homes and sought his protection. In fact, in the works of the five preeminent composers of the late nineteenth century—Wagner, Verdi, Liszt, Bruckner, and Brahms—there is no great outpouring of music that is nationalistic *per se*.

Wagner and Verdi concentrated on opera, and their masterworks brought that genre to unprecedented heights. Liszt coupled virtuosity with solid musicianship and promoted piano playing. He also created compositions that enriched piano and orchestral literature. Bruckner and Brahms were outstanding performers on keyboard instruments. Neither of them wrote program music, and both produced excellent symphonies and superb choral works. Brahms enriched chamber music literature also.

RICHARD WAGNER

Wagner (1813–83), ninth child of Johanna and Karl Wagner, was born in Leipzig. Karl died shortly after Richard was born, and Johanna married Ludwig Geyer (1779–1821), an actor employed at the Dresden court theater. In Dresden, Wagner received a general education, and some music lessons, and he had bit parts in operas and plays. In 1827 Frau Geyer moved her family back to Leipzig, where Wagner attended *Nicolaigymnasium*. By then, the theater had captured his attention, and he wrote a play. He determined to learn more about music, tried to teach himself composition, then arranged for harmony lessons. In 1830 he studied at Thomasschule; a year later he entered Leipzig University to study music but soon gave that up in favor of private lessons from the

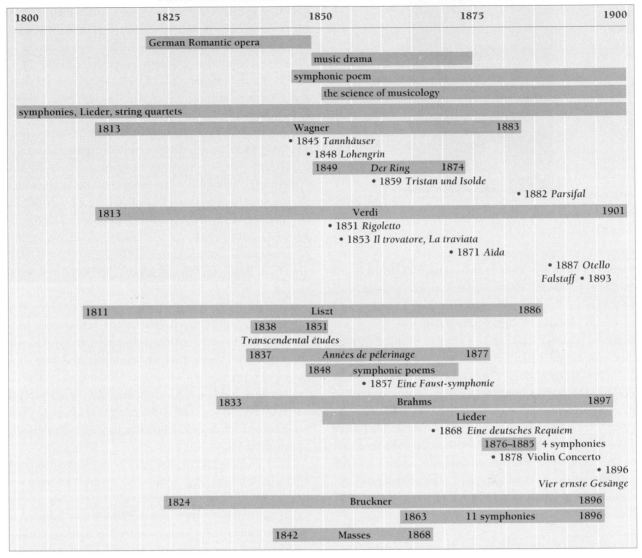

| 1800 | 1825 | 1850 | 1875 | 1900 |

German Romantic opera

music drama

symphonic poem

the science of musicology

symphonies, Lieder, string quartets

1813 Wagner **1883**
- 1845 *Tannhäuser*
- 1848 *Lohengrin*
1849 *Der Ring* 1874
- 1859 *Tristan und Isolde*
- 1882 *Parsifal*

1813 Verdi **1901**
- 1851 *Rigoletto*
- 1853 *Il trovatore, La traviata*
- 1871 *Aïda*
- 1887 *Otello*
Falstaff • 1893

1811 Liszt **1886**
1838 1851
Transcendental études
1837 *Années de pèlerinage* 1877
1848 symphonic poems
- 1857 *Eine Faust-symphonie*

1833 Brahms **1897**
Lieder
- 1868 *Eine deutsches Requiem*
1876–1885 4 symphonies
- 1878 Violin Concerto
- 1896
Vier ernste Gesänge

1824 Bruckner **1896**
1863 11 symphonies 1896
1842 Masses 1868

Thomaskirche Kantor. Those lessons fostered several compositions, including two piano sonatas (B♭ major, A major), a *Fantasia* (F♯ minor), some overtures, and a symphony (C major).

Primarily, Wagner was interested in stage music. In 1832 he wrote a libretto and composed an opera, *Die Hochzeit* (The Wedding). Later, he destroyed part of it. He looked for a suitable libretto for another opera but, after reading some, decided that only he could write his libretti. On that, he never changed his mind.

During 1833 Wagner worked at Würzburg as chorus master and was involved in the production of French rescue operas and German Romantic operas. There he composed *Die Feen* (The Fairies; 1833–34), a Romantic fairy-tale opera in the tradition of Marschner and Weber. Next, he wrote *Das Liebesverbot* (Forbidden love; 1834–36), based on Shakespeare's *Measure for Measure*.

In 1834 Wagner began writing articles on various aspects of drama, art, and music. Throughout his life he wrote essays of this kind for such journals as *Neue Zeitschrift für Musik* and *Gazette musicale*. He became music director of Bethmann's theatrical company in 1834 and moved to Magdeburg to be near actress Minna

Richard Wagner. Photograph taken in 1880. *(Courtesy of the Free Library of Philadelphia)*

Planer (1809–66). They married in 1836. In 1834–36 Wagner produced operas and learned a great deal about them.

Briefly, in 1837 Wagner was music director at Königsberg Theater, then held a similar position at Riga where he began a grand opera, *Rienzi* (1837–40). When his work at Riga ended (1839), he was heavily in debt and left the country secretly. He and Minna embarked on a schooner for London, then went to Paris, where he completed *Rienzi* and wrote *Der fliegende Hollander* (The flying Dutchman; 1840–41). In 1842 he returned to Dresden. *Rienzi,* performed there in October, was his first operatic triumph. Wagner was offered and accepted the position of conductor at Dresden. In 1844 he composed some music for Weber's interment services (see p. 436).

At Dresden, Wagner wrote *Tannhäuser* (1842–45) and *Lohengrin* (1845–48), but only *Tannhäuser* was performed there (1845). Wagner had strong feelings about political conditions in Germany, published his revolutionary writings, and was active in the revolutionary *Vaterlandsverein*. He became deeply involved in political intrigue, and, after participating in the uprising in May 1849, he had to flee to avoid imprisonment. He went to Weimar, where Liszt aided him, then fled to Zurich. While Wagner was in Switzerland, Liszt conducted the première of *Lohengrin* at Weimar (1850).

In Zurich, Wagner wrote some of his most significant essays on music, art, and drama, including *Die Kunst und die Revolution* (Art and Revolution, 1849), *Das Kunstwerk der Zukunft* (The Artwork of the Future, 1849), and *Oper und Drama* (Opera and Drama, 1851). His essay *Jewry in Music* (1850) was blatantly anti-Semitic, and portions of some of his operas could be construed similarly. Though Adolph Hitler (1889–1945) owned manuscripts of several of Wagner's operas, his admiration for Wagner was not based solely on his music.

In Zurich, Wagner prepared the libretti for a cycle of music dramas based on material from the Icelandic *Edda* and the German *Nibelungenlied* (Song of the Nibelung). He did not compose the operas in the order in which they appear in the finished cycle, nor did he originally give them the titles they now bear: *Das Rheingold* (The Rhinegold), *Die Walküre* (The Walkyrie), *Siegfried,* and *Götterdämmerung* (Twilight of the Gods). Together those works constitute *Der Ring des Nibelungen* (The Nibelung's Ring). Composition of the series took Wagner more than a quarter of a century (1848–74), yet the music dramas are remarkably unified. He had completed the first two and part of the third by 1856, then other projects attracted him: five songs on poems by Mathilde Wesendonk (1857), *Tristan und Isolde* (1857–59), and *Die Meistersinger von Nürnberg* (sketched 1845; comp. 1861–67). Then he resumed work on *Siegfried* and *Götterdämmerung* (completed 1874).

After Wagner had begun *Das Rheingold,* he designed a special kind of tuba, with tone quality midway between that of horn and trombone. In *Der Ring . . .* he used a quartet of those horns, which are known as **Wagner tubas.** Bruckner, Mahler, Stravinsky, and R. Strauss included Wagner tubas in some orchestral works, and they have been used in some film and television music.

Meanwhile, in 1864 King Ludwig II of Bavaria paid Wagner's debts, directed him to come to Munich, and granted him a yearly allowance. But again in 1865 Wagner had to seek refuge in Switzerland for political reasons. In 1866 Minna died, and Wagner was free to marry Cosima Liszt von Bülow, with whom he had had an affair for several years. Cosima left her husband in 1868 and, with the two of her daughters who were Wagner's, joined Wagner in Switzerland. Their son Siegfried was born in 1869. In 1870 Cosima obtained a divorce from von Bülow and married Wagner.

Wagner wanted a theater whose design would meet the needs of his stage works. In 1871 he acquired land in Bayreuth, and in 1872–76 his ideal theater was constructed. In 1876 the first Bayreuth Festival was held in the new theater, and *Der Ring des Nibelungen* was performed in its entirety.

In 1857 Wagner began sketching the music for *Parsifal;* he completed it in 1882. It was his last stage work and is the only one of them designed specifically for the Bayreuth theater.

Wagner had suffered from angina pectoris for several years, and he frequently spent the winter months in Italy. While in Venice on 13 February 1883 he suffered a fatal heart attack.

His Contributions

Wagner carried to completion the work in German Romantic opera begun by Weber and went beyond it to create music drama and approach the kind of *Gesamtkunstwerk* in stage music that Weber had striven toward—a work in which all the arts merged to achieve a common artistic goal. Wagner was extremely critical of the term *music drama* and would not have condoned its application to his stage works, yet he did not offer a more acceptable term. He concentrated on opera but also wrote orchestral pieces, chamber music, choral music, and songs. His C-major Symphony (1832) was performed several times during his lifetime and was the last work he conducted in public (1882), *Siegfried Idyll* (December 1870) was a birthday gift to his wife, and *Grosser Festmarsch* (Grand Festival March; 1876) was commissioned for the centennial celebrating the American colonies' declaration of independence from Britain and was performed in Philadelphia. He devised a new tuba and planned the theater at Bayreuth.

His Music

Wagner was involved in every step of the creation of many of his stage works, from the time the idea for a new work came to him until the curtain fell at the conclusion of its première. He knew exactly what was meant by each word of the libretto and could accurately express in his music the dramatic truth of the text.

His early operas follow traditional lines. Only fragments of *Die Hochzeit* survive. *Die Feen* and *Das Liebes-*verbot reflect the French and German operas that he had conducted. *Rienzi* is a grand opera in the style of Spontini's *Fernand Cortez* and Halévy's *La Juive.*

Der fliegende Hollander, a German Romantic opera of the redemption type, is based on a legend by Heine. It is a through-composed **scene opera** (i.e., a work comprised of separate scenes that succeed one another). The heart of this opera is Senta's ballad (in Act II), wherein she narrates the tale of the flying Dutchman. In this opera Wagner used only a few recurrent motives and used them as reminiscence motives.

For *Tannhäuser* Wagner combined the tale of Tannhäuser in *Des Knaben Wunderhorn* and E. T. A. Hoffmann's tale of the guild singers' contest at Wartburg. *Tannhäuser* is a German Romantic opera of the redemption type with some elements of grand opera. The plot relates how Tannhäuser, after spending a year enjoying sensual pleasures at Venusberg, seeks absolution from those sins; that absolution comes through the sacrificial death of Elisabeth, whose hand he wins in a singers' contest. The spectacular scenes in *Tannhäuser* are direct outgrowths of the story: the Venusberg ballet, the choruses sung by persons on pilgrimages to Rome, the song contest. There are numbers (set pieces) in *Tannhäuser;* this is typical of a song contest. Wagner wrote Tannhäuser's narrative of his pilgrimage to Rome in the kind of flexible, semideclamatory style of arioso that Weber had used in *Euryanthe.* Wagner used this expressive semideclamatory style of writing extensively in his later operas; he called it *Sprechgesang* (speech song).

Lohengrin, considered the last important German Romantic opera, is based on Wolfram von Eschenbach's epic poem *Parzivál* (p. 101) and Grimm's fairy tale of the Swan Knight, with historical elements added to justify the opera's tragic ending. In the nineteenth century, a tragic ending was acceptable only in historical works. Elements of both white and black magic are present. Taken literally, the plot deals with the trials of Elsa's love for Lohengrin, whose name she is not permitted to know. However, the character Lohengrin has been viewed as symbolically representing divine love descending in human form to give its blessing to humanity whose faith is too weak to accept it unquestioningly. The Prelude is interpreted as portraying the descent of the Holy Grail and its ascent back into heaven. *Lohengrin* contains elements of grand opera—pageantry, processions, and tableaux. Choruses are important; chorus members serve either as participants in the action or as spectators who sometimes comment. The music is generally diatonic, with specific keys assigned to the major characters—A major (the key of the Prelude) for Lohengrin, E♭ or A♭ major for Elsa, F♯ minor for Ortrud and for evil. Besides similarities in plot, *Lohengrin* has in common with Weber's *Euryanthe* the use of a few recurrent themes or associative *Leitmotifs* and semi-declamatory arioso. In *Lohengrin* the music is more continuous and greater use is made of scenes than in *Tannhäuser.*

Tristan und Isolde is music drama, concerned with human character and emotions, and is devoid of spectacle. The libretto is based on a medieval Celtic poem that relates the tragic love story. In *Tristan und Isolde* Wagner uses *Leitmotifs* that are allegorical and associative and that are related to and derived from one another. Frequently, one Leitmotif is the inversion of another (e.g., Yearning and Suffering). Motives may be melodic, harmonic, or a combination of both. The Yearning motive is not self-sufficient but is dependent on its underlying harmony. The same is true of the Love-potion motive, which is presented with the "Tristan chord."

The term *Tristan chord* derives from the first chord in *Tristan und Isolde,* f–b–d♯′–g♯′, or an enharmonic spelling of that chord (ex. 23.1). In functional harmony, the chord is an altered diminished seventh, with resolution effected by chromatic movement from g♯′ to a′, thus forming another seventh. The feeling of yearning generated by the prelude's first measures is not fully resolved until the opera's conclusion, in the *Liebestod* ("Love death"), which is sometimes referred to as Isolde's transfiguration. The Tristan chord did not originate with Wagner; however, he sounded it without preparation, whereas other composers wove it into the musical fabric more subtly. For example, Gottschalk achieved a similar sound in his religious meditation *The Last Hope* (Op. 16, piano; 1854) by writing a French sixth and resolving it to a dominant seventh by chromatic movement of the top pitch upward (ex. 23.2). Gottschalk used the passage sequentially, as Wagner did later in the *Prelude* to *Tristan und Isolde* (DWMA160).

The Tristan chord is of special harmonic and dramatic significance in *Parsifal* also. The entire harmonic vocabulary Wagner used in *Tristan und Isolde,* a harmonic vocabulary filled with daring chromatic progressions and bold accented appoggiaturas, is of historical significance in the breakdown of functional harmony and the advent of pantonality, atonality, and dodecaphony (see Chap. 25). A characteristic of Wagner's harmony in *Tristan und Isolde* is the ambiguous character of the chromatically altered chords. Wagner's chromaticism is founded in harmony, and there is the possibility that resolution of a chromatically altered chord could be effected in several ways. In other words, Wagner's harmony is tonal, but his use of altered chords and his unorthodox resolution of chromaticism pushed key tonality to the brink of dissolution. In chordal ambiguity lies the power of Wagnerian harmony in *Tristan und Isolde.*

In *Tristan und Isolde* Wagner does not realize the full potential of Leitmotifs as essential building blocks; that remained for *Der Ring des Nibelungen.* The music of *Tristan und Isolde* is continuous throughout each act, though scenes are distinguishable. The orchestration becomes very dense. In Isolde's final aria, *Liebestod,* the text is embedded in the symphonic sound, and the voice becomes another tone color in the orchestral fabric.

Wagner began the libretto for *Die Meistersinger von Nürnberg* at Dresden in 1845; he composed the music in 1861–62. The story concerns a sixteenth-century Meistersinger guild's public singing contest in which Walther and Beckmesser are the chief competitors for

EXAMPLE 23.1 The Prelude to *Tristan und Isolde* opens (mm. 1–6) with the Love-potion Leitmotif culminating in the Tristan chord.

the prize. Wagner's music is appropriate to the plot and its historical era. There are numbers and scenes in *Die Meistersinger,* and each act concludes with a massed finale, as in grand opera. The music is diatonic with conventional harmonies. Much use is made of aab structure, the bar form commonly used by the medieval Meistersinger.

Wagner modeled the character Hans Sachs after Meistersinger Hans Sachs (1494–1576), a master shoemaker who was a vital force in the activities of the guild at Nuremberg. Wisely, Wagner used some authentic Meistersinger music (e.g., the guild march) and set Sachs's song *Wach' auf, es nahet gen dem Tag* (Awaken, the day approaches) in an approximation of Meistersinger style. In recognition of the historical Sachs's activity during the Lutheran Reformation, Wagner opened the opera with a chorale. Moreover, he has the character Sachs comment on the fact that Walther's song "sounded so old and yet was so new." Thus, Wagner linked historical past with controversial present; Sachs's comment could be applied to the music of *Die Meistersinger.* Part of that old sound is due to the fact that Wagner suppressed chromaticism; when it is present, it is not often obvious. Some of the music is sentimental—many Meistersinger songs were. There is motivic linking between themes, and there are some recurring motives (e.g., the motive used at the very end of the opera is the one with which the crowd mocked Beckmesser earlier). The opera conveys the idea of conflict between the old and the new in the art of music, a conflict that was present in Wagner's life at the time. The rules of the guild are presented as antiquated, designed to preserve the old music; the expressive new music is regarded as unacceptable. The character Hans Sachs is a proponent of the new art, as is the Knight Walther von Stolzing. Sixtus Beckmesser, severe critic and town clerk who keeps the score, is against innovation; supposedly, he represents the critic Eduard Hanslick, who was outspoken in criticism of Wagner. In the

music of *Die Meistersinger* Wagner presented the conflict between the old and the new, the historical past and the then present, and combined the musical techniques of the past with those of his own time.

Der Ring des Nibelungen is Wagner's masterpiece. *Das Rheingold,* the first music drama in the series, explains the origin of the magic ring and the need for a hero. The music dramas forming the trilogy about Siegfried were intended to be performed in succession on the next three days (or evenings). *Der Ring des Nibelungen* relates mythological events in the lives of Germanic gods and goddesses, humans, dwarfs, giants, and other beings, most of whom are greedy for gold and for the power wielded by a gold ring crafted from the stolen Rhinegold. Alberich, the dwarf who had the ring made, imbued it with a curse of death when he relinquished it. Everyone who wears the ring perishes, even the gods. Ultimately, the ring is restored to the Rhinemaidens, rightful guardians of the gold.

Behind the obvious story lies a symbolic one representing the creation and the end of the world and, in a much smaller way, symbolizing the beginning, the living, and the end of a single human life. The greed for the ring fashioned from the Rhinegold and the struggles to attain it are symbolic of the human desire for money, worldly success, and power and may be related to the biblical statement that "the love of money is the root of all evil." Siegfried's destiny is death; redemption is secured through Brünnhilde's sacrifice of herself in Siegfried's funeral flames.

Der Ring des Nibelungen is a unified symphonic network of sound created from Leitmotifs that Wagner used in every imaginable way—at various times they succeed one another, overlap or interlock, and are rhythmically altered, transformed, transposed, and/or combined. In manipulating Leitmotifs Wagner used the contrapuntal techniques of Bach and the motivic development devices of Beethoven. There are Leitmotifs of association, presentiment, reminiscence,

EXAMPLE 23.2 This excerpt from Gottschalk's piano solo *The Last Hope* includes chords similar to the Tristan chord with similar resolution.

and presence. They represent characters, places, things, thoughts, premonitions, and have other associations. The Leitmotifs are essential structural factors, the building stones of the musical edifice. The path of the gold can be traced musically through its Leitmotif: from the Rhinemaidens to Alberich and Mime's forge, to Wotan, to the giant Fasolt and his brother (who becomes the dragon Fafner), to Siegfried, and back to the Rhinemaidens.

The vocal lines add their special timbres to the symphonic network to form the total musical picture. For Wagner, there was never a question of priority between text and music, voice and orchestra; they were of equal importance, and he treated them as such. Very often, the vocal line doubles an instrumental line (or vice versa). Leitmotifs may appear in the orchestra and not in the vocal line. Wagner used a very large orchestra in order to have available the instrumentation capable of producing the special timbres and effects that he needed in the music dramas.

Leitmotifs do not of themselves unify the music dramas or make Wagner's music great. Formal structure and keys are unifying factors also. Frequently, sections of acts are organized in AAB or ABA form. In *Siegfried* there are ABA, AABA, and rondo forms. Each of the characters and important objects has an assigned key, and the relationships between characters, and between characters and objects, are reflected in the keys assigned to them. For example, when prophesied, Siegfried is in C minor, as hero he has B♭ major, and at death returns to C minor; Brünnhilde has E♭ major; the Rhinegold first appears in G major. Very few of the female characters are assigned major keys. The overall key of *Der Ring* is D♭ major, the key of the chief god, Wotan.

Gluck and others had advocated the use of continuous music from the time the first note of the overture sounded until the curtain was pulled on the last scene. Wagner advocated not merely continuous or endless melody but what he termed **infinite melody**—continuous expressive melody. To Wagner it was not the endless melody itself that was important but the expressive quality of that music at all times. He achieved this in *Der Ring*.

Parsifal (1882), Wagner's last theatrical work, presents a legend of the Holy Grail, with a theme of redemption through self-denial and sacrifice. Much of the presentation is by way of tableaux, with narration sung by the characters. Parsifal's reactions are as important as his actions—sometimes more so. *Parsifal* is constructed symmetrically, in *Bogen* (arch) form, with Acts I and III considered A and Act II, B. Choruses are important, and Wagner's choral writing is excellent. His use of separated choirs creates an effect resembling that of the *cori spezzati* of Gabrieli. For the Grail Leitmotif Wagner borrowed an old *Amen* formula that was sung at Dresden Hofkapelle when he conducted there; the Prelude's first theme (the Last Supper Leitmotif), resembles Gregorian chant.

There are great contrasts in the music of *Parsifal*. The music of Amfortas, befitting the agony he endures, is sometimes very dissonant and chromatic to the brink of atonality. The sorcery and intrigues of Klingsor and Kundry vary from extreme chromaticism to lush Romanticism. The music of the Grail is diatonic and at times churchlike. Within those different areas, Wagner makes even finer distinctions, for example, that made in the diatonic music to differentiate the guilelessness of Parsifal, the purity of the Grail, and the elevation of Parsifal to a position of leadership and guardianship of the Grail.

Wagner's genius as a composer of theatrical music is unparalleled. He used every historical and traditional musical technique that would serve his purposes and shaped them and merged them expressively to create music so new that it was considered radical. Wagner's music had a marked effect on later musical developments. His use of orchestral color, treatment of motives, the minimizing of divisions and subdivisions to the point where they were inaudible, and the symphonic character of his music dramas affected the work of symphonists as well as composers of operas. His treatment of key tonality and chromaticism, producing at times a measure of polytonality and verging on atonality, provided incentive for later composers to move into dodecaphony and pantonality/atonality.

GIUSEPPE VERDI

Verdi (1813–1901) was born in the village of Le Roncole, near Busseto, in Parma. When he was barely a toddler, he showed an interest in music, and his father arranged for him to have lessons from the local church organist. Verdi attended school in Busseto, where he received an excellent general education and had composition lessons from the municipal music director. Verdi expected to enter Milan Conservatory but was denied admission because he failed to meet keyboard performance requirements. Disappointed, he arranged for private lessons with a composer who had written operas for La Scala.

In 1836 Verdi returned to Busseto as municipal music master. Most of the music he wrote then is lost. His first published compositions—songs—appeared in 1838. That year he worked on his opera *Oberto*. Its performance at La Scala in 1839 brought him a commission for three operas. The first, the comedy *Un giorno di regno* (King for a day; 1840), was a failure. That may have turned Verdi against comedy; all his other operas except the last one are serious. However, after 1850 he occasionally included comic roles in his serious operas. Verdi's third opera, *Nabucco* (Nebuchadnezzar; 1842), was an outstanding success. The role of Abigaille was created by soprano Giuseppina Strepponi (1815–97), who, before she met Verdi, had been influential in

getting his first opera produced. *I lombardi alla prima crociata* (The Lombards on the first crusade; 1843) was another success.

Between 1842 and 1849 Verdi wrote 11 operas, all dealing with heroism. Those works constitute the first of four distinctive groupings of Verdi's operas: (1) works concerned with heroism, (2) works relating to personal life (predicaments of ordinary people in everyday life, divorce, unmarried persons living together), (3) works showing French influence, and (4) masterpieces based on Shakespeare's works.

Verdi's association with Francesco Piave (1810–76), librettist for 10 of his 28 operas, began with *Ernani* (1844) and continued intermittently until 1862. Piave and Verdi were intensely patriotic. A visible thread of patriotism is woven into all the operas Verdi wrote before 1871. Italians who attended performances of his operas were keenly aware of this. As Verdi's operas became more and more popular, Italians used his name as a slogan for unification of Italy under rule of the king of Sardinia. The cry "Viva VERDI!" not only paid homage to a favorite native son but also expressed political

Giuseppe Verdi. Photograph, 1888.

Giuseppina Strepponi Verdi. Anonymous portrait in the Verdi home, Villa Sant'Agata, Busseto, Italy.

hope: "Viva *Vittorio Emanuele, Re D'Italia!*" Verdi was a member of the Italian Parliament from 1861 to 1865.

In the summer of 1847 Verdi went to London for the première of *I masnadieri* (The robbers). Soprano Jenny Lind, nicknamed "the Swedish nightingale," created the role of Amalie. From London Verdi went to Paris to supervise some rehearsals. While there he contacted Giuseppina Strepponi, who had retired from singing opera and was teaching singing. Their friendship deepened, and they lived together openly for years before marrying in 1859. Giuseppina constantly encouraged Verdi; when he spoke of retiring, it was she who coaxed him into composing another opera.

The second major period in Verdi's opera composition covers the operas *Luisa Miller* (1849), *Stiffelio* (1850), *Rigoletto* (1851), *Il trovatore* (The troubadour; 1853), and *La traviata* (The fallen woman, 1853). Most of these opera plots contain something very close to a situation in Verdi's own life.

A period of French influence in Verdi's opera composition began in 1853 when he composed his first grand opera, *Les vêpres siciliennes* (Sicilian vespers). Other important operas from this period are *Simon Boccanegra* (1857), *Un ballo in maschera* (A masked ball, 1859), *La forza del destino* (The force of destiny, 1862), *Don Carlos* (1867), and *Aïda* (1871).

Verdi's operas were performed internationally, and he was invited to write new works for major opera houses all over Europe. He rejected requests to compose a new opera for Cairo until he saw a synopsis of A. E. Mariette's scenario for *Aïda*. After investigating the quantity and quality of performing resources at Cairo, Verdi decided to compose *Aïda*. Antonio Ghislanzoni prepared the libretto. Within two years of its première (Cairo, 1871), *Aïda* became an established part of international opera repertoire.

In 1873, for his own pleasure, Verdi wrote a string quartet in E minor. That year novelist Alessandro Manzoni died. Verdi deeply mourned the loss of his friend and proposed that Milan honor Manzoni with a memorial on the first anniversary of his death. For that occasion Verdi composed his *Messa da Requiem*. Verdi was a professed atheist, yet this Mass seems to be a sincere expression of Catholic religious faith.

After writing the Requiem, Verdi lived in semiretirement. In 1880 he composed an *Ave Maria* and a *Pater noster*. For almost six years he wrote no operas. In 1879 Arrigo Boito (1842–1918) prepared an *Otello* libretto and suggested that Verdi set it. Verdi was interested, but it took Giuseppina's persuasion to convince him to write the opera. With *Otello,* Verdi brought Italian tragic opera to its peak.

Verdi was not permitted to rest on those laurels. Boito gave him another Shakespearean libretto, *Falstaff,* based on *The Merry Wives of Windsor* and *Henry IV.* Verdi could not resist. When completed in 1893, Verdi's *Falstaff* took its place beside *Otello* as one of the great masterpieces of all time; with *Falstaff* Italian operatic comedy was brought to its peak.

Verdi's last contribution to opera was a short ballet written for the Paris première of *Otello* in 1894. In 1889 he wrote another *Ave Maria;* he deemed it (rightly) inconsequential and did not want it performed. Between composition of *Otello* and *Falstaff,* he wrote *Laudi alla Vergine Maria* (Praises to the Virgin Mary) and in 1895–97 composed a *Stabat Mater* and a *Te Deum laudamus.* These three pieces are excellent. All four sacred compositions were published as *Quattro pezzi sacri* (Four sacred pieces; 1898).

Verdi's last contribution was not a musical composition. He financed the construction of Casa di Riposo per Musicisti, a home for aged retired musicians, in Milan. Verdi died on 27 January 1901 after having suffered a stroke a few days earlier.

His Music

A list of Verdi's works includes 28 operas, 3 major choral works (*Messa da Requiem, Pater noster,* and *Quattro pezzi sacri*), 3 instrumental compositions, and several vocal pieces. Since 1950, Verdi's operas have experienced a revival in the United States. Until the 1920s, only *Otello* and *Falstaff* received serious consideration.

Verdi consistently chose libretti based on literary works by major authors; he used works by Romantic writers but did not limit himself to that era. He chose authors from various countries, and poetry, prose, and drama all supplied material. When choosing a libretto, Verdi sought a subject that was bold, with emotional situations that could move at a fast pace. He worked closely with his librettists, but he was demanding and made his requirements clear to them. Verdi reserved for himself the final determination of affairs—he checked every word of the script carefully, often changing words, paring phrases, or carving away entire sections that did not suit him, and he demanded that certain things be said in a certain way. Word choice was extremely important to Verdi, as was the proper musical setting of those words. He insisted that opera must not be acting or mere presentation of drama-in-song but the representation of persons involved in and reacting to realistic situations and events; this lies at the core of his success.

Verdi took a vital interest in all aspects of the production of his operas. He made sketches in the libretto margins (fig. 23.1) and prepared production manuals wherein he indicated precisely scene by scene such things as the placement of properties and the position of singers at key points in a scene.

There is in Verdi's operas a strong but unobtrusive strand of Italian patriotism. Not only is patriotism present in his choice of subjects, but it is in some of the lines his characters sing—lines filled with double meaning, suited to the character roles in the operas but also conveying his own intense patriotism. For Italians, the double meaning of those patriotic lines was obvious.

A basic skeletal structural scheme is common to almost all of Verdi's operas. Most of them are constructed in four acts, in three acts with a prologue, or in three acts so organized that a fourfold division of structure is visible. In the first main division (prologue or first act), one of the principal characters other than the heroine sings a solo with chorus; in the second or third scene, the heroine is introduced in a solo (usually of narrative character) with chorus. In either the second or third act, there is a large duet; both middle acts conclude with ensemble finales, one of which might center on a stirring duet. At or near the beginning of the last act, there is a prayer scene for the heroine, and there is a death scene for the hero or a rondo finale for the heroine. This scheme is basic and was varied in many ways. The scheme was not peculiar to Verdi; many other composers followed it.

The principal male singing voices basic to Verdi's cast were a strong baritone, a lyric tenor, and a firm bass. The type of soprano varied according to the characteristics of the heroine; the nature of the supporting female role determined that voice type.

FIGURE 23.1 Page from a copy of the printed libretto of Verdi's *Aïda* with his autograph notations made in 1872 concerning the position of singers on stage and matters of interpretation. *(The Mary Flaggler Cary Collection in the Pierpont Morgan Library, New York)*

Verdi drafted a large-scale harmonic plan for his operas but modified that plan after he observed carefully the singers' optimum points. He used traditional tonal musical language, colored by the enriched harmonies of Romanticism. Frequently he used repeated figurations to arrive at the desired tonality, then reiterated a pitch until the key was firm. He might use a diminished-seventh chord to pivot into a new key or move by a series of melodic thirds over a $^6_4$ chord.

Characteristically, as Verdi planned his operas, he made notations as to possible instrumental combinations for accompaniments. Frequently, he wrote a number that was orchestrated with only a few instruments of light tone quality. He used bits of instrumental solo prominently—harp, violin, flute, or 'cello. His vocal duets are distinctive in that he gave the participants dissimilar rather than similar material. Often he wrote baritone-soprano, father-daughter duets. The aria types he used vary considerably; usually his music moves fluidly from dramatic or free declamation through arioso to aria.

In the works Verdi wrote in 1839–c. 1850, the influences of Rossini, Donizetti, and Saverio Mercadante (1795–1870) are the most significant. Mercadante, whose 60 operas never found a permanent place in standard repertoire because he was completely overshadowed by Verdi, provides a link in the development of Italian opera during those few years in the 1830s when Rossini was no longer composing operas and Bellini was deceased, when Donizetti was beginning to achieve fame, and when Verdi's star had not yet risen. Mercadante's writing was uneven, but in some operas his orchestration was imaginative, his ensemble writing remarkable. In Verdi's early works, the influence of Donizetti is seen especially in the unison writing for chorus and in the regular and smoothly flowing melodies. Rossini and Mercadante possibly influenced the rapid-paced ensembles. From the time of Mayr, Italian composers had placed the aria within a scene and had linked recitative and aria with arioso or choral interjections.

Verdi's use of recurrent themes is particularly apparent in *Rigoletto, Un ballo in maschera,* and *La forza del destino.* Themes recur within an opera, and sometimes there is thematic similarity or recurrence between operas.

Verdi considered *Rigoletto* a landmark in his writing. Based on Victor Hugo's *Le roi s'amuse* (The king is amused), the libretto had to be altered before it was suitable for performance in Italy. The jester Rigoletto is directly related to the dwarfs Isabella d'Este maintained for entertainment. In this opera Verdi included some satire, some comic touches. Two of the solos are popular favorites: Gilda's *Cara nome* (Dear name), a *romanza,* and the philandering Duke's *La donna e mobile* (Woman is fickle). Duets are an important feature of *Rigoletto,* and Verdi again wrote a father-daughter, baritone-soprano duet. The semideclamatory recitative used in *Rigoletto* appears in Verdi's later operas, especially *Otello.*

Aïda is a number opera but has remarkable continuity. It contains much dramatic declamatory recitative, and spectacular divertissements make it a monumental grand opera. Radames's *romanza, Celeste Aïda* (Heavenly Aïda), is impressive.

In *Otello,* to achieve unity of time and place Boito omitted Act I of Shakespeare's play; thus, all the action could take place in Cyprus. The three main characters are introduced in the first act, but none of them has a solo aria. It is apparent at the outset that the leading characters are important because of their roles in the drama and not because they are singers. Every part of a scene contributes to propelling the drama (e.g., the *brindisi* [drinking scene] is a dramatic ensemble). Verdi accorded supremacy to voice, but he used instruments and orchestral techniques to enhance the text and the characterization. Iago's sinister personality is portrayed not only through his words and his actions but also through well-placed chromaticism and ornaments: acciaccaturas, appoggiaturas, and a long trill followed by the drop of a fifth (DWMA161). In *Otello* Verdi produced a kind of "music drama" with continuous music and some associative figures (*not* Leitmotifs) used to characterize persons, but his music drama was still within the bounds of traditional Italian opera and was quite different from those of Wagner.

Falstaff seems shorter than it actually is because it moves along so rapidly. It is a witty comedy filled with puns and musical subtleties that play on those puns—humor that can be appreciated most by persons who really know the Italian language. The humor is not only in the words and action; it is in the orchestration as well (e.g., 'celli and piccolo playing four octaves apart in *Se Falstaff s'assottiglia*). In *Falstaff* Verdi skillfully combined recitative with aria, letting the music flow from one to the other, so there is no sense of recitative or aria *per se.* The opera abounds in melodic phrases and exhibits a kind of writing that Giuseppina described as "a new combination of poetry and music." In the last act there is a song within a song, and much of the Windsor Forest scene is reminiscent of *A Midsummer Night's Dream.* The opera ends exuberantly with an ensemble finale—a fugue begun by Falstaff, *Tutto nel mondo è burla* (Everything in the world is a joke).

Verdi must be considered a Classic-Romanticist. Romantic traits infiltrated his writing, but they were used to further the drama—the human actions and reactions—and were not exploited. He followed the traditional lines of Italian opera established by Monteverdi and developed through the work of Steffani, Alessandro Scarlatti, Hasse, Mozart, Rossini, and Donizetti. Their work culminated in Verdi's masterpieces, *Otello* and *Falstaff.* In his insistence on realistic details and staging, and in his regard for the presentation of events as human experiences with human reactions, Verdi paved the way for the *verismo* operas of Puccini.

FRANZ LISZT

The life of Franz Liszt (1811–86) was filled with opposites, as was the Romantic era in which he lived. He had the kind of personality that accepted and carried out responsibilities yet wanted freedom, that sought a priestly life yet wanted all the world had to offer. He was restless and versatile, with a multifaceted career as virtuoso pianist, composer, author, and teacher.

Liszt's first piano teacher was his father, an Esterházy court official who also played 'cello in the court orchestra. In 1821 the Liszt family moved to Vienna, where Franz studied piano with Czerny and had composition lessons from Salieri. At the age of 11, Liszt played in his first concert, in Vienna. In 1823 he began to concertize throughout Europe. Customarily, several performers shared a concert program, assisting one another or being assisted by an orchestra. By 1827 Liszt had wearied of performing and wanted to become a priest. However, the death of his father (1827) and his own precarious health deterred him from religious studies. For a while, he taught piano in Paris. In 1827–30 he composed little music—for a young virtuoso pianist this is not surprising.

In 1831 Liszt heard Paganini for the first time. His technical prowess so astounded Liszt that he determined to achieve comparable technical facility on the piano. Using the *La campanella* (The little bell) melody from Paganini's B-minor Violin Concerto, Liszt composed *Grand fantasia de bravoure* (pub. as Op. 2; 1834).

Liszt met Berlioz and Chopin in 1833. His observations of Chopin's playing brought more Romanticism into his own playing. He made transcriptions of some of Berlioz's works, including *Symphonie fantastique*. Throughout his life, Liszt made transcriptions and arrangements of other composers' works—more than 400 of them survive. He captured the orchestration fairly accurately—for some large orchestral works, such as those of Berlioz, that was not easy. Schumann commended Liszt on his piano transcriptions of symphonies.

Franz Liszt. *(Courtesy of the Free Library of Philadelphia)*

In 1834 Liszt met Countess Marie d'Agoult. Soon they began an affair. Around that time Liszt began to write articles on music for various European journals; he discussed his material with Marie, who gave him valuable assistance. In 1835 she left her husband and lived with Liszt for about nine years. They had three children: Blandine (1835–62), Cosima (1837–1930), and Daniel (1839–59). When the countess and Liszt separated in 1844, he took their children to Paris to be educated.

Liszt was at the height of his concert career in 1838. He is credited with being the first to perform a complete *solo* recital; he did so in London in 1840. That year, Liszt had his first experience conducting. In 1842 he was appointed Grand Ducal Director of Music Extraordinary at Weimar.

There were mistresses in Liszt's life after the countess, but he did not form another lasting liaison until he met Princess Carolyne Sayn-Wittgenstein in 1847. Though she requested a divorce so that she and Liszt might marry, she could not obtain the pope's consent. The princess's husband died in 1864, but by then Carolyne and Liszt no longer thought of marriage. Carolyne persuaded Liszt to give up his performance career and concentrate on composition. Once that decision was made, he accepted the conducting post at Weimar as a permanent position. Between 1847 and 1858 he wrote most of the compositions that established his reputation as a major composer and for which he is now known. At Weimar Liszt conducted major works by contemporary composers as well as those of past generations. Because of his willingness to perform works of promising composers, he attracted many of the avant-garde. That created some difficult situations in connection with his court position. For example, he championed Wagner's music when Wagner was a political refugee in Switzerland.

Besides composing and conducting, Liszt taught. One of his pupils was Hans von Bülow, a fine pianist and an excellent conductor. Liszt's daughter Cosima married von Bülow but later left him for Wagner (see p. 498). That affair caused a serious (but not permanent) rupture in Liszt's friendship with Wagner. Though Liszt was party to affairs in his own life, he did not condone his daughter's.

In December 1858 Liszt resigned his position at Weimar. In 1859 his son died, and Liszt expressed his grief in the funeral ode *Les morts* (The dead).

Late in 1861, Liszt moved to Rome to begin religious studies. He still composed but concentrated on religious music. In 1855 he had written a setting of Psalm 13 (How long wilt Thou forget me, O Lord?; tenor soloist, chor., orch.) and a *Missa solemnis* for the consecration of the basilica at Gran in 1856. He revised his settings of Psalms 23 and 137 and made settings of Psalms 116 and 129. He composed a *Missa choralis* (1865) based on Gregorian chants, completed the oratorio *Die Legende von der heiligen Elisabeth* (1857–62), composed *Christus* (1862–67), and wrote *Via Crucis* (Stations of the Cross; 1879). When his daughter Blandine died, he composed, as memorial to her, variations on the passacaglia theme from Bach's Cantata No. 12.

In 1863 Liszt entered Oratorio della Madonna del Rosario and in 1865 took minor orders in the Catholic Church, but he never became a priest. He continued to compose sacred music, including a Mass for the coronation of Emperor Franz Josef of Austria (r. 1848–1916) as King of Hungary (1867).

Teaching still interested Liszt. Annually he conducted master classes in Weimar. From time to time, noted composers visited him in Rome and sought his advice. Occasionally, he performed in charity concerts. His last public performance was in Luxembourg in 1885. In July 1886 he attended performances of several operas at Bayreuth, where Cosima maintained some control in the management of Wagner's interests.

While in Bayreuth, Liszt became ill, pneumonia developed, and he died on 31 July 1886.

STYLE

In addition to Czerny, who, as teacher, transmitted to Liszt Beethoven's playing style, the most significant influences on Liszt's piano playing and compositional styles were Hungarian gypsy music, Field, Chopin, and Paganini. In his playing, Liszt strove to make the piano transcend its limitations. He could caress the keys and draw forth intimate, delicate tones or elicit from the instrument full, almost orchestral, sonorities. Emulating Paganini's violin virtuosity and showmanship, Liszt became the "Paganini of the piano." He played with brilliance and clarity, and his technique, shaped by Czerny, was flawless. He was as skilled on organ as he was on piano.

Much of Liszt's music is monothematic, with the material for a work being derived from thematic transformation of an initial theme or a germinal motive. He treated traditional formal patterns freely, particularly large forms. His harmonies are Romantic, and that Romanticism gradually increased as he used more tritones, diminished and augmented chords, and chromaticism. After c. 1860, whole-tone scales appear more frequently in his works. Sometimes his harmonies clash to the extent that it seems he completely dispensed with the traditional rules governing harmony in key tonality—perhaps in some instances he did.

KEYBOARD MUSIC

The type of piano music Liszt composed was directly related to his principal interests during a particular period in his life. His most virtuosic works were composed when he was concertizing actively. In pieces created for his own use, he exploited all the piano's resources, sometimes notating the piano music on three staves, as he did in *Mazeppa* (ex. 23.3), the fourth of his 12 *Études d'exécution transcendante* (Transcendental études). He composed and published simple versions of those études in 1827, then expanded them, increasing the degree of difficulty to make them "transcendental."

Liszt composed 11 collections of character pieces. Of these the most significant are the volumes entitled *Années de Pélerinage* (Years of pilgrimage); they contain some of his finest piano solos. *Première année: Suisse* (First year: Switzerland; 1848–54, pub. 1855) holds nine short character pieces; one of the finest pieces in this set is *Au Bord d'une Source* (At the edge of a spring). Each piece in *Seconde année: Italie* (Second year: Italy; 1837–49, pub. 1858) was inspired by an Italian poem or work of art. Included in that volume are piano arrangements of three settings of Petrarch sonnets Liszt had written earlier. The largest piece in the volume is *Après une lecture de Dante, Fantasia quasi sonata* (After reading Dante, fantasia like a sonata), a multisection, cyclic work that contains some very difficult passages. *Troisième année* (Third year; 1867–77, pub. 1883) was inspired in Italy. The pieces related to Villa d'Este are the finest in this compilation. *Les jeux d'eaux à la Villa d'Este* (The fountains at Villa d'Este; DWMA162) is an important precursor of Ravel's (1875–1937) *Jeux d'eau* (Fountains; 1901) and of Impressionism (see p. 565).

Among Liszt's excellent individual character pieces for piano are three comparatively little-known works: *Nuages gris* (Grey clouds; 1881; pub. 1927; DWMA163), *La lugubre gondola* (The ominous gondola; 1882, pub. 1916), and *Schlaflos! Frage und Antwort* (Sleepless! Question and answer; 1883), a nocturne. These pieces are significant because of their experimental harmonies and unexpected chromatic modulations.

Few piano sonatas were written during the middle and late nineteenth century. Liszt wrote only one, Sonata in B minor (1852–53). It is divided into three sections—Lento assai–Allegro energico, Andante sostenuto, and Allegro energico—but is actually one continuous movement. Three themes, stated in the first section, undergo thematic transformation throughout the work. Structurally, the sonata resembles a symphonic poem (see p. 510).

Liszt wrote a number of piano pieces in dance forms. He composed a great deal of Hungarian music, resembling gypsy rather than authentic folk or nationalistic music. There are 20 *Hungarian Rhapsodies*, of which the 2nd, 11th, and 12th are pianists' favorites. Liszt's favorite was the 13th; it is one of the finest, but is seldom performed. The 15th is a version of his *Rákóczy March*.

Of Liszt's 11 works for organ, the most significant are *Fantasie und Fuge über den Choral "Ad nos, ad*

EXAMPLE 23.3 Liszt: *Mazeppa*, mm. 7–12.

salutarem undam" (Fantasia and Fugue on the Chorale *Ad nos, ad salutarem undam;* 1850) and the *Präludium und Fuge über den Namen BACH* (Prelude and Fugue on the name Bach; 1855, rev. 1870).

The hundreds of piano arrangements and transcriptions that Liszt made of symphonies, operatic selections, and other large works are an important contribution to the literature. By performing and publishing such works, Liszt made those compositions available to many persons who were unable to attend live performances of the original works.

Liszt's music for piano and orchestra consists of three concerti (No. 1, E♭ major, 1849; No. 2, A major, 1839; No. 3, E♭ major; c. 1839); three Fantasias, one of them an expansion of the 14th *Hungarian Rhapsody* for solo piano; and *Totendanz* (Dance of death; 1849). Concertos Nos. 1 and 2 were revised several times. Concerto No. 1 has four movements, thematically linked and designed to be played without a break. Thematic transformation is present. Liszt knew Schubert's *Wandererfantasie* and obviously was influenced by it. Concerto No. 2 is a single-movement multisectional work, bearing more resemblance to a rhapsody than to a traditional concerto. Concerto No. 3, located in manuscript c. 1989, is a single-movement multisectional work exhibiting thematic transformation and other techniques that Liszt used in symphonic poems years later. *Totentanz*, a *danse macabre*, is a set of variations on *Dies irae*.

ORCHESTRAL AND CHAMBER MUSIC

Liszt did not write purely orchestral works until he became court conductor at Weimar. While he held that post (1848–61), he composed 2 symphonies and 12 single-movement programmatic works that he called **symphonic poems.** His other orchestral works include *Two episodes from Lenau's Faust* (c. 1861), one being the *First Mephisto Waltz; Trois odes funèbres* (Three funeral odes; 1860–66); *Second Mephisto Waltz* (1880–81); the short occasional piece *Von der Wiege bis zum Grabe* (From the cradle to the grave; 1881–82); and five marches, one of them the *Rákóczy March* (1865).

For each symphonic poem Liszt provided a synopsis so that the listener would know what the music was supposed to express. The poems were not meant or be pictorial or to tell a story, though at times they depict scenes realistically. Rather, Liszt sought to express his views relative to the extramusical material and considered the musical content more important than referential depiction. This coincides with Beethoven's view of his Sixth Symphony. Though the symphonic poem was a product of nineteenth-century Romanticism, it had roots in such works as Beethoven's *Overture to Egmont.* Several of Liszt's poems originated as introductions or overtures to other works or are expanded versions of earlier compositions. *Mazeppa* is an expanded version of the *Transcendental Étude.* All the symphonic poems exist also as arrangements for piano duet or for two pianos.

Hamlet (1858), planned as an overture to Shakespeare's play, is the shortest of Liszt's symphonic poems and one of his finest. Here, Liszt painted a psychological portrait of Prince Hamlet.

The best known of Liszt's symphonic poems is *Les préludes.* It was originally written (1848) as introduction to *Les quatres élémens* (The four elements; unpub.), a collaborative choral setting of four poems by Joseph Autran. When Liszt decided to use the introduction as a separate piece, he looked for a new literary program for it and selected these lines from Alphonse Lamartine's (1790–1869) *Nouvelles méditations poétiques* (New poetic meditations): "What is life? Only a series of preludes to that unknown song whose first solemn note is sounded by death." Liszt mentioned also Lamartine's poem *Les préludes;* its four large sections seem to conform to the sections of Liszt's music. The principle of thematic transformation is a feature of *Les préludes.* From one germinal motive Liszt derived many others (ex. 23.4).

In *Eine Faust-Symphonie in drei Charakterbildern* (A Faust symphony in three character pictures; 1854–57) Liszt portrayed the three main characters in Goethe's *Faust.* The symphony was conceived in three movements: *Faust, Gretchen,* and *Mephistopheles,* but three years after they were completed Liszt added a choral *Epilogue,* for which organ, tenor soloist, and male chorus were needed. The slow introduction presents two of the symphony's main themes; thematic transformation is a feature of the Allegro impetuoso Faust movement that follows. The characterization of Gretchen is delicate, tender, and youthful in sound. The Mephistopheles movement has no new themes; instead, in keeping with Mephistopheles's character, Faust's themes are parodied, and a short phrase is bor-

EXAMPLE 23.4 (*a*) Germinal motive and (*b*) three of the themes it generated in Liszt's *Les préludes.*

rowed from *Malédiction,* an early work for piano and strings. The text of the choral epilogue is the *Chorus mysticus* from Goethe's *Faust.*

Liszt planned *Eine Symphonie zu Dantes Divina commedia* (A symphony on Dante's *Divine Comedy;* 1855–56) in three movements to correspond with the divisions of Dante's poem: *Inferno, Purgatorio,* and *Paradiso.* Wagner convinced him that it was impossible to portray Paradise musically, so he concluded the symphony with a Magnificat for women's voices.

Liszt wrote only a few pieces of chamber music. Most of them are for violin and piano, including a sonata based on Chopin's *Mazurka in C♯ minor.*

VOCAL MUSIC

Liszt wrote approximately 70 songs setting German, French, Italian, and Hungarian poems; one song has an English text. Among the Italian songs are three Petrarch sonnets, which exist in two versions. Liszt composed several secular cantatas and began but never finished an opera. Among Liszt's sacred choral works are numerous Psalms settings and liturgical works. There are two oratorios, *Christus* and *Die Legende von der heiligen Elisabeth.* The oratorios are too long—*Christus* contains some magnificent music but takes over four hours to perform. The Masses include the *Missa solemnis* performed at Gran, the *Hungarian Coronation Mass,* a *Missa choralis,* and a *Requiem Mass* (1868) that is filled with whole-tone themes and harmonies. An excellent composition from Liszt's late years is *Via Crucis* (soloists, choir, organ or piano).

CONTRIBUTIONS

Liszt contributed to the development of music through his piano playing, his piano arrangements and transcriptions of major works by other composers, and his original compositions. He encouraged and assisted others by programming and conducting their works. He is credited with originating the symphonic poem; his poems influenced others to create single-movement programmatic orchestral works. Among them were Bedřich Smetana (see p. 538); César Franck (1822–90) with *Psyché* (1888); and Camille Saint-Saëns (1835–1921) with *Le rouet d'Omphale* (Omphale's spinning-wheel, 1872) and *Danse macabre* (1874).

ANTON BRUCKNER

Schoolteaching, the monastery of St. Florian, and music were the main interests of Anton Bruckner (1824–96). He received his first music lessons at the age of 4 from his schoolmaster-organist father. He learned to play violin, spinet, and organ, and by the time he was 10 he could substitute for his father as church organist. At the age of 11, Bruckner received his first theory lessons from an organist-schoolmaster cousin—mainly, learning to realize figured bass at the organ. At that time, Bruckner first heard a Mozart Mass and Haydn's oratorios. After his father died (1837), Bruckner entered St. Florian monastery as a chorister. There, in addition to general education, he studied music and had organ and violin lessons. In 1839 his voice broke, but he served as violinist at St. Florian for another year, then took the one-year teacher-training course at Linz. Music lessons were part of that curriculum. In addition, he studied organ with cathedral organist August Dürrnberger (1800–80), author of a text on harmony and figured bass.

From 1841 to 1845 Bruckner worked as schoolmaster in small Austrian villages. He studied organ and theory and composed a few organ preludes, some small sacred choral pieces, and two Masses. In 1845–55 he was on the faculty at St. Florian, first as teacher and then as organist. All the while, he took theory and organ lessons, concentrating on Bach's works. Bruckner's first notable works were written as memorials to

Anton Bruckner. *(Kulturamt der Stadt Steyr)*

friends: a Requiem Mass in D minor (1848) for Franz Sailer and *Vor Arneths Grab* (At Arneth's grave; male chorus, 3 trombones; 1854) and *Libera me* (Deliver me; mixed choir, 3 trombones, organ; 1854) for Michael Arneth. For the installation of Arneth's successor at St. Florian in 1854, Bruckner composed a *Missa solemnis* (B♭ minor; soloists, choir, orch., org.). Bruckner considered himself a schoolmaster and obtained additional teacher's training diplomas: in high-school teaching and in organ playing and improvisation.

From 1855 to 1867 Bruckner was organist at Linz Cathedral. Immediately after moving to Linz, he arranged for private lessons in composition from Simon Sechter (1788–1867) of Vienna Conservatory. Sechter demanded that Bruckner compose no music other than that for his lessons. In 1861, when Sechter declared Bruckner's training completed, he obtained from Vienna Conservatory a diploma qualifying him to teach in music academies.

Bruckner was not yet satisfied with himself as composer—he never was—and studied with Otto Kitzler (1834–1915). Until he worked with Kitzler, Bruckner was a conservative craftsman, well versed in Classic, Baroque, and late Renaissance techniques. He could improvise a Baroque organ fugue and write a polyphonic motet or a Classic Mass, but Kitzler put him in touch with the musical styles of his own century. He introduced Bruckner to the styles of Beethoven, Mendelssohn, and other nineteenth-century composers; taught him orchestration and the principles of sonata form; and encouraged him to write orchestral music.

Not until he encountered Wagner's music did Bruckner's compositional style change appreciably. After studying the score of *Tannhäuser* and hearing some of Wagner's music, Bruckner was convinced that Wagner's style was to be emulated. However, Bruckner was not, nor did he consider himself to be, a revolutionary. He wrote a Symphony in F minor (unnumbered; 1863) and an overture that showed changes taking place in his style—more unconventional harmonies, greater vitality in the music. In 1863–64 he composed a Symphony in D minor that he later labeled *Die Nullte* (0). Bruckner's individual, mature style is first seen in the Mass in D minor, which he called Mass No. 1 (1864; SATB soloists, SATB choir, orch., organ); he had previously composed eight Masses, two of them Requiems. From that time on, Bruckner subjected his works to constant revision. Not only was he extremely critical of his work, but his self-esteem was low, an attitude fostered by the rejection of his symphonies by the Vienna Philharmonic and his friends' adverse comments.

Bruckner attended all performances of Wagner's operas given in Linz, went to the première of *Tristan und Isolde*, met Wagner, and became his friend. As the years passed, Bruckner allied himself with Wagner, met with him frequently, and attended the premières of *Der Ring* and *Parsifal*. Eventually, critics placed Bruckner in the "Wagner camp" and criticized his symphonies severely.

For more than a decade, Bruckner had spent long hours at his work. Eventually, he pushed himself to the limit of his endurance and in 1867 experienced a nervous breakdown. When he had regained his health, he was offered a professorship at Vienna Conservatory, as successor to Sechter, but not until 1868 could his friends persuade him to accept that appointment. Later, he was named imperial court organist.

Bruckner was a quiet person, deeply religious, intelligent, sincere, trusting, and sometimes naive. He was often filled with self-doubt and insecurity, though he was an excellent musician and a craftsman composer. His reputation as a superb organist spread rapidly as he participated in international organ competitions and performed recitals. On recital programs he played his own compositions and improvised a great deal. He never notated those organ works; according to published reviews, they were magnificent. Only a few insignificant preludes and a fugue for organ survive.

In 1870 Bruckner was appointed teacher of theory, organ, and piano at the college of St. Anna, in Vienna. He continued to compose liturgical music (see p. 513) but spent most of his creative time composing symphonies. He wrote No. 1 in 1865–66, Nos. 2 through 5 in 1871–76, and Nos. 6 through 8 in 1879–87; he worked on No. 9 from 1889 until the day of his death in 1896 and had not yet written the last movement. As a whole, the symphonies were not successful during his lifetime. The Vienna Philharmonic rejected them as "too daring" or "unperformable," and most conductors were unwilling to program them. When a symphony was performed, the audience's and critics' reactions were equally unfavorable. This, together with urging by friends and pupils, caused Bruckner to make some drastic, and not always wise, revisions. Symphony No. 7 was received favorably when performed by Leipzig's Gewandhaus Orchestra in 1884, and gradually other orchestras performed his symphonies, albeit in newly revised rather than original versions.

Bruckner died on 11 October 1896. His body was interred in the crypt beneath the organ at St. Florian Monastery.

His Music

The music Bruckner composed before he was 39 is, for the most part, conservative and Classic in style, modeled after Mozart and Haydn. He could write liturgical music in Palestrina-style Renaissance polyphony and improvise or notate counterpoint in the Baroque style of J. S. Bach. Throughout his life, when composing, Bruckner used figured bass. His style changed considerably after he heard Wagner's music, and his mature, individual style gradually became manifest. After he began to compose symphonies, he allowed himself to be persuaded by friends and pupils that his works were too long, his harmonies too radical, his instrumentation incorrect—interference that caused him to make drastic changes, often with unsatisfactory results. For this reason, the early published editions of Bruckner's works (some publications issued as late as 1904 and some editions made in the 1930s) are considered unreliable. Fortunately, Bruckner saved the original versions of many of his works and willed the sealed packet to the Vienna Court Library with instructions to forward the manuscripts to specified reliable firms for publication. In 1927 the International Bruckner Society was founded and began to prepare Bruckner's preferred versions of his symphonies for publication. The publications the Society issued after 1945 are considered the most authentic, for they are based on the manuscripts and sketches Bruckner preserved and on materials with corrections made in his handwriting.

VOCAL WORKS Bruckner wrote 19 accompanied secular choral pieces and 29 a cappella ones. Most of them are for male voices—most of the choral ensembles in Germany and Austria were exclusively male. Only 2 of the surviving accompanied works are cantatas. Many of the accompanied works use trombones and/or keyboard. Bruckner's last completed composition was the symphonic chorus *Helgoland* (G minor; 1893; male chor., orch.). *Abendzauber* (Evening magic; G♭ major; 1878) is a representative example of Bruckner's Romantic writing for male chorus. Austrian folk elements abound in works of this kind and also are tucked into scherzo movements in some of Bruckner's symphonies. Six solo songs by Bruckner are extant, three for alto, three for tenor, and all have piano accompaniment.

There survive approximately 40 small sacred works on liturgical texts. One of the earliest of Bruckner's mature works in this category is a seven-voice *Ave Maria* written in Palestrina-style counterpoint. Quite a few of Bruckner's motets are written in ecclesiastical modes rather than in key tonalities. Five of his motets are superb: (1) the Gradual *Locus iste* ([How awesome is] this place; C major; *a cappella* mixed choir; 1869), (2) the deeply moving Gradual *Os justi* (Lydian mode; 8-vc. *a cappella* mixed choir; 1879), (3) the Antiphon *Tota pulchra es* (All beautiful thou art; Aeolian; tenor solo, SATB choir, organ; 1878), (4) the Tract *Virga Jesse floruit* (The rod of Jesse blossomed; Lydian; *a cappella* mixed choir; 1885), and (5) the hymn *Vexilla regis* (Phrygian; *a cappella* mixed choir; 1892). In the Alleluia that concludes the motet *Virga Jesse floruit* (DWMA164), Bruckner requires the tenors to leap an octave and sing a passage in falsetto, while basses reiterate sustained E pitches.

Of Bruckner's five psalm settings, *Psalm cl* (1892) is the finest. There survive also *Te Deum laudamus* (C major; 1881–84) and a Magnificat (B♭ major; 1852).

Six complete Masses and a Requiem Mass (D minor; 1848–49) by Bruckner are extant; fragments and sketches of others survive. His first Mass (unnumbered; C major; 1842) is for alto soloist, two horns, and organ. The Mass in E minor (No. 2; 1866), written for the dedication of the new Linz Cathedral, was first performed in the open air; therefore, Bruckner chose wind band to accompany the eight-part choir. The Masses in D minor (No. 1; 1864) and F minor (No. 3; 1867–68) are often called symphonic Masses. Each is for SATB soloists, mixed choir, with full orchestra and organ accompaniment.

INSTRUMENTAL WORKS Bruckner's surviving instrumental works comprise 10 piano solos, 2 piano duets, a few preludes and a fugue for organ, 5 pieces of chamber music, several marches for band, an orchestral overture (G minor; 1862–63), and 11 symphonies and fragments of others.

Among his chamber music is a string quartet (C minor; 1862) that was located after World War II and was first performed in 1951; it is a student work of little consequence. The String Quintet (F major; 1879; 2 vlns., 2 vlas., vcl.) is excellent. It is in four movements, with Scherzo second and a lovely, rich Adagio third. Some of Bruckner's most beautiful instrumental music occurs in his Adagio movements.

Bruckner's symphonies are an important contribution to orchestral literature. The symphony that he numbered *Die Nullte* (0) has been performed several times by major orchestras since 1975. His other numbered symphonies are as follows: No. 1, C minor (1865–66); No. 2, C minor (1871–72); No. 3, D minor (1873–77); No. 4, the "Romantic" Symphony, E♭ major (1874); No. 5, B♭ major (1875–76); No. 6, A major (1879–81); No. 7, E major (1881–83); No. 8, C minor (1884–87); and the unfinished No. 9, D minor (1891–96). With Symphony No. 3, Bruckner's genius for symphonic writing became apparent. Most of his symphonies were written for the standard-sized orchestra of his time. He never used English horn, bass clarinet, or piccolo, and rarely used contrabassoon, but included Wagner tubas in his last three symphonies. Bruckner orchestrated in blocks of sound, with changes of instrumental color effected by using contrasting sections of the orchestra and sudden changes of dynamics.

The general characteristics of Bruckner's symphonic writing are as follows: (1) use of traditional four-movement complete sonata structure with sonata form (or an altered version thereof) as first and fourth movements; (2) with the exception of Symphony No. 5, no introduction *per se* to begin the symphony; instead, the first movement begins with string tremolo, a *nebula*, that seems to be drawn from the air and gradually increases in volume; (3) thematic material presented according to standard procedure in the exposition of sonata-form movements, with theme groups rather than single themes; (4) frequently, themes in the second group presented simultaneously rather than successively; (5) predilection for contrapuntal treatment of thematic material, with augmentation, diminution, and inversion; (6) combination of thematic material (e.g., simultaneous use of a theme and its inversion or a variant, or combining motives, phrases, and melodies); (7) usually, recapitulation does not return material in its original state but presents a transformation of that material; (8) very long codas that sum up all that has gone before and, in first movements, that usually conclude with a statement of the main theme (No. 8 is an exception) and, in finales, use the first theme of the first movement with the first theme of the finale; (9) lest the great length of the coda overbalance the other sections of the sonata-form movement, section lines are minimized by telescoping the end of the development with the beginning of recapitulation (e.g., No. 9); (10) frequent use of rhythmic figure combining a duplet with a triplet, e.g., $\frac{4}{4}$ ♩ ♩ ♩♩♩(3) or $\frac{4}{4}$ ♩♩♩(3) ♩ ♩ ; (11) in Adagio movements, use of two groups of themes, the second, which Bruckner called *Gesange-thema* (song theme), being more lyrical than the first; (12) strong thematic relationships between material in all movements, sometimes exact quotations of material previously used, sometimes variant or related material; and (13) a penchant for concluding a section with a rest that is a great window of sound (e.g., No. 7, Finale, m. 212), but Bruckner wrote smooth transitions, also.

Despite the fact that these characteristics are common to Bruckner's symphonies, no two of the symphonies are structured exactly alike in every respect. Bruckner used quotations from his other works in a symphony movement (e.g., the Adagio of Symphony No. 9 contains references to the D-minor Mass and to Symphonies Nos. 7 and 8). The Finale of Symphony No. 5 is a fusion of sonata form with double fugue.

Bruckner dedicated his Symphony No. 9 "To my dear Lord," prayed daily that he would live long enough to complete it, and referred to it as his "farewell to life." The work exhibits most of the characteristics of his symphonic writing. The first movement (*Feierlich, Misterioso*) begins with a blur of sound created by strings producing a D tremolo that is soon strengthened by winds. From this "nebula" there emerges a horn call, then a horn melody to which strings reply *marcato*. Their response is extended by sequential repetition. The combination of gradual crescendo and string tremolo gives an impression of increased tempo and intensity. The first theme is stated majestically by full orchestra in unison. Immediately after the cadence Bruckner placed the first of many strategic General

Pauses. He telescoped development and recapitulation. The last theme in the first group is not returned in the recapitulation but is reserved for the coda. Portions of the movement resemble pastoral scenes painted by Smetana or Dvořák.

The Scherzo/Trio second movement commences with one and two-thirds measures of rest. The D-minor tonality of the Scherzo is colored by a dissonant chord (e–g♯–b♭–c♯) stated and sustained at the outset by three clarinets and oboe and reiterated by violins and 'celli in pizzicato arpeggiation. The Trio (F♯ major) proceeds at a much faster tempo than the Scherzo—a reversal of Bruckner's usual practice. The Adagio third movement begins with music that is rich yet desolate, with a profundity concealing gloom, Wagnerian in its breadth of sound. A quietly beautiful coda, which refers to the symphony's first theme, to the Adagio of the Eighth Symphony, and to the opening of the Seventh Symphony brings the movement to a serene conclusion.

Bruckner was the first composer to really extend the scope of the symphony beyond what Beethoven expressed in his Ninth Symphony. Thus, he stood in direct opposition to many of his contemporaries, who believed that Beethoven had attained the ultimate in symphonic writing in Symphony No. 9.

JOHANNES BRAHMS

Brahms (1833–97) was the second of the three children in the family of J. J. Brahms, a string bass player in the Hamburg city orchestra. Both Johannes and his brother Fritz became musicians. At an early age, Johannes had piano lessons, and in 1843 he performed in a public recital. When it was suggested that he go on tour as a prodigy, his teacher intervened to prevent it. In 1846 Brahms began composition lessons with Eduard Marxsen (1896–87) and soon found a job arranging music for a small local orchestra. He gave his first solo piano concert in 1848.

During the revolutions of 1848, many Hungarian refugees came to Hamburg, and Brahms became interested in Hungarian gypsy music. He learned more about it when he accompanied violinist Eduard Reményi (1828–98) on a concert tour in 1853; Reményi taught Brahms how to play in Hungarian gypsy style and how to play *rubato* properly.

Another lifelong interest of Brahms was early music. In his childhood he began to visit libraries to copy and study music manuscripts, and as a youth he began to collect folk songs. Later, among his friends were some of the leading musicologists of his time, and he could intelligently discuss with them problems of performance practice and methods of editing early music (Insight, "Musicology").

In the 1850s Brahms formed a lifelong friendship with violinist Joseph Joachim. Joachim and Brahms devised counterpoint lessons for each other, exchanging assignments weekly. Joachim introduced Brahms to Liszt and to Robert and Clara Schumann. When the Schumanns heard Brahms play some of his own compositions, they recognized his genius, and Robert wrote the article *Neue Bahnen* (New Paths) praising Brahms's talents and predicting his success with large orchestral and choral works. Brahms became a staunch friend of all members of the Schumann family and was a

Johannes Brahms. *(Courtesy of the Free Library of Philadelphia)*

mainstay to them during Robert's illness. Brahms composed *Alt-Rhapsodie* as a wedding song for the Schumanns' daughter, Julie.

From 1859 to 1862 Brahms lived in Hamburg, where he founded and conducted a women's chorus and wrote music for that group. Also, he wrote some vocal solos with piano accompaniment. In 1856 he composed several fine organ works (see p. 518). In 1858 he completed the Piano Concerto, Op. 15 (D minor), and he performed it several times in 1859 and 1860. His Serenades No. 1 (D major, Op. 11; 1857–58) and No. 2 (A major; Op. 16; 1858–59) appeared in print in 1860.

Brahms moved to Vienna in 1862. He taught some piano lessons and concertized. For the 1863 season, he conducted the Vienna Singakademie; in 1872–75 he conducted concerts of the Vienna *Gesellschaft der Musikfreunde.*

The successful performance of *Ein deutsches Requiem* in 1869 established Brahms as a composer. In 1873 his *Variations on a Theme by Haydn* (Op. 56) appeared. Soon he had more than 60 published works and was financially secure. In 1876 Brahms and Joachim were offered honorary doctorates by Cambridge University: Brahms declined, but he sent with Joachim the Symphony No. 1 (C minor, Op. 68), which was performed on the occasion.

At the time of Schumann's final illness, Brahms developed deep romantic feelings for Clara that eventually settled into firm friendship and veneration for her. At various times in his life he evidenced strong interest in other women (e.g., Agathe von Siebold and Elisa-

beth von Herzogenberg), but he never married. He was pleased when Joachim married Amalie Weis (1839–98), famous mezzo-soprano, and was concerned when they experienced marital difficulties.

During 1877–78 Brahms concertized a great deal and wrote much music. His Symphony No. 2 (D major, Op. 73; 1877) and Violin Concerto (D major, Op. 77; 1878) were performed at concerts commemorating the fiftieth anniversary of the Hamburg Philharmonic Society. In 1879 he accepted an honorary doctorate from the University of Breslau and wrote for them the *Academic Festival Overture.* It contains a number of student songs, including *Gaudeamus igitur.* In 1880 he composed the *Tragic Overture.*

Brahms formed a number of friendships that were beneficial to his career. For example, in 1881 Hans von Bülow offered him the services of the Meiningen court orchestra as a rehearsal group. Other associations, such as that with 'cellist Robert Hausmann (1852–1909), inspired new works. In 1885 Hausmann's performance of Brahms's E-minor Sonata for 'Cello and Piano (Op. 38) inspired Brahms to compose the F-major Sonata for 'Cello/Piano (Op. 99). Brahms then composed two Violin/Piano Sonatas (Op. 100, A major; Op. 108, D minor); and the Piano Trio in C Minor (Op. 101), with the talents of Joachim, Hausmann, and himself in mind. The Concerto for Violin and Violoncello (A minor; 1887) was designed for Hausmann and Joachim. After hearing clarinetist Richard Mühlfeld (1856–1907) perform Weber's clarinet compositions, Brahms wrote the Trio in A minor (Op. 114) for clarinet, 'cello, and piano, the Clarinet Quintet in B minor (Op. 115), and two Clarinet/Piano Sonatas (F minor, and E♭ major, Op. 126).

In 1896 Brahms composed 11 chorale preludes for organ (pub. 1902); some of them are the finest written since those of J. S. Bach. At the time of Clara Schumann's final illness, Brahms composed *Vier ernste Gesänge* (Four serious songs, Op. 121; see p. 523). Though Brahms was not aware of it at the time, he was afflicted with cancer; he died on 3 April 1897.

STYLE

Though Brahms's music contains elements of Romanticism (e.g., rich harmonies and lyric melodies), basically he composed in Classic style. Probably, he should be considered a Romantic-Classicist. Yet, Brahms's handling of music's elements may be viewed as a harbinger of twentieth-century developments. For example, his combining modality and key tonality (as he did in Symphony No. 4) may be seen as an antecedent to the pantonality Schönberg sought and that he achieved by means of serialism. Indeed, Schönberg knew Brahms's music and was influenced by it.

Brahms was a craftsman, with solid musicianship, and disliked flamboyance, brilliance, and bravura as showmanship. Everything in his music contributes to the innate musical coherence of the entire composition. Brahms had high regard for Classic forms and materials and was deeply interested in music of the past. Not only did he study early music, he incorporated some of its theory and principles into his own works. His understanding of the value of counterpoint as a compositional technique is seen first in his desire to master it and then in his effective use of it. Several of his compositions reflect his appreciation and knowledge of Bach's works (e.g., the cantatas, chorale preludes, preludes and fugues, and those variations written as passacaglia/chaconne). Brahms was a master of rhythmic intricacies and rhythmic innovation. Frequently, he placed triplets against duplets, devised syncopations, or shifted metric accents. Sometimes he wrote phrases of irregular lengths, and frequently he wrote chains of thirds.

Brahms wrote no program music. He did write some character pieces for piano (e.g., ballades and intermezzi). His music is filled with rich, velvety sonorities, and he especially favored the lower registers, at times omitting violins from his orchestration.

Most of Brahms's music is for voice, but throughout his life he composed purely instrumental music. He was one of the finest pianists of his day. His personality is reflected in his works. Basically reserved, he was a deep thinker; though he sought the advice of friends, he relied on his own judgment when making decisions. He needed sincere, warm friendships and made long-lasting ones, but he also required times of solitude—his music reflects both aspects.

SOLO KEYBOARD MUSIC

Brahms's keyboard works were designed primarily to suit his talent and that of Clara Schumann. Many of them are rhythmically complex, abounding in polyrhythms, syncopations, and rhythmic transformations.

Counterpoint is present in abundance. Often, he used two melodic lines simultaneously, stating one simply and weaving the other into figuration; his Op. 116 *Intermezzi* provide examples. He began by writing piano sonatas, then moved to variations and character pieces. It took him several years to compose each piano concerto, and a space of 20 years separates the two. Because he preferred to play only his own compositions in concert, it seems that, when concertizing, he was more comfortable playing variations, character pieces, and stylized dances—or that his audiences responded more favorably to those kinds of pieces. Brahms was a master of variation technique, a practice closely associated with improvisation. In large works he often used thematic variation.

Most of Brahms's early works are for piano and include three piano sonatas (No. 1, C major, Op. 1; No. 2, F♯ minor, Op. 2; No. 3, F minor, Op. 5); a Scherzo in E♭ minor; four Ballades (Op. 10, D minor, D major, B minor, B major); Piano Concerto No. 1 (D minor, Op. 15; 1854–58); some gavottes; and several sets of variations, including *Variations and Fugue on a Theme by G. F. Handel* (B♭ major, Op. 24; 1861). The piano sonatas are filled with rhythmic vitality and exhibit passages in thirds, parallel sixths, imitation, and canon—all traits present in his mature style. The *Ballades* resemble rhapsodies; all are in some kind of ternary form (ABA, ABC).

The *Variations and Fugue on a Theme by G. F. Handel* is a masterpiece of variation technique. Handel's theme, used in the last section of his *Suite in B♭ major* for harpsichord, was equipped with five variations. Brahms wrote 25 and in them used all kinds of contrapuntal and harmonic devices. The composition climaxes with a masterly fugue.

During Brahms's first 12 to 15 years in Vienna, he wrote very little piano music. When he resumed composing piano solos, he wrote chiefly variations and character pieces. The *Variations on a Theme by Paganini* (Op. 35; 1862–63) are based on the twenty-fourth of Paganini's *Caprices for Unaccompanied Violin*. Brahms wrote 28 variations, divided them into two sets, and provided each set with a finale. When all the variations are performed, the finale at the end of the first set and the statement of the theme at the beginning of the second set should be omitted. Brahms subtitled the variations *Studien;* indeed, they are concert études. This composition is extremely difficult technically.

An element of Hungarian gypsy music infiltrates many of Brahms's works. He arranged some Hungarian Dances as piano solos and duets, made orchestral arrangements of three of those duets, and composed a few Hungarian dances. Because he had collected and studied folk songs, he was able to arrange or write Hungarian dances that preserve the melodies, harmonies, and rhythms characteristic of gypsy music but that present the gypsy music with a higher degree of artistry than it has in its original folk-music status.

In 1892–93 Brahms published four collections (Opp. 116, 117, 118, 119) containing a total of 20 character pieces, each in ternary form. The pieces are very concentrated. In the Intermezzi there is simplicity of form, some rhythmic and harmonic elaboration, counterpoint, and thematic variation. Occasionally, Brahms placed the melody in an inner voice (e.g., in Op. 119, No. 3). The last of the 4 pieces in Op. 119 is a magnificent *Rhapsody*.

For organ, Brahms wrote a Fugue in A♭ minor (1856; pub. 1864), the chorale prelude and fugue *O Traurigkeit, O Herzeleid* (O sorrow, O heartache; 1856; pub. 1882), 2 Preludes and Fugues (A minor, G minor; 1856–57, pub. 1927), and 11 *Chorale Preludes* (Op. 122; 1896, pub. 1902). It is believed that he wrote others, but they have not been located. The chorale prelude *O Welt ich muss dich lassen* (O world, I now must leave thee), which concludes the set, was Brahms's last composition. In general, the chorales are somber and convey an impression of preparation for impending death.

CHAMBER MUSIC

After composing the piano sonatas, Brahms reserved sonata form and complete sonata structure for his orchestral and chamber music works. Many of the chamber music pieces were composed for friends and are suited to their special talents. When writing for violin, Brahms frequently consulted Joachim. There are extant 24 chamber music works by Brahms. Those without piano include 2 string sextets (B♭ major, G major; 2 vlns., 2 vlas., 2 vcl.), 3 string quartets, 2 string quintets (F major, G major; 2 vlns., 2 vlas., vcl.), and the clarinet quintet, Op. 115 (B minor). The latter is a masterpiece comparable wjth Mozart's clarinet quintet. Brahms's quintet amply displays the complete range and the artistic capabilities of the clarinet without treating it virtuosically; throughout the composition

the clarinet remains on a par with the other participants in the ensemble.

It is believed that Brahms wrote at least 24 string quartets. Only 3 have survived: the C-minor and A-minor quartets, Op. 51 (c. 1873), and the B♭-major quartet, Op. 67 (1876). They are the finest composed in the nineteenth century after Beethoven's death. The Op. 51 quartets are in contrasting moods: the A-minor work is delicate and tender until one arrives at the finale, which contains a bit of *czardas*; the C-minor composition is more dramatic, rich, and with a hint of melancholy. The B♭-major quartet is the most light-hearted of all Brahms's chamber music works.

Brahms was dissatisfied with an early string quintet in F minor and rewrote it as a sonata for two pianos. Still not pleased, he remolded it as the Piano Quintet, Op. 34. The String Quintet in F major, Op. 88, has only three movements. The fugal exposition of the finale suggests the influence of Beethoven's Op. 59 No. 3 finale.

In 1853–54 Brahms wrote a Piano Trio in B major, Op. 8; more than 25 years later, he composed two more Piano Trios, Op. 87 in C major (1880–82) and Op. 101 in C minor (1886). The Clarinet Trio in A minor, Op. 114, is not outstanding. Brahms intended the Horn Trio, Op. 40 (E♭ major; 1865), for natural horn. Much of the charm of this Trio is due to its blend of timbres; the mellow tone quality of the horn colors the entire composition with a feeling for Nature.

Seven of Brahms's chamber music works are duos for piano and another instrument: three violin/piano sonatas (Op. 78, G major, 1878–79; Op. 100, A major, 1886; Op. 108, D minor, 1886–88), two 'cello/piano sonatas (Op. 38, E minor, 1862–65; Op. 99, F major, 1886), and two clarinet/piano sonatas (Op. 120, F minor, E♭ major; 1894). Of the violin/piano sonatas, the D-minor is finest. In formal structure, the sonatas differ considerably from Brahms's other chamber music works. Only three of the sonatas have four movements: Opp. 99, 108, and 120, No. 1. Each of the others has three. The clarinet/piano sonatas are masterpieces.

ORCHESTRAL WORKS

The list of Brahms's orchestral works is not lengthy. There are two serenades, two concert overtures, four symphonies, a set of variations, two piano concerti, a violin concerto, and a double concerto (violin, cello). In addition, there are three *Hungarian Dances* (arr. from piano duets): No. 1 in G minor, No. 3 in F major, and No. 10 in F major. Most of these works were composed within the space of 14 years.

After much deliberation, Brahms decided in 1854 to compose a symphony. However, the projected symphony became Piano Concerto No. 1 (1854–58). In Piano Concerto No. 2 (Op. 83, B♭ major; 1878–81), soloist and orchestra are treated as equal partners; however, in several places the soloist must be aggressive to avoid being relegated to the position of accompanist to the orchestra. The concerto has four movements—Brahms inserted a Scherzo as second movement. All movements have structural innovations (e.g., the first movement opens with an introduction in which soloist and orchestra engage in dialogue).

The Violin Concerto (D major, Op. 77; 1878) is one of the great concerti in standard repertoire. Here again Brahms wrote expressive, substantial music, not bravura display. He demands of the violinist exceptional technique but not virtuosity. The concerto follows the traditional three-movement scheme, commencing with an Allegro non troppo in sonata-concerto form. Brahms supplied the minor cadenzas for the concerto but left the major one for Joachim to improvise; the one Joachim created (and notated) is Brahmsian in style. The Adagio second movement (F major) is brief; the violin part consists almost entirely of arabesques. The D-major rondo Finale, an Allegro *giocoso,* has melodies suggestive of Hungarian origin.

The double concerto (Op. 102, A minor; 1887) is less gratifying for the soloists. When the work was being composed, Joachim and Hausmann urged Brahms to make their parts more difficult. This concerto was Brahms's last orchestral composition.

Serenade No. 1 was originally intended for eight solo instruments; later, Brahms arranged the six-movement work for full orchestra. Serenade No. 2 is a divertimento, with five short movements. Its orchestration contains no violins, trumpets, or drums and includes only two horns. Much of the music is in the instruments' low registers.

Variations on a Theme of Haydn (B♭ major, Op. 56a; 1873) was inspired when Brahms saw the manuscript of an unpublished Partita that it was believed Haydn had composed for the Esterházy troops. (Current research assigns the Partita to Haydn's pupil, Ignaz Pleyel; the chorale theme is anonymous.) Brahms used the second movement, a harmonization of the *Chorale St. Antonii,* as theme for the Variations. Brahms made only one change in instrumentation—because the serpent had become obsolete, he had to substitute contrabassoon (Insight, "Serpent"). In Brahms's orchestral work, eight winds state the theme, a rounded binary in B♭, with both halves repeated. In the variations, the chorale theme is present but not always apparent. The Finale is based on an ostinato that Brahms constructed from skeletal pitches of the first five bars of the theme. Though presented continuously in the bass, the ostinato sometimes appears imitatively in other voices. In conclusion, the chorale theme is stated in augmentation against rapid scales.

Unquestionably, Brahms was the greatest nineteenth-century symphonist after Beethoven. Brahms's four symphonies are absolute music, Classic in form, Romantic in expression and lyricism, and masterworks that deservedly are standard symphonic repertoire. The symphonies abound in characteristics of Brahms's mature musical style: rhythmic intricacies, shifting metric accents, triplets against duplets, melodies combined in contrary motion, harmonies that omit the fifth of the chord but with octave-doubling of the root, avoidance of obvious cadences by devices such as elision or overlapping phrases, "learned" counterpoint used nonpedantically, chains of thirds, and, at times, ambiguity of tonality (e.g., combining modality and key tonality). Like Beethoven, Brahms was adept at motivic development, often modulated to mediant or submediant keys, and frequently related movements and sections of a work by thirds. Each of Brahms's symphonies contains four movements: the first in sonata form, the second in slow tempo, the third a modified scherzo or having some characteristics thereof, and the finale (in all but the Fourth Symphony; see p. 521) sonata form or a modification of it.

One of Brahms's contributions to the development of the symphony is his modification of the formal structure of the third movement. More important is his rejection of referential or programmatic concepts and his confirmation and reestablishment of the validity of abstract musical materials as basic building blocks of the symphony. Stylistically, Brahms's use of motives as basic concepts from which to build a work

Serpent

The serpent is a large bass-register woodwind instrument equipped with a cup-shaped mouthpiece made of ivory, bone, or horn. Constructed from approximately seven feet of conical, wide-bore wooden tubing, the instrument was serpentine-shaped from necessity—to keep its fingerholes in a position easily accessible for playing. There are six open side holes, arranged in two groups of three, with the groups spaced about 12 inches apart. The mouthpiece is connected with the small end of the wooden tubing by a 12-inch metal crook that is curved almost at right angles. Like other instruments with cup-shaped mouthpieces, the serpent is capable of sounding partials of the harmonic series. A player could modify the pitches considerably. By lip adjustment, a player could lower a pitch a fourth. Because of the considerable latitude in pitch available by lip adjustment, compass of the instrument varied between two and one-half and three octaves. It is surmised that the fundamental pitch of the earliest serpents was E, but most

French instruments were built with D as fundamental, and in England the fundamental was C. The instrument is held vertically when played.

Invention of the serpent is attributed to Canon Edmé Guillaume of Auxerre, France, in 1590. At first, it was used solely for ecclesiastical purposes, primarily to double (at the unison) and support male voices singing liturgical chant. But by the middle of the eighteenth century, the serpent was being used in military bands. At some time in the seventeenth century, instrument makers gradually equipped the serpent with keys, and by 1800 three-keyed serpents were more or less standard. There were serpents in the wind band at the Esterházy estate when Haydn worked there.

Originally, a serpent was made in halves—carved from two large blocks of wood (usually walnut), shaped and hollowed out—and then fitted and glued together to make a tube that was covered with leather. Later, serpents were constructed by fitting together small segments whose

halves were glued together; these, too, were covered with leather, and both ends of the wooden conical tube were strengthened with brass mountings. The serpent fell into disuse during the nineteenth century. Most of the serpents in existence in the late twentieth century are in historical instrument collections.

---

is comparable with Wagner's use of Leitmotifs as building blocks in the creation of the symphonic web of his music dramas. Both composers transformed their motives. Both men were using similar contemporary procedures, but the manner in which they used them differed: Brahms believed and proved that the music itself was sufficient for the task; Wagner imbued the motives with associative features and used a greater number of motives to create a complex symphonic web.

Brahms composed his Symphony No. 1 (C minor, Op. 68; 1855–76) only after he had spent much time studying Beethoven's symphonies. The first movement of Brahms's symphony is intense and serious; it commences with a massive, slow introduction that

presents the basic motives from which the movement's themes are created (ex. 23.5). The development section is comparatively short. The subsections of the movement's Classic formal structure are not obviously delineated. The lyrical Andante sostenuto second movement (E major) is a ternary (ABA) with coda. The third movement, an Allegretto (A♭ major) with trio (B major), is treated as a kind of alternating form (fig. 23.2), although material is returned incomplete or altered. The abridged sonata-form finale commences with an Adagio introduction that presents the main themes. There is no development *per se*; the recapitulation returns the thematic material considerably varied.

Brahms's Symphony No. 2 (D major, Op. 73; 1877) is lighter, more idyllic in character, and uses fewer

EXAMPLE 23.5 The four basic motives of Brahms's Symphony No. 1, mvt. 1, all presented in the movement's introduction.

FIGURE 23.2 Diagram of formal structure of Brahms's Symphony No. 1, mvt. 3.

themes than his First. Movements 1, 2, and 4 are in sonata form. All movements use simple, lyrical melodies and motivic relationships. The Adagio is serenely beautiful. In the third movement, a short Allegretto in triple meter alternates with two trios in *presto* tempo, one in $\frac{2}{4}$ meter, the other in $\frac{3}{8}$; thus, it forms a rondo (ABACA) with temporal, metric, and thematic contrasts. In commencing this movement, Brahms again combined material in two contrasting tonalities—an E-minor melody with Aeolian modal tendencies is fitted with G-major harmonies. The Finale is thematically complex.

In Symphony No. 3 (F major, Op. 90; 1883) Brahms's personal motto F–A–F serves as germinal motif for thematic material in all four movements. A full F-major chord commences the majestic pronouncement of Brahms's motto, which is altered by a flatted A. The second theme, in A major, consists of several variations of a single $\frac{9}{4}$ measure. The Andante second movement (ABA form) features winds; when returned, the A material is treated freely and supplied with new figuration. The third movement is a lyrical song with trio. The Finale is dramatic, with violent changes of mood. In the development, themes undergo augmentation and transformation of all kinds; the rhythm of the transition theme sounded by brasses

is reminiscent of the motive of Beethoven's Fifth Symphony. In the coda, the emotion that has colored the symphony subsides; with restatement of the motto and the material that began the symphony, the music draws to a serene close.

Symphony No. 4 (E minor, Op. 98; 1884–85) is the most economical of Brahms's symphonies. In addition to exhibiting many of Brahms's compositional traits, it evidences his study of early music and his ability to apply its techniques competently. Moreover, it disturbs the long-held image of Brahms as being totally Romantic-Classic in outlook and reveals him as a progressive composer who combined old—even ancient—procedures with Classic and current ones and, in the process, produced results that were a harbinger of twentieth-century practices such as pantonality and serialism (see p. 595–96).

The basic tonal relationships in Symphony No. 4 are E and C keys and modes. This mingling is logical, for C serves as dominant in Phrygian mode and is submediant to E in key tonality; moreover, the C-major and Ionian modal scales are identical. Violins and woodwinds open the sonata-form first movement (Allegro non troppo; E minor; DWMA165) by stating the first segment of the principal theme quasi-canonically against arpeggiated accompaniment and a tonic pedal. When reduced to proximity, the widely spaced pitches of the violin melody form a descending chain of thirds. Woodwinds introduce the second theme with a subdued fanfare (m. 53) that becomes accompaniment (mm. 55–56). A new figure appearing early in the development (m. 157) is increasingly significant. The movement concludes with a sustained E-minor chord, thus preparing the ear for the Phrygian-mode horn call with which the Andante moderato second movement commences. The E modality changes to E-major tonality at measure 5, where that melody, placed a third higher, is harmonized. Phrygian mode returns in the coda, and the movement closes with a true Phrygian cadence that ends on an E-major chord. Movement 3 (Allegro giocoso; C major) is a scherzo-like developmental form with considerable thematic transformation. The Finale (E minor) is a chaconne whose theme and continuous variations are structured as sonata form with coda. Brahms's composition of this movement was influenced by the chaconnes in Bach's Cantata No. 150 (*Nach Dir, Herr, verlanget mich;* For

EXAMPLE 23.6 Chaconne theme, Symphony No. 4, mvt. 4.

you, Lord, I long) and D-minor Sonata for unaccompanied violin. Brahms transformed Bach's theme into an eight-measure phrase and inserted a chromatic A♯, thereby creating a leading tone to the dominant B of the theme (ex. 23.6). The chaconne theme is not confined to ground-bass status but permeates the entire orchestral fabric through Brahms's use of the principle of developing variation. This movement is unique in symphonic literature.

MUSIC FOR SOLO VOICE(S)

Brahms wrote approximately 300 songs for solo voice and piano, 20 duets, and numerous quartets. Throughout his life he composed Lieder. He had great interest in German folk songs, collected them, and made arrangements of them for solo voice and piano. Three large collections of his arrangements were (1) *Volks-Kinderlieder* (Children's Folk songs; 1858), 14 songs; (2) 28 *Deutsche Volkslieder* (German Folk songs; arr. 1858, pub. 1926); and (3) 49 *Deutsche Volkslieder* (German Folk songs; 1894). Brahms published 18 *Liebeslieder* waltzes (Love songs; Op. 52) and 15 *Neue Liebeslieder* waltzes (New love songs; Op. 65) for vocal quartet with optional four-hand piano accompaniment. For 9 of the Op. 52 *Liebeslieder* he furnished optional orchestral accompaniment. Also, he wrote a set of 11 *Ziegeunerlieder* (Gypsy songs, Op. 103; 1887) for vocal quartet and included 4 others in the Six Quartets, Op. 112 (pub. 1891).

The Lieder of Schubert and Schumann were Brahms's models. After Brahms had chosen a text, he wrote the melody and bass line; they determined the form and tonal plan of the Lied. In his sketches, he indicated the harmonies by figured bass. His formal options were the same as those open to Schubert: ballad, with elements of narrative recitative and arioso; strophic; modified strophic; and through-composed. He used all of them. Usually, for folk-song texts and melodies with folk-song flavor, he chose strophic settings; for other Lieder he seemed to favor modified strophic structure. A number of Brahms's songs are set-

tings of folk-song texts or of editions of such texts in published collections (e.g., *Des Knaben Wunderhorn*).

Brahms's earliest surviving Lied, *Heimkehr* (Returning home, Op. 7 No. 6; 1851), contains elements of accompanied recitative and arioso and thus resembles some of the early ballad settings. Other works representative of his early Lieder are in the Opp. 3, 6, and 7 compilations. Remarkable for its tone color is *An eine Äolsharfe* (An Aeolian harp, Op. 19 No. 5; 1858) in A♭ minor/major.

One of Brahms's humorous Lieder is *Vergebliches Ständchen* (Unsuccessful serenade, Op. 84 No. 4; 1881), a slightly modified strophic setting of a traditional folk poem. Brahms labeled alternate stanzas *Er* (He) and *Sie* (She) and included the Lied in a group of songs to be sung by one or two voices, but whether he intended it to be sung by two persons is debatable; it is challenging to a soloist to be asked to characterize two roles when the vocal line has few differences. Brahms's interest in folk song is apparent in many of his Lieder; for example, *Wiegenlied* (Cradle Song, Op. 49 No. 4; 1868), popularly known as "Brahms's Lullaby," was a folk poem that he set characteristically with pedal tones and open fifths. Woven into the accompaniment is the melody of an Upper-Austrian waltz song. Brahms enjoyed combining melodies and could do it unobtrusively in vocal music by tucking tunes into accompaniments, especially if the accompaniments involved figurations. Many times his use of that kind of polyphony—polyphony hidden in homophony—goes unnoticed.

Die Mainacht (May Night, Op. 43 No. 2) is one of Brahms's most beautiful and most serene songs. Another in the same Classic vein is *Sapphische Ode* (Sapphic Ode, Op. 94 No. 4). Equally lovely, but unusual, are the two songs of Op. 91, for alto, accompanied by viola and piano: *Gestillte Sehnsucht* (When I yearn no more) and *Geistliches Wiegenlied* (Sacred cradle song, or The Virgin's lullaby). *Geistliches Wiegenlied* is remarkable for its use of cantus firmus technique, its emotional profundity, and its unusual timbres.

Most of Brahms's songs are serious, and his late works are filled with contemplations on death. Outstanding examples are *Der Tod, das ist die kühle Nacht* (Death is like cool night, Op. 96 No. 1); *Auf dem Kirchhofe* (In the churchyard, Op. 105 No. 4), in which Brahms incorporated the Lutheran chorale *O*

Haupt voll Blut und Wunden; and *Immer leiser wird mein Schlummer* (literally, Ever lighter becomes my slumber; sometimes given the English title, Fretful is my slumber; Op. 105 No. 2).

Brahms's masterpiece of solo song is *Vier ernste Gesänge,* on texts he selected from the German Bible. The dark mood of the first two songs is pessimistic; the third song tells of the blessedness of death for the world-weary person; the concluding song (DWMA166), through the love text from I Corinthians 13, extols the great power of love and asserts that love conquers even death. The vocal line is declamatory and varies between recitative and arioso in character; the piano part often sounds orchestral.

CHORAL WORKS

Brahms composed many choral works, sacred and secular, accompanied and unaccompanied, for various kinds of ensembles, but he wrote no operas or stage works. He composed one large secular cantata, *Rinaldo* (Op. 50; 1863–68), on a text by Goethe.

His important accompanied choral works are (1) *Ein deutsches Requiem* (Op. 45; 1857–68); (2) *Alt-Rhapsodie* (Op. 53; 1869); (3) *Schicksalslied* (Song of Destiny, Op. 54; 1868–71), for SATB chorus and orchestra; (4) *Triumphlied* (Song of triumph, Op. 55; 1871), based on Revelation 19, for baritone solo, eight-part chorus, and orchestra; (5) *Nänie* (Op. 82; 1881), a lamentation, four-part chorus, and orchestra; and (6) *Gesang der Parzen* (Song of the Fates, Op. 89; 1882), six-part chorus and orchestra.

Alt-Rhapsodie (contralto, male chor., orch.) is one of the most beautiful choral works ever written. Three stanzas from Goethe's *Harzreise im Winter* (Winter journey to the Harz mountains) form the text. The first stanza is a recitative-like solo with orchestral accompaniment; the second is an aria in three sections. The chorus enters after the soloist has begun the third stanza, which contains a moving invocation to the "Loving Father." To maintain the dark, rich sonorities of the work, the soloist must have a wide range that does not become thin in the upper register. Amalie Weis Joachim, whose voice was acclaimed for its rich tone quality, sang the solo when the work was first performed.

Ein deutsches Requiem (S, Bar., SATB chor., orch.; org. optional) is Brahms's greatest achievement in choral music. It was first performed in its entirety (i.e., after the insertion of mvt. 5) in February 1869. Though not overtly Christian, its texts were drawn from the Lutheran German Bible and Apochrypha and include quotations from and references to Christ (e.g., Matt. 5:4; John 16:24; I Cor. 15:51–55; Rev. 4:11). This Requiem is not a prayer for eternal peace for the souls of the dead, as is the Catholic Requiem Mass, but seeks to console the living and help them reconcile death and life. The Requiem Mass, when the *Dies irae* is included (and it was standard until 1965), conveys the idea of Judgment after death; Brahms's Requiem conveys hope, confidence, and promise. A Requiem Mass is a religious service intended to be sung in church; Brahms's Requiem was intended for concert performance. German Requiems had been composed previously, but they were closely related in text and mood to the Latin Requiem Mass. *Ein deutsches Requiem* attests Brahms's ability to compose orchestral music, his mastery of counterpoint, and his study of early music, particularly the cantatas of Schütz and Bach.

Textually and tonally, Brahms's Requiem is symmetrical, in *bogen* (arch) form (fig. 23.3). Its text seeks to comfort the bereaved and sorrowing, offsets the inevitability of death with the promise of resurrection, counterbalances lamentation with deliverance, and centers on the beauty and joy of dwelling in the house of the Lord. Harmonically, the work proceeds from F major through its subdominant and submediant keys to center on E-flat (the key that Baroque composers related to the Trinity), then moves through secondary dominant and dominant keys to return to F and, before concluding, deviates through A to include, perhaps as signature, Brahms's personal motto, F–A–F. *Ein deutsches Requiem* is filled with counterpoint; fugues appear in movements 2 and 3, and a great double fugue concludes movement 6. Movements 1 and 7 conclude with the same music.

Brahms indicated that his Requiem was based on a chorale; the work's opening melody and that of the funeral march (mvt. 2) are thematically related to the chorale *Wer den lieben Gott lässt walten* (Whom only the loving God allows to rule) and to Bach's Cantatas BWV27 *Wer weiss, wie nahe mir mein Ende!* (Who knows how near [is] my end!) and BWV106 *Gottes Zeit ist der allerbeste Zeit* (God's time is the very best time; ex. 23.7). In the latter, a funeral cantata, Bach sought to reconcile people with the thought of death

FIGURE 23.3 Diagram of the symmetrical structural plan of *Ein deutsches Requiem*.

Movement	Key(s)	Text; Message	Medium
1	F	"Blessed are they that mourn . . . they shall be comforted" Solace	Chorus
2	B♭ min./maj.	"All flesh is as grass . . ." Funeral march Universal mortality	Chorus
3	D min./maj.	"Lord, make me know the measure of my days . . ." Lamentation; life's frailty	Baritone; Chorus
4	E♭	"How lovely is Thy dwelling place" Beauty of heavenly home; Bliss	Chorus
5	G	"Ye now have sorrow . . . shall be joyful" Deliverance; joy	Soprano; Chorus
6	C min./maj.	"On earth . . . no continuing place . . . seek one to come" Promised resurrection; Hope	Baritone; Chorus
7	F–A–F	"Blessed are the dead who die in the Lord" Rest from labor; Works remain	Chorus

EXAMPLE 23.7 (*a*) Motive spanning a fourth by means of a third and a second as it appears in Brahms's Requiem, mvt. 1, mm. 15–17; (*b*) Chorale melody on which the Requiem theme is based; (*c*) Theme, *Ein deutsches Requiem*, mvt. 1, mm. 3–4, 'cello I.

and the promise of a better world beyond the grave. There are similarities of scoring, instrumentation, and format between Bach's work and Brahms's. In the first movement of his Requiem, Brahms omitted violins, clarinets, and trumpets from the orchestra and divided violas and 'celli. Muted violins are used in movement 2; much of the time they are in middle to low register. (Bach did not use violins in BWV106.) *Ein deutsches Requiem* contains many of Brahms's compositional traits—apparent is his penchant for mediant and submediant relationships, chains of thirds, long pedals, a mingling of modality and key tonality, and frequent use of a motive encompassing a fourth by means of movement upward or downward through a third and a second or vice versa (ex. 23.7).

Brahms was probably the most versatile and most accomplished composer in the nineteenth century after Beethoven. He produced masterpieces of solo song, accompanied choral music, symphonies, and chamber music. He was the successor to Schubert and Schumann in the composition of Lieder and song cycle and to Beethoven in the areas of string quartet and symphony. In the composition of absolute music, he followed in the tradition of Haydn, Mozart, and Beethoven, but he also incorporated in his music some principles used by earlier composers and some innovative procedures that inspired and influenced twentieth-century composers.

SUMMARY

Throughout his life, Richard Wagner was interested in the theater and its music and made important contributions in those areas. He became well versed in every aspect of opera. From the first, he wrote his own libretti. Eventually he designed and built at Bayreuth a theater complex ideally suited to the production of his works. Wagner carried to completion the work in German Romantic opera begun by Weber and went beyond that to create music drama. With *Der Ring des Nibelungen,* Wagner approached the kind of *Gesamtkunstwerk* Weber had been striving toward. Wagner was an eclectic composer, using every historical and traditional musical technique that would serve his purpose, but he shaped, merged, and manipulated those techniques in new ways to create music that some critics considered radical. From beginning to end, *Der Ring . . .* is a unified symphonic network of sound created from Leitmotifs used in every imaginable way musically. Wagner's use of orchestral color, treatment of motives and Leitmotifs, obscuring of dividing lines, and the symphonic character of his music dramas affected symphonists as well as opera composers. His treatment of key tonality and chromaticism, frequently producing polytonality and at times verging on atonality, was a step toward the dodecaphony and pantonality of later composers. *Der Ring . . .* is a landmark in the development of music.

Giuseppe Verdi, too, concentrated on opera. Verdi took a vital interest in the way libretti were written and was involved in all aspects of the production of his operas. He followed the traditional lines of Italian opera but permitted Romantic traits to infiltrate when they furthered the drama. For Verdi, the prime purpose of the music was to support and reinforce expressively the human actions and reactions that constituted the drama. In insisting on being realistic in details and staging, and in his regard for the presentation of events as human experiences with human reactions, he paved the way for *verismo* operas. Verdi carried Italian opera to unprecedented heights with *Otello* and *Falstaff.* In *Otello,* Verdi produced a kind of music drama with continuous music and some associative musical figures (not Leitmotifs) used to characterize persons, but his work was still within the bounds of traditional Italian opera and was quite different from the music dramas of Wagner.

Franz Liszt's closest approach to music drama was in his secular cantatas and oratorios. He first became famous as a virtuoso pianist and contributed a great deal to the development of piano playing and piano repertoire. Admiration for Paganini's virtuosity inspired Liszt to exhibit a comparable degree of technical proficiency and virtuosic display in his own playing. Like Chopin, Liszt strove to make the piano transcend its limitations. Liszt's piano arrangements and transcriptions of symphonies and operas by other composers form another significant contribution. To orchestral literature Liszt added a new genre, the symphonic poem, a single-movement programmatic composition of symphonic proportions. Throughout his life, Liszt was deeply religious, and he composed some fine sacred music, including some Psalms settings, Masses, the Requiem Mass, and *Via crucis.*

Anton Bruckner was renowned throughout Europe as a concert organist. Unfortunately, he improvised most of his organ compositions and never notated them. He composed some of the finest sacred choral music written in the late nineteenth century. His symphonies, like Brahms's, are absolute music and are an important contribution to orchestral literature. His Ninth Symphony is exceptionally fine. Bruckner was the first composer to extend the scope of the symphony beyond what Beethoven expressed in his Ninth Symphony.

Johannes Brahms was a superb concert pianist and was one of the most accomplished nineteenth-century composers. Most of his music is for voice. He never wrote an opera, though he was interested in the genre. He created masterpieces in the areas of solo song, accompanied choral music, symphonies, and chamber music. He was the successor to Schubert and Schumann in the composition of Lied and song cycle and to Beethoven in string quartet and symphony. Brahms reinforced the position of absolute music in the concert hall. His four symphonies are absolute music, Classic in form, Romantic in expression and lyricism, progressive in treatment of material—masterworks that deservedly are in standard symphonic repertoire. His Symphony No. 4 may be viewed as a harbinger of twentieth-century pantonality and serial techniques. Brahms's Violin Concerto is one of the greatest of all time. *Alt-Rhapsodie* is one of the most beautiful choral works ever written, but Brahms's greatest achievement in choral music is *Ein deutsches Requiem.*

NATIONALISM IN NINETEENTH-CENTURY MUSIC

24

The last third of the nineteenth century was colored by the growth of nationalism, both politically and culturally. There was a trend toward expansion—in business, in population, in aggressive territorial expansion (particularly into Africa and Asia), and in greatly increased performing resources called for by some composers. In several countries there was a move toward democracy, with control firmly in the hands of parliamentary governments based on equal male suffrage. (In Germany and Austria-Hungary the parliaments did not control the government.) Elementary education was compulsory in most western European countries, a fact that advanced literacy and increased the reading public.

In music, composers had several paths from which to choose. Some post-Romanticists followed Wagner for a time; others, observing the extent of Wagner's expanded tonalities, were extremely innovative. Of course, some composers were conservative. Increased awareness of the accomplishments of great masters of the historical past provided techniques to emulate and incorporate in contemporary compositions and, in some cases, intimidated composers. This was particularly true of Beethoven's symphonies. The preeminence of Germanic composers began to fade, challenged mainly by nationalism and a new school of composition that arose in France (discussed in Chap. 25).

NATIONALISM

Three kinds of nationalism are apparent in nineteenth-century music: (1) a nation's revival of its own folk song and the absorption of that folk song into the art music being composed, such as occurred in Germany early in the century; (2) a composer's use of a national element as an accessory to a basically cosmopolitan style or form of music (e.g., Liszt's rhapsodies on Hungarian gypsy tunes); and (3) a composer's use of national elements as subjects for and as basic features of a composition (e.g., Glinka's *A Life for the Tsar*' and Smetana's *Má Vlast* [My fatherland]). In nations such as Russia that had relied heavily on or had been dominated by foreign music and musicians, native-born composers consciously endeavored to write music colored by or incorporating national and folk elements. Composers chose their nation's history, legends, and folklore as subjects for opera and program music, quoted snatches of folk song in compositions, used folk melodies as themes in orchestral works, and collected and published folk songs of their own lands. Distinctive features of nationalistic music—modal scales, harmonies, motives, melodies, rhythms, and forms peculiar to or characteristic of national idioms—gradually infiltrated the cosmopolitan music of Western Europe, and new styles of music arose.

RUSSIA

Until well into the nineteenth century, music in Russia was dominated by foreigners. Tsar Peter the Great (r. 1689–1725), desiring to modernize his country, imported science, industry, art, and music from the West. During the reigns of Tsarinas Anne (r. 1730–40) and Elizabeth (r. 1741–62), Italian opera, translated into Russian, gained a real foothold. Catherine II ("the Great"; r. 1762–96) maintained a magnificent theater at court and imported Italian singers and composers. Talented Russians went to Italy to study and returned to Russia to write inconsequential Italianate operas. Alexander I (r. 1801–25) preferred French opera and brought Boieldieu, as well as Germans and Italians, to work at court. Muzio Clementi and John Field went to Russia to concertize, and Field remained there for more than a decade, to teach and concertize. Catterino Cavos (1776–1840), who worked in St. Petersburg from 1797–1840, was the first to really explore Russian history and legends as source material for operas (e.g., in *Ivan Susanin* [1815]). However, no Russian musical compositions of real worth were created before Glinka (1804–57).

GLINKA, DARGOMÏZHSKY

Mikhail Glinka's exposure to music was restricted to Russian folk songs until 1810; then he heard operas and Haydn and Mozart symphonies. Around 1817, Glinka was sent to school in St. Petersburg. He learned to sing and play piano, and he composed *Andante cantabile and Rondo* for orchestra (c. 1823, pub. 1955), two overtures (c. 1822–26, pub. 1955), several sets of variations and a few character pieces for piano, and many songs. Six of his early songs could be mistaken for folk songs.

After visiting Italy and Berlin in 1830–33 Glinka composed an opera about the Russian peasant-hero Ivan Susanin. Tsar Nicholas I (r. 1825–55) renamed that work *A Life for the Tsar'* (1836). Basically, the music is Western, with elements of Italian and French opera (ballet), but new to Russian opera was Glinka's

use of recitative; previous Russian operas used spoken dialogue. There are some recurring themes. The opera sounds as though it contains more authentic folk music than it does—there are only two borrowed melodies. Glinka's orchestration is excellent. *A Life for the Tsar'* is a cornerstone in the history of Russian art music. Its success brought Glinka an appointment as *maître de chappelle* of the Imperial Chapel. He found the court singers in a deplorable state. By training them and by recruiting additional singers, he ultimately produced a magnificent choral ensemble of male voices, capable of performing eight-part harmony from very deep bass (down to A♭′ or G′) to fairly high soprano.

Glinka based his second opera, *Ruslan i Ludmila* (Ruslan and Ludmila; 1842), on a Pushkin fairy tale that is not specifically Russian and that is not really suitable for opera. The music evidences Glinka's liking for thematic variation, mediant relationships, the flatted sixth degree, descending chromaticism used for color or for sharp dissonance, and changing-background technique (i.e., keeping a folk melody constant while changing the accompaniment background each time the melody is repeated). The only Leitmotif is the whole-tone scale associated with Chernomor.

Glinka spent 1844–48 in Spain, where he composed two orchestral works on Spanish melodies. In 1848 he visited Warsaw, where he wrote his only other major work, *Kamarinskaya* (orch.). In it he incorporated and juxtaposed the dance tune *Kamarinskaya* and the song "From behind the mountains." Two techniques are used in the work: the changing-background principle and variation.

The next important Russian composer was Alexander Dargomïzhsky (1813–69), who was employed in government service but had an adjunct career in music. A talented pianist, he taught himself composition by studying Glinka's composition notebooks. Dargomïzhsky wrote many songs and seriously studied Russian folk song. The value of his study is apparent in his third opera, *Rusalka* (1855). In many respects, it is Italianate, with recitatives, arias, set numbers, and choruses; however, the recitatives are basically declamatory with simple harmonic accompaniment. Russia was experiencing social upheaval, and *Rusalka* is sometimes viewed as a vehicle designed to express the contemporary reaction against social inequality. Perhaps it

1860	1870	1880	1890	1900	1910	1920	1930

Growth of nonmilitaristic nationalism in art, literature, music
seen in opera, symphony, symphonic (tone) poem

• c. 1888 symphonic suite

• c. 1908 symphonic song cycle

Revival of *Märschenoper* in Germany

Realism in literature

Verismo in Italian literature and opera

Paris the cultural capital of Europe

Impressionism in art;

Symbolism in French poetry;

Impressionism/Symbolism in music

Increased interest in collecting folk songs; ethnomusicology

• 1875 Harvard University establishes chair of music

Minstrel shows   Cakewalk; Ragtime; Blues; Jazz

RUSSIA:

Dargomïzhsky (d. 1869)

(1837)   Balakirev, the leader and mentor   1910

(1835)   Cui   1918

• 1880 *Musique en Russie*

(1839)   Musorgsky   1881

• 1869 *Boris Godunov*

• 1874 *Pictures at an Exhibition*

(1844)   Rimsky-Korsakov   1908

• 1888 *Scheherezade*, symphonic suite

(1833)   Borodin   1887

• 1869–87 *Prince Igor*

(1840)   Tchaikovsky   1893

symphonies and ballets

1892   Scriabin   1915

color-music relationship

• 1910 *Prométhée*

CZECHOSLOVAKIA:

(1824)   Smetana   1884

nationalistic operas; symphonic poem cycle

• (1872–80) *Má Vlast*

(1841)   Dvořák   1904

symphonies; operas; chamber music

(1854)   Janáček   1928

collecting folk songs; composing operas, choral and instr. music

---

was, but more probably Dargomïzhsky chose the Russian legend because of its dramatic possibilities.

In the mid-1860s, Dargomïzhsky began his opera *Kamennïy gost* (The stone guest), Pushkin's version of the Don Juan story. Dargomïzhsky set Pushkin's words virtually unchanged, as declamation, and hoped to avoid everything Italianate in structure. When Dar-

gomïzhsky's health failed, he requested César Cui to finish the piano score and Modest Musorgsky to orchestrate the work. Cui wrote the Prelude and finished the first scene. When performed (1872), *The Stone Guest* was a failure, but it was one of the most influential failures in the development of music, for it affected not only Russian music but that of the Western European

1860	1870	1880	1890	1900	1910	1920	1930

SCANDINAVIA:

(1843) Grieg 1907

1865 Nielsen (1931)

1865 Sibelius (1957)
nationalistic tone poems; symphonies (no works after 1930)

SPAIN: Opera, *zarzuela*, liturgical music

(1823) Barbieri 1894

(1841) Pedrell 1922
critical writings; editions of Spanish liturgical music

(1850) Bréton 1923

(1845) Chueca 1906

(1851) Chapí 1909
• 1875 *La hija de Jeftá*   • 1897 *La revoltosa*

1860 Albéniz 1909
• 1906–9 *Suite Iberia*

1867 Granados 1916
• 1911 *Goyescas*

GERMANY, AUSTRIA:

1860 Hugo Wolf 1903
Lieder

1860 Mahler 1911
Lieder; symphonies; symphonic song cycle
integration of Lied and symphony

1864 Richard Strauss (1949)
• 1889–98 tone poems; 1900–41 operas

FRANCE:

Cosmopolitan, traditional music (Franck, d'Indy)
French traditional music (Saint-Saëns, Fauré)
Impressionism in art; Symbolism in poetry

Impressionism/Symbolism in music (Debussy)

1862 Debussy 1918
• c. 1894 *Prélude à l'après-midi d'un faune*

1875 Ravel (1937)

1917–22 Les Six

BRITAIN: Interest in oratorio, music festivals continued

UNITED STATES:

Paine, MacDowell, Parker active

1874 Charles Ives (1954)
individualistic style; experimental

Ragtime (Joplin)

Rise of Jazz

composers who knew it. Dargomïzhsky sought to escape the bonds of key tonality and wrote the entire score without key signatures; he used some whole-tone scales and harmonizations, some unusual modulations, and some radical harmonies. Italianate recitative and French phrases are minimal.

529   NATIONALISM IN NINETEENTH-CENTURY MUSIC

MOGUCHAYA KUCHKA, "MIGHTY HANDFUL"

During the 40 years after the death of Nicholas I (d. 1855), Russia expanded in many ways: population, industry, agriculture, and education of the people. In the 1860s there were strong feelings of nonmilitaristic nationalism, expressed in art, literature, and music. The main sources of materials for this new kind of nationalism were history (medieval Russia, Byzantium, the Eastern Orthodox Church, the Tatar Orient) and the common man (his surroundings, work, folk tales, folk songs, and folk dances). Russian artists, authors, and composers relied on all of these.

Many musicians, both native and foreign, were active in Russia during those decades. The most significant Russians were the five men whom critic Vladimir Stasov (1824–1906) called the *moguchaya kuchka* (mighty handful, powerful fist): Mily Balakirev (1837–1910), the acknowledged leader and mentor of the group; César Cui (1835–1918); Modest Musorgsky (1839–81); Nikolai Rimsky-Korsakov (1844–1908); and Alexander Borodin (1833–87). They never referred to themselves by Stasov's term, nor was the term used in Russia by anyone other than Stasov. Actually, Stasov was as mighty a force as the others not only through his many writings on art, literature, and music but also through the assistance he provided the composers—suggesting subjects for compositions and ferreting out source materials.

Balakirev's mother was his first piano teacher. When he was 10, he had piano lessons from A. Dubuque, a pupil of John Field. Later, Balakirev studied theory with Karl Eisrich, who introduced him to Alexander Ulïbïshev, a wealthy landowner. Balakirev lived in Ulïbïshev's home and at the age of 15 was permitted to conduct rehearsals of his private orchestra. Among Balakirev's earliest compositions are *Grand Fantaisie on Russian Folksongs* (1852; pno., orch.), some songs (pub. 1908), and the first movement of a Piano Concerto in F♯ minor (1855–56). In 1855 Ulïbïshev introduced him to Glinka, who supplied him with themes for some compositions, checked the completed works, and introduced him to Stasov.

In 1857–58 Balakirev played some of his piano works in concerts. At a private concert, he met César Cui, an officer in the Engineering Corps. Balakirev introduced him to Dargomïzhsky, at whose home Cui met Modest Musorgsky, a military officer who was interested in musical composition. Cui introduced Musorgsky to Balakirev. In 1861 Théodore Canille, who was teaching Nikolai Rimsky-Korsakov, a naval cadet, introduced him to Balakirev, who encouraged Rimsky-Korsakov to compose. In 1862 Borodin, a chemistry student and a friend of Musorgsky, met Balakirev, who guided his compositional endeavors. Thus, the *moguchaya kuchka* was formed.

In general, the Five upheld these principles: (1) the music of the Russian people, religious and folk, should be used as a basis for art music—this was the new Russian nationalism; (2) strict German counterpoint and other techniques of Western European music might be ignored to allow a composer more freedom in creating art music; (3) realism was advocated; and (4) the spirit and style of nineteenth-century Romanticism was favored and Classicism rejected.

In 1860 Balakirev began collecting Russian folk songs; he harmonized a number of them and published two collections (1866, 1898). In 1862 he was instrumental in founding the Free School of Music in St. Petersburg. His work there, plus the hours he spent helping other composers in his circle, left little time for his own composing. Short works he completed; larger works bogged down, and some he never finished. He worked on his Symphony No. 1 (C major) for 33 years. His insistence on national themes, his general advocacy of musical nationalism, and his teaching that composers had the right to ignore the traditional rules of Western European music caused antagonism among musicians and made for him many enemies. Between 1870 and 1881 he was involved in mysticism, and his compositional activity slackened. After 1894 he resumed composing; in the next decade he wrote about 3 dozen piano pieces and at least 20 songs in which he used traditional forms, though he altered them somewhat. His Piano Sonata in B♭ minor (1905) comprises a sonata-form Andantino first movement, followed by stylized Mazurka, nocturne-like Intermezzo, and fast Finale.

Thus, Balakirev experienced two short periods of creativity, separated by 25 years of silence. His surviving music includes 11 choral works, most of them for women's voices; 6 anthems for mixed chorus, 1 being *Cherubim Song;* 2 incomplete piano concertos;

The Russian Five, "The Mighty Handful," with Stasov. *Top row:* Balakirev, Stasov, Musorgsky; *bottom row:* Rimsky-Korsakov, Borodin, Cui.

2 symphonies (C major; D minor); 4 nationalistic concert overtures; 3 orchestral suites; *Romance* for violin/piano; approximately 50 piano works; and 45 vocal solos with piano accompaniment. One of his most significant compositions is the *Second Overture on Russian Themes* (1864), which he renamed *1000 let'* (1000 years) to commemorate Russia's chiliad (1,000th anniversary of its founding). The overture, revised, was published in 1882 as the symphonic poem *Russia*. Another important work is the virtu-osic Oriental fantasy *Islamey* for piano (1869). It is based on three themes (Caucasian, Armenian) and has tremendous rhythmic drive. *Islamey* shows the influence of Liszt and in its turn influenced Debussy and Ravel.

Balakirev did a great deal for Russian music by instilling in his colleagues and students the belief that Russian composers could rival Western Europeans. In his own works he did not completely reject tradi-tional Western European methods but merged the Russian and Near Eastern with them. From Glinka he received training in the proper instrumental treatment of folk-music materials, then expanded and built on that training and transmitted what he learned to other Russian composers (e.g., Borodin, Musorgsky, and Rimsky-Korsakov). Balakirev was dictatorial—he did not merely suggest subjects to his colleagues but also supplied themes, insisted on certain keys, and reworked portions of their compositions. He believed that great composers should be teachers and should pass their techniques on to their students. So firmly did he impress this on his colleagues and students that, from Balakirev's time to the present, great Russian com-posers have taught. In no other country is there such a continuous chain of music pedagogy.

César Cui, a fortifications expert, was the weakest member of the Five, yet his critical articles were influ-ential in Russian music for more than 50 years. He composed much music: 15 operas, 4 of them children's operas (e.g., *The Snow Giant*); more than 200 songs; some cantatas and other choral works; 3 string quar-tets and some other chamber music; at least a dozen orchestral pieces; and many piano pieces. His best works are miniatures, particularly the delicate ones, such as *Orientale,* one of the 24 violin/piano pieces in *Kaleydoskop* (Kaleidoscope, Op. 50; 1893). Cui was an ardent proponent of nationalism, but not all his works are nationalistic. His operatic writing was highly respected by Dargomïzhsky (see p. 528). Cui wrote the first comprehensive book on Russian music, *Musique en Russie* (pub. Paris, 1880). His book *The Russian Song: A Study of its Development* appeared in 1896.

Alexander Borodin, son of a Georgian prince, received an excellent general education, learned several languages, and played flute, piano, and 'cello. He graduated from the Academy of Medicine in St. Petersburg, earned a doctorate in chemistry (1858), and in 1864 became professor of organic chemistry at the Academy. Borodin was internationally known in his field and published several important scientific papers. He was among the first to advocate the admission of women to the medical profession in Russia.

For Borodin, music was necessarily an avocation, but he composed whenever he could find time. Because he worked long hours in the laboratory and at the Academy, it took him several years to complete a large composition. The first large work he composed after meeting Balakirev was Symphony No. 1 (E♭ major; 1862–67). Borodin next wrote some songs. An opera-farce and an opera, *The Tsar's Bride* (1867–69), have not survived. Borodin used unusual key relationships in Symphony No. 2 (1869–76): sonata-form first movement in B minor, scherzo/trio in F major, slow movement in D♭ major, and Finale in B major.

Stasov supplied the scenario for *Prince Igor,* and Borodin wrote the libretto. He worked on the music intermittently and composed other works—songs, chamber music, orchestral pieces, piano solos, and Act IV of the opera-ballet *Mlada* (1872). *Prince Igor* (1869–87) was not finished at the time of Borodin's sudden death from heart failure; it was completed by Alexander Glazunov (1865–1936), with assistance from Rimsky-Korsakov. Glazunov had discussed *Prince Igor* with Borodin and knew something of his plans. Glazunov wrote the overture by piecing together sketches Borodin had made, relying on his memory of the overture as Borodin had improvised it for him, and adding a few measures of his own. It was a remarkable achievement for Glazunov. Composition of *Prince Igor* extended over 18 years, and it was assembled and completed by two composers who were not involved in planning the work; it is not surprising that the opera seems to be a series of tableaux rather than a unified drama. Some of the arias are excellent (e.g., those sung by Yaroslavna). The *Polovtsian Dances* (Act II) are frequently performed in orchestral concerts; one of the dances supplied the melody for the twentieth-century popular song *Stranger in Paradise.*

Another excellent work by Borodin is the short orchestral piece *V sredney Azii* (In central Asia; 1882), one of a dozen works commissioned for background music for living tableaux illustrating events during the reign of Alexander II (r. 1855–81).

Modest Musorgsky was the most talented and the most nationalistic of Balakirev's disciples. When he met Balakirev, Musorgsky knew a great deal about Russian folklore but very little about musical composition. As a child, he had piano lessons but was taught nothing about form or harmony. In 1852 he entered Cadet School of the Guards at St. Petersburg. He sang in the school choir, began to compose music, and studied the works of Bortniansky and other early nineteenth-century Russian composers. In 1857 with Balakirev's guidance, Musorgsky wrote some songs and piano pieces; in 1858 he composed two piano sonatas (E♭ major; F♯ minor; lost) and two Scherzi for piano (C♯ minor; B♭ major) and began an opera that he abandoned.

In 1858 Musorgsky experienced nervous difficulties and resigned his military commission. From time to time, nervous disorders disrupted his career; those attacks may have been the early stages of epilepsy. Russian serfs were emancipated in 1861, and for the next two years Musorgsky helped his brother manage the family estate. When funds ran low in 1863, he entered civil service, where he held responsible positions until his dismissal in 1867. He wrote a few songs and began another opera that he never completed. Shortly after his mother's death in 1865, Musorgsky had his first serious bout with alcoholism. Both diseases worsened over the years, and the combination of alcoholism and epilepsy eventually claimed his life. Many of his works remained unfinished; a number of them were completed by Rimsky-Korsakov and other composers.

Of Musorgsky's completed compositions, the following are extant: the opera *Boris Godunov* (first version, 1868–69; rev. 1871–72); 4 choral works; 5 orchestral pieces, 1 being *St. John's Night on the Bare Mountain* (1867); approximately a dozen piano pieces; at least 50 songs; and 3 song cycles, *Detskaya* (The Nursery; 1870–72), *Bez solntsa* (Sunless; 1874), and *Pesni i plyaski smerti* (Songs and dances of death; 1874).

Musorgsky's songs rank among the finest written in the nineteenth century. Reportedly, he sang them most effectively at private gatherings. His songs portray various moods, among them devotional (*Prayer;* 1865), satirical (*Oh, you, drunken sot!;* 1866), tender (*Lullaby;* 1865), and comical (*Mephistopheles's song of the flea;* 1879). Some convey sobering messages (e.g., *The Field-marshal* from *Songs and Dances of Death*). For many songs Musorgsky wrote his own texts (e.g., *The Nursery*); for others he used poems by noted Russian authors and translations of works by Goethe, Heine, and Rückert. All Musorgsky's songs are in Russian. His music fits the natural declamation of normal Russian speech perfectly, and the songs lose much in translation. Phrases are usually asymmetrical and of uneven lengths. Melodic lines may be lyrical, or declamatory, or nonlyrical and individualistic, typical of the speech of the characters in the song (e.g., the satirical *Seminarist* [The Seminarian; 1866]). Much of Musorgsky's music is modal or hints at modality. Frequently he used pedal points and sometimes short ostinato patterns. Musorgsky used chord streams 30 years before Debussy did so. Debussy heard some of Musorgsky's music in Russia and was influenced by it.

The best known of Musorgsky's piano pieces is *Pictures at an Exhibition* (1874; pub. 1886), a suite inspired by an exhibit of architect-artist Victor Hartmann's works. From the more than 400 pieces on exhibit, Musorgsky chose 10 to depict musically and linked them by a *Promenade* that describes himself, as viewer, walking about the exhibit. Musorgsky owned two of the drawings he translated into music; both have disappeared. *Pictures at an Exhibition* has been orchestrated by several persons; the best is that made by Maurice Ravel in 1921.

Musorgsky developed his libretto for *Boris Godunov* from Pushkin's play *Boris Godunov* (1825) and Karamzin's *History of the Russian State* (1818). The story is based on the long-held belief (since proven false) that Tsar Boris (regent for Fyodor, 1584–98; r. 1598–1605) murdered his nephew Dmitry, heir to the throne. The opera commences with Boris's coronation, then relates how a monk pretends to be Dmitry and attempts to usurp the throne. Boris broods about his crime and, after he hears of a miracle that occurred at Dmitry's grave, he collapses and dies.

Musorgsky's construction of the opera in scenes, rather than continuous drama, conforms with the structure of many literary works of the late nineteenth century. The final version of the opera contains four acts with prologue. Basically, *Boris Godunov* is a historical grand opera, with spectacular crowd scenes that are essential to the story. Musorgsky created characters that are perceived by the audience as real people rather than as characters enacting a drama. *Boris Godunov* presents not only a personal tragedy but the suffering of the Russian people, the masses. The people are the losers—the real heroes. The subject matter is extremely nationalistic, and it is so presented with folk song and Russian Orthodox church music and many realistic details. The fierceness of medieval Russia, still existing in the sixteenth century, lives again in Musorgsky's music. This is musical realism.

The Coronation Scene in *Boris Godunov* is magnificent (fig. 24.1; DWMA167). The crowd praises Boris with the melody of the folk song *Slava* (Glory); the whole-tone scale is prominent (ex. 24.1). The pealing of many bells, representing Moscow's cathedrals and churches, is most effective. The music is vigorous and vibrant. Boris's solo is an excellent example of Musorgsky's ability to write in a style that is both expressive and flexible. Here, he united text with music so well that Boris's prayer has the effect of religious chant. The role of Boris requires a deep bass singer who can interpret expressively and convey an impression of great strength and power.

Acting in good faith, with the aim of making *Boris Godunov* acceptable to the public and less difficult to perform and to produce, Rimsky-Korsakov revised the work. His drastic alterations destroyed much of the originality of Musorgsky's harmonies, modulations, and melodic lines. He removed many of Musorgsky's harmonic innovations—the harsh dissonances, chords

FIGURE 24.1 Musorgsky: *Boris Godunov*, Prologue, Scene 2, the coronation scene, which takes place in the square inside the Kremlin's walls. From the Bolshoi Theater performance, 1948. (*The Society for Cultural Relations with the USSR*)

EXAMPLE 24.1 The Russian melody *Slava* (Glory).

structured in fourths and fifths, and unorthodox and uninhibited modulations—that sounded strange but added dramatic power and color. Rimsky-Korsakov also revised *St. John's Night on the Bare Mountain*. His versions present Musorgsky's music much more conventionally than it really was—Musorgsky was a daring, innovative, avant-garde composer. However, Rimsky-Korsakov did put *Boris Godunov* back into the repertoire in Russia. In 1908 musicologists expressed much dissatisfaction with Rimsky-Korsakov's revisions. As a result of agitation for publication of the works with Musorgsky's original texts (unaltered), the Russian State Music Corporation began in 1928 to prepare an edition of Musorgsky's complete works that presents his original versions and all the variant versions published by editors. Only when all Musorgsky's music is available in its original form will his genius be fully recognized.

Rimsky-Korsakov's autobiography, *Chronicle of My Musical Life* (published by his son Andrey in 1909) reveals much about musical activities in Russia during the years the Five were active. Though Nikolai's musical talent was apparent when he was quite young, his real interest was aroused when he heard Bortnian-sky's sacred music at a nearby monastery. While at the College of Naval Cadets (1856–62), he attended performances of operas and heard for the first time Beethoven symphonies and Mendelssohn overtures. Glinka was his favorite composer. During his cadet years, Rimsky-Korsakov had piano lessons from Théodore Canille, and through him was drawn into Balakirev's circle. Rimsky-Korsakov was trying to compose a symphony in E♭ minor, and Balakirev insisted that he continue to work on it. The first movement, scherzo, and finale were completed by 1862, but the slow movement was not finished until after Rimsky-Korsakov returned from two and one-half years of naval duty abroad. In 1866 Rimsky-Korsakov discussed music with Dargomïzhsky and Balakirev's circle and composed the *Overture on Russian Themes,* some songs, and some dances. Then he wrote the symphonic poem *Sadko,* based on the legend of the minstrel Sadko (1867; rev. 1869, 1892). The composition contains borrowings from works by Glinka, Balakirev, Dargomïzhsky, and Liszt. (In 1894–96, Rimsky-Korsakov wrote the opera *Sadko.*)

In 1868 the Balakirev group regularly attended *soirées* at Dargomïzhsky's home and performed portions of *The Stone Guest* as they were completed. Among the musicians attending those *soirées* were the Purgold sisters, one of whom, Nadezhda, married Rimsky-Korsakov. Discussions of opera at the *soirées* increased Rimsky-Korsakov's interest in that genre, and he composed *The Maid of Pskov* (1868–72; rev. 1876, 1898). Rimsky-Korsakov constantly revised his compositions, and when he completed works left unfinished because of the deaths of his colleagues, he revised their works.

In 1871 Rimsky-Korsakov was appointed professor of composition and instrumentation at St. Petersburg Conservatory. He knew very little about harmony, counterpoint, and form but he learned the basics in those areas and studied to keep ahead of his students. For a time, he wrote abstract music along traditional lines, but it did not satisfy him, nor did he think he did it well. Most of his 16 chamber music works are nonprogrammatic, contain a fair amount of counterpoint, and follow traditional lines. His love of fantasy, folklore, and Russian history made program music and opera better areas in which to work.

From 1873 to 1884 Rimsky-Korsakov was Inspector of Bands for the Navy. In order to learn as much as possible about the various instruments, he learned to play them. This, plus thorough study of Berlioz's treatise on instrumentation, made Rimsky-Korsakov a brilliant orchestrator. He could orchestrate well because he knew the various instrumental techniques, ranges, tone colors, and capabilities. He orchestrated some of his colleagues' works, helped Cui and Dargomïzhsky, finished and edited Musorgsky's compositions, and worked with Glazunov in completing Borodin's *Prince Igor.* However, in working with the music of these composers, he altered it considerably.

In 1874 Rimsky-Korsakov succeeded Balakirev as director of the Free School of Music, and in 1883 he became assistant superintendent of music at the Imperial Chapel. In 1884 his *Textbook of Harmony* was published. Then he wrote *Principles of Orchestration* (pub. 1913), illustrated with more than 300 excerpts from his works. It is still used at some universities as an orchestration text.

Rimsky-Korsakov published two substantial collections of Russian folk songs and composed a great deal of music: operas, orchestral works, some chamber music, piano pieces, and many songs. Over a 40-year period, he composed 14 operas and 1 opera-ballet, most of them unknown outside Russia. None of his operas is as fine as *Boris Godunov.* However, Rimsky-Korsakov's finest vocal writing is in his operas. Only *The Snow Maiden* (1880–81, rev. 1895), *Sadko* (1895–96), and *The Golden Cockerel* (1906–7) have been accepted internationally.

The Golden Cockerel is based on Pushkin's satire. The opera, in which the King kills the Astrologer, and in retaliation the Astrologer's cockerel attacks and kills the King, had political overtones in Russia. The satirical depiction of the aristocracy fit conditions in Russia at the time, and government censors demanded deletion of some lines. Rimsky-Korsakov's music reveals his knowledge of Wagnerian principles; Leitmotifs associated with the main characters are deftly woven into the symphonic fabric of the opera. Rimsky-Korsakov's characters are delightful caricatures, and his scenic depictions are excellent.

Rimsky-Korsakov's reputation in the Western world rests on three orchestral works: *Spanish Capriccio* (*Capriccio espagnole;* 1887), *Scheherazade* (1888), and the overture *Russian Easter Festival* (1888). *Spanish Capriccio* resulted from his desire to use Spanish themes for a virtuosic violin solo with orchestral accompaniment. The work has five short movements: (1) *Alborada,* a morning serenade; (2) Theme with variations; (3) *Alborada* for orchestra, a variation of the first movement; (4) *Scene and Gypsy Song,* containing cadenzas for flute, clarinet, harp, and violin; and (5) *Fandango and Asturias,* stylized dance music. The work is exciting, buoyant, and vividly brilliant, filled with figurations suited to each solo instrument and to each section of the orchestra.

Romantic composers had written numerous short pieces based on fairy tales and legends but nothing symphonic in scope. Rimsky-Korsakov wanted to write a multimovement orchestral programmatic work that combined the characteristic features of symphony, symphonic poem, and the nineteenth-century suite, a set of related pieces. He called this kind of work a **symphonic suite.**

Scheherazade is a symphonic suite based on episodes from *A Thousand and One Nights.* The movements have these titles: (1) *The Sea and Sinbad's*

Ship; (2) *The Tale of Prince Kalender;* (3) *The Young Prince and the Young Princess;* and (4) *Festival at Bagdad—The Sea—The Ship is Wrecked on a Rock Surmounted by a Bronze Warrior—Conclusion.* The suite is unified by cadenza-like introductions to movements 1, 2, and 4 and a cadenza-intermezzo in movement 3, all for solo violin with harp accompaniment, representing Scheherazade telling her fascinating (and lifesaving) tales to the Sultan. The work is Romantic in its exotic Eastern colors and fairy-tale basis. Rimsky-Korsakov handled the instrumentation expertly, combining unlike instruments to produce new tonal colors and effects, contrasting the basic tone color of the same instruments in different registers, and contrasting individual instruments or groups of different instruments. To some extent, *Festival at Bagdad* foreshadows twentieth-century treatment of rhythm—in some sections rhythmic changes occur every few measures.

In *Russian Easter Festival* Rimsky-Korsakov aimed to depict the spectacle of a typical Easter morning service at a cathedral of Russian Orthodox faith and to convey the deeper meaning of that service, a combination of Isaiah's prophecy of resurrection, the gospel story of Jesus' resurrection, and the pagan symbolism and merrymaking that invaded Easter ritual. The very idea of composing an orchestral work based on Russian Orthodox liturgical materials was daring—for 1,000 years church edicts had banned musical instruments from the sanctuary. Most of the themes used in *Russian Easter Festival* were derived from the *obikhod,* a collection of the most important canticles in the Russian Orthodox liturgy. Among those Rimsky-Korsakov used are "Let God arise!," "An angel wailed," "Let them also that hate Him flee before Him," and, in the coda, "Christ is risen!" *Russian Easter Festival* is Romantic in its presentation of ritualistic pageantry, yet is a deeply devotional presentation of all that the Easter ritual represents.

Rimsky-Korsakov wrote traditional and Romantic, abstract and program, nationalistic and nonnationalistic music. His musical language was also dual, sometimes diatonic and lyrical, sometimes filled with chromaticism or based on artificial whole-tone scales. His orchestrations are superb. The main influences in his style were Glinka, Balakirev, Liszt, and Berlioz. That he was an excellent composition and orchestration teacher is evident from the success of his pupils. His influence is apparent in some of the compositions of Debussy, Ravel, Dukas, and Respighi.

OTHER RUSSIAN COMPOSERS

Rimsky-Korsakov passed on to his students the legacy he received from Dargomïzhsky and Balakirev and that they had inherited from Glinka. Among Rimsky-Korsakov's composition students were Alexander Glazunov (1865–1936), Anatoli Liadov (1855–1914), Mikhail Ippolitov-Ivanov (1859–1935), Igor Stravinsky (1882–1971), Sergey Prokofiev (1891–1953), and Nikolai Miaskovsky (1881–1950).

Some Russian composers wrote mainly along traditional Western lines but produced some nationalistic music, as did Pyotr Tchaikovsky (1840–93; discussed in Chap. 25). Anton Rubinstein (1829–94) occupied a controversial position.

Anton Rubinstein was one of the nineteenth century's finest pianists, comparable with Liszt, and enjoyed international acclaim as a concert pianist. He and Henryk Wieniawski (1835–80), Polish violinist-composer, toured North America in 1872, presenting 215 concerts. In 1859 Rubinstein and Grand Duchess Elena founded the Russian Musical Society, which became St. Petersburg Conservatory in 1862. As director of the Conservatory (1862–67; 1887–93), Rubinstein did much to improve the status of musicians in Russia and to raise standards of performance, particularly in piano playing. However, in the 1860s he occupied a controversial position because of his espousal of Western European teaching methods and his outspoken attitude against nationalism in opera. Nevertheless, his advocacy of government-supported conservatories and opera theaters in every important Russian city and his ideas concerning the teaching of music in Russian schools are the basis for twentieth-century educational practices in Russia.

Only a few of Rubinstein's many works have achieved lasting popularity, among them the piano pieces *Melody in F* (Op. 3, No. 1) and *Kamennïyostrov* (Rocky island), Piano Concerto No. 4, and, in Russia, the opera *Demon* (The demon; 1871), which has some nationalistic tendencies. Most of his music is Western

European in style, reflecting particularly the influence of Mendelssohn and Meyerbeer. Rubinstein was the first Russian to achieve success as an interpreter (pianist, conductor) of other composers' works and as composer.

CZECHOSLOVAKIA

The country known as Czechoslovakia was created in 1918 from the Habsburg territories of Bohemia, Moravia, and Slovakia. Slovakia had been conquered by the Magyars in 906 and had become part of Hungary. The kingdom of Bohemia, under strong Přemyslid rulers, dominated Moravia and formally incorporated it as a margravate in 1029. Bohemia suffered from imperial invasions and Hussite wars during the fifteenth century but remained autonomous, even after Emperor Ferdinand I was crowned King of Bohemia (1527). During the sixteenth century, emperors and nobility maintained excellent musical chapels at their castles in Prague. In 1620, after the Habsburgs defeated the Bohemian nobility at the Battle of Blaník, Bohemia and Moravia were taken into the Habsburg Empire as virtual provinces and were forced to adopt the imperial language (German) and religion (Catholicism). The Imperial Court at Vienna attracted the leading Bohemian musicians. There was an undercurrent of resentment in the Bohemian people that did not surface until the nationalistic movement in the nineteenth century. The Bohemian language (which eventually became the Czech language) was not used by musicians until the beginning of the nineteenth century, though its use in the arts was openly encouraged in 1862 when a Provisional Theater for Czech drama and music opened in Prague and Count Harrach sponsored a competition for operas and libretti. In May 1919, by formal decree, "Czech" (Bohemian) became the official language of "Czecho-Slovakia." In Moravia there was interest in folk song. In 1835 František Sušil published his first collection of Moravian folk songs. His work was continued by František Bartoš and Leoš Janáček. Czechoslovakia's first great nationalist composer was the Bohemian Bedřich Smetana.

BEDŘICH SMETANA

Smetana (1824–84) was raised in a German-language household, attended schools that taught in German, and did not learn to read and write the Bohemian language until the 1860s. His father taught him to play violin, and he had piano lessons from local musicians. At the gymnasium in Plzeň in 1840–43, Smetana studied diligently, but he also played piano for dancing at homes of the wealthy. At that time he met Kateřina Kolářová, with whom he played piano duets and for whom he composed many piano solos and duets (lost); in 1849 he and Kateřina married. Meantime, Smetana decided to become a professional musician and moved to Prague. In 1844–47 he was resident piano teacher to the family of Count Thun. During those years, Smetana studied harmony, theory, and composition. He was a virtuoso pianist, yet his concerts in Bohemia were not well attended. Nor did he have success when he opened a music institute. He had been composing piano music and dedicated *Six characteristic pieces* (Op. 1; 1847–48) to Liszt, who arranged for their publication.

The June 1848 Revolution in Prague failed. Smetana was unhappy with the political situation, and in 1856 he went to Sweden, where he concertized, directed a choral society, opened a singing school for ladies, and composed some character pieces and dance music. Liszt's symphonic poems inspired Smetana to write *Richard III* (1852; Shakespeare), *Wallensteins Lager* (1859; Schiller), and *Hakon Jarl* (1859–60; Oehlenschläger). Each symphonic poem is directly related to the drama and presents musically a series of

Bedřich Smetana. *(Historical Pictures Collection/Stock Montage)*

episodes from it, with descriptive themes representing important characters.

Kateřina died in 1859; the following year Smetana married Bettina Ferdinandova. In 1861, when he learned of plans for a Provisional Theater for Czech plays and operas and of a competition for a national opera, Smetana returned to Prague. There were few Czech operas— František Škroup's (1801–62) *Drátnik* (The Tinker; 1826), the first, is Mozartean in style. Jiři Macourek's *Žižka's Oak* (1847), concerning the warrior Jan Žižka, is more nationalistic.

Smetana's opera *Braniboři v Čechách* (The Brandenburgers in Bohemia; 1863) has a historical plot. The opera is sung throughout; the orchestral music is continuous, and the music does not resemble folk song. Smetana's opera was awarded the prize but disappointed the critics, who expected folklike entertainment and received drama. Smetana believed that composers of nationalistic music should not adhere strictly to folk songs but should employ contemporary compositional techniques and forms. He promoted late nineteenth-century music as well as nationalism in Bohemia.

Smetana designed his second opera for entertainment. Originally written in two acts, with spoken dialogue, the comedy *Prodana nevěsta* (The bartered bride; 1863–66) was a success from the outset. It is the only one of Smetana's operas to become popular outside Czechoslovakia. In 1870 Smetana expanded it to three acts, with recitatives replacing the spoken dialogue. Part of the opera's charm is its apparent simplicity, with melodies reminiscent of Bohemian folk song and realistic characters with individual personalities. There is a drinking chorus, and there are national dances. Smetana's achievement is remarkable when one realizes that at that time he did not know the Bohemian language well.

In 1866–74 Smetana was principal conductor of the Provisional Theater. He increased the repertoire, adding 16 Czech operas (2 were his) and 42 major works by European composers. After the diversion of *The Bartered Bride*, Smetana returned to his original aim: to compose a series of operas that would feed nationalistic sentiments and glorify his native land. For his next opera he chose the legend *Dalibor* (1865–67), in which he achieved unity through recurring themes and used thematic transformation effectively.

Smetana's fourth opera, *Libuše* (1869–72), commemorates the founding of the first Bohemian dynasty. Smetana specified that *Libuše* not be placed in opera repertoire but be reserved for special national festivals and commemorations. So effective is Smetana's nationalism in this opera that its performance was banned while Nazis occupied the country and again when the Soviet Union took over Czechoslovakia. The music of *Libuše* reflects Wagner's influence—themes are associated with characters in the manner of Leitmotif. *Libuše* is a magnificent work, and despite Smetana's directive, its performance should not be restricted to national commemorations.

While working on *Libuše*, Smetana was inspired to write *Má vlast* (My fatherland; 1872–80), a cycle of symphonic poems depicting Czech legend, history, and scenery. He planned nine but completed only six: (1) *Vyšehrad*, the old royal castle; (2) *Vltava*, the Moldau River; (3) *Šarka*, the legendary Amazon heroine; (4) *Z českých luhuv a háju* (From Bohemian fields and groves); (5) *Tábor*, the city and Hussite events there; and (6) *Blaník*, White Mountain. Two themes used in *Vyšehrad* recur in the cycle; these themes open and close the cycle. In the first symphonic poem whole-tone progressions are used. *Vltava* is a picture of nature with fleeting glimpses of Czech customs and history revealed as one follows the course of the river from its sources in the Šumava forest until it joins the Elbe beyond Prague. Both *Tábor* and *Blaník* are based on the fifteenth-century chorale *All ye warriors of God*, one of the oldest Hussite hymns. While working on *Vyšehrad*, Smetana's hearing began to fail; before he had completed *Blaník* he was totally deaf.

His next three operas are not particularly nationalistic, though they contain folk songs. *Dvě vdovy* (The Two Widows; 1873–74) is a comedy; *Hubička* (The Kiss; 1876) is romantic, with humor and pathos; and *Tajemství* (The Secret; 1877–78) is a comedy about a secret that was broadcast. Smetana's last completed opera, *Čertova stěna* (The Devil's Wall; 1879–82), satirizes those in the church who scheme to get power and wealth. In all Smetana's operas, except the original version of *The Bartered Bride*, he used continuous orchestral music, *accompagnato* recitative, declamatory arioso, and aria.

Smetana's compositions include orchestral music (absolute as well as program), sacred and secular choral works, solo songs with piano accompaniment, and chamber music. His two string quartets, in E minor and D minor, respectively, are excellent. The first quartet is autobiographical, *Z mého života* (From my life).

Smetana was concerned primarily with establishing a repertoire of nationalistic music for his native land. He cared little whether it was performed outside Czech boundaries. Antonin Dvořák (1841–1904) was also a sincere patriot and nationalist composer but achieved his greatest success outside Bohemia.

ANTONIN DVOŘÁK

Dvořák's ancestors were butchers and innkeepers and he was expected to follow one of those trades. Nevertheless, he had lessons on viola and organ and in music theory. He assisted in his father's butcher shop for a short time and then decided, at whatever cost, to be a musician. In 1857 he entered Prague Organ School to train as church musician. When he graduated in 1859, he had his certificate and second prize but no position, no piano, and no money for purchasing study scores. He found work in a small orchestra that played in restaurants and for dances. In 1862 he was hired as violist in the opera orchestra at the Provisional Theater, where, under Smetana's direction, he learned a great deal about nineteenth-century music by performing it.

By 1865 Dvořák had composed two operas, two symphonies, a Mass (B♭ major; lost), a song cycle, a 'cello concerto with piano accompaniment, some chamber music, and some piano pieces. In 1874 he submitted 15 compositions in the Austrian competition for poor young artists and was awarded the prize. Brahms influenced Simrock to publish some of Dvořák's works, and Simrock commissioned others. By 1880 Dvořák had written 4 more symphonies, a piano concerto, a violin concerto, a set of orchestral *Slavonic Dances,* the *Slavonic Rhapsodies,* 10 string quartets and numerous other chamber music works, many keyboard pieces, a *Stabat mater,* other sacred and secular choral works, some songs, and 4 more operas. His one-act comic operas with plots about peasants were especially popular.

During 1884–92 Dvořák concertized throughout Europe as conductor and violist. In 1884–85 he composed for the London Philharmonic what he considered his finest symphony, No. 7, in D minor. It follows traditional structure: sonata-form first movement, a

Antonin Dvořák. *(Shaffer Archive)*

melancholy Poco Adagio second, a Scherzo resembling a *furiant* third, and a powerful Finale that concludes on a major chord. The symphony is filled with intense emotional expression. Technically, it shows Dvořák to be a master of thematic manipulation. Dvořák composed, on commission, a Requiem Mass for performance at Birmingham (1891) and a *Te Deum laudamus* for New York celebrations commemorating the fourth centenary of the discovery of America (1892). He came to New York in 1892 to serve as director of the National Conservatory of Music and spent most of the next three years in the United States. He visited Bohemian communities throughout the country, especially that at Spillville, Iowa, and became interested in the music of black Americans. How much his music was influenced by that of black Americans cannot be determined, for previously he had used "Scottish snap" rhythm, minor keys with flatted seventh degree, and some pentatonic scales. While in the United States, Dvořák composed Symphony No. 9, *Z nového světa* (From the New World; E minor; 1893), the "American" String Quartet (No. 12, F major; 1893), and "American" String Quintet (E♭ major; 2 vln., 2 vla., vcl.; 1893). Symphony No. 9 is a cyclic work; its motto theme appears in every movement (ex. 24.2). A melody closely resembling the

EXAMPLE 24.2 Dvořák: Symphony No. 9, "From the New World," mvt. 1, theme 1, the motto theme.

spiritual *Swing low, sweet chariot* is heard in the first movement. The broad, lyrical melody of the Largo has become the song "Goin' home." In the Finale, themes from the previous movements are recalled in the manner of Beethoven's Ninth Symphony's Finale. Despite the evidence of American-inspired themes, such factors as modal melodies, use of the flatted seventh scale degree, and dronelike accompaniment lend a Bohemian touch to this symphony. Dvořák wrote for the standard symphony orchestra of his time. He thoroughly understood and effectively used the timbres and techniques of orchestral instruments.

Between 1895 and 1904 Dvořák composed his thirteenth and fourteenth string quartets, a 'cello concerto, his first symphonic poems, some songs, and five operas. The quartets, in G major and A♭ major, are some of his finest chamber music. In his last three operas, *Čert a Káča* (The Devil and Kate; 1899), *Rusalka* (1900), and *Armida* (1902–3), he eliminated formal recitative and used Leitmotifs and thematic transformation effectively.

From time to time, the influence of other composers can be detected in Dvořák's music, but Brahms exerted the greatest influence on his career. All Dvořák's music, whether program or absolute, contains elements that mark it Bohemian. National characteristics appear in his dance pieces, in the rhythms of dance movements or dance sections of his chamber music, in his programmatic overtures, in the subjects of some of his operas, and in many of his songs. One of Dvořák's contributions was making the music of Bohemian composers known outside the boundaries of his own country.

LEOŠ JANÁČEK

As composer, educator, theorist, and authority on Moravian folk music, Janáček (1854–1928) contributed a great deal to the music of Czechoslovakia. His organ school and its curriculum laid the foundation for Brno Conservatory. His theoretical writings are little known today, primarily because his terminology is difficult to

Leoš Janáček.

understand. His work with folk music stimulated research by others.

Janáček attended the choir school at the Augustinian monastery in Old Brno, Moravia, when the school was under the influence of the Cecelian movement; no instrumental music was taught, and vocal music was *a cappella*. He spent three years at the German College, completed the teaching curriculum at Czech Teachers' Institute, taught without pay for the required two years at the Institute School, and then studied for two years at Prague Organ School. In 1875 he returned to Brno to conduct the monastery choir and the male choral society. Soon he admitted women to the choral society. By supplementing that group with the monastery choir and Institute pupils, he had sufficient forces to perform large choral works.

Janáček's earliest works were liturgical pieces and a Mass (c. 1870; lost). In 1877 he composed an *a cappella* Offertory *Exaudi Deus* and a *Suite* for string orchestra. He spent 1879–80 in Leipzig studying composition; in 1880–81 he studied at Vienna Conservatory. Then he returned to Brno and founded and became director of the Organ School that later became Brno Conservatory. Not until 1885 did he resume composing. He dedicated to Dvořák four choruses for male voices, works whose bold modulations shocked Dvořák. Next Janáček composed the opera *Šarka* (1887–88; perf. 1925).

In 1888 Janáček helped František Bartoš (1837–1906) collect Moravian folk songs and assisted in preparing that collection for publication. Janáček made arrangements of some folk song melodies (e.g., *V Lašské tance* [Dances from Lašsko]) and used some folk songs in *Suite* for orchestra (Op. 3, 1891), a folk ballet, and the one-act opera *Počátek románu* (The beginning of a romance; 1891). The opera music was chiefly folk dances with vocal lines added.

In his next opera, *Jenůfa* (also called *Její pastorkyňa,* Her foster-daughter; 1894–1903), Janáček relied heavily on musical monologue; there are some choruses but few duets and ensembles. Folk melodies are well integrated. While writing *Jenůfa* he studied carefully the patterns of speaking voices to determine their "speech-melody"—the rhythms and pitch inflections of voices in normal speech—and incorporated what he learned into the writing of musical monologues in his operas. He preferred prose libretti. Much of the time, the orchestral and vocal lines differ—yet, at important points, they are united lyrically and rhythmically.

During the next 12 years Janáček wrote three more operas, a Mass and several other liturgical settings, some secular choruses, a few cantatas, a symphonic poem, and a little chamber music. Recognition did not come to Janáček until 1915–16, when the Prague National Opera accepted *Jenůfa* into its repertoire.

During the last decade of his life Janáček created the operas *Kaťa Kabanová* (1919–21), *Příhody Lišky Bystroušky* (The adventures of the vixen Bystrouška; 1921–23), *Věc Makropulos* (The Makropulos affair; 1923–25), and *Z mrtvého domu* (From the house of the dead; 1927–28). In *The adventures of the vixen Bystrouška,* he specified the use of children's voices because of the animals; in his other operas he did not want children's voices used. In his vocal music he showed decided preference for soprano and high tenor parts and tended to use alto solo voices sparingly.

After 1905, Janáček preferred to notate his music without key signatures; his string quartets, violin sonata, and other works do not have specified keys. Because of his interest in Moravian folk songs, he was predisposed toward modality and pentatonic scales. Also borrowed from Moravian folk song are mirror rhythms and the technique of immediately repeating a phrase or melody but displacing the rhythm in the repetition.

One of Janáček's outstanding choral works is *Glagolská mše* (Glagolitic Mass; 1928), setting an Old Slavic text. His finest instrumental works are the two string quartets (No. 1, 1923; No. 2, 1928), the Violin Sonata (1921), *Mládí* (Youth; 1924; wind sextet), and *Vojenská Symfonietta* (Military Sinfonietta; 1926), his last completed orchestral work, created for the Sokol festival. The symphony *Dunaj* (Danube, 1923–28), unfinished when Janáček died, was completed in 1948 by his pupil Osvald Chlubna (1893–1971) and was given its North American première by the St. Louis Symphony in May 1988.

Scandinavia

Sweden

In Sweden, during the first half of the nineteenth century, most of the musical activity was in the hands of the middle class. Music societies existed in major cities, and music publishing firms were active. By 1866 Stockholm Conservatory was providing a good music curriculum. Around midcentury, Romantic elements entered a Swedish style that had been primarily Classic. In the late nineteenth century, the outstanding Swedish composer was Johan A. Söderman (1832–76), who wrote incidental music for 80 plays. Most of his other extant works are vocal; a few orchestral pieces, a piano quartet, and a piano fantasia survive. His works are historically significant because of his incorporation of elements of Swedish folk music.

The first symphony orchestras were established in Sweden c. 1900. Almost all the music of Hugo Alfvén (1872–1960) is programmatic, much of it descriptive of Sweden and colored by folk music. *Midsommarvaka* (Midsummer vigil; orch.; 1903) is an example. Wilhelm Stenhammar's (1871–1927) music is tinged with Swedish color but without quotations from folk material. His *Serenade* (F major; orch.; 1911–13, rev. 1919) contains Impressionistic passages.

Norway

Norway achieved independence from Denmark in 1814 but was united with Sweden from 1814 to 1905. During the nineteenth century, Norwegian nationalism increased, with periodic agitation for independence. Virtuoso violinist Ole Bull (1818–70) concertized throughout the world, published a collection of folk songs arranged for piano (1852), and helped found the Norwegian Society for the Advancement of the National Element in Art and Literature (1859). In some of his ensemble pieces (e.g., *Norges fjelde* [Norway's mountains; 1832]) he included the Hardanger fiddle, a kind of violin with sympathetic strings, and incorporated some Norwegian folk songs and the *slåtter,* a Norwegian dance. Bull was intensely patriotic, wanting independence for Norway and supporting Norwegian culture by encouraging native authors and composers, by founding a national theater, and by advocating a national conservatory of music.

Richard Nordraak's (1842–66) music is strongly nationalistic. His extant works constitute six songs, five *a cappella* choruses, some piano solos, and the Norwegian national anthem, *Ja, vi elsker dette landet* (Yes, we love this land; 1864).

Norway's most important nationalist-Romantic composer was Edvard Hagerup Grieg (1843–1907). His first music lessons were from his mother, Gesine Hagerup Grieg, an excellent amateur pianist. Edvard's father was British consul at Bergen, and musical gatherings were held regularly at the Grieg home. Edvard's piano playing attracted the attention of Ole Bull, who influenced the Griegs to send Edvard to Leipzig Conservatory.

Grieg knew almost nothing about Norwegian nationalism and Norwegian folk music until he spent the summer of 1864 with Ole Bull at Osterøy. After meeting Nordraak in 1865, Grieg wrote nationalistic-Romantic Norwegian music. His first compositions influenced by folk idioms are *Humoresker* (4 Humoresques, Op. 6, piano; 1865). The Piano Sonata, Op. 7 (E minor; 1865), and piano/violin Sonata No. 1 (F major; 1865) are not nationalistic, but national traits reappear in the first set of *Lyric Pieces* (Op. 12, piano; 1867). One of Grieg's finest works for piano is *Ballade in Form von Variationen* . . . (G minor, Op. 24; 1875–76), theme and variations on the folk song *Den nordlandske bondestand* (The northern peasantry). Some of his best work is his incidental music for plays, especially the 23 pieces for Ibsen's *Peer Gynt* (1874–75)—music for solo voices, chorus, and orchestra. When heard consecutively, in the order in which they occur in the play, those 23 pieces have tremendous dramatic impact. This is not apparent in the arrangement of the 8 pieces that form the two orchestral *Peer Gynt Suites.*

Other significant works by Grieg include the Piano Concerto (A minor, 1868), 10 sets of *Lyric Pieces, Folkelivsbilleder* (Pictures from country life, Op. 19; 1870–71), 3 piano/violin sonatas (F major, 1865; G major, 1867; C minor, 1886–87), and the string quartet in G minor (1877–78). Grieg, in his quartet, used chromatically altered chords within functional tonal harmony, occasionally wrote parallel chords and chord streams, and sustained chords as pedals for moving parts. The entire quartet is based on a bit of melody from *Spillemaend* (Minstrel), one of the six settings of Ibsen's poems comprising Grieg's Op. 25 (1876). The quartet was the model for Debussy's string quartet, also in G minor (1893).

National characteristics appearing in Grieg's works are the Hardanger fiddle, drone basses, modal tendencies in melodies and sometimes in harmonies (particularly Lydian and Aeolian), and national dance rhythms, especially the *slåtter,* in which $\frac{3}{4}$ and $\frac{6}{8}$ meter rhythms are combined.

The principal Danish composer at the end of the nineteenth century was Carl Nielsen (1865–1931), son of painter Niels Jørgensen. In accordance with Danish custom, Carl's surname was derived from his father's given name (son of Niels = Nielsen). Nielsen's parents were amateur musicians; he heard a great deal of music at home. He learned to play violin, cornet, and piano. In 1884–86, Nielsen studied at Copenhagen Conservatory and concentrated on violin. The few compositions that he wrote before 1886 are Haydnesque. In 1889 Nielsen worked as a violinist in the royal chapel. In 1890–91 he traveled in Europe; in Paris he met Anne Brodersen, a sculptress, and they married. When they returned to Denmark, he completed his Symphony No. 1 (G minor, Op. 7; 1890–92), in which Brahms's influence is apparent.

Around 1900 Nielsen's personal compositional style began to emerge—a style rooted in Classicism and strongly influenced by the village music he heard as a child. His early works show a preference for tonal functional harmony with rather fast harmonic rhythm. In the 1890s, in an endeavor to create music that had more intense expression, he began to use what he termed "extended tonality"—to consider all 12 semitones within a key as being autonomous, each pitch directly related to the tonic. This allowed free use of chromaticism within a key. Thus, Nielsen regarded his music as being in a certain key, but he could modulate freely from one key to another because he was not dealing with functional harmony. Intervals, too, were considered equal—there was no functional difference between major and minor thirds or between major and minor sevenths. Because of this, his music sometimes sounds quite modal. Polytonal and atonal passages appear in his late works. He created themes first and preferred concise motives to melodies; the themes then dictated the harmonies. He was adept at motivic development and thematic variation and transformation, and he was skilled at counterpoint. Nielsen's treatment of phrasing underwent change also. In his early works, he used symmetrical phrases, usually four measures long; gradually, he worked toward the metrically free phrasing that appears in his late works. Polyphony became more important to Nielsen, and in his Symphonies No. 4 ("The Inextinguishable"; 1916) and No. 5 (1922) he wrote "group polyphony," treating groups of orchestral instruments polyphonically.

Nielsen composed operas, incidental music for plays, cantatas, songs, choral works, chamber music, concertos, and orchestral works. His finest orchestral work and the one that best exemplifies his mature style is *Symphony No. 3: Sinfonia espansiva* (Expansive symphony, Op. 27; 1910–11). His string quartets, Op. 14 (E♭ major; 1898) and Op. 44 (F major; 1919), are excellent; his best-known work is probably Symphony No. 5 (Op. 50, 1922).

FINLAND

Finland had no significant composers of art music until after 1750; then, the composers studied in Germany and wrote music that was Germanic. During the Reformation, Finland had become Lutheran, and the chorale occupies a central place in Finnish church services. In 1809, Finland became a grand duchy in the Russian empire. There were strong feelings of Finnish nationalism, but not until 1917 did Finland achieve independence.

The two leading Finnish composers in the 1880s were Robert Kajanus (1856–1933) and Martin Wegelius (1846–1906). Wegelius founded Helsinki Music College (1882) and taught Jean Sibelius, Kajanus founded the first permanent orchestra in Helsinki (1882). His symphonic poem *Aino* (1885), based on Finland's epic poem *Kalevala,* inspired Sibelius to compose music based on the *Kalevala.*

Jean Sibelius (1865–1957) began serious study of the violin when he was 14. He played in the family trio and hoped to become a virtuoso soloist. His first compositions were chamber music: a violin/'cello piece written when he was 10, a Piano Trio (A minor), a Piano Quartet (E minor), and a violin/piano Sonata (D minor), all written in 1881–82.

Sibelius had always been interested in Swedish nature poetry, Norse legend, and the saga of Finland, *Kalevala.* After hearing Kajanus's *Aino,* Sibelius decided to write some orchestral music, turned to the *Kalevala* for inspiration, and wrote *Kullervo,* a large five-movement symphony whose central movement, "Kullervo and his Sister," incorporates soprano and baritone solos and male chorus. From the quality of the vocal writing and the dramatic propulsion of that movement, it is apparent that Sibelius could have written opera had he chosen to do so. Sibelius's feelings of nationalism were strong and deep-seated; he expressed them through program music rather than by consciously incorporating folk materials into his music. Folk music colored some of his compositions, but he did not collect folk music and did not deliberately use it in his works.

After the première of *Kullervo* (1892) Sibelius was recognized as Finland's leading composer. His next orchestral works were *En saga* (1892); the tone poems *Skogsrået* (The wood-nymph; 1894) and *Vårsång* (Spring song; 1895), both unpublished; and *Lemminkäissarja* (Lemminkäinen suite; 1895). That suite is a powerful symphonic work, consisting of four large movements: *Lemminkäinen and the island maidens, Lemminkäinen in Tuonela, The swan of Tuonela,* and *Lemminkäinen's return.* Usually, *The swan of Tuonela* is performed as an independent piece. Sibelius wrote four works based on Viktor Rydberg's poem *Skogsrået:* a song setting it, a piano piece, a tone poem, and a melodrama (narrator, pno., 2 hns., stgs.), all Op. 15. These works were relocated early in 1996 and recorded for the first time.

Late in 1897 the Finnish government awarded Sibelius a small pension, then extended it to a life pension. In 1899, for a pageant presented at the Press Pension Celebrations, Sibelius wrote *Scènes historiques* (Historical scenes) and *Finlandia.* Finnish patriotism was running high, and some of the celebrations amounted to rallies. *Finlandia* fueled the patriotic fires considerably. A portion of that symphonic poem has become a hymn and is included in many Protestant hymnals.

Sibelius composed seven symphonies, some overtures and other orchestral pieces, a violin concerto (D minor; 1903), 2 violin/piano sonatas (D minor, F major), almost two dozen other works for violin and piano, some string quartets and other chamber music, incidental music for plays, more than 100 songs, and many choral works. His last string quartet, *Voces intimae* (Intimate voices, D minor, 1909), is excellent. Important programmatic orchestral works, besides those already mentioned, are the fantasia *Pohjolan tytär* (Pohjola's daughter; 1906) and *Tapiola* (1926). His finest symphony is No. 6, but it is seldom performed.

Sibelius's symphonic achievements are summed up in Symphony No. 7 (C major, Op. 105; 1924), which he called *Fantastica sinfonica* (Fantastic symphony). It is a highly unified work whose single movement cannot be squeezed into any stereotyped formal pattern. The music undergoes changes in character and tempo, suggesting now a scherzo, then a slow movement or an intermezzo, merged so skillfully that one can only approximate the point at which the changes actually occur. Sibelius's mastery of thematic metamorphosis is evident.

In general, Sibelius's music is sombre, serious, grand, majestic, and at times, sweeping. In some works he wrote phrases that are seemingly conversational between two solo instruments and some long solo passages. Some of the compositions he wrote c. 1908–9, when he underwent several operations for suspected throat cancer and had to give up alcohol and cigar smoking, are austere. In 1914 he visited the United States, taught at the New England Conservatory for a short time, and composed *Aallottaret* (The oceansides). During World War I, the October 1918 Revolution in Finland, and the ensuing civil war instigated by Finnish communists, Sibelius composed very little. In the 1920s he wrote much music but only four major works: two symphonies, incidental music for Shakespeare's *The Tempest,* and *tapiola.* Supposedly, he completed an Eighth Symphony in 1929, but it has been lost or destroyed. No later works are known.

SPAIN

In the early nineteenth century, Italian opera infiltrated Spain; however, Spanish popular taste was not favorably inclined toward drama that was sung throughout, and composers had greater success with zarzuela, in which music was important but intermittent. Francisco Barbieri (1823–94), musicologist and composer, was a vital force in eradicating foreign elements from Spanish theater. Though he enjoyed opera and wrote some, he concentrated on zarzuela and wrote more than 70 of them, infusing them with characteristic elements of Spanish folk music. He organized symphonic groups also and located a large amount of fifteenth- and sixteenth-century Spanish music that he edited and published as *Cancionero musical de Palacio.*

Both Federico Chueca (1845–1906) and Ruperto Chapí (1851–1909) worked in Madrid. Chueca composed catchy melodies but often relied on others to orchestrate them. His tuneful zarzuelas appealed to Madrid's lower-class folk; Chapí's attracted the middle- and upper-class populace. In 1873 Chapí wrote the zarzuela *Abel y Cain* and the symphonic suite *La corte de Granada* (The Granada Court), a four-movement Moorish fantasia; in 1875 his opera *La hija de Jeftá* (Jephta's daughter) appeared. Commencing with *Musica clasica* (1880), a stream of zarzuelas—more than 100 of them—poured from his pen. *La revoltosa* (The rebellious; 1897) and *La tempesta* (The tempest; 1882; melodrama) are still popular favorites. Frequently, in his zarzuelas he used dance rhythms, and sometimes he included popular songs (e.g., the *guijaras,* which is notated in $\frac{6}{8}$ but accented as if in $\frac{3}{4}$ meter). His style was distinctive—Spanish composers refer to it as *estilo chapiano.*

Tomás Bréton (1850–1923) composed nine operas with Spanish librettos but created zarzuela and *sainete* (comedy) masterpieces e.g., *La verbena de la paloma* (The dove festival; 1897), which was very popular in Spain and South America and is considered a classic.

Felipe Pedrell (1841–1922) was a chorister at Tortosa Cathedral; except for that training, he was self-taught in music. In 1873 he became deputy director of Barcelona's Teatro Circo Light Opera Company and began to compose operas; however, during an extended stay in Rome (1876–77), he became interested in early music and in 1882 abandoned composition for musicology, concentrating on Spanish music. He edited the *opera omnia* of Victoria, and his many critical writings and editions of Spanish liturgical music contributed significantly to the revival of interest in that genre. Pedrell was an inspiration to younger Spanish composers and a major influence on the work of Albéniz and Granados.

Isaac Albéniz (1860–1909), a child prodigy, first performed in public as pianist at age 4 and made his first concert tour with his father in 1868. Though Isaac was enrolled in conservatories, at least twice he ran away to concertize, first in Spain, then in the Americas. He returned to Madrid briefly in 1877; in 1883 he settled in Barcelona. His early virtuosic compositions for piano show Liszt's influence, but the many piano works Albéniz composed after he met Pedrell (c. 1883) reflect his Spanish heritage, and after 1890 his works exhibit elements of Spanish folk music increasingly. Albéniz's most significant theater works are the zarzuela *San Antonio de la Flórida* (1894) and the comedy *Pepita Jiménez* (1896). His piano music is of higher quality, especially his masterwork, *Suite Iberia* (4 books; 1906–9), a series of technically complex works in which, at times, piano simulates guitar or castanets. Two piano works left unfinished at the time of his death, *Navarra* and *Azalejos*, were completed by de Sévérac and Granados, respectively.

Enrique Granados (1867–1916) enjoyed a career as concert pianist and achieved his first success as a composer with the zarzuela *María del Carmen* (1898). Composition lessons with Pedrell had directed him toward a nationalistic style. Yet Schumann's influence is apparent in some of Granados's small pieces for piano, and, though the music is Spanish, the overall literary themes of the song cycles *Tonadillas* and *Canciones Amatorias* are remarkably similar to those of Schumann's *Frauenliebe und -leben* and *Dichterliebe*. Granados was an excellent painter; he was particularly interested in Goya's etchings and expressed his admiration for them in the piano suite *Goyescas* (first perf. 1911). The pieces are linked musically to *Tonadillas* and evidence the influence of D. Scarlatti's *essercizi* also. Granados's opera *Goyescas*, based on the suite music, was premiered by the New York Metropolitan Opera in January 1916. Immediately thereafter, Granados presented a piano recital at the White House. Then, he and his wife embarked for Spain by way of London and were among the casualties when the steamer Sussex was torpedoed in the English Channel on 24 March.

Musically, Granados expressed his view of Spain as it existed at the end of the eighteenth century; Albéniz,

in *Iberia*, presented a more contemporary view. What Barbieri, Bréton, Chueca, and Chapí accomplished for Spanish music locally, Albéniz and Granados achieved internationally.

BRITAIN

In Britain, nationalism was more prominent in the music of Ireland and Scotland than in England itself. The Irish and Scottish hope for their own kingdoms never died, and their pride in their national background was preserved in their literature and folk music. Music in England was cosmopolitan and had been dominated by foreigners since the time of Handel. There had been little opportunity anywhere for British composers. Near the end of the nineteenth century the tide began to turn.

The folk element was always present in the music of Wales. The Welsh treasure their Celtic heritage and have maintained links with their historical past through their unique language and their music. Thus, Welsh music was conscious nationalism with a different purpose than that of most countries in the nineteenth century. The *eisteddfod* (session), a competitive festival mainly for music and literature, originated in medieval times but became popular in the eighteenth century. The National Eisteddfod was established in 1880 and has been held annually since that time. The most important prizes are Chief Choral and Chief Male Voice. In the twentieth century, Welsh communities in the United States have held annual *Cymanfa Ganu* (hymn sing) sessions early in September.

Welsh composer Joseph Parry (1841–1903) composed songs and glees with Welsh texts and wrote the first Welsh opera, *Blodwen* (1878). He composed five operas, most of them on Welsh and English subjects; several oratorios and cantatas; some orchestral music; and edited and harmonized a six-volume collection of Welsh songs. The most famous of his approximately 400 hymn tunes is *Aberystwyth* (1879).

Other Welsh composers who made significant contributions to choral music repertoire are David Evans (1834–1913) and David Jenkins (1849–1915). David V. Thomas (1873–1934) set medieval Welsh poetry to music, and the works of David de Lloyd (1883–1948) were influenced by Welsh folk music.

Both Irish and English elements are present in the works of Charles V. Stanford (1851–1924). Among his orchestral works are five Irish Rhapsodies (1901–14), two sets of Irish dances, *Symphony No. 3, "Irish,"* and *Irish Concertino* (vln., vcl., orch.). He published three volumes of Irish folk song arrangements (130 songs). Stanford's compositions include a Mass, several choral works, seven symphonies, and six operas.

Alexander Mackenzie (1847–1935) prepared and published arrangements of Scottish folk songs, and many of his compositions contain folk-music elements. Among such works are the *Pibroch Suite* (vln., orch.; 1889), the *Highland Ballad* (vln., orch., 1893), *Scottish Concerto* (pno., orch.; 1897), three orchestral rhapsodies (*Scottish Rhapsody No. 1* [1880], *Burns, Scottish Rhapsody No. 2* [1881], and *Tam o'Shanter, Scottish Rhapsody No. 3* [1911]), and the piano suite *In the Scottish Highlands* (1881). In addition, he composed *Canadian Rhapsody* (1905), the suite *London Day by Day,* and several excellent cantatas and oratorios.

UNITED STATES

The music of American Indians influenced the work of Arthur Farwell (1877–1952) and Charles W. Cadman (1881–1946). Cadman was interested in Indian music, spent several months on Omaha and Winnebago reservations, made recordings of Indian songs, and arranged and published some of them. "At Dawning" and "From the Land of the Sky-blue Water" from *Four American Indian Songs* were very popular. He organized and presented a series of lecture-recitals with Omaha Indian Princess Tsianina Redfeather, mezzo-soprano, a descendant of Tecumseh. Cadman used Indian melodies in many of his compositions. His most successful work was the opera *Shanewis or The Robin Woman* (1918), based on the life of Redfeather. *Shanewis* was performed by The Metropolitan Opera in 1918 and 1919.

Farwell's primary interest was American Indian music, but he worked with Anglo-American folk song and the music of Spanish-Americans, blacks, and cowboys also. Failing to find a publisher for *American Indian Melodies* (1900), he founded Wa-Wan Press, which published music by contemporary American composers. Farwell's compositions range from *Navajo*

War Dance No. 1 to settings of Emily Dickinson poems, from preludes and fugues to *Polytonal Studies.*

SUMMARY

In the last third of the nineteenth century, three kinds of nationalism were apparent in music: a nation's revival of its folk music and absorption of it into art music, use of a national element as accessory to a basically cosmopolitan style, and use of national elements as basic features of a composition.

Russians and Czechoslovakians were foremost among nationalist composers. Until well into the nineteenth century, music in Russia was dominated by foreigners. No Russian musical compositions of real worth were created before Glinka's *A Life for the Tsar'* (1836). More influential was Dargomïzhsky, who sought to avoid everything Italianate and used the Russian language, whole-tone scales and harmonizations, and notation without key signatures. Also significant were the composers whom Stasov called the *moguchaya kuchka:* Balakirev, Cui, Musorgsky, Rimsky-Korsakov, and Borodin. The *moguchaya kuchka* is often viewed as a highly organized group that worked aggressively for Russian nationalism and totally rejected all aspects of Western European and traditional music. Such was not the case. The talents of the members of the group were not equal, and their interests were diverse. They did not totally reject the forms and techniques of traditional European music and break out new paths. Balakirev helped develop the talents of each of those he drew into his circle, but each of "The Five" promoted Russian nationalism in his own way. Balakirev instilled in his colleagues and students the belief that Russian composers could rival Western European composers and that great composers should teach and pass on their techniques to their students. Musorgsky was the most talented and the most nationalistic of Balakirev's disciples; his opera *Boris Godunov* is a landmark in Russian music. Rimsky-Korsakov wrote a textbook on orchestration and was influential as the teacher of Glazounov and Stravinsky.

Czechoslovakia's first great nationalist composer was Smetana, who encouraged the composition of Czech operas and is especially honored for his cycle of nationalistic symphonic poems, *Má Vlast.* Smetana was concerned primarily with establishing a repertoire of nationalistic music for his country; Dvořák made the music of Bohemian composers known outside of Czechoslovakia. Janáček worked with Bartoš in collecting, editing, and publishing Moravian folk songs; founded an Organ School that was the basis for Brno Conservatory; and wrote some excellent music.

In Scandinavia, the most important composers were Södermann and Alfvén in Sweden, Grieg in Norway, and Nielsen in Denmark. Both Kajanus and Sibelius, the two leading composers in Finland, composed music based on Finland's legends and epic poetry.

Spanish popular taste favored the zarzuela, hundreds of which were written in the late nineteenth century. Those by Chueca appealed to the lower classes; those by Chapí attracted middle- and upper-class audiences. Barbieri was a vital force in eradicating foreign elements from Spanish theater; Pedrell's scholarly writings and editions of Spanish liturgical music contributed to the revival of interest in that genre. The zarzuelas written by Barbieri, Bréton, Chueca, and Chapí were known throughout Spain; the works of Albéniz and Granados were acclaimed internationally.

The folk element was always present in the music of Wales. The Welsh have maintained links with their historical past through their unique language and their music.

In the United States, few composers were inspired by or tapped the wealth of indigenous material that surrounded them—Indian tribal melodies, black spirituals, New England hymns, and gospel songs. The music of Farwell and Cadman reflects their interest in the music of the American Indians.

LATE NINETEENTH-CENTURY AND EARLY TWENTIETH-CENTURY MUSIC

Modern nationalism was evident politically in the late nineteenth century. Italy was united, and Rome was its capital (instead of being capital of the papacy); a German nation was formally established; and an Austro-Hungarian empire was set up with limited self-government for its two halves, each of which desired democracy. This was an era of increased exploration and colonization to expand for economic reasons, especially into Africa and Asia. Society was increasingly becoming more literate and more democratic, and artists and composers were more dependent on bourgeois patronage than on aristocracy. In general, composers fared better than artists in marketing their wares. Some of the great symphony orchestras were founded, and the interpretive art of orchestral conducting became a lucrative career choice and a source of adulation. In the mid-nineteenth century there was a trend in the fine arts toward depiction of political events and cultural conditions realistically, as Honoré Daumier (1808–79) did in *Rue Transnonain, April 14, 1834* and *The Third-Class Carriage* (c. 1862). As the century advanced, the movement expanded into literature, and European authors created works on subjects that varied from the romantic bohemianism of garret living and casual sex life to morbid and more shocking topics expressed in brutal passions, fierce hatred, and murder. Characters were drawn from bourgeois and lower social classes, and the writings were filled with strong local color. This movement is known as Realism. Realism is apparent in the novels of Émile Zola and Thomas Hardy, the short stories of Guy de Maupassant, and the plays of Henrik Ibsen. But the Symbolist school of French poets—Stéphane Mallarmé (1842–98) was one—favored allusion rather than literal depiction. Personal independence was prized, and individual initiative led to innovations, especially in the arts.

Paris was the cultural capital of Europe. International expositions there in 1889 and 1900 presented much that was spectacular, including the Eiffel Tower, the engineering triumph of A. G. Eiffel (1832–1923), and the Gallery of Machines (now demolished). The 1889 exhibit featured non-Western musics performed by native Asiatic ensembles, including Indonesian gamelan. Innovations are visible in the Impressionistic art of Monet, Cézanne, Renoir, Degas, and Pissaro and in the restless energy expressed by many of Auguste Rodin's (1840–1917) sculptures.

RUSSIAN COMPOSERS

Some Russian composers worked along traditional Western lines, writing programmatic and/or absolute Romantic music and occasionally including some national characteristics but not to the extent that the composers or their music could be called nationalistic. Two such composers were Pyotr Il'yich Tchaikovsky (1840–93) and Sergey Rakhmaninov (1873–1943).

PYOTR TCHAIKOVSKY

Tchaikovsky was exposed to Western European music from his infancy—the family owned an orchestrion, a kind of automatophon controlled by pinned cylinders or punched cards that played orchestral music and excerpts from operas. When the family moved to St. Petersburg in 1848, Pyotr had piano lessons, and in 1850 he saw Glinka's *A Life for the Tsar'*. Tchaikovsky was educated at the School of Jurisprudence and, at the age of 19, became a government clerk in the Ministry of Justice. That work provided his living, but he was interested in music and enrolled in classes at the Russian Musical Society. He studied composition with Rubinstein and in 1863 resigned from the Ministry of Justice to become a full-time student at St. Petersburg Conservatory. To help meet expenses, he taught piano and theory lessons privately. In 1865 his graduation exercise, a cantata on Schiller's *An die Freude* (To Joy), won a silver medal. The following year, Tchaikovsky became professor of theory at Moscow Conservatory. In Moscow he met his future publisher and made friends who became powerful allies. He composed in earnest, often finding it very hard work. Frequently, he consulted other composers about his works. Balakirev caused him to revise the *Overture-fantasy Romeo and Juliet* three times, and that work became Tchaikovsky's first real success. Much as he valued Balakirev's criticism, Tchaikovsky never joined his circle.

In 1868–74 Tchaikovsky regularly contributed articles on music criticism to Moscow journals, and in 1871 his *Guide to the Practical Study of Harmony* was published. He made numerous trips to major European music centers and in 1891 visited the United States. During c. 1876–c. 1890 he enjoyed the patronage of Nadezhda von Meck, a wealthy widow who provided him an annual subsidy and commissioned works. Tchaikovsky and Meck never met; their association was maintained entirely by correspondence.

For all his adult life, Tchaikovsky's homosexuality was a great concern to him and ultimately interfered with his career. His brief marriage to Antonina Milyukova, which he hoped might offer some solution to his problems, only added to his anguish. It is presumed that his death, on 6 November 1893, nine days after he completed Symphony No. 6, was suicide.

Tchaikovsky's surviving works include 10 operas; 3 ballets; 6 numbered symphonies and the programmatic symphony *Manfred*; the symphonic poem *Fatum* (Fate; C minor; 1868); several concert overtures, orchestral fantasias, suites, and marches; 3 piano concerti; a violin concerto; *Variations on a Rococo Theme* ('cello, orch.); 3 string quartets and a piano trio; and numerous vocal works and piano solos. Many of his works are standard repertoire: Symphonies Nos. 4 (F minor; 1877), 5 (E minor; 1888), and 6 (B minor; 1893); the ballets *Swan Lake* (1875–76), *The Sleeping Beauty* (1888–89), and *The Nutcracker* (1891–92); Piano Concerto No. 1 (B♭ major; 1874–75); the Violin Concerto (D major; 1878); *Overture-fantasy Romeo and Juliet* (B minor; 1869); *Serenade* (C major; 1880; strings); and *Variations on a Rococo Theme* (A major; 1876). His Violin Concerto is one of the finest and one of the most difficult in the repertoire.

Every Christmas season *The Nutcracker* ballet is performed hundreds of times in the United States alone. In the *Danse de la fée dragée* (Dance of the sugarplum

Pyotr I. Tchaikovsky *(Courtesy of the Free Library of Philadelphia)*

fairy) Tchaikovsky featured the *célesta,* a keyboard metallophone patented by Auguste Mustel in 1886. Tchaikovsky had seen the instrument in Paris and was the first to write an orchestral part for it.

Much of Tchaikovsky's music is orchestral or involves orchestra. His symphonic writing is a mixture of absolute and program music. His symphonic poems are programmatic, but the fact that some of his symphonies bear titles does not mean that they have programs. *Manfred,* based on Byron's drama, was modeled after Berlioz's *Harold en Italie* and *Symphonie fantastique.* The opening theme of *Manfred* appears in each movement much in the manner of the *idée fixe* of *Symphonie fantastique* and the theme in *Harold in Italy.* *Manfred* contains some of Tchaikovsky's finest orchestral writing and deserves to be heard more often. Symphonies Nos. 4, 5, and 6 are frequently performed.

Five of the six symphonies have four movements; No. 3 has five. The finales of all but No. 6 are festive. The first symphony, "Winter Daydreams," has programmatic origins; its first two movements bear subtitles, and the folk melody "The gardens bloomed" appears in the finale. Symphony No. 2, named "Little Russian" by a critic in 1896, contains some Ukrainian folk tunes. Though Symphony No. 4 opens with a statement of the motto theme that Tchaikovsky termed "Fate," the work is absolute music. Subjective programmatic sketches exist for Nos. 5 and 6. An outline that Tchaikovsky made in 1892 for a "program symphony" on "Life"—a work beginning with passion and activity and ending with collapse and death—has been linked to No. 6, which seems to express his depressing, fatalistic view of life. Symphony No. 5 is cyclic—its motto theme, borrowed from Glinka's *A Life for the Tsar',* appears in all four movements (ex. 25.1). Tchaikovsky's liking for the waltz is apparent in his treatment of some thematic material in the first movement, and the third movement is a waltz. In Symphony No. 6, which Tchaikovsky labeled *Pathétique,* the coloring of the first and last movements is dark and the mood gloomy; in the first movement trombones sound a portion of the Russian Orthodox Requiem.

Nationalism is present in Tchaikovsky's operas *Evgeny Onegin* (Eugene Onegin; 1877–78) and *Charodeyka* (The sorceress; 1885–87). Folk songs and other Russian materials appear in some of his other works but not as conscious nationalism. Dance tunes and rhythms, especially waltzes, characterize all his music except the sacred works. Tchaikovsky had a gift for writing broad, lyrical melodies of great beauty, which he harmonized and orchestrated effectively. Such melodies usually are not suitable for thematic development, and this explains, in part, the long-standing criticism that one of Tchaikovsky's weaknesses is his inability to manipulate material in thematic development. His music is rhythmically strong, and he enjoyed using unusual meters (e.g., the $\frac{5}{4}$ of the waltzlike second movement of Symphony No. 6).

The textures and harmonies Tchaikovsky used are basically Western European; in his later works he increasingly included seventh chords. His chromaticism is decorative rather than fundamental, but frequently, in a major key, he built a triad on the flatted submediant. Tchaikovsky was a master of instrumental color and adeptly combined instrumental timbres to achieve the exact tone color he wanted, as in blending English horn and viola on the second theme in *Romeo and Juliet.* Tchaikovsky's music has remained popular in Russia and always had approval of the Soviet government.

Sergey Rakhmaninov

Rakhmaninov was one of the finest pianists of his time and is considered the last of the great Russian Romantic composers. The third of six children, he received his first piano lessons from his mother, then studied at St. Petersburg Conservatory. When his concern for his parents' marital difficulties caused him emotional disturbances and interfered with his studies, he was transferred to Moscow Conservatory and lived in the home of Nicolay Zverev, whose musical circle included Anton Rubinstein and Tchaikovsky. Their influence is seen in Rakhmaninov's early works. He graduated in piano in 1891 and in composition in 1892; his graduation composition was the one-act opera *Aleko,* based

EXAMPLE 25.1 Tchaikovsky: Symphony No. 5, mvt. 1, mm. 1–6 of clarinet part, the first presentation of the motto theme.

on Pushkin's poem *Tsigani* (The gypsies). That year Rakhmaninov signed a publishing contract. His first successful composition was the Prelude in C♯ minor, Op. 3 No. 2 (1892); the next to succeed was Piano Concerto No. 2 (1901). Both pieces have remained popular.

In 1902 Rakhmaninov married his cousin Natalya Satina. That year he began a triple-faceted career as piano soloist and conductor (at the Bolshoi Theatre and Moscow Philharmonic Society) and as composer. Because of the political unrest in Russia, he worked in Dresden part of each year; there he composed, among other works, Symphony No. 2 (1906–7) and the symphonic poem *Isle of the Dead* (1909), inspired by Arnold Böcklin's painting. The somber music depicts the sea, the rocky isle, and the gloomy atmosphere of death portrayed in the painting.

At the time of the Bolshevik revolution, Rakhmaninov accepted an invitation to concertize in Sweden, then he and his family emigrated to the United States, where they lived for the next 25 years. Rakhmaninov maintained a villa in Switzerland also; there he composed his *Rhapsody on a Theme of Paganini* (1934) and Third Symphony (1935).

The piano figures prominently in Rakhmaninov's works; he wrote idiomatically and expressively for it. Besides piano pieces and piano/orchestra works, his compositions comprise operas, chamber music, sacred and secular choral works, and purely orchestral music. He had a gift for melodic invention, thoroughly understood orchestration, and used individual instrumental tone qualities to advantage (e.g., he used alto saxophone in his last composition, *Symphonic Dances* [1940]). Frequently, he included liturgical chant in his works (e.g., the Russian Orthodox chant "Blessed be the Lord" and the *Dies irae* appear in several of his instrumental works).

ALEXANDER SCRIABIN

Scriabin's music is in no way related to the new nationalism. He studied piano from early childhood and became a concert pianist, but he was not a virtuoso. The music of Chopin and Liszt considerably influenced Scriabin's style, especially in the works written before 1903 (e.g., *Twenty-four Preludes*, Op. 11 [1888–96]). As a result of temporary injury to his right hand, Scriabin became interested in developing left-hand technique and composed two pieces for the left hand (Op. 9; 1894). In 1898 he joined the faculty of Moscow Conservatory and wrote *Rêverie* (orch.) and two symphonies that show Tchaikovsky's influence.

Around 1900, Scriabin became interested in the writings of Nietszche and the theosophical teachings of Mme Blavatsky and Annie Besant, and his way of life and his compositional style changed. In 1903 he resigned from the Conservatory, left his family, and concertized in Europe and America for six years. Many of the piano pieces that he wrote then bear such titles as *Enigme* (Enigma) and *Caresse dansé* (Danced caress).

For his early music, Scriabin chose keys far removed from C major. Habitually, he began a piece with harmonies remote from the work's tonal center, then moved into it. During c. 1903–7 he gravitated toward C major, perhaps because that key has no sharps or flats. Eventually, he dispensed with key signatures entirely and based a work on a few selected pitches that form a set (or series) that he manipulated linearly and chordally. A few of the pieces Scriabin wrote in 1903–7 are decidedly Impressionistic (e.g., *Poème languide* [Languid poem]). (Impressionism is discussed on p. 564–65). Scriabin's music abounds in fourths, tri-tones, and all kinds of sixth chords—French, German, and the so-called Scriabin sixth consisting of an augmented triad with an added whole tone (ex. 25.2). He frequently used the ♭II chord. Whole-tone scales

EXAMPLE 25.2 Beginning of Scriabin's *Poème fantasque,* Op. 45, No. 2. The "Scriabin sixth" chord is indicated by an x.

with an added nonharmonic pitch also figure prominently in his writing.

Scriabin was a superb miniaturist. This is apparent from his Preludes, the finest of which are Op. 11 and Op. 74, written at the beginning and end of his career (DWMA168; Op. 74 No. 3). For longer works he favored single-movement structure, often with a semblance of sonata form; in multimovement works, he usually moved from one movement to another without pause. An example is *The Divine Poem* (Symphony No. 3, Op. 43; 1904), in three linked movements that share thematic material, recurrent or related figurations, and harmonies. This work requires a very large orchestra, with four of each woodwind instrument, the horn section doubled, and subdivided strings. *Le poème de l'extase* (Poem of ecstasy; 1905–8) is a transitional work exhibiting a blend of his early and mature styles.

Rimsky-Korsakov and Scriabin had discussed the color possibilities of music; both composers related musical pitches to colors but in different ways. Scriabin expressed his views of color-music relationship in *Prométhée, le poème de feu* (Prometheus, poem of fire, Op. 60; 1908–10), for piano, orchestra, textless voices, and *clavier à luce* (light-keyboard), though a keyboard of colored lights did not exist. The music for the light-keyboard is in two-part notation: The lower part is like pedal point, designed to fill the room with a basic atmosphere of light whose color changes portray a "spiritual evolution" taking place in the listeners as the music is performed. The upper part reflects actual harmonic changes in the music.

Scriabin's program for *Prométhée* does not adhere to the myth about the Titan who stole fire (the flame of wisdom) from the gods and gave it to mankind. Rather, Scriabin filled his music with theosophical symbolism. The work opens with a widespread chord (the "mystic chord") sounded *pianissimo* for several measures—a representation of the Mists (or Original Chaos) from which the universe was shaped. Scriabin formed this "mystic chord" by selecting six pitches from the natural harmonic series of C and rearranging them to form a chord structured in fourths (ex. 25.3). The "mystic chord" appears either literally or transposed in several of Scriabin's mature works. *Prométhée* was given its first satisfactory performance in September 1975 by the University of Iowa orchestra, with colors and pitches

coordinated according to Scriabin's scheme (fig. 25.1) and projected by laser apparatus devised by Lowell Cross.

After 1908, Scriabin seems to have based each of his works on a set of selected pitches and a chord structured from them, or vice versa, certainly an avant-garde procedure at that time. In his mature works he used no key signature—at times his music approached pantonality/atonality. Harmonies were no longer func-

EXAMPLE 25.3 Scriabin's mystic chord and its derivation from the harmonic series.

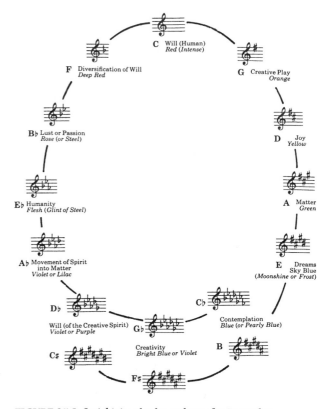

FIGURE 25.1 Scriabin's color-key scheme for *Prométhée*.

tional, and in some pieces rhythm also dissolved. Forms became more condensed; he worked almost exclusively in single movements. The musical language Scriabin used during his last eight years was unique. His omission of key signatures may have stemmed originally from his knowledge of Dargomïzhsky's *The Stone Guest;* possibly his use of fourths is related to Musorgsky's daring harmonies.

GERMAN AND AUSTRIAN COMPOSERS

During the last decades of Romanticism in Germany and Austria, significant contributions were made by Hugo Wolf (1860–1903), Gustav Mahler (1860–1911), and Richard Strauss (1864–1949).

HUGO WOLF

The composition of Lieder was brought to another peak by Wolf. He aspired to write opera—he did not want to be just a songwriter, for he considered songs an inferior form of art music. Yet, history remembers Wolf as a great composer of songs.

Wolf was born in Styria, Yugoslavia, but worked mainly in Vienna. From childhood until within a few years of his death he was poverty stricken. His family was musical, and his father gave him violin and piano lessons; he learned some theory from his teacher at the village primary school, and he and his teacher played in the Wolf household orchestra. When Wolf was 8 he

Hugo Wolf. Photograph, 1895.

attended an opera performance for the first time, and it made a lasting impression on him. He attended several schools for short periods of time; he was not a good student, was inattentive, was regarded as being too independent, and sometimes was a discipline problem. He composed some absolute music along Classic lines; reportedly, it was not very good, but it convinced his father that Hugo should study at Vienna Conservatory.

In 1875 Wolf began to write songs. He considered worthy of publication only 15 of the many songs he wrote before 1888. The first of those was *Morgentau* (Morning dew; June, 1877; pub. 1888). Many of the texts he set in 1877 are by early nineteenth-century poets and concern romantic love or world-weariness (more aptly described by the German word *Weltschmerz*). Wolf stated in letters to friends that in composing Lieder he was following in the tradition of Schubert and Schumann. Indeed, Wolf's early Lieder reveal those influences, especially that of Schumann.

Around the middle of 1878, Wolf chose more serious texts, sometimes even gloomy poetry, filled with renunciation and remorse. At that time he was being treated for syphilis. Throughout his life, Wolf's choice of texts and subjects for his music was directly related to circumstances in his personal life and his attitudes toward those circumstances. When he was romantically involved, he wrote Lieder about love and sexual passion; when syphilis recurred, he became depressed and derogatory toward women and chose material that blamed women for evils brought on men. His personality had always been moody; however, his periods of severe depression, antagonism toward former friends, and extended periods of solitude were all related to the encroachment of disease on his central nervous system. Also, he deeply resented his short stature; his height was five feet, one and one-half inches, comparable with that of Schubert.

In 1883 Wolf considered composing an opera, along Wagnerian lines, but could find no libretto that suited him. Instead, he composed a symphonic poem, *Penthesilea,* depicting the story of the Amazon queen who led her warriors to Troy, where she fell in love with Achilles, was defeated by him, and in retaliation incited her war hounds to shred him to bits. Wolf's symphonic poem shows Liszt's influence in its thematic transformation and treatment of harmonies.

In 1884 Melanie Köchert and her husband secured Wolf's appointment as music critic of the *Wiener Salonblatt*. For three years, that Sunday journal published his outspoken articles on compositions and composers. He was highly critical of Brahms and very supportive of Wagner. Wolf's knowledge of Wagner's operas was thorough, and his articles on them are important.

Wolf and Melanie became lovers, and in 1888 he experienced a year of song like that of Schumann in 1840–41. By early 1889, he had set 13 Eichendorff texts and 51 Goethe poems; in 1890 he composed settings for German translations of 44 Spanish songs. The Lieder are excellent. He had learned to write piano accompaniments independent of the declamatory vocal line, and he could effectively manipulate motives in the accompaniment; thus, his Lieder became more expressive and more dramatic. In 1888 he began to publish his Lieder, and his songs were first sung in public recitals. His music received favorable recognition, and from that time his fame spread.

In 1892–94 Wolf was ill. In 1895 he composed *Der Corregidor*; its text blames women for men's injuries. Wolf's last songs, settings of German translations of Michelangelo poems, were written in March 1897. Then he became insane. Initial treatment proved ineffective; he attempted to drown himself and had to be institutionalized for the remainder of his life (cf. Schumann, p. 473). He died on 22 February 1903.

Wolf's mature compositional style first appeared in his settings of poems by Mörike (1887–88). Wolf considered the poetry more important than the music, published most of his Lieder under such titles as *Gedichte von Mörike* (Poems of Mörike), and usually printed at the head of a Lied the poem that formed its text. He regarded his music as translations of poetry rather than settings of it; each volume was a musical translation of poetry, not a volume of songs. For each volume of Lieder he had an overall plan—the volume was his large-scale work, and the individual Lieder were its movements or sections. Motivic relationships link some of the Lieder. Wolf's talent had to be as great as that of the poets, or he could not have created such masterful settings.

Wolf set only those poems that he believed had not been set adequately by other composers or that had not been set previously. His settings differ from those of other composers in formal structure, treatment of the vocal line, types of harmonies and rhythms used, and general interpretation or expression of the meaning of the text. Wolf intended his music to expressively dramatize the poem. The vocal line has no greater importance than the accompaniment; in fact, the accompaniment maintains the continuity of the Lied through interludes that link the vocal phrases. This Wolf had learned from studying Wagner's operas. Wolf, like Wagner, considered the voice another tonal color in the total fabric of the music.

Wolf's music is tonal; he let the structure of the poetry dictate the harmonies, and within a key he used chromaticism and dissonance to create expressive intensity as dictated by the poem. His music abounds in nonfunctional augmented sixth chords. Sometimes he effected harmonic changes subtly through enharmonic modulations. In some songs he used progressive tonality (e.g., commencing in C and moving through E♭ to conclude in G). Rarely, a song has two tonal centers in keys a third apart (e.g., *In dem Schatten meiner Locken* [In the shadow of my tresses]). Wolf associated a key with a specific mood and had the expression of a poetic text in mind when he chose a key for a Lied. Therefore, when one of Wolf's songs is transposed, it loses part of the specific expression with which he imbued it. Most of Wolf's mature songs contain psychological details whose expressive intricacies in the musical interpretation are not immediately apparent. Many of his Lieder have a basic four-part (not four-voice) texture. This can be seen in *Anakreons Grab* (Anakreon's grave; Goethe poem; 1888; DWMA169), which is one of a few songs that Wolf orchestrated.

Among Wolf's published Lieder are volumes of poetry by Mörike (53 songs), Eichendorff (20 songs), Goethe (51 songs), Michelangelo (3 songs), 2 *Spanisches Liederbucher* (Spanish Songbooks; one containing 10 sacred songs, the other 34 secular songs), and 2 *Italienisches Liederbucher* (Italian Songbooks, one containing 22 songs, the other 24). Besides Lieder, *Der Corregidor,* and *Penthesilea,* Wolf composed a String Quartet (D minor; 1878–84), *Intermezzo* (E♭ major, str. qrt.; 1886), *Italienische Serenade* (Italian Serenade; str. qrt.; 1887), a few piano solos, and 5 unaccompanied and 14 accompanied choral works.

GUSTAV MAHLER

Lieder interested Mahler also. His compositional talent was concentrated in two spheres: the Lied and the symphony, and his work enriched both areas—the Lied was supplied with orchestral accompaniment, and the symphony was infiltrated by the Lied. Mahler was an excellent conductor and in his interpretations insisted on accuracy down to the most minute detail. His compositions are filled with intricate directives relative to dynamics, *tempi,* and other matters pertaining to performance.

Mahler grew up in a Bohemian village culturally rich in music and art. As a child, he learned many folk songs and received piano and music theory lessons. In 1875 he enrolled at the Vienna Conservatory and pursued the composition course; for graduation in 1878 he submitted a Scherzo for piano quintet (lost). In Vienna he became acquainted with Wagner's music and joined a Wagnerite circle.

During 1878–81 Mahler composed the dramatic cantata *Das klagende Lied* (The song of sorrow). In 1880 he composed three Lieder for tenor and piano on his own poems (first perf. 1934). Two of those Lieder have the kind of progressive tonality that characterizes many of his works: *Im Lenz* (In spring) begins in F major and ends in A♭ major, and *Winterlied* (Winter song) commences in A major and concludes in F major. The third song, *Maitanz im Grünen* (May dance on the green), is in D major. In 1880–83 Mahler composed the first volume of *Lieder und Gesänge* (Lieder and songs, 3 vols., pub. 1892).

From 1883 to 1897 Mahler worked as a conductor or director of theaters in various cities. In Leipzig, he saw Weber's sketches for *Die drei Pintos;* Mahler completed

Gustav Mahler.

that opera. In 1888 he met Richard Strauss, and a life-long friendship developed. From 1897 to 1907 Mahler was director of the Vienna Opera. There he did a great deal to change the tastes of audiences who favored French grand opera. In 1901 he fell in love with Alma Schindler (1879–1964; Insight, "Alma Schindler Mahler"), who was studying composition in Vienna; they married in 1902. In 1907 Mahler was appointed principal conductor of the Metropolitan Opera, New York;

INSIGHT

Alma Schindler Mahler

Alma Schindler studied counterpoint and composition with Josef Labor (1842–1924) and Alexander von Zemlinsky (1871–1942), both of whom taught Schoenberg. Alma met Mahler in 1901. He knew she was writing Lieder but had never seen any of her work. Apparently, he surmised that it was of some worth, for, when a serious relationship developed between them, he advised her by letter that she would have to give up composing because a compositional rivalry between husband and wife would be bizarre. She complied with his request but always resented it; she did not destroy all her compositions but kept some in a portfolio. As with most couples, there were times of marital crisis. At such a time in summer 1910, Alma came on her husband playing some of her Lieder. Subsequently, he encouraged her to compose and arranged for publication of five songs she had written c. 1901 (*Fünf Lieder*). Four years after Gustav's death, she married architect Walter Gropius; their marriage ended in divorce, and in 1929 she married the writer Franz Werfel (1890–1945). Alma's *Vier Lieder* (Four Lieder) was published in 1915, and 1924 *Fünf Gesänge* (Five Songs) appeared. Because she did not date her work, it is difficult to determine when the songs were composed. However, *Der Erkennende* is a setting of a poem Werfel wrote in 1915. If she composed other songs, they have not survived. Alma Mahler's music is tonal but at times greatly expanded by chromatic alterations. Her ability to write effective counterpoint is evident. Usually, the vocal line is independent of the accompaniment, and often it is completely surrounded by accompaniment harmonies.

in 1909 he became conductor of the New York Philharmonic. From 1907 he had suffered from a heart ailment that was complicated by a bacterial infection in 1911, causing his death on May 18.

MAHLER'S MUSIC   Mahler's works include nine completed symphonies, the symphonic song cycle (sometimes called a song-symphony) *Das Lied von der Erde* (The song of the earth; 1908–9), three song cycles for voice and orchestra, the dramatic cantata *Das klagende Lied,* and several volumes of Lieder. A tenth symphony, unfinished at the time of his death, was constructed from his sketches by Deryck Cooke in 1951 (perf. 1976). The song cycles are *Lieder eines fahrenden Gesellen* (Songs of a wayfarer; 4 songs; 1883–85), *Des Knaben Wunderhorn* (The boy's magic horn; 12 songs; 1892–98), and *Kindertotenlieder* (Songs about the deaths of children; 5 settings of Rückert poems; 1901–4). Volumes 2 and 3 of *Lieder und Gesänge,* for voice and piano, are also settings of *Des Knaben Wunderhorn* poems.

In its medieval setting, depiction of nature, and use of magic, *Das klangende Lied* reflects the influence of German Romanticism, Weber's operas, and Wagner's music. Mahler used different keys to represent certain events. For this cantata he used a large orchestra and in the last scene combined an offstage band playing festive music with the catastrophe presented by those visible on stage. Many of the vocal melodies in *Das klagende Lied* are directly related to Bohemian folk song.

In *Lieder eines fahrenden Gesellen,* the key changes as the hero travels; this gave rise to the term *narrative key tonality. Progressive* and *narrative* tonality are different names for the same practice—changing keys as the music unfolds and concluding in a key other than that which begins the work. The practice evidences composers' search for greater expression than that afforded them through adherence to the rules of traditional harmony.

In *Kindertotenlieder* there is a richness expressive of the depth of love of father for child, deep emotion over tragic loss, and calm serenity in the assurance of God's protection and the promise of eternal life. Orchestral interludes between phrases of text seem to indicate soul-searching reflection; they occur frequently, do not disrupt the train of thought of the lyrics, and are vital to the continuity of the compositions. In these songs Mahler proved that a selective instrumentation need not imply a thin orchestration (No. 5, DWMA170).

The Arnim and Brentano collection *Des Knaben Wunderhorn* provided Mahler material for several sets of songs that, in turn, yielded source material for other compositions. The Second, Third, and Fourth Symphonies are closely linked with his *Des Knaben Wunderhorn* songs.

Mahler's Lieder and symphonies are interrelated. He based symphonies and symphony movements on some of his Lieder, used Lieder in his symphonies, and borrowed from Lieder for symphony themes. The progressive tonality that occurs in many of his Lieder appears in his symphonies also. Symphonies Nos. 1, 6, and 8 are the only Mahler symphonies that begin and end in the same key. Most of Mahler's symphonies are programmatic, though he removed traces of programs from some of them. A few symphonies require enormous performing resources. Other scores call for a very large orchestra, but he does not use all the instruments at the same time; the instrumental forces are available for special instrumental combinations. In Symphonies Nos. 1, 2, and 8, he placed some instruments offstage. Only Symphonies Nos. 1, 4, 6, and 9 have the traditional four movements. When he used sonata form for a symphony movement, he might return to the proper key for the recapitulation, but usually he did not return the thematic material in the order in which it was originally presented. He followed Beethoven, Berlioz, and Liszt in using vocalists in some symphonies: Nos. 2, 3, and 8 have parts for soloists and chorus, No. 8 uses two choruses, and No. 4 requires a soprano soloist.

Mahler originally planned his first symphony as a kind of tone poem in two parts, with five movements in all, and gave each part and each movement a programmatic title. Later he deleted the titles and at one time named the symphony *Titan.* At another time, he stated that the symphony represented victory achieved by every gifted man in overcoming his Roquairol, his self-reflecting, scoffing, imperiling spirit. After a few performances he removed the original second movement, *Blumine* (Flowers). Since 1966, several orchestras have performed the symphony as a five-movement work, with *Blumine* as second movement. Songs figure prominently in this symphony, but it is purely instrumental.

Symphonies Nos. 5, 6, and 7 are closely related to the *Kindertotenlieder* cycle as well as to *Des Knaben Wunderhorn*. The symphonic song cycle *Das Lied von der Erde* was originally conceived as the eighth symphony. The work is based on seven poems from Hans Bethge's translation of *The Chinese Flute,* which Mahler set for tenor and alto soloists and orchestra. Mahler's actual Symphony No. 8 is sometimes called "Symphony of a Thousand" because of its enormous performing resources. It is the first completely choral symphony. In it Mahler made two statements: in Part I, an affirmation of Christian faith and belief in the power of the creative Holy Spirit, through use of the ninth-century hymn *Veni, Creator Spiritus;* in Part II, a belief in the redemption of mankind through love, as Goethe presented it in Part II of *Faust,* in the *Chorus mysticus.* (Liszt had used this in his *Faust Symphony.*) Mahler's polyphonic treatment of the *Veni, Creator Spiritus* stemmed from his interest in the works of J. S. Bach; that influence is seen also in the inclusion of boys' choir and in Mahler's choice of E♭ as the overall key of the symphony, the key Bach associated with the Trinity. Much of the Baroque, as Mahler viewed it, is present in the symphony's first movement.

Throughout much of his life, Mahler was preoccupied with thoughts of death. Several of his symphonies and *Das Lied von der Erde* are often viewed in this light. The "Farewell" motive used by Beethoven appears in several of Mahler's works, and in the fourth movement of the unfinished Tenth Symphony Mahler wrote the words *Leb' wohl* (Farewell) several times. His Ninth Symphony is sometimes regarded as expressing his premonition of his own death. Perhaps it does, but possibly he considered it a requiem for his daughter.

Mahler's music is tonal, with many of the melodies in his orchestral works borrowed from songs. His increased use of counterpoint after 1900 resulted from his study of Bach's works. In his symphonic writing, Mahler built on the work of his nineteenth-century predecessors, especially Beethoven, Berlioz, Liszt, and Bruckner, in the inclusion of voices, thematic transformation, and expanded form and tonality. Mahler ex-tended the symphony beyond the massive proportions and programmatic content of post-Romanticism, and through the incorporation of the Lied, use of expanded harmonies and progressive tonality, he elevated the symphony to an unprecedented height.

RICHARD STRAUSS

Strauss (1864–1949) grew up in a musical atmosphere. His father was horn player in the Munich Court Orchestra, and, from an early age, Richard attended rehearsals and performances of Classic and early Romantic music. He had piano and violin lessons and at the age of 11 received instruction in theory, harmony, and instrumentation. But he wrote his first composition when he was 6, and for the rest of his life he composed music, though he was almost middle-aged before he thought of himself as a composer. His primary career was conducting.

Richard Strauss. *(Courtesy Free Library of Philadelphia)*

At Munich University, Strauss studied philosophy, art history, and esthetics. In Munich he heard Wagner's music for the first time. His admiration for Wagner's music was lifelong, yet he did not compose music in that style.

By 1885, Strauss had written two symphonies (D minor, F minor), some overtures and orchestral serenades, a violin concerto, a horn concerto, a 'cello/piano sonata, a string quartet, some piano trios and other chamber music, some choral music, and some Lieder. One of these songs, *Allerseelen* (All Soul's day), ranks among his finest.

In 1885 Strauss was appointed assistant conductor to Hans von Bülow at Meiningen and within weeks succeeded von Bülow, who resigned. Strauss read Wagner's writings and delved into Schopenhauer's philosophy. He was impressed with the idea of couching new music in new forms, was attracted to Liszt's symphonic poems, and decided to try composing works of that kind. In 1886 he wrote *Aus Italien* (From Italy), descriptive of his visit to Italy that summer. He called the work a symphonic fantasy—it is a four-movement programmatic orchestral work that lies midway between symphony and symphonic poem.

STRAUSS'S TONE POEMS In *Macbeth* (1886–88) Strauss's handling of symphonic poem is immature, but *Don Juan* (1888–89) shows his mastery of the structure, which he called **tone poem.** *Macbeth* and *Don Juan* are single-movement works in sonata form, with self-contained episodes in the development section. *Macbeth* is a psychological study of Macbeth, not a musical retelling of Shakespeare's play. *Don Juan* is based on three philosophical excerpts from Nikolaus Lenau's unfinished *Don Juan* poem. The hero is a man in ceaseless pursuit of the unattainable—the ideal woman, the perfect love. Several features of the work became trademarks of Strauss's style: a broad, upward-sweeping opening passage; use of solo instruments or of a section playing in unison to introduce thematic material; and presentation of an important melody relatively late in the work. When Strauss employs a solo violin in dialogue with the orchestra, the soloist remains an integral part of the ensemble rather than being set apart from the group.

Strauss stated that *Tod und Verklärung* (Death and transfiguration; 1889) portrays an artist on his death-bed who recalls his youth and unfulfilled idealism; at death, his soul is transfigured.

Strauss's next four orchestral works—*Till Eulenspiegels lustige Streiche,* . . . (Till Eulenspiegel's merry pranks, . . . ; 1894–95), *Also sprach Zarathustra* (Thus spake Zarathustra; 1895–96), *Don Quixote* (1896–97), and *Ein Heldenleben* (A Hero's life; 1897–98)—brought him recognition as the leading German composer of his day. He was considered a "modern" composer because of the large orchestra, the realistic effects that he used, and the changes in formal structure in his works. Strauss' choice of rondo structure is appropriate for *Till Eulenspiegels lustige Streiche,* for, though Till resolves to reform, he remains a prankster; the rondo theme, representing Till, unifies the episodes. Extra instruments (e.g., clarinets in different keys) are required for the orchestra.

Also sprach Zarathustra is based on Nietzsche's poem expressing the superman doctrine. Formally, Strauss's composition is a free fantasia unified by the motive C–G–C. There is artificiality in the fugue theme, contrived to contain all 12 pitches of the chromatic scale and thus represent the omniscience of *Wissenschaft* (science).

Don Quixote, fantastische Variationen über ein Thema ritterlichen Charakters (Don Quixote, fantastic variations on a knightly character's theme), based on Cervantes' novel, describes the adventures of Don Quixote and his faithful companion, Sancho Panza. A solo 'cello represents the knight; Panza's theme is stated by bass clarinet and bass tuba. The music is conversational at times and resembles sinfonia concertante as well as symphonic poem. The personalities of Don Quixote and Sancho Panza are altered by their experiences; therefore, Strauss's choice of theme and variation with thematic transformation is appropriate. In depicting Don Quixote's encounter with the sheep, Strauss used a technique of maintaining a constant pitch but changing its color kaleidoscopically by having various instruments enter and drop out. Schoenberg used the technique more than a decade later and termed it ***Klangfarbenmelodie*** (tone-color-melody; see p. 597).

In *Ein Heldenleben,* Strauss is the Kapellmeister whose professional life is depicted; his wife is represented by solo violin. *Sinfonia domestica* (Domestic symphony; 1902–3), a one-movement work, portrays

PLATE 21 Anne-Louis Girodet. *The Burial of Atala*, 1808, oil on canvas, approx. 6′11″ × 8′9″. Atala vowed lifelong virginity but fell in love with a young savage. Rather than break her vows, she committed suicide; her lover and a priest bury her in the shadow of the cross. *(The Louvre, Paris. Réunion des Musées Nationaux)*

PLATE 22 Francesco Goya. *The Third of May, 1808*, painted in 1814, oil on canvas, approx. 8′8″ × 11′3″. *(Museo del Prado, Madrid)*

PLATE 23 Felix Mendelssohn. Aquatint landscape painted at Thun 11 July 1847. Original in Mendelssohn-Archivs der Staatsbibliothek, Preussischer Kulturbesitz, Berlin. *(Courtesy Allen County Public Library, Fort Wayne, Indiana, owner of Mendelssohn Aquarellenalbum No. 660)*

PLATE 24 Cloister scene, Act III, of Meyerbeer's *Robert le Diable*. Original in Bibliothèque de l'Opera, Paris. *(© Erich Lessing/Magnum Photos)*

PLATE 25 Claude Monet. *Impression: Soleil levant* (Sunrise), 1872, oil on canvas, 19⅝″ × 25½″. The painting was stolen but has been recovered. It is now in Musée Marmottan, Paris.

PLATE 26 Hilaire-Germain-Edgar Degas. *Rehearsal on the Stage*, c. 1873, pastel over brush-and-ink drawing on paper. 21″ × 28½″.

(*The H. O. Havemeyer Collection, The Metropolitan Museum of Art, New York City. Bequest of Mrs. H. O. Havemeyer, 1929*)

PLATE 27 Marc Chagall. *Music and Art*, panels 1 and 2 (left bay) from *America windows*, 1977, stained glass, 240 × 342 cm. Original at The Art Institute of Chicago. Gift of the Auxiliary Board of The Art Institute of Chicago in memory of Richard J. Daley. (© *ARS, New York/ADAGP Paris*)

PLATE 28 Three panels from *The Isenheim Altarpiece,* painted by Matthias Grünewald c. 1510–15: (*a*) Engelkonzert (Angelic Concert); (*b*) Grablegung (Entombment); and (*c*) Versuchung des heiligen Antonius (The Temptation of St. Anthony). *(Sources: (a) and (c) © Scala/Art Resource, New York; (b) © Giraudon/Art Resource, New York)*

the Strauss family's home life. *Eine Alpensinfonie* (An Alpen symphony; 1911–15) describes a full day spent in the mountains. All of Strauss's orchestral works from *Don Quixote* through *Eine Alpensinfonie* require a very large orchestra.

OPERA CONDUCTOR AND COMPOSER   From 1886 to 1889 Strauss was third conductor at the Munich Court Opera; then he went to Bayreuth and Weimar to conduct. During the 1890s and 1900s, he was recognized as one of the three great Austro-Germanic conductors, the others being Mahler and Felix Weingartner (1863–1942). At Weimar Strauss met Pauline de Ahna (1862–1950); they married in 1894. A talented soprano, de Ahna sang leading operatic roles at Bayreuth and concertized. For her, Strauss wrote many excellent Lieder, commencing with the four songs, Op. 27, that were his wedding gift to her. One of the finest of his more than 200 Lieder is *Traum durch die Dämmerung* (Dream in the twilight, one of three songs in Op. 29; 1895). Strauss's Lieder deserve wider recognition than they have been accorded.

Strauss's work as opera conductor and his association with Pauline caused him to write opera. For his first, *Guntram,* which centers on redemption through a woman, he prepared his own libretto and designed the heroine (Freihild) role for Pauline. The opera was not successful. To retaliate for the criticism he received, Strauss wrote another, the one-act *Feuersnot* (lit., distress caused by fire; 1900–1), a satire on Munich's philistinism. For his opera *Salome* (1 Act; 1903–5) he used a libretto by Wilde, a fantasy on the biblical account of Herod's execution of John the Baptist. The music in *Salome* is beautiful, but the plot is gruesome (e.g., Salome's singing a soliloquy to John's bloody disembodied head, which she caresses and kisses). Strauss's themes are short; Leitmotifs woven into the musical fabric create dissonant polyphony. The orchestra is unusually large; Strauss used instrumental timbres effectively and colored the music with harsh dissonances. He worked within established tonality and assigned keys, but in many places dissonance completely obliterates any sense of the designated key. *Salome* drew mixed reactions. Critics and audience were both shocked, but whereas critics were repelled by the violence and lust and considered the opera blasphemous, audiences were attracted by it.

Salome was followed by another one-act opera with dramatic female roles and bloody violence, *Elektra.* The libretto was by Hugo von Hofmannsthal (1874–1929), with whom Strauss established a working relationship that lasted until Hofmannsthal died. *Elektra* presents the mythological story of Electra and Orestes, who avenge their father's murder by slaying their mother. In *Elektra,* dissonances are even sharper than those in *Salome,* and repetition, dynamics, and accentuation reinforce them. Actually, *Elektra* is music drama. Strauss wrote continuous music and used Leitmotifs systematically—example 25.4a shows that for Elektra, with a tritone progression. Strauss assigned special keys to characters: B♭ major for Agamemnon, E♭ major for Chrysosthemis, and bitonality with Elektra, sometimes A major/E♭ minor, and C major/E major with her triumph. As Liszt and Scriabin had done, Strauss generated the harmonies from a single germinal chord (ex. 25.4b).

Performance of *Elektra* evoked reactions similar to those for *Salome.* At this point, critics considered Strauss a talented, daring, modern composer who wrote unconventional music filled with ugly, cacophonous sounds. But it was not this that caused Strauss to effect a change of style in his next opera. Rather, it was the realization that he could not top what he had done in *Elektra.* He and Hofmannsthal next collaborated on the three-act comedy *Der Rosenkavalier* (The Knight of the rose; 1909–10), a witty, romantic, farcical opera. In style, it reverts to eighteenth-century Classicism, with Mozartean melody and lightness. Strauss's inclusion of waltz in the opera is, of course, anachronous. There are three important soprano roles in the opera; Oktavian is a trousers role. Strauss's change of style was totally unexpected, and his continued composition of operas along the same lines earned for him a new reputation—conservative composer. *Der Rosenkavalier* was well received, his later operas were not. However, his last

(a)   (b)

EXAMPLE 25.4 (*a*) Motive representing *Elektra.* (*b*) Germinal chord for musical material in *Elektra.* (*Source: Strauss* Elektra, *copyright © 1908. A. Furstner, renewed 1936*) opera, *Capriccio* (1 Act; 1941), is economical, elegant, and refined and almost as delightful as *Der Rosenkavalier.*

Strauss worked in and around court all his life but paid relatively little attention to political activities. In 1933, for the first time, he experienced political difficulties with the Nazis under Hitler's chancellorship. Joseph Goebbels, the Nazi minister of propaganda, established a state music bureau and, without consulting Strauss, named him president of it. When Hitler and Goebbels learned that Strauss was working with a Jewish librettist, Stefan Zweig (1881–1942), Strauss's position was terminated. For a time, Strauss and his household—his daughter-in-law was Jewish—had to leave the area. Then, as casualties of World War II, came the destruction of opera houses in several major cities. After the war, Strauss composed *Metamorphosen* (1945) as an elegy for the previous German musical life he had known. The work is a study for 23 solo stringed instruments and is Neoclassic in style. Neoclassicism is visible in several of Strauss's late works. His last compositions are *Vier letzte Lieder* (Four last songs; 1948; S or T, orch.). Strauss died quietly, of heart failure, on 8 September 1949.

MINOR COMPOSERS

In the late nineteenth century there was a revival of interest in Germany in **Märschenoper** (fairy-tale opera). Engelbert Humperdinck (1854–1921) wrote several of them, including *Hänsel und Gretel* (Hansel and Gretel; 1893) and *Dornröschen* (Sleeping Beauty; 1902). His finest works are *Hänsel und Gretel* and his incidental music to Shakespeare plays. *Hänsel und Gretel,* based on Grimm's fairy tale, originated as songs Humperdinck wrote for his sister in 1890. He expanded them into a Singspiel, then into a three-act **Märschenspiel** (fairy-tale opera with spoken dialogue; 1893). Humperdinck had met Wagner in Italy in 1880 and had worked closely with him in 1881–82. Mingled with the folklike simplicity of Humperdinck's melodies is a Wagnerian influence, seen in the choice of harmonies, some contrapuntal textures, and some recurrent motives.

The music of Max Reger (1873–1916) has remained little known outside of Germany and Russia. Reger's music mingles Baroque, Classic, and Romantic elements. An excellent organist, he understood Renaissance and Baroque polyphonic styles, had a predilection for counterpoint, and was adept at fugue and variation techniques. Reger greatly admired Bach. Though Reger was a devout Catholic, he based many works on Lutheran chorales, including several large choral fantasias and three volumes of chorale preludes. Some of the preludes are very easy, whereas others are quite difficult. Reger used chromaticism as an adjunct to functional harmony, thus expanding key tonality without destroying it. His combination of chromaticism with counterpoint makes his large organ works tremendously difficult technically, for example, *Chorale Fantasia "Ein' feste Burg ist unser Gott"* (Op. 27; 1898) and *Chorale Fantasia "Wie schon leucht't uns der Morgenstern"* (How brightly shines the morning star, Op. 52; 1900). At places in these fantasias the chromaticism pushes key tonality to its very limits but still does not destroy it.

Reger wrote in all genres except opera. Much of his chamber music reflects his admiration for and knowledge of the music of Beethoven and Brahms. Two excellent works for two pianos are *Variations and Fugue on a Theme of Beethoven* (Op. 86; 1904) and *Variations and Fugue on a Theme of Mozart* (Op. 132a; 1914), the latter based on the theme from Mozart's Piano Sonata, K. 331, mvt. 1. Another fine work is the orchestral *Variationen und Fuge über ein lustigs Thema von J. A. Hiller* (Variations and Fugue on a merry theme of J. A. Hiller, Op. 100, E major; 1907).

ITALY—*VERISMO*

In the late nineteenth century there was a trend toward naturalism, or realism, in European literature. This is seen in the writings of Émile Zola (1840–1902) in France, Giovanni Verga (1840–1922) in Italy, Henrik Ibsen (1828–1906) in Norway, Leo Tolstoy (1828–1910) and Anton Chekhov (1860–1904) in Russia, and other European authors. Composers of operas sought to duplicate the realism of spoken drama and the realism of life itself. Realism is apparent in Dargomïzhsky's *The Stone Guest* and Musorgsky's *Boris Godunov.* Italians used the term **verismo** for their works of this kind. Frequently, they chose characters from the lower classes, or from a "bohemian" kind of life, involved in situations generating violent and brutal passions, especially hatred, lust, and murder. Strong local color is present in all operas of this kind.

In a competition held in 1888 for a one-act opera, Pietro Mascagni (1863–1954) won first prize with *Cavalleria rusticana* (Rustic chivalry). Because of the tremendous popularity of that opera, Mascagni's name has been associated almost exclusively with *verismo;* only 2 of his 15 operas are that type. He composed secular and sacred choral music, including a Mass, Requiem Mass, and other liturgical works; about a dozen songs; a symphony, a symphonic poem, and other orchestral pieces; some chamber music; and several piano pieces.

Another verismo opera that has remained in the repertoire is *I Pagliacci* (The Clowns; 1892) by Ruggero Leoncavallo (1857–1919). The opera presents a play within a play and a situation in which dramatic art becomes reality. The plot concerns a troupe of *commedia dell'arte* players whose leader plays the clown role. He is a sensitive, suffering person who must always present a happy attitude to the world. The play within the play closely parallels a situation in his private life; he acts realistically and kills his wife. Then he sings, "I am not a clown, but a man," and, in a stupor, announces, "The comedy is ended."

In his music, Leoncavallo used many seventh chords, and there is much movement by thirds. The melody *Ridi, Pagliaccio!* (Laugh, clown!) appears three times in the opera. Originally, Leoncavallo intended *I Pagliacci* as a one-act opera, but the enthusiastic applause after *Vesti la giubba* (Put on the smock) caused him to divide the work into two acts.

PUCCINI

The chief exponent of verismo was Giacomo Puccini (1858–1924). When he was 10 he joined the choir at San Martino, in Lucca, and four years later became organist there. At the age of 17 he began composing, writing and improvising for church service use organ pieces in which he included bits of Tuscan folk songs and melodies from operas. After performance of his one-act opera *Le villi* (The Willis; 1884), Puccini received commissions for operas. The tremendous success of *Manon Lescaut* (1893) brought Puccini to the attention of audiences outside Italy. Besides operas, Puccini composed other vocal music, a few orchestral pieces, and some chamber music.

Puccini wrote a total of 12 operatic works, if one counts as 3 works the triptych comprising the one-act operas *Il tabarro* (The tabard), *Suor Angelica* (Sister Angelica), and *Gianni Schicchi* (Johnny Schicchi), first performed at the Metropolitan Opera, New York, 1918. Among Puccini's works in standard repertoire are *Manon Lescaut, La bohème*, ("Bohemian" life; 1895), *Tosca* (1900), and *Madama Butterfly* (1904). In *La bohème* Puccini paints a romantic picture of "bohemian" life in Paris c. 1830, through the activities of a young poet, a painter, a philosopher, a musician, and a poor seamstress suffering from tuberculosis. Other Puccini operas frequently performed in the late twentieth century are *La fanciulla del West* (The Girl of the [golden] West; first perf. New York, 1910) and *Gianni Schicchi.*

A characteristic of Puccini's orchestral writing is double or multiple reinforcement of the vocal melody, a technique known as **violinata,** used also by Rossini, Bellini, and Donizetti. Puccini's orchestra supplies continuous music but is not symphonic. The music expresses and enhances the local color of the opera's setting (e.g., the bohemianism of Paris's Latin Quarter in *La bohème*, the Japanese locale of *Madama Butterfly*). The orchestration and instrumentation are always appropriate to the details of the opera's plot, sometimes delicate, sometimes brilliant. Puccini viewed opera as *musical drama*—the drama more important than the music—but he insisted that every element of the production be meticulously coordinated to produce a unified work of art.

FRANCE

At the close of the Franco-Prussian War, there was a kind of musical renaissance in France that at first was nationalistic. In February 1871 a group of French composers founded the Société Nationale de Musique for the purpose of encouraging French composers. The organization was motivated by a sincere desire to improve the quality of French music, to divest it of superficiality, and to promote it as a serious art with solid craftsmanship. César Franck was the leader of the group. The Society sponsored its first concert in November 1871. Other concert series were established and were designed to promote the performance of contemporary orchestral and chamber music. The most influential conductor-directors of these were Jules Pasdeloup, Édouard Colonne, and Charles Lamoureux.

During the 1890s, there was also a revival of interest in music of the past. Editions of the works of F. Couperin, Rameau, Palestrina, and other noted early composers were prepared, and their music was performed. In 1894 the Schola Cantorum was founded in Paris by Vincent d'Indy, Charles Bordes, and Alexandre Guilmant. The school was intended to provide instruction in plainchant and Palestrina-style religious music, but gradually the curriculum was expanded to include all areas of music. The Schola Cantorum admitted all who could qualify, not just French citizens. By 1900 it had become a decided challenge to the Paris Conservatoire.

All this activity in composition, performance, education, and scholarship elevated France to a position of world leadership in music in the first half of the twentieth century.

There were several overlapping and interdependent lines of development in French music after 1871. Two were basic: one followed cosmopolitan traditions and is seen in the work of Franck and his pupils, especially d'Indy; the other, adhering to specifically French traditions, is apparent in the work of Camille Saint-Saëns and his pupils, particularly Gabriel Fauré. Later, a third line of development appeared, based on French tradition and influenced by the ideas of Symbolist writers and Impressionist artists. Its principal exponent was Claude Debussy.

CÉSAR FRANCK

As a youngster, Belgian-born César Franck (1822–90) studied at Paris Conservatoire, where in 1872 he became professor of organ. Despite his colleagues' disapproval, he taught composition to the students in his organ classes, including Vincent d'Indy, Ernest Chausson, Gabriel Pierné, Henri Duparc, and Louis Vierne.

Much of the music Franck wrote before 1858 is of little significance. From 1858 to 1872 he was organist at Ste. Clothilde and was concerned with church music. His finest compositions are the symphonic, chamber music, and keyboard works written during the last dozen years of his life. The important keyboard pieces include *Prélude, choral et fugue* (1884; pno.), *Prélude, aria et final* (1887; pno.), and *Trois chorals* (Three chorales; E major, B minor, A minor; 1890; organ). The chorales are highly developed fantasias on original themes, the kind of music Franck improvised at the conclusion of Service at Ste. Clothilde. *Prélude, choral et fugue* was originally planned as a prelude and fugue in the style of Bach; then Franck inserted the chorale. The composition is a masterpiece.

With his last three chamber music works—the Piano Quintet (F minor; 1879), the violin/piano Sonata (A major, 1886), and the String Quartet (D major; 1889)—Franck laid the foundation for modern French chamber music. These works, and his *Symphonie* (D minor; 1888), are cyclical. Frequently, Franck generated themes from two germinal motives for contrast, as he did in the *Symphonie* and *Variations symphoniques* (1885; pno., orch.). Only a few of Franck's works are programmatic, the most significant being the symphonic poems *Le chasseur maudit* (The accursed hunter; 1882) and *Phyché* (orch., chor.; 1888).

VINCENT D'INDY

In 1869 Vincent d'Indy (1851–1931), who had been a child prodigy as a pianist, decided to become a professional musician. The Franco-Prussian War intervened, and he served France in the National Guard. He studied composition with Franck in 1872–80 and later transmitted Franck's methods and cosmopolitan ideals to his own students. D'Indy actively supported the Société Nationale de Musique from the time of its inception and succeeded Franck as its president.

D'Indy was greatly interested in music education. In 1893 he helped reorganize teaching methods at Paris Conservatoire. That experience led to the founding of the Schola Cantorum, where students learned Gregorian chant and Palestrina-style composition and received thorough grounding in the music of Bach, Beethoven, Rameau, and other masters. D'Indy published his instructional methods in a multivolume *Cours de composition musicale* (Course in music composition; 1903–33).

D'Indy did much to further the cause of symphonic composition in France. His most important compositions are *Symphonie sur un chant montagnard français* (Symphony on a French mountain air; 1886, his second symphony though not so numbered) for piano and orchestra; *Istar* (1896); Symphony No. 2 (B♭; 1903); the Violin/Piano Sonata (C major; 1904), and the opera *Fervaal* (1897). That d'Indy used Leitmotifs in *Fervaal* reflects his appreciation of Wagner's techniques.

Istar is a set of symphonic variations depicting the legend of that Assyrian goddess: To free her lover from Hades, Istar must walk through seven gates and gradually disrobe as she passes through them; after walking through the last gate, she is nude. Consequently, d'Indy began his composition with the most complex variation and concluded the work with orchestral unison statement of the theme.

CAMILLE SAINT-SAËNS

Saint-Saëns (1835–1921) received piano lessons at the age of two and a half, evidenced talent for musical composition at the age of three, and before he was seven was playing organ and piano in public programs. He studied composition with Pierre Maleden (1806–c. 1848), who taught Gottfried Weber's (1779–1839) principles of harmonic theory. Those principles, which were more lax than Rameau's with regard to treatment of altered chords and resolution of dissonance, made a lasting imprint on Saint-Saëns's compositional style. In 1848 he entered Paris Conservatoire to study organ and composition. By 1853 he had written a number of large works, including cantatas and symphonies. From 1857 to 1876 he was organist at La Madeleine and in 1861–65 taught at École Niedermeyer. Gabriel Fauré was one of his students. A close friendship developed between Saint-Saëns and Fauré that lasted for many years, with Saint-Saëns eventually being considered a kind of older relative in the Fauré family.

Saint-Saëns was one of the founders of the Société Nationale de Musique, but he withdrew from the organization in 1908 when the Society began to perform works by contemporary foreign composers. His own music was basically that of the French tradition, conservative, with order and restraint, and couched in Classic forms. His orchestral writing attests his mastery of counterpoint and his ability to write full sonorities. He was eclectic, and at times Romantic elements colored his music. His finest and most representative compositions were written in the 1870s and 1880s.

They include Piano Concerto No. 4 (C minor; 1875); Violin Concerto No. 3 (B minor; 1880); Symphony No. 3, the "Organ Symphony" (C minor, 1886); Sonata No. 1 for violin and piano (D minor; 1885); Sonata No. 1 for 'cello and piano (C minor, 1872); and *Le carnaval des animaux* (The carnival of animals; chamber orch., 2 pnos.; 1886). Both the piano concerto and the symphony commence in C minor and conclude in C major, use thematic transformation, and contain chorale melodies. The symphony is scored for a large orchestra, with two pianos and an organ. *Le carnaval des animaux*, a series of delightful parodies of well-known compositions, reveals Saint-Saëns's wit and his knowledge of instrumental techniques. It has become one of his most popular pieces. Also significant are the opera *Samson et Dalila* (Samson and Delilah; 1877) and the symphonic poems *Le rouet d'Omphale* (Omphale's spinning wheel; A major; 1872) and *Danse macabre* (G minor; 1874), which marks an early use of xylophone as an orchestral instrument.

GABRIEL FAURÉ

Fauré (1845–1924) entered École Niedermeyer as a boarding student in 1854 and remained there 11 years. The curriculum was oriented toward training students to be church organists and choirmasters and consisted mainly of organ and piano lessons, chant, counterpoint, and Renaissance polyphony. After the death of Niedermeyer (1861), Saint-Saëns taught the piano classes and expanded the course to include contemporary music and composition. Fauré studied with him there for 5 years. The training Fauré received at École Niedermeyer, with its emphasis on chant and modes and its special way of teaching harmony, according to Gottfried Weber's theoretical principles, strongly influenced his compositional style. Those principles favor the use of altered chords in a manner that alludes to remote keys without actual modulation to them.

Fauré began his professional career as church organist at Rennes (1866–70). During the Franco-Prussian War he served in the infantry; thereafter he held organist and choirmaster posts in various Paris churches. In 1896 he was appointed professor of composition at Paris Conservatoire and in 1905–20 was director of that school. Among his pupils were Charles Koechlin,

Maurice Ravel, and Nadia Boulanger. Through Boulanger's teaching, Fauré's influence was extended to many twentieth-century composers.

Fauré is highly regarded in France; elsewhere only his Requiem Mass (1887), some of his chamber music, and a few of his songs are performed. In the area of chamber music he made some real contributions, and several of his works are standard repertoire: Sonata No. 1 for violin and piano (A major; 1875–76), Piano Trio (D minor; 1923), Piano Quintet No. 2 (C minor; 1921), and String Quartet (E minor; 1924).

Fauré is seen at his best in chamber music, piano pieces, and songs. His earliest compositions (1861– 62) are songs of the romance type, and his first pieces are three *romances sans paroles* (romances without words; c. 1863). His piano pieces consist of character pieces, principally nocturnes, barcarolles, preludes, impromptus, and valse-caprices. Until the 1890s Fauré wrote single song settings; then he began to compose song cycles, the first being *Cinq mélodies 'de Venise'* (Five melodies from Venice; 1891). Throughout his career, Fauré wrote songs and piano music, and the changes in his style over the years are apparent in those genres. His early music is Romantic, showing the influence of Schumann, Mendelssohn, and Saint-Saëns, with formal clarity and basic Romantic harmonies. Then Liszt's influence became apparent. In the late 1880s, there appear reflections of the ideas of Impressionist painters and the Symbolist poets whose stanzas he set (e.g., Verlaine's *Clair de lune* [Moonlight; 1887]). Gradually, Fauré's harmonies became bolder and more expressive, as seen in *La bonne chanson* (The good song; 1892–94) and the opera *Prométhée* (1900). Fauré's style, in his final period, became more economical and at times austere, with increasing harmonic boldness and more use of polyphony.

Some characteristics of Fauré's writing remained constant. His music is tonal, but he blended modality into it and treated harmonies rather freely. Many of his melodies are modal, but he seldom used the whole-tone scale. The flatted seventh scale degree and the plagal cadence figure prominently; major and minor seventh chords appear frequently. He did not consider seventh and ninth chords dissonant; thus, they required no resolution. Nor did an altered chord indicate an impending modulation—he often used altered chords and foreign notes without changing key. Because of his facility

with altered chords, he could and did modulate to remote keys swiftly and was able to return to the tonic key just as suddenly. However, he did not modulate as frequently as is generally believed. Typical of his harmony is alteration of the mediant with no thought of vacillating between major and minor and no intention of changing the tonality. At times he substituted the fourth for the third in a triad and blended the dissonance into a common pitch in the next chord. Fauré's treatment of rhythm is equally interesting. In many of his songs he established a rhythmic ostinato figure and used it so skillfully that it did not become monotonous. He used syncopation subtly; frequently he combined duple and triple rhythmic patterns in cross rhythms.

Fauré was a master of French song, the *mélodie,* and wrote more than a hundred of them. (The term **mélodie** was used after c. 1840 to denote a French solo song with accompaniment.) Three principal collections were published (1879, 1897, 1908), each containing 20 songs. His best-known *mélodies* are *Lydia* (1865), *Après un rêve* (After a dream; 1865), *Clair de lune* (Moonlight; 1887), and *Au cimitière* (At the cemetery; 1888). The little-known *Le don silencieux* (The silent gift; pub. 1906) is excellent. However, Fauré is seen at his finest in the song cycles *Cinq mélodies, La bonne chanson, La chanson d'Eve* (Eve's song; 1906–10), and *L'horizon chimérique* (The chimerical horizon; 1921). In most of these cycles, unity is achieved by two means: (1) the poems are arranged so that they tell a story, and (2) the songs share some common musical motives. In *La bonne chanson* the nine *mélodies* are linked thematically by common motives, and the last song, *L'Hiver a cessé* (Winter is over; DWMA171), recapitulates material from some of the other songs and concludes the cycle with an expression of great joy. The overall form of the cycle and the manner of its unification were innovations. When *La bonne chanson* first appeared, it created quite a furor. Many persons were shocked at the harmonic innovations, the degree of expression, the unusual treatment of the vocal lines, and the importance given the piano accompaniment.

IMPRESSIONISM

The first use of the term "Impressionism" as a label for a distinctive artistic style was by critic Louis Leroy, who, after viewing an art exhibit in Paris in 1874, published a derogatory article in which he referred to the artists as "Impressionists." The title of one of the paintings exhibited contributed to that term—Claude Monet's *Impression: soleil levant* (Impression: sunrise, 1872; plate 25). Within a few years, those exhibitors, who included Monet (1849–1926), Édouard Manet (1832–83), Edgar Degas (1834–1917); plate 26), August Renoir (1841–1919), and Camille Pissarro (1830–1903), were commonly referred to as Impressionists, and the style of their work Impressionism. Characteristics of that style are avoidance of sharp outlines and formal precision, reliance on the effect of light and color, and a certain fluidity of design. The paintings manifest both blurring and brilliance. They are representational but not graphic and usually not realistic. Impressionist painting existed in France prior to 1872 but was at its height in 1874–86.

There was a comparable movement in French poetry known as *Le Symbolisme.* Precursor of the movement was Pierre Baudelaire (1821–67), who, in works like the sonnet *Correspondances,* expressed his theories about the music of poetry and the symbolic relationships between sound and color. The movement gained ground in the 1880s, when Verlaine's *Romances sans paroles* (Romances without words; 1874), Mallarmé's *L'Après-midi d'un faune* (The afternoon of a faun; 1876), and similar poems became known. The extreme Symbolist movement of which Mallarmé was leader was at its height c. 1890. Symbolist poets sought to convey impressions and suggestions; the function of their poetry was not to describe but to evoke. Words were chosen for color, harmony, and evocative power; fluidity of line and strophe was important. Fauré, Debussy, and Ravel were among the composers who made settings of Symbolist poetry.

When first applied to music, the term "Impressionism" was used in a disparaging sense. The Académie des Beaux Arts, after examining Claude Debussy's symphonic suite *Printemps* (Spring; orch., female chor.; 1887), which he submitted as evidence of his work in Rome, recorded that the composition exhibited "vague impressionism" and lacked formal clarity. Debussy was cautioned against excessive use of color but did not heed that admonition. Generally, he has been considered the chief exponent of Impressionist music, though that is only one aspect of his style. He strongly opposed the label "Impressionism" and iden-

tified his work as "Symbolism." Impressionistic music is characterized by irregular phrases and blurring of formal outlines, avoidance of traditional harmonic progressions, use of streams of chords in parallel motion and altered chords with unresolved dissonances, and choice of instruments for their coloristic possibilities. Though the music is tonal, modality frequently appears within it, and often the leading tone is suppressed. Composers wanted to create an atmosphere, to suggest rather than define, to hint rather than to state. Therefore, Impressionistic music *is* vague and may seem as elusive and fragile as gossamer.

ACHILLE-CLAUDE DEBUSSY

Debussy's influence has been far-reaching, touching almost every significant composer working during the first half of the twentieth century and a good many after that time. Debussy (1862–1918) did not come from a musical family. As a child, he received piano lessons and in 1872 was accepted in piano at Paris Conservatoire. In the summer of 1880, Nadezhda von Meck engaged Debussy as household pianist, and he spent several summers in her employ, in Italy, Vienna, and Moscow. Also in 1880, he enrolled in composition courses at Paris Conservatoire; in 1884 he was awarded the Prix de Rome for his cantata *L'enfant prodigue* (The prodigal son).

At the Paris World Exhibition in 1889 Debussy again heard Russian orchestral music and Musorgsky's songs and was introduced to the sound of gamelan. All influenced his work to some extent. An example

Claude Debussy. *(Courtesy Free Library of Philadelphia)*

is *Nuages* (Clouds; from *Nocturnes*; 1897–99), whose opening measures resemble portions of Musorgsky's "The idle noisy day is ended" (No. 3 in *Sunless*; 1874; ex. 25.5) and whose middle section simulates the distinctive gamelan sound. *Nocturnes* comprises three orchestral pieces: *Nuages, Fêtes* (Festivals), and *Sirènes* (Sirens), the latter including textless vocalization by female chorus.

By 1889 Debussy had become acquainted with several Symbolist writers and had set some of their poetry. He had written a number of works but was relatively unknown until his *La damoiselle élue* (*The Blessed Damosel*; S, female chor., orch.; 1888) was performed by the Société Nationale in 1893. At that time he was already working on *Prélude à l'après-midi d'un faune* (orch.; 1892–94; DWMA172), based on Mallarmé's poem. The music is chromatic, vague, and fluid, and becomes intensely emotional. It is more attuned to Symbolism than Impressionism, with the flute symbol-

izing the faun's panpipes and the music his emotional release (fig. 25.2). This symphonic poem is a free treatment of sonata form, a kind of statement-departure-return with an element of rhapsody. The orchestration includes two harps and uses no bright brasses, and the only percussion instruments are antique cymbals (small discs that are struck together very softly and allowed to vibrate) sounded near the end of the piece. Much of the time the strings play very softly, are muted, or bow over the fingerboard.

One way in which Debussy influenced twentieth-century music was his treatment of the orchestra. He had learned a great deal about instrumentation and orchestration from Rimsky-Korsakov's works. Debussy used an orchestra of average size and included only those instruments whose colors would effectively paint the picture he wanted portrayed. Most often, he favored winds over strings, and he seldom doubled melodic lines. For effect, he relied on understatement.

EXAMPLE 25.5 (*a*) Musorgsky: *Okonchen prazdnij, shumnij den'* (1874), mm. 16–21; (*b*) Debussy: *Nuages* (1893), mm. 1–4, clarinet and bassoon parts.

(a)

(b)

In 1893 Debussy saw Maurice Maeterlinck's (1862–1949) symbolist drama *Pelléas et Mélisande* and decided to make an opera of it. *Pelléas et Mélisande* (vocal score 1893–95; orchestration 1901–2) is a landmark in French opera. Debussy gave text primacy over the music—he believed music was usually too predominant in opera. He wrote no arias and included no dances; the singing is a kind of recitative. Some recurrent themes and motifs are used, representing states of mind, but there is no extensive use of Leitmotifs. The music is soft and atmospheric. Tonality and modality are mingled in the harmonies. The opera is an expression of Debussy's philosophy that music should be a free art, truly representative of the fact that it cannot be contained but exists in time and is borne on air. That freedom meant a relaxation of restrictions such as those that normally governed form, harmonic progressions, and rhythm. He expressed those ideas in articles he wrote as well as in his music. *Pelléas et Mélisande* may be considered, both musically and psychologically, a forerunner of Alban Berg's *Wozzeck*.

Pelléas et Mélisande is the only opera Debussy completed. He planned operas on some of Edgar Allan Poe's (1809–49) stories, particularly *The Devil in the Belfry* and *The Fall of the House of Usher,* but did not complete them. For the latter opera he planned three scenes; the two that he completed (*La chute de la maison Usher;* 1908–17) were performed at Yale University in 1977.

Debussy's *La Mer* (The Sea; 1903–5) comprises the three symphonic sketches *De l'aube à midi sur la mer* (From dawn to noon on the sea); *Jeux de vagues* (Play of waves), a study of light; and *Dialogue du vent et de la mer* (Dialogue of the wind and sea), a study of color and space. His other important orchestral work, *Images* (1905–12), comprises *Gigues, Ibéria,* and *Rondes du printemps* (Spring round-dances), all containing French folk songs. *Gigues* and *Rondes du printemps* foreshadow Stravinsky's *Le sacre du printemps* (The Rite of Spring; see p. 610) The fusion of timbres, unexpected dissonances, combinations of tonality and modality, and the unusual scales Debussy used in the work were shocking to many persons, but those factors influenced later twentieth-century music.

Many of Debussy's songs were written before 1885. His most important songs are *Fêtes galantes* (Galant festivals; two sets; 1891, 1904), *Chansons di Bilitis* (Songs of Bilitis; 1898), and *Trois ballades de Villon* (Three ballades of Villon; 1910).

Debussy was one of the most important composers of piano music in the early twentieth century. Most of his piano music was written after 1900. His only significant early piano pieces are *Suite Bergamasque* (1890, rev. 1905), which contains *Clair de lune* (Moonlight), and *Suite: Pour le piano* (Suite: For piano; 1894–1901). His mature style is apparent in the collection *Estampes* (Prints; 1903), comprising *Pagodes* (Pagodas), *Soirée dans Granade* (Evening in Granada), and *Jardins sous la Pluie* (Gardens in the rain). This is Impressionistic music, as are the two sets of *Images* for piano (1905–7). The two books of *Préludes* (1910, 1912) provide an excellent cross-section of Debussy's piano writing. Each book contains 12 titled pieces, both individualistic and programmatic (e.g., *Voiles* [Sails, or Veils], *La fille aux cheveux de lin* [The girl

(a)

(b)

FIGURE 25.2 (*a*) Sketch of a faun playing panpipes. (*b*) One solo flute, representing the faun, plays this melody in *Prélude à l'après-midi d'un faune*, mm. 1–4.

with the flaxen hair], and *La cathédral engloutie* [The engulfed cathedral]). Each of the two books of *Études* (1915) holds six serious technical studies that are highly musical. Debussy's humor is seen in *Children's Corner* (1906–8; 6 pcs.), which satirizes Czerny in *Doctor Gradus ad Parnassum* and Wagner in *Golliwog's Cake-walk*. The suite *En blanc et noir* (In white and black; 1915) has three pieces for two pianos.

Nor did Debussy neglect chamber music and solo instrumental music. Important contributions are the unaccompanied flute solo *Syrinx* (1913), the String Quartet (1893), and three sonatas ('cello/piano, 1915; fl., vla., harp, 1915; violin/piano, 1917).

MAURICE RAVEL

After Debussy's death, Ravel (1875–1937) was considered the leading French composer. Viewed overall, Ravel's music is less Impressionistic than Debussy's, and their musical styles differ considerably. Ravel mingled Impressionism and Classicism. He was more objective than Debussy and more traditional in choice and treatment of form. Ravel preferred modal (Phrygian and Dorian, especially) rather than whole-tone scales, and he did not write dominant ninth chords and augmented triads to the extent that Debussy did. Ravel's music is colored by chromaticisms, and his harmonies are complex but, for the most part, diatonic and functional. He was generous with major sevenths and supertonic ninths and did not always resolve dissonances. Frequently, he wrote streams of parallel triads or other chords. Organum-like passages of consecutive fourths or fifths appear in several of his works (e.g., the song *Ronsard à son âme* [Ronsard to his soul; 1923–24]). Other traits are the interval of a falling fourth and the reiteration of an accompaniment figure or a single pitch.

Maurice Ravel.

Many things influenced Ravel's music. During his childhood and youth, private lessons from distinguished pianists in Paris gave him technical facility on the piano. At Paris Conservatoire (1889–95; 1897–1900), in Fauré's classes, he acquired the mastery of composition that made him a superb craftsman, attentive to minute details, and writing with clarity of form. Ravel's style was affected by gamelan and Russian music he heard at the Paris World Exhibition in 1889. He was a brilliant orchestrator and was knowledgeable concerning the coloristic possibilities of all instruments, and he used instrumental timbres effectively. However, he was primarily a pianist, and many of his orchestral works were conceived for piano, then orchestrated.

Partially, Ravel's interest in Iberian music was inherited from his mother; yet, his works reflect the pure Spanish music of Andalusia and of flamenco rather than the Basque of her region. Ravel's friendship with his Conservatoire classmate, Spanish pianist Ricardo Viñes (1875–1943), was another influential factor.

Some characteristics of Ravel's compositional style are present in his earliest works: use of traditional form for *Menuet antique* (1895; pno.), the Spanish idiom of *Habanera* (1895; 2 pnos.), and the consecutive parallel intervals in *Entre cloches* (Amid bells; 1897; 2 pnos.). Later, he used *Habanera,* orchestrated, as the third movement in *Rapsodie espagnole* (Spanish rhapsody; 1907–8). Other works with Spanish flavor are the comic opera *L'heure espagnole* (Spanish hour; 1907–8), *Alborada del gracioso* (Morning song of the buffoon) from *Miroirs* (Mirrors; 1904–5; pno.), and *Boléro* (orch.; 1928) written for dancer Ida Rubenstein. *Boléro* was, to Ravel, an essay in orchestration, with continual repetition of two 16-bar phrases (harmonized) over an ostinato rhythmic figure; the only variety is the orchestral crescendo effected by the cumulative entrances of instruments as well as by increased volume.

Ravel's most Impressionistic compositions are *Jeux d'eau* (Fountains; 1901), *Miroirs* (Mirrors; 1904–5), *Gaspard de la nuit* (1908), all for piano, and *Daphnis et Chloé* (1910–12), a choreographic symphony that requires a very large orchestra, a wind machine, and a chorus singing textless melody.

Ravel wrote some of his finest piano music in the literature. *Jeux d'eau* (DWMA173) was a natural outgrowth of his interest in the piano music of Liszt and the latter's depiction of the fountains at Villa d'Este. *Jeux d'eau* may have influenced Debussy's *Jardin sous la pluie* and *Reflets dans l'eau.*

Ravel's other major piano works are Neoclassic: *Pavane pour une Infante défunte* (Pavane for a deceased Infanta; 1899), *Sonatine* (1905), *Valses nobles et sentimentales* (Noble and sentimental waltzes; 1911), and *Le tombeau de Couperin* (Lament for Couperin; 1917). *Pavane* is the best known of these works, especially in its orchestral version (1910), but *Le tombeau de Couperin* is Ravel's finest achievement for solo piano. The composition resembles a harpsichord suite of Couperin's time. In two respects the suite is nationalistic—it honors Couperin, and each movement is dedicated to the memory of a World War I victim. For piano and orchestra, Ravel composed two concerti, one in D major (1929–30) for left hand only, commissioned by Paul Wittgenstein, Austrian concert pianist who lost his right arm in World War I; the other, in G major (1929–31), for Marguerite Long. The D-major concerto has one movement (Allegro with Lento introduction) and contains a quasi-improvisatory episode with elements of jazz. *Concerto for Left Hand* is an extraordinary work; it does not sound as though the performer is using only one hand.

Classicism is apparent in Ravel's chamber music: a cyclic String Quartet in F major (1903), a Piano Trio (1914), a violin/piano Sonata (1922), and a 'cello/piano Sonata (1927). The Piano Trio contains some elements of Impressionism.

Ravel wrote a considerable amount of vocal music, much of it for solo voice with piano. The two groups of solos for which he supplied chamber ensemble accompaniment—*Trois poèmes de Stéphane Mallarmé* (Three poems by Stéphane Mallarmé; 1913) and *Chansons madécasses* (Songs of Madagascar; 1926)—are his most significant contribution to vocal solo literature. The Mallarmé settings were inspired by Schoenberg's *Pierrot Lunaire,* which Ravel had heard in Berlin, but Ravel did not use *Sprechstimme* (speech-song).

From time to time, Ravel harmonized folk songs of various lands and made orchestral arrangements of other composers' works. The most notable of the latter is his orchestration of Musorgsky's *Pictures at an Exhibition* (1922).

OTHER IMPRESSIONISTS

Impressionism is found in the work of other composers including Albert Roussel (1869–1937), Florent Schmitt (1870–1958), and Déodat de Séverac (1873–1921) in France, Ottorino Respighi (1879–1936) in Italy, Charles Griffes (1884–1920) in the United States, and the English composer Frederick Delius (1862–1934). One of Griffes's best-known Impressionistic works is *The White Peacock,* from *Roman Sketches,* Op. 7 (1915–16). Respighi's greatest success came with *Le fontane di Roma* (The fountains of Rome; 1917) and *I pini di Roma* (The pines of Rome; 1924) both for orchestra. The insertion of a phonograph recording of a nightingale's song in *I pini di Roma* was an innovation.

LILI BOULANGER

Lili Boulanger's (1893–1918) father and his parents had been awarded prizes at Paris Conservatoire; her father taught there; her sister Nadia (see p. 613) was talented. Lili had private lessons on several instruments and studied composition with Georges Caussade and Paul Vidal at the Conservatoire. In 1913 she was awarded the Prix de Rome for her cantata *Faust et Hélène* (Faust and Helen); she was the first woman to receive that award. Her stay in Rome was cut short by ill health.

Lili's finest works are *Du fond de l'abîme* (Out of the depths, setting Ps. 130; 1914–17; A, T, chor., orch., organ), a work that shows her capable of handling solo voices and large ensembles admirably; *Vieille prière bouddhique* (Old Buddhist prayer; 1917; T, chor., orch.); and *Piè Jesu* (Holy Jesus; 1918; Mez., str. qrt., harp, organ). Her instrumental works include chamber music, two symphonic poems, pieces for small orchestra, songs, piano solos, *Ave Maria* for organ, and some instrumental solos for violin/piano and flute/piano. *Nocturne* (vln., pno., 1911) is delicate, with Impressionistic tendencies, and shows Debussy's influence. An opera, *La princess Maleine* (Princess Maleine), was unfinished at the time of her death.

ERIK SATIE

The eccentric composer Erik Satie (1866–1925) was neither Impressionistic nor anti-Impressionistic but was extremely individualistic. Elements of his late style were as avant-garde as some music of the 1960s.

Satie studied at Paris Conservatoire but accomplished little. After completing military service (1886–87), he composed a few piano pieces, including three *Sarabandes* (1887) and *Trois Gymnopédies* (Three Gymnopédies; 1888). In 1890, *Gnossiennes* (Gnostics) appeared. Then Satie joined the "Rose + Croix" movement. Music he composed while active in the group (1891–95) has an aura of mysticism and contains unresolved ninth chords, successions of first-inversion triads, and melodies in ancient Greek modes.

Then he began writing satirical pieces with humorous titles and bizarre directives for the performers. Among these are the piano duets *Trois morceaux en forme de poire* (Three pieces in pear form; c. 1903) and the piano solos *Embryons desséchés* (Dessicated embryos; 1913) and *Descriptions automatiques* (Automatic descriptions; 1913). The music is spare of texture, frequently written in only two parts; the sound is dry, capricious, and witty. The notation of such pieces is avant-garde, sometimes with black notes on red staves, without bar lines, and without key signatures.

Some of Satie's best work is in his ballets, *Parade* (1917), *Relâche* (Theater closed; 1924), and in the symphonic drama *Socrate* (Socrates; 1918; 4 sopranos, chamber orch.) In *Relâche* jazz is included, perhaps for the first time in Paris.

Satie's music was misunderstood because he was so avant-garde. To some degree, his miniatures and sparse textures forecast the very compressed pieces of Webern, and the spatial separation of performers predicts similar requests by composers active after 1945. Satie's influence extended beyond the young composers around him and affected the work of Ravel, Varèse, Cage, and others later in the century.

LES SIX FRANÇAIS

In 1917 six students at the Paris Conservatoire began sharing ideas and gave joint concerts of new music. In the group were George Auric (1899–1983), Louis Durey (1888–1979), Arthur Honegger (1892–1955), Darius Milhaud (1892–1974), Francis Poulenc (1899–1963), and Germaine Tailleferre (1892–1983). They called themselves *Les nouveaux jeunes* (The new youth). Jean Cocteau (1889–1963) promoted their work in his articles, and they were attracted to Erik Satie, whose work embodied some of their precepts.

In 1920 journalist Henri Collet referred to this group as *Les six français* (The French Six). He wrote of them in the same sentence with the Russian Five, and he was not incorrect, for the two groups had in common a desire to compose music devoid of German

Les Six, with Cocteau. Left to right: Milhaud, Auric, Honegger, Tailleferre, Poulenc, Durey, and Cocteau at the piano. *(Photograph by Lipnitzki, 1952)*

characteristics. In addition, the Six advocated (1) choosing subjects from everyday life for use in program music, operas, and ballets; (2) using machines as instruments or source material; (3) writing for nonconventional as well as conventional instruments; and (4) learning about styles other than those suited to the concert hall (e.g., circus band, jazz band, or café-cabaret entertainment) and writing in those styles if they so desired. They thought compositions should be brief, dry, and straightforward. They collaborated in producing *Album des Six* (piano pieces) and *Les mariés de la tour Eiffel* (The wedding party at the Eiffel Tower; 1921), a ballet-farce on a text by Cocteau. In *Les mariés . . .* , two speaking voices, representing phonographs, describe the mime of the ballet. The Six did not remain active as a group, but all continued to compose to some degree (see p. 605).

BRITAIN

In England, there was continued interest in oratorio, opera, music festivals, madrigal singing, and old music. Societies were formed to publish particular works: the Purcell Society (Purcell's complete works), the Plainsong and Mediaeval Music Society (Sarum chant books), and the Musical Antiquarian Society (works of Byrd, Gibbons, Weelkes, and Wilbye). John Stainer published some chansons by Du Fay and his contemporaries. Music festivals and the London Philharmonic commissioned works by many European composers. English composers active during 1870–1920 include Edward Elgar (1857–1934), Ethel Smyth (1858–1944), Frederick Delius (1862–1934), Ralph Vaughan Williams (1872–1958), and Gustavus (von) Holst (1874–1934).

GUSTAVUS (VON) HOLST

From early childhood Holst practiced piano under his father's supervision. Gustav had poor eyesight, suffered from asthma, and during his teens developed neuritis in his right arm. Finally, his father realized that Gustav could never be a concert pianist and permitted him to study composition at Oxford, where he met and became a close friend of Vaughan Williams; throughout their lives, they shared with one another sketches of works in progress.

While at Oxford, Holst conducted a choir that met at poet William Morris's (1834–96) home. There he met Isobel Harrison, whom he married in 1901, and he was introduced to Hindu literature and philosophy. He became proficient in Sanskrit, read stories from the *Ramayana* and *Mahābharata,* and translated hymns from the *Rig Veda* (see p. 3). Hindu mysticism influenced several of Holst's works: *Hymns from the Rig Veda* (9 hymns; vc., pno.; 1907–8), *Choral Hymns from the Rig Veda* (4 sets; chor., instrs.; 1908–12), the chamber opera *Sāvitri* (from *Mahābharata;* 1908), the opera *Sita* (from *Ramayana;* 1900–6), and some songs. From 1905 to 1934 Holst was music director at St. Paul's Girls' School, Hammersmith. Besides teaching, he conducted amateur choral ensembles, orchestras, and festivals; he was responsible for the first performance in England of some of Bach's cantatas.

Acquaintance with modal folk songs removed from Holst's style much of the chromaticism that colored his early works. This is apparent in *A Somerset Rhapsody* (orch.; 1906–7). He made choral settings of 12 Welsh folk songs (1930–31), at least two dozen English ones, and some traditional English Christmas carols.

Holst considered *Egdon Heath* (1927) his best work, but his best-known work is *The Planets* (1914–16), a suite of seven orchestral pieces, one for each planet then known to be in our galaxy. *The Hymn of Jesus* (1917), for two choruses, female semichorus, and orchestra, is a masterpiece. Holst incorporated in it the chants *Pange lingua* and *Vexilla regis* (see p. 91) and used as fundamental text this passage from the apocryphal *Acts of St. John:* "Ye who dance not know not what we are knowing." The music contains some sharp dissonances but conveys an overall sense of great exultation (DWMA174).

Imogen Holst (1907–84) prepared the thematic catalog of her father's works and wrote a biography of him and a book about his music. She formed the Purcell Singers in 1953 and conducted them until 1967. She was one of the first women in Britain to conduct brass and military bands.

EDWARD ELGAR

Elgar's only formal training in music consisted of a few violin lessons, but he learned a great deal from observation, at church, at his father's music store, and at meetings of choral societies. He played violin and bassoon well enough to participate in ensembles, substituted for his father as organist at church, and conducted instrumental and choral ensembles in public programs.

Elgar attained recognition with *Variations on an Original Theme* (*Enigma Variations;* 1898–99). He explained carefully that, in addition to his original theme, which has 14 variations, another larger theme goes through the entire work, but he never revealed that theme or its meaning. Most of the variations are headed by the initials of the one portrayed.

Elgar composed works in all genres. The piece that is heard most often is the first of his five marches titled *Pomp and Circumstance* (D major, 1901). Of his five oratorios, the finest is *The Dream of Gerontius* (1900; Mez., T, Bar. soloists, chor., orch.). The text concerns a man facing imminent death, judgment, and eternity. Elgar used representative motives, and the influence of Wagner's *Parsifal* is apparent. Gerontius's solos vary from natural speech-rhythms to lyricism.

Elgar did not quote folk songs in his works but did depict programmatically some English scenes and events. Some of his works evidence strong patriotism, as does *The Spirit of England* (1915–17; S or T solo, chor., orch.). Contributing to the "English" sound of his music are characteristic traits of late medieval English music, such as cross-relations and passages in parallel thirds.

Minor Composers

Ethel Smyth knew as a child that she wanted to be a musician, and she was determined to study music in continental Europe. In 1877 she entered Leipzig Conservatory but, like many others, was not pleased with the teaching there and arranged for private instruction. Her first compositions were a String Quintet (1884), a violin/piano Sonata (1887), a 'cello/piano Sonata (1887), and two sets of Lieder (c. 1886). In 1891 she composed a Mass in D major (SATB soloists, chor., orch.), which was performed by the Royal Choral Society, London. After seeing the Mass, the conductor Hermann Levi (1839–1900) urged her to write an opera. Her first opera, *Fantasio* (1892–94), was performed in Weimar in 1898. Her second, *Der Wald* (The Forest; 1899–1901), has the forest setting of a German Romantic opera and a Wagnerian-type theme of salvation through death. Smyth's third opera, *Les Naufrageurs* (The Wreckers; 1903–4), is her finest and best-known work. It shows Wagner's influence in use of Leitmotifs, the style of the counterpoint, and the large orchestral resources. In places, choral hymn-singing offstage accompanies singers on stage.

Smyth wrote three more operas, choral works with orchestra, a concerto for horn and violin with orchestra, about a dozen solo songs, and some chamber music. Her last composition, *The Prison* (1930), is a symphonic work for two soloists, chorus, and orchestra. Smyth's style is eclectic, not distinctly personal. Her operas clearly show the influence of Wagner and Arthur Sullivan.

Frederick Delius was not a nationalistic composer, and his works do not sound particularly English, though he wrote program music on English subjects (e.g., *Brigg Fair: An English Rhapsody* [orch.; 1907]). He composed several operas, incidental music for plays, concerti, orchestral works, chamber music, and vocal pieces. His best works are for soloists, chorus, and orchestra, such as *Sea Drift* (Bar., chor., orch.; 1903–4) and *A Mass of Life* (SATBar. solos, chor., orch.; 1904–5).

Delius's best-known work is the tone poem *On Hearing the First Cuckoo in Spring* (1912), one of two works published as *Pieces for Small Orchestra*. The other piece, *Summer Night on the River* (1911), is Impressionistic. So is *In a Summer Garden* (1908), an orchestral rhapsody, free in form, with some sensuous harmonies and at times rather pointillistic in the depiction of light and shade. In several of Delius's works for orchestra and chorus, the choral singing is textless (e.g., *A Song of the High Hills* [1911] and *Songs to be sung of a Summer Night on the Water* [SATTBB chorus; 1917]).

United States

During the 1860s, the United States experienced Civil War and the assassination of President Lincoln, and after 1865 many areas of the country needed reconstruction. These circumstances influenced popular rather than serious art music, for most of America's composers were still European trained and wrote music that reflected European styles. Very few American composers were inspired by or tapped for resources the wealth of indigenous material that surrounded them—Indian tribal melodies, black spirituals, New England hymns, and gospel songs. James Bland (1854–1911), one of the few who did, composed more than 700 popular songs, such as *Carry Me Back to Old Virginny.* Between 1860 and 1920 American conservatories of music were founded, and private citizens financed the building of concert halls in major cities. European virtuosi and opera troupes concertized in the United States, noted composers came to teach for a while, and American concert programs were filled with music by European composers. The most important American composers during the last decades of the nineteenth century were James Knowles Paine (1839–1906) and Edward MacDowell (1860–1908).

PAINE, MACDOWELL

Paine received his early musical training from Herman Kotzschmar, a German musician living in Maine. Then, in 1858–61, he studied in Berlin. Paine joined the faculty of Harvard University in 1862, and, in 1875, when Harvard became the first American university to establish a professorship of music, Paine was appointed to that post. Besides many organ works, his compositions include incidental music for plays, two operas, numerous choral works, a few songs, two symphonies, a symphonic poem, and some chamber music. Bach was the model for Paine's early organ works but many of Paine's compositions reflect the influence of German early Romanticists. The works written after c. 1880 show increased chromaticism and Chopinesque figurations, not always used to advantage (e.g., Symphony No. 2). One of Paine's finest late works is the incidental music to Sophocles's *Oedipus tyrannus* (King Oedipus; 1880–81), particularly the Prelude, in which he effectively used thematic transformation.

As a child, Edward MacDowell studied piano with Juan Buitrago and Teresa Carreño (1853–1917); Carreño recognized the measure of his talent and encouraged study abroad. In 1876–78 MacDowell studied at Paris Conservatoire, then went to Germany for piano, counterpoint, advanced theory, and composition lessons. For several years he enjoyed a successful career in Europe as teacher, composer, and concert pianist. He returned to the United States in the autumn of 1888

and began his American concert career in Boston. When Columbia University established a chair of music in 1896, MacDowell was appointed to that professorship and retained it until 1904.

MacDowell's earliest works date from 1876; many of them were published under the pseudonym Edgar Thorn. He composed nothing after 1902, when his health began to deteriorate. MacDowell's compositions for piano include 2 concerti (A minor, D minor), 16 sets of character pieces, 4 sonatas, and some études. He wrote 2 orchestral suites, 4 symphonic poems, at least 42 solo songs, and more than 20 choral works. His music is tonal and shows the influence of Liszt and Grieg. Most of MacDowell's instrumental compositions are Romantic program music. Some of the piano pieces are quite simple; others are virtuosic. Perhaps his best-known work is *To a Wild Rose,* from 10 *Woodland Sketches* (1896). Other sets of character pieces for piano are *Sea Pieces* (1898) and *New England Idyls* (1901–2). In 1887 MacDowell wrote several collections of piano pieces interpreting poems: *6 Idyls after Goethe, Sechs Gedichte nach Heinrich Heine* (Six poems of Heinrich Heine), and *Vier kleine Poesien* (Four little poems).

Though MacDowell musically portrayed some New England scenes, he rarely used indigenous American materials in his compositions. Theodore Baker's *Über die Musik der Nordamerikanischer Wilden* (About the music of the North American savages) provided thematic material for MacDowell's orchestral *Suite No. 2, "Indian,"* but chromatic harmonies and thick texture often obscure the Indian melodies. MacDowell was supportive of American music, but he believed strongly that the music should stand on its own merits and not be performed simply because its composer was American.

After MacDowell's death, his widow, pianist Marian Nevins MacDowell (1857–1956), converted their summer home into a working retreat—The MacDowell Colony—for artists, composers, and writers. She helped support that retreat, which is still in operation, by performing concerts of her husband's music.

AMY CHENEY BEACH

Amy Cheney (1867–1944) made her concert début as pianist in 1883 in Boston, and in October 1885 she performed Chopin's Concerto No. 2 with the Boston

Symphony. In December 1885 she married Dr. H. H. A. Beach and thereafter used her married name in her career. She was the first American woman to achieve recognition as a composer of large forms. Her works include Mass in E♭ (1890), *Gaelic Symphony* (E minor; 1896), Piano Concerto (C♯ minor; 1899), the opera *Cabildo* (1932), a violin/piano Sonata (A minor; 1896), Piano Quintet (F♯ minor; 1898), Piano Trio (A minor; 1938), and numerous other piano pieces, choral works, and songs. Beach's Mass in E♭, premiered by the Boston Handel and Haydn Society in 1892, was that society's first performance of a composition by a woman. Her *Gaelic Symphony,* based on Irish folk melodies, is the first symphony composed by an American woman. The first performances of the *Gaelic Symphony* (1896) and the Piano Concerto (1899) were by the Boston Symphony, with Beach as soloist in the concerto. After her husband's death (1910), she concertized in Europe for four years; in the 1920s she spent several summers at The MacDowell Colony. Her most popular song was *The Year's at the Spring* (1899). The Sonata is Brahmsian, and the influence of Brahms and Liszt is seen in her piano works.

Where music written and/or performed by women is concerned, Boston, in the 1890s, seems to have occupied a position comparable with that of the Medici court at Ferrara in the late sixteenth century. In 1893–96 the Boston Symphony played several of Margaret Lang's (1867–1972, age 104) works: *Dramatic Overture,* the overtures *Totila* and *Wichitis,* and three arias for solo voice and orchestra. Helen Hood, Helen Hopekirk, and Mabel Daniels were active in Boston early in the twentieth century.

FOOTE, CHADWICK, PARKER

Among the New England composers adhering to Classic-Romantic traditions were Arthur Foote (1853–1937), George Chadwick (1854–1931), and Horatio Parker (1863–1919). Foote studied with Paine at Harvard and earned the first master's degree in music granted by that university (1875). Some of Foote's finest works are *Ballad* (vln., pno.), Piano Trio No. 2 (B♭ major), and the Piano Quartet (1890). Most of his orchestral pieces were first performed by the Boston Symphony. Some have never been published (e.g., the overture *In the Mountains* [1886], which was per-

formed also at the Paris Exposition in 1889). Foote wrote more than 100 solo songs, the best known being *The Night Has a Thousand Eyes, In Picardie,* and *I Know a Little Garden Path.* Other works by Foote include cantatas, numerous keyboard pieces (piano, organ), three string quartets and other chamber music, a 'cello concerto, the symphonic poem *Francesca da Rimini,* and several suites.

Chadwick began his career by serving for a year (1876) as head of the music department of Olivet College, Michigan, then spent several years studying organ and composition in Europe. In 1882 he joined the faculty of New England Conservatory and in 1897–1930 was director of that school. Many of Chadwick's works follow traditional Germanic lines, but he did not limit himself to that style. In several works he incorporated popular melodies and Afro-Caribbean syncopated dance rhythms; in Symphony No. 2 (B♭ major; 1883–85) he used a Negro melody. His opera *The Padrone* is the first American verismo opera. Chadwick advocated using the natural rhythms of American prose. Those rhythms appear in several of his works. Representative of his non-Germanic style is the orchestral suite *Symphonic Sketches* (A major; 1895–1904).

Parker received organ and piano lessons from his mother, then studied with Chadwick at New England Conservatory and went to Munich for further training in organ and composition. In 1894 he was appointed professor of theory at Yale University and was dean of the School of Music there in 1904–19. Most of his compositions are choral works on religious or medieval subjects and include Latin motets, cantatas, oratorios, anthems, and occasional pieces. Also, he wrote songs, hymns, chamber music, operas and incidental music, orchestral works, a few piano pieces, and numerous organ works. His masterpiece is the oratorio *Hora novissima* (The last hour; 1893). He was awarded prizes for his operas *Mona* (1912) and *Fairyland* (1915). On the whole, Parker's music is conservative and tonal, with well-defined melodies, diatonic harmonies, and traditional key relationships and formal structures. Only a few works written in 1901–11 show tendencies toward tonally evasive harmonies and chromaticism (e.g., the concert aria *Crépuscle* [Mez., orch.] and *Mona.*).

CHARLES IVES

Ives (1874–1954) was an individualistic composer who did not teach and who founded no school. His works were strongly influenced by transcendentalist philosophies and by the ideas about music instilled in him by his father, who was his first teacher. George E. Ives (1845–94) thoroughly understood traditional harmony, counterpoint, and the music of Bach; moreover, he was interested in quarter tones, polytonality, acoustics, and the effect of space in relation to performance. He gave Charles thorough grounding in all these things, as well as lessons on organ, piano, drums, and cornet. In addition, Charles absorbed all features of the music that was part of the small town in which he lived. Frequently, George required Charles to sing or play a melody in one key while playing the accompaniment in another. Charles retained an interest in polytonality and later wrote some four-voice fugues with each voice in a different key (e.g., *The Shining Shore* [1897]).

By the time Ives was 12, he was composing. When he was 14, he was a salaried organist at Danbury Baptist Church; for the next 16 years, he was a church organist in whatever city he lived. Quotations from hymns are a feature of his compositions. Ives was adept at improvising and at making variations. One of his early compositions for organ is a set of *Variations on "America,"* first improvised, then notated c. 1891.

During 1894–98 Ives pursued a business degree at Yale and also enrolled in Horatio Parker's music courses there. Ives and Parker did not always agree on compositional procedures, for Ives considered music confined to traditional harmonies "stupid music." From his teens, Ives's works were characterized by musical quotations, strong dissonance, and bitonality or polytonality. He could and did write music that followed the rules of traditional harmony but not by preference. His *First Symphony*, written at Yale, follows tradition, but his second has five movements and is filled with musical quotations and dissonance. Ives believed that not every dissonance required resolution. In his terminology, to write music without strong dissonance was to be "lily-livered." However, he did not sacrifice melody for dissonance.

After graduating from Yale, Ives worked in a New York insurance firm, secured a position as a church or-

Charles Ives. *(Bettman Newsphotos)*

ganist, and spent his free time writing music. In 1902, he resigned his organist post. After 1902, his music became more experimental and more aurally challenging. He tended to write orchestral works in sets, one of the most famous being *I. A Contemplation of a Serious Matter or The Unanswered Question. II. A Contemplation of Nothing Serious or Central Park in the Dark "In the Good Old Summertime"* (1905). The set requires two orchestras and two conductors, unsynchronized, and juxtaposes tonal and atonal music.

A heart problem forced Ives to take a vacation from business in 1906; then, he and Julian Myrick started their own insurance firm. Ives never considered music his vocation. At that time he did not care whether his works were ever performed—in his opinion, it is impossible to perform some of his music. In the "Postface" to *114 Songs* he stated that if the rights of some of the songs were observed, they would not be sung. Ives once said, "What has sound to do with music?" It sufficed for Ives to hear his music mentally and to express it by sketching out the notation. Many of his works have been lost or survive only in fragments. Not until after he suffered a serious heart attack in 1918 did he consider sharing his music, sort through his sketches, and make fair copies of some of his works. By then, he had written several orchestral sets, 4 symphonies, 4 violin/piano sonatas, some string quartets and other chamber music, 2 piano sonatas and other keyboard works, numerous choral works and part-songs, and over 100 solo songs. He made a fair copy of the *Second Piano Sonata: "Concord, Mass. 1840–60,"* wrote *Essays before a Sonata* to accompany the music, had both printed (1920), and gave copies to persons he thought might be interested in them. Next, he assembled a collection of his vocal solos, had

114 Songs printed (1922), and distributed those copies. The texts of several songs were by his wife, Harmony Twitchell Ives (1876–1969).

In 1927 Ives met Henry Cowell (1897–1965). They had several things in common: their musical innovations had not been influenced by avant-garde European composers, their use of tone clusters as a viable compositional device had occurred independently of each other, and their music was affected to some extent by vernacular and popular music. By 1927 Ives had almost stopped composing; his creativity had waned considerably. Cowell printed some of Ives's works in *New Music Quarterly* and introduced Ives to Nicolas Slonimsky (1894–1995), who conducted the first performances of Ives's *Three Places in New England* (c. 1912).

Around 1927, John Kirkpatrick (1905–91) determined to learn the *Concord Sonata,* a task that took several years. When he performed the sonata in 1939, the work received a favorable review, and a recital of Ives's music was presented in New York. From then on, Ives began to be recognized as a great American avant-garde composer.

The *Concord Sonata* comprises the programmatic movements "Emerson," "Hawthorne," "The Alcotts," and "Thoreau." Ives aimed to present musically the spirit of the philosophical and literary views of the transcendentalists of Concord. The sonata is a cyclic work based on two principal motives that appear in various permutations in all movements: the four-note motive that dominates Beethoven's Fifth Symphony and a descending five-note figure that is first stated in octaves (ex. 25.6).

In the first three movements of the sonata, meter signatures and bar lines appear infrequently; when a bar line is used, it points up a significant musical event. In the last movement there are no key signatures, no meter signatures, and no bar lines. The "Hawthorne" movement, designated Scherzo, is a little lighter in character than the first movement. Tone clusters occur frequently, sometimes in rapid succession (ex. 25.7a). In one section of the movement, a board 14¾ inches long is used to depress silently the piano keys covering an expanse of two octaves and a second so that an echo chamber is created within the piano and those strings can vibrate freely and produce harmonics when other chords are played normally (ex. 25.7b).

"The Alcotts" (DWMA175) is simpler in texture, in accord with activities in the Alcott home, and includes portions of hymns, *Loch Lomond,* and the "Wedding March" from *Lohengrin.* The key signatures used near the beginning of the movement openly indicate bitonality. Several chords in the "Thoreau" movement represent echoes over Walden Pond. In the last two-thirds of the movement, an ostinato figure recurs periodically. One instance is in conjunction with an *ad libitum* flute melody that is intended to convey the sound of music floating over Walden Pond. Ives's associative use of quotations parallels literary authors' "stream of consciousness" technique—as writers used words, phrases, and quotations from other literary works to invoke associations in the reader's mind, so Ives used musical quotations.

In some works Ives does not quote at all, as in the songs *The Cage* (1906) and *Soliloquy, or a Study in 7ths*

EXAMPLE 25.6 In *"Concord" Sonata,* mvt. 1, mm. 1–3, Ives presents the sonata's two basic motives: (*a*) the first five bass notes and (*b*) the three repeated notes (the accented e pitches) and a descent of a third.

and *Other Things* (1907). *The Cage* resulted from Ives's observation of a boy watching a leopard pace back and forth in its cage. The song is without bar lines or meter signature. The vocal melody moves stepwise in a persistent rising and falling pattern that depicts the monotony of the animal's pacing in its confined quarters. The last eight notes of the melody are a repetition of the first eight. To most listeners *The Cage* sounds atonal.

In Ives's musical style, no consistent line of development can be traced. He expressed his thoughts without regard for traditional rules of composition. He based at least one piece on a tone row, wrote some ragtime, and experimented freely. His music is truly American, for he used indigenous musical material from various sources, and American literature, philosophy, and traditions were embedded in his esthetic.

HENRY COWELL

Cowell, pianist-composer and writer on music, maintained a lifelong interest in Irish folk melodies and legends. Among his innovative procedures was the use of large clusters of tones, which he called **tone clusters** and which he produced in *The Tides of Manaunaun* (c. 1912) by striking groups of piano keys with his hand or entire forearm. The tone clusters are in the bass register, supporting a modal melody. The total effect is atonal. Cowell's use of tone clusters affected other composers' work, especially that of Bartók.

Before 1914 Cowell had written more than 100 pieces of music. In several works written during 1915–19, he initiated **indeterminancy,** chance factors in performance. In *Quartet Romantic* (2 fl., vln., vla.; 1915–17) and *Quartet Euphometric* (str. qrt.; 1916–19), Cowell provided harmonic guidance through the basic structure of a simple four-part theme, but most of the pitches are to be chosen freely. Indeterminancy was developed to a greater degree in some of Cowell's later works, and he transmitted the principle directly to his student John Cage.

It was Cowell who first had the idea of playing on the strings of the piano and then of placing foreign objects among the piano strings to create unusual

EXAMPLE 25.7 *"Concord" Sonata,* mvt. 2: (*a*) portion of passage of tone clusters played faster and faster; (*b*) clusters requiring use of a board. (Piano Sonata No. 2 by Charles Ives. Copyright © 1947 (renewed) Associated Music Publishers, Inc. (BMI). International Copyright Secured. All Rights Reserved. Used by Permission of Associated Music Publishers, Inc.)

(a)

(b)

sounds and new timbres. In the hands of John Cage, the latter technique developed into **prepared piano.** Cowell included music incorporating his experiments in his recital in Carnegie Hall in 1924. Among his early works requiring the performer to play on the piano strings are *The Aeolian Harp* (1923) and *The Banshee* (1925). In *The Aeolian Harp*, piano keys are depressed silently with one hand while the other hand strums or plucks the piano strings. *The Banshee* requires an assistant to hold down the damper pedal while the performer plays on the piano strings (DWMA176).

Between c. 1935 and 1950 Cowell's music became increasingly conservative and tonal, with emphasis on folk music and early American hymnody. In general, conditions in America were economical, for the country was struggling to recover from the Great Depression. After 1950 Cowell endeavored to synthesize ethnic influences and his early innovative styles. Approximately 700 of his compositions survive.

JAZZ

Jazz emerged early in the twentieth century in the southern United States, but some of its roots extend far back over the centuries into the complex polyrhythms of African tribal music and the call-response (or leader-audience) nature of musical performance in African societies. Other factors in the development of jazz are the creation and manner of singing spirituals, gospel songs, and secular songs dealing with all kinds of personal situations and feelings—difficult working conditions, infidelity, loneliness, and others. The songs were improvised, then learned and (in variant forms) transmitted orally from one locality to another, from one generation to the next. Such songs were forerunners of the 12-measure **blues** that is fundamental in the development of jazz.

Blues are songs dealing with human problems—love, sex, poverty, and death. Somewhat more complex than ordinary work songs, a blues is constructed in 12 measures, divided into 3 equal phrases. Usually the formal pattern is AAB, the second phrase being exact textual and melodic repetition of the first. Harmonically, the first line is totally in the tonic, the second line moves from tonic to subdominant, and the last line uses a I–V–IV–I progression. Certain notes in the melody—the third and seventh degrees of the scale and sometimes the fifth degree—are inflected or

"bent" downward from their standard pitch; these are "blue notes" (ex. 25.8). The accompaniment is a vital part of a blues song and is constructed from the I, IV, and V chords of the normal major scale. Probably the earliest blues songs were accompanied by guitar. Guitarists can adjust tuning and bend tones, but when the accompaniment is supplied by piano, a harmonic clash is created between melody and accompaniment.

A blues is sung simply, often with considerable freedom because of the singer's individual vocal inflections of the melody. It conveys an impression of improvisation and that the performer is personally identified with its message. A well-known blues singer was Bessie Smith (1894–1937), whose finest performances were with Louis Armstrong in 1925. One of the last of the great blues singers was Alberta Hunter (1895–1984), who, in her 89th year, was still acclaimed for her public performances of blues.

Also important in the development of jazz were the blackface minstrel shows popular around the middle of the nineteenth century, the cakewalk, and ragtime. The **cakewalk** was a processional dance done by couples parading or strutting around a square and improvising high stepping and other lively movements as they turned the corners. These "walkarounds," danced to fiddle and banjo tunes that were quite syncopated, became a feature of the parody-dances regularly held as part of black slaves' Sunday entertainments. Customarily, a prize—usually a cake—was given the couple whose movements in the walkaround were judged the most innovative. Thus, that dance became known as "cakewalk." The cakewalk became a fad in the 1890s, and cakewalk music was composed and published as sheet music. The cakewalk was known in Europe early in the twentieth century; Debussy included it in his *Children's Corner* suite.

Ragtime was developed by black pianists and is akin to march music. The name derives from the fact that the rhythm is ragged; that is, the pianist's right hand plays

EXAMPLE 25.8 A blues scale.

syncopated rhythms against a steady rhythm maintained by the left hand. Ragtime is formally structured music intended to be performed exactly as notated. A ragtime piece usually consists of four **strains** (melodies), each 16 measures long, and each strain repeated (e.g., AA BB CC DD). The left hand maintains a steady rhythm in duple meter throughout the piece while the right hand syncopates. Obviously, a rag contains no blue notes, because the piano is a structured instrument and cannot "bend" notes. The most famous rag is Scott Joplin's (1868–1917) *Maple Leaf Rag* (1899).

Jazz is generally believed to have emerged in New Orleans early in the twentieth century, when small ensembles (bands) playing ragtime incorporated elements of blues. There was little recorded or notated jazz during the first quarter of the twentieth century. Early jazz relied heavily on improvisation, and improvisation is still considered a vital element of jazz. Supposedly, cornetist Charles ("Buddy") Bolden (1868–1938) was the first instrumentalist to play in jazz style. If this is true, jazz was in evidence before 1907, for Bolden's performing career ended in that year. After Bolden came "King" Oliver (1885–1938), Louis Armstrong (1900–71), and others. Around 1910, the characteristic jazz ensemble consisted of cornet, clarinet/saxophone, trombone, and rhythm section. By 1920 jazz elements were being included in works of European composers. The New Orleans style of jazz reached a peak with Louis Armstrong and his "Hot Five" c. 1925. Armstrong was probably the greatest solo player in jazz. His cornet playing—his technique, expression, vibratos, and "shakes"—served as a model for other jazz soloists. Another brilliant jazz trumpeter was Miles Davis (1926–91), who began playing jazz in the 1940s and, over several decades, introduced audiences to cool jazz, hard bop, modal playing, free-form exploration, and the use of electronics in fusion jazz.

SUMMARY

In the late nineteenth century, composers could choose conservatism, post-Romanticism, nationalism, or Impressionism or be innovative in a variety of ways.

In Russia, Tchaikovsky and Rakhmaninov sometimes included nationalistic traits in their music, but mainly they wrote works in the Western tradition. Skriabin's music is devoid of nationalism; his late works are avant-garde.

In Austria and Germany, contributions were made by Wolf, Mahler, and Richard Strauss. Wolf brought the composition of Lieder to another peak. Mahler's talents were concentrated on the Lied and the symphony, and his work enriched both areas—the Lied was supplied with orchestral accompaniment, and the symphony was infiltrated by the Lied. He extended the symphony beyond the massive proportions and programmatic content of post-Romanticism and, through the incorporation of the Lied and the use of expanded harmonies and progressive tonality, elevated the symphony to an unprecedented height. Strauss is remembered primarily for his tone poems and a few of his operas. *Salome* and *Elektra* established his reputation as a daring composer whose music shattered conventions. With *Der Rosenkavalier,* he effected a complete change of style—to Neoclassicism—that surprised the musical world and altered his reputation to that of conservative composer. Most of Strauss's tone poems have either purely descriptive or philosophical programs.

During the last two decades of the nineteenth century, Germany experienced a revival of fairy-tale opera. Humperdinck wrote several. Another development in opera in several countries was verismo. Its leading Italian exponent was Puccini.

There were several overlapping and interdependent lines of musical development in France after 1871. Two were basic: one followed cosmopolitan traditions and is seen in the work of Franck and his pupils, especially d'Indy; the other, adhering specifically to French traditions, appears in the work of Saint-Saëns

Louis Armstrong. *(The Bettman Archive)*

and his pupils, particularly Fauré. Later, another line of development appeared, based on French tradition and influenced by the ideas of Symbolist writers and Impressionist artists; its principal exponents were Debussy and Ravel. The term *Impressionism* was first applied to music in a disparaging sense, usually implying that a composition was vague and lacked formal and harmonic clarity. Impressionistic music is characterized by irregular phrases, blurring of formal outlines, avoidance of traditional harmonic progressions, use of streams of chords in parallel motion and altered chords with unresolved dissonances, and choice of instruments for their coloristic possibilities. The music is tonal, but modality frequently appears within it, and often the leading tone is suppressed. Composers aimed to create an atmosphere, to suggest rather than to define.

Satie was an eccentric composer with an extremely individualistic style. Some of his music was very avant-garde. A group of young composers associated with Satie in Paris in 1917 became known as *Les Six*: Auric, Durey, Honegger, Milhaud, Poulenc, and Tailleferre. Like the Russian Five, they advocated writing music devoid of German characteristics, but were not nationalistic. The Six did not remain active as a group, and their ideas about music changed somewhat, but all remained active to some degree.

In England, there was continued interest in oratorio, opera, music festivals, madrigal singing, and old music. Composers active during 1870–1920 include Elgar, Smyth, Delius, Vaughan Williams, and Holst.

In the United States, between 1860 and 1920 the first American conservatories of music were founded, and concert halls were built in major cities, but concert programs were filled with music written by Europeans. The most important American composers during the last decades of the nineteenth century were Paine and MacDowell. Their compositions were tonal and, in general, show the influence of nineteenth-century European composers of Romantic music.

Where music written and/or performed by women is concerned, Boston, in the 1890s, seems to have occupied a position comparable with that of the Medici court at Ferrara in the late sixteenth century. Mrs. H. H. A. Beach appeared as piano soloist with the Boston Symphony and was the first American woman recognized as a composer of large forms—Mass, symphony, piano concerto, and some chamber music. Other New England composers adhering to Classic-Romantic traditions were Foote, Chadwick, and Parker. One of America's most important and most individualistic composers was Ives. Ives and Cowell were innovative, had not been influenced by avant-garde European composers, used tone clusters, and to some extent were influenced by vernacular and popular music. In Ives's musical style, no consistent line of development can be traced. He wrote for self-satisfaction, without regard for traditional rules of composition. Cowell named tone clusters, and his use of them affected the work of other composers, especially Bartók. In some works written in 1915–19, Cowell incorporated chance factors. He was first to play on the strings of the piano and to place foreign objects among the strings to create unusual sounds and new timbres.

Jazz emerged early in the twentieth century in southern United States, but some of its roots extend back into the complex polyrhythms of African tribal music and the call-response nature of musical performance in African societies. Other factors in the development of jazz include spirituals, gospel songs, secular songs dealing with personal situations and feelings, blues, cakewalk, and ragtime. Jazz is generally believed to have originated in New Orleans early in the twentieth century, when small ensembles playing ragtime incorporated elements of blues. Early jazz relied heavily on improvisation, and improvisation is still considered a vital element of jazz. The New Orleans style of jazz reached a peak with Armstrong and his "Hot Five" c. 1925. Thereafter, a number of variant jazz styles appeared.

DEVELOPMENTS BETWEEN THE WORLD WARS

26

The curtain opened on the twentieth century to reveal national pride, imperialism, and unrest—the anti-Western Boxer uprisings in China; the British fighting the Boers, who wanted to establish an independent republic in South Africa; and labor problems that culminated in strikes in France. Each large European nation exhibited a sense of security that was individualistic and that was not to last. Rivalries for colonial and industrial power led to military alliances, and, though political leaders hoped that a major war would not occur, the major European nations prepared for it. In 1914 the assassination of Austrian Archduke Francis Ferdinand and his wife in Sarajevo was the spark that ignited World War I—falsely dubbed the "war to end all wars." But World War I did not bring lasting peace. There were a few years of prosperity after the war, but most of Western Europe experienced some degree of trouble during the 1920s—a general strike in Britain (1926), inflation in France, and civil unrest and turmoil in Spain, a country that had remained neutral during World War I. Then, in 1929, the Great Depression began.

The quarter-century following the Treaty of Versailles (1919) was marked by increased nationalism in several countries and by an intense rivalry among the major powers for political world power, which created international tension. Naturally, each country considered its own ideology the best. In Russia, the Bolshevik Revolution of 1917 had toppled the tsar. Under Lenin's leadership, Russia became the Union of Soviet Socialist Republics on 30 December 1922. After Lenin's death (1924), an internal power struggle ensued; eventually, Joseph Stalin (1879–1953) became the recognized leader. The Stalinist government aimed to suppress so-called capitalist imperialism and professed the fraternity and equality of man but without spiritual or political freedom. In Italy, in 1919, Fascism was established by dictator Benito Mussolini (1883–1945). Fascism was characterized by the utmost nationalism, its aims being national unity, militaristic national expansion, class unity, and primacy of government and state. Violence, considered morally desirable, was fostered. In Germany, World War I had destroyed the old political hierarchy. A number of working-class movements arose, and the anti-Semitic National Socialist party (Nazi) emerged. Adolph Hitler (1889–1945) rose to party leadership and, by the Enabling Act of 1933, became dictator of Germany. His goals were narrow and determined, colored by Nietzsche's theory of a super race. The Hitler régime was filled with brutality and horror. Nazism in Germany and, to some degree, Fascism in Italy were suppressed at the expense of World War II (1939–45), more violent and horrible than the first because of powerful new weapons.

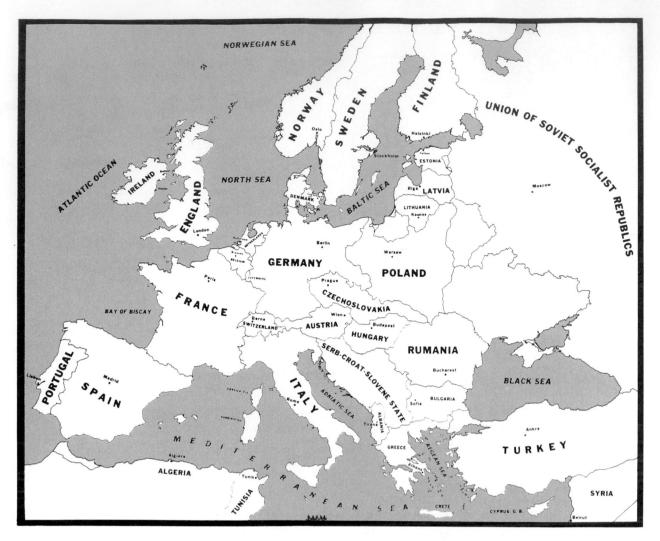

FIGURE 26.1 Europe in 1920.

Northern France had suffered much desolation during World War I, but Paris still exuded a magetism that attracted artists from all over the world. As political conditions and varying degrees of artistic censorship in Nazi and fascist countries became intolerable, composers and artists fled first to Paris and then to the United States.

The cultural arts were not immune from these earth-shattering events. Political and economic happenings always affect the arts to some extent and find expression in them. As the European political, social, and economic systems changed, so did the arts. Liberalism, rationalism, and irrationalism are all represented. Various styles are present in the artwork of Pablo Picasso

(1881–1973). New movements in art included Dadaism (lit., "hobby-horse"), which was grotesque and often nonsensical; Surrealism ("super-reality"), an attempt to express subconscious feelings in weird, fantastic shapes, seen in the work of Salvador Dali (1904–89); Expressionism, of which Marc Chagall (1887–1986; plate 27) was an exponent; and Abstraction, such as the nonrepresentational geometric works of Piet Mondrian (1872–1944). In modern architecture, the principal creators were Frank Lloyd Wright (1869–1959), Walter Gropius (1883–1969), and Le Corbusier (Charles Édouard Jeanneret; 1887–1965).

In music, the economic conditions brought by World War I were reflected in the limited performing

1910	1920	1930	1940	1950

• World War I (1914–18) Depression World War II (1939–45)

• 1917 Bolshevik Revolution

1917 ← Lenin → 1924 ← Stalin → (1953)

1919 Fascism in Italy; Mussolini 1945

Rise of Nazi Party in Germany; 1933 Hitler, dictator → 1945

ART: Dadism fl. Surrealism Expressionism Abstraction

Continuation of nationalism in music; folk music research: Janáček, Bartók, Kodály

Bartók: Synthesis of folk idioms in art music 1945

percussive piano music; string quartets; *Mikrokosmos*

Orff: complete or "total" theater

Vaughan Williams: operas (1924–29); symphonies (1912–57)

1941 Britten (1971)
operas, chamber operas

• 1932 Union of Soviet Composers, isolation from West

1917 Prokofiev: *Classical Symphony* Symphony No. 5, 1944

1925 Shostakovich: 15 symphonies (1971)

Second Viennese School: Schoenberg, Berg, Webern

Schoenberg: pantonal Expressionism; twelve-tone, serialism (1951)

Sprechstimme:
• 1913 *Pierrot Lunaire*

Berg: Expressionist opera *Wozzeck* 1922; *Lulu* (1928–35); Violin concerto 1935

Webern: Pointillism; Expressionism 1945

Les Six, as a group 1917–22; then separately

Durey: politically Communistic music
Auric: stage and theater music
Tailleferre: traditional music
Honegger: stage and dramatic works; vocal effects, *Sprechstimme*
Poulenc: *mélodie;* religious choral music
Milhaud; lyrical, contrapuntal, polytonal works

Neoclassicism

• 1932–35 Hindemith: *Mathis der Maler*
symphony and opera

Stravinsky: ballets;
• 1913 *Le sacre du printemps* (polytonal, primitivism)

1920 *Pulcinella* (Neoclassicism) *The Rake's Progress* 1951

Nadia Boulanger, master teacher

Copland: ballets *Appalachian Spring* 1944
symphonies; *Fanfare for the
Common Man,* 1942

Gershwin: • 1924 *Rhapsody in Blue;* • 1935 *Porgy and Bess*

• 1931 R. Crawford Seeger: String Quartet

• 1928 Thomson: *Four Saints in Three Acts*

W. G. Still Harris, Piston, Sessions

Villa-Lobos

Ginastera

Chávez: Development of music in Mexico

resources called for by some of the major composers. The rejection of traditional principles governing composition and the radical experimentation that characterized art invaded the realm of music. There was also Neoclassicism, a style in which the traditional and the new were synthesized. Nationalism, both overt patriotism and the conscious use of folk music, continued to be a major factor in the work of some composers. Others used folk music only incidentally, and still others did not use it at all. One distinctive school of composition arose—the Second Viennese School, which explored principles of dodecaphonic (twelve-tone) music advanced by Arnold Schoenberg. There were a few composers (e.g., Igor Stravinsky) whose work followed a path through many styles but espoused no single one of them permanently.

INTEGRATION OF FOLK AND ART MUSIC STYLES

Folk music was an important aspect of the expression of nationalism. Composers quoted folk songs and dance tunes in their works and sought to absorb other elements of folk music into traditional styles. Popular music resembling folk song and dance found its way into compositions. The availability of acoustic recording devices made collecting folk music easier and more accurate, so the material gathered could be studied objectively through ethnomusicological methods. Interest in and serious study of folk material became more widespread—many persons made regional collections, which they organized, edited, and published. One of the earliest scientific studies of folk music was done by Janáček among the Moravians. The most extensive scholarly research in central European folk music was accomplished by Zoltán Kodály (1881–1967) and Béla Bartók (1882–1945), who studied Magyar folk music first, then that of neighboring regions. Gradually, as scientific investigation of folk materials revealed the nature of those melodies, rhythms, harmonies, and forms and as the idiosyncrasies of the various regional musics became apparent, composers applied that knowledge in creating art music. Thus, the study of folk idioms generated new musical styles, and the scope of tonality was enlarged through the incorporation of the modal, pentatonic, or other scale patterns found in folk music. The most complete synthesis of folk idioms and art music was achieved by Bartók.

HUNGARY

Under the Compromise of 1867, Austria and Hungary had become a dual monarchy with Emperor Franz Joseph I of Austria (r. 1848–1916) as King of Hungary and with Vienna as one capital and Budapest as the other. Magyars were the largest ethnic group in Hungary but constituted slightly less than 50 percent of the population. Among the other ethnic groups were the Croats, Serbs, and Slovenes. Many Magyars were discontent with the dual arrangement, wanted independence for Hungary, and actively worked to "Magyarize" Hungary. By 1900 more than 90 percent of the officials and judiciary were Magyar; the Ugrian dialect of the Magyars became the official language and was used in the schools, though German was spoken in many homes. Feelings of Hungarian nationalism and the desire for independence increased during 1900–10. In 1907 teachers might be dismissed if their students had not mastered the Ugrian language.

BÉLA BARTÓK

Nationalism is closely interwoven with the career of Bartók. He was a virtuoso pianist who concertized, taught, composed, and made significant contributions as ethnomusicologist. Folk music, particularly that of his native Hungary, was one of his lifelong interests. Another was the piano and its music. Bartók's mother, a piano teacher, provided his first instruction. At the Budapest Academy of Music (1899–1903), he trained for a career as a concert pianist; he was an excellent accompanist and played chamber music well. Composition was considered as an adjunct career.

While a student at the Academy, Bartók was disturbed by the fact that Hungarian composers of nationalist music used pseudo rather than authentic Hungarian folk materials as models for their works. In the early 1900s he wrote down a few songs that he heard Hungarian peasants singing, and c. 1905 he collaborated with Zoltán Kodály in gathering and cataloging ethnic musics of Hungary, Rumania, and other nearby Slavic countries. The cataloging system Bartók developed is still in use. Gradually, he expanded his research into other central European countries and into Turkey and North Africa. He published his editions of folk music, made arrangements of many folk songs, and assimilated folk materials into his own compositions.

In 1907 Bartók was appointed professor of piano at the Budapest Academy of Music, a position that provided a measure of financial security yet allowed him time to perform, compose, and continue folk-music research. For 27 years, he taught at the Academy and concertized, establishing his reputation internationally as a concert pianist. Usually, in concerts he performed only his own compositions. He wrote some purely pedagogical pieces. *Mikrokosmos* (1926–37), originally intended for the instruction of his son Peter, is a six-volume progressive course in piano technique. The 153 pieces in the series range from simple one- and two-part pieces to extremely difficult works with complicated asymmetrical rhythms and bitonality. *Mikrokosmos* is a compendium of Bartók's style and of many of the compositional devices in use during the first half of the twentieth century.

Before 1902 Bartók wrote mainly piano pieces and songs; most of them are short, Romantic in style, and relatively unimportant. Between 1902 and 1907, his attitude and his works became increasingly nationalistic. Among the original nationalistic works he composed then are a violin/piano Sonata in E minor (1903), a Piano Quintet (1903–4), and the symphonic poem *Kossuth* (1903) honoring Lajos Kossuth (1802–94), the Hungarian nationalist leader during the Revolution of 1848. Bartók's first compositions with *opus* numbers appeared in 1904: *Rhapsody,* Op. 1 (pno.), and *Scherzo,* Op. 2 (pno., orch.). In 1907 Kodály introduced Bartók

to Debussy's music. Bartók was fascinated by the elements of folk music in it and by Debussy's coloristic, nonfunctional treatment of chords.

Elements of Bartók's individual style began to manifest themselves soon after he began collecting folk music and became increasingly apparent in his works in 1908–11. Throughout his life he relied heavily on folk music; often his innovations were stimulated by his research. Around 1908 he began to write melodies and harmonies based on modal and pentatonic scales; to combine modes or, as he described it, to color one with another; to construct chords by stacking fourths instead of thirds or to use simultaneously the major and minor third (though he always placed the minor third uppermost); to use palindromic formal patterns; and to apply in his works the Fibonacci series of numbers and the "golden section." Among the scales Bartók used are the pentatonic; the whole tone; the acoustic, formed, for example, of a lower Lydian pentachord joined to a Mixolydian upper part; and the octatonic, which is comparable with that Messiaen termed "mode 2 of limited transposition" (ex. 26.1). Many of these features appear in the 14 *Bagatelles* (Op. 6; 1908) for piano. Other significant works written by Bartók during these years are String Quartet No. 1 (Op. 7), *Two Pictures* (Op. 10; orch.; 1910); *Duke Bluebeard's Castle* (1911), his first one-act opera; and *Allegro barbaro* (1911; pno.), which exemplifies primitivism. *Allegro barbaro* is percussive piano music, with driving rhythms, harsh chords in persistent ostinato patterns, melody of narrow range, and many repeated notes.

The libretto for *Duke Bluebeard's Castle* is by Symbolist poet Béla Balázs, who adapted the Bluebeard

Bela Bartók. *(Courtesy Free Library of Philadelphia)*

EXAMPLE 26.1 Some of the scale patterns Bartók used: (*a*) pentatonic, (*b*) acoustic, and (*c*) octatonic.

legend to present symbolically humans' thirst for knowledge and a moral—Curiosity can kill. (Balázs was also implying that in a marital relationship some past events should remain behind closed doors.) The opera has only two singing roles, Judith and Bluebeard; a Prologue is spoken by the Bard. Bartók wrote chromatic Romantic music for Judith and pentatonic, folklike music for Bluebeard. In the garden scene Bartók used an acoustic scale. Treatment of the vocal lines shows Bartók's knowledge of Debussy's *Pelléas et Mélisande*. Symbolic motives recur, and there is a quotation from Bach's *St. Matthew Passion*.

During 1912–19 Bartók concentrated on teaching and folk music. Of his few new works, the most important is String Quartet No. 2 (Op. 17; 1915–17), which contains a good deal of folk material. In 1919 he resumed concertizing and wrote the piano score for the pantomime *The Miraculous Mandarin* (orchestrated in 1923). The music is tonal but includes slow string *glissandi* designed to produce quarter tones. Political conditions in Hungary in 1920 hampered Bartók's career. He wanted to concertize abroad but was prevented from leaving the country until 1922. Performances of *Duke Bluebeard's Castle* and the ballet *The Wooden Prince* (1914–16) were prohibited in Hungary because Balázs was a political exile. In 1923 Bartók and other leading Hungarian composers were commissioned to write music for a Festival Concert commemorating the fiftieth anniversary of the merging of Pest, Buda, and Óbuda into the city of Budapest. For that concert Bartók composed *Dance Suite* for orchestra.

In 1926 Bartók began to use traditional forms and a great deal of counterpoint. *Out of Doors* (1927), a five-movement piano suite, is significant for the style of its fourth movement, "Night music," which Bartók simulated in several later works—the piano concertos, the Sonata for piano and percussion, and *Music for Strings, Percussion, and Celesta.* The Piano Sonata (1926), Piano Concerto No. 1 (1926), and Piano Concerto No. 2 (1930–31) were for his own performances. Bartók attributed his use of tone clusters in Piano Concerto No. 1 to Henry Cowell (see p. 577). *Rhapsody No. 1* and *No. 2* (vln., pno.; 1928) were written for concerts Bartók played with Hungarian violinists Joseph Szigeti (1892–1973) and Zoltán Székely (b. 1903); later Bartók wrote orchestral accompaniments for both rhapsodies.

Between 1927 and 1939 Bartók composed String Quartets Nos. 3–6. As the *Mikrokosmos* provides a summary of Bartók's style through his writing for piano, so the six string quartets provide a summary of his style through chamber music. Bartók's string quartets are among the finest written since Beethoven's. String Quartet No. 4 is in five movements, arranged in palindromic arch form, and is cyclic. The performers are required to play some difficult multiple stops and execute a variety of unusual techniques, including snap pizzicato, pizzicato glissando, pizzicato *sul ponticello,* and *col legno* chords. There is a good deal of counterpoint and some bitonality. String Quartet No. 5 contains five movements also; its central movement is a Scherzo flanked by slow movements. That Scherzo is written in $^{4+2+3}_8$ meter; its Trio, in very fast tempo, uses $^{3+2+2+3}_8$ meter.

Cantata profana (1930), for tenor and baritone soloists, double chorus, and orchestra, is Bartók's most important nonoperatic vocal work. Its text was derived from two versions of a Rumanian *colinda* (song). The music sounds as though it is filled with folk materials but actually contains none. Ostensibly in D, and beginning and ending in that key, it contains passages that are Mixolydian or that use the acoustic scale D–E–F♯–G♯–A–B–C–D or its inversion. Structurally, the composition is symmetrical—what Bartók called *Brückenform* (bridge form). Symmetry is found also in invertible counterpoint (ex. 26.2).

Many of the works Bartók wrote in the 1930s were commissioned, including String Quartet No. 5; *Music for Strings, Percussion, and Celesta* (1937); *Divertimento* (1939); Sonata for two pianos and percussion (1937); Violin Concerto (1937); and *Contrasts* (1938; cl., vln.; pno.), which was first performed by Szigeti and Benny Goodman with Bartók at the piano. Clarinetist and violinist each need two instruments, for *Contrasts* uses *scordatura* as well as *accordatura* tuning of the violin, and the B♭ and A clarinets.

In the 1930s Bartók's open opposition to fascism created problems for him. He wanted to emigrate but did not do so until after his mother died. He came to the United States in 1940 for performances with Szigeti and Goodman and returned later that year to reside. Besides concertizing, he cataloged Yugoslav folk music at Harvard University. For two years he composed nothing. Then he became ill with polycythae-

EXAMPLE 26.2 In *Cantata profana*, mvt. 1, mm. 35–37, Bartók used invertible counterpoint and canon in the chorus parts. *(CANTATA PROFANA © Copyright 1934 by Universal Edition; Copyright Renewed. Copyright and Renewal assigned to Boosey & Hawkes, Inc. Reprinted by permission.)*

mia, a type of blood cancer. In 1943, he wrote *Concerto for Orchestra* (rev. 1945), commissioned by Koussevitsky, and in 1944 wrote the Sonata for solo violin, but his quarter-tone version of the sonata's last movement remains unpublished. Bartók's last two works were Piano Concerto No. 3 (1945), written for his second wife, Ditta Pásztory (1902–82), and Viola Concerto (1945), commissioned by William Primrose. Bartók had not quite finished them when he died; violist Tibor Serly (1901–78) completed them.

The compositions Bartók wrote after 1937 are tonal, with much counterpoint. His use of thematic development and thematic transformation stems from Beethoven and Liszt, and from Liszt he learned to use germinal motives. As did Beethoven, Bartók often modulated to a mediant or submediant tonality instead of moving to the dominant. Frequently he used foreign chords in a nonfunctional, nonmodulatory manner. The tritone is important in many of his works. Most of his compositions written after 1908 were influenced in some way by folk materials. Bitonality and polytonality appear in many of his compositions, but Bartók wrote neither atonal music nor twelve-tone serial music. Several of his late works contain most of the techniques that characterize his style for example, *Music for Strings, Percussion, and Celesta.*

The celesta is by no means a featured solo instrument in *Music for Strings, Percussion, and Celesta.* The work is for two five-part string ensembles, side drums, cymbals, tam-tam, bass drum, tympani, celesta, harp, and piano. To ensure the blend of tone qualities he desired, Bartók provided an ensemble seating plan. The entire composition is colored by tritone relationships, contrapuntal intricacies, and mirror and contrary motion techniques. The Andante tranquillo first movement (DWMA177) is a fugue whose subject (ex. 26.3a) is presented in successive entries that move alternately in contrary motion around the circle of fifths from A to E♭ (i.e., A–E–D–B–G and so on); then the subject is inverted, and the tonality progresses from E♭ back to A. The tritone relationship between A and E♭, which is the secondary tonal center (rather than the dominant), is reinforced in the movement's last three measures (ex. 26.3b). The dynamic level of the first movement gradually increases in intensity from the *pp* of muted strings at measure 1 to *fff* when E♭ is attained, then diminishes to conclude *ppp.* The second movement is a sonata-form Allegro in C. The third movement, an Adagio in F♯ (a tritone away from the C of mvt. 2), is bridge form—Introduction–ABCBA–coda. The movement ends on the C–F♯ tritone. The fourth movement, Allegro molto, exhibits

EXAMPLE 26.3 Bartók: *Music for Strings, Percussion, and Celesta*, mvt. 1: (*a*) mm. 1–4, the subject; (*b*) the last three measures (mm. 86–88).

(*MUSIC FOR STRINGS, PERCUSSION & CELESTE © Copyright 1937 by Universal Edition; Copyright Renewed. Copyright and Renewal assigned to Boosey & Hawkes, Inc., for the USA. Reprinted by permission.*)

(a)

(b)

many characteristics of Bartók's style: elements of Magyar folk music, driving rhythms, ostinato, and tone clusters.

ZOLTÁN KODÁLY

After Bartók emigrated to America, Kodály worked alone collecting, scientifically studying, and codifying folk music, especially in Magyar and Slavic regions. In addition, Kodály did a great deal to advance the degree of musical literacy of young persons. He was concerned primarily with vocal music education, and many of the materials he used were derived from folk music. In teaching sight-singing, he used mainly polyphony and for that purpose composed hundreds of two- and three-part exercises. The "Kodály method" is currently in use in many places in the Western world.

Folk elements infiltrated Kodály's compositions, but he made no direct quotations from folk music. Rather, his mature works are an amalgamation of many influences—Bach-style counterpoint, the choral writing of Palestrina, Gregorian chant, and Hungarian folk music, including *verbunkos*. (*Verbunkos* originated as a Hungarian soldiers' dance consisting of two or more sections, alternating slow quasi-introductory material with very fast, wild music. Later, *verbunkos* became a ceremonial dance.) Kodály's music is basically tonal and diatonic, colored by modality, and is more narrowly nationalistic than that of Bartók. Kodály attracted international attention with *Psalmus hungaricus* (1923; T, chor., orch.), commissioned for the Budapest 50th Anniversary Festival Concert. The most popular of Kodály's compositions are the Singspiel *Háry János* (1926), based on the national legend of Háry János, teller of tall tales, and the orchestral suite (1927) derived from that comedy.

GERMANY

CARL ORFF

Orff (1895–1982), a German composer, was also greatly interested in the music education of elementary-school children and was especially concerned with rhythmic proficiency and fluidity of movement. After becoming acquainted with Jaques-Dalcroze eurhythmics, a method that correlated music and movement, Orff determined to use similar didactic methods in Germany and decided to train young adults as teachers of eurhythmics. To that end, he and Dorothee Günther (1896–1975) founded the Güntherschule in Munich in 1924 and prepared a curriculum in which music, dance, and gymnastics were highly coordinated. With that curriculum, Orff used a wide variety of percussion instruments that are easy to play. Improvisation is a vital part of Orff's curriculum. He simplified the Jaques-Dalcroze methods so that they were suitable for elementary-school children, and he prepared a collection of carefully graded music exercises: *Orff-Schulwerk* (Schoolwork; 1930–35), and *Musik für Kinder* (Music for Children; 1950–54). His didactic procedures were adopted in Germany first, then spread throughout the world.

Orff's principal interest was complete or "total" theater, in which all aspects of words, music, and movement formed a cohesive whole. His models were ancient Greek drama and early Baroque Italian *rappresentazione* and opera. He adapted some Monteverdi works, one being *Klage der Ariadne* (Lament of Ariadne; 1925; rev. 1940), then wrote Christmas and Easter plays, Bavarian peasant plays, and works based on Greek tragedies.

Orff's most famous work is *Carmina burana* (see p. 93). Also well known are the operas *Der Mond* (The moon; 1939) and *Die Kluge* (The wise woman; 1943), based on Grimm's fairy tales; and *Antigonae* (1949) and *Oedipus der Tyrann* (King Oedipus; 1959), drawn from Sophocles. Orff's vocal lines are declamatory and rhythmically accented; orchestral accompaniments use simple harmonies in block chords.

ENGLAND

RALPH VAUGHAN WILLIAMS

Vaughan Williams (1872–1958) was composer, editor, arranger, author, teacher, conductor, and collector of folk song. The most important influence in his music was his English heritage (especially folk song), music of the Elizabethan and Jacobean eras, and hymnody. Literature, the music of Handel, Bach, Ravel, and Debussy, and Vaughan Williams's friendship with Holst, were important factors, too.

Throughout his life, Vaughan Williams maintained an interest in choral music. Some of his earliest compositions were unaccompanied part-songs; *A Sea Symphony* (1903–9) is for soprano and baritone soloists, SATB chorus, and orchestra. From 1905 to 1953 Vaughan Williams was principal conductor of the annual Leith Hill Music Festival and wrote choral works specifically for them. Many of the performers at the festivals were amateurs who were receiving their first

Ralph Vaughan Williams. *(The Bettmann Archive)*

acquaintance with the choral music of Bach, Handel, Mendelssohn, and other outstanding composers. Several of Vaughan Williams's instrumental works were designed for performance by amateurs. His *Household Music* (1941), three preludes on Welsh hymn tunes, is for string quartet or other available instruments, and a section of his *Concerto Grosso* (1950) uses only open strings.

In 1904 Vaughan Williams became a member of the Folk Song Society. Over the years, he collected hundreds of folk songs. Some he incorporated in his compositions, some he arranged as choral works or accompanied vocal solos, and others he edited and published in collections. The modality and simplicity of folk song influenced his compositions considerably. He arranged and published several collections of traditional English carols and was coeditor of *The Oxford Book of Carols* (1928), to which he contributed some original carols. He was music editor of *The English Hymnal* (1904–6) and included in the book some of his own hymns, one being *Sine nomine* (Nameless; known as "For all the saints"; 1905). The opening notes of that hymn follow a downward curve that became characteristic of many of Vaughan Williams's melodies. In fact, it may be considered a trademark of his style (ex. 26.4).

EXAMPLE 26.4 Melodic curves typical of Vaughan Williams's writing: (*a*) Melody of the hymn *Sine nomine*; (*b*) *Toward the Unknown Region*, mm. 1–3. *(Source: Example a copyright © 1906 Oxford University Press. New York, NY; example b copyright © 1918 Breitkopf and Härtel, Leipzig.)*

(a)

(b)

The years 1909–14 cover the first period of Vaughan Williams's mature writing. The benefit of his study with Ravel (in 1908) is seen in the chord streams, the rippling arpeggiated figurations, expressive chromaticisms, colorful musical imagery, and skillful orchestration. Vaughan Williams's style was unified, and elements of folk song had been assimilated into it. One of the most representative works of this period is the song cycle *On Wenlock Edge* (1908–9; T, pno., str. qrt.). The music is filled with streams of parallel chords—first-inversion triads, root-position triads, seventh chords, and octaves with open fifths. The sound recalls the English penchant for the full sonority achieved by complete triads and the parallel $^6_3$ chords of fifteenth-century English discant. A sense of the dramatic is present, fostered by the judicious use of chromaticism and dissonance as well as by the vocal line, which is simple but demanding.

Four other works from this period are significant: *Fantasia on a Theme by Thomas Tallis* (1910) for two string orchestras, *A London Symphony* (1912–13), the opera *Hugh the Drover* (1910–14), and *The Lark Ascending* (1914; violin, orch.). Based on a hymn tune, the *Fantasia* mingles key tonality and modality, polyphony and homophony, and reflects somewhat the music of the Elizabethan era in which Tallis lived.

A London Symphony, Vaughan Williams's second symphony, is purely orchestral. It is traditional in form, with four movements, the third being a scherzo labeled *Nocturne* and the fourth called *Epilogue.* The first movement opens with a Lento introduction whose theme is basis for the *Epilogue.* Vaughan Williams structured five of his nine symphonies with epilogues reflecting first-movement introductions.

England had no tradition of native opera. In fact, it seemed almost as though there was a barrier against English opera. Vaughan Williams penetrated that barrier with *Hugh the Drover* (perf. 1924), which he called a ballad opera. The songs are not limited to ballads, though the opera contains at least 10 well-known tunes. In 1924–29 Vaughan Williams composed 3 more operas: *Sir John in Love, Riders to the Sea,* and *The Poisoned Kiss. Sir John in Love,* based on Shakespeare's *The Merry Wives of Windsor,* requires 20 soloists. Included in the opera is a Fantasia on *Greensleeves* that is frequently performed as a separate piece.

During the years immediately following World War I, Vaughan Williams worked on the *Pastoral Symphony* (No. 3, completed 1921), in which he included voice. At the beginning and near the end of the Finale, he placed a pentatonic, textless melisma for solo soprano, a feature that resembles the long melismas of pure vocal sound found near the end of English motets written during the Elizabethan era.

Several compositions Vaughan Williams wrote between World Wars I and II have a religious association, though only a few are liturgical. The neo-modal *a cappella* Mass in G minor (1920–21; SATB soloists, eight-part choir) was written when there was renewed interest in Byrd's music and the polyphony produced by other English composers of that era who worked at Westminster Cathedral. The oratorio *Sancta civitas* (The Holy City; 1923–25), for tenor and baritone soloists, SATB chorus, semichorus, and distant chorus, takes its principal text from Revelation. *Job* (1927–30) is a masque for dancing and is not churchly. *Flos campi* (Flower of the field; 1925), for viola, chamber orchestra, and small SATB chorus singing textless music, is an interpretation of verses from *Song of Solomon*. The opening of the piece is bitonal, and much of the music sounds improvised. *Flos campi* is the finest of the several works featuring solo instrument that Vaughan Williams created during this period.

Although Vaughan Williams stated that his fourth, fifth, and sixth symphonies are absolute music, many persons have considered them related to World War II: No. 4, in F minor (1931–34), as prophecy of it; No. 5, D major (1938–43), as the hope for peace, especially seen in the serenity of its Finale; and No. 6, E minor (1944–47), as descriptive of war.

In 1905–13 Vaughan Williams composed incidental music for nine stage works. In the 1940s he wrote music for three radio dramas, and in 1940 he began composing music for films. His most significant film score was that for *Scott of the Antarctic*. That score inspired a seventh symphony, *Sinfonia antartica* (1949–52), a five-movement work for soprano, small SSA chorus, and orchestra. The orchestra includes a wind machine, and quotations from Scott's journal are in the epilogue.

Vaughan Williams's last two symphonies, No 8 in D minor (1953–55) and No. 9 in E minor (1956–57), are purely instrumental, neither has an epilogue, and sonata form was not used for the first movement of either of them. Both symphonies have parts for unusual instruments—vibraphone in the Eighth Symphony and three saxophones and a flugelhorn in the Ninth. Other unusual works from Vaughan Williams's last period are the Concerto in F minor for bass tuba and orchestra (1954) and the *Romance* in D♭ major (1951) for harmonica, strings, and piano, which was written for Larry Adler (b. 1914).

Vaughan Williams's style is English, nationalistic in character without being tied to folk song, and at the same time highly personal. In his works archaic procedures from the Tudor era blend with those of his own time. Counterpoint and homophony, modes and keys, are handled with equal skill, often incorporating shifts between major and minor harmonies and including some polytonality. Vaughan Williams laid the groundwork for a tradition of English opera and did a

great deal to establish the symphony as an important form in English music.

BENJAMIN BRITTEN

Britten's (1913–76) principal contributions were solo songs, choral works, and operas. He also wrote a large amount of challenging music for amateurs and children and some orchestral and chamber music.

In the mid-1930s, when Britten composed the music for a series of documentary films, he met poet W. H. Auden (1907–73). Britten set a number of Auden's poems, and Auden supplied the libretto for *Paul Bunyan* (1941), Britten's first opera. A homosexual relationship and long-lasting musical partnership developed between Britten and tenor Peter Pears (1910–86) as a result of a series of recitals of English music the two men presented in 1937. Pears, who inspired a number of Britten's vocal works, sang the leading tenor roles in most of Britten's operas. In 1939, when war was impending, Britten and Pears came to the United States; Auden had already emigrated to America. In 1942 Britten returned to England, where, as a conscientious objector, he was exempted from military service. While in the United States, he composed at least a dozen works, including the Violin Concerto (1939), the song cycles *Les illuminations* (T, strings; 1939) and *Seven Sonnets of Michelangelo* (T, pno.; 1940), *Sinfonia da Requiem* (Requiem Symphony; 1940), and String Quartet No. 1 (D major; 1941). *Sinfonia da Requiem* is programmatic, with movements entitled *Lachrymosa, Dies irae*, and *Requiem aeternam*. Quite a number of Britten's works concern death. Before 1942, Britten's output was mainly instrumental; thereafter, most of his compositions were vocal music.

Until the advent of Vaughan Williams and Britten, England had no native-born composer of the stature of Henry Purcell. Several of Britten's compositions reflect his knowledge of and appreciation for Purcell's works: String Quartet No. 2 (C major; 1945), written in tribute to Purcell; the song cycle *The Holy Sonnets of John Donne* (T, pno.; 1945); *Rejoice in the Lamb* (SATB soloists, chor., org.; 1943); and *The Young Person's Guide to the Orchestra* (1945), variations on a theme of Purcell followed by a fugue on an original theme by Britten. After 1945, the only purely instrumental compositions Britten wrote were for specific individuals, for example, a Sonata (C major; 'cello/piano; 1961), three Suites for unaccompanied 'cello (1964, 1967, 1971), and *Symphony in D for 'Cello and Orchestra* (1963), written for Mstislav Rostropovitch (b. 1927).

Shortly before Britten returned to England in 1942, the Koussevitsky Foundation commissioned an opera from him, and he wrote *Peter Grimes* (1944–45). That opera concerns moral issues—innocence being the prey of violence and the adverse effect of a community's unfounded suspicions—and graphically depicts living conditions in a small English seaside community. Peter Grimes, a rough fisherman, is suspected of having killed his apprentice. Peter is innocent, but most of the villagers consider him guilty, and their actions reflect their beliefs. Britten set the narrative portions of the opera as *secco* recitative and used arioso and aria for solos. Besides accompanying, the orchestra plays mood-setting interludes between scenes and acts. There are some recurrent motives and figures. The harmonies are basically triadic and traditional, but Lydian and Phrygian modes color the melodies. *Peter Grimes* is Britten's best-known opera.

In 1945 Britten decided to write chamber operas—works that require only a few singers and an orchestra of solo instruments and that can be performed on small stages. After composing *The Rape of Lucretia* (1946) and *Albert Herring* (1947), Britten formed a chamber opera company, the English Opera Group, and in 1948 Eric Crozier (1914–91), Pears, and Britten founded the Aldeburgh Festival, with facilities for producing chamber opera. By 1950 Britten's success as a chamber opera composer was established. The large-scale opera *Billy Budd,* commissioned for the Festival of Britain in 1951, has become part of English opera repertoire. Other significant operas are *Gloriana,* written for the coronation of Queen Elizabeth II in 1953, *The Turn of the Screw* (1954), *A Midsummer Night's Dream* (1960), *Death in Venice* (1973), and the one-act children's opera *Noye's Fludde* (1960). For television in 1971 Britten composed *Owen Wingrave,* a study in pacificism. Fundamentally, most of Britten's operas deal with social issues; *Albert Herring* is his only comic opera. Britten's works laid a firm foundation for the future of English opera.

Britten interspersed composition of operas and other works, most of them vocal. The most notable of the latter are the *War Requiem* (1961) and the cantata *Phaedra* (Mez., small orch.; 1975). The *War Requiem,* performed at the consecration of the new Coventry Cathedral, is both a denunciation of war and a tribute to the British who died in World War II. The traditional liturgical Requiem text alternates with poems by Wilfred Owen, a war victim.

RUSSIA

In Russia after the Bolshevik Revolution in 1917, cultural conditions differed vastly from those in Western Europe. Education of the masses was a prime concern of the government under Lenin and Trotsky. Composers were expected to write music that supported and reinforced government ideals rather than create works for purely esthetic reasons. All the arts were placed under state supervision in 1921, but composers were permitted some individuality of expression. The Union of Soviet Composers was formed in 1932; by Resolution it decreed that all music should be socialistic and should be easily understood by the masses. The use of folk material was advocated, as was the expression of "national feelings." Western modern music was banned, and performance of individualistic works, especially those with modern techniques, by Russian composers was prohibited. Thus, Russia sought to isolate itself from the West.

News of the suppression of works, or composers' withdrawal of them because of severe criticism, reached the West. In 1936 several works by Dmitry Shostakovich (1906–75) were condemned; in 1948 some works by Shostakovich, Sergei Prokofiev (1891–1953), Aram Khachaturian (1903–78), Dmitry Kabalevsky (1904–87), and others were declared antidemocratic and in violation of regulations. All art was supposed to be "socially significant communication."

Conditions gradually improved after the death of Stalin and were appreciably better when Nikita Krushchev (1894–1971) came into power. In 1958 the Communist Party's reversal of Stalin's 1948 decree lifted the ban on music by censured composers. Cultural agreements with other countries made possible the performance of new Western music in the Soviet Union, and Russian composers who had emigrated were permitted to visit their native land.

Much of the music written by composers living in the Soviet Union is related to specific revolutionary events, heroes, or anniversaries. Other works implicitly convey Soviet ideology. Comparatively few of those works have been accepted into Western repertoire, and the pieces most frequently performed are instrumental. A large body of music by Russian composers was created for films, and suites were derived from these scores. Most of that music is unknown outside Russia. Conditions continued to improve in the Soviet Union. The arts were not without censorship, but some modern music, with atonal, serial, or aleatoric features, was written by some avant-garde composers and is performed there as well as abroad.

The most significant of the composers living in Russia in 1917–45 are Prokofiev, Shostakovich, Khachaturian, and Kabalevsky. Works by them are in Western repertoire. Khachaturian received international acclaim for his Piano Concerto (1936), Violin Concerto (1940), and the ballet *Gayane* (1942). He was particularly successful in Russia because his music incorporates regional materials, promotes Russian tradition, adheres to standard forms, and is not innovative. Many of his works reinforced Soviet ideology. In 1954 Khachaturian was named People's Artist of the Soviet Union. His wife was composer Nina Makarova (1908–76), whose numerous compositions include a symphony and an opera. Her music is Romantic, with some Impressionistic touches.

Kabalevsky, poet, painter, and musician, began his career in music as an accompanist and a piano teacher. He wrote his first compositions for his piano pupils. He entered the Moscow Conservatory in 1925 because he wanted to be able to compose more effective teaching pieces; later, he became professor of composition there. His works exemplify the ideals of the Soviet Russian school of musical composition: diatonic melodies, harmonies basically tonal but not without dissonance, energetic rhythms, and traditional forms. In Russia Kabalevsky is best known for his vocal works (operas, cantatas, songs); in Western countries his reputation rests on his instrumental music (symphonies, symphonic poems, concerti, and piano sonatas and preludes).

SERGEI PROKOFIEV
Prokofiev began composing at the age of 5 and before he was 10 had written several piano pieces, a symphony, and two operas. From 1904 to 1914 he was a student at St. Petersburg Conservatory, where he received from Nikolay Myaskovsky (1881–1950) the advice and encouragement that he needed concerning his compositions. By the time Prokofiev graduated, he had written a number of works, the most important being Piano Concerto No. 1 (D♭ major; 1911). Though controversial at the time, it has remained in the repertoire, as has Piano Concerto No. 3 (C major; 1917–21). In 1914 Prokofiev visited Paris, became intrigued with ballet, and met Sergey Diaghilev (1872–1929), who commissioned a work. That ballet, *Ali i Lolli*, was a failure, but from it evolved the *Scythian Suite* (1915; orch.), which related to ancient Russian sun worship and was strongly primitive.

Prokofiev's next significant work was the *Classical Symphony* (Op. 25; D major; 1916–17), notable for foreshadowing the Neoclassic trend in early twentieth-century music that emerged a few years later. Actually, Prokofiev was merely attempting to write a symphony as Haydn might have, had he been living in 1917. The name "Classical" conveyed Prokofiev's hope that his work would become a "classic." Structured in four movements (sonata, ternary, gavotte with trio, rondo) and transparent in texture, this work has the angular melody and ostinato that became characteristic of Prokofiev's style. Prokofiev did not continue writing Neoclassic music.

In 1918–36, Prokofiev lived outside Russia. His opera *The Love for Three Oranges* (1919) was first performed by the Chicago Opera Company in 1921. Frequently performed works written during those years are the symphonic suite *Lieutenant Kijé* (1934) and *Peter and the Wolf* (1936; spoken narration, orch.), a "symphonic fairy tale" for children.

After the Union of Soviet Composers was established, Prokofiev received some Soviet commissions for works. He believed that he could comply with the general guidelines that the Soviets had set up for composers, and in 1936 he returned to Russia. Yet, some of his works were severely criticized and rejected, and he had to rewrite several compositions to please Soviet and Union officials.

In 1938, after Prokofiev studied film music techniques in California, Mosfilm commissioned from him the film score for *Alexander Nevsky*. Later, Prokofiev edited that music as a cantata.

Prokofiev wrote numerous works in all genres. Of his seven symphonies, the *Classical* and the Fifth (B♭ major; 1944) are outstanding. Symphony No. 5 is an excellent example of Prokofiev's style, which may be described as follows: Nationalism is present but is mingled with Classic and modern features. He used traditional forms and was adept at motivic development. His music is tonal, with lyrical but angular melodies, strong motor rhythm, and sudden modulations to unexpected keys. Basso ostinato occurs frequently. The instrumental writing is idiomatic. Often, in places where the basic texture is thin, fuller sonority is achieved by having dissimilar instruments double the passages. Most of the symphonies include piano and harp.

DMITRY SHOSTAKOVICH

Shostakovich received his first musical training from his mother, a professional pianist. In 1919 he entered the Petrograd Conservatory, where he concentrated on piano and composition. He graduated in piano in 1923 and in composition in 1925. As graduation composition, he submitted his Symphony No. 1 (F minor), a four-movement work modern in style. Both first and second movements hint at serialism, with themes containing 11, 9, and 12 pitches, but the symphony is tonal throughout.

Shostakovich composed 15 symphonies. In them his stylistic traits are clearly revealed. *Symphony No. 2: "To October"* (C major; 1927) and *Symphony No. 3: "May First"* (E♭ major; 1930) are politically oriented one-movement works with chorus. His other symphonies are multimovement compositions, and only two of them (Nos. 13 and 14) include voices. Symphonies Nos. 2, 3, 7, 8, 11, and 12 are decidedly Russian in tone; the others are more contemporary and somewhat individualistic. Thus, there is visible in Shostakovich's work a dualism that reflects his vacillation between writing the kind of music he wanted to and fulfilling his moral and political obligations as a loyal Soviet citizen. In his last three symphonies, he seems to have returned to his youthful daring and experimentation. In fact, of the last three "symphonies," only No. 15 is truly orchestral. It is Neoclassic, concisely written, and is in four movements with Scherzo third.

Seven of Shostakovich's symphonies are in minor keys, and most of them end in tonic major. The Third Symphony is especially dissonant. The Thirteenth and Fourteenth are closer to song cycle than symphony.

Dmitry Shostakovich. *(Historical Pictures Collection/Stock Montage)*

Shostakovich became interested in writing stage works and composed the satirical opera *The Nose* (1927) and the ballet *The Golden Age* (1930), equally satirical. His opera *Lady Macbeth of the Mtsensk District* (1930–32), the ballet *The Limpid Stream* (1934–35), and Symphony No. 4 (C major; 1936) drew harsh criticism and public condemnation from Russian political and cultural authorities. All three works were withdrawn. *Lady Macbeth* reappeared in 1956, completely revised, as *Katerina Izmaylova,* and was favorable received.

Supposedly, Shostakovich wrote Symphony No. 5 (D minor; 1937) as acknowledgment of and in response to the "justified" criticism of his previous works. Actually, he made no concessions. The work contains no folk materials and is not nationalistic. However, it was favorably received and has remained one of his most frequently performed works. Symphony No. 5 opens with a Moderato in sonata form. Characteristically, bass instruments present the first theme; the second theme is introduced by violins. The Scherzo second movement is in ternary form, a lyrical Largo is third movement, and the Finale is a festive sonata-form Allegro non troppo.

Symphony No. 7 (C major; 1941), the "Leningrad Symphony," was Shostakovich's reaction to Hitler's invasion of Russia. The symphony quickly gained acceptance and became a symbol of Allied resistance against Nazism. Symphony No. 10 (E minor; 1953) is performed frequently; some persons consider it Shostakovich's finest symphony. Shostakovich personalized a number of his works, including the Tenth and Fifteenth symphonies, by placing within them his musical monogram, a transliteration of his Cyrillic first and

EXAMPLE 26.5 Shostakovich's musical monogram as used in Symphony No. 10, mvt. 3: closing measures, monogram stated by flutes and piccolos. *(Source: Dmitri Shostakovich, Symphony No. 10, Kalmus Miniature Score No. 158, Columbia Pictures/Belwin-Mills Publishing Corporation, Miami, FL.)*

last initials into German: D–SCH (D–Es–C–H), or D–E♭–C–B♮ in musical notation (ex. 26.5).

Many persons consider Shostakovich the greatest symphonist of the mid-twentieth century. His Fourteenth and Fifteenth Symphonies are masterpieces but are relatively unknown. His 15 string quartets are a valuable addition to the repertoire; of them, Nos. 7 and 8 are the finest. The Piano Quintet (G minor; 1940) is also excellent.

EXPRESSIONISM

The movement known as Expressionism appeared in art and literature in Germany and in Paris early in the twentieth century. The philosophy fundamental to Expressionism is that the artist's or writer's personal feelings and emotional reaction to a subject are more important than objective representation of it. Rather than objectively and accurately portraying a subject, the artist used bold color and strong linear patterns to express his emotional reaction to that subject. Exaggeration and distortion are features of Expressionism. German Expressionist artists, in addition to using strong color and linear pattern(s), chose subjects of highly emotional character. Some of Edvard Munch's (1863–1944) early works may be viewed as forerunners of true Expressionist art (e.g., *The Scream,* whose lone human's silent scream evokes in the viewer empathetic terror, mental anguish, and ear-splitting sound). As Expressionism developed, subjectivity of presentation increased, and representation of external reality weakened and disappeared. The first completely nonobjective paintings were created c. 1909 by the Russian painter Vesily Kandinsky (1844–1944), who was working in Berlin (e.g., the works he titled *Improvisation*). In music, Expressionism is seen in atonal/pantonal compositions that distort or ignore the conventions of traditional harmony and formal patterns

and are abstract and intense. Schoenberg, who was an accomplished amateur painter and who knew Kandinsky in Berlin, wrote some Expressionistic music. Undoubtedly, Schoenberg influenced Webern and others of the Second Viennese School to compose works in that style.

THE SECOND VIENNESE SCHOOL

The name "Second Viennese School" has been applied to Arnold Schoenberg and his few private pupils at Vienna, especially Alban Berg and Anton Webern. From this small "school" there emerged a new style of music called **dodecaphony,** or **twelve-tone music** (from Greek *dodeca,* 12; *phonos,* sound), an atonal or pantonal style in which all 12 of the chromatic pitches in the octave were regarded as equals and none had any special function. (Schoenberg considered dodecaphonic music pantonal, i.e., a blend of all key tonalities, but most persons refer to it as atonal.) Two of the principal factors generating the new style were (1) the increasingly abundant use of dissonances in post-Romantic music, particularly dissonances that remained unresolved and that were unrelated and unjustifiable in traditional harmony, and (2) a greater interest in and an ever-increasing use of linear counterpoint, whose motives and melodies dictated harmonies that, less and less frequently, followed the rules governing functional harmonies of key tonality.

During the first two decades of the twentieth century several composers, including Scriabin, Schoenberg, and Berg, wrote atonal music and music in which they considered the octave's 12 tones as being on a par. (This has led to the music being referred to sometimes as "total chromaticism.") Largely due to Schoenberg's efforts, an organizational system was developed that was put into operation in the 1920s and became known as **serialism.** The name derives from the fact that a composer prearranged the order in which the 12 chromatic pitches were to be used, thus establishing a **Series** or **Tone Row**—the Original Row (O), which Schoenberg called *Grundgestalt* (basic pattern). The pitches were to be used in the specific order in which they appeared in the row, but the position of any one of them on the staff might be displaced by the distance of one or more octaves (octave displacement). Any two or more successive pitches might be combined to form a harmonic interval or chord. The row might be used in retrograde (R), in inversion (I), or in retrograde inversion (RI). Moreover, any or all of the four versions of the row might be transposed to any step of the chromatic scale. Thus, 48 possible versions of the row were available. A **matrix** (also called a **grid**) of those possibilities is shown in figure 26.2. It should be readily apparent that what might seem, at the outset, to be extremely limiting, actually allows a composer considerable freedom.

Schoenberg was not the only composer in Vienna in 1913–23 who was seeking to develop a workable system for atonal music, though his principles were those generally accepted. Another system, less efficient, was developed by Josef Hauer (1883–1959), who, for each composition, arbitrarily divided the 12 chromatic pitches into two hexachords but did not regulate the order of the pitches within each hexachord. In other words, he specified content but not order.

Berg and Webern adopted Schoenberg's principles but used them in modification. Berg did not adhere to a single row for an entire composition or movement and often combined tonal and nontonal elements in a work. Webern strictly adhered to serial principles, used one row per movement, and wrote highly ordered counterpoint that was concentrated in extremely compressed forms. He used serial principles scientifically, creating rows whose variant forms, in transposition, reverted to the Original, and rows in which the intervals of the second hexachord, in retrograde, exactly duplicated those of the first hexachord. And what of Schoenberg himself? In his last style period, he tried to reconcile the principles of tonality and atonality. From time to time, he sought to return to the traditional tonal system but found himself using atonality and serialism.

At this point some clarification of terminology must be made. The terms **atonal** and **pantonal** are both used

FIGURE 26.2 Matrix (or grid) for the Row Schoenberg used in *Suite für Klavier*, Op. 25.

to describe music in which key centers of tonality are not clearly audible. Technically, those two terms are not synonymous. Atonal indicates the total absence of any center of key tonality, whereas pantonal indicates the presence of all tonal centers with none distinctive enough to be recognized or strong enough to exercise a tonal gravitation to itself. Schoenberg considered his works pantonal. *Dodecaphony,* meaning *twelve-tone music,* is the term applied to music based on series, sets, or rows containing all 12 chromatic pitches in the octave. A dodecaphonic composition is not necessarily atonal/pantonal; it may be written in a key tonality. A composer can construct a series or row that reinforces rather than negates key tonality. Conversely, an atonal/pantonal composition is not necessarily dodecaphonic. A composition that is not based on twelve-tone techniques may be written in such a manner that no tonal center can be detected. These several terms must be clearly differentiated if one is to understand the music of many composers active after c. 1924.

Arnold Schoenberg

Schoenberg (1874–1951) had some violin lessons when he was 8 years old but was largely a self-taught musician. He became proficient enough on violin and 'cello to play in ensembles with friends and in an

Arnold Schoenberg. *(Historical Pictures Collection/Stock Montage)*

amateur orchestra conducted by Alexander Zemlinsky (see p. 555), and he learned a great deal about musical composition by studying the scores of great composers. His first compositions were piano pieces and songs. In 1894 he began to take counterpoint lessons from Zemlinsky. By 1897 Schoenberg was composing works of sufficient quality to merit public performance. He earned his living by conducting small choral groups and by preparing orchestrations (e.g., for operettas). In 1901 he married Mathilde Zemlinsky (1877–1923). In 1902–3 they lived in Berlin. In Vienna in 1904 he advertised for pupils and attracted Alban Berg and Anton Webern. Schoenberg knew the music of Wagner, Strauss, Mahler, and Brahms, and their influences may be seen in Schoenberg's music from time to time. He considered Brahms a progressive composer and was interested in the way he combined modality and tonality and the manner in which he formed themes from two- and three-note motifs.

Schoenberg's career as composer may be divided into five periods: (1) 1895–1908, characterized by tonal works that are post-Romantic in style, containing much chromaticism and reflecting the influence of Wagner, Mahler, and Richard Strauss; (2) 1909–14, when he dared to be different and composed dissonant pantonal Expressionistic works that defied or ignored the principles of traditional harmony; (3) 1914–23, a time of experimentation during which he formulated the twelve-tone method and serial principles but composed nothing for publication; (4) 1923–33, a period of dodecaphonic composition; and (5) 1934–51, when he sought to reconcile dodecaphony and key tonality

and, by his own statement, wanted to return to composing according to traditional principles of tonality but from time to time found himself slipping back into pantonality.

The first work to indicate that Schoenberg's music would be distinctive was *Verklärte Nacht* (Transfigured Night, Op. 4; 1899; 2 vlns., 2 vlas., 2 vcl.). Containing sudden modulations and filled with chromaticism clearly related to that of Wagner's *Tristan und Isolde, Verklärte Nacht* is an emotionally intense programmatic work. To write that kind of program music for string sextet was unusual.

Other post-Romantic tonal works from Schoenberg's first period include the symphonic poem *Pelleas und Melisande* (1902–3), *Acht Lieder für Klavier und Singstimme* (Eight songs for piano and voice, Op. 6; 1904–5), *Sechs Orchesterlieder* (Six Songs with orchestra, Op. 8; 1903–5), and *Gurre-Lieder* (Songs of Gurre; 1900–11). *Pelleas und Melisande* is an extremely polyphonic work for a large orchestra. The cantata *Gurre-Lieder* is a massive work for five soloists, three four-part male choruses, an eight-part mixed chorus, and a huge orchestra. Apparent in the music is the influence of Wagner's *Die Walküre.* The last soloistic piece in *Gurre-Lieder,* presented just before the final chorus, is melodrama.

Schoenberg's compositions grew increasingly more chromatic, with an abundance of highly dissonant chords that are not resolved. Then he moved into the pantonality/atonality that characterizes his second period. His first truly atonal works were *Drei Klavierstücke* (Three Piano Pieces, Op. 11; 1909) and *Das Buch der hängenden Gärten* (The book of the Hanging Gardens; 1908–9; vc., pno.). In these works, consonance is no longer primal, with dissonance being required to resolve to it. Rather, dissonance has become independent, on a par with consonance. Next Schoenberg applied his atonal style to orchestral music. Each of the *Five Orchestral Pieces* (Op. 16; 1909) has a programmatic title. The third piece, "Summer Morning by the Lake," was at various times entitled "Chord Colors" and "The Changing Chord." The opening and concluding sections of the piece contain sustained chords whose instrumentation continually changes, unobtrusively, thus producing a flow of different tone colors. This is a form of **Klangfarbenmelodie** (tone-color melody; see also p. 558), the technique of creating a melody from changing tone colors rather than from a succession of different pitches. Schoenberg used it frequently to point up motives.

Schoenberg wrote two important one-act dramatic works during this period. *Erwartung* (Expectation, Op. 17; 1909) is a surrealist **monodrama** for female voice and large orchestra. (In a monodrama, one person is responsible for unfolding the entire drama.) Much of the time, the woman sings in dialogue with orchestral instruments as though with persons. Tone colors are extremely important. The other work, *Die glückliche Händ* (The lucky hand, Op. 18; 1910–13), was a dramatic experiment. It requires a man and a woman who mime the action, a high baritone singer, six men and six women for the chorus, and a very large orchestra. Only the faces of the chorus are visible, painted green (or illuminated to appear green) and protruding through holes in purple velvet backdrop drapery. The chorus, whose function is similar to that of the citizens chorus in ancient Greek tragedy, delivers its texts in a mixture of *Sprechstimme* (speech-song) and song. Expressionist works were not intended to be beautiful, pleasing, or realistic. Rather, every detail of such a work is exploited to convey, as penetratingly as possible, inner thoughts, emotions, and experiences.

Schoenberg's unusual treatment of the voice that began in a small way with the melodrama in *Gurre-Lieder,* and continued through the various vocal shadings in the monodrama *Erwartung* and the choral mingling of *Sprechstimme* and singing in *Die glückliche Hand,* culminated in *Pierrot Lunaire* (Moonstruck Pierrot, Op. 21; 1912), the major work of this pantonal period. *Pierrot Lunaire* is probably Schoenberg's best-known work. The composition is a set of 21 melodramas presented in *Sprechstimme* by a vocalist-reciter against instrumental accompaniment that varies from piece to piece. Five instrumentalists are needed, 3 of them doubling: piano, 'cello, flute switching to piccolo, clarinet to bass clarinet, violin to viola. Schoenberg arranged the poems in 3 groups of 7. Each of the poems has 13 lines arranged in Renaissance rondeau form, but the musical settings do not follow rondeau form. Schoenberg wrote the vocal line of all 21 pieces in *Sprechstimme* using normal notation that indicates precise pitch and duration of each note but with an x through each note's stem to indicate that a special kind of delivery was required: ♩. He supplied written instructions for singing *Sprechstimme* in which he indicated that the rhythm must be absolutely strict but that the notated pitch is merely touched on at the outset of the note's value, then immediately rises or falls. He cautioned the reciter-singer never to really sing the pitches and never to "singsong" them. "It must not be reminiscent of song," he stated. For the instrumentalists, accuracy of dynamics and maintenance of strict rhythm is extremely important. In each piece, a short initial motive generates the music for that entire piece. In No. 8, *Nacht* (Night; DWMA178a), which is a passacaglia, the generative motive contains 10 notes. Though a 3-note ostinato figure is ever-present, its note values are modified much of the time. The song is dark in color, well suited to the gloomy text. Song No. 18, *Der Mondfleck* (The Moonspot; DWMA178b), is the most contrapuntally complex piece of the entire cycle. A double canon *cancrizans*—one between the strings, the other between the winds—turns retrograde at the middle of the tenth measure. Simultaneously with the canon, the pianist plays a 3-voice fugue whose subject is an augmented version of the canonic melody between the winds. The piano music and the vocal line do not turn retrograde.

Between 1908 and 1913 Schoenberg's works gradually became more dissonant, and most of them were not well received. Therefore, for almost a full decade, he worked behind the scenes, so to speak, and shared his compositions with the public only after he had devised a new style of composition to offer them. His first works in that style were completed in 1923. In *Fünf Klavierstücke* (Five piano pieces, Op. 23) and *Serenade* (Op. 24; chamber ensemble) the twelve-tone method was still experimental. The first composition in which Schoenberg used a single twelve-note row throughout was *Suite für Klavier* (Piano Suite, Op. 25; 1923). Not until he composed the orchestral *Variations,* Op. 31 (1927–28), were the possibilities of his twelve-tone system fully realized (ex. 26.6). A detailed analysis of that work, which consists of Introduction, nine variations, and Finale (DWMA179), could serve as a textbook on serial techniques.

After Hitler was elected chancellor of Germany, Schoenberg emigrated to the United States and taught at California universities. In many of the compositions he wrote in America he combined serial techniques with tonality. The Violin Concerto (Op. 36;

EXAMPLE 26.6 Forms of the Row Schoenberg used in *Variations*, Op. 31.

Alban Berg. *(Historical Pictures Collection/Stock Montage)*

1936) and String Quartet No. 4 (Op. 37; 1936) are strictly serial atonal compositions.

Among the musical expressions of Schoenberg's Jewish faith are settings of several Psalms in Hebrew and *Kol Nidre* (Op. 39; 1938), a tonal work. *A Survivor from Warsaw* (Op. 46; 1947; narrator, male vcs., orch.) was written in response to a report of courageous Jews singing the *Shema Yisroel,* the Creed, during the Warsaw uprising.

Unfinished at the time of Schoenberg's death was the opera *Moses und Aron* (Moses and Aaron). Schoenberg had composed Acts I and II in 1930–32 but had not written Act III. He based the entire opera on a single tone row. The work requires six soloists, chorus, and a large orchestra. Acts I and II have been performed, in a concert version (1954) and staged (1957). They are magnificent music.

Certain stylistic characteristics are visible in Schoenberg's compositions in all periods of his career: (1) melodies containing wide leaps; (2) the use of small motifs, as Brahms had done; (3) the absence of vigorous, propelling rhythms; (4) emphasis on counterpoint, especially in twelve-tone works; and (5) a penchant for constantly changing tone colors, particularly in orchestral works. In many pieces, the rhythmic beat is deliberately obscured through such techniques as dense texture, placement of rests on primary beats, frequent tempo changes, and sustained tones.

ALBAN BERG

As a youngster, Berg (1885–1935) played piano and enjoyed writing songs, though he had no formal training in composition. After completing his general education, he obtained clerical work in a government office. In 1904 he noticed Schoenberg's advertisement for pupils, contacted him for lessons, and studied with him for six years.

The compositions Berg wrote during his first years of study with Schoenberg—the *Sieben frühe Lieder* (Seven early songs; 1905–8) and the one-movement Piano Sonata (Op. 1; 1907–8)—are Romantic and tonal. Atonality and originality emerged in the last of Berg's *Vier Lieder* (Four Songs, Op. 2; 1909–10) and the String Quartet (Op. 3; 1910). Some features of the quartet became characteristic of Berg's works: use of scales that are largely (but not completely) wholetone, prolongation of a passage by melodic expansion of an interval (e.g., widening an interval from a second to a third to a fourth), combining atonality with traditional forms, and suggesting tonality in what is actually atonality.

Berg's *Fünf Orchesterlieder nach Ansichtskartentexten von Peter Altenberg* (Five orchestral songs after picture postcard texts by Peter Altenberg, Op. 4; orch. with voice; 1911), the "Altenberg Songs," are miniatures for a large orchestra. The very brief *Vier Stücke* (Four pieces, Op. 5; 1913; cl., pno.), when viewed overall, form a miniature sonata, with movements 12, 9, 18, and 20 measures long. A feature of Berg's mature works, and a factor that creates a kind of tension (between old and new), is the use of traditional form with powerful new music.

During World War I, Berg was employed by the War Ministry but found the time to compose *Drei Stücke* (Three Pieces, Op. 6; 1913–15; orch.) and to work on the opera *Wozzeck* (1917–22). The opera concerns a soldier whose frustrations ultimately drive him to murder his unfaithful mistress and then commit suicide.

Berg constructed a three-act opera, with five scenes per act, each act being a cyclic self-contained form and each scene a self-contained movement or compositional form. Act I is a suite of five character pieces, in which Scene 1 is a stylized version of a Bach *French Suite.* Act II could be viewed as a five-movement symphony. Act III consists of five inventions (DWMA180, Scene 2). Analysis reveals other formal patterns and traditional techniques: fugue, rondo, rhapsody, isorhythm, variations, and so on. Though *Wozzeck* is considered the first full-length atonal opera, there are semblances of tonality within it (e.g., in Act II, Scene 1). The music is continuous in *Wozzeck,* and Leitmotifs are a unifying device. Another unifying device is the use of the same music at the opera's end and at the close of Act I. Berg hoped that no one in the audience would be aware of the music *per se,* but attention would be concentrated on the social problems presented through the drama.

Thematic material for the *Kammerkonzert* (Chamber concerto; pno., vln., 13 wind instrs.; 1923–25), a three-movement serial work, is derived from the letters of musical pitches in the names Arnold Schönberg, Anton Webern, and Alban Berg, a technique resembling the *soggetto cavato* used by Josquin (see p. 162). The *Lyrische Suite* (Lyric Suite; 1925–26) was commissioned by the Kolisch Quartet. In 1928 Berg arranged the suite's second, third, and fourth movements for string orchestra; that version is frequently performed. At some time he wrote a vocal finale for the work for mezzo-soprano solo with string quartet; this movement was discovered and first performed in 1979.

In 1928 Berg began another Expressionist opera, *Lulu.* He had composed the entire opera but had not finished orchestrating the third act before his untimely death (1935) from systemic poisoning caused by an abscessed insect bite. Berg's widow refused to release his manuscript for Act III; only after her death (1976) was the orchestration completed and the entire opera performed (1979). Berg's music for *Lulu* is a combination of atonal, serial, and nondodecaphonic elements. Each act was designed as a musical form: Act I, sonata form; Act II, rondo; and Act III, theme and variations. Within the acts are autonomous pieces, as in a number opera. Lulu represents female sexuality. In Act I she is seductive, powerful, and a murderess; in Act III she is murdered. Some persons in the cast play dual roles—each of Lulu's victims in the first half of the opera becomes an avenger-character in the final scene. To reinforce that fact, Berg brought back, as highly telescoped recapitulation, the music of the first half of the opera.

Berg's last completed composition is the Violin Concerto. It is in two movements, each containing two sections—Andante-Allegretto and Allegro-Adagio—and each section having a distinct formal pattern. Notated without a key signature and with almost every note in the score preceded by a ♮, ♭, or ♯, the music is serial atonality so carefully structured that it permits Berg to allude to tonality. Some portions of the concerto are clearly tonal (e.g., that including Bach's chorale harmonization [ex. 26.7]). The Andante commences with an introduction consisting of arpeggiations closely akin to the pitches of the four open strings of the violin. The soloist presents the row, which consists principally of four arpeggiated triads (alternately minor and major) constructed on the pitches of the violin's open strings, plus a whole-tone tetrachord, all joined conjunctly (ex. 26.8a). The whole-tone tetrachord, in various guises, appears throughout the concerto. The work is cyclic; the row appears in all four sections and in the finale is combined with the chorale *Es ist genug!* (It is enough!) as harmonized by Bach in his Cantata No. 60. That chorale melody commences with a whole-tone tetrachord; the row concludes with a whole-tone tetrachord (ex. 26.8b). The concerto concludes with five string soloists successively stating the row, their statements commencing with contrabass open-string E and extending upward to violin g‴. While the violin soloist sustains that high pitch, there is heard in the orchestra, very softly, as from a distance, the downward arpeggiation of the six perfect fifths that began the concerto.

Berg's principal works are *Wozzeck, Lulu,* and the Violin Concerto. Though an exponent of atonality, Berg never completely relinquished Romanticism and tonality. In his treatment of twelve-tone music he differed from Schoenberg and Webern in several respects, principally in that he (1) used dodecaphonic and nondodecaphonic episodes in the same work, sometimes in the same movement; (2) frequently supported a tone row with harmony in or suggesting a key; (3) sometimes used different rows (or sets) in the same work

(a)

(b)

EXAMPLE 26.7 (*a*) Beginning of J. S. Bach's harmonization of the chorale *Es ist genug!*; (*b*) piano reduction of orchestral presentation of the chorale as used by Berg in mm. 142–45 of the Violin Concerto. Berg used Bach's harmonization transposed up a semitone. *(Example b Berg VIOLIN CONCERTO © Copyright 1938 by Universal Edition. A. G., Vienna. Copyright renewed. All Rights Reserved. Used by permission of European American Music Distributors Corporation, sole U.S. and Canadian agent for Universal Edition Vienna.)*

and even in the same movement; (4) used retrograde and retrograde inversions of a row only in palindromes; and (5) usually wrote lyrical music.

ANTON WEBERN

Webern (1883–1945), a native of Vienna, was Schoenberg's first pupil, studying with him in 1904–8. Webern played piano and 'cello and studied harmony and counterpoint at the University of Vienna; however, he concentrated on musicology and earned his Ph.D. in 1906. His dissertation on Heinrich Isaac's *Choralis Constantinus II* (see p. 165) led to his edition of that liturgical music (pub. in *DTÖ*, Volume xxxii; 1909) and influenced the motivic treatment in some of his works. After graduating, Webern worked as a conductor, taught privately, lectured, and composed. Few of his works were published. He remained relatively obscure as a composer throughout his lifetime. Some of

(a)

(b)

EXAMPLE 26.8 Berg, Violin Concerto: (*a*) the Row, as introduced by solo violin; (*b*) first phrase of the chorale, parallel in tonal structure to last four notes of the Row.

his lectures on dodecaphony were published in 1960 as *Der Weg zur neuen Musik* (The way to the new music). When Nazism caused the loss of some of his sources of income, Webern secured routine work from

Universal Edition that he could do at home. He and his wife spent most of the World War II years at Mödling; near the end of the war they moved to Mittersill to be near their daughters. There, on 15 September 1945, Webern was accidentally shot and killed by an American soldier investigating black-market activities in the neighborhood.

Webern's output comprises 31 works with *opus* numbers and approximately an equal number of other pieces of various kinds. The compositions with *opus* numbers may be separated into two groups, representing the two major periods of his compositional career: (1) Opp. 1–16, including 2 tonal works (Opp. 1 and 2) and 14 atonal ones, composed in 1908–23, and (2) Opp. 17–31, the dodecaphonic serial works composed in 1924–45. Once Webern renounced key tonality, he did not recant; after he began to use serial techniques, he continued along that path. He sought to express inner thoughts through abstract music, and he did so succinctly. Some of his pieces and movements are very short; for example, Op. 10 No. 4 has six and one-third measures, Op. 11 No. 3 has 10. His compositions bear generic titles—Four Songs, String Quartet, Symphony, and so on.

Webern reserved the designation "Op. 1" for the orchestral *Passacaglia* he composed in 1908. He was justified in doing so; the music he wrote before studying with Schoenberg is of little consequence. Among the atonal works in the first group of pieces with *opus* numbers are eight sets of solo songs with accompaniment; two sets of pieces for string quartet, including *Six Bagatelles* (Op. 9; 1911–13); two orchestral sets, one being *Five Pieces* (Op. 10; 1911–13); *Four Pieces* for violin and piano (Op. 7; 1910); and *Three Little Pieces* (Op. 11; 1913) for 'cello and piano. The compositions are concise and pointillistic, and they emphasize dissonant intervals such as the minor second and major ninth. The word **pointillism** is used to describe athematic music seemingly constructed of isolated notes. The term was borrowed from art, where it connotes paintings consisting of dots or points of color that are blended into shapes by the viewer's eyes. Tone color was important to Webern, and the variation of timbres became a feature of his atonal pieces for instrumental ensembles. An instance of this occurs at the end of *Five Pieces* for orchestra, Op. 10, No. 1 (ex. 26.9). Webern

Anton Webern. (*The Bettmann Archive*)

varied tone color to differentiate motives or to point up polyphonic entrances and used different articulations, mutes, and other devices. Despite the changing timbres and registers, continuity of line is present, and he stressed the fact that the performer(s) *must* maintain that continuity. Variation of timbres considerably enriched the economy of means that characterizes Webern's works. He included instruments for their timbral sonorities in particular passages rather than using them in orchestral ensemble. Webern recognized the significance of silence; rests play an important role in his works.

Between 1914 and 1924, Webern concentrated on vocal music. By 1924, serial techniques had been developed, and he used them as extensions of variation technique. In his second group of *opus* numbers, the works are highly contrapuntal and often contain canons, palindromes, and variations. He combined serial techniques with traditional ones and incorporated them in traditional forms; in this sense, his work is Neoclassic. Gradually, in orchestral works, he eliminated nonpitched percussion instruments and stopped writing harmonics and *col legno* in string parts. In his serial writing, Webern, like Schoenberg, sometimes reiterated a pitch. Frequently, he constructed a row from a series of small motives, or sets; then, he might work with only a portion of the row, or with one of the motives, before going on to the next.

Webern imposed strict structural limitations on himself yet provided ample freedom to be creative. His *Symphonie* (Op. 21; 1928) exemplifies this. The work is in two movements, the first in sonata form, the

EXAMPLE 26.9 Webern: *Fünf Stücke für Orchester*, I, last 6 measures. To conclude the piece, the same note is sounded successively by different instruments, producing *Klangfarbenmelodie*.

second in theme and variations with coda (DWMA 181). He made sketches for a third movement but never completed it. Scored for chamber orchestra of nine solo instruments, the music is highly concentrated, with a texture that never goes beyond four-part writing. Webern established a twelve-tone row whose retrograde is identical with the original transposed up an augmented fourth. He used only the original and its inversion in the first movement and only the original and its retrograde in the second movement. The first movement, in addition to being in sonata form, is a four-voice double canon with the original row and its inversion as subjects. The row that he established for

the second movement and that forms the theme that is varied is constructed so that its second half is the retrograde of the first half transposed up an augmented fourth. The fact that the entire theme is presented by clarinet, accompanied by horns and harp—in a single timbral combination—is unusual in Webern's music.

Webern's last completed composition was Cantata No. 2 (Op. 31; 1941–43; S, B soloists, SATB chor., orch.). It is one of his longest works, requiring about 10 minutes for performance. It is in six sections: bass recitative, bass aria, female chorus with soprano solo, soprano recitative, soprano aria with chorus and violin obbligato, and final chorale for mixed chorus. The chorale directly reflects Webern's study of Isaac's music. Webern stated that the cantata is "basically a Missa brevis."

The most obvious features of Webern's mature style are the brevity and conciseness of the compositions and the presence of silence. Textural clarity and harmonic simplicity are evident also. Less apparent but equally significant are motivic organization, symmetry, and intervallic structure, particularly the use of the semitone. Webern, like Brahms and Schoenberg, understood the value of using two-, three-, or four-note motifs as structural units in a melody, theme, or composition, and he seems to have been more concerned with constructing a tone row or series by assembling small motifs than with creating an extended melodic theme. Recurrent patterns—short motifs—small sets play an important role in Webern's compositions. He seems not to have used total serialization—in none of his known works do all the elements of music follow an established preset order.

Not until after Webern's death was the significance of his work realized. As the value of his contributions to serial technique became more apparent, he was recognized as a leader, and his work was emulated by avant-garde composers internationally.

SPAIN

In Spain, in the early twentieth century, the term *art* meant the plastic arts, and *culture* connoted primarily literature and philosophy—music occupied a sideline position, though writers and musicians/composers often were close friends, as were de Falla and Lorcá. In general, Spanish opera was not successful; the zarzuela survived during the first part of the century but almost disappeared for a time after the Civil War (1936–39). The establishment of philharmonic societies, symphony orchestras, and permanent choruses in 1904–15 stimulated composition of works suitable for performance by such groups. Conservatories were a center of musical life, and reliable critics kept the interested public aware of composers' creations. The most important composer was Manuel de Falla (1876–1946). Five others of his generation are significant: Conrado del Campo (1878–1953), Oscar Esplá (1886–1976), Julio Gómez (1886–1973), Jesús Guridi (1886–1961), and Joaquín Turina (1882–1949). Though their at-

tempts to establish a national opera failed, they contributed immensely by laying the foundation for Spanish symphonic and chamber music, whose repertoires rose from virtual nonexistence to brilliance because of their works. Campo's twelve string quartets have been called "a striking body of music."

MANUEL DE FALLA

Manuel de Falla, a native of Cádiz, received his first music training from his mother, then studied at the Madrid Conservatory, where he won first prize in piano in 1899. After meeting Pedrell in 1902, de Falla studied with him and composed music influenced by Spanish tradition—music with a nationalistic flavor but without quotations from folk music, for example, the Andalusian song *Tus ojillos negros* (Your dark eyes; 1902) and *Allegro de concierto* (1903; pno.). Both works are performed frequently.

Only one of the five zarzuelas that de Falla composed was staged. His lyric drama *La vida breve* (The short life; 1904–5), which contains folklike music and some authentic folk dances, was awarded first prize in a competition sponsored by the Real Academia de Bellas Artes but was not performed as promised. In 1907 de Falla moved to Paris, where he translated *La vida breve* into French, and Dukas helped him secure performance of it (1913). In Paris he became friends with Debussy, Ravel, Albéniz, and Viñes; Viñes premiered many of de Falla's piano works.

When World War I threatened, de Falla returned to Spain. During 1914–20 he composed several significant works, including the Impressionistic symphonic suite *Noches en los jardines de España* (Nights in the gardens of Spain; pno., orch.), which sounds Spanish but contains no actual folkloric elements, and *El amor brujo* (Love, the magician; spectacle/ballet), in which, by using elements derived from *cante jondo* (a primitive Andalusian song type) but without quoting actual folk material, he created an Andalusian gypsy world whose vibrant rhythms and depth of color are Expressionistic. Then de Falla composed a two-scene pantomime, *El corregidor y la molinera* (The corregidor and the miller) that later became the ballet *El sombrero de tres picos*. Its second scene is "Neo-Scarlatti" in style.

After the deaths of his parents in 1919, de Falla settled in Granada. As a child, he had played with a small puppet theater; in 1923 he wrote an excellent chamber opera for marionettes, three puppets, and small orchestra, *El retablo de Maese Pedro* (The altarpiece of Master Peter), based on an episode in Cervantes's *Don Quixote*. The music is a synthesis of historical material, street vendors' cries, and popular ballads. *Psyché* (1924; vc., 5 instrs.), depicting an eighteenth-century court concert, is Neoclassic.

On occasion, during 1920–36, de Falla composed several works titled "Homage" that later were orchestrated. The first of these, *Homenaje 'Le tombeau de Debussy'* (Homage "Lament for Debussy"; 1920; guitar), is a landmark in guitar literature. Several well-known keyboard artists commissioned works from de Falla. The *Concerto para clavicémbalo y cinco instrumentos* (Concerto for harpsichord and five instrs.; 1923–26), written for Wanda Landowska, was described by Ravel as "a masterwork of modern chamber music."

In 1926 de Falla began composing *Atlàntida* (oratorio; soloists, chor., orch.) and worked on it intermittently over the years; in it he aimed to present the essence of Spanish music (especially Catalan) from the Middle Ages to his present. The work, still unfinished at the time of his death, was completed by Ernesto Halffter (1905–89).

NEOCLASSICISM

Near the end of World War I a reaction began to set in against late Romanticism. This movement, usually referred to as Neoclassicism, gathered momentum in the 1920s and remained strong until after 1945. It is characterized by a preference for absolute music, greater emphasis on counterpoint, economy of performing resources, and a revival of eighteenth-century traditional forms, with thematic material subject to techniques and compositional processes then favored. The prefix *neo* indicates that the early music style was modified by twentieth-century features, such as expanded tonality, modality, or atonality/pantonality. At times there was direct quotation of portions of an early work rather than allusion to or parody of it.

As a movement, Neoclassicism began in 1920 with the performance of Igor Stravinsky's *Pulcinella* (ballet with song, 1919–20), written in Preclassic style and borrowing from Pergolesi and other composers of that era. In general, Stravinsky's style between 1920 and 1951 (*The Rake's Progress*) is Neoclassic. Many com-

posers turned to Neoclassicism after having explored other styles. Paul Hindemith (1895–1963) began writing Neoclassic music in the 1930s and continued in that style for the remainder of his life. Hindemith and Stravinsky are the chief exponents of Neoclassicism.

The significance of Neoclassicism lies in the historical awareness of early music by twentieth-century composers and the fact that their appreciation and parodying of eighteenth-century music led to the revival of forms and characteristic styles of previous eras. Moreover, an unwillingness to accept twentieth-century musical sounds as suitable for church music caused composers to use as models sixteenth- and seventeenth-century styles and techniques. In addition to the general back-to-Bach-and-Handel movement, composers in each country were motivated by nationalism to turn to the musical styles of the historical past in their own countries—the English to the music of Byrd and Tallis, the Italians to Monteverdi, Gabrieli, and Palestrina.

LES SIX—LATER

Of the six young French composers whom critic Collet dubbed *Les Six* (see Chap. 25), the most enduring music was written by Milhaud, Honegger, and Poulenc. The Six worked together only a few years, then each took a separate path.

Many of Louis Durey's (1888–1979) pieces are miniatures. He wrote some fine chamber music and some excellent songs (e.g., *Le printemps au fond de la mer* [Spring at the bottom of the sea; 1920]). Durey joined the French Communist Party in 1936. As Secretary-General of the Fédération Musicale Populaire (1937–56) and the Association Française des Musiciens Progressistes (1948–79) and as music critic for the Paris Communist newspaper, he urged composers to write nationalistic music based on folk songs, to be "democratic" in their choice of forms, and to avoid individuality. Among his communist-oriented works is *La longue marche* (The long march; T, chor., orch.; 1949; text by Mao Tse-tung).

Georges Auric was one of the four pianists premiering Stravinsky's ballet *Les noces* (The Wedding) in 1923. Sergei Diaghilev (1872–1929) commissioned Auric to compose several works for the Ballet Russe. Particularly successful were *Les fâcheux* (The bores; 1923), based on Molière's play, and *Les matelots* (The sailors; 1924). Both ballets are Neoclassic in style, with touches of humor. In the 1920s Auric wrote incidental music for at least eight plays and in 1930–55 composed scores for a dozen films. He wrote ballets until 1960. Works created in the 1950s reveal his awareness of avant-garde techniques. Both tonality and atonality are found in the ballet *Chemin de lumière* (Path of light; 1951).

From 1954 to 1977 Auric was president of the Société d'Auteurs, Compositeurs et Editeurs de Musique. As director of the Paris Opéra and Opéra-Comique in 1962–68, he did much to revitalize opera in France. After retiring from the directorship, he wrote only a few works, all instrumental: *Imaginées I–IV* (I, fl., pno., 1968; II, vcl., pno., 1969; III, cl., pno., 1971; IV, vla., pno., 1973) and *Double-jeux I–III* (2 pianos; 1970–71). Those pieces are atonal but thematic and attest that Auric remained in tune with current developments without relinquishing individuality or originality.

Germaine Tailleferre's compositions follow traditional lines established by Fauré and continued by Ravel, with whom she studied orchestration. She worked mainly in large forms—ballet, opera, opéra comique, concerto, sonata, and string quartet—but wrote a few songs and single-movement instrumental pieces. Some of her keyboard pieces show Couperin's influence. She married an American author and visited the United States briefly in 1927. Her *Concertino for Harp and Orchestra* (1926) was written for and first performed by Boston Symphony Orchestra. Most representative of her style are her first violin/piano Sonata (1921), the ballet *Le marchand d'oiseaux* (The bird merchant; 1923), and *Ouverture* (orch.; 1932).

Arthur Honegger composed music in all genres. In 1917–30 he wrote a number of works with programmatic titles such as, the *Symphonic Movements* subtitled *Pacific 231* (1923) and *Rugby* (1928), which he considered absolute music. Lest *Mouvement symphonique No. 3* (1932–33) be misunderstood, he did not subtitle it. Honegger's finest orchestral writing is in his five symphonies, all absolute music. Stage and dramatic works make up the bulk of Honegger's music: operas and operettas, dramatic oratorios, incidental music for plays, ballets and pantomimes, and radio and film scores. In 1923 a concert performance of the dramatic psalm *Le roi David* (King David; 1921; staged 1921; rev. 1923) brought Honegger international recognition. The work is a Neoclassic number oratorio. In subsequent stage works Honegger wrote more demanding speaking and singing parts, including *Sprechstimme,* humming, whispering, and screaming. In the dramatic oratorio *Jeanne d'Arc au bûcher* (Joan of Arc at the stake; 1934–35), there are five speaking and five vocal solo roles, mixed chorus that speaks and sings, children's chorus, and a large orchestra. Designed to be staged, the work contains some highly dramatic scenes with tremendous emotional impact. Some of the music is quite dissonant, but into that dissonance Honegger blended dance tunes, folk songs, and Gregorian chant.

Francis Poulenc was a master of the *mélodie,* and wrote approximately 150 of them. Among his finest are the nine love songs constituting the cycle *Tel jour, telle nuit* (Such a day, such a night; 1936–37). Many of Poulenc's songs and piano pieces require "*beaucoup de pedale*" (much pedal) to produce the results he intended. The prime factor in his music is melody; it is supported by simple diatonic harmonies with passing dissonances in basically homophonic texture.

Another area in which Poulenc excelled is religious choral music. His work in this field was done after the untimely death of a close friend in 1935 caused Poulenc to draw closer to the Catholic faith. After visiting Notre Dame de Rocamadour, he composed *Litanies à la vierge noire* (Litanies to the black Virgin; 1936; female chor., organ). Also notable are the Mass in G (1937; SATB chor.) and the *Gloria* (1961; S, chor., orch.).

Poulenc wrote several ballets and incidental music for about a dozen plays. In 1944 he composed an opera bouffe based on Apollinaire's play *Les mamelles de Tirésias* (The breasts of Tirésias). The opera, which preserves Apollinaire's message against equality for women, reveals Poulenc's talent for musical satire. He waited almost a decade, then wrote the religious opera *Dialogues des carmélites* (Dialogues of the Carmelites; 1953–56) and the monodrama *La voix humaine* (The human voice; 1958).

Darius Milhaud's voluminous output and the rapidity and facility with which he composed rival that of Telemann and Mozart. His works include operas, ballets, incidental music for plays, film and radio scores, orchestral compositions, chamber music, music for brass band, choral works, songs, keyboard works (piano, organ), and music for children. Several works have small dimensions: six chamber symphonies (1917–23) and three *opéras minutes* (miniature operas, about 10 minutes in duration; 1927–28) parodying classical myths.

Milhaud's deep appreciation of his Provençal heritage, the pastoral scenes of the region, and its folk music is apparent in a number of his compositions, especially, the orchestral *Suite provençale* (1936). As Paul Cézanne (1839–1906) painted Provençal landscapes, so Milhaud translated the Provençal atmosphere into music.

Milhaud's association with Francis Jammes (1868–1938) and Paul Claudel (1868–1955) greatly influenced his career. While Claudel was French minister to Brazil (1916–18), he employed Milhaud as secretary. After returning to France, Milhaud composed *Saudades do Brasil* (Souvenirs of Brazil; 1920–21), two suites of six dances each, written in two versions—orchestral and piano. He incorporated Brazilian music in the ballet *Le boeuf sur le toit* (The ox on the roof; 1919) and the two-piano work *Scaramouche* (1927). Although Milhaud suffered severely from rheumatoid arthritis, he traveled a great deal, and various musics of the countries he visited found their way into his compositions. He experienced authentic jazz played by black musicians when he visited Harlem, New York, in 1922. That inspired him to write the ballet *Le création de la monde* (The creation of the world; 1923), in which he included saxophones and elements of ragtime, blues, and jazz. This may be the earliest use of jazz and blues in an orchestral score.

Another influence in Milhaud's music was his pride in and reverence for his Jewish heritage. He expressed this in several works, the finest being *Poèmes juïfs* (8 Jewish poems; 1916), *Service sacré* (Sacred Service; 1947), portions of the ballet *Moïse* (Moses; 1940), the five-act biblical opera *David* (1952), and his last work, the cantata *Ani maamin, un chant perdu et retrouvé* (Ani maamin, a song lost and found again; soprano, 4 reciters, chor., orch.; 1973).

Milhaud's music is objective, characterized by lyrical melodies, formal clarity, skillful use of counterpoint, and bitonality or polytonality. He stated that he used polytonal chords primarily to enhance diatonic melody (i.e., as an artist uses color to point up specific things). Generally, in instrumental ensembles, he minimized polytonal dissonance by maintaining the tonal planes in different instrumental timbres. Once he discovered bi- and polytonality, that became a permanent feature of his music. A panorama of Milhaud's style is visible in his operas. A masterpiece, the opera-oratorio *Christophe Columbe* (Christopher Columbus; 1928), requires massive performing resources: 45 soloists, non-singing actors, a very large chorus, and film inserts. The music incorporates elements of Symbolism and Expressionism, uses some Leitmotifs, and in places uses chorus in the manner of the ancient Greeks. The work was first performed in Berlin in 1930, then lay untouched for almost 40 years, until Milhaud revised it drastically for a 1969 staging in Graz.

PAUL HINDEMITH

Hindemith (1895–1963) had a multifaceted career as performer, composer, theorist, teacher, and author and made significant contributions in each of those areas. He was virtuosic on violin and viola and exceptionally accomplished on several other instruments. In 1915 he was first violinist in the Frankfurt Opera orchestra and second violinist in the Rebner quartet. His career was interrupted in 1917 when he was called into military service, but for much of the time he was assigned to a regimental band. When World War I ended, he returned to both of his previous positions.

Around 1912 Hindemith became seriously interested in composition. In 1919 he presented a public concert entirely of his own music that included two sonatas, a piano quartet, and the String Quartet, Op. 10. In compositions written in 1918–23 he seems to have been exploring stylistic possibilities and seeking innovations. Most of his early works are chamber

Paul Hindemith. *(Historical Pictures Collection/Stock Montage)*

music, the most important being *Kleine Kammermusik* (Little chamber music pieces; 1922) for wind quintet. In 1921 the performances of Hindemith's one-act operas *Mörder, Hoffnung der Frauen* (Murderer, hope of women; 1919) and *Sancta Susanna* (St. Susanna; 1921) attracted attention as much for their attitude toward sexuality as their innovative music. However, Hindemith did not adopt the Expressionist style of those operas. By 1923, his works show a tendency to favor the forms, counterpoint, and rhythmic vitality that characterized Baroque music. This is apparent in the song cycle *Das Marienleben* (The life of Mary; 1922–23; S, pno.; rev. 1936–48).

Hindemith's style changed in several respects during 1924–33. For about two years, he wrote neo-Baroque works, with considerable linear counterpoint that deprived the bass line of much of its usual harmonic function. This is apparent in *Kammermusiken Nrs. 2–7*. At times he altered orchestral balance by scoring works for an ensemble in which the number of winds and brasses equals that of strings. This is the case in *Concerto for Orchestra* (1925) and the opera *Cardillac* (1926; rev. 1952).

In 1927 Hindemith became professor of composition at the Berlin Hochschule für Musik. His work there had important results. It aroused in him a desire to write music for instruments with minimal or deficient repertoire; he planned at least 25 sonatas but actually wrote 16. It generated the text *Unterweisung im Tonsatz* (Instruction in Composition, 3 vols., 1937, 1939, 1970), published in English as *The Craft of Musical Composition*. It effected a change in his compositional style, bringing more lyrical melody, less dissonant counterpoint, and greater use of functional tonal harmonies, and in general it led toward the Neoclassicism that remained typical of his music from 1933 to the end of his life. The change to more lyrical melody is visible in *Konzertmusik* (Opp. 48–50; 1930). It shaped and strengthened his philosophy of music, which he expressed in the Charles Eliot Norton Lectures at Harvard University (1949–50) and in the book *A Composer's World* (1952). Some knowledge of that philosophy is vital to understanding the music he composed after 1927.

First, he believed that music must be understood as a means of communication between composer and the consumer of the music (i.e., between composer and performer and between composer and audience with performer as intermediary). Music understood by and gratifying only its composer is not viable. It is the composer's responsibility to ascertain the needs and desires of the consumers of his product and to gratify them to the best of his ability. With the intent of narrowing the gap between composer and amateur performer, Hindemith wrote some music specifically for amateurs (e.g., *Spielmusik* [1927] and *Sing- und Spielmusiken für Liebhaber und Musikfreunde* [Vocal and instrumental music for amateurs and music-lovers; 1928–29]). He created several works specifically for children (e.g., the musical play *Wir bauen eine Stadt* [Let's build a city; 1930] and *Plöner Musiktag* [A day at summer music camp; 1932]). Somehow, the word *Gebrauchsmusik* (music for use)—a term Hindemith thoroughly disliked—became associated with works of this kind. Closely related to "music for use" is didactic music, and Hindemith contributed to that category. Especially notable is *Ludus tonalis* (Game of tonalities; piano; 1942), which comprises a Prelude; a cycle of 12 fugues, 1 in each key, linked by modulatory interludes; and a Postlude. In tonality the Prelude proceeds from C to F♯; the Postlude presents the music of the Prelude inverted and retrograde and thus moves from F♯ to C.

Second, Hindemith was convinced that a composer must be a performing musician and must have acquired familiarity with instruments through participation in ensembles. Only through practical experience can a composer understand how to write idiomatically and effectively for instruments. Theory without practice is fruitless.

Third, Hindemith considered key tonality unavoidable. The manner in which the various pitches are naturally generated, as partials or overtones of a fundamental tonality, establishes their functional relationship to that central pitch and to each other. He explained this in *Unterweisung im Tonsatz*.

Finally, he wholeheartedly endorsed the theory expressed in the writings of Plato, Ptolemy, Boethius, and other ancient and medieval philosophers that the principles of order governing the acoustical ratios of musical intervals and the order within a musical composition symbolize and reflect, as microcosm to macrocosm, the principles that govern the orderly behavior of the universe. Hindemith expressed this part of his philosophy musically in his five-act opera *Die Har-*

monie der Welt (The harmony of the world; 1956–57). The story concerns the endeavors of astronomer-mathematician Johannes Kepler (1571–1630) to discover the harmony of the world, and the name of the opera derives from the title of Kepler's treatise *Harmonices mundi* (The harmony of the world; 1619). Hindemith prepared a companion symphony to the opera and entitled its three movements according to Boethius's threefold classification of music (see p. 22).

Hindemith's masterpiece is the opera *Mathis der Maler* (Mathias the painter; 1932–35), concerning Mainz court painter Matthias Grünewald (c. 1480–1528). The opera is in seven scenes, each clearly in one overall key. Though essentially it is a number opera, its continuity is maintained by links of recitative or arioso. At appropriate places, Hindemith incorporated chant and folk song. Hindemith's first symphony, also titled *Mathis der Maler* (1934), is a companion piece to the opera and was completed before the opera was finished. The symphony is programmatic and tonal. Each of its three movements ("Angelic Concert," "Entombment," and "The Temptation of St. Anthony") represents a panel of the altarpiece Grünewald painted (1510–15) for the monastic order of St. Anthony at Isenheim (plate 28) and is at the same time a quotation from the opera. Formally, melodically, and harmonically, the symphony is an amalgamation of traditional and twentieth-century musical resources. The movements are arranged in fast-slow-fast order: the first movement in sonata form, the second, ABA′ with coda, and the third, a complex ternary with elements of rondo.

The symphony *Mathis der Maler* provides an excellent preview of Hindemith's mature style, which is a synthesis of traditional and modern and reflects influences of major German composers from the sixteenth through the nineteenth centuries. Hindemith was very prolific and wrote works in every genre. Many of his compositions were written for specific performers. Among the works frequently performed in America are *Mathis der Maler* symphony, *Symphonic Metamorphoses on Themes of Carl Maria von Weber* (1943), and the dance legend *Nobilissima visione* (Noblest vision; 1938) concerning St. Francis of Assisi.

During the Hitler régime, Hindemith's concerts and his music were boycotted in Germany because he performed in ensembles with Jewish musicians. More-over, his wife was Jewish. Hindemith was never expelled from Germany but thought it best to leave that country. He came to America and in 1946 became a U.S. citizen. From 1941 to 1953 he taught at Yale University and for the next several years divided his time between Yale and the University of Zurich. He died in Frankfurt on 28 December 1963.

IGOR STRAVINSKY

Stravinsky (1882–1971) was one of the twentieth century's most outstanding composers. His father, Fyodor Stravinsky (1843–1902), one of the principal bass singers at the imperial opera theater, provided his children with music lessons and encouraged them to attend opera and ballet performances. Igor studied piano and had lessons in counterpoint and harmony. Nevertheless, he enrolled at St. Petersburg University to study law. One of his friends there was Vladimir Rimsky-Korsakov, who invited Stravinsky to visit in his home. Thus, Stravinsky met Nicolai Rimsky-Korsakov, who became his mentor and strongly influenced many of his compositions. Stravinsky dedicated his Symphony No. 1 (Op. 1; E♭ major; 1905–7) to Rimsky-Korsakov, and when Rimsky-Korsakov died Stravinsky composed a dirge for wind instruments in his memory. That music is lost. Stravinsky considered that dirge his finest work prior to *L'oiseau de feu* (The firebird; 1909–10). From Rimsky-Korsakov, Stravinsky learned to write

Igor Stravinsky. *(Historical Pictures Collection/Stock Montage)*

DEVELOPMENTS BETWEEN THE WORLD WARS

harmonies and melodies based on the augmented fourth to portray supernatural characters and to use diatonicism with modal overtones for the principal human characters. He became adept at expressing psychological states and physical movements musically.

In 1909 Stravinsky visited Paris, where Diaghilev asked him to orchestrate some pieces for the Ballet Russe and commissioned *L'oiseau de feu*. Though Stravinsky was almost 30, his career as a professional composer was just beginning. The success of *L'oiseau de feu* brought him commissions for other ballets: *Petrushka* in 1911 and *Le sacre du printemps* (The rite of spring) in 1913.

Petrushka and *Le sacre du printemps* differ vastly, each in its own way, from Stravinsky's earlier works. The Oriental exoticism that colored *L'oiseau de feu* is no longer present. The character Petrushka is Slavic counterpart of the French Pierrot. The ballet depicts a puppet who, endowed with life, is scorned by the Ballerina he loves and is destroyed in a struggle with his rival, the Moor. In portraying interaction between characters with such different personalities, Stravinsky superimposed scales, harmonies, melodies, and rhythms and used contrasting instrumentation. For example, in the third tableau, contrasting instrumental combinations present, superimposed, the $\frac{3}{4}$ waltz rhythm of the graceful Ballerina and the $\frac{2}{4}$ rhythm of the rather clumsy Moor. That tableau simultaneously presents material in C major and F♯ major (in the scoring for B♭ clarinets the latter is written as G♭ major). The simultaneous arpeggiations of the tonic chords of these keys gave rise to the epithet "Petrushka chord." Stravinsky composed at a muted piano, and his choice of these tonalities for contrasting voices may have been prompted by the fact that one passage uses only white and the other only black keys on the keyboard. However, the bitriadic "Petrushka chord" is rooted in the octatonic scale on C (C–C♯–D♯–E–F♯–G–A–A♯). Not all of *Petrushka* is bitonal. For some of the music Stravinsky used conventional diatonic harmonies. He included Russian folk song modal melodies, a popular French air, and a waltz. Ostinato patterns appear often—they became a characteristic of Stravinsky's style.

In *Le sacre du printemps* Stravinsky used polytonality, polyrhythm, ostinati, and contrasting instrumental timbres extensively. Strongly dissonant, with savage, pulsating rhythms, *Le sacre du printemps* was a musical

counterpart to the primitivism being expressed in artworks at that time. So were Debussy's orchestral *Gigues*, with its pounding rhythm, and *Rondes de printemps*, with its distinctive timbres, unexpected dissonances, combined tonalities, and unusual scales—works that Stravinsky knew. Those works foreshadowed *Le sacre du printemps* but are mild in comparison with it.

Stravinsky presents the scenes of pagan Russia in two Parts: "The Adoration of the Earth" (Introduction and 7 Scenes) and "The Sacrifice of the Chosen One" (6 Scenes). Within each Part, the scenes proceed without pause. Basically, the ballet symbolizes primitive pagan tribes' adoration of the Earth as the Mother of all, the association of fertility with Spring, and the belief that death ensures the renewal of life, as evidenced by the earth's biological cycles. The première of *Le sacre du printemps* (29 May 1913) caused one of the largest theatrical riots Paris had known. The choreography, costumes, stage settings, and, to a lesser degree, the music were considered ugly and were offensive to many in the audience. Probably, they had come expecting to view beautiful costumes and scenery, to hear music typifying Spring, but received primitivism. Actually, the scenery, costumes, and musical style were dictated by the subject matter and were appropriate to it. There were those present who applauded the innovations, and undoubtedly there were as many shouts of approval as there were cries of derision. The critical outcry in artistic circles after the première of *Le sacre du printemps* was comparable with that occasioned by Pablo Picasso's painting *Les demoiselles d'Avignon* in 1907. Scathing reviews of the ballet and its music appeared. But in 1914 when a concert version of the *Le sacre du printemps* was performed, critics praised it.

Stravinsky scored *Le sacre du printemps* for a very large orchestra, with a greatly expanded woodwind section, and extra brass and percussion instruments. The various instrumental choirs are treated as distinct entities, each having at times its own ostinato and its own key. Most of the different instruments have solo passages, often in extreme ranges. The Introduction (DWMA182) is begun by bassoon voicing in its high register a Lithuanian folk melody in Aeolian mode. Gradually, the distinctive timbres of other winds are added, sometimes challenging the tonality—the c♯ of the horns in measure 2, and the "black-key" melody of English horn at measure 10 challenging the "white-key" folk tune of the solo bassoon and generating the three bassoons' chromaticism at the *più mosso*. Many of the melodic fragments that appear later in the music have some relationship to the opening Lithuanian melody.

In Stravinsky's polytonality, one key seems to be fundamental, with the other(s) superimposed temporarily. For example, in the Introduction to Part II, the fundamental key is D minor. Frequently, Stravinsky used the bitonality of chords with roots a semitone apart, for example, in the opening of "Augurs of Spring" with the simultaneous sounding of an F♭-major chord (enharmonically, E major) and a seventh chord on E♭ (ex. 26.10). This bitonality bears the same significance for *Le sacre du printemps* as the bitonal clarinet arpeggiations had for *Petrushka*. As he had done in *Petrushka*, Stravinsky used the octatonic scale and bitriadic harmonies in *Le sacre du printemps*. (Bitriadic chords are sometimes analyzed as subsets of an octatonic scale.)

In *Le sacre du printemps* there is counterpoint of melodic fragments and ostinati and counterpoint of timbres, tonalities, and rhythms. Rhythm is probably the most outstanding feature of the work. As the music proceeds, the rhythm becomes increasingly significant until, in the sacrificial dance, the frenetic rhythms dominate the music. A number of persons have stated that in *Le sacre du printemps* Stravinsky emancipated music from the tyranny of the bar line. He did not dispense with bar lines but, by continually shifting accents and/or changing meter signatures, made the bar line the servant rather than the master of his music. Underlying those shifting accents and changing meter signatures is a basic pulse—the unit of beat remains the same, though the number of beats per measure and the placement of accents change. Observance of this basic pulse is of vital importance to the choreographer and the dancers. Stravinsky used rhythm according to the additive manner of the ancient Greeks, in multiples of a *minimum* or basic unit (see Chap. 1). This kind of treatment produced a different result from that in traditional music written since c. 1600, when composers began to think of rhythm as subdivisions of a *maximum* value that filled a measure in which, predictably, the first beat was strong and the second weak. (For example, instead of thinking of a whole note as being divided into eighth notes, Stravinsky considered an eighth note as basic unit and used multiples of

EXAMPLE 26.10 Stravinsky, *Le sacre du printemps*, "Augurs of Spring," mm. 1–2, ostinato of F♭-major chord and first inversion of E♭ seventh-chord sounded simultaneously. *(THE RITE OF SPRING © 1927 by Edition Russe de Musique; Copyright Renewed. Copyright and Renewal assigned to Boosey & Hawkes, Inc., for all countries. Reprinted by permission.)*

them, placing bar lines where he needed them.) Some sections of *Le sacre du printemps* are much easier to play if the performer disregards meter signatures and bar lines and simply thinks in terms of the basic underlying beat—the eighth note or the sixteenth note, whichever it happens to be.

During World War I Stravinsky lived in Switzerland. His most important work from those years is *Les noces* (The wedding; 1914–17), a stylized portrayal of a Russian peasant wedding. The libretto uses Russian folk-song texts. *Les noces* is in four choreographic scenes for four vocal soloists, four-part chorus, four pianos, and large percussion ensemble. Rhythm is the most significant feature of the composition. Throughout the work, each rhythmic change is proportionally related to that which it follows as well as to a basic pulse that underlies the entire work.

An economy of resources is apparent in most of the compositions Stravinsky wrote in 1913–23. Undoubtedly, this reflects wartime general economy to some extent, but it stemmed primarily from Stravinsky's desire to make contemporary art music available to people living in small communities. With that in mind, he decided in 1918 to write a stage work that could be performed by a few persons in small concert halls. *L'histoire du soldat* (The soldier's tale), which is to be "read, played, and danced," requires three actors, a female dancer, and seven instrumentalists who are representative of the various orchestral families—violin, string bass, clarinet, bassoon, cornet, trombone, and percussion. The instrumentalists are to be seen as well as heard, for they and their music participate in the action. The story relates the adventures of a soldier who sells his violin (his soul) to the devil in exchange for a book that contains the answer to every question.

Stravinsky wrote only one more work strongly colored by Russian nationalism—*Mavra,* a one-act opera buffa. It was the first of several works in which Stravinsky used a preponderance of wind instruments. His writing for winds includes *Symphonies of Wind Instruments* (23 winds; 1920) and *Octet* (1922–23). In *Chronicle of My Life,* Stravinsky discussed *Mavra* and nationalism in the arts. He stated that Pushkin, Glinka, and Tchaikovsky were essentially cosmopolitan in their outlook but produced nationalistic works naturally and instinctively because they were Russian. On the other hand, the kind of nationalism expressed by The Five and others was deliberate and cultivated, "a doctrinaire catechism which they wished to impose." Stravinsky did not condone remaking an art that originally was an instinctive creation of the people.

Though he had no firsthand experience with ragtime, he dabbled in it and wrote *Rag-time* for 11 orchestral instruments (1918) and *Piano-rag-music* (1919). Then Diaghilev commissioned him to arrange for ballet some music attributed to Pergolesi. That ballet, *Pulcinella,* with chamber orchestra accompaniment, is a forerunner of the Neoclassic period in Stravinsky's writing, a period that actually began with the *Octet* for winds and continued through the opera *The Rake's Progress* (1948–51).

In the early 1920s, Stravinsky needed to earn more money and decided to perform more often as pianist and conductor. He wrote a number of piano pieces for himself: Sonata (1924); *Serenade* (A major; 1925); Concerto for piano with orchestra of winds, string bass, and timpani (1923–24); and *Capriccio* (pno., orch.; 1928–29). For performance with his son Soulima (1910–94), a professional pianist, Stravinsky wrote the Concerto for two pianos (no orch.; 1931–35). American violinist

Samuel Dushkin (1891–1976) commissioned the Violin Concerto (D major; 1931), and Stravinsky wrote the *Duo concertante* (vln., pno.; 1931–32) to perform with Dushkin.

Stage works attracted Stravinsky's attention again in the late 1920s. He composed the opera-oratorio *Oedipus rex* (Oedipus the king; 1927) and two ballets, *Apollon musagète* (Apollo, leader of the Muses; 1927–28; rev. 1947) and *Le baiser de fée* (The fairy's kiss; 1928).

As a youth, Stravinsky left the Russian Orthodox Church. In 1926, he rejoined the church and expressed the renewal of his faith in three sacred choruses on Slavonic liturgical texts. For the fiftieth anniversary celebration of the Boston Symphony Orchestra, he composed *Symphony of Psalms* (1930), an outstanding contribution to choral literature. The connotation of "symphony" is closely akin to Schütz's and Gabrieli's understanding of the word—a harmonious blend of voices and instruments—for Stravinsky intended that these "two elements should be on an equal footing." *Symphony of Psalms* is a setting of selected Latin verses from Psalms 38, 39, and 150 in the Vulgate (39, 40, 150 in KJV). The orchestral complement to the SATB chorus contains no violins or violas; includes a harp, two pianos, and brass instruments; and relies heavily on woodwinds (5 flutes, 4 oboes, English horn, 3 bassoons, contrabassoon). The work's three movements present, respectively, lamentation and supplication, faith, and praise. The second movement (DWMA183) is a large bitonal double fugue—one in C minor for orchestra, one in E♭ major for chorus.

Most of Stravinsky's compositions written during 1927–45 were commissioned, including *Jeu de cartes* (The card party; 1936) for the American Ballet Company, *"Dumbarton Oaks" Concerto* (chamber orch.; 1937–38), *Symphony in C* (1939–40), and *Symphony in Three Movements* (1942–45). Stravinsky taught at Harvard University in 1939–40. Those lectures, which became his book *Poétique musicale* (Musical poetic; 1942), state his philosophy and musical esthetics. He asserted that, in composing music, the more constraints a composer imposes on himself, the greater is his freedom. In his own work, he established certain limitations at the outset and moved within them as freely as possible. Obviously, Stravinsky's self-imposed limitations did not shackle his creative spirit.

In 1939 Stravinsky decided to make his home in the United States, and in 1945 he became a naturalized citizen. While living on the West Coast, he wrote some music for films. For some time he had wanted to write a liturgical Roman Catholic Mass, and in 1944–48 he composed one. Liturgical though the Mass is, rarely has it been used in a church service; its first performance was at La Scala, Milan.

Next, he wrote *The Rake's Progress,* based on Hogarth's artwork. It is a Neoclassic morality opera, dealing with the conflict of good and evil, and is replete with satire on many social customs of the time. The music consists of separate recitatives, arias, and ensembles in the traditional eighteenth-century manner; harpsichord is specified for the continuo used with the secco recitatives. There is some melodrama. *The Rake's Progress* is one of the finest Neoclassic compositions.

Stravinsky was wary of serialism and approached it cautiously when he experimented with the techniques. He did not change his compositional style; he merely blended serial techniques into it. At first, he used rows of only 4, 5, or 6 notes. (For *In memoriam Dylan Thomas,* he used a five-note row.) Only after he had used a full twelve-note series in some short movements of a work did he employ serial techniques throughout a composition.

Canticum sacrum ad honorem Sancti Marci nominis (Sacred song to honor the name of St. Mark; 1955; T, B, choir, orch.) was specifically designed for performance in St. Mark's. As prelude, the soloists sing the Latin dedication to Venice, accompanied by two trombones. *Canticum sacrum* has a biblical text and is in five short movements. The composition is symmetrical, as are many of the works of J. S. Bach. The fifth movement is the retrograde of the first. In the three middle movements Stravinsky used two twelve-note rows that are interrelated, and the middle movement contains *cancrizans. Canticum sacrum* is filled with symbolism of all kinds, including a structural relationship with the edifice of St. Mark's.

Stravinsky visited Russia in 1962, after an absence of almost 50 years. When he returned to America, he wrote his first completely serial composition—*Threni: id est Lamentationes Jeremiae prophetae* (Lamentations of Jeremiah the prophet; 1962–63).

Most of the compositions Stravinsky wrote after 1953 are choral. A number of them are elegies, including *Elegy for J. F. K.* (Elegy for John F. Kennedy; 1964; Bar. solo, 3 clarinets). With his own death in mind, Stravinsky composed *Requiem canticles* (1965–66), using selected texts from the Requiem Mass.

Stravinsky had mastery of all available compositional techniques. A survey of his compositions, with particular regard to style, reveals diversity. Yet, underlying that diversity there is unity. Though he moved from one genre and style to another, keeping in touch with contemporary trends, some things remained constant. He never completely abandoned key tonality. Many times, he worked with opposing tonal poles, and he used modality, bitonality, polytonality, and dodecaphonic techniques. Rhythm is perhaps the most important feature of all his works. He based rhythms on the constancy of a minimum value and used multiples of that, making whatever adjustments were necessary in meter signatures and bar line placement. The bar line was subservient to his purposes. Silence was important, and he used rests effectively. Ostinato patterns figure prominently in his music, as does syncopation. Stravinsky understood instrumental and vocal tone colors and was a master of orchestration. Throughout his life, he built on the excellent foundation he had received from Rimsky-Korsakov.

NADIA BOULANGER

Boulanger (1887–1979) was a master teacher who influenced the careers of composers from many countries. Her paternal grandparents and her father were highly talented musicians; when he was 20, her father had received the Grand Prix de Rome for his cantata *Achille.* Ernest Boulanger (1815–1900) was 62 when he married 18-year-old Russian Princess Raissa Mychetskaya; Nadia, their second child, studied at Paris Conservatoire and was awarded several prizes, including the second Grand Prix in composition for her cantata *La Sirène* (The siren). After the death of Raoul Pugno (1852–1914), she completed his opera *La Ville morte* (The dead city). For a number of years she was organist at La Madeleine, Paris.

Boulanger began teaching in 1909; she was assistant in the organ class at Paris Conservatoire and also had private pupils. Her teaching was the principal source of income for the Boulanger family. From 1920 to 1939 she taught music history and other subjects at École Normale de Musique, Paris, and when the American Conservatory was founded at Fontainebleau in 1921, she joined the faculty as teacher of harmony. In addition, she taught a large number of private pupils at her home, where lessons covered all aspects of music, especially analysis, composition, and conducting. Boulanger was an excellent conductor. She conducted the première of Stravinsky's *"Dumbarton Oaks" Concerto* in Washington, D.C. (1938), and some concerts of the Boston Symphony and the New York Philharmonic. During World War II, Boulanger lectured and taught at several schools in the United States. In 1946 she returned to Paris and resumed teaching responsibilities at the American Conservatory; four years later she became its director. She continued private teaching until she was well into her eighties.

Nadia Boulanger was the most influential woman in the history of music pedagogy. Her masterly teaching was a shaping force in the lives of many composers, including Aaron Copland, Virgil Thomson, Walter Piston, Roy Harris, and Elliott Carter. With regard to contemporary music, Boulanger had definite preferences. She admired the work of Stravinsky, Debussy, and Ravel; she did not like Schoenberg's music. Not all of Boulanger's students agreed with her musical tastes; Philip Glass was one who, after studying with her, followed his own dictates into Eastern music and minimalism (p. 653). Boulanger was much interested in the music of Bach and those who preceded him. During the 1920s and 1930s, she was influential in promoting performances of Monteverdi madrigals in Paris and frequently conducted or performed works by French composers of the Renaissance and Baroque eras.

UNITED STATES

During the years between World War I and World War II significant changes occurred in the United States relative to music. There was an appreciable increase in the number of American composers creating major works comparable with those of European composers. Gradually, there dawned an awareness of the excellent training available in American schools in all areas of music. From time to time, the quality teaching done by Americans was supplemented by guest lecturers from Europe. A number of European composers emigrated to America to escape impending or actual persecution and, at some time, taught in American schools. Among those composers were the cream of Europe's crop—Rakhmaninov, Prokofiev, Schoenberg, Bartók, Stravin-

Nadia Boulanger with her American former students Aaron Copland, Virgil Thomson, and Walter Piston. *(From Fred and Rose Plaut Archives, Music Library of Yale University)*

sky, Milhaud, Hindemith, and others. Some became naturalized United States citizens. Perhaps the most outstanding native American composer during this era was Aaron Copland.

AARON COPLAND

Copland (1900–90) was born in Brooklyn, New York. As a child, he was strongly attracted to music, learned to play piano, and by 1917 had decided to be a composer. He studied harmony and counterpoint with Rubin Goldmark (1872–1936) and wrote a few pieces, most of them for solo piano. In 1920 Copland went to Paris for further study. Shortly before he left Brooklyn, he composed a short piano piece entitled *Humoristic scherzo: The Cat and the Mouse* (1920). It was his first published work—in Paris he sold it to Durand.

In France Copland attended many concerts and observed the styles of many composers. He enrolled at the American Conservatory and was urged by a student to visit Boulanger's harmony class. Once Copland visited her class, he too became excited about her teaching. He studied with Boulanger for four years, and they became lifelong friends. While studying in Paris, Copland wrote a few songs, a choral work, some piano pieces, and a ballet, *Grohg,* portions of which he arranged as *Dance Symphony* (1930). When he returned to the United States in 1924, he earned his living by teaching piano privately but also composed. Then, Walter Damrosch invited Boulanger to concertize in America, and Serge Koussevitzky (1874–1951) commissioned Copland to write the *Symphony for Organ and Orchestra* (1924) for the Boston Symphony Orchestra. In 1928 Copland revised the work, and it became his Symphony No. 1.

Copland wanted his music to be as clearly American as that of Musorgsky and Stravinsky was Russian. For that reason, he began to incorporate ragtime, blues, and jazz elements in his works (e.g., in the suite *Music for the Theatre* [1925] and the Piano Concerto [1926]). To promote the performance of new music by American composers, Copland and Roger Sessions (1896–1985) presented the Copland-Sessions Concerts in New York (1928–31). Also, in 1927–37, at the New School for Social Research, Copland lectured to laypersons on various aspects of music. Those lectures provided the material for his books *What to Listen for in Music* (pub. 1939) and *Our New Music* (pub. 1941). The latter, revised and enlarged, was issued in 1968 as *The New Music, 1900–1968.* In 1952 Copland was appointed Norton Professor of Poetics at Harvard. From those lectures came the book *Music and Imagination* (1952).

At the invitation of composer Carlos Chávez, Copland visited Mexico. He returned there many times and found inspiration for several orchestral works, including his *Short Symphony* (1932) and *El Salón México* (1933–36). Memories of a visit to Havana inspired *Danzón cubana* (2 pnos.; 1942; orch., 1944). The *danzón* is a stately dance, usually performed in alternation with more animated Latin American dances such as the rhumba and tango. Other visits to Latin America are reflected in *Latin American Sketches* (1972).

Commencing in 1938, Copland received commissions for several ballets, including *Billy the Kid* (1938); *Rodeo* (1942), written for Agnes de Mille (1905–93); and *Appalachian Spring* (1943–44), written for Martha Graham (1894–1991). The *Clarinet Concerto* (1947–48; cl., strings, harp, pno.) that Copland wrote for Benny Goodman (1909–86) provided the music for the ballet *Pied Piper.* Orchestral suites were derived from all the ballets. *Appalachian Spring Suite* has been Copland's most popular orchestral work, receiving a Pulitzer Prize in 1945. For the ballet, the music was scored for a 13-piece chamber ensemble. *Appalachian Spring* depicts the celebration of spring and the wedding of a young couple in a rural community in Pennsylvania in the early nineteenth century. The ballet comprises eight scenes. The seventh scene (DWMA184), portraying daily activities of the young married couple, consists of theme and variations on the Shaker song *Simple Gifts,* which originated c. 1837–47 (ex. 26.11). The section culminates in a hymn. Copland's ballet music is vibrant and appealing, not without technical sophistication, and frequently sounding much simpler than it really is.

Copland wrote for all musical media and in all genres. His full-length opera *The Tender Land* (1952–54; rev. 1955) was severely criticized by the concert-going public and reviewers. In 1938–61 Copland wrote eight film scores, the most important being for *Of Mice and Men* (1939), *Our Town* (1940), and *The Red Pony* (1948). Occupying a unique position among

'Tis the gift to be sim-ple, 'tis the gift to be free, 'Tis the

gift to some down where we ought to be, And

when we find our-selves in the place just right, 'Twill

be in the val-ley of love and de-light. When true sim-

pli-ci-ty is gained, To bow and to bend we

shan't be a-sham'd, To turn, turn will

be our de-light, 'till by turn-ing, turn-ing we come round right.

EXAMPLE 26.11 The Shaker song *Simple Gifts*.

Copland's works is *Lincoln Portrait* (1942; speaker, orch.). Written as part of a series of musical portraits of American heroes, the music includes tunes from Lincoln's time, and the text presents excerpts from Lincoln's letters and addresses. *Lincoln Portrait* has been performed frequently; poet Carl Sandburg (1878–1967) and statesman Adlai Stevenson have effectively read the text.

During World War II, conductor-composer Eugene Goossens (1893–1962) decided to open each of the Cincinnati Symphony concerts in the 1942–43 season with a different fanfare by an American composer. Copland wrote *Fanfare for the Common Man* (1942), which has been performed many times at all kinds of public events and has been subjected to numerous arrangements for various ensembles. Copland reused the fanfare in the introduction to the Finale of Symphony No. 3 (1944–46), a four-movement cyclic work. When the Third Symphony was first performed, Copland wrote the program notes and, in addition to analyzing the composition, pointed out that it is absolute music and contains no folk or popular material.

From time to time Copland experimented with serial techniques. The first work in which he used serialism to any extent is the Piano Quartet (1950). Some features of dodecaphony appear in other works: *Twelve Poems of Emily Dickinson* (1950; vc., pno.), *Piano Fantasy* (1952–57), *Inscape* (1957; orch.), and *Connotations* (1962; orch.), written for the opening of Philharmonic Hall at Lincoln Center in New York City. In general, however, a strong sense of tonality is present in Copland's music. At times, he wrote on two tonal levels, combining major and minor or tonic and dominant. Such writing occurs in several sections of *Appalachian Spring*. He wrote simple chords with variable spacings and was adept at writing syncopations and polyrhythms and, on occasion, devising rhythmic intricacies. Copland was an important influence in the lives and careers of many American composers.

GEORGE GERSHWIN

Gershwin (1898–1937) began his career in 1914 by playing piano for a New York publishing house to demonstrate new popular songs to prospective buyers. He had relatively little technical training for composition but possessed a gift for melodic and rhythmic invention, and within two years he was writing popular songs for publication as sheet music and for inclusion in Broadway shows. As a songwriter, his first big success came with *Swanee* (1919), popularized by singer Al Jolson.

In 1919 Gershwin wrote a musical of his own; by 1933 he had composed 28 of them. The **Broadway musical** (sometimes called *musical comedy*) is an important genre of twentieth-century American music. Recognition of that fact came when Gershwin's *Of Thee I Sing* (1931), a political satire, was awarded a Pulitzer Prize—the first musical to be accorded that honor. But Gershwin was not content with writing only popular music. In 1924 he composed *Rhapsody in Blue,* a combination of jazz elements and Romantic music for solo piano and orchestra, and performed the work with Paul Whiteman's (1890–1967) jazz ensemble in a special concert on 12 February 1924 in New York's Aeolian Hall. Thus, blues entered the concert hall in America. Ferde Grofé (1892–1972), arranger for Whiteman's band, orchestrated the *Rhapsody.* (Grofé composed a piano concerto and a number of suites, e.g., *Grand*

Canyon Suite, in which he combined jazz rhythms and ballad-like melodies.) Gershwin determined that he would orchestrate any future works himself and demonstrated his ability to do so in his Piano Concerto (F major; 1925) and symphonic poem *An American in Paris* (1928).

Gershwin's ambition to compose a full-length opera was realized in 1935 with *Porgy and Bess,* written for black singers. It is generally referred to as a "folk opera," but it contains no actual folk music. At first, reviews of *Porgy and Bess* were mixed—some praising, some condemning the work. For a time, the opera was seldom performed, but several songs from it became popular: "Summertime," "It Ain't Necessarily So," and "Bess, You Is My Woman Now." The opera was revived in the 1950s and has been acclaimed internationally.

RUTH CRAWFORD SEEGER

Ruth Crawford (1901–53) began teaching piano at the School of Musical Arts in Jacksonville, Florida, as soon as she graduated from high school. In 1920 she entered the American Conservatory of Music in Chicago to prepare for a concert career. When problems with muscular tension in her arms made piano playing increasingly more difficult, she concentrated on composition. While working on her masters degree (1924), she taught piano at the Conservatory. During those years she composed, among other things, *Five Preludes for Piano* (1924–25), Sonata for violin and piano (1926), several chamber music suites, and *The Adventures of Tom Thumb* (1925; pno., narrator) for children's entertainment.

Through clarinetist (later, music critic) Alfred Frankenstein, Crawford met poet Carl Sandburg, who stimulated her interest in folk song and in preparing books for children. Almost all her songs are settings of Sandburg's poems.

Crawford spent the summer of 1929 at The MacDowell Colony, where she wrote the songs *Joy, Sunsets,* and *Loam.* In the vocal lines declamation and lyricism alternate; there are some tone clusters and whole-tone scales. At the end of the summer she moved to New York. Henry Cowell, cognizant of her talent, persuaded composer Charles Seeger (1886–1979) to accept her as a student. The first fruits of that study were *Diaphonic Suites Nos. 1–4,* dissonant

Ruth Crawford Seeger. *(From the estate of Carl Crawford)*

chamber music. In 1930 Crawford was awarded a Guggenheim Foundation Fellowship to study composition in Europe for a year; she was the first woman to receive such a grant. That year she created her most important compositions: *Three Chants for Women's Chorus* and the String Quartet. *Three Chants,* settings of meaningless phonemes, are filled with dissonant counterpoint and, in the third chant, intricate polyrhythms. The String Quartet (1931) placed Crawford firmly among the avant-garde composers of the time. In the third movement, constant legato and continually changing dynamic patterns, different in each part, produce a kind of "dynamic counterpoint." The fourth movement closely approaches total serialism, for all the musical elements are organized according to preset patterns. The second half of the movement is a transposed retrograde of the first half. Such use of retrograde motion occurs in many of Crawford's compositions, as do strong dissonance and ostinato patterns.

When Crawford returned to the United States, her marriage to Seeger altered her priorities, pushing composition into the background. She and Seeger decided to collect and study American folk music. Soon they joined John and Alan Lomax in their similar endeavors and made translations of field recordings for their publications. While the Seegers lived in Washington, D.C., in the 1940s, Ruth became interested in teaching young children, for whom she compiled and published several books of folk songs, arranged for voice and piano: *American Folk Songs for Children* (1948), *Animal Folk Songs for Children* (1950), and *Christmas Folk Songs for Children* (1953). In this she was a pioneer.

Crawford completed only a few original compositions after her marriage, the most important being *Rissolty, Rossolty* (1939; orch.), based on three folk songs, and the *Suite for Wind Quintet* (1952), which is in the abstract, dissonant, contrapuntal style of her early works.

OTHER AMERICAN COMPOSERS

A number of American-born composers were active during the decades between the two world wars. Several included folk music or specifically American idioms such as blues and jazz elements in their works; others set texts relating to American topics or wrote program music on American subjects. The works of some composers were not at all nationalistic.

Virgil Thomson (1896–1989) is best known for his opera *Four Saints in Three Acts* (1927–28), on a libretto by Gertrude Stein (1874–1946). The work is a series of tableaux and processions without a central plot. His opera *The Mother of us all* (1947; Stein libretto) concerns Susan B. Anthony and the woman's suffrage movement and includes some nineteenth-century American music. Thomson provided nationalistic music for the documentary films *The Plow that Broke the Plains* (1936), *The River* (1937), and *Louisiana Story* (1948). Most of his music is characterized by basically diatonic harmonies, though some bitonality is present, and by quotations from folk tunes, hymns, patriotic songs, and dances. His operas are witty and entertaining, but most of them are not deeply emotional. Thomson wrote several books on contemporary music, including *The State of Music* (1939), *The Musical Scene* (1945), and *American Music since 1910* (1971).

Roy Harris (1898–1979) wrote mainly choral music and orchestral works. He composed a few works specifically for band (e.g., *Cimarron* [1941] and *West Point Symphony* [1952]). Harris particularly liked the poetry of Walt Whitman (1819–92) and set many of his works. The finest of his 14 symphonies is the Third Symphony (1937). It contains many elements that became characteristic of his style; a broad opening motive; melody in long lines and, frequently,

modal melody; emphasis on harmonic counterpoint; contrapuntal devices favored over motivic development; and diverse rhythmic patterns. Harris did not use key signatures, but his music conveys a strong sense of tonality. The first of his works to include folk music was *When Johnny Comes Marching Home* (1935; chorus); he used much of it in *Folksong Symphony* (1940; chor., orch.).

William Grant Still (1895–1978) studied composition at Oberlin Conservatory, Ohio, and later with Edgard Varèse and George W. Chadwick. Still's early works include the symphonic poem *Darker America* (1924), the suite *From the Black Belt* (1926), and *Afro-American Symphony* (1930), the first of his five symphonies. In some works he used jazz and blues idioms. Occasionally, he included authentic Negro folk melodies, but usually he fabricated themes that simulated them.

In the output of most American composers, non-nationalistic works far outnumber those that are decidedly nationalistic. Roger Sessions first attracted attention with his orchestral suite *The Black Masters* (1923). One of his finest works is his cantata setting Walt Whitman's *When Lilacs Last in the Door-Yard Bloom'd*. Whitman wrote the poem as an elegy for Abraham Lincoln; Sessions's work (for S, A, Bar. soloists, chor., orch.; 1970) is a memorial to Martin Luther King Jr. and Robert Kennedy.

Many of Walter Piston's (1894–1976) works are Neoclassic. Piston came to the attention of the musical world with the ballet suite *The Incredible Flutist*; his reputation spread after the première of his Symphony No. 2 (1944). Piston preferred to write in the large forms that were favored during the late eighteenth and nineteenth centuries, but his complex harmonies are not from those eras.

Howard Hanson's (1896–1981) opera *The Maypole of Merry Mount* (1933) is one of his few compositions on American subjects. Another is *A Sea Symphony* (Sym. No. 7; 1977; orch., chor.). Hanson's music is basically Romantic in style (e.g., *Symphony No. 2: Romantic*). Many of his compositions (e.g., *Symphony No. 1: Nordic*) reflect the influence of Sibelius, whom he greatly admired. As director of the Eastman School of Music, Hanson was largely responsible for the elevation of that school to its prestigious status.

LATIN AND SOUTH AMERICAN COMPOSERS

The most significant Latin and South American composers during this era were Heitor Villa-Lobos (1887–1959) of Brazil, Alberto Ginastera (1916–83) of Argentina, and Carlos Chávez (1899–1978) of Mexico. All used traditional forms to some extent, and all were nationalistic to some degree.

Villa-Lobos was a master of 'cello and guitar. Though he incorporated authentic Brazilian rhythms and melodic types in many of his works, he refrained from quoting Brazilian songs. As a youth, he played popular music, particularly the dance form called *chôros,* with the musicians of Rio de Janeiro. In 1920–28 he composed a series of 15 *Chôros* for various instruments, ensemble and solo. Villa-Lobos seriously studied the works of Bach and transcribed several pieces from *Das wohltemperirte Clavier* for chorus and for 'cello ensemble. Later, he composed nine suites entitled *Bachianas Brasileiras* (1932–44), in which he combined Bach-style counterpoint with melodies resembling those of Brazilian folk and popular music. To each piece he gave two titles, one typical of the Baroque and the other referring to Brazilian popular music. Especially lovely is *Bachianas Brasileiras No. 5,* for soprano soloist accompanied by 'cello soloist and an ensemble of seven 'celli. *Bachianas Brasileiras No. 9* is textless, intended for vocalization by *a cappella* mixed chorus, which Villa-Lobos called "an orchestra of voices."

In Ginastera's music, nationalism (both objective and subjective), Neoclassicism, Expressionism, and serialism mingle. His twelve-tone writing is not always strict serialism. Frequently, for instrumental pieces, he used sonata form or theme and variations. Argentinian folk melodies and rhythms appear in his early works (e.g., the ballets *Panambi* [1936] and *Estancia* [1941] and the piano pieces *Danzas Argentinas* [Argentinian dances; 1937]). The excellent quality of Ginastera's work was recognized internationally after the première of String Quartet No. 2 (1958), his first entirely serial composition. Dodecaphony became a feature of his works, along with polytonality and some use of microintervals. His Piano Concerto No. 2 (1972) uses a tone-row derived from the opening of the Finale of Beethoven's Symphony No. 9. The concerto's second movement is for left hand alone. Serial techniques, unusual sound effects, and traditional forms appear in all of Ginastera's operas: *Don Rodrigo* (1964), *Bomarzo* (1967), and *Beatrix Cenci* (1971).

Carlos Chávez was a fine conductor, an excellent composer, and a remarkable educator. After the Mexican revolution (1910–21), the government assumed patronage of the arts and stressed the importance of native Indian cultures. Chávez's first important nationalistic work was *El fuego nuevo* (The new fire; 1921), written when the Mexican minister of education commissioned a ballet on an Aztec subject. During 1922–28, Chávez spent much time in the United States. When the first permanent symphony orchestra was formed in Mexico in 1928, he became its conductor and served in that capacity for 20 years. During the 6 years that Chávez was director of the National Conservatory of Music, he reformed the curriculum, instigated concert series with students as soloists, established committees to research folk and popular music, and constantly encouraged talented Mexicans to compose. Chávez was one of the founders of the Colegio de México and the Mexican Academy of the Arts. One of his best-known works is *Sinfonia India* (1936), which contains authentic Aztec themes. Many of Chávez's works convey the character of native Indian music without actually using indigenous materials. In part, he achieved that effect by including folk instruments (percussion and ocarinas). Rhythm is an important factor in his music. His skill at handling irregular meters, cross-rhythms and syncopation, and polyrhythm is apparent in *Sinfonia India*. Of Chávez's five ballets, the most remarkable is *La hija de Cólquide* (Cólquide's daughter; 1943) written for Martha Graham, with music for string quartet and wind quartet. Later that year, Chávez orchestrated the music as a symphonic suite.

SUMMARY

In the World Wars Era, nationalism was expressed musically, and folk music was an important aspect of that expression. As scientific investigation of folk music increased, more composers incorporated the peculiar attributes of regional folk musics into their works. Scholarly research on central European folk music was carried out by Janáček, Kodály, and Bartók; scientific investigations by others ensued. The most complete synthesis of folk idioms and art music was achieved by Bartók.

Primarily a virtuoso pianist, Bartók also composed and taught. His *Mikrokosmos* is a compendium of his style and of many of the compositional devices used during the first half of the twentieth century. His string quartets present a comparable summary of his style. After Bartók emigrated to America, Kodály worked alone collecting, scientifically studying, and codifying the folk music of central European peoples. He made significant contributions in the field of vocal music education, particularly the "Kodály method" of sight-singing. Kodály's music, more narrowly nationalistic than Bartók's, is an amalgamation of many influences—Bach-style counterpoint, the choral writing of Palestrina, Gregorian chant, and Hungarian folk music.

Orff was also greatly interested in the music education of elementary-school children, especially with regard to rhythmic proficiency and fluidity of movement. The *Orff-Schulwerk* graded music exercises and the "Orff instruments" are well known. Orff's principal interest was complete or "total" theater, in which all aspects of words, music, and movement form a cohesive whole.

Until the advent of Vaughan Williams and Britten, England had no native-born composer of the stature of Purcell. In the twentieth century, there was a revival of interest in Purcell's music; several of Britten's compositions reflect his knowledge of and appreciation for Purcell's works. Vaughan Williams's style is nationalistic in character, without being tied to folk song, yet is highly personal. He blended archaic procedures from the Tudor era with techniques of his own time, and he handled counterpoint and homophony, modes and keys, with equal skill. His nine symphonies did a great deal to establish that genre as an important form in English music. The operas of Vaughan Williams and Britten provided a firm foundation for the future of English opera. Britten's principal contributions are solo songs, choral works, and operas.

Cultural conditions in Russia differed vastly from those in Western Europe. All the arts were placed under state supervision in 1921, and in 1932 the Union of Soviet Composers formally resolved that all music should be socialistic and easily understood by the masses. Use of folk material and expression of "national feelings" were advocated. Western modern music was banned, and performance of individualistic works with a semblance of modern techniques was prohibited. Among composers whose works were severely criticized and censored were Shostakovich, Prokofiev, Khachaturian, and Kabalevsky, who were the most significant composers living in Russia in 1917–45. Many of Khachaturian's compositions reinforce Soviet ideology and exemplify the ideals of the Soviet school of composition: diatonic melodies, basically tonal harmonies that include dissonance, energetic rhythms, and traditional forms. Prokofiev is best known for his symphonies. In his Haydnesque *Classical Symphony* (1917), he foreshadowed the Neoclassic trend that emerged a few years later. Many persons consider Shostakovich the greatest symphonist of the mid-twentieth century.

Expressionism appeared in art, literature, and music early in the twentieth century. In that style of music, a composer sought to express inner feelings and created atonal/pantonal works in which the music is abstract and intense and traditional harmony and formal patterns are distorted or ignored. Schoenberg wrote some Expressionistic music.

The name "Second Viennese School" has been applied to Schoenberg and his few private pupils, especially Berg and Webern. From them there emerged a new style of music called dodecaphony, an atonal/pantonal style in which all twelve chromatic pitches in the octave are considered equal and none has any special function. Among the factors generating the new style were the increased use of linear counterpoint with motives and melodies that dictated harmonies and the abundant use of unresolved dissonances (nonfunctional harmonies) in post-Romantic music. Largely because of Schoenberg's efforts, an organizational system called serialism was developed, in which a composer prearranged the order in which the twelve chromatic pitches were to be used, thus establishing a Series or Row. Berg and Webern adopted Schoenberg's principles but modified them. Berg never completely relinquished Romanticism and tonality. He did not adhere to a single row for an entire composition; often he combined tonal and nontonal elements in a work. Webern strictly adhered to serial principles, used one row per movement, and wrote highly ordered counterpoint that was concentrated in extremely compressed forms. Characterized by economy of means, his compositions are extremely compressed, and some of his pieces are pointillistic (music seemingly constructed of isolated notes). After Webern's death the significance of his work was realized and was emulated by avant-garde composers internationally.

In Spain, the zarzuela survived for a time, then almost disappeared for a time after the Civil War. The establishment of symphony orchestras and choral groups stimulated composition of works suitable for their performing ensembles. The most important composer was Manuel de Falla, whose works are strongly Spanish in character without actually quoting folk materials.

Neoclassicism, a movement against late Romanticism, began near the end of World War I, gathered momentum in the early 1920s, and remained strong until after 1945. It is characterized by a preference for absolute music, greater emphasis on counterpoint, economy of performing resources, and a revival of eighteenth-century traditional forms, with thematic material subject to techniques and compositional processes then favored. Hindemith and Stravinsky were the chief exponents of Neoclassicism. Twentieth-century composers' awareness of early music led to a revival of forms and characteristic styles of previous eras. Also, an unwillingness to accept twentieth-century musical styles as suitable for church music caused composers to use as models sixteenth- and seventeenth-century styles and techniques. In addition to the general back-to-Bach-and-Handel movement, composers in each country were motivated by nationalism to turn to the musical styles of their respective countries' historical past.

In France, each of The Six took a separate path. Durey joined the French Communist Party, and his works became politically oriented. Auric's most important contributions were his stage and theater music; he did much to revitalize opera in France. Tailleferre's music followed the traditional lines established by Fauré and continued by Ravel. Honegger wrote mainly stage and dramatic works, often with demanding speaking and singing parts that included unusual vocal techniques. Poulenc was master of the *mélodie* and

wrote religious choral music. Milhaud's works, which are in all genres, are characterized by lyrical melodies, formal clarity, skillful use of counterpoint, and bitonality or polytonality.

Hindemith made significant contributions as performer, composer, theorist, teacher, and author. He believed that music must be understood as a means of communication between composer and consumer. By writing some music specifically for amateurs, he hoped to narrow the gap between composer and amateur performer. Music performed purely for enjoyment was important. Hindemith was convinced that a composer must be a performing musician, familiar with instruments through participation in ensembles. He considered key tonality unavoidable. He wholeheartedly endorsed the theory expressed in the writings of the ancient Greek philosophers that the principles of order governing the acoustical ratios of musical intervals and the order within a musical composition symbolize and reflect, as microcosm to macrocosm, the principles that govern the orderly behavior of the universe. These beliefs—Hindemith's philosophy—influenced his compositions.

Stravinsky was one of the twentieth century's most outstanding composers. From Rimsky-Korsakov, Stravinsky learned to use timbres effectively and to express psychological states and physical movements through music. His most famous composition, *Le sacre du printemps,* is filled with polytonality, polyrhythms, ostinati, contrasting instrumental timbres, and the frenetic rhythms of primitivism. Stravinsky was a versatile composer with mastery of all compositional techniques available to him. Though he moved from one genre and style to another, keeping in touch with contemporary trends, some things remained constant. He never completely abandoned tonality, though he composed some atonal pieces. Many times, he worked with opposing tonal poles; he used modality, bitonality, polytonality, and dodecaphonic techniques. Rhythm is probably the most significant feature of his works. He based his rhythms on the constancy of a minimum value and used multiples of that; the bar line was subservient to his purposes.

The teaching of Nadia Boulanger was a shaping force in the careers of many composers. Copland, one of many Americans who studied with her, wanted his music to be as clearly American as Musorgsky's was

Russian. In the 1920s he incorporated some ragtime, blues, and jazz elements into his works. He did much to promote the performance of new music by American composers and to provide greater understanding of music among the general public. Copland wrote for all musical media and in all genres. Occasionally, he experimented with serial techniques, but for the most part his music has a strong sense of tonality. A number of his works are on American subjects.

Gershwin first succeeded with popular songs. His *Of Thee I Sing* was the first Broadway musical to be awarded a Pulitzer Prize. With the performance of his *Rhapsody in Blue,* jazz and blues elements entered the concert hall in America.

A number of American-born composers were active during the World Wars Era. Several included folk music or specifically American idioms such as blues and jazz elements in their works; others set texts relating to American topics or wrote program music on American subjects, but the works of some composers were not at all nationalistic. In the output of most American composers, nonnationalistic works far outnumber those that are decidedly nationalistic. W. G. Still wrote large-scale works representative of black Americans, though he usually did not include authentic Negro melodies in them.

Most important among Latin and South American composers were Villa-Lobos of Brazil, Ginastera of Argentina, and Chávez of Mexico. All used traditional forms to some extent, and all were nationalistic to some degree. Chávez played a decisive role in the development of music in Mexico.

MUSIC SINCE 1945

27

After World War II ended, restoration was needed on many fronts—political, physical, psychological, and cultural. Nazi Germany had suffered defeat and the suicide of its leader, Hitler; the nuclear bombing of Hiroshima and Nagasaki had shocked Japan and horrified other countries. Disputes over territory and distrust of one another's intentions caused communist-capitalist national alliances to degenerate, resulting in a "cold" war. British and French colonies in Asia and Africa obtained independence at specified later dates. In 1962 the United States became involved in the internal warfare in Vietnam and for more than a decade experienced a conflict that brought true victory to no one. At the same time, within the United States there was domestic agitation for economic, political, and social justice and equality for minorities—women, blacks, and various ethnic groups. Tremendous technological achievements were realized, including the exploration of outer space, with men landing on the moon and walking in space, and the development of computers and robots for industrial use.

Where music was concerned, there were many World War II casualties, some more severe than others. Webern had been killed; some musicians and composers had experienced capture and imprisonment, and some had suffered indignities and horrors in concentration camps. When the Nazi and Fascist parties rose to power, many prominent European composers and performers had taken refuge in the United States; Bartók, Schoenberg, Hindemith, and Milhaud are a few who fled their native lands and whose talents considerably enriched American music. The works of some composers who remained at home had been subjected to their government's censorship; other composers had had royalties cut off, bank accounts frozen, other assets seized, and family members mistreated. The war had disrupted concert life, and music publishing had virtually ceased. Moreover, because of difficulties in or lack of communication during the war years, many composers were out of touch with what others were doing. That was both bad and good, for it encouraged independent initiative, and new styles and techniques came into being.

After World War II, there was an extensive search for true values. In the arts, this brought innovation and experimentation, particularly on the part of young artists and composers. Considerable diversity resulted. Not all the music that was created was good; in fact, some of it was quite bad, and much of it was mediocre, as is the case in every era.

Though the time was ripe for striking out in new directions, some composers sought restoration and continued along old paths. In communist countries of Eastern Europe,

FIGURE 27.1 Europe in 1978.

composers found the symphony a safe and suitable vehicle. That form was cultivated in Britain and America, also. Some excellent symphonies were written. In California, Stravinsky was writing in Neoclassic style, and Schoenberg continued to write Expressionistic twelve-tone music. In dealing with serialism, Schoen-berg, Berg, and Webern used fascinating, in-depth technical procedures but did not develop serialism to its fullest potential. Their work was continued by avant-garde composers in France and America, who, independently of one another, eventually achieved total serialism and created new styles—*musique concrète,*

1870	1890	1910	1930	1950	1970	1990

• 1877 Phonograph invented; wax cylinders
• 1885 Wax-covered cardboard cylinders
• 1896 Flat disc recordings 78 rpm
• c. 1924 Microphones; electrical amplifiers
• 1948 Nonbreakable discs LP (33⅓ rpm)
• 1957 Stereophonic recordings
• c. 1960 Quadraphonic sound
• c. 1980
Compact discs

• 1898 Recording on steel piano wire
• c. 1925 Recording on steel bands
• 1935 Flexible coated tape
Plastic film tapes
• 1947 Tape recordings
used in radio broadcasting
• c. 1958 Tape cartridges/cassettes
• 1965 8-track cassette tapes

• 1923 "Talking pictures"
• 1928 *The Jazz Singer*—talking picture with music
• 1960s Video tape recorder
• 1980s
Video disc systems
(1500 rpm)

• c. 1920 AM radio   • 1950 FM radio   • 1970 VHF
• 1930s BBC television service
• 1951 Color television in USA
• 1964–65 Moog synthesizer
• 1966 *Silver Apples
of the Moon*

• 1957 Computer-generated
musical score
Computer-generated sounds
Computer playing in 1980s

• c. 1920 Theremin invented
• c. 1924 Ondes Martenot invented

electronic music, indeterminacy (aleatory, chance, or choice music), and others. Several European leaders of the avant-garde music acknowledged their indebtedness to the music of Webern and to the teaching and guidance of Messiaen.

TECHNOLOGY

The twentieth century has witnessed tremendous technological advances that have affected the development of music. When the first recording devices were invented, they were valued for their ability to store materials and were of particular assistance to persons gathering folk songs. With each improvement in the recording mechanisms, the possibilities for their use loomed larger. By 1896 Edison's method of recording sounds on a wax cylinder had been supplanted by Émile Berliner's method using a flat disc. In addition to storing material, the disc could serve as a master from which multiple copies could be reproduced—a commercial advantage. Performances by outstanding musicians could be recorded and marketed, thus providing

1940	1950	1960	1970	1980	1990

Messiaen:
Quartet pour le fin de temps
- 1944 *Vingt-regards* . . .
- 1949 *Mode de valeurs et d'intensités*
- 1956 *Oiseaux exotiques*
- 1969 *Méditations sur . . . la Sainte Trinité*
  Saint François d'Assise (opera) • 1983
  Livre du saint sacrement (organ) • 1985
  Éclairs sur l'Au-Dela (orch.) • 1991

PARIS: **Musique concrète**
- 1948 Schaeffer; Henry
- 1948 Boulez, leader of young serialists in Paris
- 1952 *Le marteau san maître*
- 1957 *Piano Sonata No. 3* (chord multiplication)
- c. 1975 Founded the Institute de Recherche et Coordination de Acoustique/Musique

GERMANY:
- 1951 Eimert founded Studio für Elektronische Musik

Stockhausen: • 1953 *Kontra-Punkte*
- 1956 *Gesang der Jünglinge*

1952	*Klavierstücke I–XIV*	1985

Series of *Licht* operas | 1980 | 1997

ITALY: | 1958 | Berio: *Sequenza* series | 1985 |

| 1980 | *Chemins* series |

---

to both composers and performers a wide dissemination of their artistic talents. The early standard speed for playing such discs with reasonable fidelity was 78 rpm. By the early 1920s, Berliner's gramophone was in many homes. Microphones and electrical amplifiers were available c. 1924 and were another aid in the recording industry. Columbia Records made one of the earliest recordings with these devices in March 1925 in the Metropolitan Opera House. World War II interrupted research. In 1948 Columbia Records produced recordings on nonbreakable microgroove discs playable at 33⅓ rpm—the long-playing record, capable of storing much more material on a 12-inch disc than was possible at 78 rpm speed. By 1957 stereophonic recording and reproduction were possible. The next development was quadraphonic (four-channel) sound. By 1980 there were available digital players with laser beams scanning metal-coated discs. One side of a compact digital disc (12 cm. diameter) holds approximately one hour of stereophonic sound.

Before World War II, some composers had begun to experiment with disc recordings as a compositional

tool. By recording sounds and then manipulating or altering the recording, new sounds could be created. However, when magnetic tape became readily available, it proved to be a much more workable tool.

As early as 1898, Vladimir Poulsen had invented a means of recording sounds as patterns of magnetized domains on steel piano wire that was wound around a cylinder. The prime purpose for his research was to find a way to record telephone conversations, and he called his invention the *telegraphone*. Because round wire twisted easily, flat steel bands came into use. These could be edited, and by c. 1927–29 methods had been devised for high-frequency erasing and substitution of sounds.

Real progress in magnetic tape recording came when flexible coated tapes became available c. 1935. At first these were made of coated paper, then plastic film was used for the tape base. With this, editing was easier, for the tape could be cut and spliced; also, several tracks could be recorded simultaneously, and more material could be stored on a single tape than on a single disc. This opened up countless opportunities for composers.

1940	1950	1960	1970	1980	1990

AMERICA:

• 1950–54 Varèse: *Déserts* (tape, instrs.)

• 1957 *Poème électronique* (tape)

Babbitt: Combinatoriality; total serialization

• 1947 *Three Compositions for Piano*

• 1961 *Composition for Synthesizer*   • 1981 *Ars combinatoria*

• 1969 Wuorinen: *Time's Encomium* (tape)

Cage: Prepared piano, after Cowell

• 1946–48 *Sonatas and Interludes*

• 1951 *Music of Changes* (aleatory)

• 1953–58 *Music for Piano*

New Movements: "Happenings"   "Fluxus"

• 1961–67 Oliveros: electronic works

• 1976–86 Ivey: Tape + live performance

• 1970 Crumb: *Ancient Voices of Children*

• 1972–79 *Makrokosmos*, Vols. I–IV

• 1984 Musgrave:
Harriet, the Woman called 'Moses' (opera)

Ligeti: • 1955 *Éjszaka; Reggel*   • 1965 *Requiem Mass*

Penderecki: • 1960 *Threnody . . .*   • 1978 *Paradise Lost* (opera)

• c. 1964 Riley: *In C*; Minimalism

• 1974 Glass: *Music with Changing Parts*

• 1967 Reich: *Violin Phase* (phase shifting)

The Desert Music • 1984

Music for Percussion and Keyboard • 1984

• 1968– Del Tredici: the series of *Alice* pieces begun

Zwilich: *Concerto Grosso* • 1985

Double Concerto • 1991

Tower: *Silver Ladders* • 1987

Concerto for Orchestra • 1991

Not only could they record resource materials, they could, and eventually did, work directly with source materials to create entire compositions on tape and thus avoid the difficult task of trying to notate their works precisely so that performers would interpret them correctly and re-create them with reasonable accuracy. Rhythm and slow glissandos were especially difficult to notate. Taped compositions could be marketed, just as discs were, but not until after 1955 was there any real endeavor to do so. Of course, World War II caused delays, but by 1947 tape recording was used in radio broadcasting studios. The manufacturer of stereo disc records led to similar developments with stereophonic tapes. Then, in the late 1950s and early 1960s,

tape cartridges and cassettes were designed, and in 1965 the eight-track cassette was developed, primarily for use in automobiles. In such a cassette, the tape is a continuous loop, wound to provide the listener with uninterrupted sound. Composers used the tape loop as a compositional tool for creating ostinato passages in their tape compositions.

Recording sounds on film became a reality in 1923 when Lee de Forest (1863–1961) developed the photoelectric cell that enabled motion pictures to become "talking" pictures. The earliest successful one with music was *The Jazz Singer* (1928). At first, a sound track was put on a film through variable density optical recording to achieve reliable synchronization of sound and action. Then, magnetic recording techniques were applied to "movie" film. This opened another vista—composing for cinema. Composer-conductor John Williams (b. 1932) began his career writing background music for films and won Academy Awards for his music for *Jaws* (1975) and *Star Wars* (1977). Later developments include videotape recorders (introduced by Ampex in the 1960s), electronic video recording (1968), and video disc systems operating at 1500 rpm (in the 1980s).

Radio was another realm that opened to composers c. 1920. It has progressed from amplitude modification (AM) to frequency modulation (FM; in the 1950s) and use of very high frequency (VHF) transmission, which reduces interference noise and achieves a quiet background and thus greater fidelity of the music (or other sounds) transmitted for reception in the home. Many composers, including Aaron Copland, have written music for radio, and, since the advent of television, composers have written theme, background, and incidental music for telecasts, for example, John Williams's theme music composed in 1986 for NBC's *Today* and *Nightly News* shows and his compositions and arrangements in the 1990s for telecasts of the Olympic Games.

ELECTRONIC INSTRUMENTS

Composers sought new sounds and new means of generating them electronically and encouraged electrical engineers to invent new instruments. In 1964–65, at the instigation of composer Herbert Deutsch, Robert Moog (b. 1934) built a voltage-controlled synthesizer for composing music. Organist-composer Wendy Carlos (née Walter Carlos; b. 1939) popularized the sounds of the Moog Synthesizer by recording several of J. S. Bach's compositions as *Switched-On Bach*. At about the same time that Deutsch contacted Moog, composer Morton Subotnik (b. 1933), in California, requested electrical engineer Donald Buchla to construct some electronic music equipment for him. Subotnik installed one of Buchla's voltage-controlled Electronic Music Systems in his New York studio and used it to create *Silver Apples of the Moon* (1966), the first electronic music composition composed specifically (i.e., commissioned) for a record (Nonesuch 71174). For this piece, Subotnik used the sequencer

module, a control voltage source in the Buchla System, to perform the same functions as a tape loop more rapidly and more efficiently.

The first instance of a computer being programmed to produce the score of a musical composition occurred in 1957 at the University of Illinois when Lejaren Hiller (1924–94) and Leonard Isaacson (b. 1925) wrote *Illiac Suite for String Quartet*. Only the score was computer generated; the music was performed by a string quartet. Between 1959 and 1962 Iannis Xenakis (b. 1922), working in Paris, used computer calculations to produce the scores of seven compositions, including *Stratégie, Jeu pour deux orchestres* (Strategy, Game for two [small] orchestras). In other words, the computer was employed as a kind of composing machine to produce scores for performance on conventional instruments.

In 1957, at Bell Telephone Laboratories in New Jersey, under direction of Max Mathews, computer-generated sounds were produced through use of a digital-to-analog converter (DAC). This means that numbers, in a specific order, are input to the computer either by typing or by punched cards (cf., Ada Lovelace's ideas in 1842; p. 455). The numbers represent various elements of the music each of which the computer translates into either 0 or 1 and transmits to magnetic digital tape or disk. The disk or tape is sent through the DAC, the digital information is converted to voltages (the analog), the voltages are recorded on tape (on a conventional tape recorder), and the tape recorder head translates the voltages to sounds. Further research at Bell Laboratories produced a light pencil whose graphic representations replaced the punched cards, and in 1968 Mathews and Frederick Moore used a computer to control a synthesizer. Home computers, such as the Apple IIgs (gs, graphic sound) available in October 1986, were capable of "playing" as many as 15 lines of music sounded simultaneously and printing out the notated score by means of an Imagewriter II printer. Even more advanced are Power Macintosh computers and others with CD/ROM capabilities, software for music notation (e.g., "Finale"), and laser printers.

Bösendorfer has created an Imperial grand piano, 9'6" in length, whose 97-key keyboard extends the range down to subcontra C (fundamental frequency

16.3 hertz, or cycles per second). Regardless of whether the pianist uses the additional bass keys, all of which are black in color, the piano's extended bass bridge provides the instrument with increased resonance. Moreover, one Imperial grand model—Model 290SE—is a computer-controlled instrument. Interfaced with Macintosh computer, the piano, without the touch of human hands, can perform even the most intricate piano music impeccably. The computer can record performances on the Bösendorfer, and the piano can reproduce them precisely. By means of appropriate software (e.g., "Vision"), music initiated on the Bösendorfer or a MIDI keyboard can be encoded in a kind of bar-graph notation to form a music score that is recorded on disc. When called up on a computer monitor screen, that score is "read" by a vertical cursor sweeping from left to right across the screen, thus activating the piano to perform the music. The computer can track 128 distinct increments of key and pedal velocity as well as timings of damper, hammer, and pedal movement at a resolution of approximately one-thousandth of a second, and the Model 290SE piano can reproduce them accurately.

The original intent of recording technology—to provide a means for storing, transmitting, and faithfully reproducing live sounds—has been extended considerably. Technology has made available to composers every sound in the universe as source material. Not only the proportions of the macrocosm but the *musica mundana* (or inaudible cosmic music) about which Pythagoras, Plato, and Boethius wrote and everything within it—even its silence—has been placed within reach of those creating the microcosm, audible *musica instrumentalis*.

SERIALISM

Schoenberg began to use serialism consistently in the 1920s and continued to do so for the remainder of his life without exploring its possibilities beyond the element of pitch. Each of his pupils applied serial principles in his own way and relayed the technique to his pupils. Outside that circle of pupils, serialism had little use until after 1945. Then, in Paris, René Leibowitz (1913–72) taught Schoenberg's technique for a few years, and Pierre Boulez attended some of his classes. In the opinion of Boulez and other European avant-garde composers, the late works of Webern provided the best models for serial composition. Because of Webern's economy, it was easy to follow his procedures. Moreover, his use of counterpoint was intriguing.

For a time, Messiaen decried serialism, then began to use it with discrimination. After he applied serial principles to rhythm in *Quatre études de rhythme* and composed some of those pieces while teaching summer courses at Darmstadt, other composers became interested in his procedures, particularly those in *Mode de valeurs et d'intensités*. (However, *Mode de valeurs . . .* is not a serial piece; see p. 632.) Boulez, Karel Goeyvaerts (b. 1923), Karlheinz Stockhausen (b. 1928), and Luigi Nono (1924–90) wrote compositions directly influenced by *Mode de valeurs et d'intensités*. Through continued experimentation with multiple serialism, the scope of that technique was extended until eventually total serialism was attained. Boulez, Stockhausen, and Goeyvaerts explored use of serial principles in *musique concrète* and electronic music. Meantime, in the United States, Milton Babbitt had analyzed and studied the late works of Schoenberg and Webern and in 1947 had arrived at serialization of rhythm and dynamics as well as pitch. None of the composers used precisely the same procedures, yet each, working individually, achieved results comparable with those of the others. One of the features of serialism—perhaps its most exciting facet—is the fact that no two composers used precisely the same procedures or produced music that sounds the same.

OLIVIER MESSIAEN

French composer Olivier Messiaen (1908–92) was one of the twentieth century's most individualistic composers. Though he adhered to no single style, his personal techniques of composition remained more or less constant. Since the mid-1940s, Messiaen was highly influential as teacher and composer, but his teaching and his works have affected his students and other composers differently.

Messiaen's parents encouraged Olivier but did not consider him a prodigy, even when, at age 9, he composed piano pieces. When Olivier was 11, he entered

Olivier Messiaen. *(© François Lochon/Gamma-Liaison)*

Paris Conservatoire. He was a brilliant student, winning first prizes in several subjects in successive years. His earliest published compositions, *Le banquet céleste* (The heavenly banquet; organ; 1928) and eight *Préludes* (pno.; 1929), were products of his student years but exhibit some features of his mature style.

In 1931 Messiaen was appointed organist at L'Église de la Sainte Trinité, Paris, and also began teaching at L'École Normale de Musique and the Schola Cantorum. During 1932–36, he and three others formed *La Jeune France* (Young France), a group that aimed to promote modern French music. Among the works Messiaen created in the 1930s are *La nativité du Seigneur* (The Nativity of the Lord; organ; 1935) and two song cycles written for his wife, violinist Claire Delbos (1910–59), *Poèmes pour Mi* (Poems for "Mi"; vc., pno.; 1936) and *Chants de terre et de ciel* (Songs of earth and sky; 1938).

During World War II, Messiaen was a prisoner at Görlitz, Silesia, where he composed *Quatuor pour le fin du temps* (Quartet for the end of time; vln., vcl., cl., pno.; 1940), which he and three other prisoners performed at Stalag VIIIA in January 1941. Later that year Messiaen was repatriated and resumed his position at Trinité. In 1942 he was appointed professor of harmony at Paris Conservatoire; the following year he began teaching semiprivate classes in analysis at the home of Guy-Bernard Delapierre, whom he had met at prison camp. Pierre Boulez (b. 1925), Yvette Grimaud (b. 1920), and Yvonne Loriod (b. 1924) were among those attending his seminars. Messiaen was not teaching serial techniques, so some of his pupils went to Leibowitz for private lessons in serial music. Leibowitz, who had studied with Schoenberg and Webern, was the chief exponent of twelve-tone music in France in the 1940s.

Messiaen's semiprivate teaching ceased when he was appointed professor of analysis and rhythm at Paris Conservatoire in 1947. Though the Conservatoire was aware that Messiaen was becoming an important influence in avant-garde music after 1945 and recognized his compositional talents, not until 1966 was he named professor of composition there. He did not found a school of composition, for he encouraged his students to be individualistic in their writing. None of them copied his style. Commencing in 1947, Messiaen began to teach and to lecture outside France for short periods.

Messiaen's religious philosophies and the Roman Catholic faith were always extremely important to him and colored many of his compositions. He set some biblical texts and sought to express musically the meaning of others. He wrote vocal lines in the style of psalm tones, combined melodic motives in the manner of centonization, followed the formal patterns of chants in some of his works, and used phrases of music and texts of liturgical chants as basis for or within compositions. His eight-movement *Quatuor pour le fin du temps* depicts events of the apocalypse and in the two very slow movements (fifth and eighth) praises the eternity and immortality of Jesus. The two excellent piano works that followed the quartet are also deeply religious. *Visions de l'amen* (Amen visions; 2 pnos.; 1943) thoroughly explores all registers of the keyboard. *Vingt regards sur l'enfant Jésus* (Twenty contemplations of the infant Jesus; 1944) comprises 20 movements that express contemplations of the infant Jesus by various spiritual and human beings and symbolic or immaterial entities: God, Holy Spirit, angels, Mary, Wise Men, the Star, the Cross, Time, and others. Messiaen's last work concerns Eternity.

In 1942 Messiaen explained the characteristics of his musical style up to that point in *Technique de mon langage musical* (Technique of my musical language), which he illustrated with examples from his compositions. Perhaps the most unusual characteristic of his music is his treatment of rhythm. While a student, he became interested in the rhythms of ancient Greek poetry, then studied the thirteenth-century treatise

Sāngīta-Ratnākara (Ocean of Music), in which theorist Sārṅgadeva listed and discussed the 120 *desī-talas* (provincial rhythms) used in Hindu music. Both kinds of rhythms found permanent places in Messiaen's compositional style. In some works, he identified the unusual rhythms he used, for example, the Greek Cretic pattern ♩ ♪ ♩ and the Hindu *rāgavardhana* pattern ♫♩.♫ ♩. in *Couleurs de la cité céleste* (Colors of the heavenly city; pno., winds, perc.; 1963). For Messiaen, much of the time, rhythm amounted to an accumulation of durations rather than a division of time into equal parts. Many of his works are ametrical, with bar lines placed only to indicate phrasing; probably, this is an influence of chant. Sometimes he used bar lines as in measures but without meter signatures. In those instances, the performer relies on a basic unit of beat, comparable with the *chronos protos* of the ancient Greeks.

Messiaen altered rhythmic patterns by means of added values, that is, by adding a short note, inserting a short rest, or lengthening the value of one of the notes (ex. 27.1). Augmentation or diminution of rhythms was effected by means other than doubling or halving values. The augmentation or diminution might be uneven or cumulative (ex. 27.2a, b), or it might be brought about by increasing or diminishing all notes proportionately (ex. 27.2c, d, e).

Messiaen also used nonretrogradable rhythms, or rhythmic palindromes (ex. 27.3). These are rhythmic patterns designed so that they read the same backward and forward. They are comparable with word or phrase palindromes, such as "kayak," "Madam, I'm Adam," or "able was I ere I saw Elba." (Cf. Machaut, ex. 8.1, p. 113.)

Another contrivance Messiaen used is rhythmic ostinato, which he termed "rhythmic pedal." This is identical with the device of isorhythm used by Machaut and other late Medieval and early Renaissance composers. In "*Liturgie de cristal*," the first movement of *Quatuor pour le fin du temps*, Messiaen used a combination of melodic and rhythmic ostinati that do not coincide, a procedure similar to Machaut's use of *color* and *talea* in isorhythm (see Chap. 8). There is isorhythm in the first movement of Messiaen's *Turangalîla-symphonie* (1946–48). Of course, the combination of different rhythmic pedals in several voices creates polyrhythm, as does the rhythmic canon that Messiaen sometimes used.

EXAMPLE 27.1 Examples of rhythmic patterns altered by means of added values at the place in the measure marked with +: (*a*) short note added; (*b*) short rest inserted; (*c*) note lengthened in value.

EXAMPLE 27.2 Some types of augmentation and diminution used by Messiaen: (*a*) inexact or uneven augmentation; (*b*) cumulative augmentation; (*c*) augmentation by one-fourth of original note value; (*d*) augmentation by one-half of original note value; (*e*) diminution by three-fourths of original value.

EXAMPLE 27.3 Rhythmic palindromes.

Still another device used by Messiaen is rhythmic interversion. He arranged note values "chromatically" in order of duration and numbered them as though forming a row. Then, commencing at the center of that arrangement, he took numbers in order from each side to form the first interverted row:

Original Series:	12	11	10	9	8	7	6	5	4	3	2	1
Interversion I:	6	7	5	8	4	9	3	10	2	11	1	12
Interversion II:	3	9	10	4	2	8	11	5	1	7	12	6
Interversion III:	11	8	5	2	1	4	7	10	12	9	6	3
Interversion IV:	7	4	10	1	12	2	9	5	6	8	3	11

Succeeding interversions were formed in the same manner. Such interversion is limited, for the tenth permutation (interversion) reproduces the original rhythmic row. Also, in the third and eighth columns of the rhythm grid, two rhythmic values alternate.

Messiaen's melodies were strongly influenced by chant and folk song, particularly Russian folk song, which are modal and evidence use of centonization. He invented modal scale patterns, containing 6, 8, 9, or 10 pitches per octave, with tones and semitones in various arrangement (ex. 27.4). He called these "modes of limited transposition" for the obvious reason that after a few transpositions pitches recur. One of these scales is actually an octatonic scale (see Bartók, p. 585). He used major and minor scales also. Messiaen's modes of limited transposition are counterparts to his nonretrogradable rhythms. The rhythms present horizontally what transposition of the modes realizes vertically. Another complementary relationship exists between his rhythms with added values and chords with added notes. For him, such complementary relationships possessed "the charm of impossibilities."

Where harmonies are concerned, Messiaen stated that he envisioned colors as he wrote or heard harmonies. This accounts for some of the complex chords that he wrote. Certain aggregations of pitches, designed as "resonance chords," include several overtones of a fundamental pitch—the overtones Messiaen heard as "natural resonance of a sounding body." He used these prisms in sound to produce what he termed "rainbows," or "stained-glass window" effects (ex. 27.5). Messiaen made considerable use of the added sixth and the augmented fourth (the tritone); this was an influence of Debussy and Musorgsky.

Timbres were varied by using many different percussion instruments or new instruments such as ondes Martenot (Insight, "Theremin and Ondes Martenot") or by including transcribed birdsongs. Later, in some vocal music, the text contains phonemes or vocalized sounds instead of actual words (e.g., in *Cinq rechants* [Five songs reset; chorus; 1949]).

During 1949–52 Messiaen ventured into serialism and wrote some experimental music that proved to be

influential: *Cantéyodjayâ* (Song with *djayâ* refrains; pno.; 1948) and *Quatre études de rythme* (Four rhythmic studies; pno.; 1949–50). A passage in *Cantéyodjayâ* is three-voice polyphony with each voice in its own mode and each pitch in each mode assigned a specific duration and dynamic level. This was a move toward **total serialism,** along lines explored by Milton Babbitt in America two years earlier. (Total serialism is the application of the rules of serial composition to all possible musical parameters.)

Messiaen carried the principle of serialization further in *Quatre études de rythme.* In the étude *Neumes rythmiques* (Rhythmic neumes), strophes constructed of rhythmic neumes alternate with two refrains. The neumes (name derived from plainchant neumes) are short rhythmic groups with structured pitches and intensities (ex. 27.6). Another étude, *Mode de valeurs et d'intensités* (Mode of values and intensities), is a three-voice piece in which the mode in each voice contains all 12 pitches of the chromatic scale, and each pitch has an assigned constant duration, register, and articulation. But *Mode de valeurs . . .* is *not* a serial piece. The preface to the work explains its structure. The other rhythmic études, *Île de feu I* and *Île de feu II* (Isle of fire I, II; 1950), have rhythmic interversion and

EXAMPLE 27.5 **Resonance chords of the sort Messiaen used.**

EXAMPLE 27.6 **Three rhythmic neumes, one neume per "measure," used by Messiaen in *Neumes rhythmiques.*** (*Source: Olivier Messiaen, Neumes rhythmiques, Durand Publishers, Paris, France*)

EXAMPLE 27.4 **Two of the modal scale patterns Messiaen used in his music.**

Theremin and Ondes Martenot

The theremin and ondes Martenot are electronic monophonic instruments—electronic oscillators generate the tones. An **oscillator** is a device (or circuit) capable of producing an alternating current or waveform. An oscillator may have a fixed frequency, or variable frequency, producing different pitches in response to a keyboard or other pitch-designating device. Both theremin and ondes Martenot use two supersonic oscillators, one fixed and one variable, and a tone is produced by the heterodyne action of the two oscillators. (To **heterodyne** is to combine radio oscillations in a manner that results in the production of beats whose frequency is the difference, or the sum, of the frequencies of the oscillators. In other words, pitches are produced as either difference tones or summation tones, not directly generated.) The resulting pitch is amplified and emitted from the instrument's loudspeaker. However, the manner of activating

tone production differs in the two instruments.

The theremin, originally called "aetherophone," was invented c. 1920 by Léon Thérémin (1896–1993), a physicist in Petrograd, and was first used in an orchestral work by Russian composer Andrei Pashchenko in 1924. The theremin is unique in that the performer does not touch any part of it to produce tones. The instrument's variable frequency oscillator is connected to an antenna (a metal rod) that projects vertically from the instrument. The frequency of the pitch produced and emitted from the instrument's speaker depends on the proximity of the player's hand to that antenna. Pitch changes are caused by moving the hand back and forth and varying its distance from the antenna. The player controls volume by moving the left hand in relation to a metal loop on the instrument. Different timbres are available, selected by manipulating controls governing a system of filters

that vary the harmonics (fig. 27.2).

The ondes Martenot (also called *ondes musicales,* musical waves) was invented in Paris c. 1928 by Maurice Martenot (1898–1980). The instrument is equipped with a seven-octave keyboard—a separate unit from the speaker cabinet—that controls the frequency of the variable oscillator. The player's right hand operates the keyboard but can produce only one pitch at a time; if the player depresses more than one key, as in a dyad or chord, only the lowest pitch sounds. Each key can be slightly moved laterally to create a vibrato (cf., clavichord *Bebung*). A wide glissando sweep is produced by an alternative method of tone production—the player moves a finger ring that is attached to a metal ribbon, and the sliding ribbon controls the frequency. The player's left hand varies the dynamics and timbres by manipulating switches that control filters (fig. 27.3). Jeanne Loriod is an exponent of ondes Martenot.

FIGURE 27.2 L. Thérémin with a theremin.

FIGURE 27.3 John Morton with his ondes Martenot.

rhythm-pitch associations but incorporate only a few assigned intensities and kinds of attack.

In only one piece did Messiaen use the conventional matrix pattern of twelve-tone serialism, *Pièce en trio I* (Trio piece I) in *Livre d'Orgue* (Organ Book; 1951). Like Bach's trio sonatas for organ, the trio consists of the two manuals and the pedalboard of the organ. The principal melody is in the pedals. A unique quality in Messiaen's serial music is its ability to retain a sense of modality. This is particularly apparent in *Pièce en trio I* and may be due to Messiaen's emphasis on the tritone. Some aspects of serial technique appear in *Messe de la Pentecôte* (Pentecost Mass; 1950), an organ Mass. That Mass is a summation of all of Messiaen's compositional techniques up to 1950. Though he did not pursue serialism in his own music beyond a few years of experimentation, his nonserial *Mode de valeurs . . .* greatly influenced the work of some of his pupils and colleagues (e.g., Stockhausen, Goeyvaerts, Michel Fano, and Boulez).

Messiaen collaborated with Pierre Henry in creating a piece of electronic music: *Timbres-durées* (Timbres-durations; tape; 1952). Messiaen did not compose another.

From his youth, Messiaen was interested in birdsong. He was a member of several ornithological societies and collected and transcribed hundreds of birdsongs. (Ornithology is the branch of zoology dealing with birds.) He first included birdsongs in his music in *Quatuor pour le fin du temps*. From 1950, they became an integral part of many of his compositions. His principal works based chiefly on birdsongs are *Réveil des oiseaux* (Awakening of birds; pno., orch.; 1953), *Oiseaux exotiques* (Exotic birds; pno., winds, perc.; 1955–56), *Catalogue d'oiseaux* (Catalog of birds; pno.; 1959), and *La fauvette des jardins* (The garden warbler; pno.; 1970). Yvonne Loriod, Messiaen's second wife, was piano soloist in the premiéres of those works. *Oiseaux exotiques* is a collage or counterpoint of approximately 40 birdsongs (all identified) from various countries with which Messiaen at times combined authentic Greek and Hindu rhythms. The composition strongly resembles a piano concerto whose form is an overall arch with two main sections. Each main section commences with a *tutti* and continues with subsections that alternately feature soloist and ensemble. The last two subsections are, respectively, a piano cadenza and a coda that is an abridged version of the introduction.

Color figures prominently in many of Messiaen's compositions. The large orchestra for *Chronochromie* (The color of time; 1960), one of his few works without piano, uses gamelan-type pitched percussion. Pitches are less important to the composition than durations and colors. With the exception of *Chronochromie* and *Sept Haïkaï* (Seven Haiku poems; small orch.; 1962), Messiaen's works of the 1960s have religious connotations. In addition to Christian symbolism and Gregorian chant melodies, the compositions contain birdsongs, color-chords, and Hindu and Greek rhythmic patterns. In *Couleurs de la cité céleste* Messiaen wrote in the score the colors he associated with the chords. For *Méditations sur le mystère de la Sainte Trinité* (Meditations on the mystery of the Holy Trinity; organ; 1969; DWMA185), Messiaen created a communicable musical language based on an alphabet of pitches. He began with the German pitch associations A through H (B = B♭; H = B♮), then gave letter names to pitches in other registers and assigned a fixed duration to each pitch used in forming words. His message is conveyed through musical nouns, adjectives, and verbs only; special motivic formulas connote "God," "to be," and "to have." Though Messiaen supplied all the information for deciphering the musical language, the true message is still concealed, as is the mystery of the Holy Trinity.

In the 1970s, Messiaen created two major works: *Des canyons aux étoiles* (From the canyons to the stars; pno., orch.; 1971–74), a 12-movement suite that commences in a desert in Utah and concludes with a combination of Zion Park and the Celestial City, and the opera *Saint François d'Assise* (Saint Francis of Assisi; 1975–83; perf. November 1983). The opera is in eight scenes presented in three acts. It requires 9 soloists (all male except the angel, a soprano), a 10-part chorus of 150, and an orchestra of 120 players, with very large wind and percussion sections and 3 ondes Martenots. Each major character has a special theme, and often the vocal solo lines resemble modal chant. Color is important—Messiaen specified the colors for costumes, and colored lighting plays a significant part in the production. In the final scene, after Francis's body is carried off the stage, dazzling light fills the place where it had lain, and the orchestra and chorus present a resurrection chorale that ends in C major. The powerful C-major conclusion of the opera reminds one of Haydn's great C-major chord on the word "light" in the *The Creation.*

Messiaen's *Livre du saint sacrement* (Book of the blessed sacrament; organ; 1984–85) had its world première on 1 July 1986 in Detroit, Michigan; Messiaen was present. The composition comprises 18 movements of various lengths. The first 4 movements represent acts of adoration before the hidden God, the unseen Christ; movement 5 concerns the Nativity, and movements 6 through 11 deal with events in Jesus' life and with his words. In movements 12 ("The Transubstantiation") through 16 ("Prayer after Communion") Messiaen refers to the Communion sacrament. Movement 17 ("The Presence multiplied") portrays Christ's eternal presence in all consecrated hosts on earth. The work concludes with *Offrande et Alleluia final* (Offering and final Alleluia), an offering to God of the prayers of all the saints, and a brilliant, joyous toccata that includes passages of alleluias. For each movement Messiaen provided a quotation that is the key to what he said musically. All characteristic features of Messiaen's music are present in *Livre du saint sacrement,* including plainsong and liturgical references, birdsongs, color-chords, and rhythmic precision.

Messiaen's last completed large-scale work was *Éclairs sur l'Au-Delà* (Illuminations of the Beyond; 1987–91; 12 mvts., orch.). It was commissioned by the New York Philharmonic, which gave the work its world première on 5 November 1992 as part of that orchestra's 150th anniversary celebration. The last movement is entitled "Christ, Light of Paradise." *Éclairs . . .* contains all of Messiaen's compositional traits.

According to Messiaen, all of his music is an expression of his faith, just as J. S. Bach's music was. Messiaen divided music into three basic categories. From the lowest level to the highest, these are (1) liturgical music, which consists solely of plainsong; (2) religious music, which comprises all sacred music other than chant; and (3) "sound-color and dazzlement" music—music whose colors merge into dazzling light like that mentioned in Revelation and carry a person to unprecedented heights in an approach to true Faith. Messiaen's

music is an individually conceived composite of many styles and many cultures. The full impact of his influence may not be realized for another half century. Certainly he was one of the twentieth century's greatest composers.

FRANCE—*MUSIQUE CONCRÈTE*

Musique concrète (concrete music) was the term Pierre Schaeffer (b. 1910) used to describe music he composed directly on disc or tape by recording natural sounds that he manipulated by reversal, changes of speed, or other editing. The term was intended to denote that the sounds were from natural (concrete) sources and that the compositions were created directly on tape (concretely) rather than through notation that had to be interpreted by performers. Schaeffer, who invented the technique in 1948, was a telecommunications engineer. He had worked at Radiodiffusion Française and in 1942 helped found the Studio d'Essai, which became the center for the Resistance movement in French radio during World War II.

At first Schaeffer manipulated disc recordings (varying speeds, altering the grooves, playing sections backward); when the tape recorder became readily available, he worked with magnetic tape. In 1948 he created the first *musique concrète* compositions: *Étude violette* (Violet study), *Étude au piano* (Study with piano), *Étude aux chemins de fer* (Study with railroads), and others. Then he shared his techniques and collaborated with others, notably Pierre Henry (b. 1927). Together, Schaeffer and Henry prepared *musique concrète* for ballet, radio, pantomime, and the opera *Orphée 53* (Orpheus 1953). One of their collaborations is *Symphonie pour un homme seul* (Symphony for one man; 1950, rev. 1953), whose 12 short movements were created from sounds made by the human body. In the 1960s, Schaeffer taught electronic techniques and wrote about them; in 1968 he was appointed professor of electronic composition at Paris Conservatoire.

Pierre Henry joined the Groupe de Recherche de Musique Concrète (Group for research in *musique concrète*) in 1951 and headed the Groupe in 1952–58. He formulated an index of sounds of all kinds that could be used in creating music on tape. In 1952 he prepared *musique concrète* for the film *Astrologie*

(Astrology), the first electronic music compositions used in commercial cinema in France.

In 1958, Henry and Jean Baronnet established the Apsone-Cabasse Studio, the first private electronic music studio in France. Then Henry no longer restricted his compositions to natural sounds but combined *concrète* and purely electronic techniques. The first of his works to explore such a synthesis were *Coexistence* (1959) and *Investigations* (1959). Henry prepared electronic music for several Béjart ballets and composed several religious works, including *La messe de Liverpool* (Mass for Liverpool; 1967–68), created from sounds produced by a voice, a 'cello, a flute, and synthesized sounds. Though much of the music is complex, the text is intelligible. *L'apocalypse de Jean* (The apocalypse of John; 1968) is a dense polyphony of electronic sounds, but the narration of the biblical text comes through clearly.

In the 1970s, Henry tried various approaches to recorded composition. For *Gymkhana* (1970) he reverted to sounds produced by conventional instruments. Then he experimented with lighting effects and created audiovisual works as in *Mise en musique du corticolart* (Cortex art set to music; 1971), which depicts brain waves as electronic sound and light. *La dixième* (The tenth; 1973) is based on electronic reproduction and manipulation of material borrowed from Beethoven's symphonies.

PIERRE BOULEZ

Boulez, a pianist, studied harmony with Messiaen at Paris Conservatoire in 1942 and had private lessons in counterpoint from Andrée Vaurabourg (1894–1980). Boulez became a superb analyst and a fine composer. He regarded music from a scientific viewpoint and was firmly convinced of the necessity for atonality. When Leibowitz offered instruction in serial techniques, Boulez joined the class. After the death of Schoenberg, Boulez publicly decried Schoenberg's failure to develop serialism to its fullest and affirmed that Webern was the serialist composer to emulate.

Boulez has withdrawn all his earliest works except Piano Sonata No. 1 (1946) and *Sonatine* (fl., pno.; 1946). *Sonatine,* a single movement, is divided into sections comparable with those of a four-movement sonata. The arrangement of pitches in the row gave rise to melodic motives or cells that Boulez treated as thematic

Pierre Boulez. *(AP/Wide World Photos)*

material; such motivic treatment is a feature of many of his works. (Cf. Brahms p. 519, 524, Webern p. 604.)

By 1948 Boulez was recognized as the leader of the young serialist composers working in Paris. That year he wrote Piano Sonata No. 2 and provided the music for a radio broadcast of René Char's (1907–88) play *Le soleil des eaux* (The sunlight of the waters). In 1950 Boulez transformed the play music into a cantata. Piano Sonata No. 2, modeled on Beethoven's Classic four-movement sonatas, uses two different pitch series, one row for movements 1 and 3, another for movements 2 and 4. The finale concludes with a section based on the pitches H–C–A–B. Though serial, the rows are segmented, and the music relies heavily on motivic cells. The piano is treated percussively, and the mood of much of the sonata is violent.

For *Structures, livre 1* (Structures, book 1; 2 pnos.; 1952), Boulez borrowed the pitch series from Messiaen's *Mode de valeurs et d'intensités* and serialized attacks and dynamics. He assigned registers to the pitches and arranged tempo changes as palindromes. Though the musical elements are well organized, Boulez carefully mixed them so that his scheme is not easily recognized. Of the three pieces in the volume (labeled *Ia, Ib,* and *Ic*), *Ib* was composed last and is extremely complex.

Boulez's best-known composition, and one that is probably his most expressive musically, is *Le marteau sans maître* (The hammer without a master; 1952–54, rev. 1957). The work is in nine short movements, for alto voice and a chamber ensemble composed of alto flute, viola, guitar, vibraphone, xylorimba, and unpitched percussion. Boulez's choice of instrumentation was prompted by relationships between them: voice

EXAMPLE 27.7 (*a*) Chord multiplication as used by Boulez in *Blocs I* of *Constellation-Miroir*: The four pitches of the row between the small arrows form the chord +, and that chord squared forms the chord ++. (*b*) The process of chord multiplication: To determine the square of a chord, transpose the chord to the tonal level of each of its component pitches, and form a chord by combining the pitches of all transpositions. *(From Paul Griffiths, Boulez. Copyright © 1978 Oxford University Press, Oxford, England. Reprinted by permission.)*

(a)

(b)

and flute are in alto range and produce sounds by means of breath, alto flute and viola can sustain tones, viola played *pizzicato* has affinity with guitar, and so on. The settings of three verses by Char that lie at the heart of the work (mvts. 3, 5, 6) generated the other movements that complement them. The ninth movement is essentially a variation of the fifth but recalls short passages from the other two vocal movements. The remaining movements are instrumental: first and seventh serve as prelude and postlude to the third (DWMA186); second, fourth, and eighth are commentaries on the sixth. With the exception of movements 6 and 9, which use all performing resources, no two movements are scored the same. The vocal line contains wide intervals, grace notes, melismas, glissandos, and *Sprechstimme*. The flute part includes harmonics and flutter tonguing.

It is important to realize that Boulez considered a series as source material capable of providing small motivic cells and countless possibilities for treatment of a basic idea. A series could be handled strictly, or it might be carefully contrived so that it allowed the composer considerable freedom. Most often, he chose to do the latter.

Boulez's aim was to expand musical composition perpetually. With this in mind, he created some works that allow the performer(s) some choice in what is played. Piano Sonata No. 3 (1955–57) has five movements, to be played in any order, and choices are to be made within the movements. For example, the move-

ment named *Trope* is supplied with interpolations (tropes) that, at the discretion of the performer, may be performed or omitted. (Cf., Chap. 4, tropes; Chap. 2, troparia.)

Boulez's next contribution to serialism was chord multiplication. A chord can be squared (multiplied by itself) by transposing it to the level of each of its pitches and then combining all the small chords to form one large new one (ex. 27.7). The same procedure is used to multiply one chord by another chord. Multiplied chords appear in the *Constellation-Miroir* movement of Piano Sonata No. 3.

Several of Boulez's works were influenced by poetry or philosophies of poets. Among these are *Pli selon pli* (Fold by fold; sop., orch.; 1957–62), an unfolding of Mallarmé's esthetic philosophies, and *e. e. cummings ist der Dichter* (e. e. cummings is the poet; 1970–76), a chamber cantata. *Messagesquisse* (1977), for 'cello solo and an ensemble of six 'cellos, is based on pitches derived from the name Sacher (Paul Sacher, Swiss conductor, b. 1906). *Rituel* (Ritual; orch.; 1974–75) was written as an epitaph for Italian conductor Bruno Maderna (1920–73).

Around 1975 Boulez founded the Institut de Recherche et de Coordination Acoustique/Musique, located in the center of Paris, "next door and underground" from the Pompidou museum for contemporary art. As director of the Institut, Boulez has at his disposal the most advanced and extensive studios for electronic computer-generated music in the world.

637

GERMANY—ELECTRONIC MUSIC

In Germany, developments in electronic music occurred independently of and almost simultaneously with those in France. Herbert Eimert (1897–1972), composer and theorist, led the German movement. While studying at the Cologne Conservatory (1919–24), Eimert became interested in atonal music. Working independently, Eimert wrote *Atonale Musiklehre* (Atonal music textbook; 1923), in which he systematically described dodecaphonic technique and supplied music examples illustrating his principles. He then composed *Five Pieces* (1923–25), twelve-tone pieces for string quartet. Eimert continued to work with serial techniques, using them in his ballet *Der weisse Schwan* (The white swan; 1926; fl., sax., mech. instrs.). From 1927 until the war, Eimert worked in radio broadcasting at Cologne; in 1945 he resumed that work at Westdeutscher Rundfunk (West German Radio). In 1951 he founded the Studio für Elektronische Musik and was its director until 1962. His *Vier Stücke* (Four pieces; tape; 1952–53) are among the earliest compositions created from purely synthetic sounds. Eimert directly influenced Stockhausen's career and stimulated the work of other young composers. From 1965 to 1971 Eimert taught electronic music at Cologne Hochschule für Musik. He published several texts on twelve-tone music and, with Stockhausen, edited the journal *Die Reihe* (The Row).

KARLHEINZ STOCKHAUSEN

While a student at the University of Cologne, Stockhausen became interested in contemporary music and, encouraged by Eimert, attended Messiaen's summer class at Darmstadt in 1951. There he met Goeyvaerts and Nono and was influenced by Messiaen's *Mode de valeurs et d'intensités*. When Stockhausen returned to Cologne, he composed *Kreuzspiel* (Cross-play; 1951), for piano, with oboe, bass clarinet, and three percussion instruments. In this piece, pitch, duration, and intensity are serialized; timbre is not. The title is derived from Stockhausen's treatment of register—he began at opposite ends of the instruments' available range, moved to the center, then crossed over, with cross-play of pitch register between instruments. An important feature of *Kreuzspiel* is pointillistic treat-

Karlheinz Stockhausen, October 1994, in Studio für Elektronische Musik of WDR Köln during the production of the Electronic Music from FREITAG aus LICHT. Photo by Kathinka Pasveer. *Courtesy Stockhausen-Verlag, Köln, Germany.*

ment of the pitches—each note is an important point individually and is not related to a motive or a melody.

Stockhausen applied the same technique to groups or units of pitches. At first he was disappointed in the results because the pieces seemed too thematic. *Punkte* (Points; orch.; 1952) underwent three revisions before being performed in 1962. However, *Kontra-Punkte* (Counter-points; 1952, rev. 1953), for piano and nine conventional orchestral instruments, was performed at Cologne in 1953 and was Stockhausen's first published composition. In this one-movement work, the antitheses of individual notes, temporal relationships, and timbres are resolved into homogeneity. Counter-points occur in this manner: (1) Stockhausen first presents single pitches (points) sounded by various individual instruments and ultimately combines the first six pitches to form a chord (a counter-point) sounded by one instrument, the piano. (2) There is a counterpoint of timbres. The instruments are arranged in six groups or families of related instruments; gradually, instruments drop out until only the piano remains. (3) The pointillistic style found at the beginning of the piece gradually changes to a counterpoint of groups. After the successful performance of *Kontra-Punkte,* Stockhausen was recognized as the leader of the young avant-garde composers.

In 1953 Stockhausen became codirector of the electronic music studio at Cologne. There, he composed two *Elektronische Studien* (Electronic Studies)

EXAMPLE 27.8 Stockhausen: *Studie II*, page 14 of score. *(Copyright 1956 by Universal Edition (London) Ltd., London. Copyright renewed. All Rights Reserved. Used by permission of the Stockhausen Verlag, 51515 Kürten, Germany.)*

on single-track tape. *Studie I* (1953; unpub.) is built entirely from **sine-wave sounds** (pure frequency tones) organized serially. *Studie II* (1954) commences with **white noise** (all possible frequencies sounding simultaneously), then sounds are gradually filtered out until Stockhausen has isolated those he wants to use in his composition. *Studie II* was the first electronic music composition to be published in score. Preparing scores for electronic music compositions gave rise to new kinds of music notation involving graphic symbols (ex. 27.8).

Stockhausen composed music for conventional instruments while experimenting with electronic music. During 1955–56 he wrote major works in both areas: *Zeitmasze* (Time measures) for woodwind quintet and *Gesang der Jünglinge* (Song of the youths) on tape. *Zeitmasze* calls for the simultaneous performance of music written in different tempi. Stockhausen used this technique on a larger scale in *Gruppen* (Groups; 1955–57), for three orchestras, each with its own conductor.

In 1953–56 Stockhausen studied phonetics, acoustics, and communications theory with Werner Meyer-

Eppler at the University of Bonn and became interested in using the sound of the human voice in electronic compositions. For *Gesang der Jünglinge,* he recorded a boy's treble voice reciting Bible verses from the apocrypha to the Book of Daniel, then manipulated the recorded words by splitting them into vowels and phonemes and duplicating them synthetically. Next, he rearranged the component parts of the words, forming synthetic words and garbling the text. The resultant word-sounds were mingled with and completely embedded in purely electronic sounds. Finally, a mixture of electronic sounds, intelligible text excerpts, and manipulated text was recorded on five single-track tapes. (Later, Stockhausen rerecorded the composition on a single four-track tape.) The work was intended for performance in Cologne Cathedral, with the music to issue antiphonally from five groups of loudspeakers that were spatially separated. As Gabrieli had used *cori spezzati* in St. Mark's (see p. 224), so Stockhausen employed physical space as a component part of *Gesang der Jünglinge.* For the first time, space was an important element in electronic composition. In combining the human voice and electronic sounds, Stockhausen merged the techniques of the Parisian *musique concrète* and the Cologne electronic music studios. A factor in the merger was his belief that, to be truly expressive, music needed more than precisely regulated serialism.

Stockhausen composed a series of *Klavierstücke* (Piano Pieces). *Klavierstücke I–IV* (1952–53) are complex and are extremely difficult rhythmically; *Klavierstücke V–X* (1954–55) are a little less demanding of the pianist. Stockhausen's use of the Fibonacci numbers series (see p. 249) is apparent in several *Klavierstücke*. *Klavierstück III* is an example—it contains 55 notes, uses 34 different pitches, and covers a range of 50 semitones (3 + 5 + 8 + 13 + 21 = 50). In *Klavierstück XI* (1956) the performer's choices determine the form of the piece. Stockhausen notated 19 musical "groups" and instructed the pianist to play them in random order, making spontaneous choices as the performance proceeds.

In 1957 Stockhausen began to teach composition at Darmstadt, and in 1963 he founded the Cologne Courses for New Music, the nucleus of the Cologne Institute for New Music. He was recognized internationally, and he traveled widely in response to invitations to lecture or to teach. *Telemusik* (1966), prepared on four-track tape in Tokyo's NHK radio studios, combines folk music of various countries with electronically produced sounds. The composition is designed in 32 sections, each announced by the sounding of an Oriental temple instrument, as is customary in Japanese Noh drama. *Mantra* (1969–70; 2 pnos., woodblock, crotales, and 2 ring modulators for sine tones) is also concerned with a ritual of Japanese Noh drama. A **mantra** is a special melodic formula associated with ritual. *Mantra* is Stockhausen's first composition to be based on a specific melodic formula.

In 1977, Stockhausen began a cycle of seven operas, under the common title *Licht* (Light; subtitled The Seven Days of the Week), and has completed *Donnerstag aus Licht* (Thursday from Light; 1978–80), *Samstag aus Licht* (Saturday from Light; 1981–83), *Montag aus Licht* (Monday from Light; 1984–88), *Dienstag aus Licht* (Tuesday from Light; 1977–90), and *Freitag aus Licht* (Friday from Light; 1991–94), and in progress *Mittwoch aus Licht* (Wednesday from Light). Performance forces for these operas include solo voices, solo instruments, solo dancers, choirs, orchestras, ballet and mimes, and electric and concrete music. The cycle contains borrowings from various cultures, especially exotic ones, and is intended to be representative of the entire world. In its wideness of scope, the cycle has been likened to Wagner's *Der Ring*, but in sound and techniques Stockhausen's operas are quite different from Wagnerian music drama.

Stockhausen wants to write music that is representative of the entire universe. One of his endeavors to depict activity outside the planet Earth is *Sternklang* (Star sound; 1971), which is park music designed for five groups of performers (21 singers and instrumentalists). As names of stars or constellations are called out by the director, a group looks at the night sky and is supposed to read and perform the music emanating from that star or constellation. Thus, in **aleatory** (chance) music, a connection may be made, through meditation and inspiration, with the music of the spheres about which Kepler, Boethius, and Plato wrote.

Since 1966, when Stockhausen composed *Telemusik* (Electronic music) and *Hymnen* (Anthems), his music has been associated with the concept of "world music," but he describes his combination of abstract sound shapes with musical forms of national and folk awareness and folkloric patterns as being a "unification that developed into a planetary music"—music of Planet Earth. This development continued in *Montag aus Licht,* in which, he states, "one travels about in time as if in a time machine, backwards and forwards, to all eras and to all cultures on this planet."

Stockhausen has received many awards and honors, and in 1996 the Free University of Berlin awarded him an honorary Doctor of Philosophy degree.

MUSIC IN AMERICA

EDGARD VARÈSE

Varèse (1883–1965), a native of France, spent most of his life in the United States and is usually regarded as an American composer. He was educated in science and technology in Turin and in music in Paris at the Schola Cantorum and Conservatoire. For several years he lived in Berlin, where in 1912 he heard Schoenberg's *Pierrot Lunaire* and became interested in nonserial twelve-tone music. In 1913 Varèse moved to Paris but left almost all of his manuscripts in storage in Berlin, where they were destroyed by fire. Reportedly, those works were Romantic in style. Around 1913–14, the music of Debussy and Stravinsky interested him; Debussy's influence is evident in Varèse's works written in the 1920s and 1930s.

In 1915 Varèse came to America. He was dissatisfied with the sounds produced by conventional means, sought new resources, and wanted new musical instruments. He seldom wrote for strings because he disliked vibrato. He never liked the term "music" and called his work "organized sound." His earliest published composition, *Amériques* (Americas; c. 1918–21), requires a huge orchestra with harp, two sets of timpani, and a siren, the latter replaced in 1929 by ondes Martenot. Varèse used sirens in his works to produce long, slow glissandos and could not achieve the precise effect he wanted by other means.

In the 1920s Varèse began writing for groups of percussion and was especially interested in the effects obtainable from nonpitched percussion. Representative of his pieces for winds and percussion are *Hyperprism* (1922–23; 9 winds, 7 percussionists) and *Integrales* (1924–25; 11 winds, 4 percussionists). Most of *Ionisation* (1929–31; 13 percussionists, pno.) is for unpitched instruments; only in the last few measures are definite pitches sounded.

For some time, Varèse had been wanting electronic instruments. He knew Thérémin had invented an electronic instrument called "theremin" and c. 1932 requested him to make two of them for use in *Ecuatorial* (1932–34). However, when the composition was performed, two ondes Martenot were substituted for theremin. With electronic instruments Varèse was able to extend the range to e⁗.

After writing *Density 21.5* (1936) for Georges Barrère to play on his platinum flute, Varèse did not compose for a decade. During that time, he taught composition and orchestration in several schools and promoted performances of Renaissance and Baroque choral music in the United States. In 1947 his *Étude pour Espace* (Étude for space; chor., 2 pnos., perc.) appeared, then he lapsed into compositional silence for several years. In 1953 he acquired an Ampex tape recorder and began to collect the sounds that he used in the tape portions of *Déserts* (c. 1950–54), the earliest major composition created on tape. He completed the tape portions of the piece in Schaeffer's studio at RTF in 1954, and the composition was broadcast on French radio later that year. According to Varèse, the title refers to all deserts—on earth, in space, in city streets, and in the minds of humans. The composition contrasts sounds of conventional instruments with tapes of real (i.e., not electronically generated or otherwise artificially produced) sounds that cannot be obtained from conventional musical instruments. The sounds on magnetic tape are on two channels, transmitted stereophonically, to convey to the listener a sense of spatial distribution. The contrast of timbres makes the piece a kind of alternating form: ABABABA, the A sections being performed on conventional instruments and the B sections being taped organized sounds transmitted stereophonically. The first and last tape interpolations are organized sounds gathered from industrial sources (factories) and electronically manipulated—filtered, transposed, mixed, transmuted, and so on. Sounds for the second B section were produced by percussion ensemble. The sections become shorter, higher pitched, and more intense until a climax is attained in the last two sections; then the music fades to a *pianissimo* conclusion. The piece is atonal but not serial. Despite the lack of recognizable thematic material, there is unity and continuity in the work.

At Philips Research Laboratories in Eindhoven in 1957, Varèse created *Poème électronique* on three-track tape. The work was designed for performance in the Philips pavilion at the 1958 World Exhibition in Brussels. Spatial effects were obtained by transmitting the tape through strategically placed loudspeakers so that the listener was surrounded by sound. A control tape regulated special lighting effects that came from a variety of sources in the pavilion. *Poème électronique* was the last composition Varèse completed. After 1925, he began several pieces, using conventional means of tone production, but never finished them. Among those works are *Nocturnal* (1961; completed by one of his students in 1973) and *Nocturnal II* (1961–65). Of Varèse's output, only 14 complete pieces survive. He was highly respected by avant garde composers and was influential through his desire for new sound sources and his writing for unpitched percussion instruments.

He composed two of the earliest major compositions created on tape.

MILTON BABBITT

The interests of Babbitt (b. 1916) lie in mathematics as well as in music. Arithmetic served as a compositional tool in structuring his works. At first, he was interested in the music of Stravinsky and Varèse, then was attracted by the serialism of Schoenberg and Webern. In studying their construction of tone rows, Babbitt found that in some of them the unordered six-note set in the first hexachord of the row could be inverted and transposed, or used retrograde and transposed, and still not duplicate any of the pitches in the original hexachord. Obviously, the same would be true of the unordered six-note set in the second hexachord of the original row (ex. 27.9). The hexachords from such rows could be combined in a variety of ways and still produce a complete dodecaphonic row. Not all rows have this special property, which Babbitt termed **combinatoriality.** Schoenberg used rows of this kind in *Klavierstück,* the *Violin Concerto,* and *Variations* for orchestra. Babbitt developed the principle of combinatoriality extensively.

Babbitt's *Three Compositions for Piano,* No. 1 (1947; DWMA187), uses a row constructed so that it is **all-combinatorial**—that is, a hexachord of the original row may be combined with its transposed inversion, retrograde, or retrograde-inversion to form a complete dodecaphonic series. In this piece, Babbitt serialized rhythm and dynamics independently of the pitch series. The serialization of rhythm was based on constancy of the 16th note, and he established a rhythmic row with the arrangement of 16th-note values in groups of 5, 1, 4, 2, thus forming a 5 1 4 2 series that could be manipulated (ex. 27.10). He devised a method of inverting the rhythm series by subtraction, in this case by subtracting the numbers from 6. Thus, the inversion of his 5 1 4 2 series is 1 5 2 4, and a retrograde inversion is 4 2 5 1. *Three Compositions for Piano* provides the first real example of rhythmic serialization. Babbitt "transposed" rhythms by delaying them. *Three Compositions for Piano,* No. 1, contains six sections (marked off musically by rests or sustained pitches), the last of which is symmetrical with the first.

For *Composition for Twelve Instruments* (1948), Babbitt devised another system of rhythm serialization, using a set of 12 durations and 12-note rows. Each of the 12 instruments has its own pitch series. In *All Set* (1957), for an eight-piece jazz ensemble, Babbitt combined an all-combinatorial set with jazzlike solos.

For some time, Babbitt had been interested in the possibilities of synthesizer as an aid to musical composition, primarily because it offered absolute control of

Milton Babbitt. *(Courtesy of Milton Babbitt)*

all musical events. The fact that the synthesizer could produce new sounds was of lesser importance. When, in the 1950s, he joined RCA as composer-consultant, he became the first composer to work with the Mark II synthesizer, with which he created *Composition for Synthesizer* (1961), his first totally synthesized composition. Next came *Vision and Prayer* (1961), for soprano and synthesizer (tape). Other compositions using tape followed, including *Ensembles for Synthesizer* (1962–64), *Concerti* (1974; vln., small orch., tape), and *Ars combinatoria* (Combinatorial art; 1981).

Babbitt has not used any aspects of chance in composition or performance. His music is precise and should be performed with precision. He has indicated that he wants each of his compositions to be as much as it possibly can be; this accounts for the complexity of many of his works. He has become involved with synthesizer but has not limited his compositions to works on or including tape. *Relata I* (1965) is for a large orchestra, treated as families of timbres: four trios of woodwinds, three quartets of brass instruments, and two string sextets, one of them bowed, the other plucked. The polyphony of timbres richly enhances the serialism of that work. Other works using conventional sources are *A Solo Requiem* (1976–77; S, 2 pnos.) and *The Head of the Bed* (1982; S, fl., cl., vln., vcl.).

Among those who have been influenced by Babbitt are Peter Westergaard (b. 1931) and Charles Wuorinen (b. 1938). Some of Westergaard's pieces are quite economical, as is the *Quartet* (1960; vln., vibraphone, A cl.,

vcl.), in which the twelve-tone row governs the succession of pitches through all four lines of the polyphony. In *Variations for Six Players* (1963), he directs the performers to match sonorities through the method of attack used (e.g., violin harmonic matches glockenspiel tone). His other works include a cycle of cantatas and the chamber opera *Mr. and Mrs. Discobbolos* (1965).

Wuorinen, a virtuoso pianist and brilliant composer, has written well over 100 works, including *Symphony III* (1959) for orchestra and tape, *Concerto* (1972) for amplified violin and orchestra, a percussion symphony (1976), and numerous chamber music works. *Time's Encomium* (1969), for tape, is probably his best-known work. In it, he took full advantage of electronic means to control all musical happenings. The Mark II synthesizer at RCA was used in preparing the work, which combines pure synthesized sounds with electronically processed synthesized material supplemented by reverberation. Wuorinen ventured into theater music with the masque *The Politics of Harmony* (1966–67; ATB soloists, 12-pc. chamber orch.). Among his more recent large works are Piano Concerto No. 3 (1984), *Rhapsody* (1984; vln., orch.), the oratorio *The Celestial Sphere* (1980), and a Mass (1982). Wuorinen attempts to differentiate clearly between taped music and music for live performance. His works for conventional instruments have more grandeur and stronger rhythms than his electronic pieces.

JOHN CAGE

Cage (1912–92) studied music with Schoenberg in California and with Cowell in New York; their influence is apparent in the pieces Cage wrote in the 1930s. His early compositions are based on organized arrangements of the pitches in the chromatic scale. After he observed Cowell introducing foreign objects among the strings of a piano to produce unusual timbres, Cage became interested in **prepared piano.** For dancer Syvilla Fort (c. 1917–75) in Seattle, he composed *Bacchanale* (1938), using one prepared piano as substitute for percussion ensemble. Essentially, "preparing" a piano transforms the instrument into a kind of one-person percussion ensemble. Cage wrote *Metamorphosis* for prepared piano in 1938, then created nine works for percussion ensemble (1939–42). By 1948 Cage had written, among other things, almost three dozen works for prepared piano. *Sonatas and Interludes* (16 sonatas,

EXAMPLE 27.9 Combinatoriality in the row that Schoenberg used in *Variations* for orchestra: (*a*) Original Row; (*b*) Inversion, transposed down a minor third; (*c*) Retrograde Inversion of the transposition.

EXAMPLE 27.10 Babbitt's rhythmic row established for *Three Compositions for Piano*, No. 1.

John Cage. (© *Steve Vagan/Photo Researchers, Inc.*)

4 interludes; 1946–48) brought him several awards. The score of that work gives instructions for altering 45 of the piano's pitches to produce new, percussive sounds. Cage used a number sequence to determine rhythm in the various pieces. All the *Sonatas and Interludes* are intended to portray traditional Indian ideas of "permanent emotions"—pain, mirth, heroism, tranquility, and others. To plan the durations in the works, Cage prepared matrices. Such plans aided in unifying a piece and in avoiding metric regulation and "tyranny of the bar line."

Cage used number sequences to determine the structure of rhythm in several other works, including *String Quartet in Four Parts* (1950) and *Concerto* for prepared piano and chamber orchestra of 22 soloists (1951). In the quartet, the "parts" are the four movements, which express the American Indians' connotations of the four seasons: summer as preservation; autumn, destruction; winter, peace; and spring, creation. Much of the quartet sounds polyphonic, but Cage considered the music an unaccompanied melodic line, even though it contains triads and other aggregates of pitches produced by more than one instrument. The harmonies are not functional but are unrelated sonorities designed as elements of color. *Concerto* harmonies follow the same principle.

Meantime, Cage had studied Zen, a Buddhist philosophy, and he determined to express musically the idea of zero thought. Endeavoring to create purposeless music, he composed *Imaginary Landscape no. 4* (1951) for 12 radio receivers. So that none of his personal preferences would enter into the composition, he used the element of chance to determine the choices of wavelengths, duration, and volume (numbers on the radio dial). The choices were determined by procedures comparable with those outlined in the Chinese *I Ching: The Book of Change,* for divining answers to problems. Cage used charts based on *I Ching* and tossed three coins. Though he precisely notated the choices chance determined, he stated that his work was indeterminate of composition and indeterminate of performance, meaning that chance operations produced the score and the performers' choices (the radio receivers) produced the sounds. To this type of composition Cage applied the term **indeterminacy.** Other composers who used the element of chance or choice in their works referred to the music as **aleatory** (from Latin *alea,* dice). Another aleatory work that Cage created through *I Ching* charts and coin tossing is *Music of Changes* (1951), four volumes of piano music.

Cage wanted to produce some music in which he said nothing—music that would let silence itself speak.

Eventually he did so, with *4'33"* (1952), a piece entirely *tacet,* to be performed by one or more instrumentalists who sit in silence on the stage for 4 minutes and 33 seconds. Cage's aim was, in his words, "to let sounds be themselves in a space of time." The audience is expected to listen attentively to all sounds that occur during the allotted time span.

In 1951 Vladimir Ussachevsky (1911–90) began to experiment with electronic music at Columbia University. Cage, too, became interested in creating pieces on magnetic tape and, working in a private recording studio, applied his aleatory methods in preparing the tape compositions *Imaginary Landscape no. 5* (1952) and *Williams Mix* (1952). For *Imaginary Landscape no. 5* the source material consists of any 42 recordings. *Williams Mix* uses sounds gathered from six broad categories, such as "city sounds," "country sounds," and "wind-produced sounds." Cage used tape primarily as a means of assembling a musical collage; Ussachevsky used tape to manipulate and alter sounds as well as to record them.

Cage's next innovation was music created from "happenings"—actions and presentations, musical and nonmusical, that are simultaneous but uncoordinated. He also created "theater music," such as *Water Music* (1952), whose performance requires of a pianist actions not related to the piano (e.g., pouring water and blowing whistles that are under water). The visual events are an important part of the composition. Cage's music from "happenings" was a forerunner of the **Fluxus** movement in New York in 1960–65, which presented concerts of "music" created from unusual sources and often humorous happenings. One of the leaders of the Fluxus group was George Brecht (b. 1924), who created *Drip Music,* a live presentation consisting entirely of water dripping from a source into a container. Action/happening composition drew a satirical response from Ligeti in works such as *Poème symphonique* for 100 metronomes (see p. 650).

The idea of indeterminacy led Cage to write pieces with open form—works that allowed the performer(s) to choose the order in which movements or portions of movements were played. He wrote several groups of numbered pieces that might be performed individually or combined by one or more pianists: *Music for Piano 4–19* (1953), *Music for Piano 21–36* (1955), *Music for Piano 37–52* (1955), *Music for Piano 53–68* (1956),

and *Music for Piano 69–84* (1956). Perhaps the ultimate in work with open form is Cage's *Concert for Piano and Orchestra* (1957–58), in which: the music for each of the orchestral parts was determined by chance operations, each person chooses the pages he or she will play and the sequence in which those pages will be played, and the conductor has no score but uses his arms as the hands of a clock to indicate elapsed time.

Cage's work has been highly influential, especially with regard to chance operations and indeterminacy. He continued to write experimental music of all kinds—chance music involving the audience; action pieces for any number of people performing any kind of actions (*Variations III;* 1963); music indeterminate as to number of performers and instrumentation (*Variations II* [1961] and *IV* [1963]); and sounds derived from plants, animals, various inanimate sources, electronic means, and music of the cosmos (*Études astrales,* Star studies; 32 pieces for piano; 1974–75). Cage worked with computers in the production of highly integrated compositions. He collaborated with Lejaren Hiller (1924–94) in preparing *HPSCHD* (1967–69), to be performed on 1 to 7 amplified harpsichords and using 1 to 51 electronic tapes each played through its own amplifier. The tapes contain computer-generated sounds and may be combined in various ways to produce different arrangements. As prepared, *HPSCHD* consists of 7 harpsichord solos created from computer-generated sounds. Only the first solo is completely original music; the others use material from works by Mozart, Beethoven, Chopin, Schumann, Gottschalk, Busoni, Schoenberg, Cage, and Hiller. Not only does *HPSCHD* combine techniques of quotation, collage, and indeterminacy, but its performance becomes a multimedia event, for the music is enhanced by colored lights, films, and slides.

Why did Cage create such unusual works? Judging from remarks he made, his response to that question might have been, To affirm the reality of life and living in our world, to break down the distinctions and barriers between art and living, to make persons realize that we are surrounded by sounds and that everything we do is music.

On 13 May 1993 the Wexner Prize, presented annually to the contemporary artist(s) whose "highly original and influential work has consistently challenged convention," was awarded jointly to John Cage and choreographer Merce Cunningham (b. 1919), whose artistic collaboration lasted almost 50 years.

PAULINE OLIVEROS

From childhood, Oliveros (b. 1932) has been intrigued by all kinds of sounds and, in her compositions, has sought new sonorities, even subliminal ones. Her earliest works were for conventional instruments, but she wrote unconventional harmonies. Soon, she became interested in electronic music. The San Francisco Tape Music Center was established in 1959, and in 1961 Oliveros participated in musical experiments there. In 1966–67 she was director of the Center. Between 1961 and 1967, Oliveros created a great deal of electronic music. Not all her electronic pieces have been produced through studio techniques—several of her works have involved live electronics. *I of IV* (1966) could be performed live, for it was created on tape in "real" time (i.e., without tape editing or splicing). To compose that work she connected 12 oscillators to a keyboard, amplified and reverberated the sounds, and used two tape recorders to produce double feedback loops and time delays.

Pauline Oliveros. *(1979 photograph, © Becky Cohen)*

In *Sound Patterns* (1961), a textless choral work, Oliveros explored various vocal techniques in the production of sound masses. Some of her works, written with the intent of inducing sonic meditation, are filled with vocalizations that vary from quiet murmuring to exuberant ululation. In her search for the unusual, she ventured into action (happening) music and theatrical scenes, requiring musicians to assume all kinds of nonmusical roles, from being page turners and piano movers to barking like dogs. Most of Oliveros's works are in mixed media, combining theater, art, and music to create unusual scenic events. For a short time during the 1960s, her mixed media works seemed to be carrying activities to extremes, bordering on the ridiculous. In the early 1970s, she introduced a psychic element into her works. Since 1975 most of her writing has been for voices and instruments without electronics, but she has not abandoned electronic music composition.

JEAN EICHELBERGER IVEY

Ivey (b. 1923), founder and director of the electronic music studio at the Peabody Conservatory, has composed works in various styles—tonal, Neoclassic, dodecaphonic, and electronic—and in most media, vocal and instrumental, solo and ensemble, including music for films and television. Influences of the music of Ravel and Bartók are audible in several of her works, electronic as well as conventional. Some of Ivey's electronic pieces are for tape alone, as are *Continuous Form* (1969), a work of indeterminate length, and *Pinball* (1965), whose material was derived entirely from pinball machine sounds. In other works she combined tape and live performance, including *Testament of Eve* (1976; Mez., orch., tape), *Sea-Change* (1982; orch., tape), and *Terminus* (1986; Mez., tape).

Testament of Eve is based on the biblical story of Eve and the Tree of Knowledge. Ivey said that she depicted Eve as a heroic woman who chose "knowledge and growth for herself and her children instead of remaining a pampered pet in the Garden of Eden." The (taped) voice of Lucifer, disembodied and coming out of turbulent winds, represents also Eve's awareness of her self and her awakened desire for personal growth. The words Eve sings were written by Ivey.

Sea-Change was based on several lines from one of Ariel's songs in Shakespeare's *The Tempest*:

Full fathom five thy father lies;
   Of his bones are coral made;
Those are pearls that were his eyes;
   Nothing of him that doth fade
But doth suffer a sea-change
Into something rich and strange.

Taped electronic sounds enter the piece four times, sometimes mingling with the orchestral playing, sometimes sounding alone. The taped music is transmitted through four loudspeakers placed in the four corners of the hall so that the audience is surrounded by music. The sounds resemble water, seabirds, bells tolling under water, and fairy voices and are intended to represent some of the rich changes wrought by the sea. Some of the electronic sounds resemble textless choral singing, but the piece contains no actual singing. The music, which is a changing kaleidoscope of delicate colors, is basically quiet and contemplative but works up to one major climax. Some passages reflect the influence of Debussy and Ravel.

Nonelectronic works by Ivey include the SATB *a cappella* motets *Lord, Hear my Prayer, O Come Bless the Lord,* and *Entreat me not to Leave Thee* and the song cycle *Woman's Love* (Sara Teasdale poems; Mez., pno.).

Italy—Luciano Berio

The works of Berio (b. 1925) exhibit a variety of musical styles including (among others) twelve-tone serialism, electronic music, multimedia, and eclecticism. In his early works, for example, *Due pezzi* (Two pieces; 1951; vln., pno.), he followed the standard 12-note serial procedures. Then he began to treat serialism freely; his String Quartet (1956) is an example of this.

In 1955, Berio joined Bruno Maderna at Studio di Fonologia, Milan, and experimented with electronic music techniques. From 1956 to 1960 Berio edited the publication *Incontri musicali* and, with Maderna, managed the *Incontri musicali* concert series. At Studio di Fonologia Berio created *Thema: Omaggio a Joyce* (Theme: Homage to Joyce; 1958; 2-track tape), based on a portion of Joyce's *Ulysses*. *Thema* commences with spoken recitation of the complete text, unaltered. The remainder of the work is a development of that material through tape manipulations of the words

out of context and filtering to suppress overtones and change timbres. A cadential effect is achieved through soft hissing sounds. In *Circles* (1960; voice, harp, 2 percussionists), there is a mixture of spoken and sung text, of meaningful words and phonetic sounds, and of physical gestures. The piece was written for American vocalist Cathy Berberian (1928–83), whom Berio considered the best interpreter of his vocal music. (From 1950 to 1966 Berberian and Berio were married.)

In 1961 Berio moved to the United States, where he taught and worked with synthesizers and computers at Columbia University and Bell Telephone Company Laboratories. In 1972 he returned to Italy, where he continued research, composed for television, and served as artistic director of Accademia Filarmonica Romana. In 1958–85. Berio composed a series of virtuosic solo works entitled *Sequenza* (Sequence) for conventional instruments. The first was for flute; the series continued with pieces for harp, female voice, piano, trombone, viola, oboe, violin, clarinet, saxophone, trumpet, and guitar. The solos for violin and clarinet present a melodic theme and variations. As counterparts of the *Sequenza* pieces, Berio has begun a series entitled *Chemins* (Paths) for solo instrument and small orchestra, each *Chemins* based on a *Sequenza*. *Chemins V* (1980) is for clarinet and electronics.

Sinfonia (1968; mvt. 5 added 1969; 8 solo vcs., orch.) contains a variety of textual quotations and numerous recognizable musical ones, sometimes mingled. In the middle movement, Berio quoted the entire Scherzo from Mahler's Symphony No. 2 as basic material but, with it, uses material from other composers' works. The movement is, in a way, a kind of historical résumé—a presentation of excerpts from compositions written during the previous two and a half centuries—woven into the fabric of Mahler's Scherzo according to Berio's plan. By comparison, Berio's treatment of voices and instruments in the first and last movements of *Sinfonia* seem to be references to music's primitive stages.

Berio's later works confirm that he is still writing in several styles and for different media. Among these works are Concerto for piano and orchestra (1977), *Coro* (1975–76; 40-vc. chor., 40-pc. orch.), *Duo* (1977; violin/'cello), *Chants parallèle* (1974–75; tape), and two operas (*La vera storia*, 1972; *Un re in ascolto,*

1984) in which he explores ways in which stories can be told musically. *La vera storia* (The true story) includes acrobats and features textless music for soprano soloist.

COMPOSERS WORKING OUTSIDE ELECTRONICS

Not all composers were intrigued by electronic music. Some did not subscribe to any avant-garde techniques. Others, like George Crumb, obtained new sounds by ingenious choices of sound sources and unusual combinations of instruments: mingling Occidental and Oriental instruments from various cultures (Japanese, Chinese, Tibetan, Balinese, African), adapting conventional instruments (prepared piano), including toys (toy piano), instruments sometimes considered "primitive rural" or "backwoods" (harmonica), and household tools (musical saw) and other objects usually considered nonmusical. György Ligeti created unusual sound masses with voices. Still other composers, such as Thea Musgrave, have written a few electronic pieces but have relied basically on conventional means of sound production.

GEORGE CRUMB

Crumb (b. 1929) received much of his musical training at home, began composing while still in school, and heard some of his earliest works performed by the Charleston, West Virginia, Symphony. He continued his music study in college, then began teaching piano and composition. He cites Debussy, Bartók, and Mahler as major influences in his music. In his vocal works, Crumb has set mainly verses by Frederico García Lorcá (1899–1936) and regards these settings as an extended cycle. Crumb's vocal music is exceptionally demanding, requiring the vocalist to sing microintervals as well as very wide leaps, to produce special sound effects (by tongue clicking, singing through a tube or into the piano, shrieking, hissing, and so on) and unusual timbres (imitate various muted trumpet sounds) and to sing and shout phonemes and nonsense syllables. An example is *Ancient Voices of Children* (1970), a song cycle for soprano, boy soprano, oboe, mandolin, harp, electric

piano, and toy piano. In some pieces, Crumb included quotations from well-known works by other composers; he did this in *Ancient Voices of Children*. *Black Angels: 13 Images from the Dark Land* (1970; amplified string quartet) is a kind of parable, with God and the devil in polarity, and incorporates such musical associations as *diabolus in musica* (the tritone), the *Dies irae* in chant, Tartini's *Trillo di diavolo* (Devil's Trill, vln./pno. sonata), and, from numerology, the numbers 7 and 13.

Performers are spatially separated for some of Crumb's pieces. *Star-Child* (1977), for soprano, two antiphonal choirs of children, male speaking choir, bell ringers, and huge orchestra, requires coordination of four conductors.

Crumb wrote four volumes entitled *Makrokosmos* (cf., Boethius, p. 22; Bartók, *Mikrokosmos*, p. 585). Volumes I and II are each subtitled *12 Fantasy-Pieces after the Zodiac,* the first volume for piano (1972), the second for amplified piano (1973). Volume III, *Music for a Summer Evening* (1974), is for two amplified pianos and percussion; Volume IV, *Celestial Mechanics* (1979), for amplified piano, four hands, constitutes cosmic dances. Among his later works are *Processional for Piano* (1983) and *A Haunted Landscape* (orch.; 1984).

Crumb designed several works for virtuoso mezzo-soprano Jan DeGaetani (1933–89), who was internationally acclaimed for her ability to sing unusual intervals accurately, to produce the finest gradations of dynamic nuances, and to interpret texts with keen insight. She recorded several of Crumb's compositions, including *Ancient Voices of Children* and *Apparition* (1979; S, pno.; DWMA188), based on Whitman's *When Lilacs Last in the Dooryard Bloom'd.*

THEA MUSGRAVE

Musgrave (b. 1928), who studied with Boulanger in 1950–54, wrote her earliest compositions in predominantly diatonic harmonies. After filling commissions for vocal works in Scotland in 1953–54, she became interested in opera. Her chamber opera, *The Abbott of Drimock* (1955) is in conventional nineteenth-century lyrical style. Gradually, Musgrave's music became more chromatic and more abstract, and by 1960 she was writing serial music. Many of her works in the

1960s are instrumental—solos, accompanied solos, chamber music, and orchestral pieces. Opera interested her greatly, and in 1964–65 she composed *The Decision* (perf. 1967). Since then, most of her compositions have been commissioned instrumental works. Perhaps the most significant of these are the Horn Concerto (1971) and the Viola Concerto (1973). Only occasionally has she included tape in her works: *Soliloquy* (1969; guitar, tape), *From One to Another* (1970, vla., tape; 2d version, vla., stgs., 1979–80), and the ballet *Orfeo* (1975; dancer, flute, tape).

The three-act opera *Mary, Queen of Scots* (Musgrave libretto) was commissioned by the Scottish Opera for the 1977 Edinburgh Festival. In 1978–79 Musgrave wrote the two-act opera *A Christmas Carol*. Her finest opera is *Harriet, The Woman Called 'Moses'* (1984), the story of Harriet Tubman (1820–1913), "conductor" of the Underground Railroad network used by slaves seeking transportation into free territory. Musgrave had heard a group of black singers perform in New York in 1980 and wanted to write an opera for them. The opportunity came when she received a joint commission from London Royal Opera and Virginia Opera Association. She incorporated well-known black songs, such as *Go down, Moses*, into the opera. The work is remarkable for Musgrave's ability to set the black speech patterns correctly. At times, the slave chorus participates in the action; at other times, it stands at the side and offers comment, as did the citizens chorus in ancient Greek plays. The opera contains some dancing and requires a large orchestra.

GYÖRGY LIGETI

From 1945–49 Hungarian composer Ligeti (b. 1929) was a student at the Budapest Academy of Music. For the next year, he did field research in Rumanian folk music, then returned to the Academy as professor of harmony, counterpoint, and analysis. He became interested in serialism as practiced by Schoenberg and Webern and began to develop an individualistic style of composition. Until the death of Stalin, political conditions in Hungary prevented publication or performance of some of his most adventuresome works. Only the pieces he based on folk or peasant songs were acceptable. Most of the music Ligeti composed in 1945–56 is tonal, though he seldom used key signatures. Typi-

cal of his writing in the 1950s are the choruses *Éjszaka* (Night; SSAATTBB; 1955; DWMA189) and *Reggel* (Morning; S, Mez., ATB; 1955). *Éjszaka* uses a theme that commences as a C-major scale and is treated as canon at the unison at the distance of one measure, a procedure that produces a long procession of cluster chords through most of the piece. The composition closes with a C-major chord sung *ppp*. Three things present in *Éjszaka* became characteristic of Ligeti's compositional style: clusters, extremely soft sustained chords, and canon.

After the Russian invasion of Hungary in 1956, Ligeti worked in the Westdeutscher Rundfunk electronic music studios in Cologne. He composed very few pieces on tape; he was more interested in the avant-garde extensions of serialism, but, eventually, he concluded that serial principles were self-defeating. He focused on the development of musical textures to the extent that the importance of other elements of music was pushed into the background in several of his works. In the orchestral pieces *Apparitions* (1959) and *Atmosphères* (1961) he concentrated on chromatic complexes, with pitches in sustained clusters, and avoided any feeling of harmony, rhythmic pulse, or definite durations. However, the scores for these works are in precise conventional notation.

The most characteristic features of Ligeti's works are clusters and "clouds"—the whisperlike *ppp* and *pppp* sustained chords and passages marked *pppppp*. His use of clusters was highly influential in the work of other composers during the 1960s and 1970s, for example, Penderecki's use of "sound masses."

Ligeti uses canon often. It is an important structural factor in some sections of his Requiem Mass (1963–65), and his choral *Lux aeterna* (1966) is constructed entirely as strict canon. There are clusters in the Requiem, and there is evidence that harmony was a definite consideration, but for the most part it is well concealed and surfaces only momentarily.

Harmonies are evident in *Lontano* (Distant; orch.; 1967). *Mélodien* (Melodies; small orch.; 1971) contains many small melodies that appear fleetingly. In several works Ligeti used microtones: *Ramifications* (1968–69) for two groups of string instruments tuned a quarter tone apart, String Quartet No. 2 (1968), and the Double Concerto for flute and oboe with orchestra (1972).

Ligeti was aware of new developments in other composers' music. Those with which he disagreed or of which he disapproved he sometimes satirized, as in *Poème symphonique* (1962) for 100 metronomes, whose different metrical tickings become quite complex layers at times. Ligeti recognized some new techniques, such as minimalism (see p. 653), by incorporating them in one or more of his works. Though Ligeti had arrived at the technique of frequent repetition independently, he paid tribute to the work of American minimalists in the central piece of the triptych *Monument—Selbstporträt mit Reich und Riley (und Chopin ist auch dabei)—Bewegung* (Monument—Self-portrait with Reich and Riley, and Chopin is also near—Movement; 2 pnos.; 1976), in which small bits of music are repeated incessantly and blur the harmonies. Numerous repeated figurations in the first part of *Bewegung* conceal some canon, and the movement concludes with a chorale that is an eight-voice mirror canon.

Though Ligeti stated that he would not write a traditional opera because he considered opera incompatible with late twentieth-century music, he did write a work for performance in an opera house (*"Opernhaus Stück"*). Several analysts consider that opera house piece, *Le grand macabre* (The great gruesome [one]; 1974–77), quite close to a traditional opera. Ligeti has begun an opera, *The Tempest* (1985–).

Ligeti's significance lies in the fact that he moved away from the areas that attracted the attention of many avant-garde composers—serialism and expansions thereof and electronic music—into other technical developments that have influenced a younger generation of composers.

KRZYSTOF PENDERECKI

Penderecki (b. 1933), of Poland, attracted attention in 1958 with *Psalmy Dawida* (Psalms of David; chorus, perc.) and *Strophe* (Strophes; reciter, sop., 10 instrs.), a multilingual work with texts taken from the Bible, Omar Khayyám, Sophocles, and Menander. International recognition came in 1960 after performances of *Anaklasis* for 42 strings and percussion and *Tren pamieci ofiarom Hiroszimy* (Threnody in memory of victims of Hiroshima) for 52 stringed instruments. *Threnody* is filled with sound masses and concludes on a massive two-octave tone cluster. The music focuses on textures and timbres; many of the sonorities are

expressively agonizing. The performers are asked to produce sounds by unconventional means, for example, by rubbing, tapping, or snapping fingertips against the body of the instrument or obtaining extremely high pitches by stopping a string between fingerboard and bridge.

Many of Penderecki's compositions are large works for vocal soloists, chorus, and orchestra and are liturgical or on religious subjects. He seems to favor topics with dramatic situations characterized by mourning, conflict, or victory. Among his liturgical text settings are *Stabat mater* (1962; 3 choruses), *Dies irae* (1967; solo vcs., chor., orch.), *De profundis* (1977; chor., orch.), *Te Deum* (1979; solo vcs., chor., orch.), and a *Magnificat* (1973–74; bass solo, boys' chor., chor., orch.). The *Dies irae* concerns the Auschwitz killings during World War II. Penderecki's music is more restrained in *Passio et mors domini nostri Jesu Christi secundum Lucam* (1963–65). *Utrenja* (Morning prayer; 1970–71) is a two-part work: (1) *Zlozeni* (The laying in the tomb) and (2) *Zmartwychwstanie* (The Resurrection). *Utrenja* is based on Orthodox liturgy and contains some quotations of Orthodox chant; its text is in old Slavonic. In several large-scale vocal works, Penderecki effectively mingled materials from Roman and Orthodox liturgies, texts in ancient and modern languages, and sources as diverse as ancient Greek plays, prisoners' letters, and astronauts' comments. His

Krzystof Penderecki. *(Courtesy of Chicago Lyric Opera)*

music is designed to be dramatic, and he exploits all available sonic resources.

In the early 1960s and again in the early 1970s, Penderecki prepared a few pieces on tape, then abandoned that kind of composition. *Concerto for Violino Grande and Orchestra* (1967) requires a specially constructed five-string violin. His other concerti are for conventional instruments: a violin concerto (1976), two 'cello concerti (1972, 1981–82), and a viola concerto (1982–83). *Partita* (1971) features solo harpsichord and four electrically amplified solo instruments with chamber orchestra. In 1973 he wrote his first symphony; his second, *Christmas Symphony* (1979–80), was first performed in New York on 1 May 1980. Penderecki's stage works include the opera *Diably z Loudun* (The devils of Loudun; 1968); *Paradise Lost* (1975–78), a *sacra rappresentazione* after John Milton's (1608–74) epic poem; and the opera *Ubu roi* (King Ubu; 1985–91).

Paradise Lost was written for the Chicago Lyric Opera Company, which gave its world première on 27 November 1978. The fact that Penderecki labeled the work *sacra rappresentazione* links it with Cavalieri's allegorical *Rappresentatione di anima, et di corpo* (1600). In *Paradise Lost,* Sin and Death are personified as offspring of Satan. *Paradise Lost* is as much oratorio as opera. Though staged as an opera, with scenery, costumes, acting, and ballet, some scenes resemble tab-

leaux, and the role of John Milton, designed to be spoken rather than sung, is that of a narrator explaining the circumstances for and events in his poem. The man portraying Milton also proclaims the words of God, who, unseen, speaks through dazzling light to create, admonish, command, and condemn. The roles of Adam and Eve are double, each requiring a dancer and a singer; both pairs may be on stage at the same time (fig. 27.4a). The chorus participates in the drama as unseen voices, a celestial chorus, Satan's fallen angels, and an angelic guard moving through Eden, and also sings from two scaffolding towers positioned at the sides of the stage. In fact, the choral portions are the finest music in the composition. Performing forces for the work are colossal: a chorus of 100, a children's choir of 35, a 90-piece orchestra, 45 dancers, and 20 soloists. The music is a mixture of tonality and atonality, with some borrowings from chant, Bach, and Wagner. The scenery is minimal—a huge glass dome rises and falls as needed, and the action occurs either on a bare dark stage or in clouds of smoke from hell (fig. 27.4b).

Three other Polish composers whose careers were delayed or otherwise inhibited by political upheaval were Witold Lutosławski (1913–94), Andrzej Panufnik (b. 1914), and Henryk Górecki (b. 1933). The styles of all three men are more or less individualistic, and many of their works show the influence of folk

(a)

(b)

FIGURE 27.4 Two scenes from Penderecki's opera *Paradise Lost:* (*a*) Adam and Eve, double roles, with both pairs on stage at the same time; (*b*) stage setting using the huge glass dome. 1978 performance, Chicago Lyric Opera. *(Courtesy of Chicago Lyric Opera)* music. Lutosławski, who worked with Panufnik for a time, first wrote diatonic melodies based on folk music and used nonfunctional harmony; later, he employed dodecaphonic serial techniques but allowed one chord to predominate. Panufnik's *Sinfonia sacra* (1963) commemorates the millenium of Christianity in Poland; its four movements constitute three Visions and a Hymn, the latter based on and quoting *Bodzurodzica,* a chant sung in church and on the battlefield.

SPAIN

Culturally and politically, for two decades Spain was virtually isolated from the rest of the world, first because of the Spanish Civil War, then by Fascist ideology, World War II, and a blockade. Thereafter, musical institutions had to be rebuilt, new faculties assembled, and orchestras and choral groups reestablished. For a time there was increased interest in nationalism, then came a return to eighteenth-century Neoclassicism (neo-Scarlatti) as viewed by aristocracy. A number of composers claimed to follow de Falla's style but actually were following that of earlier composers; some persons combined careers as performers or teachers with composing. Barcelona and Madrid are the only cities with stable musical structure. Government-supported Orquesta Nacional and Orquesta Sinfónica de Radiotelevision Español (RTVE) have replaced Madrid's two former orchestras; chamber music groups are privately supported. Among the significant composers active in the late twentieth century are Cristóbal Halffter, Luis de Pablo, Miguel Angel Coria, and Miguel Roig-Francolí.

Cristóbal Halffter (b. 1930), nephew of Ernesto, studied at the Madrid Conservatory, taught composition there in 1962, and in 1964 became its director. In 1966 he resigned to concentrate on composition and conducting and has been successful internationally. In 1993 he was director of the electronic studio at the Südwestfunk, Freiburg, Germany. Halffter's early works are traditional and are Spanish in flavor. After much reflection, he turned to avant-garde styles—to dodecaphonic and serial music in the Violin Sonata (1959) and *Cinco Microformas* (1960) and to aleatory in *Formantes* (1961; 2 pnos.). In a number of works he expressed his concern for human, political, or social conditions, including *Yes, Speak Out* (1968; soloists, 2 chor., 2 orch.,

2 conductors), commissioned by the United Nations. Representative of his chamber music are *Oda* (1969; chmbr. orch.) and *Fibonacciana* (1969; fl., orch.). In the area of church music, he composed *Officium defunctorum* (Office for the dead; 1978; soloists, chor., orch.). *Jarchas de dolor de ausencia* (Jarchas of sorrow and absence; 1978; chor.) concerns popular strophic medieval Arabic poems and songs; flamenco elements are present in *Debla* (1981; fl.) and *Tiento* (1981; orch.). Though Halffter's music is complex, it is highly expressive.

Luis de Pablo (b. 1930), a very prolific composer, considered composition "an activity for investigation and invention" and wrote in a variety of styles. His early works are traditional; then he turned to atonality and serialism, for example, in *Cuatro invenciones* (Four inventions; 1955; rev. 1960, 1962; orch.), and to expressionism in *Ein Wort* (A word; 1965). In the mid-1960s, in a series of five works titled *Módulo,* he worked with modules, or "closed units of autonomous expressive meaning," that could be combined; that technique led to aleatory music in two works named *Imaginario* (1967). Next he combined preexisting modules with citations from works by other composers, for example, *Quasi una fantasia* (1969; orch.), for which Schoenberg's *Verklärte Nacht* was background. *Vielleicht* (1973; perc. ens.), based on a Beethoven Bagatelle, is lovely. Pablo's two piano concertos (1979) differ in style, degree of difficulty, accompanying ensembles, and concentration but are complementary. Pablo taught composition at the University of New York, Buffalo, in 1973–74 and at the University of Ottawa in 1975–76 and is currently on the faculty at Madrid Conservatory.

Miguel Angel Coria (b. 1937) was not a prolific composer and seemed to prefer writing small-scale works. His early compositions exhibit the conciseness and symmetry of Webern's music; then he became interested in the expressive possibilities of timbres. Representative of his early works are *Juego de densidades* (Game of densities; 1962; pno.) and *Interacción* (1963). In 1966 he studied at the State University of Utrecht, became interested in electronic music, and composed such works as *Collage* (1967) and *Joyce's Portrait* (1968). When he returned to Spain, Coria taught private lessons, worked professionally in television, and served as a director of several music organizations.

One of Spain's most promising young composers in the late 1970s and early 1980s, Miguel Roig-Francolí (b. 1953), a native of Ibíza, studied composition with Miguel Angel Coria and, along with his teacher, was a pioneer in the return to consonant harmonic music in Spain. Sometimes referred to as "neotonality" or "neomodality," this music aimed to express beauty of sound through the use of consonant harmonies that were not bound by the rules of functional Romantic harmonic theory. Expressive harmonies, colorful timbres, and harmonic counterpoint are features of Miguel's compositions. His most significant works are *Quasi variazioni* (1979; chamber ensemble), *Cinco piezas para orquesta* (Five pieces for orchestra; 1980), and the *Cantata on Dante's Vita nuova* (Cantata on Dante's New Life; Bar., chor., orch.; 1983), written for and performed by the Spanish National Orchestra and Chorus. The music of *Cinco piezas* was the basis for the ballet *La Espera* (The Awaiting; 1987; choreographed by Ray Barra), which is frequently performed by the National Ballet of Spain. In 1982 Miguel came to the United States to pursue graduate studies in music theory at Indiana University at Bloomington, where he earned his doctorate, and is currently teaching music theory at the Eastman School of Music.

MINIMALISM

Minimalism is the name given to the style of music that is characterized by the repetition of short figures, tonal harmony, slow harmonic rhythm, and more or less regular pulsation. A minimal amount of musical material is used, but the composition may be quite long. La Monte Young (b. 1935) is considered the founder of minimalism. Since c. 1964, his music has been characterized by repetitive figures, static harmonies, and just intonation.

Some minimal works consist entirely of prolonged chanting on one note, such as Philip Corner's (b. 1933) *Om Breath*. In other pieces, a single figure or a single measure is reiterated numerous times. One of the best-known minimal works is Terry Riley's (b. 1935) *In C* (1964), for an ensemble of an unspecified number of musicians, including piano. The work is both minimal and aleatoric. The notated score comprises 53 small figures (ex. 27.11); the piano part, not notated, consists entirely of the pulsation of eighth-note octaves

EXAMPLE 27.11 First six figures (the first line of the score) of Riley's *In C*. *(Copyright 1964 by Terry Riley. Reprinted by permission.)*

drummed out on the top two C's of the keyboard. Against this background, each member of the ensemble plays the 53 minimal motives "in sync with the pulse," moving consecutively from 1 through 53. Each player decides for himself when to move from figure to figure, where to place the primary accent, and how often to repeat each figure. Performance time of the piece varies from 45 to 90 minutes. (Available recording, ARG 430 380.) In *Poppy Nogood's Phantom Band* (1966), short fragments played on soprano saxophone are repeated by means of tape loops—one saxophonist's playing forms the "band."

Philip Glass (b. 1937), in his harmonically static works, not only reiterates motives but, after several repetitions of a figure, lengthens or shortens it by the addition or deletion of a rhythmic unit. Such is the case in *Music in Similar Motion* (1969; ex. 27.12). Glass's early minimal works are characterized by parallel motion—chord streams, and passages in octaves or fifths that resemble ninth-century organum, (e.g., *Music in Fifths* [1970]). Later works, such as *Music with Changing Parts* (1974), exhibit greater harmonic variety. Since 1975 Glass has concentrated on music for dance, film, and theater. Among his several operas are *Satyagraha* (1980), *The Photographer* (1982), *Akhnaten* (1983), and *The Voyage* (1992). The latter was commissioned by the Metropolitan Opera and premiered on Columbus Day 1992. Glass's science-fiction music drama *1000 Airplanes on the Roof*, commissioned for the Donau Festival, was premiered at Vienna International Airport, Hangar 3, on 15 July 1988. In the 1990s, Glass seems to be turning away from minimalism. He has been working with film, on a Cocteau trilogy: *Orfée* was the first; *La belle et la bête* (Beauty and the beast; 1994) was the second, using film and live music; and *Les enfants terribles* is projected to be film, dance, and theater related.

The extensive repetition of small figures in ostinato fashion can also be found in nonminimal works.

EXAMPLE 27.12 Four excerpts from Glass: *Music in Similar Motion*. In performance, each motivic unit is repeated until the composer signals his ensemble to proceed to the next unit. Units 2 and 3 contain all notes of the previous unit and add several notes.

John Williams's *Scherzo for* TODAY, commissioned by NBC for use as theme music for the *Today* television program, is an example. The reiterated motives serve at times as vamp preceding a melody, at other times as background for a melody.

STEVE REICH

Reich (b. 1936) is one of the principal exponents of minimalism. At the beginning of his career, he was interested in jazz and drumming and studied African music and Balinese gamelan music. Then he worked with tape loops and became fascinated with possibilities involved in repetition, especially **phase shifting,** which places parts out of synchronization. For example, tape 1 and tape 2, containing the same material, are lined up to commence in unison; then tape 2 is gradually moved out of phase (out of synchronization) with tape 1 so that tape 2 lags farther and farther behind. Reich used phase shifting with tape loops containing a few spoken words in *It's Gonna Rain* (1965). Through such shifting, the continuity of the individual line disappears; what remains audible are isolated elements being repeated. In 1967 Reich transferred the phase shifting idea to music performed on conventional instruments, in *Piano Phase* and *Violin Phase* (ex. 27.13). Reich next applied his phase shifting idea to canon, treating the melodic lines as though they were tapes moving out of phase with one another. This occurs in *Tehillim* (Psalms; 3 sopranos, 1 alto, orch.; 1981), a setting of four passages from Psalms, in Hebrew. The work is in four sections, the first and last of which contain canonic vocal passages that simulate phasing (DWMA190).

Reich's interest in repetitive figures and patterns led him to minimalism and a considerably reduced harmonic vocabulary in a work. He has created compositions from a single chord (*Four Organs;* 1970) or from a few words (*Come Out;* 1966). Reich referred to some

EXAMPLE 27.13 Excerpt from Reich: *Violin Phase*, showing the effect of phase shifting. *(Reich VIOLIN PHASE © Copyright 1979 by Universal Edition (London) Ltd., London. All Rights Reserved. Used by permission of European American Music Distributors Corporation, sole U.S. and Canadian agent for Universal Edition, London.)*

of his music as being related to that of Pérotin and the *ars antiqua* of the Notre Dame school. Indeed, some of Reich's parallelisms sound like Pérotin's organum.

During the 1970s, Reich turned to writing more melodic music, including submelodies within repetitive patterns. His music has evidenced a greater interest in tonality of a new, nonfunctional kind. For a time during the 1970s he abandoned electronic music in favor of writing for conventional instruments, for example, *Variations for Winds, Strings, and Keyboards* (1979; small orch.; 1980, full orch.) and *Octet* (1979; str. qrt., 2 pnos., 2 cls. doubling on bass cl. and fl.). He did not completely forego composition on tape, however; *Vermont Counterpoint* (1982) is for 11 flutes, 10 of them recorded on tape. Reich's compositions of the mid-1980s include *The Desert Music* (1983; chor., orch.), *Music for Percussion and Keyboards* (1984), and *New York Counterpoint* (1985), juxtaposing two small ensembles (cl., b.cl., tape / cls., b.cls.).

AFTER 1970

During the 1970s, changes took place in composers' attitudes toward music. There was still a search for the new and different, and experimentation never ceased. Serial music was still being written, but it was no longer a dominant force, and in 1977 Messiaen stated that it was "over and done with." For a time, it seemed that serialism would be replaced by minimalism, for minimalism gained adherents. Its influence can be seen in the use of repetitive material by composers whose work cannot be specifically classed as minimalism. Yet, some composers are turning from minimalism and seem to be seeking new techniques.

The compositions of John Adams (b. 1947) provide several examples of various uses of minimalist features: the lyric *Phrygian Gates* (1977; pno.), whose repeated figures continually modulate to different modes; *Shaker Loops* (1978; str. septet); and *Harmonielehre* (1985; orch.), a three-movement work that, in addition to the repetitive figures of minimalism, evidences the influence of Schoenberg's *Gurre-Lieder* and Sibelius's symphonies. *Harmonium* (1980; chor., orch.) uses poetry by John Donne and Emily Dickinson; *El Dorado* is "an orchestral landscape." Adams's opera *Nixon in China* (1987), depicting Nixon's historic meeting with the Chinese government, was followed by *The Death of Klinghoffer* (1991), relating the 1985 hijacking of the cruise ship Achille Lauro and the murder of American tourist Leon Klinghoffer. In the latter opera, distinct characterization is avoided to present collective identity of participants; Adams conveys "shared expression, shared grief, and shared hope" through soliloquies rather than dramatization. The chorus is important.

A number of composers were eclectic, choosing from styles of all centuries and mingling traits from different stylistic movements and eras. Philip Glass's combination of minimalism with the parallelism of medieval organum is one example; others are Penderecki's and Musgrave's treatment of opera chorus in the manner of the citizens chorus in ancient Greek drama. Frequently, composers quoted from the works of others, as Ives had done. Crumb and Berio are eclectic composers who have used quotation extensively in major works.

Another eclectic is Ellen Taaffe Zwilich (b. 1939), whose music reflects the influence of jazz, Bartók, Berg, and Stravinsky. In 1972 Zwilich abandoned her orchestral violinist career to become a professional composer. By 1975 her works had attracted attention, particularly *Symposium* (1973; orch.) and *String Quartet* (1974). In 1983 her *Symphony No. 1: 3 Movements for Orchestra* (1982) was awarded a Pulitzer Prize. In *Concerto Grosso 1985* (DWMA191), commissioned to commemorate the 300th anniversary of Handel's birth,

Zwilich quoted the entire first movement of Handel's Sonata in D major (vln., hpschd.) and combined Baroque and twentieth-century styles. She has composed several concerti, including *Concerto for Flute and Orchestra* (1990) and *Concerto for Violin, Violoncello, and Orchestra* (1991).

The early works of Joan Tower (b. 1938) rely on serial techniques, for example, *Hexachords* (1972; fl.), based on a six-tone unordered chromatic series. After 1975 her works are more lyrical, as in *Wings* (1981; cl.), inspired by a falcon's flight. Ascending passages are a feature of *Silver Ladders* (1986), written for the St. Louis Symphony. Tower acknowledged the influence of Beethoven and Stravinsky by writing *Piano Concerto: Homage to Beethoven* (1985) and *Petroushskates* (1980; fl., cl., vln., vcl., pno.). Her several concerti include *Concerto for Orchestra* (1991) for the St. Louis Symphony and the brief (18 min.) *Violin Concerto* (1992), "a fantasy for violin and orchestra" dedicated to Elmar Oliviera. Other works by Tower are *Sequoia* (1991; orch.); four pieces entitled *Fanfare for the Uncommon Woman* (I, 1986; II, 1989; III, 1991; IV, 1992); *Night Fields* (1994; stg. qrt.), which makes reference to Bartók's quartets; and *Ducts*, which she commences with pairs of instruments and gradually adds others to form a small orchestra.

Gradually, more emphasis has been placed on melody and on tonality, but it is a different kind of tonality from that of the nineteenth century. The first and fifth scale degrees no longer possess the tonal pull, the functional direction they held in traditional key tonality. Instead, chordlike arpeggiations of pitches form harmonies that succeed one another without the feeling that functional relationships exist between them. Pieces are written without designation of a "key tonality," but tonal centers appear within the work, and movement from one tonal center to another is achieved without the traditional processes of modulation. However, some composers still use diatonic harmonies and key tonality as they were used traditionally.

The term *Neoromanticism* has been used to describe many composers' return to the forms and genres used during the Romantic period, to a greater emphasis on melody, and to the appearance of tonal centers within the music. Among the Americans writing Neoromantic music is David Del Tredici (b. 1937). He was trained as a concert pianist, and his early compositions are for keyboard. During 1959–66 he wrote mainly settings of James Joyce's poetry, with music that is Expressionistic and highly dissonant and uses canon and palindromes. In 1968, when he was inspired by Lewis Carroll's (1832–98) *Alice's Adventures in Wonderland* (1865) and *Through the Looking-Glass* (1871), Del Tredici's style changed, primarily because of the nineteenth-century style of Carroll's writing. To balance that writing style, Del Tredici wrote Neoromantic music that has some resemblance to R. Strauss's orchestral style but with strong dissonances. In the "Alice" compositions written between 1968 and 1976, to reflect Carroll's puns and word play Del Tredici juxtaposed soprano soloist and full orchestra against a small instrumental ensemble, either a folk group or a rock group. The vocal line, which is amplified, often contains highly virtuosic passages. Included in the "Alice" series are *Pop-Pourri* (1968), *An Alice Symphony* (1969), *Adventures Underground* (1971), *Vintage Alice* (1972), *Final Alice* (1976), *Child Alice* (1977–81), and *Heavy Metal Alice. Final Alice,* originally intended to be the last composition in the series, deals with events in the concluding chapters of *Alice in Wonderland,* presented as narrative with orchestral music, recitatives, and arias. Thematic transformation and Leitmotifs are used. *Child Alice* presents Del Tredici's unrealistic view of Carroll's memories of hours he spent with the child Alice Liddell. Near the end of most of the "Alice" pieces, Del Tredici's musical signature appears: some players count from 1 to 13 in Italian, with special emphasis on *tredici.* A recent work by Del Tredici is *Opposites Attract* (1996; pno.), in which he contrasts themes and styles of composers often considered to be musically antagonistic to one another, particularly Wagner and Brahms.

Increasingly, in the late twentieth century there has been a tendency for composers to base works on compositions of earlier composers or to borrow from, quote from, or musically allude to compositions of earlier composers. Among the many persons who have done so are Ellen Zwilich, Joan Tower, John Corigliano, Hiram Titus, and John Tavener.

Tavener (b. 1944), an organist, was educated at London's Royal Academy of Music. He has written some instrumental music, but most of his works are vocal, principally on religious subjects (e.g., several cantatas and Requiems). His interest in mysticism and spirituality is apparent in his music. A number of his works are colored by Byzantine and Slavic liturgical chants. His harmonies are basically Romantic, and, to some extent, he is eclectic. Some of his early works show Stravinsky's influence, others suggest that of Messiaen, one relates to Machaut, and several works contain borrowings from Bach's B-minor Mass. Among Tavener's late works are *Two Hymns for the Mother of God* (1985), *Annunciation* (1992; *a cappella* massed choirs), and *Innocence* (1995).

John Corigliano (b. 1938) has composed a great deal of vocal music, most of it for SATB choir, and a wide variety of instrumental music, usually in traditional forms with tonal harmonies (e.g., concertos and symphonies). *Troubadours* (1993) constitutes variations for guitar and orchestra. He used nontraditional performing forces and some serial techniques in *Naked Carmen* (1 Act; 1970), a recorded "electric rock opera" based on Bizet's *Carmen.* Corigliano's second opera, *The ghosts of Versailles* (2 Acts, 1980–87; Wm. Hoffman libretto), was commissioned by the New York Metropolitan Opera and was premiered by it in 1991. The drama is set in three worlds—historical, theatrical, and ghostly—and presents a love story as well as dealing with revolution. The characters are drawn from *La mère coupable* (the third drama in Beaumarchais's trilogy) and include the ghostly Beaumarchais, Marie Antoinette, and persons from the eighteenth-century Versailles court. In addition to quoting from operas and other music of earlier eras, parodying the Beaumarchais operas of Mozart and Rossini, and alluding to R. Strauss's operas, Corigliano used some dodecaphonic techniques and quarter-tone dissonances.

In the same year that Corigliano began his opera, Hiram Titus composed the chamber opera *Rosina* (1980; Barbara Field libretto), which has only six characters and an orchestra of 12 players. *Rosina* is, in essence, a sequel to Mozart's *The Marriage of Figaro.* Titus's music is tonal and Neoclassic. He makes one brief reference to Rossini's *The Barber of Seville* and musical allusions to Stravinsky's *The Rake's Progress,* Poulenc's *Carmelites,* and R. Strauss's *Ariadne.*

The last quarter of the twentieth century has been characterized by diversity and continued experimentation. This is true of popular as well as classical music. Popular music has included styles as diverse as

FIGURE 27.5 Europe as of January 1993.

country music, jazz, rock, and **rap.** Among musicals playing on Broadway are representatives of all of these styles. Rap, which emerged in New York discothèques c. 1975, consists of poetry rhythmically spoken against a musical background that, in the 1970s, was often borrowed from preexistent recordings. However, rap was not really new—it has existed for many years and is apparent in chants and taunts of children playing on the streets of Chicago and other large cities and the biting commentary of persons concerned about ghetto living conditions. Rap is closely related to the songs created by the slaves.

Some composers have found a certain style that expresses what they have to say and have worked almost exclusively in that style. Other composers have been eclectic, choosing the styles in which they wish to write, moving from one to another, or freely mingling elements of several styles if that pleases them. The diversity of the era is comparable with that prevalent during the middle third of the eighteenth century. Late twentieth-century historians can speak of the present era only as an Age of Diversity and Experimentation; they are too close to the period to be objective in assigning it a definitive name.

In America many composers have been active, creating especially commissioned orchestral works, concerti, and operas, some of the latter concerning current events. United States's involvement in the brief Kuwait-Iraq war—"Operation Desert Storm"—did not curtail artistic creativity. However, in continental Europe political and economic conditions have not fostered musical composition. In some respects, conditions in 1989 paralleled those of 1848, when a chain of revolutions erupted against monarchial rule, and there was a wave of nationalism that, in Germany and Italy, sought unification. In 1848 soldiers battled armed mobs, and the revolutions failed; in 1989 citizens' effective demonstrations—and meetings in which Kurt Mazur was a vital force—brought down the Berlin Wall, and Germany was reunited. Poland, too, achieved independence. In a "Velvet Revolution" led by playwright Václav Havel, Czechoslovakia freed itself from Communist domination, but Slovakia broke away from the Czechs. On 26 January 1993 Havel was elected president of the Czech Republic.

With the realization and admission that Communism was not a viable form of government came the collapse of the Soviet Union. Though a coup against Mikhail Gorbachev failed and he resigned as head of government, the newly elected president, Boris Yeltsin, could not unify the Soviet states. Some states demanded and achieved autonomy; a few united to form the Commonwealth of Independent States under Yeltsin. In Yugoslavia bitter fighting resulted when individual states sought release from Serbian domination. Many Old World countries and cities have changed their names.

Richard Strauss once remarked that new music should be couched in new forms. Perhaps the politico-economic upheaval prevalent in the early 1990s will be reflected in the emergence of new forms of music as well as in the subject matter of old forms.

SUMMARY

The twentieth century has witnessed technological advances that affected the development of music: devices for recording on discs and magnetic tape and putting sound tracks on movie film, radio, television, computer, synthesizer, and other electronic instruments. The original intent of recording technology—to provide a means for storing, transmitting, and faithfully reproducing live sounds—has been extended considerably. Technology has made available to composers every sound in the universe as source material.

The principles of serialism, applied to pitch by Schoenberg and his pupils, were extended to other elements of music, and ultimately total serialization was attained. By 1947, Babbitt had arrived at serialization of rhythm and dynamics as well as pitch. Messiaen used serial techniques only briefly. He was one of the twentieth century's greatest and most influential composers and teachers, though his style—an individually conceived composite of many styles and many cultures—was not copied by any of his pupils. One of them, Boulez, became leader of the young serialist composers working in Paris in 1948. Working independently of Babbitt, Boulez also serialized musical elements other than pitch.

Musique concrète was the term Schaeffer used to describe music composed directly on disc or tape by recording natural sounds that are manipulated by various means. In Germany, developments in electronic music occurred independently and almost simultaneously with those in France. The German movement was led by Eimert, who was joined by Stockhausen, one of Messiaen's pupils. Stockhausen composed music for conventional instruments even while experimenting with electronic music, and he wrote major works in both areas. In some works, he mingled manipulated word sounds with electronic sounds. As Gabrieli had used *cori spezzati,* so Stockhausen employed physical space in some of his works.

Varèse, working in America, began writing for groups of wind and percussion instruments in the 1920s and wanted electronic instruments. When theremin and ondes Martenot became available, he included them in ensembles. Around 1950 Varèse began writing compositions that mingled taped sounds with the sonorities of conventional instruments. He composed two of the earliest major works created on tape.

Babbitt used arithmetic as a compositional tool in structuring his works. Intrigued by the manner in which Schoenberg and Webern constructed tone rows, particularly those in which unordered hexachords formed combinatorial sets, Babbitt developed the principle of combinatoriality further. He was interested in the possibilities of synthesizer as an aid to composition, primarily because it offered absolute control of all musical events. He was the first composer to work with RCA's Mark II synthesizer.

Cage is usually associated with prepared piano, a technique he learned from Cowell. Cage was an experimentalist, seeking new sounds and new media, and was influential with regard to chance operations and indeterminacy in music. Among his works are theater music, happenings, aleatory music, and computer-generated pieces.

Berio worked with electronics in Italy, then came to the United States, where he worked with synthesizers and computers but also composed for conventional instruments. American women composing music by electronic means include Ivey and Oliveros.

Not all composers were intrigued by electronic music. Some did not subscribe to any avant-garde techniques. Others, like Crumb, obtained new sounds by ingenious choices of sound sources and unusual combinations of instruments, including those from Africa and the Orient, and even toys. Thea Musgrave is well known for her operas.

Ligeti's works are characterized by large tone clusters and whisperlike sustained "clouds." He was aware of new developments in other composers' music and incorporated some of them in a few of his works. But he moved away from serialism and expansions thereof and electronic music into other technical developments, such as the frequent repetition of figures or short passages.

In a number of his works, Penderecki asks performers to produce sounds from conventional instruments by unusual means. Many of his compositions are large works for vocal soloists, chorus, and orchestra and are liturgical or on religious subjects. His *Paradise Lost,* though staged as an opera, with scenery, costumes, acting, and ballet, contains tableaux and a major role for narrator.

Minimalism, the style of music that is based on the repetition of short figures using a minimal amount of musical material, had as its principal exponents Young, Riley, Glass, and Reich, but Glass has begun to move away from that style.

During the 1970s and 1980s experimentation and diversity continued. Serial music was still being written but was no longer a dominant force. Minimalism gained some adherents and influenced some composers writing in other styles to include repetitive figures in works. A number of composers have been eclectic, choosing from styles of all centuries and mingling characteristics from different movements. Two such composers are Zwilich and Tower.

Gradually, more emphasis has been placed on melody and on tonality, but it is a kind of tonality in which there is no tonal pull by tonic or dominant, and functional relationships between chords seem to be lacking. The term Neoromanticism has been used to describe many composers' return to the forms and genres used during the Romantic period, to a greater emphasis on melody, and to the appearance of some tonal centers within the music.

POSTLUDE

It is the task of a music historian to record and recount facts—a musicologist is expected to evaluate them. Throughout the twentieth century, as in others, composers have created works of varying degrees of quality. A great deal of bad music has been written, and much that is mediocre. Although there are excellent compositions by fine composers, it seems that since 1945 the bad and the mediocre have outweighed the excellent. During the last 50 years, musical composition has been characterized by experimentation and diversity. To a great extent, technology has fostered this—magnetic tape, recording devices, synthesizer, electronic instruments, and computers are valuable compositional aids, and experiments with them have resulted in diverse types of music being composed. It is true that successful experimentation promotes progress, but the various new styles that have been produced have been relatively short-lived, and much of the music created after 1945 has had little appeal for music devotees. One wonders if some of it can honestly be considered "art music" and if it would be classified more accurately as "organized sound." Perhaps Varèse was correct in using that term, though his works *are* musical. Certainly, changing cultural conditions and the availability of technological devices have had something to do with the types of music being composed, but they are not solely responsible for the dearth of enduring musical styles. The responsibility for the quality of the music lies mainly with composers, their choices of the elements used in constructing their compositions, and their aims. For example, opera can be a moral force—it can be used to deal with the important human and political issues of an era. However, to get the message across to the populace, the drama must be presented in music that will attract audiences, as Mozart, Cherubini, Britten, and Adams have done.

During the last 50 years, there have been no composers of the stature of Brahms or Beethoven, whose talents were recognized during their lifetimes and whose works are still performed, appreciated, and acclaimed. (Messiaen may be an exception—he may be considered "the Bach of the twentieth century.") Where have today's composers missed the mark? Certainly, they do not lack talent. Rather, in being attracted to new paths and following side roads, they seem to have lost sight of all references to the main highway. Serialism, atonality, aperiodicity, and aleatoric styles seem to have run their course. But surely, there is still much to be said musically. Perhaps the time has come for a composer to be daring enough to compose new melodies and harmonies by using traditional methods, materials, and performing forces and thereby create quality music that will appeal to today's audiences.

Appendix

GUIDE TO PRONUNCIATION OF LITURGICAL LATIN ACCORDING TO ROMAN USE

SYLLABLES

There are as many syllables in Latin words as there are vowels or diphthongs. In the division of words into syllables:

1. A single consonant goes with the following vowel.
2. Division is made between double consonants, and each of the consonants must be sounded clearly, e.g., bello = behl-loh, *not* as in English word *bellow*.
3. If two or more consonants are between two vowels, the division is *generally* made before the last consonant, e.g., ma-gis-ter. Exceptions are: (a) If the last consonant of the group is h, l, or r, the last two consonants go with the following vowel, e.g., pa-tria. (b) Compound words are divided into their original parts, e.g., de-scen-do. (c) x goes with the preceding vowel, e.g., dux-i.

VOWELS

1. a as in *father:* Ma-ri-a = Mah-ree-ah.
2. e as in *met:* Chris-te = Krees-teh (generally sung Kree-steh).
   Avoid the diphthong sound ay-ee as in *stay.*
3. i as in *marine:* Fi-li-i = fee-lee-ee.
4. y is the same as i: Ky-ri-e = Kee-ree-eh.
5. o as in *for:* cor-po = kawr-poh; no-mi-ne = naw-mee-neh.
6. u as in *moon:* lu-na = loo-nah.
   Avoid the diphthong sound ee-oo.
   When u is preceded by q, the combination qu is pronounced kw as in *square:* qui = kwee.
7. When two vowels come together, each vowel is pronounced, except in diphthongs ae and oe. In singing, the first vowel is sustained, and the second vowel is sounded on passing to the next syllable: a-it = ah-eet.

DIPTHONGS

1. ae and oe are pronounced like e: sae-cu-lum = seh-koo-loom.
2. au and eu are pronounced as a single syllable, but each vowel must be distinctly heard. In singing, the first vowel is sustained as in other combinations of two vowels: la-u-da = lah-oo-dah.

CONSONANTS

1. b, d, f, l, m, n, p, and v are pronounced the same as in English.
2. c before e, i, y, ae, oe is pronounced ch as in *church:* coe-lum = cheh-loom; otherwise, c is pronounced k as in *can:* sa-crum = sah-kroom.
3. cc before e, i, y, ae, ce is pronounced t-ch: ec-ce = et-cheh.
4. ch is pronounced as k: che-ru-bim = keh-roo-beem.
5. g is soft before e, i, ae, oe, y, as in *generous:* ge-mi-nus = jeh-mee-noos; otherwise, g is hard, as in *get:* ga-rum = gah-room. The word *gigas* contains both sounds: jee-gahs.
6. gn is pronounced as ny in *canyon:* a-gnus = ah-nyoos.
7. h is mute, except in mi-hi = mee-kee, and in ni-hil = nee-keel.
8. j is pronounced as i or y: e-jus = eh-yoos, or ju-bi-lus = yoo-bee-loos.
9. q is always followed by u and another vowel and is pronounced as in *square:* quam = kwahm; qualis = kwah-lees.
10. r is slightly rolled on the tongue and is never given a hard sound such as ar.
11. sc before e, i, ae, oe, y, is pronounced sh as in *shed:* de-scen-dit = deh-shehn-deet.

12. th is pronounced t: ther-ma = tehr-mah.

13. ti is pronounced tzee when followed by an-
    other vowel and not following s, x, t: gra-ti-a =
    grah-tzee-ah.

14. x is pronounced ks as in *vex:* ex-cla-mat =
    eks-klah-maht.

15. xc before e, ae, oe, i, y is pronounced ksh:
    ex-cel-sis = ek-shel-sees; xc before other vowels
    has the hard sound of ksk: ex-cus-so-rum =
    eks-koos-saw-room.

16. z is pronounced dz: za-mi-a = dzah-mee-ah.

Glossary

This glossary provides a brief definition for most terms appearing in bold print in the text. The page number refers to a significant description of the term in the text; other references may be located by consulting the index. Each term that appears in bold face has its own entry and definition in this glossary. A more detailed explanation may be found in a music dictionary.

A

absolute music (284, 459)   Music composed in purely musical forms (e.g., binary, sonata form, fugue) withoug sung or chanted words and without depiction of or reference to nonmusical events.

accent neumes (58)   A ninth-century style of chant notation that consists of various symbols indicating the general rise and fall of the melodic line rather than designating specific pitches.

affections (228)   Emotional states such as anger, fear, or love, which Baroque composers sought to express and also to arouse in listeners' minds.

agréments (275)   Grace notes and other small melodic ornaments, and the symbols for them, that were devised and developed into a system by French lutenist-composers during the Baroque era.

air, or **air de cour** (185)   A French secular, strophic song sung at court for entertainment between 1572 and c. 1650. Polyphonic airs were composed for four or five unaccompanied voices; airs for solo voice had lute accompaniment.

Alberti bass (331)   An accompaniment figure consisting of a broken three-pitch chord whose notes are played in this order: lowest, highest, middle, highest.

aleatory music (640, 644)   Music whose composition or performance is determined by deliberate use of chance, choice, or indeterminacy; also referred to as *chance music.*

all-combinatorial (642)   A **twelve-tone** term indicating that half the tone row (hexachord) may be combined with its transposed inversion, retrograde, or retrograde inversion without duplicating pitches.

allemande (274)   The first core dance in the Baroque **suite.** It is characterized by binary form, moderate tempo, duple meter, and polyphonic texture, and usually commences with an **anacrusis.**

alternatim Mass (165)   A Mass setting in which polyphonic sections are interspersed with sections sung in chant or performed on organ.

anacrusis (274)   The upbeat preceding the first strong downbeat of a phrase. It may consist of more than one note.

anthem (200)   A choral work with devotional text in English, it is the Anglican version of the **motet** used in the Roman Catholic Mass.

antiphon (39)   A liturgical chant performed in the manner of a refrain before, after, and sometimes between individual verses of a psalm or canticle.

antiphonal chants (33)   Chants with sections or phrases sung by alternating choirs.

antiphonal rendition (27)   Performance in alternation; see **antiphonal chants.**

arietta (351)   A short, through-composed vocal solo, less elaborate than an aria. Used in opera in the eighteenth century.

ariette (430)   The French term for a simple, melodious vocal solo with light-textured orchestral accompaniment used in opéra comique c. 1820.

arioso (252)   A style of text setting that lies between the speech-style of recitative and the lyricism and metrical regularity of aria.

atonal (596)   The total absence of any center of key tonality.

ayre (187)   A term used by English Renaissance composers to denote a solo song with lute accompaniment. Also called **lute song.**

B

ballad opera (352)   A play, usually comic, in which spoken prose dialogue is interspersed with verses set to traditional tunes or popular melodies.

ballade (96)   One of the medieval **formes fixes,** its musical structure uses the pattern aabC, with C being a refrain that concludes each of the three poetic stanzas.

ballata (119)   A medieval Italian song form similar to but more elaborate than the **virelai,** using AbbaA musical form.

balletto (180)   An Italian instrumental form intended to accompany dancing, composed principally for lute c. 1560–90 and for chamber ensemble after 1620. A version for vocal ensemble (fl. 1591–1620) uses a rhythmic, homophonic strophic setting, and sometimes includes nonsense syllables such as fa-la-la.

bar form (101)   The term for AAB form. The Meistersinger called the A sections *Stollen* and the B section *Abgesang.*

Baroque (226)   The term denoting the historical period between c. 1600 and c. 1750 and the style of the music composed during that era.

basso continuo (230)   The independent bass line played throughout a **Baroque** composition to provide the foundation for the unnotated harmonic structure of the work.

basso ostinato (272)   A continuously repeated sequence of notes in the bass line used as framework for melodic or harmonic variation as well as supporting freely constructed melodies.

basso seguente (229)   A bass line formed by the keyboard player extracting the lowest-sounding pitches of a polyphonic composition and performing them as harmonic basis for the work.

bicinium (195)   A two-voice composition. The Renaissance bicinium was often based on a chorale melody, which was placed in the bottom voice.

blues (578)   A popular musical style that emerged early in the twentieth century. It generally includes three basic elements: a text pattern of aab; a 12-measure harmonic sequence based on I, IV, and V chords; and melodic notes inflected or bent downward for expressive purposes.

broken consort (212)   A Renaissance term for an ensemble consisting of instruments from various family groups.

burden (122)   A refrain sung at the beginning and end of each stanza in an English carol.

C

cabeletta (449)   A short operatic aria that intensifies the momentum of the drama. Characteristics include persistent rhythm and a repeated vocal section with embellishments improvised by the soloist.

caccia (119)   Medieval three-voice composition written in strict canon at the unison for two equal voices, supported harmonically by an instrumental lower line.

cadence rhyme (115, 332)   Use of the same cadential figures, transposed, at the conclusion of different sections of a work; the rhyme often includes several measures prior to the cadence.

cakewalk (578)   A strutting, high-stepping processional dance that was performed in competition for a cake as prize.

canon (276)   A polyphonic work composed through the exact repetition (imitation) of a melody in subsequent voices. Inversion, retrograde, and other procedures (as well as literal repetition) can be employed. The technique can be used as a developmental process within a larger work.

cantata (267)   Initially described **strophic variations** for solo voice with **basso continuo** accompaniment. It developed into an extended composition alternating recitatives and arias.

cantilena style (115)   Medieval musical texture wherein a lyrical solo voice is accompanied by an instrumental tenor and contratenor.

cantus firmus (68)   Lit., fixed song. The melody on which a polyphonic composition was based.

cantus firmus variation (272)   While the basic melody remains unchanged, each repetition of it is surrounded or supported by different counterpoint.

canzona (219)   Originally an instrumental arrangement of a polyphonic chanson. Around 1650, sections were lengthened into independent movements with contrasting melodic and rhythmic character. The terms *sonata* and *canzona* were used interchangeably during the early Baroque era.

canzonetta (180)   An Italian treble-dominated, homophonic, secular song for three to five voices that was popular in the 1580s.

catholicon (153)   A composition that can be sung in more than one **mode.**

cavatina (324, 448)   A short aria in simpler vocal style than da capo aria and lacking da capo repetition of the opening section.

centonization (32)   The creation of a melody or chant by assembling melodic formulas.

chamber music (374)   Prior to the Classic era, the term referred to nontheatrical secular music, such as **sonata da camera.** During the last half of the eighteenth century, it described music, either orchestral or for small ensembles, performed in an intimate setting such as an aristocrat's private apartment. Early in the nineteenth century, it came to describe ensemble music performed by one person per part.

chanson (140)   A generic term for French secular song.

character piece (401)   A short, programmatic composition for piano evoking a mood suggested by the work's title.

choirbook notation (86)   Medieval manuscript style in which the **duplum** and **triplum** are notated separately in parallel columns; the **tenor** line is on a staff across the bottom of the page.

choral, or **dramatic Passion** (263)   A **responsorial Passion** that sets the words of Christ and the *turba* in polyphony. The remainder of the text is monophonic.

chorale (194)   A German hymn comprising a text and a melody, intended for congregational singing in the Lutheran church.

chorale motet (195)   A motet-style composition using a chorale melody as the **cantus firmus.**

clausula (78)   A section of **organum** in which both voices are written in **discant-style counterpoint** and proceed at approximately the same rate.

clefs (59)   Symbols assigning specific pitches to staff lines.

collegium musicum (303)   A predominantly amateur group of musicians that gives public concerts. In the Baroque era, such an ensemble performed contemporary music.

color (110)   The melody or repeated melodic segment of an isorhythmic voice.

coloration (109)   An ars nova technique to signify certain deviations from normal note values by writing those notes in red ink.

combinatoriality (642)   The same as **all-combinatorial** except that the combination is limited to one other set.

concert (330)   A public nontheatrical performance of music. Concerts were almost nonexistent until the mid-Baroque and public concerts did not become common until the nineteenth century.

concertino (285)   The small ensemble of soloists featured in a **concerto grosso.**

concerto (285)   After 1650, the term denotes a multimovement composition for one or more soloists and orchestra.

concerto grosso (285)   A Baroque **concerto** contrasting a **concertino** with a larger ensemble known variously as concerto grosso, tutti, or ripieno.

conductus (69)   A polyphonic setting of a metrical Latin poem, usually using a newly composed tenor. It is performed as an introduction to a liturgical chant.

conductus motet (85)   A **motet** style of the Notre Dame school. The upper voices sing the same text homorhythmically while the **tenor,** derived from chant, has a different text **incipit** and rhythm.

consort song (187)   Late Renaissance and early Baroque English vocal music for one or more solo voices with instrumental accompaniment intended for a consort of viols.

contrafactum (143)   A vocal composition in which the original text has been replaced by another. In Renaissance practice, a sacred text was usually substituted for a secular one.

contratenor bassus (112)   In fourteenth-century 4-voice polyphony, the part placed below the tenor; it was predecessor of the modern bass voice part.

cori spezzati (168, 224)   Lit., spaced choirs. The practice of spatially separating choral and/or instrumental ensembles of contrasting sonorities for antiphonal performance of music. Associated with the Venetian polychoral tradition at St. Mark's.

corrente (274)   A fast, homophonic, triple-meter Italian dance that was frequently interchanged with the **courante** in the **Baroque suite.**

counterpoint (109)   In the fourteenth century, note-against-note writing. Currently, the term is used to describe the melodic, rhythmic, and harmonic character of a polyphonic composition.

courante (274)   A French dance commonly included in the **Baroque suite.** It is written in triple meter and moderate tempo, with dotted rhythms that reflect the hopping character of the dance.

course (216)   A group of (usually two) lute strings tuned in unison or as an octave and sounded simultaneously to obtain increased volume.

cyclic mass (135)   A Mass in which the same cantus firmus melody appears in all movements of the Ordinary.

D

da capo (253)   An instruction placed at the end of the B section of a composition designating that repetition of the A section is required.

dal segno al fine (253)   An instruction placed at the end of the B section of a composition indicating that repetition of the A section is to commence at the sign rather than the beginning of the composition.

direct psalmody (27)   The intonation or chanting of scriptural or liturgical texts from beginning to end by one individual or one choir.

direct rendition (33)   Singing of a chant from beginning to end by one individual or one choir.

discant (68)   A style of **organum** in which all voices use the same text and move in note-against-note or **neume**-against-neume polyphony.

divertissement (258)   A section or scene within a large stage work that consists of vocal solos, ensembles, and dances, and may or may not be essential to the plot.

dodecaphony (595)   Term synonymous with **twelve-tone music.**

dominants (tenors) (57)   The **reciting notes** of medieval modal scales.

dots of division (87)   A medieval notation device used by Petrus de Cruce to indicate grouping of notes into semibreves.

double (274)   The notated ornamented version of a slow movement of a Baroque suite.

double leading-tone cadence (120)   A cadential figure frequently appearing in the works of Landini, Machaut, and other ars nova composers. The tenor moves down by step to the root of the cadence chord (2–1), the inner voice ascends by a semitone to the fifth (♯4–5), and the top voice frequently ornaments its rise to the octave with a 7–6–8 melodic succession.

double motet (83)   A **motet** with two texts sung simultaneously by different voices.

dramma giocoso (351)   A comic opera containing elements of tragedy while remaining basically humorous.

duplum (68)   The upper, newly composed voice in two-part **organum.**

E

English discant (122)   Term used to describe homorhythmic passages of ⅜ chords in smooth succession occurring in English medieval polyphony. English "discanting" is the practice of improvising around a notated cantus firmus melody to create a parallel line a fourth above the cantus firmus and another a third below it, thus producing a stream of ⅜ chords.

episode   In a **fugue,** sections that are modulatory and wherein the subject does not appear in its entirety (276). In opera, a scene or tableau that appears without regard for dramatic continuity (479).

epitaphium (91)   A poem or song performed at a funeral.

equal temperament (213)   A tuning system that divides the octave into 12 equally spaced semitones.

ethnomusicology (515)   The scientific study of folk and non-Western art music, emphasizing sociological and comparative analysis.

ethos (12)   Greek philosophy that believed the specific character of each mode or tuning affected the morals and character of the people in a certain way.

étude (337)   A composition featuring at least one consistently recurring problem of musical or technical difficulty.

exercise (337)   A mechanical note pattern of undetermined length designed for the player's drill on a specific technical aspect of performing on the instrument.

exposition   The opening section of a **fugue** in which the subject is introduced by each voice in succession (276). The opening section of **sonata form** that establishes the tonic key and then moves to the dominant; it also presents the themes of the movement (335).

F

falsobordone (246)   A *cappella* 4-voice homophonic setting of a chant, generally notated as a succession of root position triads following the form, melody, and phrase structure of a Gregorian chant psalm tone.

familiar style (151)   A sixteenth-century term for polyphonic composition employing a homorhythmic texture and syllabic text setting.

fantasia (274)   A composition evoking the style of free improvisation and therefore lacking standard length, form, or meter.

fausse reprise (374)   A false recapitulation occurring in the development section of **sonata form.** The first theme returns as though commencing the recapitulation but is abandoned in favor of continued development before the actual recapitulation occurs.

faux bourdon (133)   A continental technique in which two notated voices move in parallel sixths and octaves and a middle voice is improvised by duplicating the top voice a fourth lower.

figured bass (230)   Arabic numerals or symbols for chromatic alterations placed above or below the **basso continuo** notes to convey the composer's intention with regard to realization of the harmony.

final (57)   The concluding pitch of a chant in one of the eight church modes.

fine (253)   Lit., end. The word indicates the end of a work and is placed at the conclusion of an A section indicating the final cadence of the composition.

fluxus (645)   An avant-garde movement in New York City and Europe c. 1960–65 that presented concerts of "music"

created from experimental, unusual, and often humorous "happenings."

formes fixes (95)   Poetic forms that dominated and directly affected the musical structure of French secular music during the late medieval and early Renaissance periods. The three most important were **ballade, rondeau,** and **virelai.**

French overture (258)   A **Baroque** form usually in two sections. The first is slow and homophonic, emphasizing dotted rhythms; the second is fast, using imitative polyphony. A third section that returns to the style of the opening is not uncommon.

frottola (174)   A late fifteenth- and early sixteenth-century strophic Italian secular song. The main melody is usually placed in the top voice of the three- or four-part homorhythmic texture, and often the song concludes with a refrain.

fuge (395)   The second section of a **fuging-tune.** It begins with successive contrapuntal entrances in an imitative style and usually concludes with a refrain.

fuging-tune (394)   A hymn or psalm tune is presented in two sections: the first is a simple 4-part harmonization of the theme with the tune in the tenor; the second section, usually repeated, presents the **fuge.**

fugue (276)   A composition in imitative counterpoint based on a theme, called the *subject,* which can be manipulated through a variety of techniques, such as augmentation, diminution, inversion, and stretto. Although fugues lack a consistent formal structure, they begin with an **exposition,** after which statements of the subject alternate with **episodes.**

full anthem (200)   An Anglican **anthem** that is choral throughout and is usually contrapuntal in texture. Many appear to be *a cappella* but may have been accompanied when performed.

G

gigue (274)   Frequently the concluding dance of a **Baroque suite,** it is a rapid dance in either compound duple or triple meter. Features of the melody are wide leaps and triplets.

grand opera (432, 479)   Nineteenth-century French opera based on historical subject matter and emphasizing spectacular dramatic scenes. It is sung throughout. Solos may be interrupted by choral or ensemble interjections.

Great Service (200)   See **Service.**

grid (596)   See **matrix.**

ground (272)   Synonymous with **basso ostinato.**

gymel (122)   English 2-voice polyphony in parallel thirds or sixths.

H

head motive (123)   A melodic motive presented at the beginning of each movement or section as a unification device.

heighted neumes (67) Chant notation in which **neumes** are placed in a vertically relative position in the staffless space above the text, making pitch differences discernible.

heterodyne (633) A technique used in electronic music referring to the combined sound frequency produced by two radio oscillators. The resulting pitch is either a difference tone or a summation tone.

heterophony (64) Texture resulting from the simultaneous performance of two different versions of the same melody.

hocket (89) Individual or small groups of notes from a single melody are performed by two voices or instruments in alternation so that one voice is always silent when the other is singing.

I

In nomine (219) An English instrumental composition derived from the Benedictus section of John Taverner's 6-voice Mass *Gloria tibi Trinitas*.

in score (67) Parts of a composition notated one below the other on different staves.

incipit (83) The first few words and/or notes with which a composition or piece of literature begins.

indeterminancy (577) The element of chance in music.

infinite melody (502) Wagner's term for melody that was continuously expressive of dramatic content, not simply ceaseless from the first note of the overture to the closing curtain.

intermedio (182, 236) A mythological or allegorical interlude presented between the acts of a play by soloists performing in a style midway between recitation and singing. In the late sixteenth century the performances became more elaborate, with scenery and embellished solos.

isorhythm (110) A twentieth-century term describing the structural principle that served as the basis for the polyphony of the fourteenth-century motet. It consists of an extended rhythmic pattern, called **talea,** that is reiterated one or more times in the **tenor** and a melodic segment, known as **color,** that is superimposed on the **talea.**

Italian overture (250) Italian opera overture consisting of three distinct sections in fast-slow-fast order of tempo.

J

just intonation (213) A tuning system based on acoustically pure major thirds or fifths but resulting in one fifth that will be painfully out of tune. This tuning occurs naturally in *a cappella* singing.

K

Klangfarbenmelodie (597) A melody created not simply by successive pitches but by changing instrumental timbre. This alternation of color may occur within a single pitch as well as between individual notes or short motives.

L

Landini cadence (115) A medieval cadence in which suspension is combined with an escape note in a melodic progression 7–6–8.

laude, or **laude spirituali** (100) Medieval Italian monophonic songs with nonliturgical religious texts. The songs are strophic and commence with a refrain that recurs after each strophe.

Leisen (194) German Lutheran hymns in which the refrain *Kyrieleison* or *Kyrieleise* concludes each stanza.

Leitmotif (352, 437) A theme or coherent musical idea representing or symbolizing a person, thing, place, idea, state of mind, or even a supernatural force. It is an important unifying device in many German operas.

libretto (239) The book or text of an **opera** or **oratorio** that is set to music.

Lied (pl., **Lieder**) (189) The generic term for German art song.

ligatures (76) A notation style used in the medieval and early Renaissance periods that combined the pitch and rhythm of two or three notes in one symbol.

liturgy (27) The prescribed ritual or format for worship in the church.

lute song (185, 187) A solo song with lute accompaniment.

M

madrigal In the medieval period, a form of Italian secular polyphony characterized by a strophic setting and a **ritornello** (118). In the Renaissance period, a through-composed setting of one poetic stanza intended for *a cappella* performance (175). Because the music was meant to enhance the meaning of the poetry, **text painting** and formal irregularities were common.

madrigal cycle (238) A series of **madrigals** presenting an uncomplicated plot through descriptive music and, on occasion, dialogue.

madrigali ariosi (182) Late sixteenth century solo **madrigals** performed in a highly ornamented manner.

madrigali spirituali (177) Sixteenth-century **madrigals** with a devotional text in Italian.

magadizing (64) A term describing the simultaneous presentation of a melody in octaves when sung by male and female voices.

manneristic style (120) A late medieval style of composition characterized by extremely intricate rhythms and notation. Modern scholarship has replaced the term with *Ars subtilior.*

masque (258) English aristocratic entertainment blending the art of poetry, dance, song, and instrumental music into a dramatic form and often staged in an elaborate setting.

matrix (596)   A graph delineating the 48 possible versions of a **tone row.**

mean-tone (213)   A tuning system frequently employed for keyboard instruments in use c. 1500. It uses pure major thirds but fifths are slightly contracted and whole tones are equal in size.

measures (232)   A mid-seventeenth-century invention that used bar lines to mark off regularly recurring rhythmic patterns of strong and weak beats.

Meisterlieder (188)   Monophonic German songs created and performed by members of a Meistersinger guild.

melismatic chant (33)   A style of chant in which numerous notes occur for each syllable of text.

melismatic (florid) organum (67)   An organum style in which several or many notes of the organal voice occur for each note of the rhythmically extended chant.

mélodie (564)   A term used after 1840 to designate French solo song with accompaniment.

minimalism (653)   A twentieth-century style characterized by the repetition of short motives, tonal harmony, slow harmonic rhythm, and a more or less regular pulsation.

mode(s) (57)   The organization of pitches into a diatonic scale pattern of whole and half steps, such as Dorian or Phrygian.

monodrama (598)   A drama wherein one person is responsible for unfolding the entire work.

monody   In ancient Greece, a lyrical solo song performed by an actor in a play and accompanied by the aulos (11). A twentieth-century term for a type of Italian accompanied solo secular song popular between c. 1600–40 (235). The vocal line emphasized text expression through correct declamation, flexible rhythm, and appropriate use of ornamentation.

motet   In the medieval period, a polyphonic secular composition for three or four voices based on a slow-moving tenor line normally derived from a phrase of chant. The upper voices move in a more rapid rhythm and may contain multiple texts in either Latin or French (82). In the Renaissance period, a polyphonic setting of a sacred Latin text other than the Ordinary of the Mass (140).

motetus (112)   The vocal line placed immediately above the tenor in medieval motets.

motto aria (252)   A style wherein the opening phrase of the vocal solo is restated after a brief rest before continuing with new material.

motto Mass (135)   A Mass using a **head motive** as a unifying device.

murky bass (331)   A keyboard accompaniment figuration consisting of broken octaves.

musica ficta (90)   Notes in medieval and Renaissance music that were chromatically altered during performance to produce pitches not in the hexachord system.

musica reservata and **musica secreta** (182)   Music performed for the Este family in Ferrara, Italy, by the *concerto delle donne*. This ensemble had a secret repertoire for their private concerts.

musicology (515)   Broadly refers to the scientific study of music but is more commonly associated with the historical study of Western art music.

musique mesurée (186)   A short-lived attempt in late Renaissance to apply quantitative principles of Greek verse to French music, using two values, long and short.

mutation (60)   The medieval practice of modulating from the hexachord of one mode into the hexachord of another. It is comparable with the modern process of modulating to a different key by means of a pivot chord.

N

neumes (31)   Symbols used to notate chant.

neumatic (33)   A chant style in which one **neume** (two or three notes) is sung to each syllable of the text.

O

occursus (65)   The harmonic convergence on the unison at the end of a phrase in **organum.**

opera (236)   A drama in which all or most of the text is sung and intended for a staged performance. The instrumental ensemble serves to enhance the dramatic mood as well as provide accompaniment for the singers.

opéra-ballet (258)   French Baroque opera consisting of loosely connected or independent acts, each containing a **divertissement.**

opera buffa (350)   A full-length comic opera that developed during the eighteenth century. It uses a large cast of characters, including some of the stock characters of *commedia dell'arte,* uses some regional dialects, exploits the bass voice, and employs an **ensemble finale.**

opera seria (346)   Late Baroque and early Classic opera sung in Italian. The **libretto,** generally purged of all comic elements, is based on heroic stories from the mythology and history of ancient Greece and Rome.

operetta (481)   Musical theatrical work with songs, spoken dialogue, and some dancing. It was a popular form of entertainment during the late nineteenth and early twentieth centuries.

oratorio (260)   A large-scale composition resembling an opera and containing operatic style **recitatives** and **arias** but, unlike opera, usually has a narrator, places great emphasis on the chorus, and is presented without stage action, scenery, or costumes. Oratorio may be sacred or secular.

oratorio Passion (263)   A Passion set in the style of an oratorio.

oratorio volgare (261)   An oratorio set in a vernacular text instead of Latin.

Ordinary (40) Texts of the Mass that remain constant throughout the liturgical year: the Kyrie, Gloria, Credo, Sanctus/Benedictus, Agnus Dei, and Ite missa est.

organ Mass (217, 278) A series of polyphonic compositions for organ designed to alternate with choral passages of the **Ordinary** and **Proper.** Each organ movement is based on a chant corresponding with that movement of the Mass.

organum (64) An elaboration of chant through the addition of polyphonic lines. The chant melody, called *vox principalis* is typically the lower voice, whereas a newly composed part, *vox organalis,* generally lies above the original and usually matches each pitch of the *principalis* with a consonant interval: octave, fifth, or fourth.

organum duplum (68), or **organum triplum,** and **organum quadruplum** (78) Organum composed for two, three, and four voices, respectively.

organum purum (78) A term for late twelfth- and early thirteenth-century **melismatic organum.**

oscillator (633) An electronic device capable of producing audio frequencies in response to a keyboard or other pitch-designating device.

P

pantonal (596) The presence of all tonal centers with none distinctive enough to achieve preeminence over any of the others.

paraphrase variation (272) A technique in which the contrapuntal harmony remains constant while the melody, usually retained in the uppermost part, is given different embellishments.

Parisian chanson (184) A Renaissance homophonic **chanson** with a light rhythmic texture, often with passages of repeated notes, and a musical structure that corresponds to that of the poem.

parody (156, 166) A Renaissance practice of basing a polyphonic composition on all lines of a preexistent work but supplementing and modifying them to create a new composition.

parte (272) A variation section; a single statement of the harmonic pattern in a **partita.**

partial signatures (124) A late-fourteenth-century practice of placing a flat at the beginning of only one of the polyphonic voices of a work.

partita (272) A late Renaissance and early Baroque term for a set of variations, often variations on a **ground.**

Passion (262) The story of the Crucifixion as recorded in the Gospels. Most often it is based on a single Gospel account. It includes the words of Christ, a narrator, and a *turba* (crowd).

pastorale (238) Music, literature, or drama depicting characters and scenes of an idealized rural life.

pervading imitation (161) Imitation used throughout a composition, usually appearing in every part.

Picardian (151) The term for the major chord that concludes a minor key composition.

planctus (91) The medieval term for a lament.

point neumes (58) **Heighted neumes** that resemble dots and clearly indicate pitch differences.

pointillism (602) Athematic music constructed from isolated notes often highlighted by different timbres.

point of imitation (151) A portion of a polyphonic composition in which a single musical subject, used to set a phrase of text, is treated imitatively. The beginning of one such imitative phrase overlaps the conclusion of another, thus providing smooth transition between phrases.

polyphony (64) Texture resulting from the simultaneous combination of two or more independent melodic lines.

prebend (108) Endowment or monetary allowance provided by a cathedral or large church for the living expenses of a clergyman.

prelude (274) A self-contained movement in an improvisatory style without a set form.

prepared piano (578) Placement of foreign objects (such as paper, rubber, and metal objects) among the piano strings to create unusual sounds and new timbres.

primary sources (5) Compositions through which music can be studied.

program (459) The extramusical content of a work. See **program music.**

program music (428) Music that, without words, describes, characterizes, or was inspired by a nonmusical subject. A title, explanatory remarks, or prefatory material provided by the composer usually conveys the idea to the performer(s) and audience. Most **program music** is instrumental, but some referential music comprising vocalized sounds without words exists.

Proper (40) The sections of the Mass that are appropriate only to specific days and seasons of the liturgical year.

psalm tones (33) The nine melodic patterns used in chanting psalms.

psalmody (27) The musical intonation or chanting of psalm verses or scriptural texts.

R

ragtime (578) A twentieth-century genre, originally for piano, characterized by highly syncopated melodies in the right hand while the left maintains a steady rhythmic pulse.

rap (657) The term for a twentieth-century style of popular music in which poetry is rhythmically spoken against a musical background.

razo (99) A prose paraphrase of a song used by a *joglar* as an introduction to the performance.

realization (230) The process of improvising an accompaniment from a **figured bass** or **basso continuo** line.

recitative (239)   A style of vocal music designed to imitate natural speech rhythms and inflections. Used in opera to convey the action or narrative of the drama.

recitativo accompagnato (253)   A **recitative** accompanied by the orchestra, used for dramatically intense situations.

recitativo semplice (secco) (252)   A **recitative** accompanied only by the **basso continuo** (played by the harpsichord and a sustaining bass instrument), it allows for the rapid presentation of lengthy passages of dialogue.

reciting note (33)   The pitch on which the major potion of each psalm verse is chanted in a kind of monotone.

reminiscence motive (432)   A recurring motive, most often played by the orchestra, suggestive of a dramatic element in the opera. Term associated with Méhul's operas.

rescue opera (352)   A type of opera that relates the story of a person in peril of death who is saved through the heroic endeavors of a devoted friend.

responsorial chant (33)   Chant sung by a soloist with response by the choir.

responsorial Passion (263)   A **passion** in which only the portions of the text representing the *turba* are set in motet-style polyphony.

retrograde (116)   The notes of a melody in reverse order.

rhythmic modes (76)   Rhythmic notation used by the composers of the Notre Dame school. The six patterns matched those of six common poetic meters.

rhythmic palindrome (113)   A structure that produces the same rhythmic pattern whether played forward or backward.

ricercar (167)   The instrumental counterpart of the motet. Instrumental music based on the compositional principles of the Renaissance **motet,** with imitative treatment of one or more themes.

ritornello (241, 290)   A short passage of music that recurs several times as a kind of refrain, unifying a movement. In **Baroque** music it is performed by the orchestra as interludes between vocal statements in an aria or between **concertino** sections in a **concerto grosso.**

romance   In the Renaissance era, a Spanish ballad with a narrative text set in a homophonic, strophic form (190). In the eighteenth century, a strophic song usually recounting an ancient love story or a historic event of gallantry (354).

rondeau (96)   One of the medieval **formes fixes,** set in ABaAabAB pattern.

rondellus (89)   The English technique of duple or triple voice exchange (phrase exchange). A composition written entirely by rondellus technique.

rota (89)   Medieval canon or round. Term associated with *Sumer is icumen in.*

rounded binary (332)   A form in which a substantial portion of the first section returns in its original key in the final portion of the second section, |:A:|:BA:| structure.

S

sacramentary (34)   The liturgical book used by the celebrant at Mass, it contains the **Proper** prayers, Collect, Secret, and other formulas and benedictions.

salmi spezzati (168)   Settings of psalm verses for **antiphonal rendition** by a divided choir.

sarabande (274)   One of the core dances of the **Baroque suite,** it is a slow triple-meter dance that characteristically emphasizes the second beat of each measure.

scene opera (499)   An opera composed of separate scenes that succeed one another.

scordatura (286)   Unconventional tuning of a stringed instrument to obtain special tone colors, chords, or notes not ordinarily possible on that instrument.

secondary sources (9)   Items such as instruments, literary writing and treatises, artifacts, and iconography (e.g., painting and sculpture) that enable scholars to draw conclusions about music.

serialism (595)   A compositional style in which a composer prearranges the order in which the 12 chromatic pitches are to be used.

series (596)   Synonymous with **tone row.**

Service (200)   The Anglican version of the Roman Catholic Mass, the liturgy for Morning and Evening Prayer and Communion. A Service using contrapuntal, melismatic music is termed a **Great Service** and one using syllabic, homorhythmic music a **Short Service.** Both contain the same number of musical items—the only difference is the setting.

sine-wave sounds (638)   Pure frequency tones used in electronic music.

Singspiel (259, 354)   German light opera consisting of spoken dialogue and strophic songs.

solmization (60)   The practice of singing or designating pitches by syllables instead of letter names.

sonata   In the Baroque era, it is a sectional or multimovement instrumental composition (e.g., **sonata da camera, trio sonata**) (284). In the Classic era, the term designated a multimovement composition of chamber music that usually used the symphonic structures of **sonata form, theme and variations,** and rondo (335).

sonata da camera (284)   A multimovement instrumental work intended for secular performance, comprised of a group of stylized dances that often began with a nondance introduction or prelude. The difference between sonata da camera and **Baroque suite** is negligible.

sonata da chiesa (284)   A multimovement instrumental work intended for performance in church. The movements are labeled only by tempo markings.

sonata-concerto form (363)   Developed in the Classic era, it combines the thematic and harmonic elements of **sonata**

form and the **ritornello**-solo alternation of the Baroque concerto.

sonata form (332)   The principal instrumental form of the Classic era. The exposition modulates from tonic to dominant or relative major key; the development manipulates previously stated thematic material and modulates to remote tonal areas; and the recapitulation restates the thematic material presented in the exposition but the entire section remains in the tonic or parallel major key.

stile concitato (244)   Lit., excited style. A **Baroque** technique developed by Monteverdi to evoke the emotions of anger and excitement by means of measured tremolo.

stile rappresentativo (238)   An early **Baroque** manner of singing that was more expressive than ordinary speech but not as lyrical as song. It is characterized by declamatory melody with flexible rhythms and irregular phrasing sung over a static bass line.

stile recitativo (235)   Lit., recited style. A vocal style closely related to speaking in tones, it was intended to imitate the natural speech inflections of an orator and to support and enhance the meaning of the text.

Stimmtausch (80)   The German term for voice exchange (phrase exchange).

strain (579)   An 8- or 16-measure phrase that commonly provides the melody for nineteenth-century marches and ragtime compositions.

stretta (449)   A **cabeletta** in rapid tempo used in opera in the finale of an act, where there is mounting excitement.

strophic (11)   Using the same music to set all stanzas of a text.

strophic dithyramb (11)   A wildly emotional ancient Greek song in honor of Dionysus.

strophic variation (235)   A vocal form wherein the bass line remains constant while the melody of each strophe is varied to suit the expressive needs of each poetic stanza.

style brisé (275)   Lit., broken style. A Baroque style developed by French lutenists. Chords are arpeggiated so that notes of the melody and harmony are distributed throughout the various registers of the instrument in a continuous flow of notes.

substitute clausula (78)   A different clausula based on the same section of chant, altering the duration of **organum** without affecting the liturgical propriety of the service.

suite (273)   A multimovement composition based on stylized dance forms. The movements usually include four core dances (**allemande, courante, sarabande, gigue**) that are in the same key. After 1850 the term was applied to music extracted from larger works such as ballets for performance in the concert hall.

summa Passion (263)   A **Passion** setting incorporating text from all four Gospels, thus including all words of Christ on the cross.

syllabic chant (33)   A chant with one note of music for each syllable of text.

symphonic poem (510)   A programmatic single-movement orchestral composition. The musical structure is often uniquely suited to each composition. Synonymous with **tone poem.**

symphonic suite (535)   A programmatic multimovement orchestral work combining the characteristic features of a symphony, symphonic poem, and nineteenth-century suite.

symphonie concertante (364)   A three-movement composition featuring two or more instrumental soloists with orchestra. It often uses **sonata-concerto form.**

T

tablature (212)   A term for a variety of notation systems in which pitches are indicated by letters, numbers, or symbols rather than notes on a staff.

talea (110)   A continuously repeated rhythmic pattern that provides part of the structural foundation in an **isorhythmic motet;** most often placed in the tenor of the motet.

tempo rubato (462)   A slight variation or flexibility in the tempo for expressive purposes. On piano, the hand playing the accompaniment relaxes the tempo, then unobtrusively accelerates it in order to resume synchronization with the accompaniment, which has retained steady rhythm.

tenor (68)   The principal voice in medieval polyphony. It was often constructed by sustaining the pitches of a phrase of chant and served as the **cantus firmus** of a composition.

Tenorlied (146)   The principal type of German polyphonic **Lied** during the Renaissance. A preexistent Lied melody was used as tenor **cantus firmus** and two or three more active lines provided polyphonic accompaniment.

tessitura (32)   The average range consistently required for the performance of a work rather than the composition's total range.

tetrachord (14)   A series of four pitches that span the interval of a perfect fourth.

thematic transformation (417)   Modifying a theme so substantially that it appears to be unrelated even though it is created from and includes the same elements.

theme and variation (271)   A structure consisting of a set of variations based on a stated theme.

through-composed (11)   A vocal form in which new music is provided for each stanza of text.

through-composed or **motet Passion** (263)   A **responsorial Passion** in which the complete text has a polyphonic setting.

time signature (232)   Symbol indicating the metrical organization of a composition.

toccata (274, 276)   A sectional composition for a keyboard instrument, frequently in a virtuosic, quasi-improvisational, rhapsodic style.

tone cluster (577)   A group of dissonant, closely spaced notes sounded simultaneously on the piano with the hand or forearm to create atonal harmony.

tone poem (558)   R. Strauss's term for **symphonic poem.**

tone row (596)   The arrangement of the 12 pitches of the chromatic scale as a sequence that serves as the basis of a **twelve-tone** composition. The pitches of the row must be used in order, but the row can be manipulated through a variety of techniques including but not limited to octave displacement, transposition, retrograde, and retrograde inversion.

total serialism (632)   The application of the rules of **serial** or **twelve-tone music** to all possible musical parameters.

tricinium (195)   A three-voice composition. The Renaissance tricinium was often based on a chorale melody, which was placed in the bottom voice.

trio sonata (285)   A sectional or multimovement Baroque chamber music composition written for four instruments playing three lines of music: two treble solo instruments and a **basso continuo** consisting of a harpsichord and a sustaining bass instrument such as viola da gamba.

triple motet (83)   A three-voice motet with three different texts to be sung simultaneously.

triplum (112)   The uppermost newly composed voice in three-voice **organum.**

twelve-tone music (595)   Initially an **atonal** or **pantonal** style in which all 12 of the octave's chromatic pitches were regarded as equals and none had any special function. It soon came to refer to the ordering of the 12 pitches into a **series** or **tone row** unique to each composition that furnished the basis for the work.

V

variation suite (297)   A **Baroque suite** in which each movement expands the thematic relationships through progressive variation.

vaudeville (352)   A French song based on a preexistent popular tune with a **contrafactum** text satirizing current political events. In the late Renaissance the term was often synonymous with **voix de ville.**

vaudeville final (352)   The concluding event of each act in opéra comique. All important characters assemble on stage, where each sings a stanza or two of a **vaudeville.**

verismo (560)   A type of opera depicting the realism of life. Characters were often drawn from lower social classes or those living a "bohemian" kind of life, the plot emphasized violent and emotional situations, and the drama's environment was portrayed realistically.

vers mesurée (185)   Late Renaissance French poetry in which poets attempted to apply an accentual version of the quantitative principles of Greek and Latin poetry to the French language.

verse anthem (200)   An Anglican **anthem,** usually with organ accompaniment, with alternating sections for soloist(s) and choir.

verset or **verse** (218)   A short organ solo that was substituted for chant in some sections of the Proper of the Mass or Offices.

versus (69)   One of the earliest polyphonic compositions not based on chant, it was a newly composed setting of a Latin sacred text sung as an extraliturgical addition to a Mass on an important feast day. Versus were set in **discant style.**

villancico (190)   A Renaissance Spanish song for three or four voices, its structure resembles that of medieval **ballata** and **virelai.**

villanella (175)   A light, witty, sophisticated Italian Renaissance song intended for aristocratic audiences. The simple homophonic setting enhances the melody in the top voice and often contains a series of parallel fifths.

violinata (561)   Double or multiple reinforcement of a vocal melody by the orchestral accompaniment. Used by Puccini, Rossini, and other opera composers.

virelai (96)   One of the three important **formes fixes,** it uses AbbaA structure.

virginal (221)   A small harpsichord with only one set of strings and one manual (keyboard). It was popular in England during the Renaissance.

voix de ville (184)   Sometimes called **vaudeville.** A French Renaissance courtly poem in which several short stanzas are given strophic setting. The treble melody is supported by a simple homophonic accompaniment.

Volkslied (433)   A term coined in the late eighteenth century to designate German folk song.

votive (39)   A chant, Mass, or Office honoring a particular saint.

W

Wagner tubas (498)   A special tuba developed for Wagner's operas. Its tone quality is between that of French horn and trombone.

white noise (639)   All possible frequencies sounding simultaneously, resulting in a hissing sound.

whole consort (212)   A Renaissance term for an ensemble in which all instruments belong to the same family.

word (text) painting (164)   Depiction of the meaning of a word or phrase through its musical setting.

Z

zarzuela (260)   A Spanish dramatic form that combines singing, dancing, and spoken dialogue. To some extent it is patterned after early Baroque opera.

Select Bibliography for Further Reading

GENERAL

Detailed bibliography of collected works and editions: (a) "Editions, Historical," *The New Harvard Dictionary of Music*, ed. Don M. Randel (Cambridge, MA: Harvard U. Press, 1986), pp. 264–76. (b) "Editions, Historical," *The New Grove Dictionary of Music and Musicians*, 20 vols., ed. Stanley Sadie (London: Macmillan, 1980–81), Vol. 5, pp. 848–69.

Detailed bibliography of primary source materials: "Sources," *The New Grove Dictionary of Music and Musicians*, 20 vols., ed. Stanley Sadie (London: Macmillan, 1980–81), Vol. 17, pp. 590–753.

Biblia sacra, Vulgate edition (Paris: Librairie Garnier Frères, 1868).

Austin, William W. *Music in the Twentieth Century: From Debussy through Stravinsky* (New York: Norton, 1966).

————, ed. *New Looks at Italian Opera* (Westport, CT: Greenwood Press, 1976).

Béhague, Gerard. *Music in Latin America: An Introduction* (Englewood Cliffs, NJ: Prentice-Hall, 1979).

Bowers, Jane, and Judith Tick. *Women Making Music: The Western Art Tradition, 1150–1950* (Urbana: U. of Illinois Press, 1986).

Bukofzer, Manfred. *Music in the Baroque Era: From Monteverdi to Bach* (New York: Norton, 1947).

Bulfinch, Thomas. *Bulfinch's Mythology* (New York: Crowell, n.d.).

Claudon, Francis, J. Mongrédien, C. de Nys, and K. Roschitz. *Histoire de L'Opéra en France* (Paris: Nathan, 1986).

Clough, Shepard B., et al. *European History in a World Perspective,* 2 vols., 3d ed. (Lexington, MA: Heath, 1975).

Egan, Edward W., C. B. Hintz, and L. F. Wise, comp. and eds. *Kings, Rulers, and Statesmen,* rev. ed. (New York: Sterling Publishing, 1976).

Farmer, Henry G. *A History of Music in Scotland* (London: Hinrichsen, 1947; repr. New York: Da Capo Press, 1970).

Ferguson, Donald N. *Image and Structure in Chamber Music* (Minneapolis: U. of Minnesota Press, 1964).

Gardner, Helen. *Gardner's Art Through the Ages,* 6th ed., rev. by H. de la Croix and R. G. Tansey (New York: Harcourt Brace Jovanovich, 1975).

Gies, Frances, and Joseph Gies. *Women in the Middle Ages* (New York: Crowell, 1978).

Gillespie, John. *Five Centuries of Keyboard Music: An Historical Survey of Music for Harpsichord and Piano* (Belmont, CA: Wadsworth, 1965).

Grout, Donald J. *A Short History of Opera,* 3d ed. (New York: Columbia U. Press, 1988).

Grun, Bernard. *The Timetables of History,* 3d rev. ed. (New York: Simon & Schuster, 1991).

Harrison, Frank Ll. *Music in Medieval Britain,* 2d ed., ed. Egon Wellesz (London: Routledge and Kegan Paul, 1963).

Hitchcock, H. Wiley. *Music in the United States: A Historical Introduction,* 3d ed. (Englewood Cliffs, N.J.: Prentice-Hall, 1988).

Hope-Wallace, Philip. *A Picture History of Opera* (London: Hulton, 1959).

Hoppin, Richard H. *Medieval Music* (New York: Norton, 1978).

Hughes, Andrew. *Medieval Music: The Sixth Liberal Art* (Toronto: U. of Toronto Press, 1980).

Kirby, Frank E. *A Short History of Keyboard Music* (New York: Free Press, 1966).

Kralik, Heinrich. *The Vienna Opera,* trans. Richard Rickett. (London: Methuen, 1963).

Leonard, Richard A. *A History of Russian Music* (New York: Macmillan, 1956; repr. New York: Minerva Press, 1968; repr. Westport, CT: Greenwood Press, 1977).

Livermore, Ann. *A Short History of Spanish Music* (New York: Vienna House, 1972).

Longyear, Rey M. *Nineteenth-Century Romanticism in Music,* 3d ed. (Englewood Cliffs, NJ: Prentice-Hall, 1988).

MacKerness, Eric D. *A Social History of English Music* (Westport, CT: Greenwood Press, 1976).

Marcuse, Sibyl. *Musical Instruments: A Comprehensive Dictionary* (New York: Doubleday, 1964).

Marco, Tomás. *Spanish Music in the Twentieth Century,* trans. Cola Franzen. (Cambridge, MA: Harvard U. Press, 1993).

McGee, Timothy J. *The Music of Canada* (New York: Norton, 1985).

Meggett, Joan M. *Keyboard Music by Women Composers: A Catalog and Bibliography* (Westport, CT: Greenwood Press, 1981).

Neuls-Bates, Carol, ed. *Women in Music: An Anthology of Source Readings from the Middle Ages to the Present* (New York: Harper & Row, 1982).

The New Grove Dictionary of Music and Musicians, 20 vols., ed. Stanley Sadie (New York: Macmillan, 1980–81).

The New Oxford History of Music, 10 vols., ed. Jack A. Westrup, Gerald Abraham, et al. (London: Oxford U. Press, 1954–).

Newmarch, Rosa. *The Music of Czechoslovakia* (London: Oxford U. Press, 1972; repr. New York: Da Capo Press, 1978).

Plantinga, Leon. *Romantic Music* (New York: Norton, 1984).

Raynor, Henry. *Music & Society Since 1815* (New York: Schocken, 1976).

————. *A Social History of Music: From the Middle Ages to Beethoven* (New York: Schocken, 1972).

Reese, Gustave. *Music in the Middle Ages* (New York: Norton, 1940).

―――. *Music in the Renaissance,* rev. ed. (New York: Norton, 1959).

Roberts, Alexander, and James Donaldson, eds. *The Ante-Nicene Fathers,* Vol. VIII [Apocryphal Books of *The Bible*] (Buffalo, NY: The Christian Literature Co., 1886).

Salzman, Eric. *Twentieth-Century Music,* 3d ed. (Englewood Cliffs, NJ: Prentice-Hall, 1988).

Simms, Bryan. *Music of the Twentieth Century: Style and Structure* (New York: Schirmer Books, 1986).

Strunk, Oliver. *Source Readings in Music History* (New York: Norton, 1950).

Subira, José. *Historia de la Música española e Hispano Americana* (Barcelona and Madrid: Salvat Editoreo, 1953).

Sumner, William L. *The Organ: Its Evolution, Principles of Construction and Use,* 3d ed. (London: Macdonald, 1962).

Trevelyan, Janet P. *A Short History of the Italian People,* 3d ed. (New York: Pitman, 1956).

Ulrich, Homer. *Symphonic Music: Its Evolution Since the Renaissance* (New York: Columbia U. Press, 1952).

―――. *Chamber Music,* 2d ed. (New York: Columbia U. Press, 1966).

Walker, Ernest. *A History of Music in England,* 3d ed., rev. by J. A. Westrup (Oxford: Clarendon, 1952).

CHAPTER 1: HERITAGE FROM ANTIQUITY

GENERAL

Quasten, Johannes. *Music & Worship in Pagan & Christian Antiquity* (Munster: Aschendorff, 1973), Eng. trans. Boniface Ramsey, O. P. (trans. 1973; pub. Washington, D.C.: National Association of Pastoral Musicians, 1983).

Sachs, Curt. *The Rise of Music in the Ancient World* (New York: Norton, 1943).

Wellesz, Egon, ed. *Ancient and Oriental Music,* Vol. I of *The New Oxford History of Music,* 10 vols., ed. J. A. Westrup et al. (London: Oxford U. Press, 1957).

GREEK MUSIC

Anderson, Warren D. *Ethos and Education in Greek Music* (Cambridge, MA: Harvard U. Press, 1966).

Aristotle. *The Works of Aristotle,* ed. W. D. Ross, trans. J. J. Beare et al. (Oxford: Oxford U. Press, 1908–52), especially *Politics,* Book VIII.

Aristoxenus. *Harmonics,* ed. and trans. Henry S. Macran, pub. as *The Harmonics of Aristoxenus* (Oxford: Clarendon Press, 1902).

Barker, Andrew, ed. *Greek Musical Writings,* Vol. I, *The Musician and His Art* (Cambridge: Cambridge U. Press, 1984).

Crocker, Richard. "Pythagorean Mathematics and Music," *Journal of Aesthetics and Art Criticism* 22 (1963–64), pp. 189–98, 325–35.

Lippmann, Edward. *Musical Thought in Ancient Greece* (New York: Columbia U. Press, 1964).

Mountford, James Frederick. "The Harmonics of Ptolemy and the Lacuna in II,14" *Transactions and Proceedings of the American Philological Association,* ed. Joseph W. Hewett, 57 (1926) (Middletown, CT: American Philological Association), pp. 71–95.

Plato. *Republic,* trans. Desmond Lee (Harmondsworth, England, and Baltimore: Penguin, 1974), esp. Book III.

―――. *Timaeus,* trans. Robert G. Bury, bilingual ed., *The Loeb Classics Library* (Cambridge, MA: Harvard U. Press, 1929; repr. 1981).

HEBREW

Vantoura, Suzanne Haïk. *La Musique de la Bible Révélée* [book and cassette tape] (Paris: Dessin et Tolra, 1978).

INDIA

Kaufmann, Walter. *The Rāgas of North India* (Bloomington: Indiana U. Press, 1968).

Wade, Bonnie C. *Music in India: The Classical Traditions* (Englewood Cliffs, NJ: Prentice-Hall, 1979).

NEAR AND MIDDLE EAST

Bibikov, Sergey N. *The Oldest Musical Complex, Made of Mammoth Bones* (Kiev: Iadatelstvo "Naukova Dumka," 1981).

Kilmer, Anne Draffkorn, Richard L. Crocker, and Robert R. Brown. *Sounds from Silence* (Berkeley, CA: Bit Enki Publications, 1976).

CHAPTER 2: THE EARLY CHRISTIAN ERA

GENERAL

Cattin, Giulio. *Music of the Middle Ages I,* trans. Steven Botterill (Cambridge: Cambridge U. Press, 1984).

Levi, Peter. *The Frontiers of Paradise: A Study of Monks and Monasteries* (New York: Weidenfeld & Nicolson, 1988).

BOETHIUS, CASSIODORUS

Boethius, A. M. S. *Consolation of Philosophy,* trans. H. F. Stewart and E. K. Rand, bilingual ed., in *The Loeb Classics Library* (Cambridge, MA: Harvard U. Press, 1946; repr. 1953).

―――. *De institutione musica,* trans. Calvin M. Bower, pub. as *Fundamentals of Music* (New Haven, CT: Yale U. Press, 1989).

Carpenter, N. C. *Music in the Medieval and Renaissance Universities* (Norman: U. of Oklahoma Press, 1958).

Rand, Edward K. *Founders of the Middle Ages* (Cambridge, MA: Harvard U. Press, 1929; repr. New York: Dover, 1957), Chapter 5.

Schrade, Leo. "Music in the Philosophy of Boethius," *The Musical Quarterly* 23 (1947), pp. 188–200.

BYZANTINE

Strunk, Oliver. *Essays on Music in the Byzantine World* (New York: Norton, 1977).

Wellesz, Egon. *Eastern Elements in Western Chant* (Oxford: Byzantine Institute, 1947).

―――. *A History of Byzantine Music and Hymnody,* 2d ed. (Oxford: Clarendon, 1961; repr. 1971).

―――. "Music of the Eastern Churches," *The New Oxford History of Music,* Vol. II, ed. Anselm Hughes, 2d ed., rev. (London: Oxford U. Press, 1955), pp. 14–51.

CHRISTIAN CHURCH

Augustinus, Aurelius [Saint Augustine]. *Confessions,* trans. Edward B. Pusey, Vol. 7 in *The Harvard Classics* (New York: Collier, 1909). Also, *Confessions of St. Augustine,* trans. E. M. Blaiklock (Nashville: T. Nelson, 1983).

Backhouse, Janet. *The Lindisfarne Gospels* (Oxford: Phaidon Press, 1981).

Chabannes, Jacques. *St. Augustine* (Paris: Empire, 1961), trans. Julie Kernan (Garden City, NY: Doubleday, 1962).

Jungmann, Josef A. *The Early Liturgy to the Time of Gregory the Great* (Notre Dame, IN: U. of Notre Dame Press, 1959).

McCann, Justin, ed. and trans. *The Rule of St. Benedict in Latin and English* (London: Burns, Oates, 1952).

Migne, Jacques Paul, ed. *Patrologiae cursus completus . . . Series Graeca,* 161 vols. (Paris: J. P. Migne, 1857–87), re: writings of St. John Chrysostomus and other church fathers.

————. *Patrologiae cursus completus . . . Series latina,* 221 vols. (Paris: J. P. Migne, 1841–79), re: writings of specific church fathers.

Oates, Whitney J. *Basic Writings of Saint Augustine* (New York: Random House, 1948).

Roberts, Alexander, and James Donaldson, eds. *The Ante-Nicene Fathers: Translations of the Writings of the Fathers down to A.D. 325,* 10 vols. (New York: Scribner's, 1899–1900).

Treitler, Leo. "Homer and Gregory: The Transmission of Epic Poetry and Plainchant," *The Musical Quarterly* 55 (1974), pp. 333–74.

Gregory the Great

Dudden, Frederick H. *Gregory the Great: His Place in History and Thought,* 2 vols. (London: Longmans, Green, 1905; repr. New York: Russell & Russell, 1967).

Richards, Jeffrey. *Consul of God: The Life and Times of Gregory the Great* (London: Routledge & Kegan Paul, 1980).

HEBREW

Idelsohn, A. Z. *Jewish Music in its Historical Development* (New York: Schocken Books, 1967).

Rothmuller, Aron M. *The Music of the Jews,* new, rev. ed. (Cranbury, NJ: A. S. Barnes, 1975).

Werner, Eric. *The Sacred Bridge,* Vol. I: *Liturgical Parallels in Synagogue and Early Church* (New York: Columbia U. Press, 1959; Schocken Books, 1970; repr. Da Capo Press, 1979); Vol. II: *The Interdependence of Liturgy and Music in Synagogue and Church during the First Millennium* (New York: KTAV Publishing House, 1984).

CHAPTER 3: ECCLESIASTICAL CHANT

Music

Benedictines of Solesmes, eds. *The Liber Usualis* (Tournai, Belgium: Desclée & Co., 1960).

Frere, Walter H., ed. *Antiphonale Sarisburiense,* 17 vols. (London: The Plainsong & Mediaeval Music Society, 1901–26; rcpr. 1966).

————. *Graduale Sarisburiense* (London: The Plainsong & Mediaeval Music Society, 1894; repr. Farnborough, Eng.: Gregg, 1966).

————. *The Use of Sarum* (Cambridge: Cambridge U. Press, 1898, 1900).

Legg, J. W., ed. *The Sarum Missal* (Oxford: Clarendon, 1916; repr. 1969).

Paléographie musicale: Les principaux manuscrits de chant Grégorien, Ambrosien, Mozarabe, Gallican [Facsimiles of the principal manuscripts of chant] (Solesmes, France: Imprimerie St.-Pierre, and Tournai, Belgium: Desclée, Lefebure, 1889–), 2 series.

Suñol, G. M., ed. *Antiphonale missarum juxta ritum Sanctae Ecclesiae Mediolanensis* [Ambrosian Antiphonale] (Rome, 1935).

————. *Canti ambrosiani per il popolo* (Milan, 1936).

For Further Reading

Anglès, H. "Latin Chant before St. Gregory," *New Oxford History of Music,* Vol. II (1954), pp. 58–91.

Apel, Willi. *Gregorian Chant* (Bloomington: Indiana U. Press, 1958; 3d ed., 1966).

Backhouse, Janet. *The Lindisfarne Gospels* (Oxford: Phaidon Press, 1981).

Cattin, Giulio. *Music of the Middle Ages I,* trans. Steven Botterill (Cambridge: Cambridge U. Press, 1984).

Harrison, Frank L. *Music in Medieval Britain* (London: Routledge & Kegan Paul, 1958; 2d ed., 1963).

Hughes, David. "Evidence for the Traditional View of the Transmission of Gregorian Chant," *Journal of the American Musicological Society* 40 (1987), pp. 377–404.

Jungmann, Josef A. *The Early Liturgy to the Time of Gregory the Great* (Notre Dame, IN: U. of Notre Dame Press, 1959).

Lechner, R. F. "Mozarabic Rite," and Wortman, I., "Mozarabic Rite, Chants of," in *New Catholic Encyclopedia* 10 (New York: McGraw-Hill, 1967), pp. 58–60.

Levy, Kenneth. "Charlemagne's Archetype of Gregorian Chant," *Journal of the American Musicological Society* 40 (1987), pp. 1–30.

Porter, William S. *The Gallican Rite, Studies in Eucharistic Faith and Practice,* Vol. IV (London: Mowbray, and New York: Morehouse-Gorham, 1958).

CHAPTER 4: THE ROMAN LITURGY

LITURGICAL BOOKS

Abbatiae Sancti Petri de Solesmis and Consociatio Internationalis Musicae Sacrae. *Liber cantualis* (Solesmes, France: Abbaye Saint-Pierre, and Tournai, Belgium: Desclée, 1978).

Abbaye Saint-Pierre de Solesmes. *Graduale Sacrosanctae Romanae Ecclesiae de tempore & de sanctis* (Solesmes, France: Abbaye Saint-Pierre, and Tournai, Belgium: Desclée, 1979).

————. *Graduale Triplex* (Solesmes, France: Abbaye Saint-Pierre, and Tournai, Belgium: Desclée, 1979).

————. *The Gregorian Missal for Sundays* (Solesmes, France: Abbaye Saint-Pierre, and Tournai, Belgium: Desclée Publishing Co., 1990).

Benedictines of Solesmes, eds. *The Liber Usualis* (Tournai, Belgium: Desclée & Co., 1960).

Lectionary for Mass, Eng. trans., American version, being *The Roman Missal* revised by decree of The Second Vatican Council and published by authority of Pope Paul VI (New York: Catholic Book Publishing Co., 1970).

The Rites of the Catholic Church as Revised by The Second Vatican Council and published by Authority of Pope Paul VI, Eng. trans., The International Commission on English in the Liturgy (New York: Pueblo Publishing Co., 1976).

The Sacramentary, Eng. trans. by The International Commission on English in the Liturgy, revised by decree of The Second Vatican Council and published by authority of Pope Paul VI (New York: Catholic Book Publishing Co., 1974).

For Further Reading

Abbott, Walter M., S. J., gen. ed. *The Documents of Vatican II,* trans. Msgr. Joseph Gallagher (The America Press, 1967).

Handschin, Jacques. "Trope, Sequence, and Conductus," *Early Medieval Music up to 1300,* ed. Dom Anselm Hughes, Vol. II of *New Oxford History of Music,* rev. ed. (London: Oxford U. Press, 1955), pp. 128–74.

Jungmann, Josef A. *The Mass: An Historical, Theological, and Pastoral Survey,* trans. Julian Fernandes, ed. Mary E. Evans (Collegeville, MN: Liturgical Press, 1976).

———. *The Mass of the Roman Rite: Its Origins and Development,* 2 vols., trans. Francis A. Brunner (New York: Benziger, 1951–55; repr. 1986).

Marty, Martin E. *A Short History of Christianity* (New York: Meridian, 1959).

McKinnon, J. W., ed. *Music in Early Christian Literature* (Cambridge: Cambridge U. Press, 1987).

Richstatter, Thomas, O. F. M. *Liturgical Law: New Style, New Spirit* (Chicago: Franciscan Herald Press, 1977).

Liturgical Drama
Music
Coussemaker, Edmond de. *Drames liturgique du moyen-âge* [Liturgical dramas of the Middle Ages], an anthology (New York: Broude, 1964).

Greenberg, Noah, ed. *The Play of Daniel* (New York: Oxford U. Press, 1959).

———. *The Play of Herod* (New York: Oxford U. Press, 1965).

For Further Reading
Bevington, David. *Medieval Drama* (Boston: Houghton Mifflin, 1975).

Lipphardt, Walther. *Lateinische Osterfeiern und Osterspiele* [Latin Easter plays] (Berlin: DeGruyter, 1975–).

Young, Karl. *The Drama of the Medieval Church* (Oxford: Clarendon, 1933).

Notker
Crocker, Richard L. *The Early Medieval Sequence* (Berkeley: U. of California Press, 1977).

Steinen, Wolfrem von den. *Notker der Dichter und seine geistige Welt,* 2 vols., bilingual (Bern: A. Francke, 1948).

———, ed. *Notkeri Poetae Liber Ymnorum* [Book of Hymns of Notker, Poet] (Bern: Francke, 1960).

Chapter 5: Early Middle Ages

General
Barraclough, Geoffrey. *The Crucible of Europe* (Berkeley: U. of California Press, 1976).

Caldwell, John. *Medieval Music* (Bloomington: Indiana U. Press, 1978), pp. 114–30.

Coussemaker, C. Edmond de. *Scriptorum de musica medii aevi nova series* (Paris: A. Durand, 1864–76; repr. Hildesheim: G. Olms, 1963).

Gerbert, Martin. *Scriptores ecclesiatici de musica sacra,* 3 vols. (St. Blasien, 1784; repr. Hildesheim: Olms, 1963).

Henderson, Ernest F., ed. and trans. *Select Historical Documents of the Middle Ages* (London: George Bell and Sons, 1892; repr. New York: AMS Press, 1968).

Hoppin, Richard. *Medieval Music* (New York: Norton, 1978), pp. 187–214.

Hughes, Dom Anselm. "The Birth of Polyphony," and "Music in the Twelfth Century," *Early Medieval Music up to 1300,* vol. II of *The New Oxford History of Music* (London: Oxford U. Press, 1954; rev. 1955).

Munrow, David. *Instruments of the Middle Ages and Renaissance* (London: Oxford U. Press and EMI Records, 1976).

Ogg, Frederic A., ed. *A Source Book of Mediaeval History: Documents . . . from the German Invasions to the Renaissance* (New York: American Book Co., 1907).

Palisca, Claude, ed. *Hucbald, Guido and John on Music* (New Haven, CT: Yale U. Press, 1978).

Reese, Gustave. *Music in the Middle Ages* (New York: Norton, 1940), pp. 249–71, 387ff.

Stoddard, Whitney S. *Monastery and Cathedral in France* (Middletown, CT: Wesleyan U. Press, 1966).

Guido
Chailley, Jacques. "*Ut queant laxis* et les Origines de la Gamme," [*Ut queant laxis* and the origins of the scale], *Acta Musicologica* 56 (1984), pp. 48–58.

Waesberghe, Joseph Smits van. "Guido of Arezzo and Musical Improvisation," *Musica Disciplina,* 5 (1951), pp. 55–63.

———. "The Musical Notation of Guido of Arezzo," *Musica Disciplina* 5 (1951), pp. 15–53.

Organum
Anonymous. *Ad Organum faciendum & Item de Organo,* ed. and trans. Jay A. Huff (Brooklyn, NY: The Institute of Mediaeval Music, 1969).

Anonymous. *Musica enchiriadis,* trans. Leonie Rosenstiel (Colorado Springs: Colorado College, 1976).

Anonymous. *Scolica enchiriadis,* trans. Nancy C. Phillips (Diss., Ann Arbor, MI: University Microfilms, 1985).

Frere, W. H. *The Winchester Troper* (London: Henry Bradshaw Society, 1894).

Britain
Baxter, J. H., ed. *An Old St. Andrews Music Book,* facsimile ed. (London: St. Andrews U. Publications, 1931).

Galpin, Francis W. *Old English Instruments of Music* (London: Methuen, 1910; repr. 1978).

Harrison, Frank L. *Music in Medieval Britain* (London: Routledge & Kegan Paul, 1958; 2d ed., 1963), Chapter 3.

Planchart, Alejandro. *The Repertory of Tropes at Winchester,* 2 vols. [music] (Princeton, NJ: Princeton U. Press, 1977).

Santiago de Compostela
Wagner, Peter, ed. *Die Gesänge der Jakobusliturgie zu Santiago de Compostela aus dem Sog. Codex Calixtinus* [The songs of the Jacobus Liturgy at Santiago de Compostela in the so-called Codex Calixtinus] (Freiburg, Switz.: Universitaets-Buchhandlung, 1931).

Whitehill, Walter M., and G. Prado. *Liber Sancti Jacobi, Codex Calixtinus,* 3 vols. [facsimile, transcriptions, commentary] (Santiago de Compostela, 1944).

St. Martial
Treitler, Leo. "The Polyphony of St. Martial," *Journal of the American Musicological Society* 17 (1963), pp. 29–42.

Chapter 6: The Middle Ages—*Ars Antiqua*

General

Barraclough, Geoffrey. *The Crucible of Europe* (Berkeley: U. of California Press, 1976).

Caldwell, John. *Medieval Music* (Bloomington: Indiana U. Press, 1978), pp. 131–58.

Henderson, Ernest F., ed. and trans. *Select Historical Documents of the Middle Ages* (London: George Bell & Sons, 1892; repr. AMS Press, 1968).

Kubach, Hans Erich. *Romanesque Architecture* (New York: Harry N. Abrams, 1975).

Ogg, Frederick A., ed. *A Source Book of Mediaeval History* (New York: American Book Co., 1907).

Reese, Gustave. *Music in the Middle Ages* (New York: Norton, 1940), pp. 272–330.

Temko, Allan. *Notre-Dame of Paris* (New York: Viking Press, 1955).

Notation, Theory

Apel, Willi. *The Notation of Polyphonic Music, 900–1600,* 5th ed. (Cambridge, MA: Medieval Academy of America, 1961), pp. 282–324.

Parrish, Carl. *The Notation of Medieval Music* (New York: Norton, 1957, 1959), pp. 60–140.

Franco of Cologne

Franco of Cologne. *Ars cantus mensurabilis,* trans. and annotated, in Oliver Strunk: *Source Readings in Music History* (New York: Norton, 1950), pp. 139–59.

Hocket

Grocheo, Johannes de. *De musica,* trans. A. Seay, pub. as *Johannes de Grocheo: Concerning Music* (Colorado Springs: Colorado College, 1967; 2d ed., 1973).

Sanders, Ernest H. "The Medieval Hocket in Practice and Theory," *The Musical Quarterly* 60 (1974), pp. 246–56.

Notre Dame School

Music

Manuscript: Wolfenbüttel Helmstedt 628 (formerly 677), [W$_1$]. Facsimile: *An Old St. Andrews Music Book,* ed. J. H. Baxter (London: St. Andrews U. Publications, 1931).

Manuscript: Wolfenbüttel Helmstedt 1099 (formerly 1206), [W$_2$]. Facsimile: *Wolfenbüttel 1099,* ed. Luther Dittmer (Brooklyn, NY: Institute of Medieval Music, 1960).

Manuscript: Pluteus 29.1, Biblioteca Medicea-Laurenziana, Florence. Facsimile: *Firenze, Biblioteca Medicea-Laurenziana, pluteo 29.1* [sic], 2 vols., ed. L. Dittmer, pub. as Vols. 10–11 of *Publications of Medieval Music Manuscripts* (Brooklyn, NY: Institute of Mediaeval Music, 1966–67).

Husmann, Heinrich, ed. *Die drei- und vierstimmige Notre-Dame Organa* [The three- and four-voice Notre Dame organa] (Leipzig: Breitkopf & Härtel, 1940; repr. Hildesheim: G. Olms, 1967).

Thurston, Ethel, ed. *The Conductus Collection of MS Wolfenbüttel 1099,* 3 vols. (Madison, WI: A-R Editions, 1980).

———. *The Works of Perotin* (New York: Kalmus, 1970).

For Further Reading

Anonymous IV, trans. and ed. Luther Dittmer, Vol. I of *Musical Theorists in Translation* (Brooklyn, NY: Institute of Mediaeval Music, 1959).

Guérard, Paul. *Collection des Cartulaires de France,* Vol. IV, *Cartulaire de l'Église Notre-Dame de Paris,* Tome I [Documents of the Church of Notre Dame of Paris, unedited] (Paris: Crapelet, 1850).

Hoppin, Richard. *Medieval Music* (New York: Norton, 1978), pp. 215–55.

Husmann, H. "The Origin and Destination of the *Magnus liber organi,*" *The Musical Quarterly* 49 (1963), pp. 311–30.

Roesner, Edward H. "The Origins of W$_1$," *Journal of the American Musicological Society* 29 (1976), pp. 337–80.

Sanders, E. H. "The Question of Perotin's Oeuvre and Dates," *Festschrift für Walter Wiora,* ed. L. Finscher and C.-H. Mahling (Kassel: Bärenreiter, 1967), pp. 241–49.

Tischler, Hans. "The Dates of Perotin," *Journal of the American Musicological Society* 16 (1963), pp. 240ff.

———. "The Evolution of the *Magnus liber organi,*" *The Musical Quarterly* 70 (1984), pp. 163–74.

———. "The Structure of Notre Dame Organa," *Acta Musicologica* 49 (1977), pp. 193ff.

Waite, William G. *The Rhythm of Twelfth-Century Polyphony* (New Haven, CT: Yale U. Press, 1954).

Wright, Craig. "Leoninus, Poet and Musician," *Journal of the American Musicological Society* 49 (1986), pp. 21–52.

Motet

Bamberg Codex. (a) Manuscript: Lit.115 (formerly Ed.IV.6), Staatliche Bibliothek, Bamberg, West Germany (Federal Republic of Germany). (b) Editions: Aubrey, Pierre. *Cent motets du XIIIe siècle: publiés d'après le manusrit Ed.IV.6 de Bamberg* (Paris: A. Rouart, Lerolle & Cie, P. Guethner, 1908), 3 vols. (1, facsimile; 2, transcription; 3, commentary). Anderson, G., ed. *Compositions of the Bamberg Manuscript,* Vol. 75 of *Corpus mensurabilis musicae,* American Institute of Musicology (Neuhausen-Stuttgart: Hänssler, 1977).

Las Huelgas Codex. (a) Manuscript at Monasterio de Las Huelgas, Burgos, Spain. (b) Edition: Anglès, Higini. *El codex musical de Las Huelgas* (Barcelona: Institut d'estudis Catalans, Biblioteca de Catalunya, 1931), 3 vols. (1, commentary; 2, facsimile; 3, transcription).

Montpellier Codex. (a) Manuscript: H 196, Faculté de médecine, Montpellier, France. (b) Editions: Rokseth, Yvonne. *Polyphonies du XIIIe siècle: Le manusrit H 196 de la Faculté de Medicine de Montpellier* (Paris: Éditions de l'Oiseau Lyre, 1935–39), 4 vols. (1, facsimile; 2, 3, transcription; 4, commentary). Tischler, hans, ed. *The Montpellier Codex,* 3 vols. (Madison, WI: A-R Editions, 1978).

Tischler, Hans. *The Earliest Motets (to circa 1270): A Complete Comparative Edition* (New Haven, CT: Yale U. Press, 1982), 3 vols.

Britain

Harrison, Frank L. *Music in Medieval Britain,* 2d ed. (London: Routledge & Kegan Paul, 1963), pp. 115–49.

Wooldridge, H. E., and H. V. Hughes, eds. *Early English Harmony from the 10th to the 15th Century,* 2 vols., Plainsong and Mediaevel Music Society (London: Quaritch, 1897–1913).

Chapter 7: Medieval Monophony

Latin Songs

Bingen, Hildegard von. *Lieder,* ed. Prudentiana Barth, M. Immaculata Ritscher, and Joseph Schmidt-Görg (Salzburg: Otto Müller Verlag, 1969).

Bruel, Karl, ed. *The Cambridge Songs* (Cambridge: Cambridge U. Press, 1915; repr. AMS, 1973, 1978).

Raby, F. J. E. *A History of Secular Latin Poetry in the Middle Ages,* 2 vols. (Oxford: Clarendon, 1934; repr. 1957).

Waddell, Helen. *Songs of the Wandering Scholars,* ed. Felicitas Corrigan (London: The Folio Society, 1982).

ENGLAND

Armstrong, Robert B. *English and Irish Instruments,* 2 vols. (Edinburgh: D. Douglas, 1904–8; repr. Shannon: Irish U. Press, 1969, and New York: Praeger, 1970).

Galpin, Francis W. *Old English Instruments of Music: Their History and Character* (London: Methuen, 1910).

Trend, J. B. "The First English Songs," *Music and Letters* 9 (1928), pp. 111–27.

FRANCE

Adam de la Halle

Manuscript: MS 657 (formerly 139), Bibliothèque municipale, Arras. Facsimile: *Le Chansonnier d'Arras,* ed. Alfred Jeanroy (Paris, 1925; repr. New York: Johnson, 1968).

Adam de la Halle. *Works,* Vol. 44, *Corpus mensurabilis musicae,* ed. A. Carapetyan (Rome: American Institute of Musicology, 1947).

Coussemaker, E. de, ed. *Oeuvres complètes de Adam de la Halle: poésies et musique* (Paris, 1871); repr. as *Complete Works of the Troubadour Adam de la Halle* (New York: Broude, 1964).

Gennrich, F., ed. *Adam de la Halle: Le jeu de Robin et de Marion; Li Rondel Adam* (Frankfurt am Main: Langen, 1962).

Troubadours, Trouvères

Manuscript: MS 5198 (formerly B.L.F. 63), Bibliothèque de l'Arsenal, Paris. Facsimile, with some transcriptions: *Le Chansonnier de l'Arsenal,* ed. Pierre Aubry (Paris: P. Guethner, 1909–10).

Manuscript: MS fr.844, Bibliothèque nationale, Paris. Facsimile: *Le Manuscrit du Roi,* 2 vols., ed. Jean Beck and L. Beck (Philadelphia: U. of Pennsylvania Press, 1938).

Manuscript: fr.846 (Cangé 66), Bibliothèque nationale, Paris. Facsimile: *Le Chansonnier Cangé,* 2 vols. (1, facsimile; 2 transcriptions), ed. Jean Beck (Philadelphia: U. of Pennsylvania Press, 1927).

Briffault, R. *The Troubadours* (Bloomington: Indiana U. Press, 1965).

Gennrich, F., ed. *Troubadours, Trouvères, Minne- und Meistergesang,* Vol. II of *Das Musikwerk,* ed. K. G. Fellerer (Cologne: Arno Volk, and London: Leeds Music, 1951); Eng. trans. pub. as *Anthology of Music* (1960).

Page, Christopher. *Voices and Instruments of the Middle Ages: Instrumental practice and songs in France 1100–1300* (Berkeley: U. of California Press, 1986).

Van der Werf, Hendrik. *The Chansons of the Troubadours and Trouvères* (Utrecht: A. Ousthoek, 1972).

Trobairitz

Bogin, Meg [Magda]. *The Women Troubadours* (London: Paddington Press, 1976).

Coldwell, Maria V. "Jougleresses and Trobairitz: Secular Musicians in Medieval France," *Women Making Music: The Western Art Tradition, 1150–1950,* ed. Jane Bowers and Judith Tick (Urbana: U. of Illinois Press, 1986).

Gies, Frances, and Joseph Gies. *Women in the Middle Ages* (New York: Crowell, 1978; repr. Barnes & Noble, 1980).

Neuls-Bates, Carol, ed. *Women in Music: An Anthology of Source Readings from the Middle Ages to the Present* (New York: Harper & Row, 1982), pp. 11–36.

GERMANIC LANDS

Moser, H., and Müller-Blattau, eds. *Deutsche Lieder des Mittelalters* [German Songs of the Middle Ages] (Stuttgart: Klett, 1968).

Taylor, R. J., ed. *The Art of the Minnesinger,* 2 vols. (Cardiff: U. of Wales Press, 1968).

(Also see Gennrich, above.)

IBERIA

Manuscripts: (1) MS b.I.2 (also known as j.b.2), Real Monasterio de El Escorial; (2) MS T.j.I, Real Monasterio de El Escorial; (3) MS 10069, Biblioteca national, Madrid.

Anglés, Higinio. *La Música de las cantigas de Santa María del rey Alfonso el Sabio* [The music of *Las cantigas de Santa Maria* of King Alfonso the Wise], 3 vols. (1, MS b.I.2 facsimile; 2, MS b.I.2 transcription; 3, other cantigas) (Barcelona: Biblioteca Central, Sección de Música, 1943–64).

Stevenson, Robert. *Spanish Music in the Age of Columbus* (The Hague: M. Nijhoff, 1960).

ITALY

Liuzzi, Fernando, ed. *La Lauda e i primordi della melodia italiana,* 2 vols. (Rome: Libreria dello Stato, 1935).

CHAPTER 8: LATE MEDIEVAL MUSIC

GENERAL

Music

Manuscript: MS Pal. 87 (Squarcialupi Codex), Biblioteca Medicea Laurenziana, Florence. Facsimile: *Der Squarcialupi Codex Pa. 87 der Biblioteca Medicea Laurenziana zu Florenz,* ed. Johannes Wolf (Lippstadt: Fr. Kistner & C. F. W. Siegel & Co., 1955).

Manuscript: fr.146 (*Roman de Fauvel*), Bibliothèque nationale, Paris. Text: Gervais du Bus, *Le Roman de Fauvel,* ed. Arthur Langfors (Paris: Didot et Cie., 1914). Transcription: *Polyphonic Music of the Fourteenth Century,* Vol. 1, ed. L. Schrade (Monaco: L'Oiseau-Lyre, 1956).

Corpus mensurabilis musicae, ed. A. Carapetyan (Rome: American Institute of Musicology, 1947–), Vols. 2, 13, 29, 36, 37, 39, 53.

French Secular Compositions of the Fourteenth Century, ed. Willi Apel (Cambridge, MA: Mediaeval Academy of America, 1950); also, as Vol. 53 of *Corpus mensurabilis musicae* (Rome: American Institute of Musicology, 1970).

Les monuments de l'Ars nova: la musique polyphonique de 1320 à 1400 environ, ed. G. de Van (Paris: L'Oiseau-Lyre, 1938). [Only 1 volume published; series continued in *Polyphonic Music of the Fourteenth Century.*]

Polyphonic Music of the Fourteenth Century, 24 vols. to date. (Monaco: Éditions de L'Oiseau-Lyre, 1956–). [Vol. 1, *Roman de Fauvel*; 2, 3, Machaut; 4, Landini; 5, Ivrea MS; 6–14, Italian music; 15–17, English music; 18, 19, MSS of Chantilly, Musée Condé.]

For Further Reading

Boorman, Stanley, ed. *Studies in the Performance of Late Mediaeval Music* (Cambridge: Cambridge U. Press, 1983).

Carli, Enzo. *Giotto and His Contemporaries,* trans. Susan Bellamy (New York: Crown Publishers, 1958).

Günther, Ursula. "The Fourteenth-Century Motet and Its Development," *Musica Disciplina* 12 (1958), pp. 27ff.

Harman, Alec. *Man & His Music,* 3 vols., *Part One: Mediaeval and Early Renaissance Music* (New York: Schocken Books, 1969).

Swann, Win. *The Late Middle Ages: Art and Architecture from 1350 to the Advent of the Renaissance* (Ithaca, NY: Cornell U. Press, 1977).

Van Puyvelde, Leo. *L'Agneau mystique d'Hubert et Jean van Eyck* [The mystic lamb, i.e., the Ghent Altarpiece] (Brussels: Meddens, 1964).

MACHAUT
Music
Guillaume de Machaut: Musikalische Werke, ed. Friedrich Ludwig, 4 vols.; Vol. 4 rev. by H. Besseler (Leipzig: Breitkopf & Härtel, 1926–54; repr. 1954–62; repr. 1968).

Machaut, Guillaume de. *Works,* Vols. 2, 3, of *Polyphonic Music of the Fourteenth Century,* ed. Leo Schrade (Monaco: Éditions de L'Oiseau-Lyre, 1956).

For Further Reading
Gombosi, Otto. "Machaut's *Messe Notre-Dame,*" *The Musical Quarterly* 36 (1950), pp. 204–24.

Levarie, Siegmund. *Guillaume de Machaut,* ed. John J. Becker (New York: Sheed and Ward, 1954; repr. New York: Da Capo Press, 1969).

Macabey, A. *Guillaume de Machaut: la vie et l'oeuvre musicale* [Guillaume de Machaut: Life and musical works] (Paris, 1955).

Perle, George. "Integrative Devices in the Music of Machaut," *The Musical Quarterly* 34 (1948), pp. 169–76.

Reaney, Gilbert. *Guillaume de Machaut* (London: Oxford U. Press, 1971).

THEORISTS
Schrade, Leo, ed. *The Works of Philippe de Vitry,* Vol. I of *Polyphonic Music of the Fourteenth Century* (Monaco: L'Oiseau-Lyre, 1956).

Strunk, Oliver, ed. *Source Readings in Music History* (New York: Norton, 1950), pp. 160–92; excerpts from: (a) Marchetto da Padua, *Pomerium;* (b) Jean de Muris, *Ars novae musicae;* (c) Jacob of Liège, *Speculum musicae.*

Vitry, Philippe de. *Ars nova,* trans. Leon Plantinga, *Journal of Music Theory* 5 (1961), pp. 204–23.

ENGLAND
Greene, R. L. *The Early English Carols* (Oxford: Clarendon, 1935; repr. 1977).

Hughes, Andrew, and M. Bent. "The Old Hall Manuscript," *Musica Disciplina* 21 (1967), pp. 97–147.

Kenney, S. W. " 'English Discant' and Discant in England," *The Musical Quarterly* 45 (1959), p. 26ff.

McPeek, Gwynn S., ed. *The British Museum Manuscript Egerton 3307* (London: Oxford U. Press, and Chapel Hill: U. of North Carolina Press, 1963).

The Old Hall Manuscript, ed. Andrew Hughes and Margaret Bent, Vol. 46 of *Corpus mensurabilis musicae,* ed. A Carapetyan (Rome: American Institute of Musicology, 1969).

Ramsbotham, A., H. B. Collins, and Anselm Hughes, eds. *The Old Hall Manuscript,* 3 vols. (London: The Plainsong and Mediaevel Music Society, 1933–38).

Stevens, John, ed. *Medieval Carols,* Vol. 4 of *Musica Britannica* (London: Stainer & Bell, 1952).

Dunstable
J. Dunstable: Complete Works, ed. Manfred Bukofzer, Vol. 8, *Musica Britannica* (London: Stainer & Bell, 1953; 2d ed., rev. by M. Bent, I. Bent, and B. Trowell, 1970).

ITALY
L'Ars nova italiana del trecento, 3 vols. (Certaldo, 1959–60).

Landini, Francesco. *Complete Works,* 2 vols., ed. Leo Schrade (Monaco: L'Oiseau-Lyre, 1958; repr. 1982).

———. *Works,* ed. L. Ellinwood (Cambridge, MA: Mediaeval Academy of America, 1939; repr. New York: Kraus, 1970).

Marrocco, Thomas, ed. *Fourteenth-Century Italian Cacce* (Cambridge, MA: Mediaeval Academy of America, 1942; 2d ed., 1961).

———. *The Music of Jacopo da Bologna* (Berkeley: U. of California Press, 1954).

CHAPTER 9: TRANSITION TO THE RENAISSANCE

GENERAL
Codex Tridentinus 87–93 [Trent Codices], facsimile ed. (Rome: Bibliopola, 1969–70).

Fenlon, Iain, ed. *Music in Medieval and Early Modern Europe: Patronage, Sources, and Texts* (Cambridge: Cambridge U. Press, 1981).

Hamm, Charles, and A. B. Scott. "A Study and Inventory of the Manuscript Modena, Biblioteca Estense, α.X.1.11," *Musica disciplina* 26 (1972), pp. 101–43.

Hanen, Martha. *The Chansonnier El Escorial, IV.a.24,* 3 vols., Vol. 1, commentary; Vols. 2–3, transcriptions (Henryville, PA: Institute of Medieval Music, 1983).

Kottick, Edward. "The Chansonnier Cordiforme," *Journal of the American Musicological Society* 20 (1967), pp. 10–27.

Lane, Frederic C. *Venice: A Maritime Republic* (Baltimore: The Johns Hopkins U. Press, 1973).

Marix, Jeanne. *Histoire de la musique et des musiciens de la cour de Bourgogne sous le règne de Philippe le Bon (1420–1467)* [History of the music and musicians at the Burgundian court during the reign of Philippe the Good (1420–1467)] (Strasbourg: Heitz, 1939).

———, ed. *Les musiciens de la cour de Bourgogne au XVe siècle* [The musicians at the Burgundian court in the Fifteenth Century] (Paris: L'Oiseau-Lyre, 1937).

Sparks, Edgar H. *Cantus Firmus in Mass and Motet 1420–1520* (Berkeley: U. of California Press, 1963; repr. New York: Da Capo Press, 1975).

Strohm, Reinhard. *Music in Late Medieval Bruges* (Oxford: Clarendon Press, 1985).

BINCHE (BINCHOIS)
Die Chansons von Gilles Binchois (1400–1460), ed. W. Rehm, *Musikalisches Denkmäler,* Vol. 2 (Mainz: Schott, 1957).

Parris, A. *The Sacred Works of Gilles Binchois* (Diss., Bryn Mawr College, 1965).

BUSNE (BUSNOIS)
Brooks, C. "Antoine Busnois, Chanson Composer," *Journal of the American Musicological Society* 6 (1953), p. 111ff.

GUILLAUME DU FAY (DUFAY)

Music

G. *Dufay: Opera omnia,* ed. Guglielmus de Van and Heinrich Besseler, *Corpus mensurabilis musicae* 1 (Rome: American Institute of Musicology, 1947).

Stainer, J. F. R., and C. Stainer. *Dufay and His Contemporaries* (Amsterdam: Frits A. M. Knuf, 1966).

For Further Reading

Fallows, David. *Dufay* (London: Dent, 1982).

Hamm, Charles. *A Chronology of the Works of Guillaume Dufay* (Princeton, NJ: Princeton U. Press, 1964).

Houdoy, Jules. *Histoire artistique de la cathédrale de Cambrai, ancienne église métropolitaine de Notre-Dame: comptes, inventaires et documents inédits* [Artistic history of Cambrai Cathedral, ancient metropolitan church of Notre-Dame] (Lille: Mémoires de la Société des Sciences, de l'Agriculture et des Arts de Lille, 4th series, Vol. VII, 1880).

Millon, Henry A., ed. *Key Monuments of the History of Architecture* (New York: Henry N. Abrams, 1965).

Papers of the Dufay Quincentenary Conference: Brooklyn College, Brooklyn, NY, 1974, ed. Allan W. Atlas (Brooklyn: Music Dept., Brooklyn College of the City University of New York, 1976).

Planchart, Alejandro E. "Guillaume Dufay's Masses: Notes and Revisions," *The Musical Quarterly* 58 (1972), pp. 1–23.

Warren, Charles W. "Brunelleschi's Dome and Dufay's Motet," *The Musical Quarterly* 59 (1973), pp. 92–105.

Wright, Craig. "Dufay at Cambrai: Discoveries and Revisions," *Journal of the American Musicological Society* 28 (1975), pp. 175–229.

ENGLAND

The Eton Choirbook, transcribed by F. Ll. Harrison, *Musica Brittanica* 10–12, Royal Music Association (London: Stainer & Bell, 1951).

Kenney, Sylvia W. *Walter Frye and the Contenance Angloise* (New Haven, CT: Yale U. Press, 1964).

CHAPTER 10: THE RENAISSANCE: FRANCO-NETHERLANDS COMPOSERS

GENERAL

Music

Corpus mensurabilis musicae, ed. A. Carapetyan (Rome: American Institute of Musicology, 1947–), including Clement (Clemens non papa), vol. 4; Gombert, 6; Isaac, 65; Mouton, 43; Pipelare, 34; Willaert, 3.

The Chanson Albums of Marguerite of Austria, ed. Martin Picker (Berkeley: U. of California Press, 1965).

The Medici Codex of 1518, ed. Edward E. Lowinsky, Vols. 3–5 in *Monuments of Renaissance Music* (Chicago: U. of Chicago Press, 1968).

The Mellon Chansonnier, facsimile and modern edition, ed. Leeman Perkins and Howard Garey (New Haven, CT: Yale U. Press, 1979).

Slim, H. Colin, ed. *A Gift of Madrigals and Motets* (Chicago: U. of Chicago Press, 1972).

For Further Reading

Blume, Friedrich. *Renaissance and Baroque Music: A Comprehensive Survey,* trans. M. D. Herter Norton (New York: Norton, 1967), pp. 3–82.

Brown, Howard M. *Music in the Renaissance* (Englewood Cliffs, NJ: Prentice-Hall, 1976).

Bukofzer, Manfred. *Studies in Medieval and Renaissance Music* (New York: Norton, 1950), Chapters 5, 6, and 7.

Burckhardt, Jacob. *The Civilization of the Renaissance in Italy* (1860), 2 vols. (New York: Harper & Brothers, 1958).

Glareanus, Henricus [Henrich Loris]. *Dodecachordon* (Basle, 1547), facsimile ed. (New York: Broude, 1967).

Lowinsky, Edward E. *Secret Chromatic Art in the Netherlands Motet* (New York: Columbia U. Press, 1946).

Reese, Gustave. *Music in the Renaissance* (New York: Norton, 1954; 2d rev. ed. 1959), Part I.

Sparks, E. H. *Cantus Firmus in Mass and Motet, 1420–1520* (Berkeley: U. of California Press, 1963).

Stevenson, R. *Spanish Cathedral Music in the Golden Age* (Berkeley and Los Angeles: U. of California Press, 1961).

CLEMENT (CLEMENS; CLEMENS NON PAPA)

Clemens non Papa. *Souterliedekens,* Bks. I–III (Antwerp, 1556–57), facsimile ed., Vols. 16–18 in Corpus of Early Music in Facsimile (Brussels: Éditions Culture et Civilisation, 1972).

ISAAC

H. *Isaac: Choralis Constantinus,* 3 vols., I, ed. E. Bezecny and W. Rabl, *Denkmäler der Tonkunst in Österreich* 10 (Vienna: Artaria, 1898); II, ed. A. von Webern, *Denkmäler der Tonkunst in Österreich* 32 (Leipzig: Breitkopf & Härtel, 1909); III, ed. Louise Cuyler (Ann Arbor: U. of Michigan Press, 1956).

H. *Isaac: Messen,* ed. M. Staehelin, *Musikalische Denkmäler* 7, 8 (Mainz: B. Schott, 1970–73).

H. *Isaac: Opera omnia,* ed. E. R. Learner, 7 vols., *Corpus mensurabilis musicae* 65 (Rome: American Institute of Musicology, 1974–84).

JOSQUIN

Josquin Desprez: Werken, ed. A. Smijers et al. (Amsterdam: Uitgaven der Vereniging voor nederlanse muziekgeschiedenis, 1921–69).

Lowinsky, Edward E., with Bonnie J. Blackburn, eds. *Josquin des Prez* [sic]: *Proceedings of the International Josquin Festival-Conference, New York, 1971* (London: Oxford U. Press, 1976).

LA RUE

P. *de La Rue: Liber missarum,* ed. A. Tirabassi (Malines: Maison Dessain, 1941).

MORALES

C. *de Morales: Opera omnia,* 8 vols., ed. H. Anglés, *Monumentos de la música española* (Rome: Escuela Española de Historia y Arquelogia, 1952–).

Stevenson, R. "Cristóbal de Morales: A Fourth-centenary Biography," *Journal of the American Musicological Society* 6 (1953), pp. 3–42.

OBRECHT

Werken von Jacob Obrecht, 8 vols., ed. J. Wolf (Amsterdam: Alsbach, and Leipzig: Breitkopf & Härtel, 1912–21; repr. Gregg International, 1968).

Jacob Obrecht: Opera omnia, 5 vols., ed. A. Smijers and M. van Crevel (Amsterdam: Alsbach, 1953–).

News Obrecht edition, gen. ed. C. Maas (Amsterdam: Uitgaven der Vereniging voor nederlanse muziekgeschiedenis, 1983–).

Murray, Bain, "Jacob Obrecht's Connection with the Church of Our Lady in Antwerp," *Revue belge de musicologie* 11 (1957), p. 329ff.

———. "New Light on Jacob Obrecht's Development—A Biographical Study," *The Musical Quarterly* 43 (1957), p. 500ff.

OCKEGHEM

J. Ockeghem: Sämtliche Werke (Messen I–VIII), ed. Dragan Plamenac, *Publikationen älterer Musik* (Leipzig, 1927), rev. as *J. Ockeghem: Collected Works: I, Masses I–VIII; II, Masses and Mass Sections IX–XVI,* ed. D. Plamenac (New York: American Musicological Society, 1947; 2d, corrected ed., 1959, 1966).

Plamenac, Dragan. "A Postscript to Volume ii of the Collected Works of Johannes Ockeghem," *Journal of the American Musicological Society* 3 (1950), p. 33ff.

Van Ockeghem tot Sweelinck, ed. A. Smijers. Amsterdam: Uitgaven der Vereniging voor nederlanse muziekgeschiedenis (1949–56).

WILLAERT

Willaert, Adrian. *Musica nova* (Venice: A. Gardano, 1559), ed. H. Colin Slim, *Monuments of Renaissance Music* 1 (Chicago and London: U. of Chicago Press, 1964).

PETRUCCI

Harmonice Musices Odhecaton A (Venice: Petrucci, 1504; repr. New York: Broude, 1973). Also, edition by Helen Hewitt (Cambridge, MA: Medieval Academy of America, 1946).

Canti B (Venice: Petrucci, 1502; repr. New York: Broude, 1975). Also, *O. Petrucci: Canti B numero cinquante (Venice, 1502),* ed. Helen Hewitt, *Monuments of Renaissance Music* 2 (Chicago: U. of Chicago Press, 1967).

Canti C (Venice: Petrucci, 1504; repr. New York: Broude, 1978).

Boorman, S. "The 'First' edition of the *Odhecaton A,*" *Journal of the American Musicological Society,* 30 (1977), p. 183ff.

Norton, Frederick J. *Italian Printers 1501–1520* (London: Bowes & Bowes, 1958).

Reese, Gustave. "The First Printed Collection of Part-music (the *Odhecaton*)," *The Musical Quarterly* 20 (1934), pp. 39–76.

CHAPTER 11: THE RISE OF REGIONAL STYLES

GENERAL

Music

Corpus mensurabilis musicae, ed. A. Carapetyan (Rome: American Institute of Musicology, 1947–), including Arcadelt, 31, Crequillon, 63; Festa, 25; Marenzio, 72; Rore, 15; Sermisy, 52; Verdelot, 28; Vincentino, 26; Wert, 24; Willaert, 3.

Slim, H. Colin, ed. *A Gift of Madrigals and Motets* (Chicago: U. of Chicago Press, 1972).

ITALY

Music

D'Accone, Frank, ed. *Music of the Florentine Renaissance,* Vols. 11 and 32 in *Corpus mensurabilis musicae,* ed. A. Carapetyan (Rome: American Institute of Musicology, 1966–69).

Cardamone, Donna, ed. *Canzone villanesche alla Napolitana and Villotte: Adrian Willaert and His Circle,* Vol. 30, *Recent Researches in Music of the Renaissance* (Madison, WI: A-R Editions, 1978).

For Further Reading

D'Accone, Frank. "The Musical Chapels at the Florentine Cathedrals and Baptistry during the First Half of the Sixteenth Century," *Journal of the American Musicological Society* 24 (1971), pp. 1–50.

Anglès, H. "The Musical Notation and Rhythm of the Italian Laude," *Essays in Musicology: A Birthday Offering for Willi Apel* (Bloomington: Indiana U. Press, 1968), p. 51ff.

Einstein, Alfred. *The Italian Madrigal* (Princeton, NJ: Princeton U. Press, 1949; repr. 1971).

Fenlon, Iain. *Music and Patronage in Sixteenth-century Mantua,* 2 vols. (Cambridge: Cambridge U. Press, I, 1980; II, 1982).

Haar, James, ed. *Chanson and Madrigal, 1480–1530* (Cambridge, MA: Harvard U. Press, 1981).

———. *Essays on Italian Poetry and Music in the Renaissance, 1350–1600* (Berkeley: U. of California Press, 1986).

———. "Isabella d'Este and Lucretia Borgia as Patrons of Music: The Frottola at Mantua and Ferrara," *Journal of the American Musicological Society* 38 (1985), pp. 1–33.

Lockwood, Lewis. *Music in Renaissance Ferrara 1400–1505* (Cambridge, MA: Harvard U. Press, 1984).

Newcomb, Anthony. *The Madrigal at Ferrara 1579–1597,* 2 vols. (Princeton, NJ: Princeton U. Press, 1980).

Prizer, William. *Courtly Pastimes: The Frottole of Marchetto Cara* (Ann Arbor, MI: UMI Research Press, 1981).

Roche, Jerome. *The Madrigal* (New York: Scribner's, 1972).

Canti Carnascialeschi

Music

Gallucci, Joseph G., Jr., ed. *Florentine Festival Music 1480–1520* (Madison, WI: A-R Editions, 1981).

Ghisi, Federico. *I canti carnascialeschi nelle fonti musicali del xv e xvi secolo* (Florence: Olschki, 1937).

———. *Feste musicali della Firenze medicea 1480–1589* (Florence: Vallecchi, 1939; repr. 1969).

Italian Madrigalists

Marenzio

Marenzio, Luca. *Sämtliche Werke,* ed. A. Einstein (Leipzig: Breitkopf & Härtel, 1929–31; repr. Hildesheim: Olms, 1967).

Arnold, Denis. *Marenzio* (London: Oxford U. Press, 1965).

Chater, J. *Luca Marenzio and the Italian Madrigal, 1577–1593* (Ann Arbor, MI: UMI Research Press, 1981).

Monte

Monte, Philippe de. *Opera, New Complete Edition,* ed. R. B. Lenaerts (Louvin: Leuven U. Press, 1975–81).

Mann, Brian. *The Secular Madrigals of Filippo di Monte, 1521–1603* (Ann Arbor, MI: UMI Research Press, 1983).

FRANCE

Music

Janequin, C. *Chansons polyphoniques: Oeuvres complètes,* ed. A. T. Merritt and François Lesure (Monaco: Éditions de L'Oiseau-Lyre, 1965–71).

Lesure, François. *Anthologie de la chanson parisienne au XVIe siècle* (Monaco: Éditions de L'Oiseau-Lyre, 1953).

Picker, Martin. *Chanson Albums of Marguerite of Austria* (Berkeley: U. of California Press, 1965).

For Further Reading

Brown, Howard M. *Music in the French Secular Theater, 1400–1550* (Cambridge, MA: Harvard U. Press, 1963).

Heartz, Daniel. "A New Attaignant Book and the Beginnings of French Music Printing," *Journal of the American Musicological Society* 14 (1961), p. 9ff.

————. *Pierre Attaignant, Royal Printer of Music: A Historical Study and Bibliographical Catalogue* (Berkeley: U. of California Press, 1969).

Walker, D. P. "The Aims of Baïf's *Academie de poésie et de musique,*" *Journal of Renaissance and Baroque Musique* 1 (1946–47), p. 91ff.

ENGLAND
Music
The Collected Lute Music of John Dowland, ed. Diana Poulton and B. Lam (London: Faber, 1974; repr. New York: Dover).

The English Madrigal School, ed. E. H. Fellowes, 36 vols. (London: Stainer & Bell, 1913–24); rev. ed. published as *The English Madrigalists,* ed. Thurston Dart (1956–).

The English School of Lutenist Song Writers, ed. E. H. Fellowes, 32 vols. (London: Stainer & Bell, 1920–32); rev. ed. pub. as *The English Lute-songs,* ed. T. Dart (London: Stainer & Bell, 1956–66).

Ledger, Philip, ed. *The Oxford Book of English Madrigals* (London: Oxford U. Press, 1979).

Musica Britannica, Vols. 6 [Dowland]; 9, 22, 40 [Consort music]; 23 [Weelkes]; 18 [Court music, Henry VIII]; 36 [Early Tudor Music, ed. J. Stevens], Royal Music Association (London: Stainer & Bell, 1951–).

For Further Reading
Fellowes, E. H. *The English Madrigal* (Oxford: Oxford U. Press, 1925; 2d ed., 1948; repr. Salem, NH: Ayer, 1984).

————. *The English Madrigalist Composers,* 2d ed. (London and New York: Oxford U. Press, 1948).

Kerman, Joseph. *The Elizabethan Madrigal* (New York: American Musicological Society, 1962).

Poulton, Diana. *John Dowland* (London: Faber & Faber, 1972).

IBERIA
J. del Encina: L'opera musicale, ed. Clemente Terni (Florence: Casa Editrice d'Anna, 1974).

Chase, Gilbert. *The Music of Spain* (New York: Norton, 1941; repr. New York: Dover, 1959).

Stevenson, Robert. *Spanish Music in the Age of Columbus* (The Hague: Nijhoff, 1960; repr. 1987).

CHAPTER 12: REFORMATION AND COUNTER-REFORMATION

GENERAL
Reese, Gustave. *Music in the Renaissance* (New York: Norton, 1954; 2d rev. ed., 1959), esp. Chapters 8, 9, 11, 13, and 15.

REFORMATION
Appel, Richard. *Music of the Bay Psalm Book, 9th ed.* (Brooklyn, NY: Institute for Studies in American Music, 1975).

The Bay Psalm Book [*The Whole Book of Psalmes Faithfully Translated into English Metre*], facsimile ed. (Chicago: U. of Chicago Press, 1956).

Blume, Friedrich. *Protestant Church Music* (New York: Norton, 1974).

Pidoux, Pierre, comp. *Le Psautier Huguenot du XVIᵉ siècle, mélodies et documents* (Basle: Bärenreiter, 1962).

Pratt, Waldo S. *The Music of the French Psalter of 1562* (New York: Columbia U. Press, 1939).

Riedel, J. *The Lutheran Chorale: Its Basic Traditions* (Minneapolis: Augsburg, 1967).

Luther
Music
Das Acht Lieder Buch (1524), facsimile ed., ed. Konrad Ameln (Kassel & Basel: Bärenreiter, 1957).

Luther, Martin. *Deudsche Messe* (1526), facsimile ed. (Kassel: Bärenreiter, 1934).

Luther's Works, 55 vols., gen. eds. Jaroslav Pelikan and Helmut T. Lehmann, Vol. 53, *Liturgy and Hymns,* ed. Ulrich S. Leupold (Philadelphia: Fortress Press, 1965).

For Further Reading
Bainton, Roland H. *Here I Stand: A Life of Martin Luther* (New York: Abingdon-Cokesbury Press, 1950).

Rhau (Rhaw)
G. Rhau: Musikdrucke aus den Jahren 1538 bis 1545 in praktischer Neuausgabe (Kassel: Bärenreiter, 1955–).

Rhau, Georg. *Musikdrucke VI: Bicinia gallica, latina, germanica, Tomus I, II* (1545), ed. Bruce Bellingham (Kassel: Bärenreiter, and St. Louis, MO: Concordia Publishing House, 1980).

Walter (Walther)
J. Walter: Sämtliche Werke, ed. O. Schröder (Kassel: Bärenreiter, 1953–73).

Walter, Johann. *Geystliches gesangk Buchleyn* (Wittenberg, 1524), in Vol. 7 (Jg. vi), *Publikationen älterer praktischer und theoretischer Musikwerke, vorzugsweise des XV. und XVI. Jahrhunderts,* 29 vols. in 33 Jg., ed. R. Eitner (Berlin: Bahn & Liepmannssohn, 1873–1905; repr. 1967).

COUNTER-REFORMATION
Barthel, Manfred. *The Jesuits: History and Legend of the Society of Jesus,* trans. and adapted by Mark Howson (New York: William Morrow, 1984).

Culley, T. *Jesuits and Music: A Study of the Musicians connected with the German College in Rome during the 17th Century and of Their Activities in Northern Europe* (Rome: Jesuit Historical Institute Press, 1970).

Stevenson, Robert. *Spanish Cathedral Music in the Golden Age* (Berkeley and Los Angeles: U. of California Press, 1961).

Lassus
O. de Lassus: Sämtliche Werke, ed. F. X. Haberl and A. Sandberger (Leipzig: Breitkopf & Härtel, 1894–1927; repr. Broude, 1974).

O. de Lassus: Sämtliche Werke, neue Reihe, ed. S. Hermelink, W. Boetticher, et al. (Kassel: Bärenreiter, 1956–).

Roche, Jerome. *Lassus* (London: Oxford U. Press, 1982).

Palestrina
G. P. da Palestrina: Werke, ed. F. X. Haberl, T. de Witt, et al. (Leipzig: Breitkopf & Härtel, 1862–1903; repr. Farnborough, Eng.: Gregg International, 1968).

G. P. da Palestrina: Le opere complete, ed. R. Casimiri and L. Virgili (Rome: Fratelli Scalera, 1939–).

Jeppesen, Knud. *Palestrinastil med saerligt henblik paa dissonansbehandlingen* (Copenhagen, 1923); Eng. trans. Edward J. Dent, as *The Style of Palestrina and the Dissonance* (London: Oxford U. Press, 1927, 2d ed., 1946).

Victoria

T. L. de Victoria: Opera omnia, ed. F. Pedrell (Leipzig: Breitkopf & Härtel, 1902–13; repr. Farnborough, Eng.: Gregg Press, 1968).

T. L. de Victoria: Opera omnia, corrected, augmented, ed. H. Anglès, *Monumentos de la Música Española,* Vols. 25, 26, 30 and 31 (Rome: Escuela Española de Historia y Arquelogia, Consejo Superior de Investigaciones Científicas, Delegacíon de Rome, 1965–68).

ENGLAND: REFORMATION AND COUNTER-REFORMATION
Music
Early English Church Music, ed. F. Ll. Harrison, British Academy (London: Stainer & Bell, 1972–).

Tudor Church Music, ed. P. C. Buck, E. H. Fellowes, et al., 10 vols. (London and elsewhere: Oxford U. Press, 1922–29; appendix 1948; repr. New York: Broude, 1963).

For Further Reading
Fellowes, E. H. *English Cathedral Music,* 5th ed., rev. Jack A. Westrup (London: Methuen, 1969).

Le Huray, Peter. *Music and the Reformation in England, 1549–1600* (London and New York: Oxford U. Press, 1967).

Stevens, Denis. *Tudor Church Music* (New York: Merlin, 1955; repr. New York: Da Capo, 1973; 2d ed., London: Faber & Faber, and New York: Norton, 1966).

Byrd
Music
The Collected Works of William Byrd, ed. E. H. Fellowes (London: Stainer & Bell, 1937–50); rev. T. Dart et al. (London: Stainer & Bell, 1962–).

For Further Reading
Brett, Philip. *The Music of William Byrd,* Vol. 2, *The Songs, Services, and Anthems of William Byrd* (in preparation).

Fellowes, E. H. *William Byrd* (London: H. Milford and Oxford U. Press, 1936; 2d ed., Oxford U. Press, 1948).

Kerman, Joseph. *The Music of William Byrd,* Vol. 1, *The Masses and Motets of William Byrd* (Berkeley: U. of California Press, 1980).

Neighbour, Oliver W. *The Music of William Byrd,* Vol. 3, *The Consort and Keyboard Music of William Byrd* (London: Faber, 1978).

Tallis, Taverner, Tye
Music
T. Tallis: English Sacred Music, I: Anthems, ed. L. Ellinwood, rev. P. Doe, Early English Church Music 12, 2d ed.; *II: Service Music,* ed. L. Ellinwood, rev. P. Doe, *Early English Church Music 13,* 2d ed. (London: Stainer & Bell, 1974).

J. Taverner: I. The Six-part Masses, ed. H. J. Benham, *Early English Church Music 20* (London: Stainer & Bell, 1978).

J. Taverner: II. The Votive Antiphons, ed. H. J. Benham, *Early English Church Music 25* (London: Stainer & Bell, 1981).

C. Tye: The Latin Church Music, ed. J. Satterfield (Madison, WI: A-R Editions, 1977).

C. Tye: The English Sacred Music, ed. J. Morehen, *Early English Church Music 19* (London: Stainer & Bell, 1977).

For Further Reading
Davison, N. "The Western Wind Masses," *The Musical Quarterly* 57 (1971), p. 427ff.

Doe, Paul. *Tallis* (London: Oxford U. Press, 1968).

Donington, Robert, and Thurston Dart. "The Origin of the *In Nomine,*" *Music and Letters* 30 (1949), p. 101ff.

Hand, Colin. *John Taverner: His Life and Music* (London: Eulenberg, 1978).

Josephson, D. S. *John Taverner, Tudor Composer* (Ann Arbor, MI: UMI Research Press, 1979).

Reese, Gustave. "The Origins of the *In Nomine,*" *Journal of the American Musicological Society* 2 (1949), p. 7ff.

Stevens, D. "The Background of the English *In Nomine,*" *The Monthly Musical Record* 84 (1954), p. 199ff.

CHAPTER 13: RENAISSANCE INSTRUMENTAL MUSIC

GENERAL
Apel, Willi. *The History of Keyboard Music to 1700,* trans. and rev. Hans Tischler (Bloomington: Indiana U. Press, 1972).

Arnold, Denis. *Giovanni Gabrieli and the Music of the Venetian High Renaissance* (London: Oxford U. Press, 1979).

Baines, Anthony. *Brass Instruments: Their History and Development* (London: Faber, 1976).

———. *European and American Musical Instruments* (London: Batsford, 1966).

———, ed. *Musical Instruments through the Ages* (Harmondsworth, Eng.: Penguin Books, 1961).

———. *Woodwind Instruments and Their History* (London: Faber, 1957; 3d ed., 1967).

Blades, James. *Percussion Instruments and Their History* (New York: Praeger, 1970).

Boyden, David D. *The History of Violin Playing from Its Origins to 1761* (London: Oxford U. Press, 1965).

Dart, Thurston. "The Fretted Instruments, III: The Viols," *Musical Instruments through the Ages,* ed. A. Baines (Harmondsworth, Eng.: Penguin Books, 1961; 2d ed., rev. 1966), p. 184ff.

Gillespie, John. *Five Centuries of Keyboard Music: An Historical Survey of Music for Harpsichord and Piano* (Belmont, CA: Wadsworth, 1965).

Kirby, Frank E. *A Short History of Keyboard Music* (New York: Free Press, 1966), pp. 1–62.

Marcuse, Sybil. *Musical Instruments: A Comprehensive Dictionary* (Garden City, NY: Doubleday, 1964).

———. *A Survey of Musical Instruments* (London: David & Charles, and New York: Harper & Row, 1975).

Munrow, David. *Instruments of the Middle Ages and Renaissance* (London: Oxford U. Press, 1976).

Praetorius, Michael. *Syntagma musicum,* Vol. II (*De Organographia*) (Wolfenbüttel, 1618); reprint of Parts I and II, plus *Theatrum organorum,* trans. Harold Blumenfeld (New York: Da Capo Press, 1980).

Russell, R. *The Harpsichord and Clavichord* (London: Faber, 1959; 2d ed., rev. 1973).

Selfridge-Field, Eleanor. *Venetian Instrumental Music from Gabrieli to Vivaldi* (Oxford: Blackford, 1975).

Sumner, William L. *The Organ* (London: Macdonald, 1952; 3d ed., rev. and enlarged, 1962).

Virdung, Sebastian. *Musica getutscht und aussgezogē* (Basle, 1511), facsimile ed. (New York: Broude, 1966).

GABRIELI
Music
A. and G. Gabrieli: La musica striamentale in San Marco, 2 vols., ed. G. Benvenuti, Istituzioni e monumenti dell'arte musicale italiana (Milan: Ricordi, 1931–41).

G. Gabrieli: Opera omnia, ed. Denis Arnold, Vol. 12 in *Corpus mensurabilis musicae*, ed. A. Carapetyan (Rome: American Institute of Musicology, 1956–).

G. Gabrieli: Opera omnia, ed. Fondazione Giorgio Cini, Venice (Mainz: Universal, 1969–).

G. Gabrieli: Canzoni e sonate, ed. M. Sanvoisin, *Le Pupitre*, Vol. 21 (Paris: Heugel, 1971).

For Further Reading
Arnold, Denis. *Giovanni Gabrieli and the Music of the Venetian High Renaissance* (London: Oxford U. Press, 1979).

Kenton, Egon. *The Life and Works of Giovanni Gabrieli, Musicological Studies and Documents*, Vol. 16, A. Carapetyan (Rome: American Institute of Musicology, 1967).

CHAPTER 14: THE BAROQUE ERA

Arnold, Frank. *The Art of Accompaniment from a Thorough-Bass as Practiced in the XVIIth and XVIIIth Centuries*, 2 vols. (New York: Dover, 1965).

Blume, Friedrich. *Renaissance and Baroque Music: A Comprehensive Survey*, trans. M. D. Herter Norton (New York: Norton, 1967), pp. 83–167.

Bukofzer, Manfred F. *Music in the Baroque Era* (New York: Norton, 1947).

Palisca, Claude V. *Baroque Music*, 2d ed. (Englewood Cliffs, NJ: Prentice-Hall, 1981).

CHAPTER 15: BAROQUE VOCAL MUSIC

EARLY OPERA
Series of facsimile editions: *Italian Opera, 1640–1770*, gen. ed. Howard M. Brown (New York: Garland, 1978–).

Donington, Robert. *The Rise of Opera* (London: Faber & Faber, 1981).

Grout, Donald J. *A Short History of Opera*, 3d ed. (New York: Columbia U. Press, 1988).

Marco, Guy A. *Opera: A Research and Information Guide* (New York: Garland, 1984).

Murata, Margaret. *Operas for the Papal Court, 1631–1668* (Ann Arbor, MI: UMI Research Press, 1981).

Pirrotta, Nino. "Early Italian Opera and Aria," *Music and Theatre from Poliziano to Monteverdi*, trans. K. Eales (Cambridge: Cambridge U. Press, 1982).

Porter, William. "Peri and Corsi's *Dafne*: Some New Discoveries and Observations," *Journal of the American Musicological Society* 28 (1965), pp. 170–96.

Walker, D. P., ed. *Les fêtes du mariage de Ferdinand de Médicis et de Christine de Lorraine, Florence, 1589* [The festivities for the marriage of Ferdinand de Medici and Christine of Lorraine] (Paris: Éditions du Centre national de la recherche scientifique, 1963).

Worsthorne, Simon T. *Venetian Opera in the Seventeenth Century* (Oxford: Clarendon Press, 1954).

FLORENCE: THE CAMERATA
Galilei, Vincenzo. *Dialogo della musica antica, et della moderna* (Florence: Giorgio Marescotti, 1581), facsimile ed. (New York: Broude Brothers, 1967).

Palisca, Claude V. *Girolamo Mei: Letters on Ancient and Modern Music to Vincenzo Galilei and Giovanni Bardi* (Neuhausen-Stuttgart: American Institute of Musicology, 1960; 2d ed., 1977).

Caccini
Music
Caccini, Giulio. *Le nuove musiche* (Florence: 1600/1601), facsimile ed. (New York: Broude Bros., 1973). Modern transcription, ed. H. Wiley Hitchcock (Madison, WI: A-R Editions, 1970).

————. *Nuove musiche e nuova maniera di scriverle* (Florence, 1614), ed. H. Wiley Hitchcock (Madison, WI: A-R Editions, 1978).

Cavalieri
Music
Cavalliere [sic], Emilio del. *Rappresentatione di Anima, et di Corpo* (Rome: Nicolò Mutij, 1600), facsimile ed. (Farnborough, Eng.: Gregg International, 1967).

Peri
Peri, Jacopo. *Euridice*, ed. Howard M. Brown (Madison, WI: A-R Editions, 1981).

MONTEVERDI
Music
C. Monteverdi: Tutte le opere, ed. G. F. Malipiero (Asolo: Malipiero, 1926–42; rev. 1954; suppl. 1966).

C. Monteverdi: Opera Omnia, ed. R. Monterosso, Fondazione Claudio Monteverdi (Cremona: Athenaeum cremonense, 1970–).

For Further Reading
Arnold, Denis. *Monteverdi* (London: Dent, 1963; rev. 1975).

Arnold, Denis, and Nigel Fortune, eds. *The Monteverdi Companion* (New York: Norton, 1968, 1972).

————. *The New Monteverdi Companion* (London: Faber, 1985).

Redlich, Hans F. *Claudio Monteverdi and His Works*, trans. Kathleen Dale (London: Oxford U. Press, 1952; repr. Westport, CT: Greenwood Press, 1970).

Schrade, Leo. *Monteverdi: Creator of Modern Music* (New York: Norton, 1950; repr. 1964, 1969; repr. New York: Da Capo Press, 1979).

Whenham, John, ed. *Claudio Monteverdi: Orfeo* (New York: Cambridge U. Press, 1986).

SCARLATTI, A.
Music
The Operas of Alessandro Scarlatti, 8 vols., gen. ed. Donald J. Grout (Cambridge, MA: Harvard U. Press, 1974–83).

For Further Reading
Dent, Edward J. *Alessandro Scarlatti: His Life and Work* (London, 1905); rev. with additions by Frank Walker (London: Edward Arnold, 1960; repr. 1962).

Grout, Donald J. *Alessandro Scarlatti: An Introduction to His Operas* (Berkeley: U. of California Press, 1979).

FRANCE
Music
Les chefs d'oeuvres classiques de l'opéra français, 40 vols., ed. J. B. Weckerlin et al. (Paris: T. Michaelis, 1878–83; repr. New York: Broude, 1972).

For Further Reading

Anthony, James R. *French Baroque Music from Beaujoyeulx to Rameau,* rev. ed. (New York: Norton, 1978).

Isherwood, Robert M. *Music in the Service of the King: France in the Seventeenth Century* (Ithaca, NY: Cornell U. Press, 1973).

Lully
Music

J.-B. Lully: Oeuvres complètes, ed. Henri Prunières, 10 vols. (Paris: Éditions de La Revue Musicale, 1930–39; rev. M. Sanvoisin, New York: Broude Brothers, 1935–66; repr. 1972).

For Further Reading

La Laurencie, Lionel de. *Lully* (Paris: Alcan, 1911; repr. New York: Da Capo, 1977).

Newman, J. E. W. *Jean-Baptiste de Lully and His Tragedies lyriques* (Ann Arbor, MI: UMI Research Press, 1979).

ENGLAND
Music

Blow, John. *Venus and Adonis,* ed. A. Lewis (Monaco: Éditions de l'Oiseau-Lyre, 1949).

Shirley, Davenant, and Lawes. *Trois masques à la cour de Charles Ier d'Angleterre,* ed. M. Lefkowitz (Paris: Éditions de Centre National de la Recherche Scientifique, 1970).

The Works of Henry Purcell, ed. The Purcell Society (London: Novello, 1878–1965; rev. 1961–).

For Further Reading

Fellowes, Edmund. *English Cathedral Music* (London: Methuen, 1941; rev. by Jack A. Westrup, 1969).

Moore, Robert E. *Henry Purcell & the Restoration Theatre* (London: Heinemann, 1961; repr. Westport, CT: Greenwood Press, 1974, 1976).

Zimmerman, F. B. *Henry Purcell: His Life and Times* (London: Macmillan, 1967; 2d rev. ed., Philadelphia: U. of Pennsylvania Press, 1983).

SPANISH OPERAS

Calderón de la Barca, Pedro. *Celos aun del aire matan,* ed., with intro., trans. and notes by Matthew D. Stroud (San Antonio, TX: Trinity U. Press, 1981).

Torrejón y Velasco, Tomás. *La Púrpura de la Rosa,* trans. Robert Stevenson (Lima, Peru: Organización de los Estados Americanos, 1976).

ORATORIO

Smither, Howard E. *A History of the Oratorio,* 3 vols. (Chapel Hill, NC: U. of North Carolina Press, 1977–87); Vol. 1: *The Oratorio in the Baroque Era: Italy, Vienna, Paris.*

Carissimi
Music

G. Carissimi: Le opere complete, ed. L. Bianchi et al. (Rome: Pubblicazioni dell'Istituto italiano per la storia della musica, Monumenti, 3, 1951–73).

For Further Reading

Rose, Gloria. "The Cantatas of Carissimi," *The Musical Quarterly* 68 (1962), p. 204ff.

Smither, H. E. "Carissimi's Latin Oratorios: Their Terminology, Functions, and Position in Oratorio History," *Analecta Musicologica* 17 (1976), p. 54ff.

SCHÜTZ
Music

H. Schütz: Sämtliche Werke, 18 vols., ed. P. Spitta et al. (Leipzig: Breitkopf & Härtel, 1885–1927; repr. 1968–73).

H. Schütz: Sämtliche Werke, ed. G. Graulich et al. (Kassel: Bärenreiter, 1955–).

H. Schütz: Sämtliche Werke, ed. G. Graulich et al. (Stuttgart: 1971–).

For Further Reading

Moser, Hans Joachim. *Heinrich Schütz,* trans. C. F. Pfatteicher (St. Louis, MO: Concordia Publishing House, 1959).

Skei, Allen. *Henrich Schütz: A Guide to Research* (New York: Garland, 1981).

Smither, H. E. *A History of the Oratorio,* vol. 2, *The Oratorio in the Baroque Era: Protestant Germany and England* (Chapel Hill: U. of North Carolina Press, 1977).

CANTATA

The Italian Cantata in the Seventeenth Century [facsimiles], gen. ed. Carolyn Gianturco (New York: Garland, 1986–).

CHAPTER 16: BAROQUE INSTRUMENTAL MUSIC

GENERAL

Anthony, James R. *French Baroque Music from Beaujoyeulx to Rameau,* rev. ed. (New York: Norton, 1978).

Apel, Willi. *The History of Keyboard Music to 1700,* trans. and rev. Hans Tischler (Bloomington: Indiana U. Press, 1972).

Boyden, David D. *The History of Violin Playing from Its Origins to 1761* (London: Oxford U. Press, 1965).

Farga, Franz. *Violins and Violinists,* trans. Egon Larsen (London: Rockliff, 1950; repr. 1955).

Fux, J. J. *Gradus ad Parnassum* (Vienna, 1725), facsimile ed. *Monuments of Music and Music Literature in Facsimile,* Series 2, Vol. 24 (New York: Broude, 1966); Eng. trans. pub. as *Steps to Parnassus: The Study of Counterpoint from Johann Joseph Fux's Gradus ad Parnassum,* trans. and ed. Alfred Mann and J. Edmunds, rev. ed. (New York: Norton, 1965).

Gillespie, John. *Five Centuries of Keyboard Music: An Historical Survey of Music for Harpsichord and Piano* (Belmont, CA: Wadsworth, 1965).

Horsley, Imogene. *Fugue: History and Practice* (New York: Free Press, 1966).

Hutchings, Arthur J. B. *The Baroque Concerto* (London: Faber & Faber, 1961).

Kirby, Frank E. *A Short History of Keyboard Music* (New York: Free Press, 1966).

Newman, William S. *The Sonata in the Baroque Era* (Chapel Hill: U. of North Carolina Press, 1959; 3d ed., New York: Norton, 1972).

Selfridge-Field, Eleanor. *Venetian Instrumental Music from Gabrieli to Vivaldi* (Oxford: Blackford, 1975).

Smithers, Don L. *The Music and History of the Baroque Trumpet before 1721* (London: Aldine Press, Letchworth & Herts, 1973; Syracuse, NY: Syracuse U. Press, 1973).

Sumner, William L. *The Organ,* 3d ed., rev. and enlarged (London: Macdonald, 1962).

Wasielewski, Jos. Wilh. von, ed. *Anthology of Instrumental Music from the End of the Sixteenth to the End of the Seventeenth Century*

(Berlin: Liepmannssohn, n.d.; repr. New York: Da Capo Press, 1974).

See also *Das Musikwerk,* ed. K. G. Fellerer (Cologne: Arno Volk-Verlag, 1951–); Eng. trans. published as *Anthology of Music;* Vols. 7, 15, 17, 23 (Cologne: Arno Volk, 1959–75).

BUXTEHUDE

D. Buxtehude: Klaverwaerker, ed. E. Bangert (Copenhagen: W. Hansen, 1942).

D. Buxtehude: Orgelwerke, ed. J. Hedar (Copenhagen: W. Hansen, 1952).

D. Buxtehude: Sämtliche Orgelwerke, ed. K. Beckmann (Wiesbaden: Breitkopf & Härtel, 1971–72).

Hutchins, F. K. *Dietrich Buxtehude: The Man, His Music, His Era* (Paterson, NJ: Music Textbook Co., 1955).

Snyder, Kerala J. *Dietrich Buxtehude: Organist in Lübeck* (New York: Schirmer Books, 1987).

CABANILLES

J. B. Cabanilles: Opera omnia, Vols. I–IV, ed. H. Angles, in Biblioteca Central Sección de Musica *Publicaciones,* Vols. 4, 8, 13, 17 (Barcelona: Biblioteca de Catalunya, 1927–56).

CORELLI

A. Corelli: Historisch-kritische Gesamtausgabe der musikalischen Werke, 5 vols., gen. ed. Hans Oesch (Cologne: Arno Volk, 1976–); supplement, ed. Hans J. Marx (Cologne: Arno Volk, 1980).

A. Corelli: Les oeuvres de Arcangelo Corelli, ed. J. Joachim and F. Chrysander (London: Augener, 1888–91; repr. 1952).

Pincherle, Marc. *Corelli: His Life, His Music,* trans. Hubert E. M. Russell (New York: Norton, 1956; repr. 1968).

COUPERIN, F.

Music

F. Couperin: Oeuvres complètes, ed. M. Cauchie, P. Brunold, et al. (Paris: Éditions de l'Oiseau-Lyre, 1932–33). New critical edition, ed. K. Gilbert et al. (Monaco: Éditions de l'Oiseau-Lyre, 1980–).

F. Couperin: Pièces de clavecin, ed. K. Gilbert, in *Le Pupitre: Collection de musique ancienne* 21–24 (Paris, Heugel, 1969–72).

F. Couperin: Pièces de violes (1728), ed. L. Robinson, in *Le Pupitre* 51 (Paris: Heugel, 1974).

Couperin, F. *L'Art de toucher le clavecin* (Paris, 1716); ed., trans. A. Linde and M. Roberts (Leipzig: Breitkopf & Härtel, 1933).

———. *L'Art de toucher le clavecin* (Paris, 1716); ed., trans. Margery Halford (Sherman Oaks, CA: Alfred Publishing, 1974).

For Further Reading

Mellers, Wilfred, *François Couperin and the French Classical Tradition* (London: Denis Dobson, 1950; New York: Dover, 1968).

Tunley, David. *Couperin* (London: British Broadcasting Corporation, 1982).

FRESCOBALDI

G. Frescobaldi: Opere Complete, ed. O. Mischiati and L. F. Tagliavini, *Monument musicali italiani* (Milan: Edizioni Suvini Zerboni, 1975–).

G. Frescobaldi: Orgel- und Klavierwerke, ed. P. Pidoux (Kassel: Bärenreiter, 1949–54).

Hammond, Frederick. *Girolamo Frescobaldi* (Cambridge, MA: Harvard U. Press, 1983).

FROBERGER

J. J. Froberger: Orgel- und Klavierwerke (Organ and Keyboard Works), ed. G. Adler, in *Denkmäler der Tonkunst in Österreich,* Vols. 8 [Jg. 4/1], 13 [Jg. 6/2], and 21 [Jg. 10/2] (Vienna: Artaria, 1897–1903).

J. J. Froberger: Oeuvres complètes (Complete Works), ed. H. M. Schott, *Le Pupitre* (Paris: Heugel, 1979–).

GAULTIER

Gaultier, Denis. *La Rhétorique des Dieux et aultres Pieces de Luth de Denis Gaultier,* transcr. by André Tessier, Vol. 6 in Series I of *Publications de la Société Française de Musicologie* (Paris: Droz, 1932).

JACQUET DE LA GUERRE

Jacquet de La Guerre, Elisabeth. *Pièces de clavecin,* ed. Thurston Dart (Monaco: Éditions de L'Oiseau-Lyre, n.d.).

Bates, Carol H. *The Instrumental Music of Elisabeth-Claude Jacquet de la Guerre* (Diss., Indiana U., 1978).

Borroff, Edith. *An Introduction to Elisabeth-Claude Jacquet de La Guerre* (Brooklyn, NY: Institute of Mediaeval Music, 1966).

KUHNAU

Kuhnau, J. *Klavierwerke,* ed. K. Päsler, Vol. 4 in *Denkmäler deutscher Tonkunst* (Leipzig: Breitkopf & Härtel, 1958).

———. *Six Biblical Sonatas for Keyboard (1700),* ed., trans., and annotated by Kurt Stone (New York: Broude, 1953).

MUFFAT

Muffat, Georg. *Florilegium . . .* (1695), ed. Heinrich Rietsch, Vols. 2 (Jg. 1/2) and 4 (Jg. 2/2) in *Denkmäler der Tonkunst in Österreich,* ed. Guido Adler (Graz: Akademische Druck- und Verlagsanstalt, 1959).

PURCELL

The Works of Henry Purcell, ed. The Purcell Society (London: Novello, 1878–1965; rev. 1961–).

Westrup, Jack A. *Purcell* (New York: Collier, 1962).

Zimmerman, F. B. *Henry Purcell: His Life and Times* (London: Macmillan, 1967; 2d rev. ed., Philadelphia: U. of Pennsylvania Press, 1983).

SWEELINCK

J. P. Sweelinck: Opera omnia, editio altera, ed. R. Lagas, G. Leonhardt, et al., Vol. I: *The Instrumental Works,* Uitgaven der Vereeniging voor Nederlandse Muziekgeschiedenis (Amsterdam: Alsbach, 1968; 2d rev. ed., 1974).

J. P. Sweelinck: Werken, ed. M. Seiffert et al. (The Hague: Nijhof; Leipzig: Breitkopf & Härtel, 1894–1901; repr. 1968); rev., enlarged (Amsterdam: Alsbach, 1943).

CHAPTER 17: EMINENT COMPOSERS OF THE EARLY EIGHTEENTH CENTURY

J. S. BACH

Music

J. S. Bach: Werke, ed. Bach-Gesellschaft, 61 vols. [in 47 Jahrgänge] (Leipzig: Bach Gesellschaft, 1851–99; repr. [except Jg. 47] Ann Arbor, MI: J. W. Edwards, 1947). *Neue Bach-Ausgabe sämtliche Werke,* ed. Johann-Sebastian-Bach-Institut, Göttingen, and Bach-Archiv, Leipzig (Kassel: Bärenreiter, 1954–). *Faksimile-Reihe Bachser Werke und Schriftstücke* (Leipzig: Verlag für Musik, 1955–). J. S. Bach, *Organ Chorales from the Neumeister*

Collection [MS LM4708, at Yale U.] (Kassel: Bärenreiter, and New York: Yale U. Press, 1985).

For Further Reading

Boyd, Malcolm. *Bach* (London: J. M. Dent, 1983).

David, Hans, and Arthur Mendel. *The Bach Reader* (New York: Norton, 1966).

Dickinson, A. E. F. *Bach's Fugal Works, with an Account of Fugue before and after Bach* (London: Pitman & Sons, 1956; repr. Westport, CT: Greenwood Press, 1979).

Emery, Walter. *Bach's Ornaments* (London: Novello, 1953).

Geiringer, Karl. *The Bach Family: Seven Generations of Creative Genius* (London: G. Allen Unwin, 1954; repr. New York, 1971).

————. *Johann Sebastian Bach: The Culmination of an Era* (New York: Oxford U. Press, 1966).

Leaver, Robin A., ed. *J. S. Bach and Scripture,* with intro. and notes by Leaver (St. Louis, MO: Concordia, 1985).

Marshall, Robert. *The Compositional Process of J. S. Bach: A Study of the Autograph Scores of the Vocal Works* (Princeton, NJ: Princeton U. Press, 1978).

Schwendowius, Barbara, and Wolfgang Dömling, eds. *J. S. Bach: Life, Times, Influence* (Kassel: Bärenreiter, 1976).

Stauffer, George, and Ernest May, eds. *J. S. Bach as Organist* (Bloomington: Indiana U. Press, 1986).

Stiller, Günther. *Johann Sebastian Bach and Liturgical Life in Leipzig,* trans. H. J. A. Buman et al., ed. Robin A. Leaver (St. Louis, MO: Concordia Publishing House, 1984).

Terry, C. S. *Bach's Chorales,* 3 vols. (Cambridge: Cambridge U. Press, 1917–21).

Williams, Peter, ed. *Bach, Handel, Scarlatti: Tercentenary Essays* (Cambridge: Cambridge U. Press, 1985).

————. *The Organ Music of J. S. Bach,* 2 vols. (Cambridge: Cambridge U. Press, 1980–84).

HANDEL

Music

G. F. *Handels Werke: Ausgabe der Deutschen Handelgesellschaft,* ed. F. W. Chrysander, vols. 1–48, 50–94, with 6 suppl. vols. (Leipzig: Breitkopf & Härtel, 1858–1903; repr. Ridgewood, NJ: Gregg International, 1965–66). *Hallische Händel-Ausgabe,* ed. M. Schneider, R. Steglich, et al. (Kassel: Bärenreiter, 1955–).

For Further Reading

Dean, Winton. *Handel's Dramatic Oratorios and Masques* (London: Oxford U. Press, 1959).

————. *Handel and the Opera Seria* (Berkeley: U. of California Press, 1969).

Dean, Winton, and J. Merill Knapp. *Handel's Operas, 1724–1726* (Oxford and New York: Clarendon Press, 1987).

Deutsch, Otto E. *Handel: A Documentary Biography* (New York and London: Adam and Charles Black, 1955).

Landon, H. C. Robbins. *Handel and His World* (London: Weidenfeld & Nicolson, 1984).

Lang, Paul H. *George Frideric Handel* (New York: Norton, 1966).

Williams, Peter, ed. *Bach, Handel, Scarlatti: Tercentenary Essays* (Cambridge: Cambridge U. Press, 1985).

RAMEAU

Music

J.-P. *Rameau: Oeuvres complètes,* ed. C. Saint-Saëns, C. Malherbe, et al. (Paris: A Durand et fils, 1895–1924; repr. New York, 1968).

Writings

Jean-Philippe Rameau: Complete Theoretical Writings, ed. E. Jacobi, 6 vols. (Rome: American Institute of Musicology, Series Misc. 3, 1967–72).

Rameau, J. P. *Traité de l'harmonie reduite à ses principes naturels* (Paris, 1722), trans., with intro. and notes, Philip Gossett (New York: Dover, 1971).

For Further Reading

Anthony, James R. *French Baroque Music from Beaujoyeulx to Rameau* (New York: Norton, 1974).

Claudon, Francis, Jean Mongrédien, Carl de Nuys, and Karlheinz Roschitz. *L'Histoire de l'Opéra en France* (Paris: Fernand Nathan, 1984).

Delmuth. N. *French Opera: Its Development to the Revolution* (Sussex: Artemis Press, 1963).

Girdlestone, Cuthbert. *Jean-Philippe Rameau: His Life and Work* (London: Cassell & Co., 1957; repr. New York: Dover, 1969).

TELEMANN

Music

G. P. *Telemann: Musikalische Werke* (Kassel & Basel: Bärenreiter, 1950–).

G. P. *Telemann: Orgelwerke,* ed. T. Fedtke (Kassel, 1964).

For Further Reading

Petzoldt, Richard. *Georg Philip Telemann,* trans. H. T. Fitzpatrick (New York: Oxford U. Press, 1974).

VIVALDI

Music

Scholarly edition of Vivaldi's works, by Istituto Italiano Antonio Vivaldi (Milan: Ricordi, 1982–). Collected practical edition of Vivaldi's works, ed. A. Fanna (Rome: Edizioni Ricordi, 1947–), with thematic catalog of the instrumental works by A. Fanna (Milan: Ricordi, 1968). A. *Vivaldi: Motetti a canto solo con stromenti,* ed. R. Blanchard, *Le pupitre* 7 (Paris: Heugel, 1968). Thematic catalog: Ryom, P. *Verzeichnis der Werke Antonio Vivaldis,* 2d ed. (Leipzig: VEB Deutscher Verlag für Musik, 1977).

For Further Reading

Collins, M., and E. Kirk, eds. *Opera and Vivaldi* (Austin: U. of Texas Press, 1984, 1971).

Kolneder, Walter. *Vivaldi,* trans. B. Hopkins (Berkeley: U. of California Press, 1971).

Pincherle, Marc. *Vivaldi, Genius of the Baroque,* 2 vols. (Paris: Floury, 1948), trans. Christopher Hatch (New York: Norton, 1957).

Talbot, Michael. *Vivaldi* (London: J. M. Dent, 1978).

CHAPTER 18: EIGHTEENTH-CENTURY PRECLASSIC MUSIC

GENERAL

Burney, Charles. *The Present State of Music in Germany, the Netherlands, and United Provinces* (London: T. Becket, 1773; 2d ed., 1775), and *The Present State of Music in France and Italy* (London: T. Becket, 1771); ed. Percy Scholes as *Dr. Burney's Musical Tours* (London and New York: Oxford U. Press, 1959; repr. Westport, CT: Greenwood Press, 1979).

Duckles, Vincent, and Minnie Elmer. *Thematic Catalog of a Manuscript Collection of Eighteenth-Century Italian Instrumental Music in the University of California, Berkeley, Music Library* (Berkeley: U. of California Press, 1963).

Helm, E. Eugene. *Music at the Court of Frederick the Great* (Norman: U. of Oklahoma Press, 1960).

Lang, Paul H. "Rococo—Style galant—Empfindsamkeit," *Music in Western Civilization* (New York: Norton, 1941), pp. 530–617.

Newman, William. *The Sonata in the Classic Era* (Chapel Hill: U. of North Carolina Press, 1983).

Sheldon, D. A. "The Galant Style Revisited and Re-evaluated," *Acta Musicologica* 47 (1975), pp. 240–69.

Stolba, K Marie. *A History of the Violin Étude to about 1800* (repr. New York: Da Capo Press, 1979).

PERFORMANCE PRACTICE
Treatises
Bach, C. P. E. *Versuch über die wahre Art das Clavier zu spielen, mit Exempeln . . .* (Berlin: Winter, 1753), trans. ed. William J. Mitchell, as *Essay on the True Art of Playing Keyboard Instruments* (New York: Norton, 1949).

Mozart, Leopold. *Versuch einer gründlichen Violinschule* (Augsburg: Lotter, 1756), facsimile ed. (Leipzig: H. L. Grahl, 1956), trans. Editha Knocker as *A Treatise on the Fundamental Principles of Violin Playing,* 2d ed. (London and New York: Oxford U. Press, 1951).

Quantz, Johann Joachim. *Versuch einer Anweisung die Flöte traversière zu spielen* (Essay on Playing the Transverse Flute; Berlin: C. F. Voss, 1752); facsimile of 3d ed., Breslau, 1789 (Kassel: Bärenreiter, 1953); trans. Edward R. Reilly, *On Playing the Flute* (New York: Schirmer Books, 1966; rev. ed., 1985).

Tartini, Giuseppe. *Traité des Agréments de la Musique* (Treatise on Ornaments in Music), trans. Pierre Denis (Paris: Denis, 1771), and *Regole per arrivare a saper ben suonar il violino* (MS compiled by G. F. Nicolai, in Conservatorio di Musica Benedetto Marcello, Venice), ed. Erwin R. Jacobi and pub. in multilingual edition (Celle and New York: Moeck, 1961). Also, *Libro de regole, ed Esempi necessari per ben suonare,* MS It. 00987, Music Library, U. of California, Berkeley.

Other Writings
Boyden, David D. "Dynamics in Seventeenth- and Eighteenth-Century Music," *Essays on Music in Honor of Archibald Thompson Davison* (Cambridge, MA: Harvard U. Press, 1957), p. 185ff.

Williams, P. "The Harpsichord Acciaccatura: Theory and Practice in Harmony, 1650–1750," *The Musical Quarterly* 54 (1968), p. 503ff.

J. S. BACH'S SONS
Barford, Philip. *The Keyboard Music of C. P. E. Bach* (London: Barrie & Rockliff, 1965; repr. New York: October House, 1966).

Geiringer, Karl. *The Bach Family: Seven Generations of Creative Genius* (London: G. Allen Unwin, 1954; repr. New York, 1971).

Newman, William S. "Emanuel Bach's Autobiography," *The Musical Quarterly* 51 (1965), pp. 363–73.

Schulenberg, David. *The Instrumental Music of C. P. E. Bach* (Ann Arbor, MI: UMI Research Press, 1984).

Terry, Charles S. *John Christian Bach* (London: Oxford U. Press, 1929); 2d rev. ed., by H. C. R. Landon, 1967 (Westport, CT: Greenwood Press, 1980).

Warburton, E. "J. C. Bach's Operas," *Proceedings of the Royal Musical Association* 92 (1965–66), p. 95ff.

Young, Percy M. *The Bachs, 1500–1850* (New York: Crowell, 1970).

D. SCARLATTI
Music
Opere complete per clavicembalo di Domenico Scarlatti, 10 vols. and suppl., ed. A. Longo (Milan: 1906–08; New York: Ricordi, 1947–51). *D. Scarlatti: Sixty Sonatas,* 2 vols., ed. R. Kirkpatrick (New York: G. Schirmer, 1953). *D. Scarlatti: Complete Keyboard Works in Facsimile,* 18 vols., ed. R. Kirkpatrick (New York: Johnson Reprint, 1971–72). *Domenico Scarlatti: 100 Sonatas,* 3 vols., ed. Eiji Hashimoto (New York: G. Schirmer, 1975).

For Further Reading
Boyd, Malcolm. *Domenico Scarlatti—Master of Music* (New York: Schirmer Books, 1987, cpr. 1986).

Kirkpatrick, Ralph. *Domenico Scarlatti* (New York: Crowell, 1968; new ed., Princeton, NJ: Princeton U. Press, 1953; rev. 1968; new ed., 1983).

OPERA
Anonymous. [Benedetto Marcello]. *Il Teatro alla Moda* (Venice, c. 1720; repr. Milan: Ricordi, 1956). Translation by R. G. Pauly, in *The Musical Quarterly* 34 (1948), pp. 371–403; 35 (1949), pp. 85–105.

Charlton, David. *Grétry and the Growth of Opéra-comique* (Cambridge: Cambridge U. Press, 1986).

Dent, E. J. "Italian Opera in the Eighteenth Century and its Influence on the Music of the Classic Period," *Sammelbände der Internationalen Musik-Gesellschaft* 14 (1912–13), p. 500ff.

Gagey, E. M. *Ballad Opera* (New York: Columbia U. Press, 1937).

Pitou, Spire. *The Paris Opera,* Vol. 2, *Rococo and Romantic, 1715–1815* (Westport, CT: Greenwood Press, 1985).

PARIS
Brook, Barry S. *La Symphonie française dans la seconde moitié du XVIIIe siècle,* 3 vols. (Paris: Institut de musicologie de l'Université de Paris, 1962).

Launay, D., ed. *La Querelle des Bouffons,* repr. of pamphlets pub. Paris and The Hague, 1752–54 (Geneva, 1974).

Macdonald, R. J. *François-Joseph Gossec and French Instrumental Music in the Second Half of the Eighteenth Century* (Diss., U. of Michigan, 1968).

McClellan, Michael E. "Counterrevolution in Concert: Music and Political Dissent in Revolutionary France," *The Musical Quarterly* 80 (1996), pp. 31–52.

PERGOLESI
Opera omnia di Giovanni Battista Pergolesi, 26 vols., ed. F. Caffarelli (Rome: Gli Amici della Musica da Camera, 1939–42; repr. in 5 vols., 1953). [New edition in progress, Pergolesi Research Center, City U. of New York.]

CHAPTER 19: THE CLASSIC ERA

GENERAL
Blume, Friedrich. *Classic and Romantic Music: A Comprehensive Survey,* trans. M. D. Herter Norton (New York: Norton, 1970), pp. 3–94.

Landon, H. C. Robbins. *Essays on the Viennese Classical Style: Gluck, Haydn, Mozart, Beethoven* (New York: Macmillan, 1970).

Pauly, Reinhard. *Music in the Classic Period,* 2d ed. (Englewood Cliffs, NJ: Prentice-Hall, 1973).

Rosen, Charles. *The Classical Style: Haydn, Mozart, Beethoven* (New York: Viking Press, 1971; New York: Norton, 1972).

———. *Sonata Forms* (New York: Norton, 1980).

Ratner, Leonard. *Classic Music: Expression, Form, and Style* (New York: Schirmer Books, 1980).

Webster, James. "Towards a History of Viennese Chamber Music in the Early Classical Period," *Journal of the American Musicological Society* 27 (1974), pp. 212–47.

GLUCK
Music
C. W. *Gluck: Sämtliche Werke,* ed. R. Gerber, G. Croll, et al. (Kassel & Basel: Bärenreiter, 1951–). Edition of operas, commencing with *Orfeo ed Euridice,* pub. in 7 vols., by J. Pelletan et al. (Leipzig, 1873–96).

For Further Reading
Cooper, Martin. *Gluck* (New York: Oxford U. Press, 1935).

Einstein, Alfred. *Gluck* (London: J. M. Dent, 1936; repr. New York: Collier, 1962).

Newman, Ernest. *Gluck and the Opera* (London: 1895; repr. 1964).

HAYDN
Music
J. *Haydn: Werke,* ed. J. Haydn-Institut, Cologne, directed by J. P. Larsen (1958–61) and G. Feder (1962–), 59 vols. (Munich and Duisberg: G. Henle, 1958–). *J. Haydn: Kritische sämtliche Symphonien,* 12 vols., ed. H. C. R. Landon, Philharmonia series (Vienna, 1965–68).

For Further Reading
Barrett-Ayres, Reginald. *Joseph Haydn and the String Quartet* (New York: Schirmer Books, 1974).

Brown, A. Peter. *Joseph Haydn's Keyboard Music: Sources and Style* (Bloomington: Indiana U. Press, 1986).

Geiringer, Karl. *Haydn: A Creative Life in Music* (Berkeley: U. of California Press, 1968, 3d rev. ed., 1982).

Hughes, Rosemary. *Haydn,* rev. ed. (London: J. M. Dent, 1974).

———. *Haydn String Quartets* (Seattle: U. of Washington Press, 1969; rev. 5th ed., 1975).

Keller, Hans. *The Great Haydn String Quartets: Their Interpretation* (London: J. M. Dent, 1986).

Landon, H. C. Robbins. *Haydn: Chronicle and Works,* 5 vols. (Bloomington: Indiana U. Press, 1976–80).

———. *Haydn: A Documentary Study* (New York: Rizzoli, 1981).

———. *The Symphonies of Joseph Haydn* (London: Universal Edition, 1955; supplement, Barrie & Rockliff, 1961).

W. A. MOZART
Music
W. A. *Mozarts Werke,* ed. L. von Köchel et al., 14 series incl. supplements (Leipzig: Breitkopf & Härtel, 1877–1910; repr. Ann Arbor: Edwards, 1951–56; repr. in miniature, New York: Kalmus, 1969). *W. A. Mozart: Neue Ausgabe sämtlicher Werke,* ed. E. P. Schmid et al. (Kassel: Bärenreiter, 1955–).

For Further Reading
Abert, Hermann. *W. A. Mozart,* 2 vols. (Leipzig: Breitkopf & Härtel, 1956; rev. 1975).

Badura-Skoda, Eva, and Paul Badura-Skoda. *Interpreting Mozart on the Keyboard,* trans. Leo Black (London: Barrie & Rockliff, 1962).

Dearling, Robert. *The Music of W. A. Mozart: The Symphonies* (Rutherford, NJ: Fairleigh Dickinson U. Press, 1982).

Dent, E. J. *Mozart's Operas,* 2d ed. (London: Oxford U. Press, 1960).

Deutsch, Otto E. *Mozart: A Documentary Biography,* 2d ed., trans. E. Blom et al. (London: Adam & Charles Black, 1965).

Einstein, Alfred. *Mozart: His Character, His Work,* trans. Arthur Mendel and N. Broder (New York: Oxford U. Press, 1945; 4th ed., 1961).

Girdlestone, Cuthbert M. *Mozart's Piano Concertos* (London: Cassell, 1958; 3d ed., 1978).

Godwin, Joscelyn. "Layers of Meaning in *The Magic Flute.*" *The Musical Quarterly* 65 (1979), pp. 471–92.

Hutchings, Arthur. *Mozart: The Man, the Musician* (London: Thames & Hudson, 1976).

King, A. Hyatt. *Mozart* (London: Bingley, 1970).

———. *Mozart Chamber Music* (London: British Broadcasting Corporation, 1968; Seattle: U. of Washington Press, 1969).

Landon, H. C. Robbins. *Mozart and the Masons: New Light on the Lodge "Crowned Hope"* (New York: Thames & Hudson, 1983).

Levey, Michael. *The Life & Death of Mozart* (New York: Stein & Day, 1971).

Liebner, János. *Mozart on the Stage* (New York: Praeger, 1972).

Mann, William. *The Operas of Mozart* (London: Oxford U. Press, 1960).

Nettl, Paul. *Mozart and Masonry* (New York: Philosophical Society, 1957; repr. New York: Da Capo Press, 1970; repr. New York: Dorset, 1987).

Rothschild, Fritz. *Musical Performance in the Times of Mozart & Beethoven* (London: Adam & Charles Black, 1961).

Saint-Foix, Georges de. *The Symphonies of Mozart,* trans. Leslie Orrey (London: Dennis Dobson, 1947; repr. New York: Dover, 1968).

Solomon, Maynard. *Mozart: A Life* (New York: HarperCollins Publishers, 1995).

AMERICAN MUSIC
Antes
Kroeger, Karl. "John Antes at Fulneck," *Moravian Music Journal* 30/1 (1985), p. 12ff.

McCorkle, Donald M. *John Antes, American Dilettante* (Winston-Salem, NC: Moravian Music Foundation, 1956; rev. 1980).

Stolba, K. M. "Evidence for Quartets by John Antes, American-born Moravian Composer," *Journal of the American Musicological Society* 33 (1980), p. 565ff.

Billings
W. *Billings: Complete Works,* 4 vols.; Vols. 1, 3, 4, ed. Karl Kroeger, Vol. 2, ed. H. Nathan (Charlottesville, VA: American Musicological Society and University Press of Virginia, 1977–81).

Nathan, Hans. *William Billings: Data and Documents* (Detroit: 1976).

Hopkinson, Lyon
Sonneck, Oscar G. T. *Francis Hopkinson and James Lyon* (Washington, D.C., 1905; repr. New York: Da Capo Press, 1967).

CHAPTER 20: FROM CLASSICISM TO ROMANTICISM

THE LONDON SCHOOL
Music
J. L. *Dussek: Sämtliche Werke für Klavier* [*Oeuvres de J. L. Dussek*] (Leipzig: Breitkopf & Härtel, 1813–17; repr. New York: Da Capo Press, 1978).

The London Pianoforte School: 1766–1860, 20 vols., Nicholas Temperley, gen. ed. (New York: Garland, 1985).

Muzio Clementi: Complete Works (Leipzig: Breitkopf & Härtel, 1803–19; repr. New York: Da Capo Press, 1973).

For Further Reading
Clementi
Plantinga, Leon, *Muzio Clementi: His Life and Music* (London: Oxford U. Press, 1977).

Dussek
Klima, S. V. "Dussek in England," *Music and Letters* 41 (1960), p. 146ff.

Kraw, H. A. *A Biography and Thematic Catalog of the Works of J. L. Dussek (1760–1812)* (Diss., U. of Southern California, 1964).

Field
Piggott, Patrick. "John Field and the Nocturne," *Proceedings of the Royal Musical Association* 95 (1968–69), p. 55ff.

———. *The Life and Music of John Field* (London: Faber, 1973).

Southall, Geneva. *John Field's Piano Concertos: An Analytical and Historical Study* (Diss., U. of Iowa, 1966).

Temperley, Nicholas. "John Field and the First Nocturne," *Music and Letters* 56 (1975), p. 335ff.

———. "John Field's Life and Music," *The Musical Times* 95 (1974), p. 386ff.

BOHEMIAN PIANISTS
Sachs, J. "A Checklist of the Works of Johann Nepomuk Hummel," *Notes* 30 (1973–74), p. 732ff.

Tomášek: Principal MS collection of works is in Prague: Národni Muzeum, Music Division.

Hummel
Davis, R. "The Music of J. N. Hummel, its Derivation and Development," *The Music Review* 26 (1965), p. 169ff.

Sachs, J. *Hummel in England and France: A Study in the International Musical Life of the Early Nineteenth Century* (Diss., Columbia U., 1968).

Voříšek
DeLong, K. G. *The Music of Jan Hugo Voříšek: A Stylistic Study* (Diss., Stanford U.).

Simpson, Adrienne. "A Profile of Jan Václav Voříšek," *Proceedings of the Royal Musical Association* 97 (1970–71), p. 125ff.

BEETHOVEN
Music
Ludwig van Beethovens Werke, 24 series and suppl. (Leipzig: Breitkopf & Härtel, 1864–90; repr. Ann Arbor: J. W. Edwards, 1949; repr. in miniature, New York: Kalmus, 1971). *Supplement zur Gesamtausgabe,* ed. W. Hess (Wiesbaden: Breitkopf & Härtel, 1959–71). *Neue Ausgabe sämtlicher Werke,* ed. J. Schmidt-Görg (Munich & Duisburg: Henle, 1961–).

For Further Reading
Abraham, G., ed. *The Age of Beethoven, 1790–1830* (New York: Oxford U. Press, 1982).

Anderson, Emily, ed., trans. *The Letters of Beethoven,* 3 vols. (New York: St. Martin's Press, 1961).

[A. W.] Thayer's Life of Beethoven, rev. and ed. Elliot Forbes, 2 vols. (Princeton: Princeton U. Press, 1969; 1-vol. paperbd. ed., 1970).

Cooper, Martin. *Beethoven: The Last Decade, 1817–1827* (London: Oxford U. Press, 1970).

Grove, Sir George. *Beethoven and His Nine Symphonies* (London: Novello, 1884; repr. New York: Dover, 1962).

Landon, H. C. Robbins. *Beethoven: A Documentary Study* (London: Macmillan, 1970).

Lang, Paul H., ed. *The Musical Quarterly Special Issue Celebrating the Bicentennial of the Birth of Beethoven,* Vol. 56, No. 4 (New York: G. Schirmer, October 1970).

Newman, William S. *Performance Practices in Beethoven's Piano Sonatas: An Introduction* (New York: Norton, 1971).

Schindler, Anton. *Beethoven as I Knew Him* (Münster, 1840), ed. D. W. McArdle, trans. C. S. Jolly (Chapel Hill: U. of North Carolina Press, 1966; repr. New York: Norton, 1972).

Solomon, Maynard. *Beethoven* (New York: Schirmer Books, 1977).

Szigeti, Joseph. *The Ten Beethoven Sonatas for Piano & Violin,* ed. Paul Rolland (Urbana, IL: American String Teachers Association, 1965).

Tovey, Donald F. *A Companion to Beethoven's Pianoforte Sonatas* (London: The Associated Board of the Royal Schools of Music, 1931; repr. New York: AMS Press, 1976).

CHAPTER 21: EARLY NINETEENTH-CENTURY MUSIC

GENERAL
Abraham, Gerald. *A Hundred Years of Music* (London: Duckworth, 1964; 4th ed., Duckworth, 1974).

Abrams, Meyer H. *The Mirror and the Lamp: Romantic Theory and the Critical Tradition* (New York: Oxford U. Press, 1953).

Blume, Friedrich. *Classic and Romantic Music: A Comprehensive Survey,* trans. M. D. Herter Norton (New York: Norton, 1970), pp. 95–194.

Durant, Will, and Ariel Durant. *The New Age of Napoleon* (New York: Simon & Schuster, 1975).

Einstein, Alfred. *Music in the Romantic Era* (New York: Norton, 1947).

Longyear, Rey M. *Nineteenth-Century Romanticism in Music* (Englewood Cliffs, NJ: Prentice-Hall, 1969; 2d ed., 1973).

Newman, William S. *The Sonata Since Beethoven* (Chapel Hill: U. of North Carolina Press, 1970; 3d ed., New York: Norton, 1983).

Plantinga, Leon. *Romantic Music* (New York: Norton, 1984).

Tischler, Hans. "Classicism, Romanticism and Music," *The Music Review* 14 (1953), pp. 108–205.

OPERA
Claudon, Francis, Jean Mongrédien, Carl de Nuys, and Karlheinz Roschitz. *L'Histoire de l'Opéra en France* (Paris: Fernand Nathan, 1984).

Crosten, William L. *French Grand Opera: An Art and a Business* (New York: King's Crown Press, 1948; repr. New York: Da Capo Press, 1972).

Dent, Edward J. *The Rise of Romantic Opera,* ed. Winton Dean (Cambridge: Cambridge U. Press, 1976).

Grout, Donald J. *A Short History of Opera,* 3d ed. (New York: Columbia U. Press, 1988).

Pitou, Spire. *The Paris Opera*, Vol. 2, *Rococo and Romantic, 1715–1815* (Westport, CT: Greenwood Press, 1985).

GARCÍAS
Levien, John J. N. *The Garcia Family* (London: Novello, 1932; 2d rev. ed., pub. as *Six Sovereigns of Song,* 1948).

Mattfeld, Julius. *A Hundred Years of Grand Opera in New York, 1825–1925* (New York: New York Public Library, 1937; repr. New York: AMS Press, 1976).

Sterling-Mackinlay, M. *García the Centenarian and his Times* (Edinburgh: W. Blanchard, 1908; repr. New York: Da Capo Press, 1976).

Subira, José. *Historia de la musica española e hispano-americana* (Barcelona: Salvat, 1953; repr. Salvat, 1987), p. 628ff.

LOEWE
Carl Loewes Werke: Gesamtausgabe der Balladen, Legenden, Lieder und Gesänge, ed. M. Runze (Leipzig: Breitkopf & Härtel, 1899–1904; repr. 1970).

Loewe, Carl. *Selbstbiographie,* ed. Karl H. Ritter (Berlin: W. Müller, 1870; repr. Hildesheim: Olms, 1976).

For Further Reading
Brown, Maurice J. E. "Carl Loewe, 1796–1869," *The Musical Times* 110 (1969), p. 357ff.

ROSSINI
Stendhal, Mme [Marie Henri Beyle]. *Vie de Rossini* (Life of Rossini; Paris: 1824); trans. R. N. Coe (New York: Orion Press, 1970; repr. Seattle: U. of Washington Press, 1972).

Weinstock, Herbert. *Rossini: A Biography* (New York: Knopf, 1968).

SCHUBERT
Music
F. Schuberts Werke: Kritisch durchgeschene Gesamtausgabe, ed. J. Brahms, E. Mandyczewski, et al. (Leipzig: Breitkopf & Härtel, 1884–97; repr. New York; Dover, 1964–69; repr. in miniature, New York: Kalmus, 1971).

F. Schubert: Neue Ausgabe sämtlicher Werke, ed. W. Dürr, C. Landon, et al. (Kassel and New York: Bärenreiter, 1964–).

F. Schubert: Lieder, 7 vols. (Frankfurt and New York: C. F. Peters, 1985–88).

For Further Reading
Abraham, Gerald, ed. *The Music of Schubert* (Washington, DC, and New York: Kennikat Press, 1969).

Brown, Maurice J. E. *Schubert: A Critical Biography* (London: Macmillan, 1958; repr. New York: Da Capo Press, 1977).

———. "Schubert: Discoveries of the Last Decade," *The Musical Quarterly* 47 (1961), p. 293ff.

———. "Schubert: Discoveries of the Last Decade," *The Musical Quarterly* 57 (1971), p. 351ff.

Capell, Richard. *Schubert's Songs,* 3d ed. (London: Duckworth, 1973).

Deutsch, Otto E. *Schubert: A Documentary Biography,* trans. E. Blom (London: Dent, 1946; repr. New York: Da Capo Press, 1977).

———. *The Schubert Reader: A Life of Franz Schubert in Letters and Documents,* trans. E. Blom (New York: Norton, 1947).

Marek, George R. *Schubert* (New York: Viking, 1985).

SPOHR
Spohr, Louis. *Selbstbiographie,* 2 vols. (Kassel: City of Kassel, 1860–61), Eng. trans. (London: Longmans, Green, 1865; repr. New York: Da Capo Press, 1969).

WEBER
Warrack, John H. *Carl Maria von Weber* (London: Hamilton, 1968; New York: Macmillan, 1968; 2d ed., Cambridge: Cambridge U. Press, 1976).

Weber, Max Maria von. *Carl Maria von Weber: ein Lebensbild,* 2 vols. (Leipzig: E. Keil, 1864–65; Eng. trans. London: Chapman & Hall, 1865; repr. Westport, CT: Greenwood Press, 1969).

CHAPTER 22: NINETEENTH-CENTURY MUSICAL EXPANSION

GENERAL
Claudon, Francis, Jean Mongrédien, Carl de Nuys, and Karlheinz Roschitz. *L'Histoire de l'Opéra en France* (Paris: Fernand Nathan, 1984).

Crosten, William L. *French Grand Opera: An Art and a Business* (New York: King's Crown Press, 1948; repr. New York: Da Capo Press, 1972).

Lovelace, Ada. *Notes upon the Memoire, Sketch of the Analytical Engine invented by Charles Babbage* (Geneva, 1842) reprinted in *Charles Babbage and His Calculating Engines,* ed. Philip Morrison and Emily Morrison (New York: Dover, 1961).

Pitou, Spire. *The Paris Opera,* Vol. 2, *Rococo and Romantic, 1715–1815* (Westport, CT: Greenwood Press, 1985).

BELLINI
Orrey, Leslie. *Bellini* (London: J. M. Dent & Sons; New York: Farrar, Straus & Giroux, 1969).

Weinstock, Herbert. *Vincenzo Bellini: His Life and His Operas* (New York: Knopf, 1971).

BERLIOZ
Music
H. Berlioz: Werke, 20 vols., ed. C. Malherbe and F. Weingartner (Leipzig: Breitkopf & Härtel, 1900–10). *New Berlioz Edition,* ed. H. Macdonald et al. (Kassel: Bärenreiter, 1967–).

Writings
Grand traité d'instrumentation et d'orchestration modernes (Treatise on Instrumentation and Orchestration), Op. 10 (Paris, 1843; 2d ed., 1855; rev. and enl. by Richard Strauss, 1905, trans. Theodore Front, New York: Kalmus, 1948, and Melville, NY: Belwin Mills, 1948).

Memoires de Hector Berlioz from 1803 to 1865 (Paris, 1870); Eng. trans. by Holmes rev. by Ernest Newman (New York: Knopf, 1932; repr. New York: Dover, 1966).

For Further Reading
Barzun, Jacques. *Berlioz and His Century* (Boston: Little, Brown & Co., 1969).

———. "Berlioz a Hundred Years After," *The Musical Quarterly* 56 (1970), p. 1ff.

Cairns, D. "Spontini's Influence on Berlioz," *From Parnassus: Essays in Honor of Jacques Barzun,* ed. Dora B. Weines and Wm. R. Keylor (New York: Harper & Row, 1976).

Comboroure, C. "Harriet Smithson, 1828–37," *Berlioz Society Bulletin,* No. 86 (1975), p. 15ff.

Dickinson, Alan E. F. *The Music of Berlioz* (London: Faber, 1972).

Macdonald, Hugh. *Berlioz* (London: Dent, 1982).

Primmer, Brian. *The Berlioz Style* (London: Oxford U. Press, 1973).

Rushton, Julian. *The Musical Language of Berlioz* (Cambridge: Cambridge U. Press, 1973).

BIZET

Curtiss, Mina. *Bizet and His World* (New York: Knopf, 1958).

Dean, Winton. *Georges Bizet: His Life and His Work* (London: Dent, 1948; 3d ed., 1975).

CHOPIN
Music

F. F. *Chopin: Dziela wszytkie* (Complete Works), ed. I. J. Paderewski et al. (Warsaw: Institut Fryderyka Chopina, 1949–61).

For Further Reading

Abraham, Gerald. *Chopin's Musical Style* (London: Oxford U. Press, 1939).

Hedley, A. *Chopin* (London: Dent, 1947); rev. by Maurice J. E. Brown (London: Dent, 1974).

Kelley, Edgar S. *Chopin, the Composer* (New York: Cooper Square Publishers, 1969).

Melville, Derek. *Chopin* (London: Clive Bingley, 1977; Hamden, CT: Linnet Books, 1977).

Walker, Alan, ed. *The Chopin Companion* (New York: Norton, 1973).

Weinstock, Herbert. *Chopin: The Man and His Music* (New York: Knopf, 1949; 4th repr. 1969).

DONIZETTI

Ashbrook, William. *Donizetti* (London: Cassell, 1965).

———. *Donizetti and His Operas* (Cambridge: Cambridge U. Press, 1982).

Weinstock, Herbert. *Donizetti and the World of Opera in Italy, Paris, and Vienna in the First Half of the Nineteenth Century* (New York: Pantheon Books, 1963; repr. Octagon, 1979).

HENSEL

Citron, Marcia J. *The Letters of Fanny Hensel to Felix Mendelssohn* (New York: Pendragon Press, 1987).

———. "The Lieder of Fanny Mendelssohn Hensel," *The Musical Quarterly* 69 (1983), pp. 570–93.

Hensel, Sebastian. *Die Familie Mendelssohn 1729–1847, nach Briefen und Tagebüchern* [The Mendelssohn Family, 1729–1847, according to Letters and Diaries] (Berlin, 1879; 18th repr. 1959; Eng. trans., 1882, repr. New York: Haskell House, 1969).

Sirota, Victoria R. *The Life and Works of Fanny Mendelssohn Hensel* (Ann Arbor, MI: University of Microfilms, 1981).

MENDELSSOHN
Music

F. *Mendelssohn-Bartholdy: Werke: kritisch durchgesehene Ausgabe,* 35 vols., ed. J. Rietz (Leipzig: Breitkopf & Härtel, 1874–77; repr. Farnborough, Eng.: Gregg International, 1967; repr. in miniature, New York: Kalmus, 1971). *Leipziger Ausgabe der Werke Felix Mendelssohn Bartholdys,* ed. Internationale Felix-Mendelssohn-Gesellschaft (Leipzig: Deutscher Verlag für Musik, 1960–).

Paintings

Mendelssohn Bartholdy, Felix. *Aquarellenalbum* [Album of Watercolor Paintings] (Berlin: Staatsbibliothek Preussischer Kuklturbesitz, 1968).

Writings

Elvers, R., ed. *Felix Mendelssohn Bartholdy Briefe* (Frankfurt am Main, 1984), trans. C. Tomlinson and pub. as *Felix Mendelssohn: A Life in Letters* (New York: Fromm International, 1986).

Mendelssohn, Felix. *Reisebriefe aus den Jahren 1830 bis 1832* (Letters from the years 1830 to 1832), ed. P. Mendelssohn Bartholdy (Leipzig, 1871). Also, *Briefe aus den Jahren 1830 bis 1847* (Letters from the years 1830 to 1847), comp. J. Rietz (Leipzig, 1861–63).

For Further Reading

Blunt, Wilfred. *On Wings of Song: A Biography of Felix Mendelssohn* (New York: Scribner's Sons, 1974).

Jacob, Heinrich E. *Mendelssohn and His Times,* trans. Richard and Clara Winston (Englewood Cliffs, NJ: Prentice-Hall, 1963).

Radcliffe, Philip. *Mendelssohn* (London: J. M. Dent & Sons; New York: Farrar, Strauss & Giroux, 1967; rev. ed., 1976).

PAGANINI

Courcy, Geraldine I. C. de. *Chronology of Nicolò Paganini's Life* (Wiesbaden: Erdmann Musik Verlag, 1961).

———. *Paganini, the Genoese,* 2 vols. (Norman: U. of Oklahoma Press, 1957; repr. 1977).

Kendall, Alan. *Paganini* (London: Chappell, 1982).

SCHUMANN, CLARA WIECK

Litzmann, B. *Clara Schumann: Ein Künstlerleben* [Clara Schumann: An Artist's Life] (Leipzig: Breitkopf & Härtel, 1902–8; repr. 1971; Eng. trans. 1913, repr. New York: Da Capo Press, 1979).

Meichsner, A. *Friedrich Wieck und seine beiden Töchter Clara Schumann, geb. Wieck, und Marie Wieck* [Friedrich Wieck and his two Daughters, Clara Wieck Schumann and Marie Wieck] (Leipzig: 1875).

Reich, Nancy B. *Clara Schumann: The Artist and the Woman* (Ithaca, NY: Cornell U. Press, 1985).

SCHUMANN, ROBERT
Music

R. *Schumann: Werke,* ed. Clara Schumann, Johannes Brahms, et al. (Leipzig: Breitkopf & Härtel, 1881–93; repr. in miniature, New York: Kalmus, 1971).

Writings

Schumann, Robert. *Gesammelte Schriften über Musik und Musiker* [Collected Writings on Music and Musicians] (Leipzig: G. Wiegand, 1854; repr. 1968; Eng. trans. 1877; new Eng. trans. [selections], 1947).

———. *Tagenbücher, 1827–38* [Diaries] (Leipzig: Deutscher Verlag für Musik, 1971).

For Further Reading

Abraham, Gerald, ed. *Schumann: A Symposium* (London: Oxford U. Press, 1952).

Brion, Marcel. *Schumann and the Romantic Age,* trans. Geoffrey Sainsbury (New York: Macmillan, 1956).

Chissell, Joan. *Schumann* (New York: Collier Books, 1962; rev. ed., London: Dent, 1977).

Ostwald, Peter. *Schumann: Music and Madness* (London: Victor Gollancz, 1985).

Plantinga, Leon. *Schumann as Critic* (New Haven, CT: Yale U. Press, 1967; repr. 1977).

Sams, Eric. "Schumann's Hand Injury," *The Musical Times* 112 (1971), pp. 1156–59.

———. *The Songs of Robert Schumann*, 2d ed. (London: Methuen, 1975).

Walker, A. ed. *Robert Schumann: The Man and His Music* (London: Barrie & Jenkins, 1972; 2d ed., 1976).

AMERICAN COMPOSERS
Foster
Howard, John T. *Stephen Foster: America's Troubadour* (New York: Crowell, 1934; rev. 3d ed., 1962).

Smith, S. B. *A Tribute to Stephen Collins Foster* (Bardstown, KY: Smith, 1976). [Includes facsimiles.]

Gottschalk
The Piano Works of Louis Moreau Gottschalk, ed. Vera B. Lawrence (New York: Arno Press, 1969).

Gottschalk, L. M. *Notes of a Pianist*, ed. Clara Gottschalk Peterson (Philadelphia: Lippincott, 1881), ed. J. Behrend (New York: Knopf, 1964; repr. New York: Da Capo Press, 1979).

Lowens, Irving. "The First Matinée Idol: Louis Moreau Gottschalk," *Musicology* 2 (1948); repr. in *Music and Musicians in Early America* (New York: Norton, 1964), p. 223ff.

Marrocco, W. T. "America's First Nationalist Composer: Louis Moreau Gottschalk (1829–1869)," *Scritti in onore di Luigi Ronga* (Milan and Naples: R. Ricciardi, 1973), p. 293ff.

Mason
Pemberton, C. A. *Lowell Mason: His Life and Work* (Diss., U. of Minnesota, 1971).

Rich, A. L. *Lowell Mason* (Chapel Hill: U. of North Carolina Press, 1946).

Thayer, A. W. "Lowell Mason," *Dwight's Journal of Music* 39 (1879), pp. 186, 195.

CHAPTER 23: PREEMINENT COMPOSERS OF THE LATE NINETEENTH CENTURY

BRAHMS
Music
Johannes Brahms sämtliche Werke, 26 vols. (Leipzig: Breitkopf & Härtel, 1926–27; repr. Ann Arbor, MI: J. W. Edwards, 1949; repr. in miniature, New York: Kalmus, 1970).

For Further Reading
Burnett, James. *Brahms: A Critical Study* (New York: Praeger, 1972).

Frisch, Walter. *Brahms and the Principle of Developing Variation* (Berkeley: U. of California Press, 1984).

Gal, Hans. *Johannes Brahms: His Work and Personality,* trans. Joseph Stein. (New York: Alfred A. Knopf, 1963).

Geiringer, Karl. *Brahms: His Life and Work,* 2d ed., rev. (Garden City, NY: Doubleday & Co., Inc., 1961).

Harrison, Max. *The Lieder of Brahms* (New York: Praeger, 1972).

Horton, John. *Brahms Orchestral Music* (Seattle: U. of Washington Press, 1969).

MacDonald, Malcolm. *Brahms* (New York: Schirmer Books, 1990).

Mason, Daniel G. *The Chamber Music of Brahms,* 2d ed. (New York: Macmillan, 1950).

Musgrave, Michael. *The Music of Brahms* (Boston: Routledge & Kegan Paul, 1985).

Newman, W. S. "A Basic Motive in Brahms's German Requiem," *The Music Review* 24 (1963), p. 70.

Schoenberg, Arnold. "Brahms the Progressive," *Style and Idea* (New York: Philosophical Library, 1950).

BRUCKNER
Music
Anton Bruckner: Sämtliche Werke, kritische Gesamtausgabe, ed. L. Nowak et al. (Vienna: Musikwissenschaftlicher Verlag, 1951–).

For Further Reading
Doernberg, Erwin. *The Life and Symphonies of Anton Bruckner* (London: Barrie & Rockliff, 1960; repr. New York: Dover Publications, 1968).

Redlich, H. F. *Bruckner and Mahler,* rev. ed. (London: J. M. Dent & Sons, 1963).

Schönzeler, Hans-Hubert. *Bruckner* (New York: Grossman, 1970).

Simpson, Robert. *The Essence of Bruckner* (New York: Crescendo Publishing, 1967).

Watson, Derek. *Bruckner* (London: J. M. Dent & Sons, 1975).

LISZT
Music
F. Liszt: Musikalische Werke, ed. F. Busoni, P. Raabe, et al., 34 vols. [but incomplete] (Leipzig: Breitkopf & Härtel, 1907–36; repr. 1967).

F. Liszt: Neue Ausgabe sämtlicher Werke, ed. Z. Gárdonyi, I. Sulyok, et al. (Kassel and Budapest: Bärenreiter, 1970–).

For Further Reading
Beckett, Walter. *Liszt,* rev. ed. (London: J. M. Dent & Sons, 1963).

Perényi, E. *Liszt: The Artist as Romantic Hero* (Boston: Little, Brown & Co., 1974).

Searle, Humphrey. *The Music of Liszt,* 2d rev. ed. (New York: Dover, 1966).

Walker, Alan, comp. *Franz Liszt: The Man and His Music,* 2d ed. (London: Barrie & Jenkins, 1976).

———. *Franz Liszt: The Virtuoso Years, 1811–1847* (New York: Knopf, 1983).

VERDI
Music
"Complete Works" not published. "Study scores" of *Rigoletto, La traviata, Un ballo in maschera, Aïda, Otello,* and *Falstaff* published by Ricordi, in 1930s; repr. in miniature by Kalmus, New York. Full score of *Otello* and *Falstaff* repr. by Dover, New York, 1988.

For Further Reading
Budden, Julian. *The Operas of Verdi,* 3 vols. (New York: Praeger, 1973–82).

Godefroy, Vincent. *The Dramatic Genius of Verdi: Studies of Selected Operas,* 2 vols. (New York: St. Martin's Press; I, 1975; II, 1977).

Hussey, Dyneley. *Verdi* (London: J. M. Dent & Sons, 1963).

Martin, George. *Verdi: His Music, Life and Times* (New York: Dodd, Mead & Co., 1963).

Toye, Francis. *Giuseppe Verdi: His Life and Works* (London: Heinemann, 1931; repr. New York: Vienna House, 1972).

Walker, Frank. *The Man Verdi* (New York: Knopf, 1962).

Weaver, William, comp., ed., trans. *Verdi, a Documentary Study* (London: Thames & Hudson, 1977).

Weaver, William, and Martin Chusid, eds. *The Verdi Companion* (New York: W. W. Norton, 1981).

WAGNER

Music
Richard Wagners Werke [incomplete edition], ed. M. Balling (Leipzig: Breitkopf & Härtel, 1912–29). *R. Wagner: Sämtliche Werke*, ed. C. Dahlhaus (Mainz: B. Schott's Söhne, 1970–). Full scores of *Der Ring des Nibelungen, Die Meistersinger, Lohengrin, Parsifal, Tannhäuser,* and *Tristan und Isolde,* pub. by Dover, New York.

For Further Reading
Barth, Herbert, Dietrich Mack, and Egon Voss, eds. *Wagner: A Documentary Study,* trans. P. R. J. Ford and M. Whittall (New York: Oxford U. Press, 1975).

Burbridge, Peter, and Richard Sutton, eds. *The Wagner Companion* (Cambridge and New York: Cambridge U. Press, 1979).

Dahlhaus, Carl. *Richard Wagner's Music Dramas,* trans. Mary Whittall (Cambridge and New York: Cambridge U. Press, 1979).

Jacobs, Robert L. *Wagner,* rev. ed. (London: J. M. Dent & Sons, 1965).

Mander, Raymond, and Joe Mitchenson. *The Wagner Companion* (New York: Hawthorn Books, 1978).

Newman, Ernest. *Life of Richard Wagner,* 4 vols. (London: Cassell, 1933–47; repr. 1976).

Westernhagen, C. von. *Wagner: A Biography,* 2 vols., trans. Mary Whittall (Cambridge: Cambridge U. Press, 1979).

CHAPTER 24: NATIONALISM IN NINETEENTH-CENTURY MUSIC

RUSSIA
General
Abraham, Gerald. *Studies in Russian Music* (London: W. Reeves, 1935; rev. 1969).

Leonard, Richard A. *A History of Russian Music* (New York: Macmillan, 1956; repr. London: Minerva Press, 1968; repr. Westport, CT: Greenwood Press, 1977).

Seaman, Gerald. *History of Russian Music:* Vol. 1, *From its Origins to Dargomïzhsky* (New York: Praeger, 1967).

Balakirev
Garden, Edward. *Balakirev: A Critical Study of His Life and Music* (London: Faber & Faber, and New York: St. Martin's Press, 1967).

Borodin
Calvocoressi, Michel D. "Alexander Borodin," in M. D. Calvocoressi and Gerald Abraham, *Masters of Russian Music* (London: Duckworth, 1936), p. 155ff.

Cui
Cui, César, *La musique en Russie* [Music in Russia] (Paris: Fischbacher, 1880; trans. and repr. 1974).

Dargomïzhsky
Baker, J. "Dargomïzhsky, Realism and *The Stone Guest,*" *The Music Review* 37 (1976), p. 193ff.

Taruskin, Richard. *Opera and Drama in Russia as Preached and Practiced in the 1860s* (Ann Arbor, MI: UMI Research Press, 1981).

Glinka
Brown, David. *Mikhail Glinka: A Biographical and Critical Study* (London and New York: Oxford U. Press, 1974).

Musorgsky
Calvocoressi, M. D. *Modest Mussorgsky: His Life and Works* (London: Rockliff, 1956; repr. Boston: Crescendo, 1967).

————. *Mussorgsky* [sic] (1946), rev. G. Abraham (London: Dent, 1946; rev. London: Dent, 1974, 1977).

Leyda, Jay, and S. Bertensson, eds. *The Musorgsky Reader: A Life of M. P. Musorgsky in Letters and Documents* (New York: Norton, 1947; repr. 1970).

Lloyd-Jones, David. *Boris Godunov: Critical Commentary* (London: Oxford U. Press, 1975).

Orlova, A. *Musorgsky's Days and Works: A Biography in Documents* (Moscow, 1963), trans. and ed. R. J. Guenther (Ann Arbor, MI: UMI Research Press, 1983).

Serov, Victor I. *Modest Musorgsky* (New York: Funk & Wagnalls, 1968).

Rimsky-Korsakov
Writings
Rimsky-Korsakov, N. *Chronicle of My Musical Life* (St. Petersburg, 1909); Eng. translation by J. Joffe pub. as *My Musical Life* (New York: Knopf, 1923; repr. 1974).

————. *Principles of Orchestration* (St. Petersburg, 1913); Eng. trans. Edward Agate, ed. Maximilian Steinberg (New York: Dover, 1964).

For Further Reading
Abraham, Gerald. *Rimsky-Korsakov: A Short Biography* (London: Duckworth, 1945).

CZECHOSLOVAKIA
Abraham, Gerald. *Slavonic and Romantic Music* (New York: St. Martin's Press, 1968).

Eckstein, Pavel. *Czechoslovak Opera: A Brief Outline* (Prague: Theatre Institute, 1964).

Newmarch, Rosa. *The Music of Czechoslovakia* (London and New York: Oxford U. Press, 1942; repr. New York: Da Capo Press, 1978).

Dvořák
Writings
Dvořák, Antonín. *Letters and Reminiscences,* ed. Otakar Sourek, trans. Roberta Samsour (Prague: Artia, 1958; repr. New York: Da Capo Press, 1983).

For Further Reading
Clapham, John. *Antonin Dvořák* (London: Faber and New York: St. Martin's Press, 1966; rev. ed., New York: Norton, 1979).

Layton, Robert. *Dvořák's Symphonies and Concertos* (London: British Broadcasting Corporation, 1978).

Robertson, Alec. *Dvořák* (London: Dent, 1943; repr. New York: Collier, 1962; rev. London: Dent, 1974).

Janáček
Ewans, Michael. C. *Janáček's Tragic Operas* (Bloomington and London: Indiana U. Press, 1977).

Vogel, J. *Leoš Janáček: His Life and Works* (Kassel, 1958); trans. Geraldine Thomsen-Munchova (London: P. Hamlyn, 1962); rev. and ed. by K. Janovický (New York: Norton, 1981).

Smetana
Clapham, John. *Smetana* (London: Dent, 1972).

Karásek, Bohumil. *Bedřich Smetana* (Prague: Státni hudební vydavatelstuí, 1966), trans. (Prague: Editio Supraphon, 1967).

Large, Brian. *Smetana* (London: Duckworth, and New York: Praeger, 1970; repr. New York: Da Capo Press, 1985).

Malý, Miloslav. *Bedřich Smetana* (Prague: Orbis, 1954), trans. (Orbis, 1956; 1976).

SCANDINAVIA
General
Hodgson, A. *Scandinavian Music: Finland and Sweden* (Rutherford, NJ: Fairleigh Dickinson Press, and London: Associated University Presses, 1984).

Grieg
Abraham, Gerald, ed. *Grieg: A Symposium* (London: Lindsay Drummond, 1948; repr. Westport, CT: Greenwood Press, 1972).

Horton, J. *Grieg* (London: Dent, 1974).

Johansen, David M. *Edvard Grieg,* trans. Madge Robertson (Princeton, NJ: Princeton U. Press, 1938; repr. 1967; repr. New York: Kraus Reprint, 1972).

Nielsen
Simpson, Robert. *Carl Nielsen, Symphonist* (London: Dent, 1964).

FINLAND
Sibelius
Burnett, James. *The Music of Sibelius* (Rutherford, NJ: Fairleigh Dickinson Press, 1983).

Layton, Robert. *Sibelius* (London: Dent, 1965; 2d ed., 1978).

Tawaststjerna, Erik. *Sibelius* (Helsingfors: Söderstroms, 1976); trans. Robert Layton (London: Faber & Faber, 1976).

CHAPTER 25: LATE NINETEENTH-CENTURY AND EARLY TWENTIETH-CENTURY MUSIC

RUSSIA
Scriabin
Baker, James M. *The Music of Alexander Scriabin* (New Haven, CT: Yale U. Press, 1986).

Bowers, Faubion. *The New Scriabin: Enigma and Answers* (New York: St. Martin's Press, 1973).

———. *Scriabin: A Biography of the Russian Composer, 1871–1915,* 2 vols. (Tokyo and Palo Alto, CA: Kodansha International, 1969).

Hull, Arthur Eaglefield. *A Great Russian Tone-Poet: Scriabin* (London: Kegan Paul, Trench, Trubner & Co., 1918; repr. New York: AMS Press, Inc., 1970).

Macdonald, Hugh. *Skryabin* [sic] (London: Oxford U. Press, 1978).

Schloezer, Boris de. *Scriabin: Artist and Mystic,* trans. N. Slonimsky (Berkeley: U. of California Press, 1982).

Swan, Alfred J. *Scriabin* (London: John Lane, 1923; repr. New York: Da Capo Press, 1969).

Tchaikovsky
Brown, David. *Tchaikovsky: A Biographical and Critical Study,* Vol. I, *The Early Years, 1840–1874* (New York: Norton, 1978); Vol. II, *The Crisis Years, 1874–1878* (New York: Norton, 1982); Vol. III, *The Years of Wandering, 1878–1885* (London: Gollancz, 1986).

Garden, Edward. *Tchaikovsky* (London: Dent, 1973).

GERMANY, AUSTRIA
Mahler, G.
Blaukopf, Kurt. *Mahler: A Documentary Study* (New York: Oxford U. Press, 1976).

Cooke, Deryck. *Gustav Mahler: An Introduction to His Music* (London: Faber & Faber, 1980).

Greenberg, Egon. *Mahler: The Man and His Music* (New York: Schirmer Books, 1978).

Kennedy, Michael. *Mahler* (London: Dent, 1974).

La Grange, Henri-Louis de. *Mahler* (Garden City, NY: Doubleday, 1973).

Lea, Henry A. *Gustav Mahler: Man on the Margin* (Bonn: Bouvier, 1985).

Mitchell, Donald. *Gustav Mahler: The Early Years* (London: Rockliff, 1958), rev. ed. P. Banks and D. Mathews (Berkeley: U. of California Press, 1980).

———. *Gustav Mahler: The Wunderhorn Years* (Boulder, CO: Westview Press, 1976).

Werfel, Alma Mahler. *Mahler: Memories and Letters,* 3d ed., rev., ed. D. Mitchell and K. Martner, trans. B. Creighton (Seattle: U. of Washington Press, 1975).

Mahler, A.
Monson, Karen. *Alma Mahler: Muse to Genius* (Boston: Houghton Mifflin, 1983).

Strauss, R.
Armstrong, T. *Strauss's Tone Poems* (London: Oxford U. Press, 1931).

Del Mar, Norman. *Richard Strauss: A Critical Commentary on His Life and Work,* 3 vols. (Philadelphia: Chilton Books, 1969–73; repr., corrected, 1978).

Jefferson, Alan. *The Lieder of Richard Strauss* (New York: Praeger, 1972).

Krause, Ernst. *Richard Strauss: The Man and His Work,* trans. J. Coombs (London: Collett's, 1964).

Mann, William. *Richard Strauss: A Critical Study of His Operas* (London: Cassell, 1964).

Wolf
Sams, Eric. *The Songs of Hugo Wolf* (London: Methuen, 1961; 2d ed., 1981).

Walker, Frank. *Hugo Wolf, A Biography* (London: Dent, 1951; 2d ed., enlarged, 1968).

VERISMO
Dahlhaus, Carl. *Realism in Nineteenth-Century Music,* trans. Mary Whittall (Cambridge and New York: Cambridge U. Press, 1985).

Puccini
Ashbrook, William. *The Operas of Puccini* (New York: Oxford U. Press, 1968).

Carner, Mosco. *Puccini: A Critical Biography* (London: Duckworth, 1958; 2d ed., 1974).

Kaye, Michael. *The Unknown Puccini: A Historical Perspective on the Songs* (London: Oxford U. Press, 1987).

FRANCE
Cooper, Martin. *French Music from the Death of Berlioz to the Death of Fauré* (London: Oxford U. Press, 1951).

Shattuck, Roger. *The Banquet Years: The Arts in France, 1885–1918* (London: Flammarion, 1959; rev. 1968).

L. Boulanger
Rosenstiel, Leonie. *The Life and Works of Lili Boulanger* (Rutherford, NJ: Fairleigh Dickinson U. Press, 1978).

Debussy
Writings

Debussy, Claude. *Monsieur Croche, anti-dilettante* (Paris, 1923), collected by François Lesure, trans. and ed. R. L. Smith, and pub. as *Debussy on Music* (New York: Knopf, 1977).

Lockspeiser, Edward, comp. *Debussy et Edgar Poe: Manuscrits et Documents ineditées* [Manuscripts and unedited documents] (Monaco: Éditions Rocher, 1962).

For Further Reading

Lockspeiser, Edward. *Debussy* (London: Dent, 1936; rev. ed., 1963).

———. *Debussy: His Life and Mind,* 2 vols., 2d ed. (London: Cassell, 1965–66).

Vallas, Léon. *Claude Debussy: His Life and Works,* trans. M. and G. O'Brian (London: Oxford U. Press, 1933).

Wenk, Arthur B. *Claude Debussy and Twentieth-Century Music* (Boston: Twayner, 1983).

———. *Debussy and the Poets* (Berkeley and Los Angeles: U. of California Press, 1976).

Fauré

Koechlin, Charles. *Gabriel Fauré* (London: Dobson, 1945; repr. New York: AMS Press,1976).

Orledge, Robert. *Gabriel Fauré* (London: Eulenberg, 1979).

Suckling, Norman. *Fauré* (London: Dent, and New York: Dutton, 1946).

Vuillermoz, Émile. *Gabriel Fauré* (Paris: Flammarion, 1960), trans. Kenneth Schapin (Philadelphia: Chilton Book Co., 1969; repr. New York: Da Capo Press, 1983).

Franck

Davies, Laurence. *César Franck and His Circle* (London: Barrie & Jenkins, 1970).

———. *Franck* (London: Dent, 1973).

Demuth, Norman. *César Franck* (London: Dobson, and New York: Philosophical Library, 1949).

d'Indy

Davies, Laurence. *César Franck and His Circle* (London: Barrie & Jenkins, 1970).

Demuth, Norman. *Vincent d'Indy* (London: Rockliff, 1951).

Paul, G. B. "Rameau, d'Indy, and French Nationalism," *The Musical Quarterly* 58 (1972), p. 46ff.

Ravel

Demuth, Norman. *Ravel* (London: Dent, 1947; repr. New York: Collier Books, 1962).

Myers, Rollo H. *Ravel: His Life and Works* (London: Duckworth, 1960; repr. Westport, CT: Greenwood Press, 1973).

Orenstein, A. *Ravel, Man and Musician* (New York: Columbia U. Press, 1975).

Saint-Saëns

Harding, James. *Saint-Saëns and His Circle* (London: Chapman & Hall, 1965).

Rolland, Romain. *Camille Saint-Saëns,* in *Musiciens français d'aujourd'hui* series (Paris, 1908; repr. 1946, trans. 1915; repr. 1969).

BRITAIN
Elgar

Burley, Rosa, and Frank C. Carruthers. *Edward Elgar: The Record of a Friendship* (London: Barrie & Jenkins, 1972).

McVeagh, Diana. *Edward Elgar: His Life and Music* (London: Dent, 1955; repr. Westport, CT: Hyperion Press, 1979).

Parrott, Ian. *Elgar* (London: Dart, 1971; repr. 1977).

Young, Percy. *Elgar O. M.: A Study of a Musician* (London: Collins, 1955; rev. ed., Westport, CT: Greenwood Press, 1973).

Holst

Holst, Imogen. *Gustav Holst: A Biography* (London: Oxford U. Press, 1938; 2d ed., 1969).

———. *Holst's Music Remembered* (New York: Oxford U. Press, 1986).

———. *The Music of Gustave Holst* (London: Oxford U. Press, 1951; 3d ed., rev., 1975).

AMERICA

Chase, Gilbert. *America's Music,* 2d ed. (New York: McGraw-Hill, 1966).

Hamm, Charles. *Music in the New World* (New York: Norton, 1983).

Hitchcock, H. Wiley. *Music in the United States: A Historical Introduction* (Englewood Cliffs, NJ: Prentice-Hall, 1969, 1974; 3d ed., 1988).

Ives
Writings

Ives, Charles. *Essays Before a Sonata and Other Writings,* ed. H. Boatwright (New York: Norton, 1961).

For Further Reading

Burkholder, J. P. *Charles Ives: The Ideas Behind the Music* (New Haven, CT: Yale U. Press, 1985).

Cowell, Henry, and Sidney Cowell. *Charles Ives and His Music* (New York: Oxford U. Press, 1955).

Hitchcock, H. Wiley. *Ives* (London and New York: Oxford U. Press, 1955; repr. 1974).

Hitchcock, H. Wiley, and Vivian Perlis, eds. *An Ives Celebration: Papers and Panels of the Charles Ives Centennial Festival Conference* (Urbana: U. of Illinois, 1977).

Kirkpatrick, John, ed. *Charles E. Ives, Memoirs* (New York: Norton, 1972).

Perlis, Vivian. *Charles Ives Remembered* (New Haven, CT: Yale U. Press, 1976).

Rossiter, Frank. *Charles Ives and His America* (New York: Liveright, 1975).

Wooldridge, David. *From the Steeples and Mountains: A Study of Charles Ives* (New York: Knopf, 1974).

MacDowell

Gilman, Lawrence. *Edward MacDowell: A Study* (New York and London: J. Lane, 1908; repr. New York: Da Capo Press, 1969).

Jazz

Gridley, Mark C. *Jazz Styles: History and Analysis,* 3d ed. (Englewood Cliffs, NJ: Prentice-Hall, 1988).

Taylor, Billy. *Jazz Piano: A Jazz History* (Dubuque, IA: Wm. C. Brown Publishers, 1983).

Tirro, Frank. *Jazz: A History* (New York: Norton, 1977).

CHAPTER 26: DEVELOPMENTS BETWEEN THE WORLD WARS

GENERAL

Austin, William W. *Music in the Twentieth Century from Debussy through Stravinsky* (New York: Norton, 1966).

Collaer, Paul. *A History of Modern Music* (Brussels: Elsevier, 1955), trans. Sally Abeles (Cleveland and New York: The World Publishing Co., 1961).

Simms, Bryan. *Music of the 20th Century: Style and Structure* (New York: Schirmer Books, 1986).

Whittall, Arnold. *Music Since the First World War* (London: St. Martin's Press, 1977).

ENGLAND
Britten
Evans, Peter. *The Music of Benjamin Britten* (Minneapolis: U. of Minnesota Press, 1979).

Herbert, David, ed. *The Operas of Benjamin Britten* (London: H. Hamilton, 1979).

Howard, P. *The Operas of Benjamin Britten* (London: Barrie & Rockliff, 1969; New York: Praeger, 1969).

Kennedy, Michael. *Britten* (London: J. M. Dent & Sons, 1981).

Palmer, Christopher, ed. *The Britten Companion* (London: Faber & Faber, 1984).

White, Eric W. *Benjamin Britten: His Life and Operas,* 2d ed. (Berkeley: U. of California Press, 1981).

Vaughan Williams
Writings
Vaughan Williams, Ralph. *National Music and Other Essays* (London: Oxford U. Press, 1963; repr. 1972, 1987).

For Further Reading
Howes, Frank. *The Music of Ralph Vaughan Williams* (London and New York: Oxford U. Press, 1954; repr. Westport, CT: Greenwood Press, 1975, 1977).

Kennedy, Michael. *The Works of Ralph Vaughan Williams* (London: Oxford U. Press, 1964; rev. ed., 1982).

Ottaway, H. *Vaughan Williams* (London: Novello, 1966).

———. *Vaughan Williams Symphonies* (London: British Broadcasting Corp., 1972; repr. Seattle: U. of Washington Press, 1973).

Schwartz, Elliott S. *The Symphonies of Ralph Vaughan Williams* (Amherst: U. of Massachusetts Press, 1964; repr. New York: Da Capo Press, 1982).

FRANCE
N. Boulanger
Campbell, Don G. *Master Teacher Nadia Boulanger* (Washington, DC: The Pastoral Press, 1984).

Kendall, Alan. *The Tender Tyrant: Nadia Boulanger* (London: Macdonald and Janes, 1976; repr. Wilton, CT: Lyceum Books, 1977).

Rosensteil, Leonie. *Nadia Boulanger: A Life in Music* (New York: Norton, 1982).

LES SIX
Writings
Honegger, Arthur. *Je suis compositeur* [I am a composer] (Paris: Editions du Conquistador, 1951), trans. O. Clough (London: Faber & Faber, 1966).

Milhaud, Darius. *Notes Without Music* (Paris: Julliard, 1949), trans. Donald Evans, ed. Rollo H. Myers (London: Dobson, 1952; New York: Knopf, 1953; repr. New York: Da Capo Press, 1970).

For Further Reading
Bernac, Pierre. *Francis Poulenc: The Man and His Songs* (London: V. Gollancz, 1977), trans. Winifred Radford (New York: Norton, 1977).

Collaer, Paul. "Eric Satie and the Six," and "Milhaud, Honegger, Auric, Poulenc: After the Six," *A History of Modern Music* (Brussels: Elsevier, 1955), trans. Sally Abeles (Cleveland and New York: The World Publishing Co., 1961), pp. 201–73.

Daniel, Keith W. *Francis Poulenc: His Artistic Development and His Musical Style* (Ann Arbor, MI: UMI Research Press, 1982).

Palmer, Christopher. *Milhaud* (London, 1976).

Robert, F. *Louis Durey: l'ainé des Six* [Louis Durey: Oldest of The Six] (Paris: L'Editeurs français réunis, 1968).

GERMANY
Orff
Liess, Andreas. *Carl Orff: Idee und Werk* (Zurich: Atlantis Verlag, 1955), trans. Adelheid and Herbert (New York: St. Martin's Press, 1966; 2d ed., 1971).

Hindemith
Writings
Hindemith, Paul. *A Composer's World: Horizons and Limitations* (Cambridge: Harvard U. Press, 1952; repr. Garden City, NY: Anchor Books, Doubleday & Co., 1961).

———. *The Craft of Musical Composition* (New York: Associated Music Publishers, 1954).

For Further Reading
Neumeyer, David. *The Music of Paul Hindemith* (New Haven, CT: Yale U. Press, 1986).

Skelton, Geoffrey. *Paul Hindemith: The Man Behind the Music* (London: Gollancz, 1975; New York: Crescendo, 1975).

HUNGARY
Bartók
Antokoletz, Elliott. *The Music of Béla Bartók: A Study of Tonality and Progression in 20th-Century Music* (Berkeley: U. of California Press, 1984).

Crow, Todd, ed. *Bartók Studies* (Detroit, MI: Information Coordinators, 1976).

Griffiths, Paul. *Bartók* (London: J. M. Dent & Sons, 1984).

Lendvai, Erno. *Béla Bartók: An Analysis of His Music* (London: Kahn & Averill, 1971).

———. *The Workshop of Bartók and Kodály* (Budapešt: Editio Musica, 1983).

Stevens, Halsey. *The Life and Music of Béla Bartók* (New York: Oxford U. Press, 1953; rev. ed., 1964; rev. 1968).

Kodály
Writings
Kodály, Zoltán. *Folk Music of Hungary,* trans. R. Tempest and C. Jolly (London: Barrie & Jenkins, 1971).

For Further Reading
Eösze, L. *Zoltán Kodály: Chronicle of His Life* (Budapešt: Corvina Kiadó, 1977).

———. *Zoltán Kodály: His Life and Work* (London: Collet's, 1962; New York: Crescendo, 1962).

Lendvai, Erno. *The Workshop of Bartók and Kodály* (Budapešt: Editio Musica, 1983).

Szabó, Helga. *The Kodály Concept of Music Education* (London and New York: Boosey & Hawkes, 1969).

Stevens, Halsy. "The Choral Music of Zoltán Kodály," *The Musical Quarterly* 54 (1968), p. 147ff.

RUSSIA
Abraham, Gerald. *Eight Soviet Composers* (New York: Oxford U. Press, 1943).

Brown, Malcolm H., ed. *Russian and Soviet Music: Essays for Boris Schwarz* (Ann Arbor, MI: UMI Research Press, 1984).

Krebs, Stanley D. *Soviet Composers and the Development of Soviet Music* (London and New York: Allen & Unwin, 1970).

Schwarz, Boris. *Music and Musical Life in Soviet Russia, Enlarged Edition, 1917–1981* (Bloomington: Indiana U. Press, 1983).

Prokofiev

Nest'yev, Izrael V. *Prokofiev: His Musical Life* (Moscow: Gos. muz, 1957), enlarged, trans. F. Jonas (Stanford, CA: Stanford U. Press, 1960; repr. 1971).

Robinson, Harlow. *Prokofiev: A Biography* (New York: Viking, 1987).

Shostakovich

Blokker, Roy, with Robert Dearling. *The Music of Dmitri Shostakowich: The Symphonies* (London: Tantivy Press, 1979; Rutherford, NJ: Fairleigh Dickinson U. Press, 1979).

Norris, Christopher, ed. *Shostakovich: The Man and His Music* (London: Lawrence & Wishart, 1982; Boston and London: Marion Boyars, 1982).

Seroff, Victor. *Dmitri Shostakovich: The Life and Background of a Soviet Composer* (New York: Knopf, 1943; repr. 1947; repr. Freeport, NY: Books for Libraries Press, 1970).

SECOND VIENNESE SCHOOL

Berg

Carner, Mosco. *Alban Berg: The Man and the Work* (London: Duckworth, 1975); 2d ed. (London: Duckworth, and New York: Holmes & Meier, 1983).

Jarman, Douglas. *The Music of Alban Berg* (Berkeley: U. of California Press, 1979).

Perle, George. *The Operas of Alban Berg: Wozzeck* (Berkeley: U. of California Press, 1980).

Redlich, Hans. *Alban Berg: The Man and His Music* (Vienna: University Edition, and New York: Abelard-Schumann, and London: Calder, 1957).

Reich, Willi. *Alban Berg* (Zurich: Atlantis Verlag, 1965), trans. Cornelius Cardew (New York: Harcourt, Brace & World, 1965; repr. New York: Da Capo Press, 1981).

Schmalfeldt, Janet. *Berg's Wozzeck: Harmonic Language and Dramatic Design* (New Haven, CT: Yale U. Press, 1983).

Schoenberg

Berg, Alban, et al. *Arnold Schönberg* (München: R. Piper & Co., 1912).

Leibowitz, René. *Schoenberg and His School: The Contemporary Stage of the Language of Music* (Paris: Éditions du Seuil, 1947), trans. Dika Newlin (New York: Philosophical Library, 1949).

Newlin, Dika. *Schoenberg Remembered: Diaries and Recollections (1938–76)* (New York: Pendragon Press, 1980).

Payne, Anthony. *Schoenberg* (London: Oxford U. Press, 1968; repr. 1974).

Reich, Willi. *Schoenberg: A Critical Biography,* trans. Leo Black (London: Longman and New York: Praeger, 1971; repr. New York: Da Capo Press, 1981).

Rosen, Charles. *Arnold Schoenberg* (New York: Viking Press, 1975).

Smith, Joan. *Schoenberg and His Circle: A Viennese Portrait* (New York: Schirmer Books, 1986).

Wellesz, Egon: *Arnold Schönberg,* trans. W. H. Kerridge (London: J. M. Dent & Sons, 1925; repr. New York: Da Capo Press, 1969).

Webern

Kolneder, Walter. *Anton Webern: An Introduction to His Works* (Rodenkirchen: P. J. Tonger, 1961), trans. Humphrey Searle (London: Faber & Faber, 1968; repr. Westport, CT: Greenwood Press, 1982).

Moldenhauer, Hans. *Anton von Webern: Chronicle of His Life and Works* (New York: Knopf, 1979).

———. *The Death of Anton Webern: A Drama in Documents* (London: Vision, and New York Philosophical Library, 1961; repr. New York; Da Capo Press, 1989).

Stravinsky

Writings

Stravinsky, Igor. *An Autobiography,* Eng. trans. (New York: Simon & Schuster, 1936; repr. New York: Norton, 1962; repr. Calder & Boyars, 1975).

———. *Poétique musicale,* Eng. trans. (Cambridge, MA: Harvard U. Press, 1947; 3d ed., 1966).

For Further Reading

Craft, Robert. *Stravinsky: Chronicle of a Friendship 1948–1971* (London: Gollancz, 1972; New York: Knopf, 1973).

———. *A Stravinsky Scrapbook 1940–1971* (New York: Thames & Hudson, 1983).

Druskin, Mikhail S. *Igor Stravinsky: His Life, Works, and Views* (Leningrad: "Sov. kompozitor," 1974; rev. 1979), trans. Martin Cooper (Cambridge and New York: Cambridge U. Press, 1983).

Griffiths, Paul. *Igor Stravinsky, The Rake's Progress* (Cambridge and New York: Cambridge U. Press, 1982).

Tansman, Alexandre. *Igor Stravinsky: The Man and His Music,* trans. Therese and Charles Bleefield (New York: G. P. Putnam's Sons, 1949).

Van en Toorn, Peter C. *The Music of Igor Stravinsky* (New Haven, CT: Yale U. Press, 1983).

Vlad, Roman. *Stravinsky,* 2d ed., trans. Frederick and Ann Fuller (London: Oxford U. Press, 1967).

White, Eric W. *Stravinsky: The Composer and His Works* (London: Faber, 1966); rev., enlarged (London: Faber, and Berkeley: U of California Press, 1979).

UNITED STATES

Copland

Writings

Copland, Aaron. *Copland on Music* (Garden City, NY: Doubleday, 1960).

———. *Music and Imagination* (Cambridge: Harvard U. Press, 1952).

———. *Our New Music* (New York: McGraw-Hill, 1941); rev. ed. pub. as *The New Music 1900–1960* (New York: Norton, 1968).

———. "The Role of the Composer," *Canadian Composer,* No. 63 (1971), p. 24ff.

———, with Vivian Perlis. *Copland: 1900–1942* (New York: St. Martin's Press, 1984).

For Further Reading

Berger, Arthur. *Aaron Copland* (New York: Oxford U. Press, 1953).

Butterworth, Neil. *The Music of Aaron Copland* (London: Toccata Press, 1985, and New York: Universe Books, 1986).

Skrowronsky, J. *Aaron Copland: A Biobibliography* (Westport, CT: Greenwood Press, 1985).

Gershwin

Goldberg, I. *George Gershwin: A Study in American Music* (New York: Simon & Schuster, 1931); rev., enlarged ed. (New York: Simon & Schuster, 1958).

Jablonski, Edward. *Gershwin* (New York: Doubleday, 1987).

Schwartz, Charles. *Gershwin: His Life and Music* (Indianapolis: Bobbs & Merrill, 1973; repr. New York: Da Capo Press, 1979).

Ruth Crawford Seeger

Gaume, Matilda. *Ruth Crawford Seeger: Her Life and Works* (Diss., Ann Arbor, MI: University Microfilms, 1973).

Sessions

Daniel, Oliver, et al. *Roger Sessions* (New York: Broadcast Music, Inc., 1965).

Olmstead, Andrea. *Roger Sessions and His Music* (Ann Arbor, MI: UMI Research Press, 1985).

Still

Haas, R., ed. *William Grant Still and the Fusion of Cultures in American Music* (Los Angeles: Black Sparrow Press, 1972; repr. 1975).

Southern, Eileen. *The Music of Black Americans: A History* (New York: Norton, 1971; 2d ed., 1983), p. 422ff.

Thomson
Writings

Thomson, Virgil. *American Music Since 1910* (London: Weidenfeld & Nicolson, 1967).

———. *The Art of Judging Music* (New York: Knopf, 1948).

———. *Virgil Thomson* (New York: Knopf, 1966; repr. 1977).

———. *A Virgil Thomson Reader* (Boston: Houghton-Mifflin, 1981; repr. New York: E. P. Dutton, 1984).

For Further Reading

Hoover, Kathleen, and John Cage. *Virgil Thomson: His Life and Music* (New York: T. Yoseloff, 1959).

Meckna, Michael. *Virgil Thomson: A Bibliography* (New York: Greenwood Press, 1986).

Jazz

Gridley, Mark C. *Jazz Styles: History and Analysis,* 3d ed. (Englewood Cliffs, NJ: Prentice-Hall, 1988).

Tirro, Frank. *Jazz: A History* (New York: Norton, 1977).

LATIN AND SOUTH AMERICA
Chávez
Writings

Chávez, Carlos. *Musical Thought* (Cambridge, MA: Harvard U. Press, 1961).

———. "The Music of Mexico," (1933), in *American Composers on American Music,* ed. Henry Cowell, 2d ed. (New York: F. Ungar, 1962).

———. *Toward a New Music: Music and Electricity,* trans. H. Weinstock (New York: Norton, 1937; repr. New York: Da Capo Press, 1975).

For Further Reading

Copland, Aaron. "Composer from Mexico," in *The New Music: 1900–1960* (New York: Norton, 1968).

Cowell, Henry. "Chávez," in *The Book of Modern Composers,* ed. David Ewen, 2d ed. (New York: Knopf, 1942); 3d ed., rev., enlarged, pub. as *The New Book of Modern Composers* (New York: Knopf, 1967).

Villa-Lobos

Mariz, Vasco. *Heitor Villa-Lobos* (Rio de Janiero: Serfviço de Publicações, 1949); Eng. trans. (Gainesville: U. of Florida Press, 1963; repr. 1970).

Romero, M. "Heitor Villa-Lobos," *Inter-American Music Bulletin,* 15 (1960), p. 4ff.

Sprague-Smith, C. "H. Villa-Lobos (1889–1959)," *Inter-American Music Bulletin,* 15 (1960), p. 1ff.

Wright, S. "Villa-Lobos: The Formation of his Style," *Soundings,* 9 (1979–80), p. 55ff.

CHAPTER 27: MUSIC SINCE 1945

GENERAL

Brindle, Reginald S. *The New Music: The Avant-Garde Since 1945* (London: Oxford U. Press, 1975; repr. 1987).

Cope, David. *New Directions in Music,* 4th ed. (Dubuque, IA: Wm. C. Brown Publishers, 1984).

Griffiths, Paul. *Modern Music: The avant garde since 1945* (New York: George Braziller, 1981).

———. *Modern Music: A Concise History from Debussy to Boulez* (New York: Thames & Hudson, 1978).

———. *The Thames and Hudson Encyclopaedia of 20th-Century Music* (New York: Thames & Hudson, 1986).

Lang, Paul Henry, ed. *Problems of Modern Music,* a reprint of *The Musical Quarterly,* April 1960 issue (New York: Norton, 1962).

Martin, William R., and Julius Drossin. *Music of the Twentieth Century* (Englewood Cliffs, NJ: Prentice-Hall, 1980).

Rockwell, John. *All American Music: Composition in the Late Twentieth Century* (New York: Knopf, 1983).

Ruhe, Harry, ed. *Fluxus, the Most Radical and Experimental Art Movement of the Sixties* (Amsterdam: "A," 1979).

Salzman, Eric. *Twentieth-Century Music: An Introduction,* 3d ed. (Englewood Cliffs, NJ: Prentice-Hall, 1988).

Simms, Bryan R. *Music of the Twentieth Century: Style and Structure* (New York: Schirmer Books, 1986).

Vinton, John, ed. *Dictionary of Contemporary Music* (New York: Dutton, 1974).

ELECTRONIC MUSIC

Ernst, David. *The Evolution of Electronic Music* (New York: Schirmer Books, 1977).

Griffiths, Paul. *A Guide to Electronic Music* (London and New York: Thames & Hudson, 1979).

MINIMALISM

Mertens, Wim. *American Minimal Music: La Monte Young, Terry Riley, Steve Reich, Philip Glass,* trans. J. Hautekiet (London and New York: Kahn & Averill, 1983).

Nyman, Michael. *Experimental Music: Cage and Beyond* (New York: Schirmer Books, 1974).

Reich, Steve. *Writings about Music* (Halifax: Press of Nova Scotia Art and Design, 1974).

Schwarz, K. Robert. "Steve Reich: Music as a Gradual Process," *Perspectives of New Music,* Fall/Winter 1980 and Spring/Summer 1981, pp. 373–92; Fall/Winter 1981 and Spring/Summer 1982, pp. 225–86.

BOULEZ

Writings

Boulez, Pierre. *Boulez on Music Today,* trans. Susan Bradshaw and Richard R. Bennett (Cambridge, MA: Harvard U. Press, 1971).

————. *Notes of an Apprenticeship,* compiled by Paula Thévenin, trans. Herbert Weinstock (New York: Knopf, 1968).

For Further Reading

Glock, William, ed. *Pierre Boulez: A Symposium* (London: Eulenberg, 1986).

Griffiths, Paul. *Boulez* (Oxford and New York: Oxford U. Press, 1978).

Peyser, Joan. *Boulez: Composer, Conductor, Enigma* (New York: Schirmer Books, 1976).

CAGE

Writings

Cage, John. *Empty Words* [writings, 1973–78], (Middletown, CT: Wesleyan U. Press, 1979).

————. *M* [writings, 1967–72], (Middletown, CT: Wesleyan U. Press, 1973).

————. *Notations* (West Glover, VT: Something Else Press, 1969).

————. *Silence* (Middletown, CT: Wesleyan U. Press, 1961).

————. *A Year from Monday: New Lectures and Writings* (Middletown, CT: Wesleyan U. Press, 1967).

For Further Reading

Gena, Peter, and Jonathan Brent, eds. *A John Cage Reader: In Celebration of his 70th Birthday* (New York: Peters, 1983).

Griffiths, Paul. *Cage* (London: Oxford U. Press, 1981).

Kostelanetz, Richard, ed. *John Cage* (New York: Praeger, 1970).

LIGETI

Griffiths, Paul. *György Ligeti* (London: Robson Books, 1983).

MESSIAEN

Writings

Messiaen, Olivier. *The Technique of My Musical Language,* 2 vols., trans. John Satterfield (Paris: Leduc, 1944; repr. 1966).

For Further Reading

Bell, Carla Huston. *Olivier Messiaen* (Boston: Twayne, 1984).

Griffiths, Paul. *Olivier Messiaen and the Music of Time* (Ithaca, NY: Cornell U. Press, 1985).

Johnson, Robert Sherlaw. *Messiaen* (Berkeley: U. of California Press, 1975; repr. 1980).

Kaufmann, Walter. *The Rāgas of North India* (Bloomington: Indiana U. Press, 1968).

Nichols, R. *Messiaen* (Oxford: Oxford U. Press, 1985).

Rössler, Almut. *Contributions to the Spiritual World of Olivier Messiaen,* "with original texts by the composer" (Duisberg, W. Ger.: Gilles & Francke Verlag, 1986).

Wade, Bonnie C. *Music in India: The Classical Traditions* (Englewood Cliffs, NJ: Prentice-Hall, 1979).

STOCKHAUSEN

Harvey, Jonathan. *The Music of Stockhausen* (Berkeley: U. of California Press, 1975).

Maconie, Robin. *The Works of Karlheinz Stockhausen* (London and New York: Oxford U. Press, 1976).

Wörner, Karl H. *Stockhausen: Life and Work,* trans. and ed., Bill Hopkins (Berkeley: U. of California Press, 1973).

VARÈSE

Bernard, Jonathan. *The Music of Edgard Varèse* (New Haven, CT: Yale U. Press, 1987).

Van Solkema, Sherman, ed. *The New Worlds of Edgard Varèse* (Brooklyn, NY: Institute for Studies in American Music, 1979).

Varèse, Louise. *Varèse: A Looking-Glass Diary* (New York: Norton, 1972).

Index

Monteverdi, C., 248–250
Stravinsky, I., 610
Tchaikovsky, P., 549
Ballet de Casandre, 256
Ballet de cour (dance), 221, 257, 258, 268
Ballet de la nuit, 256
Balletti, gighe, correnti, alemande, e sarabande
    (D. Gabrielli), 289
Balletti a cinque voci . . . (Gastoldi), 180
Balletto, Italian Renaissance, 180
Balletts to Five Voyces (Morley), 180, 186
Ballo delle ingrate, Il, 242, 243, 244, 248
Ballo in maschera, Un, 504, 506
Bamberg Codex, 83
Banchetto musicale, 273, 297
Banchieri, Adriano, 238
Banister, John, 330
Banjo, Le, 493
Banquet Céleste, Le, 630
Banshee, The, 578
Barbaia, Domenico, 441, 449
Barbapiccola, Nicolo, 254
Barbe-bleu, 481
Barberini, Cardinal Antonio, 251
Barberini family, 252
Barbier de Séville, Le (Beaumarchais), 449
Barbiere di Siviglia, Il (Rossini), 449, 450,
    451, 656
Barbiere di Siviglia ovvero La precauzione inutile
    (Paisiello), 351, 449
Barbieri, Francisco, 544
Barbosa, Domingos, 452
Barcarolle, 462
Bardi, Giovanni de', 235, 237, 238
Bar form, 101, 501
Baronnet, Jean, 636
Baroque era, 226–234
    affections, 228–229
    basso continuo texture, 229–231
    idiomatic instrumental composition, 228
    key tonality, 231, 292
    notation, 231–234
    printed music, 233
    rhythm, 231
    styles and practices, 228
    violin making, 285
Baroque era composers,
    Bach, J. S., 311–319
    Handel, G., 319–326
    Rameau, J.-P., 305–311
    Telemann, G., 302–305
    Vivaldi, A., 299–302
Baroque instrumental music, 270–298
    Bach, J. S., 315–319
    clavier keyboard instruments, 280–283
    ensemble music, 284–297
    French lute music, 275
    Handel, G., 325–326
    organ music, 275–280
    Rameau, J.-P., 307
    Telemann, G., 304–305
    types of, 270–275
    Vivaldi, A., 300–302
Baroque vocal music, 235–269
    Bach, J. S., 312–315
    cantata, 267–268
    Handel, G., 323–325
    monody, 235–236
    opera (*see* Opera)
    oratorio, 240–241, 260–262
    passion, 262–263
    Rameau, J.-P., 306–307
    Telemann, G., 304
Barra, Ray, 653
Barrère, Georges, 641
Bartered Bride, The, 538

Bartók, Béla, 584–588, 614, 623
    photo, *585*
Bartolino da Padova, 118
Bartoš, František, 537, 540
Barzeletta, 174
Basile, Adriana, 242
Basil of Caesarea, Saint, 23, 24
Bass (voice), 112, 144, 153, 154
Basse danse (dance), 141–142, 221, 222, 272,
    colorplate 14
Basso continuo, 229–231
Bassoon concerto (Weber), 435
Basso ostinato, 272
Basso seguente, 229, 231, 247
Bastien und Bastienne, 381, 385
Baudelaire, Charles-Pierre, 565
Bay Song Book, 146
Beach, Amy M. Cheney (Mrs. H. H. A.), 573–574
Béatitudes, Les, 459
Beatrice et Benedict, 486
Beatritz, Countess of Dia, 99
Beatrix Cenci, 619
Beaumarchais, P. A., 328, 385, 386, 656
Beccaria, Cesare, 329
Becker, Carl F., 469
Becker, Cornelius, 265
Becker Psalter, 265, 266
Beethoven, Johann van, 403
Beethoven, Karl, 405
Beethoven, Kaspar Anton Karl, 403, 405
Beethoven, Ludwig van, 340, 341, 345, 359, 394,
    401, 402, 442
    life, 403–405
    music,
        chamber music, 410–415
        general, 406–407
        piano sonatas, 409–410
        piano variations, 410
        for solo instruments and orchestra, 421–422
        style periods, 407–409
        symphonies, 415–421, 459
        vocal works with orchestra, 422–423
    personal characteristics, 405–406
    portrait, *403*
Beethoven, Nikolaus Johann, 403, 405
Beggar's Opera, The, 322, 353
Beglückte Florindo, Der, 320
Beiden Grenadiere, Die, 473, 475
Beiden Pädagogen, Die, 468
Béjart, 636
Bella ninfa fuggitiva, 239
Bellarmonic (instrument), 395
Belle bonne, 121, colorplate 11
Belle et la bête, La, 653
Belle Hélène, La, 481
Bellermann, Friedrich, 9
Bellini, Vincenzo, 479, 488, 489, 490, 506
Belshazzar, 323
Benda, Franz, 355
Benda, Georg, 354
Bendidio, Isabella, 180
Bendidio, Lucrezia, 180
Benedicamus domino, 68, 69, 79
Benedict of Nursia, 24
Benedict XI, Pope, 104
Benedict XII, Pope, 107
Benedict XIII, Pope, 46, 47
Benedict XIV, Pope, 367
Benedictus Dominus Deus (Tromboncino), 175
Benincori, Angelo, 433
Bennet, John, 187
Bentivoglio, Vittoria Cybo, 180
Benvenuto Cellini, 483, 485
Beowulf, 62, 93
Berberian, Cathy, 647
Berg, Alban, 567, 595, 596, 597, *599*–601, 624

Berger, Ludwig, 464
Bergerettes, 143
Bergomasca (dance), 221, 279
Berio, Luciano, 647–648, 655
Berliner, Émile, 625, 626
Berlioz, Louis-Hector, 345, 369, 432, 437, 459,
    469, 471, 488, 507, 535, 550
    life, 482–483
    music
        choral works, 486–487
        instrumental music, 483–485
        operas, 485–486
        style characteristics, 479, 483
    photo, *482*
    written works, 487, 535
Bernardi, Bartolomeo, 260
Bernart de Ventadorn, 94, 97
Berry, Jean, Duke of, 106, 112, 130, colorplate 13
Bertran de Born, 94, 97, 99
Besant, Annie, 551
"Bess, You Is My Woman Now," 617
Bez Solntsa, 533
Bethge, Hans, 557
Bethmann, 497
Bèze, Théodore de, 197
Bianca e Fernando, 490
Bianchi, Antonia, 488
Bianco e dolce cigno, Il, 175
Biauté qui toutes autre, 116
Biber, Heinrich Ignaz Franz von, 296
Biblischer Historien, 281
Bieris de Romans, 99
Bigot, Marie Kiéné, 464, 465
Bigot, Paul, 465
Billings, William, 394, 395
Billy Budd, 592
Billy the Kid, 615
Binary form, evolution of sonata form from,
    332, 333
Binchois (Gilles de Binches), 130, *131,* 140,
    142–143
    chansons, 142
    sacred works, 142–143
Bingen, Hildegard von, 91, 92, *93,* 236
Bird string quartet (Haydn), 375
Bizet, Georges, 480–481
Black Angels, 648
Black Masters, The, 618
Blahoslav, Jan, 192
Blanchet family, 280
Bland, James, 573
Blaník, 538
Blessed Damosel, The, 566
Blondel de Nesle, 97
Blow, John, 258, 268, 294
Blues, 578
Blutige und sterbende Jesus, Der, 263
Boccaccio, Giovanni, 105, 149
Boccherini, Luigi, 393
Bocklet, Karl Maria von, 442
Bodzurodzica, 652
Boethius, Anicius, 22, 57, 58, 159, 608, 629, 640
Boeuf sur le toit, Le, 607
Bohème, La, 561
Bohemia, 327, 343
    late 18th/early 19th-century pianists from,
    402–403
    opera in, 260
Bohemian Brethren, 192
Bohemian Girl, The, 491
Boieldieu, Francois-Adrien, 430, 433, 527
Boito, Arrigo, 504, 506
Böklin, Arnold, 551
Bolden, Charles "Buddy," 579
Bolero (Chopin), 462
Boléro (Ravel), 568

Gedichte von Mörike, 554
Geduldige Socrates, Der, 304
Geisslerlieder, 100
Geistliches Wiegenlied, 522
Geminiani, Francesco, 294
General History of Music ... (Burney), 400
General History of the Science and Practice of Music,
    A (Hawkins), 400
Génération harmonique, 317
Genevan Psalter, 197
Genius of Christianity, 484
Genoveva, 472, 475
George I, England, 321, 327
George II, England, 322
Gerhardt, Paul, 195, 263
Germanico sul Reno, 253
German Requiem, A (Brahms). See
    Deutsches Requiem
Germany and Germanic lands. See also Austria;
    names of individual composers
    baroque ensemble (chamber) music, 296–297
    baroque organ music, 275–280
    early 19th-century Romantic music in Austria
        and, 433–447
    electronic music in, 638–640
    late 19th/early 20th-century music in Austria
        and, 553–560
    lieder (see Lieder)
    medieval vernacular monophony, 100–102
    mid-19th-century music in Austria and,
        460–477
    music after 1945, 638–640
    music between the World Wars, 607–609
    national beginnings, 55
    opera, 259–260, 497
    Renaissance music, 188–190
    secular song, 18th-century, 354–355
    singspiel, 354
    symphony composition in Mannheim, 343–344
    transition to Renaissance music, 146–147
Gershwin, George, 616–617
Gerusalemme liberata, 178, 238, 484
Gesamtkunstwerk, 433, 434, 469
Gesang der Geister uber den Wassern, 441, 444
Gesang der Junglinge, 639
Gesang der Parzen (Brahms), 523
Geschöpfe des Prometheus, Die, 406, 407
Gestillte Sehnsucht, 522
Gesualdo, Carlo, 178, 179, 228, 278
Getreue Musikmeister, Der, 304
Geystliches gesangk Buchleyn, 193, 196
Ghent Altarpiece, 106, 108, colorplate 6
Gherardello da Firenze, 118, 119
Ghosts of Versailles, The, 656
Gianni Schicci, 561
Giasone, 251
Gibbons, Christopher, 258
Gibbons, Orlando, 201, 221, 233
Gigue (dance), 273, 274
Gigues (Debussy), 567
Gilbert, Kenneth, 336
Gilbert, W. S., 491
Ginastera, Alberto, 619
Ginevra di Scozia, 448
Giochi di Sansone, 262
Giorno di regno, Un, 503
Giotto di Bondone, 106, 119, 149, colorplate 7
Giovanni da Cascia, 118
Girodet, Anne Louis, 426, colorplate 21
Giulio Cesare in Egitto (Handel), 321, 323, 324
Giuoco della cieca, Il, 238
Giuseppe: oratorio per la Settimana Santa, 261
Giustiniana, 175
Giustino, Il, 252, 253
Glagolská m še, 541
Glareanus. See Loris, Henrich (Glareanus)

Glass, Philip, 614, 653, 654, 655
Glass harmonica, Benjamin Franklin's, 395, 396
Glazunov, Alexander, 535, 536
Gleeman, 101
Glees, 492
Glinka, Mikhail, 526, 527, 531, 534, 549, 550, 612
Glogauer Liederbuch songbook, 146
Gloria, of Mass, 45, 46
Gloria, laus et honor (Binchois), 142
Gloriana (Britten), 592
Gloria tibi Trinitas, 219, 295
Gluck, Christoph Willibald, 243, 332, 335, 352,
    361, 366–369, 383, 394, 432, 478, 502
    portrait, 357
    reform operas, 368–369, 447
Glückliche Hand, Die, 598
Glückwünschende Freudensdarstellung, 268
Gnossiennes, 570
Go, Congregation, Go—Surely He has borne our
    griefs, 396
"Go crystall teares," 188
Go down, Moses, 649
Godric, Saint, 101
Goebbels, Joseph, 560
Goethe, Johann Wolfgang, 328, 402, 408, 422,
    426, 438, 439, 465, 470, 472, 523, 554
Goeyvaerts, Karel, 629, 634
Goldberg, J. T., 316
Goldberg Variations, 156, 310, 316, 411
Golden Age, The, 594
Golden Cockerel, The, 535
Golden equations, 12
Golden Section, theory of, 249, 585
Goldoni, Carlo, 351
goliards, 92–93
Golliwog's Cake-walk, 568
Gombert, Nicholas, 167, 184
Gómez, Julio, 604
Gondoliers, The, 491
Gonzaga, Ferrante, 208
Gonzaga, Francesco, 175, 242, 244, 245
Gonzaga, Guglielmo, 182
Gonzaga, Margherita, 177, 182
Gonzaga, Vincenzo, 183
Gonzaga, Vincenzo I, 242, 243, 244, 245
Goodman, Benny, 586, 615
Goostly psalmes and spirituall songs, 201
Góecki, Henryk, 651
Gossec, François-Joseph, 343, 344–345, 364, 416,
    431, 432
Gothic. See Middle Ages, Ars Antiqua period
Götterdämmerung (Wagner), 498
Gott! erhalte Franz den Kaiser, 371
Gottes Zeit ist der allerbeste Zeit, 523
Gottschalk, Louis Moreau, 459, 493, 501
Goudimel, Claude, 197
Gounod, Charles, 450, 481, 491
Goya, Francesco, 426, 545, colorplate 22
Goyescas, 545
Grab, Das, 394
Gradual, of Mass, 45
Graduale Romanum, 38, 42
Gradualia, 201
Gradus ad Parnassum (Clementi), 401
Gradus ad Parnassum (Fux), 203, 228, 355
Graf, Konrad, 402
Graham, Martha, 615
Granados, Enrique, 545
Grand Canyon Suite (Grofé), 616
Grand Concertos (Handel), 325
Grand duo concertant (Weber), 436
Grand Duo sonata (Schubert), 442
Grand macabre, Le, 650
Grande Messe des Morts (Berlioz), 458, 483, 486
Grande symphonie funèbre et triomphale
    (Berlioz), 485

Grand Fantaisie on Russian Folksongs, 530
Grand fantasia de bravoure (Liszt), 507
Grandi, Alessandro, 235, 267
Grand opera
    in mid-19th-century France, 477–480
Grand Polonaise (Weber), 435
Grand Sonatas (Pinto), 401
Grand traité d'instrumentation et d'orchestration
    modernes (Berlioz), 483
Grassi, Cecilia, 349
Graun, J. G., 343
Graun, K. H., 355
Graupner, Gottlieb, 453
Grazianini, Caterina, 262
Great C-Major Symphony (Schubert), 442, 443,
    446, 465, 472
Great Depression, 578, 581
Greater Perfect System, 7, 14, 15, 16
Great Organ Mass (Haydn), 372
Great Schism, 104, 120, 127, 192
Great Service (Byrd), 200, 201
Great Service, Anglican, 200
Greece, music in ancient, 8–13
    cultural view of, 10–13
    instruments, 9–10
    music theory, 14–17
    mythological origins of, 4
    philosophy and ethos doctrine, 12–13
Greensleeves, 590
Gregorian chant, 23
    church modes, 32
    classes and forms, 33–34
    notation, 30–32
    in regional liturgies, 34
    rhythm, 29–30
Gregorian Missal for Sundays, 38, 44
Gregory I, Pope, 22, 23, 46
Gregory VII, Pope, 57
Gregory XI, Pope, 104
Gregory XIII, Pope, 203, 208, 261
Gretchen am Spinnrade, 439, 444, 445
Grétry, Andre-Ernest-Modest, 352, 411, 433
Grid, 596
    Messiaen's interversion permutation, 631
Grieg, Edvard Hagerup, 477, 542
Griffes, Charles, 569
Grigny, Nicolas de, 282
Grillo, Carlo, 162
Grillo e buon cantore, El, 162
Grillparzer, 442, 443
Grimani, Cardinal, 254
Grimani, Doge Marino, 251
Grimani, Maria Margherita, 262
Grimaud, Yvette, 630
Grimm Brothers fairy tales, 434, 499, 560
Griselda, La, 254, 255
Grofé, Ferde, 616
Grohg, 615
Gropius, Walter, 582
Grosse fugue (Beethoven), 413
Grosser Festmarsch, 499
Ground, harmonic, 272
Groupe de Recherche de Musique Concrète, 635
Grünewald, Matthias, 609, colorplate 28
Gruppe aus dem Tartarus, 440
Gruppen, 639
Guarini, Anna, 182
Guarini, G. B., 177, 182, 238, 247
Guarneri, Andrea, 285, 318
Guarneri, Giuseppe, 285
Guerin, Alipson, 94
Guerre, La, 184, 207
Guerre, Marin de la, 281
Guerre des chansons, 353
Guide to the Practical Study of Harmony
    (Tchaikovsky), 549

Nero (Handel), 320
Nerval, Gérard de, 482, 486
Netherlands
    Reformation in, 197–198
    Renaissance composers (see Franco-
        Netherlands composers, Renaissance)
Neue Arien, 268
Neue Bahnen, 473, 515
Neue Leipziger Zeitschrift für Musik, 471
Neue Liebeslieder, 522
Neue Zeitschrift Für Musik, 471, 472, 497
Neumatic Biblical text settings, 33
Neumeister, Erdmann, 303
Neumes, 31, 32
    accent, 58
    compound, 31
    heighted, 67
    ligatures, 76, 77
    point, 58
    staffless, *92*
Neumes rythmiques, 632
Newe deudsche geistliche Gesenge CXX ..., 196
New England Idyls, 537
New-England Psalm-Singer, The, 395
New Music: 1900–1968, The, 615
New Music Quarterly, 576
Newton, Isaac, 329
New York Counterpoint, 654
Niagara Symphony, 493
Niccolo da Perugia, 118
Nicene Creed, 23, 46
Nicholas I, Pope, 57
Nicholas I, Russia, 527, 530
Nicholas II, Pope, 57
Nicholas V, Pope, 127, 132, 287
Nicolai, Giovanni Francesco, 345
Nicolai, Otto, 438
Nicomachus, 22
Niejevelt, Willem van Zuylen van, 166
Nielsen, Carl, 542–543
Nietzsche, Friedrich Wilhelm, 558
Night Fields, 655
Night has a Thousand Eyes, The, 574
Nightmare, The, 332, colorplate 20
Nineteenth-century music
    in Austria and Germanic lands, 460–477
    classic era in early (see Classic music)
    in Czechoslovakia, 537–541
    in Denmark, 487, 542–543
    in England, 490–491
    in France, 477–487
    Impressionism, 564–565, 569
    instrumental music, 459–460
    in Italy, 487–490
    nationalism, 526–527
    in North America, 491–494
    preeminent composers of late, 496–525
    romanticism (see Romantic music)
    in Russia, 527–536
    transition from classic to romantic, 399–424
    verismo (realism) in late, 480, 560–561
    vocal music, 458–459
    in Wales, Ireland and Scotland, 544–546
Nixon in China, 655
Nobilissima visione, 609
Noces, Les (Stravinsky), 605, 611
Noches en los jardines de España, 604
Nocturnal (Varèse), 641
Nocturne, 401
Nocturne (L. Boulanger), 569
Nocturne, Op. 27, No. 1 (Chopin), *463*
Nocturne in A flat major (Chopin), 463
Nocturne in A major (Field), 463
Nocturne in E flat (Chopin), 462, 463
Nocturnes (Debussy), 566
Non al suo amante, 118

None but the lonely heart, 442
Non moriar, sed vivam, 193
Nonne, Die, 470
Nono, Luigi, 629
Non schivar, non parar, 245, *246*
Nordraak, Richard, 542
Norges fjelde, 541
Norma, 490
Norway, music in, 541–542
Nose, The, 594
Notation. *See also* Tablature
    agréments, 275
    alla breve signature, 176
    ancient Greek instrumental, 17
    baroque, 231
    cabalistic numerological symbolism in, 159
    C mensuration sign, 176
    coloration, 109, 110
    early middle ages, 58–59
    ecclesiastical chant
        Gregorian, 30–32
    Iberian 18th-century, 338
    key signature, 232
    motet
        choirbook, *86*
        dots of division, 87
        Franconian, 87
        successive, *86*
    Renaissance, 151
    time signature, 232
    12th-century polyphony, 67, 70
    Vitry, P. de, codification of, 108
Notenbüchlein für Anna Magdalena Bach, 315
Notker Balbulus, 49, 50
Notre Dame Cathedral, Cambrai, *133*
Notre Dame Cathedral, Paris, 73–75
Notre Dame of Paris, 493
Notturno. *See* Divertimento
Nouveau système de musique théorique
        (Rameau), 305
Nouveaux concerts (Couperin), 296
Nouvelles méditations poétiques (Lamartine), 510
Nouvelles suites de pieces de clavecin (Rameau), 306
Noveletten, 473
Noye's Fludde, 592
Nozze d'Enea con Lavinia, Le, 245, 249
Nozze di Figaro, Le (Mozart), 383, 385, 386, 656
Nuages (Debussy), 566
Nuages gris (Liszt), 409
Nuit des tropiques, La, 493
Nuits d'été, Les, 483, 487
Nullte, Die, 512, 514
Nunc dimittis, 39
Nunes García, José Mauricio, 452
Nun komm' der Helden Heiland, 195, 277
Nuove musiche, Le, 235, 240
Nuper rosarum flores-Terribilis est lucus iste, 134,
        136–137
Nursery, The, 533
Nur wer die Sehnsucht kennt, 442
Nussbaum, Der, 473, 475
Nutcracker, The, 435, 549
Nyevelt, Willem Zuylen van, 197
Nylandensis, Theodoricus Petri, 197

O

O Admirabile veneris (Cambridge Songs), 91, *92*
Oberon, 436
Oberto (Verdi), 503
Oboe Quartet (Mozart), 382
Obrecht, Jacob, 144, 149, 151, 158–161
    sacred music, 158–161
        masses, 159–160
        motets, 160–161
    secular music, 158
O Canada, 493

Occursus, 65
Ockeghem, Johannes, 131, 142, 143, 145, 149,
        151–157, 158, 161, colorplate 8,
        colorplate 16
    sacred music, 153–157
        masses, 154–157
        motets, 157
    secular music, 152–153
O Come Bless the Lord, 647
Octet (Mendelssohn), 465, 467
Octet (Reich), 654
Octet (Stravinsky), 612
Octet in F major (Schubert), 442, 446
Ode for St. Cecilia's Day, 294, 322
Odes
    ancient Greek, 11
    German Renaissance, 189
    of kanōn, 26
Odington, Walter, 82, 89
Odovacar, 20
Odyssey, 11
Oedipus der Tyrann (Orff), 589
Oedipus rex (Stravinsky), 610
Oedipus tyrannus (Paine), 573
Oehlenschläger, 537
Offenbach, Jacques, 435, 481
Offertoria totius anni, 206
Offices (Canonical Hours) of the Church, 38, 42
Officium defunctorum, 652
O florens rosa, 146
Of Mice and Men, 615
Of Thee I Sing, 616
O gloriosa Domina, 221
O gloriosissimi, 93
O Gott, du frommer Gottm 277
O Haupt voll Blut und Wunden, 195, 281, 314, 523
Oh, you, drunken sot!, 533
Oiseau de feu, L' (Stravinsky), 609, 610
Oiseaux exotiques, 634
O Jesu Christe, Gottes Sohn, 263
O Jesu fili David, 162
Okonchen prazdnij, shumnij den', 566
Oktōēchos, 26, 32, 57
Old Folks at Home, 492
Old Hall Manuscript, 122
"Old Hundredth," 197
Old Roman liturgy and chant, 34
Old Saint Andrews Manuscript, 88
Oleg, Kievan king, 57
Olimpiade, L', 347
Olimpie, 432
Oliphant (instrument), 64
Oliver, "King," 579
Oliveros, Pauline, *646*
Olivet, 491
O magnum mysterium, 207
Om Breath, 653
Ondes Martenot (instrument), 632, *633*, 634
114 Songs (Ives), 575
I of IV (Oliveros), 646
1000 Airplanes on the Roof, 653
1000 let' (Balakirev), 531
On Hearing the First Cuckoo in Spring, 572
On parole-A Paris-Frese nouvele, 84
On Wenlock Edge, 590
Open Thy Lattice, Love, 492
Opera
    all-sung, 432–433
    ballad, 352–354
    Berlioz, L.-H., 485–486
    buffa (see Opera buffa, Operetta)
    castrati, 242, 243
    comique (see Opera comique)
    Debussy, C., 567
    in England, 258–259, 352–354
    fairy tale (Marschenoper), 560